P9-CFA-430

BIOGRAPHICAL DICTIONARY OF MATHEMATICIANS

PUBLISHED UNDER THE AUSPICES OF
THE AMERICAN COUNCIL OF LEARNED SOCIETIES

The American Council of Learned Societies, organized in 1919 for the purpose of advancing the study of the humanities and the humanistic aspects of the social sciences, is a nonprofit federation comprising fifty national scholarly groups. The Council represents the humanities in the United States in the International Union of Academies, provides fellowships and grants-in-aid, supports research-and-planning conferences and symposia, and sponsors special projects and scholarly publications.

BIOGRAPHICAL DICTIONARY OF MATHEMATICIANS

REFERENCE BIOGRAPHIES FROM THE
Dictionary of Scientific Biography

Volume 1

NEILS ABEL – RENÉ DESCARTES

Charles Scribner's Sons
NEW YORK

Collier Macmillan Canada
TORONTO

Maxwell Macmillan International
NEW YORK, OXFORD, SINGAPORE, SYDNEY

Library of Congress Cataloging-in-Publication Data

Biographical Dictionary of Mathematicians: reference biographies from the Dictionary of scientific biography.
p.cm.
"Published under the auspices of the American Council of Learned Societies."
Includes bibliographical references and index.
ISBN 0-684-19282-9. – ISBN 0-684-19288-8 (v. 1)
1. Mathematicians–Biography–Dictionaries. I. American Council of Learned Societies. II. Dictionary of scientific biography.
QA28.B534 1991
510'.92'2–dc20 90-52920
[B] CIP

Charles Scribner's Sons
Macmillan Publishing Company
866 Third Ave.
New York, New York 10022

Collier Macmillan Canada, Inc.
1200 Eglington Ave. East
Suite 200
Don Mills, Ontario M3C 3N1

5 7 9 11 13 15 17 19 20 18 16 14 12 10 8 6 4

Printed in the United States of America.

Editorial Staff

PREFACE

The *Biographical Dictionary of Mathematicians* collects all the essays on mathematicians that were originally published in the fourteen-volume *Dictionary of Scientific Biography* and Supplements I and II. By reprinting these biographies in clusters, we hope to make the scholarship of the larger work more widely available to smaller libraries as well as to individual scholars who are primarily interested in just one field or era of science.

The initial question of which scientists to include in these volumes raised a number of issues. We started by reviewing the list of scientists by field which appears in the index volume of the *Dictionary of Scientific Biography*. Immediately we saw the danger of including only those scientists who had been labeled as "mathematicians," for it was obvious that the science of numbers has been enriched by many intellectual giants outside the formal profession of mathematics. We therefore sought the advice of several historians of science in order to add those figures (such as Plato and Thales) who might not otherwise have been included. The result is the present compilation of 1023 biographies.

Entries such as "Aristotle" and "Leonardo da Vinci" posed special questions. The original essays were divided into several sections, each addressing contributions to different branches of science. Although the mathematics sections might have stood alone in the present work, we chose instead to retain the full biographies so as to preserve the scope of these great figures' intellectual legacies and the narrative integrity of the original essays, some of which are themselves the work of distinguished scholars.

The Publishers

ABEL, NIELS HENRIK (*b.* Finnöy, an island near Stavanger, Norway, 5 August 1802; *d.* Froland, Norway, 6 April 1829)

Abel's father, Sören Georg Abel, was a Lutheran minister and himself the son of a minister. He was a gifted and highly ambitious theologian, educated at the University of Copenhagen, which was at that time the only such institution in the united kingdom of Denmark-Norway. He had married Ane Marie Simonson, the daughter of a wealthy merchant and shipowner in the town of Risör, on the southern coast. Finnöy was the first parish for pastor Abel; it was small and toilsome, comprising several islands. The couple had seven children, six sons and a daughter; Niels Henrik was their second child.

In 1804 Sören Georg Abel was appointed successor to his father in the parish of Gjerstad, near Risör. The political situation in Norway was tense. Because of its alliance with Denmark the country had been thrown into the Napoleonic Wars on the side of France, and a British blockade of the coast created widespread famine. Pastor Abel was prominent in the nationalistic movement, working for the creation of separate Norwegian institutions—particularly a university and a national bank—if not for outright independence. At the conclusion of the peace treaty of Kiel, Denmark ceded Norway to Sweden. The Norwegians revolted and wrote their own constitution, but after a brief and futile war against the Swedes under Bernadotte, they were compelled to seek an armistice. A union with Sweden was accepted, and Abel's father became one of the members of the extraordinary Storting called in the fall of 1814 to write the necessary revision of the new constitution.

Niels Henrik Abel and his brothers received their first instruction from their father, but in 1815 Abel and his older brother were sent to the Cathedral School in Christiania (Oslo). This was an old school to which many public officials in the province sent their children; some fellowships were available. The Cathedral School had been excellent, but was then at a low ebb, because most of its good teachers had accepted positions at the new university, which began instruction in 1813.

Abel was only thirteen years old when he left home, and it seems probable that deteriorating family life expedited his departure. During the first couple of years his marks were only satisfactory; then the quality of his work declined. His brother fared even worse; he began to show signs of mental illness and finally had to be sent home.

In 1817 an event took place at the school that was destined to change Abel's life. The mathematics teacher mistreated one of the pupils, who died shortly afterward, possibly as a consequence of the punishment. The teacher was summarily dismissed and his place was taken by Bernt Michael Holmboe, who was only seven years older than Abel. Holmboe also served as an assistant to Christoffer Hansteen, professor of astronomy and the leading scientist at the university.

It did not take Holmboe long to discover young Abel's extraordinary ability in mathematics. He began by giving him special problems and recommending books outside the school curriculum. The two then started to study together the calculus texts of Euler, and later the works of the French mathematicians, particularly Lagrange and Laplace. So rapid was Abel's progress that he soon became the real teacher. From notebooks preserved in the library of the University of Oslo one sees that even in these early days he was already particularly interested in algebraic equation theory. By the time he finished school, he was familiar with most of the important mathematical literature. Holmboe was so delighted by the mathematical genius he had discovered that the rector of the school made him moderate his statements about Abel in the record book. But the professors at the university were well informed by Holmboe about the promising young man and made his personal acquaintance. Besides Hansteen, who also taught applied mathematics, there was only one professor of mathematics, Sören Rasmussen, a former teacher at the Cathedral School. Rasmussen, a kindly man, was not a productive scholar; his time was largely taken up by tasks assigned to him by government, particularly in his post as an administrator of the new Bank of Norway.

During his last year at school Abel, with the vigor and immodesty of youth, attacked the problem of the solution of the quintic equation. This problem had been outstanding since the days of del Ferro, Tartaglia, Cardano, and Ferrari in the first half of the sixteenth century. Abel believed that he had succeeded in finding the form of the solution, but in Norway there was no one capable of understanding his arguments, nor was there any scientific journal in which they could be published. Hansteen forwarded the paper to the Danish mathematician Ferdinand Degen, requesting its publication by the Danish Academy.

Degen could not discover any fault in the arguments, but requested that Abel illustrate his method by an example. Degen also found the topic somewhat sterile and suggested that Abel turn his attention to a topic "whose development would have the greatest consequences for analysis and mechanics. I refer to the elliptic transcendentals [elliptic integrals]. A serious investigator with suitable qualifications for research of this kind would by no means be restricted to the many beautiful properties of these most remarkable functions, but could discover a Strait of Magellan leading into wide expanses of a tremendous analytic ocean" (letter to Hansteen).

Abel began constructing his examples for the solution of the fifth-degree equation, but discovered to his dismay that his method was not correct. He also followed Degen's suggestion about the elliptic transcendentals, and it is probable that within a couple of years he had in the main completed his theory of the elliptic functions.

In 1818 pastor Abel was reelected to the Storting, after an unsuccessful bid in 1816. But his political career ended in tragedy. He made violent unfounded charges against other representatives and was threatened with impeachment. This, together with his drunkenness, made him the butt of the press. He returned home in disgrace, a disillusioned man. Both he and his wife suffered from alcoholism, and the conditions at the vicarage and in the parish became scandalous. It was generally considered a relief when he died in 1820. His widow was left in very straitened circumstances, with a small pension barely sufficient to support her and her many children.

The penniless Abel entered the university in the fall of 1821. He was granted a free room at the university dormitory and received permission to share it with his younger brother Peder. But the new institution had no fellowship funds, and some of the professors took the unusual measure of supporting the young mathematician out of their own salaries. He was a guest in their houses and became particularly attracted to the Hansteen home, and to Mrs. Hansteen and her sisters.

Abel's first task at the university was to satisfy the requirements for the preliminary degree, *Candidatus Philosophiae.* Once this was achieved, after a year, Abel was entirely on his own in his studies. There were no advanced courses in mathematics and the physical sciences, but this does not seem to have been a handicap; in a letter from Paris a little later he stated that he had read practically everything in mathematics, important or unimportant.

He devoted his time to advanced research and his efforts received a strong impetus when Hansteen started a scientific periodical, *Magazin for Naturvidenskaben.* In 1823 this journal published Abel's first article, in Norwegian, a study of functional equations. Mathematically it was not important, nor was his second little paper. The subscribers to the magazine had been promised a popular review, however, and Hansteen, probably after criticism, felt obliged to apologize for the character of these papers: "Thus I believe that the *Magazin* in addition to scientific materials should also further the tools serving for their analysis. It will be reckoned to our credit that we have given the learned public an opportunity to become acquainted with a work from the pen of this talented and skillful author" (*Magazin,* **1**). Abel's next paper, "Opläsning afet Par Opgaver ved bjoelp af bestemte Integraler" ("Solution of Some Problems by Means of Definite Integrals"), is of importance in the history of mathematics, since it contains the first solution of an integral equation. The paper, which went unnoticed at the time, in part because it was in Norwegian, deals with the mechanical problem of the motion of a mass point on a curve under the influence of gravitation. During the winter of 1822–1823 Abel also composed a longer work on the integration of functional expressions. The paper was submitted to the university Collegium in the hope that that body would assist in its publication. The manuscript has disappeared, but it seems likely that some of the results obtained in it are included in some of Abel's later papers.

Early in the summer of 1823 Abel received a gift of 100 daler from Professor Rasmussen to finance a trip to Copenhagen to meet Degen and the other Danish mathematicians. His letters to Holmboe reveal the mathematical inspiration that he received. He stayed in the house of his uncle and here made the acquaintance of his future fiancée, Christine Kemp.

Upon his return to Oslo, Abel again took up the question of the solution of the quintic equation. This time he took the reverse view and succeeded in solving the centuries-old problem by proving the impossibility of a radical expression that represents a solution of the general fifth- or higher-degree equation. Abel fully realized the importance of his result, so he had it published, at his own expense, by a local printer. To reach a larger audience, he wrote it in French: "Mémoire sur les équations algébriques où on démontre l'impossibilité de la résolution de l'équation générale du cinquième degré." To save expense the whole pamphlet was compressed to six pages. The resulting brevity probably made it difficult to understand; at any rate, there was no reaction from any of the foreign mathematicians—including the great C. F. Gauss, to whom a copy was sent.

It had become clear that Abel could no longer live on the support of the professors. His financial problems had been increased by his engagement to Christine Kemp, who had come to Norway as a governess for the children of a family living near Oslo.

Abel applied for a travel grant, and after some delays the government decided that Abel should receive a small stipend to study languages at the university to prepare him for travel abroad. He was then to receive a grant of 600 daler for two years of foreign study.

Abel was disappointed at the delay but dutifully studied languages, particularly French, and used his time to prepare a considerable number of papers to be presented to foreign mathematicians. During the summer of 1825 he departed, together with four friends, all of whom also intended to prepare themselves for future scientific careers; one of them later became professor of medicine, and the three others became geologists. Abel's friends all planned to go to Berlin, while Abel, upon Hansteen's advice, was to spend his time in Paris, then the world's principal center of mathematics. Abel feared being lonely, however, and also decided to go to Berlin, although he well knew that he would incur the displeasure of his protector.

Abel's change of mind turned out to be a most fortunate decision. On passing through Copenhagen, Abel learned that Degen had died, but he secured a letter of recommendation from one of the other Danish mathematicians to Privy Councilor August Leopold Crelle. Crelle was a very influential engineer, intensely interested in mathematics although not himself a strong mathematician.

When Abel first called upon Crelle, he had some difficulty in making himself understood, but after a while Crelle recognized the unusual qualities of his young visitor. The two became lifelong friends. Abel presented him with a copy of his pamphlet on the quintic equation, but Crelle confessed that it was unintelligible to him and recommended that Abel write an expanded version of it. They talked about the poor state of mathematics in Germany. In a letter to Hansteen, dated from Berlin, 5 December 1825, Abel wrote:

> When I expressed surprise over the fact that there existed no mathematical journal, as in France, he said that he had long intended to edit one, and would presently bring his plan to execution. This project is now organized, and that to my great joy, for I shall have a place where I can get some of my articles printed. I have already prepared four of them, which will appear in the first number.

Journal für die reine und angewandte Mathematik, or *Crelle's Journal,* as it is commonly known, was the leading German mathematical periodical during the nineteenth century. The first volume alone contains seven papers by Abel and the following volumes contain many more, most of them of preeminent importance in the history of mathematics. Among the first is the expanded version of the proof of the impossibility of the solution of the general quintic equation by radicals. Here Abel develops the necessary algebraic background, including a discussion of algebraic field extensions. Abel was at this time not aware that he had a precursor, the Italian mathematician Paolo Ruffini. But in a posthumous paper on the equations which are solvable by radicals Abel states: "The only one before me, if I am not mistaken, who has tried to prove the impossibility of the algebraic [radical] solution of the general equations is the mathematician Ruffini, but his paper is so complicated that it is very difficult to judge on the correctness of his arguments. It seems to me that it is not always satisfactory." The result is usually referred to as the Abel-Ruffini theorem.

After Abel's departure from Oslo an event took place that caused him much concern. Rasmussen had found his professorship in mathematics too burdensome when combined with his public duties. He resigned, and shortly afterward the faculty voted to recommend that Holmboe be appointed to fill the vacancy. Abel's Norwegian friends found the action highly unjust, and Abel himself probably felt the same way. Nevertheless, he wrote a warm letter of congratulation to his former teacher, and they remained good friends. But it is evident that from this moment Abel worried about his future and his impending marriage; there was no scientific position in sight for him in his home country.

During the winter in Berlin, Abel contributed to *Crelle's Journal*; among the notable papers are one on the generalization of the binomial formula and another on the integration of square root expressions. But one of his main mathematical concerns was the lack of stringency in contemporary mathematics. He mentioned it repeatedly in letters to Holmboe. In one of these, dated 16 January 1826, he wrote:

> My eyes have been opened in the most surprising manner. If you disregard the very simplest cases, there is in all of mathematics not a single infinite series whose sum has been stringently determined. In other words, the most important parts of mathematics stand without foundation. It is true that most of it is valid, but that is very surprising. I struggle to find the reason for it, an exceedingly interesting problem.

A result of this struggle was his classic paper on power series which contains many general theorems and also, as an application, the stringent determination of the sum of the binomial series for arbitrary real or complex exponents.

During the early spring of 1826, Abel felt obliged to proceed to his original destination, Paris. Crelle had promised to accompany him, and on the way they intended to stop in Göttingen to visit Gauss. Unfortunately, pressure of business prevented Crelle from leaving Berlin. At the same time, Abel's Norwegian friends were planning a geological excursion through central Europe, and, again reluctant to be separated from them, he joined the group. They traveled by coach through Bohemia, Austria, northern Italy, and the Alps. Abel did not reach Paris until July, low on funds after the expensive trip.

The visit to Paris was to prove disappointing. The university vacations had just begun when Abel arrived, and the mathematicians had left town. When they returned, he found that they were aloof and difficult to approach; it was only in passing that he met Legendre, whose main interest in his old age was elliptic integrals, Abel's own specialty. For presentation to the French Academy of Sciences Abel had reserved a paper that he considered his masterpiece. It dealt with the sum of integrals of a given algebraic function. Abel's theorem states that any such sum can be expressed as a fixed number p of these integrals, with integration arguments that are algebraic functions of the original arguments. The minimal number p is the genus of the algebraic function, and this is the first occurrence of this fundamental quantity. Abel's theorem is a vast generalization of Euler's relation for elliptic integrals.

Abel spent his first months in Paris completing his great memoir; it is one of his longest papers and includes a broad theory with applications. It was presented to the Academy of Sciences on 30 October 1826, under the title "Mémoire sur une propriété générale d'une classe très-étendue de fonctions transcendantes." Cauchy and Legendre were appointed referees, Cauchy being chairman. A number of young men had gained quick distinction upon having their works accepted by the Academy, and Abel awaited the referees' report. No report was forthcoming, however; indeed, it was not issued until Abel's death forced its appearance. Cauchy seems to have been to blame; he claimed later that the manuscript was illegible.

Abel's next two months in Paris were gloomy; he had little money and few acquaintances. He met P. G. L. Dirichlet, his junior by three years and already a well-known mathematician, through a paper in the Academy sponsored by Legendre. Another acquaintance was Frédéric Saigey, editor of the scientific revue *Ferrusac's Bulletin,* for whom Abel wrote a few articles, particularly about his own papers in *Crelle's Journal.* After Christmas he spent his last resources to pay his fare to Berlin.

Shortly after his return to Berlin, Abel fell ill; he seems to have then suffered the first attack of the tuberculosis that was later to claim his life. He borrowed some money from Holmboe, and Crelle probably helped him. Abel longed to return to Norway but felt compelled to remain abroad until his fellowship term had expired. Crelle tried to keep him in Berlin until he could find a position for him at a German university; in the meantime he offered him the editorship of his *Journal.*

Abel worked assiduously on a new paper: "Recherches sur les fonctions elliptiques," his most extensive publication (125 pages in the *Oeuvres complètes*). In this work he radically transformed the theory of elliptic integrals to the theory of elliptic functions by using their inverse functions corresponding in the most elementary case to the duality

$$y = \text{arc} \sin x = \int \frac{dx}{\sqrt{1 - x^2}} \qquad x = \sin y.$$

The elliptic functions thereby become a vast and natural generalization of the trigonometric functions; in the wake of Abel's work they were to constitute one of the favorite research topics in mathematics during the nineteenth century. Abel had already developed most of the theory as a student in Oslo, so he was able to present the theory of elliptic functions with a great richness of detail, including double periodicity, expansions in infinite series and products, and addition theorems. The theory led to the expressions for functions of a multiple of the argument with the concomitant determination of the equations for fractional arguments and their solution by radicals, much in the way that Gauss had treated the cyclotomic equations; Abel's letters to Holmboe (from Paris in December 1826 and from Berlin on 4 March 1827) indicate that he was particularly fascinated by a determination of the condition for a lemniscate to be divisible into equal parts by means of compass and ruler, analogous to Gauss's construction of regular polygons. The last part deals with the so-called theory of complex multiplication, later so important in algebraic number theory.

Abel returned to Oslo on 20 May 1827, to find that the situation at home was as gloomy as he had feared. He had no position in prospect, no fellowship, and an abundance of debts. His application to have his fellowship prolonged was turned down by the Department of Finance, but the university courageously awarded him a small stipend out of its meager funds. This action was criticized by the department, which reserved the right to have the amount deducted from any future salary he might receive.

Abel's fiancée found a new position with friends of Abel's family, the family of the owner of an ironworks at Froland, near Arendal. During the fall Abel eked out a living in Oslo by tutoring schoolboys and probably with the help of friends. At the new year the situation became brighter. Hansteen, a pioneer in geomagnetic studies, received a large grant for two years to examine the earth's magnetic field in unexplored Siberia. In the meantime Abel became his substitute both at the university and at the Norwegian Military Academy.

The first part of the "Recherches" was published in *Crelle's Journal* in September 1827, and Abel completed the second part during the winter. He lived in isolation at Oslo; there was no package mail during the winter, and he had no inkling of the interest his memoir had created among European mathematicians. Nor did he know that a competitor had appeared in the field of elliptic functions until early in 1828, when Hansteen showed him the September issue of the *Astronomische Nachrichten.* In this journal a young German mathematician, K. G. J. Jacobi, announced without proofs some results concerning the transformation theory of elliptic integrals. Abel hurriedly added a note to the manuscript of the second part of the "Recherches," showing how Jacobi's results were the consequence of his own.

Abel was keenly aware that a race was at hand. He interrupted a large paper on the theory of equations that was to contain the determination of all equations that can be solved by radicals; the part that was published contained the theory of those equations that are now known as Abelian. He then wrote, in rapid succession, a series of papers on elliptic functions. The first was "Solution d'un problème général concernant la transformation des fonctions elliptiques." This, his direct response to Jacobi, was published in *Astronomische Nachrichten*; the others appeared in *Crelle's Journal.* In addition, Abel prepared a book-length memoir, "Précis d'une théorie des fonctions elliptiques," which was published after his death. Jacobi, on the other hand, wrote only brief notices which did not reveal his methods; these were reserved for his book, *Fundamenta nova theoriae functionum ellipticarum* (1829).

Much has been written about the early theory of elliptic functions. There seems to be little doubt that Abel was in possession of the ideas several years before Jacobi. On the other hand, it is also an established fact that Gauss, although publishing nothing, had discovered the principles of elliptic functions long before either Abel or Jacobi.

The European mathematicians watched with fascination the competition between the two young mathematicians. Legendre noticed Jacobi's announcements and also received a letter from him. In a meeting of the French Academy in November 1827, he praised the new mathematical star; the speech was reproduced in the newspapers and Legendre sent the clipping to Jacobi. In his reply Jacobi, after expressing his thanks, pointed out Abel's "Recherches" and its general results. Legendre responded: "Through these works you two will be placed in the class of the foremost analysts of our times." He also expressed his disappointment over Jacobi's method of publication and was irritated when Jacobi confessed that in order to derive some of his results he had had to rely on Abel's paper. About this time also, Abel began a correspondence with Legendre and poured out his ideas to him.

All that the European mathematicians knew about Abel's condition in Norway was that he had only a temporary position and had recently been compelled to tutor schoolboys to make a living. The main source of their information was Crelle, who constantly used his influence to try to obtain an appointment for Abel at a new scientific institute to be created in Berlin. Progress was very slow, however. In September 1828 four prominent members of the French Academy of Sciences took the extraordinary step of addressing a petition directly to Bernadotte, now Charles XIV of Norway-Sweden, calling attention to Abel and urging that a suitable scientific position be created for him. In a meeting of the Academy, on 25 February 1829, Legendre also paid tribute to Abel and his discoveries, particularly to his results in the theory of equations.

In the meantime Abel, in spite of his deteriorating health, wrote new papers frantically. He spent the summer vacation of 1828 on the Froland estate with his fiancée. At Christmas he insisted on visiting her again, notwithstanding that it required several days' travel in intense cold. He was feverish when he arrived, but enjoyed the family Christmas celebration. He may have had a premonition that his days were numbered, however, and he now feared that the great paper submitted to the French Academy had been lost forever. He therefore wrote a brief note, "Demonstration d'une propriété générale d'une certaine classe de fonctions transcendantes," in which he gave a proof of the main theorem. He mailed it to Crelle on 6 January 1829.

While waiting for the sled that was to return him to Oslo, Abel suffered a violent hemorrhage; the doctor diagnosed his illness as tuberculosis and ordered prolonged bed rest. He died in April, at the age of twenty-six, and was buried at the neighboring Froland church during a blizzard. The grave is marked by a monument erected by his friends. One of them, Baltazar Keilhau, wrote to Christine Kemp,

ABRAHAM BAR ḤIYYA

without ever having seen her, and made her an offer of marriage which she accepted. Two days after Abel's death Crelle wrote jubilantly to inform him that his appointment in Berlin had been secured.

On 28 June 1830, the French Academy of Sciences awarded its Grand Prix to Abel and Jacobi for their outstanding mathematical discoveries. After an intensive search in Paris the manuscript of Abel's great memoir was rediscovered. It was published in 1841, fifteen years after it had been submitted. During the printing it again disappeared, not to reappear until 1952 in Florence.

Crelle wrote an extensive eulogy of Abel in his *Journal* (**4** [1829], 402):

> All of Abel's works carry the imprint of an ingenuity and force of thought which is unusual and sometimes amazing, even if the youth of the author is not taken into consideration. One may say that he was able to penetrate all obstacles down to the very foundations of the problems, with a force which appeared irresistible; he attacked the problems with an extraordinary energy; he regarded them from above and was able to soar so high over their present state that all the difficulties seemed to vanish under the victorious onslaught of his genius. . . . But it was not only his great talent which created the respect for Abel and made his loss infinitely regrettable. He distinguished himself equally by the purity and nobility of his character and by a rare modesty which made his person cherished to the same unusual degree as was his genius.

BIBLIOGRAPHY

I. ORIGINAL WORKS. Abel's complete works are published in two editions, *Oeuvres complètes de N. H. Abel, mathématicien,* ed. and annotated by B. Holmboe (Oslo, 1839), and *Nouvelle édition,* M. M. L. Sylow and S. Lie, eds., 2 vols. (Oslo, 1881).

II. SECONDARY LITERATURE. Materials on Abel's life include *Niels Henrik Abel: Mémorial publié à l'occasion du centenaire de sa naissance* (Oslo, 1902) which comprises all letters cited in the text; and O. Ore, *Niels Henrik Abel; Mathematician Extraordinary* (Minneapolis, Minn., 1957).

OYSTEIN ORE

ABRAHAM BAR ḤIYYA HA-NASI, also known as **Savasorda** (*fl.* in Barcelona before 1136)

In Arabic he was known as Ṣāḥib al-Shurṭa, "Elder of the Royal Suite," denoting some type of official position; this title later gave rise to the commonly used Latin name of Savasorda. He was also known as Abraham Judaeus. Savasorda's most influential work by far is his Hebrew treatise on practical geometry, the *Ḥibbūr ha-meshīḥah we-ha-tishboret.* Translated into Latin as *Liber embadorum* by Plato of Tivoli, the work holds an unusual position in the history of mathematics. It is the earliest exposition of Arab algebra written in Europe, and it contains the first complete solution in Europe of the quadratic equation, $x^2 - ax + b = 0$.

The year the *Ḥibbūr* was translated (1145) also saw the Robert of Chester translation of al-Khwārizmī's algebra and so may well be regarded as the birth year of European algebra. Thus the *Ḥibbūr* was among the earliest works to introduce Arab trigonometry into Europe, and it was also the earliest to treat of Euclid's *Book of Divisions.* Leonardo Fibonacci was influenced by Savasorda and devoted an entire section of his *Practica geometriae* to division of figures. Savasorda made a novel contribution when he included the division of geometric figures in a practical treatise, thus effecting a synthesis of Greek theory with the pragmatic aspects of mathematics.

Savasorda himself recommended Euclid, Theodosius of Bithynia, Menelaus, Autolycus, Apollonius of Perga, Eudemus of Rhodes, and Hero of Alexandria for study in geometry. He knew well al-Khwārizmī and al-Karajī. Following Hero and not Euclid he did not accept the Pythagorean figurate numbers in his explanation of plane and square numbers. In general, Savasorda preferred those definitions and explanations that may be aligned more easily and closely with reality.

To understand this approach, it is necessary to go back to the earliest known Hebrew geometry, the *Mishnat ha-Middot* (*ca.* A.D. 150). This work may be considered as a link in the chain of transmission of mathematics between Palestine and the early medieval Arab civilization. The Arab mathematicians al-Khwārizmī and al-Karajī, and later Savasorda, followed the methodological lines of this old *Mishna.* Savasorda himself provided a new cross-cultural bridge a thousand years after the *Mishna.* In his *Encyclopedia* there is the same teaching of both theory and practice, including not only the art of practical reckoning and business arithmetic but also the theory of numbers and geometric definition. This book is probably the earliest algorismic work written in Western Europe, but knowledge of the work is not apparent in the arithmetical works of either Abraham ibn Ezra or Levi ben Gerson, although they may have had a common origin.

In the history of decimal theory and practice, the two mainstreams of development in the Middle Ages came from the Jewish and Christian cultures. Savasorda, however, did not belong definitely to any one mathematical group. He spent most of his life in

Barcelona, an area of both Arab and Christian learning, and was active in translating the masterpieces of Arab science. In an apologetic epistle on astrology to Jehuda ben Barsillae al-Barceloni, he deplored the lack of knowledge of Arab science and language among the people of Provence. He wrote his own works in Hebrew, but he helped translate the following works into Latin: al-ʿImrānī's *De horarum electionibus* (1133–1134), al-Khayyāt's *De nativitatibus* (1136), and Almansori's *Judicia seu propositiones* . . . (1136). Savasorda may have worked on translations of the *Quadripartitum* of Ptolemy, the *Spherics* of Theodosius, the *De motu stellarum* of al-Battānī, and others, with Plato of Tivoli. It is also possible that he worked with Rudolf of Bruges on the *De astrolabia.*

BIBLIOGRAPHY

I. ORIGINAL WORKS. Savasorda's *Ḥibbūr*, Michael Guttman, ed., was published in Berlin (1912–1913); a Catalan translation was done by J. Millás-Vallicrosa (Barcelona, 1931). Three treatises of Savasorda constitute a complete astronomical work: *Ẓurat ha-ereẓ* ("Form of the Earth," Bodleian MS 2033) is concerned with astronomical geography and general astronomy; *Ḥeshbon mahlakot ha-kokhabim* ("Calculation of the Movement of the Stars," Leiden MS 37 Heb.) covers astronomical calculations; and *Luḥot ha-nasi* ("Tables of the Prince," Berlin MS 649; Bodleian MS 443, 437) follows al-Battānī's work. His work on the calendar, *Sefer ha-'ibbur* ("Book on Intercalation," H. Filipowski, ed., London, 1851), written 1122–1123, exerted great influence on Maimonides and Isaac Israeli the Younger. Savasorda's philosophical works include *Megillat ha-megalleh* ("Scroll of the Revealer," A. Poznanski and J. Guttmann, eds., Berlin, 1924) and *Hegyon ha-nefesh* ("Meditation of the Soul," E. Freimann, ed., Leipzig, 1860). See also J. Millás-Vallicrosa, ed., *Llibre de Geometria* (Barcelona, 1931), *Llibre revelador* (Barcelona, 1929), and *La obra enciclopédica yĕsodé ha-tĕbuná u-migdal ha-ĕmuná* (Madrid-Barcelona, 1952); and A. Poznanski and J. Guttmann, eds., *Megillat ha-nefesh* (Berlin, 1924).

II. SECONDARY LITERATURE. For other studies of mathematics and Savasorda's contributions, see F. Baer, *Die Juden im Christlichen Spanien*, I (Berlin, 1929), 81, n. 1; M. Curtze, "Der *Liber Embadorum* des Abraham bar Chijja Savasorda in der Übersetzung des Plato von Tivoli," in *Abhandlungen zur Geschichte der mathematischen Wissenschaften*, **12** (1902), 1–183; I. Efros, "Studies in Pre-Tibbonian Philosophical Terminology," in *Jewish Quarterly Review*, **14** (1926–1927), 129–164, 323–368; S. Gandz, "The Invention of Decimal Fractions . . . ," in *Isis*, **25** (1936), 17, and "*Mishnat ha-Middot*," in *Quellen und Studien zur Geschichte der Mathematik, Astronomie und Physik*, Abt. A, 2 (Berlin, 1932). See also B. Goldberg and L. Rosenkranz, eds., *Yesod Olam* (Berlin, 1846–1848); J. M. Guttmann, *Chibbur ha-Meschicha weha-Tischboreth* (Berlin, 1913); M. Levey, "Abraham Savasorda and His Algorism: A Study in Early European Logistic," in *Osiris*, **11** (1954), 50–63, and "The Encyclopedia of Abraham Savasorda: A Departure in Mathematical Methodology," in *Isis*, **43** (1952), 257–264. Additional studies are by P. A. Sorokin and R. K. Merton, "The Course of Arabian Intellectual Development, 700–1300 A.D., A Study in Method," in *Isis*, **22** (1935), 516–524; M. Steinschneider, *Gesammelte Schriften* (Berlin, 1925), p. 345; H. Suter, "Die Mathematiker und Astronomen der Araber und Ihre Werke," in *Abhandlungen zur Geschichte der mathematischen Wissenschaften*, **10** (1900); J. Tropfke, "Zur Geschichte der quadratischen Gleichungen ueber dreieinhalb Jahrtausend," in *Jahresbericht der Deutschen Mathematiker-vereinigung*, **43** (1933), 98–107; **44** (1934), 95–119.

MARTIN LEVEY

ABŪ KĀMIL SHUJĀʿ IBN ASLAM IBN MUḤAMMAD IBN SHUJĀʿ (*b. ca.* 850, *d. ca.* 930)

Often called al-Ḥāsib al-Miṣrī ("the reckoner of Egypt"), Abū Kāmil was one of Islam's greatest algebraists in the period following the earliest Muslim algebraist, al-Khwārizmī (*fl. ca.* 825). In the Arab world this was a period of intellectual ferment, particularly in mathematics and the sciences.

There is virtually no biographical material available on Abū Kāmil. He is first mentioned by al-Nadīm in a bibliographical work, *The Fihrist* (987), where he is listed with other mathematicians under "The New Reckoners and Arithmeticians," which refers to those mathematicians who concerned themselves with the practical algorisms, citizens' arithmetic, and practical geometry (see Bibliography). Ibn Khaldūn (1322–1406) stated that Abū Kāmil wrote his algebra after the first such work by al-Khwārizmī, and Ḥajjī Khalīfa (1608–1658) attributed to him a work supposedly concerned with algebraic solutions of inheritance problems.

Among the works of Abū Kāmil extant in manuscripts is the *Kitāb al-ṭarā'if fi'l-ḥisāb* ("Book of Rare Things in the Art of Calculation"). According to H. Suter[1] this text is concerned with integral solutions of some indeterminate equations; much earlier, Diophantus (*ca.* first century A.D.) had concerned himself with rational, not exclusively integral, solutions. Abū Kāmil's solutions are found by an ordered and very systematic procedure. Although indeterminate equations with integral solutions had been well known in ancient Mesopotamia, it was not until about 1150 that they appeared well developed in India. Aryabhata (*b.* A.D. 476) had used continued fractions in solutions, but there is uncertain evidence that this knowledge had been passed on in any ordered form to the Arabs by the time of Abū Kāmil.

A work of both geometric and algebraic interest is the *Kitāb . . . al-mukhammas wa'al-mu'ashshar* . . . ("On the Pentagon and Decagon"). The text is algebraic in treatment and contains solutions for a fourth-degree equation and for mixed quadratics with irrational coefficients. Much of the text was utilized by Leonardo Fibonacci (1175–*ca.* 1250) in his *Practica geometriae*.[2] Some of the equations solved by Abū Kāmil in this work read as follows:

$$s_{15} = \sqrt{\frac{s}{32}d^2 \sqrt{\frac{s}{1024}d^4} + \sqrt{\frac{3}{64}d^2}} - \sqrt{\frac{15}{64}d^2}$$
$$= \frac{r}{4}\left(\sqrt{10 + 2\sqrt{5}} + \sqrt{3} - \sqrt{15}\right),$$

with s the side of a regular polygon inscribed in a circle. Also

$$S_5 = \sqrt{5d^2 - \sqrt{20d^4}} = 2r\sqrt{5 - 2\sqrt{5}},$$

with S the side of a regular polygon (pentagon here) which has an inscribed circle.[3]

The outstanding advance of Abū Kāmil over al-Khwārizmī, as seen from these equations, is in the use of irrational coefficients.[4] Another manuscript, which is independent of the *Ṭarā'if*, mentioned above, is the most advanced work on indeterminate equations by Abū Kāmil. The solutions are not restricted to integers; in fact, most are in rational form. Four of the more mathematically interesting problems are given below in modern notation. It must be remembered that Abū Kāmil gave all his problems rhetorically; in this text, his only mathematical notation was of integers.

(1) $x^2 - 8x - 30 = y^2$

(2) $x + x^2 = y^2$
$x - x^2 = z^2$

(3) $20 + x = y^2$
$50 - (10 - x) = z^2$

(4) $10 + x^2 = y^2$
$10 - x^2 = z^2$

Many of the problems in *Kitāb fi'l-jabr wa'l-muqābala* had been previously solved by al-Khwārizmī. In Abū Kāmil's work, a solution[5] for x^2 was worked out directly instead of first solving for x. Euclid had taken account of the condition x less than $p/2$ in $x^2 + q = px$, whereas Abū Kāmil also solved the case of x greater than $p/2$ in this equation.

Abū Kāmil was the first Muslim to use powers greater than x^2 with ease. He used x^8 (called "square square square square"), x^6 (called "cube cube"), x^5 (called "square square root"), and x^3 (called "cube"), as well as x^2 (called "square"). From this, it appears that Abū Kāmil's nomenclature indicates that he added "exponents." In the Indian nomenclature a "square cube" is x^6, in contradistinction. Diophantus (*ca.* A.D. 86) also added "powers," but his work was probably unknown to the Arabs until Abu'l Wafā' (940–998) translated his work into Arabic (*ca.* 998).

Abū Kāmil, following al-Khwārizmī, when using *jadhr* ("root") as the side of a square, multiplied it by the square unit to get the area ($x \cdot 1^2$). This method is older than al-Khwārizmī's method and is to be found in the *Mishnat ha-Middot*, the oldest Hebrew geometry, which dates back to A.D. 150.[6] This idea of root is related to the Egyptian *khet* ("cubit strip").[7]

The Babylonians stressed the algebraic form of geometry as did al-Khwārizmī. However, Abū Kāmil not only drew heavily on the latter but he also derived much from Heron of Alexandria and Euclid. Thus he was in a position to put together a sophisticated algebra with an elaborated geometry. In actuality, the resulting work was more abstract than al-Khwārizmī's and more practical than Euclid's. Thus Abū Kāmil effected the integration of ancient Mesopotamian practice and Greek theory to yield a wider approach to algebra.

Some of the more interesting problems to be found in the *Algebra*, in modern notation, are:[8]

(No. 57) $\dfrac{x \cdot \sqrt{10}}{2 + \sqrt{3}} = x - 10$

(No. 60) $x + \sqrt{x} + \sqrt{2x} + \sqrt{5x^2} = 10$

(No. 61) $x + y + z = 10;\ x < y < z$
$x^2 + y^2 = z^2$
$xz = y^2$

(No. 63) $\dfrac{10}{x} + \dfrac{10}{10 - x} = 6\dfrac{1}{4}$

It is possible that Greek algebra was known to Abū Kāmil through Heron of Alexandria, although a direct connection is difficult to prove. The influence of Heron is, however, definite in Abraham bar Ḥiyya's work.[9] That Abū Kāmil influenced both al-Karajī and Leonardo Fibonacci may be demonstrated from the examples they copied from his work. Thus through

Abū Kāmil, mathematical abstraction, elaborated together with a more practical mathematical methodology, impelled the formal development of algebra.

NOTES

1. "Das Buch der Seltenheiten."
2. See also Suter, "Die Abhandlung des Abū Kāmil."
3. *Ibid.*, p. 37. Levey will soon publish the Arabic text of "On the Pentagon and Decagon," discovered by him.
4. At least twenty of these problems from this text may be found in Leonardo Fibonacci, *Scritti*, Vol. I, sect. 15; Vol. II.
5. Tropfke, *Geschichte der Elementar-Mathematik*, pp. 74–76; 80–82; Weinberg, "Die Algebra des abu Kamil."
6. S. Gandz, "On the Origin of the Term 'Root.'"
7. M. Levey, *The Algebra of Abū Kāmil*, pp. 19–20. P. Schub and M. Levey will soon publish Abū Kāmil's advanced work on indeterminate equations, newly discovered in Istanbul.
8. *Ibid.*, pp. 178, 184, 186, 202.
9. M. Levey, "The Encyclopedia of Abraham Savasorda" and "Abraham Savasorda and His Algorism."

BIBLIOGRAPHY

I. ORIGINAL WORKS. The following manuscripts of Abū Kāmil are available: *Kitāb fi'l-jabr wa'l-muqābala* ("Book on Algebra," Paris BN MS Lat. 7377A; Munich Cod. MS Heb. 225; Istanbul-MS Kara Mustafa 379), trans. into Hebrew by Mordecai Finzi *ca.* 1460. See also *Kitāb al-ṭarā'-if fi'l ḥisāb* ("Book of Rare Things in the Art of Calculation," Leiden, MS Arabic 1003, ff. 50r–58r; translations are found in Munich Cod. MS Heb. 225 and in Paris BN MS Lat. 7377A); *Kitāb . . . al-mukhammas wa'l-mu'ashshar . . .* ("On the Pentagon and Decagon," Paris BN MS Lat. 7377A; Munich Cod. MS Heb. 225; Istanbul-MS Kara Mustafa 379, ff. 67r–75r); *Al-wāṣāyā bi'l-judhūr* (MS Mosul 294) discusses the ordering of roots. Works of Abū Kāmil listed in *The Fihrist* of al-Nadīm (p. 281) include *Kitāb al-falāḥ* ("Book of Fortune"), *Kitāb miftāḥ al-falāḥ* ("Book of the Key to Fortune"), *Kitāb fi'l-jabr wa'l-muqābala* ("Book on Algebra"), *Kitāb al-misāḥa wa'l-handasa* ("Book on Surveying and Geometry"), *Kitāb al-kifāya* ("Book of the Adequate"), *Kitāb al-ṭayr* ("Book on Omens"), *Kitāb al-'asīr* ("Book of the Kernel"), *Kitāb al-khaṭa'ayn* ("Book of the Two Errors"), *Kitāb al-jam' wa'l-tafrīq* ("Book on Augmentation and Diminution").

II. SECONDARY LITERATURE. For works on both Arab mathematics and Abū Kāmil see the following: H. T. Colebrooke, *Algebra with Arithmetic and Mensuration from the Sanskrit* (London, 1817); G. Fluegel, ed. and trans., *Lexicon bibliographicum et encyclopedicum a Haji Khalfa compositum* (Leipzig, 1835–1858); W. Hartner, "Abū Kāmil Shudjā'," in the *Encyclopedia of Islam*, 2nd ed., I (Leiden, 1960), 132–133; II (Leiden, 1962), 360–362; *Ibn Khaldūn The Muqaddimah*, Franz Rosenthal, trans., 3 vols. (New York, 1958); Leonardo Fibonacci, *Scritti di Leonardo Pisano*, 2 vols: Vol. I, *Liber abaci;* Vol. II, *Practica geometriae;* S. Gandz, "On the Origin of the Term 'Root,'" in *American Math. Monthly*, **35** (1928), 67–75; M. Levey, *The Algebra of Abū Kāmil (Kitāb fi'l-jabr wa'l-muqābala) in a Commentary by Mordecai Finzi* (Madison, Wisc., 1966), "The Encyclopedia of Abraham Savasorda: A Departure in Mathematical Methodology," in *Isis* **35** (1952), 257–264; and "Abraham Savasorda and His Algorism: A Study in Early European Logistic," in *Osiris*, **11** (1954), 50–63.

For additional material see G. Libri, *Histoire des sciences mathématiques en Italie* (Paris, 1938), pp. 253–297; 2nd ed. (Paris, 1865), pp. 304–369; al-Nadīm, *Fihrist al-'ulūm*, G. Fluegel, ed. (Leipzig, 1871–1872); M. Steinschneider, *Die Hebraeischen Uebersetzungen des Mittelalters und die Juden als Dolmetscher*, a reprint (Graz, 1956), pp. 584–588; and H. Suter, "Die Abhandlung des Abū Kāmil Šoja' b. Aslam über das Fünfeck und Zehneck," in *Bib. Math.*, **10** (1909–1910), 15–42; "Das Buch der Setenheiten der Rechenkunst von Abū Kāmil el-Misrī," in *Bib. Math.*, Ser. 3, **11** (1910–1911), 100–120; "Die Mathematiker und Astronomen der Araber und ihre Werke," in *Abhandlungen z. Gesch. d. Math. Wissenschaften*, **10** (1900). See also J. Tropfke, *Geschichte der Elementar-Mathematik*, Vol. III (Berlin, 1937); J. Weinberg, "Die Algebra des abū Kāmil Šoǧā' ben Aslam" (doctoral diss., Munich, 1935); A. P. Youschkevitch, *Geschichte der Mathematik im Mittelalter* (Basel, 1964).

MARTIN LEVEY

ABŪ'L-WAFĀ' AL-BŪZJĀNĪ, MUḤAMMAD IBN MUḤAMMAD IBN YAḤYĀ IBN ISMĀ'ĪL IBN AL-'ABBĀS (*b.* Būzjān [now in Iran], 10 June 940; *d.* Baghdad [now in Iraq], 997 or July 998)

Abū'l-Wafā' was apparently of Persian descent. In 959 he moved to Baghdad, which was then the capital of the Eastern Caliphate. There he became the last great representative of the mathematics-astronomy school that arose around the beginning of the ninth century, shortly after the founding of Baghdad. With his colleagues, Abū'l-Wafā' conducted astronomical observations at the Baghdad observatory. He continued the tradition of his predecessors, combining original scientific work with commentary on the classics—the works of Euclid and Diophantus. He also wrote a commentary to the algebra of al-Khwārizmī. None of these commentaries has yet been found.

Abū'l-Wafā''s textbook on practical arithmetic, *Kitāb fī mā yaḥtaj ilayh al-kuttāb wa'l-'ummāl min 'ilm al-ḥisāb* ("Book on What Is Necessary From the Science of Arithmetic for Scribes and Businessmen"), written between 961 and 976, enjoyed widespread fame. It consists of seven sections (*manāzil*), each of which has seven chapters (*abwāb*). The first three sections are purely mathematical (ratio, multiplication and division, estimation of areas); the last four contain the solutions of practical problems concerning payment for work, construction estimates, the exchange and sale of various grains, etc.

ABŪ'L-WAFĀ'

Abū'l-Wafā' systematically sets forth the methods of calculation used in the Arabic East by merchants, by clerks in the departments of finance, and by land surveyors in their daily work; he also introduces refinements of commonly used methods, criticizing some for being incorrect. For example, after indicating that surveyors found the area of all sorts of quadrangles by multiplying half the sums of the opposite sides, he remarks, "This is also an obvious mistake and clearly incorrect and rarely corresponds to the truth." Abū'l-Wafā' does not introduce the proofs here "in order not to lengthen the book or to hamper comprehension," but in a series of examples he defines basic concepts and terms, and also defines the operations of multiplication and division of both whole numbers and fractions.

Abū'l Wafā''s book indicates that the Indian decimal positional system of numeration with the use of numerals—which Baghdad scholars, acquainted with it by the eighth century, were quick to appreciate—did not find application in business circles and among the population of the Eastern Caliphate for a long time. Considering the habits of the readers for whom the textbook was written, Abū'l-Wafā' completely avoided the use of numerals. All numbers and computations, often quite complex, he described only with words.

The calculation of fractions is quite distinctive. Operation with common fractions of the type m/n, where m, n are whole numbers and $m > 1$, was uncommon outside the circle of specialists. Merchants and other businessmen had long used as their basic fractions—called *ra's* ("principal fractions") by Abū'l-Wafā'—those parts of a unit from 1/2 to 1/10, and a small number of *murakkab* ("compound fractions") of the type m/n, with numerators, m, from 2 to 9 and denominators, n, from 3 to 10, with the fraction 2/3 occupying a privileged position. The distinction of principal fractions was connected with peculiarities in the formation of numerical adjectives in the Arabic language of that time. All other fractions m/n were represented as sums and products of basic fractions; businessmen preferred to express the "compound" fractions, other than 2/3, with the help of principal fractions, in the following manner:

$$\frac{2}{5} = \frac{1}{3} + \frac{2}{3} \cdot \frac{1}{10} \cdot \frac{9}{10} = \frac{1}{2} + \frac{1}{3} + \frac{2}{3} \cdot \frac{1}{10}.$$

Any fraction m/n, the denominator of which is a product of the sort $2^r\,3^q\,5^k\,7^s$, can be expanded into basic fractions in the above form. In the first section of his book, Abū'l-Wafā' explains in detail how to produce such expansions with the aid of special rules and auxiliary tables. Important roles in this operation are played by the expansion of fractions of the type $a/60$ and the preliminary representations of the given fraction m/n in the form $m \cdot 60/n \div 60$ (see below). Since usually for one and the same fraction one can obtain several different expansions into sums and products of basic fractions, Abū'l-Wafā' explains which expansions are more generally used or, as he wrote, more "beautiful."

If the denominator of a fraction (after cancellation of the fraction) contains prime factors that are more than seven, it is impossible to obtain a finite expansion into basic fractions. In this case approximate expansions of the type $3/17 \approx (3 + 1) \div (17 + 1) = 2/9$ or $3/17 \approx 3\tfrac{1}{2} \div 17\tfrac{1}{2} = 1/5$—or still better, $3/17 \approx 3\tfrac{1}{7} \div 17\tfrac{1}{7} = 1/6 + 1/6 \cdot 1/10$—were used.

Instead of such a method, which required the skillful selection of a number to be added to the numerator and denominator of a given fraction, Abū'l-Wafā' recommended the regular method, which enables one to obtain a good approximation with reasonable speed. This method is clear from the expansion

$$\frac{3}{17} = \frac{180}{17} \div 60 = \frac{10 + \frac{10}{17}}{60} \approx \frac{11}{60} = \frac{1}{6} + \frac{1}{6} \cdot \frac{1}{10}.$$

Analogously, one can obtain

$$\frac{3}{17} \approx \frac{1}{10} + \frac{1}{2} \cdot \frac{1}{9} + \frac{1}{6} \cdot \frac{1}{8}$$

or

$$\frac{3}{17} \approx \frac{1}{10} + \frac{1}{2} \cdot \frac{1}{9} + \frac{1}{6} \cdot \frac{1}{8} + \frac{1}{2} \cdot \frac{1}{6} \cdot \frac{1}{10} \cdot \frac{1}{10} \cdot \frac{1}{10}.$$

The error of this last result, as Abū'l-Wafā' demonstrates, equals

$$\frac{1}{4} \cdot \frac{1}{9} \cdot \frac{1}{10} \cdot \frac{1}{10} \cdot \frac{1}{10} \cdot \frac{1}{17}.$$

The calculation described somewhat resembles the Egyptian method, but, in contrast with that, it (1) is limited to those parts of a unity $1/q$, for which $2 \leq q \leq 10$; (2) uses products of the fractions $1/q_1 \cdot 1/q_2$ and $2/3 \cdot 1/q$; and (3) does not renounce the use of compound fractions m/n, $1 < m < n \leq 10$. Opinions differ regarding the origin of such a calculation; many think that its core derives from ancient Egypt; M. I. Medovoy suggests that it arose independently among the peoples living within the territory of the Eastern Caliphate.

In the second section is a description of operations with whole numbers and fractions, the mechanics of the operations with fractions being closely con-

ABŪ'L-WAFĀ'

nected with their expansions into basic fractions. In this section there is the only instance of the use of negative numbers in Arabic literature. Abū'l-Wafā' verbally explains the rule of multiplication of numbers with the same ten's digit:

$$(10a + b)(10a + c) = [10a + b - \{10(a + 1) - (10a + c)\}]10(a + 1) + [10(a + 1) - (10a + b)] \cdot [10(a + 1) - (10a + c)].$$

He then applies it where the ten's digit is zero and $b = 3$ and $c = 5$. In this case the rule gives

$$3 \cdot 5 = [3 - (10 - 5)] \cdot 10 + [10 - 3] \cdot [10 - 5] = (-2) \cdot 10 + 35 = 35 - 20.$$

Abū'l-Wafā' termed the result of the subtraction of the number 10 − 5 from 3 a "debt [*dayn*] of 2." This probably reflects the influence of Indian mathematics, in which negative numbers were also interpreted as a debt (*kśaya*).

Some historians, such as M. Cantor and H. Zeuthen, explain the lack of positional numeration and "Indian" numerals in Abū'l-Wafā''s textbook, as well as in many other Arabic arithmetic courses, by stating that two opposing schools existed among Arabic mathematicians: one followed Greek models; the other, Indian models. M. I. Medovoy, however, shows that such a hypothesis is not supported by fact. It is more probable that the use of the positional "Indian" arithmetic simply spread very slowly among businessmen and the general population of the Arabic East, who for a long time preferred the customary methods of verbal expression of whole numbers and fractions, and of operations dealing with them. Many authors considered the needs of these people; and, after Abū'l-Wafā', the above computation of fractions, for example, is found in a book by al-Karajī at the beginning of the eleventh century and in works by other authors.

In the third section Abū'l-Wafā' gives rules for the measurement of more common planar and three-dimensional figures—from triangles, various types of quadrangles, regular polygons, and a circle and its parts, to a sphere and sectors of a sphere, inclusive. There is a table of chords corresponding to the arcs of a semicircle of radius 7, which consists of $m/22$ of the semicircumference ($m = 1, 2, \cdots, 22$), and the expression for the diameter, d, of a circle superscribed around a regular n-sided polygon with side a:

$$d = \sqrt{a^2\left[(n-1)\frac{n}{2} + 3\right]\frac{2}{g}}$$

Abū'l-Wafā' thought this rule was obtained from India; it is correct for $n = 3, 4, 6$, and for other values of n gives a good approximation, especially for small n. At the end of the third section, problems involving the determination of the distance to inaccessible objects and their heights are solved on the basis of similar triangles.

Another practical textbook by Abū'l-Wafā' is *Kitāb fī mā yaḥtaj ilayh al-ṣāni' min al-a'māl al-handasiyya* ("Book on What is Necessary From Geometric Construction for the Artisan"), written after 990. Many of the two-dimensional and three-dimensional constructions set forth by Abū'l-Wafā' were borrowed mostly from the writings of Euclid, Archimedes, Hero of Alexandria, Theodosius, and Pappus. Some of the examples, however, are original. The range of problems is very wide, from the simplest planar constructions (the division of a segment into equal parts, the construction of a tangent to a circle from a point on or outside the circle, etc.) to the construction of regular and semiregular polyhedrons inscribed in a given sphere. Most of the constructions can be drawn with a compass and straightedge. In several instances, when these means are insufficient, intercalation is used (for the trisection of an angle or the duplication of a cube) or only an approximate construction is given (for the side of a regular heptagon inscribed in a given circle, using half of one side of an equilateral triangle inscribed in the same circle, the error is very small).

A group of problems that are solved using a straightedge and a compass with an invariable opening deserves mention. Such constructions are found in the writings of the ancient Indians and Greeks, but Abū'l-Wafā' was the first to solve a large number of problems using a compass with an invariable opening. Interest in these constructions was probably aroused by the fact that in practice they give more exact results than can be obtained by changing the compass opening. These constructions were widely circulated in Renaissance Europe; and Lorenzo Mascheroni, Jean Victor Poncelet, and Jakob Steiner developed the general theory of these and analogous constructions.

Also in this work by Abū'l-Wafā' are problems concerning the division of a figure into parts that satisfy certain conditions, and problems on the transformation of squares (for example, the construction of a square whose area is equal to the sum of the areas of three given squares). In proposing his original and elegant constructions, Abū'l-Wafā' simultaneously proved the inaccuracy of some methods used by "artisans."

Abū'l-Wafā''s large astronomical work, *al-majisṭī*, or *Kitāb al-kāmil* ("Complete Book"), closely follows Ptolemy's *Almagest*. It is possible that this work, available only in part, is the same as, or is included in, his *Zīj al-Wāḍiḥ,* based on observations that he and his colleagues conducted. The *Zīj* seems not to be extant. Abū'l-Wafā' apparently did not introduce anything essentially new into theoretical astronomy. In particular, there is no basis for crediting him with the discovery of the so-called variation of the moon (this was proved by Carra de Vaux, in opposition to the opinion expressed by L. A. Sédillot). E. S. Kennedy established that the data from Abū'l-Wafā''s observations were used by many later astronomers.

Abū'l-Wafā''s achievements in the development of trigonometry, specifically in the improvement of tables and in the means of solving problems of spherical trigonometry, are undoubted. For the tabulation of new sine tables he computed sin 30′ more precisely, applying his own method of interpretation. This method, based on one theorem of Theon of Alexandria, gives an approximation that can be stated in modern terms by the inequalities

$$\sin\frac{15^\circ}{32}+\frac{1}{3}\left(\sin\frac{18^\circ}{32}-\sin\frac{15^\circ}{32}\right)<\sin 30'$$

$$<\sin\frac{15^\circ}{32}+\frac{1}{3}\left(\sin\frac{15^\circ}{32}-\sin\frac{12^\circ}{32}\right).$$

The values $\sin 15^\circ/32$ and $\sin 18^\circ/32$ are found by using the known values of $\sin 60^\circ$ and $\sin 72^\circ$, respectively, with the aid of rational operations and the extraction of a square root, which is needed for the calculation of the sine of half a given angle; the value $\sin 12^\circ/32$ is found as the sine of the difference $72^\circ/32 - 60^\circ/32$. Setting $\sin 30'$ equal to half the sum of the quantities bounding it above and below, with the radius of the circle equal to 60, Abū'l-Wafā' found, in sexagesimal fractions, $\sin 30' = 31^{I}\ 24^{II}\ 55^{III}\ 54^{IV}\ 55^{V}$. This value is correct to the fourth place, the value correct to five places being $\sin 30' = 31^{I}\ 24^{II}\ 55^{III}\ 54^{IV}\ 0^{V}$.

In comparison, Ptolemy's method of interpolation, which was used before Abū'l-Wafā', showed error in the third place. If one expresses Abū'l-Wafā''s approximation in decimal fractions and lets $r = 1$ (which he did not do), then $\sin 30' = 0.0087265373$ is obtained instead of 0.0087265355—that is, the result is correct to 10^{-8}. Abū'l-Wafā' also compiled tables for tangent and cotangent.

In spherical trigonometry before Abū'l-Wafā', the basic means of solving triangles was Menelaus' theorem on complete quadrilaterals, which in Arabic literature is called the "rule of six quantities." The application of this theorem in various cases is quite cumbersome. Abū'l-Wafā' enriched the apparatus of spherical trigonometry, simplifying the solution of its problems. He applied the theorem of tangents to the solution of spherical right triangles, priority in the proof of which was later ascribed to him by al-Bīrūnī. One of the first proofs of the general theorem of sines applied to the solution of oblique triangles also was originated by Abū'l-Wafā'. In Arabic literature this theorem was called "theorem which makes superfluous" the study of complete quadrilaterals and Menelaus' theorem. To honor Abū'l-Wafā', a crater on the moon was named after him.

BIBLIOGRAPHY

I. ORIGINAL WORKS. The text on practical arithmetic has never been published in any modern language; however, discussions of it may be found in Woepcke, Luckey, and Medovoy (see below). Manuscripts of this work are preserved at the library of the University of Leiden (993) and the National Library, Cairo ([1]V, 185). Besides these, there exist the manuscript of a work containing the fundamental definitions of theoretical arithmetic: "Risāla fī'l-aritmāṭīqī," at the Institute of Oriental Studies of the Academy of Sciences of the Uzbek S.S.R. in Tashkent (4750/8), which is described by G. P. Matvievskaja (see below); an unstudied arithmetical manuscript at the Escorial (Casiri, 933); and an unstudied arithmetical manuscript at the Library Raza, Rampur (I, 414). The text on geometric constructions has been studied in a Persian variant (Paris, Bibliothèque Nationale, pers. anc., 169) by Woepcke; Suter has studied the Milan manuscript (Biblioteca Ambrosiana, arab. 68); and a Russian translation by Krasnova of the Istanbul manuscript (Aya Sofya, 2753) has appeared. Eleven of the thirteen chapters of the latter are extant. The manuscript of the *al-Majisṭī,* only part of which has survived, is in Paris (Bibliothèque Nationale, ar. 2497) and has been studied by Carra de Vaux (see below). MS Istanbul, Carullah, 1479, is unstudied.

II. SECONDARY LITERATURE. General works concerning Abū'l-Wafā' are A. von Braunmühl, *Vorlesungen über Geschichte der Trigonometrie,* I (1900), 45–61; C. Brockelmann, *Geschichte der arabischen Litteratur,* I, 2nd ed. (Leiden, 1943), 255; Supp. I (Leiden, 1937), p. 400; M. Cantor, *Vorlesungen über Geschichte der Mathematik,* 2nd ed., I (Leipzig, 1894), 698–704, Index; Ibn al-Nadīm (Abū'l-Farāj Muḥammad Ibn Isḥāq), *Kitāb al-Fihrist,* G. Flügel, Y. Rödiger, and A. Müller, eds., I (Leipzig, 1871), 266, 283; H. Suter's translation of the *Fihrist,* "Das Mathematikerverzeichnis im Fihrist des Ibn Abī Ya'kūb al-Nadīm," in *Abhandlungen zur Geschichte der mathematischen Wissenschaften,* **6** (1892), 39; A. Youschkevitch, *Geschichte der Mathematik im Mittelalter* (Leipzig, 1964), Index; G. Sarton, *Introduction to the History of Science,* I, 666–667; H. Suter, *The Encyclopaedia of Islam,* new ed., I (Leiden–London, 1954), 159, and *Die Mathematiker und Astronomen der Araber* (Leipzig, 1900–1902), 71–72; Supp.,

166-167; and Joh. Tropfke, *Geschichte der Elementar-Mathematik*, 2nd ed., VII (Leipzig, 1921-1924), Index.

The first attention to Abū'l-Wafā''s work was F. Woepcke's "Analyse et extraits d'un recueil de constructions géométriques par Aboûl Wefâ," in *Journal asiatique*, 5th ser., **5** (1855), 218-256, 309-359, which deals with the Paris (Persian) manuscript. For an analysis of Abū'l-Wafā''s practical arithmetic, see P. Luckey, *Die Rechenkunst bei Ǧamšid b. Mas'ūd al-Kāši mit Rückblicken auf die ältere Geschichte des Rechnens* (Wiesbaden, 1951). There are two detailed investigations of the arithmetic text by M. I. Medovoy: "Ob odnom sluchae primenenija otritsatel'nykh chisel u Abu-l-Vafy" ("On One Case of the Use of Negative Numbers by Abū'l-Wafā'"), in *Istoriko-matematicheskie issledovanija* ("Studies in the History of Mathematics"), **11** (1958), 593-598, and "Ob arifmeticheskom traktate Abu-l-Vafy" ("On the Arithmetic Treatise of Abū'l-Wafā'"), *ibid.*, **13** (1960), 253-324; both articles constitute the first detailed investigation of this work. On the Tashkent manuscript, see G. P. Matvievskaja, *O matematicheskikh mkopissiakh iz sobranija instituta vostokovedenija AN Uz. S.S.R.* ("On the Mathematical Manuscripts in the Collection of the Institute of Oriental Studies of the Academy of Sciences of the Uzbek S.S.R."), Publishing House of the Academy of Sciences of the Uzbek S.S.R. Physical and Mathematical Sciences Series, pt. 9 (1965), no. 3, and *Uchenije o chisle na siednevekovom Vostoke* ("Number Theory in the Orient During the Middle Ages"); (Tashkent, 1967). An exposition of the Milan geometric manuscript is H. Suter, "Das Buch der geometrischen Konstruktionen des Abûl Wefâ," in *Abhandlungen zur Geschichte der Naturwissenschaften und Medizin* (1922), pp. 94-109. A Russian translation of the Istanbul geometric manuscript, with commentary and notes, has been done by S. A. Krasnova: "Abu-l-Vafa al-Buzdzhani, Kniga o tom, chto neobkhodimo remeslenniku iz geometricheskikh postroenij" ("Abū'l-Wafā' al-Būzjānī, 'Geometrical Constructions for the Artisan'"), in *Fiziko-matematicheskie nauki v stranakh vostoka* ("Physics and Mathematics in the Orient"), I (IV) (Moscow, 1966), 42-140.

The astronomical and trigonometrical works of Abū'l-Wafā' are discussed in Carra de Vaux, "*L'Almageste* d'Abū-l-Wéfā al-Būzjānī," in *Journal asiatique*, 8th ser., **19** (1892), 408-471; E. S. Kennedy, "A Survey of Islamic Astronomical Tables," in *Transactions of the American Philosophical Society*, n.s. **46** (1956), 2; and F. Woepcke, "Sur une mesure de la circonférence du cercle due aux astronomes arabes et fondée sur un calcul d'Aboûl Wefâ," in *Journal asiatique*, 5th ser., **15** (1860), 281-320.

A. P. YOUSCHKEVITCH

ADAMS, JOHN COUCH (*b.* Laneast, Cornwall, England, 5 June 1819; *d.* Cambridge, England, 21 January 1892)

John Couch Adams was born at Lidcot farm, seven miles from Launceston. He was the eldest son of Thomas Adams, a tenant farmer and a devout Wesleyan, and Tabitha Knill Grylls. The family circumstances were modest but respectable: Tabitha Adams' cousin was the headmaster of a private school in Devonport, and in 1836 her adoptive mother left her some property and a small income which helped support John's education.

Adams had his first schooling in a Laneast farmhouse. In 1827 he was tutored in calligraphy, Greek, and mathematics, but quickly outpaced his teacher. He developed an early interest in astronomy, inscribing a sundial on his window sill and observing solar altitudes with an instrument he built himself. In 1831 he was sent to his cousin's academy, where he distinguished himself in classics, spending his spare time on astronomy and mathematics. Teaching himself, he finished the standard texts on conic sections, differential calculus, theory of numbers, theory of equations, and mechanics. Adams' precocity convinced his parents that he should be sent to a university, and in October 1839 he sat for examinations at St. John's College, Cambridge University, and won a sizarship. He went on to win the highest mathematical prizes in his college and took first prize in Greek testament every year that he was at Cambridge.

In July 1841, Adams, having read about the irregularities in the motion of the planet Uranus, decided to investigate them as soon as he had taken his degree. He graduated from Cambridge in 1843 as senior wrangler in the mathematical tripos and first Smith's prizeman; shortly afterward he became a fellow and tutor of his college. At the beginning of the next long vacation he returned to Lidcot and began the long-deferred investigation of Uranus.

By October 1843 Adams had arrived at a solution of the inverse perturbation problem: given the mass of a body and its deviations from the path predicted for it by Newtonian mechanics, find the orbit and position of another body perturbing it through gravitational attraction. This problem required, among other procedures, the solution of ten simultaneous equations of condition for as many unknowns. Although Adams' first result was approximate, it convinced him that the disturbances of Uranus were due to an undiscovered planet.

In February 1844, Adams applied through James Challis to the astronomer royal, Sir George Biddell Airy, for more exact data on Uranus. Using figures supplied by Airy, Adams computed values for the elliptic elements, mass, and heliocentric longitude of the hypothetical planet. He gave his results to Challis in September 1845, and after two unsuccessful attempts to present his work to Airy in person, he left a copy of it at the Royal Observatory on 21 October 1845. Although Airy wrote to Adams a few weeks later criticizing his paper, he did not institute a search for the planet until July 1846.

In the meantime a French astronomer, Urbain Jean Joseph Leverrier, independently published several papers on the theory of Uranus and reached the same conclusions as Adams had regarding an exterior planet. Although Leverrier began his investigation later, he pressed his case more aggressively, and on 23 September 1846 the perturbing body—Neptune—was discovered as a result of his efforts. Johann Gottfried Galle, an astronomer at the Berlin Observatory, found the planet less than one degree distant from the point where Leverrier predicted it would lie.

Leverrier was immediately showered with honors and congratulations. Adams' earlier prediction, which agreed closely with Leverrier's, was thus far unpublished. It was first publicized in a letter from Sir John Herschel to the London *Athenaeum* on 3 October 1846 and provoked a long and bitter controversy over priority of discovery. The two principals took little part in the feud, but the issue became a public sensation. It still seems remarkable that Airy suppressed Adams' work for so long and that Adams was so reticent about pressing his claims. This behavior was, however, characteristic of Adams. The modesty that temporarily cost him some glory endeared him to colleagues and friends throughout his life.

The disparity between the credit accorded to Leverrier and that accorded to Adams was not made up for some years, but the two men met at Oxford in 1847 and became good friends. Adams was offered a knighthood by Queen Victoria in 1847 but declined it; the following year the Adams Prize, awarded biennially for the best essay in physics, mathematics, or astronomy, was instituted at Cambridge. The Royal Society gave Adams its highest award, the Copley Medal, in 1848.

In 1851 Adams was elected president of the Royal Astronomical Society and shortly afterward began to work on lunar theory. After much laborious calculation he finished new tables of the moon's parallax which corrected several errors in lunar theory and gave more accurate positions. In the meantime, since he had not taken holy orders, his fellowship at St. John's expired in 1852. He was elected a fellow of Pembroke College in 1853, and shortly afterward he presented to the Royal Society a remarkable paper on the secular acceleration of the moon's mean motion. This quantity was thought to have been definitively investigated by Pierre Simon de Laplace in 1788, but Adams showed that Laplace's solution was incorrect. In particular, Laplace had ignored a variation in solar eccentricity that introduces into the differential equations for the moon's motion a series of additional terms. Adams calculated the second term of the series, on which the secular acceleration depends, as $3771/64\,m^4$; the value computed from Laplace's work was $2187/128\,m^4$. The effect of the correction was to reduce the figure for the moon's secular acceleration by about half, from 10″.58 to 5″.70.

This paper caused a sharp scientific controversy, marked by angry chauvinism on the part of several French astronomers. Their attacks stimulated a number of independent investigations of the subject, all of which confirmed Adams' result. The matter was definitely settled in his favor by 1861, but not without hard feelings.

In 1858 Adams occupied the chair of mathematics at the University of St. Andrews, vacating it the following year to accept the appointment as Lowndean professor of astronomy and geometry at Cambridge. In 1861 he succeeded James Challis as director of the Cambridge Observatory, and in 1863, when he was forty-four, he married Eliza Bruce of Dublin. In 1866 the Royal Astronomical Society awarded Adams a gold medal for his work on lunar theory.

The brilliant Leonid meteor shower of November 1866 stimulated Adams to investigate the elements of the Leonid system. By dividing the orbit into small segments, he calculated an analysis of perturbations for the meteor group, resulting in improved values for its period and elements. This work provided another demonstration of Adams' extraordinary ability to manipulate equations of great length and complexity without error.

In 1870 the Cambridge Observatory acquired a Simms transit circle. In order to exploit it fully, Adams undertook—a rarity for him—the direction of a program of observational astronomy. The circle was used to map a zone lying between 25° and 30° of north declination for the *Astronomische Gesellschaft* program. This work was first published in 1897.

In 1874 Adams was elected to a second term as president of the Royal Astronomical Society. His scientific interest at this time turned to mathematics. Like Euler and Gauss, Adams enjoyed the calculation of exact values for mathematical constants. In 1877 he published thirty-one Bernoullian numbers, thus doubling the known number. With sixty-two Bernoullian numbers available, he decided to compute a definitive value of Euler's constant; this required the calculation of certain logarithms to 273 decimal places. Using these terms, Adams extended Euler's constant to 263 decimal places. This result was published in the *Proceedings* of the Royal Society in 1878; in the same year Adams published expressions for the products of two Legendrian coefficients and for the integral of the product of three.

Adams was a fervent admirer of Isaac Newton. In 1872, when Lord Portsmouth presented Newton's scientific papers to Cambridge University, Adams willingly undertook to arrange and catalog those dealing with mathematics. He was also an omnivorous reader in other fields, especially botany, history, and fiction. He usually kept a novel at hand when working on long mathematical problems.

In retrospect Adams' many mathematical and astronomical achievements pale in comparison to his analysis of the orbit of Uranus and his prediction of the existence and position of Neptune at the age of twenty-four. Much of his later work has been superseded, but as the co-discoverer of Neptune he occupies a special, undiminished place in the history of science.

BIBLIOGRAPHY

I. ORIGINAL WORKS. Works by Adams include MSS on the perturbations of Uranus, 1841-1846, St. John's College Library, Cambridge, England; *Lectures on the Lunar Theory* (Cambridge, England, 1900); and William Grylls Adams, ed., *The Scientific Papers of John Couch Adams*, 2 vols. (Cambridge, England, 1896-1900).

II. SECONDARY LITERATURE. See Morton Grosser, *The Discovery of Neptune* (Cambridge, Mass., 1962); Urbain Jean Joseph Leverrier, MS of the memoir "Recherches sur le mouvement de la planète Herschel (dite Uranus)," in the library of the Paris Observatory; W. M. Smart, "John Couch Adams and the Discovery of Neptune," in *Occasional Notes of the Royal Astronomical Society* (London), 2 (1947), 33-88.

MORTON GROSSER

ADELARD OF BATH (*b.* Bath, England; *fl.* 1116-1142)

Among the foremost of medieval English translators and natural philosophers, Adelard of Bath was one of the translators who made the first wholesale conversion of Arabo-Greek learning from Arabic into Latin. He traveled widely, first journeying to France, where he studied at Tours and taught at Laon. After leaving Laon, he journeyed about for seven years, visiting Salerno, Sicily (before 1116, perhaps before 1109), Cilicia, Syria, and possibly Palestine. It seems probable that he spent time also in Spain, on the evidence of his manifold translations from the Arabic (particularly his translation of the astronomical tables of al-Khwārizmī, from the revised form of the Spanish astronomer Maslama al-Majrīṭī).

It may be, however, that he learned his Arabic in Sicily and received Spanish-Arabic texts from other Arabists who had lived in or visited Spain, for example, Petrus Alphonsus and Johannes Ocreatus. He is found in Bath once more in 1130 when his name is mentioned in the Pipe Roll for 31 Henry I as receiving 4*s.* 6*d.* from the sheriff of Wiltshire. There are several indications in his writings of some association with the royal court. The dedication of his *Astrolabe* to a young Henry (*regis nepos*) seems to indicate a date of composition for that work between 1142 and 1146, and no later date for his activity has been established. F. Bliemetzrieder[1] has attempted to show that Adelard made a later trip to Salerno and Sicily, where he undertook the translation from the Greek of the *Almagest* of Ptolemy (completed about 1160), but a lack of any positive evidence and an improbable chronology militate against acceptance of this theory.

Adelard's modest contributions to medieval philosophy are found in two of his works: *De eodem et diverso* (1), written prior to 1116 and dedicated to William, bishop of Syracuse, and *Quaestiones naturales* (6), certainly written before 1137 and probably much earlier. [The numbers assigned here to the works of Adelard are those used by Haskins.[2] The author of this article has divided no. (5) into three parts, (5*a*), (5*b*), and (5*c*), and also has added a no. (15), which may reflect a further possible work.]

In the first work no trace of Arabic influence is evident, and he speaks as a quasi Platonist. From the *Timaeus*, he drew the major theme of *Philosophia* as representing "the same" and *Philocosmia* "the diverse." To the problem of universals, Adelard proposed as a kind of harmonizing of Plato and Aristotle his theory of *respectus*, that is, that the names of individuals, species, and genus are imposed on the same essence but under different aspects. ("Nam si res consideres, eidem essentiae et generis et speciei et individui nomina imposita sunt, sed respectu diverso."[3])

Both in *De eodem et diverso* and *Quaestiones naturales*, Adelard exhibits eclectic tendencies rather than strictly Platonic views. The *Natural Questions*, a dialogue with his unnamed nephew, comprises seventy-six chapters covering such manifold subjects as the nature and growth of plants (with attention to the doctrine of the four elements and four qualities); the nature of animals (including the question of whether animals have souls, which is answered in the affirmative); the nature of man (including his psychology and physiology); and meteorology, physics, and astrology.

Although professedly written to reveal something of his recent Arabic studies, no Arabic author is mentioned by name or quoted directly. Still the work shows traces of Arabic influence. The nephew describes a pipette-like vessel with holes in both ends. Water is prevented from flowing out of the holes in the lower end by covering the holes in the upper end with the thumb; "but with the thumb removed from the upper perforations the water [is] wont to flow immediately through the lower holes."[4] This is not unlike the vessel described in Hero's *Pneumatica* or in Philo of Byzantium's *Pneumatica*, which was translated from the Arabic in the twelfth century. Adelard explains this phenomenon by using a theory of the continuity of elements; no element will leave its place unless another element succeeds it; but with the upper holes covered and a vacuum formed, no air can enter the tube to replace the water. Hence the water cannot fall from the open holes below until the upper holes are uncovered and air can enter and replace it.

While there is some tendency to exaggerate Adelard's use of observation and experiment, it is clear that the *Natural Questions* exhibits a naturalistic trend, a tendency to discuss immediate natural causation rather than explain natural phenomena in terms of the supernatural.[5] This was also to become the practice of later writers such as William of Auvergne and Nicole Oresme. Adelard expressly prefers reason to authority, calling authority a *capistrum* ("halter") like that used on brutes.[6] He claims in the final chapter of the *Natural Questions* that he will write (7) on pure elements, simple forms, and the like, which lie behind the composite things treated in the *Natural Questions;* but no such work has been found.

There is extant, however, the tract *On Falcons* (8), which harkens back to the *Natural Questions.* According to Haskins, it is the "earliest Latin treatise on falconry so far known."[7] Perhaps also indicative of his interest in natural phenomena is the enlarged edition of the work on chemical recipes, *Mappae clavicula* (12), which is attributed to him.[8] However, the pristine version of that work is far earlier than Adelard. It is possible that some miscellaneous notes (14) that appear in a manuscript at the British Museum are by Adelard.[9] These are philosophical, astronomical, cosmological, and medical notes that seem to conform to Adelard's wide naturalistic interests, and the lunar cycle therein is that of 1136–1154.

Adelard's chief role in the development of medieval science lay, as has been noted, not so much in his contributions to natural philosophy as in the various translations he made from the Arabic. His translations were of a crucial and seminal nature in several areas.

Adelard gave the Latin Schoolmen their first example of the work of one of the most important Arabic astrologers with his *Ysagoga minor Iapharis matematici in astronomicam per Adhelardum bathoniensem ex arabico sumpta* (10), a translation of Abū Maʿshar's *Shorter Introduction to Astronomy.*[10] Consisting of some astrological rules and axioms, it was abridged by Abū Maʿshar from his longer *Introductorium maius.* Adelard's translation may well have served to whet the appetite of the Schoolmen for the longer work, which was twice translated into Latin: by John of Seville in 1135 and five years later by Hermann of Carinthia. Adelard also translated an astrological work of Thābit ibn Qurra on images and horoscopes, *Liber prestigiorum Thebidis (Elbidis) secundum Ptolomeum et Hermetem per Adelardum bathoniensem translatus* (11).[11]

In astronomy Adelard's most significant achievement was his translation of the *Astronomical Tables* of al-Khwārizmī, *Ezich Elkauresmi per Athelardum bathoniensem ex arabico sumptus* (3). At the end of chapter 4, the Arabic date A.H. 520 Muḥarram 1 is said to be 26 January 1126,[12] and this has usually been taken as the approximate date of translation. However, a manuscript at Cambridge gives examples for 1133 and 1134 and mentions a solar eclipse in 1133, throwing some doubt on the date.[13] These additional examples may, of course, be accretions not present in the original translation. How dependent this translation was on a possible earlier translation of the *Tables* by Petrus Alphonsus cannot definitely be determined from the available evidence. Millás-Vallicrosa has proposed that Petrus composed an earlier translation or adaptation of al-Khwārizmī's work, which Adelard then retranslated in 1126 with the assistance or collaboration of Petrus himself.[14]

At any rate, the *Tables* (comprising some 37 introductory chapters and 116 tables in the edition published by Suter) provided the Latin West with its initial introduction (in a considerably confused form) to the complex of Hellenistic-Indian-Arabic tabular material, including, among others, calendric tables; tables for the determination of the mean and true motions of the sun, moon, and planets; and trigonometric tables. (Tables 58 and 58*a* were very probably the first sine tables to appear in Latin.) In addition to this basic translation, Adelard also composed a tract on the *Astrolabe* (9),[15] continuing a line of work that began with translations from the Arabic as early as the middle of the tenth century. It is in this work that he cites his *De eodem et diverso,* his translation of the *Tables* of al-Khwārizmī, and his rendering of the *Elements* of Euclid.

Adelard's earliest efforts in arithmetic appear in a work entitled *Regule abaci* (2), which was apparently a work composed prior to his study of Arabic mathematics, for it is quite traditional and has Boethius and Gerbert for its authorities. But another work, the

ADELARD OF BATH

Liber ysagogarum Alchorismi in artem astronomicam a magistro A. compositus (4), based in part on Arabic sources, might well have been composed by him. Manuscript dates and internal evidence point to a time of composition compatible with the period in which Adelard worked. Hence the "magister A." is usually thought to be Adelard. The first three books of this work are concerned with arithmetic; the remaining two consider geometry, music, and astronomy. The subject of Indian numerals and the fundamental operations performed with them is introduced as follows: ". . . since no knowledge (*scientia*) goes forth if the doctrine of all the numbers is neglected, our tract begins with them, following the reasoning of the Indians."[16] (The section on geometry is, however, based on the Roman-Latin tradition rather than the Arabic-Indian tradition. The astronomical section returns to Arabic and Hebrew sources.) It has been suggested that the first three books on Indian reckoning have been drawn from an early Latin translation of al-Khwārizmī's *De numero Indorum* (not extant in its pristine state) or from a version of that translation revised sometime before 1143, which is preserved in an incomplete state at Cambridge and which has the incipit "Dixit algorizmi laudes deo rectori. . . ."[17] This work has been published three times: in transcription by B. Boncompagni,[18] in transcription and facsimile by K. Vogel,[19] and in facsimile only by A. P. Youschkevitch.[20] It has been suggested by Vogel[21] and Youschkevitch,[22] without any decisive evidence, that the original Latin translation of the *De numero Indorum* was executed by Adelard.

Adelard of Bath in all likelihood was the first to present a full version, or versions, of the *Elements* of Euclid in Latin and thus to initiate the process that led to Euclid's domination of high and late medieval mathematics. Prior to Adelard's translation (*5a–5c*) from the Arabic, the evidence exists that there were only grossly incomplete translations from the Greek, such as that of Boethius. Adelard's name is associated in twelfth-century manuscripts with three quite distinct versions. Version I (*5a*) is a close translation of the whole work (including the non-Euclidean Books XIV and XV) from the Arabic text, probably that of al-Hajjāj. No single codex contains the whole version, but on the basis of translating techniques and characteristic Arabicisms the text has been pieced together.[23] Only Book IX, the first thirty-five propositions of Book X, and the last three propositions of Book XV are missing.

The second treatment of the *Elements* bearing Adelard's name, Version II (*5b*), is of an entirely different character. Not only are the enunciations differently expressed but the proofs are very often replaced by instructions for proofs or outlines of proofs. It is clear, however, that this version was not merely a paraphrase of Version I but derives at least in part from an Arabic original since it contains a number of Arabicisms not present in Version I. It may be that Version II was the joint work of Adelard and his student Johannes Ocreatus or that Ocreatus revised it in some fashion since some manuscripts of Version II include a statement specifically attributed to "Joh. Ocrea," i.e., Ocreatus.[24] (In another work, addressed "to his master Adelard of Bath," Ocreatus' name is given as "N. Ocreatus.") It was Version II that became the most popular of the various translations of the *Elements* produced in the twelfth century. Apparently this version was the one most commonly studied in the schools. Certainly its enunciations provided a skeleton for many different commentaries, the most celebrated of which was that of Campanus of Novara, composed in the third quarter of the thirteenth century. Version II also provided the enunciations for Adelard's Version III (*5c*).

Version III does not appear to be a distinct translation but a commentary. Whether or not it is by Adelard, it is attributed to him and distinguished from his translation in a manuscript at the Bibliothèque National in Paris;[25] and judging from a twelfth-century copy at Oxford,[26] it was written prior to 1200. This version enjoyed some popularity and was quoted by Roger Bacon, who spoke of it as Adelard's *editio specialis.* Still another quasi commentary, consisting of a hodgepodge of geometrical problems, is found in a Florence manuscript, *Bachon Alardus in 10 Euclidis* (15).[27] It may be based in some way on a work of Adelard. Incidentally, the set of proofs for the *Elementa de ponderibus*, which were almost certainly composed by Jordanus de Nemore, is assigned in one manuscript to "Alardus."[28] Finally, in the area of geometry, note should be made of a thirteenth-century reference to a commentary on the *Spherica* of Theodosius, *Dicti Theodosii liber de speris, ex commentario Adelardi* (13), in the *Biblionomia* of Richard de Fournival.[29] No such work has been found, and the fact that the *Spherica* was translated only later by Gerard of Cremona makes it quite unlikely that Adelard did a commentary. The foregoing is an impressive list of geometrical translations and compositions; and, if by any chance, Bliemetzrieder should be proven correct concerning Adelard's role as the translator of the *Almagest* of Ptolemy, then the recently discovered translation from the Greek of the *Elements*[30] would also have to be assigned to Adelard since both translations exhibit identical translating techniques and styles.

The conclusion that must be drawn from the widespread translating activity described above is that Adelard should be considered, along with Gerard of Cremona and William of Moerbeke, as one of the pivotal figures in the conversion of Greek and Arabic learning into Latin.

NOTES

1. Bliemetzrieder, *Adelhard von Bath*, pp. 149-274.
2. Haskins, *Studies in Medieval Science*, ch. 2.
3. *De eodem*, edit. of Willner, p. 11, ll. 20-21.
4. *Quaestiones naturales*, edit. of Müller, ch. 58, p. 53.
5. *Ibid.*, ch. 4, p. 8.
6. *Ibid.*, ch. 6, p. 11.
7. Haskins, p. 28.
8. Brit. Mus., Royal MS 15.C.iv., Table of Contents.
9. Brit. Mus., Old Royal and King's Collections, MS 7.D.xxv.
10. Oxford, Bodleian Lib. MS Digby 68, 116r. The opening paragraphs are published in Richard Lemay, *Abu Maʿshar*, p. 355.
11. MS Lyons 328, 70r-74r, is among the extant MSS.
12. Edit. of Suter in Björnbo et al., ch. 4, p. 5.
13. Oxford, Corpus Christi Coll. MS 283, f. 142r.
14. Millás-Vallicrosa, *Nuevos estudios*, p. 107.
15. Cf. Cambridge, Fitzwilliam Mus., McClean MS 165, ff. 81r-88r, and Brit. Mus. Arundel MS 377, ff. 69r-74r.
16. *Liber ysagogarum*, edit. of Curtze, p. 18.
17. Cambridge Univ. Lib. MS Ii.6.5.
18. *Trattati d'aritmetica*, pp. 1-23.
19. *Mohammed ibn Musa Alchwarizmi's Algorismus*.
20. "Über ein Werk," pp. 1-63; cf. his earlier paper, in Russian, cited on p. 22, n. 2.
21. *Op. cit.*, p. 43.
22. *Op. cit.*, p. 22.
23. Clagett, "The Medieval Latin Translations," p. 18.
24. *Ibid.*, p. 21.
25. Paris, BN MS Lat. 16648, f. 58r.
26. Oxford, Balliol Coll. MS 257.
27. Biblioteca Nazionale Centrale Conv. Soppr. J.IX.26, 46r-55r.
28. Oxford, Corpus Christi Coll., MS 251, 10r-12v.
29. Haskins, p. 31.
30. Cf. Paris, BN MS Lat. 7377 and Florence, Biblioteca Nazionale Centrale Conv. Soppr. C.I.448.

BIBLIOGRAPHY

Among the works of Adelard of Bath available in modern editions and in manuscript form are the following: *De eodem et diverso*, edit. of H. Willner, in *Beiträge zur Geschichte der Philosophie des Mittelalters*, **4**, Heft 1 (1903); (?) *Liber ysagogarum Alchorismi in artem astronomicam a magistro A. compositus*, MSS Paris, BN Lat. 16208, ff. 67r-71r; Milan, Ambrosian Lib., A. 3 sup., ff. 1r-20r; Munich, Staatsbibliothek, Cod. 13021, ff. 27r-68v, Cod. 18927, ff. 31r *seq.*; Vienna, Nationalbibliothek, Cod. 275, f. 27r; first three books, edit. of M. Curtze, in *Abhandlungen zur Geschichte der Mathematik*, Heft 8 (1898), 1-27; *Quaestiones naturales*, edit. of M. Müller, in *Beiträge zur Geschichte der Philosophie und Theologie des Mittelalters*, **31**, Heft 2 (1934); *Regule abaci*, edit. of B. Boncompagni, in *Bullettino di bibliografia e di storia delle scienze matematiche e fisiche*, **14** (1881), 1-134.

For the texts of Adelard's translations and studies on his activities, see A. Björnbo, R. Besthorn, and H. Suter, *Die astronomischen Tafeln des Muhammed ibn Mūsā al-Khwārizmī in der Bearbeitung des Maslama ibn Ahmed al-Madjrītī* (Copenhagen, 1914); F. Bliemetzrieder, *Adelhard von Bath* (Munich, 1935); B. Boncompagni, *Trattati d'aritmetica, I. Algoritmi de numero Indorum* (Rome, 1857), pp. 1-23; M. Clagett, "The Medieval Latin Translations from the Arabic of the *Elements* of Euclid, with Special Emphasis on the Versions of Adelard of Bath," in *Isis*, **44** (1953), 16-42; C. H. Haskins, *Studies in the History of Mediaeval Science*, 2nd ed. (Cambridge, Mass., 1927), pp. 20-42; R. Lemay, *Abu Maʿshar and Latin Aristotelianism in the Twelfth Century* (Beirut, 1962), p. 355; and J. M. Millás-Vallicrosa, "La aportación astronómica de Pedro Alfonso," in *Sefarad*, **3** (1943), 65-105, and *Nuevos estudios sobre historia de la ciencia española* (Barcelona, 1960), pp. 105-108; O. Neugebauer, *The Astronomical Tables of al-Khwārizmī. Translation with Commentaries of the Latin Versions edited by H. Suter supplemented by Corpus Christi College MS 283* (Copenhagen, 1962); T. Phillipps, "The *Mappae Clavicula*; a Treatise on the Preparation of Pigments During the Middle Ages," in *Archaeologia*, **32** (1847), 183-244; G. Sarton, *Introduction to the History of Science*, II (Baltimore, 1931), 167-169; L. Thorndike, *A History of Magic and Experimental Science*, II (New York, 1923), 19-49; K. Vogel, *Mohammed ibn Musa Alchwarizmi's Algorismus* (Aalen, 1963); A. P. Youschkevitch, "Über ein Werk des ʿAbdallah Muḥammad ibn Mūsā al-Ḫuwārizmī al-Maǧūsī zur Arithmetik der Inder," in *Beiheft 1964 zur Schriftenreihe Geschichte der Naturwissenschaften, Technik und Medizin*, pp. 1-63.

MARSHALL CLAGETT

ADRAIN, ROBERT (*b.* Carrickfergus, Ireland, 30 September 1775; *d.* New Brunswick, New Jersey, 10 August 1843)

Adrain was a teacher in Ireland and took part in the rebellion of 1798. With his wife, Ann Pollock, he escaped to America, where he first served as a master at Princeton Academy, then moved to York, Pennsylvania, as principal of the York County Academy. In 1805 he became principal of the academy in Reading, Pennsylvania. From 1809 to 1813 Adrain was professor of mathematics at Queen's College (now Rutgers), New Brunswick, New Jersey, and from 1813 to 1826 at Columbia College, New York. He then returned to Queen's College for a short while. He taught from 1827 to 1834 at the University of Pennsylvania in Philadelphia, where in 1828 he became vice-provost. From 1836 to 1840 he taught at the grammar school of Columbia College, after which he returned to New Brunswick. It is reported that in the classroom he often showed impatience with ill-prepared students. He had seven children, one of whom, Garnett Bowditch Adrain (1815–1878), was a Democratic member of Congress from New Brunswick between 1857 and 1861.

Adrain's first mathematical contributions were in George Baron's *Mathematical Correspondent* (1804), in which he solved problems and wrote on the steering of a ship and on Diophantine algebra. He continued the latter subject in *The Analyst* (1808), a short-lived periodical that he published himself. Here we find Adrain's most interesting mathematical paper, a study of errors in observations with the first two published demonstrations of the normal (exponential) law of errors. Gauss's work was not published until 1809. This volume also contains Adrain's paper on what he calls isotomous curves, inspired by Rittenhouse's hygrometer. If a family of curves (e.g., circles or parabolas) are all tangent at a point A, then an isotomous curve cuts these curves at equal arcs measured from A. Another article deals with the *catenaria volvens,* the form taken by a homogeneous, flexible, nonelastic string uniformly revolving about two points, without gravity.

Adrain shares with his contemporary Nathaniel Bowditch the honor of being the first creative mathematician in America. Like Bowditch, he was an ardent student of Laplace, and his paper on errors is in the spirit of Laplace.

Adrain became a member of the American Philosophical Society in 1812, and six years later he published in its *Transactions* a paper on the figure of the earth, in which he found 1/319 as its ellipticity (Laplace had 1/336; the modern value is 1/297). In the same issue of the *Transactions* he also published a paper on the mean diameter of the earth. Both papers were inspired by Laplace.

BIBLIOGRAPHY

I. Original Works. Adrain's papers include "A Disquisition Concerning the Motion of a Ship Which Is Steered in a Given Point of the Compass," in *Mathematical Correspondent,* **1** (1804), 103–114; "Research Concerning the Probabilities of the Errors Which Happen in Making Observations," in *The Analyst,* **1** (1808), 93–109; "Researches Concerning Isotomous Curves," *ibid.,* 58–68; "Investigation of the Figure of the Earth and of the Gravity in Different Latitudes," in *Transactions of the American Philosophical Society,* n.s. **1** (1818), 119–135; and "Research Concerning the Mean Diameter of the Earth," *ibid.,* 352–366. He also contributed to *Portico,* **3** (1817); *Scientific Journal and Philosophical Magazine* (1818–1819); *Ladies and Gentleman's Diary* (1819–1822); and *The Mathematical Diary* (1825–1833), of which he edited the first six issues. In addition, Adrain prepared American editions of T. Keith, *A New Treatise on the Use of Globes* (New York, 1811); and C. Hutton, *Course in Mathematics* (New York, 1812).

II. Secondary Literature. The most easily available source of information on Adrain is J. L. Coolidge, "Robert Adrain and the Beginnings of American Mathematics," in *American Mathematical Monthly,* **33** (1926), 61–76, with an analysis of Adrain's mathematical work. On his theory of errors, see also O. R. Seinin, "R. Adrain's Works in the Theory of Errors and Its Applications," in *Istoriko-matematicheskie issledovaniya,* **16** (1965), 325–336 (in Russian). An early source is an article in *United States Magazine and Democratic Review,* **14** (1844), 646–652, supposedly written by Adrain's son Garnett. See also G. E. Pettengill, in *Historical Review of Berks County (Penna.),* **8** (1943), 111–114; and D. E. Smith, in *Dictionary of American Biography,* I (1928), 109–110.

Coolidge mentions the existence of manuscript material of Adrain's on which M. J. Babb of Princeton was working. These papers seem to have been lost after Babb's death in 1945. The library of the American Philosophical Society has some letters by and concerning Adrain to John Vaughan in Philadelphia, and a letter written to Adrain by M. Roche in 1831.

D. J. Struik

AEPINUS, FRANZ ULRICH THEODOSIUS

(*b.* Rostock, Germany, 13 December 1724; *d.* Dorpat, Russia [now Tartu, Estonian Soviet Socialist Republic], 10 August 1802)

Aepinus came from a family long distinguished for its learning. His great-grandfather, who had translated the family name, Hoeck, into Greek, had been an important evangelical theologian. His father held the chair of theology and his elder brother that of oratory at the University of Rostock. Aepinus studied medicine and mathematics at Jena, particularly under the guidance of G. E. Hamberger, and at Rostock, where he took his M.A. in 1747 with a dissertation on the paths of falling bodies. Until 1755 he taught mathematics at Rostock, as a junior lecturer, and published only on mathematical subjects: the properties of algebraic equations, the integration of partial differential equations, the concept of negative numbers. In 1751–1752 one of his auditors was J. C. Wilcke, who had come to Rostock to study under Franz's brother. With Franz's encouragement and instruction, Wilcke concentrated on physics and mathematics, and soon decided against the clerical career for which his father had intended him. A few years later Wilcke played an equally important role in reorienting his mentor's professional career.

In the spring of 1755 Aepinus became director of the observatory in Berlin and a member of the Academy of Sciences there. These appointments were apparently merely a device for establishing Aepinus, who had begun to acquire a reputation, in Frederick's capital: he was neither especially interested nor experienced in astronomy, and his closest published approach to the subject during his Berlin sojourn was a mathematical analysis of a micrometer adapted to a quadrant circle. His main preoccupation at the time was the study of the tourmaline, to which he was introduced by Wilcke, who had followed him to Berlin. Aepinus' first researches on the thermoelectric properties of this stone, which was then of extreme rarity, were fundamental. He recognized the electrical nature of the attractive power of a warmed tourmaline and attempted, not altogether successfully, to reduce its apparent capriciousness to rule. He was particularly struck by the formal similarity between the tourmaline and the magnet in regard to polarity, which inspired him to reconsider the possibility, then occasionally discussed, that electricity and magnetism were basically analogous. This thought became the theme for his masterwork, *Tentamen theoriae electricitatis et magnetismi* (1759).

In experimenting on the tourmaline Aepinus was often assisted by Wilcke, who was then preparing a dissertation on electricity. Their closeness made it natural for Wilcke to bring to Aepinus' attention certain phenomena he had discovered that apparently conflicted with Franklin's principles. In seeking an explanation, Aepinus came to the anti-Franklinian idea of a Leyden jar without the glass. The success of this air condenser eventually helped to persuade many to abandon Franklin's special assumptions about electrical atmospheres and the electricity of glass, and to prepare the ground for more general views of the kind Aepinus urged in his *Tentamen.*

In October 1756 Aepinus asked to be relieved of his positions in Berlin in order to accept the directorship of the observatory and the professorship of physics, vacant since the death of Richmann, at the Imperial Academy of St. Petersburg. Euler, with whom he boarded in Berlin, warmly recommended him for the job and interceded with Frederick to procure his release, which occurred in the spring of 1757. The Petersburg academicians expected that Aepinus, as befitted Richmann's successor, would continue to work on electricity. They were not disappointed. Late in 1758 Aepinus completed the lengthy *Tentamen,* which the Academy rushed into print before its author could finish his polishing.

The *Tentamen* is one of the most original and important books in the history of electricity. It is the first reasoned, fruitful exposition of electrical phenomena based on action-at-a-distance. Aepinus emphatically rejects the current notion of electrical atmospheres. Not that he believes that bodies act where they are not: he merely takes literally Newton's precepts about natural philosophy, and deduces the phenomena from certain assumed forces, without inquiring into the manner in which the forces themselves might be effected. Three such forces, according to him, create all the appearances of electricity: a repulsion between the particles of the electric fluid, an attraction between them and the corpuscles of common matter, and a repulsion between the corpuscles. This last is necessary to prevent unelectrified bodies—bodies with their normal complement of electrical fluid—from attracting one another. Aepinus observes that although such a repulsion might appear to conflict with universal gravitation there is no reason not to suppose several types of forces between matter corpuscles, and in fact the phenomena require it. As for the law of force, it is proportional to the excess or deficiency of fluid, and the same for all pairs of particles and corpuscles. Aepinus does not pretend to know its precise form. Analogy, he thinks, favors the inverse square, which he uses in one numerical application; but generally he leaves the matter open, the great unanswered question in electrical theory.

Aepinus does not need the precise law, however, to explain the phenomena qualitatively. He is particularly successful with induction effects, which had puzzled philosophers since Canton's experiments of 1752; his explanations, with appropriate terminological changes, are essentially those used in elementary electrostatics today. Although his exposition is not quantitative, it is mathematical, with symbols used to indicate the excess or deficiency of fluid and the associated forces. Assuming that the forces decrease with distance, he is able to anticipate the direction of electrical interactions. In this way he predicts apparently paradoxical phenomena, e.g., that if two bodies with like charges of greatly different strengths are pushed together, their repulsion will at some point change to attraction. The magnetic theory of the *Tentamen* operates on the same principles, except that the magnetic fluid can freely penetrate all substances but iron, in which it is so tightly held that it can neither increase nor decrease. A piece of iron is thus to the magnetic fluid what a perfect insulator would be to the electric. All magnetic phenomena depend on the displacement of the magnetic fluid within iron. Aepinus' analysis of magnetization is exactly analogous to his treatment of electrical induction; it is adequate to all problems he considers except the formation of two magnets by the halving of one. Most notably it leads him to improve on Canton's and Michell's method of preparing artificial magnets, and on the usual disposition of armatures.

In 1760 or 1761 Aepinus became instructor to the Corps of Imperial Cadets, a position that left him too little time to fulfill his duties at the academy. The observatory was seldom used, and the equipment in the physics laboratory deteriorated. These circumstances gave Lomonosov the opportunity for a furious attack on Aepinus, whose haughtiness toward Russian scientists and quick preferment at court had already irritated him. Despite such unfavorable conditions, Aepinus continued for a few years to produce papers on various mathematical and physical subjects. He published the most important and coherent of these, several dissertations on the tourmaline, along with some criticism and corrections of his earlier work, as *Recueil des différents mémoires sur la tourmaline* (1762). Among the more occasional pieces, perhaps the most interesting are a masterful discussion of the mercurial phosphorus and a critical examination of Mayer's theory of magnetism, both of which appeared in the *Novi commentarii* of the Petersburg Academy for 1766–1767. About that time Aepinus' scientific activity ceased almost entirely. He became preceptor to the crown prince, a member of the prestigious Order of St. Anne, an educational reformer, a diplomat, a courtier, and finally a privy councillor. In 1798, after forty years in Russia, he resigned his offices and retired to Dorpat.

Except for his work on the tourmaline, which established a new subject, it is difficult to assess Aepinus' immediate influence. He had no distinguished students besides Wilcke. His contributions to mathematics, astronomy, and optics were competent but not outstanding. The *Tentamen* was at first not widely read. It was not easy to find (Beccaria had not seen a copy as late as 1772), and it was not easy to read (it demanded greater mathematical facility than most physicists then possessed). Although it was known and praised by Volta, Cavendish, and Coulomb, those physicists appear largely to have developed their own views before they came across it. But, less directly, the *Tentamen* was of great importance. Most of its content became easily available in 1780 in the excellent nonmathematical epitome composed by R. J. Haüy, who managed to preserve the spirit and clarity of the original. A much less adequate notice appeared in Priestley's *History*. Through such means the message of the *Tentamen* became widely diffused. Those who returned to the original then discovered in it a model for the application of mathematics to electricity and magnetism, and a store of apposite experiments. As one can see from P. T. Riess's *Die Lehre von der Reibungselektricität* (1853), the *Tentamen* remained an important source until the middle of the nineteenth century.

BIBLIOGRAPHY

I. Original Works. Aepinus' most important works are "Mémoire concernant quelques nouvelles expériences électriques remarkables," in *Histoire de l'Académie Royale des Sciences de Berlin* (1756), 105–121; *Tentamen theoriae electricitatis et magnetismi* (St. Petersburg, 1759); *Recueil des différents mémoires sur la tourmaline* (1762); and the discussions of phosphorus and Mayer's theory of magnetism in *Novi commentarii* of the Imperial Academy (1766–1767). The best bibliography is in Poggendorff, to which should be added *Commentatio de notatione quantitatis negativae* (Rostock, 1754); and "Two Letters on Electrical and Other Phenomena," in *Transactions of the Royal Society of Edinburgh*, **2** (1790), 234–244. In addition, there are a few essays, in Russian, listed in Ia. G. Dorfman, ed., *Teoriia elektrichestva i magnetizma* (Moscow, 1951), a modern translation of the *Tentamen* and of Aepinus' contributions to the *Recueil*. Notes on Aepinus' lectures in Rostock, taken by Wilcke, are preserved in the library of the Swedish Academy of Sciences; other manuscripts may exist in the Soviet Union.

II. Secondary Literature. Biographical information about Aepinus is sparse and scattered. The older, standard biographical entries are summarized and slightly expanded in W. Lorey's notice in *Allgemeine deutsche Biographie* and in H. Pupke, "Franz Ulrich Theodosius Aepinus," in *Naturwissenschaften*, **37** (1950), 49–52. For other data, see Euler's correspondence, particularly A. P. Youschkevitch and E. Winter, eds., *Die Berliner und die Petersburger Akademie der Wissenschaften im Briefwechsel Leonhard Eulers. I. Der Briefwechsel L. Eulers mit G. F. Müller* (Berlin, 1959); A. A. Morosow, *Michail Wassilyewitsch Lomonossow 1711–1765* (Berlin, 1954); and E. Winter, ed., *Die Registres der Berliner Akademie der Wissenschaften 1746–1766* (Berlin, 1957).

For Aepinus' work, see Dorfman's essay in *Teoriia* (above); Haüy's abridgment, *Exposition raisonée de la théorie de l'électricité et du magnetisme d'après les principes de M. Aepinus* (Paris, 1787); C. W. Oseen, *Johan Carl Wilcke. Experimental-fysiker* (Uppsala, 1939); Joseph Priestley, *The History and Present State of Electricity*, 2 vols., 3rd ed. (London, 1775); and P. T. Riess, *Die Lehre von der Reibungselektricität*, 2 vols. (Berlin, 1853).

John L. Heilbron

AGNESI, MARIA GAETANA (*b.* Milan, Italy, 16 May 1718; *d.* Milan, 9 January 1799)

Maria Gaetana Agnesi, the first woman in the Western world who can accurately be called a mathematician, was the eldest child of Pietro Agnesi and Anna Fortunato Brivio. Her father, a wealthy Milanese who was professor of mathematics at the University of Bologna, encouraged his daughter's interest in scientific matters by securing a series of distinguished professors as her tutors and by establishing in his home a cultural salon where she could present theses on a variety of subjects and then defend them in academic disputations with leading scholars. Agnesi invited both local celebrities and foreign noblemen to his soirées. During the intermissions between Maria Gaetana's defenses, her sister, Maria Teresa, a composer and noted harpsichordist, entertained the guests by playing her own compositions.

In all her discourses at these gatherings, Maria Gaetana demonstrated her genius as a linguist. At age five she spoke French fluently. At age nine, she translated into Latin, recited from memory, and released for publication a lengthy speech advocating higher education for women. By age eleven, she was thoroughly familiar with Greek, German, Spanish, and Hebrew. The disputations were conducted in Latin, but during the subsequent discussions a foreigner would usually address Maria in his native tongue and would be answered in that language. The topics on which she presented theses covered a wide range—logic, ontology, mechanics, hydromechanics, elasticity, celestial mechanics and universal gravitation, chemistry, botany, zoology, and mineralogy, among others. Some 190 of the theses she defended appear in the *Propositiones philosophicae* (1738), her second published work.

Although the 1738 compilation does not contain any of Agnesi's purely mathematical ideas, various other documents indicate her early interest in mathematics and her original approach to that subject. At fourteen she was solving difficult problems in analytic geometry and ballistics. Her correspondence with some of her former tutors indicates that, as early as age seventeen, she was beginning to shape her critical commentary on the *Traité analytique des sections coniques* of Guillaume de L'Hospital, a leading mathematician of the Newtonian era. The manuscript material that she prepared, although judged excellent by all the professors who examined it, was never published.

In 1738, after the publication of the *Propositiones philosophicae,* Agnesi indicated that the constant public display of her talents at her father's gatherings was becoming distasteful to her, and she expressed a strong desire to enter a convent. Persuaded by her father not to take that step, she nevertheless withdrew from all social life and devoted herself completely to the study of mathematics. In the advanced phases of the subject she was guided by Father Ramiro Rampinelli, a member of the Olivetan order of the Benedictines, who later became professor of mathematics at the University of Pavia. A decade of concentrated thought bore fruit in 1748 with the publication of her *Istituzioni analitiche ad uso della gioventù italiana,* which she dedicated to Empress Maria Theresa of Austria. This book won immediate acclaim in academic circles all over Europe and brought recognition as a mathematician to Agnesi.

The *Istituzioni analitiche* consisted of two huge quarto volumes containing more than a thousand pages. Its author's objective was to give a complete, integrated, comprehensible treatment of algebra and analysis, with emphasis on concepts that were new (or relatively so) in the mid-eighteenth century. In this connection one must realize that Newton was still alive when Agnesi was born, so that the development of the differential and integral calculus was in progress during her lifetime. With the *gioventù* (youth) in mind, she wrote in Italian rather than in Latin and covered the range from elementary algebra to the classical theory of equations, to coordinate geometry, and then on to differential calculus, integral calculus, infinite series (to the extent that these were known in her day), and finally to the solution of elementary differential equations. She treated finite processes in the first volume and infinitesimal analysis in the second.

In the introduction to the *Istituzioni analitiche,* Agnesi—modest as she was, with too great a tendency to give credit to others—had to admit that some of the methods, material, and generalizations were entirely original with her. Since there were many genuinely new things in her masterpiece, it is strange that her name is most frequently associated with one small discovery which she shared with others: the formulation of the *versiera,* the cubic curve whose equation is $x^2y = a^2(a-y)$ and which, by a process of literal translation from colloquial Italian, has come to be known as the "witch of Agnesi." She was apparently unaware (and so were historians until recently) that Fermat had given the equation of the curve in 1665 and that Guido Grandi had used the name *versiera* for it in 1703.

Agnesi's definition of the curve may be stated as follows: If C is a circle of diameter a with center at $(O, 1/2\,a)$, and if the variable line OA through the origin O intersects the line $y = a$ at point A and the circle at point B, then the *versiera* is the locus of point P, which is the intersection of lines through A and B parallel to the Y axis and X axis, respectively. The curve, generated as the line OA turns (Latin *vertere,* hence the name *versiera*), is bell-shaped with the X axis as asymptote. There are interesting special properties and some applications in modern physics, but these do not completely explain why mathematicians are so intrigued by the curve. They have formulated a *pseudo-versiera* by means of a change in the scale of ordinates (a similarity transformation). Even Giuseppe Peano, one of the most formidable figures in modern axiomatics and mathematical logic, could not resist the temptation to create the "*visiera* of Agnesi," as he called it, a curve generated in a fashion resembling that for the *versiera.*

The tributes to the excellence of Agnesi's treatise were so numerous that it is impossible to list them all, but those related to translations of the work will be noted. The French translation (of the second volume only) was authorized by the French Academy of Sciences. In 1749 an academy committee recorded its opinion: "This work is characterized by its careful organization, its clarity, and its precision. There is no other book, in any language, which would enable a reader to penetrate as deeply, or as rapidly, into the fundamental concepts of analysis. We consider this treatise the most complete and best written work of its kind."

An English translation of the *Istituzioni analitiche* was made by John Colson, Lucasian professor of mathematics at Cambridge, and was published in 1801 at the expense of the baron de Masères. In introducing the translation, John Hellins, its editor, wrote: "He [Colson] found her [Agnesi's] work to be so excellent that he was at the pains of learning the Italian language at an advanced age for the sole purpose of translating her book into English, that the British Youth might have the benefit of it as well as the Youth of Italy."

The recognition of greatest significance to Agnesi was provided in two letters from Pope Benedict XIV. The first, dated June 1749, a congratulatory note on the occasion of the publication of her book, was accompanied by a gold medal and a gold wreath adorned with precious stones. In his second letter, dated September 1750, the pope appointed her to the chair of mathematics and natural philosophy at Bologna.

But Agnesi, always retiring, never actually taught at the University of Bologna. She accepted her position as an honorary one from 1750 to 1752, when her father was ill. After his death in 1752 she gradually withdrew from all scientific activity. By 1762 she was so far removed from the world of mathematics that she declined a request of the University of Turin to act as referee for the young Lagrange's papers on the calculus of variations.

The years after 1752 were devoted to religious studies and social work. Agnesi made great material sacrifices to help the poor of her parish. She had always mothered her numerous younger brothers (there were twenty-one children from Pietro Agnesi's three marriages), and after her father's death she took his place in directing their education. In 1771 Agnesi became directress of the Pio Albergo Trivulzio, a Milanese home for the aged ill and indigent, a position she held until her death.

BIBLIOGRAPHY

I. ORIGINAL WORKS. Agnesi's main works are *Propositiones philosophicae* (Milan, 1738) and *Analytical Institutions,* an English translation of the *Istituzioni analitiche* by the Rev. J. Colson (London, 1801).

II. SECONDARY LITERATURE. Further information about Agnesi and her work may be found in L. Anzoletti, *Maria Gaetana Agnesi* (Milan, 1900); A. F. Frisi, *Elogio storico di Domina Maria Gaetana Agnesi milanese* (Milan, 1799); and A. Masotti, "Maria Gaetana Agnesi," in *Rendiconti del seminario matematico e fisico di Milano,* **14** (1940), 1–39.

EDNA E. KRAMER

AGUILON, FRANÇOIS D' (*b.* Brussels, Belgium, 1546; *d.* Antwerp, Belgium, 1617)

The son of the secretary to Philip II, Aguilon became a Jesuit in 1586. After having taught syntax and logic, then theology, he was charged with organizing in Belgium the teaching of the exact sciences, which were useful in commerce, geography, navigation, and architecture, as well as military activities. This project led to the composition of a master treatise on optics that synthesized the works of Euclid, Ibn al-Haytham (Alhazen), Vitellion, Roger Bacon, Pena, Ramus (Pierre de la Ramée), Risner, and Kepler. Its organization into three sections was determined by the manner in which the eye perceives objects (directly, by reflection on polished surfaces, and by refraction through transparent bodies). Aguilon's death prevented the publication of the second and third sections, on catoptrics, dioptrics, and telescopes. Only the first part exists, with six frontispieces drawn by Rubens: *Francisci Aguilonii e Societate Jesu Opticorum libri sex juxta ac mathematicis utiles* (1613).

Aguilon treated, successively, the eye, the object, and the nature of vision; the optic ray and horopter; the general ideas that make possible the knowledge of objects; errors in perception; luminous and opaque bodies; and projections.

The sixth book, on orthographic, stereographic, and scenographic projections, remains important in the history of science. It accounts for a third of the treatise and was meant for the use of astronomers, cosmographers, architects, military leaders, navigators, painters, and engravers. It places particular emphasis on stereographic projection—a type of projection, used by Ptolemy, in which the portion of the sphere to be represented is projected from the pole onto the plane of the equatorial circle.

The balance of the treatise is of interest for the history of optics: description of the eye; controversies on the nature of light and its action; the application of mathematics to optics; the analysis of the concepts of distance, quantity, shape, place, position, continuity, discontinuity, movement, rest, transparency, opacity, shadow, light, resemblance, beauty, and deformity; and explanation of the various errors of perception linked to distance, size, position, shape, place, number, movement, rest, transparency, and opacity.

Book 5, in spite of an Aristotelian concept of light, studies the propagation of light, the limit of its action, the phenomena produced by the combinations of light sources, and the production of shadows. Aguilon proposes an experimental apparatus, drawn by Rubens, that made it possible to study the variations of intensity according to variations in distance and to compare lights of different intensities. This attempt to apply mathematics to the intensity of light was continued by Mersenne, then by Claude Milliet de Chales, and resulted in Bouguer's photometer.

BIBLIOGRAPHY

Aguilon's only work is *Francisci Aguilonii e Societate Jesu Opticorum libri sex juxta ac mathematicis utiles* (Antwerp, 1613; Würzburg, 1685; Nuremberg, 1702).

Writings on Aguilon or his work are P. Alegambe, *Bibliotheca scriptorum Societatis Jesu* (Antwerp, 1643), p. 112; A. de Backer, *Bibliothèque des écrivains de la Compagnie de Jésus* (Liège, 1853); Michel Chasles, *Aperçu historique sur l'origine et le développement des méthodes en géométrie* (Brussels, 1837), pp. 222, 517; F. V. Goethals, *Histoire des lettres, des sciences et des arts en Belgique et dans les pays limitrophes*, I (Brussels, 1840), 149, 153; J. E. Morère, "La photométrie: Les sources de l'Essai d'optique sur la gradation de la lumière de Pierre Bouguer, 1729," in *Revue d'histoire des sciences*, **18**, no. 4 (1965), 337-384; L. Moréri, *Dictionnaire historique* (Paris, 1749), I, 231; V. G. Poudra, *Histoire de la perspective ancienne et moderne* (Paris, 1864), pp. 68-70; Adolphe Quetelet, *Histoire des sciences mathématiques chez les Belges* (Brussels, 1864), pp. 192-198; E. Quetelet, "Aíguillon" [*sic*], in *Biographie nationale*, I (Brussels, 1866), 140-142; and C. Sommervogel, *Bibliothèque de la Compagnie de Jésus*, I (Louvain, 1890), 90.

J. E. MORÈRE

AḤMAD IBN YŪSUF (*b.* Baghdad, Iraq [?]; *fl. ca.* 900-905; *d.* Cairo, Egypt, 912/913 [?])

Aḥmad ibn Yūsuf ibn Ibrāhīm ibn al-Dāya al Miṣrī was the son of an Arab scholar, Yūsuf ibn Ibrāhīm. Yūsuf's home was in Baghdad, but in 839/840 he moved to Damascus, and later to Cairo; hence his son was known as an Egyptian. Aḥmad's birth date is not known, although it seems probable that he was born before the move to Damascus. His death date is likewise in doubt, although the most probable date is 912/913.

Aḥmad's father, sometimes referred to as *al-ḥāsib* ("the reckoner"), was one of a group of learned and influential men. A work on the history of medicine, another on the history of astronomy, and a collection of astronomical tables are attributed to him, although no written work of his survives today.

In Egypt, Aḥmad ibn Yūsuf was a private secretary to the Ṭūlūn family, which ruled Egypt from 868 to 905. In his writing, Aḥmad made several references to one Hudā ibn Aḥmad ibn Ṭūlūn. This was probably Abu'l-Baqā' Hudā, the thirteenth son of Aḥmad ibn Ṭūlūn, and probably Aḥmad ibn Yūsuf's employer.

Aḥmad ibn Yūsuf wrote a treatise on ratio and proportion, a work on similar arcs, a commentary on Ptolemy's *Centiloquium,* and a work on the astrolabe. All the works survive in Arabic manuscript, and all but the work on the astrolabe exist in Latin translation. While it is impossible to distinguish absolutely the work of the father from that of the son, there seems to be little doubt of Aḥmad's authorship of the above four works. A number of other works are attributed to him, but these cannot be authenticated.

Aḥmad's most significant work is the treatise on ratio and proportion. This was translated from the Arabic into Latin by Gerard of Cremona and then extensively copied. Manuscript copies of the Latin version exist today in at least eleven libraries in England, Spain, Austria, France, and Italy, thus testifying to the wide interest in the treatise in medieval times. Arabic versions of the work are in manuscript form in Cairo and Algiers libraries. The work is largely an expansion of and commentary on Book V of Euclid's *Elements.* Aḥmad developed and expanded Euclid's definitions of ratio and proportion in a long dialectic argument. Having clarified the meaning of these terms, he went on to show in great detail various methods for finding unknown quantities from given known quantities when the knowns and unknowns existed in certain proportional relationships.

By applying the Euclidean definitions of composition, separation, alternation, equality, and repetition to the given proportional relationships, Aḥmad found eighteen different cases: six when there are three different quantities in the proportion, eight when there are four quantities, and four when there are six. The discussion and geometrical interpretation of these eighteen cases form the nucleus of the treatise. Since many of his proofs referred to variations on a single triangular figure, later authors have referred to his work as the eighteen cases of the divided figure.

Besides his obvious dependence on Euclid, Aḥmad acknowledged his indebtedness to Ptolemy. The latter part of the treatise on ratio and proportion is actually an extension of two lemmas from Book I, chapter 13, of Ptolemy's *Almagest.* Aḥmad also made reference to, and quoted from, Archimedes, Hero, Plato, Empedocles, and Apollonius, indicating that he was acquainted with at least some of their works.

Writing as he did at the beginning of the tenth century, not only was Aḥmad ibn Yūsuf profoundly influenced by his Greek predecessors, but also in his turn he exerted an influence on the works of several medieval mathematicians. Leonardo Fibonacci, in his *Liber abacci,* mentioned the work of Aḥmad (Ametus in the Latin form) in the eighteen cases of proportion, and he used Aḥmad's methods in the solution of tax problems. Some traces of Aḥmad's influence have been seen in the work of Jordanus de Nemore, *Arithmetica in decem libris demonstrata.* Aḥmad was cited as an authority by Thomas Bradwardine in his differentiating between continuous and discontinuous proportions. Pacioli listed Aḥmad (Ametus), along with such well-known scholars as Euclid, Boethius, Jordanus, and Bradwardine, as one of those whose work on proportions was of major significance.

On the somewhat negative side, Aḥmad was guilty of a grave logical error. Campanus of Novara, in his commentary on the definitions of Book V of Euclid's *Elements,* devoted considerable attention to Aḥmad's method of proof and pointed out a subtle but real bit of circular reasoning. In his eagerness to establish definitions and postulates, Aḥmad did, at one point in his treatise, accept as a postulate a principle that he later was to prove as a theorem. This logical error does not detract from the value of his careful classification and solution of the various cases of proportional quantities. In fact, it is for this that he is remembered: his eighteen cases of the divided figure.

BIBLIOGRAPHY

Latin MSS of the *Epistola de proportione et proportionalitate* are in Paris, Bibliothèque Nationale, MS Lat. 9335, ff. 64r–75v; Florence, Biblioteca Medicea-Laurenziana, MS San Marco 184, ff. 90r–112v; and Vienna, Oesterreichische Nationalbibliothek, MS 5292, ff. 158r–179v. Arabic MSS, with the title *Risāla fi 'l-nisba wa 'l-tanāsub,* are in Algiers, MS 176 R. 898e + 684, ff. 54r–73r; and Cairo, National Library, MS 39 Riyāḍa mīm, ff. 1–25r.

Works containing information on Aḥmad ibn Yūsuf are Abū Muḥammad ʿAbd Allāh ibn Muḥammad al-Madīnī al-Balawī, *Sīrat Aḥmad ibn Ṭūlūn,* Muḥammad Kurd ʿAlī, ed. (Damascus, 1939); C. Brockelmann, *Geschichte der arabischen Litteratur,* supp. I (1937), 229, and I, 2nd ed. (1943), 155; George Sarton, *Introduction to the History of Science,* I, 598; M. Steinschneider, "Iusuf ben Ibrahim und Ahmed ben Iusuf," in *Bibliotheca mathematica* (1888), 49–117, esp. 52, 111; H. Suter, "Die Mathematiker und Astronomen der Araber und ihre Werke," in *Abhandlungen zur Geschichte der mathematischen Wissenschaften,* **10** (1900), 42–43; and Yāqūt, *Irshād al-arīb ilā maʿrifat al-adīb,* D. S. Margoliouth, ed., II (Leiden, 1909), 157–160.

DOROTHY V. SCHRADER

AIDA YASUAKI, also known as **Aida Ammei** (*b.* Yamagata, Japan, 10 February 1747; *d.* Edo [now Tokyo], Japan, 26 October 1817)

Aida studied mathematics under Yasuyuki Okazaki in Yamagata when he was fifteen. When he was twenty-two, he went to Edo, determined to become the best mathematician in Japan, and worked as a field supervisor of engineering, river improvement, and irrigation under the Edo shogunate. His coworkers in the civil service included Teirei Kamiya, who was one of the ablest disciples of the famous mathematician Sadasuke Fujita. Aida wanted to become Fujita's pupil, and asked Kamiya for an introduction. Fujita did not receive Aida as a pupil, however, perhaps because of a falling-out occasioned by Fujita's pointing out mistakes in the problems inscribed on a tablet donated to a temple by Aida (these tablets, called *sangaku,* were hung on the walls of shrines and temples by recognized mathematicians as votive offerings—they further served as an exhibition of scholarship and as a supplement to textbooks). Aida then devoted his efforts to composing and publishing his *Kaisei sampo* (1781), in which he criticized and revised Fujita's highly regarded *Seiyo sampo* of 1781. Kamiya accordingly lost face, because he had introduced Aida to Fujita who then was insulted by him; he retaliated by publicly pointing out the faults in Aida's book. Kamiya's criticism of Aida initiated a series of polemics that, conducted in private correspondence and in more than ten published mathematical works, lasted for the next twenty years.

In this dispute Naonobu Ajima, who was a friend of Fujita, sided with Kamiya. Ajima and Fujita had both been pupils of Nushizumi Yamaji, a master of the Seki school, and the private feud was thus transformed into a rivalry between the Seki school of mathematicians and the Saijyo school established by Aida. The Seki school was the most popular of the many schools of mathematics in Japan. Yoriyuki Arima (1714–1783), Lord of Kurume, was one of its leaders and was the first to publish its secret theories of algebra. Arima personifies the anomaly of a member of a hereditary warrior class drawn, in a time of enforced peace, to mathematics of the mostly highly abstract and purely aesthetic sort; he, too, had been a pupil of Yamaji, and he took Fujita under his protection and assisted him in the publication of *Seiyo sampo*. (Arima's own *Shuki sampo* was as popular in its time as Fujita's work, and Aida drew heavily upon both books.)

In 1788 Aida published *Sampo tensei shinan,* a collection of conventional geometry problems which were, however, presented in a new and simplified symbolic notation. The same year saw the coronation of a new shogun, and Aida was released from his post to face the social and cultural dislocation of the masterless samurai. He then decided that it was heaven's will that he concentrate on mathematics; he would live on his savings and devote himself to the perfection of his studies. He also took pupils, including many from the northeastern provinces; these returned to teach in their native regions, where Aida is still revered as a master of mathematics.

In *Sampo tensei shinan,* Aida compiled the geometry problems presented in Arima's *Shuki sampo* and Fujita's *Seiyo sampo* and *Shinpeki sampo.* These were largely the problems of *yo jutsu,* the inscribing in circles or triangles of other circles, a mainstay of traditional Japanese mathematics. In his book, Aida also showed how to develop formulas for ellipses, spheres, circles, regular polygons, and so on, and explained the use of algebraical expressions and the construction of equations.

Aida was well acquainted with the mathematical literature of his time, and edited several other books. In the course of his research he developed a table of logarithms, transmitted from China, that differed substantially from that of Ajima, being calculated to the base of two.

Aida also worked in number theory and gave an explanation of approximate fractions by developing a continued fraction (a simplification of the methods of Seki and Takebe). And, by expanding $x_1^2 + x_2^2 + x_3^2 + \cdots x_n^2 = y^2$, he obtained the integral solutions of $x_1^2 + k_2 x_2^2 + \cdots + k_n x_n^2 = y^2$.

Aida was hard-working and strong-willed and produced as many as fifty to sixty works a year. Nearly 2,000 works survived him, including many on nonmathematical subjects. He was a distinguished teacher of traditional mathematics and a successful popularizer of that discipline.

KAZUO SHIMODAIRA

AJIMA NAONOBU, also known as **Ajima Chokuyen** (common name, **Manzo;** pen name, **Nanzan**) (*b.* Shiba, Edo [now Tokyo], Japan, *ca.* 1732; *d.* Shiba, 1798)

Ajima was born at the official residence of the Shinjo family, and was later stationed in Edo as a retainer of that clan. He remained there until his death, and is buried in the Jorin-ji Temple, Mita, Tokyo.

Ajima first studied mathematics under Masatada Irie of the Nakanishi school, and later he studied both mathematics and astronomy under Nushizumi Yamaji, who initiated him into the secret mathematical principles of the Seki school. He was apparently over thirty when he began his studies with Yamaji; his career before then (save for his studies with Masatada) is largely a matter of conjecture. Ajima wrote several works on astronomy soon after becoming Yamaji's pupil; it is presumed that during this time he was also engaged in helping his master to compile an almanac. After Yamaji's death, Ajima began to write on mathematics.

In the traditional succession of the Seki school, Ajima is in the fourth generation of masters. None of his books were published in his lifetime; they existed solely as copies handwritten by his students, perhaps because of the esoteric nature of the discipline. Most of the essential points of his work are summarized in his *Fukyu sampo,* a book that Ajima intended as an emendation of Sadasuke Fujita's *Seiyo sampo,* which was then a popular textbook. His pupil Makoto Kusawa wrote a preface to this book in 1799, a year after Ajima's death: although Kusawa planned to publish the work, he did not do so. Kusawa succeeded Ajima as a master of the Seki school. Masatoda Baba and Hiroyasu Sakabe were also students of Ajima; as did Kusawa, they had their own pupils, many of whom became first-rate mathematicians and continued the tradition of the Seki school until the Meiji restoration (an arithmetic book in the European style was published in Japan in 1856, and marked the end of the native forms of mathematics).

The mathematics originated by Takakazu Seki was refined by his successive pupils and tentatively completed and systematized by Yoshisuke Matsunaga and Yoriyuki Arima, who was the first to publish it. Upon this base Ajima began to develop a new mathematics; his works reflect an innovative trend toward geometry within a tradition that was basically algebraic and numerical in approach.

This trend is exemplified in the development of *yenri,* a method for determining the area of a circle, of a sphere, or of plane figures composed of curved lines.

Seki's technique for calculating the length of an arc of a circle depended upon giving a fixed number to the diameter of the circle, and was not much more sophisticated a method than that of Archimedes. His pupil Takebe used letters instead of numbers to represent a diameter and found infinite series, expressed exponentially. Matsunaga improved Takebe's method and increased the number of types of infinite series capable of representing the different elements of circles.

The *yenri* process began with the inscription in the circle of a regular polygon to divide the circle or arc into equal parts; this method was, however, by definition limited, and could not be expanded to include curves other than circles and their arcs. Ajima expanded the process by dividing the diameter or chord into equal, small segments, initiating a technique somewhat similar to the definite integration of European mathematics. The earlier Japanese mathematicians had been concerned with subdividing the circle or arc directly; it was Ajima's contribution to proceed from the subdivision of the chord. He introduced his method in his *Kohai jutsu kai,* and used it for the basis of further calculations.

Japanese mathematicians were accustomed to using exponential notation for convenience in dealing with large numbers. Integration was also easier if an exponent were used, and double integrals were thus easily obtained. In the same year that Ajima developed his *yenri* method, he discovered a way to obtain the volume common to two intersecting cylinders by using double integration, which he presented in *Enchu kokuen jutsu.* Ajima's new method was a logical outgrowth of the method he described in *Kohai jutsu kai,* and required the application of the earlier technique.

For his work with logarithms, Ajima drew upon *Suri seiran,* a book published in China in 1723 that almost certainly incorporated some of the Western principles brought to China by the Jesuits. *Suri seiran* introduced the seven-place logarithmic table into Japan, and also showed how to draw up such a table. It is apparent that Ajima knew this book, since he used the same terminology in setting up his own table of logarithms (actually antilogarithms). Ajima's table and its uses are described in *Fukyu sampo,* and there is also a copybook of the table only. The Chinese logarithmic table was useful for multiplication and division; Ajima's was not. Ajima used his table to find the tenth root, and it was also useful in finding the power of a number. Before this table could be used, however, it was necessary to find the logarithm by division. The setting up of Ajima's table, as explained in *Fukyu sampo,* is based upon $\log 10 = 1$, $\log^{10} \sqrt{10} = 0.1$; therefore, the logarithm of $^{10}\sqrt{10} = 1$, while the value of 0.1 is 258925411. Ajima's tables permitted the calculation of a logarithm to twelve places.

Ajima drew upon Japanese mathematical tradition for *yo jutsu,* problems involving transcribing a number of circles in triangles and squares. Ajima wrote a major work on this subject, which included the problem described by Malfatti in 1803: in a given triangle, inscribe three circles, each tangent to the other and to two sides of the triangle. Although this problem became known as "Malfatti's question," it is obvious that Ajima's work preceded Malfatti's, although it is not known when Ajima published his problem. Malfatti approached the problem analytically, while Ajima was concerned with finding the diameters of the circles, but it is apparent that the problems are essentially identical.

BIBLIOGRAPHY

Ajima's works include *Fukyu sampo*; *Kohai jutsu kai*; and *Enchu kokuen jutsu.*

SHIN'ICHI OYA

AKHIEZER, NAUM IL'ICH (*b.* Cherikov, Belorussia, 6 March 1901; *d.* Kharkov, U.S.S.R., 3 June 1980)

Akhiezer graduated from the Kiev Institute of People's Education in 1923, then continued his studies for the candidate degree at the University of Kiev under D. A. Grave, who was well known in the field of algebra. In his candidate's thesis, on his aerodynamic research, he applied methods of complex analysis to aerodynamic problems. He was the first to obtain a formula for the conformal mapping of a double-connected polygonal domain onto a ring.

Akhiezer was very much involved in problems of approximation theory. In 1928 he solved a difficult problem: Among all the polynomials of degree n with three fixed senior coefficients, find the least deviation from the zero polynomial in a given interval of the real axis. Akhiezer showed that the solution of this problem can be obtained with the help of Schottky's functions. This result gave impetus to further development of the classical theory of the least deviation from the zero polynomials of P. L.

Chebyshev, N. E. Zolotarev, and V. A. Markov. Akhiezer later showed that the problem of the least deviation from the zero polynomial in the case where k senior coefficients are fixed can be reduced to the problem of finding some domain that is the complex plane with k segmental sections along the real axis, and to the construction of the Green function of this domain.

In 1933 Akhiezer moved to Kharkov, where he was head of the complex analysis department and president of the Kharkov Mathematical Society for many years. In 1934 he was elected corresponding member of the Ukrainian Academy of Sciences. At that time Akhiezer and M. G. Krein began to investigate the L-moments problem: Find a density $\rho(t)$ $(-\infty \leq a \leq t \leq b \leq \infty)$ of a mass distribution with given moments that satisfies an additional condition $0 \leq \rho(t) \leq L$. Their researches in this field were summarized in *Some Questions in the Theory of Moments* (1933). They also found the precise value of a constant in the theorem of Dunham Jackson concerning the approximation of a periodic function by trigonometric polynomials (this value was obtained independently by Jean Favard).

During World War II, Akhiezer was at the Alma-Ata Mining Institute (1941–1943) and the Moscow Power Engineering Institute (1943–1947). He returned to Kharkov in 1947, the year in which his book on approximation theory was published. In it he combined new ideas of functional analysis with classical methods and presented his own results. In 1949 Akhiezer was rewarded by the Chebyshev Prize for this book.

Further investigations were inspired by S. N. Bernstein, one of the founders of approximation theory, who in 1924 had formulated the following problem: Let $\phi(x)(-\infty\ x < \infty)$ be a function such that $\inf_{-\infty<x<\infty}\phi(x) > 0$ and $\lim_{|x|\to\infty} x^{2n}/\phi(x) = 0$ $(n = 0, 1, 2, \cdots)$. Let us introduce the space C_ϕ of continuous functions $f(t)$ such that $\lim_{|x|\to\infty} f(x)/\phi(x) = 0$ and let $\|f\| = \sup_{-\infty<x<\infty} \frac{|f(x)|}{\phi(x)}$ be the norm in C_ϕ. Find the necessary and sufficient conditions on ϕ such that polynomials will form a dense set of C_ϕ. In their joint work on this problem, Akhiezer and K. I. Babenko studied an important class M_ϕ of polynomials $P(x)$ satisfying the inequality $|P(x)| \leq \phi(x)$ and introduced the expression

$$J_\phi = \sup_{Q\in M_\phi} \int_{-\infty}^{+\infty} \frac{\ln|P(x)|}{1+x^2}\,dx.$$

In 1953 Akhiezer and Bernstein found that the condition $J_\Psi = \infty$, where $\Psi = (1 + x^2)^{1/2}\phi \times$, is a sufficient and necessary condition for the completeness of the set of polynomials in C_ϕ. This result established the complete solution of Bernstein's problem. In another group of works Akhiezer studied the following problem: Among all the entire functions of a finite degree with given values or derivatives at a finite set of given points in the complex plane, find the least deviation from the zero entire function. Akhiezer also obtained a generalization of Bernstein's inequality for the derivative of an entire function of a finite degree. Later he and B. Ia. Levin extended these results to important classes of many-valued functions. In 1961 another important book, *The Classical Moment Problem*, was published. At the same time Akhiezer worked on problems connected with "continual analogues" of the classical problem of moments. He also further developed a work by Mark Kac on the Fredholm determinants of the Wiener-Hopf equation with a hermitian kernel.

Akhiezer investigated the orthogonal polynomials with respect to a weight function on a set of arcs of a circle or on a set of intervals of the real axis; he then applied these methods to inverse problems in spectral analysis. Let

$$L = -\frac{d^2}{dx^2} + q(x)\,(x \geq 0, y(0) + hy'(0) = 0)$$

be a Sturm-Liouville operator, where $q(x)$ is a real continuous function and h is a real constant. Let us assume that the spectrum of L has g gaps. Akhiezer constructed and studied a hyperelliptical Riemannian surface of genus g, associated with the operator L; the corresponding Bloch function $E(\lambda; x)$ on this surface is single-valued with respect to λ. The set $\{P_1(x), \cdots, P_g(x)\}$ of its zeros plays an important role; B. A. Dubrovin later showed that the potential $q(x)$ can be expressed explicitly with the help of the functions $\{P_1(x), \cdots, P_g(x)\}$. These results are presented in the appendix to the third edition of *Theory of Operators in Hilbert Space*. Using the above results, S. P. Novikov, B. A. Dubrovin, and more recently V. A. Marchenko obtained solutions of remarkable classes of nonlinear partial differential equations of the Korteweg–de Vries type in an explicit and effective form.

BIBLIOGRAPHY

I. Original Works. Akhiezer wrote 130 papers and 8 books. The latter include *Theory of Approximation*, Charles J. Hyman, trans. (New York, 1956); *Some Questions in the Theory of Moments*, W. Fleming and D. Prill, trans. (Providence, R.I., 1962), written with M. G. Krein; *The Classical Moment Problem*, N. Kemmer, trans. (New

York, 1965); and *Theory of Operators in Hilbert Space*, 2 vols., E. R. Dawson, trans. and W. N. Everitt, ed. (Boston, 1981; 3rd ed., 1987), written with I. M. Glassman.

II. SECONDARY LITERATURE. M. Berezanskii, A. N. Kolmogorov, M. G. Krein, B. Ia. Levin, B. M. Levitan, and V. A. Marchenko, "Naum Il'ich Akhiezer (k semidesiatiletiiu so dnia rozhdeniia" (. . . to the seventieth birthday), in *Uspekhi matematicheskikh nauk*, **26**, no. 6 (1971), 257–261; M. G. Krein and B. Ia. Levin, "Naum Il'ich Akhiezer (k shestidesiatiletiiu so dnia ruzhdeniia)" ([. . . to the sixtieth birthday]), *ibid.*, **16**, no. 4 (1961), 223–232; and, V. A. Marchenko, *Nonlinear Equations and Operator Algebra*, V. I. Rublinetskii, trans. (Dordrecht and Boston, 1988).

MOSHE LIVŠIĆ

ALBERT, ABRAHAM ADRIAN (*b.* Chicago, Illinois, 9 November 1905; *d.* Chicago, 6 June 1972)

Adrian Albert was the second of three children of Elias and Fannie Fradkin Albert. Albert's parents, originally from Russia, both immigrated to the United States, but his father's route to America had begun long before he met and married Fannie Fradkin, who was twenty years his junior. At the age of fourteen Elias ran away from his home in Vilnius for a new life in England. On his arrival he abandoned his Russian name (which remains unknown) and assumed the English surname Albert in honor of the prince consort. Although Elias taught school in England, on coming to the United States he worked as a retail merchant. This allowed him to provide a reasonably comfortable life for the family he insisted on raising in a formally orthodox Jewish, if not deeply religious, atmosphere.

Except for the years 1914 to 1916, when his family lived in Iron Mountain, Michigan, Adrian received all of his elementary, secondary, and university education in Chicago. In 1922 he entered the University of Chicago, obtaining his B.S. degree in 1926, his M.S. in 1927, and his Ph.D., under Leonard E. Dickson, in 1928. On 18 December 1927 Albert married Frieda Davis, and they took his National Research Council fellowship to Princeton for the academic year 1928–1929. Following a two-year instructorship at Columbia University, the Alberts returned to the University of Chicago permanently in 1931. Beginning as an assistant professor of mathematics, Albert moved steadily through the academic ranks, rising to the rank of full professor in 1941. In 1943 he was elected to the National Academy of Sciences, and in 1960 his university honored him with the E. H. Moore Distinguished Service Professorship. At Chicago, Albert served as the chairman of the mathematics department from 1958 to 1962 and as dean of the Division of Physical Sciences from 1962 to 1971. Albert was recognized for his leadership and service to mathematics in 1965 when he was elected president of the American Mathematical Society (AMS), a position he held through 1966. After he stepped down from his deanship in 1971, at the mandatory retirement age of sixty-five, he swiftly succumbed to the diabetes that had plagued him for many years.

Albert's contributions to mathematics ranged over three related algebraic areas: associative and nonassociative algebras and Riemann matrices. In the late 1920's Dickson's presence at the University of Chicago made it a world center for the study of algebras. In his 1923 book *Algebras and Their Arithmetics*, and in its more influential German translation of 1927, Dickson extended the theory of algebras that Joseph H. M. Wedderburn had so elegantly set up in his paper "On Hypercomplex Numbers." Wedderburn showed that the classification of finite-dimensional associative algebras over a field essentially reduced to a classification of the division algebras. From 1928 to 1932 researchers in this area pushed toward the classification of the finite-dimensional division algebras over the field of rational numbers Q. Albert was edged out in the race for this result in 1932 by the German team of Richard Brauer, Helmut Hasse, and Emmy Noether after independently hitting upon many of their ideas, most notably that of the Brauer group. At Hasse's urging, he and Albert coauthored a paper for the *Transactions of the American Mathematical Society* later in 1932 detailing Albert's contributions to this result.

Putting this setback behind him, Albert continued to work actively on associative algebras and focused most notably on determining whether all finite-dimensional central division algebras are crossed products, a question finally settled by Shimshon Amitsur in 1972. Albert's book, *Structure of Algebras*, published as a colloquium volume by the AMS in 1939, remains a definitive work on the theory of algebras and testifies to his achievements in this field.

In spite of his interest in associative algebras, however, Albert profited perhaps more from his contact with the geometer Solomon Lefschetz than with the increasingly reclusive Wedderburn during his year at Princeton. Lefschetz introduced Albert to multiplication algebras of Riemann matrices, constructs from algebraic geometry that Hermann Weyl made formally algebraic in his 1934 paper "On Generalized Riemann Matrices," published in the *Annals of Mathematics*. In a series of articles that also appeared in the *Annals* in 1934 and 1935, Albert gave necessary and sufficient conditions for a division algebra over Q to be the multiplication algebra of a Riemann matrix, the main research problem in the area. For this work he was awarded the Cole Prize in algebra by the AMS in 1939.

During the war years Albert continued his pure research efforts, concentrating on nonassociative algebras. In 1932 the physicist Pascual Jordan had defined the so-called Jordan algebra over a field for use in quantum mechanics. The algebra J over a field F of characteristic unequal to two is a Jordan algebra provided that for a, b in J, $ab = ba$ and $(a^2b)a = a^2(ba)$. Thus Jordan algebras are commutative but nonassociative. In the spirit of Wedderburn before him, Albert developed the basic structure theory of these algebras and published his main results in 1947. In addition Albert contributed to the war effort through his participation in the Applied Mathematics Group at Northwestern University, serving as its associate director in 1944 and 1945. He was also interested in the interrelations between pure mathematics and cryptography and lectured on this subject at the AMS regional meeting in 1941 at Manhattan, Kansas.

Throughout the 1950's and 1960's Albert continued his research on nonassociative algebras and frequently returned to associative questions. It was also during these decades that he contributed significantly to mathematics at the political level. He was instrumental in the late 1940's in securing government research grants for mathematics commensurate with those awarded in the other sciences. In 1950 he served on the committee to draft the mathematics budget for the newly formed National Science Foundation, and from January 1955 to June 1957 he chaired the "Albert Committee," which evaluated training and research potential in the mathematical sciences in the United States. He acted as consultant to the Rand Corporation and to the National Security Agency, and as trustee to both the Institute for Advanced Study and the Institute for Defense Analysis, after having directed the latter's Communications Research Division at Princeton from 1961 to 1962. At the international level Albert was elected vice president of the International Mathematical Union in 1970 to serve a four-year term beginning on 1 January 1971.

Although Albert's research on Riemann matrices and especially on nonassociative algebras was important, he made his primary contribution to mathematics in the field of associative algebras. His work in that area completed a major chapter in the history of algebra that had begun in 1907 with the foundational results of Joseph H. M. Wedderburn.

BIBLIOGRAPHY

I. Original Works. Albert wrote or edited eight books and 141 papers during his career. Many American graduate students in mathematics received their first introduction to advanced algebraic concepts from Albert's classic text, *Modern Higher Algebra* (Chicago, 1937), while specialists consulted his treatise *Structure of Algebras* (Providence, R.I., 1939), a work that remains one of the standard sources on the theory of algebras. Indicative of his deep interest in teaching, five of his other books were textbooks on algebra and geometry aimed at college students of various levels of sophistication.

Albert's original research focused primarily on three algebraic topics: associative and nonassociative algebras and Riemann matrices. Among his most noteworthy contributions to these areas are "A Determination of All Normal Division Algebras in Sixteen Units," in *Transactions of the American Mathematical Society*, **31** (1929), 253–260; "On Direct Products," *ibid.*, **33** (1931), 690–711; "Normal Division Algebras of Degree Four over an Algebraic Field," *ibid.*, **34** (1932), 363–372; "A Determination of All Normal Division Algebras over an Algebraic Number Field," *ibid.*, 722–726, written with Helmut Hasse; "On the Construction of Riemann Matrices: I," in *Annals of Mathematics*, 2nd ser., **35** (1934), 1–28; "Normal Division Algebras of Degree 4 over F of Characteristic 2," in *American Journal of Mathematics*, **56** (1934), 75–86; "A Solution of the Principal Problem in the Theory of Riemann Matrices," in *Annals of Mathematics*, 2nd ser., **35** (1934), 500–515; "On the Construction of Riemann Matrices: II," *ibid.*, **36** (1935), 376–394; "Normal Division Algebras of Degree p^e over F of Characteristic p," in *Transactions of the American Mathematical Society*, **39** (1936), 183–188; "Simple Algebras of Degree p^e over a Centrum of Characteristic p," *ibid.*, **40** (1936), 112–126; "Non-associative Algebras: I. Fundamental Concepts and Isotopy," in *Annals of Mathematics*, 2nd ser., **43** (1942), 685–707; "A Structure Theory for Jordan Algebras," *ibid.*, 2nd ser., **48** (1947), 546–567; "A Theory of Power-Associative Commutative Algebras," in *Transactions of the American Mathematical Society*, **69** (1950), 503–527; "A Construction of Exceptional Jordan Division Algebras," in *Annals of Mathematics*, 2nd ser., **67** (1958), 1–28; and "On Exceptional Jordan Division Algebras," in *Pacific Journal of Mathematics*, **15** (1965), 377–404.

II. Secondary Literature. Four obituary notices appeared in American journals. Nathan Jacobson's article in the *Bulletin of the American Mathematical Society*, n.s. **80** (1974), 1075–1100, systematically details Albert's most significant research and concludes with a complete bibliography of Albert's works. Irving Kaplansky contributed a less mathematical and more biographical sketch to *Biographical Memoirs. National Academy of Sciences*, **51** (1980), 3–22, which included a list of Albert's twenty-nine doctoral students. One of these students, Daniel Zelinsky, wrote a more personal memoir for the *American Mathematical Monthly*, **80** (1973), 661–665. Finally, the issue of *Scripta Mathematica*, **29** (1973), which was to have been dedicated to Albert on his sixty-fifth birthday, served instead as a memorial volume and was prefaced by a short tribute to his life and work by his longtime friend and colleague I. N. Herstein.

See also Shimshon Amitsur, "On Central Division Algebras," in *Israel Journal of Mathematics*, **12** (1972), 408–420; David Kahn, *The Codebreakers: The Story of Secret Writing* (London, 1967); and Joseph H. M. Wedderburn, "On Hypercomplex Numbers," in *Proceedings of the London Mathematical Society*, 2nd ser., **6** (1907), 77–118.

KAREN HUNGER PARSHALL

ALBERT OF SAXONY (*b.* Helmstedt, Lower Saxony, *ca.* 1316; *d.* Halberstadt, Saxony, 8 July 1390)

The family name of Albert of Saxony was de Ricmestorp; his father, Bernard de Ricmestorp, was a well-to-do burgher of Helmstedt. A brother, John, was a master of arts at the University of Paris in 1362, while Albert himself was still there. Of Albert's youth and early schooling nothing is known, although there is some evidence to indicate that he studied at Prague before going to Paris, where he obtained the degree of master of arts in 1351.

He quickly achieved renown as a teacher on the faculty of arts at Paris and was made rector of the university in 1353. During most of the period of Albert's study and teaching at Paris, the most influential figure on the faculty of arts was Jean Buridan, and Albert's own lectures on natural philosophy, represented by his books of questions on Aristotle's *Physics* and *De caelo et mundo,* were modeled closely on those of Buridan. Nicole Cresme, another pupil of Buridan, also taught at Paris at this time, and there is evidence that he influenced Albert in the direction of mathematical studies. Albert apparently studied theology also but never received a theological degree.

It is believed that he left Paris by the end of 1362, going to Avignon and spending the next two years carrying out various commissions for Pope Urban V. The pope obtained for him a benefice at Mainz, later made him parochial priest at Laa, and shortly afterward canon of Hildesheim. Albert played a major role in obtaining the authorization of the pope for the establishment of a university at Vienna and in drawing up its statutes. When the university was established in June 1365, Albert was its first rector. But he held this position for only a year; at the end of 1366 he was appointed bishop of Halberstadt and his academic career came to an end. His twenty-four years as bishop were marred by political and financial difficulties, and at one point he was even accused of heresy by some inimical clergy of his own region who intimated that he was "more learned in human science than in divine wisdom," and that he had openly taught an astrological determinism with denial of human freedom of choice. Surviving these vicissitudes, he held the bishopric until he died at the age of seventy-six. He was buried in the cathedral of Halberstadt.

Albert's writings, which were probably composed during the years when he was teaching at Paris, consist mostly of books of questions on Aristotle's treatises and of some treatises of his own on logic and mathematical subjects. Extant in early printed editions are questions on Aristotle's *Physics, De caelo et mundo, De generatione et corruptione, Posterior Analytics,* and on the "old logic" (Porphyry's *Predicables* and Aristotle's *Categories* and *De interpretatione*); a complete textbook of logic published in 1522, under the title *Logica Albertutii;* an extensive collection of logical puzzles, entitled *Sophismata;* and a treatise on the mathematical analysis of motion, entitled *Tractatus proportionum.* In unpublished manuscripts there are sets of questions on Aristotle's *Meteora, Ethics, De sensu et sensato,* and *Oeconomica;* a book of questions on John of Sacrobosco's *De sphaera;* and two short treatises on the mathematical problems of "squaring the circle" and of determining the ratio of the diameter of a square to its side. Suter's ascription of the second of these mathematical treatises to Albert has been questioned by Zoubov (see Bibliography), who attributes it to Oresme. It does in fact echo passages found in one of Oresme's known works, but since Albert often paraphrased the content of works whose ideas he borrowed, this does not prove that the work was not written by Albert. There is much uncertainty concerning the attribution of a number of these manuscript works to Albert. It has been shown that his *Questions on the Ethics,* although written by Albert as his own work, is an almost literal plagiarism of the corresponding work of Walter Burley.

Albert's significance in the history of science is primarily that of a transmitter and an intelligent compiler of scientific ideas directly drawn from the works of Buridan, Thomas Bradwardine, William of Ockham, Burley, Oresme, and other writers in the medieval scientific tradition. His works in physics are heavily dependent on the corresponding works of Buridan, to the extent that all but a few of the questions devoted to the *Physics* and the *De caelo et mundo* correspond directly to those of Buridan's works of similar title, both in form and in content. Most of the questions that Albert adds, and which are not found in Buridan's works, draw their materials from the Oxford tradition of Bradwardine and his Mertonian pupils, or, in a few cases, from the early thirteenth-century works on statics and hydrostatics associated with Jordanus de Nemore. Albert's *Tractatus proportionum* is modeled directly on Bradwardine's treatise *De proportionibus velocitatum in motibus,* although it adds some refinements in terminology and in the analysis of curvilinear motions that reflected the later Mertonian developments and probably also the influence of Oresme.

Despite his lack of originality Albert contributed many intelligent discussions of aspects of the problems dealt with, and he had the particular merit of seeing the importance of bringing together the mathematical treatments of motion in its kinematic aspect, stemming from the Oxford tradition of Bradwardine, with the dynamical theories that Buridan had developed without sufficient concern for their mathematical formulation. As a transmitter of Buridan's work, Albert played an important part in making known the explanations of projectile motion and of gravitational acceleration provided by Buridan's theory of impetus, although he tended to blur the distinction between Buridan's quasi-inertial concept of impetus and the older doctrine of the self-expending "impressed virtue." Unlike Buridan, he introduced an error into the analysis of projectile motion, by supposing that there is a short period of rest between the ascent of a projectile hurled directly upward and its descent. Yet this led him to initiate a fruitful discussion by raising the question of the trajectory that would be followed by a projectile shot horizontally from a cannon. He supposed that it would follow a straight horizontal path until its *impetus* ceased to exceed the force of its gravity, but that it would then follow a curved path for a short period in which its lateral impetus would be compounded with a downward impetus caused by its gravity, after which it would fall straight down. Leonardo da Vinci took up the problem, but it remained for Nicolò Tartaglia to show that the entire trajectory would be a curve determined by a composition of the two forces.

Albert's textbook of logic is one of the best organized of the late medieval works in the field. In its first three sections it presents the analysis of the signification and supposition of terms, and the internal analysis and classification of propositional forms, provided by the work of Ockham and Buridan. The fourth section, on "consequence," shows influence by Burley and Buridan, developing the theory of inference on the foundation of the logic of unanalyzed propositions, exhibiting the syllogism as a special type of consequence, and ending with a very full treatment of modal syllogisms and a shorter formulation of the rules of topical argumentation. The last two sections deal with logical fallacies, with the "insoluble" (or paradox of self-reference), and with the rules of disputation known as *Obligationes.* There is little that is not directly traceable to the sources Albert used, but these materials are skillfully integrated, reduced to a uniform terminology, and presented with systematic elegance.

Despite its excellence as a textbook, this work did not achieve the popularity or influence attained by Albert's *Tractatus proportionum* and by his questions on the physical treatises of Aristotle. These, printed in many editions at Venice, Padua, and Pavia, became the principal means by which the contributions of the northern Scholastics of the fourteenth century to the science of mechanics were made known to the physicists and mathematicians of Italy, from Leonardo da Vinci to Galileo himself.

BIBLIOGRAPHY

I. ORIGINAL WORKS. *Expositio aurea et admodum utilis super artem veterem . . . cum quaestionibus Alberti parvi de Saxonia* (Bologna, 1496); *Quaestiones subtilissimae Alberti de Saxonia super libros Posteriorum* (Venice, 1497); *Logica Albertutii* (Venice, 1522); *Sophismata Alberti de Saxonia* (Paris, 1490, 1495); *Tractatus obligationum* (Lyons, 1498; with Albert's *Insolubilia,* Paris, 1490, 1495); *Subtilissimae quaestiones super octo libros Physicorum* (Venice, 1504, 1516); *Quaestiones in libros de caelo et mundo* (Pavia, 1481; Venice, 1492, 1497, 1520); *Quaestiones in libros de generatione et corruptione* (Venice, 1504, 1505, 1518); *Quaestiones et decisiones physicales insignium virorum . . .,* Georgius Lockert, ed. (Paris, 1516, 1518), contains Albert's questions on the *Physics* and the *De caelo et mundo; Tractatus proportionum* (Bologna, 1502, 1506; Padua, 1482, 1484, 1487; Venice, 1477, 1494, 1496; Paris, *s.a.*).

II. SECONDARY LITERATURE. Philotheus Boehner, *Medieval Logic* (Chicago, 1952); B. Boncompagni, "Intorno al Tractatus proportionum di Alberto de Sassonia," in *Bolletino di bibliografia e di storia delle scienze matematiche e fisiche,* **4** (1871), 498 ff.; Maximilian Cantor, *Vorlesungen über die Geschichte der Mathematik,* II, 2nd. ed. (1900), 137-154; Marshall Clagett, *The Science of Mechanics in the Middle Ages* (Madison, Wis., 1959); Pierre Duhem, *Études sur Léonard de Vinci,* Vols. I-III (Paris, 1906-1913); A. Dyroff, "Ueber Albertus von Sachsen," in *Baeumker-Festgabe* (Münster, 1913), pp. 330-342; G. Heidingsfelder, "Albert von Sachsen: Sein Lebensgang und sein Kommentar zur Nikomachischen Ethik des Aristoteles," in *Beiträge zur Geschichte der Philosophie und Theologie des Mittelalters,* **22,** 2nd ed. (Münster, 1926); M. Jullien, "Un scolastique de la décadence: Albert de Saxe," in *Revue Augustinienne,* **16** (1910), 26–40; Anneliese Maier, *Zwei Grundprobleme der scholastischen Naturphilosophie* (Rome, 1951), pp. 259-274; C. Prantl, *Geschichte der Logik im Abendlande,* **4** (Leipzig, 1870), 60–88; H. Suter, "Der Tractatus 'De quadratura circuli' des Albertus de Saxonia," in *Zeitschrift für Mathematik und Physik,* **29** (1884), 81–102 (reedited and translated in M. Clagett, *Archimedes in the Middle Ages* [Madison, Wis., 1964], pp. 398–432); H. Suter, "Die Quaestio 'De proportione dyametri quadrati ad costam eiusdem' des Albertus de Saxonia," in *Zeitschrift für Mathematik und Physik,* **32** (1887), 41–56; V. P. Zoubov, "Quelques Observations sur l'Auteur du Traité Anonyme 'Utrum dyameter alicuius quadrati sit commensurabilis costae ejusdem,'" in *Isis,* **50** (1959), 130–134.

ERNEST A. MOODY

ALBERTI, LEONE BATTISTA (*b.* Genoa, Italy, 18 February 1404; *d.* Rome, Italy, April 1472)

In the twelfth century Alberti's ancestors were feudal lords of Valdarno who settled in Florence, where they became judges and notaries and were members of the wealthy bourgeoisie. In the fourteenth century they engaged in commercial and banking enterprises, organizing a firm with branches scattered all over Europe; their wealth enriched Florence. At the same time, the Albertis became involved in politics. Toward the end of the fourteenth and the beginning of the fifteenth centuries, this led to the family's exile; they sought refuge in the foreign branches of their firm. Thus Leone Battista Alberti, the son of Lorenzo Alberti, came to be born in Genoa. It is possible that he was illegitimate.

From his early childhood Alberti is said to have been precocious; little else is known about his youth. Fleeing the plague, his father went to Venice, the site of perhaps the most important branch of the house of Alberti. The father died suddenly, leaving his children in the care of their uncle, who disappeared soon thereafter. It is possible that unscrupulous relatives liquidated the Venice branch in order to make themselves rich at the orphans' expense.

Alberti seems to have started his advanced education at Padua. At any rate, after 1421 he continued it at Bologna, where he began the study of law. Overwork caused him to fall ill, and he had to interrupt his studies; nevertheless, he received a doctorate in canon law. For relaxation he took up the study of mathematics, natural sciences, and physics, subjects that he pursued to a rather advanced level. Subsequently, the decrees of exile against his family having been revoked, Alberti undoubtedly returned to Florence, or at least to Tuscany. In Florence he met Brunelleschi, who became a good friend. Between 1430 and 1432 he was in the service of a cardinal, who took him with his entourage to France, Belgium, and Germany.

In 1432 Alberti arrived in Rome, where he became a functionary at the papal court. In Rome he discovered antiquity and became the artist we know today—painter, sculptor, and then architect. His paintings and sculptures, however, have never been found or identified. As part of the papal court, he necessarily shared all its tribulations. In 1437 he was in Bologna and Ferrara with Pope Eugene IV, who was roaming all over northern Italy. He was often in Rome, yet he also served those humanistic families who ruled small, more or less independent principalities. Thus he certainly spent some time at the court of Rimini, with the Malatesta family. Here Alberti conceived and partially executed his most important architectural work, the Malatesta Temple, a chapel designed to shelter their tombs.

Alberti was, we are told, amiable, very handsome, and witty. He was adept at directing discussions and took pleasure in organizing small conversational groups. Alberti represented, perhaps even better than Brunelleschi, the first scholar-artists of the Renaissance, more inquisitive than given to realization, more collectors of facts and ideas than imaginative and creative. Still close to the expiring Middle Ages, Alberti had trouble freeing himself of its shackles on the scientific level. He was possessed of a perpetual need to know—and a perpetual need to expound his ideas—as well as a desire to mingle with intellectual equals. It is certain that from these encounters at the courts of rulers like the Malatestas, a new scientific spirit arose. In this sense Alberti occupies a place of particular importance in the history of thought. At the end of his life, aside from architectural works or such engineering projects as the attempt to refloat the Roman galleys in Lake Nemi in 1447 (on which he wrote a short treatise, now lost), he was occupied with these meetings and with the editing of his written works, which were numerous.

Unfortunately, a large part of Alberti's scientific work has been lost. It is not impossible, however, that some of his works may be submerged in the scientific literature of the age without being known. Like all of his contemporaries, Alberti inherited a fragmentary science. He seems to have been interested in isolated problems which furnished subjects for discussion but which individually could not result in anything important. It was difficult to give them a personal emphasis, for these questions had already been debated, discussed, and restated many times.

Alberti's mathematics is exactly that of his times. He wrote, at least on an advanced level, only a small treatise, the *Ludi matematici,* dedicated to his friend Meliadus d'Este, himself an accomplished mathematician. Only twenty problems were involved, some of which had to do with mathematics only remotely. Only one of them touched on an abstract question—lunules in "De lunularum quadratura," in which he furnished an elegant solution to the problem but lost his way in the squaring of the circle. On all other points he shared the preoccupation of a great number of fifteenth-century scholars, considering mathematics as a tool rather than an independent science. Often he merely applied formulas. Thus, geometry was used to calculate the height of a tower, the depth of a well, the area of a field. In this work we find notions of the hygrometer which is simply the hygrometer of Nicholas of Cusa. Alberti wrote a book of mathematical commentaries that may have contained more precise ideas, but unfortunately the manuscript has never been found.

Not much is known about Alberti's physics. He wrote *De motibus ponderis,* which has been lost also. In some of his works we can find some references to physics, but they are rather elusive ones. Some years ago the *Trattati dei pondi, lieve e tirari,* long attributed to Leonardo da Vinci, was reattributed to Alberti. It concerns gravity, density (harking back to the works of Archimedes), hydrostatics, and heat. There are only vague, undoubtedly traditional ideas on the preservation of labor. His optics is more pragmatic than theoretical, although he sets forth a theory of vision. In his opinion bodies, even dark ones, emit in all directions rays that move in a straight line. They converge toward the eye and together form a visual pyramid. This theory is also completely traditional. The camera obscura, which may be his greatest discovery, deeply impressed his contemporaries, although he perhaps borrowed this device from Brunelleschi, to whom he was greatly indebted for his studies on perspective. In his *Elementa picturae,* however, he contributed nothing more than applied geometry. He worked from the idea that the construction of similar figures was the basis for all figure representation.

Alberti displayed the same attitude in his writings on the natural sciences, in which he speculated on nature rather than on scientific data. Like many others, he admitted the roundness of the earth, and also wrote briefly on the development of its crust. He seemingly spoke knowledgeably of earthquakes, atmospheric erosion, water circulation, the action of plants on soil, plant decomposition and formation of humus, sedimentary layers, and the formation of deltas. He considered fossils merely a freak of nature.

Alberti's best-known work, containing many of his scientific ideas, is his *De re aedificatoria,* which was presented to Pope Nicolas V about 1452. The work was printed in 1485 and exerted a certain influence. It was to be a treatise on the art of engineering, but this aim was not completely achieved. Alberti dealt with lifting devices, grain bins and "other conveniences that albeit of little esteem nevertheless bring profit," water supply, ways of quarrying rock and cutting through mountains, the damming of the sea or of rivers, the drying up of swamps, machines of war, and fortresses. In this work he was concerned less with architecture per se and architectural techniques than with an actual attempt at town planning. His ideas of a city were still largely inspired by the Middle Ages, but they also contained elements clearly belonging to the Renaissance, such as the respect for urban aesthetics, perspective, and orderly arrangement. Something that certainly seems new—but we hardly know his predecessors—is the application of the entire range of scientific knowledge to town planning and architectural practice. Alberti applied his knowledge of the natural sciences to building materials; his knowledge of physics was applied to equilibrium of buildings, the flexibility of beams, and the construction of engines; and that of mathematics (still very simple mathematics) was shown in the very Pythagorean layout of cities and the arrangement of fortresses.

As was typical of his time, Alberti was preoccupied with various machines and apparatuses, some in current use and some the subject of scattered and almost confused observation which made it impossible to draw the parallels and comparisons necessary to develop a technology. He spoke of balances, clocks, sundials, pulleys, water mills and windmills, and canal locks. He developed topographical instruments and envisaged the odometer and the "sulcometer," which measured distances traveled by ships. He studied the methods of sounding in deep waters. In all of this work he manifested more interest in manual crafts than in true science.

Alberti is difficult to place in both the history of science and the history of technology. Contemporary works in these fields almost invariably cite him in their lists of scholars, but he is not credited with anything really new. He contributed no new principles, but he seems to have had a very profound knowledge. In short, he seems to have regarded science as a means for action rather than as a system of organized knowledge. On many occasions he admitted his interest in knowledge, but more for reasons of efficiency than as an abstract science, as power rather than as intellectuality. He knew only the perspective and natural science that serve the artist or the architect, and only the mathematics and physics of use to the engineer and the technician. Nevertheless, he perceived certain directions for research. He was well aware of the difference between sensation (common observation) and scientific ideas: "Points and lines are not the same for the painter as for the mathematician." Observation was a point of departure for scientific hypothesis, which must be verified by systematic observation. In the last analysis, although Alberti contributed nothing but a supplementary collection of special cases to scientific progress, he nevertheless outlined some promising avenues for future work.

BIBLIOGRAPHY

I. Original Works. In most cases only very old editions of Alberti's works are extant. *De re aedificatoria* was first published in Florence in 1485; there were many subsequent editions in Italian, and a French version appeared in Paris in 1553. *Opere volgari dei L. B. Alberti,* IV (Florence, 1847), contains *Ludi matematici. Opera inedita et pauca separatim impressa* (Florence, 1890) includes *Elementa picturae;* it also contains a treatise on perspective incorrectly attributed to Alberti. *Trattati dei pondi, lieve e tirari* was published as an appendix to Vasari (Florence, 1917).

II. Secondary Literature. There are few works on Alberti. The essential work is P. H. Michel, *La pensée de L. B. Alberti* (Paris, 1930), with an exhaustive bibliography of works published until then. There is a good chapter on Alberti in L. Olschki, *Geschichte der neuspralichen Literatur* (Leipzig, 1919). The technological aspects of Alberti's work are discussed by B. Gille in *Les ingénieurs de la Renaissance* (Paris, 1967), pp. 80–84.

Bertrand Gille

ALBERTUS MAGNUS, SAINT, also known as **Albert the Great** and **Universal Doctor** (*b.* Lauingen, Bavaria, *ca.* 1200; *d.* Cologne, Prussia, 15 November 1280)

Albert was born in the family castle and probably spent his childhood at the family manor in nearby Bollstädt—whence he is variously referred to as Albert of Lauingen and Albert of Bollstädt. His birth date could have been as early as 1193 or as late as 1206 or 1207. His family was wealthy and powerful, of the military nobility, and he received a good education.

He studied liberal arts at Padua, where, over strong opposition from his family, he was recruited into the Dominican Order by its master general, Jordan of Saxony—identified by some (but probably falsely) as Jordanus de Nemore, the mechanician. He likely studied theology and was ordained a priest in Germany, where he also taught in various priories before being sent to the University of Paris *ca.* 1241. In Paris he was the first German Dominican to become a master of theology and to lecture in the chair "for foreigners" (1245–1248). In the summer of 1248 he went to Cologne to establish a *studium generale*: among his students were Thomas Aquinas, Ulrich of Strassburg, and Giles (Aegidius) of Lessines.

He began the administrative phase of his career as provincial of the German Dominicans (1253–1256). Subsequently he became bishop of Regensburg (1260), a post he resigned in 1262. The latter part of his life was spent in preaching and teaching, mainly at Cologne. He took part in the Council of Lyons (1274) and journeyed to Paris in an unsuccessful attempt to block the famous condemnation of 1277, where some of Aquinas' teachings were called into question. His health was good and he had great powers of physical endurance, even to old age, although his eyesight failed during the last decade of his life. Albert was canonized by Pope Pius XI on 16 December 1931 and was declared the patron of all who cultivate the natural sciences by Pope Pius XII on 16 December 1941.

Albert's principal importance for the history of modern science derives from the role he played in rediscovering Aristotle and introducing Greek and Arab science into the universities of the Middle Ages. Before his time, what was to become the subject matter of modern science was usually treated in encyclopedias, which assembled a curious mélange of fact and fable about nature, or in theological treatises, which described the cosmos in terms of the six days of creation, as recounted in Genesis and variously analyzed by the church fathers. Aristotle, of course, had already made his entry into the Latin West through the translations of Gerard of Cremona and James of Venice, among others; but Christendom was generally hostile to the teachings of this pagan philosopher, particularly as contained in his *libri naturales* ("books on natural science"). In 1210, the ecclesiastical authorities at Paris had condemned Aristotle's works on natural philosophy and had prohibited their being taught publicly or privately under pain of excommunication. Although this condemnation was revoked by 1234, it had a general inhibiting effect on the diffusion of Greek science in the schools of the Middle Ages.

Albert seems to have become acquainted with the Aristotelian corpus while at the Paris priory of St.

Jacques in the 1240's. Here too he probably began his monumental paraphrase of all the known works of Aristotle and Pseudo-Aristotle, to which are allotted seventeen of the forty volumes in the Cologne critical edition of Albert's works (see Bibliography). The project was undertaken by Albert, then studying and teaching theology, at the insistence of his Dominican brethren, who wished him to explain, in Latin, the principal physical doctrines of the Stagirite so that they could read his works intelligently. Albert went far beyond their demands, explaining not only the natural sciences but also logic, mathematics, ethics, politics, and metaphysics, and adding to Aristotle's exposition the discoveries of the Arabs and of whole sciences that were not available to him. The gigantic literary production that this entailed was recognized as one of the marvels of his age and contributed in no small measure to Albert's outstanding reputation. Roger Bacon, a contemporary who was not particularly enamored of the German Dominican, complained of Master Albert's being accepted as an authority in the schools on an equal footing with Aristotle, Avicenna, and Averroës—an honor, he protested, "never accorded to any man in his own lifetime."

Like all medieval Aristotelians, Albert incorporated considerable Platonic thought into his synthesis, and even commented on a number of Neoplatonic treatises. In several places he represents himself as merely reporting the teachings of the Peripatetics and not as proposing anything new; some historians charge him, on this basis, with being a compiler who was not too judicious in his selection of source materials. Those who have studied his works, however, detect there a consistent fidelity to Aristotle's basic theses, a clear indication of his own views when he thought Aristotle in error, a repudiation of erroneous interpretations of Aristotle's teaching, and an explicit rejection of Platonic and Pythagorean physical doctrines—all of which would seem to confirm his Aristotelianism. J. A. Weisheipl, in particular, has stressed the differences between thirteenth-century Oxford masters such as Robert Grosseteste, Robert Kilwardby, and Roger Bacon (all of whom were more pronouncedly Platonist in their scientific views) and Paris masters such as Albert and Aquinas (who were more purely Aristotelian). Whereas the former held that there is a successive subalternation between physics, mathematics, and metaphysics (so that the principles of natural science are essentially mathematical, and the principle of mathematics is the unity that is identical with Being), the latter held for the autonomy of these sciences, maintaining that each has its own proper principles, underived from any other discipline.

Albert's early identification as a precursor of modern science undoubtedly stemmed from his empiricist methodology, which he learned from Aristotle but which he practiced with a skill unsurpassed by any other Schoolman. From boyhood he was an assiduous observer of nature, and his works abound in descriptions of the phenomena he noted, usually in great detail. Considering that his observations were made without instruments, they were remarkably accurate. Some of the "facts" he reported were obviously based on hearsay evidence, although he was usually at pains to distinguish what he had himself seen from what he had read or been told by others. *Fui et vidi experiri* ("I was there and saw it happen") was his frequent certification for observations. Sometimes, as Lynn Thorndike has well illustrated in his *A History of Magic and Experimental Science,* even these certifications test the reader's credulity; what is significant in them, however, is Albert's commitment to an empiricist program. He stated that evidence based on sense perception is the most secure and is superior to reasoning without experimentation. Similarly, he noted that a conclusion that is inconsistent with the evidence cannot be believed and that a principle that does not agree with sense experience is really no principle at all. He was aware, however, that the observation of nature could be difficult: much time, he remarked, is required to conduct an experiment that will yield foolproof results, and he suggested that it be repeated under a variety of circumstances so as to assure its general validity.

On the subject of authority, he pointed out that science consists not in simply believing what one is told but in inquiring into the causes of natural things. He had great respect for Aristotle, but disagreed with the Averroists of his day on the Stagirite's infallibility. "Whoever believes that Aristotle was a god, must also believe that he never erred. But if one believes that he was a man, then doubtless he was liable to error just as we are." His *Summa theologica,* for example, contains a section listing the errors of Aristotle, and in his *Meteorology* he observes that "Aristotle must have spoken from the opinions of his predecessors and not from the truth of demonstration or experiment."

Albert recognized the importance of mathematics for the physical sciences and composed treatises (unfortunately lost) on its pure and applied branches. Yet he would not insist that the book of nature is written in the language of mathematics, as Galileo was later to do, and as Roger Bacon intimated in his own lifetime. Rather, for Albert, mathematics had only a subsidiary role to play in scientific activity, insofar as it assisted in the discovery of physical causes. Mathematics is itself an abstract science, prescinding from motion and sensible matter, and thus its applications must be evaluated by the science that studies nature as it really exists, *in motu et inabstracta* ("in motion and in concrete detail").

The mechanics of Albert was basically that of Aristotle, with little innovation in either its kinematical or its dynamical aspects. One part of Albert's teaching on motion, however, did assume prominence in the late medieval period and influenced the emerging new science of mechanics. This was his use of the expressions *fluxus formae* and *forma fluens* to characterize the scholastic dispute over the entitative status of local motion. Arab thinkers such as Avicenna and Averroës had pursued the question whether this motion, or any other, could be located in the Aristotelian categories; the question quickly led to an argument whether motion is something really distinct from the terminus it attains. Local motion, in this perspective, could be seen in one of two ways: either it was a *fluxus formae* (the "flowing" of successive forms, or locations) or a *forma fluens* (a form, or absolute entity, that is itself a process). Although Albert made no clear dichotomy between these two views and allowed that each described a different aspect of motion, later writers came to be sharply divided over them. Nominalists, such as William of Ockham, defended the first view: this equivalently denied the reality of local motion, equating it simply with the distance traversed and rejecting any special causality in its production or continuance—a view that stimulated purely kinematical analyses of motion. Realists, such as Walter Burley and Paul of Venice, on the other hand, defended the second view: for them, local motion was an entity really distinct from the object moved and from its position, and thus had its own proper causes and effects—a view that stimulated studies of its more dynamical aspects.

Albert mentioned the term *impetus* when discussing projectile motion, but spoke of it as being in the medium rather than in the projectile, thus defending the original Aristotelian teaching; certainly he had no treatment of the concept to match that found in the work of fourteenth-century thinkers. His analysis of gravitational motion was also Aristotelian: he regarded the basic mover as the generator of the heavy object, giving it not only its substantial form but also its gravity and the motion consequent on this. He knew that bodies accelerate as they fall, and attributed this to their increasing propinquity to their natural place.

The cause of sound, for Albert, is the impact of two hard bodies, and the resulting vibration is propagated in the form of a sphere whose center is the point of percussion. He speculated also on the cause of heat, studying in detail how light from the sun produces thermal effects; here his use of simple experiments revealed a knowledge of the method of agreement and difference later to be formulated by J. S. Mill. He knew of the refraction of solar rays and also of the laws of refraction of light, although he employed the term *reflexio* for both refraction and reflection, as, for example, when discussing the burning lens and the burning mirror. His analysis of the rainbow was diffuse in its historical introduction, but it made an advance over the theory of Robert Grosseteste in assigning individual raindrops a role in the bow's formation, and undoubtedly prepared for the first correct theory of the rainbow proposed by another German Dominican, Dietrich von Freiberg, who was possibly Albert's student. In passing, he corrected Aristotle's assertion that the lunar rainbow occurs only twice in fifty years: "I myself have observed two in a single year."

Although he had no telescope, he speculated that the Milky Way is composed of stars and attributed the dark spots on the moon to configurations on its surface, not to the earth's shadow. His treatise on comets is notable for its use of simple observation to verify or falsify theories that had been proposed to explain them. He followed Grosseteste in correlating the occurrence of tides with the motion of the moon around its deferent. He favored the mathematical aspects of the Ptolemaic theory of the structure of the solar system, contrasting it with that of al-Biṭrūjī, although he acknowledged the superiority of the latter's theory in its physical aspects. Albert accepted the order of the celestial spheres commonly taught by Arabian astronomers; he knew of the precession of the equinoxes, attributing knowledge of this (falsely) to Aristotle also. Like most medieval thinkers, Albert held that heavenly bodies are moved by separated substances, but he denied that such substances are to be identified with the angels of Christian revelation, disagreeing on this point with his celebrated disciple Thomas Aquinas.

On the structure of matter, when discussing the presence of elements in compounds, Albert attempted to steer a middle course between the opposed positions of Avicenna and Averroës, thereby preparing for Aquinas' more acceptable theory of "virtual" presence. In a similar vein, he benignly viewed Democritus' atoms as equivalent to the *minima naturalia* of the Aristotelians. He seems to have experimented with alchemy and is said to have been the first to isolate the element arsenic. He compiled a list of some hundred minerals, giving the properties of each. During his many travels, he made frequent sidetrips to mines and excavations in search of specimens. He was acquainted with fossils, and made accurate observations of "animal impressions" and improved on

ALBERTUS MAGNUS

Avicenna's account of their formation. Albert suggested the possibility of the transmutation of metals, but he did not feel that alchemists had yet found the method to bring this about.

Extensive as was Albert's work in the physical sciences, it did not compare with his contributions to the biological sciences, where his powers of observation and his skill at classification earned for him an unparalleled reputation. Some aspects of his work have been singled out by A. C. Crombie as "unsurpassed from Aristotle and Theophrastus to Cesalpino and Jung." His *De vegetabilibus et plantis,* in particular, is a masterpiece for its independence of treatment, its accuracy and range of detailed description, its freedom from myth, and its innovation in systematic classification. His comparative study of plants extended to all their parts, and his digressions show a remarkable sense of morphology and ecology. He drew a distinction between thorns and prickles on the basis of their formation and structure, classified flowers into the celebrated three types (bird-form, bell-form, and star-form), and made an extensive comparative study of fruits. His general classification of the vegetable kingdom followed that proposed by Theophrastus: he ranged plants on a scale reaching from the fungi to the flowering types, although, among the latter, he did not explicitly distinguish the monocotyledons from the dicotyledons. He seems to have been the first to mention spinach in Western literature, the first to note the influence of light and heat on the growth of trees, and the first to establish that sap (which he knew was carried in veins—like blood vessels, he said, but without a pulse) is tasteless in the root and becomes flavored as it ascends.

On plant evolution, Albert proposed that existing types were sometimes mutable and described five ways of transforming one plant into another; he believed, for example, that new species could be produced by grafting. Here he registered an advance over most medieval thinkers, who accounted for the succession of new species not by modification but by generation from a common source such as earth.

Albert's *De animalibus* includes descriptions of some fabulous creatures, but it also rejects many popular medieval myths (e.g., the pelican opening its breast to feed its young) and is especially noteworthy for its sections on reproduction and embryology. Following Aristotle, Albert distinguished four types of reproduction; in sexual reproduction among the higher animals he taught that the material produced by the female was like a seed (a *humor seminalis*), differentiating it from the catamenia (*menstruum*) in mammals and the yolk of the egg in birds, but incorrectly identifying it with the white of the egg. The cause of the differentiation of the sexes, in his view, was that the male "vital heat" could "concoct" semen out of surplus blood, whereas the female was too cold to effect the change.

He studied embryology by such simple methods as opening eggs at various intervals of time and tracing the development of the embryo from the appearance of the pulsating red speck of the heart to hatching. He was acquainted, too, with the development of fish and mammals, and understood some aspects of fetal nutrition. His studies on insects were especially good for their descriptions of insect mating, and he correctly identified the insect egg. He showed that ants lose their sense of direction when their antennae are removed, but concluded (wrongly) that the antennae carry eyes.

Among the larger animals, he described many northern types unknown to Aristotle, noting changes of coloration in the colder climates, and speculating that if any animals inhabited the poles they would have thick skins and be of a white color. His knowledge of internal anatomy was meager, but he did dissect crickets and observed the ovarian follicles and tracheae. His system of classification for the animal kingdom was basically Aristotelian; occasionally he repeated or aggravated the Stagirite's mistakes, but usually he modified and advanced Aristotle's taxonomy, as in his treatment of the ten genera of water animals. His anthropology was more philosophical than empirical in intent, but some have detected in it the adumbration of methods used in experimental psychology.

Apart from these more speculative concerns, Albert made significant contributions also to veterinary and medical science, dentistry included. In anatomy, for example, he took the vertebral column as the basis for structure, whereas in his day and for long afterward most anatomists began with the skull. He was reported to have cures for all manner of disease, and despite his own repudiation of magic and astrology came to be regarded as something of a magician. Many spurious works, some utterly fantastic, were attributed to him or published under his name to assure a wide diffusion—among these are to be included the very popular *De secretis mulierum* ("On the Secrets of Women") and other occult treatises.

Albert's productivity in science was matched by a similar output in philosophy and theology. In these areas his teachings have been overshadowed by those of his most illustrious disciple, Thomas Aquinas. The latter's debt to Albert is, of course, considerable, for Aquinas could well attribute the extent of his own vision to the fact that he stood on the shoulders of a giant.

BIBLIOGRAPHY

I. MAJOR WORKS AND WRITINGS. Standard editions include *Omnia opera*, B. Geyer, ed. (Cologne, 1951–), a critical edition, in progress, 40 vols.; Vol. XII (1955) is the only work of direct scientific interest to appear thus far; it contains the *Quaestiones super de animalibus* and other treatises related to Albert's work in zoology; *Omnia opera*, A. Borgnet, ed. (Paris, 1890–1899), 38 quarto vols.; *Omnia opera*, P. Jammy, ed. (Lyons, 1651), 21 folio vols., available on microfilm positives from the Vatican Library; his *Book of Minerals* is translated from the Latin by Dorothy Wychoff (Oxford, 1967). Special texts include H. Stadler, ed., "Albertus Magnus De animalibus libri XXVI," in *Beiträge zur Geschichte der Philosophie des Mittelalters*, **15–16** (Münster, 1916; 1921); L. Thorndike, *Latin Treatises on Comets Between 1238 and 1368 A.D.* (Chicago, 1950), pp. 62–76; J. A. Weisheipl, "The Problema Determinata XLIII ascribed to Albertus Magnus (1271)," in *Mediaeval Studies*, **22** (1960), 303–354.

II. SECONDARY LITERATURE. For a compact summary of Albert's life and works, with bibliography, see J. A. Weisheipl, "Albert the Great (Albertus Magnus), St.," in the *New Catholic Encyclopedia* (New York, 1967). Biographies include S. M. Albert, *Albert the Great* (Oxford, 1948) and T. M. Schwertner, *St. Albert the Great* (Milwaukee, 1932), a fuller biography with indication of sources. Works concerned with scientific teachings include H. Balss, *Albertus Magnus als Biologe* (Stuttgart, 1947); M. Barbado, *Introduction à la psychologie expérimentale*, P. Mazoyer, trans. (Paris, 1931), pp. 114–189; C. B. Boyer, *The Rainbow: From Myth to Mathematics* (New York, 1959), esp. pp. 94–99; A. C. Crombie, *Medieval and Early Modern Science*, I (New York, 1959), esp. 147–157; A. C. Crombie, *Robert Grosseteste and the Origins of Experimental Science* (Oxford, 1953), esp. pp. 189–200; E. J. Dijksterhuis, *The Mechanization of the World Picture*, C. Dikshoorn, trans. (Oxford, 1961); P. Duhem, *Le système du monde*, III (Paris, 1914; reprinted, 1958), 327–345; A. Maier, *Die Vorlaüfer Galileis im 14. Jahrhundert*, Edizioni di Storia e Letteratura, **22** (Rome, 1949), 11–16, 183–184; L. Thorndike, *A History of Magic and Experimental Science*, II (New York, 1923), esp. pp. 517–592; J. A. Weisheipl, *The Development of Physical Theory in the Middle Ages* (London, 1959); J. A. Weisheipl, "Celestial Movers in Medieval Physics," in *The Thomist*, **24** (1961), 286–326. See also *Serta Albertina*, a special issue of the Roman periodical *Angelicum*, **21** (1944), 1–336, devoted to all branches of Albert's science; includes a bibliography classified by fields.

WILLIAM A. WALLACE, O. P.

ALEKSANDROV (OR ALEXANDROFF), PAVEL SERGEEVICH (*b*. Bogorodsk [formerly Noginsk], Russia, 7 May 1896; *d*. Moscow, U.S.S.R., 16 November 1982)

Pavel Sergeevich Aleksandrov was the youngest of six children (four sons, two daughters) of Sergei Aleksandrovich Aleksandrov, a rural government doctor, and of Tsezariia Akimovna Aleksandrova (née Zdanovskaia), whose main concern was the education of her children. Both parents instilled in him an intense interest in science and music. His mother taught him German, in which he was as proficient as in his native Russian, and French. Aleksandrov's early education was in the public schools of Smolensk, where his family moved in 1897 when his father became senior doctor in the Smolensk state hospital. The development of Aleksandrov's mathematical abilities and interest in the fundamental problems of mathematics were encouraged by his grammar school mathematics teacher, Aleksandr Romanovich Eiges. (In 1921 Aleksandrov was married for a brief time to Ekaterina Romanovna Eiges, sister of his teacher.)

Aleksandrov matriculated in the mathematics department of Moscow University in September 1913, intending to become a teacher. In the fall of 1914 he attended a lecture given by the brilliant young mathematician Nikolai Nikolaevich Luzin and became his first student. In 1915 Aleksandrov obtained his first mathematical result on the structure of Borel sets. When it was initially explained to him, Luzin doubted that the method Aleksandrov employed would work and suggested that another approach be taken. Aleksandrov persisted, however. The result he obtained may be stated as follows: every nondenumerable Borel set contains a perfect subset.

Enjoying the success of this first project, Aleksandrov energetically embarked on his second project: the continuum hypothesis. It is now known that Cantor's famous hypothesis cannot be proved or disproved within the framework of the theory of sets, so that Aleksandrov's efforts to obtain a definitive result were doomed to failure. His lack of complete success led him to conclude that his mathematical career was ended, and he left the university to go to Novgorod-Severskii, where he worked as a producer in the local theater, and then to Chernigov, where he helped to establish the Chernigov Soviet Dramatic Theater in the spring of 1919.

Life during the years 1918 to 1920 was filled with turmoil following the October Revolution of 1917. Aleksandrov was arrested and jailed for a brief time in 1919 by a group opposing the new Soviet government, but he was released when the Soviet army reoccupied Chernigov. In addition to his work in the theater, he embarked upon a series of public lectures on literature and mathematics. In December 1919, following a six-week illness, he decided to go to Moscow University and resume his study of

ALEKSANDROV

mathematics.

After returning to Moscow in September 1920, Aleksandrov prepared for his master's examinations by studying with Pavel Samuilovich Uryson. Their association blossomed into a deep friendship. During the summer of 1922 the two P.S.'s (as they were referred to by their fellow students) and several friends rented a dacha on the banks of the Klyaz'ma. The two young mathematicians embarked on the study of topology, a recently formed field of mathematics. Their work of that summer and fall was guided by a mere handful of articles, among them the pioneering work of Maurice Fréchet (1906) and Felix Hausdorff's monumental *Grundzüge der Mengenlehre* (1914). Their primary concern was to obtain necessary and sufficient conditions for a topological space to be metrizable. The outcome of their research was the lengthy and authoritative paper "Mémoire sur les espaces topologiques compacts," which, because of various problems, was not published until 1929.

Their search for a metrization theorem was successful, but their formulation made its application difficult. The search for a workable result continued until one of Aleksandrov's students, Yuri M. Smirnov, as well as J. Nagata and R. H. Bing, independently achieved a workable formulation (1951–1952). Using modern terminology, the condition that Aleksandrov and Uryson derived may be stated as follows: A topological space is metrizable if and only if it is paracompact and has a countable refining system of open coverings.

Encouraged by their work, the two young men visited Göttingen, the intellectual hotbed of German mathematics. (To finance their journey, they gave a series of lectures in and around Moscow on the theory of relativity.) During the summer of 1923, the two presented their results, which were enthusiastically received by such mathematicians as Emmy Noether, Richard Courant, and David Hilbert. This summer not only marked the first time since the revolution that Soviet mathematicians had traveled outside their country, but it also set the stage for mathematical exchanges between Moscow and Göttingen. In fact, Aleksandrov returned to Göttingen every summer until 1932, when such exchanges became impossible because of the restrictiveness of regulations imposed by the German government.

Aleksandrov and Uryson returned to Göttingen in the summer of 1924; they also visited with Felix Hausdorff in Bonn and with L. E. J. Brouwer in Holland. After their time with Brouwer, the two young Soviets went to Paris and then to the Atlantic coast of France for a period of work and relaxation. In Batz, France, their tour ended tragically on 17 August 1924 when Uryson drowned.

The death of his friend seemed to intensify Aleksandrov's interest in topology and in the seminar which the two had begun organizing in the spring of 1924. One of the first students in this seminar was the first of Aleksandrov's students to make substantial contributions to mathematics in general and to topology in particular. Andrei Nikolaevich Tikhonov developed the concept of the product of an infinite number of topological spaces (at least for infinitely many copies of the closed unit interval [0,1]). He developed the concept to solve a problem posed by Aleksandrov: Is every normal space embeddable as a subspace of a compact Hausdorff space?

After the death of Uryson, Aleksandrov returned to Moscow and made plans to spend the academic year 1925–1926 in Holland with Brouwer. One of the reasons was that during their visit with Brouwer in 1924, Aleksandrov and Uryson had been persuaded by him to have their topological work published in *Verhandelingen der Koninklijke akademie van wetenschappen*. Due to a series of delays, this monumental work was not published until 1929. The original version was in French; since then it has appeared in Russian three times (1950, 1951, 1971), each time with footnotes by Aleksandrov updating contributions by mathematicians answering questions posed by the work.

Aleksandrov formed lifelong friendships during his summers in Göttingen, the most important of which, with Heinz Hopf, began in 1926. Their friendship grew during the academic year 1927–1928, which they spent at Princeton University. When they returned to conduct a topological seminar at Göttingen during the summer of 1928, they were asked by Richard Courant to write a topology book as part of his Yellow Collection for Springer. This request resulted in a seven-year collaboration that culminated in 1935 with the publication of *Topologie*, a landmark textbook on topology. Two additional volumes had originally been planned, but the war prevented completion of the project.

Aleksandrov loved to swim and to take long walks with his students while discussing mathematical problems. His athletic inclinations were restricted by his eyesight, which had been poor from his youth. (He was totally blind during the last three years of his life.)

In 1935 Aleksandrov and his close friend Andrei Nikolaevich Kolmogorov acquired a century-old dacha in the village of Komarovka, outside Moscow. They shared the house and its surrounding garden until death separated them. It not only became a convenient and popular place for Aleksandrov and his students to gather but also sheltered many renowned mathematicians who came to meet and work with Aleksandrov or Kolmogorov.

Aleksandrov's achievements were not limited to pure mathematics. From 1958 to 1962 he was vice president of the International Congress of Mathematicians. He held the chair of higher geometry and topology at Moscow State University, was head of the mathematics section of the university, and served as head of the general topology section of the Steklov Institute of Mathematics of the Soviet Academy of Sciences. For thirty-three years Aleksandrov was president of the Moscow Mathematical Society; he was elected honorary president in 1964. In addition to serving as editor of several mathematical journals, he was editor in chief of *Uspekhi matematicheskikh nauk* (*Russian Mathematical Surveys*). In 1929 he was elected a corresponding member of the Soviet Academy of Sciences, and a full member in 1953. He was a member of the Göttingen Academy of Sciences, the Austrian Academy of Sciences, the Leopoldina Academy in Halle, the Polish Academy of Sciences, the Academy of Sciences of the German Democratic Republic, the National Academy of Sciences (United States), and the American Philosophical Society, and an honorary member of the London Mathematical Society. He was awarded honorary doctorates by the Dutch Mathematical Society and Humboldt University in Berlin.

In his last years Aleksandrov supervised the editing of a three-volume collection of what he considered his most important works: *Teoriia funktsii deistvitel'nogo peremennogo i teoriia topologicheskikh prostranstv* ("The Theory of Functions of Real Variables and Theory of Topological Spaces"; 1978), *Teoriia razmernosti i smezhnye voprosy: Stat'i obshchego kharaktera* ("Dimension Theory and Related Questions: Articles of a General Nature"; 1978), and *Obshchaia teoriia gomologii* ("The General Theory of Homology"; 1979).

In addition Aleksandrov wrote his autobiography, portions of which appeared in two parts under the title "Stranitsii avtobiografii" ("Pages from an Autobiography") in *Russian Mathematical Surveys* along with papers presented at an international conference on topology in Moscow (June 1979) of which he was the prime organizer.

Aleksandrov's mathematical results were substantial and diverse. Through his joint work with Uryson he is credited with the definition of compact spaces and locally compact spaces (originally described as bicompact spaces). In 1925 he first formulated the modern definition of the concept of topological space. The concept of compact space undoubtedly led to the definition of a locally finite covering of a space that he used to prove that every open cover of a separable metric space has a locally finite open cover, or, in modern terminology, that every separable metric space is paracompact. This idea appeared later in the result of A. H. Stone that every metric space is paracompact, a fact used by Smirnov, Nagata, and Bing in their metrization theorem.

In the period 1925 to 1929 Aleksandrov is credited with laying the foundations of the homology theory of general topological spaces. This branch of topology is a blend of topology and algebra, his study of which was inspired by Emmy Noether during his Göttingen summers and during a visit she made to Brouwer (while Aleksandrov was working with him) in the winter of 1925 to 1926. It was during this visit that Aleksandrov became interested in the concept of a Betti group, which he was to use in his work. (He coined the term "kernel of a homomorphism," which appeared in print for the first time in an algebraic supplement to *Topologie*.)

Aleksandrov's arguments used the concept of the nerve of a cover that he had introduced in 1925. The nerve of a cover ω of a topological space X is a simplicial complex N_ω whose vertexes are in a one-to-one correspondence with the elements of ω, and any vertexes $e_1, \ldots, e_k$ of N_ω form a simplex in N_ω if and only if the elements of ω corresponding to these vertexes have a nonempty intersection. Based upon this, one may define a simplicial transform $\Pi_\omega^{\omega'}$ (ω' being a cover contained in or succeeding ω), which is called the "projection" of the nerve N_{ω}' into N_ω.

For a compact space X, the collection of all such projections formed by letting ω range over the directed family of all the finite open covers of X is the projective spectrum S of X. This projective spectrum is the directed family of complexes N_ω, which are linked by the projections $\Pi_\omega^{\omega'}$. The limit space of the projective spectrum is homeomorphic to X, which implies that the topological properties of the space X may be reduced to properties of the complexes and their simplicial mappings. Among other results, this work led to Aleksandrov's theorem that any compact set of a given dimension lying in a Hilbert space can, for any $\epsilon > 0$, be transformed into a polyhedron of equal dimension by means of an ϵ-deformation, that is, a continuous deformation in which each point is displaced by at most ϵ.

These concepts led to the creation of the homological theory of dimension in 1928 to 1930. Aleksandrov's works frequently seemed to be springboards for other mathematicians, including many of his own students: A. N. Tikhonov, L. S. Pontriagin, Y. M. Smirnov, K. A. Sitnikov, A. V. Arkhangel'skii, V. I. Ponomarev, V. I. Zaitsev, and E. V. Shchepin, to name only a few.

In his autobiography Aleksandrov broke down his mathematical life and the associated papers into six periods:

1. The summer of 1915—the structure of Borel sets and the *A*-operation

2. May 1922–August 1924—basic papers on general topology

3. August 1925–spring 1928—the definition of the nerve of a family of sets and the establishment of the means of the foundations of homology theory of general topological spaces by a method that permitted him to apply the methods of combinatorial topology to point-set topology

4. The first half of 1930—the development of homological dimension theory, which built upon his spectral theory

5. January–May 1942—Because of World War II, Aleksandrov, Kolmogorov, and other scientists were sent to Kazan in July 1941. Although Aleksandrov returned to Moscow for the start of the fall session at the university, he was told to go back to Kazan. There, during the winter of 1941, he wrote a work devoted to the study of the form and disposition of a closed set (or complex) in an enveloping closed set (or complex) by homological means. One important by-product of this paper was the concept of an exact sequence, an important algebraic tool used in many branches of mathematics

6. The winter of 1946–1947—duality theorems for nonclosed sets; he regarded the paper containing these results as his last important work

In the late 1940's and early 1950's, Aleksandrov and his pupils built upon this last work with the construction of homology theory for nonclosed sets in euclidean spaces. At all times his works seemed motivated and guided by geometric ideas undoubtedly stemming from his youthful fascination with the subject.

One of the pervasive elements in Aleksandrov's works is the theory of continuous mappings of topological spaces, beginning with his theory of the continuous decompositions of compacta, which led to the theory of perfect mappings of arbitrary, completely regular spaces. Included in this development is Aleksandrov's theorem on the representation of each compactum as a continuous image of a perfect Cantor set. This result gave rise to the theorem that every compactum is a continuous image of a zero-dimensional compactum of the same weight, and is part of the foundation of the theory of dyadic compacta.

Most of Aleksandrov's life was spent in university teaching and research, and in many ways was structured around education and his students. It included visits to Kamarovka, musical evenings at the university, public talks, and private concerts. The last twenty-five years of his life seem to have been devoted to his students and education in general, as indicated by the survey articles he wrote during this period. He seemed to radiate the same kind of magnetism and contagious fervor for mathematics and life that first drew Aleksandrov, Uryson, and other young students to cluster around Luzin in their student years.

BIBLIOGRAPHY

I. Original Works. "Some Results in the Theory of Topological Spaces, Obtained Within the Last Twenty-five Years," in *Russian Mathematical Surveys*, **15**, no. 2 (1960), 23–84; *Teoriia funktsii deistvitel'nogo peremennogo i teoriia topologicheskikh prostranstv* ("The Theory of Functions of Real Variables and Theory of Topological Spaces"; Moscow, 1978); *Teoriia razmernosti i smezhnye voprosy: Stat'i obshchego kharaktera* ("Dimension Theory and Related Questions: Articles of a General Nature"; Moscow, 1978); "The Main Aspects in the Development of Set-Theoretical Topology," in *Russian Mathematical Surveys*, **33**, no. 3 (1978), 1–53, with V. V. Fedorchuk; *Obshchaia teoriia gomologii* ("The General Theory of Homology"; Moscow, 1979); "Pages from an Autobiography," in *Russian Mathematical Surveys*, **34**, no. 6 (1979), 267–302, and **35**, no. 3 (1980), 315–358.

II. Secondary Literature. A. V. Arkhangelskii *et al.*, "Pavel Sergeevich Aleksandrov (On His 80th Birthday)," in *Russian Mathematical Surveys*, **31**, no. 5 (1976), 1–13; and *Russian Mathematical Surveys*, **21**, no. 4 (1966), an issue dedicated to Aleksandrov, with a biographical introduction by A. N. Kolmogorov *et al.*

Douglas Ewan Cameron

ALEMBERT, JEAN LE ROND D' (*b.* Paris, France, 17 November 1717; *d.* Paris, 29 October 1783)

Jean Le Rond d'Alembert was the illegitimate child of Madame de Tencin, a famous salon hostess of the eighteenth century, and the Chevalier Destouches-Canon, a cavalry officer. His mother, who had renounced her nun's vows, abandoned him, for she feared being returned to a convent. His father, however, located the baby and found him a home with a humble artisan named Rousseau and his wife. D'Alembert lived with them until he was forty-seven years old. Destouches-Canon also saw to the education of the child. D'Alembert attended the Collège de Quatre-Nations (sometimes called after Mazarin, its founder), a Jansenist school offering a curriculum in the classics and rhetoric—and also offering more than the average amount of mathematics. In spite of the efforts of his teachers, he turned against a religious career and began studies of law and medicine before he finally embarked on a career as a mathematician. In the 1740's he became part of the *philosophes,* thus joining in the rising tide of criticism of the social and intellectual standards of the day. D'Alembert published many works on mathematics and mathematical physics, and was the scientific editor of the *Encyclopédie.*

D'Alembert never married, although he lived for a number of years with Julie de Lespinasse, the one love of his life. A slight man with an expressive face, a high-pitched voice, and a talent for mimicry, he was known for his wit, gaiety, and gift for conversation, although later in life he became bitter and morose. D'Alembert spent his time much as the other *philosophes* did: working during the morning and afternoon and spending the evening in the salons, particularly those of Mme. du Deffand and Mlle. de Lespinasse. He seldom traveled, leaving the country only once, for a visit to the court of Frederick the Great. D'Alembert was a member of the Académie des Sciences, the Académie Française, and most of the other scientific academies of Europe. He is best known for his work in mathematics and rational mechanics, and for his association with the *Encyclopédie.*

D'Alembert appeared on the scientific scene in July 1739, when he sent his first communication to the Académie des Sciences. It was a critique of a mathematical text by Father Charles Reyneau. During the next two years he sent the academy five more *mémoires* dealing with methods of integrating differential equations and with the motion of bodies in resisting media. Although d'Alembert had received almost no formal scientific training (at school he had studied Varignon's work), it is clear that on his own he had become familiar not only with Newton's work, but also with that of L'Hospital, the Bernoullis, and the other mathematicians of his day. His communications to the academy were answered by Clairaut, who although only four years older than d'Alembert was already a member.

After several attempts to join the academy, d'Alembert was finally successful. He was made *adjoint* in astronomy in May 1741, and received the title of *associé géometre* in 1746. From 1741 through 1743 he worked on various problems in rational mechanics and in the latter year published his famous *Traité de dynamique.* He published rather hastily (a pattern he was to follow all of his life) in order to forestall the loss of priority; Clairaut was working along similar lines. His rivalry with Clairaut, which continued until Clairaut's death, was only one of several in which he was involved over the years.

The *Traité de dynamique,* which has become the most famous of his scientific works, is significant in many ways. First, it is clear that d'Alembert recognized that a scientific revolution had occurred, and he thought that he was doing the job of formalizing the new science of mechanics. That accomplishment is often attributed to Newton, but in fact it was done over a long period of time by a number of men. If d'Alembert was overly proud of his share, he was at least clearly aware of what was happening in science. The *Traité* also contained the first statement of what is now known as d'Alembert's principle. D'Alembert was, furthermore, in the tradition that attempted to develop mechanics without using the notion of force. Finally, it was long afterward said (rather simplistically) that in this work he resolved the famous *vis viva* controversy, a statement with just enough truth in it to be plausible. In terms of his own development, it can be said that he set the style he was to follow for the rest of his life.

As was customary at the time, d'Alembert opened his book with a lengthy philosophical preface. It is true that he was not always faithful to the principles he set down in the preface, but it is astonishing that he could carry his arguments as far as he did and remain faithful to them. D'Alembert fully accepted the prevailing epistemology of sensationalism. Taken from John Locke and expanded by such men as Condillac, sensationalism was to be d'Alembert's metaphysical basis of science. The main tenet of this epistemology was that all knowledge was derived, not from innate ideas, but from sense perception. In many ways, however, d'Alembert remained Cartesian. The criterion of the truth, for example, was still the clear and simple idea, although that idea now had a different origin. In science, therefore, the basic concepts had to conform to this ideal.

In developing his philosophy of mechanics, d'Alembert analyzed the ideas available to him until he came to those that could be analyzed no further; these were to be his starting points. Space and time were such. So simple and clear that they could not even be defined, they were the only fundamental ideas he could locate. Motion was a combination of the ideas of space and time, and so a definition of it was necessary. The word "force" was so unclear and confusing that it was rejected as a conceptual building block of mechanics and was used merely as a convenient shorthand when it was properly and arbitrarily defined. D'Alembert defined matter as impenetrable extension, which took account of the fact that two objects could not pass through one another. The concept of mass, which he defined, as Newton had done, as quantity of matter, had to be smuggled into the treatise in a mathematical sense later on.

In the first part of the *Traité,* d'Alembert developed his own three laws of motion. It should be remembered that Newton had stated his laws verbally in the *Principia,* and that expressing them in algebraic form was a task taken up by the mathematicians of the eighteenth century. D'Alembert's first law was, as Newton's had been, the law of inertia. D'Alembert, however, tried to give an a priori proof for the law, indicating that however sensationalistic his thought might be he still clung to the notion that the mind could arrive at truth by its own processes. His proof was based on the simple ideas of space and time; and the reasoning was geometric, not physical, in nature. His second law, also proved as a problem in geometry, was that of the parallelogram of motion. It was not until he arrived at the third law that physical assumptions were involved.

The third law dealt with equilibrium, and amounted to the principle of the conservation of momentum in impact situations. In fact, d'Alembert was inclined to reduce every mechanical situation to one of impact rather than resort to the effects of continual forces; this again showed an inheritance from Descartes. D'Alembert's proof rested on the clear and simple case of two equal masses approaching each other with equal but opposite speeds. They will clearly balance one another, he declared, for there is no reason why one should overcome the other. Other impact situations were reduced to this one; in cases where the masses or velocities were unequal, the object with the greater quantity of motion (defined as mv) would prevail. In fact, d'Alembert's mathematical definition of mass was introduced implicitly here: he actually assumed the conservation of momentum and defined mass accordingly. This fact was what made his work a mathematical physics rather than simply mathematics.

The principle that bears d'Alembert's name was introduced in the next part of the *Traité.* It was not so much a principle as it was a rule for using the previously stated laws of motion. It can be summarized as follows: In any situation where an object is constrained from following its normal inertial motion, the resulting motion can be analyzed into two components. One of these is the motion the object actually takes, and the other is the motion "destroyed" by the constraints. The lost motion is balanced against either a fictional force or a motion lost by the constraining object. The latter case is the case of impact, and the result is the conservation of momentum (in some cases, the conservation of *vis viva* as well). In the former case, an infinite force must be assumed. Such, for example, would be the case of an object on an inclined plane. The normal motion would be vertically downward; this motion can be resolved into two others. One would be a component down the plane (the motion actually taken) and the other would be normal to the surface of the plane (the motion destroyed by the infinite resisting force of the plane). Then one can easily describe the situation (in this case, a trivial problem).

It is clear that the use of d'Alembert's principle requires some knowledge beyond that of his laws. One must have the conditions of constraint, or the law of falling bodies, or some information derived either empirically or hypothetically about the particular situation. It was for this reason that Ernst Mach could refer to d'Alembert's principle as a routine form for the solution of problems, and not a principle at all. D'Alembert's principle actually rests on his assumptions of what constitutes equilibrium, and it is in his third law of motion that those assumptions appear. Indeed, in discussing his third law (in the second edition of his book, published in 1758) d'Alembert arrived at the equation $\phi = dv/dt$, which is similar to the standard expression for Newton's second law, but which lacks the crucial parameter of mass. The function ϕ was to contain the parameters for specific problems. For example (and this is d'Alembert's example), should the assumption be made that a given deceleration is proportional to the square of the velocity of an object, then the equation becomes $-gv^2 = dv/dt$. The minus sign indicates deceleration, and the constant g packs in the other factors involved, such as mass. In this fashion d'Alembert was able to avoid dealing with forces.

It has often been said that d'Alembert settled the *vis viva* controversy in this treatise, but such a view must be qualified. In the preface d'Alembert did discuss the issue, pointing out that in a given deceleration the change in velocity was proportional to the time. One could therefore define force in terms of the velocity of an object. On the other hand, if one were concerned with the number of "obstacles" that had to be overcome to stop a moving body (here he probably had in mind 'sGravesande's experiments with objects stopped by springs), then it was clear that such a definition of force depended on the square of the velocity and that the related metric was distance, not time. D'Alembert pointed out that these were two different ways of looking at the same problem, that both methods worked and were used with success by different scientists. To use the word "force" to describe either mv or mv^2 was therefore a quarrel of words; the metaphysical notion of force as a universal causal agent was not clarified by such an argument. In this way d'Alembert solved the controversy by declaring it a false one. It involved convention, not reality, for universal causes (the metaphysical meaning of the idea of force) were not known, and possibly not even knowable. It was for this reason that d'Alembert refused to entertain the possibility of talking of forces in mechanics. He did not throw the word away, but used it only when he could give it what today would be called an operational definition. He simply refused to give the notion of force any metaphysical validity and, thus, any ontological reality.

In this way d'Alembert was clearly a precursor of positivistic science. He employed mathematical abstractions and hypothetical or idealized models of physical phenomena and was careful to indicate the shortcomings of his results when they did not closely match the actual events of the world. The metaphysician, he warned in a later treatise, too often built systems that might or might not reflect reality, while the mathematician too often trusted his calculations, thinking they represented the whole truth. But just as metaphysics was suspect because of its unjustified claim to knowledge, so mathematics was suspect in its similar claim. Not everything could be reduced to calculation.

> Geometry owes its certainty to the simplicity of the things it deals with; as the phenomena become more complicated, the results become less certain. It is necessary to know when to stop, when one is ignorant of the thing being studied, and one must not believe that the words *theorem* and *corollary* have some secret virtue so that by writing QED at the end of a proposition one proves something that is not true [*Essai d'une nouvelle théorie de la résistance des fluides*, pp. xlii–xliii].

D'Alembert's instincts were good. Unfortunately, in this case they diverted him from the path that was eventually to produce the principle of the conservation of energy.

A major question that beset all philosophers of the Enlightenment was that of the nature of matter. While d'Alembert's primary concern was mathematical physics, his epistemology of sensationalism led him to speculate on matter theory. Here again, he was frustrated, repeating time after time that we simply do not know what matter is like in its essence. He tended to accept the corpuscular theory of matter, and in Newton's style; that is, he conceived of the ideal atom as perfectly hard. Since this kind of atom could not show the characteristic of elasticity, much less of other chemical or physical phenomena, he was sorely perplexed. In his *Traité de dynamique,* however, he evolved a model of the atom as a hard particle connected to its neighbors by springs. In this way, he could explain elasticity, but he never confused the model with reality. Possibly he sensed that his model actually begged the question, for the springs became more important that the atom itself, and resembled nothing more than a clumsy ether, the carrier of an active principle. Instead of belaboring the point, however, d'Alembert soon returned to mathematical abstraction, where one dealt with functional relations and did not have to agonize over ontology.

In 1744 d'Alembert published a companion volume to his first work, the *Traité de l'équilibre et du mouvement des fluides.* In this work d'Alembert used his principle to describe fluid motion, treating the major problems of fluid mechanics that were current. The sources of his interest in fluids were many. First, Newton had attempted a treatment of fluid motion in his *Principia,* primarily to refute Descartes's *tourbillon* theory of planetary motion. Second, there was a lively interest in fluids by the experimental physicists in the eighteenth century, for fluids were most frequently invoked to give physical explanations for a variety of phenomena, such as electricity, magnetism, and heat. There was also the problem of the shape of the earth: What shape would it be expected to take if it were thought of as a rotating fluid body? Clairaut published a work in 1744 which treated the earth as such, a treatise that was a landmark in fluid mechanics. Furthermore, the *vis viva* controversy was often centered on fluid flow, since the quantity of *vis viva* was used almost exclusively by the Bernoullis in their work on such problems. Finally, of course, there was the inherent interest in fluids themselves. D'Alembert's first treatise had been devoted to the study of rigid bodies; now he was giving attention to the other class of matter, the fluids. He was actually giving an alternative treatment to one already published by Daniel Bernoulli, and he commented that both he and Bernoulli usually arrived at the same conclusions. He felt that his own method was superior. Bernoulli did not agree.

In 1747 d'Alembert published two more important works, one of which, the *Réflexions sur la cause générale des vents,* won a prize from the Prussian Academy. In it appeared the first general use of partial differential equations in mathematical physics. Euler later perfected the techniques of using these equations. The pattern was to become a familiar one: d'Alembert, Daniel Bernoulli, or Clairaut would pioneer a technique, and Euler would take it far beyond their capacity to develop it. D'Alembert's treatise on winds was the only one of his works honored by a prize and, ironically, was later shown to be based on insufficient assumptions. D'Alembert assumed that wind patterns were the result of tidal effects on the atmosphere, and he relegated the influence of heat to a minor role, one that caused only local variations from the general circulation. Still, as a work on atmospheric tides it was successful, and Lagrange continued to praise d'Alembert's efforts many years later.

D'Alembert's other important publication of 1747 was an article in the *Mémoirs* of the Prussian Academy dealing with the motion of vibrating strings, another problem that taxed the minds of the major mathematicians of the day. Here the wave equation made its first appearance in physics. D'Alembert's mathematical instincts led him to simplify the boundary conditions, however, to the point where his solution, while correct, did not match well the observed phenomenon. Euler subsequently treated the same problem more generally; and although he was no more correct than d'Alembert, his work was more useful.

During the late 1740's, d'Alembert, Clairaut, and Euler were all working on the famous three-body problem, with varying success. D'Alembert's interest in celestial mechanics thus led him, in 1749, to publish a masterly work, the *Recherches sur la précession des équinoxes et sur la nutation de la terre.* The precession of the equinoxes, a problem previously attacked by Clairaut, was very difficult. D'Alembert's method was similar to Clairaut's, but he employed more terms in his integration of the equation of motion and arrived at a solution more in accord with the observed motion of the earth. He was rightly proud of his book.

D'Alembert then applied himself to further studies in fluid mechanics, entering a competition announced by the Prussian Academy. He was not awarded the prize; indeed, it was not given to anybody. The Prussian Academy took this action on the ground that nobody had submitted experimental proof of the theoretical work. There has been considerable dispute over this action. The claim has been made that d'Alembert's work, although the best entered, was marred by many errors. D'Alembert himself viewed his denial as the result of Euler's influence, and the relations between the two men deteriorated further. Whatever the case, the disgruntled d'Alembert published his work in 1752 as the *Essai d'une nouvelle théorie de la résistance des fluides.* It was in this essay that the differential hydrodynamic equations were first expressed in terms of a field and the hydrodynamic paradox was put forth.

In studying the flow lines of a fluid around an object (in this case, an elliptical object), d'Alembert could find no reason for assuming that the flow pattern was any different behind the object than in front of it. This implied that whatever the forces exerted on the front of the object might be, they would be counteracted by similar forces on the back, and the result would be no resistance to the flow whatever. The paradox was left for his readers to solve. D'Alembert had other difficulties as well. He found himself forced to assume, in order to avoid the necessity of allowing an instantaneous change in the velocity of parts of the fluid moving around the object, that a small portion of the fluid remained stagnant in front of the object, an assumption required to prevent breaking the law of continuity.

In spite of these problems, the essay was an important contribution. Hunter Rouse and Simon Ince have said that d'Alembert was the first "to introduce such concepts as the components of fluid velocity and acceleration, the differential requirements of continuity, and even the complex numbers essential to modern analysis of the same problem." Clifford Truesdell, on the other hand, thinks that most of the credit for the development of fluid mechanics must be granted to Euler; thus historians have continued the disputes that originated among the scientists themselves. But it is often difficult to tell where the original idea came from and who should receive primary recognition. It is certain, however, that d'Alembert, Clairaut, Bernoulli, and Euler were all active in pursuing these problems, all influenced one another, and all deserve to be remembered, although Euler was no doubt the most able of the group. But they all sought claims to priority, and they guarded their claims with passion.

D'Alembert wrote one other scientific work in the 1750's, the *Recherches sur différens points importants du systeme du monde.* It appeared in three volumes, two of them published in 1754 and the third in 1756. Devoted primarily to the motion of the moon (Volume III included a new set of lunar tables), it was written at least partially to guard d'Alembert's claims to originality against those of Clairaut. As was so often the case, d'Alembert's method was mathematically more sound, but Clairaut's method was more easily used by astronomers.

The 1750's were more noteworthy in d'Alembert's life for the development of interests outside the realm of mathematics and physics. Those interests came as a result of his involvement with the *Encyclopédie.* Denis Diderot was the principal editor of the enterprise, and d'Alembert was chosen as the science editor. His efforts did not remain limited to purely scientific concerns, however. His first literary task was that of writing the *Discours préliminaire* of the *Encyclopédie,* a task that he accomplished with such success that its publication was largely the reason for his acceptance into the Académie Française in 1754.

The *Discours préliminaire,* written in two parts, has rightly been recognized as a cardinal document of the Enlightenment. The first part is devoted to the work as an *encyclopédie,* that is, as a collection of the knowledge of mankind. The second part is devoted to the work as a *dictionnaire raisonnée,* or critical dictionary. Actually, the first part is an exposition of the epistemology of sensationalism, and owes a great deal to both John Locke and Condillac. All kinds of human knowledge are discussed, from scientific to moral. The sciences are to be based on physical perception, and morality is to be based on the perception of those emotions, feelings, and inclinations that men can sense within themselves. Although d'Alembert gives lip service to the truths of religion, they are clearly irrelevant and are acknowledged only for the sake of the censors. For this reason, the *Discours préliminaire* came under frequent attack; nevertheless, it was generally well received and applauded. It formed, so to say, the manifesto of the now coalescing party of *philosophes;* the body of the *Encyclopédie* was to be the expression of their program.

The second part of the *Discours préliminaire* is in fact a history of science and philosophy, and clearly shows the penchant of the *philosophes* for the notion of progress through the increased use of reason. As a history, it has often quite properly been attacked for its extreme bias against the medieval period and any form of thought developed within the framework of theology, but this bias was, of course, intentional. At the end of this history, the *philosophes'* debt to Francis Bacon is clearly acknowledged in the outline of the organization of knowledge. A modified version of Bacon's tree of knowledge is included and briefly explained. All knowledge is related to three functions of the mind: memory, reason, and imagination. Reason is clearly the most important of the three. Bacon's emphasis on utility was also reflected in the *Encyclopédie,* although more by Diderot than by d'Alembert. D'Alembert's concept of utility was far wider than that of most people. To him, the things used by philosophers—even mathematical equations—were very useful, even though the bulk of the public might find them mysterious and esoteric.

In the midst of this activity, d'Alembert found time to write a book on what must be called a psychophysical subject, that of music. In 1752 he published his *Élémens de musique théorique et pratique suivant les principes de M. Rameau.* This work has often been neglected by historians, save those of music, for it was not particularly mathematical and acted as a popularization of Rameau's new scheme of musical structure. Yet it was more than simply a popularization. Music was still emerging from the mixture of Pythagorean numerical mysticism and theological principles that had marked its rationale during the late medieval period. D'Alembert understood Rameau's innovations as a liberation; music could finally be given a secular rationale, and his work was important in spreading Rameau's ideas throughout Europe.

As time went on, d'Alembert's pen was increasingly devoted to nonscientific subjects. His articles in the *Encyclopédie* reached far beyond mathematics. He wrote and read many essays before the Académie Française; these began to appear in print as early as 1753. In that year he published two volumes of his *Mélanges de littérature et de philosophie.* The first two were reprinted along with two more in 1759; a fifth and last volume was published in 1767. The word *mélanges* was apt, for in these volumes were essays on music, law, and religion, his treatise on the *Élémens de philosophie,* translations of portions of Tacitus, and other assorted literary efforts. They make an odd mixture, for some are important in their exposition of Enlightenment ideals, while others are mere polemics or even trivial essays.

In 1757 d'Alembert visited Voltaire at Ferney, and an important result of the visit was the article on Geneva, which appeared in the seventh volume of the *Encyclopédie.* It was clearly an article meant to be propaganda, for the space devoted to the city was quite out of keeping with the general editorial policy. In essence, d'Alembert damned the city by praising it. The furor that resulted was the immediate cause of the suspension of the license for the *Encyclopédie.* D'Alembert resigned as an editor, convinced that the enterprise must founder, and left Diderot to finish the task by himself. Diderot thought that d'Alembert had deserted him, and the relations between the men became strained. Rousseau also attacked d'Alembert for his view that Geneva should allow a theater, thus touching off another of the famous controversies that showed that the *philosophes* were by no means a totally unified group of thinkers.

D'Alembert's chief scientific output after 1760 was his *Opuscules mathématiques,* eight volumes of which appeared from 1761 to 1780. These collections of mathematical essays were a mixed bag, ranging from theories of achromatic lenses to purely mathematical manipulations and theorems. Included were many new solutions to problems he had previously attacked—including a new proof of the law of inertia. Although the mathematical articles in the *Encyclopédie* had aired many of his notions, these volumes provide the closest thing to a collection of them that exists.

As Carl Boyer has pointed out, d'Alembert was almost alone in his day in regarding the differential as the limit of a function, the key concept around which the calculus was eventually rationalized. Unfortunately, d'Alembert could never escape the tradition that had made geometry preeminent among the sciences, and he was therefore unable to put the idea of the limit into purely algorithmic form. His concept of the limit did not seem to be any more clear to his contemporaries than other schemes invented to explain the nature of the differential.

It has often been said that d'Alembert was always primarily a mathematician and secondarily a physicist. This evaluation must be qualified. No doubt he sensed the power of mathematics. But, as he once said, "Mathematics owes its certainty to the simplicity of the things with which it deals." In other words, d'Alembert was never able to remove himself to a world of pure mathematics. He was rather in the tradition of Descartes. Space was the realization of geometry (although, unlike Descartes, d'Alembert drew his evidence from sense perception). It was for this reason that he could never reduce mathematics to pure algorithms, and it is also the reason for his concern about the law of continuity. In mathematics as well as physics, discontinuities seemed improper to d'Alembert; equations that had discontinuities in them gave solutions that he called "impossible," and he wasted no time on them. It was for this reason that the notion of perfectly hard matter was so difficult for him to comprehend, for two such particles colliding would necessarily undergo sudden changes in velocity, something he could not allow as possible.

It was probably the requirement of continuity that led d'Alembert to his idea of the limit, and it also led him to consider the techniques of handling series. In Volume V of the *Opuscules* he published a test for convergence that is still called d'Alembert's theorem. The mathematical statement is:

If $\lim_{n\to\infty} |S_{n+1}/S_n| = r$, and $r < 1$, the series $\sum_{n=1}^{\infty} S_n$ converges. If $r > 1$, the series diverges; if $r = 1$, the test fails.

But in spite of such original contributions to mathematical manipulation, d'Alembert's chief concern was in making this language not merely descriptive of the world, but congruent to it. The application of mathematics was a matter of considering physical situations, developing differential equations to express them, and then integrating those equations. Mathematical physicists had to invent much of their procedure as they went along. Thus, in the course of his work, d'Alembert was able to give the first formulation of the wave equation, to express the first partial differential equation, and to be the first to solve a partial differential equation by the technique of the separation of variables. But probably the assignment of "firsts" in this way is not the best manner of evaluating the development of mathematics or of mathematical physics. For every such first, one can find other men who had alternative suggestions or different ways of expressing themselves, and who often wrote down similar but less satisfactory expressions.

More important, possibly, is the way in which these ideas reflect the mathematicians' view of nature, a view that was changing and was then very different from that of a mathematical physicist today. D'Alembert's very language gives a clue. He used, for example, the word *fausse* to describe a divergent series. The word to him was not a bare descriptive term. There was no match, or no useful match, for divergence in the physical world. Convergence leads to the notion of the limit; divergence leads nowhere—or everywhere.

D'Alembert has often been cited as being oddly ineffective when he considered probability theory. Here again his view of nature, not his mathematical capabilities, blocked him. He considered, for example, a game of chance in which Pierre and Jacques take part. Pierre is to flip a coin. If heads turns up on the first toss, he is to pay Jacques one *écu.* If it does not turn up until the second toss, he is to pay two *écus.* If it does not turn up until the third toss, he is to pay four *écus,* and so on, the payments mounting in geometric progression. The problem is to determine how many *écus* Jacques should give to Pierre before the game begins in order that the two men have equal chances at breaking even. The solution seemed to be that since the probability on each toss was one-half, and since the number of tosses was unlimited, then Jacques would have to give an infinite number of *écus* to Pierre before the game began, clearly a paradoxical situation.

D'Alembert rebelled against this solution, but had no satisfactory alternative. He considered the possibility of tossing tails one hundred times in a row.

Metaphysically, he declared, one could imagine that such a thing could happen; but one could not realistically imagine it happening. He went further: heads, he declared, must *necessarily* arise after a finite number of tosses. In other words, any given toss is influenced by previous tosses, an assumption firmly denied by modern probability theory. D'Alembert also said that if the probability of an event were very small, it could be treated as nothing, and therefore would have no relevance to physical events. Jacques and Pierre could forget the mathematics; it was not applicable to their game.

It is no wonder that such theorizing caused d'Alembert to have quarrels and arguments with others. Moreover, there were reasons for interest in probability outside games of chance. It had been known for some time that if a person were inoculated with a fluid taken from a person having smallpox, the result would usually be a mild case of the disease, followed by immunity afterward. Unfortunately, a person so inoculated occasionally would develop a more serious case and die. The question was posed: Is one more likely to live longer with or without inoculation? There were many variables, of course. For example, should a forty-year-old, who was already past the average life expectancy, be inoculated? What, in fact, was a life expectancy? How many years could one hope to live, from any given age, both with and without inoculation? D'Alembert and Daniel Bernoulli carried on extensive arguments about this problem. What is significant about d'Alembert's way of thinking is that he expressed the feeling that the laws of probability were faint comfort to the man who had his child inoculated and lost the gamble. To d'Alembert, that factor was as important as any mathematical ratio. It was not, as far as he was concerned, irrelevant to the problem.

Most of these humanitarian concerns crept into d'Alembert's work in his later years. Aside from the *Opuscules,* there was only one other scientific publication after 1760 that carried his name: the *Nouvelles expériences sur la résistance des fluides* (published in 1777). Listed as coauthors were the Abbé Bossut and Condorcet. The last two actually did all of the work; d'Alembert merely lent his name.

In 1764 d'Alembert spent three months at the court of Frederick the Great. Although frequently asked by Frederick, d'Alembert refused to move to Potsdam as president of the Prussian Academy. Indeed, he urged Frederick to appoint Euler, and the rift that had grown between d'Alembert and Euler was at last repaired. Unfortunately, Euler was never trusted by Frederick, and he left soon afterward for St. Petersburg, where he spent the rest of his life.

In 1765 d'Alembert published his *Histoire de la destruction des Jésuites.* The work was seen through the press by Voltaire in Geneva, and although it was published anonymously, everyone knew who wrote it. A part of Voltaire's plan *écraser l'infâme,* this work is not one of d'Alembert's best.

In the same year, d'Alembert fell gravely ill, and moved to the house of Mlle. de Lespinasse, who nursed him back to health. He continued to live with her until her death in 1776. In 1772 he was elected perpetual secretary of the Académie Française, and undertook the task of writing the eulogies for the deceased members of the academy. He became the academy's most influential member, but, in spite of his efforts, that body failed to produce anything noteworthy in the way of literature during his preeminence. D'Alembert sensed his failure. His later life was filled with frustration and despair, particularly after the death of Mlle. de Lespinasse.

Possibly d'Alembert lived too long. Many of the *philosophes* passed away before he did, and those who remained alive in the 1780's were old and clearly not the vibrant young revolutionaries they had once been. What political success they had tasted they had not been able to develop. But, to a large degree, they had, in Diderot's phrase, "changed the general way of thinking."

BIBLIOGRAPHY

I. Original Works. There have been no collections made of d'Alembert's scientific works, although reprints of the original editions of his scientific books (except the *Opuscules mathématiques*) have recently been issued by Éditions Culture et Civilisation, Brussels. There are two collections of d'Alembert's *Oeuvres* which contain his literary pieces: the Bélin ed., 18 vols. (Paris, 1805); and the Bastien ed., 5 vols. (Paris, 1821). The most recent and complete bibliographies are in Grimsley and Hankins (see below).

II. Secondary Literature. The following works are devoted primarily to d'Alembert or accord him a prominent role: Joseph Bertrand, *D'Alembert* (Paris, 1889); Carl Boyer, *The History of the Calculus and Its Conceptual Development* (New York, 1949), ch. 4; René Dugas, *A History of Mechanics* (Neuchâtel, 1955), pp. 244-251, 290-299; Ronald Grimsley, *Jean d'Alembert* (Oxford, 1963); Maurice Müller, *Essai sur la philosophie de Jean d'Alembert* (Paris, 1926); Hunter Rouse and Simon Ince, *A History of Hydraulics* (New York, 1963), pp. 100-107; Clifford Truesdell, *Continuum Mechanics,* 4 vols. (New York, 1963-1964); and Arthur Wilson, *Diderot: The Testing Years* (New York, 1957). Of the above, Boyer, Dugas, Rouse and Ince, and particularly Truesdell, deal specifically and in detail with d'Alembert's science.

Three recent doctoral dissertations on d'Alembert are J. Morton Briggs, *D'Alembert: Mechanics, Matter, and Morals* (New York, 1962): Thomas Hankins, *Jean d'Alembert, Scientist and Philosopher* (Cornell University, 1964); and Harold Jarrett, *D'Alembert and the Encyclopédie* (Durham, N. C., 1962).

J. MORTON BRIGGS

ALZATE Y RAMÍREZ, JOSÉ ANTONIO (*b.* Ozumba, Mexico, 1738; *d.* Mexico City, Mexico, 1799)

Born into a wealthy country family, Alzate attended San Ildefonso College and graduated in 1753 with a bachelor of arts degree. In 1756, he received a bachelor of divinity degree from the University of Mexico, and was subsequently ordained as a Roman Catholic priest.

An enthusiastic naturalist and man of letters, Alzate was a member of the Sociedad Económica Vascongada, the Real Jardín Botánico de Madrid, and the Académie Royale des Sciences de Paris. He embraced the ideas of the Enlightenment and devoted his life to the study of all branches of natural science. On various occasions, he was commissioned by the colonial government to solve problems affecting the public interest. His principal aim was to transcend the Aristotelian philosophy of his day and to promote the development of technology in New Spain. The value of his scientific production was not consistent, however, for his work covered a great many fields and was often conducted in an unfavorable atmosphere.

Aggressive by nature, Alzate was continually involved in scientific polemics, and his sarcasm aroused the animosity of his colleagues. He struggled to contradict the European opinions regarding the inferiority of American scientific knowledge. When Charles III of Spain sent a botanical expedition to New Spain, Alzate touched off a lengthy controversy by defending the advanced botanical knowledge of the ancient Mexicans and criticizing the Spaniards' application of Linnaean methods and principles.

Using his own limited economic resources, Alzate founded several scientific periodicals: *Diario literario de México* (1768); *Asuntos varios sobre ciencias y artes* (1772); *Observaciones sobre la fisica, historia natural y artes utiles* (1787); and *Gazeta de literatura* (1788–1795). On the basis of these journals, all of which were designed to improve the country's welfare through technology, Alzate is considered to be one of the pioneers of scientific journalism in the western hemisphere.

As a result of his continuous efforts to promote the scientific advancement of his countrymen and his successful fight to abolish the scholastic systems used in the colonial institutions, Alzate is regarded as one of the forerunners of Mexican independence. In 1884, the Sociedad Científica Antonio Alzate (now known as the Academia Nacional de Ciencias) was founded in Mexico City. Many Mexican intellectuals consider Alzate to be the father of modern natural science in Mexico.

BIBLIOGRAPHY

For information on Alzate's life and work, see F. Fernández del Castillo, "Apuntes para la biografía del Presbítero Bachiller J. A. F. de Alzate y Ramírez," in *Memorias de la Sociedad científica "Antonio Alzate,"* **48** (1927), 347–375; J. Galindo y Villa, "El Pbro. J. A. Alzate y Ramírez. Apuntes biográficos y bibliográficos," *ibid.,* **3** (1889–1890), 125–183, and "El enciclopedista Antonio Alzate," in *Memorias de la Academia nacional de ciencias "Antonio Alzate,"* **54** (1934), 9–14; A. Gómez Orozco, "Don Antonio Alzate y Ramírez," in *Humanidades,* **1** (1943), 169–177. See also R. Moreno Montes de Oca, "Alzate y la conciencia nacional," in *Memorias de la Academia nacional de ciencias "Antonio Alzate,"* **57** (1955), 561–572, and "Alzate y su concepción de la ciencia," in *Memorias del primer coloquio mexicano de historia de la ciencia,* **2** (1965), 185–200; B. Navarro, "Alzate, símbolo de la cultura ilustrada mexicana," in *Memorias de la Academia nacional de ciencias "Antonio Alzate,"* **57** (1952), 176–183.

ENRIQUE BELTRÁN

AMPÈRE, ANDRÉ-MARIE (*b.* Lyons, France, 22 January 1775; *d.* Marseilles, France, 10 June 1836)

Ampère's father, Jean-Jacques, was a merchant of independent means who, soon after his son's birth, moved the family to the nearby village of Poleymieux, where André-Marie grew up. The house is today a national museum. Jean-Jacques Ampère had been greatly influenced by the educational theories of Rousseau and was determined to educate his son along the lines laid down in *Émile.* The method he seems to have followed was to expose his son to a considerable library and let him educate himself as his own tastes dictated. One of the first works Ampère read was Buffon's *Histoire naturelle,* which stimulated his lifelong interest in taxonomy. Probably the most important influence on him was the great *Encyclopédie*—even thirty years later he could recite many of the articles from memory. In his father's library he also discovered Antoine Laurent Thomas's eulogy of Descartes, which convinced him of the nobility of a life in science. It also introduced him to metaphysics, the one passion he sustained throughout his life.

Almost incidentally Ampère discovered and perfected his mathematical talents. As an infant, he was fascinated by numbers and taught himself the elements of number theory. Like the young Pascal, having been forbidden the rigors of geometry because of his tender years, he defied parental authority and worked out the early books of Euclid by himself.

When the librarian in Lyons informed him that the works by Euler and Bernoulli that he wished to read were in Latin, Ampère rushed home to learn this language. He soon became adept enough to read the books that interested him, but continued his studies to the point where he could write quite acceptable Latin verse.

Ampère's early education was also conducted in a deeply religious atmosphere. His mother, the former Jeanne Desutières-Sarcey, was a devout woman who saw to it that her son was thoroughly instructed in the Catholic faith. Throughout his life, Ampère reflected the double heritage of the *Encyclopédie* and Catholicism. He was almost constantly assailed by the doubts sown by the Encyclopedists and, just as constantly, renewed his faith. From this conflict came his concern for metaphysics, which shaped his approach to science.

Ampère's childhood ended in 1789 with the outbreak of the French Revolution. Although Poleymieux was a rural backwater, the events in Lyons soon involved the Ampère family. Jean-Jacques was called upon by his fellow citizens to assume the post of *juge de paix,* a post with important police powers. He met the threat of a Jacobin purge head-on by ordering the arrest of Joseph Chalier, the leading Jacobin of Lyons. Chalier was executed. When Lyons fell to the troops of the Republic, Jean-Jacques Ampère was tried and guillotined on 23 November 1793. The event struck André-Marie like a bolt of lightning. The world had always been remote; now it had moved to the very center of his life, and this sudden confrontation was more than he could immediately bear. For a year he retreated within himself, not speaking to anyone and trying desperately to understand what had happened. His contact with the outside world was minimal; only an interest in botany, stimulated by a reading of Rousseau's letters on the subject, seemed to survive.

It was in this extremely vulnerable emotional state that Ampère met the young lady who was to become his wife. Julie Carron was somewhat older than Ampère and as a member of a good bourgeois family must have seen Ampère's suit in a somewhat unfavorable light. Although the Ampères and the Carrons lived in neighboring villages and shared a common economic and social background, marriage seemed impossible. At twenty-two, Ampère had only a small patrimony and no trade or other special skill. He was also homely and rustic, characteristics that were hardly likely to attract someone accustomed to the society and usages of Lyons. Ampère's courtship, carefully documented in his journal, reveals an essential aspect of his character: he was an incurable romantic whose emotional life was both intense and simple. Having lost his heart to Julie, he had no choice but to pursue her until she finally consented to marry him. His joy, like his despair at the death of his father, was immoderate. So, in his science, Ampère was possessed by his own enthusiasm. He never laid out a course of experiments or line of thought; there would be a brilliant flash of insight that he would pursue feverishly to its conclusion.

On 7 August 1799 Ampère and Julie were wed. The next four years were the happiest of Ampère's life. At first he was able to make a modest living as a mathematics teacher in Lyons, where on 12 August 1800 his son, Jean-Jacques, was born. In February 1802 Ampère left Lyons to become professor of physics and chemistry at the *école centrale* of Bourg-en-Bresse, a position that provided him with more money and, more important, with the opportunity to prepare himself for a post in the new *lycée* that Napoleon intended to establish at Lyons. In April of that year he began work on an original paper on probability theory that, he was convinced, would make his reputation. Thus, everything concurred to make him feel the happiest of men. Then tragedy struck. Julie had been ill since the birth of their son, and on 13 July 1803 she died. Ampère was inconsolable, and began to cast about desperately for some way to leave Lyons and all its memories.

On the strength of his paper on probability, he was named *répétiteur* in mathematics at the École Polytechnique in Paris. Again his emotional state was extreme, and again he fell victim to it. Bored by his work at the École Polytechnique, lonely in a strange and sophisticated city, Ampère sought human companionship and was drawn into a family that appeared to offer him the emotional warmth he so desperately craved. On 1 August 1806 he married Jeanne Potot. The marriage began under inauspicious circumstances: his father-in-law had swindled him out of his patrimony and his wife had indicated that she was uninterested in bearing children. The marriage was a catastrophe from the very beginning. After the birth of a daughter, Albine, his wife and mother-in-law made life so unbearable for Ampère that he realized that his only recourse was a divorce. Albine joined Jean-Jacques in Ampère's household, now presided over by his mother and his aunt, who had come to Paris from Poleymieux.

In 1808 Ampère was named inspector general of the newly formed university system, a post he held, except for a few years in the 1820's, until his death. On 28 November 1814 he was named a member of the class of mathematics in the Institut Impérial. In September 1819 he was authorized to offer a course in philosophy at the University of Paris, and in 1820 he was named assistant professor (*professeur suppléant*) of astronomy. In August 1824 Ampère was elected to the chair of experimental physics at the Collège de France.

During these years, Ampère's domestic life continued in turmoil. His son, for whom he had great hopes, fell under the spell of Mme. Recamier, one of the great beauties of the Empire, and for twenty years was content to be in her entourage. His daughter, Albine, married an army officer who turned out to be a drunkard and a near maniac. There was, too, a constant anxiety about money. In 1836 Ampère's health failed and he died, alone, while on an inspection tour in Marseilles.

Ampère's personal misery had an important effect on his intellectual development. His deep religious faith was undoubtedly strengthened by the almost constant series of catastrophes with which he was afflicted. Each successive tragedy also reinforced his desire for absolute certainty in some area of his life. His son later remarked on this characteristic of his father's approach; he was never content with probabilities but always sought Truth. It is no coincidence that his first mathematical paper, "Des considérations sur la théorie mathématique du jeu" (1802), proved that a single player inevitably would lose in a game of chance if he were opposed by a group whose financial resources were infinitely larger than his own. The outcome was certain.

In science Ampère's search for certainty and the exigencies of his faith led him to devise a philosophy that determined the form of his scientific research. The dominant philosophy in France in the early years of the nineteenth century was that of the Abbé de Condillac and his disciples, dubbed *Idéologues* by Napoleon. It maintained that only sensations were real, thus leaving both God and the existence of an objective world open to doubt. Such a position was abhorrent to Ampère, and he cast about for an alternative view. He was one of the earliest Frenchmen to discover the works of Immanuel Kant. Although Kant's philosophy made it possible to retain one's religious faith, Ampère felt that his treatment of space, time, and causality implied the doubtful existence of an objective reality at a fundamental level. Space and time, as Ampère interpreted Kant, became subjective modes of the human understanding, and Ampère, as a mathematician, could not accept this.

He therefore constructed his own philosophy. Its foundation was provided by his friend Maine de Biran, who felt he had successfully refuted David Hume's conclusion that *cause* simply meant succession of phenomena in time. The act of moving one's arm provided a firm proof that a cause explained an act and was not simply a description of succession. One wills the arm to move and one is conscious of the act of willing; the arm then moves. Therefore the arm moves *because* one wills it to. Ampère used this argument to prove the existence of an external world. If one's arm cannot move because it is, say, under a heavy table, then one becomes conscious of causes external to oneself. The arm does not move because the table prevents it from doing so. Thus Ampère carried causation from the psychological world to the physical world. Moreover, the resistance of the table proved, to Ampère's satisfaction, that matter does exist, for this external cause must be independent of our sensation of it. With similar arguments, Ampère was able to prove that the soul and God also must exist.

Ampère's philosophy permitted him to retain both a belief in God and a belief in the real existence of an objective nature. The next step was to determine what could be known about the physical world. Here again, Ampère's analysis contained highly idiosyncratic views on the nature of scientific explanation which were to be clearly illustrated in his own work. There are (and here the influence of Kant is obvious) two levels of knowledge of the external world. There are phenomena, presented to us directly through the senses, and there are noumena, the objective causes of phenomena. Noumena, according to Ampère, are known through the activity of the mind, which hypothesizes certain real, material entities whose properties can be used to account for phenomena. These two aspects of reality, however, are not all that we can know. We also can know relations (*rapports*) between phenomena and relations between noumena, and these relations are just as objectively real as the noumena. One example may suffice to illustrate this. It had been known since the end of the eighteenth century that two volumes of hydrogen combined with one volume of oxygen to form two volumes of water vapor. This is knowledge of a specific phenomenon.

In 1808 Gay-Lussac discovered that all gases combine in simple ratios, and thus was able to announce his law of combining volumes. The law states a relationship between phenomena and thereby extends our knowledge of the phenomenal world. In 1814 Ampère published his "Lettre de M. Ampère à M. le comte Berthollet sur la détermination des proportions dans lesquelles les corps se combinent d'après le nombre et la disposition respective des molécules dont leurs particules intégrantes sont composées."[1] It was an attempt to provide the noumenal, and therefore deeper, explanation of the phenomenal relations. From the theory of universal attraction used to account for the cohesion of bodies and the fact that light easily passes through transparent bodies, Ampère concluded that the attractive and repulsive forces associated with each molecule hold the ultimate molecules of bodies at distances from one another that are, as Ampère put it, "infinitely great in comparison to the dimensions of these molecules." This is knowledge of the noumena. It explains certain basic qualities of the observable world in terms of theoretical entities whose properties can be hypothesized from phenomena.

From the science of crystallography Ampère borrowed the idea of the integral particle, that is, the smallest particle of a crystal that has the form of the crystal. Ampère's molecules now were assumed to group themselves in various ways to form particles that had specific geometric forms. Thus there would be particles composed of four molecules that formed tetrahedrons (oxygen, nitrogen, and hydrogen), of six molecules that formed an octahedron (chlorine), etc. These geometrical forms were of the greatest importance in Ampère's theory, for they allowed him to deal with the problem of elective affinity and also to deduce Avogadro's law. Ampère's particles were compound and could, therefore, be broken down into smaller parts. Thus, oxygen was composed of four molecules that could, and did, separate under certain conditions, with two molecules going one way and two the other. The rule was that only compounds whose molecules were regular polyhedrons could be formed. If a tetrahedron met an octahedron, there could not be a simple combination, for the result would be a bizarre (in Ampère's terms) geometrical figure. Two tetrahedrons could combine with one octahedron, however, since the result would be a dodecahedron.

Ampère's philosophy and its influence on his science are obvious here. The relations of noumena, in this case the association of molecules to form a geometrically regular form, are simply assumed. If Ampère had been asked what evidence he had for the existence of such forms, he would have replied that no evidence could be offered. One hypothesizes noumena and relations between them in order to give causal explanations of phenomena. There can be no "evidence" for the noumena; there can be only the greater or lesser success of the noumenal hypothesis in explaining what can be observed. The point is of central importance, for it permitted Ampère to assume whatever he wished about the noumena. His assumption of an electrodynamic molecule followed this pattern exactly.

Ampère's philosophical analysis also provided him with the key for his classification of the sciences, which he considered the capstone of his career. Like Kant, he was concerned with relating precisely what man could know with the sciences that dealt with each part of man's ability to know. The chart appended to the first volume of his *Essai sur la philosophie des sciences* (1834) seems, at first glance, to be a fantastic and uncorrelated list of possible objects of investigation. If Ampère's philosophical views are attended to, however, they all fall into a rather simple pattern. We may use general physics as an example. In Ampère's classification this is divided into two second-order sciences—elementary general physics and mathematical physics. Each of these, in turn, has two divisions. Elementary general physics consists of experimental physics and chemistry; mathematical physics is divided into stereonomy and atomology (Ampère's neologisms). Experimental physics deals with phenomena, i.e., with the accurate description of physical facts. Chemistry deals with the noumenal causes of the facts discovered by experimental physics. Stereonomy concerns the relations between phenomena, e.g., laws of the conduction of heat through a solid. Atomology explains these laws by demonstrating how they may be deduced from relations between the ultimate particles of matter. All other sciences are treated in this fashion and have exactly the same kind of fourfold division.

This classification reveals Ampère's far-ranging mind and permits us to understand his occasional excursions into botany, taxonomy, and even animal anatomy and physiology. He was, in large part, seeking confirmation for his philosophical analysis, rather than setting out on new scientific paths. By the time of his death, Ampère had found, to his great satisfaction, that his scheme did fit all the sciences and, in his *Essai sur la philosophie des sciences,* he maintained that the fit was too good to be coincidence; the classification must reflect truth. Once again he had found certainty where his predecessors had not.

Although the one continuing intellectual passion of Ampère's life from 1800 to his death was his philosophical system, these years were also devoted to scientific research of considerable originality. From 1800 to about 1814, he devoted himself primarily to mathematics. As his mathematical interests declined, he became fascinated with chemistry and, from 1808 to 1815, spent his spare time in chemical investigations. From 1820 to 1827, he founded and developed the science of electrodynamics, the scientific work for which he is best known and which earned him his place in the first rank of physicists.

Ampère was not a truly outstanding mathematician. His first paper showed considerable originality and, more revealingly, great ability as an algorist. Like Leonhard Euler, Ampère had the uncanny ability, found only in the born mathematician, to discover mathematical relations. His largest mathematical memoir, "Mémoire sur l'intégration des équations aux différences partielles" (1814), was on various means of integrating partial differential equations. Although one should not underestimate the utility of such works, they should not be put in the same class as, say, the invention of quaternions by Sir William Rowan Hamilton or the laying of rigorous foundations of the calculus by Augustin Cauchy.

Ampère's failure to achieve the early promise he had shown in mathematics was undoubtedly the result of his passion for metaphysics and the necessity of earning a living. But there was also the fact, worth noting here, that the French scientific system forced him to do mathematics when his interests were focused elsewhere. Having been classified as a mathematician, Ampère found himself unable to gain recognition as anything else until after his epoch-making papers on electrodynamics. The security that came with election to the Academy of Sciences was achieved by Ampère only at the cost of putting aside his chemical interests and writing a mathematical memoir for the express purpose of gaining entry to the Academy. Original mathematical work is rarely done under such conditions.

Ampère's interest in chemistry had been aroused in the days when he gave private lessons at Lyons. This interest continued to grow at Bourg-en-Bresse, where he mastered the subject, and it became most intense about 1808, when Humphry Davy was shaking the foundations of the orthodox chemistry of the French school. Ampère once described himself as credulous in matters of science, and this again reflected his philosophy. A new scientific idea could be immediately accepted as a hypothesis even if there was no evidence for it, just as a fundamental assumption could be made without evidence: the main criterion was whether it worked or not. Ampère was not committed to Lavoisier's system of chemistry.

When Davy announced the discovery of sodium and potassium, the orthodox were startled, if not dismayed. How could oxygen be the principle of acidity, as Lavoisier had insisted, if the oxides of potassium and sodium formed the strongest alkalies? For Ampère there was no problem; he simply accepted the fact. If this fact were true, however, then the oxygen theory of acids was probably wrong. And if this were so, then the great riddle of muriatic acid could easily be solved. The green gas that was given off when muriatic acid was decomposed need not be a compound of some unknown base and oxygen; it could be an element. Thus, at the same time that Davy was questioning the compound nature of chlorine, Ampère had also concluded that it was an element. Unfortunately, and much to his later regret, he had neither the time nor the resources to prove this point, and the credit for the discovery of chlorine as an element went to Davy. Ampère was forestalled once again by Davy in 1813, when he brought Davy a sample of a new substance that Bernard Courtois had isolated from seaweed. Ampère had already seen its similarities to chlorine, but it was Davy who first publicly insisted upon its elemental character and named it iodine.

The noumenal aspect of chemistry fascinated Ampère. Although his derivation of Avogadro's law came three years after Avogadro had enunciated it, the law is known today in France as the Avogadro-Ampère law. This was Ampère's first excursion into molecular physics, and was followed almost immediately by a second. In 1815 he published a paper demonstrating the relation between Mariotte's (Boyle's) law and the volumes and pressures of gases at the same temperature. The paper is of some interest as a pioneer effort, along with Laplace's great papers on capillarity, in the application of mathematical analysis to the molecular realm.

In 1816 Ampère turned to the phenomenal relations of chemistry in a long paper on the natural classification of elementary bodies ("Essai d'une classification naturelle pour les corps simples"). Here he drew attention to the similarities between Lavoisier's and his followers' classification of elements in terms of their reactions with oxygen and Linnaeus' classification of plants in terms of their sexual organs. Bernard de Jussieu had successfully challenged Linnaeus with his natural system that took the whole plant into account and sought affinities between all parts of the plant, not just the flowers, as the basis of classification. Ampère now wished to do the same thing for chemistry. By discovering a natural classification, i.e., one that tied the elements together by real rather than artificial relations, Ampère hoped to provide a new insight into chemical reactions. His classificatory scheme, therefore, was not merely an ordering of the elements but, like the later periodic table of Dmitri Mendeleev, a true instrument of chemical research.

Unfortunately, Ampère's system was as artificial as Lavoisier's. Although he looked for more analogies among elements than Lavoisier had, the ones he selected offered little insight into the relations between the groups founded on them. The paper may be noted, however, as an early attempt to find relationships between the elements that would bring some order into the constantly growing number of elementary bodies.

By 1820 Ampère had achieved a certain reputation as both a mathematician and a somewhat heterodox chemist. Had he died before September of that year, he would be a minor figure in the history of science. It was the discovery of electromagnetism by Hans Christian Oersted in the spring of 1820 which opened up a whole new world to Ampère and gave him the opportunity to show the full power of his method of discovery. On 4 September 1820 François Arago reported Oersted's discovery to an astonished and skeptical meeting of the Académie des Sciences. Most of the members literally could not believe their ears; had not the great Coulomb proved to everyone's satisfaction in the 1780's that there could not be any interaction between electricity and magnetism? Ampère's credulity served him well here; he immediately accepted Oersted's discovery and turned his mind to it. On 18 September he read his first paper on the subject to the Académie; on 25 September and 9 October he continued the account of his discoveries. In these feverish weeks the science of electrodynamics was born.

There is some confusion over the precise nature of Ampère's first discovery. In the published memoir, "Mémoire sur l'action naturelle de deux courants électriques . . ." (1820), he stated that his mind leaped immediately from the existence of electromagnetism to the idea that currents traveling in circles through helices would act like magnets. This may have been suggested to him by consideration of terrestrial magnetism, in which circular currents seemed obvious. Ampère immediately applied his theory to the magnetism of the earth, and the genesis of electrodynamics may, indeed, have been as Ampère stated it. On the other hand, there is an account of the meetings of the Académie des Sciences at which Ampère spoke of his discoveries and presented a somewhat different order of discovery. It would appear that Oersted's discovery suggested to Ampère that two current-carrying wires might affect one another. It was this discovery that he announced to the Académie on 25 September.[2] Since the pattern of magnetic force around a current-carrying wire was circular, it was no great step for Ampère the geometer to visualize the resultant force if the wire were coiled into a helix. The mutual attraction and repulsion of two helices was also announced to the Académie on 25 September. What Ampère had done was to present a new theory of magnetism as electricity in motion.

From this point on, Ampère's researches followed three different but constantly intertwining paths. They conform exactly to his ideas on the nature of science and scientific explanation. The phenomenon of electromagnetism had been announced by Oersted; the relations of two current-carrying wires had been discovered by Ampère. It remained to explore these relations in complete and elaborate detail. Then, following his own philosophy, it was necessary for Ampère to seek the noumenal causes of the phenomena, which were found in his famous electrodynamic model and theory of the nature of electricity. Finally, Ampère had to discover the relations between the noumena from which all the phenomena could be deduced. Between 1820 and 1825 he successfully completed each of these tasks.

Ampère's first great memoir on electrodynamics was almost completely phenomenological, in his sense of the term. In a series of classical and simple experiments, he provided the factual evidence for his contention that magnetism was electricity in motion. He concluded his memoir with nine points that bear repetition here, since they sum up his early work.

> 1. Two electric currents attract one another when they move parallel to one another in the same direction; they repel one another when they move parallel but in opposite directions.
>
> 2. It follows that when the metallic wires through which they pass can turn only in parallel planes, each of the two currents tends to swing the other into a position parallel to it and pointing in the same direction.
>
> 3. These attractions and repulsions are absolutely different from the attractions and repulsions of ordinary [static] electricity.
>
> 4. All the phenomena presented by the mutual action of an electric current and a magnet discovered by M. Oersted . . . are covered by the law of attraction and of repulsion of two electric currents that has just been enunciated, if one admits that a magnet is only a collection of electric currents produced by the action of the particles of steel upon one another analogous to that of the elements of a voltaic pile, and which exist in planes perpendicular to the line which joins the two poles of the magnet.
>
> 5. When a magnet is in the position that it tends to take by the action of the terrestrial globe, these currents move in a sense opposite to the apparent motion of the sun; when one places the magnet in the opposite position so that the poles directed toward the poles of the earth are the same [S to S and N to N, not south-seeking to S, etc.] the same currents are found in the

same direction as the apparent motion of the sun.

6. The known observed effects of the action of two magnets on one another obey the same law.

7. The same is true of the force that the terrestrial globe exerts on a magnet, if one admits electric currents in planes perpendicular to the direction of the declination needle, moving from east to west, above this direction.

8. There is nothing more in one pole of a magnet than in the other; the sole difference between them is that one is to the left and the other is to the right of the electric currents which give the magnetic properties to the steel.

9. Although Volta has proven that the two electricities, positive and negative, of the two ends of the pile attract and repel one another according to the same laws as the two electricities produced by means known before him, he has not by that demonstrated completely the identity of the fluids made manifest by the pile and by friction; this identity was proven, as much as a physical truth can be proven, when he showed that two bodies, one electrified by the contact of [two] metals, and the other by friction, acted upon each other in all circumstances as though both had been electrified by the pile or by the common electric machine [electrostatic generator]. The same kind of proof is applicable here to the identity of attractions and repulsions of electric currents and magnets.[3]

Here Ampère only hinted at the noumenal background. Like most Continental physicists, he felt that electrical phenomena could be explained only by two fluids and, as he pointed out in the paper, a current therefore had to consist of the positive fluid going in one direction and the negative fluid going in the other through the wire. His experiments had proved to him that this contrary motion of the two electrical fluids led to unique forces of attraction and repulsion in current-carrying wires, and his first paper was intended to describe these forces in qualitative terms. There was one problem: how could this explanation be extended to permanent magnets? The answer appeared deceptively simple: if magnetism were only electricity in motion, then there must be currents of electricity in ordinary bar magnets.

Once again Ampère's extraordinary willingness to frame *ad hoc* hypotheses is evident. Volta had suggested that the contact of two dissimilar metals would give rise to a current if the metals were connected by a fluid conductor. Ampère simply assumed that the contact of the molecules of iron in a bar magnet would give rise to a similar current. A magnet could, therefore, be viewed as a series of voltaic piles in which electrical currents moved concentrically around the axis of the magnet. Almost immediately, Ampère's friend Augustin Fresnel, the creator of the wave theory of light, pointed out that this hypothesis simply would not do. Iron was not a very good conductor of the electrical fluids and there should, therefore, be some heat generated if Ampère's views were correct. Magnets are not noticeably hotter than their surroundings and Ampère, when faced with this fact, had to abandon his noumenal explanation.

It was Fresnel who provided Ampère with a way out. Fresnel wrote in a note to Ampère that since nothing was known about the physics of molecules, why not assume currents of electricity around each molecule. Then, if these molecules could be aligned, the resultant of the molecular currents would be precisely the concentric currents required. Ampère immediately adopted his friend's suggestion, and the electrodynamic molecule was born. It is, however, a peculiar molecule. In some mysterious fashion, a molecule of iron decomposed the luminiferous ether that pervaded both space and matter into the two electrical fluids, its constituent elements. This decomposition took place *within* the molecule; the two electrical fluids poured out the top, flowed around the molecule, and reentered at the bottom. The net effect was that of a single fluid circling the molecule. These molecules, when aligned by the action of another magnet, formed a permanent magnet. Ampère did not say why molecules should act this way; for him it was enough that his electrodynamic model provided a noumenal foundation for electrodynamic phenomena.

There was no doubt that Ampère took his electrodynamic molecule seriously and expected others to do so too. In an answer to a letter from the Dutch physicist Van Beck, published in the *Journal de physique* in 1821, Ampère argued eloquently for his model, insisting that it could be used to explain not only magnetism but also chemical combination and elective affinity. In short, it was to be considered the foundation of a new theory of matter. This was one of the reasons why Ampère's theory of electrodynamics was not immediately and universally accepted. To accept it meant to accept as well a theory of the ultimate structure of matter itself.

Having established a noumenal foundation for electrodynamic phenomena, Ampère's next steps were to discover the relationships between the phenomena and to devise a theory from which these relationships could be mathematically deduced. This double task was undertaken in the years 1821–1825, and his success was reported in his greatest work, the *Mémoire sur la théorie mathématique des phénomènes électrodynamique, uniquement déduite de l'expérience* (1827). In this work, the *Principia* of electrodynamics, Ampère first described the laws of action of electric currents, which he had discovered from four extremely ingenious experiments. The measurement of electrodynamic forces was very difficult, although it could be done, as J.-B. Biot and Félix Savart had shown in their formulation of the Biot-Savart law. Ampère realized, however, that much greater accuracy could be achieved if the experiments could be null experiments, in which the forces involved were in equilibrium.

The first experiment, to quote Ampère, "demonstrated the equality of the absolute value of the attraction and repulsion which is produced when a current flows first in one direction, then in the opposite direction in a fixed conductor which is left unchanged as to its orientation and at the same distance from the body on which it acts." The second "consists in the equality of the actions exerted on a mobile rectilinear conductor by two fixed conductors situated at equal distances from the first of which one is rectilinear and the other bent or contorted in any way whatsoever. . . ." The third case demonstrated "that a closed circuit of any form whatsoever cannot move any portion of a conducting wire forming an arc of a circle whose center lies on a fixed axis about which it may turn freely and which is perpendicular to the plane of the circle of which the arc is a part." Ampère rather casually mentioned at the end of the *Mémoire* that he had not actually performed the fourth experiment, which was intended to determine certain constants necessary for the solution of his mathematical equation. These constants, it would appear, had been found by measuring the action of a magnet and a current-carrying wire upon one another and were sufficiently accurate to permit Ampère to continue his researches.

From these cases of equilibrium, Ampère was able to deduce certain necessary consequences that permitted him to apply mathematics to the phenomena. It was time to turn to the noumena once again and to complete the edifice by deducing from the noumenal elements those mathematical relationships that had been indicated by experiment. The flow of an electrical current, it will be remembered, was a complicated process in Ampère's theory. Positive electricity was flowing in one direction in the wire while negative electricity flowed in the opposite direction. The luminiferous ether was a compound of these two fluids, so that it was constantly being formed from their union, only to be decomposed as each fluid went its way. Thus, at any moment in the wire there were elements of positive electricity, negative electricity, and the ether. Ampère's current element (*ids*), therefore, was not a mathematical fiction assumed out of mathematical necessity, but a real physical entity. What his experiments had done was to tell him the basic properties of this element. The force associated with the element is a central force, acting at a distance at right angles to the element's direction of flow. From this fact it was easy to deduce that the mutual action of two lengths of current-carrying wire is proportional to their length and to the intensities of the currents. Ampère was now prepared to give precise mathematical form to this action. As early as 1820, he had deduced a law of force between two current elements, *ids* and *i'ds'*. He gave the formula

$$F = \frac{i \cdot i' \cdot ds \cdot ds'}{r^2} [\sin\theta \cdot \sin\theta' \cdot \cos\omega + k \cos\theta \cdot \cos\theta']$$

for the force between two current elements, making angles θ and θ' with the line joining them and the two planes containing this line and the two elements respectively making an angle ω with each other. At that time he had been unable to evaluate the constant k. By 1827 he was able to show that $k = -1/2$. The formula above could now be written

$$F = \frac{i \cdot i' \cdot ds \cdot ds'}{r^2} [\sin\theta \cdot \sin\theta' \cdot \cos\omega - 1/2 \cos\theta \cdot \cos\theta'].$$

When integrated around a complete circuit (as in practice it must be), this formula is identical with that of Biot and Savart.

It was now possible for Ampère to attack the theory of magnetism quantitatively. He could show that his law of action of current elements led to the conclusion that the forces of a magnet composed of electrodynamic molecules should be directed toward the poles. He was also able to deduce Coulomb's law of magnetic action. In short, he was able to unify the fields of electricity and magnetism on a basic noumenal level. The theory was complete.

Not everyone accepted Ampère's theory. His primary opponent was Michael Faraday, who could not follow the mathematics and felt that the whole structure was based on *ad hoc* assumptions for which there was no evidence whatsoever. The phenomenal part was accepted; even in France the electrodynamic molecule was regarded with considerable suspicion. The idea, however, did not die with Ampère. It was accepted later in the century by Wilhelm Weber and became the basis of his theory of electromagnetism.

After 1827 Ampère's scientific activity declined sharply. These were the years of anxiety and fear for his daughter's well-being, as well as years of declining health. He produced an occasional paper but, by and large, after the great 1827 memoir Ampère's days as a creative scientist were ended. He turned instead to the completion of his essay on the philosophy of science and his classification of the sciences. He must have derived some satisfaction from the fact that he had, almost single-handedly, created a new science to be placed in his taxonomic scheme.

NOTES

1. *Annales de chimie,* **90** (1814), 43 ff.
2. See *Bibliothèque universelle des sciences, belles-lettres, et arts,* **17** (1821), 83.
3. *Mémoires sur l'électrodynamique,* I (Paris, 1885), 48.

BIBLIOGRAPHY

I. Original Works. The most important source for the life and work of Ampère is the forty cartons of documents in the archives of the Académie des Sciences in Paris. This material has been catalogued but never used. For Ampère's correspondence, see Louis de Launay, ed., *Correspondance du Grand Ampère,* 3 vols. (Paris, 1936–1943). It should be used with care, for there are many errors of transcription and it is not complete. It does, however, have a complete bibliography of Ampère's works at the end of the second volume. One should also consult *André-Marie Ampère et Jean-Jacques Ampère: Correspondance et souvenirs (de 1805 à 1864) recuellis par Madame H. C.*[*heuvreux*], 2 vols. (Paris, 1875), and Mme. Cheuvreux's *Journal et correspondance d'André-Marie Ampère* (Paris, 1872). These volumes should be used with great caution, for Mme. Cheuvreux was not a scholar and changed the order of whole passages, sometimes inserting part of one letter in another for artistic reasons. Ampère's papers on electrodynamics were reprinted by the Société Française de Physique as *Mémoires sur l'électrodynamique,* 2 vols. (Paris, 1885–1887). The *Mémoire sur la théorie mathématique des phénomènes électrodynamiques, uniquement déduite de l'expérience* (Paris, 1827) was republished with a foreword by Edmond Bauer (Paris, 1958). Portions of this work and others of Ampère's papers on electrodynamics have been translated and appear in R. A. R. Tricker, ed., *Early Electrodynamics: The First Law of Circulation* (Oxford, 1965). This volume contains a long commentary by the editor that is of great value in explaining Ampère's theory.

For Ampère's philosophical development, see *Philosophie des deux Ampère publiée par J. Barthélemy Saint-Hilaire* (Paris, 1866), which contains a long essay by Jean-Jacques Ampère on his father's philosophy.

II. Secondary Literature. There is no adequate biography of Ampère. C. A. Valson, *André-Marie Ampère* (Lyons, 1885), and Louis de Launay, *Le grand Ampère* (Paris, 1925), are the standard biographies, but neither discusses Ampère's work in any detail. The eulogy by François Arago provides a survey of Ampère's scientific achievement from the perspective of a century ago. See his *Oeuvres,* 17 vols. (Paris, 1854-1862), II, 1 ff. For some modern appreciations of Ampère's work, see the *Revue général de l'électricité,* **12** (1922), supplement. The entire issue is devoted to Ampère's work. For an interesting account of Ampère's early career, see Louis Mallez, *A.-M. Ampère, professeur à Bourg, membre de la Société d'Émulation de l'Ain, d'après des documents inédits* (Lyons, 1936).

For various aspects of Ampère's career, see Borislav Lorenz, *Die Philosophie André-Marie Ampères* (Berlin, 1908); and Maurice Lewandowski, *André-Marie Ampère. La science et la foi* (Paris, 1936). The *Bulletin de la Société des Amis d'André-Marie Ampère,* which appears irregularly, contains much Ampère lore. Two interesting sketches of Ampère are Henry James, "The Two Ampères," in *French Poets and Novelists* (London, 1878); and C. A. Sainte-Beuve, "M. Ampère," in *Portraits littéraires,* 3 vols. (Paris, 1862), I.

A discussion of Ampère's electrodynamic molecule is to be found in L. Pearce Williams, "Ampère's Electrodynamic Molecular Model," in *Contemporary Physics,* **4** (1962), 113 ff. For Ampère's relations with England, see K. R. and D. L. Gardiner, "André-Marie Ampère and His English Acquaintances," in *The British Journal for the History of Science,* **2** (1965), 235 ff.

L. Pearce Williams

AMSLER (later **AMSLER-LAFFON**), **JAKOB** (*b.* Stalden bei Brugg, Switzerland, 16 November 1823; *d.* Schaffhausen, Switzerland, 3 January 1912)

The son of a farmer, Amsler was educated at local schools before going on to study theology at the universities of Jena and Königsberg. At Königsberg he came under the influence of Franz Neumann, whose lectures and laboratory sessions he attended for seven semesters. After earning his doctorate in 1848, Amsler spent a year with Plantamour at the Geneva observatory; he went from there to Zurich, where he completed his *Habilitation* and began his teaching career. For four semesters he lectured on various topics in mathematics and mathematical physics, then in 1851 accepted a post at the Gymnasium in Schaffhausen. From this he hoped to gain some financial independence as well as an opportunity for more research. In 1854 Amsler married Elise Laffon, the daughter of a Schaffhausen druggist who was well known in Swiss scientific circles. Henceforth he used the double form Amsler-Laffon. The change applied to Jakob alone and was not adopted by his children.

Until 1854 Amsler's interests lay in the area of mathematical physics; he published articles on magnetic distribution, the theory of heat conduction, and the theory of attraction. One result of his work was a generalization of Ivory's theorem on the attraction of ellipsoids and of Poisson's extension of that theorem. In 1854 Amsler turned his attention to precision mathematical instruments, and his research resulted in his major contribution to mathematics: the polar planimeter, a device for measuring areas enclosed by plane curves. Previous such instruments, most notably that of Oppikofer (1827), had been based on the Cartesian coordinate system and had combined bulkiness with high cost. Amsler eliminated these drawbacks by basing his planimeter on a polar coordinate system referred to a null circle as curvilinear axis. The instrument, described in "Ueber das Polarplanimeter" (1856), adapted easily to the determination of static and inertial moments and of the coefficients of Fourier series; it proved especially useful to shipbuilders and railroad engineers.

To capitalize on his inspiration, Amsler established his own precision tools workshop in 1854. From 1857 on, he devoted full time to the venture. At his death, the shop had produced 50,000 polar planimeters and 700 momentum planimeters. The polar planimeter marked the height of Amsler's career. His later research, mostly in the area of precision and engineering instruments, produced no comparable achievement, although it did bring Amsler recognition and prizes from world exhibitions at Vienna (1873) and Paris (1881, 1889), as well as a corresponding membership in the Paris Academy (1892). From 1848 until his death, Amsler was an active member of the Naturforschende Gesellschaft in Zurich.

BIBLIOGRAPHY

I. ORIGINAL WORKS. Amsler's writings include: "Zur Theorie der Verteilung des Magnetismus im weichen Eisen," in *Abhandlungen der naturforschenden Gesellschaft in Zürich* (1847), reprinted in *Neue Denkschriften der allgemeinen schweizerischen Gesellschaft für die gesammten Naturwissenschaften,* **10** (1849); "Methode, den Einfluss zu kompensieren, welchen die Eisenmassen eines Schiffes infolge der Verteilung der magnetischen Flüssigkeiten durch den Erdmagnetismus auf die Kompassnadel ausüben," in *Verhandlungen der schweizerischen naturforschenden Gesellschaft* (1848); "Ueber die klimatologischen Verhältnisse der Polargegenden" and "Ueber die Anwendung von Schwingungsbeobachtungen zur Bestimmung der spezifischen Wärme fester Körper bei konstantem Volumen," in *Mitteilungen der naturforschenden Gesellschaft in Zürich,* **2** (1850–1852), 314–315; "Neue geometrische und mechanische Eigenschaft der Niveauflächen," "Zur Theorie der Anziehung und der Wärme," and "Ueber die Gesetze der Wärmeleitung im Innern fester Körper, unter Berücksichtigung der durch ungleichförmige Erwärmung erzeugten Spannung," in *Crelle's Journal,* **42** (1851), the last reprinted in *Neue Denkschriften,* **12** (1852); "Ueber das Polarplanimeter," in *Dingler's Journal,* **140** (1856); "Ueber die mechanische Bestimmung des Flächeninhaltes, der statischen Momente und der Trägheitsmomente ebener Figuren, insbesondere über einen neuen Planimeter," in *Vierteljahrsschrift der naturforschenden Gesellschaft in Zürich,* **1** (1856), also printed separately (Schaffhausen, 1856); "Anwendung des Integrators (Momentumplanimeters) zur Berechnung des Auf- und Abtrages bei Anlage von Eisenbahnen, Strassen und Kanälen," a pamphlet (Zurich, 1875); "Der hydrometrische Flügel mit Zählwerk und elektrischer Zeichengebung," a pamphlet (Schaffhausen, 1877), reprinted in *Carls Repertorium,* **14** (1878); "Neuere Planimeterkonstruktionen," in *Zeitschrift für Instrumentkunde,* **4** (1884); and "Die neue Wasserwerksanlage in Schaffhausen und einige darauf bezügliche technische Fragen," in *Schweizerische Bauzeitung,* **16** (1890).

II. SECONDARY LITERATURE. See Poggendorf, Vols. III, IV, and V. The present article is based on the necrology by Ferdinand Rudio and Alfred Amsler in *Vierteljahrsschrift der naturforschenden Gesellschaft in Zürich,* **57** (1912), 1-17, and on the extensive study by Fr. Dubois, "Die Schöpfungen Jakob und Alfred Amsler's auf dem Gebiete der mathematischen Instrumente anhand der Ausstellung im Museum Allerheiligen systematisch dargestellt," in *Mitteilungen der naturforschenden Gesellschaft Schaffhausen,* **19** (1944), 209-273.

M. S. MAHONEY

ANATOLIUS OF ALEXANDRIA (*b.* Alexandria; *d.* Laodicea; *fl. ca.* A.D. 269)

The historian Eusebius, whose *Ecclesiastical History* provides what we know of Anatolius' life, says, "For his learning, secular education and philosophy [he] had attained the first place among our most illustrious contemporaries." Learned in arithmetic, geometry, astronomy, and other sciences both intellectual and natural, Anatolius was also outstanding in rhetoric. The Alexandrians deemed him worthy of heading the Aristotelian school in that city.

Bishop Theotecnus of Caesarea consecrated Anatolius as his successor, and he held office for a while in Caesarea. About A.D. 280, however, as he passed through Laodicea on his way to Antioch, he was retained by the inhabitants as their bishop, the previous bishop, also called Eusebius, having died. He remained bishop of Laodicea until his death some years later.

Anatolius' Christian and humanitarian character was much admired. During a siege of the Greek quarter of Alexandria by the Roman army, he attempted to make peace between the factions. He failed, but he succeeded in winning safe conduct from the besieged quarter for all noncombatants.

Anatolius put his knowledge of astronomy at the

service of his religion in a treatise on the date of Easter. Eusebius gives the title of the work as *The Canons of Anatolius on the Pascha* and quotes several paragraphs that display Anatolius' grasp of astronomy in the discussion of the position of the sun and moon in the zodiac at the time of Easter. According to Eusebius, Anatolius did not write many books; but those that he did write were distinguished for eloquence and erudition, which is evident through his quotation of Philo, Josephus, and two of the seventy who translated the Old Testament into Greek during the third and second centuries B.C.

The only other work of Anatolius known to us by name is his *Introduction to Arithmetic*. In ten books, it seems to have been excerpted by the author of the curious writing entitled *Theologoumena arithmetica*. A Neoplatonic treatise, uncertainly attributed to Iamblichus, it is a discussion of each of the first ten natural numbers. It mixes accounts of truly arithmetical properties with mystical fancies. Many parts of the discussion are headed "of Anatolius." The character of its arithmetical lore may be illustrated by the following quotation from a part attributed to Anatolius: "[Four] is called 'justice' since its square is equal to the perimeter [i.e., $4 \times 4 = 16 = 4 + 4 + 4 + 4$]; of the numbers less than four the perimeter of the square is greater than the area, while of the greater the perimeter is less than the area."

In contrast with the flights of fancy preserved in *Theologoumena arithmetica*, some paragraphs of a writing of Anatolius are found in manuscripts of Hero of Alexander in which Anatolius deals soberly and sensibly, and in Aristotelian terms, with questions about mathematics, its name, its philosophical importance, and some of its methods. The structure of *Theologoumena arithmetica* and its selection of material from Anatolius suggest that Anatolius' *Introduction to Arithmetic* may have dealt with each of the first ten natural numbers. The Pythagoreanism or Neoplatonism manifested here was in the spirit of the times. Despite the number mysticism, however, Anatolius' competence in mathematics is clear and justifies the esteem in which Eusebius says he was held in Alexandria.

BIBLIOGRAPHY

No individual works of Anatolius' are known to exist today. Some paragraphs of a work by him are found in *Heronis Alexandrini geometricorum et stereometricorum reliquiae*, F. Hultsch, ed. (Berlin, 1864), pp. 276-280. A seeming use of excerpts from Anatolius' *Introduction to Arithmetic* is *Theologoumena arithmetica*, V. De Falco, ed. (Leipzig, 1922). Two sources of information on the life of Anatolius are Eusebius, *The Ecclesiastical History*, H. J. Lawlor, trans., II (Cambridge-London, 1942), 228-238; and Pauly-Wissowa, eds., *Real-Enzyklopädie der Klassischen Altertumswissenschaft*, XII (Stuttgart, 1894-), col. 2073 f.

JOHN S. KIEFFER

ANDERSON, OSKAR JOHANN VIKTOR (*b.* Minsk, Russia, 2 August 1887; *d.* Munich, German Federal Republic, 12 February 1960)

After studying for one term at the mathematical faculty of Kazan University, Anderson entered the economics faculty of the Petersburg Polytechnical Institute in 1907. He graduated in 1912 as a candidate in economics. His dissertation, in which he developed the variance-difference method for analyzing time series, was published in *Biometrika* (1914) almost simultaneously with similar work by W. S. Gosset.

Anderson was a pupil and an assistant of A. A. Tschuprow and always, even during the general excessive enthusiasm aroused by Karl Pearson's methods, considered himself a representative of the "Continental direction" of mathematical statistics exemplified by Lexis, Bortkiewicz, and Tschuprow. From 1912 until he left Russia in 1920, Anderson taught in commercial colleges at St. Petersburg and Kiev, and engaged in research. He participated in a study of the agriculture of Turkestan in 1915 using sampling methods—he was a pioneer in this field—and worked at the Demographical Institute of the Kiev Academy of Sciences in 1918.

After he left Russia, Anderson spent four years in Hungary, continuing his pedagogic and scientific activities. From 1924 to 1942 he lived in Bulgaria, where he was extraordinary professor of statistics and economic geography at the Varna Commercial College until 1929 and full professor from then on; a member of the Supreme Scientific Council of the Central Board of Statistics; and from 1935 director of the Statistical Institute of Economic Researches of Sofia University. Anderson was engaged mainly in the application of statistics to economics, and published a review of the general status of Bulgarian economics (1938). Subsequent economical-statistical investigations in Bulgaria were always conducted in the spirit of Andersonian traditions, and in this sense he founded a school in that country. Anderson also became internationally known: he published a primer (1935), delivered lectures at the London School of Economics in 1936, and was an adviser to the League of Nations and a charter member of the Econometric Society. He was also an honorary member of the Royal and West German Statistical Societies, the

International Statistical Institute, and the American Statistical Association.

In 1942 Anderson accepted a professorship at the University of Kiel; from 1947 until his death he held the chair of statistics at the economics faculty of the University of Munich and was the recognized leader of West German statisticians. His pedagogic activities resulted in higher standards of statistical education for student economists in West Germany.

Besides developing the variance-difference method, Anderson did research in the quantity theory of money and in the index-number theory from the statistical viewpoint. Seeing no significant advantage in the application of classical mathematics to economics, he advocated the application of mathematical statistics. Anderson believed that the application of statistics distinguished modern economics from economics based on Robinson Crusoe theories and the *homo oeconomicus.* He especially believed that statistics, based on the law of large numbers and the sorting out of random deviations, is the only substitute for experimentation, which is impossible in economics. Sensibly estimating the difficulties inherent in economics as a science, Anderson was opposed to the use of "refined" statistical methods and to accepting preconditions regarding laws of distribution. This led him to nonparametric methods and to the necessity of causal analysis in economics.

BIBLIOGRAPHY

I. ORIGINAL WORKS. Anderson published some eighty books, papers, reports to national and international bodies, reviews, and obituaries, mainly in German and Bulgarian. He published three papers in Russian.

His books are *Einführung in die mathematische Statistik* (Vienna, 1935); *Struktur und Konjunktur der bulgarischen Volkswirtschaft* (Jena, 1938); and *Probleme der statistischen Methodenlehre in den Sozialwissenschaften,* 4th ed. (Würzburg, 1962). These books provide a sufficient overall notion of Anderson's work. Intended for a broad circle of readers with a preuniversity mathematical background, they are less known outside the German-speaking countries than they deserve to be.

Aside from the books, Anderson's main writings are in his selected works: *Ausgewählte Schriften,* 2 vols. (Tübingen, 1963). Forty-six works by Anderson are reprinted there, with translations into German if the originals are in Bulgarian. Vol. II contains a list of his other works (thirty-two items). This list is not complete, however, for Anderson published at least two more works.

II. SECONDARY LITERATURE. General information about Anderson can be found in Capelli, ed., *Bibliografie con brevi cenni biografici, Biblioteca di statistica,* II, pt. 1 (1959); and *Kürschners deutscher Gelehrten-Kalender* (Berlin, 1961). About fifteen obituaries of Anderson are listed with a biography in Vol. I of the *Ausgewählte Schriften.* Among the obituaries are E. M. Fels, in *Econometrica,* **29,** no. 1 (1961), 74–80; G. Tintner, in *American Statistical Association, Quarterly Publication,* **56,** no. 294 (1961), 273–280; and H. Wold, in *Annals of Mathematical Statistics,* **32,** no. 3 (1961), 651–660.

The most recent biography of Anderson is E. M. Fels, in the *International Encyclopedia of the Social Sciences* (New York, 1968).

O. B. SHEYNIN

ANDOYER, HENRI (*b.* Paris, France, 1 October 1862; *d.* Paris, 12 June 1929)

Andoyer taught astronomy at the Sorbonne for thirty-seven years. His research dealt with celestial mechanics: perturbation theory, special cases of the three-body and of the *n*-body problem, and the motions of the moon. He developed special methods for use in computing ephemerides, the most elaborate one—for the moon—approximating E. W. Brown's definitive treatment but at a fraction of the labor.

Andoyer's interest in manipulating numbers began very early; his father's work as chief clerk at the Banque de France may have influenced him. He graduated at the top of his class in mathematical science at the École Normale Supérieure in 1884 and wrote his doctoral thesis (1887) on the theory of intermediate orbits as applied to the moon.

His first job took him to Toulouse, where besides continuing his theoretical studies he worked at the telescope, preparing a photographic map of the sky. In "Formules générales de la méchanique céleste" he showed how to solve the general equations of motion to any desired degree of accuracy in terms of trigonometric functions alone.

In 1892 Andoyer returned to Paris, where he began as a *maître de conférence* at the Sorbonne and became a full professor in 1903. Here he worked on special cases of the three-body problem, showing, for example, how to use the Lagrangian libration points (null points in a two-body gravitational field where a third body, of negligible mass, can remain more or less indefinitely) to make the periodic terms of the solution independent of time.

Next he attacked the problem of asteroids that, like Hecuba, move almost exactly twice as fast as Jupiter and hence are strongly perturbed. There followed an analysis of *n* bodies close to equilibrium points, which has been applied to problems of the general stability of the solar system.

In 1910 Andoyer became a member of the Bureau des Longitudes, where he succeeded to the editorship of *Connaissance des temps*, the French nautical almanac. During World War I, with most of the staff mobilized, he prepared many of the ephemerides himself. His *Nouvelles tables trigonométriques fondamentales*, prepared as an aid to computers, have values to fifteen decimal places. He must indeed have been, in the words of one of his students, *un calculateur formidable.*

In 1919 Andoyer became a member of the Académie des Sciences.

BIBLIOGRAPHY

I. ORIGINAL WORKS. Andoyer's doctoral thesis, "Contributions à la théorie des orbites intermédiares," appeared in *Annales de la Faculté des Sciences de Toulouse*, **1** (1887), M.1-M.72. Other papers include "Sur les formules générales de la méchanique céleste," *ibid.*, **4** (1890), K.1-K.35; "Sur le calcul des équations de perturbations," in *Bulletin astronomique* (Paris), **19** (1902), 49-61; "Contribution à la théorie des petites planètes dont le moyen mouvement est sensiblement double de celui de Jupiter," *ibid.*, **20** (1903), 321-356; and "Sur les solutions périodiques voisines des positions d'équilibre relatif, dans le problème des *n* corps," *ibid.*, **23** (1906), 129-146.

The *Nouvelles tables trigonométriques fondamentales* was published in three volumes (Paris, 1915-1918). His lunar theory, a revision of Charles Delaunay's earlier work, appeared in four installments under the general title "Sur la théorie analytique du mouvement de la lune," in *Mémoires de l'Académie des Sciences*, 2nd series, **58**, no. 1 (1926), 1-30; **58**, no. 2 (1926), 1-69; **59**, no. 1 (1928), 1-98; and **59**, no. 3 (1928), 1-59.

Andoyer's lectures at the Sorbonne resulted in eight textbooks: four on mathematics, published in Paris from 1894 to 1898—*Cours de géométrie, Cours d'arithmétique, Cours d'algèbre,* and *Leçons élémentaires sur la théorie des formes et applications géométriques*; and four on astronomy —*Cours d'astronomie, Part I* (Paris, 1906; 3rd ed., 1923) and *Part II*, written with A. Lambert (Paris, 1907; 2nd ed., 1924), and *Cours de méchanique céleste, Part I* (Paris, 1923) and *Part II* (Paris, 1926).

II. SECONDARY LITERATURE. An obituary, with a portrait and a list of sixty-seven publications, appeared in *Bulletin astronomique* (Paris), 2nd series, **6** (1930), 129-145; two shorter memorials, with anecdotes, are in *Journal des observateurs* (Marseilles), **12** (15 November 1929), 193-198, and **13** (April 1930), 61-64.

SALLY H. DIEKE

ANGELI, STEFANO DEGLI (*b.* Venice, Italy, 21 September 1623; *d.* Venice, 11 October 1697)

Born Francesco degli Angeli, he entered the Order of the Gesuati of Saint Jerolamen. At twenty-one he was appointed reader of literature, philosophy, and theology in the faculty of his order at Ferrara. He remained in Ferrara for about three years, although he was in poor health, until his physicians concluded that the climate of the city was harmful to him. He was then transferred to Bologna, where he developed a deep interest in mathematics under the guidance of a member of the same religious order, Bonaventura Cavalieri, who taught at the University of Bologna. Cavalieri was soon able to appreciate Angeli's ability, and encouraged him in his studies and mathematical researches.

Toward the end of his life, when he was gravely ill, Cavalieri entrusted Angeli with the task of correcting and publishing his last work, *Exercitationes geometricae sex* (1647). After Cavalieri's death in 1647, Angeli was offered the opportunity to succeed his master as professor of mathematics, but he was too modest to accept. Instead, he went to Rome, where he zealously continued his mathematical studies and his religious activity. About 1652 he was appointed prior of the monastery of the Gesuati in Venice, and shortly afterward he was given the post of provincial definer, a position he held until Pope Clement IX suppressed the order in 1668. On 2 January 1663 the Republic of Venice offered him the professorship of mathematics at the University of Padua, a post that had been held by Galileo, which he filled until his death. The mathematician Jacopo Riccati was among Angeli's pupils.

Angeli's studies in mathematics include a further development of the methods of indivisibles—methods introduced by Cavalieri and Evangelista Torricelli—to solve problems dealing with infinitesimals and with the areas, volumes, and centers of gravity of given geometric figures. His mathematical works echo the polemics that took place in the seventeenth century between supporters of the method of indivisibles and those such as Paul Guldin and Andreas Tacquet, who defended the more rigorous but less cogent exhaustive method of the ancients. "Lectori benevolo," the introduction to Angeli's *De infitinitis parabolis* (1654), is interesting in this connection. To those who opposed Cavalieri's method by asserting that the continuous is not composed of indivisibles, Angeli replied, in agreement with his master, that the method in question does not depend on the composition of the continuous.

Angeli's work on mathematics, *De infinitorum spiralium spatiorum mensura* (1660), deals with curves that constitute a generalization of Archimedes' spiral. A moving point describes one of these curves when it is acted upon by two movements, one uniform and rectilinear starting from a point *A*, and the other rotational around the same point *A*. If the rotational motion is also uniform, one obtains Archimedes' spiral; if, on the other hand, it varies, the general condition studied by Angeli results. In particular, if the angles described by the rotational motion are proportional to the squares of the times, one obtains a quadratic spiral; if these angles are proportional to the cubes of the times, one obtains a cubic spiral, and so on. The *De infinitorum spiralium* is devoted to the areas of the figures bounded by arcs of these curves and to the centers of gravity of the figures themselves.

In his *De infinitarum cochlearum mensuris ac centris gravitatis* (1661), Angeli begins with the definition of the solid that he called a *cochlea* and with the results of the problem published by Torricelli:[1] Consider in a given plane a figure, *F*, with nonzero area, and a straight line, *a*. Let *F* be subjected to a double motion; a rotational motion around *a* and a translation motion along the *a* direction. The solid thus obtained is a cochlea. Torricelli concluded that the volume of the cochlea is equivalent to that of a rotational solid; he had intended to devote a small volume to the later developments of the cochlea, especially regarding centers of gravity, but he died before completing it. In *De infinitarum cochlearum* Angeli seeks to carry out Torricelli's plan.

In questions dealing with infinitesimals, Angeli remained faithful to the indivisibles of the school of Galileo. Indeed, he proves to be unfamiliar with the points of view that follow from the analytic geometry of Descartes and the infinitesimal calculus of Newton and Leibniz, even though he had read Newton's *Naturalis philosophiae principia mathematica.*

Four of Angeli's minor works, in the form of dialogues that reflect Galileo's style, form a lively but cautious polemic on the problems of the Ptolemaic and Copernican cosmological systems. G. B. Riccioli, in his *Almagestum novum,* had formulated some arguments against the Copernican system. Angeli asserted that "the earth is motionless, but Riccioli's reasons do not prove the point," and he devoted the first of these studies (1667) to demonstrating that Riccioli's anti-Copernican arguments were without foundation. Angeli replied to Riccioli's arguments with another work in 1668. G. A. Borelli, who later participated in the polemic, rejected Riccioli's arguments and pointed out that if Angeli's views were correct, falling bodies should follow a vertical trajectory in the hypothesis of the earth's motion as well. In addition, he held that there must be a deviation to the east (as was experimentally proved by G. B. Guglielmini in 1791).[2]

Angeli's *Della gravità dell'aria e fluidi* is largely experimental in character. In it he examines the fluid statics, based on Archimedes' principle and on Torricelli's experiments. It also contains theories of capillary attraction.

In Angeli's works on physics, there are many references to Galileo's mechanics, as well as his acceptance of the experimental method.

NOTES

1. Torricelli's *Opere,* I, pt. 1 (Faenza, 1919), 223–230.
2. M. Gliozzi, *Storia della fisica,* Vol. II of *Storia delle scienze* (Turin, 1962), p. 89.

BIBLIOGRAPHY

I. Original Works. Angeli's works, all of which are in the library of the University of Padua, are *De infinitis parabolis, de infinitisque solidis* (Venice, 1654); *Problemata geometrica sexaginta* (Venice, 1658); *Miscellanaeum hyperbolicum et parabolicum* (Venice, 1659); *De infinitorum spiralium spatiorum mensura, opusculum geometricum* (Venice, 1660); *Miscellanaeum geometricum* (Venice, 1660); *De infinitarum cochlearum mensuris ac centris gravitatis* (Venice, 1661); *De superficie ungulae et de quartis liliorum parabolicorum et cycloidalium* (Venice, 1661); *Accessionis ad steriometriam, et mecanicam,* I (Venice, 1662); *De infinitis parabolis liber quintus* (Venice, 1663); *Considerationi sopra la forza di alcune ragioni fisico-mattematiche, addotte dal M. R. P. Gio. Battista Riccioli, . . . nel suo Almagesto nuovo, et astronomia riformata contro il sistema copernicano* (Venice, 1667); *De infinitis spirabilibus inversis, infinitisque hyperbolis* (Padua, 1667); *Seconde considerationi sopra la forza dell'argomento fisico-mattematico del M. R. P. Gio. Battista Riccioli, . . . contro il moto diurno della terra* (Padua, 1668); *Terze considerationi sopra una lettera del molto illustre et eccellentissimo Signor Gio. Alfonso Borelli* (Venice, 1668); *Quarte considerationi sopra la confermatione d'una sentenza del Signor Gio. Alfonso Borelli* (Padua, 1669); *Della gravità dell'aria e fluidi* (Padua, 1671–1672).

II. Secondary Literature. Works on Angeli are J. E. Montucla, *Histoire des mathématiques* (Paris, 1758), I, 537; II, 69; A. G. Kästner, *Geschichte der Mathematik,* III (Göttingen, 1798), 212–215; P. Magrini, "Sulla vita e sulle opere del P. Stefano degli Angeli," in *Giornale arcadico di scienze lettere ed arti,* **190** (July-August 1864), 205–237, also printed separately (Rome, 1866); M. Cantor, *Vorlesungen über Geschichte der Mathematik,* II (Leipzig, 1892), 820–821; P. Riccardi, *Biblioteca matematica italiana* (Modena, 1893), I, cols. 33–36 and IV, s.6 col. 181; G. Favaro, "Amici e corrispondenti di G. Galilei," in *Atti dell'Istituto veneto,* **72**, no. 2 (1912–1913), 46, and "I successori di Galileo nello studio di Padova," in *Nuovo archivio veneto,* n. s. **33** (1917), 117–121; G. Loria, *Storia delle matematiche,* II (Turin, 1931), 417–418, 425, 429;

A. A. Michieli, "Un maestro di Jacopo Riccati," in *Atti dell'Istituto veneto, classe di scienze morali e lettere,* **107** (1948–1949), 73–81; and M. Gliozzi, "Angeli, Stefano degli," in *Dizionario biografico degli Italiani,* III (Rome, 1961), 205–206.

ETTORE CARRUCCIO

ANTHEMIUS OF TRALLES (*fl.* sixth century A.D., in the time of Justinian)

The son of Stephanus, a physician, Anthemius came from a learned family of Tralles in western Asia Minor. One of his brothers, Metrodorus, was a man of letters; another, Olympius, was a lawyer; and two others, Dioscorus and Alexander, were physicians. Together with Isidorus of Miletus and under the patronage of Justinian, Anthemius undertook in A.D. 532 the replacing of the old church of Hagia Sophia in Constantinople. Anthemius and Isidorus are said also to have been employed by Justinian in the repair of the flood defenses at Daras. An anecdote relates that Anthemius persecuted a neighbor and rival, Zenon, by reflecting sunlight into his house. He also produced the impression of an earthquake in Zenon's house by the use of steam led under pressure through pipes connected to a boiler.

Anthemius' interest in conic sections as well as in reflectors is shown by the work *On Remarkable Mechanical Devices* (first edited in modern times by L. Dupuy in 1777, although it was known to Ibn al-Haytham [Alhazen] and Vitello). A mathematical fragment from Bobbio concerned with parabolic burning mirrors is sometimes attributed to Anthemius but may well be of early Hellenistic origin. Eutocius dedicated his *Commentaries* on Books I to IV of the *Conics* of Apollonius to Anthemius. The problem of how to contrive that at any hour and season a ray of the sun, passing through a small aperture, shall fall in a given spot without moving away was solved by Anthemius. He describes the construction of an elliptical reflector with one focus at the aperture and the other at the point to which the ray is to be reflected. Both winter and equinoctial rays are considered. In his treatment, Anthemius incidentally mentions the construction of an ellipse by means of a loop of string drawn closely around the foci. He also uses a proposition not made explicit in the *Conics*: that the straight line joining the focus to the intersection of two tangents bisects the angle between the two straight lines joining the focus to the two points of contact. Another construction shows how parallel rays may be reflected to one point at the focus of a parabolic reflector.

BIBLIOGRAPHY

Procopius, *De aedificiis,* edit. of H. B. Dewing, in Loeb Classical Library, Vol. VII (London-Cambridge, Mass., 1960). Agathias, *Historiae* 5. 6–9; F. Hultsch, in Pauly-Wissowa, *Real-Encyclopädie,* I, pt. 2 (Stuttgart, 1894), cols. 2368–2369; J. L. Heiberg, *Mathematici Graeci Minores* (Copenhagen, 1927); G. L. Huxley, *Anthemius of Tralles* (Cambridge, Mass., 1959); T. L. Heath, *Bibliotheca Mathematica,* **7**, ser. 3 (1907), 225–233.

G. L. HUXLEY

ANTIPHON (lived in Athens in the second half of the fifth century B.C.)

Antiphon was the first native Athenian to be classed as a "Sophist" in the sense of "professional teacher of young men." Unfortunately little is known for certain of his life, or even of his identity. The grammarian Didymus Chalcenterus, writing in the late first century B.C., distinguished two "Sophistic" Antiphons at Athens in the fifth century B.C. The first was Antiphon the orator, sometimes called Antiphon of Rhamnus, the author of the surviving *Tetralogies,* which are specimen outline speeches for the prosecution and the defense in certain real or imaginary cases of murder; he took part in Athenian politics and was condemned to death in 410 B.C. after the overthrow of the oligarchic conspiracy at Athens (Thucydides VIII, 68). The other was Antiphon the diviner and interpreter of dreams, author of the treatises *On Truth, On Concord,* and *The Statesman.*

This distinction between two Antiphons was repeated by Hermogenes in the second century A.D., but he based the distinction on a supposed difference in the style of writing in the *Tetralogies* compared with the other works; he may have had no other grounds. Caecilius of Calacte, probably writing just slightly later than Didymus, seems to have known nothing of such a distinction, and he is the source of the alternative tradition preserved in Pseudo-Plutarch's *Lives of the Ten Orators,* which assumes a single Antiphon who was the subject of conflicting stories.

Modern scholars are divided, and some follow the approach of Didymus, distinguishing at least three different Antiphons, who, it is supposed, were later confused. Others adopt a view like that of Caecilius, concluding that at least the orator and the Sophist were one and the same person. Something is known of the political career of Antiphon the orator, and if the identification is sound, we would at least know that the Sophist had belonged to the extreme right wing in politics and probably met his death in 410 B.C. The identification must remain uncertain, however, and virtually nothing is known of the life of

Antiphon the Sophist if he was not the same person as the orator.

Four works are clearly ascribed to Antiphon the Sophist (*On Truth, On Concord, The Statesman, On Interpretation of Dreams*), and a fifth (*The Art of Avoiding Pain*) may also be his. Of these works only brief quotations remain, aside from some important papyrus fragments of *On Truth* found at Oxyrhynchus in Egypt; but it seems likely that most of them were still known in the first century A.D.

On Truth comprised two books. Its title suggests the first part of Parmenides' poem "On Nature" (written at least a generation before Antiphon), commonly referred to as "The Way of Truth" and dealing with the doctrine of One Being as the sole reality, as against the (unreal) multiplicity of the phenomenal world. But since Protagoras the Sophist, roughly contemporary with Antiphon, also used the title *Truth* for a work in which he rejected the One Being of Parmenides and preferred instead the "truth" of every individual's sensations, we cannot infer from the title what position Antiphon adopted about the status of the phenomenal world. The first surviving fragment of Antiphon in the collection by Hermann Diels and Walther Kranz may hold the answer to this question, but the text is so corrupt that its meaning must remain wholly uncertain.

More helpful as evidence is the attempt to square the circle recorded by Aristotle (*Physics* A, 185a14). It is clear from Aristophanes (*The Birds,* 1004) that the squaring of the circle was a standard problem in the late fifth century B.C. The problem was to construct, by means of compass and ruler only, a square with an area equal to that of a given circle. Since any rectilinear figure could quite easily be converted into a square of the same area, the problem in practice was that of reducing the area of a circle to an equal area bounded by straight lines. In the third century B.C., Archimedes, in his *On the Measurement of the Circle* (Prop. I), showed that this requirement was satisfied by a right-angled triangle with one side adjacent to the right angle equal to the radius and the other adjacent side equal to the circumference. The problem is now known to be incapable of solution by the use of ruler and compass alone.

Aristotle was aware of three attempts to solve this problem in its original form. One he seems to have attributed, perhaps mistakenly (see full discussion in W. D. Ross, *Aristotle's Physics* [Oxford, 1936], pp. 463–466), to Hippocrates of Chios about the middle of the fifth century B.C. According to this attempt, it was mistakenly concluded from the possibility of squaring the lune on the side of the square inscribed in a circle that the circle could be completely divided into lunes similar to the one thus squared. Another was by a certain Bryson, who simply argued that since a polygon inscribed within a circle is smaller than the circle and a polygon circumscribing a circle will be larger than the circle, there must be a polygon intermediate in size that will be equal to the circle; however, he did not have anything to say about how such a polygon could be constructed diagrammatically. Antiphon's method is explained slightly differently by each of two commentators on Aristotle. According to Simplicius, he proposed to inscribe a polygon such as a square within the circle and, on each of its sides, to build two chords meeting midway on the circumference above the side. The process must be continued with each of the sides of the resulting octagon, and so on with subsequent polygons, until the sides are so small that they coincide with their respective sections of the circumference. According to the Neoplatonist Themistius (A.D. 320–390), the polygon is an equilateral triangle, but otherwise his account of the procedure is the same.

In modern times it has often been supposed that Antiphon was simply making a bad mistake in geometry by supposing that any approximation could ever amount to coincidence between a polygon with however many sides and the continuously curved circumference of a true circle. At the same time, his method has been considered of interest as anticipating the method of exhaustion used by Euclid (XII, 2) and the method of approximation of Archimedes. This may not be the right view to take. Antiphon appears to have believed that complete coincidence could be achieved by his method, and Aristotle treats this not as a mistake in geometry, but as nongeometrical in its approach, in that it did not proceed on geometrical assumptions. This may mean that Antiphon regarded the circle itself as a polygon with a very large (or possibly infinite) number of sides. Such a view is implied in the doctrine of Protagoras that the tangent touches a circle not at a single point only, but over a series of points, as we see with our eyes in the case of drawn tangents and circles. This would suggest that Antiphon, like Protagoras, may have considered the world of phenomena more real than the "truth" of Parmenides.

It is probable that Antiphon, like most of the pre-Socratics, discussed in detail the physical formation of the universe and the nature of the heavenly bodies, but only small details of his doctrines survive. He seems to have related the rising and setting of the sun to changes in the air surrounding the earth (fr. 26); he regarded the moon as the source of its own light (fr. 27) and as undergoing eclipse by some kind of turning of its bowl (fr. 28). He appears to have held a doctrine of opposite qualities (such as hot and cold) acting as primary substances or elements (frs. 26, 29, 32) and also as determining human physiology (fr. 29*a*; Diels and Kranz II, 426).

Antiphon's most famous doctrine is his opposition of nature and convention. In fr. 15 he opposes manufactured articles to the "natural" materials of which they are made; and he is often interpreted as preferring things that exist by nature to those that exist merely by convention and, thus, as setting up the selfish "natural" impulses of the individual as norms superior to the laws of the community. But in *On Concord* he defends the authority of the community as a safeguard against anarchy (fr. 61) and recommends the ideals of concord and self-restraint both within communities and within the individual soul. Most probably he was only concerned to criticize the laws of a city by asking whether or not they satisfy the "natural" needs of the individual. Thus, in *On Truth* he argues that there is a basic human nature common to Greeks and barbarians, and in the *Art of Avoiding Pain*, if it is his, he was probably also concerned with ways in which the individual could achieve the fulfillment of his nature without having to suffer.

BIBLIOGRAPHY

I. Original Works. For fragments and testimonia in Greek, see Hermann Diels and Walther Kranz, eds., *Die Fragmente der Vorsokratiker*, 7th ed., II (Berlin, 1954), 334-370. Antonio Battegazzore and Mario Untersteiner, eds., *Sofisti, testimonianze e frammenti* (Florence, 1962), fasc. IV, has, in addition to the Greek, a bibliography, Italian translation, and commentary. An English translation of the fragments can be found in Kathleen Freeman, *Ancilla to the Pre-Socratic Philosophers* (Oxford, 1948). For text and English translation of the *Tetralogies* of Antiphon the orator, see Kenneth John Maidment, *Minor Attic Orators*, Vol. I (London-New York, 1941), which is part of the Loeb Classical Library.

II. Secondary Literature. For interpretations, see Ettore Bignone, *Studi sul pensiero antico* (Naples, 1938), chs. 1-3; and, in English, Mario Untersteiner, *The Sophists* (Oxford, 1954).

G. B. Kerferd

APOLLONIUS OF PERGA (*b:* second half of third century B.C.; *d.* early second century B.C.)

Very little is known of the life of Apollonius. The surviving references from antiquity are meager and in part untrustworthy. He is said to have been born at Perga (Greek Πέργη), a small Greek city in southern Asia Minor, when Ptolemy Euergetes was king of Egypt (i.e., between 246 and 221 B.C.)[1] and to have become famous for his astronomical studies in the time of Ptolemy Philopator, who reigned from 221 to 205 B.C.[2] Little credence can be attached to the statement in Pappus that he studied for a long time with the pupils of Euclid in Alexandria.[3] The best evidence for his life is contained in his own prefaces to the various books of his *Conics*. From these it is clear that he was for some time domiciled at Alexandria and that he visited Pergamum and Ephesus.

The prefaces of the first three books are addressed to one Eudemus of Pergamum. Since the Preface to Book II states that he is sending the book by the hands of his son Apollonius, he must have been of mature age at the time of its composition.[4] We are told in the Preface to Book IV that Eudemus is now dead;[5] this and the remaining books are addressed to one Attalus. The latter is commonly identified with King Attalus I of Pergamum (reigned 241-197 B.C.); but it is highly unlikely that Apollonius would have neglected current etiquette so grossly as to omit the title of "King" (*βασιλεύς*) when addressing the monarch, and Attalus was a common name among those of Macedonian descent. However, a chronological inference can be made from a passage in the Preface to Book II, where Apollonius says, ". . . and if Philonides the geometer, whom I introduced to you in Ephesus, should happen to visit the neighborhood of Pergamum, give him a copy [of this book]."[6] Philonides, as we learn from a fragmentary biography preserved on a papyrus and from two inscriptions, was an Epicurean mathematician and philosopher who was personally known to the Seleucid kings Antiochus IV Epiphanes (reigned 175-163 B.C.) and Demetrius I Soter (162-150 B.C.). Eudemus was the first teacher of Philonides. Thus the introduction of the young Philonides to Eudemus probably took place early in the second century B.C. The *Conics* were composed about the same time. Since Apollonius was then old enough to have a grown son, it is reasonable to accept the birth date given by Eutocius and to place the period of Apollonius' activity in the late third and early second centuries B.C. This fits well with the internal evidence which his works provide on his relationship to Archimedes (who died an old man in 212-211 B.C.); Apollonius appears at times to be developing and improving on ideas that were originally conceived by Archimedes (for examples see p. 189). It is true that Apollonius does not mention Archimedes in his extant works; he does, however, refer to Conon, an older (?) contemporary and correspondent of Archimedes, as a predecessor in the theory

APOLLONIUS OF PERGA

of conic sections.[7]

Of Apollonius' numerous works in a number of different mathematical fields, only two survive, although we have a good idea of the content of several others from the account of them in the encyclopedic work of Pappus (fourth century A.D.). But it is impossible to establish any kind of relative chronology for his works or to trace the development of his ideas. The sole chronological datum is that already established, that the *Conics* in the form that we have them are the work of his mature years. Thus the order in which his works are treated here is an arbitrary one.

The work on which Apollonius' modern fame rests, the *Conics* (*κωνικά*), was originally in eight books. Books I–IV survive in the original Greek, Books V–VII only in Arabic translation. Book VIII is lost, but some idea of its contents can be gained from the lemmas to it given by Pappus.[8] Apollonius recounts the genesis of his *Conics* in the Preface to Book I[9]: he had originally composed a treatise on conic sections in eight books at the instance of one Naucrates, a geometer, who was visiting him in Alexandria; this had been composed rather hurriedly because Naucrates was about to sail. Apollonius now takes the opportunity to write a revised version. It is this revised version that constitutes the *Conics* as we know it.

In order to estimate properly Apollonius' achievement in the *Conics*, it is necessary to know what stage the study of the subject had reached before him. Unfortunately, since his work became the classic textbook on the subject, its predecessors failed to survive the Byzantine era. We know of them only from the scattered reports of later writers. It is certain, however, that investigation into the mathematical properties of conic sections had begun in the Greek world at least as early as the middle of the fourth century B.C., and that by 300 B.C. or soon after, textbooks on the subject had been written (we hear of such by Aristaeus and by Euclid). Our best evidence for the content of these textbooks comes from the works of Archimedes. Many of these are concerned with problems involving conic sections, mostly of a very specialized nature; but Archimedes makes use of a number of more elementary propositions in the theory of conics, which he states without proof. We may assume that these propositions were already well known. On occasion Archimedes actually states that such and such a proposition is proved "in the Elements of Conics" (*'εν τοῖς κωνικοῖς στοιχείοις*).[10] Let us leave aside the question of what work(s) he is referring to by this title; it is clear that in his time there was already in existence a corpus of elementary theorems on conic sections. Drawing mainly on the works of Archimedes, we can characterize the approach to the theory of conics before Apollonius as follows.

The three curves now known as parabola, hyperbola, and ellipse were obtained by cutting a right circular cone by a plane at right angles to a generator of the cone. According to whether the cone has a right angle, an obtuse angle, or an acute angle at its vertex, the resultant section is respectively a parabola, a hyperbola, or an ellipse. These sections were therefore named by the earlier Greek investigators "section of a right-angled cone," "section of an obtuse-angled cone," and "section of an acute-angled cone," respectively; those appellations are still given to them by Archimedes (although we know that he was well aware that they can be generated by methods other than the above). With the above method of generation, it is possible to characterize each of the curves by what is known in Greek as a *σύμπτωμα*, i.e., a constant relationship between certain magnitudes which vary according to the position of an arbitrary point taken on the curve (this corresponds to the equation of the curve in modern terms). For the parabola (see Figure 1), for an arbitrary point K, $KL^2 = 2\,AZ \cdot ZL$ (for suggested proofs of this and the *σύμπτωμα* of hyperbola and ellipse, see Dijksterhuis, *Archimedes*, pp. 57–59, whom I follow closely here). In algebraic notation, if $KL = y$, $ZL = x$, $2\,AZ = p$, we get the characteristic equation of the parabola $y^2 = px$. Archimedes frequently uses this relationship in the parabola and calls the parameter p "the double of the distance to the axis" (*ʽα διπλασία τᾶς μέχρι τοῦ 'άξονος*)[11] exactly describing $2\,ZA$ in Figure 1 ("axis" refers to the axis of the *cone*). For the hyperbola and ellipse the following *σύμπτωμα* can be derived (see Figures 2 and 3):

$$\frac{KL^2}{ZL \cdot PL} = \frac{2\,ZF}{PZ};$$

in algebraic notation, if $KL = y$, $ZL = x_1$, $PL = x_2$, $2\,ZF = p$, $PZ = a$,

$$\frac{y^2}{x_1 x_2} = \frac{p}{a} = \text{constant.}$$

This is found in Archimedes in the form equivalent to

$$\frac{y^2}{x_1 x_2} = \frac{y'^2}{x'_1 x'_2}.$$ [12]

APOLLONIUS OF PERGA

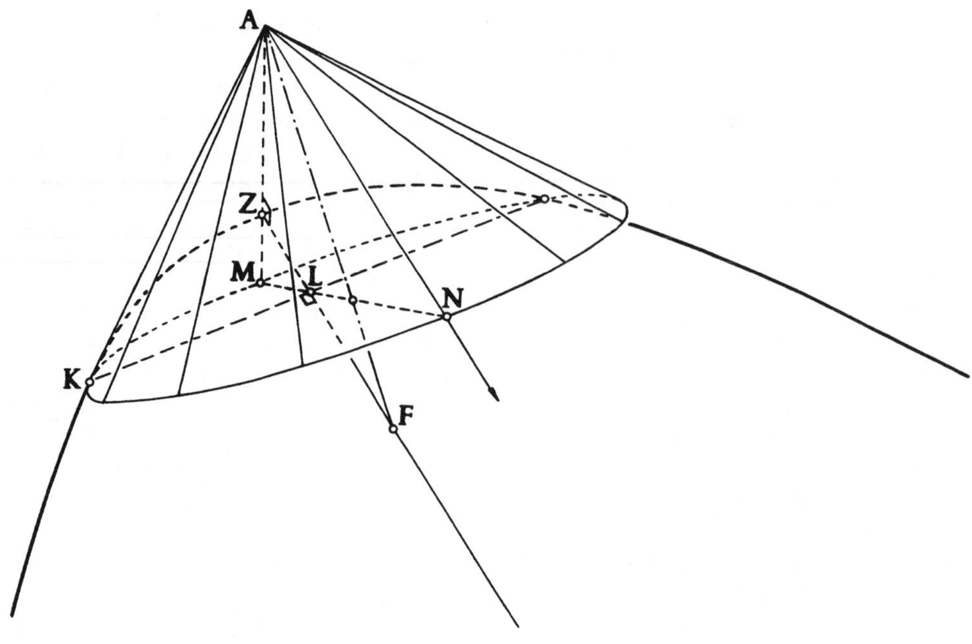

FIGURE 1

It is to be noted that in this system ZL always lies on the axis of the section and that KL is always at right angles to it. In other words, it is a system of "orthogonal conjugation."

Apollonius' approach is radically different. He generates all three curves from the double oblique circular cone, as follows: in Figures 4, 5, and 6 ZDE is the cutting plane. We now cut the cone with another plane orthogonal to the first and passing through the axis of the cone; this is known as the axial triangle (ABG); the latter must intersect the base of the cone in a diameter (BG) orthogonal to the line in which

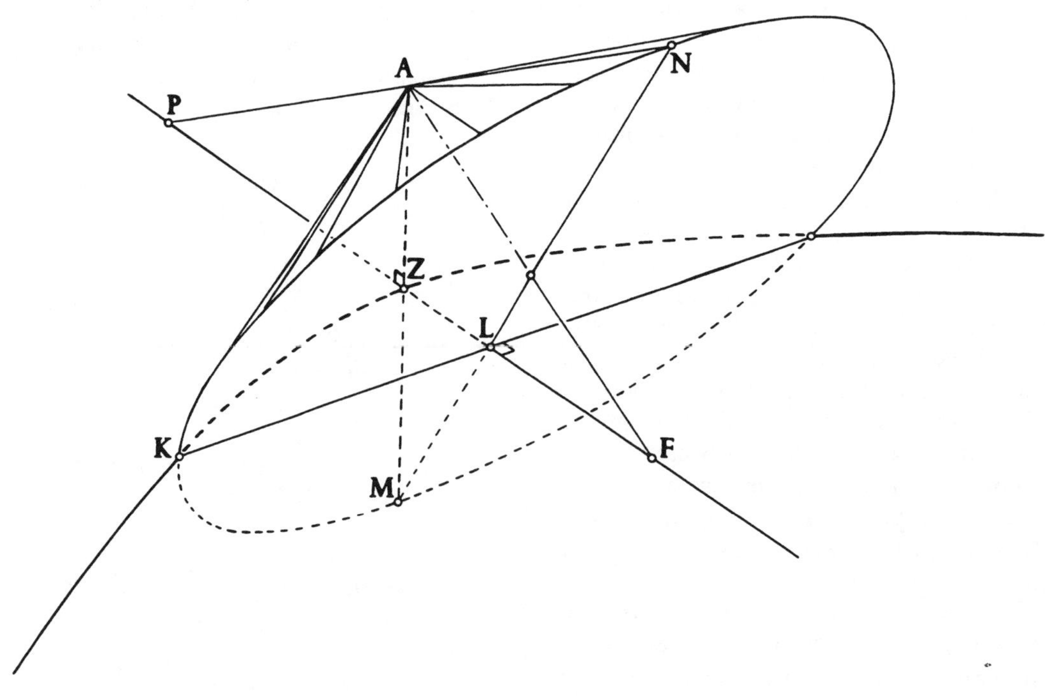

FIGURE 2

 APOLLONIUS OF PERGA

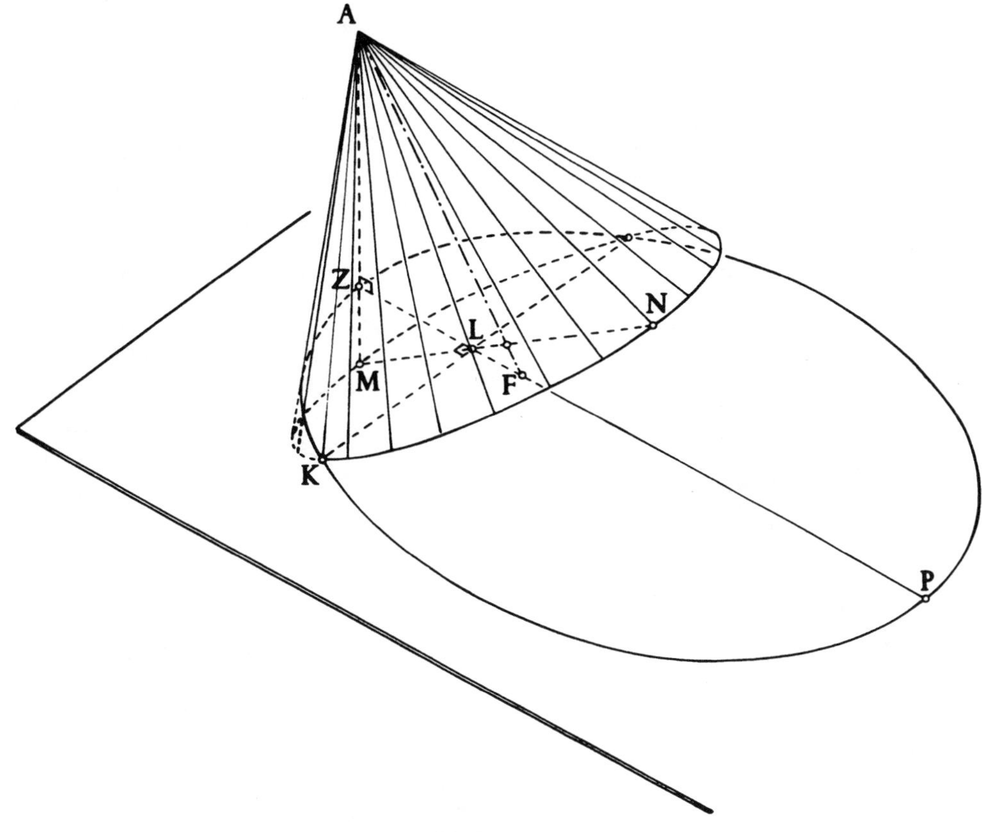

FIGURE 3

the cutting plane intersects it (or its extension); it intersects the cutting plane in a straight line ZH. Then, if we neglect the trivial cases where the cutting plane generates a circle, a straight line, a pair of straight lines, or a point, there are three possibilities:

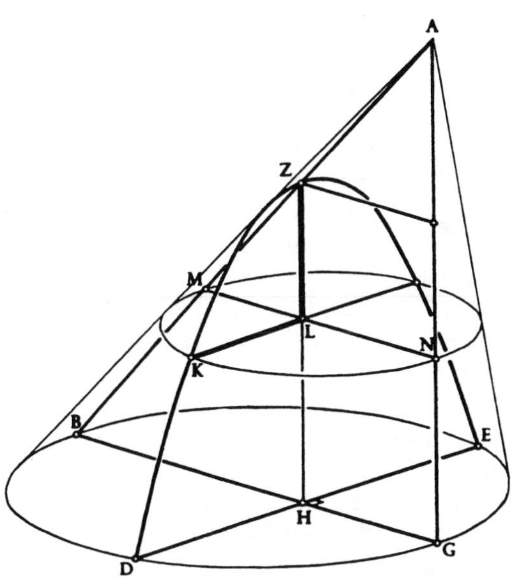

FIGURE 4

(*a*) The line ZH in which the cutting plane intersects the axial triangle intersects only one of the two sides of the axial triangle, AB, AG; i.e., it is parallel to the other side (Figure 4).

(*b*) ZH intersects one side of the axial triangle below the vertex A and the other (extended) above it (Figure 5).

(*c*) ZH intersects both sides of the axial triangle below A (Figure 6).

In all three cases, for an arbitrary point K on the curve,

$$(1) \qquad KL^2 = ML \cdot LN.$$

Furthermore, in case (*a*),

$$(2) \qquad \frac{ML}{LZ} = \frac{BG}{AG} \text{ and } \frac{LN}{BG} = \frac{AZ}{AB}.$$

If we now construct a line length Θ such that $\Theta = BG^2 \cdot AZ/AB \cdot AG$, it follows from (1) and (2) that $KL^2 = LZ \cdot \Theta$. Since none of its constituent parts is dependent on the position of K, Θ is a constant. In algebraic terms, if $KL = y$, $LZ = x$, and $\Theta = p$, then $y^2 = px$. In cases (*b*) and (*c*),

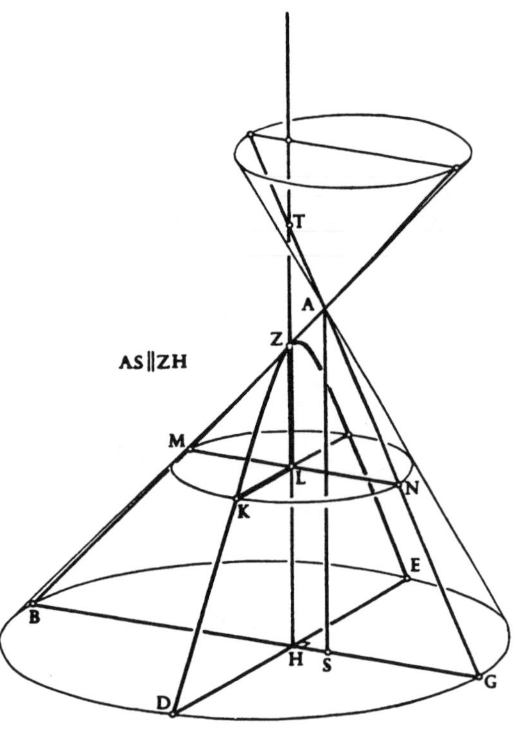

FIGURE 5

(3) $$\frac{ML}{LZ} = \frac{BS}{AS} \text{ and } \frac{LN}{LT} = \frac{SG}{AS}.$$

If we now construct a line length Ξ such that $\Xi = BS \cdot SG \cdot ZT/AS^2$, it follows from (1) and (3) that

$$KL^2 = \Xi \cdot \frac{LZ \cdot LT}{ZT}.$$

Thus

$$KL^2 = \Xi \cdot \frac{LZ(LZ + ZT)}{ZT} \text{ for case } (b)$$

and

$$KL^2 = \Xi \cdot \frac{LZ(LZ - ZT)}{ZT} \text{ for case } (c).$$

In algebraic terms, if $KL = y$, $LZ = x$, $\Xi = p$, and $ZT = a$,

$$y^2 = x\left(p + \frac{p}{a}x\right) \text{ for case } (b),$$

$$y^2 = x\left(p - \frac{p}{a}x\right) \text{ for case } (c).$$

The advantage of such formulation of the συμπτώματα of the curves from the point of view of classical Greek geometry is that now all three curves can be determined by the method of "application of areas," which is the Euclidean way of geometrically formulating problems that we usually express algebraically by equations of second degree. For instance, Euclid (VI, 28) propounds the problem "To a given straight line to apply a parallelogram equal to a given area and falling short of it by a parallelogrammic figure similar to a given one." (See Figure 7, where for simplicity rectangles have been substituted for parallelograms.) Then the problem is to apply to a line of given length b a rectangle of given area A and side x such that the rectangle falls short of the rectangle bx by a rectangle similar to another with sides c, d. This is equivalent to solving the equation

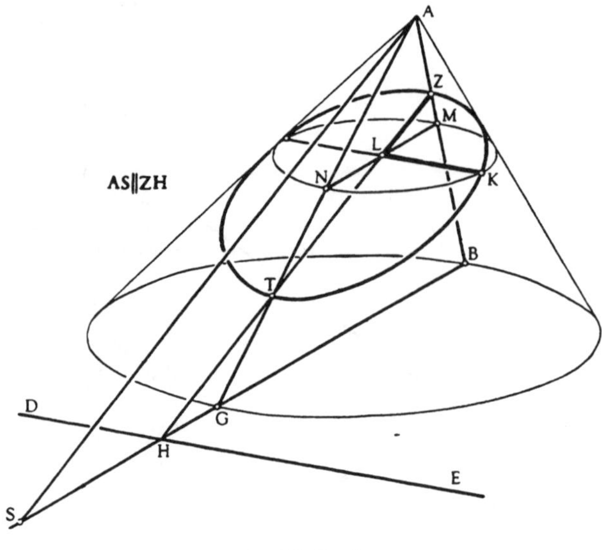

FIGURE 6

$$bx - \frac{c}{d}x^2 = A.$$

Compare the similar problem Euclid VI, 29: "To a given straight line to apply a parallelogram equal to a given area and exceeding it by a parallelogrammic figure similar to a given one."

This method is used by Apollonius to express the συμπτώματα of the three curves, as follows (see Figures 8–10).

For case (a) (Figure 8), a rectangle of side x (equal to the abscissa) is applied (παραβάλλεται) to the line-length p (defined as above): this rectangle is equal to the square on the ordinate y. The section is accordingly called parabola (παραβολή, meaning "exact application").

For case (b) (Figure 9), there is applied to p a rectangle, of side x, equal to y^2 and exceeding

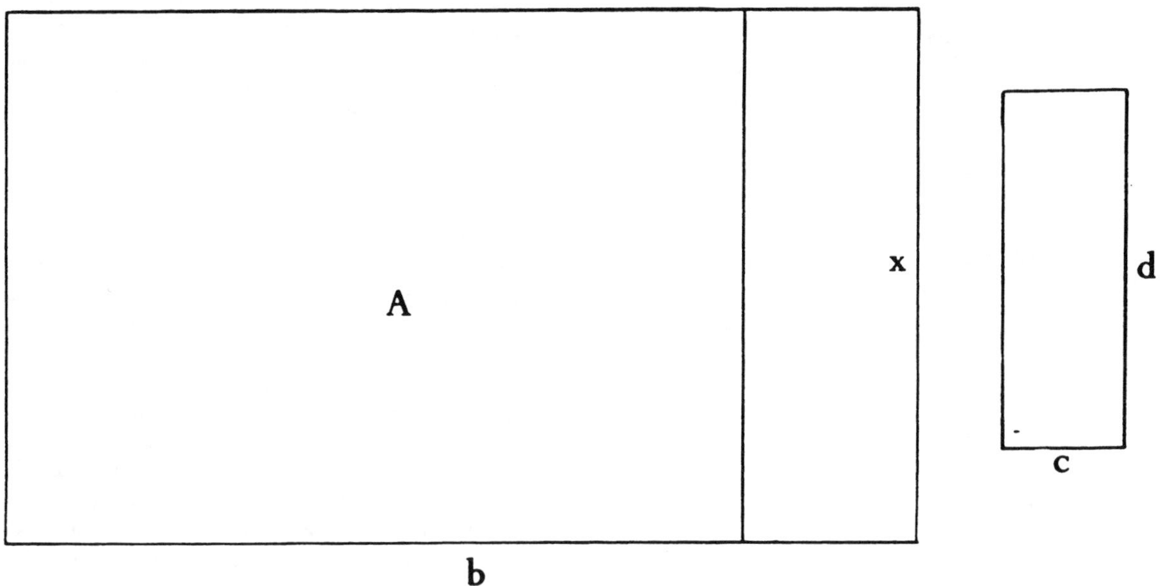

FIGURE 7

(ὑπερβάλλον) p by a rectangle similar to p/a. The section is accordingly named hyperbola (ὑπερβολή, meaning "excess").

For case (*c*) (Figure 10) there is applied to p a rectangle of side x, equal to y^2 and falling short (ἐλλεῖπον) of p by a rectangle similar to p/a. The section is accordingly named ellipse (ἔλλειψις, meaning "falling short").

This approach has several advantages over the older one. First, all three curves can be represented by the method of "application of areas" favored by classical Greek geometry (it has been appropriately termed "geometrical algebra" in recent times); the older approach allowed this to be done only for the parabola. In modern terms, Apollonius refers the equation of all three curves to a coordinate system of which one axis is a given diameter of the curve and the other the tangent at one end of that diameter. This brings us to a second advantage: Apollonius' method of generating the curves immediately produces oblique conjugation, whereas the older method produces orthogonal conjugation. As we shall see, oblique conjugation was not entirely unknown to earlier geometers; but it is typical of Apollonius' approach that he immediately develops the most general formulation. It is therefore a logical step, given this approach, for Apollonius to prove (I,50 and the preceding propositions) that a σύμπτωμα equivalent to those derived above can be established for any diameter of a conic and its ordinates: in modern terms, the coordinates of the curves can be transposed to any diameter and its tangent.

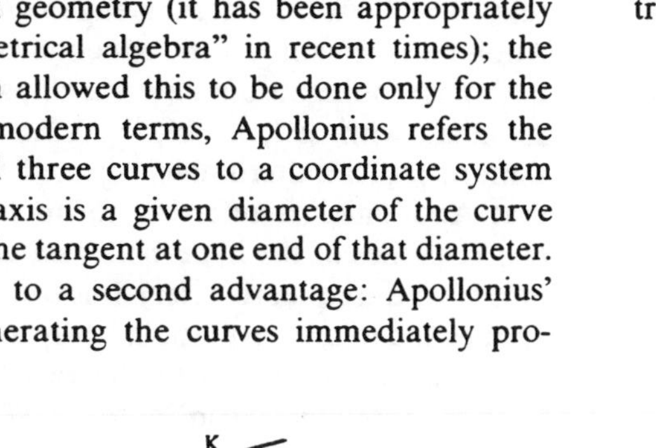

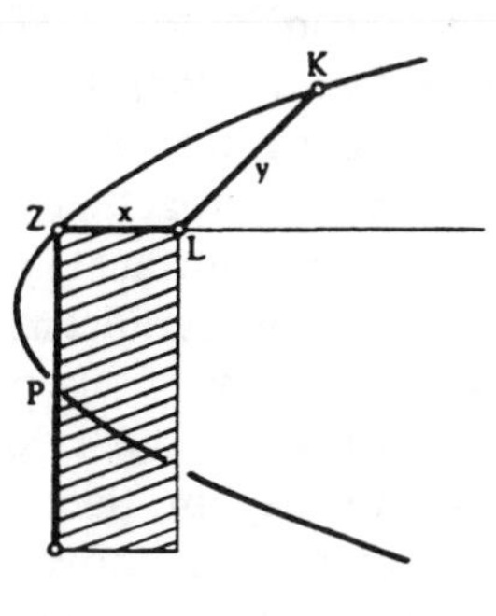

FIGURE 8

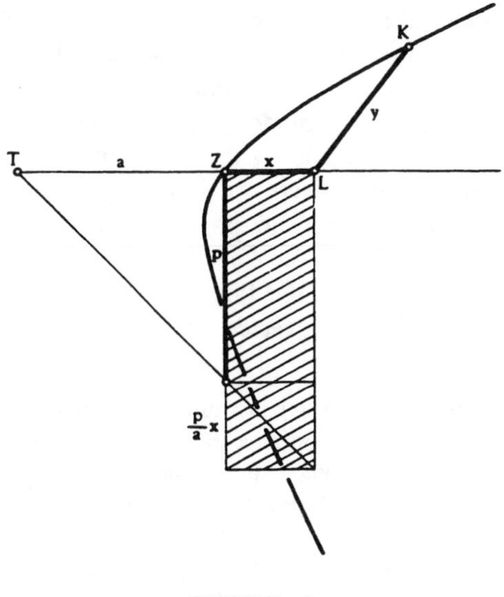

FIGURE 9

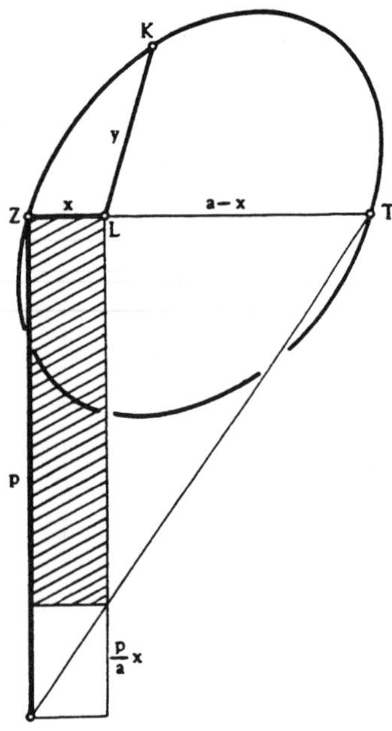

FIGURE 10

We cannot doubt that Apollonius' approach to the generation and basic definition of the conic sections, as outlined above, was radically new. It is not easy to determine how much of the *content* of the *Conics* is new. It is likely that a good deal of the nomenclature that his work made standard was introduced by him; in particular, the terms "parabola," "hyperbola," and "ellipse" make sense only in terms of Apollonius' method. To the parameter which we have called *p* he gave the name ʾορθία ("orthogonal side" [of a rectangle]), referring to its use in the "application": this term survives in the modern *latus rectum.* He defines "diameter" as *any* line bisecting a system of parallel chords in a conic, in accordance with the new generality of his coordinate system: this differs from the old meaning of "diameter" of a conic section (exemplified in Archimedes), which is (in Apollonian and modern terminology) the axis. But though this new terminology reflects the new approach, it does not in itself exclude the possibility that many of Apollonius' results in the *Conics* were already known to his predecessors. That this is true at least for the first four books is suggested by his own Preface to Book I. He says there:[13]

> The first four books constitute an elementary introduction. The first contains the methods of generating the three sections and their basic properties (συμπτώματα), developed more fully and more generally (καθόλουμᾶλλον) than in the writings of others; the second contains the properties of the diameter and axes of the sections, the asymptotes, and other things . . . ; the third contains many surprising theorems useful for the syntheses of solid loci and for determinations of the possibilities of solutions (διορισμούς); of the latter the greater part and the most beautiful are new. It was the discovery of these that made me aware that Euclid has not worked out the whole of the locus for three and four lines,[14] but only a fortuitous part of it, and that not very happily; for it was not possible to complete the synthesis without my additional discoveries. The fourth book deals with how many ways the conic sections can meet one another and the circumference of the circle, and other additional matters, neither of which has been treated by my predecessors, namely in how many points a conic section or circumference of a circle can meet another. The remaining books are particular extensions (περιουσιαστικώτερα); one of them [V] deals somewhat fully with minima and maxima, another [VI] with equal and similar conic sections, another [VII] with theorems concerning determinations (διοριστικῶν), another [VIII] with determinate conic problems.

From this one gets the impression that Books I–IV, apart from the subjects specifically singled out as original, are merely reworkings of the results of Apollonius' predecessors. This is confirmed by the statement of Pappus, who says that Apollonius supplemented the four books of Euclid's *Conics* (which Pappus *may* have known) and added four more books.[15]

Apollonius also claims to have worked out the methods of generating the sections and setting out their συμπτώματα "more fully and more generally" than his predecessors. The description "more generally" is eminently justified by our comparison of the two methods. However, it is not clear to what "more fully" (ʾεπὶ πλέον) refers. Neugebauer suggests that Apollonius meant his introduction of conjugate hyperbolas (conjugate diameters in ellipse and hyperbola are dealt with in I, 15–16).[16] At least as probable is a more radical alternative, rejected by Neugebauer, that Apollonius is referring to his treatment of the two branches of the hyperbola as a unit (exemplified in I, 16 and frequently later). It is true that Apollonius applies the name "hyperbola" only to a single branch of the curve (he refers to the two branches as the "opposite *sections*" [τομαὶ ʾαντικείμεναι]); it is also true that in his own Preface to Book IV[17] he reveals that at least Nicoteles among his predecessors had considered the two branches together; but Apollonius' very definition of a conic surface[18] as the surface *on both sides* of the vertex is significant in this context; and it is unlikely that any of his predecessors had *systematically* developed the theory of both branches of the hyperbola. Here again, then, we may reasonably regard Apollonius as an innovator in his *method.* But we are not justified in assuming that any of the

APOLLONIUS OF PERGA

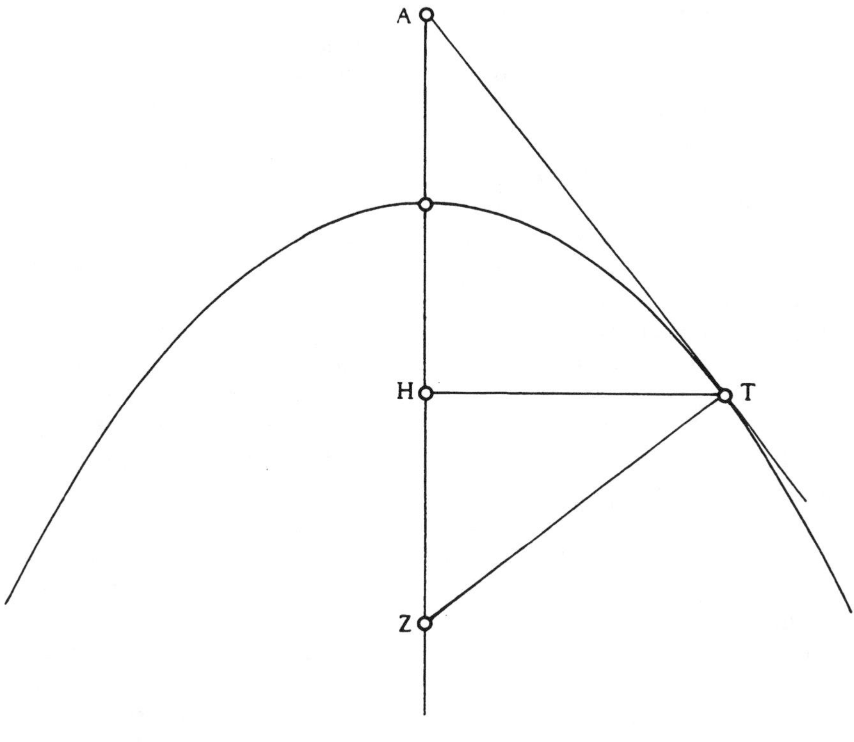

FIGURE 11

results stated in the first four books were unknown before Apollonius, except where he specifically states this. In this part of the work we must see him rather as organizing the results of his predecessors, consisting in part of haphazard and disconnected sets of theorems, into an exposition ordered rationally according to his own very general method. His mastery is such that it seems impossible to separate different sources (as one can, for instance, in the comparable work of Euclid on elementary geometry).

Nevertheless, we may suspect that Archimedes, could he have read Books I–IV of the *Conics,* would have found few results in them that were not already familiar to him (although he might well have been surprised by the order and mutual connection of the theorems). The predecessors of Archimedes were already aware that conic sections could be generated by methods other than that described on p. 180. Euclid states that an ellipse can be produced by cutting a cylinder by a plane not parallel to the base.[19] Archimedes himself certainly knew that there were many different ways of generating the sections from a cone. The best proof of this is *De conoidibus et sphaeroidibus* VII–IX, in which it is shown that for any ellipse it is possible to find an *oblique* circular cone from which that ellipse can be generated. Furthermore, it is certain that the essential properties of the oblique conjugation of at least the parabola were known to Apollonius' predecessors; for that is the essence of propositions I–III of Archimedes' *Quadrature of the Parabola,* which he states are proved "in the Elements of Conics."[20] In *De conoidibus et sphaeroidibus* III, Archimedes states "If two tangents be drawn from the same point to *any* conic, and two chords be drawn inside the section parallel to the two tangents and intersecting one another, the product of the two parts of each chord [formed by the intersection] will have the same ratio to one another as the squares on the tangents. . . . this is proved in the Elements of Conics."[21] It is plausible to interpret this, with Dijksterhuis, as treatment of all three sections in oblique conjugation.[22]

It is probable then that much of the contents of Books I–IV was already known before Apollonius. Conversely, Apollonius did not include in the "elementary introduction" of Books I–IV all theorems on conics known to his predecessors. For example, in a parabola the subnormal to any tangent formed on the diameter (*HZ* in Figure 11) is constant and equal to half the parameter *p*. This is assumed without proof by Archimedes[23] and by Diocles (perhaps a contemporary of Apollonius) in his proof of the focal property of the parabola in his work *On Burning Mirrors.*[24] We can therefore be sure that it was a well-known theorem in the *Elements of Conics.* Yet in Apollonius it can be found only by combining the results of propositions 13 and 27 of Book V, one of the "particular extensions."

If Apollonius omitted some of his predecessors' results from the elementary section, we must not be surprised if he omitted altogether some results with which he was perfectly familiar: his aim was not to compile an encyclopedia of all possible theorems on conic sections, but to write a systematic textbook on the "elements" and to add some more advanced theory which he happened to have elaborated. The question has often been raised in modern times why there is no mention in the *Conics* of the focus of the parabola. The focal properties of hyperbola and ellipse are treated in III, 45–52: Apollonius proves, *inter alia,* that the focal distances at any point make equal angles with the tangent at that point and that their sum (for the ellipse) or difference (for the hyperbola) is constant. There is no mention of directrix, and from the *Conics* we might conclude that Apollonius was totally ignorant of the focus-directrix property of conic sections. However, it happens that Pappus proves at length that if a point moves in such a way that the ratio of its distance from a fixed point and its orthogonal distance from a fixed straight line is constant, then the locus of that point is a conic section; and that according as the ratio is equal to, greater than, or less than unity, the section will be respectively a parabola, a hyperbola, or an ellipse.[25] This amounts to the generation of the sections from focus and directrix. Pappus gives this proof as a lemma to Euclid's (lost) book *On Surface Loci;* hence, it has been plausibly concluded that the proposition was there stated without proof by Euclid.[26] If that is so, here is a whole topic in the theory of conics that must have been completely familiar to Apollonius, yet which he omits altogether. Thus the lack of any mention of the focus of the parabola in the *Conics* is not an argument for Apollonius' ignorance of it. I agree with those who argue on a priori grounds that he must have known of it.[27] Since he very probably dealt with it in his work(s) on burning mirrors (see p. 189) there was all the more justification for omitting it from the *Conics.* In any case, we now have a proof of it, by Diocles, very close to the time of Apollonius. Since Diocles further informs us that a parabolic burning mirror was constructed by Dositheus, who corresponded with Archimedes, it is highly probable that the focal property of the parabola was well known *before* Apollonius.

For a detailed summary of the contents of the *Conics,* the reader is referred to the works of Zeuthen and Heath listed in the Bibliography. Here we will only supplement Apollonius' own description quoted above by noting that Book III deals with theorems on the rectangles contained by the segments of intersecting chords of a conic (an extension to conics of that proved by Euclid for chords in a circle), with the harmonic properties of pole and polar (to use the modern terms: there are no equivalent ancient ones), with focal properties (discussed above), and finally with propositions relevant to the locus for three and four lines (see n. 14). Of Books V–VII, which are, to judge from Apollonius' own account, largely original, Book V is that which has particularly evoked the admiration of modern mathematicians: it deals with normals to conics, when drawn as maximum and minimum straight lines from particular points or sets of points to the curve. Apollonius finally proves, in effect, that there exists on either side of the axis of a conic a series of points from which one can draw only one normal to the opposite side of the curve, and shows how to construct such points: these points form the curve known, in modern terms, as the *evolute* of the conic in question. Book VII is concerned mainly with propositions about inequalities between various functions of conjugate diameters. Book VIII is lost, but an attempt at restoration from Pappus' lemmas to it was made by Halley in his edition of the *Conics.* If he is right, it contained problems concerning conjugate diameters whose functions (as "determined" in Book VII) have given values.

For a modern reader, the *Conics* is among the most difficult mathematical works of antiquity. Both form and content are far from tractable. The author's rigorous rhetorical exposition is wearing for those used to modern symbolism. Unlike the works of Archimedes, the treatise does not immediately impress the reader with its mathematical brilliance. Apollonius has, in a way, suffered from his own success: his treatise became canonical and eliminated its predecessors, so that we cannot judge by direct comparison its superiority to them in mathematical rigor, consistency, and generality. But the work amply repays closer study; and the attention paid to it by some of the most eminent mathematicians of the seventeenth century (one need mention only Fermat, Newton, and Halley) reinforces the verdict of Apollonius' contemporaries, who, according to Geminus, in admiration for his *Conics* gave him the title of The Great Geometer.[28]

In Book VII of his mathematical thesaurus, Pappus includes summaries of and lemmas to six other works of Apollonius besides the *Conics.* Pappus' account is sufficiently detailed to permit tentative reconstructions of these works, all but one of which are entirely lost. All belong to "higher geometry," and all consisted of exhaustive discussion of the particular cases of one or a few general problems. The contrast with

Apollonius' approach in the *Conics,* where he strives for generality of treatment, is notable. A brief indication of the problem(s) discussed in these works follows.

(1) *Cutting off of a Ratio* (λόγου ἀποτομή), in two books, is the only surviving work of Apollonius apart from the *Conics.* However, it is preserved only in an Arabic version which, by comparison with Pappus' summary, appears to be an adaptation rather than a literal translation. Pappus describes the general problem as follows: "To draw through a given point a straight line to cut off from two given straight lines two sections measured from given points on the two given lines so that the two sections cut off have a given ratio."[29] Apollonius discusses particular cases before proceeding to the more general (e.g., in every case discussed in Book I the two given lines are supposed to be parallel) and solves every case by the classical method of "analysis" (in the Greek sense). That is, the problem is presumed solved, and from the solution is deduced some other condition that is easily constructible. Then, by "synthesis" from this latter construction, the original condition is constructed. We may presume that Apollonius followed the same method in all six of these works, especially since Book VII of Pappus was named ἀναλυόμενος ("Field of Analysis"). In the *Cutting off of a Ratio* the problem was reduced to one of "application of an area." Zeuthen[30] points out the relevance of this work to *Conics* III, 41: If one regards the theorem proved there as a method of drawing a tangent to a given point in a parabola by determining the intercepts it makes on two other tangents to the curve, that is exactly the problem discussed by Apollonius in this work. Although there is no mention in it of conic sections, the connection is surely not a fortuitous one. In fact, many of the problems discussed by Apollonius in the six works summarized in Book VII of Pappus can be reduced to problems connected with conics. (This helps to explain the great interest shown in this part of Pappus' work by mathematicians of the sixteenth and seventeenth centuries.)

(2) *Cutting off of an Area* (χωρίου ἀποτομή), in two books, has a general problem similar to that of the preceding work. But in this case the intercepts cut off from the two given lines must have a given product (in Greek terms, contain a given rectangle) instead of a given proportion.[31] Here again Zeuthen has shown that *Conics* III, 42 and 43, which concern tangents drawn to ellipse and hyperbola, are equivalent to particular cases of the problem discussed by Apollonius in this work.[32]

(3) *Determinate Section* (διωρισμένη τομή) deals with the following general problem: Given four points—A, B, C, D—on a straight line l, to determine a point P on that line such that the ratio $AP \cdot CP / BP \cdot DP$ has a given value.[33] Since this comparatively simple problem was discussed at some length by Apollonius, Zeuthen conjectured—plausibly—that he was concerned to find the limits of possibility of a solution for the various possible arrangements of the points (e.g., when two coincide).[34] We know from Pappus' account that it dealt, among other things, with maxima and minima. Whether, as Zeuthen claims, the work amounted to "a complete theory of involution" cannot be decided on existing evidence. But it is a fact that the general problem is the same as determining the intersection of the line l and the conic that is the "locus for four lines," the four lines passing through A, B, C, and D; and Apollonius must have known this. Here again, then, is a connection with the theory of conics.

(4) *Tangencies* (ἐπαφαί), in two books, deals with the general problem characterized by Pappus[35] as follows: "Given three elements, either points, lines or circles (or a mixture), to draw a circle tangent to each of the three elements (or through them if they are points)." There are ten possible different combinations of elements, and Apollonius dealt with all eight that had not already been treated by Euclid. The particular case of drawing a circle to touch three given circles attracted the interest of Vieta and Newton, among others. Although one of Newton's solutions[36] was obtained by the intersection of two hyperbolas, and solutions to other cases can also be represented as problems in conics, Apollonius seems to have used only straight-edge and compass constructions throughout. Zeuthen provides a plausible solution to the three-circle problem reconstructed from Pappus' lemmas to this work.[37]

(5) *Inclinations* (νεύσεις), in two books, is described by Pappus on pages 670–672 of the Hultsch edition. In Greek geometry, a νεῦσις problem is one that consists in placing a straight line of given length between two given lines (not necessarily straight) so that it is inclined (νεύει) toward a given point. Pappus tells us that in this work Apollonius restricted himself to certain "plane" problems, i.e., ones that can be solved with straight-edge and compass alone. The particular problems treated by Apollonius can be reconstructed with some probability from Pappus' account.

(6) *Plane Loci* (τόποι ἐπίπεδοι), in two books, is described on pages 660–670 of Pappus. "Plane loci" in Greek terminology are loci that are either straight lines or circles. In this work, Apollonius investigated

 APOLLONIUS OF PERGA

certain conditions that give rise to such plane loci. From them one can easily derive the equation for straight line and circle in Cartesian coordinates.[38]

A number of other works by Apollonius in the field of pure mathematics are known to us from remarks by later writers, but detailed information about the contents is available for only one of these: a work described by Pappus in Book II of his *Collectio*.[39] Since the beginning of Pappus' description is lost, the title of the work is unknown. It expounds a method of expressing very large numbers by what is in effect a place-value system with base 10,000. This way of overcoming the limitations of the Greek alphabetic numeral system, although ingenious, is not surprising, since Archimedes had already done the same thing in his *ψαμμίτης* (or "Sand Reckoner").[40] Archimedes' base is $10{,}000^2$. It is clear that Apollonius' work was a refinement on the same idea, with detailed rules of the application of the system to practical calculation. Besides this we hear of works on the cylindrical helix (*κοχλίας*);[41] on the ratio between dodecahedron and eicosahedron inscribed in the same sphere;[42] and a general treatise (*καθόλου πραγματεία*).[43] It seems probable that the latter dealt with the foundations of geometry, and that to it are to be assigned the several remarks of Apollonius on that subject quoted by Proclus in his commentary on the first book of Euclid (see Friedlein's Index).

Thus Apollonius' activity covered all branches of geometry known in his time. He also extended the theory of irrationals developed in Book X of Euclid, for several sources mention a work of his on unordered irrationals (*περὶ τῶν ᾽ατάκτων ᾽αλόγων*).[44] The only information as to the nature of this work comes from Pappus' commentary on Euclid X, preserved in Arabic translation;[45] but the exact connotation of "unordered irrationals" remains obscure. Finally, Eutocius, in his commentary on Archimedes' *Measurement of a Circle*,[46] informs us that in a work called *᾽ωκυτόκιον*, meaning "rapid hatching" or "quick delivery," Apollonius calculated limits for π that were closer than Archimedes' limits of 3-1/7 and 3-10/71. He does not tell us what Apollonius' limits were; it is possible to derive closer limits merely by extending Archimedes' method of inscribing and circumscribing regular 96-gons to polygons with an ever greater number of sides (as was frequently done in the sixteenth and seventeenth centuries).[47] Very probably this was Apollonius' procedure, but that cannot be proved.

In applied mathematics, Apollonius wrote at least one work on optics. The evidence comes from a late Greek mathematical work preserved only fragmentarily in a palimpsest (the "Bobbio Mathematical Fragment"). Unfortunately, the text is only partly legible at the crucial point,[48] but it is clear that Apollonius wrote a work entitled *On the Burning Mirror* (*περὶ τοῦ πυρ⟨ε⟩ίου*), in which he showed to what points parallel rays striking a spherical mirror would be reflected. The same passage also appears to say that in another work, entitled *To the Writers on Catoptrics* (*πρὸς τοὺς κατοπτρικούς*), Apollonius proved that the supposition of older writers that such rays would be reflected to the center of sphericity is wrong. The relevance of his work on conics to the subject of burning mirrors is obvious. We may conjecture with confidence that Apollonius treated of parabolic as well as of spherical burning mirrors. But the whole history of this subject in antiquity is still wrapped in obscurity.

Several sources indicate that Apollonius was noted for his astronomical studies and publications. Ptolemaeus Chennus (see n. 2) made the statement that Apollonius was called Epsilon, because the shape of the Greek letter ϵ is similar to that of the moon, to which Apollonius devoted his most careful study. This fatuous remark incidentally discloses some valuable information. "Hippolytus," in a list of distances to various celestial bodies according to different authorities, says that Apollonius stated that the distance to the moon from the earth is 5,000,000 stades (roughly 600,000 miles).[49] But the only specific information about Apollonius' astronomical studies is given by Ptolemy (fl. A.D. 140) in the *Almagest*.[50] While discussing the determination of the "station" of a planet (the point where it begins or ends its apparent retrogradation), he states that Apollonius proved the following theorem. In Figure 12, O is the observer (earth), the center of a circle on the circumference of which moves an epicycle, center C, with (angular) velocity v_1; the planet moves on the circumference of the epicycle about C with velocity v_2, and in the same sense as C moves about O. Then Apollonius' theorem states that if a line $OBAD$ is drawn from O to cut the circle at B and D, such that

$$\frac{\frac{1}{2}BD}{BO} = \frac{v_1}{v_2},$$

B will be that point on the epicycle at which the planet is stationary. Ptolemy also indicates that Apollonius proved it both for the epicycle model and for an equivalent eccenter model (depicted in Figure 13; here the planet P moves on a circle, center M, eccentric to the earth O, such that $OM/MP = CD/OC$ in Figure 12; M moves about O with speed $[v_1 + v_2]$,

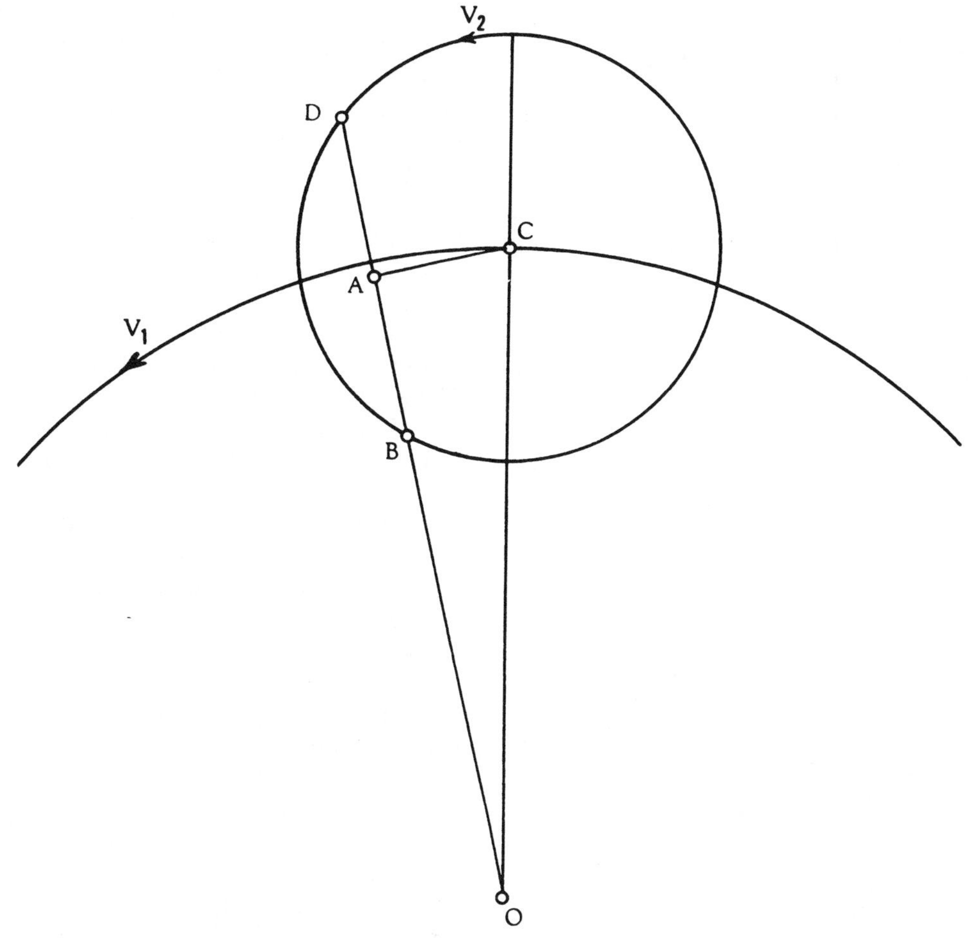

FIGURE 12

P about *M* with speed v_1). Even this much information is valuable, for it shows that Apollonius had already gone far in the application of geometrical models to explain planetary phenomena, and that he must have been acquainted with the equivalence of epicyclic and eccentric models (demonstrated by Ptolemy in *Almagest* III, 3); yet he was still operating with a simple epicycle/eccentric for the planets, although this would, for instance, entail that the length of the retrograde arc of a planet is constant, which is notoriously not the case. Neugebauer (see Bibliography) supposes, however, that the whole of the passage in which Ptolemy himself proves the above theorem is taken from Apollonius. That proof combines the two models of epicycle and eccenter in one by the ingenious device of using the same circle as both epicycle and eccenter; in other words, the epicycle model is transformed into the eccentric model by inversion on a circle. The procedure is worthy of Apollonius, and is indeed a particular case of the pole-polar relationship treated in *Conics* III, 37. But Ptolemy (who of all ancient authors is most inclined to give credit where it is due) seems to introduce this device as his own,[51] and to return to Apollonius only later.[52] Fortunately, this uncertainty does not affect the main point: that Apollonius represents an important stage in the history of the adaptation of geometrical models to planetary theories. His real importance may have been much greater than we can ever know, since not only his astronomical works, but also those of his successor in the field, Hipparchus (*fl.* 130 B.C.), are lost.

It is not clear how far Apollonius applied his theoretical astronomical models to practical prediction (i.e., assigned sizes to the geometrical quantities and velocities). For the fact that he "calculated" the absolute distance of the moon need imply no more than imitation of the crude methods of Aristarchus of Samos (early third century B.C.); for "Hippolytus" also lists figures for distances in stades between the spheres of the heavenly bodies as given by Archimedes which cannot be reconciled with any rational astronomical

APOLLONIUS OF PERGA

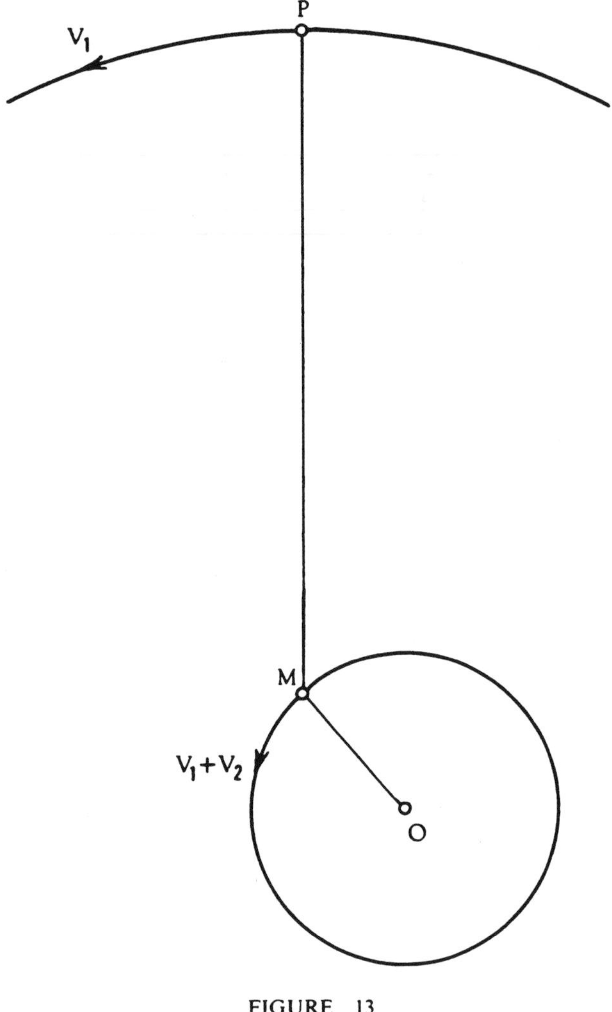

FIGURE 13

system.[53] We should not assume without evidence that Apollonius had any better basis for his lunar distance. There is, however, a passage in the astrologer Vettius Valens (*fl.* A.D. 160) that has been taken to show that Apollonius actually constructed solar and lunar tables.[54] The author says that he has used the tables of Hipparchus for the sun; of Sudines, Kidenas, and Apollonius for the moon; and also of Apollonius for both. But there is no certainty that "Apollonius" here refers to Apollonius of Perga. At least as likely is the suggestion of Kroll that it may be Apollonius of Mynda, who is known to us only from a passage of Seneca, from which it appears that he claimed to have studied with the "Chaldaeans" and that he was "very experienced in the examination of horoscopes."[55] The Apollonius of the Vettius Valens passage is also associated with Babylonian names and practices.

Although the mathematical stature of Apollonius was recognized in antiquity, he had no worthy successor in pure mathematics. The first four books of his *Conics* became the standard treatise on the subject, and were duly provided with elementary commentaries and annotations by succeeding generations. We hear of such commentaries by Serenus (fourth century A.D.?) and Hypatia (*d.* A.D. 415). The commentary of Eutocius (early sixth century A.D.) survives, but it is entirely superficial. Of surviving writers, the only one with the mathematical ability to comprehend Apollonius' results well enough to extend them significantly is Pappus (*fl.* A.D. 320), to whom we owe what knowledge we have of the range of Apollonius' activity in this branch of mathematics. The general decline of interest in the subject in Byzantium is reflected in the fact that of all Apollonius' works only *Conics* I–IV continued to be copied (because they were used as a textbook). A good deal more of his work passed into Islamic mathematics in Arabic translation, and resulted in several competent treatises on conics written in Arabic; but so far as is known, no major advances were made. (Ibn al-Haytham discusses the focus of the parabola in his work on parabolic burning mirrors;[56] but this, too, may be ultimately dependent on Greek sources.) The first real impulse toward advances in mathematics given by study of the works of Apollonius occurred in Europe in the sixteenth and early seventeenth centuries. The *Conics* were important, but at least as fruitful were Pappus' reports on the lost works, available in the excellent Latin translation by Commandino, published in 1588. (We must remember in this context that Books V–VII of the *Conics* were not generally available in Europe until 1661,[57] too late to make a real impact on the subject.) The number of "restorations" of the lost works of Apollonius made in the late sixteenth and early seventeenth centuries, some by outstanding mathematicians (e.g., Vieta, whose *Apollonius Gallus* [1600] is a reconstruction of the *Tangencies*, and Fermat, who reconstructed the *Plane Loci*) attests to the lively interest that Pappus' account excited. It is hard to overestimate the effect of Apollonius on the brilliant French mathematicians of the seventeenth century, Descartes, Mersenne, Fermat, and even Desargues and Pascal, despite their very different approach. Newton's notorious predilection for the study of conics, using Apollonian methods, was not a chance personal taste. But after him the analytic methods invented by Descartes brought about a lack of interest in Apollonius which was general among creative mathematicians for most of the eighteenth century. It was not until Poncelet's work in the early nineteenth century, picking up that of Desargues, Pascal, and la Hire, revived the study of projective geometry that the relevance of much of Apollonius' work to some basic modern theory was realized. It is no accident that the most illuminating accounts of Apollonius' geometrical work have been written by mathematicians who were themselves leading exponents of the revived "synthetic" geometry, Chasles and Zeuthen.

The contribution of Apollonius to the development of astronomy, although far less obvious to us now, may have been equally important but, unlike his geometrical work, it had an immediate effect on the progress of the subject. Hipparchus and Ptolemy absorbed his work and improved on it. The result, the Ptolemaic system, is one of the most impressive monuments of ancient science (and certainly the longest-lived), and Apollonius' work contributed some of its essential parts.

NOTES

1. Eutocius, *Commentary,* Heiberg, II, 168, quoting one Heraclius.
2. Photius, *Bibliotheca,* p. 151b18 Bekker, quoting the dubious authority Ptolemaeus Chennus of the second century A.D.
3. Pappus, *Collectio* VII, Hultsch, p. 678.
4. Heiberg, I, 192.
5. *Ibid.,* II, 2.
6. *Ibid.,* I, 192.
7. *Ibid.,* Preface to Bk. IV, II, 2, 4.
8. Pappus, *Collectio* VII, Hultsch, p. 990 ff.
9. Heiberg, I, 2.
10. *De quadratura parabolae* III, Heiberg, II², 268; *cf. De conoidibus et sphaeroidibus* III, Heiberg, I², 270.
11. E.g., *De conoidibus et sphaeroidibus* III, Heiberg, I², 272.
12. For the ellipse, see, e.g. *De conoidibus et sphaeroidibus* VIII, Heiberg, I², 294, 22–26; for the hyperbola, *ibid.* XXV, Heiberg, I², 376, 19–23.
13. Heiberg, I, 2, 4.
14. In modern terms, the locus for four lines is the locus of a point whose distances x, y, z, u from four given straight lines, measured along a given axis, satisfy the equation xz/yu = constant. This locus is a conic. (The locus for three lines is just a particular case of the above: for the distances x, y, z from three lines, xz/y^2 = constant.) This is, in modern terms, an *anharmonic* ratio: it can be shown that the theorem that this locus is a conic is equivalent to some basic theorems of projective geometry. (See Michel Chasles, *Aperçu historique,* pp. 58, 354 ff.)
15. *Collectio* VII, Hultsch, p. 672.
16. "Apollonius-Studien," p. 219.
17. Heiberg, II, 2.
18. *Ibid.,* I, 6.
19. *Phaenomena,* ed. H. Menge (*Euclidis Opera Omnia* VIII) (Leipzig, 1916), p. 6.
20. Heiberg, II², 266–268.
21. *Ibid.,* I², 270.
22. Dijksterhuis, *Archimedes,* pp. 66, n.1, 106.
23. *De corporibus fluitantibus* II, 4, Heiberg, II², 357.
24. Chester Beatty MS. Ar. 5255, f.4v.
25. *Collectio* VII, Hultsch, pp. 1006–1014.
26. See, e.g., Zeuthen, *Kegelschnitte,* p. 367 ff.
27. For a method of proving the focal property of the parabola exactly parallel to Apollonius' procedure for those of hyperbola and ellipse, see Neugebauer, "Apollonius-Studien," pp. 241–242.
28. Eutocius, *Commentary,* Heiberg, II, 170.
29. Hultsch, p. 640.
30. *Kegelschnitte,* p. 345.
31. See Pappus, ed. Hultsch, pp. 640–642.
32. *Kegelschnitte,* p. 345 ff.
33. Pappus, ed. Hultsch, pp. 642–644.
34. *Kegelschnitte,* p. 196 ff.
35. Hultsch, p. 644.
36. *Principia,* Bk., I, Lemma XVI (Motte-Cajori trans., pp. 72–73).
37. *Kegelschnitte,* p. 381 ff.
38. See T. L. Heath, *A History of Greek Mathematics,* II, 187–189.
39. Hultsch, p. 2 ff.
40. Heiberg, II², 216 ff.
41. Proclus, *Commentary on Euclid,* ed. Friedlein, p. 105.
42. "Euclid," Bk. XIV, ed. Heiberg, V, 2: the problem is solved by the author of this part of the *Elements,* a man named Hypsicles (*fl. ca.* 150 B.C.), but we cannot tell exactly how much he owes to Apollonius.
43. See the commentary on Euclid's *Data* by Marinus (fifth century A.D.), in *Euclidis opera,* ed. Heiberg-Menge, VI, 234.
44. Proclus, *op. cit.,* p. 74.
45. Ed. Junge-Thomson, p. 219.
46. *Archimedis opera,* ed. Heiberg, III², 258.
47. See E. W. Hobson, *Squaring the Circle* (Cambridge, 1913), pp. 26–28.
48. *Mathematici Graeci Minores,* ed. Heiberg, p. 88.
49. *Refutation of all Heresies* IV, 8, ed. Wendland, III, 41.
50. XII, 1, ed. Heiberg, II, 450 ff.
51. *Ibid.,* pp. 451, 22.
52. *Ibid.,* pp. 456, 9.
53. *Refutation,* ed. Wendland, pp. 41–42.
54. *Anthologiae* XI 11, ed. Kroll, 354.
55. *Quaestiones naturales* VII, 4, 1, ed. Oltramare, II, 304.
56. Ed. Heiberg-Wiedemann, in *Bibliotheca mathematica,* **10** (1910), 201–237.
57. 1661 is the date of the publication at Florence of Abraham Ecchellensis' unsatisfactory version. Some knowledge of it had trickled out before, for Mersenne mentions some of the propositions in a book published in 1644 (see Introduction, xlvi, of ver Eecke's translation of the *Conics*).

BIBLIOGRAPHY

Ancient sources for Apollonius' life include the Prefaces to Books I, II, IV, V, VI, and VII of the *Conics* (in editions of Heiberg and Halley); Eutocius, *Commentary on Apollonius* I (in Heiberg, II, 168, 170); Pappus, *Collectio* VII (Hultsch, p. 678); Photius, *Bibliotheca,* ed. Bekker (Berlin, 1824–1825), p. 151b18. The fragmentary papyrus containing the life of Philonides is edited by Wilhelm Crönert in "Der Epikureer Philonides," in *Sitzungsberichte der Königlich Preussischen Akademie der Wissenschaften zu Berlin,* Jahrgang 1900.2, pp. 942–959. Crönert there points out the importance of this text for dating Apollonius. See further R. Philippson, article "Philonides 5," in *Real-Encyclopädie,* XX.1 (Stuttgart, 1941), cols. 63 ff. A convenient summary of the evidence is given by George Huxley in "Friends and Contemporaries of Apollonius of Perge," in *Greek, Roman and Byzantine Studies,* **4** (1963), 100–103.

A critical text of books I-IV of the *Conics* (with Latin translation) and Eutocius' commentary was published by J. L. Heiberg, *Apollonii Pergaei quae Graece exstant cum commentariis antiquis,* 2 vols. (Leipzig, 1891–1893). Of the Arabic version, only part of Book V has been published, with German translation, by L. Nix, *Das Fünfte Buch der Conica des Apollonius von Perga in der Arabischen Uebersetzung des Thabit ibn Corrah* (Leipzig, 1889). For the rest of Books V–VII the basis is still Edmund Halley's Latin translation from the Arabic in the first edition of the Greek text (Oxford, 1710). The most influential translation was Commandino's Latin version of the first four books (Bologna, 1566). For other editions and early versions and a history of the text, see Heiberg, II, lvii ff. The best modern translation is the French version of all seven books (from the Greek for I–IV and from Halley's Latin for V–VII) by Paul ver Eecke, *Les coniques d'Apollonius de Perge* (Bruges, 1923; reprinted Paris, 1963); the introduction gives a good survey of the work of Apollonius. T. L. Heath's *Apollonius of Perga* (Cambridge, 1896; reprinted 1961) is a free adaptation of the *Conics* rather than a translation. The fundamental modern work on Apollonius (and the ancient theory of conics in general) is H. G. Zeuthen, *Die Lehre von den Kegelschnitten im Altertum* (Copenhagen, 1886; reprinted Hildesheim, 1966), originally published in Danish. It is indispensable for anyone who wishes to make a serious effort to understand the methods underlying the *Conics*. The Introduction of Heath's *Apollonius* is valuable for those who cannot read Zeuthen. A useful summary of the contents of the *Conics* is provided by T. L. Heath, *A History of Greek Mathematics* (Oxford, 1921), II, 126–175. O. Neugebauer's "Apollonius-Studien," in *Quellen und Studien zur Geschichte der Mathematik*, Abteilung B: Studien Band 2 (1933), pp. 215–253, a subtle analysis of some parts of the *Conics*, attempts to trace certain "algebraic" procedures of Apollonius.

On the theory of conic sections before Apollonius, Zeuthen is again the best guide. On Archimedes in particular, J. L. Heiberg, "Die Kenntnisse des Archimedes über die Kegelschnitte," in *Zeitschrift für Mathematik und Physik*, **25** (1880), Hist.-lit. Abt., 41–67, is a careful collection of the relevant passages. In English, an account of pre-Apollonian conic theory is provided by Heath, *A History of Greek Mathematics*, II, 110–126; and E. J. Dijksterhuis, *Archimedes* (Copenhagen, 1956), ch. 3, gives an illuminating comparison between the Apollonian and Archimedean approaches. Another relevant work is Diocles' "On Burning Mirrors," which is extant only in Arabic translation. The sole known manuscript is Chester Beatty Arabic no. 5255, ff. 1–26, in the Chester Beatty Library, Dublin. An edition is being prepared by G. J. Toomer.

The Arabic text of *Cutting off of a Ratio* has never been printed. Halley printed a Latin version, together with a restoration of *Cutting off of an Area*, in *Apollonii Pergaei De sectione rationis libri duo* (Oxford, 1706); see also W. A. Diesterweg, *Die Bücher des Apollonius von Perga De Sectione Rationis* (Berlin, 1824), adapted from Halley's Latin.

Ancient texts giving information on lost mathematical works of Apollonius are the commentary of Proclus (fifth century A.D.) on Euclid Book I, edited by G. Friedlein, *Procli Diadochi in primum Euclidis Elementorum librum* (Leipzig, 1873); and *The Commentary of Pappus on Book X of Euclid's Elements*, ed. G. Junge and W. Thomson (Cambridge, Mass., 1930); but the most important is in Book VII of Pappus' *Collectio*, ed. Fr. Hultsch, *Pappi Alexandrini Collectionis quae supersunt*, 3 vols. (Berlin, 1876–1878). There is a good French translation of this work by P. ver Eecke, 2 vols. (Paris-Bruges, 1933). In modern times many attempts have been made at restoration of lost works of Apollonius on the basis of Pappus' account. Here we mention only the following: for the *Determinate Section*, Willebrordus Snellius, *Apollonius Batavus* (Leyden, 1608), and Robert Simson, in *Opera quaedam reliqua* (Glasgow, 1776); for the *Tangencies*—apart from Vieta's *Apollonius Gallus* (Paris, 1600)—J. Lawson, *The Two Books of Apollonius Pergaeus Concerning Tangencies* (Cambridge, 1764); for the *Inclinations*, Samuel Horsley, *Apollonii Pergaei inclinationum libri duo* (Oxford, 1770); for the *Plane Loci*, Pierre de Fermat, *Oeuvres*, P. Tannery and C. H. Henry, eds., I (Paris, 1891), 3–51, and Robert Simson, *Apollonii Pergaei locorum planorum libri II restituti* (Glasgow, 1749).

For other restorations of all the above see the Introduction to ver Eecke's translation of the *Conics*, pp. xxii–xxxiv. A good account of the probable contents of all six works is given by Heath, *A History of Greek Mathematics*, II, 175 ff. This is heavily dependent on Zeuthen's *Kegelschnitte;* the Index to the 1966 reprint of the latter is the most convenient guide to Zeuthen's scattered treatment of these lost works. F. Woepcke, "Essai d'une restitution de travaux perdus d'Apollonius sur les quantités irrationelles," in *Mémoires présentées à l'Académie des Sciences*, **14** (Paris, 1856), 658–720, is devoted to the work on unordered irrationals; see also T. L. Heath, *The Thirteen Books of Euclid's Elements Translated*, III (2nd ed., Cambridge, 1925), 255–259.

Ancient texts relevant to Apollonius' astronomical works are "Hippolytus," *Refutatio omnium haeresium*, ed. P. Wendland, Hippolytus Werke III (Leipzig, 1916), IV 8–10; Vettius Valens, *Anthologiarum libri*, ed. W. Kroll (Berlin, 1908), IX, 11; Seneca, *Quaestiones naturales*, ed. P. Oltramare, 2 vols. (Paris, 1961), VII, 4, 1; and especially Ptolemy, *Almagest* XII, 1, ed. J. L. Heiberg, in *Claudii Ptolemaei syntaxis mathematica*, 2 vols. (Leipzig, 1898–1903).

For Apollonius' astronomical work, see O. Neugebauer, "Apollonius' Planetary Theory," in *Communications on Pure and Applied Mathematics*, **8** (1955), 641–648, and "The Equivalence of Eccentric and Epicyclic Motion According to Apollonius," in *Scripta mathematica*, **24** (1959), 5–21.

No detailed account of the influence of Apollonius on later mathematics exists. Much interesting information can be found in ver Eecke's introduction to his translation. The best guide is Michel Chasles, *Aperçu historique sur l'origine et le développement des méthodes en géométrie* (Paris, 1837; reprinted 1875), a work which is also remarkable for its treatment of Apollonius in the light of nineteenth-century synthetic geometry.

G. J. TOOMER

APPELL, PAUL (-ÉMILE) (*b.* Strasbourg, France, 27 September 1855; *d.* Paris, France, 24 October 1930)

Appell's parents, Jean-Pierre Appell and Elizabeth Müller, were Catholic Alsatians ardently loyal to revolutionary France. The family lived in a corner of the great Ritterhus, formerly a knightly lodge, where the master-dyer father and two sons by a previous marriage managed production while the mother, her sister, and a stepdaughter tended the store. Paul accepted the family ambition and patriotism but rejected Catholic piety. His character was forged by a forced move from the Ritterhus in 1866, his father's death in 1867, transfer from a religious school to the *lycée* at his own insistence in 1869, bitter experiences in the siege of Strasbourg in 1870, and a close relationship with the younger of his half brothers, Charles, who served in the Foreign Legion, fought as an irregular in 1870–1871, and in 1889 was sentenced to ten years' confinement for anti-German activities. When Appell went to Nancy in 1871 to prepare for the university and to assume French citizenship in 1872, he was carrying the hopes of his family, who remained behind in Strasbourg as German subjects.

Blessed with unbounded energy, this attractive outsider with an accent moved rapidly toward the inner circles of French mathematics. At Nancy, he and Henri Poincaré formed a friendship that lasted until the latter's death. In 1873 he entered the École Normale, from which he graduated first in the class of 1876, three months after earning his doctorate. From this time on, Appell maintained an amazing level of activity in teaching, research, editing, and public service. He typically held several teaching posts at the same time, including the chair of mechanics at the Sorbonne from 1885. He was elected to the Académie des Sciences in 1892. He served as dean of the Faculty of Science of the University of Paris from 1903 to 1920 and as rector from 1920 to 1925. In various government posts, including membership in the Conseil Supérieure d'Instruction Publique, he was an exponent of educational reform and initiator of numerous large-scale projects, including the Cité Universitaire.

In 1881 he married Amelie, daughter of the archaeologist Alexandre Bertrand, niece of the mathematicians Joseph Bertrand and Charles Hermité, and a cousin of Appell's classmate and friend Émile Picard. Their son became a deputy and undersecretary of state. Two of their three daughters married the academicians Émile Borel and J. E. Duclaux. The household included Paul's mother, who had joined him in 1877 and remained until her death in 1902. In his *Souvenirs* (p. 180) he described his life as "flowing tranquilly between teaching, mathematical work and vacations in Alsace" at the maternal home in Klingenthal, but he found energy to support vigorously the movement for women's rights, to carry from Alsace his brother's reports destined for the French War Office, and to defend his fellow Alsatian Dreyfus and serve on an expert commission whose ruling played a key role in his final rehabilitation. During World War I he founded and led the Secours National, a semiofficial organization uniting all religious and political groups to aid civilian victims. He described the return of the tricolor to Alsace as the fulfillment of his "lifelong goal" and felt that Germany had been treated too easily. He served as secretary-general of the French Association for the League of Nations.

Appell's first paper (1876) was his thesis on projective geometry in the tradition of Chasles, but at the suggestion of his teachers he turned to algebraic functions, differential equations, and complex analysis. He generalized many classical results (e.g., the theories of elliptic and of hypergeometric functions) to the case of two or more variables. From the first his work was close to physical ideas. For example, in 1878 he noted the physical significance of the imaginary period of elliptic functions in the solution of the pendulum problem, and thus showed that double periodicity follows from physical considerations. In 1880 he wrote on a sequence of functions (now called the Appell polynomials) satisfying the condition that the derivative of the nth function is n times the previous one.

In 1885 Appell was awarded half the Bordin Prize for solving the problem of "cutting and filling" (*deblais et remblais*) originally posed by Monge: To move a given region into another of equal volume so as to minimize the integral of the element of volume times the distance between its old and new positions. In 1889 he won second place (after Poincaré) in a competition sponsored by King Oscar II of Sweden: To find an effective method of calculating the Fourier coefficients in the expansion of quadruply periodic functions of two complex variables.

The flow of papers continued, augmented by treatises, textbooks, and popularizations and seemingly unaffected by other responsibilities. Although Appell never lost his interest in "pure" analysis and geometry, his activity continued to shift toward mechanics, and in 1893 Volume I of the monumental *Traité de mécanique rationnelle* appeared. Volume V (1921) included the mathematics required for relativity, but the treatise is essentially an exposition of classical mechanics of the late nineteenth century. It contains many of Appell's contributions, including his equations of motion valid for both holonomic and nonholonomic systems, which have not displaced the classical Lagrangian system in spite of undoubted advantages.

It is difficult to do justice to Appell's work because it lacks central themes, seminal ideas, and dramatic results. In 1925 he wrote: "I always had little taste for developing general theories and preferred to study limited and precise questions that might open new paths" ("Notice," p. 162). Indeed, his scientific work consists of a series of brilliant solutions of particular problems, some of the greatest difficulty. He was a technician who used the classical methods of his time to answer open questions, work out details, and make natural extensions in the mainstream of the late nineteenth century; but his work did not open new doors, as he hoped. On the contrary, he does not seem to have looked down any of the new paths that were leading to a period of unbridled abstraction and generalization. During the last half of his career he was a pillar of a backward-looking establishment that was to give way to Nicolas Bourbaki, a namesake of a general who was one of his boyhood heroes.

BIBLIOGRAPHY

I. Original Works. Appell's "Notice sur les travaux scientifiques," in *Acta mathematica,* **45** (1925), 161-285, describes 140 publications in analysis, 30 in geometry, and 87 in mechanics. The most notable are *Notice sur les travaux* (Paris, 1884, 1889, 1892), written to support his candidacy for the Académie; "Sur les intégrales des fonctions à multiplicateurs," in *Acta mathematica,* **13** (1890); *Traité de mécanique rationnelle,* 5 vols. (Paris, 1893-1921 and later eds.); *Théorie des fonctions algébriques et de leurs intégrales* (Paris, 1895, 1922), written with E. Goursat; and *Principes de la théorie des fonctions elliptiques et applications* (Paris, 1897), written with E. Lacour.

Not listed in the "Notice" are numerous elementary textbooks, popularizations, addresses and papers on history and education, and several later publications, including *Sur une forme générale des équations de la dynamique,* Mémorial des Sciences Mathématiques (Paris, 1925); *Sur les fonctions hypergéométriques de plusieurs variables, les polynomes d'Hermité et autres fonctions sphériques dans l'hyperspace, ibid.* (Paris, 1925); *Henri Poincaré* (Paris, 1925); *Fonctions hypergéométriques et hypersphériques. Polynomes d'Hermité* (Paris, 1926), written with M. J. Kampé de Feriet; *Le problème géométrique des deblais et remblais,* Mémorial des Sciences Mathématiques (Paris, 1928); *Sur la décomposition d'une fonction en éléments simples, ibid.* (Paris, 1929); and "Sur la constante d'Euler," in *Enseignement mathématique,* **29** (1930), 5-6, apparently his last paper, a follow-up to one on the same subject, *ibid.,* **26** (1927), 11-14, which had been welcomed by the editor with a note observing that "a great source of light is still burning."

II. Secondary Literature. Appell's life and work are unusually well documented by his four *notices* mentioned above; his charming and revealing autobiography, *Souvenirs d'un alsacien 1858-1922* (Paris, 1923); and E. Lebon, *Biographie et bibliographie analytique des écrits de Paul Appell* (Paris, 1910), which gives many biographical details and seems to have been written with Appell's collaboration. Other biographical articles rely on these sources, but some of them contain personal recollections or other interesting information, notably *Cinquantenaire scientifique de Paul Appell* (Paris, 1927); "Centenaire de la naissance de Paul Appell," in *Annales de l'Université de Paris,* **26**, no. 1 (1956), 13-31; A. Buhl, in *Enseignement mathématique,* **26** (1927), 5-11; **30** (1931), 5-21; **33** (1934), 229-231; T. Levi-Civita, in *Rendiconti Accademia dei Lincei,* 6th ser., **13** (1931), 241-242; and Raymond Poincaré, in *Annales de l'Université de Paris,* **5** (1930), 463-477.

Kenneth O. May

ARBOGAST, LOUIS FRANÇOIS ANTOINE (*b.* Mutzig, Alsace, 4 October 1759; *d.* Strasbourg, France, 18 April 1803)

There is no exact information on Arbogast's early years nor on his studies. He is registered as a non-pleading lawyer to the Sovereign Council of Alsace about 1780, and it is known that he taught mathematics at the Collège de Colmar about 1787. In 1789 he moved to Strasbourg, where he taught the same subject at the École d'Artillerie. He also was professor of physics at the Collège Royal, and after it was nationalized he served as director from April to October 1791. He then became rector of the University of Strasbourg. In 1790 he joined the society known as the Amis de la Constitution. He was a noted person in the Commune of Strasbourg, and in 1791 was elected a deputy to the Assemblée Législative and, in the following year, deputy from Haguenau to the Convention Nationale.

At the first of these assemblies, he and Gilbert Romme, Condorcet's closest collaborator, were on the committee of public instruction. Arbogast was the author of the general plan for public schools at all levels, which was brought before the convention but not adopted. He was responsible for the law introducing the decimal metric system in the whole of the French Republic.

Arbogast and his Alsatian colleagues were responsible for making the two assemblies aware of the efforts in Alsace toward building up a teaching force, as well as introducing the methods of pedagogy used in Germany. This information was useful in the establishment of the École Normale in the year III (1795).

Although he had been made *instituteur d'analyse* (probably professor of calculus) at the École Centrale de Paris (now École Polytechnique) in 1794, Arbogast

ARBOGAST

taught only at the École Préparatoire. In this temporary institution an accelerated course of three months was given to 392 students before they were divided into three groups, which then proceeded to finish their studies in one, two, or three years.

In July 1795 Arbogast was entrusted with the planning of the École Centrale du Bas-Rhin, which replaced the abolished university. There he held the chair of mathematics from 1796 until 1802.

Arbogast was elected corresponding member of the Académie des Sciences in 1792 and an associate nonresident member of the Institut National (mathematics section, first class) four years later.

Arbogast's interest in the history of mathematics led to his classification of papers left by Marin Mersenne. He also amassed an important collection of manuscripts that are for the most part copies, in his writing, of the originals of memoirs or letters of Pierre Fermat, René Descartes, Jean Bernoulli, Pierre Varignon, Guillaume de L'Hospital, and others. At Arbogast's death these manuscripts were collected by his friend Français. They were bought in 1839 by Guglielmo Libri, the inspector of libraries, from a bookseller in Metz. After Libri's committal for trial on charges of malfeasance, his escape, and the seizure of his property, some of Arbogast's copies were deposited at the Bibliothèque Nationale in Paris. Other documents sold by the unscrupulous historian of science to Lord Ashburnham have also come to rest there. Other copies are now in the Laurenziana Library, Florence. The collection gathered by Arbogast became extremely valuable when definitive editions of the complete works of Fermat and Descartes, and of Mersenne's correspondence, were published.

In 1787 Arbogast took part in a competition organized by the Academy of St. Petersburg on "the arbitrary functions introduced by the integration of differential equations which have more than two variables," the question being "Do they belong to any curves or surfaces either algebraic, transcendental, or mechanical, either discontinuous or produced by a simple movement of the hand? Or shouldn't they legitimately be applied only to continuous curves susceptible of being expressed by algebraic or transcendental equations?"

The Academy was thus requesting a drastic settlement of the dispute between Jean d'Alembert, who adopted the second point of view, and Leonhard Euler, partisan of the first.

Arbogast won the prize and was even bolder than Euler in his conclusions. He showed that arbitrary functions may tolerate not only discontinuities in the Eulerian sense of the term, but also "combinations of several portions of different curves or those drawn by the free movement of the hand," that is, discontinuities in the sense afterward used by Augustin Cauchy.

Two years later, Arbogast sent a report to the Académie des Sciences de Paris on the new principles of differential calculus. This was never published, but Joseph Lagrange mentions it in 1797 as setting forth the same idea that he had developed in 1772, an idea that is the fundamental principle of his theory of analytic functions, "with its own developments and applications."

In speaking of his report in the Preface to *Calcul des dérivations,* Arbogast recalled the general ideas that anticipate Cauchy's and Niels-Abel's ideas on the convergence of series. He added, "It caused me to reflect on fundamental principles . . . I then foresaw the birth of the first inkling of the ideas and methods which, when developed and extended, formed the substance of calculus of derivatives."

The principal aim of the calculus of derivatives, as Arbogast understood it, was to give simple and precise rules for finding series expansions. In order not to stay in the domain of pure theory, he used his rapid methods to find important formulas that were reached more laboriously by some of the great geometers.

Arbogast's work is dominated by a general idea that has become increasingly important in science and that until then had barely been anticipated: operational calculus. His only followers in this field were the brothers Français, then François Servois. But he was part of a vast mathematical movement that later included such names as Cauchy, George Boole, Sir William Rowan Hamilton, and Hermann Grassmann.

Arbogast clearly saw the difference that should be made between function and operation. When he defined his method of the "separation of the scale of operations," he said (*Traité des dérivations,* Preface):

> This method is generally thought of as separating from the functions of variables when possible, the operational signs which affect this function. Then of treating the expressions formed by these signs applied to any quantity whatsoever, an expression which I have called a scale of operation, to treat it, I say, nevertheless as if the operational signs which compose it were quantities, then to multiply the result by the function.

Arbogast appears in his mathematical work as a philosophical thinker whose ideas prefigured many mathematical notions of modern times, such as the introduction into analysis of discontinuous functions, the limitation of certain methods of algebra to what are today known as holomorphic functions, the necessity for care in the use of infinite series, and the conception of calculus as operational symbols, disregarding the quantities or functions on which they are based.

BIBLIOGRAPHY

I. Original Works. Arbogast's works include "Essai sur de nouveaux principes du calcul différentiel et intégral indépendant de la théorie des infiniment petits et de celle des limites; mémoire envoyé à l'Académie des Sciences de Paris au printemps 1789" (unpublished); *Mémoire sur la nature des fonctions arbitraires qui entrent dans les intégrales des équations aux dérivées partielles. Présenté a l'Académie Impériale de Pétersbourg pour concourir au Prix proposé en 1787 et couronné dans l'Assemblée du 29 novembre 1790. Par M. ARBOGAST, professeur de mathématiques à Colmar* (St. Petersburg, 1791); and *Du calcul des dérivations et de ses usages dans la théorie des suites et dans le calcul différentiel* (Strasbourg, 1800).

II. Secondary Literature. Works concerning Arbogast or his work are Paul Dupuy, *L'École Normale de l'an III* (Paris, 1895), p. 28; Maurice Fréchet, "Biographie du mathematicien alsacien Arbogast," in *Thales,* **4** (1937–1939), 43–55; Joseph Lagrange, *Théories des fonctions analytiques* (Paris, 1797), Introduction; Niels Nielsen, *Géomètres français sous la Révolution* (Copenhagen, 1929), pp. 1–5; Paul Tannery, *Mémoires scientifiques,* VI (Paris, 1926), 157; and K. Zimmermann, dissertation (Heidelberg, 1934).

JEAN ITARD

ARBUTHNOT, JOHN (*b.* Arbuthnot, Kinkardineshire, Scotland, 29 April 1667; *d.* London, 27 February 1735)

The son of a Scottish Episcopal clergyman, Arbuthnot studied at Aberdeen, took his doctor's degree in medicine at St. Andrews in 1696, and settled in London in 1697. He was elected a fellow of the Royal Society in 1704 and was appointed a physician extraordinary to Queen Anne in 1705 (he became ordinary physician in 1709). The Royal College of Physicians elected him a fellow in 1710.

Arbuthnot wrote a few scientific and medical essays, but he became especially famous for his political satires. He was a close friend of the wits and literary men of his day: with Swift, Pope, John Gay, and Thomas Parnell he was a member of the Scriblerus Club. Of the characters in his political novels, the one that has survived is John Bull.

Arbuthnot was well acquainted with the theory of probability. It is certain that he published an English translation of Christian Huygens' *De ratiociniis in ludo aleae* (probably to be identified with a work said to have appeared in 1692, and with the first edition of part of an anonymous work that appeared in a fourth edition in 1738 in London under the title *Of the Laws of Chance . . .*). His scientific importance, however, resides in a short paper in the *Philosophical Transactions of the Royal Society,* which has been taken as the very origin of mathematical statistics. Entitled "An Argument for Divine Providence, Taken From the Constant Regularity Observ'd in the Birth of Both Sexes," it begins:

> Among innumerable footsteps of divine providence to be found in the works of nature, there is a very remarkable one to be observed in the exact balance that is maintained, between the numbers of men and women; for by this means it is provided, that the species never may fail, nor perish, since every male may have its female, and of proportionable age. This equality of males and females is not the effect of chance but divine providence, working for a good end, which I thus demonstrate.

He first shows by numerical examples that if sex is determined by a die with two sides, M and F, it is quite improbable that in a large number of tosses there will be as many M as F. However, it is also quite improbable that the number of M will greatly exceed that of F. Nevertheless, there are more male infants born than female infants—clearly through divine providence—to make good the greater losses of males in external accidents. In every year from 1629 to 1710, there were more males christened in London than females—as if 82 tosses of the die would all show M. Such an event has a very poor probability: 2^{-82}. Therefore it cannot have been produced by chance; it must have been produced by providence.

Arbuthnot's argument is the first known example of a mathematical statistical inference and, in fact, is the ancestor of modern statistical reasoning. It immediately drew the attention of Continental scientists, particularly the Dutch physicist 's Gravesande, as is shown by contemporary correspondence. Daniel Bernoulli used it in 1732 to show that it could not be by chance that the planetary orbits are only slightly inclined to the ecliptic. In 1757 John Michell proved the existence of double stars by showing that stars are found close to each other more often than mere chance would allow.

Condorcet applied the argument to test the veracity of the tradition of Roman history that seven kings had reigned for a total of 257 years. Laplace, in his classic work, reconsidered such applications and added many new ones. This crude argument, although now greatly refined, is still the basis of statistical inference.

BIBLIOGRAPHY

Arbuthnot's major paper, "An Argument for Divine Providence, Taken from the Constant Regularity Observ'd in the Birth of Both Sexes," is found in *Philosophical Transactions of the Royal Society,* **27** (1710–1712), 186–190.

See also G. A. Aitken, *The Life and Works of John Arbuthnot* (Oxford, 1892); L. M. Beattie, *John Arbuthnot* (Cambridge, Mass., 1935); Daniel Bernoulli, in *Recueil des pièces qui ont remporté le prix double de l'Académie Royale des Sciences,* **3** (1734), 95–144; M. J. A. N. C. le Marquis de Condorcet, in *Histoire de l'Académie* (Paris, 1784), pp. 454–468; Hans Freudenthal, "Introductory Address," in *Quantitative Methods in Pharmacology* (Amsterdam, 1961), and "De eerste ontmoeting tussen de wiskunde en de sociale wetenschappen," in *Verhandelingen van de Koninklijke Vlaamse Akademie, Klasse Wetenschappen,* **28** (1966), 3–51; W. J. 's Gravesande, *Oeuvres philosophiques et mathématiques,* II (Amsterdam, 1774), 221–248; P. S. Laplace, *Théorie analytique de la probabilité,* 2nd ed. (Paris, 1820); John Michell, in *Philosophical Transactions of the Royal Society,* **57**, no. 1 (1767), 234–264; and I. Todhunter, *A History of the Mathematical Theory of Probability* (Cambridge, 1865; repr. New York, 1949).

HANS FREUDENTHAL

ARCHIMEDES (*b.* Syracuse, *ca.* 287 B.C.; *d.* Syracuse, 212 B.C.)

Few details remain of the life of antiquity's most celebrated mathematician. A biography by his friend Heracleides has not survived. That his father was the astronomer Phidias we know from Archimedes himself in his *The Sandreckoner* (Sect. I. 9). Archimedes was perhaps a kinsman of the ruler of Syracuse, King Hieron II (as Plutarch and Polybius suggest). At least he was on intimate terms with Hieron, to whose son Gelon he dedicated *The Sandreckoner.* Archimedes almost certainly visited Alexandria, where no doubt he studied with the successors of Euclid and played an important role in the further development of Euclidian mathematics. This visit is rendered almost certain by his custom of addressing his mathematical discoveries to mathematicians who are known to have lived in Alexandria, such as Conon, Dositheus, and Eratosthenes. At any rate Archimedes returned to Syracuse, composed most of his works there, and died there during its capture by the Romans in 212 B.C. Archimedes' approximate birth date of 287 B.C. is conjectured on the basis of a remark by the Byzantine poet and historian of the twelfth century, John Tzetzes, who declared (*Chiliad* 2, hist. 35) that Archimedes "worked at geometry until old age, surviving seventy-five years." There are picturesque accounts of Archimedes' death by Livy, Plutarch, Valerius Maximus, and Tzetzes, which vary in detail but agree that he was killed by a Roman soldier. In most accounts he is pictured as being engaged in mathematics at the time of his death. Plutarch tells us (*Marcellus,* Ch. XVII) that Archimedes "is said to have asked his friends and kinsmen to place on his grave after his death a cylinder circumscribing a sphere, with an inscription giving the ratio by which the including solid exceeds the included." And indeed Cicero (see *Tusculan Disputations,* V, xxiii, 64–66), when he was Quaestor in Sicily in 75 B.C.,

> . . . tracked out his grave. . . . and found it enclosed all around and covered with brambles and thickets; for I remembered certain doggerel lines inscribed, as I had heard, upon his tomb, which stated that a sphere along with a cylinder had been put upon the top of his grave. Accordingly, after taking a good look all around (for there are a great quantity of graves at the Agrigentine Gate), I noticed a small column arising a little above the bushes, on which there was the figure of a sphere and a cylinder. . . . Slaves were sent in with sickles. . . and when a passage to the place was opened we approached the pedestal in front of us; the epigram was traceable with about half of the lines legible, as the latter portion was worn away.

No surviving bust can be certainly identified as being of Archimedes, although a portrait on a Sicilian coin (whatever its date) is definitely his. A well-known mosaic showing Archimedes before a calculating board with a Roman soldier standing over him was once thought to be a genuine survival from Herculaneum but is now considered to be of Renaissance origin.

Mechanical Inventions. While Archimedes' place in the history of science rests on a remarkable collection of mathematical works, his reputation in antiquity was also founded upon a series of mechanical contrivances which he is supposed to have invented and which the researches of A. G. Drachmann tend in part to confirm as Archimedean inventions. One of these is the water snail, a screwlike device to raise water for the purpose of irrigation, which, Diodorus Siculus tells us (*Bibl. hist.,* V, Ch. 37), Archimedes invented in Egypt. We are further told by Atheneus that an endless screw invented by Archimedes was used to launch a ship. He is also credited with the invention of the compound pulley. Some such device is the object of the story told by Plutarch in his life of *Marcellus* (Ch. XIV). When asked by Hieron to show him how a great weight could be moved by a small force, Archimedes "fixed upon a three-masted merchantman of the royal fleet, which had been dragged ashore by the great labors of many men, and after putting on board many passengers and the customary freight, he seated himself at a distance from her, and without any great effort, but quietly setting in motion a system of compound pulleys, drew her towards him smoothly and evenly, as though she were gliding through the water." It is in connection with this story that Plutarch tells us of the supposed remark of Archimedes to the effect that "if there were another world, and he could go to it, he could move this one," a remark known in more familiar form from Pappus of Alexandria (*Collectio,* Bk. VIII, Prop. 11): "Give me a place to stand on, and I will move the earth." Of doubtful authenticity is the oft-quoted story told by Vitruvius (*De architectura,* Bk. IX, Ch. 3) that Hieron wished Archimedes to check whether a certain crown or wreath was of pure gold, or whether the goldsmith had fraudulently alloyed it with some silver.

> While Archimedes was turning the problem over, he chanced to come to the place of bathing, and there, as he was sitting down in the tub, he noticed that the amount of water which flowed over by the tub was equal to the amount by which his body was immersed. This indicated to him a method of solving the problem, and he did not delay, but in his joy leapt out of the tub, and, rushing naked towards his home, he cried out in a loud voice that he had found what he sought, for as he ran he repeatedly shouted in Greek, *heurēka, heurēka.*

Much more generally credited is the assertion of Pappus that Archimedes wrote a book *On Sphere-making,* a work which presumably told how to construct a model planetarium representing the apparent motions of the sun, moon, and planets, and perhaps also a closed star globe representing the constellations. At least, we are told by Cicero (*De re publica,* I, XIV, 21–22) that Marcellus took as booty from the sack of Syracuse both types of instruments constructed by Archimedes:

> For Gallus told us that the other kind of celestial globe [that Marcellus brought back and placed in the Temple of Virtue], which was solid and contained no hollow space, was a very early invention, the first one of that kind having been constructed by Thales of Miletus, and later marked by Eudoxus of Cnidus . . . with the constellations and stars which are fixed in the sky. . . . But this newer kind of globe, he said, on which were delineated the motions of the sun and moon and of those five stars which are called the wanderers . . . contained more than could be shown on a solid globe, and the invention of Archimedes deserved special admiration because he had thought out a way to represent accurately by a single device for turning the globe those various and divergent courses with their different rates of speed.

Finally, there are references by Polybius, Livy, Plutarch, and others to fabulous ballistic instruments constructed by Archimedes to help repel Marcellus. One other defensive device often mentioned but of exceedingly doubtful existence was a burning mirror or combination of mirrors.

We have no way to know for sure of Archimedes' attitude toward his inventions. One supposes that Plutarch's famous eulogy of Archimedes' disdain for the practical was an invention of Plutarch and simply reflected the awe in which Archimedes' theoretical discoveries were held. Plutarch (*Marcellus,* Ch. XVII) exclaims:

> And yet Archimedes possessed such a lofty spirit, so profound a soul, and such a wealth of scientific theory, that although his inventions had won for him a name and fame for superhuman sagacity, he would not consent to leave behind him any treatise on this subject, but regarding the work of an engineer and every art that ministers to the needs of life as ignoble and vulgar, he devoted his earnest efforts only to those studies the subtlety and charm of which are not affected by the claims of necessity. These studies, he thought, are not to be compared with any others; in them, the subject matter vies with the demonstration, the former supplying grandeur and beauty, the latter precision and surpassing power. For it is not possible to find in geometry more profound and difficult questions treated in simpler and purer terms. Some attribute this success to his natural endowments; others think it due to excessive labor that everything he did seemed to have been performed without labor and with ease. For no one could by his own efforts discover the proof, and yet as soon as he learns it from him, he thinks he might have discovered it himself, so smooth and rapid is the path by which he leads one to the desired conclusion.

Mathematical Works. The mathematical works of Archimedes that have come down to us can be loosely classified in three groups (Arabic numbers have been added to indicate, where possible, their chronological order). The first group consists of those that have as their major objective the proof of theorems relative to the areas and volumes of figures bounded by curved lines and surfaces. In this group we can place *On the Sphere and the Cylinder* (5); *On the Measurement of the Circle* (9); *On Conoids and Spheroids* (7); *On Spirals* (6); and *On the Quadrature of the Parabola* (2), which, in respect to its Propositions 1–17, belongs also to the second category of works. The second group comprises works that lead to a geometrical analysis of statical and hydrostatical problems and the use of statics in geometry: *On the Equilibrium of Planes,* Book I (1), Book II (3); *On Floating Bodies* (8); *On the Method of Mechanical Theorems* (4); and the aforementioned propositions from *On the Quadrature of the Parabola* (2). Miscellaneous mathematical works constitute the third group: *The Sandreckoner* (10); *The Cattle-Problem*; and the fragmentary *Stomachion*. Several other works not now extant are alluded to by Greek authors (see Heiberg, ed., *Archimedis opera*, II, 536–554). For example, there appear to have been various works on mechanics that have some unknown relationship to *On the Equilibrium of Planes*. Among these are a possible work on *Elements of Mechanics* (perhaps containing an earlier section on centers of gravity, which, however, may have been merely a separate work written before *Equilibrium of Planes*, Book I), a tract *On Balances*, and possibly one *On Uprights*. Archimedes also seems to have written a tract *On Polyhedra*, perhaps one *On Blocks and Cylinders*, certainly one on *Archai* or *The Naming of Numbers* (a work preliminary to *The Sandreckoner*), and a work on *Optics* or *Catoptrics*. Other works are attributed to Archimedes by Arabic authors, and, for the most part, are extant in Arabic manuscripts (the titles for which manuscripts are known are indicated by an asterisk; see Bibliography): *The Lemmata**, or *Liber assumptorum* (in its present form certainly not by Archimedes since his name is cited in the proofs), *On Water Clocks**, *On Touching Circles**, *On Parallel Lines*, *On Triangles**, *On the Properties of the Right Triangle**, *On Data*, and *On the Division of the Circle into Seven Equal Parts**.

But even the genuine extant works are by no means in their original form. For example, *On the Equilibrium of Planes*, Book I, is possibly an excerpt from the presumably longer *Elements of Mechanics* mentioned above and is clearly distinct from Book II, which was apparently written later. A solution promised by Archimedes in *On the Sphere and the Cylinder* (Bk. II, Prop. 4) was already missing by the second century A.D. *On the Measurement of the Circle* was certainly in a much different form originally, with Proposition II probably not a part of it (and even if it were, it would have to follow the present Proposition III, since it depends on it). The word *parabolēs* in the extant title of *On the Quadrature of the Parabola* could hardly have been in the original title, since that word was not yet used in Archimedes' work in the sense of a conic section. Finally, the tracts *On the Sphere and the Cylinder* and *On the Measurement of the Circle* have been almost completely purged of their original Sicilian-Doric dialect, while the rest of his works have suffered in varying degrees this same kind of linguistic transformation.

In proving theorems relative to the area or volume of figures bounded by curved lines or surfaces, Archimedes employs the so-called Lemma of Archimedes or some similar lemma, together with a technique of proof that is generally called the "method of exhaustion," and other special Greek devices such as *neuseis*, and principles taken over from statics. These various mathematical techniques are coupled with an extensive knowledge of the mathematical works of his predecessors, including those of Eudoxus, Euclid, Aristeus, and others. The Lemma of Archimedes (*On the Sphere and Cylinder*, Assumption 5; cf. the Preface to *On the Quadrature of the Parabola* and the Preface to *On Spirals*) assumes "that of two unequal lines, unequal surfaces, and unequal solids the greater exceeds the lesser by an amount such that, when added to itself, it may exceed any assigned magnitude of the type of magnitudes compared with one another." This has on occasion been loosely identified with Definition 4 of Book V of the *Elements* of Euclid (often called the axiom of Eudoxus): "Magnitudes are said to have a ratio to one another which are capable, when multiplied, of exceeding one another."

But the intent of Archimedes' assumption appears to be that if there are two unequal magnitudes capable of having a ratio in the Euclidian sense, then their difference will have a ratio (in the Euclidian sense) with any magnitude of the same kind as the two initial magnitudes. This lemma has been interpreted as excluding actual infinitesimals, so that the difference of two lines will always be a line and never a point, the difference between surfaces always a surface and never a line, and the difference between solids always a solid and never a surface. The exhaustion procedure often uses a somewhat different lemma represented by Proposition X.1 of the *Elements* of Euclid: "Two unequal magnitudes being set out, if from the greater there be subtracted a magnitude greater than its half, and from that which is left a magnitude greater than its half, and if this process be repeated continually, there will be left some magnitude which will be less than the lesser magnitude set out." This obviously reflects the further idea of the continuous divisibility of a continuum. One could say that the Lemma of Archimedes justifies this further lemma in the sense that no matter how far the procedure of subtracting more than half of the larger of the magnitudes set out is taken (or also no matter how far the procedure of subtracting one-half the larger magnitude, described in the corollary to Proposition X.1, is taken), the magnitude resulting from the successive division (which magnitude being conceived as the difference of two magnitudes) will always be capable of having a ratio in the Euclidian sense with the smaller of the magnitudes set out. Hence one such remainder will some time be in a relationship of "less than" to the lesser of the magnitudes set out.

The method of exhaustion, widely used by Archimedes, was perhaps invented by Eudoxus. It was used on occasion by Euclid in his *Elements* (for example, in Proposition XII.2). Proof by exhaustion (the name is often criticized since the purpose of the technique is to avoid assuming the complete exhaustion of an area or a volume; Dijksterhuis prefers the somewhat anachronistic expression "indirect passage to the limit") is an indirect proof by reduction to absurdity. That is to say, if the theorem is of the form $A = B$, it is held to be true by showing that to assume its opposite, namely that A is not equal to B, is impossible since it leads to contradictions. The method has several forms. Following Dijksterhuis, we can label the two main types: the compression method and the approximation method. The former is the most widely used and exists in two forms, one that depends upon taking decreasing differences and one that depends on taking decreasing ratios. The fundamental procedure of both the "difference" and the "ratio" forms starts with the successive inscription and circumscription of regular figures within or without the figure for which the area or volume is sought. Then in the "difference" method the area or volume of the inscribed or circumscribed figure is regularly increased or decreased until the difference between the desired area or volume and the inscribed or circumscribed figure is less than any preassigned magnitude. Or to put it more specifically, if the theorem is of the form $A = B$, A being the curvilinear figure sought and B a regular rectilinear figure the formula for the magnitude of which is known, and we assume that A is greater than B, then by the exhaustion procedure and its basic lemma we can construct some regular rectilinear inscribed figure P such that P is greater than B; but it is obvious that P, an included figure, is in fact always less than B. Since P cannot be both greater and less than B, the assumption from which the contradiction evolved (namely, that A is greater than B) must be false. Similarly, if A is assumed to be less than B, we can by the exhaustion technique and the basic lemma find a circumscribed figure P that is less than B, which P (as an including figure) must always be greater than B. Thus the assumption of A less than B must also be false. Hence, it is now evident that, since A is neither greater nor less than B, it must be equal to B. An example of the exhaustion procedure in its "difference" form is to be found in *On the Measurement of the Circle:*[1]

Proposition 1

The area of any circle is equal to a right-angled triangle in which one of the sides about the right angle is equal to the radius, and the other to the circumference, of the circle.

Let $ABCD$ be the given circle, K the triangle described.

Then, if the circle is not equal to K, it must be either greater or less.

I. If possible, let the circle be greater than K.

Inscribe a square $ABCD$, bisect the arcs AB, BC, CD, DA, then bisect (if necessary) the halves, and so on, until the sides of the inscribed polygon whose angular points are the points of division subtend segments whose sum is less than the excess of the area of the circle over K.

Thus the area of the polygon is greater than K.

Let AE be any side of it, and ON the perpendicular on AE from the centre O.

Then ON is less than the radius of the circle and therefore less than one of the sides about the right angle in K. Also the perimeter of the polygon is less than the circumference of the circle, i.e. less than the other side about the right angle in K.

Therefore the area of the polygon is less than K; which is inconsistent with the hypothesis.

Thus the area of the circle is not greater than K.

II. If possible, let the circle be less than K.

Circumscribe a square, and let two adjacent sides, touching the circle in E, H, meet in T. Bisect the arcs between adjacent points of contact and draw the tangents at the points of bisection. Let A be the middle point of the arc EH, and FAG the tangent at A.

Then the angle TAG is a right angle.

Therefore $$TG > GA$$ $$> GH.$$

It follows that the triangle FTG is greater than half the area $TEAH$.

Similarly, if the arc AH be bisected and the tangent at the point of bisection be drawn, it will cut off from the area GAH more than one-half.

Thus, by continuing the process, we shall ultimately arrive at a circumscribed polygon such that the spaces intercepted between it and the circle are together less than the excess of K over the area of the circle.

Thus the area of the polygon will be less than K.

Now, since the perpendicular from O on any side of the polygon is equal to the radius of the circle, while the perimeter of the polygon is greater than the circumference of the circle, it follows that the area of the polygon is greater than the triangle K; which is impossible.

Therefore the area of the circle is not less than K.

Since then the area of the circle is neither greater nor less than K, it is equal to it.

Other examples of the "difference" form of the exhaustion method are found in *On Conoids and Spheroids* (Props. 22, 26, 28, 30), *On Spiral Lines* (Props. 24, 25), and *On the Quadrature of the Parabola* (Prop. 16).

The "ratio" form of the exhaustion method is quite

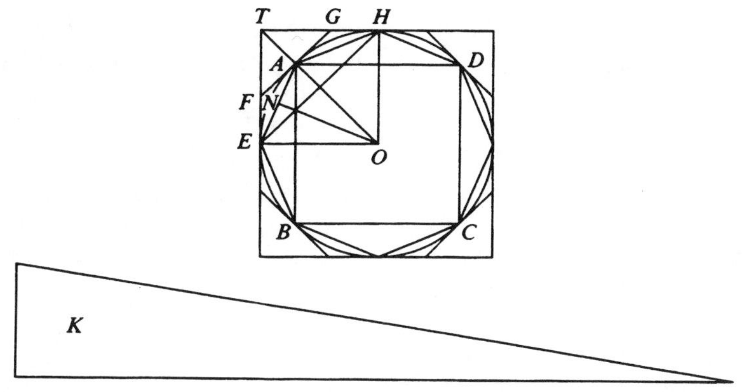

FIGURE 1

similar to the "difference" form except that in the first part of the proof, where the known figure is said to be less than the figure sought, the ratio of circumscribed polygon to inscribed polygon is decreased until it is less than the ratio of the figure sought to the known figure, and in the second part the ratio of circumscribed polygon to inscribed polygon is decreased until it is less than the ratio of the known figure to the figure sought. In each part a contradiction is shown to follow the assumption. And thus the assumption of each part must be false, namely, that the known figure is either greater or less than the figure sought. Consequently, the known figure must be equal to the figure sought. An example of the "ratio" form appears in *On the Sphere and the Cylinder* (Bk. I):[2]

Proposition 14

The surface of any isosceles cone excluding the base is equal to a circle whose radius is a mean proportional between the side of the cone [a generator] and the radius of the circle which is the base of the cone.

Let the circle A be the base of the cone; draw C equal to the radius of the circle, and D equal to the side of the cone, and let E be a mean proportional between C, D.

Draw a circle B with radius equal to E.

Then shall B be equal to the surface of the cone (excluding the base), which we will call S.

If not, B must be either greater or less than S.

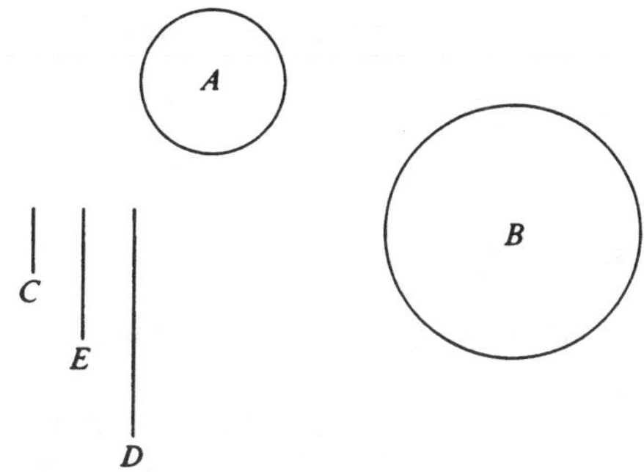

FIGURE 2

I. Suppose $B < S$.

Let a regular polygon be described about B and a similar one inscribed in it such that the former has to the latter a ratio less than the ratio $S:B$.

Describe about A another similar polygon, and on it set up a pyramid with apex the same as that of the cone.

Then (polygon about A):(polygon about B)
$= C^2:E^2$
$= C:D$
= (polygon about A):(surface of pyramid excluding base). Therefore

(surface of pyramid) = (polygon about B).

Now (polygon about B):(polygon in B) $< S:B$.

Therefore

(surface of pyramid):(polygon in B) $< S:B$,

which is impossible (because the surface of the pyramid is greater than S, while the polygon in B is less than B).

Hence $B \nless S$.

II. Suppose $B > S$.

Take regular polygons circumscribed and inscribed to B such that the ratio of the former to the latter is less than the ratio $B:S$.

Inscribe in A a similar polygon to that inscribed in B, and erect a pyramid on the polygon inscribed in A with apex the same as that of the cone.

In this case

(polygon in A):(polygon in B) $= C^2:E^2$
$= C:D$

> (polygon in A):(surface of pyramid excluding base).

This is clear because the ratio of C to D is greater than the ratio of the perpendicular from the center of A on a side of the polygon to the perpendicular from the apex of the cone on the same side.

Therefore

(surface of pyramid) > (polygon in B).

But (polygon about B):(polygon in B) $< B:S$.

Therefore, *a fortiori,*

(polygon about B):(surface of pyramid) $< B:S$;
which is impossible.

Since therefore B is neither greater nor less than S,

$$B = S.$$

Other examples of the "ratio" form of the exhaustion method are found in *On the Sphere and the Cylinder,* (Bk. I, Props. 13, 33, 34, 42, 44.)

As indicated earlier, in addition to the two forms of the compression method of exhaustion, Archimedes used a further technique which we may call the approximation method. This is used on only one occasion, namely, in *On the Quadrature of the Parabola* (Props. 18–24). It consists in approximating from below the area of a parabolic segment. That is to say, Archimedes continually "exhausts" the parabola by drawing first a triangle in the segment with the same base and vertex as the segment. On each side of the triangle we again construct triangles. This process is continued as far as we like. Thus if A_1 is the area of the original triangle, we have a series of inscribed triangles whose sum converges toward the area of parabolic segment: A_1, $1/4\,A_1$, $(1/4)^2A_1$, $\cdots$ (in the accompanying figure A_1 is $\triangle PQq$ and $1/4\,A_1$ or A_2 is the sum of triangles Prq and PRQ and A_3 is the sum of the next set of inscribed triangles—not shown on the diagram but equal to $[1/4]^2A_1$). In order to prove that K, the area of the parabolic segment, is equal to $4/3\,A_1$, Archimedes first proves in Proposition 22 that the sum of any finite number of terms of this series is less than the area of the parabolic segment. He then proves in Proposition 23 that if we have a series of terms $A_1, A_2, A_3, \cdots$ such as those given above, that is, with $A_1 = 4A_2$, $A_2 = 4A_3$, $\cdots$, then

$$A_1 + A_2 + A_3 + \cdots + A_n + \frac{1}{3}\cdot A_n = \frac{4}{3}\cdot A_1,$$

or

$$A_1\left[1 + \frac{1}{4} + \left(\frac{1}{4}\right)^2 + \cdots + \left(\frac{1}{4}\right)^{n-1} + \frac{1}{3}\cdot\left(\frac{1}{4}\right)^{n-1}\right] = \frac{4}{3}\cdot A_1$$

With modern techniques of series summation we would simply say that as n increases indefinitely $(1/4)^{n-1}$ becomes infinitely small and the series in brackets tends toward 4/3 as a limit and thus the parabolic segment equals $4/3 \cdot A_1$. But Archimedes followed the Greek *reductio* procedure. Hence he showed that if we assume $K > 4/3 \cdot A_1$ on the basis of a corollary to Proposition 20, namely, that by the successive inscription of triangles "it is possible to inscribe in the parabolic segment a polygon such that the segments left over are together less than any assigned area" (which is itself based on Euclid, *Elements* X.1), a contradiction will ensue. Similarly, a contradiction results from the assumption of $K < 4/3 \cdot A_1$. Here in brief is the final step of the proof (the reader is reminded that the terms A_1, A_2, A_3, $\cdots$, A_n, which were used above, are actually rendered by A, B, C, $\cdots$, X):[3]

Proposition 24

Every segment bounded by a parabola and a chord Qq is equal to four-thirds of the triangle which has the same base as the segment and equal height.

Suppose $$K = \frac{4}{3}\triangle PQq,$$

where P is the vertex of the segment; and we have then to prove that the area of the segment is equal to K.

For, if the segment be not equal to K, it must either be greater or less.

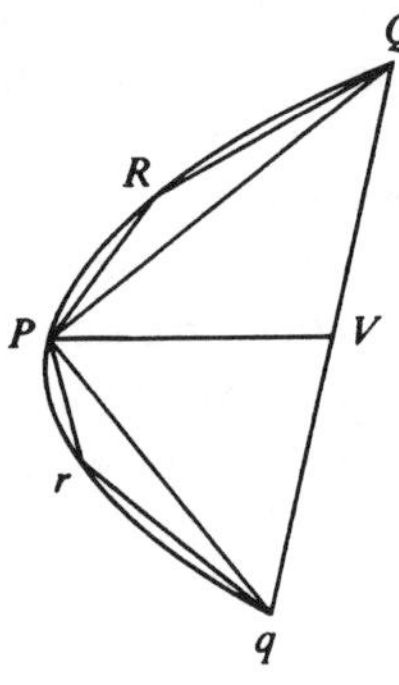

FIGURE 3

I. Suppose the area of the segment greater than K.

If then we inscribe in the segments cut off by PQ, Pq triangles which have the same base and equal height, i.e. triangles with the same vertices R, r as those of the segments, and if in the remaining segments we inscribe triangles in the same manner, and so on, we shall finally have segments remaining whose sum is less than the area by which the segment PQq exceeds K [Prop. 20 Cor.].

Therefore the polygon so formed must be greater than the area K; which is impossible, since [Prop. 23]

$$A + B + C + \cdots + Z < \frac{4}{3}A,$$

where $$A = \triangle PQq.$$

Thus the area of the segment cannot be greater than K.

II. Suppose, if possible, that the area of the segment is less than K.

If then $\triangle PQq = A$, $B = 1/4\,A$, $C = 1/4\,B$, and so on, until we arrive at an area X such that X is less than the difference between K and the segment, we have

$$A + B + C + \cdots + X + \frac{1}{3}X = \frac{4}{3}A \qquad \text{[Prop. 23]}$$
$$= K.$$

Now, since K exceeds $A + B + C + \cdots + X$ by an area less than X, and the area of the segment by an area greater than X, it follows that

$$A + B + C + \cdots + X > \text{(the segment)};$$

which is impossible, by Prop. 22. . . .

Hence the segment is not less than K.

Thus, since the segment is neither greater nor less than K,

$$\text{(area of segment } PQq) = K = \frac{4}{3} \triangle PQq.$$

In the initial remarks on the basic methods of Archimedes, it was noted that Archimedes sometimes used the technique of a *neusis* ("verging") construction. Pappus defined a *neusis* construction as "Two lines being given in position, to place between them a straight line given in length and verging towards a given point." He also noted that "a line is said to verge towards a point, if being produced, it reaches the point." No doubt "insertion" describes the mathematical meaning better than "verging" or "inclination," but "insertion" fails to render the additional condition of inclining or verging toward a point just as the name *neusis* in expressing the "verging" condition fails to render the crucial condition of insertion. At any rate, the *neusis* construction can be thought of as being accomplished mechanically by marking the termini of the linear insertion on a ruler and shifting that ruler until the termini of the insertion lie on the given curve or curves while the ruler passes through the verging point. In terms of mathematical theory most of the Greek *neuseis* require a solution by means of conics or other higher curves. *Neusis* constructions are indicated by Archimedes in *On Spirals* (Props. 5–9). They are assumed as possible without any explanation. The simplest case may be illustrated as follows:[4]

Proposition 5

Given a circle with center O, and the tangent to it at a point A, it is possible to draw from O a straight line OPF, meeting the circle in P and the tangent in F, such that, if c be the circumference of any given circle whatever,

$$FP:OP < (\text{arc } AP):c.$$

Take a straight line, as D, greater than the circumference c. [Prop. 3]

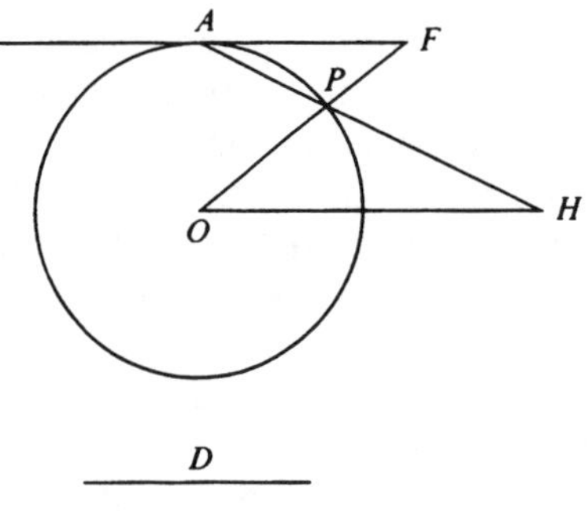

FIGURE 4

Through O draw OH parallel to the given tangent, and draw through A a line APH, meeting the circle in P and OH in H, such that the portion PH intercepted between the circle and the line OH may be equal to D [literally: "let PH be placed equal to D, verging toward A"]. Join OP and produce it to meet the tangent in F.

Then $FP:OP = AP:PH$, by parallels,
$= AP:D$
$< (\text{arc } AP):c.$

With the various methods that have been described and others, Archimedes was able to demonstrate a whole host of theorems that became a basic part of geometry. Examples beyond those already quoted follow: "The surface of any sphere is equal to four times the greatest circle in it" (*On the Sphere and the Cylinder,* Bk. I, Prop. 23); this is equivalent to the modern formulation $S = 4\pi r^2$. "Any sphere is equal to four times the cone which has its base equal to the greatest circle in the sphere and its height equal to the radius of the sphere" (*ibid.,* Prop. 34); its corollary that "every cylinder whose base is the greatest circle in a sphere and whose height is equal to the diameter of the sphere is 3/2 of the sphere and its surface together with its base is 3/2 of the surface of the sphere" is the proposition illustrated on the tombstone of Archimedes, as was noted above. The modern equivalent of Proposition 34 is $V = 4/3\ \pi r^3$. "Any right or oblique segment of a paraboloid of revolution is half again as large as the cone or segment of a cone which has the same base and the same axis" (*On Conoids and Spheroids,* Props. 21–22). He was also able by his investigation of what are now known as Archimedean spirals not only to accomplish their quadrature (*On Spirals,* Props. 24–28), but, in preparation therefore, to perform the crucial rectification of the circumference of a circle. This, then, would allow for the construction of the right triangle equal to a circle that is the object of *On the Measurement of a Circle* (Prop. I), above. This rectification is accomplished in *On Spirals* (Prop. 18): "If a straight line is tangent to the extremity of a spiral described in the first revolution, and if from the point of origin of the spiral one erects a perpendicular on the initial line of revolution, the perpendicular will meet the tangent so that the line intercepted between the tangent and the origin of the spiral will be equal to the circumference of the first circle" (see Fig. 5).

It has also been remarked earlier that Archimedes employed statical procedures in the solution of geometrical problems and the demonstration of theorems. These procedures are evident in *On the Quadrature of the Parabola* (Props. 6–16) and also in *On the Method.* We have already seen that in the latter part of *On the Quadrature of the Parabola* Archimedes demonstrated the quadrature of the parabola by purely geometric methods. In the first part of the tract he demonstrated the same thing by means of a balancing method. By the use of the law of the lever and a knowledge of the centers of gravity of triangles and trapezia, coupled with a *reductio* procedure, the quadrature is demonstrated. In *On the Method* the same statical procedures are used; but, in addition, an entirely new assumption is joined with them, namely, that a plane figure can be considered as the summation of its line elements (presumably infinite in number) and that a volumetric figure can be considered as the summation of its plane elements. The important point regarding this work is that it gives us a rare insight into Archimedes' procedures for discovering the theorems to be proved. The formal, indirect procedures that appear in demonstrations in the great body of Archimedes' works tell us little as to how the theorems to be proved were discovered. To be sure, sometimes he no doubt proved theorems that he had inherited with inadequate proof from his predecessors (such was perhaps the case of the theorem on the area of the circle, which he proved simply and elegantly in *On the Measurement of the Circle* [Prop. 1], as has been seen). But often we are told by him what his own discoveries were, and their relation to the discoveries of his predecessors, as, for example, those of Eudoxus. In the Preface of Book I of *On the Sphere and the Cylinder,* he characterizes his discoveries by comparing them with some established theorems of Eudoxus:[5]

> Now these properties were all along naturally inherent in the figures referred to . . ., but remained unknown to those who were before my time engaged in the study of geometry. Having, however, now discovered that the properties are true of these figures, I cannot feel any hesitation in setting them side by side both with my former investigations and with those of the theorems of Eudoxus on solids which are held to be most irrefragably established, namely, that any pyramid is one third part of the prism which has the same base with the pyramid and equal height, and that any cone is one third part of the cylinder which has the same base with the cone and equal height. For, though these properties also were naturally inherent in the figures all along, yet they were in fact unknown to all the many able geometers who lived before Eudoxus, and had not been observed by anyone. Now, however, it will be open to those who possess the requisite ability to examine these discoveries of mine.

Some of the mystery surrounding Archimedes' methods of discovery was, then, dissipated by the discovery and publication of *On the Method of Mechanical Theorems.* For example, we can see in Proposition 2 how it was that Archimedes discovered by the "method" the theorems relative to the area and volume of a sphere that he was later to prove by strict geometrical methods in *On the Sphere and the Cylinder:*[6]

Proposition 2

We can investigate by the same method the propositions that

(*1*) *Any sphere is* (*in respect of solid content*) *four times the cone with base equal to a great circle of the sphere and height equal to its radius; and*

(*2*) *the cylinder with base equal to a great circle of the sphere and height equal to the diameter is 1-1/2 times the sphere.*

(1) Let $ABCD$ be a great circle of a sphere, and AC, BD diameters at right angles to one another.

Let a circle be drawn about BD as diameter and in a plane perpendicular to AC, and on this circle as base let a cone be described with A as vertex. Let the surface of this cone be produced and then cut by a plane through C parallel to its base; the section will be a circle on EF as diameter. On this circle as base let a cylinder be erected with height and axis AC, and produce CA

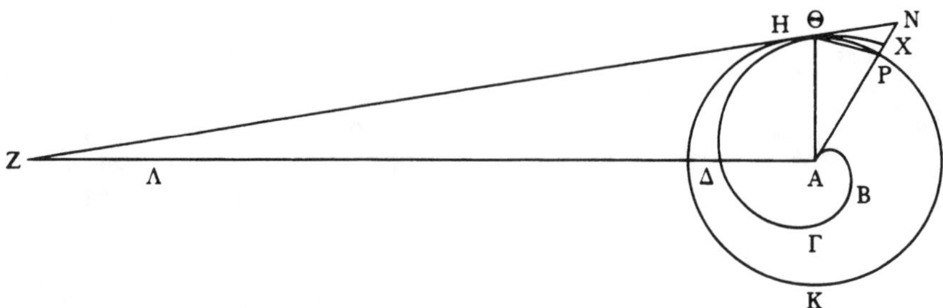

FIGURE 5

to H, making AH equal to CA.

Let CH be regarded as the bar of a balance, A being its middle point.

Draw any straight line MN in the plane of the circle $ABCD$ and parallel to BD. Let MN meet the circle in O, P, the diameter AC in S, and the straight lines AE, AF in Q, R respectively. Join AO.

Through MN draw a plane at right angles to AC; this plane will cut the cylinder in a circle with diameter MN, the sphere in a circle with diameter OP, and the cone in a circle with diameter QR.

Now, since $MS = AC$, and $QS = AS$,

$$\begin{aligned} MS \cdot SQ &= CA \cdot AS \\ &= AO^2 \\ &= OS^2 + SQ^2. \end{aligned}$$

And, since $HA = AC$,

$$\begin{aligned} HA:AS &= CA:AS \\ &= MS:SQ \\ &= MS^2:MS \cdot SQ \\ &= MS^2:(OS^2 + SQ^2), \text{ from above,} \\ &= MN^2:(OP^2 + QR^2) \\ &= (\text{circle, diam. } MN):(\text{circle, diam. } OP \\ &\quad + \text{circle, diam. } QR). \end{aligned}$$

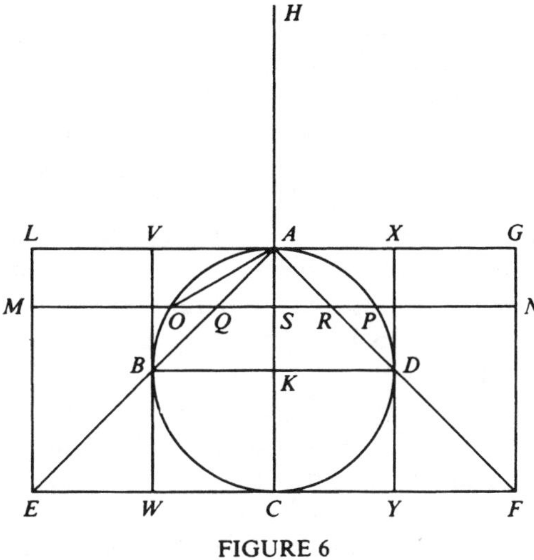

FIGURE 6

That is,
$HA:AS$ = (circle in cylinder):(circle in sphere + circle in cone).

Therefore the circle in the cylinder, placed where it is, is in equilibrium, about A, with the circle in the sphere together with the circle in the cone, if both the latter circles are placed with their centers of gravity at H.

Similarly for the three corresponding sections made by a plane perpendicular to AC and passing through any other straight line in the parallelogram LF parallel to EF.

If we deal in the same way with all the sets of three circles in which planes perpendicular to AC cut the cylinder, the sphere and the cone, and which make up those solids respectively, it follows that the cylinder, in the place where it is, will be in equilibrium about A with the sphere and the cone together, when both are placed with their centers of gravity at H.

Therefore, since K is the center of gravity of the cylinder,

$$HA:AK = (\text{cylinder}):(\text{sphere} + \text{cone } AEF).$$

But $\quad HA = 2AK;$

therefore cylinder = 2 (sphere + cone AEF).

Now $\quad$ cylinder = 3 (cone AEF); $\quad$ [Eucl. XII. 10]

therefore $\quad$ cone AEF = 2 (sphere).

But, since $EF = 2BD$,

cone AEF = 8 (cone ABD);

therefore $\quad$ sphere = 4 (cone ABD).

(2) Through B, D draw VBW, XDY parallel to AC; and imagine a cylinder which has AC for axis and the circles on VX, WY as diameters for bases.

Then

$$\begin{aligned} \text{cylinder } VY &= 2 (\text{cylinder } VD) \\ &= 6 (\text{cone } ABD) \quad \text{[Eucl. XII. 10]} \\ &= \tfrac{3}{2} (\text{sphere}), \text{ from above.} \end{aligned}$$

Q.E.D.

From this theorem, to the effect that a sphere is four times as great as the cone with a great circle of the sphere as base and with height equal to the radius of the sphere, I conceived the notion that the surface of any sphere is four times as great as a great circle in it; for, judging from the fact that any circle is equal to a triangle with base equal to the circumference and height equal to the radius of the circle, I apprehended that, in like manner, any sphere is equal to a cone with base equal to the surface of the sphere and height equal to the radius.

It should be observed in regard to this quotation that the basic volumetric theorem was discovered prior to the surface theorem, although in their later formal presentation in *On the Sphere and the Cylinder,* the theorem for the surface of a sphere is proved first. By using the "method" Archimedes also gave another "proof" of the quadrature of the parabola—already twice proved in *On the Quadrature of the Parabola*—and he remarks in his preface (see the quotation below) that he originally discovered this theorem by the method. Finally, in connection with *On the Method,* it is necessary to remark that Archimedes considered the method inadequate for formal demonstration, even if it did provide him with the theorems to be proved more rigorously. One supposes that it was the additional assumption considering the figures as the summation of their infinitesimal elements that provoked Archimedes' cautionary attitude, which he presents so lucidly in his introductory remarks to

Eratosthenes:[7]

> Seeing moreover in you, as I say, an earnest student, a man of considerable eminence in philosophy, and an admirer [of mathematical inquiry], I thought fit to write out for you and explain in detail in the same book the peculiarity of a certain method, by which it will be possible for you to get a start to enable you to investigate some of the problems in mathematics by means of mechanics. This procedure is, I am persuaded, no less useful even for the proof of the theorems themselves; for certain things first became clear to me by a mechanical method, although they had to be demonstrated by geometry afterwards because their investigation by the said method did not furnish an actual demonstration. But it is of course easier, when we have previously acquired, by the method, some knowledge of the questions, to supply the proof than it is to find it without any previous knowledge. This is a reason why, in the case of the theorems the proof of which Eudoxus was the first to discover, namely that the cone is a third part of the cylinder, and the pyramid of the prism, having the same base and equal height, we should give no small share of the credit to Democritus who was the first to make the assertion with regard to the said figure though he did not prove it. I am myself in the position of having first made the discovery of the theorem now to be published [by the method indicated], and I deem it necessary to expound the method partly because I have already spoken of it and I do not want to be thought to have uttered vain words, but equally because I am persuaded that it will be of no little service to mathematics; for I apprehend that some, either of my contemporaries or of my successors, will, by means of the method when once established, be able to discover other theorems in addition, which have not yet occurred to me.

While Archimedes' investigations were primarily in geometry and mechanics reduced to geometry, he made some important excursions into numerical calculation, although the methods he used are by no means clear. In *On the Measurement of the Circle* (Prop. 3), he calculated the ratio of circumference to diameter (not called π until early modern times) as being less than 3-1/7 and greater than 3-10/71. In the course of this proof Archimedes showed that he had an accurate method of approximating the roots of large numbers. It is also of interest that he there gave an approximation for $\sqrt{3}$, namely, $1351/780 > \sqrt{3} > 265/153$. How he computed this has been much disputed. In the tract known as *The Sandreckoner,* Archimedes presented a system to represent large numbers, a system that allows him to express a number P^{10^8}, where P itself is $(10^8)^{10^8}$ He invented this system to express numbers of the sort that, in his words, "exceed not only the number of the mass of sand equal in magnitude to the earth . . ., but also that of a mass equal in magnitude to the universe." Actually, the number he finds that would approximate the number of grains of sand to fill the universe is a mere 10^{63}, and thus does not require the higher orders described in his system. Incidentally, it is in this work that we have one of the few antique references to Aristarchus' heliocentric system.

In the development of physical science, Archimedes is celebrated as the first to apply geometry successfully to statics and hydrostatics. In his *On the Equilibrium of Planes* (Bk. I, Props. 6–7), he proved the law of the lever in a purely geometrical manner. His weights had become geometrical magnitudes possessing weight and acting perpendicularly to the balance beam, itself conceived of as a weightless geometrical line. His crucial assumption was the special case of the equilibrium of the balance of equal arm length supporting equal weights. This postulate, although it may ultimately rest on experience, in the context of a mathematical proof appears to be a basic appeal to geometrical symmetry. In demonstrating Proposition 6, "Commensurable magnitudes are in equilibrium at distances reciprocally proportional to their weights," his major objective was to reduce the general case of unequal weights at inversely proportional distances to the special case of equal weights at equal distances. This was done by (1) converting the weightless beam of unequal arm lengths into a beam of equal arm lengths, and then (2) distributing the unequal weights, analyzed into rational component parts over the extended beam uniformly so that we have a case of equal weights at equal distances. Finally (3) the proof utilized propositions concerning centers of gravity (which in part appear to have been proved elsewhere by Archimedes) to show that the case of the uniformly distributed parts of the unequal weights over the extended beam is in fact identical with the case of the composite weights concentrated on the arms at unequal lengths. Further, it is shown in Proposition 7 that if the theorem is true for rational magnitudes, it is true for irrational magnitudes as well (although the incompleteness of this latter proof has been much discussed). The severest criticism of the proof of Proposition 6 is, of course, the classic discussion by Ernst Mach in his *Science of Mechanics,* which stresses two general points: (1) experience must have played a predominant role in the proof and its postulates in spite of its mathematical-deductive form; and (2) any attempt to go from the special case of the lever to the general case by replacing expanded weights on a lever arm with a weight concentrated at their center of gravity must assume that which has to be proved, namely, the principle of static moment. This criticism has given rise to an extensive literature and stimulated some successful defenses of Archimedes, and this body of literature has been keenly analyzed by E. J. Dijksterhuis (*Archimedes*, pp. 289–304). It has been pointed out further, and with some justification, that Proposition 6 with its proof, even if sound, only establishes that the inverse proportionality of weights and arm lengths is a sufficient condition for the equilibrium of a lever supported in its center of gravity under the influence of two weights on either side of the fulcrum. It is evident that he should also have shown that the condition is a necessary one, since he repeatedly applies the inverse proportionality as a necessary condition of equilibrium. But this is easily done and so may have appeared trivial to Archimedes. The succeeding propositions in Book I of *On the Equilibrium of Planes* show that Archimedes conceived of this part of the work as preparatory to his use of statics in his investigation of geometry of the sort that we have described in *On the Quadrature of the Parabola* and *On the Method.*

In his *On Floating Bodies*, the emphasis is once more largely on geometrical analysis. In Book I, a somewhat obscure concept of hydrostatic pressure is presented as his basic postulate:[8]

> Let it be granted that the fluid is of such a nature that of the parts of it which are at the same level and adjacent to one another that which is pressed the less is pushed away by that which is pressed the more, and that each of its parts is pressed by the fluid which is vertically above it, if the fluid is not shut up in anything and is not compressed by anything else.

As his propositions are analyzed, we see that Archimedes essentially maintained an Aristotelian concept of weight directed downward toward the center of the earth conceived of as the center of the world. In fact, he goes further by imagining the earth removed and so fluids are presented as part of a fluid sphere all of whose parts weigh downward convergently toward the center of the sphere. The surface of the sphere is then imagined as being divided into an equal number of parts which are the bases of conical sectors having the center of the sphere as their vertex. Thus the water in each sector weighs downward toward the center. Then if a solid is added to a sector, increasing the pressure on it, the pressure is transmitted down through the center of the sphere and back upward on an adjacent sector and the fluid in that adjacent sector is forced upward to equalize the level of adjacent sectors. The influence on other than adjacent sectors is ignored. It is probable that Archimedes did not have the concept of hydrostatic paradox formulated by Stevin, which held that at any given point of the fluid the pressure is a constant magnitude that acts perpendicularly on any plane through that point. But, by his procedures, Archimedes was able to formulate propositions concerning the relative immersion in a fluid of solids less dense than, as dense as, and more dense than the fluid in which they are placed. Proposition 7 relating to solids denser than the fluid expresses the so-called "principle of Archimedes" in this fashion: "Solids heavier than the fluid, when thrown into the fluid, will be driven downward as far as they can sink, and they will be lighter [when weighed] in the fluid [than their weight in air] by the weight of the portion of fluid having the same volume as the solid." This is usually more succinctly expressed by saying that such solids will be lighter in the fluid by the weight of the fluid displaced. Book II, which investigates the different positions in which a right segment of a paraboloid can float in a fluid, is a brilliant geometrical tour de force. In it Archimedes returns to the basic assumption found in *On the Equilibrium of Planes, On the Quadrature of the Parabola,* and *On the Method,* namely, that weight verticals are to be conceived of as parallel rather than as convergent at the center of a fluid sphere.

Influence. Unlike the *Elements* of Euclid, the works of Archimedes were not widely known in antiquity. Our present knowledge of his works depends largely on the interest taken in them at Constantinople from the sixth through the tenth centuries. It is true that before that time individual works of Archimedes were obviously studied at Alexandria, since Archimedes was often quoted by three eminent mathematicians of Alexandria: Hero, Pappus, and Theon. But it is with the activity of Eutocius of Ascalon, who was born toward the end of the fifth century and studied at Alexandria, that the textual history of a collected edition of Archimedes properly begins. Eutocius composed commentaries on three of Archimedes' works: *On the Sphere and the Cylinder, On the Measurement of the Circle,* and *On the Equilibrium of Planes.* These were no doubt the most popular of Archimedes' works at that time. The *Commentary on the Sphere and the Cylinder* is a rich work for historical references to Greek geometry. For example, in an extended comment to Book II, Proposition 1, Eutocius presents manifold solutions of earlier geometers to the problem of finding two mean proportionals between two given lines. *The Commentary on the Measurement of the Circle* is of interest in its detailed expansion of Archimedes' calculation of π. The works of Archimedes and the commentaries of Eutocius were studied and taught by Isidore of Miletus and Anthemius of Tralles, Justinian's architects of Hagia

Sophia in Constantinople. It was apparently Isidore who was responsible for the first collected edition of at least the three works commented on by Eutocius as well as the commentaries. Later Byzantine authors seem gradually to have added other works to this first collected edition until the ninth century when the educational reformer Leon of Thessalonica produced the compilation represented by Greek manuscript A (adopting the designation used by the editor, J. L. Heiberg). Manuscript A contained all of the Greek works now known excepting *On Floating Bodies, On the Method, Stomachion,* and *The Cattle Problem.* This was one of the two manuscripts available to William of Moerbeke when he made his Latin translations in 1269. It was the source, directly or indirectly, of all of the Renaissance copies of Archimedes. A second Byzantine manuscript, designated as B, included only the mechanical works: *On the Equilibrium of Planes, On the Quadrature of the Parabola,* and *On Floating Bodies* (and possibly *On Spirals*). It too was available to Moerbeke. But it disappears after an early fourteenth-century reference. Finally, we can mention a third Byzantine manuscript, C, a palimpsest whose Archimedean parts are in a hand of the tenth century. It was not available to the Latin West in the Middle Ages, or indeed in modern times until its identification by Heiberg in 1906 at Constantinople (where it had been brought from Jerusalem). It contains large parts of *On the Sphere and the Cylinder,* almost all of *On Spirals,* some parts of *On the Measurement of the Circle* and *On the Equilibrium of Planes,* and a part of the *Stomachion.* More important, it contains most of the Greek text of *On Floating Bodies* (a text unavailable in Greek since the disappearance of manuscript B) and a great part of *On the Method of Mechanical Theorems,* hitherto known only by hearsay. (Hero mentions it in his *Metrica,* and the Byzantine lexicographer Suidas declares that Theodosius wrote a commentary on it.)

At about the same time that Archimedes was being studied in ninth-century Byzantium, he was also finding a place among the Arabs. The Arabic Archimedes has been studied in only a preliminary fashion, but it seems unlikely that the Arabs possessed any manuscript of his works as complete as manuscript A. Still, they often brilliantly exploited the methods of Archimedes and brought to bear their fine knowledge of conic sections on Archimedean problems. The Arabic Archimedes consisted of the following works: (1) *On the Sphere and the Cylinder* and at least a part of Eutocius' commentary on it. This work seems to have existed in a poor, early ninth-century translation, revised in the late ninth century, first by Isḥāq ibn Ḥunayn and then by Thābit ibn Qurra. It was reedited by Nasīr ad-Dīn al-Ṭūsī in the thirteenth century and was on occasion paraphrased and commented on by other Arabic authors (see Archimedes in Index of Suter's "Die Mathematiker und Astronomen"). (2) *On the Measurement of the Circle,* translated by Thābit ibn Qurra and reedited by al-Ṭūsī. Perhaps the commentary on it by Eutocius was also translated, for the extended calculation of π found in the geometrical tract of the ninth-century Arabic mathematicians the Banū Mūsā bears some resemblance to that present in the commentary of Eutocius. (3) A fragment of *On Floating Bodies,* consisting of a definition of specific gravity not present in the Greek text, a better version of the basic postulate (described above) than exists in the Greek text, and the enunciations without proofs of seven of the nine propositions of Book I and the first proposition of Book II. (4) Perhaps *On the Quadrature of the Parabola*—at least this problem received the attention of Thābit ibn Qurra. (5) Some indirect material from *On the Equilibrium of Planes* found in other mechanical works translated into Arabic (such as Hero's *Mechanics,* the so-called Euclid tract *On the Balance,* the *Liber karastonis,* etc.). (6) In addition, various other works attributed to Archimedes by the Arabs and for which there is no extant Greek text (see list above in "Mathematical Works"). Of the additional works, we can single out the *Lemmata* (*Liber assumptorum*), for, although it cannot have come directly from Archimedes in its present form, in the opinion of experts several of its propositions are Archimedean in character. One such proposition was Proposition 8, which employed a *neusis* construction like those used by Archimedes:[9]

Proposition 8

If we let line AB be led everywhere in the circle and extended rectilinearly [see Fig. 7], and if BC is posited as equal to the radius of the circle, and C is connected to the center of the circle D, and the line (CD) is produced to E, arc AE will be triple arc BF. Therefore, let us draw EG parallel to AB and join DB and DG. And because the two angles DEG, DGE are equal, $\angle GDC = 2\angle DEG$. And because $\angle BDC = \angle BCD$ and $\angle CEG = \angle ACE$, $\angle GDC = 2\angle CDB$ and $\angle BDG = 3\angle BDC$, and arc $BG =$ arc AE, and arc $AE = 3$ arc BF; and this is what we wished.

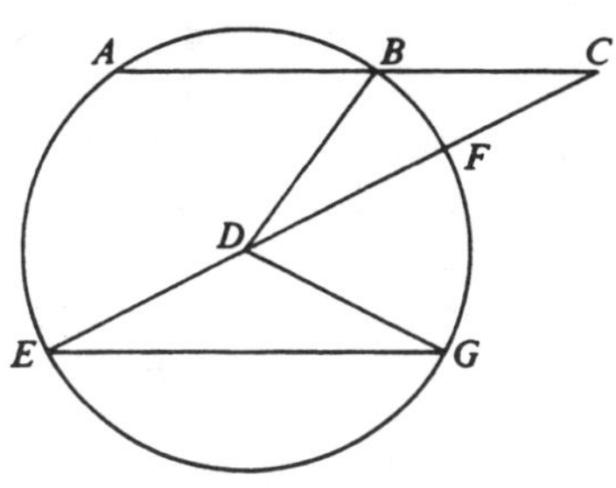

FIGURE 7

This proposition shows, then, that if one finds the position and condition of line ABC such that it is drawn through A, meets the circle again in B, and its extension BC equals the radius, this will give the trisection of the given angle BDG. It thus demonstrates the equivalence of a *neusis* and the trisection problem—but without solving the *neusis* (which could be solved by the construction of a conchoid to a circular base).

Special mention should also be made of the *Book on the Division of the Circle into Seven Equal Parts,* attributed to Archimedes by the Arabs, for its remarkable construction of a regular heptagon. This work stimulated a whole series of Arabic studies of this problem, including one by the famous Ibn al-Haytham (Alhazen). Propositions 16 and 17, leading to that construction, are given here in toto: [10]

Proposition 16

Let us construct square $ABCD$ [Fig. 8] and extend side AB directly toward H. Then we draw the diagonal

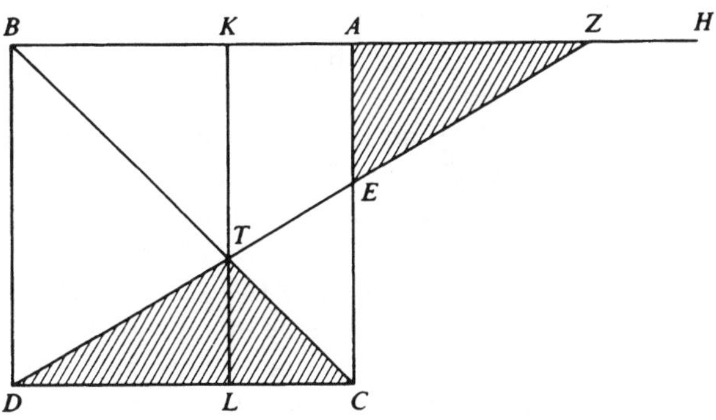

FIGURE 8

BC. We lay one end of a rule on point D. Its other end we make meet extension AH at a point Z such that $\triangle AZE = \triangle CTD$. Further, we draw the straight line KTL through T and parallel to AC. And now I say that $AB \cdot KB = AZ^2$ and $ZK \cdot AK = KB^2$ and, in addition, each of the two lines AZ and $KB > AK$.

Proof:

(1) $CD \cdot TL = AZ \cdot AE$ [given] Hence

(2) $\dfrac{CD(=AB)}{AZ} = \dfrac{AE}{TL}$

Since $\triangle ZAE \sim \triangle ZKT \sim \triangle TLD$, hence

(3) $\dfrac{AE}{TL} = \dfrac{AZ}{LD(=KB)}, \dfrac{AB}{AZ} = \dfrac{AZ}{KB}$, and

$\dfrac{TL(=AK)}{KT(=KB)} = \dfrac{LD(=KB)}{ZK}$. Therefore

(4) $AB \cdot KB = AZ^2$ and
$ZK \cdot AK = KB^2$

and each of the lines AZ and $KB > AK$. Q.E.D.

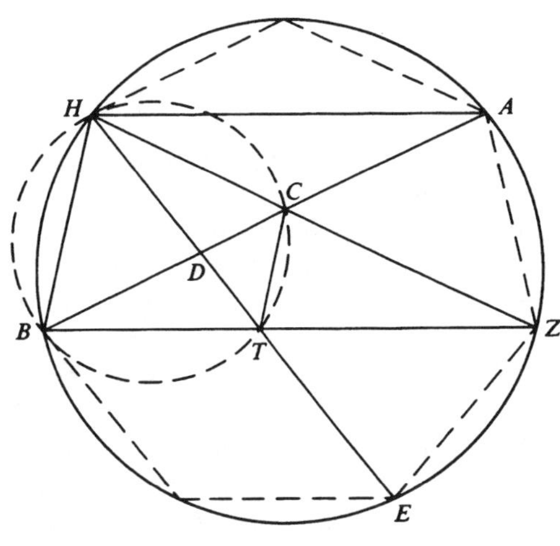

FIGURE 9

Proposition 17

We now wish to divide the circle into seven equal parts (Fig. 9). We draw the line segment AB, which we set out as known. We mark on it two points C and D, such that $AD \cdot CD = DB^2$ and $CB \cdot BD = AC^2$ and in addition each of the two segments AC and $DB > CD$, following the preceding proposition [i.e., Prop. 16]. Out of lines AC, CD and BD we construct $\triangle CHD$. Accordingly $CH = AC$, $DH = DB$ and $CD = CD$. Then we circumscribe about $\triangle AHB$ the circle $AHBEZ$ and we extend lines HC and HD directly up to the circumference of the circle. On their intersection with the circumference lie the points Z and E. We join B with Z. Lines BZ and HE intersect in T. We also draw CT. Since $AC = CH$, hence $\angle HAC = \angle AHC$, and arc $AZ =$ arc HB. And, indeed, $AD \cdot CD = DB^2 = DH^2$ and [by Euclid, VI.8] $\triangle AHD \sim \triangle CHD$; consequently $\angle DAH = \angle CHD$, or arc $ZE =$ arc BH. Hence BH, AZ and ZE are three equal arcs. Further, ZB is parallel to AH, $\angle CAH = \angle CHD = \angle TBD$; $HD = DB$, $CD = DT$, $CH = BT$. Hence, [since the products of the parts of these diagonals are equal], the 4 points B, H, C and T lie in the circumference of one and the same circle. From the similarity of triangles HBC and HBT, it follows that $CB \cdot DB = HC^2 = AC^2$ [or $HT/HC = HC/HD$] and from the similarity of $\triangle THC$ and $\triangle CHD$, it follows that $TH \cdot HD = HC^2$. And further $CB = TH$ [these being equal diagonals in the quadrilateral] and $\angle DCH = \angle HTC = 2\angle CAH$. [The equality of the first two angles arises from the similarity of triangles THC and CHD. Their equality with $2\angle CAH$ arises as follows: (1) $AHD = 2\angle CAH$, for $\angle CAH = \angle CHD = \angle CHA$ and $\angle AHD = \angle CHA + \angle CHD$; (2) $\angle AHD = \angle BTH$, for parallel lines cut by a third line produce equal alternate angles; (3) $\angle BTH = \angle DCH$, from similar triangles; (4) hence $\angle DCH = 2\angle CAH$.] [And since $\angle HBA = \angle DCH$, hence $\angle HBA = 2\angle CAH$.] Consequently, arc $AH = 2$ arc BH. Since $\angle DHB = \angle DBH$, consequently arc $EB = 2$ arc HB. Hence, each of arcs AH and EB equals 2 arc HB, and accordingly the circle $AHBEZ$ is divided into seven equal parts. Q.E.D. And praise be to the one God, etc.

The key to the whole procedure is, of course, the *neusis* presented in Proposition 16 (see Fig. 8) that would allow us in a similar fashion to find the points C and D in Proposition 17 (see Fig. 9). In Proposition 16 the *neusis* consisted in drawing a line from D to intersect the extension of AB in point Z such that $\triangle AZE = \triangle CTD$. The way in which the *neusis* was solved by Archimedes (or whoever was the author of this tract) is not known. Ibn al-Haytham, in his later treatment of the heptagon, mentions the Archimedean *neusis* but then goes on to show that one does not need the Archimedean square of Proposition 16. Rather he shows that points C and D in Proposition 17 can be found by the intersection of a parabola and a hyperbola.[11] It should be observed that all but two of Propositions 1–13 in this tract concern right triangles, and those two are necessary for propositions concerning right triangles. It seems probable, therefore, that Propositions 1–13 comprise the so-called *On the Properties of the Right Triangle* attributed in the *Fihrist* to Archimedes (although at least some of these propositions are Arabic interpolations). Incidentally, Propositions 7–10 have as their objective the formulation $K = (s - a) \cdot (s - c)$, where K is the area and a and c are the sides including the right angle and s is the semiperimeter, and Proposition 13 has as its objective $K = s(s - b)$, where b is the hypotenuse. Hence, if we multiply the two formulations, we have

$$K^2 = s(s - a) \cdot (s - b) \cdot (s - c)$$

or

$$K = \sqrt{s(s - a) \cdot (s - b) \cdot (s - c)},$$

Hero's formula for the area of a triangle in terms of its sides—at least in the case of a right triangle. Interestingly, the Arab scholar al-Bīrūnī attributed the general Heronian formula to Archimedes. Propositions 14 and 15 of the tract make no reference to Propositions 1–13 and concern chords. Each leads to a formulation in terms of chords equivalent to $\sin A/2 = \sqrt{(1 - \cos A)/2}$. Thus Propositions 14–15 seem to be from some other work (and at least Proposition 15 is an Arabic interpolation). If Proposition 14 was in the Greek text translated by Thābit ibn Qurra and does go back to Archimedes, then we would have to conclude that this formula was his discovery rather than Ptolemy's, as it is usually assumed to be.

The Latin West received its knowledge of Archimedes from both the sources just described: Byzantium and Islam. There is no trace of the earlier translations imputed by Cassiodorus to Boethius. Such knowledge that was had in the West before the twelfth century consisted of some rather general hydrostatic information that may have indirectly had its source in Archimedes. It was in the twelfth century that the translation of Archimedean texts from the Arabic first began. The small tract *On the Measurement of the Circle* was twice translated from the Arabic. The first translation was a rather defective one and was possibly executed by Plato of Tivoli. There are many numerical errors in the extant copies of it and the second half of Proposition 3 is missing. The second translation was almost certainly done by the twelfth century's foremost translator, Gerard of Cremona. The Arabic text from which he worked (without doubt the text of Thābit ibn Qurra) included a corollary on the area of a sector of a circle attributed by Hero to Archimedes but missing from our extant Greek text.

Not only was Gerard's translation widely quoted by medieval geometers such as Gerard of Brussels, Roger Bacon, and Thomas Bradwardine, it also served as the point of departure for a whole series of emended versions and paraphrases of the tract in the course of the thirteenth and fourteenth centuries. Among these are the so-called Naples, Cambridge, Florence, and Gordanus versions of the thirteenth century; and the Corpus Christi, Munich, and Albert of Saxony versions of the fourteenth. These versions were expanded by including pertinent references to Euclid and the spelling-out of the geometrical steps only implied in the Archimedean text. In addition, we see attempts to specify the postulates that underlie the proof of Proposition I. For example, in the Cambridge version three postulates (*petitiones*) introduce the text:[12] "[1] There is some curved line equal to any straight line and some straight line to any curved line. [2] Any chord is less than its arc. [3] The perimeter of any including figure is greater than the perimeter of the included figure." Furthermore, self-conscious attention was given in some versions to the logical nature of the proof of Proposition I. Thus, the Naples version immediately announced that the proof was to be *per impossibile,* i.e., by reduction to absurdity. In the Gordanus, Corpus Christi, and Munich versions we see a tendency to elaborate the proofs in the manner of scholastic tracts. The culmination of this kind of elaboration appeared in the *Questio de quadratura circuli* of Albert of Saxony, composed some time in the third quarter of the fourteenth century. The Hellenistic mathematical form of the original text was submerged in an intricate scholastic structure that included multiple terminological distinctions and the argument and counterargument technique represented by initial arguments ("principal reasons") and their final refutations.

Another trend in the later versions was the introduction of rather foolish physical justifications for postulates. In the Corpus Christi version, the second postulate to the effect that a straight line may be equal to a curved line is supported by the statement that "if a hair or silk thread is bent around circumference-wise in a plane surface and then afterwards is extended in a straight line, who will doubt—unless he is hare-brained—that the hair or thread is the same whether it is bent circumference-wise or extended in a straight line and is just as long the one time as the other." Similarly, Albert of Saxony, in his *Questio,* declared that a sphere can be "cubed" since the contents of a spherical vase can be poured into a cubical vase. Incidentally, Albert based his proof of the quadrature of the circle not directly on Proposition X.1 of the *Elements,* as was the case in the other medieval versions of *On the Measurement of the Circle,* but rather on a "betweenness" postulate: "I suppose that with two continuous [and comparable] quantities proposed, a magnitude greater than the 'lesser' can be cut from the 'greater.'" A similar postulate was employed in still another fourteenth-century version of the *De mensura circuli* called the Pseudo-Bradwardine version. Finally, in regard to the manifold medieval versions of *On the Measurement of the Circle,* it can be noted that the Florence version of Proposition 3 contained a detailed elaboration of the calculation of π. One might have supposed that the author had consulted Eutocius' commentary, except that his arithmetical procedures differed widely from those used by Eutocius. Furthermore, no translation of Eutocius' commentary appears to have been made before 1450, and the Florence version certainly must be dated before 1400.

In addition to his translation of *On the Measurement of the Circle,* Gerard of Cremona also translated the geometrical *Discourse of the Sons of Moses* (*Verba filiorum*) composed by the Banū Mūsā. This Latin translation was of particular importance for the introduction of Archimedes into the West. We can single out these contributions of the treatise: (1) A proof of Proposition I of *On the Measurement of the Circle* somewhat different from that of Archimedes but still fundamentally based on the exhaustion method. (2) A determination of the value of π drawn from Proposition 3 of the same treatise but with further calculations similar to those found in the commentary of Eutocius. (3) Hero's theorem for the area of a triangle in terms of its sides (noted above), with the first demonstration of that theorem in Latin (the enunciation of this theorem had already appeared in the writings of the *agrimensores* and in Plato of Tivoli's translation of the *Liber embadorum* of Savasorda). (4) Theorems for the volume and surface area of a cone, again with demonstrations. (5) Theorems for the volume and surface area of a sphere with demonstrations of an Archimedean character. (6) A use of the formula for the area of a circle equivalent to $A = \pi r^2$ in addition to the more common Archimedean form, $A = 1/2\,cr$. Instead of the modern symbol π the authors used the expression "the quantity which when multiplied by the diameter produces the circumference." (7) The introduction into the West of the problem of finding two mean proportionals between two given lines. In this treatise we find two solutions: (*a*) one attributed by the Banū Mūsā to Menelaus and by Eutocius to Archytas, (*b*) the other presented by the Banū Mūsā as their own but similar to the solution attributed by Eutocius to Plato. (8) The first solution in Latin of the problem of the trisection of an angle. (9) A method of approximating cube roots to any desired limit.

The *Verba filiorum* was, then, rich fare for the geometers of the twelfth century. The tract was quite widely cited in the thirteenth and fourteenth centuries. In the thirteenth, the eminent mathematicians Jordanus de Nemore and Leonardo Fibonacci made use of it. For example, the latter, in his *Practica geometrie,* excerpted both of the solutions of the mean proportionals problem given by the Banū Mūsā, while the former (or perhaps a continuator) in his *De triangulis* presented one of them together with an entirely different solution, namely, that one assigned by Eutocius to Philo of Byzantium. Similarly, Jordanus (or possibly the same continuator) extracted the solution of the trisection of an angle from the *Verba filiorum,* but in addition made the remarkably perspicacious suggestion that the *neusis* can be solved by the use of a proposition from Ibn al-Haytham's *Optics,* which solves a similar *neusis* by conic sections.

Some of the results and techniques of *On the Sphere and the Cylinder* also became known through a treatise entitled *De curvis superficiebus Archimenidis* and said to be by Johannes de Tinemue. This seems to have been translated from the Greek in the early thirteenth century or at least composed on the basis of a Greek tract. The *De curvis superficiebus* contained ten propositions with several corollaries and was concerned for the most part with the surfaces and volumes of cones, cylinders, and spheres. This was a very popular work and was often cited by later authors. Like Gerard of Cremona's translation of *On the Measurement of the Circle,* the *De curvis superficiebus* was emended by Latin authors, two original propositions being added to one version (represented by manuscript D of the *De curvis superficiebus*)[13] and three quite different propositions being added to another (represented by manuscript M of the *De curvis*).[14] In the first of the additions to the latter version, the Latin author applied the exhaustion method to a problem involving the surface of a segment of a sphere, showing that at least this author had made the method his own. And indeed the geometer Gerard of Brussels in his *De motu* of about the same time also used the Archimedean *reductio* procedure in a highly original manner.

In 1269, some decades after the appearance of the *De curvis superficiebus,* the next important step was taken in the passage of Archimedes to the West when much of the Byzantine corpus was translated from the Greek by the Flemish Dominican, William of Moerbeke. In this translation Moerbeke employed Greek manuscripts A and B which had passed to the pope's library in 1266 from the collection of the Norman kings of the Two Sicilies. Except for *The Sandreckoner* and Eutocius' *Commentary on the Measurement of the Circle,* all the works included in manuscripts A and B were rendered into Latin by William. Needless to say, *On the Method, The Cattle Problem,* and the *Stomachion,* all absent from manuscripts A and B, were not among William's translations. Although William's translations are not without error (and indeed some of the errors are serious), the translations, on the whole, present the Archimedean works in an understandable way. We possess the original holograph of Moerbeke's translations (MS Vat. Ottob. lat. 1850). This manuscript was not widely copied. The translation of *On Spirals* was copied from it in the fourteenth century (MS Vat. Reg. lat. 1253, 14r–33r), and several works were copied from it in the fifteenth century in an Italian manuscript now at Madrid (Bibl. Nac. 9119), and one work (*On Floating Bodies*) was copied from it in the sixteenth century (MS Vat. Barb. lat. 304, 124r–141v, 160v–161v). But, in fact, the Moerbeke translations were utilized more than one would expect from the paucity of manuscripts. They were used by several Schoolmen at the University of Paris toward the middle of the fourteenth century. Chief among them was the astronomer and mathematician John of Meurs, who appears to have been the compositor of a hybrid tract in 1340 entitled *Circuli quadratura.* This tract consisted of fourteen propositions. The first thirteen were drawn from Moerbeke's translation of *On Spirals* and were just those propositions necessary to the proof of Proposition 18 of *On Spirals,* whose enunciation we have quoted above. The fourteenth proposition of the hybrid tract was Proposition 1 from Moerbeke's translation of *On the Measurement of the Circle.* Thus this author realized that by the use of Proposition 18 from *On Spirals,* he had achieved the necessary rectification of the circumference of a circle preparatory to the final quadrature of the circle accomplished in *On the Measurement of the Circle,* Proposition 1. Incidentally, the hybrid tract did not merely use the Moerbeke translations verbatim but also included considerable commentary. In fact, this medieval Latin tract was the first known commentary on Archimedes' *On Spirals.* That the commentary was at times quite perceptive is indicated by the fact that the author suggested that the *neusis* introduced by Archimedes in Proposition 7 of *On Spirals* could be solved by means of an *instrumentum conchoydeale.* The only place in which a medieval Latin commentator could have learned of such an instrument would have been in that section of the *Commentary on the Sphere and the Cylinder* where Eutocius describes Nicomedes' solution of the problem of finding two mean proportionals (Bk. II, Prop. 1). We have further evidence that John of Meurs knew of Eutocius' *Commentary* in the Moerbeke translation when he used sections from this commentary in his *De arte mensurandi* (Ch. VIII, Prop. 16), where three of the solutions of the mean proportionals problem given by Eutocius are presented. Not only did John incorporate the whole hybrid tract *Circuli quadratura* into Chapter VIII of his *De arte mensurandi* (composed, it seems, shortly after 1343) but in Chapter X of the *De arte* he quoted verbatim many propositions from Moerbeke's translations of *On the Sphere and the Cylinder* and *On Conoids and Spheroids* (which latter he misapplied to problems concerning solids generated by the rotation of circular segments). Within the next decade or so after John of Meurs, Nicole Oresme, his colleague at the University of Paris, in his *De configurationibus qualitatum et motuum* (Part I, Ch. 21) revealed knowledge of *On Spirals,* at least in the form of the hybrid *Circuli quadratura.* Further, Oresme in his *Questiones super de celo et mundo,* quoted at length from Moerbeke's translation of *On Floating Bodies,* while Henry of Hesse, Oresme's junior contemporary at Paris, quoted briefly therefrom. (Before this time, the only knowledge of *On Floating Bodies* had come in a thirteenth-century treatise entitled *De ponderibus Archimenidis sive de incidentibus in humidum,* a Pseudo-Archimedean treatise prepared largely from Arabic sources, whose first proposition expressed the basic conclusion of the "principle of Archimedes": "The weight of any body in air exceeds its weight in water by the weight of a volume of water equal to its volume.") Incontrovertible evidence, then, shows that at the University of Paris in the mid-fourteenth century six of the nine Archimedean translations of William of Moerbeke were known and used: *On Spirals, On the Meas-*

urement of the Circle, On the Sphere and the Cylinder, On Conoids and Spheroids, On Floating Bodies, and Eutocius' *Commentary on the Sphere and the Cylinder.* While no direct evidence exists of the use of the remaining three translations, there has been recently discovered in a manuscript written at Paris in the fourteenth century (BN lat. 7377B, 93v–94r) an Archimedean-type proof of the law of the lever that might have been inspired by Archimedes' *On the Equilibrium of Planes.* But other than this, the influence of Archimedes on medieval statics was entirely indirect. The anonymous *De canonio,* translated from the Greek in the early thirteenth century, and Thābit ibn Qurra's *Liber karastonis,* translated from the Arabic by Gerard of Cremona, passed on this indirect influence of Archimedes in three respects: (1) Both tracts illustrated the Archimedean type of geometrical demonstrations of statical theorems and the geometrical form implied in weightless beams and weights that were really only geometrical magnitudes. (2) They gave specific reference in geometrical language to the law of the lever (and in the *De canonio* the law of the lever is connected directly to Archimedes). (3) They indirectly reflected the centers-of-gravity doctrine so important to Archimedes, in that both treatises employed the practice of substituting for a material beam segment a weight equal in weight to the material segment but hung from the middle point of the weightless segment used to replace the material segment. Needless to say, these two tracts played an important role in stimulating the rather impressive statics associated with the name of Jordanus de Nemore.

In the fifteenth century, knowledge of Archimedes in Europe began to expand. A new Latin translation was made by James of Cremona in about 1450 by order of Pope Nicholas V. Since this translation was made exclusively from manuscript A, the translation failed to include *On Floating Bodies,* but it did include the two treatises in A omitted by Moerbeke, namely, *The Sandreckoner* and Eutocius' *Commentary on the Measurement of the Circle.* It appears that this new translation was made with an eye on Moerbeke's translations. Not long after its completion, a copy of the new translation was sent by the pope to Nicholas of Cusa, who made some use of it in his *De mathematicis complementis,* composed in 1453–1454. There are at least nine extant manuscripts of this translation, one of which was corrected by Regiomontanus and brought to Germany about 1468 (the Latin translation published with the *editio princeps* of the Greek text in 1544 was taken from this copy). Greek manuscript A itself was copied a number of times. Cardinal Bessarion had one copy prepared between 1449 and 1468 (MS E). Another (MS D) was made from A when it was in the possession of the well-known humanist George Valla. The fate of A and its various copies has been traced skillfully by J. L. Heiberg in his edition of Archimedes' *Opera.* The last known use of manuscript A occurred in 1544, after which time it seems to have disappeared. The first printed Archimedean materials were in fact merely Latin excerpts that appeared in George Valla's *De expetendis et fugiendis rebus opus* (Venice, 1501) and were based on his reading of manuscript A. But the earliest actual printed texts of Archimedes were the Moerbeke translations of *On the Measurement of the Circle* and *On the Quadrature of the Parabola* (*Tetragonismus, id est circuli quadratura etc.*), published from the Madrid manuscript by L. Gaurico (Venice, 1503). In 1543, also at Venice, N. Tartaglia republished the same two translations directly from Gaurico's work, and, in addition, from the same Madrid manuscript, the Moerbeke translations of *On the Equilibrium of Planes* and Book I of *On Floating Bodies* (leaving the erroneous impression that he had made these translations from a Greek manuscript, which he had not since he merely repeated the texts of the Madrid manuscript with virtually all their errors). Incidentally, Curtius Trioianus published from the legacy of Tartaglia both books of *On Floating Bodies* in Moerbeke's translation (Venice, 1565). The key event, however, in the further spread of Archimedes was the aforementioned *editio princeps* of the Greek text with the accompanying Latin translation of James of Cremona at Basel in 1544. Since the Greek text rested ultimately on manuscript A, *On Floating Bodies* was not included. A further Latin translation of the Archimedean texts was published by the perceptive mathematician Federigo Commandino in Bologna in 1558, which the translator supplemented with a skillful mathematical emendation of Moerbeke's translation of *On Floating Bodies* (Bologna, 1565) but without any knowledge of the long lost Greek text. Already in the period 1534–1549, a paraphrase of Archimedean texts had been made by Francesco Maurolico. This was published in Palermo in 1685. One other Latin translation of the sixteenth century by Antonius de Albertis remains in manuscript only and appears to have exerted no influence on mathematics and science. After 1544 the publications on Archimedes and the use of his works began to multiply markedly. His works presented quadrature problems and propositions that mathematicians sought to solve and demonstrate not only with his methods, but also with a developing geometry of infinitesimals that was to anticipate in some respect the infinitesimal calculus of Newton and Leibniz. His hydrostatic conceptions were used to modify Aristotelian mechanics. Archimedes' influence on mechanics and mathematics can be seen in the works of such authors as Commandino, Guido Ubaldi del Monte, Benedetti, Simon Stevin, Luca Valerio, Kepler, Galileo, Cavalieri, Torricelli, and numerous others. For example, Galileo mentions Archimedes more than a hundred times, and the limited inertial doctrine used in his analysis of the parabolic path of a projectile is presented as an Archimedean-type abstraction. Archimedes began to appear in the vernacular languages. Tartaglia had already rendered into Italian Book I of *On Floating Bodies,* Book I of *On the Sphere and the Cylinder,* and the section on proportional means from Eutocius' *Commentary on the Sphere and the Cylinder.* Book I of *On the Equilibrium of Planes* was translated into French in 1565 by Pierre Forcadel. It was, however, not until 1670 that a more or less complete translation was made into German by J. C. Sturm on the basis of the influential Greek and Latin edition of David Rivault (Paris, 1615). Also notable for its influence was the new Latin edition of Isaac Barrow (London, 1675). Of the many editions prior to the modern edition of Heiberg, the most important was that of Joseph Torelli (Oxford, 1792). By this time, of course, Archimedes' works had been almost completely absorbed into European mathematics and had exerted their substantial and enduring influence on early modern science.

NOTES

1. Heath, *The Works of Archimedes,* pp. 91-93. Heath's close paraphrase has been used here and below because of its economy of expression. While he uses modern symbols and has reduced the general enunciations to statements concerning specific figures in some of the propositions quoted below, he nevertheless achieves a faithful representation of the spirit of the original text.
2. *Ibid.,* pp. 19-20.
3. *Ibid.,* pp. 251-252.
4. *Ibid.,* pp. 156-57.
5. *Ibid.,* pp. 1-2.
6. *Ibid.,* Suppl., pp. 18-22.
7. *Ibid.,* pp. 13-14.
8. Dijksterhuis, *Archimedes,* p. 373.
9. Clagett, *Archimedes in the Middle Ages,* pp. 667-668.
10. Schoy, *Die trigonometrischen Lehren,* pp. 82-83.
11. *Ibid.,* pp. 85-91.
12. Clagett, *op. cit.,* p. 27. The succeeding quotations from the various versions of *On the Measurement of the Circle* are also from this volume.
13. *Ibid.,* p. 520.
14. *Ibid.,* p. 530.

BIBLIOGRAPHY

I. Original Works.

1. *The Greek Text and Modern Translations.* J. L. Heiberg, ed., *Archimedis opera omnia cum commentariis Eutocii,* 2nd ed., 3 vols. (Leipzig, 1910-1915). For the full titles of the various editions cited in the body of the article as well as others, see E. J. Dijksterhuis, *Archimedes* (Copenhagen, 1956), pp. 40-45, 417. Of recent translations and paraphrases, the following, in addition to Dijksterhuis' brilliant analytic summary, ought to be noted: T. L. Heath, *The Works of Archimedes,* edited in modern notation, with introductory chapters (Cambridge, 1897), which together with his *Supplement, The Method of Archimedes* (Cambridge, 1912) was reprinted by Dover Publications (New York, 1953); P. Ver Eecke, *Les Oeuvres complètes d'Archimède, suivies des commentaires d'Eutocius d'Ascalon,* 2nd ed., 2 vols. (Paris, 1960); I. N. Veselovsky, *Archimedes. Selections, Translations, Introduction, and Commentary* (in Russian), translation of the Arabic texts by B. A. Rosenfeld (Moscow, 1962). We can also mention briefly the German translations of A. Czwalina and the modern Greek translations of E. S. Stamates.

2. *The Arabic Archimedes* (the manuscripts cited are largely from Suter, "Die Mathematiker und Astronomen" [see Secondary Literature], and C. Brockelmann, *Geschichte der arabischen Literatur,* 5 vols., Vols. I-II [adapted to Suppl. vols., Leiden, 1943-1949], Suppl. Vols. I-III [Leiden, 1937-1942]). *On the Sphere and the Cylinder* and *On the Measurement of the Circle;* both appear in Nāṣir al-Dīn al-Ṭūsī, *Majmū' al-Rasā'il,* Vol. II (Hyderabad, 1940). Cf. MSS Berlin 5934; Florence Palat. 271 and 286; Paris 2467; Oxford, Bodl. Arabic 875, 879; India Office 743; and M. Clagett, *Archimedes in the Middle Ages,* I, 17, n. 8. The al-Ṭūsī edition also contains some commentary on Bk. II of *On the Sphere and the Cylinder. Book of the Elements of Geometry* (probably the same as *On Triangles,* mentioned in the *Fihrist*) and *On Touching Circles;* both appear in *Rasā'il Ibn Qurra* (Hyderabad, 1947, given as 1948 on transliterated title page). *On the Division of the Circle into Seven Equal Parts* (only Props. 16-17 concern heptagon construction; Props. 1-13 appear to be the tract called *On the Properties of the Right Triangle;* Props. 14-15 are unrelated to either of other parts). MS Cairo A.-N.8 H.-N. 7805, item no. 15. German translation by C. Schoy, *Die trigonometrischen Lehren des persischen Astronomen Abu 'l-Raihân Muh. ibn Ahmad al-Bîrûnî* (Hannover, 1927), pp. 74-84. The text has been analyzed in modern fashion by J. Tropfke, "Die Siebeneckabhandlung des Archimedes," in *Osiris,* **1** (1936), 636-651. *On Heaviness and Lightness* (a fragment of *On Floating Bodies*); Arabic text by H. Zotenberg in *Journal asiatique;* Ser. 7, **13** (1879), 509-515, from MS Paris, BN Fonds suppl. arabe 952 bis. A German translation was made by E. Wiedemann in the *Sitzungsberichte der Physikalisch-medizinischen Sozietät in Erlangen,* **38** (1906), 152-162. For an English translation and critique, see M. Clagett, *The Science of Mechanics in the Middle Ages* (Madison, Wis., 1959, 2nd pr., 1961), pp. 52-55. *Lemmata* (*Liber assumptorum*), see the edition in al-Ṭūsī, *Majmū' al-Rasā'il,* Vol. II (Hyderabad, 1940). MSS Oxford, Bodl. Arabic 879, 895, 939, 960; Leiden 982; Florence, Palat. 271 and 286; Cairo A.-N. 8 H.-N 7805. This work was first edited by S. Foster, *Miscellanea* (London, 1659), from a Latin translation of I. Gravius; Abra-

ham Ecchellensis then retranslated it, the new translation being published in I. A. Borelli's edition of *Apollonii Pergaei Concicorum libri V, VI, VII* (Florence, 1661). Ecchellensis' translation was republished by Heiberg, *Opera,* II, 510–525. See also E. S. Stamates' effort to reconstruct the original Greek text in *Bulletin de la Societé Mathématique de Grèce,* new series, **6 II,** Fasc. 2 (1965), 265–297. *Stomachion,* a fragmentary part in Arabic with German translation in H. Suter, "Der Loculus Archimedius oder das Syntemachion des Archimedes," in *Abhandlungen zur Geschichte der Mathematik,* **9** (1899), 491–499. This is one of two fragments. The other is in Greek and is given by Heiberg, *Opera,* II, 416. Eutocius, *Commentary on the Sphere and the Cylinder,* a section of Bk. II. MSS Paris, BN arabe 2457, 44°; Bibl. Escor. 960; Istanbul, Fatīh Mosque Library Ar. 3414, 60v–66v; Oxford, Bodl. Arabic 875 and 895. Various tracts and commentaries *On the Sphere and the Cylinder,* Bk. II, in part paraphrased and translated by F. Woepcke, *L'Algebra d'Omar Alkhayâmmî* (Paris, 1851), pp. 91–116.

3. *The Medieval Latin Archimedes.* A complete edition and translation of the various Archimedean tracts arising from the Arabic tradition have been given by M. Clagett, *Archimedes in the Middle Ages,* Vol. I (Madison, Wis., 1964). Vol. II will contain the complete text of Moerbeke's translations and other Archimedean materials from the late Middle Ages. Moerbeke's translation of *On Spirals* and brief parts of other of his translations have been published by Heiberg, "Neue Studien" (see below). See also M. Clagett, "A Medieval Archimedean-Type Proof of the Law of the Lever," in *Miscellanea André Combes,* II (Rome, 1967), 409–421. For the Pseudo-Archimedes, *De ponderibus* (*De incidentibus in humidum*), see E. A. Moody and M. Clagett, *The Medieval Science of Weights* (Madison, 1952; 2nd printing, 1960), pp. 35–53, 352–359.

II. Secondary Literature. The best over-all analysis is in E. J. Dijksterhuis, *Archimedes* (Copenhagen, 1956), which also refers to the principal literature. The translations of Heath and Ver Eecke given above contain valuable evaluative and biographical materials. In addition, consult C. Boyer, *The Concepts of the Calculus* (New York, 1939; 2nd printing, 1949; Dover ed. 1959), particularly ch. 4 for the reaction of the mathematicians of the sixteenth and seventeenth centuries to Archimedes. M. Clagett, "Archimedes and Scholastic Geometry," in *Mélanges Alexandre Koyré,* Vol. I: *L'Aventure de la science* (Paris, 1964), 40–60; "The Use of the Moerbeke Translations of Archimedes in the Works of Johannes de Muris," in *Isis,* **43** (1952), 236–242 (the conclusions of this article will be significantly updated in M. Clagett, *Archimedes in the Middle Ages,* Vol. II); and "Johannes de Muris and the Problem of the Mean Proportionals," in *Medicine, Science and Culture, Historical Essays in Honor of Owsei Temkin,* L. G. Stevenson and R. P. Multhauf, eds. (Baltimore, 1968), 35–49. A. G. Drachmann, "Fragments from Archimedes in Heron's Mechanics," in *Centaurus,* **8** (1963), 91–145; "The Screw of Archimedes," in *Actes du VIIIe Congrés international d'Histoire des Sciences Florence-Milan 1956,* **3** (Vinci-Paris, 1958), 940–943; and "How Archimedes Expected to Move the Earth," in *Centaurus,* **5** (1958), 278–282. J. L. Heiberg, "Neue Studien zu Archimedes," in *Abhandlungen zur Geschichte der Mathematik,* **5** (1890), 1–84; and *Quaestiones Archimedeae* (Copenhagen, 1879). Most of the biographical references are given here by Heiberg. S. Heller, "Ein Fehler in einer Archimedes-Ausgabe, seine Entstehung und seine Folgen," in *Abhandlungen der Bayerischen Akademie der Wissenschaften. Mathematisch-naturwissenschaftliche Klasse,* new series, **63** (1954), 1–38. E. Rufini, *Il "Metodo" di Archimede e le origini dell'analisi infinitesimale nell'antichita* (Rome, 1926; new ed., Bologna, 1961). H. Suter, "Die Mathematiker und Astronomen der Araber und ihre Werke," in *Abhandlungen zur Geschichte der mathematischen Wissenschaften,* **10** (1892), *in toto;* "Das Mathematiker- Verzeichniss im Fihrist des Ibn Abī Ja'kûb an-Nadîm," *ibid.,* **6** (1892), 1–87. B. L. Van der Waerden, *Erwachende Wissenschaft,* 2nd German ed. (Basel, 1966), pp. 344–381. See also the English translation, *Science Awakening,* 2nd ed. (Groningen, 1961), pp. 204–206, 208–228. E. Wiedemann, "Beiträge zur Geschichte der Naturwissenschaften III," in *Sitzungsberichte der Physikalisch-medizinischen Sozietät in Erlangen,* **37** (1905), 247–250, 257. A. P. Youschkevitch, "Remarques sur la méthode antique d'exhaustion," in *Mélanges Alexandre Koyré,* I: *L'Aventure de la science* (1964), 635–653.

Marshall Clagett

ARCHYTAS OF TARENTUM (*fl.* Tarentum [now Taranto], Italy, *ca.* 375 B.C.)

After the Pythagoreans had been driven out of most of the cities of southern Italy by the Syracusan tyrant Dionysius the Elder at the beginning of the fourth century B.C., Tarentum remained their only important political center. Here Archytas played a leading role in the attempt to unite the Greek city-states against the non-Greek tribes and powers. After the death of Dionysius the Elder, he concluded, through the agency of Plato, an alliance with his son and successor, Dionysius the Younger.

Archytas made very important contributions to the theory of numbers, geometry, and the theory of music. Although extant ancient tradition credits him mainly with individual discoveries, it is clear that all of them were connected and that Archytas was deeply concerned with the foundations of the sciences and with their interconnection. Thus he affirmed that the art of calculation (λογιστική) is the most fundamental science and makes its results even clearer than those of geometry. He also discussed mathematics as the foundation of astronomy.

A central point in Archytas' manifold endeavors was the theory of means (μεσότητες) and proportions. He distinguished three basic means: the arithmetic mean of the form $a - b = b - c$ or $a + c = 2b$; the

ARCHYTAS OF TARENTUM

geometric mean of the form $a:b = b:c$ or $ac = b^2$; and the harmonic mean of the form $(a - b):(b - c) = a:c$. Archytas and later mathematicians subsequently added seven other means.

A proposition and proof that are important both for Archytas' theory of means and for his theory of music have been preserved in Latin translation in Boethius' *De musica.* The proposition states that there is no geometric mean between two numbers that are in "superparticular" (ἐπιμόριος) ratio, i.e., in the ratio $(n + 1):n$. The proof given by Boethius is essentially identical with that given for the same proposition by Euclid in his *Sectio canonis* (Prop. 3). It presupposes several propositions of Euclid that appear in *Elements* VII as well as VIII, Prop. 8. Through a careful analysis of Books VII and VIII and their relation to the above proof, A. B. L. Van der Waerden has succeeded in making it appear very likely that many of the theorems in Euclid's *Elements* VII and their proofs existed before Archytas, but that a considerable part of the propositions and proofs of VIII were added by Archytas and his collaborators.

Archytas' most famous mathematical achievement was the solution of the "Delian" problem of the duplication of the cube. A generation before Archytas, Hippocrates of Chios had demonstrated that the problem can be reduced to the insertion of two mean proportionals between the side of the cube and its double length: If a is the side of the cube and $a:x = x:y = y:2a$, then x is the side of the doubled cube. The problem of the geometrical construction of this line segment was solved by Archytas through a most ingenious three-dimensional construction. In the figure below, everything, according to the custom of the ancients, is projected into a plane.

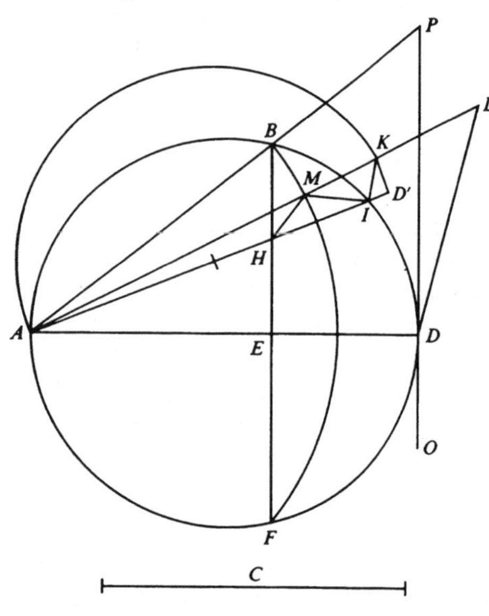

FIGURE 1

Let AD and C be the two line segments between which the two mean proportionals are to be constructed. Let a circle $ABDF$ be drawn with AD as diameter and $AB = C$ as a chord. Then let the extension of AB cut the line tangent to the circle at D at point P. Let BEF be drawn parallel to PDO. Next, imagine a semicylinder above the semicircle ABD (i.e., with ABD as its base) and above AD another semicircle located perpendicularly in the rectangle of the semicylinder (i.e., with AD as diameter in a plane perpendicular to plane $ABDF$). Let this semicircle be rotated around point A in the direction of B. Being rotated in this way, it will cut the surface of the semicylinder and will describe a curve.

If $\triangle APD$ is turned around the axis AD in the direction opposite to that of the semicircle, its side AP will describe the surface of a circular cone and in doing so will cut the aforementioned curve on the surface of the semicylinder at a point. At the same time, point B will describe a semicircle in the surface of the cone. Then, at the moment in which the aforementioned curves cut one another, let the position of the moving semicircle be determined by points AKD' and that of the moving triangle by points ALD, and let the point of intersection be called K. The semicircle described by B will then be BMF (namely, B at the moment of intersection of the curves being in M).Then drop a perpendicular from K to the plane of semicircle $ABDF$. It will fall on the circumference of the circle, since the cylinder is a right cylinder. Let it meet the circumference in I, and let the line drawn from I to A cut BF at H, and let line AL meet semicircle BMF in M (see above). Also let the connecting lines KD', MI, and MH be drawn.

Since each of the two semicircles AKD' and BMF is then perpendicular to the underlying plane ($ABDF$), their common intersection MH is also perpendicular to the plane of that circle, i.e., MH is perpendicular to BF. Hence the rectangle determined by BH, HF, and likewise that determined by AH, HI, is equal to the square on HM. Hence $\triangle AMI$ is similar to $\triangle HMI$ and AHM and $\angle AMI$ is a right angle. But $\angle D'KA$ is also a right angle. Hence $KD' \| MI$. Therefore $D'A:AK = KA:AI = AI:AM$ because of the similarity of the triangles. The four line segments $D'A$, AK, AI, and AM are therefore in continuous proportion. Thus, between the two given line segments AD and C (i.e., AB) two mean proportionals, AK and AI, have been found.

Tannery suspected and Van der Waerden, through an ingenious interpretation of *Epinomis* 990E, tried to show how the theory of means also served Archytas as a basis for his theory of music. Starting from the octave 1:2 or 6:12, one obtains the arithmetic mean 9 and the harmonic mean 8. The ratio 6:9 = 8:12 is 2:3 or, in musical terms, the fifth. The ratio 6:8 = 9:12 is 3:4 or, in musical terms, the fourth. Forming in like manner the arithmetic and harmonic means of the fifth, one obtains the ratios 4:5 and 5:6 or, in musical terms, the intervals of the major third and the minor third. Using the same procedure with the fourth, one obtains 6:7, or the diminished minor third, and 7:8, or an augmented whole tone. On these intervals Archytas built his three musical scales: the enharmonic, the chromatic, and the diatonic. The theory is also related to the theorem (mentioned above) that there is no geometric mean between two numbers in superparticular ratio. Since all the basic musical intervals are in that ratio, they can be subdivided by means of the arithmetic and the harmonic means but not by the geometric mean.

Archytas also elaborated a physical theory of sound, which he expounded in the longest extant fragment of his works. He starts with the observation that arithmetic, geometry, astronomy, and the theory of music are all related, but then proceeds to draw conclusions from empirical observations that are not subjected to mathematical analysis within the fragment. The fundamental observation is that faster motion appears to produce higher sounds. Thus, the bull-roarers used at certain religious festivals produce a higher sound when swung around swiftly than when swung more slowly. There are other easy experiments that confirm this observation. For instance, when the holes of a flute that are nearest the mouth of the flutist are opened, a higher sound is produced than when the farther holes are opened. Archytas reasoned that the air pressure in the first case ought to be higher, and therefore the air motion should be faster than in the second case. This is true of the frequencies of the air impulses produced, but Archytas appears to have concluded that the higher sounds reach the ear of the listener more quickly than the lower ones. Thus, he can hardly have applied his arithmetical theory of music consistently to his theory of the production of sound, or he would almost certainly have discovered his error.

Archytas is also credited with the invention of a wooden dove that could fly.

BIBLIOGRAPHY

The surviving fragments of Archytas' work are in H. Diels and W. Kranz, *Fragmente der Vorsokratiker,* 6th ed. (Berlin, 1951). The following are most relevant to this article: 47A16, on the musical scales; 47A19, on the superparticular ratio (also in a Latin translation in Boethius' *De musica,* III, 11); 47B1, on the mathematical foundations of astronomy; 47B2, on the three basic means; Pappus, *Synagogê,* VIII, 13 (F. Hultsch, ed., I, 85 ff.), on other means; and 47B4, on the art of calculation. A three-dimensional drawing for the doubling of the cube is in Diels and Kranz, 6th ed., I, 426.

Writings related to Archytas or his work are T. L. Heath, *A History of Greek Mathematics,* I (Oxford, 1921), 215; P. Tannery, *Mémoires scientifiques,* III (Paris, 1915), 105; M. Timpanaro Cardini, *Pitagorici. Testimonianze e frammenti,* II (Florence, 1962), 226–384; and A. B. L. Van der Waerden, "Die Harmonielehre der Pythagoreer," in *Hermes,* **78** (1943), 184 ff.; *Mathematische Annalen,* **130** (1948), 127 ff.; and *Science Awakening*.(Groningen, 1954), pp. 151, 153 f.

KURT VON FRITZ

ARGAND, JEAN ROBERT (*b.* Geneva, Switzerland, 18 July 1768; *d.* Paris, France, 13 August 1822)

Biographical data on Argand are limited. It is known that he was the son of Jacques Argand and Èves Canac; that he was baptized on 22 July (a date given by some for his birth); that he had a son who lived in Paris and a daughter, Jeanne-Françoise-Dorothée-Marie-Élizabeth, who married Félix Bousquet and lived in Stuttgart.

Argand, a Parisian bookkeeper, apparently never belonged to any group of mathematical amateurs or dilettantes. His training and background are so little known that he has often been confused with a man to whom he probably was not even related, Aimé Argand, a physicist and chemist who invented the Argand lamp.

It is remarkable that Argand's single original contribution to mathematics, the invention and elaboration of a geometric representation of complex numbers and the operations upon them, was so timed and of such importance as to assure him of a place in the history of mathematics even among those who credit C. F. Gauss with what others call the Argand diagram.

Other circumstances make Argand's story unusual. His system was actually anticipated by Caspar Wessel, a Norwegian, in 1797, but Wessel's work was without significant influence because it remained essentially unknown until 1897. Argand's own work might have suffered the same fate, for it was privately printed in 1806 in a small edition that did not even have the author's name on the title page. He received proper credit for it through a peculiar chain of events and the honesty and generosity of J. F. Français, a professor at the École Impériale d'Artillerie et du Génie, who published a similar discussion in 1813.

Argand had shown his work to A. M. Legendre before its publication, and Legendre mentioned it in a letter to Français's brother. Français saw the letter among his dead brother's papers, and was so intrigued by the ideas in it that he developed them further and published them in J. D. Gergonne's journal *Annales de mathématiques.* At the end of his article Français mentioned the source of his inspiration and expressed the hope that the unknown "first author of these ideas" would make himself known and publish the work he had done on this project.

Argand responded to this invitation by submitting an article that was published in the same volume of the *Annales.* In it he recapitulated his original work (with a change in notation) and gave some additional applications. A key to his ideas may be presented by a description and analysis of Figures 1 and 2. Figure 1 accompanies his initial discussion of a geometric representation of $\sqrt{-1}$. His motivation for this can be traced back to John Wallis' *Treatise of Algebra* (1685). In it Wallis suggested that since $\sqrt{-1}$ is the mean proportional between $+1$ and -1, its geometric representation could be a line constructed as the mean proportional between two oppositely directed unit segments.

Argand began his book, *Essai sur une manière de représenter les quantités imaginaires dans les constructions géométriques,* with a brief discussion of models for generating negative numbers by repeated subtraction; one used weights removed from a pan of a beam balance, the other subtracted francs from a sum of money. From these examples he concluded that distance may be considered apart from direction, and that whether a negative quantity is considered real or "imaginary" depends upon the kind of quantity measured. This initial use of the word "imaginary" for a negative number is related to the mathematical-philosophical debates of the time as to whether negative numbers were numbers, or even existed. In general, Argand used "imaginary" for multiples of $\sqrt{-1}$, a practice introduced by Descartes and common today. He also used the term "absolute" for distance considered apart from direction.

Argand then suggested that "setting aside the ratio of absolute magnitude we consider the different possible relations of direction" and discussed the proportions $+1:+1::-1:-1$ and $+1:-1::-1:+1$. He noted that in them the means have the same or opposite signs, depending upon whether the signs of the extremes are alike or opposite. This led him to consider $1:x::x:-1$. In this proportion he said that x cannot be made equal to any quantity, positive or negative; but as an analogy with his original models he suggested that quantities which were imaginary when applied to "certain magnitudes" became real when the idea of direction was added to the idea of absolute number. Thus, in Figure 1, if *KA* taken as positive unity with its direction from *K* to *A* is written $\overline{KA}$ to distinguish it from the segment *KA,* which is an absolute distance, then negative unity will be $\overline{KI}$. The classical construction for the geometric mean would determine $\overline{KE}$ and $\overline{KN}$ on the unit circle with center at *K*. Argand did not mention the geometric construction, but merely stated that the condition of the proportion will be met by perpendiculars $\overline{KE}$ and $\overline{KN}$, which represent $\sqrt{-1}$ and $-\sqrt{-1}$, respectively. Analogously, Argand inserted $\overline{KC}$ and $\overline{KL}$ as the mean proportionals between $\overline{KA}$ and $\overline{KE}$ by bisecting angle *AKE*.

Argand's opening paragraphs included the first use of the word "absolute" in the sense of the absolute value of a positive, negative, or complex number; of the bar over a pair of letters to indicate what is today called a vector; and of the idea that $\overline{AK} = -\overline{KA}$. Later in the *Essai* Argand used the term "modulus" (*module*) for the absolute value or the length of a vector representing a complex number. In this Argand anticipated A. L. Cauchy, who is commonly given credit for originating the term.

Argand's notation in his original essay is of particular interest because it anticipated the more abstract and modern ideas, later expounded by W. R. Hamilton, of complex numbers as arbitrarily constructed new entities defined as ordered pairs of real numbers. This modern aspect of Argand's original work has not been generally recognized. One reason for this, no doubt, is that in later letters and journal articles he returned to the more standard $a + b\sqrt{-1}$ notation. In his book, however, Argand suggested omitting $\sqrt{-1}$, deeming it no more a factor of $a\sqrt{-1}$ than is $+1$ in $+a$. He wrote $\sim a$ and $\dotplus a$ for $a\sqrt{-1}$ and $-a\sqrt{-1}$, respectively. He then observed that

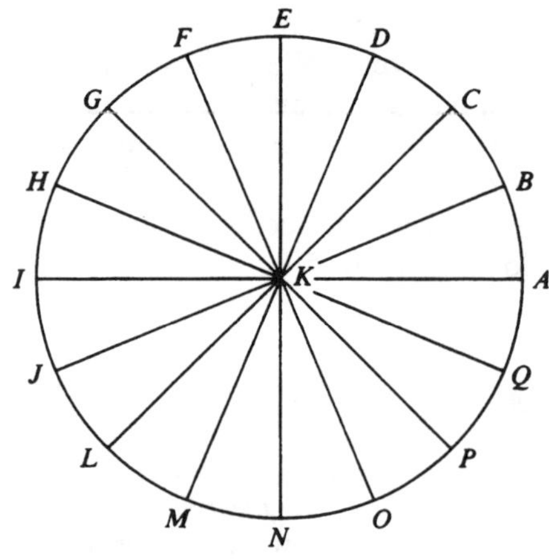

FIGURE 1

both $(\sim a)^2$ and $(\not{+}a)^2$ were negative. This led him to the rule that if in a series of factors every curved line has a value of 1 and every straight line a value of 2—thus $\sim = 1$, $- = 2$, $\not{+} = 3$, $+ = 4$—then the sign of the product of any series of factors can be determined by taking the residue modulo, 4, of the sum of the values of the symbols associated with the factors. Here he recognized the periodicity of the powers of the imaginary unit.

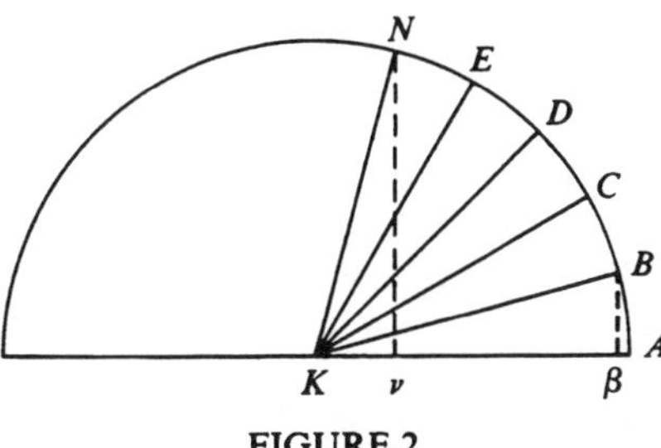

FIGURE 2

Argand generalized the insertion of geometric means between two given vectors to the insertion of any number of means, n, between the vectors $\overline{KA}$ and $\overline{KB}$ by dividing the angle between them by n. He noted that one could also find the means between $\overline{KA}$ and $\overline{KB}$ by beginning with the angles $AKB + 360°$, and $AKB + 720°$. This is a special case of de Moivre's theorem, as is more clearly and completely shown in Argand's explanation of Figure 2. In it $AB, BC, \cdots EN$ are n equal arcs. From the diagram Argand reasoned that $\overline{KN} = \overline{KB}^n$, $\overline{KN} = \overline{K\nu} + \overline{\nu N}$, and $\overline{KB} = \overline{K\beta} + \overline{\beta B}$; hence $\overline{K\nu} + \overline{\nu N} = (\overline{K\beta} + \overline{\beta B})^n$, which leads to $\cos na + \sqrt{-1} \sin na = (\cos a + \sqrt{-1} \sin a)^n$.

This result was well known before Argand, as were the uses he made of it to derive infinite series for trigonometric and logarithmic functions. As noted earlier, we know nothing of Argand's education or contacts with other mathematicians prior to 1813. It seems highly probable, however, that he had direct or indirect contact with some of the results of Wallis, de Moivre, and Leonhard Euler. Nevertheless, the purely geometric-intuitive interpretation and reasoning leading to these results seem to have been original with Argand. This geometric viewpoint has continued to be fruitful up to the present day. Argand recognized the nonrigorous nature of his reasoning, but he defined his goals as clarifying thinking about imaginaries by setting up a new view of them and providing a new tool for research in geometry. He used complex numbers to derive several trigonometric identities, to prove Ptolemy's theorem, and to give a proof of the fundamental theorem of algebra.

Argand's work contrasts with Wessel's in that the latter's approach was more modern in its explicit use of definitions in setting up a correspondence between $a + b\sqrt{-1}$ and vectors referred to a rectangular coordinate system (which neither Wessel nor Argand ever explicitly mentioned or drew). Wessel stressed the consistency of his assumptions and derived results without regard for their intuitive validity. He did not present as many mathematical consequences as Argand did.

Just as it seems clear that Argand's work was entirely independent of Wessel's, so it also seems clear that it was independent of the algebraic approach published by Suremain de Missery in 1801. Argand refuted the suggestion that he knew of Buée's work published in the *Philosophical Transactions of the Royal Society* in 1806 by noting that since academic journals appear after the dates which they bear, and that his book was printed in the same year the journal was dated, he could not have known of Buée's work at the time he wrote the book. Buée's ideas were not as clear, extensive, or well developed as Argand's.

There are obvious connections between Argand's geometric ideas and the later work of Moebius, Bellavitis, Hermann Grassmann, and others, but in most cases it is as difficult to establish direct outgrowths of his work as it is to establish that he consciously drew on Wallis, de Moivre, or Euler.

Two of the most important mathematicians of the early nineteenth century, Cauchy and Hamilton, took care to note the relationship of Argand's work to some of their own major contributions, but claimed to have learned of his work only after doing their own. Gauss probably could have made a similar statement, but he never did. Cauchy mentioned Argand twice in his "Mémoire sur les quantités géométriques," which appeared in *Exercices d'analyse et de physique mathématique* (1847). He cited Argand as the originator of the geometric interpretation of imaginary quantities, which he suggested would give clarity, a new precision, and a greater generality to algebra than earlier theories of imaginary quantities had. He also cited Argand and A. M. Legendre as authors of proofs of what Gauss termed the "fundamental theorem of algebra." Argand's proof involved considering the modulus of

$$P(x) = a_0x^n + a_1x^{n-1} + \cdots + a_{n-1}x^1 + a_n$$

when $x = a + bi$. He noted that if $|P(x)| = 0$ the theorem was true, and argued geometrically that if $|P(x)| > 0$ one could find $x' = a' + b'i$ such that $|P(x')| < |P(x)|$. Servois objected that this only showed that $P(x)$ was asymptotic to 0 for some sequence of x's. Argand replied that such behavior was associated with hyperbolas having zeros at infinity, not with polynomials. Cauchy asserted that a proof proposed by Legendre reduced to Argand's but left much to be desired, while his own method for approximating roots of $P(x) = 0$ could be used to demonstrate their existence. Gauss had published a proof of this existence in his thesis (1799). Although the geometric representation of complex numbers was implicit in this thesis, Gauss did not actually publish a discussion of it until 1832 in his famous paper "Theoria residuorum biquadraticorum." Argand, however, was the first mathematician to assert that the fundamental theorem also held if the coefficients of $P(x)$ were complex.

Hamilton used lengthy footnotes in the first edition of his *Lectures on Quaternions* (1853) to assert the priority and quality of Argand's work, especially with respect to the "multiplication of lines." He traced the roots of his own development of the algebra of couples and of quaternions, however, to John Warren's *A Treatise on the Geometrical Representation of the Square Roots of Negative Quantities* (1828). This, like C. V. Mourrey's *La vraie théorie des quantités negatives et des quantités prétendues imaginaires* (1828), seems to have been free of any dependence on Argand's work.

Argand's later publications, all of which appeared in Gergonne's *Annales,* are elaborations of his book or comments on articles published by others. His first article determined equations for a curve that had previously been described in the *Annales* (**3**, 243). Argand went on to suggest an application of the curve to the construction of a thermometer shaped like a watch. His analysis of probable errors in such a mechanism showed familiarity with the mechanics of Laplace, as presented in *Exposition du système du monde.*

His fifth article in the *Annales,* defending his proof of the fundamental theorem of algebra, showed his familiarity with the works of Lagrange, Euler, and d'Alembert, especially their debates on whether all rational functions of $(a + bi)$ could be reduced to the form $A + Bi$ where a, b, A, and B are real. Argand, oddly enough, did not accept this theorem. He apparently was not familiar with Euler's earlier reduction of $\sqrt{-1}^{\sqrt{-1}}$, for he cited this as an example of an expression that could not be reduced to the form $A + Bi$.

His last article appeared in the volume of *Annales* dated 1815–1816 and dealt with a problem in combinations. In it Argand devised the notation (m,n) for the combinations of m things taken n at a time and the notation $Z(m,n)$ for the number of such combinations.

Argand was a man with an unknown background, a nonmathematical occupation, and an uncertain contact with the literature of his time who intuitively developed a critical idea for which the time was right. He exploited it himself. The quality and significance of his work were recognized by some of the geniuses of his time, but breakdowns in communication and the approximate simultaneity of similar developments by other workers force a historian to deny him full credit for the fruits of the concept on which he labored.

BIBLIOGRAPHY

I. Original Works. There have been three editions of Argand's book (his first publication), *Essai sur une manière de représenter les quantités imaginaires dans les constructions géométriques.* The first edition (Paris, 1806) did not bear the name of the author; the second edition, subtitled *Précédé d'une préface par M. J. Hoüel et suivie d'une appendice contenant des extraits des Annales de Gergonne, relatifs à la question des imaginaires* (Paris, 1874), cites the author as "R. Argand" on the title page but identifies him as Jean-Robert Argand on page xv. The *Essai* was translated by Professor A. S. Hardy as *Imaginary Quantities: Their Geometrical Interpretation* (New York, 1881). Argand's eight later publications all appeared in Vols. **4**, **5**, and **6** (1813–1816) of J. D. Gergonne's journal *Annales de mathématiques pures et appliquées.* Hoüel lists them at the end of his preface to the second edition of the *Essai.*

II. Secondary Literature. Data on Argand's life were included by Hoüel with the second edition of the *Essai.* Verification of the dates of his birth and death is given by H. Fehr in *Intermédiare des mathématiciens,* **9** (1902), 74. Niels Nielsen, *Géomètres français sous la Révolution* (Copenhagen, 1929), pp. 6–9, discusses Argand with reference to Wessel, Français, and others. William Rowan Hamilton gives a comparative analysis of contemporary work with complex numbers while praising Argand in *Lectures on Quaternions* (Dublin, 1853), pp. 31–34, 56, 57. Augustin Louis Cauchy's appraisal is found in "Mémoire sur les quantités géometriques," in *Exercices d'analyse et de physique mathématique,* IV (Paris, 1847), and in *Oeuvres,* 2nd series, XIV (Paris, 1938), 175–202. J. F. Français's development of Argand's ideas contained in a letter to his brother, "Nouveaux principes de géometrie de position, et interpretation géométrique des symboles imaginaires," is *Annales de mathématiques,* **4** (1813–1814), 61–71.

Phillip S. Jones

ARISTAEUS (*fl. ca.* 350–330 B.C.)

Aristaeus lived after Menaechmus and was an older contemporary of Euclid. Nothing is known of his life, but he was definitely not the son-in-law of Pythagoras mentioned by Iamblichus. Pappus, whose *Collectio* (Book VII) is our chief source, calls him Aristaeus the

Elder, so presumably there was a later mathematician with the same name.

None of Aristaeus' writings have been preserved. On the other hand, Pappus (some 650 years later) had in his possession Aristaeus' treatment of conic sections as loci, the *Five Books Concerning Solid Loci.* He mentions the work in his *Treasury of Analysis.* In another place, he speaks of the solid loci of Aristaeus as "standing in relation to conic sections."[1] For that reason, and because in a scholium there is mention of *Five Books of the Elements of Conic Sections,* some have concluded that Aristaeus wrote another work of this nature. According to Heiberg's investigations, this is untrue. Pappus also reports that Aristaeus introduced the terms "section of the acute-angled, right-angled, and obtuse-angled cone."

As for its contents, it can be determined from the passages by Pappus and Apollonius that the "locus with respect to three or four lines" was treated by Aristaeus.[2] Well-founded suppositions have been expressed concerning other loci treated by him, in connection with vergings (*νεύσεις*) by means of conic sections, trisection of an angle with the aid of a hyperbola, and above all the focus-directrix property of conic sections; Pappus establishes them in a lemma to the lost *Surface Loci* of Euclid. Since Euclid evidently supposes that the principle necessary for an understanding of surface loci is well known, it could have originated with Aristaeus.

In any case, Aristaeus played a major part in the development of the conic section theory, which began with Menaechmus.[3] Zeuthen and Heath give a comprehensive presentation of his accomplishments. In 1645 Viviani undertook a revision of the *Solid Loci,* starting from the same general interpretation of the contents that was used later by Zeuthen.

Hypsicles (*ca.* 180 B.C.), the editor of Book XIV of Euclid's *Elements,* reports another work, *Concerning the Comparison of Five Regular Solids,* from which he quotes a proposition.[4] It is not certain whether Hypsicles had in mind here the author of the *Solid Loci.* One would suppose a younger Aristaeus; in that case, Euclid's dependence (in Book XIII) on Aristaeus, which has been maintained by Heath but has been denied with good reasons by Sachs, would not be a point of contention.

After Aristaeus, Euclid was the next to deal with conic sections; his work was rendered out-of-date by Apollonius and became superfluous. From a statement by Pappus one must assume that Euclid had no intention of developing further the treatment of conic sections as loci, but that he sought—as did Apollonius—to give a general, synthetic construction. The solution of the problem of the "locus with respect to three or four lines" must have been incomplete in Aristaeus' works, for the "proposition of powers" (prop. Euclid III, 36) extended to conics and the second branch of the hyperbola were still missing. Apollonius, who must have had the complete solution,[5] notes additionally that the problem could not be completely solved without the propositions he discovered. He does not give the solution, but in the third book Apollonius does prove the converse of the proposition.[6]

After Apollonius and Pappus became well known again during the Renaissance, the problem of loci again began to attract interest. It appears in letters from Golius to Mydorge (after 1629) and Descartes (1631), and in letters from Descartes to Mersenne (1632, 1634). Fermat gives (before 1637) a solution in the ancient manner; in a letter to him (4 August 1640), Roberval reports that he completely reconstructed the *Solid Loci.*[7] In Descartes's *Géométrie* (1637) the "locus with respect to three and four lines" forms the starting point for the new analytic treatment of conic sections. Descartes cites the pertinent passages in Pappus and, going beyond him, expands the problem to arbitrarily many straight lines. By means of this, he laid the foundation for a theory of the general properties of algebraic curves.

NOTES

1. *συνεχῆ τοῖς κωνικοῖς* (Pappus VII, 672). Hultsch translates it freely as *supplementum conicorum doctrinae.*
2. The proposition is as follows: If from a given point arbitrarily directed lines *a, b, c* (or *a, b, c, d*) are drawn to meet at given angles three (or four) straight lines given in position, and then if $ac:b^2$ (or $ac:bd$) is a given value, then the point lies on a conic section. Cf. Pappus VII, 678.
3. Sarton (*Introduction,* I, 125) calls him the greatest mathematician of the second half of the fourth century.
4. "The same circle circumscribes both the pentagon of the dodecahedron and the triangle of the icosahedron when both are inscribed in the same sphere." (Euclid, Heiberg ed., V, 6 f.)
5. Descartes is of still another opinion. See also Zeuthen, *Lehre,* pp. 127 ff.
6. Heath, *Apollonius,* pp. cxxxviii ff. The proposition is this: For a point of a conic section the relationship given in note 2 holds true.
7. Tannery, "Note," pp. 46 ff. From Fermat only the solution for the locus of three straight lines survived.

BIBLIOGRAPHY

Aristaeus is also discussed in J. L. Coolidge, *A History of the Conic Sections and Quadric Surfaces* (Oxford, 1945, 1947), chs. 1 (para 2), 3, 5; P. ver Eecke, *Les coniques d'Apollonius de Perge* (Paris, 1932, 1959), pp. x, xvii, 2; and *Pappus d'Alexandrie,* I (Paris-Bruges, 1933), pp. lxxxix–ci;

Euclid, *Elementa,* J. L. Heiberg, ed., V (Leipzig, 1888), 6 f.; T. L. Heath, *Apollonius of Perga* (Cambridge, 1896), pp. xxxviii, cxxxviii ff.; and *A History of Greek Mathematics,* I (Oxford, 1921), 143 f., 420; J. L. Heiberg, *Apollonii Pergaei quae Graece exstant,* I (Leipzig, 1891), 4; and *Geschichte der Mathematik und Naturwissenschaften im Altertum* (Leipzig, 1925, 1960), p. 13; F. Hultsch, trans., *Pappi Alexandrini Collectionis quae supersunt,* II (Berlin, 1877), 634, 636, 672 ff., 1004 ff.; Pauly-Wissowa, *Real-Encyclopädie,* supp. III (1918), 157 f.; E. Sachs, *Die fünf Platonischen Körper* (Berlin, 1917), pp. 107 ff.; G. Sarton, *Introduction to the History of Science,* I, 125; P. Tannery, "Note sur le problème de Pappus," in *Mémoires scientifiques,* **3** (1915), 42–50; V. Viviani, *De locis solidis secunda divinatio geometrica in quinque libros injuria temporum amissos Aristaei senioris geometrae* (Florence, 1673, 1701); and H. G. Zeuthen, *Die Lehre von den Kegelschnitten im Altertum,* R. von Fischer-Benzon, ed. (Copenhagen, 1886), repr. with foreword and index by J. E. Hofmann (Hildesheim, 1966), pp. 127 ff., 276, and *Geschichte der Mathematik im Altertum und Mittelalter* (Copenhagen, 1890), pp. 197 ff.

KURT VOGEL

ARISTARCHUS OF SAMOS (*ca.* 310–230 B.C.)

Aristarchus is celebrated as being the first man to have propounded a heliocentric theory, eighteen centuries before Copernicus. He was born on the island of Samos, close by Miletus, cradle of Ionian science and philosophy. Little is known of Aristarchus' subsequent habitation. He was a pupil of Strato of Lampsacos, third head of the Lyceum founded by Aristotle. It is more likely that he studied under Strato at Alexandria than at Athens after the latter's assumption of the headship of the Lyceum in 287 B.C. Aristarchus' approximate dates are determined by Ptolemy's record (*Syntaxis* 3.2) of his observation of the summer solstice in 280 B.C. and by Archimedes' account of his heliocentric theory in a treatise, *The Sand-Reckoner,* which Archimedes composed before 216 B.C. The sole surviving work of Aristarchus is the treatise *On the Sizes and Distances of the Sun and Moon.*

To his contemporaries Aristarchus was known as "the mathematician"; the epithet may merely have served to distinguish him from other men of the same name, although *On Sizes and Distances* is indeed the work of a highly competent mathematician. The Roman architect Vitruvius lists him with six other men of rare endowment who were expert in all branches of mathematics and who could apply their talents to practical purposes. Vitruvius also credits him with inventing the *skaphē,* a widely used sundial consisting of a hemispherical bowl with a needle erected vertically in the middle to cast shadows. Speculations as to why a reputable mathematician like Aristarchus should interest himself in the true physical orientation of the solar system thus appear to be idle. Some have pointed to the possible influence of Strato, who was known as "the physical philosopher." There is no evidence, however, to indicate that Aristarchus got his physical theories from Strato. A more likely assumption is that *On Sizes and Distances* gave him an appreciation of the relative sizes of the sun and earth and led him to propound a heliocentric system.

The beginnings of heliocentrism are traced to the early Pythagoreans, a religiophilosophical school that flourished in southern Italy in the fifth century B.C. Ancient tradition ascribed to Pythagoras (*ca.* 520 B.C.) the identification of the Morning Star and the Evening Star as the same body. Philolaus (*ca.* 440 B.C.) gave the earth, moon, sun, and planets an orbital motion about a central fire, which he called "the hearth of the universe." According to another tradition, it was Hicetas, a contemporary of Philolaus, who first gave a circular orbit to the earth. Hicetas was also credited with maintaining the earth's axial rotation and a stationary heavens. More reliable ancient authorities, however, associate the hypothesis of the earth's diurnal rotation with Heraclides of Pontus, a pupil of Plato, who is also explicitly credited with maintaining (*ca.* 340 B.C.) an epicyclic orbit of Venus—and presumably that of Mercury also—about the sun. Some Greek astronomer may have taken the next logical step toward developing a complete heliocentric hypothesis by proposing the theory advanced in modern times by Tycho Brahe, which placed the five visible planets in motion about the sun, and the sun, in turn, in motion about the earth. Several scholars have argued that such a step was indeed taken, the most notable being the Italian astronomer Schiaparelli, who ascribed the Tychonic system to Heraclides; but evidence of its existence in antiquity is lacking.

Ancient authorities are unanimous in attributing the heliocentric theory to Aristarchus. Archimedes, who lived shortly afterward, says that he published his views in a book or treatise in which the premises that he developed led to the conclusion that the universe is many times greater than the current conception of it. Archimedes, near the opening of *The Sand-Reckoner,* gives a summary statement of Aristarchus' argument:

> His hypotheses are that the fixed stars and the sun are stationary, that the earth is borne in a circular orbit about the sun, which lies in the middle of its orbit, and that the sphere of the fixed stars, having the same center as the sun, is so great in extent that the circle on which he supposes the earth to be borne has such a proportion

ARISTARCHUS OF SAMOS

to the distance of the fixed stars as the center of the sphere bears to its surface.

Plutarch (*ca.* A.D. 100) gives a similar brief account of Aristarchus' hypothesis, stating specifically that the earth revolves along the ecliptic and that it is at the same time rotating on its axis.

After reporting Aristarchus' views, Archimedes criticizes him for setting up a mathematically impossible proportion, pointing out that the center of the sphere has no magnitude and therefore cannot bear any ratio to the surface of the sphere. Archimedes intrudes the observation that the "universe," as it is commonly conceived of by astronomers, is a sphere whose radius extends from the center of the sun to the center of the earth. Accordingly, as a mathematician he imputes to the mathematician Aristarchus a proportion that he feels is implicit in his statement, namely, that the ratio that the earth bears to the universe, as it is commonly conceived, is equal to the ratio that the sphere in which the earth revolves, in Aristarchus' scheme, bears to the sphere of the fixed stars.

Modern scholars have generally supposed that Aristarchus did not intend to have his proportion interpreted as a mathematical statement, that instead he was using an expression conventional with Greek mathematical cosmographers—"having the relation of a point"—merely to indicate the minuteness of the earth's orbit and the vastness of the heavens. Sir Thomas Heath points to similar expressions in the works of Euclid, Geminus, Ptolemy, and Cleomedes, and in the second assumption of Aristarchus' extant treatise *On Sizes and Distances* (see below). Heath feels that Archimedes' interpretation was arbitrary and sophistical and that Aristarchus introduced the statement to account for the inability to observe stellar parallax from an orbiting earth. Neugebauer defends the proportion that Archimedes ascribes to Aristarchus,

$$r : R_e = R_e : R_f,$$

as mathematically sound and providing finite dimensions for the sphere of the fixed stars: the earth's radius (r) is so small in comparison with the sun's distance (R_e) that no daily parallax of the sun is discernible for determining R_e; according to Aristarchus' hypothesis, the earth moves in an orbit whose radius is R_e and no annual parallax of the fixed stars is discernible.

Why did the Greeks, after evolving a heliocentric hypothesis in gradual steps over a period of two centuries, allow it to fall into neglect almost immediately? Only one man, Seleucus of Seleucia (*ca.* 150 B.C.), is known to have embraced Aristarchus' views. The common attitude of deploring the "abandonment" of the heliocentric theory as a "retrogressive step" appears to be unwarranted when it is realized that the theory, however bold and ingenious it is to be regarded, never attracted much attention in antiquity. Aristarchus' system was the culmination of speculations about the physical nature of the universe that began with the Ionian philosophers of the sixth century, and it belongs to an age that was passing away. The main course of development of Greek astronomy was mathematical, not physical, and the great achievements were still to come—the exacting demonstrations and calculations of Apollonius of Perga, Hipparchus, and Ptolemy. These were based upon a geocentric orientation.

To a mathematician the orientation is of no consequence; in fact it is more convenient to construct a system of epicycles and eccentrics to account for planetary motions from a geocentric orientation. A heliocentric hypothesis neatly explained some basic phenomena, such as the stations and retrogradations of superior planets; but a circular orbit for the earth, about a sun in the exact center, failed to account for precise anomalies, such as the inequality of the seasons. In explanation of this inequality, Hipparchus determined the eccentricity of the earth's position as 1/24 of the radius of the sun's circle and he fixed the line of absides in the direction of longitude 65° 30′. Ptolemy adopted Hipparchus' solar data without change, unaware that the sun's orbit describes a revolving eccentric, the shift being 32′ in a century. The Arab astronomer al-Battānī (A.D. 858–929) discovered this shift. Epicyclic constructions had two advantages over eccentric constructions: they were applicable to inferior as well as superior planets and they palpably demonstrated planetary stations and retrograde motions. By the time of Apollonius it was understood that an equivalent eccentric system could be constructed for every epicyclic system. Henceforth, combinations of epicycles and eccentrics were introduced, all from a geocentric orientation. Aristarchus, too, had used a geocentric orientation in calculating the sizes and distances of the sun and moon.

It is not hard to account for the lack of interest in the heliocentric theory. The *Zeitgeist* of the new Hellenistic age was set and characterized by the abstruse erudition of the learned scholars and the precise researches of the astronomers, mathematicians, and anatomists working at the library and museum of Alexandria. Accurate instruments in use at Alexandria were giving astronomers a better appreciation of the vast distance of the sun. Putting the earth in orbit about the sun would lead to the expecta-

ARISTARCHUS OF SAMOS

tion that some variation in the position of the fixed stars would be discernible at opposite seasons. Absence of displacement would presuppose a universe of vast proportions. The more precise the observations, the less inclined were the astronomers at Alexandria to accept an orbital motion of the earth. It is the opinion of Heath that Hipparchus (*ca.* 190–120 B.C.), usually regarded as the greatest of Greek astronomers, in adopting the geocentric orientation "sealed the fate of the heliocentric hypothesis for so many centuries."

The intellectual world at large was also disinclined to accept Aristarchus' orientation. Aristotle's doctrine of "natural places," which assigned to earth a position at the bottom or center among the elements comprising the universe, and his plausible "proofs" of a geocentric orientation, carried great weight in later antiquity, even with the mathematician Ptolemy. Religious minds were reluctant to relinquish the central position of man's abode. According to Plutarch, Cleanthes, the second head of the Stoic school (263–232 B.C.), thought that Aristarchus ought to be indicted on a charge of impiety for putting the earth in motion. Astrology, a respectable science in the eyes of many leading intellectuals, was enjoying an extraordinary vogue after its recent introduction. Its doctrines and findings were also based upon a geocentric orientation.

It is interesting to note in passing that Copernicus' disappointment at being anticipated by Aristarchus has recently come to light. Copernicus deliberately suppressed a statement acknowledging his awareness of Aristarchus' theory; the statement, deleted from the autograph copy of the *De revolutionibus*, appears in a footnote in the Thorn edition (1873) of that work. Elsewhere Copernicus tells of his search for classical precedents for his novel ideas about the heavens and of his finding in Plutarch the views of Philolaus, Heraclides, and Ecphantus; but he omits mention of the clear statement about Aristarchus' theory that appears a few pages earlier. Lastly, Copernicus' almost certain acquaintance with Archimedes' *The Sand-Reckoner*, the work containing our best account of Aristarchus' theory, has recently been pointed out.

His accomplishments as an astronomer have tended to detract attention from Aristarchus' attainments as a mathematician. Flourishing a generation after Euclid and a generation before Archimedes, Aristarchus was capable of the same sort of rigorous and logical geometrical demonstrations that distinguished the work of those famous mathematicians. *On Sizes and Distances* marks the first attempt to determine astronomical distances and dimensions by mathematical deductions based upon a set of assumptions. His last assumption assigns a grossly excessive estimate to the apparent angular diameter of the moon (2°). We are told by Archimedes in *The Sand-Reckoner* that Aristarchus discovered the sun's apparent angular diameter to be 1/720 part of the zodiac circle (1/2°), a close and respectable estimate. Aristarchus uses a geocentric orientation in *On Sizes and Distances* and concludes that the sun's volume is over 300 times greater than the earth's volume. For these reasons it is generally assumed that the treatise was an early work, antedating his heliocentric hypothesis.

Aristarchus argues that at the precise moment of the moon's quadrature, when it is half-illuminated, angle *SME* is a right angle; angle *SEM* can be measured by observation; therefore it is possible to deduce angle *MSE* and to determine the ratio of the distance of the moon to the distance of the sun (Figure 1). Two obvious difficulties are involved in his procedures: the determination with any exactitude (1) of the time of the moon's dichotomy and (2) of the measurement of angle *SEM*. A slight inaccuracy in either case would lead to a grossly inaccurate result. Aristarchus assumes angle *SEM* to be 87°, when in actuality it is more than 89° 50′, and he derives a distance for the sun of 18 to 20 times greater than the moon's distance (actually nearly 400 times greater). His mathematical procedures are sound, but his observational data are so crude as to make it apparent that Aristarchus was interested here in mathematical demonstrations and not in physical realities.

Aristarchus' treatise begins with six assumptions:

(1) That the moon receives its light from the sun.

(2) That the earth has the relation of a point and center to the sphere of the moon.

(3) That when the moon appears to us to be exactly at the half the great circle dividing the light and dark portions of the moon is in line with the observer's eye.

(4) That when the moon appears to us to be at the half its distance from the sun is less than a quadrant by 1/30 part of a quadrant (87°).

(5) That the breadth of the earth's shadow (during eclipses) is that of two moons.

(6) That the moon subtends 1/15 part of a sign of the zodiac (2°).

He then states that he is in a position to prove three propositions:

(1) The distance of the sun from the earth is more than eighteen times but less than twenty times the moon's distance (from the earth); this is based on the assumption about the halved moon.

(2) The diameter of the sun has the same ratio to the diameter of the moon (i.e., assuming that the sun and moon have the same apparent angular diameter).

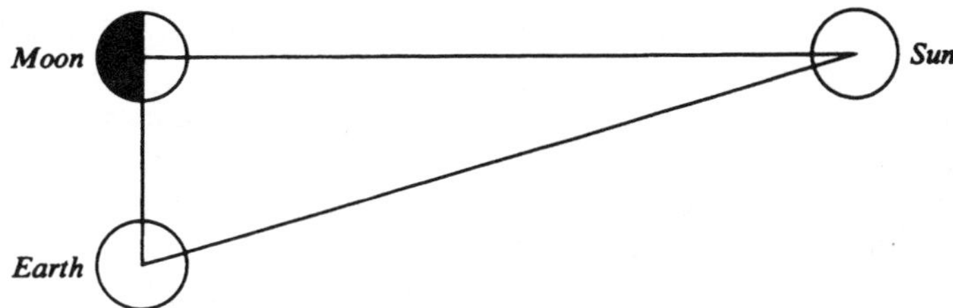

Figure 1

(3) The diameter of the sun has to the diameter of the earth a ratio greater than 19:3, but less than 43:6; this deduction follows from the ratio between the distances thus discovered, from the assumption about the shadow, and from the assumption that the moon subtends 1/15 part of a sign of the zodiac.

Then follow eighteen propositions containing the demonstrations. Heath has edited and translated the complete Greek text, together with Pappus' comments on the treatise, in his *Aristarchus of Samos* (pp. 352–414), and presents a summary account of the treatise in *A History of Greek Mathematics* (Vol. II).

Anticipating trigonometric methods that were to come, Aristarchus was the first to develop geometric procedures for approximating the sines of small angles. He deals with angles expressed as fractions of right angles and ratios of the sides of triangles, determining limits between which actual values lie. In Proposition 7, demonstrating that the distance of the sun is more than eighteen times but less than twenty times the distance of the moon, which would be expressed trigonometrically $1/18 > \sin 3° > 1/20$, he uses in his proof certain inequalities that he assumes to be known and accepted. These may be expressed trigonometrically. If α and β are acute angles and $\alpha > \beta$, then

$$\tan \alpha/\tan\beta > \alpha/\beta > \sin \alpha/\sin\beta.$$

If Aristarchus had had a correct measurement of the angle *SEM*—89 5/6° instead of 87°—his result would have been nearly correct. A century later Hipparchus was able to obtain a very close approximation of the moon's distance, expressed in terms of earth radii, by measuring the earth's shadow during lunar eclipses; but an appreciation of the vast distance of the sun had to wait upon the development of modern precision instruments.

Other dimensions deduced by Aristarchus in his treatise, all of them grossly underestimated because of his poor observational data, are:

(Prop. 10) The sun has to the moon a ratio greater than 5,832:1 but less than 8,000:1.

(Prop. 11) The diameter of the moon is less than 2/45 but greater than 1/30 of the distance of the center of the moon from the observer.

(Prop. 16) The sun has to the earth a ratio greater than 6,859:27 but less than 79,507:216.

(Prop. 17) The diameter of the earth is to the diameter of the moon in a ratio greater than 108:43 but less than 60:19.

(Prop. 18) The earth is to the moon in a ratio greater than 1,259,712:79,507 but less than 216,000:6,859.

BIBLIOGRAPHY

Thomas W. Africa, "Copernicus' Relation to Aristarchus and Pythagoras," in *Isis,* **52** (1961), 403–409; Angus Armitage, *Copernicus, the Founder of Modern Astronomy* (London, 1938); John L. E. Dreyer, *A History of the Planetary Systems from Thales to Kepler* (Cambridge, England, 1906; repr., New York, 1953); Pierre Duhem, *Le système du monde,* Vols. I-II (Paris, 1954); Sir Thomas Heath, *Aristarchus of Samos* (Oxford, 1913) and *A History of Greek Mathematics,* 2 vols. (Oxford, 1921); Otto Neugebauer, "Archimedes and Aristarchus," in *Isis,* **39** (1942), 4–6; Giovanni V. Schiaparelli, "Origine del sistema planetario eliocentrico presso i Greci," in *Memorie del'Istituto lombardo di scienze e lettere,* **18** (1898), fasc. 5; and William H. Stahl, "The Greek Heliocentric Theory and Its Abandonment," in *Transactions of the American Philological Association,* **77** (1945), 321–332.

WILLIAM H. STAHL

ARISTOTLE (*b.* Stagira in Chalcidice, 384 B.C.; *d.* Chalcis, 322 B.C.)

The following article is in four parts: Method, Physics, and Cosmology; Natural History and Zoology; Anatomy and Physiology; Tradition and Influence.

Method, Physics, and Cosmology.

Aristotle's father served as personal physician to Amyntas II of Macedon, grandfather of Alexander the Great. Aristotle's interest in biology and in the use of dissection is sometimes traced to his father's profession, but any suggestion of a rigorous family training in medicine can be discounted. Both parents died while Aristotle was a boy, and his knowledge of human anatomy and physiology remained a notably weak spot in his biology. In 367, about the time of his seventeenth birthday, he came to Athens and became a member of Plato's Academy. Henceforth his career falls naturally into three periods. He remained with the Academy for twenty years. Then, when Plato died in 347, he left the city and stayed away for twelve years: his reason for going may have been professional, a dislike of philosophical tendencies represented in the Academy by Plato's nephew and successor, Speusippus, but more probably it was political, the new anti-Macedonian mood of the city. He returned in 335 when Athens had come under Macedonian rule, and had twelve more years of teaching and research there. This third period ended with the death of his pupil, Alexander the Great (323), and the revival of Macedon's enemies. Aristotle was faced with a charge of impiety and went again into voluntary exile. A few months later he died on his maternal estate in Chalcis.

His middle years away from Athens took him first to a court on the far side of the Aegean whose ruler, Hermeias, became his father-in-law; then (344) to the neighboring island Lesbos, probably at the suggestion of Theophrastus, a native of the island and henceforth a lifelong colleague; finally (342) back to Macedon as tutor of the young prince Alexander. After his return to Athens he lectured chiefly in the grounds of the Lyceum, a Gymnasium already popular with sophists and teachers. The Peripatetic school, as an institution comparable to the Academy, was probably not founded until after his death. But with some distinguished students and associates he collected a natural history museum and a library of maps and manuscripts (including his own essays and lecture notes), and organized a program of research which *inter alia* laid the foundation for all histories of Greek natural philosophy (see Theophrastus), mathematics and astronomy (see Eudemus), and medicine.

Recent discussion of his intellectual development has dwelt on the problem of distributing his works between and within the three periods of his career. But part of the stimulus to this inquiry was the supposed success with which Plato's dialogues had been put in chronological order, and the analogy with Plato is misleading. Everything that Aristotle polished for public reading in Plato's fashion has been lost, save for fragments and later reports. The writings that survive are a collection edited in the first century B.C. (see below, Aristotle: Tradition), allegedly from manuscripts long mislaid: a few items are spurious (among the scientific works *Mechanica, Problemata, De mundo, De plantis*), most are working documents produced in the course of Aristotle's teaching and research; and the notes and essays composing them have been arranged and amended not only by their author but also by his ancient editors and interpreters. Sometimes an editorial title covers a batch of writings on connected topics of which some seem to supersede others (thus *Physics* VII seems an unfinished attempt at the argument for a prime mover which is carried out independently in *Physics* VIII); sometimes the title represents an open file, a text annotated with unabsorbed objections (e.g., the *Topics*) or with later and even post-Aristotelian observations (e.g., the *Historia animalium*). On the other hand it cannot be assumed that inconsistencies are always chronological pointers. In *De caelo* I–II he argues for a fifth element in addition to the traditional four (fire, air, water, earth): unlike them, its natural motion is circular and it forms the divine and unchanging substance of the heavenly bodies. Yet in *De caelo* III–IV, as in the *Physics,* he discusses the elements without seeming to provide for any such fifth body, and these writings are accordingly sometimes thought to be earlier. But on another view of his methods (see below, on dialectic) it becomes more intelligible that he should try different and even discrepant approaches to a topic at the same time.

Such considerations do not make it impossible to reconstruct something of the course of his scientific thinking from the extant writings, together with what is known of his life. For instance it is sometimes said that his distinction between "essence" and "accident," or between defining and nondefining characteristics, must be rooted in the biological studies in which it plays an integral part. But the distinction is explored at greatest length in the *Topics,* a handbook of dialectical debate which dates substantially from his earlier years in the Academy, whereas the inquiries embodied in his biological works seem to come chiefly from his years abroad, since they refer relatively often to the Asiatic coast and Lesbos and seldom to southern Greece. So this piece of conceptual apparatus was not produced by the work in biology. On the contrary, it was modified by that work: when Aristotle tries to reduce the definition of a species to one distinguishing mark (e.g., *Metaphysics* VII 12, VIII 6) he is a dialectician, facing a problem whose ancestry includes Plato's theory of Forms, but when he rejects such definitions in favor of a cluster of differentiae (*De partibus animalium* I 2–3) he writes as a working biologist, armed with a set of questions about breathing and sleeping, movement and nourishment, birth and death.

The starting point in tracing his scientific progress must therefore be his years in the Academy. Indeed without this starting point it is not possible to understand either his pronouncements on scientific theory

ARISTOTLE

or, what is more important, the gap between his theory and his practice.

The Mathematical Model. The Academy that Aristotle joined in 367 was distinguished from other Athenian schools by two interests: mathematics (including astronomy and harmonic theory, to the extent that these could be made mathematically respectable), and dialectic, the Socratic examination of the assumptions made in reasoning—including the assumptions of mathematicians and cosmologists. Briefly, Plato regarded the first kind of studies as merely preparatory and ancillary to the second; Aristotle, in the account of scientific and philosophical method that probably dates from his Academic years, reversed the priorities (*Posterior Analytics* I; *Topics* I 1–2). It was the mathematics he encountered that impressed him as providing the model for any well-organized science. The work on axiomatization which was to culminate in Euclid's *Elements* was already far advanced, and for Aristotle the pattern of a science is an axiomatic system in which theorems are validly derived from basic principles, some proprietary to the science ("hypotheses" and "definitions," the second corresponding to Euclid's "definitions"), others having an application in more than one system ("axioms," corresponding to Euclid's "common notions"). The proof-theory which was characteristic of Greek mathematics (as against that of Babylon or Egypt) had developed in the attempt to show why various mathematical formulae worked in practice. Aristotle pitches on this as the chief aim of any science: it must not merely record but explain, and in explaining it must, so far as the special field of inquiry allows, generalize. Thus mathematical proof becomes Aristotle's first paradigm of scientific explanation; by contrast, the dialectic that Plato ranked higher—the logical but free-ranging analysis of the beliefs and usage of "the many and the wise"—is allowed only to help in settling those basic principles of a science that cannot, without regress or circularity, be proved within the science itself. At any rate, this was the theory.

Aristotle duly adapts and enlarges the mathematical model to provide for the physical sciences. Mathematics, he holds, is itself a science (or rather a family of sciences) about the physical world, and not about a Platonic world of transcendent objects; but it abstracts from those characteristics of the world that are the special concern of physics—movement and change, and therewith time and location. So the nature and behavior of physical things will call for more sorts of explanation than mathematics recognizes. Faced with a man, or a tree, or a flame, one can ask what it is made of, its "matter"; what is its essential character or "form"; what external or internal agency produced it; and what the "end" or purpose of it is. The questions make good sense when applied to an artifact such as a statue, and Aristotle often introduces them by this analogy; but he holds that they can be extended to every kind of thing involved in regular natural change. The explanations they produce can be embodied in the formal proofs or even the basic definitions of a science (thus a lunar eclipse can be not merely accounted for, but defined, as the loss of light due to the interposition of the earth, and a biological species can be partly defined in terms of the purpose of some of its organs). Again, the regularities studied by physics may be unlike those of mathematics in an important respect: initially the *Posterior Analytics* depicts a science as deriving necessary conclusions from necessary premises, true in all cases (I ii and iv), but later (I xxx) the science is allowed to deal in generalizations that are true in most cases but not necessarily in all. Aristotle is adapting his model to make room for "a horse has four legs" as well as for "$2 \times 2 = 4$." How he regards the exceptions to such generalizations is not altogether clear. In his discussions of "luck" and "chance" in *Physics* II, and of "accident" elsewhere, he seems to hold that a lucky or chance or accidental event can always, under some description, be subsumed under a generalization expressing some regularity. His introduction to the *Meteorologica* is sometimes cited to show that in his view sublunary happenings are inherently irregular; but he probably means that, while the laws of sublunary physics are commonly (though not always) framed to allow of exceptions, these exceptions are not themselves inexplicable. The matter is complicated by his failure to maintain a sharp distinction between laws that provide a necessary (and even uniquely necessary), and those that provide a sufficient, condition of the situation to be explained.

But in two respects the influence of mathematics on Aristotle's theory of science is radical and unmodified. First, the drive to axiomatize mathematics and its branches was in fact a drive for autonomy: the premises of the science were to determine what questions fell within the mathematician's competence and, no less important, what did not. This consequence Aristotle accepts for every field of knowledge: a section of *Posterior Analytics* I xii is given up to the problem, what questions can be properly put to the practitioner of such-and-such a science; and in I vii, trading on the rule "one science to one genus," he denounces arguments that poach outside their own field—which try, for instance, to deduce geometrical conclusions from arithmetical premises. He recognizes arithmetical proofs in harmonics and geometrical proofs in mechanics, but treats them as exceptions. The same impulse leads him to map all systematic knowledge into its departments—theoretical, practical, and productive—and to divide the first into metaphysics (or, as he once calls it, "theology"), mathematics, and physics, these in turn being marked out in subdivisions.

This picture of the autonomous deductive system has had a large influence on the interpreters of Aristotle's scientific work; yet it plays a small part in his inquiries, just because it is not a model for inquiry at all but for subsequent exposition. This is the second major respect in which it reflects mathematical procedure. In nearly all the surviving productions of Greek mathematics, traces of the workshop have been deliberately removed: proofs are found for theorems that were certainly first reached by other routes. So Aristotle's theoretical picture of a science shows it in its shop window (or what he often calls its "didactic") form; but for the most part his inquiries are not at this stage of the business. This is a piece of good fortune for students of the subject, who have always lamented that no comparable record survives of presystematic research in mathematics proper (Archimedes' public letter to Eratosthenes—the *Ephodos,* or "Method"—is hardly such a record). As it is, Aristotle's model comes nearest to realization in the systematic astronomy of *De caelo* I–II (cf., e.g., I iii, "from what has been said, partly as premises and partly as things proved from these, it follows . . ."), and in the proof of a prime mover in *Physics* VIII. But these constructions are built on the presystematic analyses of *Physics* I–VI, analyses that are expressly undertaken to provide physics with its basic assumptions (cf. I i) and to define its basic concepts, change and time and location, infinity and continuity (III i). *Ex hypothesi* the latter discussions, which from Aristotle's pupils Eudemus and Strato onward have given the chief stimulus to physicists and philosophers of science, cannot be internal to the science whose premises they seek to establish. Their methods and data need not and do not fit the theoretical straitjacket, and in fact they rely heavily on the dialectic that theoretically has no place in the finished science.

Dialectic and "Phenomena." Conventionally Aristotle has been contrasted with Plato as the committed empiricist, anxious to "save the phenomena" by basing his theories on observation of the physical world. First the phenomena, then the theory to explain them: this Baconian formula he recommends not only for physics (and specifically for astronomy and biology) but for ethics and generally for all arts and sciences. But "phenomena," like many of his key terms, is a word with different uses in different contexts. In biology and meteorology the phenomena are commonly observations made by himself or taken from other sources (fishermen, travelers, etc.), and similar observations are evidently presupposed by that part of his astronomy that relies on the schemes of concentric celestial spheres proposed by Eudoxus and Callippus. But in the *Physics* when he expounds the principles of the subject, and in many of the arguments in the *De caelo* and *De generatione et corruptione* by which he settles the nature and interaction of the elements, and turns Eudoxus' elegant abstractions into a cumbrous physical (and theological) construction, the data on which he draws are mostly of another kind. The phenomena he now wants to save—or to give logical reasons (rather than empirical evidence) for scrapping—are the common convictions and common linguistic usage of his contemporaries, supplemented by the views of other thinkers. They are what he always represents as the materials of dialectic.

Thus when Aristotle tries to harden the idea of location for use in science (*Physics* IV 1–5) he sets out from our settled practice of locating a thing by giving its physical surroundings, and in particular from established ways of talking about one thing taking another's place. It is to save these that he treats any location as a container, and defines the place of X as the innermost static boundary of the body surrounding X. His definition turns out to be circular: moreover it carries the consequence that, since a point cannot lie within a boundary, it cannot strictly have (or be used to mark) a location. Yet we shall see later that his theories commit him to denying this.

Again, when he defines time as that aspect of change that enables it to be counted (*Physics* IV 10–14), what he wants to save and explain are the common ways of *telling* the time. This point, that he is neither inventing a new vocabulary nor assigning new theory-based uses to current words, must be borne in mind when one encounters such expressions as "force" and "average velocity" in versions of his dynamics. The word sometimes translated "force" (*dunamis*) is the common word for the "power" or "ability" of one thing to affect or be affected by another—to move or be moved, but also to heat or to soften or to be heated, and so forth. Aristotle makes it clear that this notion is what he is discussing in three celebrated passages (*Physics* VII 5, VIII 10, *De caelo* I 7) where later critics have discerned laws of proportionality connecting the force applied, the weight moved, and the time required for the force to move the weight a given distance. (Two of the texts do not mention weight at all.) A second term, *ischus,* sometimes rendered "force" in these contexts, is the common word for "strength," and it is this familiar notion that Aristotle is exploiting in the so-called laws of forced motion set out in *Physics* VII 5 and presupposed in VIII 10: he is relying on what a nontechnical audience would at once grant him concerning the comparative strengths of packhorses or (his example) gangs of shiphaulers. He says: let *A* be the strength required to move a weight *B* over a distance *D* in time *T*; then (1) *A* will move 1/2 *B* over 2*D* in *T*; (2) *A* will move 1/2 *B* over *D* in 1/2 *T*; (3) 1/2 *A* will move 1/2 *B* over *D* in *T*; and (4) *A* will move *B* over 1/2 *D* in 1/2 *T*; but (5) it does not follow that *A* will move some multiple of *B* over a proportionate fraction of *D* in *T* or indeed in any time, since it does not follow that *A* will be sufficient to move that multiple of *B* at all. The conjunction of (4) with the initial assumption shows that Aristotle takes the speed of motion in this case to be uniform; so commentators have naturally thought of *A* as a force whose continued application to *B* is just sufficient to overcome the opposing forces of gravity, friction, and the medium. In such circumstances propositions (3) and (4) will yield results equivalent to those of Newtonian dynamics. But then the circumstances described in (1) and (2) should yield not just the doubling of a uniform velocity which Aristotle supposes, but acceleration up to some appropriate terminal velocity. Others have proposed to treat *A* as prefiguring the later idea not of *force* but of *work,* or else *power,* if these are defined in terms of the displacement of weight and not of force; and this has the advantage of leaving Aristotle discussing the case that is central to his dynamics—the carrying out of some finite task in a finite time—without importing the notion of action at an instant which, for reasons we shall see, he rejects. But Aristotle also assumes that, for a given type of agent, *A* is multiplied in direct ratio to the size or quantity of the agent; and to apply this to the work done would be, once more, to overlook the difference between conditions of uniform motion and of acceleration. The fact is that Aristotle is appealing to conventional ways of comparing the strength of haulers and beasts of burden, and for his purposes the acceleration periods involved with these are negligible. What matters is that we measure strength by the ability to perform certain finite tasks before fatigue sets in; hence, when Aristotle adduces these proportionalities in the *Physics,* he does so with a view to showing that the strength required for keeping the sky turning for all time would be immeasurable. Since such celestial revolutions do not in his view have to overcome any such resistance as that of gravity or a medium we are not entitled to read these notions into the formulae quoted. What then is the basis for these proportionalities? He does not quote empirical evidence in their support, and in their generalized form he could not do so; in the *Physics* and again in the *De caelo* he insists that they can be extended to cover "heating and any effect of one body on another," but the Greeks had no thermometer nor indeed any device (apart from the measurement of strings in harmonics) for translating qualitative differences into quantitative measurements. Nor on the other hand does he present them as technical definitions of the concepts they introduce. He simply comments in the *Physics* that the rules of proportion require them to be true (and it may be noticed that he does not frame any of them as a function of more than two variables: the proportion is always a simple relation between two of the terms, the others remaining constant). He depends on this appeal, together with conventional ways of comparing strengths, to give him the steps he needs toward his conclusion about the strength of a prime mover: it is no part of the dialectic of his argument to coin hypotheses that require elaborate discussion in their own right.

It is part of the history of dynamics that, from Aristotle's immediate successors onward, these formulae were taken out of context, debated and refined, and finally jettisoned for an incomparably more exact and powerful set of concepts which owed little to dialectic in Aristotle's sense. That he did not intend his proportionalities for such close scrutiny becomes even clearer when we turn to his so-called laws of natural motion. Aristotle's universe is finite, spherical, and geocentric: outside it there can be no body nor even, therefore, any location or vacuum or time (*De caelo* I 9); within it there can be no vacuum (*Physics* IV 6–9). Natural motion is the unimpeded movement of its elements: centripetal or "downward" in the case of earth (whose place is at the center) and of water (whose place is next to earth), centrifugal or "upward" in the case of fire and (next below fire) air. These are the sublunary elements, capable of changing into each other (*De generatione et corruptione* II) and possessed of "heaviness" or "lightness" according as their natural motion is down or up. Above them all is the element whose existence Aristotle can prove only by a priori argument: ether, the substance of the spheres that carry the heavenly bodies. The natural motions of the first four elements are rectilinear and terminate, unless they are blocked, in the part of the universe that is the element's natural place; the motion of the fifth is circular and cannot be blocked, and it never leaves its natural place. These motions of free fall, free ascent, and free revolution are Aristotle's paradigms of regular movement,

ARISTOTLE

against which other motions can be seen as departures due to special agency or to the presence of more than one element in the moving body. On several occasions he sketches some proportional connection between the variables that occur in his analysis of such natural motions; generally he confines himself to rectilinear (i.e., sublunary) movement, as, for example, in *Physics* IV 8, the text that provoked a celebrated exchange between Simplicio and Salviati in Galileo's *Dialoghi.* There he writes: "We see a given weight or body moving faster than another for two reasons: either because of a difference in the medium traversed (e.g., water as against earth, water as against air), or, other things being equal, because of the greater weight or lightness of the moving body." Later he specifies that the proviso "other things being equal" is meant to cover identity of shape. Under the first heading, that of differences in the medium, he remarks that the motion of the medium must be taken into account as well as its density relative to others; but he is content to assume a static medium and propound, as always, a simple proportion in which the moving object's velocity varies inversely with the density of the medium. Two comments are relevant. First, in this as in almost all comparable contexts, the "laws of natural motion" are dispensable from the argument. Here Aristotle uses his proportionality to rebut the possibility of motion in a vacuum: such motion would encounter a medium of nil density and hence would have infinite velocity, which is impossible. But this is only one of several independent arguments for the same conclusion in the context. Next, the argument discounts acceleration (Aristotle does not consider the possibility of a body's speed in a vacuum remaining finite but increasing without limit, let alone that of its increasing to some finite terminal speed); yet he often insists that for the sublunary elements natural motion is always acceleration. (For this reason among others it is irrelevant to read his proportionalities of natural motion as an unwitting anticipation of Stokes's law.) But it was left to his successors during the next thousand years to quarrel over the way in which the ratios he formulated could be used to account for the steady acceleration he required in such natural motion; and where in the passage quoted he writes "we see," it was left to some nameless ancient scientist to make the experiment recorded by Philoponus and later by Galileo, of dropping different weights from the same height and noting that what we see does not answer to Aristotle's claim about their speed of descent. It was, to repeat, no part of the dialectic of his argument to give these proportionalities the rigor of scientific laws or present them as the record of exact observation.

On the other hand the existence of the natural motions themselves is basic to his cosmology. Plato had held that left to themselves, i.e., without divine governance, the four elements (he did not recognize a fifth) would move randomly in any direction: Aristotle denies this on behalf of the inherent regularity of the physical world. He makes the natural motions his "first hypotheses" in the *De caelo* and applies them over and again to the discussion of other problems. (The contrast between his carelessness over the proportionalities and the importance he attaches to the movements is sometimes read as showing that he wants to "eliminate mathematics from physics": but more on this later.)

This leads to a more general point which must be borne in mind in understanding his way of establishing physical theory. When he appeals to common views and usage in such contexts he is applying a favorite maxim, that in the search for explanations we must start from what is familiar or intelligible to us. (Once the science is set up, the deductions will proceed from principles "intelligible in themselves.") The same maxim governs his standard way of introducing concepts by extrapolating from some familiar, unpuzzling situation. Consider his distinction of "matter" and "form" in *Physics* I. He argues that any change implies a passage between two contrary attributes—from one to the other, or somewhere on a spectrum between the two—and that there must be a third thing to make this passage, a substrate which changes but survives the change. The situations to which he appeals are those from which this triadic analysis can be, so to speak, directly read off: a light object turning dark, an unmusical man becoming musical. But then the analysis is extended to cases progressively less amenable: he moves, via the detuning of an instrument and the shaping of a statue, to the birth of plants and animals and generally to the sort of situation that had exercised earlier thinkers—the emergence of a new individual, the apparent coming of something from nothing. (Not the emergence of a new *type:* Aristotle does not believe that new types emerge in nature, although he accepts the appearance of sports within or between existing types. In *Physics* II 8 he rejects a theory of evolution for putting the random occurrence of new types on the same footing with the reproduction of existing species, arguing that a theory that is not based on such regularities is not scientific physics.) *Ex nihilo nihil fit;* and even the emergence of a new individual must involve a substrate, "matter," which passes between two contrary conditions, the "privation" and the "form." But one effect of Aristotle's extrapolation is to force a major conflict between his theories and most contemporary and subsequent physics. In his view, the question "What are the essential attributes of matter?" must go unanswered. There is no general answer, for the distinction between form and matter reappears on many levels: what serves as matter to a higher form may itself be analyzed into form and matter, as a brick which is material for a house can itself be analyzed into a shape and the clay on which the shape is imposed. More important, there is no answer even when the analysis reaches the basic elements—earth, air, fire, and water. For these can be transformed into each other, and since no change can be intelligibly pictured as a mere succession of discrete objects these too must be transformations of some residual subject, but one that now *ex hypothesi* has no permanent qualitative or quantitative determinations in its own right. Thus Aristotle rejects all theories that explain physical change by the rearrangement of some basic stuff or stuffs endowed with fixed characteristics. Atomism in particular he rebuts at length, arguing that movement in a vacuum is impossible (we have seen one argument for this) and that the concept of an extended indivisible body is mathematically indefensible. But although matter is not required to identify itself by any permanent first-order characteristics, it does have important second-order properties. Physics studies the regularities in change, and for a given sort of thing at a given level it is the matter that determines what kinds of change are open to it. In some respects the idea has more in common with the field theory that appears embryonically in the Stoics than with the crude atomism maintained by the Epicureans, but its chief influence was on metaphysics (especially Neoplatonism) rather than on scientific theory. By contrast, the correlative concept of *form,* the universal element in things that allows them to be known and classified and defined, remained powerful in science. Aristotle took it from Plato, but by way of a radical and very early critique of Plato's Ideas; for Aristotle the formal element is inseparable from the things classified, whereas Plato had promoted it to independent existence in a transcendent world contemplated by disembodied souls. For Aristotle the physical world is all; its members with their qualities and quantities and interrelations are the paradigms of reality and there are no disembodied souls.

The device of extrapolating from the familiar is evident again in his account of another of his four types of "cause," or explanation, viz. the "final," or teleological. In *Physics* II 8 he mentions some central examples of purposive activity—housebuilding, doctoring, writing—and then by stages moves on to discerning comparable purposiveness in the behavior of spiders and ants, the growth of roots and leaves, the arrangement of the teeth. Again the process is one of weakening or discarding some of the conditions inherent in the original situations: the idea of purposiveness sheds its connection with those of having a skill and thinking out steps to an end (although Aristotle hopes to have it both ways, by representing natural sports and monsters as *mistakes*). The resultant "immanent teleology" moved his follower Theophrastus to protest at its thinness and facility, but its effectiveness as a heuristic device, particularly in biology, is beyond dispute.

It is worth noting that this tendency of Aristotle's to set out from some familiar situation, or rather from the most familiar and unpuzzling ways of describing such a situation, is something more than the general inclination of scientists to depend on "explanatory paradigms." Such paradigms in later science (e.g., classical mechanics) have commonly been limiting cases not encountered in common observation or discourse; Aristotle's choice of the familiar is a matter of dialectical method, presystematic by contrast with the finished science, but subject to rules of discussion which he was the first to codify. This, and not (as we shall see) any attempt to extrude mathematics from physics, is what separates his extant work in the field from the most characteristic achievements of the last four centuries. It had large consequences for dynamics. In replying to Zeno's paradox of the flying arrow he concedes Zeno's claim that nothing can be said to be moving at an instant, and insists only that it cannot be said to be stationary either. What preoccupies him is the requirement, embedded in common discourse, that any movement must take a certain time to cover a certain distance (and, as a corollary, that any stability must take a certain time but cover no distance); so he discounts even those hints that common discourse might have afforded of the derivative idea of motion, and therefore of velocity, at an instant. He has of course no such notion of a mathematical limit as the analysis of such cases requires, but in any event this notion came later than the recognition of the cases. It is illuminating to contrast the treatment of motion in the *Mechanica,* a work which used to carry Aristotle's name but which must be at least a generation later. There (*Mechanica* 1) circular motion is resolved into two components, one tangential and one centripetal (contrast Aristotle's refusal to assimilate circular and rectilinear movements, notably in *Physics* VII 4). And the remarkable suggestion is made that the proportion between these components need not be maintained for any time at all, since otherwise the motion would be in a straight line. Earlier the idea had been introduced of a point having motion and velocity, an idea that we shall find Aristotle using although his dialectical analysis of movement and location disallows it; here that idea is supplemented by the concept of a point having a given motion or complex of motions at an instant and not for any period, however small. The *Mechanica* is generally agreed to be a constructive development of hints and suggestions in Aristotle's writings; but the methods and purposes evident in his own discussions of motion inhibit him from such novel constructions in dynamics.

It is quite another thing to say, as is often said, that Aristotle wants to debar physics from any substantial use of the abstract proofs and constructions available to him in contemporary mathematics. It is a common fallacy that, whereas Plato had tried to make physics mathematical and quantitative, Aristotle aimed at keeping it qualitative.

Mathematics and Physics. Plato had tried to construct the physical world of two-dimensional and apparently weightless triangles. When Aristotle argues against this in the *De caelo* (III 7) he observes: "The principles of perceptible things must be perceptible, of eternal things eternal, of perishable things perishable: in sum, the principles must be homogeneous with the subject-matter." These words, taken together with his prescriptions for the autonomy of sciences in the *Analytics,* are often quoted to show that any use of mathematical constructions in his physics must be adventitious or presystematic, dispensable from the science proper. The province of physics is the class of natural bodies regarded as having weight (or "lightness," in the case of air and fire), heat, and color and an innate tendency to move in a certain way. But these are properties that mathematics expressly excludes from its purview (*Metaphysics* K 3).

In fact, however, the division of sciences is not so absolute. When Aristotle contrasts mathematics and physics in *Physics* II he remarks that astronomy, which is one of the "more physical of the mathematical sciences," must be part of physics, since it would be absurd to debar the physicist from discussing the geometrical properties of the heavenly bodies. The distinction is that the physicist must, as the mathematician does not, treat these properties as the attributes of physical bodies that they are; i.e., he must be prepared to explain the application of his model. Given this tie-line a good deal of mathematical abstraction is evidently permissible. Aristotle holds that only extended bodies can strictly be said to have a location (i.e., to lie within a static perimeter) or to move, but he is often prepared to discount the extension of bodies. Thus in *Physics* IV 11, where he shows an isomorphic correspondence between continua representing time, motion, and the path traversed by the moving body, he correlates the moving object with points in time and space and for this purpose calls it "a point—or stone, or any such thing." In *Physics* V 4, he similarly argues from the motion of an unextended object, although it is to be noticed that he does not here or anywhere ease the transition from moving bodies to moving points by importing the idea of a center of gravity, which was to play so large a part in Archimedes' *Equilibrium of Planes.* In his meteorology, explaining the shape of halos and rainbows, he treats the luminary as a point source of light. In the biological works he often recurs to the question of the number of points at which a given type of animal moves; these "points" are in fact the major joints, but in *De motu animalium* 1 he makes it clear that he has a geometrical model in mind and is careful to explain what supplementary assumptions are necessary to adapting this model to the actual situation it illustrates. In the cosmology of the *De caelo* he similarly makes use of unextended loci, in contrast to his formal account of any location as a perimeter enclosing a volume. Like Archimedes a century later, he represents the center of the universe as a point when he proves that the surface of water is spherical, and again when he argues that earth moves so as to make its own (geometrical) center ultimately coincide with that of the universe. His attempt in *De caelo* IV 3 to interpret this in terms of perimeter locations is correct by his own principles, but confused.

This readiness to import abstract mathematical arguments and constructions into his account of the physical world is one side of the coin whose other face is his insistence that any mathematics must be directly applicable to the world. Thus, after arguing (partly on dialectical grounds, partly from his hypothesis of natural movements and natural places) that the universe must be finite in size, he adds that this does not put the mathematicians out of business, since they do not need or use the notion of a line infinite in extension: what they require is only the possibility of producing a line n in any required ratio with a given line m, and however large the ratio n/m it can always be physically exemplified for a suitable interpretation of m. The explanation holds good for such lemmata as that applied in Eudoxus' method of exhaustion, but not of some proportionalities he himself adduces earlier in the same context or in *De caelo* I. (These proportionalities are indeed used in, but they are not the subject of, *reductio ad absurdum* arguments. In the *De caelo* Aristotle even assumes that an infinite rotating body would contain a point at an infinite distance from its center and consequently moving at infinite speed.) The same concern to make mathematics applicable to the physical world without postulating an actual infinite is evident in his treatment of the sequence of natural numbers. The infinity characteristic of the sequence, and generally of any countable series whose members can be correlated with the series of numbers, consists just in the possibility of specifying a successor to any member of the sequence: "the infinite is that of which, as it is counted or measured off, it is always possible to take some part outside that already taken." This is true not only of the number series but of the parts produced by dividing any magnitude in a constant ratio; and since all physical bodies are in principle so divisible, the number series is assured of a physical application without requiring the existence at any time of an actually infinite set of objects: all that is required is the possibility of following any division with a subdivision.

This positivistic approach is often evident in Aristotle's work (e.g., in his analysis of the location of *A* as the inner static boundary of the body surrounding *A*), and it is closely connected with his method of building explanations on the familiar case. But here too Aristotle moves beyond the familiar case when he argues that infinite divisibility is characteristic of bodies below the level of observation. His defense and exploration of such divisibility, as a defining characteristic of bodies and times and motions, is found in *Physics* VI, a book often saluted as his most original contribution to the analysis of the continuum. Yet it is worth noticing that in this book as in its two predecessors Aristotle's problems and the ideas he applies to their solution are over and again taken, with improvements, from the second part of Plato's *Parmenides.* The discussion is in that tradition of logical debate which Aristotle, like Plato, called "dialectic," and its problems are not those of accommodating theories to experimentally established facts (or vice versa) but logical puzzles generated by common discourse and conviction. (But then Aristotle thinks of common discourse and conviction as a repository of human experience.) So the argument illustrates Aristotle's anti-Platonic thesis that mathematics—represented again in this case by simple proportion theory—has standing as a science only to the extent that it can be directly applied to the description of physical phenomena. But the argument is no more framed as an advance in the mathematical theory itself than as a contribution to the observational data of physics.

Probably the best-known instance of an essentially mathematical construction incorporated into Aristotle's physics is the astronomical theory due to Eudoxus and improved by Callippus. In this theory the apparent motion of the "fixed stars" is represented by the rotation of one sphere about its diameter, while those of the sun, moon, and the five known planets are represented each by a different nest of concentric spheres. In such a nest the first sphere carries round a second whose poles are located on the first but with an axis inclined to that of the first; this second, rotating in turn about its poles, carries a third similarly connected to it, and so on in some cases to a fourth or (in Callippus' version) a fifth, the apparent motion of the heavenly body being the resultant motion of a point on the equator of the last sphere. To this set of abstract models, itself one of the five or six major advances in science, Aristotle makes additions of which the most important is the attempt to unify the separate nests of spheres into one connected physical system. To this end he intercalates reagent spheres designed to insulate the movement of each celestial body from the complex of motions propelling the body next above it. The only motion left uncanceled in this downward transmission is the rotation of the star sphere. It is generally agreed that Aristotle in *Metaphysics* XII 8 miscalculates the resulting number of agent and reagent spheres: he concludes that we need either fifty-five or forty-seven, the difference apparently representing one disagreement between the theories of Eudoxus and Callippus, but on the latest computation (that of Hanson) the figures should be sixty-six and forty-nine. The mistake had no effect on the progress of astronomy: within a century astronomers had turned to a theory involving epicycles, and Aristotle's physical structure of concentric nonoverlapping spheres was superseded. On the other hand his basic picture of the geocentric universe and its elements, once freed from the special constructions he borrowed and adapted from Eudoxus, retained its authority and can be seen again in the introductory chapters of Ptolemy's *Syntaxis.*

Conclusion. These arguments and theories in what came to be called the exact sciences are drawn principally from the *Posterior Analytics, Topics, Physics, De caelo* and *De generatione,* works that are generally accepted as early and of which the first four at least probably date substantially from Aristotle's years in the Academy or soon after. The influence of the Academy is strong on them. They are marked by a large respect for mathematics and particularly for the techniques and effects of axiomatizing that subject, but they do not pretend to any mathematical discoveries, and in this they are close in spirit to Plato's writings. Even the preoccupation with physical change, its varieties and regularities and causes, and the use of dialectic in analyzing these, is a position to which Plato had been approaching in his later years. Aristotle the meticulous empiricist, amassing biological data or compiling the constitutions of 158 Greek states, is not yet in evidence. In these works the analyses neither start from nor are closely controlled by fresh inspections of the physical world. Nor is he liable to think his analyses endangered by such inspections: if his account of motion shows that any "forced" or "unnatural" movement requires an agent of motion in constant touch with the moving body, the movement of a projectile can be explained by inventing a set of unseen agents to fill the gap—successive stages of the medium itself, supposed to be capable of transmitting movement even after the initial agency has ceased acting. In all the illustrative examples cited in these works there is nothing comparable to even the half-controlled experiments in atomistic physics and harmonics of the following centuries. His main concerns were the methodology of the sciences, which he was the first to separate adequately on grounds of field and method; and the meticulous derivation of the technical equipment of these sciences from the common language and assumptions of men about the world they live in. His influence on science stemmed from an incomparable cleverness and sensitiveness to counterarguments, rather than from any breakthrough comparable to those of Eudoxus or Archimedes.

BIBLIOGRAPHY

Aristotle is still quoted by reference to the page, column, and line of Vols. I, II of I. Bekker's Berlin Academy edition (1831–1870, recently repr.). The later texts published in the Oxford Classical Texts and in the Budé and Loeb series are generally reliable for the works quoted. The standard Oxford translation of the complete works with selected fragments occupies 12 volumes (1909–1952). The ancient commentaries are still among the best (*Commentaria in Aristotelem Graeca*, Berlin, 1882–1909). Of recent editions with commentaries pride of place goes to those by Sir David Ross of the *Metaphysics* (2nd ed., 1953), *Physics* (1936), *Analytics* (1949), *Parva naturalia* (1955), and *De anima* (1961). Others are T. Waitz, *Organon* (1844–1846); H. H. Joachim, *De generatione et corruptione* (1922).

Important modern works are W. Jaeger, *Aristotle* (2nd English ed., Oxford, 1948); W. D. Ross, *Aristotle* (4th ed., London, 1945). On the mathematics and physics, T. L. Heath, *Mathematics in Aristotle* (Oxford, 1949); P. Duhem, *Le système du monde*, I (Paris, 1913); H. Carteron, *La notion de force dans le système d'Aristote* (Paris, 1924); A. Mansion, *Introduction à la physique aristotélicienne* (2nd ed., Louvain–Paris, 1945); F. Solmsen, *Aristotle's System of the Physical World* (Ithaca, N.Y., 1960); W. Wieland, *Die aristotelische Physik* (Göttingen, 1962); I. Düring, *Aristoteles* (Heidelberg, 1966).

On the so-called laws of motion in Aristotle, I. Drabkin, *American Journal of Philology*, **59** (1938), pp. 60–84.

G. E. L. OWEN

ARISTOTLE: Natural History and Zoology.

It is not clear when Aristotle wrote his zoology, or how much of his natural history was his own work. This is unfortunate, for it might help us to interpret his philosophy if we knew whether he began theorizing in biology before or after his main philosophical formulations, and how many zoological specimens he himself collected and identified. Some believe that he began in youth, and that his theory of potentiality was directed originally at the problem of growth. Others (especially Jaeger) hold that his interest in factual research came late in life and that he turned to biology after founding the Lyceum. Most probably, however, it was in middle life, in the years 344–342 B.C., when he was living on Lesbos with Theophrastus; many of his data are reported from places in that area. This would imply that he wrote the zoology with his philosophical framework already established, and on the whole the internal evidence of the treatises bears this out. It follows that in order to understand his zoological theory, we must keep his philosophy in mind. Yet it may also be true that in thinking out his philosophy, he was conscious of biological problems in a general way.

The zoological treatises must represent many years' work, for they make up a fourth of the whole corpus, and both data and discussion are concisely presented. They owe little to Herodotus, Ctesias, Xenophon, or other extant literature; their possible debt to Democritus cannot be assessed, however, because his three zoological books are lost. Comparing the quality of Aristotle's data with previous writings, we must conclude that he sifted and rejected a great deal; even by modern standards of natural history his reports are cautious. The chief collection of data is the *Historia animalium*. Out of 560 species mentioned in all his zoology, 400 appear only in this work and only five are not included. The treatises, as we now have them, form a course of instruction in which the *Historia* is referred to as the descriptive textbook, intended to be studied first and then kept at hand. Internal evidence suggests, however, that it was in fact written after the others, and that most of it was not written by Aristotle himself. This implies that he wrote the theoretical treatises before the main collection of data. Not that the treatises lack supporting data, but most of the information was common knowledge, whereas the reports that read like new, firsthand observation are nearly all confined to the later parts of the *Historia.*

Biological data were normally quoted in cosmological arguments, not least in the Academy. The Academicians' interest was not so much in the animals for their own sake, but rather in using them as evidence for—and giving them a place within—a rational cosmology. There were two issues: to identify the formal groups of animals, and thus to classify them, and to explain their functioning as part of nature. Plato and Speusippus opposed the materialism of those like Democritus, whose lost books, entitled *Causes Concerning Animals,* were probably intended to explain biology in terms of atomism. Aristotle would have been familiar with these discussions since his youth, and his writings follow this essentially etiological approach. His earliest zoology is probably in the *De partibus animalium,* the *De incessu animalium,* and the *Parva naturalia* (all of which in their present form show signs of revision and editing), in which he sets out the "causes" of tissues and structures, and of such significant functions as locomotion, respiration, aging, and death. Here the a priori element in his theory appears strongly: for example, right is superior to left, and hence the right-hand side is the natural side to lead off with; organs properly exist in pairs, and hence the spleen (for which he found no function) exists as the partner of the liver. On the other hand, the teleological explanation, which is the main theme of *De partibus animalium,* is argued in a mature fashion with evidential support. This scientific maturity is even clearer in the next great treatise, *De generatione animalium,* in which he applies his concepts of form and matter, actuality and potentiality, to the problems of reproduction, inheritance, and growth of such inessential characters as color. On the question of classification he remains tentative and critical, as we would expect of one who rejected Plato's theory of Forms. He often returns to the problem in both early and late writings, but states no clear position.

His teleology differs from others. He argues it in *De partibus* I on the same grounds as in *Physics* B, where he states more of his opponents' case. He makes it clear that the "natural philosophers" (Empedocles, Anaxagoras, Democritus) were combating a popular teleology which presented the gods as purposive powers intervening in nature, so that "rain falls in order to make the crops grow." Against it they had argued that the "necessity" of natural causes was sufficient to explain events and that the crops happened to grow because the rain happened to fall, the real cause being the automatic interactions of the hot, the cold, and the other elements. In reply, Plato had posited a world soul and a creative "Demiurge." Aristotle, however, does not invoke a supernatural agency (for the relation between the cosmos and the Unmoved Mover is different), nor does he present nature as a quasi-conscious entity capable of purpose: his personification of nature "who does nothing in vain" is no more than a rhetorical abbreviation for "each natural substance." Neither does he posit an extra factor in nature, as modern teleologists posit a *conatus* that is not reducible to physics.

The directiveness that Aristotle sees in nature is part of the natural interactions, so that the teleological explanation coexists with the causal explanation. But he bases the teleology not primarily on directiveness but on the existence of forms. To explain an organ, he says, we must first grasp the complete animal's form and functions, what it means to be that animal, its *ousia.* Our explanation will include both the "necessary" causes and the "end" toward which development tends. This is not the temporal end or a state of equilibrium between phases of activity; indeed, it may never be reached. It is the perfect condition of the whole animal, "for the sake of which" each part develops. Thus, Empedocles was wrong to suppose that the spine is vertebrated because it gets bent: on the contrary, vertebration is necessary to the animal's functioning, and was contained potentially in the parent's seed before the embryo's vertebrae were formed. He was also wrong to think that random necessity could be a primary cause, for it could not produce the general regularity of nature, let alone the absolute regularity of the stars. Necessity in nature is secondary, or, as Aristotle calls it, "hypothetical": on the hypothesis that an animal is coming into existence, certain materials must interact, but these materials do not of themselves produce the animal any more than bricks produce a house. As the house needs a builder and a plan, the animal needs a soul and a form—factors ignored by the materialists. But whereas builder and plan are separate, soul and form are identical. The final cause of the animal is the actualization of its form, and its primary efficient cause is its soul, which "uses" the necessary movements of the materials. Aristotle's teleology therefore rests upon his theory of substantial form. The definition of a substance is logically prior to the definition of its parts, and so the final cause is prior to the necessary cause. It is prior temporally as well as logically, for Aristotle believed that the world never began—so that hen has forever preceded egg.

Although he used Plato's language ("existence is prior to coming-into-existence" and necessity is "the concomitant cause"), Aristotle did not follow Plato in positing an overall teleology or in the dualism that the *Timaeus* set up between creator and material. The few passages where Aristotle seems to imply that some species exist for the sake of man, or act for the general good as opposed to their own, cannot be meant literally. What he probably meant was a balance of nature, in which species are interdependent. The final cause of each animal is its own complete state, and nothing more. And instead of Plato's dualism, Aristotle places finality within natural interactions, not as something imposed upon them.

Within sublunary nature there are continual fresh beginnings of movement for which there are no sufficient external causes. They may be stimulated from outside, but the source of the movements in plants and animals is their souls. Only in a general way is the Unmoved Mover the prime cause. As a final and formal cause it presents the perfection that lesser beings desire to imitate. It can therefore be argued, although it is never clearly stated by Aristotle, that nature's tendency toward actualization and the *orexis* within souls are ultimately oriented toward the Unmoved Mover's perfection. As an efficient cause, the Unmoved Mover promotes general growth and decay on earth because it elicits the sun's movements in the ecliptic, and these movements cause the alternation of summer and winter. These general causes, however, do not bring about the particular starts of motion in nature. Nor, again, are souls regarded as separable entities that inhabit bodies and direct them, as Plato thought and as Aristotle may once have thought but later rejected. In his mature view, found in his biology as well as in the *Metaphysics* and *De anima,* the soul (except, possibly, for the intellect) is not an independent substance but is the form of the body. On the other hand, it is not merely a resultant form, as in the "harmonia" theory, which Aristotle refuted; rather, it is both form and source of action. In plants it causes growth and reproduction; in animals it also causes sensation (here he differs from Plato, who thought that plants had sensation); in man the soul has a third faculty, intellect, and this is its only faculty that is not the form of body and could therefore be separable.

The concept of soul as both form and efficient cause may reflect a trace of ancient hylozoism. In Aristotle's view, finality pervades nature. If there is a cosmos, this implies that the elements not only have simple motions but also combine with modified motions. Both the simple motions and their modifications are hypothetically necessary and are natural. An animal contains many motions, all natural, that by a natural coordination tend toward a specific pattern. Its soul is both the tendency and the pattern. In nonliving substances, which have no soul, the tendency to form complexes is in their nature. Aristotle accepts as his data both the observable materials and the observable forms and species; therefore the movement of nature is simultaneously necessitated and endlike.

According to the *Metaphysics,* the form toward which animals grow is their species: individual differences arise from matter and consequently are unknowable to science. In Aristotle's earlier zoology we cannot tell whether he maintains this strict view, but in *De generatione animalium* his theory of reproduction implies that individuals differ in form to some extent. He does not say so, but repeats the doctrine of *De generatione et corruptione* that sublunary beings, which cannot achieve eternity as individuals, instead achieve it as species by reproduction. Nevertheless, Aristotle's discussion is in fact about an individual's reproduction of another animal "like itself." He starts from the long-standing controversy about the origin of seed. Do both male and female contribute seed? From what part or parts of the body does it come, and what does it contain? He analyzes the problem in terms of form and matter. The male alone makes seed from his blood; it contains potentially the sensitive soul and the adult form, but actually it contains no bodily parts (here he ridicules preformism and pangenesis). The female contributes only material (the *catamenia*), whose form is nutritive soul. When the male's form has been imposed upon the female material, the somatic part of the seed is sloughed away: all that is transmitted is soul, the source of form and motion. If the fetus develops regularly, the father's form will be actualized; failing that, the mother's; failing that again, more distant ancestors successively, until eventually the form may be merely that of the species, or even just the genus *Animal* (that is, a monstrous birth).

This long and careful argument, which is supported by observed evidence, gives a brilliant impression of maturity and originality, and in several points goes beyond the biological arguments that we occasionally find in the philosophical works. Aristotle's view that the father's form is reproduced, as distinct from the species, can only mean that some individual differences are formal and apodictic. He also brings to scientific account other differences due to "necessity"—not only monstrous births but differences of coloration, voice, or sharpness of senses. Since he calls them "concomitants" arising from irregularities in the material, he may have regarded them as unpredictable, but they seem to be accountable after the event. He now argues not from the fixity of species but from the reproduction of forms. True, he does not contemplate the obsolescence or alteration of existing species (for he had no paleontology); but he does accept, within limits, the evidence for miscegenation's resulting in new forms. In fact, the emphasis on species becomes less, while the concept of necessity as hypothetical becomes more important and sophisticated than in the philosophical works, where necessity is either "simple" (axiomatic) or brute (material). The one exception among the biological works is the *Historia animalium,* from which the teleological explanation is absent. Although a discussion of causes is not to be expected here, nevertheless the account of characters and life histories involves some causal explanation; and it is noteworthy that this explanation is given only in material terms. No doubt this is because the *Historia* was mainly the work of Aristotle's successors, among whom Theophrastus ignores the final cause even in his *Causes of Plants.*

In explaining the "necessary" causes—the interaction of materials—Aristotle does not innovate so much as rationalize theories that were already current. He accepts from Plato's *Timaeus* the four elements—fire, air, water, and earth—that were common to the medical writers and can be traced back through Empedocles into popular tradition. But the tradition had confused two notions: the cosmic regions of fire, air, water, and earth, and the seasonal powers of hot, cold, wet, and dry. The two sets do not exactly match, as is obvious in the ambiguous reports of Empedocles. Aristotle systematizes them by means of a formula that survived through the Middle Ages, treating fire, air, water, and earth as combinations of hot, cold, wet, and dry: fire is hot plus dry, air is hot plus wet, and so on. In his system hot, cold, wet, and dry are the primitive qualities of matter, but cannot exist in isolation. Fire, air, water, and earth are the simplest separable bodies, and are transformable into each other.

Like his predecessors, Aristotle regards the hot as the chief active power; its characteristic action is *pepsis* ("concoction"), which transforms food into blood and blood into flesh. By its opposite, the cold, he sometimes means merely the absence of hot, but more often a power in itself. The hot means more than temperature, which he calls "the hot according to touch." Another sort of hot is that possessed by pine wood, which is not hotter to the touch than other timber but contains more heat and therefore burns better. Animals have an innate heat upon which life depends. Their droppings still contain some of it, which generates flies. While the hot is the soul's chief agent in bringing about growth, cold is also needed to solidify things. Like the medical writers, Aristotle attaches importance to the due mingling (*krasis*) of hot and cold; which does not mean a point on a temperature scale but a mixture of two powers. He follows them in extending this notion to a general "right proportion" (*symmetria*) necessary for growth and health.

The other elements—the wet or watery, and the dry or earthy—are needed to provide the fluid and the solid parts of plants and animals. Whether Aristotle really intended a fifth element, *pneuma,* is debatable. The notion was current, and soon after him it became the chief element for the Pneumatic school of medicine and the Stoics. Aristotle had his own fifth substance in the outer heaven, the *aither,* and in *De generatione animalium* he compares it with the bodily *pneuma: pneuma* is the material of the animal seed, and conveys soul and the generative warmth, which he says is different from other heat. Yet he defines *pneuma* merely as warmed air, and since warmth has various powers for him, it is probable that he means no more. So he explains spontaneous generation by the presence of a warm soul-source in the materials.

The four elements combine to form the tissues, which Aristotle calls "made of like parts" (as flesh is divisible into flesh); and the tissues form the organs, which are "made of unlike parts" (hand is not divisible into hands). Taking this distinction from Plato, he uses it in finding homologies, but he makes only general statements about the processes. The hot concocts blood into flesh here, fat there, marrow or seed somewhere else; skin, hair, bone, nails, and horn all come from the earthy. He does not explain how. Medical literature of the time contains some practical investigations, such as the action of heat upon blood, and Aristotle occasionally refers to such evidence. In *Meteorologica* IV he goes further and analyzes the actions of hot and cold into evaporating, emulsifying, dissolving, condensing, and coagulating, and differentiates many types of earthy material. But this is a late work, and may not even be his. It seems, therefore, that in his biology Aristotle is content to take these theories in a general form from current tradition, although he is careful to rationalize them. For example, he will not allow Empedocles to say that spontaneous generation results from rottenness: new life comes not from disintegration but from concoction. The heart—not the brain, as many held—is the center of sensation and of the soul's motor impulses; as the first part to develop (observed in daily openings of a clutch of eggs), it is the source of the vital heat and innate *pneuma.* In it the blood is pneumatized and then flows out to nourish the tissues. (The distinction between arteries and veins is post-Aristotelian.) The lungs admit air to replenish the *pneuma* and to moderate the heat, an excess of which brings on senescence and death. Animals without lungs are cooled by the surrounding air or water: this suffices because they are "less perfect" and therefore cooler; also, their innate store of *pneuma* is sufficient.

Classification of animals remained a difficulty, and Aristotle suggested a solution by taking an animal's vital heat as an index of its superiority. Plato had proposed *diaeresis* (division), in which a major group is progressively divided by differentiae into genera and species. This method, used by Aristotle in his early logic and later by his successors, became the basis of Linnaean systematics. In his zoology, however, Aristotle criticizes it for splitting natural groups. He shows how groupings based on habitat and locomotion, and such characters as horns and rumination, cut across each other, while many animals belong to both sides of a formal division. He also criticizes the emphasis on morphology, which he holds subordinate to function. He prefers to start from the natural genus, as defined by multiple characters, then to arrange it with other types, not in a genus-species hierarchy but in a *scala naturae* ranging from man through less perfect animals down through plants to lifeless compounds. In this he emphasizes the continuity of nature and the many borderline or overlapping types, such as the seal, the bat, and the testaceans. The degree of vital heat is indicated by method of reproduction, state at birth, respiration, posture, and other signs. But he does not produce an actual scheme, nor does he finally reject genus-species classification. For practical purposes Aristotle discusses the animals by major groups: the "blooded" (i.e., red-blooded)—man, viviparous quadrupeds, oviparous quadrupeds, cetaceans, fishes, birds; and the "bloodless"—mollusks, crustaceans, testaceans, and insects. But he points out that even these groups exclude many types, such as snakes and sponges. In fact, before any classification could succeed, far more information was needed. He may have felt this, for the *Historia animalium* was begun as a comparative study of characters, arranged under the headings *parts, activities, lives, dispositions* (i.e., psychology). Major groups were to be compared by "analogy" (as wing to fin), while within a group each structure would vary by "the more and the less" (as wings are longer or shorter).

This project, however, was not carried through; instead, the treatise became a running collection of data. As new information came in and new significant characteristics were distinguished, they were inserted at convenient places, as if into a filing cabinet. Book I gives a program of the characters to be discussed, and by comparing this with the later books, we can see that many of those proposed are never mentioned again while many more new characters come to be recognized, so much so that the whole plan of the treatise is altered. The latest additions, which can be identified in all books from the second onward, consist of dossiers or even complete descriptions of single animals, no doubt awaiting breakdown under appropriate character headings. Thus the work eventually begins to approximate a descriptive zoology, and this is how it has been taken ever since. But in judging Aristotle as a natural historian, we should remember that we are judging him as something that he never set out to be. Although the classificatory intention of the *Historia animalium* came to nothing, it remained essentially an analysis of differentiae, the ways in which animals "are like to and different from each other," in the words of the introduction. The data about animals are put there to illustrate characteristic differences, and except in the late and unassimilated additions there is no description of an animal for its own sake. The statements about a given animal are spread through the nine books of the treatise, which is arranged not by animals but by characters. It has repeated signposts helping the reader to find his way among characters, but there are none to help him find animals, and there is no index. Some animals are cited frequently to illustrate but one point—for example, the mole's blindness: Aristotle obviously examined the mole, for he describes a dissection of its concealed eyes, which is of great interest; but this is all he tells us of the mole. In fact, like all his treatises, the *Historia animalium* is a theoretical study. It is not so much about animals as about *Animal*—and the various ways it is differentiated in nature.

Aristotle names about 500 "kinds" of animals. Some of these comprise several varieties, which his reports sometimes distinguish but sometimes confuse. Altogether, between 550 and 600 species can be distinguished, and of these as many as 200 are mentioned in connection with only one character. He includes some thirty from such distant places as Libya, Ethiopia, the Red Sea, and even India. A very few are taken from travelers' tales, especially from Herodotus and Ctesias, and of these some are fabulous—for example, the flying snake and the martichoras, or manticore (a monster, perhaps derived from a garbled account of the Indian tiger, which became a favorite of the Middle Ages), of which he plainly indicates his suspicion. But most were to be seen in Greece in menageries and shows—certainly the bear, monkeys and apes, elephant, camel, and lion. Aristotle gives much information about all of these, for the very reason that they exhibited interesting differences. Some information is evidently hearsay: for example, he reports that the lion has no

ARISTOTLE

cervical vertebrae, which shows that he never examined a dead lion. But his remarks about the lion's appearance and gait show equally that he observed it in life. He describes the elephant's leg joints in order to contradict a popular belief that it sleeps standing against a tree.

However, the great majority of Aristotle's reports concern animals native to Greece, its islands, and the Greek colonies in Asia Minor. It is incorrect to accuse him of showing more interest in exotics than in what was at his own doorstep. If we compare the variety of information given on each animal, we find not only that the nearest animals are the most fully reported but also that he covers most of what was available to him. Among mammals, of which he mentions some eighty, by far the most information is given about the horse, dog, sheep, ox, and pig; next comes a group including the goat, donkey, mule, hare, deer, elephant, bear, camel, seal, and dolphin. Of 180 birds mentioned, the best-reported are the domestic fowl, the pigeons, and the partridge, and there is a good deal on the sparrow, swallow, blackbird, crows, larks, eagles, hawks, quail, and stork. On the other hand, over 100 birds are mentioned only once or twice, as examples of differences in feeding or nesting, and so on. The information on marine animals is especially good, although out of 130 fishes only twenty are cited in connection with more than a very few characters. Among over eighty insects, he gives considerable information about the flies, ants, wasps, and cicadas, and three long, separate discussions of the honeybee; there is a fair amount about the grasshoppers, gadflies, spiders, beetles, and chafers. It is true that he has relatively little on the gnats and mosquitoes, common though they were; but he reports their external structures, reproduction from larvae, feeding, and habitat—and there is, after all, little more that he could know, having no optical apparatus. Aristotle often complains that the smallness of some insects makes it impossible to discern their structures, especially the internal ones. Many features, in all groups of animals, are reported in a generalized form—"all two-winged insects have a proboscis and no rearward sting," "all fishes except selachians have gill covers"—so that if one is to assess what he knew about a given animal, these general statements have to be broken down and included. In some of them he generalizes further than the facts warrant, through faulty or deficient information.

The tests that Aristotle applies to reports are primarily observational checks, made either on the same type of animal or on "analogous" types. He shows himself well aware of the need for repeated observations, but he has not developed the refined technique of provoked and controlled observations that later (very much later) scientists learned to demand. Where observational checks are not available, he tests by inherent probability—that is, by reference to theory. The accusation that he relies on a priori argument, and not on observation, is not well founded; on the contrary, like most Greek philosophers, with the exception of Plato, he is overready to accept uncontrolled observation and to jump to large conclusions.

His chief sources of information are fishermen, farmers, stockbreeders, and hunters; to a lesser extent travelers, menageries, augurs, and drug manufacturers; and he owes a very little to such previous writers as Herodotus, Ctesias, Xenophon, Empedocles, and Democritus. There are many faulty reports that he corrects from observation. His favorite method is the counterinstance. He refutes a report that the viper does not slough its skin simply by describing an observation of the sloughing. The legend that the hyena has the genitalia of both sexes (which in fact it can appear to have externally) is refuted by inspection and dissection, and here he indicates that many specimens were examined. Fishermen said that all mullets are generated spontaneously, but he has examples of mullets with eggs ~~and~~ with sperm (although he allows that one kind of mullet is spontaneous).

Where such direct checks are not possible, he refers to analogous examples or to theory. He denies that the cuckoo is a metamorphosed hawk on the grounds that the hawk preys on the cuckoo, a thing never seen done by one bird to another of its own kind. Fishermen believed what Herodotus also said, that fishes are impregnated by swallowing the sperm; Aristotle denies this because there is no connection between stomach and uterus, and because fishes have been observed in coition—which, he remarks, is difficult to observe, and fishermen have missed it because they are not interested in acquiring knowledge. Here he has been misled by faulty observation that, unluckily, agreed with theory—a coincidence that accounts for many of the mistakes in his reports. He held that where there are separate male and female, there must be coition. He knew that the male fish sprinkles the eggs with sperm after spawning, but thought this an additional process of fertilization. Another famous example is the fishermen's report of hectocotylization—the extraordinary method by which a sperm-carrying tentacle is inserted into the female's mantle cavity and then completely detached from the male (eventually proved true): Aristotle denies that the tentacle assists reproduction, because it is not connected with the body and the spermatic channel—he was wrong because his theory could not accommodate what is, after all, a surprising fact. But in another context he makes it clear that theory must always yield to reliable observation: after his long discussion of the reproduction of bees he makes a statement that fairly represents his own practice (*De generatione animalium* 760b27):

> This, then, appears to be the method of reproduction of bees, according to theory together with the apparent facts. But the facts have not been satisfactorily ascertained, and if ever they are, then credence must be given to observation rather than to theory, and to theory only in so far as it agrees with what is observed.

Many of the reports, however, are from firsthand observation. He refers sometimes to "the dissections," evidently a collection of drawings and diagrams of internal organs; unfortunately nothing survives of them. Some of his data clearly come from deliberate dissection, while others come as clearly from casual observations in the kitchen or at augury. One of the best is a full-scale vivisection of a chameleon; and the internal organs of crabs, lobsters, cephalopods, and several fishes and birds are described from direct observation. Many of the exterior observations also presuppose a prolonged study. He speaks of lengthy investigations into the pairing of insects. He satisfies himself that birds produce wind eggs entirely in the absence of the cock. There are graphic accounts of courtship behavior, nest-building, and brood care. He records tests for sense perception in scallops, razor fish, and sponges. He watches the cuttlefish anchor itself to a rock by its two long arms when it is stormy. The detailing of structures in some crustaceans and shellfishes vividly suggests that the author is looking at the animal as he dictates. The sea urchin's mouth parts are still known as "Aristotle's lantern" from his description, and his statement that its eggs are larger at the full moon has only recently been confirmed for the Red Sea urchin. He is able to assert that two kinds of *Serranidae* are "always female" (they are in fact hermaphrodite). All such data require deliberate and patient observation. How much Aristotle himself did is not known, but it is clear enough that he caused reports to be collected and screened with great care.

The first main heading in the *Historia animalium* is "Parts of the Body." Aristotle methodically lists the external and internal structures, noting the significant differences between animal types. Through drawing an analogy between legs and fins, he holds that fishes are moved primarily by their fins; this error creates difficulties for his theory of locomotion, whereby the blooded animals are moved by two or four points and the bloodless by more than four. He classifies the forms of uterus by position: rearward and ventral in the viviparous quadrupeds, forward and dorsal in the birds and oviparous quadrupeds, rearward and dorsal in the oviparous fishes, and "in both ways" in the ovoviviparous fishes—that is, extending from a forward dorsal to a rearward ventral position, because they first produce eggs and then hatch them within the uterus. There are various mistakes, mostly concerning man (where dissection was impossible) or the rarer animals. He is prone to accept them when they fall in with theory, thus accepting that men have more sutures in the skull than women (possibly based on an unlucky observation of a female skull with sutures effaced in pregnancy), for it fits his theory that men need more heat regulation in the brain. He reports that if one blows down the windpipe, the air reaches the heart: again a faulty observation that agreed with theory (that the *pneuma* in the heart is replenished from the lungs). His account of the heart's three intercommunicating chambers, disastrous for later anatomy, was due to wrong observation in a difficult field, but it fell conveniently into his theory of the blood system.

Nevertheless, Aristotle is aware how easily observations can mislead. For example, he remarks that those who believed the lungs to be devoid of blood were misled by observing dissected animals from which the blood had escaped. Much of what he says of the lion is mistaken, as is his statement that the crocodile moves the upper jaw: in these cases external appearances have not been tested by inspection of the dead body. Some could have been better tested—for example, his reports of the incidence of the gall bladder are unreliable, probably because he trusted the augurs. But the great majority of data in this section are accurate and shrewdly observed, especially the details of alimentary canal and reproductive organs, in which he took special theoretical interest.

Under "Lives and Activities" Aristotle compares differences in reproduction, feeding, migration, hibernation, and sloughing, and variations due to season, breeding, disease, age, and habitat. His theory of reproduction, applied to all groups of animals, is argued in *De generatione animalium;* the *Historia animalium* summarizes this and adds much more information about sexual behavior, breeding methods and seasons, gestation, incubation, and brood care. He distinguishes the viviparous quadrupeds theoretically by the degree of perfection in the young at birth, and he has many details of seal and dolphin as well as land animals. The next step down is to the ovoviviparous, such as the vipers, sharks, and dogfishes. In them he describes the egg's development and its movement rearward to the position where the young are released within the uterus; in one dogfish

(*Mustelus laevis*) he notes the placentoid structure, like that of mammals, which was not rediscovered until comparatively modern times. He mistakenly generalizes that all cartilaginous fishes are ovoviviparous. He divides the ovipara into those that lay perfected eggs (birds and quadrupeds) and those whose eggs develop after laying, requiring what he took to be a second fertilizing by the male. He describes minutely the development of the eggs of birds, fishes, cephalopods, and others by opening eggs at intervals during the whole incubation period. He records many special cases: for example, the way that *Syngnathus acus* carries its eggs in a pouch, which then splits to release them (although he does not observe that it is the male which carries them). The lowest mode of reproduction in his scale of "perfectedness" is spontaneous generation, which he attributes to all testaceans, many insects, the eel, and a few fishes. He describes the spawn of whelks, but judges it to be a budding-off comparable with that of plants, not a mass of eggs; otherwise, testaceans originate from various mixtures of mud and rotting substances, the type of animal being determined by the mixture. He considers that insects (except for one butterfly) produce grubs, not eggs; although one speaks of spiders' or bees' eggs, and so on, he says that what at first looks like an egg is really a motionless larva, on the (mistaken) grounds that the subsequent animal is formed out of the whole of it. The grubs of spiders, bees, cicadas, and others develop into the parental type, but those of flies and beetles do not develop further, and originate spontaneously from a variety of materials, which he lists. Gnats and mosquitoes do not even produce grubs, but themselves arise from grubs that are spontaneously generated. He describes many types of larval development through pupa to imago, including the change of the bloodworm into the gnat. His conclusion about the honeybee (which he says is a puzzle) is tentatively that the queen produces queens and workers, the workers produce the drones, and the drones produce nothing. His view here is not exactly parthenogenesis: he holds that bees contain both male and female principles, and therefore generate without coition.

The final section on "Characters," that is, animal psychology and intelligence, contains little imputation of motives: he records strictly the observed behavior. He compares animals in compatibility, rivalry, nesting and homemaking, and miscellaneous habits of defense and self-support. Among many, for example, he reports the nests made by the octopus and the wrasse, and the brood care by the male river catfish—recently rediscovered and named after him (*Parasilurus aristotelis*). He notes that the partridge makes two nests, on one of which the male sits; and his report that some partridges cackle and others whistle led to the discovery in 1962 that two populations (rock partridge and chukar) live side by side in Thrace. Among the honeybee's habits he seems to refer to the "dance language." The section is unfinished, and the treatise in its present form ends abruptly with a distinction between birds that take dust baths and those that take water baths.

The more complete descriptions, which have been inserted throughout the treatise and seem to be the latest additions, include those of the ape, chameleon, and wryneck, and extracts from Herodotus and Ctesias on the crocodile, hippopotamus, and martichoras. But most of the fabulous or unauthenticated reports are in a separate work called *Mirabilia,* where they were perhaps held awaiting corroboration: some of them—for example, the bison—are in both treatises. For entirely new animals, Aristotle no doubt required reliable eyewitnesses. But when it comes to details reported of known animals, which is the subject matter of most of his reports, his first point of reference is the adult living animal in its natural environment. His standard of judgment is function rather than morphology, as he makes clear in *De partibus animalium.* The "analogies" that he seeks, and from which he constantly argues, are not structural but functional; and, wherever possible, his identification of differentiae is based on function. Because this is his aim in the *Historia,* he picks out the significant details better, for instance, than does Xenophon (whose excellent accounts of the hare and of horses provide the best contemporary comparison with Aristotle's reports). Its change of plan and lack of revision make the treatise seem incoherent and bewildering, but its comprehensiveness and acumen made it the outstanding descriptive zoology of ancient times, even though it was not intended to be primarily descriptive. It outlasted the work of such later encyclopedic compilers as Pliny, and combined with Aristotle's other zoological works it became—through the Arabic version translated into Latin by Michael Scot—the major ingredient in Albertus Magnus' *De animalibus,* which dominated the field until the sixteenth century.

BIBLIOGRAPHY

The standard text is Bekker's *Corpus Aristotelicum* with Latin trans. (Berlin, 1831–1870). There is also the text with English trans., intro., and brief notes in the Loeb Classical Library; see especially A. L. Peck's eds. of *De partibus animalium* (rev. 1955), *De generatione animalium* (rev.

1953), and *Historia animalium,* I (1965; remaining 2 vols. in press). *Parva naturalia* was ed. with full English commentary by W. D. Ross (Oxford, 1955). The Loeb and Ross eds. contain bibliographies of previous eds. and full accounts of the MSS.

There are also lesser works with zoological content included in the Bekker ed., but not all are by Aristotle—*De incessu animalium, De motu animalium, De spiritu, Mirabilia,* and *Problemata.* See also *The Works of Aristotle Translated Into English,* W. D. Ross, ed.: III, *De spiritu* (1931); V, *De incessu animalium* and *De motu animalium* (1912); VI, *Mirabilia* (1913); and VII, *Problemata* (1927).

D. M. BALME

ARISTOTLE: Anatomy and Physiology.

In his discussion of animals Aristotle gives great importance to the heart, the blood vessels, and the blood, making the possession of blood the basis for distinguishing one great class of animals, those with blood, from those without blood (roughly the vertebrates and invertebrates). In giving this fundamental position to the heart and blood Aristotle departs from the physiological ideas of the Hippocratic writers; in doing so he seems to have been influenced by the ideas of the Italo-Sicilian-Greek medical thinkers. The stopping of the heartbeat was a certain sign of death and thereafter the body rapidly cooled and became stiff and lifeless. In the developing chick Aristotle saw the beating heart as the first manifestation of life. From this beating heart he saw blood vessels grow out over the yolk, and within the skein of blood vessels thus formed, the body of the young chick gradually emerged. Aristotle emphasized that the heart is the center and the origin of all the blood vessels. He considered that the blood was formed in the heart and passed out from it, because from the moment that the heart became visible it was seen to contain blood and as the network of blood vessels spread out from it, in the embryo chick, the blood accompanied them.

Since the heart, blood, and blood vessels were so fundamental to the bodies of animals Aristotle undertook to discuss them first in his *Historia animalium.* Possibly because of his belief in their fundamental importance he gave one of the earliest accurate descriptions of the blood vessels as a system extending throughout the body, but with its center in the heart. References to the blood vessels by Greek writers before Aristotle emphasized superficial veins, most easily visible in emaciated men, which might be used in bloodletting. Their accounts of the internal arrangement of the blood vessels were extremely vague and fragmentary. By his full and accurate account of the cardiovascular system Aristotle may be considered a founder of detailed anatomical study.

The basis for Aristotle's success in the dissection of the blood vessels was that instead of stunning the animal and bleeding it, in the manner of butchers, he first allowed it to starve to emaciation and then strangled it, thereby retaining in the dead animal all of the blood within the blood vessels. This treatment of the animal had, however, certain physiological consequences which were to influence the character of his observations. The animal killed by strangulation dies in a state of shock which produces a constriction of the small arteries and arterioles in the lungs, thereby cutting off the supply of blood to the left side of the heart. The left ventricle of the heart contracts to empty itself of blood and cannot be refilled. Moreover, the elastic muscle walls of the arterial system contract to squeeze the blood they contain through the capillaries into the veins. Almost all the blood in the body, therefore, accumulates in the venous system, leaving the left side of the heart and the arteries nearly empty. The right side of the heart, on the other hand, is enormously swollen and engorged with blood. When the heart relaxes in death the pressure of blood in the veins will keep open the right auriculoventricular aperture. The flaps of the tricuspid valve will be pressed back against the wall of the ventricle and will be relatively inconspicuous. As a result of these circumstances the right auricle and ventricle will appear as one large chamber continuous with the superior and inferior venae cavae. Instead of four cavities, the heart will appear to have only three, the largest of which will be the united right auricle and ventricle, while the two others will be the left ventricle and the left auricle. Thus to Aristotle the vena cava or "great blood vessel" appeared as a single continuous vessel that broadened in the heart "as a river that widens out in a lake" (*Historia animalium* 513b5, Thompson, trans.). The aorta he saw arising from the middle chamber of the heart and noted that it was more sinewy than the "great blood vessel."

Aristotle did not distinguish between arteries and veins and applied the same term, *phleps* (φλεψ), to both. Neither did he describe the heart valves. He saw the pulmonary artery extending from the "largest chamber on the right" (the right ventricle) upward toward the lung, and he described how in the lung the branches of the pulmonary artery are distributed throughout its flesh and everywhere lie alongside the branches of the tubes (bronchioles) that extend from the windpipe. He traced the main branches of both the venous and arterial systems and described the blood vessels, at least in outline, as a system coextensive with the body, having a shape "like a sketch of a manikin" (*ibid.,* 515a34–515b2).

Aristotle interpreted the pulsation of the heart as the result of a kind of boiling movement in the blood which caused it to press against the walls of the heart and to pour out into the blood vessels. The heart walls were thick in order to contain the innate heat generated in it and the heat of the heart produced respiration by causing the lungs to expand and cool air to rush in. The entering air cooled the lungs so that they again subsided and the air, warmed now by the heat taken up from the blood, was expired. Thus for Aristotle respiration served the purpose of cooling and moderating the heat of the blood and the heart.

Aristotle considered the brain to be cold and to exert a cooling influence on the body in opposition to the heating influence of the heart. Since he did not know of the existence of the nervous system as a system extending throughout the body in a manner similar to the blood vessels, he could not conceive of the brain as having the same kind of central role as the heart.

BIBLIOGRAPHY

See T. H. Huxley, "On Certain Errors Respecting the Heart Attributed to Aristotle," in *Nature*, **21** (1880), 1-5; William Ogle's note to 667b in his translation of Aristotle, *De partibus animalium* (Oxford, 1910); and Arthur Platt, "Aristotle on the Heart," in C. Singer, *Studies in the History and Method of Science*, 2 vols. (Oxford, 1921), II, 520-532.

LEONARD G. WILSON

ARISTOTLE: Tradition and Influence.

An account of the Aristotelian tradition would cover, without any interruption, the whole of the intellectual history of the Western world and, in recent times, of other areas as well. On the other hand, the influence of Aristotle's works and doctrines on the cultural developments of civilization is, in most fields, elusive and undefinable. Especially in the province of science—if we use "science" in the stricter, modern sense—it may be found that Aristotle's influence is very limited, or effective only in the sense that mistakes, eliciting opposition, criticism, and new solutions to old and new problems, are the starting point of scientific progress. Positive influence and starting points for positive developments are found, for the different sciences, much more frequently in the works of Euclid and Ptolemy; of Hippocrates and Galen; of Archimedes; of al-Fārābī, Ibn Sīnā (Avicenna), and Ibn Rushd (Averroës); possibly of Boethius; and, back through Boethius, of Nicomachus of Gerasa.

Still, there are two aspects in this progress that bear the Aristotelian imprint and justify an extensive account of the spread of Aristotle's works and of their study: the methodical aspect and the conceptual-linguistic aspect. These two cannot always be separated, but they must not be confused if Aristotle's influence is to be clearly seen and properly assessed. This section will, therefore, be devoted first and foremost to such an account. We shall then consider a set of concepts and words that became essential for the elaboration of scientific problems and, indeed, for making scientific discoveries clearly expressible and understandable in the technical and, at the same time, the common language. Some exemplification will be given of the methodical aspect, insofar as it can be traced back to Aristotle's influence, and of the actual contributions derived from his works, mainly by discussion, rejection, and positive substitution of anti-Aristotelian views. In this connection it must be recorded that a very limited amount of the literature that developed around the works of Aristotle in later antiquity, in the Middle Ages, and even into the eighteenth century has been properly edited, much less has been critically read, and only a minimal proportion of it has been examined from the point of view that interests us here.

The transmission and spread of Aristotle's works can best be followed by considering the different languages or groups of languages in which it took place: basic, of course, was the Greek tradition, from which all others sprang, directly or indirectly (fourth century B.C. to our times); most important and permanent in value was the Latin (fourth century A.D. to sixteenth and seventeenth centuries); very influential, especially through elaborations and translations into Latin, was the Semitic (first Syriac, then [and mainly] Arabic, finally Hebrew [fifth century A.D. to sixteenth century]); only occasionally effective in its own right and more valuable as a help in the rebirth of the study of Greek civilization was the tradition in German, Neo-Latin, English, and, more recently, many other modern languages (tenth century to our times); limited to very narrow cultural units was the Armenian and possibly the Georgian (*ca.* fifth century A.D. to tenth century and later).

The Transmission of Aristotle's Works in Greek. Compared with the impact of what constitutes the traditional Aristotelian corpus, typically represented by the Berlin Academy edition of 1835, the influence of the other works of Aristotle—preserved, if at all, in a number of more or less extensive fragments—can be considered negligible; we cannot pursue their tradition here. The corpus, based mainly, it seems, on lectures, preparations for lectures, accounts of lectures, and elaboration of collected material (*De animalibus*), must have begun to be organized in

Aristotle's own time, by Aristotle himself and his pupils (Theophrastus, Eudemus, and others). The process continued in his school, with vicissitudes, for 250 years after his death. The quasi-final organization of Aristotle's available material seems to have been accomplished by Andronicus of Rhodes (*ca.* 70 B.C.). It may be assumed that from Andronicus' edition there derived, with minor changes and developments, the transmitted texts as we know them in Greek. From Andronicus to the middle of the sixth century, the spread of the corpus or parts of it is continuously testified by the activities in the several philosophical schools, whether mainly Peripatetic in character, or eclectic, or more purely Neoplatonic. Andronicus' pupil Boëthus of Sidon commented on Aristotle's works, making the *Physics* the basis of Aristotelian philosophy; a century after, Nicholas of Damascus expounded Aristotle's philosophy and wrote (in the mood of Aristotle's *De animalibus*) a *De plantis,* which came to be ascribed to Aristotle; and *ca.* A.D. 100, Ptolemy Chennos of Alexandria wrote a work on the life and works of Aristotle. In the second half of the second century A.D., Galen, famous for his medical work, was a critical popularizer of Aristotle's logic, physics, and metaphysics, and many other authors commented on this or that work.

The texts of Aristotle were, obviously, already popular over a wide area. When, *ca.* A.D. 200, Alexander of Aphrodisias became professor of philosophy in Athens, as a "second Aristotle," he commented upon a large proportion of the corpus and left in his works abundant evidence of the variety of readings that had been infiltrating the nearly 300-year-old transmission of the basic edition. Although only minor fragments of papyri containing Aristotle's texts from the corpus and no manuscript older than the ninth century exist, the expanding study of the works in Athens, Constantinople, Alexandria, and Pergamum justifies the statement that many manuscripts were available in many centers. The sixth century adds new evidence, since, at least in the case of some logical works, we possess not only the quotations of many Greek commentators but also the literal translations into Latin, Syriac, and Armenian: these testify to the variety of the Greek tradition, a variety that continued and became more complicated in later centuries.

The ban on pagan schools in 529 led to a reduction, if not to a halt, in the production of Greek copies of the works of Aristotle until the revival of the late eighth and ninth centuries. Then really "critical" editions of some works, and transcriptions of many, if not all, started again. The University of Constantinople became a center of studies of some of these works; the old libraries still possessed among them at least one copy of each of the writings of Aristotle. And it is possible to surmise that in form (some of them were rich in scholia extracted from the old commentaries) they were like the manuscripts of the sixth or earlier centuries. The number of extant manuscripts of the ninth and tenth centuries is very small, and does not cover the whole corpus; but the stronger revival of the eleventh century was the beginning of the uninterrupted transcription and transmission of the more popular works. This gathered momentum, not only in Constantinople but also in the numerous centers where lay and theological schools were flourishing.

By the thirteenth and fourteenth centuries publication had expanded to such an extent that about 150 manuscripts from that period still survive. There are only a few exceptions to show that not all of Aristotle was dominating the higher philosophical studies, side by side with Plato: the *Politics,* unearthed perhaps in the eleventh century and turned into a fruitful career by the Latin translator William of Moerbeke, does not appear in our collections in any manuscript older than the thirteenth century. The *Poetics* appears in late manuscripts, except for one of the eleventh century and one of the thirteenth. But the bigger collections, especially of the logical works, are relatively numerous. A new impetus to the dissemination was given in the fifteenth century by the migration of scholars from the Greek world to Italy and by the interest in Greek studies in Florence, Venice, and other cities. In the fifteenth century the number of copies of the several parts of the corpus, including the rarest works, multiplied, and the way was prepared for the printed editions, from the Aldine of 1495–1498 to those of the seventeenth century. There was then about a century of interruption: Aristotle was "out" from most points of view. By the end of the eighteenth century the new interests of learning brought about the new wave of Greek editions of Aristotle—a process that is still in full swing.

The Transmission of Aristotle's Works in Latin. No evidence has come to light to show that any work by Aristotle or any extensive paraphrase was available in Latin before *ca.* A.D. 350. Cicero's claim that his *Topica* was based directly on Aristotle's work of the same title is false. His model was the work of a rhetorician, not of a logician, and bears only vague, occasional, accidental resemblances to what Aristotle wrote. The latinization of Aristotle took place through different channels: by far the most important was the direct translation from the Greek originals; second in importance was the translation of Greek paraphrases and commentaries; third, the translation of

ARISTOTLE

some of Aristotle's works from direct or indirect Arabic versions, whether alone or accompanied by Arabic commentaries; fourth, the versions of Arabic works based, in various measure, on Aristotelian texts; finally, some translations from the Hebrew renderings of Arabic versions, commentaries, and paraphrases. All this happened in the course of four identifiable stages, very different in length, between the middle of the fourth century and the end of the sixteenth: (*a*) the first stage probably lasted only a few years and involved a few individuals belonging to two groups working in Rome; (*b*) the second corresponds to a few years in the first quarter or first half of the sixth century, with Boethius as the only person concerned with this activity in Italy, and possibly some minor contributors in Constantinople; (*c*) the third stage covers about 150 years, from *ca.* 1130 to *ca.* 1280, when the work was carried out probably in Constantinople and certainly in Sicily, Italy, Spain, Greece, England, and France by at least a score of people of many nationalities and callings—by the end of this period the whole of the Aristotelian corpus as it has reached us in Greek, with very minor exceptions, could be read and studied in Latin; (*d*) the fourth stage extended from shortly after 1400 to *ca.* 1590. Only in the third stage did the Arabic tradition contribute directly to the Latin one; and only in the fourth did it do so through the Hebrew.

(*a*) The intellectual intercourse between Greek and Latin in the third and fourth centuries, of which the most striking example outside religion was the spread of the knowledge of Plotinus' doctrines, led to the need for Latin texts of some of the works considered basic by the Greeks. It was in this Neoplatonic atmosphere (tempered by Porphyry with more Aristotelianism than Plotinus had accepted, rather than discussed and criticized) that the African Marius Victorinus, a pagan converted to Christianity, popularized the contents of Porphyry's introduction to logic, the *Isagoge*; if we accept Cassiodorus' testimony, he also translated Aristotle's *Categories* and *De interpretatione.* He certainly included Aristotelian views in his *De definitionibus,* the only work by Victorinus that contains some Aristotle and that has reached us in full (only sections of his version of the *Isagoge* survive in one of Boethius' commentaries). The attraction exercised by Themistius' school in Constantinople led to another, possibly purer, wave of Aristotelianism among the pagan revivalists, so vividly depicted in Macrobius' *Saturnalia.* Vettius Agorius Praetextatus, one of their leaders, rendered into Latin Themistius' teaching on the *Analytics.* Agorius' work was probably lost very soon, and there was no Latin text of Themistius' work on the *Analytics* until the second half of the twelfth century. This was based on an Arabic translation of part of that work (which was not translated from the Greek before the end of the fifteenth century). But Themistius' teaching of the *Categories*—a detailed exposition with additions and modernizations—found its Latin popularizer in a member of the same circle (perhaps Albinus). It is from this work, later ascribed to St. Augustine, under the title of *Categoriae decem,* that the Latin Aristotelianism of the Middle Ages started its career, never since interrupted.

(*b*) The middle and late fourth-century Aristotelianism, and much else of the cultural life of that time, was a faded, but not a lost, memory when, in the first decade of the sixth century, Boethius married a descendant of one of the prominent intellectual families, Symmachus' daughter Rusticiana. He took up what remained of that tradition, and was encouraged by his father-in-law to renew it. Cultural relations with the Greeks were not as active around 505 as around 370, but Boethius managed to obtain some Greek books, among them a copy of the collection of Aristotle's logical texts with an ample selection of notes from the greater masters of the past (Alexander, Themistius, and, mainly, Porphyry). So he probably managed to achieve what he had planned, to translate as much of Aristotle as he could get hold of: at least, we still preserve, in more or less original form, his translations of the *Categories, De interpretatione, Prior Analytics, Topics,* and *Sophistici elenchi;* he also claims to have produced a now lost translation of the *Posterior Analytics.* Since, by the fifth century, Aristotle's logical works were prefaced by Porphyry's *Isagoge,* Boethius also translated this text. He wrote that he intended to comment upon the works of Aristotle accessible to him; as it turned out, he commented on only the two shortest texts, the *Categories* and *De interpretatione*—or, better, he translated, adapted, and coordinated passages from Greek commentaries that he must have found on the margins of his Greek volume. The existence of a double recension for many sections of the *Categories, Prior Analytics,* and one short section of the *Topics;* the existence of a Latin version of a considerable collection of scholia to the *Prior Analytics* translated from the Greek and connected with one of the two recensions of this work; and a variety of evidence pointing to some editorial activity in Constantinople centering on Boethius' work in the first half of the sixth century suggest that Boethius' work as a translator in Italy had some continuation in the circle of Latin culture in Constantinople.

(*c*) The third stage is by far the most impressive,

representing as it does a variety of interests, of cultural backgrounds, of centers of progressive attitude toward the renewal, on the basis of older traditions, of the intellectual life in Europe and, to a certain extent, also representing one further step in a continuity of Aristotelian studies, hardly interrupted from the first century B.C. to the thirteenth century A.D. It is here necessary to consider separately the translators from the Greek and those from the Arabic, as well as some of the centers and people connected with this transmission of Aristotle. First of all, it cannot be emphasized too strongly that Aristotle was latinized from the Greek much more than from the Arabic and, with very few exceptions, earlier from the Greek than from the Arabic. Although competent scholars have tried to make this fact known, the commonly held view of historians of ideas and of people in general is the wrong view: that the Latin Middle Ages owed their knowledge of Aristotle first and foremost to the translations from the Arabic.

(*c*-1) The Aristotelian revival of the ninth and the eleventh centuries in the higher schools of Constantinople—particularly the second revival, due to such people as Michael Psellus, Ioannes Italus, Eustratius of Nicaea, and Michael of Ephesus—brought its fruits to the Latin revival (or, better, discovery) in the twelfth and thirteenth centuries. In the second quarter of the twelfth century James (Iacobus), a cleric with philosophical, theological, and juridical interests who seems to describe himself as Venetian-Greek, was in Constantinople and in touch with the Aristotelian corpus. He translated, either in Constantinople itself, or possibly in Italy, at least the *Posterior Analytics,* the *Sophistici elenchi,* the *Physics,* the *De anima,* parts of the *Parva naturalia,* and the *Metaphysics.* Of the translation of the last work only Books I–III and the beginning of Book IV remain; of the translation of the *Elenchi* only fragments have been recovered, mainly in contaminated texts of Boethius' version. He also translated some Greek notes to the *Metaphysics,* a short introduction to the *Physics* (known, in much of the Latin tradition, as *De intelligentia Aristotelis*), and probably *Commentaries to the Posterior Analytics* and *Elenchi* ascribed to Alexander of Aphrodisias. Finally, he himself commented at least on the *Elenchi.* James's translations, in spite of their extreme literalness, reveal a considerable knowledge of the learned Greek language of his time and interests in a variety of fields. Conscious of his limitations, which seem to be more marked when the technical language of mathematics and some philosophical terminology in Latin are concerned, he transcribes some key words in Greek letters, occasionally attempting an approximate translation. Some of his versions remained the basis, directly and through revisions, of the knowledge and study of much of Aristotle until the fifteenth and sixteenth centuries.

In 1158 Henry, nicknamed Aristippus, a Norman dignitary of the church and court in Sicily, was on an embassy at Constantinople, from which he brought back several books. With its combination of a recent Arabic past, enlightened Norman rule, and refined cultural life, Sicily was, in its own right, one of the best training grounds for a man like Henry, interested in problems of human life and death (he translated Plato's *Phaedo* and *Meno*) and curious about the workings of nature (like Empedocles, he climbed Mt. Etna to observe the volcano firsthand). He, and others around him, were conscious of the scientific tradition of Sicily; books of mechanics, astronomy, optics, and geometry were available, and attracted people from as far as England. Henry contributed to this tradition with a translation of at least Book IV of the *Meteorologics.* With less pedantry than James, he varied his vocabulary more than a work of science could admit; still, his translation remained indispensable for about a century, and what may be called Aristotle's physical chemistry was known primarily through his text.

(*c*-2) At approximately the same time, and presumably drawing on the same Greek sources of Aristotelian studies, a number of scholars with quite a good knowledge of Greek produced either new versions of texts already translated—whether the older translations were known to them cannot always be established—and versions of works previously unknown in Latin. These scholars remain anonymous, with the possible exception of a certain John, who produced, after the Venetian James, another translation of the *Posterior Analytics;* a second scholar translated anew the *Topics* and the *Prior Analytics;* a third, the *De sensu;* a fourth, the short treatises *De somno* and *De insomniis;* a fifth, the *De generatione et corruptione* and the *Nicomachean Ethics* (of which only Book I ["Ethica nova"], Books II and III ["Ethica vetus"], and fragments of Books VII and VIII ["Ethica Borghesiana"] remain); a sixth, again after James, the *Physics* (only Book I ["Physica Vaticana"] remains) and the *Metaphysics* without Book XI (the first chapter is lost); and a seventh, probably the *Rhetoric.* Some of these translations had little or no success (*Prior* and *Posterior Analytics, Topics, Rhetoric, Physics*); the others, within the limits of their survival (*De generatione et corruptione, De sensu, De somno, De insomniis, Nicomachean Ethics, Metaphysics*), remained in use, in the original form or in revisions, for three or four centuries. They all testify to the vast interest in the recovery of Aristotle in the twelfth century.

(*c*-3) While Constantinople, possibly together with minor Greek centers, was giving the Aristotelian material to the Latin scholars, the intense cultural activity of the Arab world had spread to northwestern Africa and Spain, providing Latin scholarship, especially in the part of Spain freed from Arab domination, with a vast amount of scientific and philosophical material and the linguistic competence for this to be rendered into Latin. Leaving aside for the moment the spreading of Aristotelian ideas through works of Arabic writers, mention must be made of the one translator of Aristotelian work from the Arabic, the Italian Gerard of Cremona, active in Toledo from *ca.* 1150 to his death in 1187. Being a scientist, he translated from the Arabic what was accessible to him of the more scientific works of Aristotle: the *Posterior Analytics* (theory of science by induction and deduction), *Physics, De generatione et corruptione, De caelo,* and *Meteorologics* (most of Book IV of this was either not translated or was soon lost). He also translated Themistius' paraphrase of the *Posterior Analytics.* The two of these works that did not exist in translation from the Greek (*Meteorologics* I–III and *De caelo*) were often transcribed and not infrequently studied for about sixty years in these versions from the Arabic. The others were occasionally used as terms of comparison or as additional evidence where the texts from the Greek were considered basic. It should also be mentioned that Gerard translated, under the name of Aristotle, thirty-one propositions from Proclus' *Elements of Theology* accompanied by an Arabic commentary, which formed the text (occasionally ascribed to Aristotle, more frequently left anonymous by the Latins) known under the title *Liber de causis.* Toward the end of the twelfth century, Alfred of Sareshel translated, again under the name of Aristotle (which attribution remained unchallenged for several centuries), Nicholas of Damascus' *De plantis.*

By the end of the twelfth century most of Aristotle had, therefore, found its way into Latin, but that does not mean that his works were soon widely accessible. To make them so, activity was still necessary in both transcription and translation. Some works had not yet been translated, and versions of others had been partly or completely lost; it was also realized that new versions made directly from the Greek would be necessary where only translations from the Arabic or inadequate versions from the Greek were available, and that revisions were necessary for almost every text; finally, it was felt that in order to achieve a more complete understanding of the words of Aristotle, translated by people whose knowledge of Greek was based mainly on the modernized, Byzantine usage, it was useful or necessary to give the reader of Latin access to many of the commentaries, Greek or Arabic, that linked the present with the past.

(*c*-4) The work done with these aims in view, on the basis of Greek texts, was carried out almost completely in the thirteenth century by two outstanding northerners: Robert Grosseteste, bishop of Lincoln and chancellor of Oxford University, and the Flemish Dominican William of Moerbeke, later archbishop of Corinth. A minor contribution came from a Sicilian, Bartholomew of Messina. Grosseteste, philosopher and theologian, linguist and scientist, politician and ecclesiastic, grew up at a time when it was already known how much Aristotle could help in the promotion of that Western European culture of which the foundations had been laid in the twelfth century. He was well aware of the contributions that the fading Greek renaissance could now offer, at least in books and teachers of the language. Grosseteste encouraged other Englishmen to go to Greece, southern Italy, and Sicily to collect books and men of learning. With their help, in the second quarter of the thirteenth century, he learned the language and, what concerns us here, thoroughly revised what remained of the older version of the *Nicomachean Ethics*; translated anew the major part of it, of which the older translation had been lost; and translated a large collection of commentaries on the several books of this work, some of them dating as far back as the third century, some as recent as the eleventh and twelfth. He also replaced with a translation from the Greek the *De caelo,* available until then only in a version from the Arabic, and added the translation of at least part of the vast commentary by Simplicius on the same work. Finally, he translated as Aristotelian the short treatise *De lineis insecabilibus* ("On Lines Not Made of Points").

William of Moerbeke, also a philosopher, theologian, scientist, and ecclesiastic, but in these fields a lesser man than Grosseteste, traveled from the Low Countries to Italy, Greece, and Asia Minor, widening the scope of his discoveries and of his translations to include Neoplatonic philosophy, geometry, mechanics, and medicine. His activity as an Aristotelian translator was enormous and covered approximately the third quarter of the century. He was the first to translate from Greek into Latin the Aristotelian zoological encyclopedia, the *De animalibus,* and Books I–III of the *Meteorologics;* he can almost be considered the discoverer, for our civilization, of the *Politics;* he was the first to translate into Latin the *Poetics* and Book XI of the *Metaphysics;* he translated anew the *De caelo,* the *Rhetoric* (he probably did not know of the existence of the Greco-Latin translations of these two works), and Book IV of the *Meteorologics;* he accompanied his versions of Greek commentaries with new translations of the *Categories* and *De interpretatione;* and he revised, with different degrees of thoroughness but always having recourse to Greek texts, James's versions of *Posterior Analytics, Physics, De anima, De memoria* and other minor texts of the *Parva naturalia,* Boethius' version of the *Sophistici elenchi,* and the anonymous versions of the *De generatione et corruptione,* of Books I–X and XII–XIV of the *Metaphysics,* and of the *De sensu, De somno,* and *De insomniis.* He also translated the extensive commentaries by Simplicius on the *Categories* and (again, after Grosseteste) the *De caelo,* by Alexander of Aphrodisias on the *De sensu* and *Meteorologics,* by Themistius on the *De anima,* by Ammonius on the *De interpretatione,* and by Philoponus on one part of Book III of the *De anima.* With the possible exception of the *De coloribus* (one fragment seems to be translated by him), he avoided all the works wrongly ascribed to Aristotle.

In contrast, Bartholomew of Messina, working for King Manfred around 1260, specialized in the pseudepigrapha: *De mundo, Problemata, Magna moralia, Physionomia, De mirabilibus auscultationibus, De coloribus,* and *De principiis* (Theophrastus' *Metaphysics*). The only translation of a possibly genuine Aristotelian text made by Bartholomew is that of the *De Nilo.* To complete the picture of the translations from the Greek of "Aristotelian" works before the end of the thirteenth century (or possibly a little after), we should add a second translation of the *De mundo,* by one of Grosseteste's collaborators, Nicholas of Sicily, two anonymous translations of the *Rhetorica ad Alexandrum,* and two partial translations of the *Economics.* Finally, an anonymous revision of Books I–II and part of Book III of James's translation of the *Metaphysics* was made around 1230, and an equally anonymous revision of the whole of Grosseteste's version of the *Nicomachean Ethics* was carried out probably between 1260 and 1270.

(*c*-5) The work of translating Aristotle or Aristotelian commentaries from the Arabic in the thirteenth century centered, again, mainly in Toledo and to a smaller extent in southern Italy. Most of this work was carried out by Michael Scot; other contributors were William of Luna and Hermann the German. Michael Scot was the first to make known to the Latins the *Books on Animals,* and it was his translation of most of the *Metaphysics* (parts of Books I and XII and the whole of Books XI, XIII, and XIV were not included), together with Averroës' *Great Commentary,* that provided many students of Aristotle with the bulk of this complex of Aristotelian texts: most of James's translation had probably been lost before anybody took any real interest in this work, and the anonymous Greco-Latin version (*Media*) made in the twelfth century emerged from some isolated repository *ca.* 1250. Under the title *Metaphysica nova,* Michael's version, isolated from Averroës' commentary, held its ground for about twenty years and was quite widely used for another twenty. The following translations must be ascribed to Michael Scot, some with certainty, some with great probability: the *De anima, Physics,* and *De caelo* with Averroës' *Great Commentary,* the *Middle Commentary* of the *De generatione et corruptione* and of Book IV of the *Meteorologics,* and Averroës' *Summaries* of the *Parva naturalia.*

William of Luna translated, in or near Naples, the *Middle Commentaries* to Porphyry's *Isagoge* and Aristotle's *Categories, De interpretatione,* and *Prior* and *Posterior Analytics.* Hermann the German translated Averroës' *Middle Commentaries* on the *Nicomachean Ethics, Rhetoric,* and *Poetics.* The last-mentioned was, in fact, the only source from which Latin readers acquired what knowledge they had—and that was mainly distorted—of Aristotle's *Poetics:* under the title *Poetria* (*Averrois* or *Aristotelis*) it was read quite widely; William of Moerbeke's translation from the Greek remained unknown until 1930, and the next translation from the Greek was not made until shortly before 1500.

By the end of the thirteenth century, the whole of the Aristotelian corpus as we know it, and as it has been known—if we except the relatively few fragments of early works—since the first century B.C., was available in Latin to practically everybody who cared to have access to it. The only exception consisted of the four books of the *Ethics* that are not common to the *Nicomachean Ethics* (which appears with the full complement of ten books) and to the *Eudemian Ethics* (which normally contains only the four that differ from those of the *Nicomachean*); only a small portion of this seems to have been translated, and is connected with passages of the *Magna moralia* in the so-called *De bona fortuna.* The general picture of the diffusion of Aristotle in these translations until the beginning of the sixteenth century is provided by the survival to our times of no fewer than 2,000 manuscripts containing from one to about twenty works, and by the fact that the most complete catalog of early printings (down to 1500) lists over 200 editions, without counting a large number of volumes that contain some of these translations with commentaries.

The detailed picture, when properly drawn, will show the difference in the popularity of the several works; but the difficulty in drawing such a picture derives from the fact that many works, especially minor ones, were transcribed as parts of general, mainly Aristotelian, collections without being actually taken into detailed account. Still, it may be significant that one of these collections, *Corpus Vetustius*—containing the *Physics, Meteorologics, De generatione et corruptione, De anima, Parva naturalia, De caelo,* and *Metaphysics* in the translations made before 1235—remains in slightly fewer than 100 manuscripts, all of the thirteenth (or very early fourteenth) century; a similar collection, including the same works in the new or revised translations in a more complete form (*Corpus recentius*) is preserved in about 200 manuscripts of the thirteenth, fourteenth, and fifteenth centuries. This shows that the more scientific of the works of Aristotle became indispensable in all centers of study and in private libraries. A statistical study of their provenance has not been made: it is, however, clear that France and England are most prominent in this respect for the *Corpus Vetustius;* and France, Italy, Germany, England, and Spain for the *Corpus recentius.*

If we consider the translations that most influenced Western culture and ascribe the authorship to those who produced them in the basic form, a quite accurate assessment of the individual abilities in transmitting Aristotle's works, and thus in shaping some of the philosophical, scientific, and common language of modern civilization, can be made. Their success in presenting formulations that, although not always carefully and strictly Aristotelian, have contributed a basis for discussion and polemics, and have thus led, in the dialectic of history, to much progress, can be suggested by the following list:

(1) Boethius: *Categories, De interpretatione, Prior Analytics, Topics, Sophistici elenchi;*

(2) James the Venetian-Greek: *Posterior Analytics, De anima, Physics, De memoria* (perhaps *Metaphysics* I-III);

(3) Twelfth-century anonymous translators from the Greek: *Metaphysics* IV-X, XII-XIV (perhaps I-III), *De generatione et corruptione, Nicomachean Ethics* I-III, *De sensu, De somno, De insomniis;*

(4) Michael Scot: *Metaphysics* I-X, XII, *De animalibus;*

(5) Robert Grosseteste: *Nicomachean Ethics* IV-X;

(6) William of Moerbeke: *Meteorologics, Politics, Rhetoric, De animalibus, Metaphysics* XI, *De caelo.*

An important, if sometimes misleading, role in the Latin transmission of Aristotle must be ascribed to the translators of commentaries. All of them contributed to the transmission and improvement of the technique of interpretation, as developed in the Greek schools of the second through sixth centuries. From this point of view, the greatest influence was probably exercised by the commentaries adapted from the Greek by Boethius and those of Averroës, which are linked, through an almost continuous line of scholastic discipline, with the tradition of the Greek schools. From the point of view of the contributions to the actual critical understanding of Aristotle, probably the most important of Averroës' commentaries were those on the *Metaphysics, Physics,* and *De anima.*

(*d*) The last stage in the Latin transmission of Aristotle—if we disregard the occasional translations of the seventeenth to twentieth centuries—covers what is normally called the humanistic and Renaissance period. This is the period beginning with and following the reestablishment of a more intimate collaboration between Greeks and western European scholars, which extended and deepened the understanding of the "old" Greek through a wider knowledge of the history, literature, science, etc., of the ancient world and a much more accurate understanding of the language as it was understood in ancient times. Another aspect that was soon presented as typical of the new movement in translations was the purity and perspicuity of the Latin language (purity ought to have carried with it the elimination of technical words that were not yet technical in classical Latin); but a closer study of many translations shows that the standards of knowledge of the ancient Greek background and of the Greek language were not consistently higher than in the Middle Ages, and that the need for very literal translations and technical usages of a medieval or of a new kind could not be avoided. In fact, very many new versions of Aristotle are hardly distinguishable, in their essential features, from those of the twelfth and thirteenth centuries. And what there was of a new philosophy of language applied to translations—the philosophy of meanings of contexts as against the meanings of individual words—was not always conducive to a better understanding of the original.

A complete survey of new translations down to the last quarter of the sixteenth century is impossible here. Although some of the later versions may still have exercised some influence in their own right, it seems that greater influence was exercised by some of those of the fifteenth century. And it is questionable how much even the latter ousted the medieval translations, or substituted something of great importance for them. We shall confine ourselves to a quick survey of the new versions of the fifteenth century, which were due in almost equal measure to Greek scholars attracted to Italy and to the Italians whose Greek scholarship resulted from contact with them.

The first Italian translator was a pupil of Manuel Chrysoloras, Roberto de' Rossi, who in 1406 translated the *Posterior Analytics.* Probably the greatest and most influential translator at the beginning of this movement was Leonardo Bruni of Arezzo, translator of the *Nicomachean Ethics, Politics,* and *Economics* (1416–1438). Gianozzo Manetti added to new translations of the *Nicomachean Ethics* and *Magna moralia* the first version of the *Eudemian Ethics* (1455–1460), an effort soon followed by Gregorio of Città di Castello (or Tifernate). Giovanni Tortelli again translated (*ca.* 1450) the *Posterior Analytics;* and in the 1480's Ermolao Barbaro translated, if his statements are to be taken literally, the whole of the logical works, the *Physics,* and the *Rhetoric* (only some of his versions remain). Before 1498 Giorgio Valla produced new translations of the *De caelo, Magna moralia,* and *Poetics,* and Lorenzo Laurenziano one of the *De interpretatione.*

In the meantime, from the early 1450's, the Greeks who had entered into the heritage of Latin culture were competing, or leading the way, in translation. The greatest of all, as a man of culture, collector of books, theologian, ecclesiastic, and philosopher, was Iohannes Bessarion, who translated the *Metaphysics.* His vast collection of manuscripts, among them many Greek volumes of Aristotle, was the basis of the Library of St. Mark in Venice. The most productive were John Argyropulos, translator of the *Categories, De interpretatione, Posterior* (and part of the *Prior*) *Analytics, Physics, De anima, De caelo, Metaphysics,* and *Nicomachean Ethics* (and the pseudo-Aristotelian *De mundo,* also translated shortly before by Rinucio Aretino), and George of Trebizond, translator of the *De animalibus, Physics, De caelo, De generatione et corruptione, De anima, Problemata,* and *Rhetoric.* Theodore of Gaza translated the *De animalibus* and *Problemata,* and Andronicus Callistus the *De generatione et corruptione.*

What had been done to a very limited extent in the fifteenth century was done on a large scale in the first half of the sixteenth, mainly by Italian scholars: the translation of Greek commentaries from the second to the fourteenth centuries. In this field the Renaissance obscured almost completely what had been done in the Middle Ages, something that, with a few exceptions, it failed utterly to do with the entrenched translations of Aristotle.

The Oriental Transmission of Aristotle's Works. The Greek philosophical schools of the fifth and sixth centuries were attended by people of the various nations surrounding the Mediterranean. Greek was the language of learning, but new languages were emerging to a high cultural level, especially as a consequence of the development of theology from the basic tenets and texts of the Christian faith. What had become necessary for the Greek-speaking theologian, a lay cultural basis, was necessary for the Syrian and for the Armenian. Apart from this, most probably, pure philosophical interest was spreading to other nations that were becoming proud of their nationhood. Thus, probably from the fifth century, and certainly from the sixth, Aristotelian texts started to be translated, and commentaries to be translated into, or originally written in, these languages.

The Armenian tradition, to some extent paralleled by or productive of a more limited Georgian tradition, has not been sufficiently investigated. Armenian culture continued in several parts of the world through the centuries—Armenia itself, India, Europe, and recently America—obviously depending on the culture of the surrounding nations but probably with some independence. A vast amount of unexplored manuscript material, stretching from the eighth century or earlier to the nineteenth century, is now concentrated in the National Library of Manuscripts in Yerevan, Armenian Soviet Socialist Republic. What is known in print is confined to translations of Porphyry's *Isagoge,* the *Categories* and *De interpretatione,* the apocryphal *De mundo,* and Helias' commentary to the *Categories.* A semimythical David the Unconquered (David Invictus) of the fourth or fifth century is mentioned as the author of some of these translations.

The Syriac tradition, more limited in time and space, apparently was richer both in translations of works of Aristotle and in original elaboration; apart from this, it formed the basis of a considerable proportion of the Arabic texts of Aristotle and, through them, of some of the Latin versions. The Nestorian Probus (Probha), of the fifth century, is considered the author of the surviving translations of *De interpretatione* and of *Prior Analytics* I.1–7, which may well belong to an eighth-century author. But there is no reason to doubt the ascription of translations and commentaries to Sergius of Theodosiopolis (Reshʿayna). He was a student in Alexandria and later active in Monophysite ecclesiastical and political circles in Antioch and in Constantinople, where he died *ca.* 535. He translated into Syriac the *Categories* with the *Isagoge,* and the *De mundo* (all still preserved), and possibly an otherwise unknown work by Aristotle, *On the Soul.* Toward the end of the seventh century, the Jacobite Jacob of Edessa translated the *Categories;* shortly after, George, bishop of the Arabs (*d.* 724), produced a new version of this book, of the *De interpretatione,* and of the entire *Prior Analytics.* Probably the most influential Syriac translators were two Nestorians, Ḥunayn ibn Isḥāq (*d.* 876) and his son Isḥāq ibn Ḥunayn (*d.* 910 or 911). Ḥunayn translated into Syriac the *De interpretatione, De generatione et corruptione, Physics* II (with Alexander of Aphrodisias' commentary), *Metaphysics* XI, and parts of the *Prior* and *Posterior Analytics;* his son possibly finished the version of these last two works, and translated the *Topics* into Syriac. ʿAbd al-Masih ibn Naʿima and Abū Bishr Matta translated the *Sophistici elenchi.* Isḥāq and Abū Bishr Matta also are among the translators from Greek into Arabic. Other translations into Syriac, which cannot be assigned to a definite author, include the *Poetics* (probably by Isḥāq ibn Ḥunayn), the *De animalibus,* possibly the *Meteorologics,* and a number of Greek commentaries to Aristotelian works. Not the least important feature of these translations into Syriac is the fact that numerous Arabic versions were made from the Syriac, rather than from the Greek.

Arabic translations from Aristotle were made in the ninth and tenth centuries, some by Syriac scholars, among whom the most prominent was Isḥāq ibn Ḥunayn. They were done in the latter part of the ninth century and at the beginning of the tenth, when Baghdad had become the great center of Arabic culture under al-Mamun. Of the many translations listed in the old Arabic bibliographies we shall mention only those that still exist. Those made by Isḥāq ibn Ḥunayn, presumably directly from the Greek, are *Categories, De interpretatione, Physics, De anima,* and *Metaphysics* II; by Yaḥyā ibn Abī-Manṣūr, Isa ben Zura, and ibn Naim, the *Sophistici elenchi* (Yaḥyā also translated part of *Metaphysics* XII); Abū ʿUthman ad-Dimashki and Ibrahim ibn ʿAbdallāh, the *Topics;* Abū Bishr Matta, the *Posterior Analytics* and the *Poetics* (perhaps both through the lost Syriac version by Isḥāq ibn Ḥunayn); Yaḥyā ibn al Bitriq, the *De caelo, Meteorologics,* and *De animalibus;* Astat (Eustathius), *Metaphysics* III–X; Theodorus (Abū Qurra [?]), the *Prior Analytics;* unknown translators, the *Rhetoric* and *Nicomachean Ethics* VII–X. Of the apocrypha, we have two translations of the *De mundo,* one of which was made by ʿUsa ibn Ibrahim al-Nafisi from the Syriac of Sergius of Theodosiopolis (Reshʿayna). Finally, it must be mentioned that it was in the Arab world that sections of Plotinus' work (or notes from his conversations) were edited under the title *Theology of Aristotle,* and thirty-one propositions from Proclus' *Elements of Theology* were commented upon and edited as Aristotle's *Book of Pure Goodness* (generally known under the title *De causis,* which it acquired in the Latin tradition).

Elaborations of Aristotle's Works. The transcriptions of the Greek texts, the translations into the several languages, and the multiplication of the copies of these translations were obviously only the first steps in the spread of Aristotle's pure or adulterated doctrines. The more permanent influence of those doctrines was established in the schools, through oral teaching, or on the margin of and outside the schools, through writings of different kinds at different levels. There would be, at the most elementary level, the division into chapters, possibly with short titles and very brief summaries; then occasional explanations of words and phrases in the margins or between the lines in the manuscripts of the actual Aristotelian texts (glosses or scholia), or more extensive summaries and explanations of points of particular interest at some moment or other in the history of thought.

At a higher level there would be systematic expositions or paraphrases, adhering closely to the original text but adapting the diction, the language, and the articulation of the arguments to the common scholastic pattern of this or that time, place, or school; then, expository commentaries, section by section, with or without introductory surveys and occasional recapitulations. The commentaries could aim at clarifying Aristotle's doctrine or adding doctrinal developments, criticisms, or digressions. The discussions would then take on an independent status: "questions about the *Physics,*" "questions about the *De anima,*" and so on. These would normally represent the most marked transition from the exposition of Aristotle's views—however critically they might be treated—to the original presentation of problems arising from this or that passage. Very often such *quaestiones* would not have more than an occasional, accidental connection with Aristotle: the titles of Aristotle's works would become like the headings of one or another of the main branches of philosophy, of the encyclopedia of knowledge, or of sciences. This soon led to the abandonment of the pretense of a connection with the "Philosopher's" works and doctrines or, in many cases, to the pretense of abandoning him and being original while remaining, in fact, under the strongest influence of what he had said.

Systematic works covering a wide province of philosophy, or even aiming at an exhaustive treatment of all its provinces, could take the form of a series of expositions or commentaries on the works of Aristotle, or organize the accumulated intellectual experience of the past and the original views of the author with great independence at many stages, but with explicit or implicit reference to Aristotle's corpus as it had been shaped into a whole—to a small extent by him and to a larger extent by his later followers.

Much of the philosophical literature from the first to the sixteenth centuries could be classified under headings corresponding to the ways in which Aristotle was explained, discussed, taken as a starting point for discussions, used as a model for great systematizations containing all kinds of details, or abandoned—either with or without criticism. In the Greek-speaking world, the vast commentaries by Alexander of Aphrodisias (third century) on the *Metaphysics,* the *Analytics, Topics,* and *Meteorologics;* those by Simplicius (sixth century) on the *Categories,* the *De caelo,* and the *Physics;* and those by John Philoponus (the Grammarian) on the *De anima* were among the most prominent examples of the developed, systematic, and critical commentaries of Aristotle's texts. They were matched in the Latin world of the sixth century by Boethius' commentaries on the *Categories* and *De interpretatione,* in the Arab world of the twelfth century by the "great" commentaries of Averroës, and in the Latin world of the twelfth and thirteenth centuries by those of Abailard, Robert Grosseteste, Aquinas, Giles of Rome, and many others. Themistius' paraphrases (fourth century) of the logical works and of the *De anima,* partly imitated or translated into Latin in his own time, had their counterparts in works by Syriac-, Armenian-, and Arabic-writing philosophers: al-Kindī in the ninth century, the Turk al-Fārābī in the tenth, the Persian Ibn Sīnā (Avicenna) in the eleventh, and Averroës in the twelfth contributed in this way much-needed information on Aristotle to those who would not read his works, but would like to learn something of his doctrines through simplified Arabic texts. *Summae* or *summulae* of the *Elenchi,* of the *Physics,* and of other works appeared in Latin in the twelfth and thirteenth centuries, under such names as that of Grosseteste, or have remained anonymous. The collections of scholia of Greek manuscripts were continued by such genres as *glossae* and *notulae:* such collections on the *Categories,* written in the ninth century, and on the *Posterior Analytics,* the *De anima,* and the *Meteorologics,* written between the end of the twelfth and the middle of the thirteenth centuries, became in many cases almost standard texts accompanying the "authoritative" but difficult texts of the great master. At the level of philosophical systems we find the great philosophical encyclopedia of Avicenna (eleventh century), organized on the basis of the Aristotelian corpus but enriched by the philosophical experience of Aristotelians, Platonists, and other thinkers of many centuries, and above all by the grand philosophical imagination and penetration of its author. On the other hand, in the Latin world Albertus Magnus (thirteenth century), a man of inexhaustible curiosity, and with a frantic passion for communicating as much as he knew or thought he knew as quickly as possible, followed up his discoveries in the books of others with his own cogitations and developments, and presented his encyclopedia of knowledge almost exclusively as an exposition-cum-commentary of the works by Aristotle or those ascribed to him. What he had learned from others—he was one of the most learned men of his times, and much of his reading derived from the Arabic—finds its place in this general plan.

Quaestiones (ζητήσεις) are found in the Greek philosophical literature, and one might be tempted to include in this class much of Plotinus' *Enneads.* But it is when impatience with systematic explanatory commentary (mildly or only occasionally critical) leads to independent treatment of problems that the *quaestio* comes into its own—first, perhaps, as in Abailard, in the course of the commentary itself; then, in the second half of the thirteenth and much more in the fourteenth and fifteenth centuries, independently of the commentaries. It is in many of these collections of *quaestiones* that we find the minds of philosophers, impregnated with Aristotelian concepts and methods, searching more deeply the validity of accepted statements, presenting new points of view, and inserting in the flow of speculation new discoveries, new deductions from known principles, and corrected inferences from ambiguous formulations.

Aristotle's Influence on the Development of Civilization. The influence exercised by Aristotle's writings varied from work to work and often varied for the several sections of one and the same work. It would be relatively easy to select those short writings which, in spite of their inferior and confused nature or their incompleteness—the *Categories* and the *De interpretatione* from the first century B.C. to the sixteenth, and the *Poetics* from the early sixteenth to the nineteenth—penetrated more deeply and widely into the minds of intelligent people than did the more extensive, organized, and imaginative works, such as *De animalibus, De anima,* and the *Physics.* Moreover, one could possibly select a limited number of passages that left their permanent mark because they were repeatedly quoted, learned by heart, and applied, rightly or wrongly, as proverbs, slogans, and acquired "truths" are applied. Most of all, it is possible, and essential for our purpose, to select those concepts that became common property of the civilized mind, however much they may have been elaborated and, in the course of time, transformed. And if these concepts are not all originally Aristotelian, if they have found their way into the several fields of culture in more than one (the Aristotelian) way, it is our contention that pressure of continuous study and repetition and use of those concepts in Aristotelian contexts, in the ways sketched above, are responsible more than anything else for their becoming so indispensable and fruitful.

It is enough to try to deprive our language of a certain number of words in order to see how much we might have to change the whole structure of our ways of thinking, of expressing, even of inquiring. A conceptual and historico-linguistic analysis of a definition like "mass is the quantity of matter" would show us that whatever was and is understood by these words owes much to the fact that the concepts of "quantity" and of "matter" were for two millennia inculcated into the minds of men and into their languages, more than in any other way, through the agency of Aristotle's *Categories, Physics,* and *Metaphysics.* If "energy" means something when we read it in the formula $e = mc^2$, we may forget that this "linguistic" tool is the creation of Aristotle and that it traveled through the ages with all its appendages of truths, half-truths, and hypotheses, which affected its meaning in different ways through the centuries, stimulating thoughts, experiments, and interpretations of facts, because some bits of the *Metaphysics* and of the *Physics* were the *sine qua non* condition of men's "knowledge" of the world. And if "potential" has assumed so many uses—from social and military contexts to electricity, dynamics, and what not—is it not because we have been trained to handle this term as an indispensable instrument to describe an infinite variety of situations that have something in common, as Aristotle repeated *ad nauseam,* when making "potency" (*δύναμις*) one of the basic concepts for the understanding of the structure of the world? We have used, misused, abused, eliminated, and reinstated the concepts of "substance" and "essence." "Relation" and "analogy," "form," "cause," "alteration of qualities," and "development from potentiality to actuality" are all terms that have not yet stopped serving their purpose. A writer of a detailed history of science would be hard put if he tried to avoid having recourse to Aristotle for his understanding of how things progressed in connection with them. At the very root of much of our most treasured scientific development lies the quantification of qualities; this started in the form of a general problem set by the distinction between two out of the ten "Aristotelian categories" in conjunction with Aristotle's theory of the coming into being of new "substances." It may be contended that, by his very distinction, Aristotle created difficulties and slowed progress. Perhaps there is something in that complaint; nevertheless, in this way he stimulated the search for truth and for formulations of more satisfactory hypotheses to fit, as he would say, *τὰ φαινόμενα*—to fit what we see.

His exemplification of continuous and discontinuous quantities in the *Categories* may elicit an indulgent smile from those who lack any historical sense; and it would be impertinent to skip over twenty-two and a half centuries and say that here we are, faced by the same problems that worried Aristotle, but with more sophistication: continuous waves or discontinuous quanta? But how did it happen that the problems came to be seen in this way, with this kind of alternative? No doubt Aristotle was not the only ancient sage who taught the concept of continuity to the millennia to come, but no text in which the distinction—and the problems it brought with it—appeared was learned by heart, discussed and commented upon, or became the text for examinations and testing as often and as unavoidably as the *Categories.* Do things happen by chance, or through a chain of causality? Can we determine how and why this happens—is it "essential" that it should happen or is it "accidental"? Much scientific progress was achieved by testing and countertesting, under *these,* Aristotelian, headings, what the world presents to our perception and to our mind.

Again: classification, coordination, and subordination have been and are instruments of clear thinking, of productive procedures, of severe testing of results. The terms "species" and "genus" may be outmoded in some fields, but the fashion is recent; the words have changed, yet the concepts have remained. And with them we find, not even outmoded, "property" and "difference." We have been conditioned by these distinctions, by these terms, because we come from Aristotelian stock.

It is, in conclusion, significant of Aristotle's impact on the development of culture, and particularly of science, that among the more essential elements in our vocabulary there should be the following terms, coming directly from his Greek (transliterated in the Latin or later translations) or from the Latin versions, or from texts where some of these terms had to be changed in order to preserve some equivalence of meaning when they proved ambiguous: (*a*) *category* (*class, group,* etc.) and the names of the four categories actually discussed in the *Categoriae—substance* (*essence*), *quantity, quality, relation;* (*b*) *universal* and *individual,* and the *quinque voces* (another title for Porphyry's *Isagoge,* which developed a passage of Aristotle's *Topics* and was studied as the introduction to his logic)—*genus, species, difference, property, accident* (in the sense of accidental feature); (*c*) *cause* and the names or equivalents applied to the four causes until quite recent times—*efficient, final, material,* and *formal;* (*d*) couples of correlative terms, like *matter-form* (structure), *potency-act* (energy), *substance-accident.*

Terms like "induction" and "deduction," "definition" and "demonstration" have certainly become entrenched in our language from many sources apart from Aristotle's *Analytics.* But again, the extent of their use, the general understanding of their meaning and implications, and the application in all fields of science of the methods of research and exposition that those terms summarize depend possibly more on the persistent study of Aristotle than on any other single source. All the wild anti-Aristotelianism of the seventeenth century would have been more moderate if people had realized then, as it had been realized, for instance, in the thirteenth century, how aware Aristotle was that experience, direct perception and knowledge of individual facts, is the very basis of scientific knowledge. The anti-Aristotelians were much more Aristotelian than they thought in some aspects of their methods; and that was because they had, unconsciously, absorbed Aristotle's teaching, which had seeped through from the higher level of philosophical discussion to the common attitude of people looking for truth.

It has become a truism that observation of facts was recognized as the necessary beginning of science through a revolutionary attitude which had as its pioneers such people as Roger Bacon and Robert Grosseteste. One wonders whether many realize that—because he thought Aristotle to be very often right on important matters—Aquinas insisted that a problem which, for him and his contemporaries, was of the utmost importance—the problem of the existence of God—could be solved only by starting from the observation of facts around us. If, as it happened, Aquinas was going to carry the day with his very awkward "five ways," he was also going to boost very widely the value of the basic principle on which so much depended in the development of science: observe first, collect facts, and draw your conclusions after. And it is in the course of the discussion of the *Posterior Analytics* that probably one of the main steps forward in the methodology of science was made by Grosseteste around 1230: probably not so much—as has been maintained—in passing from "experience" to "experiment" as in the discrimination of the contributory factors of a certain effect, in the search for the really effective causes, as against the circumstantial, accidental state of affairs.

One further example of the permanence of Aristotle's teaching is provided by his insistence on the old saying that nature does nothing in vain. The development from this principle of the wrongly called "Ockham's razor" is the result of a series of refinements; it may be possible (or has it already been done?) to see through which steps this principle of finality and economy of nature has established itself in all but the most independent or anarchic scientific minds.

Above all, probably, Aristotle's explicitly stated methodical doubt as a condition for the discovery of truth and his exhaustive accumulation of "difficulties" (ἀπορίαι) have trained generation after generation in the art of testing statements, of analyzing formulations, of trying to avoid sophistry. The picture of an Aristotelianism confined to teaching how to pile up syllogisms that either beg the question or, at best, make explicit what is already implicit in the premises is very far from the Aristotelianism of Aristotle, and hides most of what Aristotle has meant for the history of culture and science. It is through observation, ἀπορίαι, reasoned and cautious argument, that he thought our statements should fit the phenomena (φαινόμενα): no wonder that Aquinas himself was not troubled by the possibility that geocentrism might prove to be less "valid" than heliocentrism.

It is much more difficult to discover, isolate, and follow up the influence of Aristotle's writings on the advancement of science considered in the several fields and, what counts more, in the solution of particular problems. It is also difficult to locate exactly in time and space the several steps by which methods of inquiry, learned directly or indirectly at the Aristotelian school, have been successfully applied as Aristotelian. Out of the vast amount of evidence existing, only a small fraction has been studied. Influences have hardly ever been the result of isolated texts or of individual authors; the accumulation of interpretations, refinements, new contributions, and variations in the presentation of problems has continued for centuries, and the more striking turning points are those at which the influence has been *a contrario.* Whether it is Simplicius (sixth century) commenting on the *De caelo,* and thus contributing to the methodical transformation of the study of the heavens, or William Harvey (eleven centuries later) taking as one of his basic texts for the study of the mechanics of the living body the *De motu animalium,* there is no doubt that we can rightly speak of Aristotle's influence on the advancement of astronomy and of physiology. But determining the exact point at which that influence can be located, in what precise sense it can be interpreted, and in what measure it can be calculated would require much more than a series of textual references.

It might be suggested that one precise point in history at which Aristotle's deductive theory in the *Posterior Analytics* contributed to the mathematization of nonmathematical sciences can be found in Robert Grosseteste's commentary on that work (*ca.* 1230). Aristotle had considered optics as a science dependent on mathematics (geometry), and in his discussion of two types of demonstration, the *demonstratio quia* and the more penetrating and valuable *demonstratio propter quid,* he had used optical phenomena to exemplify the general rule that it is the higher-level science (in those particular cases, obviously, mathematics) that holds the key to the *demonstratio propter quid.* For Grosseteste the whole of nature was fundamentally light, manifesting itself in different states. It could be argued, therefore, that Grosseteste would have inferred that Aristotle's examples revealed, more than he imagined, the mathematical structure of all natural (and supernatural) sciences. One can go further and, magnifying Grosseteste's influence, state that quantification in natural sciences has its roots in the *Posterior Analytics* as interpreted by Grosseteste in the frame of his metaphysics of light. This is the kind of fallacy that results from not realizing how difficult it is to discover and assess Aristotelian influences. Nothing has so far been shown—although much has been said—to prove that statement.

Among the few fields in which many necessary inquiries have been made (through commentaries to Aristotle, *quaestiones* arising from the *Physics,* and independent treatises with an Aristotelian background) to show how (by appropriate or forced interpretation, by intelligent criticism or the process of development) modern science has to some extent come out of the study of Aristotle are those of the theories of rectilinear movement (constant velocity and acceleration), of "essential" transformations consequent to quantitatively different degrees of qualities, and of the nature and basic qualities of matter in connection with gravity. The temptation must, of course, be resisted to see Aristotle's influence wherever some connection can be established, whether *prima facie* or after detailed consideration of chains of quotations, repetitions, and slight transformations. But the pioneering studies of Pierre Duhem, the detailed analyses and historical reconstructions by Anneliese Maier, Nardi, Weisheipl; the attempts at wider historical systematizations by Thorndike, Sarton, and Crombie; and the contributions by many scholars of the last thirty years confirm more and more the view that the debt of scientists to the Aristotelian tradition is far greater than is generally accepted.

Setbacks in the Aristotelian Tradition. The progress in the spread of Aristotelian studies had its obstacles and setbacks, at different times in different spheres and for a variety of reasons. These ranged from purely philosophical opposition to purely theological convictions and prejudices, and to the interference of political and political-ecclesiastical powers with the free flow of speculation and debate. The story of the setbacks could be considered as diverse and rich as that of the actual progress; we shall mention only some of the most famous, or notorious, examples.

In 529 Justinian ordered the closing down of all philosophical schools in Athens; such people as Simplicius and Damascius became political-philosophical refugees in the "unfaithful" Persian kingdom. Greek Aristotelian studies then had over two centuries of almost total eclipse.

A similar attack on philosophy, at a very "Aristotelian" stage, was carried out in 1195 by Caliph Ya'ūb al-Manṣūr in southern Spain; one of the exiled victims was the great Averroës, who had, among other things, strongly defended philosophy against the religious mystical onslaught by al-Ghazali, the author of the *Destruction of Philosophers.* Whatever the reasons for the centuries-long eclipse of Arabic philosophy, the blow of 1195 was certainly one of the most effective contributions to it.

Much has been made by the historians of philosophy, and particularly of science, of the Roman Church's hostility to Aristotelianism, as made manifest by the decrees of 1210, 1215, and 1231—also confirmed later—"prohibiting" the study of Aristotle's works on natural philosophy and then of those on metaphysics. The prohibitions, confined first to Paris and then to a few other places, and soon limited in scope (the works in question were to be examined by a committee of specialists and, where necessary, revised), turned out to be probably one of the most important factors in the most powerful and permanent expansion of Aristotelian studies in the whole of history. Interest was intensified, obstacles were avoided or disregarded, and witch-hunting did not succeed in doing much more than alerting philosophers and scholars to the danger of expressing Aristotle's views as their own views, and of describing developments based on Aristotle's works as *the* truth rather than as logically compelling inferences from authoritative statements.

The real setbacks to the spread of Aristotelian studies—not necessarily of the kind of Aristotelian influence sketched above—came in the seventeenth and eighteenth centuries, when progress in scientific and historical knowledge; the interplay of the new interests with a sterilized, scholastic "Aristotelianism"; a passion for grand philosophical systems; refined, systematic criticism of current beliefs; and the impact of new theological disputes filled the minds of thoughtful people with problems that either were not present in Aristotle's works or had now to be expressed in a differently articulated language.

BIBLIOGRAPHY

I. Original Works. This section will be limited to the more essential references. The others will be found in works cited below under "Secondary Literature."

The tradition of the Greek texts of Aristotle is documented mainly in their critical editions; for these see the article on his "Life and Works." For the medieval Latin tradition see, above all, the *Corpus philosophorum medii aevi, Aristoteles Latinus* (Bruges-Paris, 1952–), of which the following vols. have appeared: I.1-5, *Categoriae,* L. Minio-Paluello, ed. (1961); I.6-7, *Supplementa Categoriarum* (Porphyry's *Isagoge* and Pseudo-Gilbertus' *Liber sex principiorum*), L. Minio-Paluello, ed. (1966); II.1-2, *De interpretatione,* L. Minio-Paluello, ed. (1965); III.1-4, *Analytica priora,* L. Minio-Paluello, ed. (1962); IV.1-4, *Analytica posteriora,* L. Minio-Paluello and B. G. Dod, eds. (1968); VII.2, *Physica* I ("Physica Vaticana"), A. Mansion, ed. (1957); XI.1-2, *De mundo,* 2nd ed., W. L. Lorimer *et al.,* eds. (1965); XVII.2.v, *De generatione animalium,* trans. Guillelmi, H. J. Drossaart Lulofs, ed. (1966); XXIX.1, *Politica* I-II.11, 1st vers. by William of Moerbeke, P. Michaud-Quantin, ed. (1961); and XXXIII, *Poetica,* 2nd ed., trans. Guillelmi, with Hermann the German's version of Averroës' *Poetria,* L. Minio-Paluello, ed. (1968). V.1-3, *Topica,* L. Minio-Paluello, ed., is to appear in 1969. Older eds. of most of the translations or revisions of the thirteenth century appeared from 1475 on. Among other more recent eds., the following should be recorded: *Politics,* in F. Susemihl's ed. of Greek text (Leipzig, 1872); *Rhetoric,* in L. Spengel's ed. of Greek text (Leipzig, 1867); *Metaphysica media,* in *Alberti Magni Opera omnia,* XVI, B. Geyer, ed. (Münster, 1960–); *Metaphysica,* trans. Iacobi ("Metaphysica Vetustissima"), in *Opera . . . Rogeri Baconi,* XI, R. Steele, ed. (Oxford, 1932).

The best ed. of the Armenian texts of the *Categoriae, De interpretatione,* and *De mundo* was produced by F. C. Conybeare in *Anecdota Oxoniensia,* Classical Series I.vi (Oxford, 1892). George's Syriac version of *Categoriae, De interpretatione,* and *Prior Analytics* was edited by G. Furlani in *Memorie dell'Accademia . . . dei Lincei,* Classe scienze morali, VI.5,i and iii, and VI.6.iii (Rome, 1933–1937). Most of the surviving Arabic translations of the Middle Ages were first edited or reedited by Abdurrahman Badawi in the collection Studii Islamici (then Islamica) (Cairo 1948–): these include all the works of logic, the *Rhetoric, Poetics, De anima, De caelo,* and *Meteorologics.* Of other eds. the following should be mentioned: *Metaphysics* (missing parts of Bks. I and XII, and the whole of Bks. XI and XIII-XIV), M. Bouyges, ed. (Beirut, 1938–1952); and *Poetics,* J. Tkatsch, ed. (Vienna, 1928–1932).

The extant Greek commentaries were edited by H. Diels and his collaborators in *Commentaria in Aristotelem Graeca* (Berlin, 1882–); the medieval Latin trans. are being published in the *Corpus Latinum commentariorum in Aristotelem Graecorum* (Louvain, 1957–), thus far consisting of I. *Themistius on De anima,* II. *Ammonius on De interpretatione,* III. *Philoponus on De anima,* and IV. *Alexander on De sensu*—all ed. by G. Verbeke.

The one major commentary by Averroës that is preserved in Arabic, on the *Metaphysics,* was published with the Aristotelian text by Bouyges (see above). Many of the Latin medieval trans. of the longer and shorter commentaries by Averroës were printed several times in the fifteenth and sixteenth centuries (1st ed., Venice, 1483); new trans. from the Hebrew of some of the same commentaries and of others (most importantly, the long commentary on *Posterior Analytics*) were published in the sixteenth century (first comprehensive ed., Venice, 1551–1561). Critical eds. of the medieval Latin and Hebrew trans. of Averroës' commentaries are being published in the *Corpus philosophorum medii aevi, Corpus commentariorum Averrois in Aristotelem,* the most important of which is Michael Scot's trans. of the long commentary on *De anima,* in Vol. VI.1, F. Stuart Crawford, ed. (Cambridge, Mass., 1953).

II. Secondary Literature. A list of Greek MSS of Aristotle's works and of those of his commentators, based mainly on printed catalogs, was ed. by A. Wartelle, *Inventaire des manuscrits grecs d'Aristote et de ses commentateurs* (Paris, 1963), and supplemented by D. Harlfinger and J. Wiesner in *Scriptorium,* **18,** no. 2 (1964), 238–257. A descriptive catalog of all the known MSS of Aristotle's works is being prepared by P. Moraux and his collaborators of the Aristotelian Archive at the University of Berlin. The best sources for knowledge of the printed tradition are still the general catalogs of the British Museum and of the Prussian libraries; for recent times, see also the catalog of the U.S. Library of Congress.

Nearly all the available basic information for the Latin tradition in the Middle Ages is collected in the three vols. of G. Lacombe, E. Franceschini, L. Minio-Paluello, *et al., Aristoteles Latinus, Codices:* I., Rome, 1939; II., Cambridge, 1955; *Supplem. Alt.,* Bruges, 1961. The bibliography that is in these vols. includes all the works of importance on the subject. Additional information on individual works will be found in the intros. to the eds. of texts in the *Aristoteles Latinus* series. Special mention should be made of E. Franceschini, "Roberto Grossatesta, vescovo di Lincoln, e le sue traduzioni latine," in *Atti della Reale Istituto Veneto,* **93,** no. 2 (1933–1934), 1–138; G. Grabmann, *Guglielmo di Moerbeke, il traduttore delle opere di Aristotele* (Rome, 1946); J. M. Millás Vallicrosa, *Las traducciones orientales en los manuscritos de la Biblioteca Catedral de Toledo* (Madrid, 1942); L. Minio-Paluello, "Iacobus Veneticus Grecus, Canonist and Translator of Aristotle" in *Traditio,* **8** (1952), 265–304; "Note sull'Aristotele Latino medievale," in *Rivista di filosofia neo-scolastica,* **42** ff. (1950 ff.). For the printed eds. of medieval Latin trans., see the *Gesamtkatalog der Wiegendrucke* and the library catalogs cited above.

For the humanistic and Renaissance trans. into Latin, see E. Garin, *Le traduzioni umanistiche di Aristotele nel secolo XV,* Vol. VIII in Accademia Fiorentina La Colombaria (Florence, 1951), and the *Gesamtkatalog* and the library catalogs.

For the study of Aristotle in the Middle Ages, M. Grabmann's *Mittelalterliches Geistesleben,* 3 vols. (Munich,

1926–1956), and his earlier *Geschichte der scholastischen Methode* (Freiburg im Breisgau, 1909–1911) are of fundamental importance. Among the many works of a more limited scope, see F. Van Steenberghen, *Siger de Brabant d'après ses oeuvres inédites, II: Siger dans l'histoire de l'Aristotélisme,* Vol. XII of Les Philosophes Belges (Louvain, 1942).

For the Armenian tradition, see Conybeare's ed. mentioned above; the catalogs of the more important collections of Armenian MSS (Vatican Library, British Museum, Bodleian Library, Bibliothèque Nationale); and G. W. Abgarian, *The Matenadaran* (Yerevan, 1962).

For the Syriac tradition, see A. Baumstark, *Geschichte der syrischen Literatur* (Bonn, 1922); and many articles by G. Furlani, listed in the bibliog. of his writings in *Rivista degli studi orientali,* **32** (1957).

For the Arabic tradition, see C. Brockelmann, *Geschichte der arabischen Literatur,* 2nd ed., 2 vols. (Leiden, 1943–1949) and 3 vols. of supps. (Leiden, 1937–1942); R. Walzer, "Arisṭūṭālīs," in *Encyclopaedia of Islam,* 2nd ed., I, 630–635; Abdurrahman Badawi, *Aristu ʿinda l-ʿArab* (Cairo, 1947); M. Steinschneider, "Die arabischen Uebersetzungen aus dem Griechischen," in *Zentralblatt für Bibliothekswesen,* **8** (1889) and **12** (1893), and "Die europaïschen Uebersetzungen aus dem Arabischen bis Mitte des 17 Jahrhunderts," in *Sitzungsberichte der Kaiserliche Akademie der Wissenschaften,* philos.-hist. Klasse, **149,** no. 4, and **151,** no. 1.

For the Hebrew tradition, see M. Steinschneider, *Die hebraïschen Uebersetzungen des Mittelalters und die Juden als Dolmetscher* (Berlin, 1893); and H. A. Wolfson, "Plan for the Publication of a *Corpus commentariorum Averrois in Aristotelem,*" in *Speculum* (1931), 412–427.

No comprehensive study of Aristotle's influence through the ages has ever been published. The standard histories of philosophy and science, general or specialized, contain much useful information, including bibliographies, e.g.: F. Ueberweg, *Geschichte der Philosophie,* 5 vols., 11th–13th eds. (Berlin, 1924–1928); E. Zeller, *Die Philosophie der Griechen,* 4th–7th eds. (1882–1920); I. Husik, *A History of Medieval Jewish Philosophy* (Philadelphia, 1916; 6th ed., 1946); G. Sarton, *Introduction to the History of Science,* 3 vols. (Baltimore, 1927–1948); Lynn Thorndike, *A History of Magic and Experimental Science,* 8 vols. (New York, 1923–1958); C. Singer, *Studies in the History and Method of Science* (Oxford, 1921); and A. C. Crombie, *Augustine to Galileo* (London, 1952).

Special problems, periods, or fields have been surveyed and analyzed in, e.g., P. Duhem, *Le système du monde,* 8 vols. (Paris, 1913–1916, 1954–1958), and *Études sur Léonard de Vinci* (Paris, 1906–1913); A. Maier, *Metaphysische Hintergründe der spätscholastischen Naturphilosophie* (Rome, 1951), *Zwei Grundprobleme der scholastischen Naturphilosophie,* 2nd ed. (Rome, 1951), *An der Grenze von Scholastik und Naturwissenschaft,* 2nd ed. (Rome, 1952), and *Zwischen Philosophie und Mechanik* (Rome, 1958); A. C. Crombie, *Robert Grosseteste and the Origins of Experimental Science* (Oxford, 1953); M. Clagett, *The Science of Mechanics in the Middle Ages* (Madison, Wis., 1959); and R. Lemay, *Abu Maʿshar and Latin Aristotelianism in the Twelfth Century* (Beirut, 1962).

L. MINIO-PALUELLO

ARISTOXENUS (*b.* Tarentum, *ca.* 375–360 B.C.; *d.* Athens [?])

Aristoxenus was a native of Tarentum, a Greek city in southern Italy. He flourished in the time of Alexander the Great (reigned 336–323), and can hardly have been born later than 360. His father's name was either Mnaseas or Spintharus; the latter was certainly his teacher, a musician whose wide acquaintance included Socrates, Epaminondas, and Archytas. Aristoxenus studied at Mantinea, an Arcadian city that had a strong conservative musical tradition, and later became a pupil of Aristotle in Athens. His position in the Lyceum was such that he hoped to become head of the school upon the death of Aristotle (322 B.C.); he is said to have vented his disappointment in malicious stories about his master. The date of his death is unknown, but the attribution to him of 453 published works (even if many were spurious) suggests a long life.

Of this vast production little has survived except for three books that have come down under the title *Harmonic Elements.* Modern scholars are agreed, however, that these represent two or more separate treatises. There is a substantial fragment of the second book of *Rhythmical Elements.* Aristoxenus' numerous other writings on music are all lost, except for quotations, but much of our scattered information on early Greek musical history must derive from him. He also wrote biographies (he was one of those who established this kind of writing as a tradition of the Peripatetic school); treatises on educational and political theory and on Pythagorean doctrine; miscellanies; and memoranda of various kinds.

It is proper, if paradoxical, that Aristoxenus should be included in a dictionary of scientific biography. It is proper because music under the form of "harmonics" or the theory of scales was an important branch of ancient science from the time of Plato onward, and because Aristoxenus was the most famous and influential musical theorist of antiquity. It is paradoxical because he turned his back upon the mathematical knowledge of his time to adopt and propagate a radically "unscientific" approach to the measurement of musical intervals.

When the Pythagorean oligarchs were expelled from Tarentum, Archytas, the celebrated mathematician and friend of Plato, remained in control of the new democracy and may still have been alive when Aristoxenus was born. From Archytas' pupils in Tarentum—or from the exiled Xenophilus in Athens—Aristoxenus must have become familiar with Pythagorean doctrine. The Pythagoreans recognized that musical intervals could be properly measured and expressed only as ratios (of string lengths or pipe lengths). Pythagoras himself is said to have discovered the ratios of the octave, fifth, and fourth; and the determination of the tone as difference between fifth and fourth must soon have followed. In each case the ratio is superparticular and incapable, without the aid of logarithms, of exact division in mathematical terms. Thus, "semitone" (Greek, *hemitonion*) is a misnomer; when two tones were subtracted from the fourth, the Pythagoreans preferred to call the resulting interval "remainder" (*leimma*). The Pythagorean diatonic scale, consisting of tones (9:8) and *leimmata* (256:243), was known to Plato. Archytas worked out mathematical formulations for the diatonic, chromatic, and enharmonic scales upon a different basis.

Aristoxenus, however, turned his back upon the mathematical approach and stated that the ear was the sole criterion of musical phenomena. To the ear, he held, the tone was divisible into halves (and other fractions); the octave consisted of six tones, the fifth of three tones and a half, the fourth of two tones and a half, and so on. His conception of pitch was essentially linear; the gamut was a continuous line that could be divided into any required fractions, and these could be combined by simple arithmetic. It was for the cultivated ear to decide which intervals were "melodic," i.e., capable of taking their places in the system of scales.

The division of the octave into six equal tones and of the tone into two equal semitones recalls the modern system of "equal temperament," and it is held by some authorities that Aristoxenus envisaged such a system or sought to impose it upon the practice of music. If that were so, he might well have rejected a mathematics that was still incapable of expressing it. Equal temperament, however, was devised in modern times to solve a specific problem: how to tune keyboard instruments in such a way as to facilitate modulation between keys. No comparable problem presented itself to Greek musicians: although modulation was exploited to some extent by virtuosi of the late fifth century B.C. and after, there is no reason to suppose that it created a need for a radical reorganization of the system of intervals or that such could have been imposed upon the lyre players and pipe players of the time. Furthermore, such a "temperament" would distort all the intervals of the scale (except the octave) and, significantly, the fifths and fourths; but Aristoxenus always speaks as though his fifths and fourths were the true intervals naturally grasped by the ear and his tone the true difference between them. It seems more likely, then, that he took up a dogmatic position and turned a blind eye to facts that were inconsistent with it; this would be in keeping with the rather truculent tone he sometimes adopted.

Writers on harmonics, from Aristoxenus on, fall into two schools: his followers, who reproduced and simplified his doctrines in a number of extant handbooks, and the "Pythagoreans" such as Eratosthenes, Didymus the musician, and—notably—Ptolemy, who elaborated ratios for the intervals of the scale. It is perhaps doubtful whether any writer of the mathematical school prior to Ptolemy produced a comprehensive theory of scales in relation to practical music, and it may well have been the inadequacy and limited interests of the Pythagoreans that set Aristoxenus against this approach. Nor would it be fair to deny Aristoxenus' scientific merits because of his disregard of mathematics. He was not in vain a pupil of Aristotle, from whom he had learned inductive logic and the importance of clear definition; and what he attempted was, in the words of M. I. Henderson, "a descriptive anatomy of music." His arguments are closely reasoned, but, lacking his master's breadth and receptivity, he can be suspected of sacrificing musical realities to logical clarity.

The details of his system, which can be found in standard textbooks and musical encyclopedias, are not in themselves of primary interest to the historian of science. The quality of his thinking at its best can, however, be illustrated from his work on rhythm. Earlier writers had tended to discuss rhythm in terms of poetic meters, but, since rhythm also manifests itself in melody and in the dance, there was some confusion of thought and terminology. Aristoxenus drew a clear distinction between rhythm, which was an organized system of time units expressible in ratios, and the words, melodies, and bodily movements in which it was incorporated (*ta rhythmizomena*) and from which it could be abstracted. This was a much-needed piece of clarification worthy of Aristotle.

BIBLIOGRAPHY

I. Original Works. Modern editions of Aristoxenus' works are *The Harmonics of Aristoxenus,* edited, with translation, notes, introduction, and index of words, by H. S. Macran (Oxford, 1902); and *Aristoxeni elementa harmonica,* Rosetta da Rios, ed. (Rome, 1954).

II. Secondary Literature. Works dealing with Aristoxenus include Ingemar Düring, *Ptolemaios und Porphyrios über die Musik* (Göteborg, 1934), which contains, in German translation, Ptolemy's criticisms of Aristoxenus; C. von Jan, "Aristoxenos," in Pauly-Wissowa, *Real-*

Encyclopädie, II (Stuttgart, 1895), 1057 ff.; L. Laloy, *Aristoxène de Tarente* (Paris, 1904), an outstanding work; F. Wehrli, *Die Schule des Aristoteles, Texte und Kommentar,* Vol. II, *Aristoxenos* (Basel, 1945), for the shorter fragments; and R. Westphal, *Aristoxenos von Tarent* (Leipzig, 1883–1893), which includes the fragment on rhythm.

R. P. WINNINGTON-INGRAM

ARNAULD, ANTOINE (*b.* Paris, France, 1612; *d.* Brussels, Belgium, 6 August 1694)

Arnauld was the youngest of the twenty children of Antoine Arnauld, a lawyer who defended the University of Paris against the Jesuits in 1594. He was ordained a priest and received the doctorate in theology in 1641, and entered the Sorbonne in 1643, after the death of Richelieu. In 1656 he was expelled from the Sorbonne for his Jansenist views, and spent a good part of the rest of his life in more or less violent theological dispute. He died in self-imposed exile.

Although in many of his nontheological writings Arnauld is identified with the Port-Royal school, his voluminous correspondence—with Descartes and Leibniz, among others—bears witness to his own influence and acumen. His philosophical contributions are to be found in his objections to Descartes's *Méditations,* in his dispute with Malebranche, and in the *Port-Royal Logic,* which he wrote with Pierre Nicole. The latter, a text developed from Descartes's *Regulae,* elaborates the theory of "clear and distinct" ideas and gives the first account of Pascal's *Méthode.* It had an enormous influence as a textbook until comparatively recent times.

The profound influence of the *Regulae* is shown in both the *Logic* and the *Port-Royal Grammar,* where it is assumed that linguistic and mental processes are virtually identical, that language is thus to be studied in its "inner" and "outer" aspects. This point of view underlies the project for a universal grammar and the notion of the "transparency" of language: mental processes are common to all human beings, although there are many languages. The *Grammar* and the *Logic* are based on a common analysis of signs that has brought the Port-Royal school to the attention of modern linguistic theorists, who see in it an anticipation of their own point of view.

The *Élémens* (1667) undertakes a reworking and reordering of the Euclidean theorems in the light of the contemporary literature (in which he was widely read) and Pascal's influence. It bases its claim to originality and influence on the new order in which the theorems, many of them adapted from contemporary sources, are arranged. As mathematics, it is characterized by the mastery of the contemporary literature and by its clear and fresh exposition; its virtues are pedagogical. It is interesting to compare Arnauld's order of theorems with such recent ones as that of Hilbert and Forder, whose aims are quite different. If Arnauld's pedagogical concerns are insufficiently appreciated, it may be because the role of what are properly pedagogical concerns in the habits and "methods" of modern science is insufficiently understood: its preoccupation with clarity and procedure, with formal exercises and notation, and the use of these as instruments of research.

BIBLIOGRAPHY

I. ORIGINAL WORKS. Arnauld's writings include *Grammaire générale et raisonnée* (*Port-Royal Grammar;* Paris, 1660); *La logique ou l'art de penser* (*Port-Royal Logic;* Paris, 1662), crit. ed. by P. Clair and F. Girbal (Paris, 1965); and *Nouveaux élémens de géométrie* (Paris, 1667). Collections of his work are *Oeuvres,* 45 vols. (Lausanne, 1775–1783); and *Oeuvres philosophiques,* J. Simon and C. Jourdain, eds. (Paris, 1893).

II. SECONDARY LITERATURE. Works on Arnauld are K. Bopp, "Arnauld als Mathematiker," in *Abhandlundgen zur Geschichte der mathematischen Wissenschaften,* **14** (1902), and "Drei Untersuchungen zur Geschichte der Mathematik," in *Schriften der Strassburger wissenschaftlichen Gesellschaft in Heidelberg,* no. 10 (1929), pt. 2, 5–18; H. L. Brekle, "Semiotik und linguistische Semantik in Port-Royal," in *Indogermanische Forschungen,* **69** (1964), 103–121; Noam Chomsky, *Cartesian Linguistics* (Cambridge, Mass., 1966); J. Coolidge, *The Mathematics of Great Amateurs* (Oxford, 1949); Leibniz, "Remarques sur les nouveaux Élémens de Géométrie Antoine Arnaulds," in *Die Leibniz-Handschriften zu Hannover,* E. Bodemann, ed., I (Hannover, 1895), no. 21, 287; and H. Scholz, "Pascals Forderungen an die mathematische Methode," in *Festschrift Andreas Speiser* (1945).

HENRY NATHAN

ARONHOLD, SIEGFRIED HEINRICH (*b.* Angerburg, Germany [now Węgorzewo, Poland], 16 July 1819; *d.* Berlin, Germany, 13 March 1884)

Aronhold attended the Angerburg elementary school and the Gymnasium in Rastenburg (now Kętrzyn, Poland). Following the death of his father, his mother moved to Königsberg, where the boy attended a Gymnasium. He graduated in 1841 and then studied mathematics and natural sciences at the University of Königsberg from 1841 to 1845. Among his teachers were Bessel, Jacobi, Richelot, Hesse, and Franz Neumann. When Jacobi went to Berlin, Aronhold followed him and continued his studies under Dirichlet, Steiner, Gustav Magnus, and Dove. He did not take the state examinations, but in 1851 the

University of Königsberg awarded him the *Doctor honoris causa* for his treatise "Über ein neues algebraisches Prinzip" and other studies.

From 1852 to 1854 Aronhold taught at the Artillery and Engineers' School in Berlin and, from 1851, at the Royal Academy of Architecture in Berlin, where he was appointed professor in 1863. In 1860 he joined the Royal Academy for Arts and Crafts, where, when Weierstrass became ill in 1862, he took over the entire teaching schedule. He was appointed professor in 1864. In 1869 Aronhold became a corresponding member of the Academy of Sciences in Göttingen. He was considered an enthusiastic and inspiring teacher, and was held in high esteem everywhere.

Aronhold was particularly attracted by the theory of invariants, which was then the center of mathematical interest, and was the first German to do research in this area. The theory of invariants is not, however, connected with Aronhold alone—others who worked on it were Sylvester, Cayley, and Hesse—but he developed a special method that proved to be extremely successful. In 1863 he collected his ideas in a treatise entitled "Über eine fundamentale Begründung der Invariantentheorie."

In this treatise, Aronhold offers solid proof of his theory, which he had welded into an organic entity. His method refers to functions that remain unchanged under linear substitutions. He stresses the importance of the logical development of a few basic principles so that the reader may find his way through other papers. Aronhold establishes his theory in general and does not derive any specific equations. He derives the concept of invariants from the concept of equivalency for the general linear theory of invariants. Special difficulties arise, of course, if not only general but also special cases are to be considered. His efforts to obtain equations independent of substitution coefficients led to linear partial differential equations of the first order, which also have linear coefficients. These equations, which are characteristic for the theory of invariants, are known as Aronhold's differential equations.

With these equations "Aronhold's process" can be carried out. This process permits the derivation of additional concomitants from one given concomitant. Aronhold investigates the characteristics of these partial differential equations and expands the theory to include the transformation of a system of homogeneous functions, furnishes laws for simultaneous invariants, and investigates contravariants (relevant forms), covariants, functional invariants, and divariants (intermediate forms).

Aronhold stresses that he arrived at his principles as early as 1851, citing his doctoral dissertation and the treatise "Theorie der homogenen Funktionen dritten Grades . . ." (1858). Since the subsequent theory and terminology did not yet exist, he claimed priority.

Before Aronhold developed his theory, he had worked on plane curves. The problem of the nine points of inflection of the third-order plane curve, which had been discovered by Plücker, was brought to completion by Hesse and Aronhold. Aronhold explicitly established the required fourth-degree equation and formulated a theorem on plane curves of the fourth order. Seven straight lines in a plane always determine one, and only one, algebraic curve of the fourth order, in that they are part of their double tangents and that among them there are no three lines whose six tangential points lie on a conic section.

BIBLIOGRAPHY

I. Original Works. Aronhold's writings are "Zur Theorie der homogenen Funktionen dritten Grades von drei Variabeln," in *Journal für die reine und angewandte Mathematik* (Crelle), **39** (1849); "Bemerkungen über die Auflösung der biquadratischen Gleichung," *ibid.,* **52** (1856), trans. into French as "Remarque sur la résolution des équations biquadratiques," in *Nouvelles annales de mathématiques,* **17** (1858); "Theorie der homogenen Funktionen dritten Grades von drei Veränderlichen," in *Journal für die reine und angewandte Mathematik* (Crelle), **55** (1858); "Algebraische Reduktion des Integrals ∫F(x,y) dx, wo F(x,y) eine beliebige rationale Funktion von x,y bedeutet und zwischen diesen Grössen eine Gleichung dritten Grades von der allgemeinsten Form besteht, auf die Grundform der elliptischen Transzendenten," in *Berliner Monatsberichte* (1861); "Form der Kurve, wonach die Rippe eines T-Konsols zu formen ist," in *Verhandlung der Polytechnischen Gesellschaft* (Berlin), **22** (1861); "Über eine neue algebraische Behandlungsweise der Integrale irrationaler Differentiale von der Form Π (x,y) dx, in welcher Π (x,y) eine beliebige rationale Funktion ist, und zwischen x und y eine allgemeine Gleichung zweiter Ordnung besteht," in *Journal für die reine und angewandte Mathematik* (Crelle), **61** (1862); "Über eine fundamentale Begründung der Invariantentheorie," *ibid.,* **62** (1863); "Über den gegenseitigen Zusammenhang der 28 Doppeltangenten einer allgemeinen Kurve vierten Grades," in *Berliner Monatsberichte* (1864); "Neuer und direkter Beweis eines Fundamentaltheorems der Invariantentheorie," in *Journal für die reine und angewandte Mathematik* (Crelle), **69** (1868); and "Grundzüge der kinetischen Geometrie," in *Verhandlungen des Vereins für Gewerbefleiss,* **52** (1872).

II. Secondary Literature. More detailed information on mathematics in Berlin can be found in E. Lampe, *Die reine Mathematik in den Jahren 1884–1899 nebst Aktenstücken zum Leben von Siegfried Aronhold* (Berlin,

1899), pp. 5 ff. For the theory of invariants, see Weitzenböck, *Invariantentheorie* (Groningen, 1923); *Enzyklopädie der mathematische Wissenschaften,* I, pt. 1 (Leipzig, 1898), 323 ff.; Felix Klein, *Vorlesungen über die Entwicklung der Mathematik im 19. Jahrhunderts* (Berlin, 1926–1927), I, 157, 166, 305; II, 161, 195; and Enrico Pascal, *Repertorium der höheren Analysis,* 2nd ed. (Leipzig–Berlin, 1910), ch. 5, pp. 358–420.

HERBERT OETTEL

ARTIN, EMIL (*b.* Vienna, Austria, 3 March 1898; *d.* Hamburg, Germany, 20 December 1962)

Artin was the son of the art dealer Emil Artin and the opera singer Emma Laura-Artin. He grew up in Reichenberg, Bohemia (now Liberec, Czechoslovakia), where he passed his school certificate examination in 1916. After one semester at the University of Vienna he was called to military service. In January 1919 he resumed his studies at the University of Leipzig, where he worked primarily with Gustav Herglotz, and in June 1921 he was awarded the Ph.D.

Following this, he spent one year at the University of Göttingen, and then went to the University of Hamburg, where he was appointed lecturer in 1923, extraordinary professor in 1925, and ordinary professor in 1926. He lectured on mathematics, mechanics, and the theory of relativity. In 1929 he married Natalie Jasny. Eight years later they and their two children emigrated to the United States, where their third child was born. Artin taught for a year at the University of Notre Dame, then from 1938 to 1946 at Indiana University in Bloomington, and from 1946 to 1958 at Princeton. He returned to the University of Hamburg in 1958, and taught there until his death. He was divorced in 1959. His avocations were astronomy and biology; he was also a connoisseur of old music and played the flute, the harpsichord, and the clavichord.

In 1962, on the three-hundredth anniversary of the death of Blaise Pascal, the University of Clermont-Ferrand, France, conferred an honorary doctorate upon Artin.

In 1921, in his thesis, Artin applied the arithmetical and analytical theory of quadratic number fields over the field of rational numbers to study the quadratic extensions of the field of rational functions of one variable over finite constant fields. For the zeta function of these fields he formulated the analogue of the Riemann hypothesis about the zeros of the classical zeta function. In 1934 Helmut Hasse proved this hypothesis of Artin's for function fields of genus 1, and in 1948 André Weil proved the analogue of the Riemann hypothesis for the general case.

In 1923 Artin began the investigations that occupied him for the rest of his life. He assigned to each algebraic number field k a new type of L-series. The functions

$$L(s,\chi) = \Sigma\chi(n)(Nn)^{-s}$$

—generalizations of the Dirichlet L-series—in which χ is the character of a certain ideal class group and n traverses certain ideals of k were already known. These functions play an important role in Teiji Takagi's investigations (1920) of Abelian fields K over k. Artin started his L-series from a random Galois field K over k with the Galois group G; he utilized representations of the Frobenius character χ by matrices. Further, he made use of the fact that, according to Frobenius, to each unbranched prime ideal, p, in K, a class of conjugated substitutions σ from G, having the character value χ (σ), can be assigned in a certain manner. Artin made $\chi\,(p^h) = \chi\,(\sigma^h)$ and formulated $\chi\,(p^h)$ for prime ideals p branched in K; he also defined his L-series by the formula

$$\log L(s,\chi,K/k) = \sum_{p,h} h^{-1}\chi(p^h)(Np^h)^{-s}.$$

Artin assumed, and in 1923 proved for special cases, the identity of his L-series formed of simple character and the functions $L(s,\chi)$ for Abelian groups, if at the same time χ were regarded as a certain ideal class character. The proof of this assumption led him to the general law of reciprocity, a phrase he coined. Artin proved this in 1927, using a method developed by Nikolai Chebotaryov (1924). This law includes all previously known laws of reciprocity, going back to Gauss's. It has become the main theorem of class field theory.

With the aid of the theorem, Artin traced Hilbert's assumption, according to which each ideal of a field becomes a principal ideal of its absolute class field, to a theory on groups that had been proved in 1930 by Philip Furtwaengler.

Artin had often pointed to a supposition of Furtwaengler's according to which a series k_i ($i = 1,2,\ldots$) is necessarily infinite if k_{i+1} is an absolute class field over k_i. This was disproved in 1964 by I. R. Safarevic and E. S. Gold.

In 1923 Artin derived a functional equation for his L-series that was completed in 1947 by Richard Brauer. Since then it has been found that the Artin L-series define functions that are meromorphic in the whole plane. Artin's conjecture—that these are integral if χ is not the main character—still remains unproved.

Artin had a major role in the further development of the class field theory, and he stated his results in *Class Field Theory,* written with John T. Tate (1961).

In 1926 Artin achieved a major advance in abstract algebra (as it was then called) in collaboration with Otto Schreier. They succeeded in treating real algebra in an abstract manner by defining a field as real—today we say formal-real—if in it -1 is not representable as a sum of square numbers. They defined a field as real-closed if the field itself was real but none of the algebraic extensions were. They then demonstrated that a real-closed field could be ordered in one exact manner and that in it typical laws of algebra, as it had been known until then, were valid.

With the help of the theory of formal-real fields, Artin in 1927 solved the Hilbert problem of definite functions. This problem, expressed by Hilbert in 1900 in his Paris lecture "Mathematical Problems," is related to the solution of geometrical constructions with ruler and measuring standard, an instrument that permits the marking off of a single defined distance.

In his work on hypercomplex numbers in 1927, Artin expanded the theory of algebras of associative rings, established in 1908 by J. H. Maclagan Wedderburn, in which the double-chain law for right ideals is assumed; in 1944 he postulated rings with minimum conditions for right ideals (Artin rings). In 1927 he further presented a new foundation for, and extension of, the arithmetic of semisimple algebras over the field of rational numbers. The analytical theory of these systems was treated by his student Käte Hey, in her thesis in 1927.

Artin contributed to the study of nodes in three-dimensional space with his theory of braids in 1925. His definition of a braid as a tissue made up of fibers comes from topology, but the method of treatment belongs to group theory.

Artin's scientific achievements are only partially set forth in his papers and textbooks and in the drafts of his lectures, which often contained new insights. They are also to be seen in his influence on many mathematicians of his period, especially his Ph.D. candidates (eleven in Hamburg, two in Bloomington, eighteen in Princeton). His assistance is acknowledged in several works of other mathematicians. His influence on the work of Nicholas Bourbaki is obvious.

BIBLIOGRAPHY

I. Original Works. Artin's works are in *The Collected Papers of Emil Artin,* Serge Lang and John T. Tate, eds. (Reading, Mass., 1965), and in the books and lecture notes that are listed there, including "Einführung in die Theorie der Gammafunktion" (1931); "Galois Theory" (1942); "Rings With Minimum Condition," written with C. J. Nesbitt and R. M. Thrall (1944); *Geometric Algebra* (1957); and *Class Field Theory,* written with J. T. Tate (1961). Missing from the list is "Vorlesungen über algebraische Topologie," a mathematical seminar given with Hel Braun at the University of Hamburg (1964).

II. Secondary Literature. Works on Artin are R. Brauer, "Emil Artin," in *Bulletin of the American Mathematical Society,* **73** (1967), 27–43; H. Cartan, "Emil Artin," in *Abhandlungen aus dem Mathematischen Seminar der Hamburgischen Universität,* **28** (1965), 1–6; C. Chevalley, "Emil Artin," in *Bulletin de la Société mathématique de France,* **92** (1964), 1–10; B. Schoeneberg, "Emil Artin zum Gedächtnis," in *Mathematisch-physikalische Semesterberichte,* **10** (1963), 1–10; and H. Zassenhaus, "Emil Artin and His Work," in *Notre Dame Journal of Formal Logic,* **5** (1964), 1–9, which contains a list of Artin's doctoral candidates.

Bruno Schoeneberg

ĀRYABHAṬA I (*b.* A.D. 476)

Āryabhaṭa I clearly states his connection with Kusumapura (Pāṭaliputra, modern Patna in Bihar), which had been the imperial capital of the Guptas for much of the fourth and fifth centuries. The assertion of Nīlakaṇṭha Somasutvan (*b.* 1443) that Āryabhaṭa was born in the Aśmakajanapada (this presumably refers to the Nizamabad district of Andhra Pradesh) is probably the result of a confusion with his predecessor, Bhāskara I, as commentator on the *Āryabhaṭīya.* Āryabhaṭa I wrote two works: the *Āryabhaṭīya* in 499 (see Essay V), and another, lost treatise in which he expounded the *ārddharātrika* system (see Essay VI).

The *Āryabhaṭīya* consists of three parts and a brief introduction: *Daśagītikā,* introduction with parameters (ten verses); *Gaṇitapāda,* mathematics (thirty-three verses); *Kālakriyāpāda,* the reckoning of time and the planetary models (twenty-five verses); *Golapāda,* on the sphere, including eclipses (fifty verses). It was translated into Arabic in about 800 under the title *Zīj al-Arjabhar,* and it is to this translation that all the quotations in al-Bīrūnī refer, including those that led Kaye to conclude—mistakenly—that the *Gaṇitapāda* was not written by Āryabhaṭa I.

The *Āryabhaṭīya* has been commented on many times, especially by scholars of south India, where it was particularly studied. The names of those commentators who are known are as follows:

1. Prabhākara (*ca.* 525). His commentary is lost.
2. Bhāskara I (629). His *Bhāṣya* is being edited by K. S. Śukla of Lucknow.

3. Someśvara (*fl.* 1040). His *Vāsanābhāṣya* is preserved in two manuscripts in the Bombay University Library.

4. Sūryadeva Yajvan of Kerala (*b.* 1191). There are many manuscripts of his *Bhaṭaprakāśa,* in south India.

5. Parameśvara (*fl.* 1400-1450). His *Bhaṭadīpikā,* based on Sūryadeva's *Bhaṭaprakāśa,* was published by H. Kern (see below).

6. Nīlakaṇṭha Somasutvan (*b.* 1443). His *Bhāṣya* is published in *Trivandrum Sanskrit Series* (see below).

7. Yallaya (*fl.* 1482). His *Vyākhyāna* is based on Sūryadeva's *Bhaṭaprakāśa;* there is one manuscript of it in Madras and another among the Mackenzie manuscripts in the India Office Library.

8. Raghunātha (*fl.* 1590). His *Vyākhyā* is dealt with by K. Madhava Krishna Sarma, "The *Āryabhaṭīyavyākhyā* of Raghunātharāja—A Rare and Hitherto Unknown Work," in *Brahmavidyā,* **6** (1942), 217-227.

9. Kodaṇḍarāma of the Koṭikalapūḍikula, a resident of Bobbili in the Godāvarī district of Andhra Pradesh (*fl.* 1854). Besides an *Āryabhaṭatantragaṇita,* he wrote a Telugu commentary on the *Āryabhaṭīya* entitled *Sudhātaraṅga;* it was edited by V. Lakshmi Narayana Sastri, in *Madras Government Oriental Series,* **139** (Madras, 1956).

10. Bhūtiviṣṇu. There is apparently only one manuscript (in Berlin) and its apograph (in Washington, D.C.) of his commentary (*Bhāṣya*) on the *Daśagītikā.*

11. Ghaṭīgopa. There are two manuscripts of his *Vyākhyā* in Trivandrum.

12. Virūpākṣa Sūri. There is a manuscript of his Telugu commentary in Mysore.

There also exists a Marāṭhī translation of the *Āryabhaṭīya* in a manuscript at Bombay.

There are several editions of the *Āryabhaṭīya.* That by H. Kern (Leiden, 1874) is accompanied by the commentary of Parameśvara. Kern's text and commentary were reprinted and translated into Hindi by Udaya Nārāyana Singh (Madhurapur, Etawah, 1906). A new edition of the text, with the commentary of Nīlakaṇṭha Somasutvan (who does not include the *Daśagītikā*), was published in three volumes: Vols. I and II by K. Sāmbaśiva Śāstrī and Vol. III by Suranad Kunjan Pillai, in *Trivandrum Sanskrit Series,* **101, 110,** and **185** (Trivandrum, 1930, 1931, 1957). The text has also been published accompanied by two new commentaries, one in Sanskrit and one in Hindi, by Baladeva Mishra (Patna, 1966). The *Gaṇitapāda* was translated into French by Léon Rodet, in *Journal Asiatique,* **7,** no. 13 (1879), 393-434; and into English by G. R. Kaye, in *Journal of the Asiatic Society of Bengal,* **4** (1908), 111-141. Complete English translations have been made by Baidyanath Rath Sastri (Chicago, 1925; unpub.); P. C. Sengupta, *Journal of the Department of Letters of Calcutta University,* **16** (1927), 1-56; and W. E. Clark (Chicago, 1930).

BIBLIOGRAPHY

It is intended here to include references only to those books and articles that are primarily concerned with Āryabhaṭa I and his works; the many other papers and volumes that mention and/or discuss him can be found listed in David Pingree, *Census of the Exact Sciences in India.* Listed chronologically, the references are F.-E. Hall, "On the Ārya-siddhānta," in *Journal of the American Oriental Society,* **6** (1860), 556-559, with an "Additional Note on Āryabhaṭṭa and his Writings" by the Committee of Publication (essentially W. D. Whitney), *ibid.,* 560-564; H. Kern, "On Some Fragments of Āryabhaṭa," in *Journal of the Royal Asiatic Society,* **20** (1863), 371-387; repr. in Kern's *Vespreide Geschriften,* I (The Hague, 1913), 31-46; Bhāu Dājī, "Brief Notes on the Age and Authenticity of the Works of Āryabhaṭa, Varāhamihira, Brahmagupta, Bhaṭṭotpala, and Bhāskarāchārya," in *Journal of the Royal Asiatic Society* (1865), pp. 392-418 (Āryabhaṭa only pp. 392-406, 413-414); L. Rodet, "Sur la véritable signification de la notation numérique inventée par Āryabhaṭa," in *Journal Asiatique,* ser. 7, **16** (1880), 440-485; Sudhākara Dvivedin, *Gaṇakataraṅgiṇī* (Benares, 1933; repr. from *The Pandit,* **14** [1892]), 2-7; Ś. B. Dīkṣita, *Bhāratīya Jyotiḥśāstra* (Poona, 1931; repr. of Poona ed., 1896), pp. 190-210; G. Thibaut, *Astronomie, Astrologie und Mathematik, Grundriss der indo-arischen Philologie und Altertumskunde,* III, pt. 9, (Strasbourg, 1899), 54-55; T. R. Pillai, *Ārybhaṭa or the Newton of Indian Astronomy* (Madras, 1905—not seen—reviewed in *Indian Thought* [1907], pp. 213-216); G. R. Kaye, "Two Āryabhaṭas," in *Bibliotheca mathematica,* **10** (1910), 289-292; J. F. Fleet, "Āryabhaṭa's System of Expressing Numbers," in *Journal of the Royal Asiatic Society* (1911), pp. 109-126; N. K. Mazumdar, "Āryyabhatta's Rule in Relation to Indeterminate Equations of the First Degree," in *Bulletin of the Calcutta Mathematical Society,* **3** (1911/1912), 11-19; J. F. Fleet, "Tables for Finding the Mean Place of Saturn," in *Journal of the Royal Asiatic Society* (1915), pp. 741-756; P. C. Sengupta, "Āryabhaṭa's Method of Determining the Mean Motions of Planets," in *Bulletin of the Calcutta Mathematical Society,* **12** (1920/1921), 183-188.

See also R. Sewell, "The First Arya Siddhanta," in *Epigraphia Indica,* **16** (1921/1922), 100-144, and **17** (1923-1924), 17-104; A. A. Krishnaswami Ayyangar, "The Mathematics of Āryabhaṭa," in *Quarterly Journal of the Mythic Society,* **16** (1926), 158-179; B. Datta, "Two Āryabhaṭas of al-Biruni," in *Bulletin of the Calcutta Mathematical Society,* **17** (1926), 59-74; S. K. Ganguly, "Was

Āryabhaṭa Indebted to the Greeks for His Alphabetical System of Expressing Numbers?," *ibid.*, 195-202, and "Notes on Āryabhaṭa," in *Journal of the Bihar and Orissa Research Society,* **12** (1926), 78-91; B. Datta, "Āryabhaṭa, the Author of the *Gaṇita,*" in *Bulletin of the Calcutta Mathematical Society,* **18** (1927), 5-18; S. K. Ganguly, "The Elder Āryabhaṭa and the Modern Arithmetical Notation," in *American Mathematical Monthly,* **34** (1927), 409-415; P. C. Sengupta, "Āryabhaṭa, the Father of Indian Epicyclic Astronomy," in *Journal of the Department of Letters of Calcutta University,* **18** (1929), 1-56; S. K. Ganguly, "The Elder Āryabhaṭa's Value of π," in *American Mathematical Monthly,* **37** (1930), 16-29; P. C. Sengupta, "Āryabhaṭa's Lost Work," in *Bulletin of the Calcutta Mathematical Society,* **22** (1930), 115-120; B. Datta, "Elder Āryabhaṭa's Rule for the Solution of Indeterminate Equations of the First Degree," *ibid.*, **24** (1932), 19-36; P. K. Gode, "Appayadīkṣita's Criticism of Āryabhaṭa's Theory of the Diurnal Motion of the Earth (*Bhūbhramavāda*)," in *Annals of the Bhandarkar Oriental Research Institute,* **19** (1938), 93-95, repr. in Gode's *Studies in Indian Literary History,* II, *Singhi Jain Series,* **38** (Bombay, 1954), 49-52; S. N. Sen, "Āryabhaṭa's Mathematics," in *Bulletin of the National Institute of Sciences of India,* **21** (1963), 297-319; Satya Prakash, *Founders of Sciences in Ancient India* (New Delhi, 1965), pp. 419-449.

DAVID PINGREE

ARYABHAṬA II (*fl.* between *ca.* A.D. 950 and 1100)

Of the personality of Āryabhaṭa II, the author of the *Mahāsiddhānta* (or *Āryasiddhānta*), virtually nothing is known. His date can be established only by his alleged dependence on Śrīdhara, who wrote after Mahāvīra (*fl.* 850) and before Abhayadeva Sūri (*fl.* 1050); and by his being referred to by Bhāskara II (*b.* 1114). He must be dated, then, between *ca.* 950 and 1100. Kaye's strange theories about the two Āryabhaṭas, which would have placed Āryabhaṭa II before al-Bīrūnī (963-after 1048), have been refuted by Datta. Nothing further can be said of Āryabhaṭa II; manuscripts of his work are found in Mahārāṣṭra, Gujarat, and Bengal.

The *Mahāsiddhānta* (see Essay VII) consists of eighteen chapters:

1. On the mean longitudes of the planets.
2. On the mean longitudes of the planets according to the (otherwise unknown) *Parāśarasiddhānta.*
3. On the true longitudes of the planets.
4. On the three problems relating to diurnal motion.
5. On lunar eclipses.
6. On solar eclipses.
7. On the projection of eclipses and on the lunar crescent.

8-9. On the heliacal risings and settings of the planets.

10. On the conjunctions of the planets.
11. On the conjunctions of the planets with the stars.
12. On the *pātas* of the sun and moon.

Chapters 13-18 form a separate section entitled *Golādhyāya* ("On the Sphere").

13. Questions on arithmetic, geography, and the mean longitudes of the planets.

14-15. On arithmetic and geometry.

16. On geography.
17. Shortcuts to finding the mean longitudes of the planets.
18. On algebra.

The *Mahāsiddhānta* was edited, with his own Sanskrit commentary, by MM. Sudhākara Dvivedin, in *Benares Sanskrit Series* **148-150** (Benares, 1910).

BIBLIOGRAPHY

Works dealing with Āryabhaṭa II, listed chronologically, are F. Hall, "On the Ārya-Siddhānta," in *Journal of the American Oriental Society,* **6** (1860), 556-559; G. R. Kaye, "Two Āryabhaṭas," in *Bibliotheca mathematica,* **10** (1910), 289-292; J. F. Fleet, "The Katapayadi Notation of the Second Arya-Siddhanta," in *Journal of the Royal Asiatic Society* (1912), 459-462; B. Datta, "Two Āryabhaṭas of al-Biruni," in *Bulletin of the Calcutta Mathematical Society,* **17** (1926), 59-74, and "Āryabhaṭa, the Author of the *Gaṇita,*" *ibid.*, **18** (1927), 5-18; Ś. B. Dīkṣita, *Bhāratīya Jyotiḥśāstra* (Poona, 1931; repr. from Poona, 1896), pp. 230-234.

DAVID PINGREE

ATWOOD, GEORGE (*b.* England, 1745; *d.* London, England, July 1807)

Atwood attended Westminster School and was awarded a scholarship to Trinity College, Cambridge, at the age of nineteen. He graduated with a B.A. in 1769, received his M.A. in 1772, then became a fellow and tutor at his college. His lectures were well attended and well received because of their delivery and their experimental demonstrations. These experiments, published in 1776, the year he was elected a fellow of the Royal Society, consisted of simple demonstrations to illustrate electricity, optics, and mechanics.

Among his admirers was William Pitt, who in 1784 gave Atwood an office in the treasury, at £500 a year, so that, according to an obituary in the *Gentleman's Magazine,* he could "devote a large portion of his time to financial calculation" in which he was apparently employed "to the great advantage of revenue." His only published work in this connection was *A Review of the Statutes* . . . (1801), in which he analyzed the cost of bread. The price that the baker could charge for a loaf of bread was governed by statute and was determined by the cost of grain plus an allowance for profit. Central to the problem was how much grain was required to make a loaf of bread. Atwood's work, an attempt to rationalize the standards, was based on computation as well as on the results of experiments carried out by Sir George Young in 1773.

The work for which Atwood is best known and which bears his name—Atwood's machine—is described in *A Treatise on the Rectilinear Motion* . . . (1784), which is essentially a textbook on Newtonian mechanics. Atwood's machine was designed to demonstrate the laws of uniformly accelerated motion due to gravity and was constructed with pulleys, so that a weight suspended from one of the pulleys descends more slowly than a body falling freely in air but still accelerates uniformly.

Most of Atwood's other published work consisted of the mathematical analysis of practical problems. In "A General Theory for the Mensuration . . ." (1781), he derived equations for use in connection with Hadley's quadrant; and in "The Construction and Analysis . . ." (1796) and "A Disquisition on the Stability of Ships" (1798), he extended the theories of Euler, Bougier, and others to account for the stability of floating bodies with large angles of roll. For "The Construction and Analysis . . ." he was awarded the Copley Medal of the Royal Society. His work on arches, *A Dissertation on the Construction and Properties of Arches* (1801), based on the assumption that the material of an arch is perfectly hard and rigid and that the only critical forces are those relating to the wedging action of the individual arch units, is now totally superseded. It was published with a supplement containing Atwood's questions about the proposed new London Bridge over the Thames, which was to be of iron.

BIBLIOGRAPHY

Atwood's works are *A Description of the Experiments Intended to Illustrate a Course of Lectures on the Principles of Natural Philosophy* (London, 1776); "A General Theory for the Mensuration of the Angle Subtended by Two Objects, of Which One Is Observed by Rays After Two Reflections From Plane Surfaces, and the Other by Rays Coming Directly to the Spectator's Eye," in *Philosophical Transactions of the Royal Society*, **71**, part 2 (1781), 395–434; *An Analysis of a Course of Lectures on the Principles of Natural Philosophy* (Cambridge, 1784), a revised version of *A Description of the Experiments . . . ; A Treatise on the Rectilinear Motion and Rotation of Bodies With a Description of Original Experiments Relative to the Subject* (Cambridge, 1784); "Investigations Founded on the Theory of Motion for Determining the Times of Vibration of Watch Balances," in *Philosophical Transactions*, **84** (1794), 119–168; "The Construction and Analysis of Geometrical Propositions Determining the Positions Assumed by Homogeneal Bodies Which Float Freely, and at Rest, on the Fluid's Surface; Also Determining the Stability of Ships and of Other Floating Bodies," *ibid.*, **86** (1796), 46–130; "A Disquisition on the Stability of Ships," *ibid.*, **88** (1798), 201–310; *A Dissertation on the Construction and Properties of Arches* (London, 1801); and *Review of the Statutes and Ordinances of Assize Which Have Been Established in England From the Fourth Year of King John, 1202 to the Thirty-seventh of His Present Majesty* (London, 1801).

ERIC M. COLE

AUTOLYCUS OF PITANE (*fl. ca.* 300 B.C.)

Autolycus came from Pitane in the Aeolis, Asia Minor, and was an instructor of Arcesilaus, also of Pitane, who founded the so-called Middle Academy. It is reported by Diogenes Laertius (4.29) that Arcesilaus accompanied his master on a journey to Sardis.

Autolycus was a successor to Eudoxus in the study of spherical astronomy, but was active somewhat later than the successors of the Cnidian, Callippus, and Polemarchus. It appears that he attempted to defend the Eudoxian system of concentric rotating spheres against critics, notably Aristotherus, the teacher of the astronomer-poet Aratus. The critics had pointed out that Venus and Mars seem brighter in the course of their retrograde arcs and that eclipses of the sun are sometimes annular and sometimes total, so that not all heavenly bodies remain at fixed distances from the earth. Autolycus acknowledged the difficulty in his discussion with Aristotherus and, inevitably, was unable to account for the variations by means of the Eudoxian system.

The two treatises of Autolycus, *On the Moving Sphere* and *On Risings and Settings*, are among the earliest works in Greek astronomy to survive in their entirety. *On the Moving Sphere* is almost certainly earlier than Euclid's *Phaenomena*, which seems to make use of it (*Sphere*, Ch. 11, may be compared with *Phaenomena* 7). Pappus tells us it was one of the works forming the "Little Astronomy"—the "Small Collection," in contrast with the "Great Collection" of Ptolemy.

Both Euclid and Autolycus make use of an elementary textbook, now lost, on the sphere, from which they take several propositions without proof, because the proofs were already known. In *On the Moving*

Sphere, a sphere is considered to move about an axis extending from pole to pole. Four classes of circular sections through the sphere are assumed: (1) great circles passing through the poles; (2) the equator and other, smaller, circles that are sections of the sphere formed by planes at right angles to the axis—these are the "parallel circles"; (3) great circles oblique to the axis of the sphere. The motion of points on the circles is then considered with respect to (4) the section formed by a fixed plane through the center of the sphere. A circle of class (3) is the ecliptic or zodiac circle, and (4) is equivalent to the horizon circle, which defines the visible and invisible parts of the sphere. In Euclid the great circle (4) has already become a technical term, "horizon," separating the hemisphere above the earth; Autolycus' treatment is more abstract and less overtly astronomical.

On Risings and Settings is strictly astronomical and consists of two complementary treatises or "books." True and apparent morning and evening risings and settings of stars are distinguished. Autolycus assumes that the celestial sphere completes one revolution during a day and a night; that the sun moves in a direction opposite to the diurnal rotation and traverses the ecliptic in one year; that by day the stars are not visible above the horizon owing to the light of the sun; and that a star above the horizon is visible only if the sun is 15° or more below the horizon measured along the zodiac (i.e., half a zodiacal sign or more).

The theorems are closely interrelated. Autolycus explains, for example, that the rising of a star is visible only between the visible morning rising and the visible evening rising, a period of less than half a year; similarly, he shows that the setting of a star is visible only in the interval from the visible morning setting to the visible evening setting, again a period of less than half a year. Another theorem states that the time from visible morning rising to visible morning setting is more than, equal to, or less than half a year if the star is north of, on, or south of the ecliptic, respectively.

Autolycus' works were popular handbooks and were translated into Arabic, Latin, and Hebrew.

BIBLIOGRAPHY

In addition to works cited in the text, see J. Mogenet, *Autolycus de Pitane* (Louvain, 1950); and O. Schmidt, "Some Critical Remarks About Autolycus' 'On Risings and Settings,'" in *Transactions of Den 11te Skandinaviske Matematikerkongress i Trondheim* (Oslo, 1952), pp. 202–209. See also the Mogenet edition of the Latin translation by Gerard of Cremona of *De sphaera mota,* in *Archives internationales d'histoire des sciences,* **5** (1948), pp. 139–164; and T. L. Heath, *Aristarchus of Samos* (Oxford, 1913), pp. 221–223.

G. L. HUXLEY

AUZOUT, ADRIEN (*b.* Rouen, France, 28 January 1622; *d.* Rome, Italy, 23 May 1691)

Auzout approached science with instruments rather than with mathematics. In the fall of 1647 he designed an ingenious experiment—creating one vacuum inside another—in order to prove that the weight of a column of air pressing on a barometer causes the mercury to rise inside. Auzout did not neglect mathematics, however; he criticized the treatise of François-Xavier Anyscom on the quadrature of the circle and prepared a treatise of reasons and proportions. By 1660 his career centered on astronomical instruments. He made a significant contribution to the final development of the micrometer and to the replacement of open sights by telescopic sights.

Not until after Christiaan Huygens discovered that there exists a special point (the focus) inside the Keplerian telescope, which has only convex lenses, could there be a breakthrough leading to the micrometer and to radically superior instruments. (Well before Huygens, William Gascoigne, after discovering the focal point, invented the micrometer and telescopic sights, but his inventions remained unknown to Continental astronomers until 1667.) Since an object can be superimposed on the image without distortion at the focus, precise measurements of the size of the image can be made. To do this, Huygens fashioned a crude micrometer. Cornelio Malvasia's lattice of fine wires was for Auzout, and probably Jean Picard, who worked with him, the jumping-off point for the perfection of the micrometer. They were dissatisfied with the accuracy of the lattice because images never covered exactly an integral number of squares, so they modified it. Two parallel hairs were separated by a distance variable according to the size of the image; one hair was fixed to a mobile chassis that was displaced at first by hand and later by a precision screw. By the summer of 1666 Auzout and Picard were making systematic observations with fully developed micrometers.

Soon after Huygens' discovery, Eustachio Divini and Robert Hooke replaced open sights with telescopic sights, and during the period 1667–1671 Auzout, Picard, and Gilles Personne de Roberval developed the systematic use of telescopic sights. An incomplete concept of focus caused the delay between discovery and systematic use, for Auzout, reasoning by analogy with open sights, suggested at the end of

1667 that each hair in the crosshairs be placed in a separate plane so that a line of sight might be assured. Unfortunately, after Auzout withdrew from the Académie des Sciences in 1668, he drifted into obscurity.

BIBLIOGRAPHY

I. Original Works. A complete bibliography of Auzout's work is in R. M. McKeon (see below), pp. 314–324; the claims to priority in development of the micrometer of Auzout, Picard, and Pierre Petit are discussed on pp. 63–68. Most of Auzout's published works are reprinted in the *Mémoires de l'Académie Royale des Sciences, depuis 1666 jusqu-à 1699* (Paris, 1729), **6**, 537–540; **7**, Part 1, 1–130; **10**, 451–462. The major part of his correspondence is published in E. Caillemer, *Lettres de divers savants à l'Abbé Claude Nicaise* (Lyons, 1885), pp. 201–226; Christiaan Huygens, *Oeuvres*, 22 vols. (La Haye, 1888–1950), IV, 481–482; V, *passim;* VII, 372–373 (two letters are incorrectly attributed to Auzout in VI, 142–143, 580); H. Oldenberg, *Correspondence*, A. Rupert Hall and Marie Boas, eds. and trans. (Madison, Wis., 1965–); S. J. Rigaud and S. P. Rigaud, *Correspondence of Scientific Men of the Seventeenth Century* (Oxford, 1841), I, 206–210. The manuscript copies of Auzout's letters to Abbé Charles that were in the possession of the Ginori-Venturi family of Florence—called *Épreuves* in McKeon, p. 228, n.1—were listed in the spring 1966 catalog of Alain Brieux, Paris, and were sold. (The editors of Huygens' *Oeuvres* identify Abbé Charles as Charles de Bryas [IV, 72, n.4], but Abbé Charles's horoscope, which relates that he was born at Avignon in March 1604 and formerly was employed by Cardinal Mazarin [Bibliothèque Nationale, MSS fonds français, 13028, fol. 323], rules out their identification.)

II. Secondary Literature. Writings on Auzout or his work are Harcourt Brown, *Scientific Organizations in Seventeenth Century France* (*1620–1680*) (Baltimore, 1934); C. Irson, *Nouvelle méthode pour apprendre facilement les principes et la pureté de la langue française* (Paris, 1660), pp. 317–318; and Robert M. McKeon, "Établissement de l'astronomie de précision et oeuvre d'Adrien Auzout," unpublished dissertation (University of Paris, 1965); "Le récit d'Auzout au sujet des expériences sur le vide," in *Acts of XI International Congress of the History of Science* (Warsaw, 1965), Sec. III; and "Auzout," in *Encyclopaedia universalis*, in preparation.

Robert M. McKeon

AZARA, FÉLIX DE (*b.* Barbuñales, Huesca, Spain, 18 May 1742; *d.* Huesca, 20 October 1821).

Azara was the third son of Alejandro de Azara y Loscertales and María de Perera. At the University of Huesca he studied philosophy, arts, and law from 1757 to 1761 and in 1764 became an infantry cadet. The following year he continued his mathematical training in Barcelona, and by 1769, as a second lieutenant, he was assisting in the hydrographic surveys being carried out near Madrid; afterward he taught mathematics in the army until 1774. During the assault on Argel in 1775 he received a serious chest wound.

In 1781 Azara received a commission to establish the frontier between Brazil and the neighboring Spanish colonies. Upon his arrival in Montevideo, Uruguay, he was appointed captain of a frigate by the Spanish viceroy, who then sent him to Rio Grande and later to Asunción, Paraguay; this was the area Azara was to explore as both a geographer and a naturalist for thirteen years. Félix de Azara never married but, according to Walckenaer, while on his travels he was fond of female company, particularly that of mulattoes.

Between 1784 and 1796 Azara prepared at least fifteen maps of the Brazilian frontier; the Paraná, Pequeri, and Paraguay rivers; and the territory of Mato Grosso, Uruguay, Paraguay, and Buenos Aires. During those years he filled several diaries with accounts of travels in Paraguay and the Buenos Aires viceroyalty, the geography of Paraguay and the Río de la Plata, and the natural history of the birds and quadrupeds in those areas, relying on direct observation because he was practically without books or reference collections.

Azara returned to Spain in 1801, but soon afterward he moved to Paris, where his brother José Nicolás—a man greatly admired by Napoleon—was the Spanish ambassador. He was welcomed by the French naturalists because his *Essais sur l'histoire naturelle des quadrupèdes . . . du Paraguay* had just appeared, but on the death of José Nicolás in 1804 he returned to Madrid. Azara, with his liberal ideas, declined an appointment as viceroy of Mexico, and after 1808 during the Napoleonic War in Spain he was torn between his political and patriotic beliefs. Azara retired to Barbuñales and, as mayor of Huesca, ended his days there.

Azara enlarged natural history by discovering a large number of new species. He also visualized great biological concepts expanded by Cuvier and Darwin, both of whom quoted and accepted his views; for instance, on the variation undergone by horses under domestication.

BIBLIOGRAPHY

I. Original Works. Azara's first published work was *Essais sur l'histoire naturelle des quadrupèdes de la province du Paraguay,* M. L. E. Moreau de Saint Méry, trans. (Paris,

1801), which shortly afterward was much improved and corrected (Madrid, 1802). Other works by Azara are *Apuntamientos para la historia natural de los pájaros del Paraguay y Río de la Plata* (Madrid, 1802); *Voyages dans l'Amérique méridionale,* C. A. Walckenaer, trans. (Paris, 1809), with notes by Cuvier; *Descripción e historia del Paraguay y del Río de la Plata* (Madrid, 1847); and *Memorias sobre el estado rural del Rio de la Plata en 1801 . . .* (Madrid, 1847), published by his nephew Agustín de Azara. Several other works have subsequently appeared in Madrid and Buenos Aires.

II. SECONDARY LITERATURE. Both Moreau de Saint Méry's translation of the *Essais* (1801) and C. E. Walckenaer's translation of the *Voyages* give details of Azara's life. An excellent bibliographical survey, including the manuscript material in Madrid, Rome, Rio de Janeiro, and Buenos Aires, is Luis M. de Torres, "Noticias biográficas de D. Félix de Azara y exámen general de su obra," in *Anales de la Sociedad científica argentina,* **108** (1929), 177–190. The biography of Azara and a discussion of his role as a precursor of Darwin's ideas on the origin of species and the hypothesis of successive creations is E. Álvarez López, *Félix de Azara* (Madrid, 1935).

FRANCISCO GUERRA

BABBAGE, CHARLES (*b.* Teignmouth, England, 26 December 1792; *d.* London, England, 18 October 1871)

Babbage's parents were affluent. As a child, privately educated, he exhibited unusually sharp curiosity as to the how and why of everything around him. Entering Cambridge University in 1810, he soon found that he knew more than his teachers, and came to the conclusion that English mathematics was lagging behind European standards. In a famous alliance with George Peacock and John Herschel, he began campaigning for a revitalization of mathematics teaching. To this end the trio translated S. F. Lacroix's *Differential and Integral Calculus* and touted the superiority of Leibniz's differential notation over Newton's (then widely regarded in England as sacrosanct).

After graduation, Babbage plunged into a variety of activities and wrote notable papers on the theory of functions and on various topics in applied mathematics. He inquired into the organization and usefulness of learned societies, criticizing the unprogressive ones (among which he included the Royal Society) and helping found new ones—in particular the Astronomical Society (1820), the British Association (1831), and the Statistical Society of London (1834). He became a fellow of the Royal Society in 1816, and in 1827 was elected Lucasian professor of mathematics at Cambridge. He had not sought this prestigious chair (he described his election as "an instance of forgiveness unparalleled in history") and, although he held it for twelve years, never functioned as professor. This is a little surprising, in that the position could have been used to further the pedagogic reforms he advocated. But Babbage was becoming absorbed, if not obsessed, by problems of the mechanization of computation. He was to wrestle with these for decades, and they were partly responsible for transforming the lively, sociable young man into an embittered and crotchety old one, fighting all and sundry, even the London street musicians, whose activities, he figured, had ruined a quarter of his working potential.

Babbage had a forward-looking view of science as an essential part of both culture and industrial civilization, and he was among the first to argue that national government has an obligation to support scientific activities, to help promising inventors, and even to give men of science a hand in public affairs.

Few eminent scientists have had such diversified interests as Babbage. A listing of them would include cryptanalysis, probability, geophysics, astronomy, altimetry, ophthalmoscopy, statistical linguistics, meteorology, actuarial science, lighthouse technology, and the use of tree rings as historic climatic records. Two deserve special mention: the devising of a notation that not only simplified the making and reading of engineering drawings but also helped a good designer simplify his "circuits"; and his insightful writings on mass production and the principles of what we now know as operational research (he applied them to pin manufacture, the post office, and the printing trade).

Computational aids began to haunt Babbage's mind the day he realized that existing mathematical tables were peppered with errors whose complete eradication was all but infeasible. As a creature of his era—the machine-power revolution—he asked himself, at first only half in earnest, why a table of, say, sines could not be produced by steam. Then he went on to reflect that maybe it could. He was at the time enthusiastic about the application of the method of differences to tablemaking, and was indeed using it to compile logarithms. (His finished table of eight-figure logarithms for the first 108,000 natural numbers is among the best ever made.) While still engaged in this work, Babbage turned to the planning of a machine that would not only calculate functions but also print out the results.

To understand his line of thought, we must take a close look at the method of differences—a topic in what later became known as the calculus of finite differences. The basic consideration is of a polynomial

$f(x)$ of degree n evaluated for a sequence of equidistant values of x. Let h be this constant increment. We next take the corresponding increments in $f(x)$ itself, calling these the *first* differences; then we consider the differences between consecutive first differences, calling these the *second* differences. And so forth. An obvious recursive definition of the rth difference for a particular value of x, say x_i, is

$$\Delta^r f(x_i) = \Delta^{r-1} f(x_i + h) - \Delta^{r-1} f(x_i),$$

and it is not difficult to show that, specifically,

$$\Delta^r f(x_i) = \sum_{m=0}^{r} (-1)^m \binom{r}{m} f[x_i + (r - m)h].$$

As r increases, the differences become smaller and more nearly uniform, and at $r = n$ the differences are constant (so that at $r = n + 1$, all differences are zero). A simple example—one that Babbage himself was fond of using—is provided by letting the function be the squares of the natural numbers. Here $n = 2$, and we have

x	1	2	3	4	5	6	...
$f(x)$	1	4	9	16	25	36	...
Δ^1	3	5	7	9	11	...	
Δ^2	2	2	2	2	...		

Two propositions follow. The first, perhaps not obvious but easily demonstrated, is that the schema can be extended to most nonrational functions (such as logarithms), provided that we take the differences far enough. (This is linked to the fact that the calculus of finite differences becomes, in the limit, the familiar infinitesimal calculus.) The second, originated by Babbage, is that the inverse of the schema is readily adaptable to mechanization. In other words, a machine can be designed (and it will be only slightly more sophisticated than an automobile odometer or an office numbering machine) that, given appropriate initial values and nth constant differences, will accumulate values of any polynomial, or indeed of almost any function. (For nonrational functions the procedure will be an approximation conditioned by the choice of r and h and the accuracy required, and will need monitoring at regular checkpoints across the table.)

This is what Babbage set out—and failed—to do. As the work progressed, he was constantly thinking up new ideas for streamlining the mechanism, and these in turn encouraged him to enlarge its capacity. In the end his precepts ruined his practice. The target he set was a machine that would handle twenty-decimal numbers and sixth-order differences, plus a printout device. When he died, his unfinished "Difference Engine Number One" had been a museum piece for years (in the museum of King's College, at Somerset House, London, from 1842 to 1862, and subsequently in the Science Museum, London—where it still is). What is more revealing and ironic is that, during his own lifetime, a Swedish engineer named Georg Scheutz, working from a magazine account of Babbage's project, built a machine of modest capacity (eight-decimal numbers, fourth-order differences, and a printout) that really worked. It was used for many years in the Dudley Observatory, Albany, New York.

Aside from technicalities, two factors militated against the production of the difference engine. One was cost (even a generous government subsidy would not cover the bills), and the other was the inventor's espousal of an even more grandiose project—the construction of what he called an analytical engine.

Babbage's move onto this new path was inspired by his study of Jacquard's punched cards for weaving machinery, for he quickly saw the possibility of using such cards to code quantities and operations in an automatic computing system. His notion was to have sprung feeler wires that would actuate levers when card holes allowed them access. On this basis he drew up plans for a machine of almost unbelievable versatility and mathematical power. A simplified flow diagram of the engine is shown in the accompanying figure. The heart of the machine, the mill, was to consist of 1,000 columns of geared wheels, allowing up to that many fifty-decimal-digit numbers to be subjected to one or another of the four primary arithmetic operations. Especially remarkable was the incorporation of decision-making units of the logical type used in today's machines.

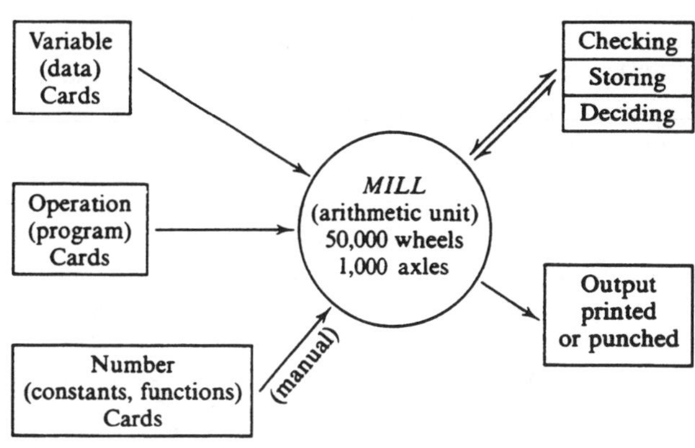

FIGURE 1

Although the analytical engine uncannily foreshadowed modern equipment, an important difference obtains: it was decimal, not binary. Babbage, not having to manipulate electronics, could not have been expected to think binarily. However, his having to use wheels meant that his system was not "purely" digital, in the modern sense.

All who understood the plans expressed unbounded admiration for the analytical engine and its conceiver. But material support was not forthcoming, and it remained a paper project. After Babbage's death his son, H. P. Babbage, sorted the mass of blueprints and workshop instructions, and, in collaboration with others, built a small analytical "mill" and printer. It may be seen today in the Science Museum, London.

BIBLIOGRAPHY

I. ORIGINAL WORKS. Babbage appended a list of eighty of his publications to his autobiographical *Passages From the Life of a Philosopher* (London, 1864), and it is reproduced in P. and E. Morrison's *Charles Babbage and His Calculating Engines* (New York, 1961). It is a poor list, with reprinted papers and excerpts separately itemized. Apart from translations and the autobiography and a few small and minor works, the only books of substance that Babbage published were *Reflections on the Decline of Science in England* (London, 1830); *Economy of Manufactures and Machinery* (London, 1832); and *The Exposition of 1851* (London, 1851). His logarithms deserve special mention: they were originally published in stereotype as *Table of the Logarithms of the Natural Numbers From 1 to 108,000* (London, 1827), with a valuable introduction dealing with the layout and typography of mathematical tables. A few years later he published *Specimen of Logarithmic Tables* (London, 1831), a 21-volume, single-copy edition of just two of the original pages printed in a great variety of colored inks on an even greater variety of colored papers, in order "to ascertain by experiment the tints of the paper and colors of the inks least fatiguing to the eye." In the same "experiment" about thirty-five copies of the complete table were printed on "thick drawing paper of various tints." In 1834 regular colored-paper editions were published in German at Vienna and in Hungarian at Budapest, by C. Nagy. Babbage's formal scientific articles number about forty. The first publication dealing with his main subject is "A Note Respecting the Application of Machinery to the Calculation of Mathematical Tables," in *Memoirs of the Astronomical Society,* **1** (1822), 309; the last is chs. 5–8 of his entertaining autobiography (see above).

II. SECONDARY LITERATURE. Practically all the significant material is either reproduced or indexed in the Morrisons' book, the only one entirely devoted to Babbage (see above). The symposium *Faster Than Thought* (London, 1953) has a first chapter (by the editor, B. V. Bowden) that is largely concerned with Babbage. Both of these books carry reprints of a translation and annotation of an article on the analytical engine written by the Italian military engineer L. F. Menabrea (Geneva, 1842). The translator was Lady Lovelace, Lord Byron's mathematically gifted daughter, and her detailed annotations (especially a sketch of how Bernoulli numbers could be computed by the engine) are excellent. It is in the course of this commentary that she finely remarks that "the Analytical Engine *weaves algebraic patterns,* just as the Jacquard-loom weaves flowers and leaves." The sectional catalog *Mathematics, I. Calculating Machines and Instruments,* The Science Museum (London, 1926), contains much useful illustrated information about Babbage's engines, as well as about allied machines, such as the Scheutz difference engine.

NORMAN T. GRIDGEMAN

BACHELIER, LOUIS (*b.* Le Havre, France, 11 March 1870; *d.* Saint-Servan-sur-Mer, Ille-et-Villaine, France, 28 April 1946)

Bachelier obtained the bachelor of sciences degree in 1898, and two years later he defended his doctoral dissertation on the theory of speculation. Encouraged by Henri Poincaré, he published three memoirs on probability: "Théorie mathématique des jeux" (1901), "Probabilités à plusieurs variables" (1910), and "Probabilités cinématiques et dynamiques" (1913). After being named lecturer at Besançon in 1919, he taught at Dijon and Rennes before returning to Besançon as professor from 1927 to 1937, when he retired.

Under the name "théorie de la spéculation" Bachelier introduced continuity into problems of probability. Making time the variable, he considered the movements of probabilities and chains of probabilities, then applied these ideas to the fluctuations of market rates and to the propagation of light and radiance. The relation between haphazard movement and diffusion was the first attempt at a mathematical theory of Brownian movement, a classic theory known today as the Einstein–Wiener theory; Wiener's rigorous study was made in 1928. Bachelier was the first to examine the stochastic methods of the Markovian type, on which A. N. Kolmogorov's theory is based. Yet lack of clarity and precision, certain considerations of doubtful interest, and some errors in definition explain why, in spite of their originality, his studies exerted no real scientific influence.

Bachelier participated in the diffusion of probabilistic thought through his articles "La périodicité du hasard" and "Quelques curiosités paradoxales du calcul des probabilités" and the book *Le jeu, la chance et le hasard.*

BIBLIOGRAPHY

Bachelier's writings include "Théorie de la spéculation," in *Annales de l'École normale supérieure,* 3rd ser., **17** (1900), 21–86; "Théorie mathématique des jeux," *ibid.,* **18** (1901), 143–210; "Théorie des probabilités continues," in *Journal de mathématiques pures et appliquées,* 6th ser., **2,** pt. 3 (1906), 259–327; "Probabilités à plusieurs variables," in *Annales de l'École normale supérieure,* 3rd ser., **27** (1910), 340–360; "Mouvement d'un point ou d'un système soumis à l'action de forces dépendant du hasard," in *Comptes rendus de l'Académie des sciences,* **151** (1910), 852–855; *Calcul des probabilités* (Paris, 1912); "Probabilités cinématiques et dynamiques," in *Annales de l'École normale supérieure,* 3rd ser., **30** (1913), 77–119; *Le jeu, la chance et le hasard* (Paris, 1924); *Les lois du grand nombre du calcul des probabilités* (Paris, 1937); *La spéculation et le calcul des probabilités* (Paris, 1938); and *Les nouvelles méthodes du calcul des probabilités* (Paris, 1939).

LUCIENNE FÉLIX

BACHET DE MÉZIRIAC, CLAUDE-GASPAR (*b.* Bourg-en-Bresse, France, 9 October 1581; *d.* Bourg-en-Bresse, 26 February 1638)

One of the ablest men of the seventeenth century, Bachet came from an ancient and noble family. His grandfather, Pierre Bachet, seigneur de Meyzériat, was counselor to King Henry II. His father was the honorable Jean Bachet, appeals judge of Bresse and counselor to the duke of Savoy; his mother was the noblewoman Marie de Chavanes. Orphaned at the age of six, the precocious Claude-Gaspar received his early education in a house of the Jesuit order that belonged to the duchy of Savoy. Presumably he studied in Padua as a young man, and he may have taught in a Jesuit school in Milan or Como. Bachet also spent a few years in Paris and in Rome, where, with his friend Claude Vaugelas, he composed a great deal of Italian verse. He was a prolific reader of poetry, history, commentary, scholarship, and mathematics.

In his fortieth year Bachet married Philiberte de Chabeu, by whom he had seven children. He suffered greatly from rheumatism and gout; when the Académie Française was founded in 1634, he was too ill to attend the inaugural ceremony. He was made a member of the Académie in the following year. His early literary works, humanist in outlook, consisted of poems in Latin, French, and Italian. Between 1614 and 1628 he published a Latin epistle from the Virgin Mary to her Son, canticles, brief sacred and profane Latin poems, translations of psalms, and a metrical translation of seven of Ovid's *Epistulae heroïdum.* He also published an anthology of French poetry, *Délices,* and the *Epistles of Ovid* (1626); the latter assured his reputation as a mythologist.

Bachet claims our attention today, however, chiefly for his contributions to the theory of numbers and to the field of mathematical recreations, in which he was one of the earliest pioneers. The two mathematical works for which he is remembered are his first edition of the Greek text of Diophantus of Alexandria's *Arithmetica,* accompanied by prolix commentary in Latin (1621), and his *Problemes plaisans et delectables qui se font par les nombres* (1612).

Diophantus had anticipated the advent of algebra and the theory of numbers. His work, which was known to the Arabs, was not appreciated until it was rediscovered in Europe during the latter part of the sixteenth century. Prior to Bachet's translation, only a few scholars had written on the work of Diophantus: Maximus Planudes, who gave an incomplete commentary on the first two books of the *Arithmetica* (*ca.* 1300); Raphael Bombelli, who embodied all of the problems of the first four books in his *Algebra* (1572); Wilhelm Holzmann, better known as Xylander, who gave a complete Latin translation (1575); and Simon Stevin, who gave a French translation of the first four books (1585). Bachet's translation, *Diophanti Alexandrini Arithmeticorum libri sex,* was based largely on the writings of Bombelli and Xylander, particularly the latter, although he admitted this with reluctance. Indeed, it is the opinion of T. L. Heath that although Bachet generally has been regarded as the only writer to interpret the contributions of Diophantus effectively, perhaps as much—if not more—of the credit is due to Xylander.

It is noteworthy that Bachet struggled with this work while suffering from a severe fever. He asserted that he corrected many errors in Xylander's version; filled in numerous omissions, such as proofs of porisms and abstruse theorems that Diophantus merely mentioned; and clarified much of the exposition. He apparently added few original contributions to number theory or Diophantine analysis, however, except for a generalization of the solution of the system $ax + v = u^2$, $cx + d = w^2$. Yet despite its imperfections, Bachet's work is commendable for being the first and only edition of the Greek text of Diophantus. It was subsequently reprinted, with the addition of Fermat's notes, in 1670; and while Fermat's notes are significant, the Greek text is inferior to that of the first edition.

Bachet's penchant for arithmetical rather than geometric problems is also obvious in the contents of his *Problemes plaisans et delectables.* These problems fall into several readily recognizable categories. The most elementary are those mildly amusing but mathematically unimportant parlor tricks of finding a number selected by someone, provided the results of certain operations performed on the number are revealed. Variations include problems involving two or three numbers, or two persons; problems depending upon the scale of notation; and tricks with a series of numbered objects, such as watch-dial puzzles and card tricks—many of these have appeared ever since in most collections of mathematical recreations. Somewhat more sophisticated is the famous problem of the Christians and the Turks, which had previously been solved by Tartaglia. (In a storm, a ship carrying fifteen Christians and fifteen Turks as passengers could be saved only by throwing half the passengers into the sea. The passengers were to be placed in a circle, and every ninth man, beginning at a certain point, was to be cast overboard. How should they be arranged so that all the Christians would be saved? Answer: CCCCTTTTTCCTCCCTCTTCCTTTCTTCCT.)

Of greater mathematical significance was Bachet's problem of the weights: to determine the least number of weights that would make possible the weighing of any integral number of pounds from one pound to forty pounds, inclusive. Bachet gave two solutions: the series of weights 1, 2, 4, 8, 16, 32; and the series 1, 3, 9, 27—depending upon whether the weights may be placed in only one scale pan or in each of the two scale pans. Last, there is the celebrated prototype of ferrying problems or difficult crossings, the problem of the three jealous husbands and their wives who wish to cross a river in a boat that can hold no more than two persons, in such a manner as never to leave a woman in the company of a man unless her husband is also present. Eleven crossings are required, but Bachet gave a solution that asserts "Il faut qu'ils passent en six fois en cette sorte." The analogous problem with four married couples cannot be solved; Bachet stated this fact without proof. It should also be noted that Bachet gave a method for constructing magic squares which is essentially that of Moschopulous (*ca.* 1300), although Bachet appears to have discovered it independently.

BIBLIOGRAPHY

I. Original Works. Bachet's translation of Diophantus' *Arithmetica* is *Diophanti Alexandrini Arithmeticorum libri sex, et de numeris multangulis liber unus. Nunc primum Graecè et Latinè editi, atque absolutissimis commentariis illustrati* (Paris, 1621); it was reprinted with the subtitle *Cum commentariis C. G. Bacheti V. C. & observationibus D. P. de Fermat senatoris Tolosani accessit doctrinae analyticae inventum novum, collectum ex variis D. de Fermat epistolis* (Toulouse, 1670). His other major work is *Problemes plaisans et delectables, qui se font par les nombres; Partie recueillis de diuers autheurs, & inuentez de nouueau auec leur demonstration. Tres-utiles pour toutes sorte de personnes curieuses, qui se seruent d'arithmetique* (Lyons, 1612). It was reprinted in several editions: *2ᵉ édition, revue, corrigée, et augmentée de plusieurs propositions, et de plusieurs problems, par le meme autheur* (Lyons, 1624; reprinted 1876); *3ᵉ édition, revue, simplifiée, et augmentée par A. Labosne* (Paris, 1874; abridged version, 1905); and *Cinquième édition, revue, simplifiée et augmentée par A. Labosne. Nouveau tirage augmenté d'un avant-propos par J. Itard* (Paris, 1959), a paperback edition.

II. Secondary Literature. Works dealing with Bachet are W. W. R. Ball and H. S. M. Coxeter, *Mathematical Recreations and Essays* (London, 1942), pp. 2–18, 28, 30, 33, 50, 116, 313, 316; Pierre Bayle, *Dictionnaire historique et critique* (Amsterdam, 1734), pp. 553–556; Moritz Cantor, *Vorlesungen über die Geschichte der Mathematik* (Leipzig, 1913), II, 767–780; C.-G. Collet and Jean Itard, "Un mathématicien humaniste: Claude-Gaspar Bachet de Méziriac (1581–1638)," in *Revue d'histoire des sciences*, **1** (1947), 26–50; and T. L. Heath, *Diophantos of Alexandria; A Study in the History of Greek Algebra* (Cambridge, 1885), pp. 49–54.

William Schaaf

BACHMANN, PAUL GUSTAV HEINRICH (*b.* Berlin, Germany, 22 June 1837; *d.* Weimar, Germany, 31 March 1920)

Bachmann's father was pastor at the Jacobi Kirche, and from his home the young Paul inherited a pious Lutheran view of life, coupled with modesty and a great interest in music. During his early years in the Gymnasium he had some trouble with his mathematical studies, but his talent was discovered by the excellent teacher Karl Schellbach. After a stay in Switzerland for his health, presumably to recover from tuberculosis, Bachmann studied mathematics at the University of Berlin until he transferred to Göttingen in 1856 to attend Dirichlet's lectures. Here he became a close friend of Dedekind, who was a fellow student.

From 1856 on, Bachmann's interests were centered almost exclusively upon number theory. He completed his studies in Berlin, where in 1862 he received his doctorate under the guidance of Ernst Kummer for a thesis on group theory. Two years later he completed his habilitation in Breslau with a paper on complex units, a subject inspired by Dirichlet. After some years as extraordinary professor in Breslau, Bachmann was appointed to a professorship in Münster.

Around 1890 Bachmann divorced his wife and resigned his professorship. With his second wife he settled in Weimar, where he combined his mathematical writing with composing, playing the piano, and serving as music critic for various newspapers. His main project, however, was a complete survey of the state of number theory, *Zahlentheorie. Versuch einer Gesamtdarstellung dieser Wissenschaft in ihren Hauptteilen* (1892–1923). It includes not only a review of known results but also an evaluation of the various methods of proof and approach, labors for which his close association with Dirichlet, Kummer, Dedekind, and Hensel made him ideally suited.

BIBLIOGRAPHY

Bachmann's writings are *Vorlesungen über die Natur der Irrationalzahlen* (Leipzig, 1892); *Zahlentheorie. Versuch einer Gesamtdarstellung dieser Wissenschaft in ihren Hauptteilen,* 5 vols. (Leipzig, 1892–1923); *Niedere Zahlentheorie,* 2 vols. (Leipzig, 1902–1910); and *Das Fermat-Problem in seiner bisherigan Entwicklung* (Leipzig, 1919), which has stimulated much research in this field.

OYSTEIN ORE

BACON, ROGER (*b.* England, *ca.* 1219; *d. ca.* 1292)

Apart from some brief references in various chronicles, the only materials for Roger Bacon's biography are his own writings. The date 1214 for his birth was calculated by Charles, followed by Little, from his statements in the *Opus tertium* (1267) that it was forty years since he had learned the alphabet and that for all but two of these he had been "in studio."[1] Taking this to refer to the years since he entered the university—the usual age was then about thirteen—they concluded that in 1267 Bacon was fifty-three and thus was born in 1214. But Crowley has argued that his statements more probably refer to his earliest education, beginning about the age of seven or eight, which would place his birth about 1219 or 1220. Of his family the only good evidence comes again from Bacon himself. He wrote in the *Opus tertium* that they had been impoverished as a result of their support of Henry III against the baronial party, and therefore could not respond to his appeal for funds for his work in 1266.[2]

After early instruction in Latin classics, among which the works of Seneca and Cicero left a deep impression, Bacon seems to have acquired an interest in natural philosophy and mathematics at Oxford, where lectures were given from the first decade of the thirteenth century on the "new" logic (especially *Sophistici Elenchi* and *Posterior Analytics*) and *libri naturales* of Aristotle as well as on the mathematical *quadrivium.* He took his M.A. either at Oxford or at Paris, probably about 1240. Probably between 1241 and 1246 he lectured in the Faculty of Arts at Paris on various parts of the Aristotelian corpus, including the *Physics* and *Metaphysics,* and the pseudo-Aristotelian *De vegetabilibus* (or *De plantis*) and the *De causis,* coincident with the Aristotelian revival there. In arguing later, in his *Compendium studii philosophie,* for the necessity of knowledge of languages,[3] he was to use an incident in which his Spanish students laughed at him for mistaking a Spanish word for an Arabic word while he was lecturing on *De vegetabilibus.* He was in Paris at the same time as Albertus Magnus, Alexander of Hales (*d.* 1245),[4] and William of Auvergne (*d.* 1249).[5]

The radical intellectual change following Bacon's introduction to Robert Grosseteste (*ca.* 1168–1253) and his friend Adam Marsh on his return to Oxford about 1247 is indicated by a famous passage in the *Opus tertium:*

> For, during the twenty years in which I have laboured specially in the study of wisdom, after disregarding the common way of thinking [*neglecto sensu vulgi*], I have put down more than two thousand pounds for secret books and various experiments [*experientie*], and languages and instruments and tables and other things; as well as for searching out the friendships of the wise, and for instructing assistants in languages, in figures, in numbers, and tables and instruments and many other things.[6]

Grosseteste's influence is evident in Bacon's particular borrowings, especially in his optical writings, but above all in the devotion of the rest of his life to the promotion of languages and of mathematics, optics (*perspectiva*), and *scientia experimentalis* as the essential sciences.

He was in Paris again in 1251, where he says in the *Opus maius*[7] that he saw the leader of the Pastoreaux rebels. This story and some later works place him there for long periods as a Franciscan. He entered the Franciscan order about 1257 and, soon afterward, he also entered a period of distrust and suspicion—probably arising from the decree of the chapter of Narbonne, presided over by Bonaventure as master general in 1260, which prohibited the publication of works outside the order without prior approval. Bonaventure had no time for studies not directly related to theology, and on two important questions, astrology and alchemy, he was diametrically opposed to Bacon. He held that only things dependent solely on the motions of the heavenly bodies, such as eclipses of the sun and moon and sometimes the weather, could be foretold with certainty. Bacon agreed with the accepted view that predictions of human affairs could establish neither certainty nor necessity over the free actions of individuals, but he held that nevertheless astrology could throw light on the future by discovering general tendencies in the influence of the stars, acting through the body, on human dispositions, as well as on nature at large. In alchemy Bonaventure was also skeptical about converting base metals into gold and silver, which Bacon thought possible.

Whatever the particular reasons for Bacon's troubles within the order, he felt it necessary to make certain proposals to a clerk attached to Cardinal Guy de Foulques; as a result, the cardinal, soon to be elected Pope Clement IV (February 1265), asked him for a copy of his philosophical writings. The request was repeated in the form of a papal mandate of 22 June 1266.[8] Bacon eventually replied with his three famous works, *Opus maius, Opus minus,* and *Opus tertium,* the last two prefaced with explanatory *epistole* in which he set out his proposals for the reform of learning and the welfare of the Church. It is reasonable to suppose that after twenty years of preparation he composed these *scripture preambule* to an unwritten *Scriptum principale* between the receipt of the papal mandate and the end of 1267. In that year he sent to the pope, by his pupil John, the *Opus maius* with some supplements, including *De speciebus et virtutibus agentium* in two versions[9] and *De scientia perspectiva,*[10] followed (before the pope died in November 1268) by the *Opus minus* and *Opus tertium* as résumés, corrections, and additions to it. The pope left no recorded opinion of Bacon's proposals.

Perhaps at this time Bacon wrote his *Communia naturalium* and *Communia mathematica,* mature expressions of many of his theories. These were followed in 1271 or 1272 by the *Compendium studii philosophie,* of which only the first part on languages remains and in which he abused all classes of society, and particularly the Franciscan and Dominican orders for their educational practices. Sometime between 1277 and 1279 he was condemned and imprisoned in Paris by his order for an undetermined period and for obscure reasons possibly related to the censure, which included heretical Averroist propositions, by the bishop of Paris, Stephen Tempier, in 1277. The last known date in his troubled life is 1292, when he wrote the *Compendium studii theologii.*[11]

Scientific Thought. The *Opus maius* and accompanying works sent to the pope by Bacon as a *persuasio* contain the essence of his conception of natural philosophy and consequential proposals for educational reform. He identified four chief obstacles to the grasping of truth: frail and unsuitable authority, long custom, uninstructed popular opinion, and the concealment of one's own ignorance in a display of apparent wisdom. There was only one wisdom, given to us by the authority of the Holy Scriptures; but this, as he explained in an interesting history of philosophy, had to be developed by reason, and reason on its part was insecure if not confirmed by experience. There were two kinds of experience, one obtained through interior mystical inspiration and the other through the exterior senses, aided by instruments and made precise by mathematics.[12] Natural science would lead through knowledge of the nature and properties of things to knowledge of their Creator, the whole of knowledge forming a unity in the service and under the guidance of theology. The necessary sciences for this program were languages, mathematics, optics, *scientia experimentalis,* and alchemy, followed by metaphysics and moral philosophy.

Bacon leaves no doubt that he regarded himself as having struck a highly personal attitude to most of the intellectual matters with which he dealt, but his writings are not as unusual as the legends growing about him might suggest. They have, on the whole, the virtues rather than the vices of Scholasticism, which at its best involved the sifting of evidence and the balancing of authority against authority. Bacon was conscious of the dangers of reliance on authority: Rashdall draws attention to the irony of his argument against authority consisting chiefly of a series of citations. Most of the content of his writings was derived from Latin translations of Greek and Arabic authors. He insisted on the need for accurate translations. When it was that he learned Greek himself is not certain, but his Greek grammar may be placed after 1267, since in it he corrected a philological mistake in the *Opus tertium.* He also wrote a Hebrew grammar to help in the understanding of Scripture.

One of the most interesting and attractive aspects of Bacon is his awareness of the small place of Christendom in a world largely occupied by unbelievers, "and there is no one to show them the truth."[13] He recommended that Christians study and distinguish different beliefs and try to discover common ground in monotheism with Judaism and Islam, and he insisted that the truth must be shown not by force but by argument and example. The resistance of conquered peoples to forcible conversion, such as practiced by the Teutonic knights, was "against violation, not to the arguments of a better sect."[14] Hence the need to understand philosophy not only in itself but "considering how it is useful to the Church of God and is useful and necessary for direct-

BACON

ing the republic of the faithful, and how far it is effective for the conversion of infidels; and how those who cannot be converted may be kept in check no less by the works of wisdom than the labour of war."[15] Science would strengthen the defenses of Christendom both against the external threat of Islam and the Tartars and against the methods of "fascination" that he believed had been used in the Children's Crusade and the revolt of the Pastoreaux, and would be used by the Antichrist.

Bacon's mathematics included, on the one hand, astronomy and astrology (discussed later) and, on the other, a geometrical theory of physical causation related to his optics. His assertions that "in the things of the world, as regards their efficient and generating causes, nothing can be known without the power of geometry" and that "it is necessary to verify the matter of the world by demonstrations set forth in geometrical lines"[16] came straight from Grosseteste's theory of *multiplicatio specierum,* or propagation of power (of which light and heat were examples), and his account of the "common corporeity" that gave form and dimensions to all material substances. "Every multiplication is either according to lines, or angles, or figures."[17] This theory provided the efficient cause of every occurrence in the universe, in the celestial and terrestrial regions, in matter and the senses, and in animate and inanimate things. In thus trying to reduce different phenomena to the same terms, Grosseteste and Bacon showed a sound physical insight even though their technical performance remained for the most part weak. These conceptions made optics the fundamental physical science, and it is in his treatment of this subject that Bacon appears most effective. Besides Grosseteste his main optical sources were Euclid, Ptolemy, al-Kindī, and Ibn al-Haytham (Alhazen). He followed Grosseteste in emphasizing the use of lenses not only for burning but for magnification, to aid natural vision. He seems to have made an original advance by giving constructions, based on those of Ptolemy for plane surfaces and of Ibn al-Haytham for convex refracting surfaces, providing eight rules (*canones*) classifying the properties of convex and concave spherical surfaces with the eye in various relationships to the refracting media. He wrote:

> If a man looks at letters and other minute objects through the medium of a crystal or of glass or of some other transparent body placed upon the letters, and this is the smaller part of a sphere whose convexity is towards the eye, and the eye is in the air, he will see the letters much better and they will appear larger to him. For in accordance with the truth of the fifth rule [Fig. 1] about a spherical medium beneath which is the object or on this side of its centre, and whose convexity is towards the eye, everything agrees towards magnification [*ad magnitudinem*], because the angle is larger under which it is seen, and the image is larger, and the position of the image is nearer, because the object is between the eye and the centre. And therefore this instrument is useful for the aged and for those with weak eyes. For they can see a letter, no matter how small, at sufficient magnitude.[18]

According to the fifth rule,[19] if the rays leaving the object, *AB,* and refracted at the convex surface of the lens meet at the eye, *E,* placed at their focus, a magnified image, *MN,* will be seen at the intersections of the diameters passing from the center of curvature, *C,* through *AB* to this surface and the projections of the rays entering the eye. As he did not seem to envisage the use of combinations of lenses, Bacon got no further than Grosseteste in speculating about magnifications such that "from an incredible distance we may read the minutest letters and may number the particles of dust and sand, because of the magnitude of the angle under which we may see them."[20] But he did make an important contribution to the history of physiological optics in the West by his exposition of Ibn al-Haytham's account of the eye as an image-forming device, basing his ocular anatomy on Ḥunayn ibn Isḥāq and Ibn Sīnā. In doing so, he seems to have introduced a new concept of laws of nature (a term found in Lucretius and numerous other authors more widely read, such as St. Basil) by his reference to the "laws of reflection and refraction" as *leges communes nature.*[21] His meaning is clarified by his discussion elsewhere of a *lex nature universalis*[22] requiring the continuity of bodies and thus giving a positive explanation, in place of the negative *horror vacui,* which he rejected, of such phenomena as water remaining in a clepsydra so long as its upper opening remained closed—an explanation comparable to one found in Adelard of Bath's *Natural Questions.* Universal nature constituted from these

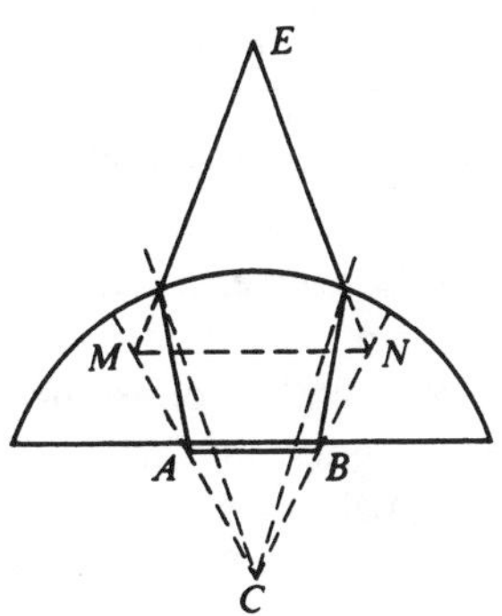

FIGURE 1

common laws, including those *de multiplicatione specierum,* was superimposed on the system of particular natures making up the Aristotelian universe—not yet the seventeenth-century concept but perhaps a step toward it.

"Having laid down the roots of the wisdom of the Latins as regards languages and mathematics and perspective," Bacon began Part VI of the *Opus maius,* "I wish now to unfold the roots on the part of *scientia experimentalis,* because without experience [*experientia*] nothing can be known sufficiently."[23] This science, "wholly unknown to the general run of students," had "three great prerogatives with respect to the other sciences."[24] The first was to certify the conclusions of deductive reasoning in existing speculative sciences, including mathematics. As an example he gave an investigation of the shape and colors of the rainbow involving both theoretical reasoning and the collection of instances of related phenomena in order to discover their common cause. The second prerogative was to add to existing sciences new knowledge that they could not discover by deduction. Examples were the discovery of the properties of the magnet, the prolonging of human life by observing what plants produced this effect naturally in animals, and the purification of gold beyond the present achievements of alchemy. The third prerogative was to investigate the secrets of nature outside the bounds of existing sciences, opening up knowledge of the past and future and the possibility of marvelous inventions, such as ever-burning lamps and explosive powders.

It is clear that Bacon's *scientia experimentalis* was not exactly what this term might now suggest, but belonged equally to "natural magic" aimed at producing astonishing as well as practically useful effects by harnessing the hidden powers of nature. His approach had been profoundly influenced by the pseudo-Aristotelian *Secretum secretorum,* of which he had produced an annotated edition variously dated between 1243 and sometime before 1257, but he also insisted that his new science would expose the frauds of magicians by revealing the natural causes of effects. The "dominus experimentorum" of the *Opus tertium,*[25] who may have been Pierre de Maricourt, the pioneer investigator of magnetism, is praised for understanding all these essential characteristics. In the *Opus minus,*[26] Bacon described possibly original experiments of his own with a lodestone held above and below a floating magnet, and argued that it was not the Nautical (Pole) Star that caused its orientation, or simply the north part of the heavens, but all four parts equally. It was in this work, and in the *Opus tertium,*[27] that he inserted his main discussion of alchemy, including the conversion of base metals into gold and silver. There is a further discussion in the *Communia naturalium,*[28] together with sketches of the sciences of medicine and agriculture. In the *Communia mathematica*[29] and the *Epistola de secretis operibus artis et naturae et de nullitate magiae,*[30] he described more wonderful machines for flying, lifting weights, and driving carriages, ships, and submarines, and so on, which he believed had been made in antiquity and could be made again.

Despite his occasional references to them, Bacon in his accredited writings deals with neither instruments nor mathematical tables in any but a superficial way. For this reason it is hard to measure his stature by comparison with that of his contemporaries whom we should call astronomers and mathematicians. We are not encouraged to set great store by the stories that while in Paris he constructed astronomical tables and supplied the new masters with geometrical problems that none of their audiences could solve.[31] His mathematics and astronomy were in fact almost wholly derivative, and he was not always a good judge of competence, preferring, for instance, al-Biṭrūjī to Ptolemy.

Bacon is often held to have achieved a deep and novel insight in regard to the role of mathematics in science, an insight that to the modern mind is almost platitudinous. In this connection it is easy to forget the large numbers of astronomers of antiquity and the Middle Ages for whom mathematics was an essential part of the science, and the smaller numbers of natural philosophers who had made use of simpler mathematical techniques than those of astronomy. It is more to the point to notice that Bacon argued for the usefulness of mathematics in almost every realm of academic activity. Part IV of the *Opus maius* is devoted to the usefulness of mathematics (1) in human affairs (this section was published separately as the *Specula mathematica*); (2) in divine affairs, such as chronology, the fixing of feasts, natural phenomena, arithmetic, and music; (3) in ecclesiastical affairs, such as the certification of faith and the emendation of the calendar; and (4) in affairs of state, under which heading are included geography and astrology. When Bacon sang the praises of mathematics, "the first of the sciences," "the door and key of the sciences," "the alphabet of philosophy," it has to be remembered that he used the word in an unusually wide sense. Bacon seemed to fear that mathematics would be dismissed as one of the blacker arts, as when arithmetic was applied to geomancy. He sought "per vias mathematice verificare omnia que in naturalibus scientias sunt necessaria"; and yet in the last resort, experience was still necessary, and in a sense supreme.[32]

So loud and long were Bacon's praises of mathematics that it is hard to avoid the conclusion that his love of the subject was unrequited. He could compose his *De communibus mathematice* and mention, in geometry, nothing beyond definitions, axioms, and methods. Apart from mathematically trivial results in such practical contexts as engineering, optics, astronomy, and the like, his works apparently contain not a single proof, not a single theorem; and we must take on trust the story of the difficult problems he devised for the young Paris masters. As for his analytical skills and his views on the citation of authority, rather than try to resolve the geometrical paradox of the doctrine of atomism—that it can make the hypotenuse and side of a square commensurable—he preferred simply to dismiss it as being contrary to Euclid.

The standard discussion of ratios in Euclid, Book V, did not include a numerical treatment of the subject, for which the standard medieval authority was the *Arithmetica* of Boethius. There the different species of ratio are tediously listed and subdivided, and the absence of a similar logical division of ratio in Euclid was complained of by Bacon in *Communia mathematica.*[33] He was not to carry out the program at which he might seem to have hinted, and not until Bradwardine's *Geometria speculativa* did the Schoolmen make any progress toward a numerical description of irrational ratios, except perhaps in some halting attempts to elucidate Proposition III of Archimedes' *De mensura circuli.*

As for the relation of logic to mathematics, Bacon inverted, in a sense, the logistic thesis of our own century: without mathematics, for instance, the categories were unintelligible.[34] Mathematics alone gave absolute certainty. Bacon was unusual in that he generally named his sources, citing such authors as Theodosius, Euclid, Ptolemy, Boethius, al-Fārābī, and—among modern writers—Jordanus de Nemore (*De triangulis* and *Arithmetica*) and Adelard. Despite his criticism of Jordanus, by any reckoning a better mathematician than Bacon, he had praise for "the only two perfect mathematicians" (of his time), John of London and Pierre de Maricourt. He also condescended to praise Campanus of Novara and a "Master Nicholas," teacher of Amauri, son of Simon de Montfort. In the last analysis, almost everything Bacon wrote under the title of mathematics is best regarded as being at a metaphysical level. His view that in mathematics we have perfect demonstration reinforced his theory of natural action. His philosophy of science, however, was inherently empiricist: rational argument may cause us to dismiss a question, but it neither gives us proof nor removes doubt.

It was held in the *Opus maius* that a more accurate knowledge of the latitudes and longitudes of places was needed for (1) knowledge of mankind and the natural world; (2) facilitation of the spiritual government of the world—missionaries, for example, would be saved from danger and from much wasted labor; (3) knowledge of the whereabouts of the ten tribes and even of the Antichrist. His geography was nevertheless a compilation of works on descriptive geography (in which he gave, as it were, an extended verbal map of the world) by such writers as Ptolemy and al-Farghānī, supplemented by the reports of Franciscan travelers, especially to the East.

In the *Opus maius*[35] he stated the possibility of voyaging from Spain to India. The passage was inserted, without reference to its source, in the *Imago mundi*[36] of Cardinal Pierre d'Ailly (*d.* 1420). Humboldt argued that this passage, quoted by Columbus in a letter of 1498 to Ferdinand and Isabella, was more important in the discovery of America than the Toscanelli letters. Thorndike suggests that Columbus probably did not read the vital work until his return from the first voyage of 1492.[37] It is immaterial, as Thorndike points out, whether Bacon was merely optimistically citing Aristotle, Seneca, Nero, and Pliny on the distance of Spain from India. In fact Bacon argued as cogently from such longitudes and latitudes as were available in the Toledan tables as he did from classical authors.

For the radius of the earth Bacon took a figure of 3,245 miles (al-Farghānī). He stated that the earth's surface was less than three-quarters water. In both cases he selected good figures from a great many authoritative but bad ones. It is clear, nevertheless, from his repetition of the method of determining the size of the earth—a method he took from al-Farghānī—that he had no appreciation whatsoever of the practical difficulties it involved.

Bacon appears to have sent a map to the pope with his *Opus maius.* Although it is now lost, from the description he gave it appears to have included the better-known towns of the world plotted by their latitudes and longitudes as found in many contemporaneous lists.[38] We have no knowledge of the projection adopted, but the description is compatible with the use of a rectangular coordinate system.

Bacon used the words "astronomia" and "astrologia" in a typically ambiguous manner, but there is no doubt that he believed in the reasonableness of what we would call astrology. In the *Opus tertium* he spoke of astrology as the most important part of mathematics, dividing it into a speculative, or theoretical, part, presumably of the sort included in Sacrobosco's *Sphere,* and a practical part, "que dicitur astronomia,"[39] concerned with the design of instruments and tables.[40] A remark in the *Opus maius,*[41] written in 1267, confirms a similar remark made four years later by Robertus Anglicus,[42] to the effect that conscious efforts were being made to drive what amounts to a clock (in Bacon's example the spherical astrolabe was to be driven) at a constant rate. This seems to confirm approximately the *terminus ante quem non* previously determined for the mechanical clock.

On many occasions Bacon emphasized at length that the two sorts of "astrology" were essential if man was to learn of the celestial influences on which terrestrial happenings depended. By reference to Ptolemy, Haly, Ibn Sīnā, Abū Ma'shar, Messahala, and others, he showed that the best astrologers had not held that the influence of the stars subjugated the human will, and that the Fathers who objected to astrology on these grounds had never denied that astrology could throw light on future events. It was possible to predict human behavior statistically but not with certainty in individual cases. Astrology might strengthen faith in the stability of the Church and foretell the fall of Islam and the coming of the Antichrist; and all these things "ut auctores docent et experiencia certificat."[43] On occasion he likened astrological influence to the influence of a magnet over iron.

In his main works Bacon did not discuss the technicalities of astronomy or astrology, but in both of the works ascribed to him with the title *De diebus creticis*[44] the standard medical astrology of the time is rehearsed. These works are not merely compilations of older authorities. Although technically they are in no sense new, they have a rational cast and even include the testimony of medical men of the time. The first of these two works is interesting because it incorporates the whole of the *De impressione aeris* attributed to Grosseteste and printed among his works by Baur. Little[45] suggests that Grosseteste (*d.* 1253) collaborated with Bacon. Internal evidence suggests a date of composition of about 1249. Some planetary positions quoted for that year are sufficiently inaccurate to suggest that the work was written before 1249 rather than after, and that the author was by no means as skilled as the best astronomers of the time.

The *Speculum astronomie,* of doubtful authorship (see below), is inconsistent with certain of Bacon's accredited writings. It is essentially a criticism of Stephen Tempier's decree of 1277 attacking 219 errors, several involving a belief in astrology. As already seen, Bacon's prison sentence was probably related to the bishop's decrees.

Bacon's astronomical influence was slight in all respects, although through Paul of Middelburg he is said to have influenced Copernicus.[46] His writings on the calendar were frequently cited.[47] Theologians treated the calendar with a respect it did not deserve, regarding it as a product of astronomy, while astronomers would have treated it with more disdain had they been detached enough to perceive it in a historical context. Here Bacon's skepticism was useful, and whatever the depth of his astronomical knowledge, he wrote on calendar reform with as much insight as anyone before Regiomontanus—Nicholas of Cusa notwithstanding. In discussing the errors of the Julian calendar, he asserted that the length of the Julian year (365 $\frac{1}{4}$ days) was in excess of the truth by about one day in 130 years, later changing this to one day in 125 years. The length of the (tropical) year implied was better than Ptolemy's, and indeed better than that accepted in the Alphonsine tables compiled a few years after the *Opus maius.* (The correct figure for Bacon's time was one day in a little over 129 years.) The Alphonsine tables imply that the Julian error is one day in about 134 years. There is no reason whatsoever to suppose, as many have done following Augustus De Morgan, that Bacon's data were his own. Thābit ibn Qurra made the length of the year shorter than the Julian year by almost exactly one day in 130 years, and according to a curious passage in the *Communia naturalium,* Thābit was "maximus Christianorum astronomus." In the *Computus,* however, Thābit is grouped with al-Battānī and others who are said to have argued for one day in 106 years, while Asophus ('Abd al-Raḥmān ibn 'Umar al-Ṣūfī) appears to have been the most probable source of influence, with his one day in 131 years.[48]

As a means of reforming the calendar, Bacon seems finally to have recommended the removal of one day in 125 years (cf. the Gregorian method of ignoring three leap years in four centuries), and in connection with Easter, since the nineteen-year cycle is in error, the astronomical calculation of the feast; otherwise a lunisolar year like that of the eastern nations should be adopted. (Grosseteste had previously made this proposal.) He tempered this rash suggestion with the pious qualification that if an astronomical calculation of Easter was to be adopted, Hebrew astronomical tables should be used. His proposals may be compared with the much less radical ones of Nicholas of Cusa, who in his *Reparatio calendarii* (pre 1437?) merely suggested a temporary patching up of the calendar, eliminating a number of days to alter the equinox suitably (Gregorian reform, supervised by Clavius, took the same superfluous step) and changing the "golden number" so as to make the ecclesiastical moon correspond for a time with reality. These solutions were inferior to Bacon's, including fewer safeguards against a future state of affairs in which Church usage and the ordinances of the Fathers might differ appreciably. It is worth noting that Stöffler proposed to omit one day in 134 years (an obviously Alphonsine parameter), while Pierre d'Ailly followed Bacon explicitly in advocating a lunisolar cycle. Again, in connection with a proposal for calendar reform in England, we find that in 1582 John Dee commended Bacon to Queen Elizabeth as one who had "instructed and admonished" the "Romane Bishopp," who was now "contented to follow so neare the footsteps of veritye."[49] Judging by the speed of English legislation in the matter of calendar reform, it seems that Bacon was a little less than five centuries ahead of most of his countrymen.

Little wrote in 1914, "The extant manuscripts of Bacon's works show that the 'Doctor mirabilis never wanted admirers,'"[50] and cited as evidence the existence of twenty-seven manuscripts of the *Perspectiva*[51] alone, dating from the thirteenth to the seventeenth centuries. Apart from his proposals for the calendar it was on Bacon's optics that most scientific value was placed, by his contemporary Witelo as well as by Francesco Maurolico, John Dee, Leonard Digges, Hobbes, and the first editors of his works. At the same time his accounts of alchemy and natural magic gave him more dubious fame, varying from the sixteenth to the nineteenth centuries with current popular prejudices.

NOTES

1. *Opus tertium,* Brewer ed., p. 65.
2. *Ibid.,* p. 16.
3. *Compendium studii philosophie,* Brewer ed., pp. 467–468.
4. *Opus minus,* Brewer ed., p. 325; *Opus tertium,* Brewer ed., p. 30; *Compendium studii philosophie,* p. 425.
5. *Opus tertium,* Brewer ed., pp. 74–75.
6. *Ibid.,* p. 59.
7. *Opus maius* (1266–1267), Bridges ed., I, 401.
8. Brewer, p. 1.
9. Cf. *Opus maius,* Bridges ed., pt. IV, dist. ii–iv; and *De multiplicatione specierum,* Bridges ed.
10. Cf. *Opus maius,* pt. V.
11. Rashdall, pp. 3, 34.
12. *Opus maius,* VI, 1.
13. *Ibid.,* Bridges ed., III, 122.
14. *Ibid.,* II, 377.
15. *Opus tertium,* Brewer ed., pp. 3–4.
16. *Opus maius,* Bridges ed., I, 143–144.
17. *Ibid.,* p. 112.
18. *Ibid.,* V.iii.ii.4 (Bridges ed., II, 157).
19. Figure 1 is redrawn and relettered from *Opus maius,* V.iii.ii.3, British Museum MS Royal 7.f.viii, 13th cent., f. 93r.
20. *Ibid.,* Bridges ed., II, 165.
21. *Opus tertium,* Duhem ed., pp. 78, 90; *Opus maius,* Bridges ed., II, 49.
22. *Ibid.,* I, 151; *De multiplicatione specierum, ibid.,* II, 453; *Communia naturalium,* Steele ed., fasc. 3, pp. 220, 224.
23. *Opus maius,* Bridges ed., II, 167.
24. *Ibid.,* p. 172.
25. Brewer ed., pp. 46–47.
26. *Ibid.,* pp. 383–384.
27. Little ed., pp. 80–89.
28. Steele ed., fasc. 2, pp. 6–8.
29. Steele ed., fasc. 16, pp. 42–44.
30. Brewer ed., p. 533.
31. *Opus tertium,* Brewer ed., pp. 7, 36, 38.
32. See, e.g., *Opus maius,* Bridges ed., II, 172–173.
33. Steele ed., fasc. 16, p. 80.
34. *Opus maius,* Bridges ed., I, 102; cf. *Communia mathematica,* Steele ed., fasc. 16, p. 16.
35. Bridges ed., I, 290 ff.
36. *Imago mundi* was first published at Louvain in 1480 or 1487.
37. *A History of Magic and Experimental Science,* II, 645.
38. Bridges ed., I, 300.
39. Cf. *Communia mathematica,* Steele ed., fasc. 16, p. 49.
40. Brewer ed., p. 106. Since in ch. XII of the same work he seems to have used the word "tables" to refer primarily to almanacs, i.e., ephemerides, and to have spoken of instruments only as a means of verifying tables, it is probable that here he meant to refer only to the astrolabe and the equatorium.
41. Bridges ed., II, 202–203.
42. See L. Thorndike, *The Sphere of Sacrobosco and Its Commentators* (Chicago, 1949), p. 72.
43. *Opus maius,* I, 385.
44. Steele ed., fasc. 9, appendices ii and iii, ed. Little.
45. Little, *ibid.,* p. xxx.
46. Bridges ed., I, xxxiii, 292.
47. See bibliography. Note that the same passage occurs, word for word, in *Opus tertium,* Brewer ed., pp. 271–292; and in *Opus maius,* Bridges ed., I, 281. Notice, however, that the *Computus,* written 1263–1265, does not contain any passage from either of these works, and that it acknowledges Arabic, rather than paying lip service to Hebrew, sources.
48. Steele ed., fasc. 6, pp. 12–18.
49. Corpus Christi College, Oxford, MS C. 254, f. 161r.
50. Pp. 30–31.
51. *Opus maius,* pt. V.

BIBLIOGRAPHY

I. ORIGINAL WORKS. A number of Baconian problems must remain unsolved until there is a complete critical edition of his works: see the bibliography by Little in *Roger Bacon: Essays* (Oxford, 1914), pp. 375–426; compare G. Sarton, *Introduction to the History of Science,* II (Baltimore, 1931), 963–967; and L. Thorndike and P. Kibre, *A Catalogue of Incipits of Mediaeval Scientific Writings in Latin* (2nd ed., Cambridge, Mass., 1963).

The earliest of Bacon's authentic works to be printed was the *Epistola de secretis operibus artis et naturae* (*De mirabili potestate artis et naturae*) (Paris, 1542; Basel, 1593); in the *Opera,* J. Dee, ed. (Hamburg, 1618); in French (Lyons, 1557; Paris, 1612, 1629); in English (London, 1597, 1659); in German (Eisleben, 1608); and other eds. After this appeared the *De retardandis senectutis accidentibus et de sensibus conservandis* (Oxford, 1590; in English, London, 1683); and *Specula mathematica* (part of *Opus maius* IV); *in qua De specierum multiplicatione earumdemque in inferioribus virtute agitur* and *Perspectiva* (*Opus maius*

V), both ed. J. Combach (Frankfurt, 1614). There were other early eds. of the doubtful *Speculum alchemiae* (Nuremburg, 1541; in French, 1557; English, 1597; German, 1608; with later reissues) and the collection *De arte chymiae scripta* (Frankfurt, 1603, 1620).

The 1st ed. of the *Opus maius* was by S. Jebb (London, 1733), followed by an improved ed. (Venice, 1750), both including only pts. I-VI. Pt. VII was included in the new ed. by J. H. Bridges, 2 vols. (Oxford, 1897), with a supp. vol. (III) of revisions and additional notes (London, 1900). This ed. was trans. into English by R. B. Burke (Philadelphia, 1928). Pt. VII of the actual MS sent to the pope has been ed. by E. Massa, *Rogeri Baconi Moralis philosophia* (Zurich, 1953). The eds. of Jebb and Bridges (Vols. II and III, pp. 183–185) both include *De multiplicatione specierum*, a separate treatise forming part of a larger work; a further section of this has been ed. with a discussion of its date and associations by F. M. Delorme, "Le prologue de Roger Bacon à son traité De influentiis agentium," in *Antionianum*, **18** (1943), 81-90.

The 1st eds. of the *Opus minus* and the *Opus tertium*, together with the *Compendium studii philosophie* and a new ed. of the *Epistola de secretis operibus*, were by J. S. Brewer in *Fr. Rogeri Bacon Opera quaedam hactenus inedita* (London, 1859). Further sections of the first two works have been ed. by F. A. Gasquet, "An Unpublished Fragment of Roger Bacon," in *The English Historical Review*, **12** (1897), 494–517, a prefatory letter and other parts of *Opus minus;* P. Duhem, *Un fragment inédit de l'Opus tertium de Roger Bacon* (Quaracchi, 1909), on optics, astronomy, and alchemy; and A. G. Little, *Part of the Opus tertium of Roger Bacon*, British Society of Franciscan Studies, IV (Aberdeen, 1912). The last two items include Bacon's *De enigmatibus alkimie*. For further parts of the *Opus minus*, including discussions of alchemy, still unpublished, see A. Pelzer, "Une source inconnue de Roger Bacon, Alfred de Sareshel, commentateur des Météorologiques d'Aristote," in *Archivium Franciscanum historicum*, **12** (1919), 44–67.

Other works have been ed. by E. Nolan and S. A. Hirsch, *The Greek Grammar of Roger Bacon, and a Fragment of His Hebrew Grammar* (Cambridge, 1902); H. Rashdall, *Fratris Rogeri Baconi Compendium studii theologii*, British Society of Franciscan Studies, III (Aberdeen, 1911); S. H. Thomson, "An Unnoticed Treatise of Roger Bacon on Time and Motion," in *Isis*, **27** (1937), 219–224; and in *Opera hactenus inedita Rogeri Baconi*, R. Steele, ed. (unless otherwise stated), 16 fasc. (Oxford, 1905-1940): (1) *Metaphysica: De viciis contractis in studio theologie* (1905); (2–4) *Communia naturalium* (1905–1913); (5) *Secretum secretorum cum glossis et notulis* (1920); (6) *Computus* (1926); (7) *Questiones supra undecimum prime philosophie Aristotelis* (*Metaphysica*, XII) (1926); (8) *Questiones supra libros quatuor physicorum Aristotelis*, F. M. Delorme, ed. (1928); (9) *De retardatione accidentium senectutis cum aliis opusculis de rebus medicinalibus*, A. G. Little and E. Withington, eds. (1928); (10) *Questiones supra libros prime philosophie Aristotelis* (*Metaphysica*, I, II, V–X) (1930); (11) *Questiones altere supra libros prime philosophie Aristotelis* (*Metaphysica*, I–IV), *Questiones supra de plantis* (1932); (12) *Questiones supra librum de causis* (1935); (13) *Questiones supra libros octo physicorum Aristotelis*, F. M. Delorme, ed. (1935); (14) *Liber de sensu et sensato, Summa de sophismatibus et distinctionibus* (1937); (15) *Summa grammatica, Sumule dialectices* (1940); and (16) *Communia mathematica* (1940). The *Chronica XXIV generalium ordinis minorum* (*ca.* 1370) was pub. in *Analecta Franciscana*, **3** (1897).

II. Secondary Literature. The best critical study of Bacon's life is T. Crowley, *Roger Bacon: The Problem of the Soul in His Philosophical Commentaries* (Louvain–Dublin, 1950). The pioneering study by E. Charles, *Roger Bacon: Sa vie, ses ouvrages, ses doctrines d'après des textes inédits* (Paris, 1861), is now mostly of historical interest. Essential general studies are A. G. Little, ed., *Roger Bacon: Essays Contributed by Various Writers* (Oxford, 1914), especially contributions by Little (life and works); L. Baur (Grosseteste's influence); Hirsch (philology); E. Wiedemann, S. Vogl, and E. Würschmidt (optics); Duhem (vacuum); M. M. P. Muir (alchemy); E. Withington (medicine); and J. E. Sandys (English literature); Little, *Franciscan Letters, Papers and Documents* (Manchester, 1943); L. Thorndike, *A History of Magic and Experimental Science*, II (New York, 1929), 616–691; S. C. Easton, *Roger Bacon and His Search for a Universal Science* (Oxford, 1952), with bibliography; and F. Alessio, *Mito e scienza in Ruggero Bacone* (Milan, 1967).

Studies of particular aspects are E. Schlund, "Petrus Peregrinus von Maricourt: Sein Leben und seine Schriften," in *Archivum Fransiscanum historicum*, **4** (1911), 445–449, 636–643; L. Baur, "Die philosophischen Werke des Robert Grosseteste," in *Beiträge zur Geschichte der Philosophie des Mittelalters*, **9** (1912), 52–63; and "Die Philosophie des Robert Grosseteste," *ibid.*, **18** (1917), 92–120; P. Duhem, *Le système du monde* (Paris, 1916–1958), III, 260–277, 411–442; V, 375–411; VIII, 121–168; A. Birkenmajer, "Études sur Witelo, i–iv," in *Bulletin international de l'Académie polonaise des sciences et des lettres*, Classe d'histoire et de philosophie (1920), 354–360; and "Robert Grosseteste and Richard Fournival," in *Mediaevalia et humanistica*, **5** (1948), 36–41; R. Carton, *L'expérience physique chez Roger Bacon, L'expérience mystique de l'illumination intérieure chez Roger Bacon, La synthèse doctrinale de Roger Bacon*, nos. 2, 3, 5 in the series Études de philosophie médiévale (Paris, 1924); C. B. Vandewalle, *Roger Bacon dans l'histoire de la philologie* (Paris, 1929); G. Meyer, "En quel sens peut-on parler de 'méthode scientifique' de Roger Bacon," in *Bulletin de littérature ecclésiastique* (Toulouse), **53** (1952), 3–25, 77–98; A. C. Crombie, *Robert Grosseteste and the Origins of Experimental Science 1100–1700*, 3rd imp. (Oxford, 1969), pp. 41, 139–162, 204–207, 213–218, 278–281, with bibliography; and "The Mechanistic Hypothesis and the Scientific Study of Vision," in *Proceedings of the Royal Microscopical Society*, **2** (1967), 20–30, 43–45; M. Schramm, "Aristotelianism: Basis and Obstacle to Scientific Progress in the Middle Ages," in *History of Science*, **2** (1963),

104–108; and A. Pacchi, "Ruggero Bacone e Roberto Grossatesta in un inedito hobbesiano del 1634," in *Rivista critica di storia della filosofia*, **20** (1965), 499–502.

A. C. CROMBIE
J. D. NORTH

AL-BAGHDĀDĪ, ABŪ MANṢŪR ᶜABD AL-QĀHIR IBN ṬĀHIR IBN MUḤAMMAD IBN ᶜABDALLAH, AL-TAMĪMĪ, AL-SHAFIᶜĪ (*b.* Baghdad; *d.* 1037)

The last two names indicate the tribe from which Abū Manṣūr was descended and the religious school to which he belonged. Born and raised in Baghdad, he left with his father for Nīshāpūr (or Nīsābūr), taking with him great wealth that he spent on scholars and scholarship. Riots broke out in Nīshāpūr, and he moved to the quieter town of Asfirāyīn. His departure was considered a great loss to Nīshāpūr. In his new home, he continued to pursue learning and to propagate it. He is reported to have lectured for years in the mosque, on several subjects, never accepting payment. Although he was one of the great theologians of his age, and many works are attributed to him, none has been studied scientifically. We are concerned here with two works on arithmetic.

The first is a small book on mensuration, *Kitāb fi'l-misāḥa*, which gives the units of length, area, and volume and ordinary mensurational rules.

The second, *al-Takmila fi'l-ḥisāb*, is longer and far more important. In the introduction Abū Mansūr notes that earlier works are either too brief to be of great use or are concerned with only one chapter (system) of arithmetic. In his work he therefore seeks to explain all the "kinds" of arithmetic in use.

The Islamic world knew three arithmetical systems: finger reckoning, the sexagesimal scale, and Indian arithmetic. Not long after the last was introduced, Greek mathematical writings became accessible and the works of Euclid, Nicomachus, and others were made known. All these elements underwent a slow unification. Abū Mansūr presents them at an intermediary stage in which each system still had its characteristics preserved but was already enriched by concepts or schemes from other systems.

Abū Manṣūr conceived of seven systems. The first two were the Indian arithmetic of integers and that of fractions. The third was the sexagesimal scale, expressed in Hindu numerals and treated in the Indian way.

The fourth was finger reckoning. Two works on Arabic finger reckoning before the time of Abū Mansūr are extant: the arithmetic of Abu'l-Wafā' and that of al-Karajī (known also as al-Karkhī). Both works devote the most space to explaining a cumbersome and complicated fractional system that lacks the idea of the unrestricted common fraction. This system does not appear in the work of Abū Manṣūr, who seems to prefer the Indian system. His finger reckoning is confined to concepts lacking in Indian arithmetic, such as shortcuts, and to topics taken from Greek mathematics, such as the summation of finite series. He provides rules for the summation of the general arithmetic, and some special geometric progressions, as well as the sequences r^2, r^3, r^4 $(2r)^2$, $(2r-1)^2$, and polygonal numbers. These rules are expressed in words and assume that the number of terms in each case is ten, a Babylonian practice presented in the works of Diophantus.

Abū Manṣūr's next two systems are the arithmetic of irrational numbers and the properties of numbers. In the first of these, Euclid's rules of the irrationals in Book X of the *Elements* are given on a numerical basis. In the second the Pythagorean theory of numbers is presented with an improvement upon Nicomachus: To determine whether n is prime, test it for divisibility by primes $\leq \sqrt{n}$. Perfect numbers, such as 6, 28, 496, and 8,128, end in 6 or 8; but there is no perfect number between 10^5 and 10^6. The first odd abundant number is 945.

This part of Abū Manṣūr's work is ten chapters long, but some folios of the manuscript are missing; only the first three chapters and a few lines of the last are extant. The latter contain an attempt to divide a cube into several cubes by using the relation $3^3 + 4^3 + 5^3 = 6^3$.

The last of Abū Manṣūr's seven systems, business arithmetic, begins with business problems and ends with two chapters on curiosities that would find a place in any modern book on recreational problems or the modulo principle. One example is given here because it is found in Greek, Indian, and Chinese sources: Your partner thinks of a number not greater than 105. He casts out fives and is left with a; he casts out sevens and is left with b; he casts out threes and is left with c. Calculate $21a + 15b + 70c$; cast out 105's, and the residue is the number. The explanation shows that the author was quite familiar with the modulo concept.

Abū Mansūr's work also seems to solve a problem encountered by historians of medieval mathematics. Latin arithmeticians of the early Renaissance were divided into abacists and algorists. The exact significance of each name was unknown. It has recently been learned that Hindu-Arabic arithmetic required the use of the abacus, thus abacists were those who used the Hindu-Arabic system, and algorists must have adhered to the older system. This agrees with the fact that a work by Prosdocimo de Beldamandi containing an outspoken denunciation of the abacus is called *Algorithmus*. "Algorist" and *Algorithmus* come from the name of al-Khwārizmī, the first Muslim to write on Indian arithmetic. His work in Arabic is lost, but we have the *Algoritmi de numero indorum*, believed to be a translation of it.

But why should those who did not use the abacus be called algorists? This question can be answered as follows: Arabic biographers attribute to al-Khwārizmī a book called *Kitāb al-jamʿ waʾl-tafrīq*, now lost. It has been commonly accepted that this was the Arabic title of al-Khwārizmī's work on Indian arithmetic. Abū Manṣūr, however, refers to this book in his *al-Takmila*, and once he quotes methods from it. These methods follow typical finger-reckoning schemes, which indicates that this book of al-Khwārizmī's was of the finger-reckoning type. It seems that those who followed this book of al-Khwārizmī's were called algorists and those who followed his work on Indian arithmetic were the abacists.

A. S. SAIDAN

BAIRE, RENÉ LOUIS (*b.* Paris, France, 21 January 1874; *d.* Chambéry, France, 5 July 1932)

Baire was one of three children in a modest artisan's family. In 1891 he entered the section for special mathematics at the Lycée Henri IV, and in 1892 was accepted at the École Normale Supérieure. During his three years there he attracted attention by his intellectual maturity.

Although he placed first in the written part of the 1895 *agrégation* in mathematics, Baire was ranked third because of a mistake in his oral presentation on exponential functions. In the course of his presentation Baire realized that his demonstration of continuity was purely an artifice, since it did not refer sufficiently to the definition of the function. This disappointment should be kept in mind, because it caused the young lecturer to revise completely the basis of his course in analysis and to direct his research to continuity and the general idea of functions.

Baire's doctoral thesis solved the general problem of the characteristic property of limit functions of continuous functions, i.e., the pointwise discontinuity on any perfect aggregate. In order to imagine this characteristic, one needed very rare gifts of observation and analysis concerning the way in which the question of limits and continuity had been treated until then. In developing the concept of semicontinuity—to the right or to the left—Baire took a decisive step toward eliminating the suggestion of intuitive results from the definition of a function over a compact aggregate. But in order to obtain the best possible results, one needed a clear understanding of the importance of the concepts of the theory stemming from aggregates.

> Generally speaking, in the framework of ideas that here concerns us, every problem in the theory of functions leads to certain questions in the theory of sets, and it is to the degree that these latter questions are resolved, or capable of being resolved, that is is possible to solve the given problem more or less completely [*Sur les fonctions*].

In this respect, Baire knew how to use the transfinite in profoundly changing a method of reasoning that had been applied only once before—and this in a different field.

> From the point of view of derivative sets that interests us here, it may be said that if α is a number of the first type, then P^{α} is the set derived from $P^{\alpha-1}$, and if α is of the second type, P^{α} is by definition the set of points that belongs to all $P^{\alpha'}$ where α' is any number smaller than α. Independently of any abstract considerations arising from Cantor's symbolism, P^{α} represents a fully determined object. Nothing more than a convenient language is contained in the use we shall be making of the term "transfinite number" [*Ibid.*, p. 36].

In line with his first results, Baire was led to approach the problem of integrating equations with partial derivatives at a time when their solution was not subjected to any particular condition of continuity. But it is in another, less specialized field that Baire's name is associated with lasting results.

Assigning to limit functions of continuous functions the name of Class 1 functions, Baire first endeavored to integrate functions of several variables into this class. Thus he considered those functions that are separately continuous in relation to each of the variables of which they are a function. Then he defined as Class 2 functions the limits of Class 1 functions, and as Class 3 functions the limits of Class 2 functions. Having established basic solutions for these three classes, he obtained a characteristic common to the functions of all classes.

Baire's work on the concept of limit and the consequences of its analysis marks a turning point in the criticism of commonplace ideas. Moreover, the class of Baire's functions remains unattainable as far as the evolution of modes of expression is concerned. This model of a brief and compact work is part of the history of the most profound mathematics.

BIBLIOGRAPHY

ORIGINAL WORKS. Baire's writings are *Sur la théorie analytique de la chaleur* (Paris, 1895), his ed. of Henri Poincaré's 1893–1894 lectures; *Sur les fonctions de variables réelles* (Milan, 1899), his doctoral thesis (Faculté des Sciences, Paris, no. 977); "Sur les séries à termes continus et tous de même signe," in *Bulletin de la Société mathématique de France,* no. 32 (1904), 125–128; *Leçons sur la théorie des fonctions discontinues,* A. Denjoy, ed. (Paris, 1905, 1930); *Théorie des nombres irrationnels, des limites et de la continuité* (Paris, 1905, 1912, 1920); "Sur la représentation des fonctions discontinues," in *Acta mathematica,* no. 30 (1906), 1–48, and no. 32 (1909), 97–176; "Sur la non-applicabilité de deux continus à n et $n + p$ dimensions," in *Bulletin des sciences mathématiques* (Darboux), no. 31 (1907) 94–99; *Leçons sur les théories générales de l'analyse,* 2 vols. (Paris, 1907–1908); and "Origine de la notion de semi-continuité," in *Bulletin de la Société mathématique de France,* no. 55 (1927), 141–142.

PIERRE COSTABEL

BALBUS (BALBUS MENSOR [?]) (*fl. ca.* A.D. 100)

For information on the life of Balbus, we must depend upon the scanty data appearing in his works. He served as an officer in the campaign that opened Dacia to the Romans (see Lachmann, p. 93). Since Balbus does not name the reigning emperor, this may have been either the war of Domitian, which started in A.D. 85, or one of the campaigns of Trajan, which terminated in A.D. 106 with the conversion of Dacia into a Roman province. The second possibility seems more likely. Immediately following his return from war, Balbus completed a treatise dedicated to a prominent engineer named Celsus, about whom nothing has come down to us.

Authenticated Works. Balbus' work in its oldest manuscript, the so-called Arcerianus B, is entitled "Balbi ad Celsum expositio et ratio omnium formarum."[1] Other manuscripts name Frontinus—or even Fronto—as the author. The work is a geometric manual for surveyors. Starting with a summary of standard measurements, it contains definitions of geometric concepts (point, line, area, types of angles, figures). The work, which refers back to the works of Hero of Alexandria (Hultsch, pp. 103 f.; Cantor, pp. 101 f.), is distorted by gaps and interpolations (see Lachmann's ed.; and Bubnov, pp. 419 f.) and undoubtedly is not preserved in full, for its contents do not match its title. Probably the end of the preserved text (Lachmann, p. 107)[2] was followed by examples of the calculation of triangles, rectangles, and polygons, such as can be found in Hero's works.

Works of Uncertain Origin. The oldest surveying codices have handed down a list of cities (*liber coloniarum I,* Lachmann, I, 209–251). Repeatedly mentioned as the source is a Balbus *mensor* (surveyor), who is said to have lived at the time of Augustus. Mommsen has demonstrated that this Balbus could not have been a contemporary of Augustus, so it is possible that this surveyor Balbus is identical with the author of *Expositio.* Nevertheless, the *liber coloniarum* does not form part of *Expositio,* since the latter almost certainly contained only geometry and not surveying material.

In 1525 Fabius Calvus of Ravenna published a short treatise on fractions (*De asse minutisque eius portiunculis*) as a fragment derived from a larger work by Balbus. However, this Balbus has no connection with the author of *Expositio:* Christ (*Sitzungsberichte der Bayerischen Akademie der Wissenschaften zu München* [1863], p. 105) and Hultsch (*Metrologicorum scriptorum reliquiae,* II [Leipzig, 1866], 14) found that the treatise on fractions originated between the time of Alexander Severus (222–235) and Constantine I (306–337).

Whether other works in the *Corpus agrimensorum* must be attributed to Balbus is uncertain.

Some chapters in the *Collection of the Surveyors* go back to Balbus (for example, Lachmann, I, 295.17–296.3). Particularly clear references to Balbus appear in the two works on geometry ascribed to Boethius: similar formulations in the five-book work on geometry have been grouped by Bubnov, p. 426. In the two-book work on geometry edited by G. Friedlein almost the entire section pp. 393.12–395.2; pp. 401.15–403.24 relates back to Balbus. At one place (p. 402.28–29 of Friedlein's edition) its anonymous author credits Frontinus with a definition actually derived from Balbus.

NOTES

1. The translation of *forma* as "geometric figure" is corroborated by Balbus' own definition (p. 104), despite the contrary views of Lachmann (*forma* as *mensura,* or "measure"; Lachmann, II, 134) and Mommsen (*forma* as *Grundriss* or "plan"; Lachmann, II, 148).
2. The text (I, 107.10–108.8 of Balbus' text, edited by Lachmann), which Lachmann himself considered spurious, is believed to be the work of Frontinus; compare C. Thulin, "Die Handschriften des *Corpus agrimensorum Romanorum,*" in *Abhandlungen der Preussischen Akademie der Wissenschaften,* Phil.-hist. Kl., no. 2 (1911), p. 23. In the London MS, BM Add. 47679, the only prehumanistic codex containing the ending of Balbus' work, this text is preceded by excerpts from Balbus and followed by abstracts from Frontinus. There are no headings. On this codex, so far neglected but a must for the reconstruction of the Balbus text, see M. Folkerts, *Zur Überlieferung der Agrimensoren: Schrijvers bisher verschollener "Codex Nansianus,"* which is to be printed in the *Rheinisches Museum für Philologie.*

BIBLIOGRAPHY

There is an edition of the *Expositio* by K. Lachmann in K. Lachmann et al., *Die Schriften der römischen Feldmesser,* I (Berlin, 1848), 91–107.

Works on Balbus are N. Bubnov, *Gerberti opera mathematica* (Berlin, 1899), pp. 400, 419–421; M. Cantor, *Die römischen Agrimensoren* (Leipzig, 1875), pp. 99–103; Gensel, in Pauly-Wissowa, II, 2820–2822; F. Hultsch, in *Ersch und Grubers allgemeine Encyclopaedie,* **92** (1872), 102–104; K. Lachmann, "Über Frontinus, Balbus, Hyginus und Aggenus Urbicus," in K. Lachmann, Blume, and Rudorff, *Die Schriften der römischen Feldmesser,* II (Berlin, 1852), 131–136; T. Mommsen, "Die *libri coloniarum,*" *ibid.,* 145–214; and Schanz and Hosius, *Geschichte der römischen Literatur,* 4th ed., II (1935), 802 f.

MENSO FOLKERTS

BALMER, JOHANN JAKOB (*b.* Lausen, Basel-Land, Switzerland, 1 May 1825; *d.* Basel, Switzerland, 12 March 1898)

Balmer was the oldest son of Chief Justice Johann Jakob Balmer and Elisabeth Rolle Balmer. He attended the district school in Liestal and the secondary school in Basel, studied mathematics at Karlsruhe and Berlin, and was granted a doctorate at Basel in 1849 with a dissertation on the cycloid. In 1868 he married Christine Pauline Rinck, who bore him six children. He taught at the girls' secondary school in Basel from 1859 until his death, and from 1865 to 1890 he also held a part-time lectureship at the University of Basel. His major field of professional interest was geometry; spectral series, the topic of his most noted contribution, was an area in which he became involved only late in life.

The earliest attempts to establish relationships between the observed lines of an elementary spectrum were organized primarily within the theoretical context of a mechanical acoustical analogy. Many investigators attempted to establish simple harmonic ratios, but in 1881 Arthur Schuster demonstrated the inadequacy of this approach. The essentially successful mathematical organization of the data began in 1885 with Balmer's presentation of the formula $\lambda = hm^2/(m^2 - n^2)$ for the hydrogen series. This formula could be used to generate, with considerable accuracy, the wavelengths of the known characteristic spectral lines for hydrogen when $n = 2$, $h = 3645.6 \times 10^{-8}$ cm., and $m = 3, 4, 5, 6, \cdots$ successively.

Initially, Balmer knew only Ångström's measurements for the first four visible hydrogen lines, but he calculated the next, or fifth, result of the formula using $m = 7$, obtaining the wavelength of a line that, if it existed, would be barely on the edge of the visible spectrum. Jakob Edward Hagenbach-Bischoff, a friend and colleague at the University of Basel who had stimulated his interest in this topic, informed him that this fifth line had been observed, and that a number of other hydrogen lines had been measured. Comparisons between the calculated results obtained using Balmer's formula for these lines and the observed values showed close agreement, differences being at most approximately one part in one thousand. Later investigators demonstrated that the formula, with a slightly altered constant, represented the whole series, including additional lines, with unusual accuracy. Balmer speculated that values for other hydrogen series in the ultraviolet and infrared regions would be generated if n were assigned integer values other than two. Such predicted series were experimentally found later and are known as the Lyman, Paschen, Brackett, and Pfund series.

Balmer's relationship was so different from the simple harmonic ratios expected on the acoustical analogy, that investigators were bewildered as to what sort of mechanism could produce such lines. In spite of this disturbing feature, Balmer's work served as a model for other series formulas, especially the more generalized formulas of Johannes Robert Rydberg (1854–1919), Heinrich Kayser (1853–1940), and Carl Runge (1856–1927). Balmer published only one further paper on spectra, in which he extended his considerations to the spectra of several other elements (1897).

BIBLIOGRAPHY

I. ORIGINAL WORKS. Balmer's major article on the hydrogen spectrum is "Notiz über die Spektrallinien des Wasserstoffs," in *Verhandlungen der Naturforschenden Gesellschaft in Basel,* **7** (1885), 548–560, 750–752; also in *Annalen der Physik,* 3rd ser., **25** (1885), 80–87. His second and only other spectral article is "Eine neue Formel für Spektralwellen," in *Verhandlungen der Naturforschenden Gesellschaft in Basel,* **11** (1897), 448–463; and in *Annalen der Physik,* 3rd ser., **60** (1897), 380–391. It is also available in *Astrophysical Journal,* **5** (1897), 199–209. A short note of historical interest is Jakob Edward Hagenbach-Bischoff's "Balmer'sche Formel für Wasserstofflinien," in *Verhandlungen der Naturforschenden Gesellschaft in Basel,* **8** (1890), 242.

II. SECONDARY LITERATURE. For discussions on aspects of Balmer's life and works, see August Hagenbach, "J. J. Balmer und W. Ritz," in *Die Naturwissenschaften,* **9** (1921), 451–455, and "Johann Jakob Balmer," in Edward Fueter, ed., *Grosse Schweizer Forscher* (Zurich, 1939), pp. 248–249; L. Hartmann, "Johann Jakob Balmer," in *Physikalische*

Blätter, **5** (1949), 11–14; and Eduard His, "Johann Jakob Balmer," in *Basler Gelehrte des 19. Jahrhunderts* (Basel, 1941), pp. 213–217.

C. L. MAIER

BANACH, STEFAN (*b.* Krakow, Poland, 30 March 1892; *d.* Lvov, Ukrainian S.S.R., 31 August 1945)

Banach's father, a railway official, and mother turned their son over to a laundress, who became his foster mother and gave him her surname. From the age of fifteen he supported himself by giving private lessons. After graduating from secondary school in Krakow in 1910, Banach studied at the Institute of Technology in Lvov but did not graduate. He returned to Krakow in 1914, and from 1916, when he met H. Steinhaus, he devoted himself to mathematics. His knowledge of the field was already fairly extensive, although it probably was not very systematic. Banach's first paper, on the convergence of Fourier series, was written with Steinhaus in 1917 and was published two years later. Also in 1919 he was appointed lecturer in mathematics at the Institute of Technology in Lvov, where, in addition, he lectured on mechanics. In the same year he received his doctorate with an unusual exemption from complete university education. Banach's thesis, "Sur les opérations dans les ensembles abstraits et leur application aux équations intégrales," appeared in *Fundamenta mathematicae* in 1922. The publication of this thesis is sometimes said to have marked the birth of functional analysis.

In 1922 Banach became a *Dozent* on the basis of a paper on measure theory (published in 1923). Soon afterward he was made associate professor, and in 1927 he became full professor at the University of Lvov. In 1924 he was elected corresponding member of the Polish Academy of Sciences and Arts. Banach's research activity was intense, and he had a number of students who later became outstanding mathematicians: S. Mazur, W. Orlicz, J. Schauder, and S. Ulam, among others. Banach and Steinhaus founded the journal *Studia mathematica*, but often Banach had little time left for scientific work because the writing of both college texts (of which the book on mechanics is of special importance) and secondary-school texts took most of his time and effort.

From 1939 to 1941 Banach was dean of the faculty at Lvov and was elected a member of the Ukrainian Academy of Sciences. In the summer of 1941, Lvov was occupied by the German army, and for three years Banach was compelled to feed lice in a German institute that dealt with infectious diseases. After the liberation of Lvov in the autumn of 1944, he resumed his work at the university. His health was shattered, however, and he died less than a year later.

Banach's scientific work comprises about fifty papers and the monograph *Théorie des opérations linéaires* (1932). Although he laid the foundations of contemporary functional analysis, most of his papers are closely connected with the field but are not precisely in it.

Banach made a significant contribution to the theory of orthogonal series, and his theorem on locally meager sets is of lasting importance in general topology. In the descriptive theory of sets and mappings, he extended to mappings some theorems previously known only for numerical functions. A number of results, many of which can now be found in textbooks, concern derivation and absolute continuity, as well as related properties. Banach made a substantial contribution to the theory of measure and integration, results that stimulated a great number of papers and, apparently, the discovery of the Radon-Nikodým theorem. The questions of the existence of measures investigated by Banach have proved to be closely connected with the axiomatic theory of sets.

Despite the great importance of these results and the unusual lucidity and force of mathematical thinking manifested in them, functional analysis is Banach's most important contribution. His work started, of course, from what was achieved during the decades following Vito Volterra's papers of the 1890's on integral equations. Before Banach there were either rather specific individual results that only much later were obtained as applications of general theorems, or relatively vague general concepts. Papers on the so-called general analysis (mainly by E. H. Moore) formed a significant trend, but these were none too comprehensible and, for that period at least, much too general. Ivar Fredholm's and David Hilbert's papers on integral equations marked the most substantial progress. The concepts and theorems they had discovered later became an integral part of functional analysis, but most of them concern only a single linear space (later called Hilbert space).

Later, more or less simultaneously with Banach, several mathematicians—O. Hahn, L. Fréchet, E. Helly, and Norbert Wiener, among others—attained many of the concepts and theorems forming the basis of Banach's theory. None of them, however, succeeded in creating as comprehensive and integrated a system of concepts and theorems and their applications as that of Banach, his co-workers, and his students.

From 1922 on, Banach introduced through his papers the concept of normed linear spaces and investigated them (and metric linear spaces), particularly regarding the assumption of completeness (complete normed linear spaces are now generally known as Banach spaces). The concept was introduced at almost the same time by Norbert Wiener (who about a quarter of a century later founded cybernetics), but he did not develop the theory, perhaps because he did not see its possible application. Banach proved three fundamental theorems of the theory of normed linear spaces: the theorem on the extension of continuous linear functionals, now called the Hahn–Banach theorem (they proved it independently, and Hahn actually did so first); the theorem on bounded families of mappings, now called the Banach–Steinhaus theorem; and the theorem on continuous linear mappings of Banach spaces. He also introduced and examined the concept of weak convergence and weak closure, and gave a series of applications of the general theorems on normed linear spaces.

Further development of functional analysis proved that metric linear spaces are not sufficient for the needs of analysis and that it is essential to use more general, and also richer and more special, objects and structures. Nevertheless, the theory of Banach spaces has—often in combination with other methods—numerous applications in analysis. The theory of these spaces is both an indispensable tool and the basis of contemporary theory of more general linear spaces; it also provided the stimulus and the starting point for other branches of functional analysis.

The fact that functional analysis originated as late as Banach and his school, although favorable conditions seemingly existed at the beginning of the century, is due largely to the way mathematics had developed until then. In fact, sufficiently detailed knowledge about the different concrete instances of linear spaces was not achieved until the 1920's. Also, by that time the applications of some methods of the theory of sets, such as transfinite construction, were clarified, and some theorems on general topology (e.g., Baire's theorem on complete metric spaces and some propositions from the descriptive theory of sets) became widely known and applied.

BIBLIOGRAPHY

I. Original Works. Banach's major work is *Théorie des opérations linéaires* (Warsaw, 1932). Numerous papers are in *Fundamenta mathematicae* and *Studia mathematica*. See also "Sur le problème de la mesure," in *Fundamenta mathematicae*, **4** (1923), 7–33; and *Mechanika w zakresie szkol akademickich*, Vols. 8 and 9 in the series Monografie Matematyczne (Warsaw–Lvov–Vilna, 1938), translated into English as *Mechanics* (Warsaw–Breslau, 1951). The first volume of his collected works, *Oeuvres* (Warsaw, 1967), contains, besides papers by Banach, up-to-date comments on almost every article.

II. Secondary Literature. A short biography, a practically complete list of scientific papers, and an analysis of Banach's work are in *Colloquium mathematicum*, **1**, no. 2 (1948), 65–102. Also see H. Steinhaus, "Stefan Banach," in *Studia mathematica*, special series, **1** (1963), 7–15; and S. Ulam, "Stefan Banach 1892–1945," in *Bulletin of the American Mathematical Society*, **52** (1946), 600–603.

Miroslav Katětov

IBN AL-BANNĀ' AL MARRĀKUSHĪ, also known as **ABŪ'L-'ABBĀS AHMAD IBN MUḤAMMAD IBN 'UTHMĀN AL-AZDĪ** (*b.* Marrakesh, Morocco, 29 December 1256; *d.* Marrakesh [?], 1321)

Some authors, following Casiri, say Ibn al-Bannā' was a native of Granada. In any case, he studied all the literary and scientific subjects that had cultural value in Fez and Marrakesh. Muḥammad ibn Yaḥyā al-Sharīf taught him general geometry and Euclid's *Elements;* Abū Bakr al-Qallūsī, nicknamed al-Fār ("the Mouse"), introduced him to fractional numbers; and Ibn Ḥajala and Abū 'Abd Allāh ibn Makhlūf al-Sijilmāsī rounded out his training in mathematics. He also studied medicine with al-Mirrīkh, but he did not delve deeply into the subject. The mystic al-Hazmirī was responsible for directing a great part of Ibn al-Bannā''s work to the study of the magic properties of numbers and letters.

He taught arithmetic, algebra, geometry, and astronomy in the *madrasa* al-'Aṭṭārīn in Fez. Among his disciples were Abū Zayd 'Abd al-Raḥmān . . . al-Lajā'ī (*d. ca.* 771/1369), teacher of Ibn Qunfudh, who left us an excellent biographical sketch of Ibn al-Bannā'; Muḥammad ibn Ibrāhīm al-Abūlī (*d.* 770/1368); Abu'l-Barakāt al-Balāfiqī (*d.* 771/1370), who had Ibn al-Khaṭīb and Ibn Khaldūn as disciples; and Ibn al-Najjār al-Tilimsānī.

H. P. J. Renaud lists eighty-two works by Ibn al-Bannā'. The most important scientific ones are an introduction to Euclid; a treatise on areas; an algebra text dedicated to Abū 'Alī al-Ḥasan al-Milyānī; a book about acronical risings and settings (*Kitāb al-anwā'*), which is not as good as his other works on astronomy, such as the *Minhāj;* and an almanac that is possibly the earliest known, in which the word *manākh* appears for the first time in its Arabic form. The works of greatest merit, however, are the *Ṭalkhīṣ* and the *Minhāj*.

The *Talkhīṣ*, as its title indicates, is a summary of the lost works of the twelfth- or thirteenth-century mathematician al-Ḥaṣṣār. It was later summarized in verse by Ibn al-Qāḍi (*d.* 1025/1616) and was often commented on and glossed. Outstanding commentaries are the *Raf῾ al-ḥijāb* by Ibn al-Bannā᾽ himself, with notes by Ibn Haydūr, and that of al-Qalaṣādī of Granada. These works contain a type of fraction that corresponds to what are today called continuing ascending fractions and an approximate method for extracting square roots that corresponds, more or less, to the third or fourth reduction in the development of the continuous fraction, and is similar to al-Qalaṣādī's

$$a + \frac{r}{2a} - \frac{\left(\frac{r}{2a}\right)^2}{2a + \frac{r}{2a}}.$$

The possible connection between this formula and that of Juan de Ortega seems evident, but the transmission has not been sufficiently proved. The works also contain sums of cubes and squares according to the formulas

$$1^3 + 3^3 + 5^3 + \cdots + (2n - 1)^3 = n^2(2n^2 - 1)$$

$$1^2 + 3^2 + \cdots + (2n - 1)^2 = \left(\frac{2n + 1}{6}\right)2n(2n - 1).$$

One cannot be sure that Ibn al-Bannā᾽ was responsible for introducing a system of mathematical notation.

The *Kitāb minhāj al-ṭālib li ta῾dīl al-kawākib* is a very practical book for calculating astronomical ephemerals, thanks to the attached tables that are based upon those that Ibn Isḥāq al-Tūnisī calculated for the year 1222. The theoretical part does not contribute anything new and sometimes gives incorrect relationships between contradictory theories.

Ibn al-Bannā᾽ is credited with a *Risāla* ("epistle") on the astrolabe called *ṣafīḥa shakāziyya,* a variation of the *ṣafīḥa zarqāliyya,* or "al-Zarqālī's plate," which is the topic of many manuscripts in the libraries of north Africa. An examination of some of these manuscripts does not show the differences that should, in theory, exist between the two instruments.

BIBLIOGRAPHY

I. Original Works. Manuscripts of works by Ibn al-Bannā᾽ are listed in Brockelmann, *Geschichte der arabischen Litteratur,* II (Berlin, 1902), 255, 710; Supp. II (Leiden, 1938), 363–364; J. Vernet, "Los manuscritos astronómicos de Ibn al-Bannā᾽," in *Actes du VIIIe Congrès International d'Histoire des Sciences* (1956), 297–298; and Griffini in *RSO,* 7 (1916), 88–106. A. Marre published a French translation of the *Talkhīṣ* in *Atti dell'Accademia pontificia de Nuovi Lincei,* **17** (5 July 1864); the commentary of al-Qalaṣādī was translated by M. F. Woepcke, *ibid.,* **12** (3 April 1859). The *Minhāj* has been edited, translated into Spanish, and studied by J. Vernet (Tetuán, 1951). The *Kitāb al-anwā᾽* was edited, translated into French, and commented on by H. J. P. Renaud (Paris, 1948).

II. Secondary Literature. The Arabic sources for Ibn al-Bannā᾽'s life are listed in al-Ziriklī, *al-A῾lām,* 2nd ed., I, 213–214; especially in H. P. J. Renaud, "Ibn al-Bannā᾽ de Marrakech, ṣūfī et mathématicien," in *Hesperis,* **25** (1938), 13–42. The *Muqaddima* of Ibn Khaldūn is fundamental; see the English translation by F. Rosenthal, 3 vols. (New York, 1958), indexes and esp. III, 121, 123, 126, 137. Also consult H. P. J. Renaud, "Sur les dates de la vie du mathématicien arabe marocain Ibn al-Bannā᾽," in *Isis,* **27** (1937), 216–218; and "Sur un passage d'Ibn Khaldoun relatif à l'histoire des mathématiques," in *Hesperis,* **31** (1944), 35–47.

Additional information can be found in George Sarton, "Tacuinum, taqwīm. With a digression on the word 'Almanac,'" in *Isis,* **10** (1928), 490–493, and *Introduction to the History of Science,* II, 998–1000; H. Suter, *Die Mathematiker und Astronomen der Araber und ihre Werke* (Leipzig, 1900), 162–164, 220, 227; J. A. Sánchez Pérez, *Biografías de matemáticos árabes que florecieron en España,* no. 44, pp. 51–54; M. Cantor, *Vorlesungen ueber Geschichte der Mathematik,* I (Leipzig, 1907), 805–810; *Encyclopaedia of Islam,* II, 367; M. Steinschneider, "Rectification de quelques erreurs relatives au mathématicien Arabe Ibn al-Banna," in *Bulletino di bibliografia e di storia delle scienze matematiche e fisiche,* **10** (1877), 313; and F. Woepcke, "Passages relatifs à des sommations de séries de cubes," in *Journal des mathématiques pures et appliquées,* 2nd ser., **10** (1865), reviewed by M. Chasles in *Comptes rendus des séances de l'Académie des Sciences* (27 March 1865).

J. Vernet

BANŪ MŪSĀ. Three brothers—**Muḥammad, Aḥmad,** and **al-Ḥasan**—always known under the one name, which means "sons of Mūsā" (*b.* Baghdad, Iraq, beginning of ninth century; *d.* Baghdad. Muḥammad, the eldest, *d.* January or February A.D. 873)

Their father, Mūsā ibn Shākir, was a robber in his youth but later became a proficient astrologer. He died during the reign of Calif al-Ma'mūn (813–833), while his children were still young. Al-Ma'mūn recognized the mental ability of the brothers and enrolled them in the House of Wisdom—the first scientific institution in the Abbasid Empire and quite similar to the modern academy—which he himself had founded. Soon the Banū Mūsā excelled in mathematics, astronomy, and mechanics and became the most active members of the House of Wisdom. With

Muḥammad ibn Mūsā al-Khwārizmī they led its scientific research. Al-Khwārizmī was the founder of the Arabic school of algebra, while the Banū Mūsā were especially interested in geometry. They also led the astronomical observations in Baghdad and organized a school of translators who rendered many Greek scientific manuscripts into Arabic. These translations were very useful in the development of science. Some important Greek works are now known only in their Arabic translations.

The most famous translators of that time worked under the guidance of the Banū Mūsā. Among them were Ḥunayn ibn Isḥāq, who became the foremost translator of medical works, and Thābit ibn Qurra, the famous scientist and translator of the ninth century, to whom are ascribed many works besides the translations of such Greek works as Euclid's *Elements* and three books of Apollonius' *Conics.* The Banū Mūsā were among the first Arabic scientists to study the Greek mathematical works and to lay the foundation of the Arabic school of mathematics. They may be called disciples of Greek mathematicians, yet they deviated from classical Greek mathematics in ways that were very important to the development of some mathematical concepts.

It is difficult to distinguish the role played by each of the brothers in their common works, but it seems that Ja'far Muḥammad was the most important. Muḥammad and al-Ḥasan were especially interested in geometry; Aḥmad was interested in mechanics. Muḥammad also did work in astronomy.

Of the many works ascribed to the Banū Mūsā, the most important was the geometrical treatise called *Book on the Measurement of Plane and Spherical Figures.* Manuscripts of this treatise are in Oxford, Paris, Berlin, Istanbul, and Rampur, India. One of these manuscripts, with a recension by the thirteenth-century mathematician Naṣīr al-Dīn al-Ṭūsī, has been published in Arabic. It was well-known in the Middle Ages in both Islam and Europe. The best evidence for this is the twelfth-century Latin translation by Gerard of Cremona, entitled *Liber trium fratrum de geometria.* Manuscripts of this translation are in Paris, Madrid, Basel, Toruń, and Oxford. The main purpose of the treatise—as stated in the introduction—was to demonstrate the most important part of the Greek method of determining area and volume. In the treatise the method was applied to the measurement of the circle and the sphere.

In *Measurement of the Circle* and *On the Sphere and Cylinder,* Archimedes found the area of the circle and the surface and volume of the sphere by means of the method of Eudoxus, which was later called the "method of exhaustion." This method was based on the same ideas that underlie the limit theory of modern mathematics. After Archimedes, this method was followed without further development. In fact, there is no evidence of work on the measurement of areas and volumes until the ninth century.

The Banū Mūsā found the area of the circle by a method different from that of Archimedes but based on his ideas of infinitesimals. They used the "method of exhaustion" but omitted the main part of it, inscribing in the circle a sequence of right polygons with 2^k sides ($k = 2, 3, \cdots, n$) and finding their areas. Then they used the method of the "rule of contraries" to find the desired result. They omitted the transition to the limit condition, however; that is, they did not find the area of such a polygon when $k \rightarrow \infty$. Instead, they depended upon a proposition whose proof included the transition. This is the sixteenth proposition of the twelfth book of the *Elements.*

Using this theorem, the Banū Mūsā proved the following: If we have a circle of circumference C and a line of length L, and if $L < C$, then we can inscribe in this circle a right polygon of perimeter P_n (n is the number of sides) such that $P_n > L$. This means that we can find an integer, N, such that $C - P_n < C - L$ for every $n > N$. In the second part of this proposition the Banū Mūsā proved that if $L > C$, then we can circumscribe a right polygon of perimeter Q_n, such that $Q_n < L$. After this the proof of $A = r \cdot 1/2\ C$ (where A is the area of the circle and r its radius) becomes easy.

It should be noted that the Banū Mūsā defined the areas and volumes as equal to the products of certain values, while in Greek geometry they were expressed as comparisons with other areas and volumes. For example, Archimedes defined the volume of the sphere as four times the volume of the cone with the radius of the sphere as its height and the great circle of the sphere as its base. The Banū Mūsā found that the volume is equal to the radius of the sphere multiplied by one third of its surface. In other words, they used arithmetical operations for determining geometrical values. It was an important step to extend the number system and make it include irrationals as well as integers and rationals. In the sixth proposition the Banū Mūsā demonstrated the method of Archimedes for the approximate determination of the value of π. By means of inscription and circumscription of right polygons of ninety-six sides, Archimedes proved that π must lie between the values 3 1/7 and 3 10/71. The Banū Mūsā wrote that this method can be continued to get nearer to the boundaries of the value of π. This means that $\pi = \lim P_n$ (where P_n is the perimeter of the inscribed or circumscribed right polygon).

Like Archimedes, the Banū Mūsā determined that

the surface of the sphere is four times its great circle, but their proof is different. Archimedes' proof is equivalent to the calculation of the definite integral

$$\int_0^\pi 2\pi r^2 \sin\phi \, d\phi = 4\pi r^2,$$

where r is the radius of the sphere. This cannot be said for the Banū Mūsā's proof, for they calculated only a finite sum of the sine series proving that

$$\cos\frac{\pi}{4n}\cdot\cot\frac{\pi}{4n} < 2\sum_{K=1}^{n}\sin\frac{K\pi}{2n} < \csc\frac{\pi}{4n};$$

they did not extend this formula to the limit condition. Instead, they used the following fact without proving it: For any two concentric spheres we can inscribe in the larger a solid generated by rotating a right polygon about the diameter of the sphere that passes through two vertexes of the polygon, such that the surface of this solid does not touch or intersect the smaller sphere. This was proved by Euclid in the seventeenth theorem of the twelfth book of the *Elements.* The Banū Mūsā calculated the volume of the solid; then, using Euclid's theorem and the rule of contraries, they proved that $A = 4C$ (where A is the surface of the sphere and C is its great circle).

In addition to the measurement of the circle and the sphere, three classical Greek problems were solved in the treatise:

(1) In the seventh proposition of the treatise the Banū Mūsā proved the following theorem: If a, b, and c are sides of any triangle and A its area, then

$$A = \sqrt{p(p-a)(p-b)(p-c)},$$

where $p = (a+b+c)/2$. This theorem is often called Hero's theorem because Europeans met it for the first time in Hero's *Metrics,* but it existed in a lost book of Archimedes, which was known to the Arabs. The Banū Mūsā's proof, however, is different from that of Hero.

(2) The determination of two mean proportionals. This problem concerns the determination of two unknowns, x and y, from the formula $a/x = x/y = y/b$, where a and b are given. This problem was solved for the first time by Archytas. The Banū Mūsā included this solution but stated that they had borrowed it from a geometrical treatise by Menelaos. Archytas found x and y through three intersecting curved surfaces: right cylinder $x^2 + y^2 = ax$, right cone $b^2(x^2 + y^2 + z^2) = a^2x^2$, and torus $x^2 + y^2 + z^2 = a\sqrt{x^2 + y^2}$. If x_0, y_0, and z_0 are the coordinates of the point of intersection of these surfaces, then it is clear that

$$\frac{a}{\sqrt{x_0^2 + y_0^2 + z_0^2}} = \frac{\sqrt{x_0^2 + y_0^2 + z_0^2}}{\sqrt{x_0^2 + y_0^2}} = \frac{\sqrt{x_0^2 + y_0^2}}{b}.$$

Therefore, $\sqrt{x_0^2 + y_0^2 + z_0^2}$ and $\sqrt{x_0^2 + y_0^2}$ are the required two mean proportionals between a and b. The Banū Mūsā gave a practical method for solving this problem by means of an instrument constructed from hinged rules. This instrument is very much like that devised by Plato for the same purpose.

(3) The trisection of the angle. Their solution to this problem, like all those given previously, is kinematic.

Thus, the contents of the Banū Mūsā's treatise are really within the boundaries of the ancient knowledge of geometry. This treatise, however, is not merely an exposition of Greek geometrical works, for it contains new proofs for the main theorems of the measurement of the circle and the sphere. Having studied the works of Greek mathematicians, the Banū Mūsā assimilated many of their methods. But in using the Greek infinitesimal method—the "method of exhaustion"—they omitted the transition to the limit conditions.

In the tenth and eleventh centuries a number of Arabic mathematical works on the measurement of figures were influenced by the Banū Mūsā's treatise, *On the Measurement of Plane and Spherical Figures.* The most important of these works were Thābit ibn Qurra's *On the Measurement of the Conic Section Named Parabola* and *On the Measurement of the Parabolic Solids,* and Ibn al-Haytham's *On the Measurement of Parabolic Solids* and *On the Measurement of the Sphere.* In the Middle Ages the treatise played a great role in spreading the tradition of Euclid and Archimedes in the Arabic countries and in Europe. Its influence upon European scientists in the Middle Ages can easily be seen in the *Practica geometrica* of Leonardo Fibonacci. In this book we can see some theorems of the Banū Mūsā that did not exist in the Greek books—for example, the theorem that says that the plane section of a right cone parallel to the base of the cone is a circle.

In addition to the treatise *On the Measurement of Plane and Spherical Figures,* the Banū Mūsā are credited with a number of other works that have been studied either insufficiently or not at all. Following is a list of the most important of these works.

(1) *Premises of the Book of Conics.* This is a recension of Apollonius' *Conics,* which was translated into

Arabic by Hilāl al-Ḥimṣī (Bks. I–IV) and Thābit ibn Qurra (Bks. V–VII). This recension was probably prepared by Muḥammad. Manuscripts of it are in Oxford, Istanbul, and Leiden.

(2) *Book of the Lengthened Circle.* This treatise, written by al-Ḥasan, seems to be on the "gardener's construction of the ellipse," that is, the construction of an ellipse by means of a string attached to the foci.

(3) *Qarasṭūn.* This is a treatise on the balance theory and its instruments.

(4) *On Mechanical Devices* (or *On Mechanics*). This treatise on pneumatic devices was written by Aḥmad. Manuscripts of it are in Berlin and the Vatican.

(5) *Book on the Description of the Instrument Which Sounds by Itself.* This work is on musical theory. A manuscript is in Beirut.

Some of these works deserve to be carefully studied, especially *Qarasṭūn* and *On Mechanical Devices.*

BIBLIOGRAPHY

I. ORIGINAL WORKS. There are two editions of the Banū Mūsā's main work, *On the Measurement of Plane and Spherical Figures: Kitāb maʿrifat misāḥat al-ashkāl al-basīṭa wa'l-kuriyya,* in *Rasā'il al-Ṭūsī,* II (Hyderabad, 1940); and *Liber trium fratrum de geometria,* M. Curtze, ed., in *Nova acta Academiae Caesareae Leopoldino Carolinae germanicae naturae curiosorum,* **49** (1885).

II. SECONDARY LITERATURE. The Banū Mūsā's contributions are discussed in Marshall Clagett, *Archimedes in the Middle Ages,* I (Madison, Wis., 1964); M. Steinschneider, "Die Söhne des Musa ben Schakir," in *Bibliotheca mathematica* (Leipzig, 1887), pp. 44–48, 71–75; H. Suter, "Mathematiker und Astronomen der Araber und ihre Werke," in *Abhandlungen zur Geschichte der Mathematik* (Leipzig, 1900), and "Die Geometria der Söhne des Musa b. Shakir," in *Bibliotheca mathematica,* **3** (1902), 259–272. Information on the life and works of the Banū Mūsā can be found in C. Brockelmann, *Geschichte der arabischen Litteratur,* I (Leiden, 1936), p. 382 of Supp. I; G. Sarton, *Introduction to the History of Science,* I, 545–546, 560; Ibn al-Nadīm, *al-Fihrist,* G. Flügel, ed. (new ed., Beirut, 1964), I, 271; II, 126–127; Ibn al-Qifṭī, *Ta'rīkh al-ḥukamā',* Julius Lippert, ed. (Leipzig, 1903), pp. 315–316, 441–443. See also E. Wiedemann, "Zur Mechanik und Technik bei der Arabern," in *Sitzungsberichte der Physikalisch-medizinischen Sozietät in Erlangen,* **38** (1906), esp. 6–8, which briefly discusses the Banū Mūsā's work on mechanics.

J. AL-DABBAGH

BARBIER, JOSEPH-ÉMILE (*b.* St.-Hilaire-Cotter, Pas-de-Calais, France, 18 March 1839; *d.* St.-Genest, Loire, France, 28 January 1889)

The son of a former soldier, Barbier was singled out in primary school for his mathematical and scientific aptitude. After secondary schooling at the Collège de St.-Omer, and then at the Lycée Henri IV in Paris, he was admitted in 1857 to the École Normale Supérieure, where he astonished his fellow students by his acute intelligence and his ability to grasp the deeper meanings of complex problems. He also had a taste for subtlety that led him to detect the errors in the most classic demonstrations.

In 1860 Barbier passed his *agrégation* and taught mathematics at the *lycée* of Nice, where he does not seem to have been appreciated by his students. Le Verrier, director of the Paris Observatory, was impressed by Barbier's keen insight and offered him a position as assistant astronomer. A good observer, Barbier showed himself also to be an able calculator. He was fully aware of the usefulness to astronomy of mathematics, physics, chemistry, and instrumental techniques, and he was thus a valuable collaborator. During this period he published numerous reports concerned with various problems in astronomy and the most diverse types of mathematics. His ingenuity led him to perfect a new type of thermometer.

But after a few years Barbier seemed to become more and more unstable and strange. In 1865 he left the observatory, and after attempting to enter a religious order broke off all contacts with his associates. Only in 1880 was he discovered in the asylum at Charenton-St.-Maurice, where he had been sequestered for several years. Joseph Bertrand, permanent secretary of the Académie des Sciences, encouraged him to return to scientific writing and was able to secure for him regular financial help from a foundation connected with the Academy. The numerous reports published thereafter were irreproachably sound and often most original. Although Barbier never recovered his sanity, the gentleness of his behavior caused him to be released, and he spent his last years in a more serene environment.

Barbier's work is scattered in thirty or more memoirs and reports, of which about two-thirds were published during his brief career as a professor and assistant astronomer (1860–1866); most of the others were published between 1882 and 1887.

Several of the studies in the first series bear on the mathematical aspects of astronomy (spherical geometry and spherical trigonometry), on the construction of new thermometers, and on other aspects of instrumental techniques. The others deal with infinitesimal calculus and elementary and infinitesimal geometry, as well as with the calculus of probabilities. The last works of Barbier dealt almost entirely with mathematics and made several interesting contributions to geometry (the theory of polyhedra, the indicatrix of Dupin), integral calculus, and the theory of numbers.

Despite the illness that ruined his career, Barbier deserves to be numbered among the good unspecialized mathematicians of the late nineteenth century.

BIBLIOGRAPHY

I. ORIGINAL WORKS. Barbier's scientific work consists of thirty or more memoirs and reports published in various French journals, particularly in *Nouvelles annales de mathématiques; Les mondes;* and *Comptes-rendus hebdomadaires de l'Académie des sciences.* Nearly complete lists of his publications are given in the *Catalogue of Scientific Papers* of the Royal Society: I (1867), 178; VII (1877), 85; IX (1891), 118–119; XIII (1914), 289; and Poggendorff, III (1898), 68, and IV (1904), 64.

II. SECONDARY LITERATURE. Articles on Barbier are J. Bertrand, in *Association des anciens élèves de l'École normale* (Paris, 1890), pp. 35–36; P. Gauja, *Les fondations de l'Académie des sciences (1881–1915)* (Hendaye, 1917), pp. 348–349; and A. M. Lautour, in *Dictionnaire de biographie française,* III (1951), col. 326.

RENÉ TATON

BARLOW, PETER (*b.* Norwich, England, October 1776; *d.* 1 March 1862)

Although he was self-educated, Barlow successfully competed for the position of assistant mathematics master at the Royal Military Academy, Woolwich, in 1801. While there he wrote mathematical articles for *The Ladies' Diary* and later for encyclopedias. He also published *An Elementary Investigation of the Theory of Numbers* (1811), *A New Mathematical and Philosophical Dictionary* (1814), and *New Mathematical Tables* (1814), later known as *Barlow's Tables.* The *Tables,* which gave the factors, squares, cubes, square roots, cube roots, reciprocals, and hyperbolic logarithms of all numbers from 1 to 10,000, was so accurate and was deemed so useful that a large part of it was reprinted and distributed by the Society for the Diffusion of Useful Knowledge (the last reprint was in 1947).

Barlow's reputation was established with the publication of his *Essay on the Strength and Stress of Timber* (1817), the result of experiments he conducted at the Woolwich dockyard and arsenal. He worked with Thomas Telford on the design of the Menai Strait suspension bridge and on the calculation of tides in the Thames as they would be affected by the removal of the old London Bridge. Barlow was made an honorary member of the Institution of Civil Engineers in 1820.

In 1819 Barlow became interested in the compass deviation caused by the iron in ships. He therefore investigated the action of terrestrial magnetism and conducted a series of experiments on the interaction of iron objects and compass needles. His results, published as *Essay on Magnetic Attractions* (1820), described a method of correcting ships' compasses by use of a small iron plate. For his discoveries in magnetism he was made a fellow of the Royal Society in 1823 and received the Copley Medal in 1825. He also received international recognition and several awards for his contribution to navigation. Barlow was also concerned with electromagnetism and unsuccessfully attempted to make an electric telegraph. Using a magnetic needle, he tried to produce a deflection by means of battery current sent through a length of wire, but the insulation failed.

Around 1827 Barlow became interested in the calculation for the curvature of achromatic object glasses, and in the course of his research he developed a telescope lens consisting of a colorless liquid between two pieces of glass. The "Barlow lens," a modification of this telescope lens, is a negative achromatic combination of flint glass and crown glass.

On several occasions in the 1830's and 1840's Barlow served as a royal commissioner of railroads. He was one of the first to conduct experiments and make calculations on the best shape for rails and the effect of gradients and curves.

BIBLIOGRAPHY

I. ORIGINAL WORKS. Forty-nine of Barlow's scientific papers are listed in the Royal Society's *Catalogue of Scientific Papers 1800–1863,* I, 182–184. He edited an edition of D. H. Mahan's *An Elementary Course of Civil Engineering* (Edinburgh-Dublin-London, 1845) and Thomas Tredgold's *Elementary Principles of Carpentry,* 5th ed. (London, 1870).

II. SECONDARY WORKS. Articles on Barlow are in *Dictionary of National Biography* and *Encyclopaedia Britannica* (1911). There is no full-length biography available.

HAROLD I. SHARLIN

BAROCIUS, FRANCISCUS, also known as **Francesco Barozzi** (*b.* Candia, Crete, 9 August 1537; *d.* Venice, Italy, 23 November 1604)

A Venetian patrician, Barocius received a humanistic education and achieved an admirable command of Greek and Latin. He studied at the University of Padua and, according to his own account, lectured there about 1559 on the *Sphere* of Sacrobosco. Barocius' edition of Proclus' commentary on the first book of Euclid's *Elements* was the first important translation of this work, for it was based on better manuscripts than previous efforts had been. The translation, published at Venice in 1560, was completed by Barocius at the age of twenty-two.

In 1572 he brought out a Latin translation of Hero's book on war machines, and in 1588 he completed his corrections, unpublished to this day, of a manuscript copy of Federicus Commandinus' translation of Pappus' *Collectio.* His translation of the Archimedean *De dimensionibus* also is still in manuscript. Barocius wrote in Italian on *rythmomachia* (1572), a number game that he attributed to Pythagoras but that appears to go back only to the eleventh century. The book is based on Boissière's work on the same subject (Paris, 1556). Barocius composed a Latin treatise on thirteen ways to draw two parallel lines in a plane (1572) and an elementary *Cosmographia* (1585), based on the *Sphere* of Sacrobosco and containing chapters on meteorology and physical geography. Barocius noted eighty-four errors in Sacrobosco's work, largely, according to Thorndike, matters of definition and order of treatment. The "errors" did not include the geocentric theory, and a marginal comment condemned as false the opinion of Aristarchus and Copernicus.

Barocius had a stormy career. In 1587 he was brought before the Inquisition on charges of sorcery, and more particularly of having caused a torrential rainstorm in Crete. He was sentenced to provide silver crosses at a cost of 100 ducats and condemned to remain in prison at the pleasure of the Holy Office (apparently a suspended sentence). After the trial the only work that he published was another edition of the *Cosmographia* (1598).

BIBLIOGRAPHY

I. ORIGINAL WORKS. Works by Barocius include *Opusculum, in quo una oratio, & duas questiones: Altera de certitudine & altera de medietate mathematicarum continentur* (Padua, 1560); *Procli Diadochi in primum Euclidis elementorum librum commentariorum libri IIII a Francisco Barocio . . .* (Padua, 1560); *Commentarius in locum Platonis obscurissimum, & hactenus a nemine recte expositum in principio dialogi octaui de Rep. ubi sermo habetur de numero geometrico, de quo prouerbium est, quod numero Platonis nihil obscurius* (Bologna, 1566); *Heronis mechanici liber de machinis bellicus, necnon liber de geodesia a Francisco Barocio . . . Latinitate donati* (Venice, 1572); *Il nobilissimo et antiquissimo givoco Pythagoreo nominato rythmomachia, cioe battaglia di consonanze di numeri, in lingua volgare a modo di parafresi composto* (Venice, 1572); *Cosmographia in quattuor libros distributa* (Venice, 1585, 1598; Italian trans., 1607); *Admirandum illud geometricum problema tredecim modis demonstratum, quod docet duas lineas in eodem plano designare, quae numquam invicem coincidant, etiam si in infinitum protahantur* (Venice, 1586). His *Descrittione dell'isola di Creta* was edited by Giuseppe Nicoletti (Venice, 1898).

Manuscripts include his corrections of Federicus Commandinus' translation of Pappus' *Collectio* (BN MS Lat. 7222[1-2]) in the Bibliothèque Nationale and two manuscripts at Trinity College in Dublin: *Savasordae Judaei liber de arcis, infinitis erroribus expurgatis atque scholis et annotationibus illustratus* and *Archimedis liber de dimensionibus a Franc. Barocio restauratus.*

II. SECONDARY LITERATURE. Works concerning Barocius are B. Boncompagni, "Intorno alla vita ed ai labori de Francesco Barozzi," in *Bullettino di bibliographia e di storia delle scienze matematiche e fisiche,* **17** (1884), 795–848; Lynn Thorndike, *A History of Magic and Experimental Science,* VI (New York, 1941), 25, 47, 154–155, 199; Athanasius Pryor Treweek, "Pappus of Alexandria. The Manuscript Tradition of the *Collectio mathematica,*" in *Scriptorium,* **11,** no. 2 (1957), 195–233; Paul Ver Eecke, ed. and trans., *Proclus de Lycie, les commentaires sur le premier livre des Éléments d'Euclide* (Bruges, 1948), pp. xxi ff.; and the entry in *Dizionario biografico degli italiani,* VI (1964), 495–499.

MARJORIE NICE BOYER

BARROW, ISAAC (*b.* London, England, October 1630; *d.* London, 4 May 1677)

Barrow's father, Thomas, was a prosperous linendraper with court connections; his mother, Anne, died when Isaac was an infant. A rebel as a dayboy at Charterhouse, Barrow came later, at Felsted, to accept the scholastic disciplining in Greek, Latin, logic, and rhetoric imposed by his headmaster, Martin Holbeach. In 1643, already as firm a supporter of the king as his father was, he entered Trinity College, Cambridge, as pensioner. There he survived increasingly antiroyalist pressure for twelve years, graduating B.A. in 1648, being elected a college fellow (1649), and receiving his M.A. (1652), the academic passport to his final position as college lecturer and university examiner. In 1655, ousted by Cromwellian mandate from certain selection as Regius professor of Greek (in succession to his former tutor, James Duport), he sold his books and set out on an adventurous four-year tour of the Continent. On his return, coincident with the restoration of Charles II to the throne in 1660, he took holy orders and was promptly rewarded with the chair previously denied him. In 1662 he trebled his slender income by concurrently accepting the Gresham professorship of geometry in London and acting as locum for a fellow astronomy professor; he was relieved of this excessive teaching load when, in 1663, he was made first Lucasian professor of mathematics at Cambridge.

During the next six years, forbidden by professorial statute to hold any other university position, Barrow devoted himself to preparing the three series of *Lectiones* on which his scientific fame rests. In 1669, however, increasingly dissatisfied with this bar to advancing himself within his college, he resigned his chair (to Newton) to become royal chaplain in London. Four years later he returned as king's choice for the vacant mastership of Trinity, becoming university vice-chancellor in 1675. Barrow never married and, indeed, erased from his master's patent the clause permitting him to do so. Small and wiry in build, by conventional account he enjoyed excellent health, his early death apparently being the result of an overdose of drugs. He was remembered by his contemporaries for the bluntness and clarity of his theological sermons (published posthumously by Tillotson in 1683–1689), although these were too literary and long-winded to make him a popular preacher. His deep classical knowledge resulted in no specialized philological or textual studies. Although he was one of the first fellows of the Royal Society after its incorporation in 1662, he never took an active part in its meetings.

As an undergraduate, Barrow, like Newton a decade later, endured a traditional scholastic course, centered on Aristotle and his Renaissance commentators, which was inculcated by lecture and examined by disputation; but from the first he showed great interest in the current Gassendist revival of atomism and Descartes's systematization of natural philosophy. (His 1652 M.A. thesis, *Cartesiana hypothesis de materia et motu haud satisfacit praecipuis naturae phaenomenis,* is based on a careful study of Descartes and Regius.) That, also like Newton, he mastered Descartes's *Géométrie* unaided is unlikely. The elementary portion of Euclid's *Elements* was part of Barrow's college syllabus, but some time before 1652 he went on to read not only Euclidean commentaries by Tacquet, Hérigone, and Oughtred, but also more advanced Greek works by Archimedes and possibly Apollonius and Ptolemy. His first published work, his epitomized *Euclidis Elementorum libri XV* (probably written by early 1654), is designed as a quadrivium undergraduate text, with emphasis on its deductive structure rather than on its geometrical content, its sole concessions to contemporary mathematical idiom being its systematic use of Oughtred's symbolism and a list "ex P. Herigono" of numerical constants relating to inscribed polyhedra. To its reedition in 1657, Barrow added a similar epitome of Euclid's *Data,* and in his 1666 Lucasian lectures expounded a likewise recast version of Archimedes' method in the *Sphere and Cylinder;* a full edition, in the same style, of the known corpus of Archimedes' works, the first four books of Apollonius' *Conics,* and the three books of Theodosius' *Spherics* appeared in 1675. Overloaded with marginal references, virtually bare of editorial amplification, and fussy in their symbolism, these texts can hardly have been easier to read than their Latin originals, and only the conveniently pocket-sized *Euclid* reached a wide public. Barrow himself commented that his Apollonius had in it "nothing considerable but its brevity." His early attempt at a modern approach to Greek mathematics was a short, posthumously edited *Lectio* in which he analyzed the Archimedean quadrature method in terms of indivisibles on the style of Wallis' *Arithmetica infinitorum.*

Barrow's Gresham inaugural, still preserved, tells little of the content of his lost London lectures: perhaps they were similar to works of his on "Perspective, Projections, Elem^ts^ of Plaine Geometry" mentioned by Collins. The first of his Lucasian series, the *Lectiones mathematicae* (given in sequence from 1664 to 1666), discourse on the foundations of mathematics from an essentially Greek standpoint, with interpolations from such contemporaries as Tacquet, Wallis, and Hobbes (usually cited only to be refuted). Such topics as the ontological status of mathematical entities, the nature of axiomatic deduction, the continuous and the discrete, spatial magnitude and numerical quantity, infinity and the infinitesimal, and proportionality and incommensurability are examined at length. Barrow's conservatism reveals itself in his artificial preservation of the dichotomy between arithmetic and geometry by classifying algebra as merely a useful logical (analytical) tool which is not a field of mathematical study in itself. The *Lectiones geometricae* were, no doubt, initially intended as the technical study of higher geometry for which the preceding course had paved the way, and the earlier lectures may indeed have been delivered as such.

About 1664, having heard (as he told Collins) that "Mersennus & Torricellius doe mencōn a generall method of finding ye tangents of curve lines by composition of motions; but doe not tell it us," he found out "such a one" for himself, elaborating an approach to plane geometry in which the elements were suitably compounded rotating and translating lines. In his first five geometrical lectures he took some trouble to define the uniformly "fluent" variable of time which is the measure of all motion, and then went on to consider the properties of curves generated by combinations of moving points and lines, evolving a simple Robervallian construction for tangents. Later lectures (6–12), evidently thrown together in some haste, are in large part a systematic generalization of tangent, quadrature, and rectification procedures gathered by Barrow from his reading of Torricelli, Descartes, Schooten, Hudde, Wallis, Wren, Fermat, Huygens, Pascal, and, above all, James Gregory; while the final *Lectio,* 13, is an unconnected account of the geometrical construction of equations. We should (despite Child) be careful not to overemphasize the originality of these lectures: the "fundamental theorem of the calculus," for example, and the *compendium pro tangentibus determinandis* in *Lectio 10* are, respectively, restylings, by way of propositions 6 and 7 of Gregory's *Geometriae pars universalis* (1668), of William Neil's rectification method (in Wallis' *De cycloide,* 1659) and of the tangent algorithm thrashed out by Descartes and Fermat in their 1638 correspondence (published by Clerselier in 1667). In theory, as Jakob Bernoulli argued in 1691, Barrow's geometrical formulations could well have been the basis on which systematized algorithmic calculus structures were subsequently erected; but in historical fact the *Lectiones geometricae* were little read even by the few (Sluse, Gregory, Newton, Leibniz) qualified to appreciate them, and their impact was small. Perhaps only John Craige (1685) based a calculus method on a Barrovian precedent, and then only in a single instance (*Lectio 11,*1).

Barrow's optical lectures, highly praised on their first publication by Sluse and James Gregory, had an equally short-lived heyday, being at once rendered obsolete by the Newtonian *Lectiones opticae,* which, both in methodology and in subject matter, they inspired. In his introduction he lays down the scarcely novel mechanical hypothesis of a lucid body (a "congeries corpusculorum ultra pene quam cogitari potest minutorum" or "collection of particles minute almost beyond conceivability") as the propagating source of rectilinear light rays. His hypothesis of color (in *Lectio 12*) as a dilution in "thickness" and swiftness, of white light through red, green, and blue to black, is no less shadowy than the Cartesian explanation to which it is preferred. Structurally, the technical portion of the *Lectiones* is developed purely mathematically from six axiomatic "Hypotheses opticae primariae et fundamentales [seu] leges . . . ab experientiâ confirmatae," notably the Euclidean law of reflection and the sine law of refraction, and presents a reasonably complete discussion of the elementary catoptrics and dioptrics of white light. Not unexpectedly, the organization and mathematical detail are Barrow's, but his topics are mostly taken from Alhazen, Kepler, Scheiner, Descartes, and others: thus, his improvement of the Cartesian theory of the rainbow (*Lectio 12,* 14) derives from Huygens by way of Sluse. The most original contributions of the work are his method for finding the point of refraction at a plane interface (*Lectio 5,* 12) and his point construction of the diacaustic of a spherical interface (*Lectio 13,* 24): both were at once subsumed by Newton into his own geometrical optics, and the latter (in ignorance) was triumphantly rediscovered by Jakob Bernoulli in 1693.

Barrow's relationship with Newton, although of considerable historical importance, has never been clarified. That Newton was Barrow's pupil at Trinity is a myth, and Barrow's name does not appear in the mass of Newton's extant early papers; nor is there good evidence for supposing that any of Newton's early mathematical or optical discoveries were in any way due to Barrow's personal tutelage. In his old age, the furthest that Newton would go in admitting a mathematical debt to Barrow was that attendance at his lectures "might put me upon considering the generation of figures by motion, tho I not now remember it." It may well be that Barrow came to know Newton intimately only after his election to senior college status in 1667. Certainly by late 1669 there was a brief working rapport between the two which, if it did not last long, at least resulted in Newton's consciously choosing to continue the theme of his predecessor's lectures in his own first Lucasian series.

BIBLIOGRAPHY

I. Original Works. The contents of Barrow's library at the time of his death are recorded in "A Catalogue of the Bookes of Dr Isaac Barrow Sent to S.S. by Mr Isaac Newton . . . July 14. 1677" (Bodleian, Oxford, Rawlinson D878, 33^{r}–59^{r}). His *Euclidis Elementorum libri XV breviter demonstrati* appeared at Cambridge in 1655; to its 1657 reedition (reissued in 1659) was appended his edition of Euclid's *Data.* Both reappeared in 1678, together with Barrow's *Lectio . . . in qua theoremata Archimedis De sphaera & cylindro per methodum indivisibilium investigata exhibentur* (Royal Society, London, MS XIX). An English edition of the *Elements; the Whole Fifteen Books* (London, 1660) was reissued half a dozen times in the early eighteenth century, and an independent English version by Thomas Haselden of the *Elements, Data,* and *Lectio* together appeared there in 1732. The manuscript of Barrow's *Archimedis opera: Apollonii Pergaei Conicorum libri IIII: Theodosii Sphaerica: Methodo novo illustrata, & succincte demonstrata* (London, 1675) is now in the Royal Society, London (MSS XVIII–XX): a proposed appendix epitomizing Apollonius' *Conics, 5–7* (from Borelli's 1661 edition) never appeared. His *Lectiones mathematicae XXIII; In quibus Principia Matheseôs generalia exponuntur: Habitae Cantabrigiae A.D. 1664, 1665, 1666* was published posthumously at London in 1683 (reissued 1684 and 1685); an English version by John Kirkby came out there in 1734. The rare 1669 edition of Barrow's *Lectiones XVIII Cantabrigiae in scholis publicis habitae; In quibus opticorum phaenomenωn genuinae rationes investigantur, ac exponuntur* was speedily followed (1670) by his *Lectiones geometricae: In quibus (praesertim) generalia curvarum linearum symptomata declarantur*: these were issued (both together and separately) at London in 1670, 1672, and 1674. Unpublished variant drafts of geometrical lectures 10, 11, and 13 are extant in private possession.

The optical lectures were reprinted, none too accurately, in C. Babbage and F. Maseres' *Scriptores optici* (London, 1823), and all three Lucasian series were collected, together with Barrow's inaugural, in W. Whewell's *The Mathematical Works of Isaac Barrow D.D.* (Cambridge, 1860). A mediocre English translation of the geometrical lectures by Edmund Stone (London, 1735) is more accurate than J. M. Child's distorted abridgment, *The Geometrical Lectures of Isaac Barrow* (Chicago-London, 1916). Alexander Napier's standard edition of Barrow's *Theological Works* (9 vols., Cambridge, 1859), based on original manuscripts in Trinity College, Cambridge, and otherwise restoring the text from Tillotson's "improvements," is scientifically valuable for the *Opuscula* contained in its final volume: here will be found the texts of Barrow's early academic exercises and college orations, as well as of his professorial inaugurals. The extant portion of Barrow's correspondence with Collins has been published several times from the originals in possession of the Royal Society, London, and the Earl of Macclesfield, notably in Newton's *Commercium epistolicum D. Johannis Collins, et aliorum de analysi promota* (London, 1712) and in S. P. Rigaud's *Correspondence of Scientific Men of the Seventeenth Century,* II (Oxford, 1841), 32–76.

II. SECONDARY LITERATURE. Existing sketches of Barrow's life (by Abraham Hill, John Aubrey, John Ward, and, more recently, J. H. Overton) are mostly collections of unsupported anecdote, both dreary and derivative. Percy H. Osmond's *Isaac Barrow, His Life and Times* (London, 1944) has few scientific insights but is otherwise a lively, semipopular account of Barrow's intellectual achievement. In "Newton, Barrow and the Hypothetical Physics," in *Centaurus,* **11** (1965), 46–56, and *Atomism in England From Hariot to Newton* (Oxford, 1966), p. 120, Robert H. Kargon argues that Barrow's scientific methodology, as expounded in the *Lectiones mathematicae,* should be interpreted as a rejection of hypothetical physics rather than as Archimedean classicism, but he is uncritical in his acceptance of Barrow's early influence on Newton.

D. T. WHITESIDE

BARTHOLIN, ERASMUS (*b.* Roskilde, Denmark, 13 August 1625; *d.* Copenhagen, Denmark, 4 November 1698)

Erasmus Bartholin was the son of Caspar Bartholin (1585–1629) and the brother of Thomas (1616–1680). He matriculated at the University of Leiden in 1646 and remained in Holland for several years, studying mathematics. Later he traveled in France, Italy (he received his M.D. at Padua in 1654), and England. Upon his return to Copenhagen, Bartholin was appointed professor of mathematics in 1656 but transferred to an extraordinary chair of medicine in 1657 and to an ordinary one in 1671. He served the University of Copenhagen as dean of the faculty of medicine, librarian, and rector, and was appointed royal physician and privy councilor.

Bartholin wrote little on medicine, although he and his brother Thomas played some part in introducing cinchona bark to Denmark; he also contributed to the journal founded and edited by Thomas, *Acta medica et philosophica Hafniensia.*

His publications in pure mathematics were fairly numerous, but not of great importance. As an exponent of the Cartesian tradition, Bartholin's main interest was in the theory of equations; in this he was directly influenced by Frans Van Schooten. Besides his own works, he issued in almost every year from 1664 to at least 1674 a *Dissertatio de problematibus geometricis* consisting of theses propounded by himself and defended by his students.

Bartholin also worked in astronomy. Like many others, he observed the comets of 23 December 1664–9 April 1665. In this effort he was assisted by Ole Rømer. He did not reach a conclusion about the true orbits, for he was skeptical of all statements about either the place of comets in the heavens (including Tycho Brahe's) or their physical nature (including Descartes's).

Also in 1664 Bartholin began, at the direction of Frederick III of Denmark, to prepare for publication the collected manuscript observations of Tycho Brahe, which the king had bought from Ludwig Kepler. In this task he was again assisted by Rømer. The king's death prevented the project's completion, and its only result was Bartholin's critique of the imperfect *Historia coelestis* of Albert Curtz.

Bartholin's major contribution to science was undoubtedly his study of Icelandic spar (specially collected by an expedition sent to Helgusta ir in Reyðarfyorðr, Iceland, in 1668). In physics, as in mathematics, Bartholin was a fervent admirer of Descartes (of whom he wrote: "Miraculum reliquum solus in orbe fuit"), as is evident in his attempt to deal with the newly discovered phenomenon of double refraction. Having shown that both rays (*solita* and *insolita*) are produced by refraction, and given a construction for determining the position of the extraordinary image, he argued that double refraction could be explained in the Cartesian theory of light by assuming that there was a double set of "pores" in the spar. This puzzling phenomenon proved to be of great theoretical interest to both Huygens and Newton. Bartholin was in fairly close touch with both French and German scientists and, through the latter (initially), with the Royal Society. The copy of his *Experimenta crystalli Islandici* that he sent to Henry Oldenburg is now in the British Museum; from it Oldenburg prepared an excellent English précis.

BIBLIOGRAPHY

I. ORIGINAL WORKS. Bartholin's works are in *Francisci à Schooten Principia matheseos universalis* (Leiden, 1651); *Dissertatio mathematica qua proponitur analytica ratio inveniendi omnia problemata proportionalium* (Copenhagen, 1657), a monograph on harmonic proportionals ($2ac = ab + bc$) leading into a short discussion of the resolution of equations; a translation of a minor Greek optical text by Damianos, or Heliodorus of Larissa (Copenhagen, 1657); a completion of two papers of Florimond de Beaune as *De aequationum natura, constitutione & limitibus*, in Descartes's *Geometria* (Amsterdam, 1659); *Auctarium trigonometriae ad triangulorum sphaericorum et rectilineorum solutiones* (Copenhagen, *ca.* 1663/1664); and *Dioristice, seu Aequationum determinationes duabus methodis propositae* (Copenhagen, 1663). The *Dissertatio, Dioristice,* and *Auctarium* (and perhaps others) were issued under the title *Selecta geometrica* (Copenhagen, 1664). Also see *De cometis anni 1664 et 1665 opusculum* (Copenhagen, 1665); his critique of Albert Curtz's *Historia coelestis* (Augsberg, 1668) in *Specimen recognitionis nuper editarum observationum astronomicarum N. V. Tychonis Brahe* (Copenhagen, 1668); and *Experimenta crystalli Islandici disdiaclastici quibus mira & insolita refractio detegitur* (Copenhagen, 1669). *De naturae mirabilibus quaestiones academicae* (Copenhagen, 1674) is a collection of reprinted essays and addresses (original dates in brackets): "The Study of the Danish Language" [1657], "The Shape of Snow" [1660], "The Pores of Bodies" [1663], "On Cartesian Physics" [1664], "On Attraction" [1665], "On Custom" [1666], "On Nature" [1666], "On Judgment and Memory" [1667], "On Experiment" [1668], "On Physical Hypotheses" [1669], "On the Shapes of Bodies" [1671], and "Secrets of the Sciences" [1673]; the article on the Danish language has attracted some interest from modern Danish scholars. *De aere Hafniensi dissertatio* (Frankfurt, 1679) is a pamphlet on climatology that alludes to medieval Iceland. There may well be other tracts by Bartholin.

II. SECONDARY LITERATURE. Works dealing with Bartholin include Axel Garboe, "Nicolaus Steno and Erasmus Bartholinus," in *Danmarks geologiske undersøgelse,* 4th ser., 3, no. 9 (1954), 38–48; V. Maar, *Den første anvendelse af kinabark i Danmark* (Leiden, 1925); Kirstine Meyer, *Erasmus Bartholin. Et Tidsbillede* (Copenhagen, 1933); and Henry Oldenburg's précis of the *Experimenta crystalli Islandici,* in *Philosophical Transactions of the Royal Society,* 6, no. 67 (16 Jan. 1671), 2039–2048.

A. RUPERT HALL

BATEMAN, HARRY (*b.* Manchester, England, 29 May 1882; *d.* Pasadena, California, 21 January 1946)

The son of Marnie Elizabeth Bond and Samuel Bateman, a druggist and commercial traveler, Bateman became interested in mathematics while at Manchester Grammar School. He attended Trinity College, Cambridge, where he received a B.A. in 1903 and an M.A. in 1906. After a tour of Europe in 1905–1906 he taught for several years, first at Liverpool University and then at Manchester. In 1910 he emigrated to the United States, where he taught for two years at Bryn Mawr College, then held a three-year research fellowship and lectured at Johns Hopkins from 1912 to 1917, taking his Ph.D. there in 1913. Although by this time he had an international reputation as a mathematician, he worked part-time on meteorology at the Bureau of Standards. In 1917 Bateman was appointed professor of mathematics, theoretical physics, and aeronautics at Throop College (which later became California Institute of Technology) in Pasadena, California, where he taught until his death. He was made a fellow of the Royal Society in 1928 and a member of the U.S. National Academy of Sciences in 1930, was elected vice-president of the American Mathematical Society in 1935, and delivered the Society's Gibbs lecture in 1943.

General theories had little attraction for Bateman; he was a master of the special instance. Much of his work consisted of finding special functions to solve partial differential equations. After some geometrical studies, he used definite integrals to extend E. T. Whittaker's solutions of the potential and wave equations to more general partial differential equations (1904). These and later results he applied to the theory of electricity and, with Ehrenfest, to electromagnetic fields (1924).

While in Göttingen in 1906, Bateman became familiar with the work of D. Hilbert and his students on integral equations. He applied integral equations to the problem of the propagation of earthquake waves, determining, from the time of contact at various surface points, the velocity of the motion at interior points. In 1910 he published a comprehensive report on research concerning integral equations.

Bateman's most significant single contribution to mathematical physics was a paper (1909) in which, following the work of Lorentz and Einstein on the invariance of the equations of electromagnetism under change of coordinates of constant velocity and constant acceleration, he showed that the most general group of transformations which preserve the electromagnetic equations and total charge of the system and are independent of the electromagnetic field is the group of conformal maps of four-dimensional space.

Bateman was one of the first to apply Laplace transform methods to integral equations (1906), but he felt that he never received recognition for this. In 1910 he solved the system of ordinary differential equations arising from Rutherford's description of radioactive decay. From 1915 to 1926 Bateman worked on problems of electromagnetism and classical atomic models that were solved by the quantum theory (1926). His interests shifted to hydrodynamics and aerodynamics; in 1934 he completed a monumental 634-page report on hydrodynamics for the National Academy of Sciences.

In 1930 Bateman set out to find complete systems of fundamental solutions to the most important equations of mathematical physics, and he wrote a text describing many of the methods of solving these equations (1932). Much of the remainder of his life was dedicated to completing the task of collecting special functions and integrals that solve partial differential equations. He developed many of these, such as Bateman's expansion and Bateman's function. Bateman kept references to the various functions and integrals on index cards stored in shoe boxes—later in his life these began to crowd him out of his office. His memory for special facts was phenomenal. Mathematicians both telephoned and wrote to him, asking about particular integrals; and after consulting his files, Bateman supplied the questioner with formulas and extensive references. After his death the Office of Naval Research assembled a team of mathematicians headed by Arthur Erdelyi to organize and publish Bateman's manuscripts. Only parts of the resulting volumes on transcendental functions and integral transforms made extensive use of Bateman's files.

BIBLIOGRAPHY

For bibliographies of Bateman's books and papers and biographical material, see Arthur Erdelyi, "Harry Bateman 1882–1946," in *Obituary Notices of Fellows of the Royal Society*, **5** (London, 1948), 591–618; and F. D. Murnaghan, "Harry Bateman," in *Bulletin of the American Mathematical Society*, **54** (1948), 88–103. The volumes resulting from the Bateman Manuscript Project are Arthur Erdelyi, ed., *Higher Transcendental Functions*, 3 vols. (New York, 1953–1955), and *Tables of Integral Transforms*, 2 vols. (New York, 1954).

C. S. FISHER

AL-BATTĀNĪ,[1] **ABŪ ʿABD ALLĀH MUḤAMMAD IBN JĀBIR IBN SINĀN AL-RAQQĪ AL-ḤARRĀNĪ AL-ṢĀBIʾ**, also **Albatenius, Albategni** or **Albategnius** in the Latin Middle Ages

One of the greatest Islamic astronomers, al-Battānī was born before 244/858,[2] in all probability at or near the city of Ḥarrān (ancient Carrhae) in northwestern Mesopotamia, whence the epithet al-Ḥarrānī. Of the other two epithets, al-Raqqī, found only in Ibn al-Nadīm's *Fihrist*,[3] refers to the city of al-Raqqa, situated on the left bank of the Euphrates, where al-Battānī spent the greater part of his life and carried out his famous observations; al-Ṣābiʾ indicates that his ancestors (al-Battānī himself was a Muslim; witness his personal name Muḥammad and his *kunya* Abū ʿAbd Allāh) had professed the religion of the Ḥarranian Ṣabians,[4] in which a considerable amount of the ancient Mesopotamian astral theology and star lore appears to have been preserved and which, tolerated by the Muslim rulers, survived until the middle of the eleventh century. The fact that al-Battānī's elder contemporary, the great mathematician and astronomer Thābit ibn Qurra (221/835–288/901) hailed from the same region and still adhered to the Ṣabian religion, seems indicative of the keen interest in astronomy that characterized even this last phase of Mesopotamian star idolatry. As for the cognomen (*nisba*) *al-Battānī*, no reasonable explanation of its origin can be given. Chwolsohn's conjecture[5] that it derives from the name of the city of Bathnae (or Batnae; Gr., Βάτναι; Syr., Baṭnān) near the ancient Edessa, was refuted by Nallino[6] with the perfectly convincing argument that the possibility of a transition of Syriac *ṭ* into Arabic *t* (Baṭnān to Battān) has to be strictly excluded; since there is no evidence of the existence of a city or town named Battān, Nallino suggests that this name, rather, refers to a street or a district of the city of Ḥarrān.

Nothing is known about al-Battānī's exact date of birth and his childhood. Since he made his first astronomical observations in 264/877, Nallino is on safe ground assuming the year 244/858 as a *terminus ante quem* for his birth. His father, in all probability, was the famous instrument maker Jābir ibn Sinān al-Ḥarrānī mentioned by Ibn al-Nadīm,[7] which would explain not only the son's keen astronomical interest but also his proficiency at devising new astronomical instruments, such as a new type of armillary sphere.

On al-Battānī's later life too the information is scanty. According to the *Fihrist*[8] and to Ibn al-Qifṭī's *Taʾrīkh al-Ḥukamāʾ*,[9] al-Battānī was

> . . . one of the illustrious observers and foremost in geometry, theoretical and practical [lit., computing]

AL-BATTĀNĪ

astronomy, and astrology. He composed an important *zīj* [i.e., work on astronomy with tables] containing his own observations of the two luminaries [sun and moon] and an emendation of their motions as given in Ptolemy's *Almagest.* In it, moreover, he gives the motions of the five planets in accordance with the emendations which he succeeded in making, as well as other necessary astronomical computations. Some of the observations mentioned in his *Zīj* were made in the year 267 H.[10] [A.D. 880] and later on in the year 287 H. [A.D. 900]. Nobody is known in Islam who reached similar perfection in observing the stars and in scrutinizing their motions. Apart from this, he took great interest in astrology, which led him to write on this subject too; of his compositions in this field [I mention] his commentary on Ptolemy's *Tetrabiblos.*

He was of Ṣabian origin and hailed from Ḥarrān. According to his own answer to Jaʿfar ibn al-Muktafī's question, he set out on his observational activity in the year 264 H. [A.D. 877] and continued until the year 306 H. [A.D. 918]. As an epoch for his [catalog of] fixed stars in his *Zīj* he chose the year 299 H. [A.D. 911].[11]

He went to Baghdad with the Banu'l-Zayyāt, of the people of al-Raqqa, on account of some injustice done them.[12] On his way home, he died at Qaṣr al-Jiṣṣ in the year 317 H. [A.D. 929].[13]

He wrote the following books: *Kitāb al-Zīj* [*Opus astronomicum*], in two recensions;[14] *Kitāb Maṭāliʿ al-Burūj* ["On the Ascensions of the Signs of the Zodiac"];[15] *Kitāb Aqdār al-Ittiṣālāt* ["On the Quantities of the Astrological Applications"], composed for Abu'l-Ḥasan ibn al-Furāt; *Sharḥ Kitāb al-Arbaʿa li-Baṭlamiyūs* ["Commentary on Ptolemy's *Tetrabiblos*"].[16]

It seems to have been a widespread belief among Western historians that al-Battānī was a noble, a prince, or even a king of Syria. Not the slightest allusion to it can be found in Arabic writers, so the source of this misunderstanding must be sought in Europe. The earliest reference quoted by Nallino[17] is Riccioli's *Almagestum novum,*[18] where al-Battānī is called "dynasta Syriae." J. F. Montucla[19] makes him a "commandant pour les califes en Syrie" and J. LaLande[20] a "prince arabe," as does J.-B. Delambre,[21] probably on LaLande's authority, since he expressly says that he used a copy, formerly in LaLande's possession, of the 1645 Bologna edition of al-Battānī's *Zīj,* although its title contains no reference to the author's alleged nobility.[22]

From al-Battānī's work, only one additional fact on his life can be derived: he mentions in his *Zīj*[23] that he observed two eclipses, one solar and one lunar, while in Antioch, on 23 January and 2 August A.D. 901, respectively.

The book on which al-Battānī's fame in the East and in the West rests is the *Zīj,* his great work on astronomy. Its original title, in all probability, was that indicated by Ibn al-Nadīm and Ibn al-Qifṭī: *Kitāb al-Zīj,* or just *al-Zīj.* Later authors also often call it *al-Zīj al-Ṣābi'* (*"The Ṣabian Zīj"*).[24] The word *zīj,* derived from the Middle Persian (Pahlavi) *zīk* (modern Persian, *zīg*), originally meant the warp of a rug or of an embroidery. As Nallino points out,[25] by the seventh century this had become a technical term for astronomical tables. In Arabic, it soon assumed the more general meaning "astronomical treatise," while for the tables themselves the word *jadwal* ("little river") came into use.[26]

Of the two recensions mentioned by Ibn al-Qifṭī, the first must have been finished before 288/900 because Thābit ibn Qurra, who died in February 901, mentions one of its last chapters.[27] Since the manuscript preserved in the Escorial[28] and the Latin version by Plato of Tivoli (Plato Tiburtinus) contain the two observations of eclipses mentioned above, the first of which occurred immediately before, and the second six months after, Thābit's death, Nallino concludes[29] that they must both have been copied (or translated) from the second recension.

In the preface to the *Zīj,*[30] al-Battānī tells us that errors and discrepancies found in the works of his predecessors had forced him to compose this work in accordance with Ptolemy's admonition to later generations to improve his theories and inferences on the basis of new observations, as he himself had done to those made by Hipparchus and others.[31] The Arabic version of the *Almagest,* on which he relied, seems to have been a translation from the Syriac, which Nallino shows on several occasions was not free from errors. All quotations from the *Almagest* are carefully made and can be verified.

A comparison of the *Zīj* with the *Almagest* at once reveals that it was far from al-Battānī's mind to write a new *Almagest.* To demonstrate this, it suffices to point out a few striking differences:

The arrangement of the fifty-seven chapters is dictated by practical rather than by theoretical considerations. Thus, contrary to al-Farghānī, who, writing half a century before al-Battānī, devotes his nine first chapters[32] to the same questions that are treated in *Almagest* I, 2–8 (spherical shape of the heavens and of the earth; reasons for the earth's immobility; the earth's dimensions and habitability; the two primary motions; etc.), al-Battānī starts his *Zīj* with purely practical definitions and problems: the division of the celestial sphere into signs and degrees, and prescriptions for multiplication and division of sexagesimal fractions. In chapter 3, corresponding to *Almagest* I, 11, he develops his theory of trigonometrical functions (see below); in chapter 4 he presents his own observations that resulted in a value for the obliquity of the ecliptic (23°35′) that is more than 16′ lower than Ptolemy's (23°51′20″; *Almagest* I, 12);[33] the next chapters (5–26), corresponding roughly to *Almagest* I, 13–16 and the whole of Book II, contain a very elaborate discussion of a great number of problems of spherical astronomy, many of them devised expressly for the purpose of finding solutions for astrological problems.

The Ptolemaic theory of solar, lunar, and planetary motion in longitude is contained in chapters 27–31. Then follows a discussion of the different eras in use and their conversion into one another (chapter 32),[34] serving as an introduction to the next sixteen chapters (33–48), in which detailed prescriptions for the use of the tables are given (chapters 39 and 40 deal with the theory of lunar parallax and the moon's distance from the earth, necessary for the computation of eclipses). Chapters 49–55 treat of the chief problems in astrology: chapter 55 has the Arabic title "Fī maʿrifat maṭāliʿ al-burūj fī-mā bayna 'l-awtād fī arbāʿ al-falak" ("On the Knowledge of the Ascensions of the Signs of the Zodiac in the Spaces Between the Four Cardinal Points of the Sphere"),[35] which is identical with Ibn al-Nadīm's title of one of al-Battānī's minor works. It is possible that this chapter actually existed as a separate treatise, but it is also possible that it was only due to an error that we find it listed separately in the *Fihrist* and in later biographies.

Of the two last chapters, 56 deals with the construction of a sundial indicating unequal hours (*rukhāma*, "marble disk"), and 57 with that of a novel type of armillary sphere, called *al-bayḍa* ("the egg"), and of two more instruments, a mural quadrant and a *triquetrum* (Ptolemy's *τεταρτημόριον*, *Almagest* I, 12, and *ὄργανον παραλλακτικόν*, *Almagest* V, 12).

Contrary to Ptolemy's procedure in the *Almagest*, the practical aspect of the *Zīj* is so predominant that it sometimes impairs the clarity of exposition and even evokes a totally wrong impression. This is felt more than anywhere else in chapter 31, which deals with the theory of planetary motion. The Arabic text consists of little more than five pages, only three of which deal with the theoretical (i.e., kinematic) aspect of the problem. Here the reader trained in Ptolemy's careful and sometimes slightly circumstantial way of exposing his arguments, and familiar with al-Farghānī's excellent *epitome*, will needs be struck by the brevity and—this is worse—by the insufficiency and inaccuracy of al-Battānī's outline. To point out some particularly bewildering features:[36] No distinction is made between, on the one hand, the theory of the three superior planets and Venus, and, on the other, the ingenious and intricate mechanism devised by

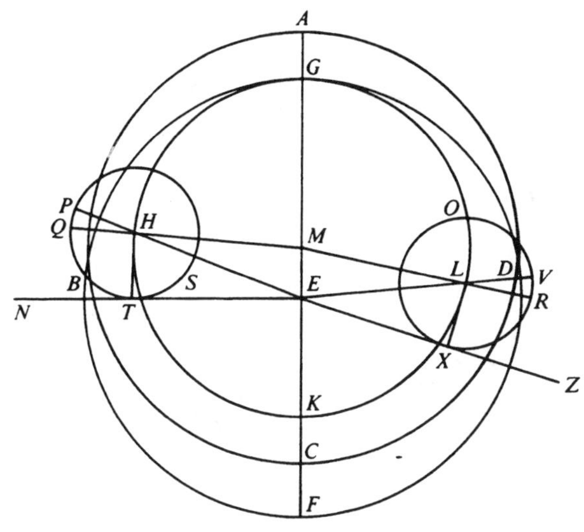

FIGURE 1

Ptolemy to represent Mercury's perplexing motion. With the aid of only one figure, which is wholly defective and misleading, al-Battānī tries—and of course fails—to demonstrate the motion of all of the five planets alike. In this figure, reproduced here (Fig. 1), the equant (*punctum aequans*), the essential characteristic of the Ptolemaic theory, is not indicated, nor is it referred to in the accompanying text, according to which the center, *M*, of the deferent itself is to be regarded as the center of mean motion (!). Moreover, the nodes of the planetary orbit are placed at right angles to the line of apsides (which of course is not true of any of the five planets), and for the planet's position in the epicycle, in the two cases indicated in the figure, the very special points are chosen in which the line earth-planet is tangent to the epicycle.

It is easy to point out all these errors and, as G. Schiaparelli has done at Nallino's request,[37] to show how the figure ought to look, were it drawn in accordance with Ptolemy's theory (Fig. 2). But Schiaparelli's surmise that al-Battānī's correct figure was distorted by some unintelligent reader or copyist does not exhaust the question. For, if so, who would dare at the same time to mutilate the text in such a way that the equant disappears from it altogether? And which uninitiated reader might have had the courage to suppress in this context the theory of Mercury, without which Ptolemy's system of planetary motions remains a torso? Since the Escorial manuscript and Plato of Tivoli's translation[38] have both the same erroneous figure and text, the alleged mutilation must have occurred, at the latest, in the eleventh century, during the lifetime of the great Spanish-Muslim astronomer al-Zarqālī (Azarquiel) or of one of his renowned

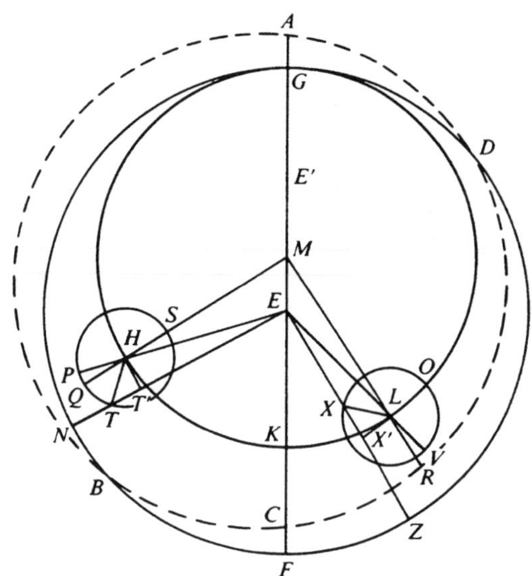

FIGURE 2

predecessors. To me it seems utterly improbable that an arbitrary disfiguring of one of the crucial chapters of al-Battānī's great *Zīj* could have escaped their attention and that no measures should have been taken to delete such faulty copies and to restore the original text. I am inclined, thus, to ascribe the matter to al-Battānī's carelessness rather than to anything else, in view of the circumstance that no other reasonable conjecture seems to square with the facts. Similar examples can be adduced from the writings even of the greatest astronomers; in this context I refer to a grave slip (although of lesser consequence) committed by al-Bīrūnī, which I have pointed out in an earlier paper.[39] It need not be emphasized that al-Battānī actually knew better; to prove this, it suffices to mention that his tables of planetary motion, far more elaborate than Ptolemy's, could not have been drawn up without a thorough familiarity with the Ptolemaic system, including all its finesses and intricacies.

While al-Battānī takes no critical attitude toward the Ptolemaic kinematics in general, he evidences, as said before, a very sound skepticism in regard to Ptolemy's practical results. Thus, relying on his own observations, he corrects—be it tacitly, be it in open words—Ptolemy's errors. This concerns the main parameters of planetary motion no less than erroneous conclusions drawn from insufficient or faulty observations, such as the invariability of the obliquity of the ecliptic or of the solar apogee.

The Islamic astronomers' interest in the question of the variability of the obliquity of the ecliptic started astonishingly early. This is the more remarkable because the effect, being on the order of magnitude of 0.5″ a year, is definitely of no practical use. According to Ibn Yūnus (*d.* 399/1009),[40] the first measurement since Ptolemy was made shortly after 160/776, yielding 23°31′, which was 4′–5′ too low;[41] after this he reports quite a number of different values, all in the vicinity of 23°33′, made during and after the time of al-Ma'mūn (*d.* 215/830). Hence, al-Battānī's determination is nothing exceptional, but it is important for us because he gives a careful description of the procedure by which his value (23°35′), which squares perfectly with the modern formula, was obtained.

In chapter 28 of the *Zīj,* al-Battānī discusses his observations of the lengths of the four seasons, from which, employing Hipparchus' method as described in *Almagest* III, 4, he infers that the sun's apogee and its eccentricity have both changed since antiquity: the apogee, found at 65°30′ by Hipparchus and erroneously claimed to be invariable by Ptolemy, had moved to 82°17′, and the eccentricity had diminished from $2^{p}29'30''$ to $2^{p}4'45''$ ($1^{p} = 1/60$ of the radius).

Despite contrary assertions, however, al-Battānī was not the first since Ptolemy to check on these values. According to al-Bīrūnī,[42] who relies on Abū Ja'far al-Khāzin's (*d. ca.* 350/961) commentary on the *Almagest,* the first observations serving the purpose of a new determination of the apogee were carried out, on the basis of the specially devised new "method of the four *fuṣūl,*"[43] in the Shammāsiyya quarter of Baghdad in A.D. 830. In spite of this methodological improvement, the result was extremely poor: it yielded a value no less than 20° too small. One year after, Thābit ibn Qurra or the Banū Mūsā, using the old Ptolemaic method, obtained the excellent value 82°45′.[44] Comparing this with Hipparchus' value (65°30′) and rejecting Ptolemy's obviously wrong confirmation of the latter, he (or they) found that the motion of the apogee amounts to 1° in sixty-six years. Then, from the fact that he had also found the same value for the motion of precession, Thābit concluded that they must of necessity be identical—in other words, that the apogee of the sun remains fixed once and for all in regard to the fixed stars (for this type of reasoning and concluding, European scholasticism has invented the term "Ockham's razor").

Al-Battānī's value for the sun's apogee (82°17′) is not quite as good as Thābit's (or the Banū Mūsā's), although the perfect accordance of the latter with the one resulting from the modern formula must be considered to some degree accidental: for A.D. 831, Leverrier's formula yields 82°50′22″ (Thābit, 82°45′); for A.D. 884, 83°45′10″[45] (al-Battānī, 82°17′). It is of interest in this context that Hipparchus' value, 65°30′ (*ca.* 140 B.C.), also squares exceedingly well with the modern, 65°21′.

Thus, it is evident that al-Battānī has no special

claim to the discovery of the motion of the solar apogee. Apart from this, he was no more able than Thābit to decide whether this motion was identical with that of precession. It was only 150 years later that al-Bīrūnī furnished the theoretical foundation for such a distinction,[46] but even he had to admit that the data at his disposal did not allow him to make a conclusive statement. The first who actually made a clear (and very correct) numerical statement concerning the proper motion—1° in 299 Julian years, or 12.04″ in one year (modern: 1.46″), was al-Zarqālī (second half of the eleventh century) of Toledo. But his result is impaired by his belief in the reality of trepidation, which he shared with Thābit.

Al-Battānī's value for the eccentricity of the solar orbit ($2^{p}4'45''$), corresponding to an eccentricity in the modern sense of 0.017326 (instead of 0.016771, according to our modern formula, for A.D. 880) must be called excellent, while Ptolemy's value (0.0208 instead of 0.0175) is much too high.[47]

Among al-Battānī's many other important achievements is his improvement of the moon's mean motion in longitude;[48] his measurements of the apparent diameters of the sun and of the moon and their variation in the course of a year, or of an anomalistic month, respectively, from which he concludes that annular solar eclipses (impossible, according to Ptolemy) must be possible;[49] and his new and elegant method of computing the magnitude of lunar eclipses.[50]

For the precession of equinoxes, he accepts and confirms Thābit's value (1° in sixty-six years), far better than Ptolemy's (1° in 100 years), but about 10 percent too fast (correct, 1° in seventy-two years). Accordingly, his tropical year ($365^{d}5^{h}46^{m}24^{s}$) is too short by $2^{m}22^{s}$ (correct, $365^{d}5^{h}48^{m}46^{s}$), while Ptolemy's ($365^{d}5^{h}55^{m}12^{s}$) is too long by $6^{m}26^{s}$.

Al-Battānī's catalog of fixed stars[51] is far less comprehensive than Ptolemy's (489 as against 1,022 stars). The latitudes and magnitudes are taken over (perhaps with a few corrections) from the *Almagest,* while the longitudes are increased by the constant amount of 11°10′, which corresponds, for the interval of 743 years between the epochs of the two catalogs (A.D. 137 and 880), to the motion of precession indicated, viz., 1° in sixty-six years.

While Ptolemy's *Almagest* is often cited, his *Tetrabiblos* is mentioned on only one occasion (end of chapter 55). It is uncertain whether al-Battānī knew and used Ptolemy's *Geography.*[52] Ptolemy's *Hypotheses* (called by later authors *Kitāb al-Iqtiṣāṣ* or *Kitāb al-Manshūrāt*)[53] are made use of in chapter 50, which deals with the distances of the planets, but al-Battānī ascribes the underlying theory of contiguous spheres, according to which the distances are computed, to "more recent scientists [who lived] after Ptolemy." Since al-Farghānī mentions no name at all in this connection,[54] it seems probable that al-Battānī's reference to "scientists after Ptolemy" reflects a passage from Proclus' *Hypotyposis,*[55] in which Ptolemy's name also does not occur, and that Ptolemy's authorship became known only when, some time before al-Bīrūnī, the *Hypotheses* were translated into Arabic.

Of other astronomical works from antiquity, only Theon of Alexandria's *Manual Tables* are mentioned. In the section of chapter 6 dealing with geographical questions,[56] al-Battānī refers to "the ancients" without further specification. Nallino[57] has shown that this expression, there, means Greco-Syriac sources.

In spite of the circumstance that al-Battānī, as demonstrated before, has a good deal in common with the Banū Mūsā, Thābit, and al-Farghānī, no reference whatever appears in his *Zīj* to his Islamic predecessors. In his terminology he abstains from using foreign (Persian or Indian) words, as found in earlier writings of his countrymen, such as *awj* for the apogee of the eccentric (circumstantially called by al-Battānī *al-buʿd al-abʿad min al-falak al-khārij al-markaz,* "the [point having] maximum distance in the eccentric"), *jayb* for the sine (al-Battānī: *watar munaṣṣaf,* "half-chord," or just *watar,* "chord"), *buht* for the (unequal) motion of a planet in the course of one day (a concept not used by al-Battānī), *jawzahar* for the ascending node (al-Battānī: *al-ra's,* "the head [of the dragon]"), *haylāj* for the astrological "significator" or "aphet" (Gr.: ἀφέτης; al-Battānī: *dalīl*), and so on.[58] His aversion to foreign terms, however, certainly springs not from any "purism of language" but, rather, from the circumstance that the words in question did not occur in the *Almagest* translations at his disposal; this explains why in some cases he does not hesitate to employ clumsy transliterations of Greek terms, such as *afījiyūn* for ἀπόγειον ("apogee") and *farījiyūn* for περίγειον ("perigee").

Al-Battānī uses the sine instead of the chord (of twice the angle), following the example of his Arab predecessors who had fused into one whole the new Indian notion (*Siddhānta*) and the old Greek notion. Besides the sine he also employs the cosine (*watar mā yabqā li-tamām . . . ilā tisʿīn,* "the sine of the complement of . . . to 90°") and the versine (R − cosine, called *watar rājiʿ,* "returning sine"), for which later authors also employed the term *jayb maʿkūs* ("inverted sine"), as opposed to *jayb mustawī* ("plain sine") or *sahm* ("arrow"), whence the medieval Latin *sagitta.* Tangents and cotangents do not occur in al-Battānī's formulas, which therefore often become as clumsy as Ptolemy's. He uses them only in his gnomonics, where they refer, as in the *Siddhāntas,* to a twelve-partite gnomon. For the cotangent, he employs the term *ẓill mabsūṭ* ("umbra extensa"; called by others also *ẓill mustawī,* "umbra recta"); for the tangent, *ẓill muntaṣib* ("umbra erecta"; called by others *ẓill maʿkūs,* "umbra versa").[59] By applying considerations based on the principle of orthographic projection, al-Battānī introduced new and elegant solutions into spherical trigonometry. In Europe, this principle was adopted and developed by Regiomontanus (1436–1476).

The epoch of al-Battānī's chief era (*Ta'rīkh Dhi'l-Qarnayn,* "Epoch of the Two-Horned [Alexander]") is Saturday (mean noon, Raqqa), 1 September 312 B.C., which precedes by thirty days the epoch *Dhu'l-Qarnayn* used by all other Arabic authors: Monday, 1 October 312 B.C. It is combined with the Julian year; for the months he uses the "Syrian" names: *aylūl* (September), *tishrīn* I and II, *kanūn* I and II, *subāṭ, ādhār, nīsān, ayyār, ḥazīrān, tammūz,* and *āb.* The epoch of the Coptic era (*Ta'rīkh al-Qibṭ*) is Friday, 29 August 25 B.C., while all other Arabs used this term to denote one of the following three: the era of Nabunassar (1 Thoth = 26 February 747 B.C.), the era of Philippus Arrhidaeus (12 November 324 B.C., mentioned in the *Almagest* as the "era of Alexander's death"), or the era of Diocletian (29 August 284, also called *Ta'rīkh al-Shuhadā',* "era of the martyrs").[60]

A Latin translation of the *Zīj* made by the English Robertus Retinensis (also cited as R. Ketenensis, Castrensis, or Cestrensis; Nallino believes the correct form to be Cataneus),[61] who flourished about the middle of the twelfth century, has not survived. The only Latin version extant is the one by Plato of Tivoli, who flourished in Barcelona in the first half of the twelfth century. This translation was printed twice. The *editio princeps* (Nuremberg, 1537) carries the title *Rudimenta astronomica Alfragrani* [sic].[62] *Item Albategnius peritissimus de motu stellarum ex observationibus tum propriis tum Ptolemaei, omnia cum demonstrationibus geometricis et additionibus Ioannis de Regiomonte;* the title of the second edition (Bologna, 1645), printed without al-Farghānī's *Elements,* is *Mahometis Albatenii de scientia stellarum liber cum aliquot additionibus Ioannis Regiomontani. Ex Bibliotheca Vaticana transcriptus.*

A Spanish translation, made at the order of King Alfonso el Sabio (1252–1284), is preserved in the Bibliothèque de l'Arsenal in Paris.[64]

Although no Hebrew translation of the *Zīj* seems to have existed, its impact on Jewish scholarship was great. It was mentioned and praised by Abrāhām bar Ḥiyyā' (*d. ca.* 1136) and Abrāhām ibn ʿEzrā (*ca.* 1090–1167). Maimonides (1135–1204) follows al-Battānī closely, but without mentioning his name, in the eighth treatise of Book III of his *Mishne Tōrā,* which bears the title "Hilkōt qiddūsh ha-ḥōdesh."[65] In chapters 12–14 the parameters used (mean motion in longitude of the sun and of the moon, mean anomalistic motion of the moon, equation of the sun) are exactly the same as in al-Battānī's tables, except that the values for the solar equation are rounded off to minutes.[66] In his prescriptions for determining the limits of visibility of the new moon, too, Maimonides closely follows the elegant method devised by al-Battānī.

Among Islamic astronomers and historians, al-Battānī holds a place of honor. The great al-Bīrūnī composed a book entitled *Jala' al-Adhhān fī Zīj al-Battānī* ("Elucidation of Genius in al-Battānī's *Zīj*"),[67] and Ibn Khaldūn (1332–1406)[68] counts his works among the most excellent in Islamic astronomy.

In Byzantine writings, al-Battānī's name is mentioned as δΠατανής, but Greek translations apparently have not existed. A great many medieval Latin authors who knew the *Zīj* or at least mention the name of its author can be enumerated. Among them are Henry Bate (1246–*ca.* 1310), who, in composing his *Magistralis compositio Astrolabii anno 1274 scripta,* makes ample use of the contents of the *Zīj*—not without giving its author due credit for it; Gerard of Sabbionetta; Albertus Magnus; Lēvi ben Gersōn (in the Latin translation of his *Astronomy*);[69] and, not least, Regiomontanus, whose keen interest in the work is evident from the great number of annotations in his handwriting found in his copy of Plato of Tivoli's version and printed as an appendix to the Nuremberg and the Bologna editions. His teacher Georg Peurbach's (1423–1461) *Theoricae planetarum,* printed and edited by Regiomontanus,[70] mentions al-Battānī's name on only one occasion (fol. 18r),[71] where he relates that "Albategni," contrary to those who defended the theory of trepidation, claimed that the stars move 1° in sixty years and four months,[72] and always toward the east. Since all Arab astronomers, in accordance with the text and the translations extant, state that al-Battānī accepted a motion of 1° in sixty-six years,[73] it is a mystery how this erroneous value, which cannot be due to a copyist's slip, could have found its way into Peurbach's book. As for his masterful presentation of planetary kinematics according to Ptolemy, it is a matter of course—in view of what I have said about al-Battānī's chapter 31[74]—that it could not be modeled after al-Battānī's fallacious chapter, while the influence of al-Farghānī seems perceptible in many places.

The indebtedness of Copernicus to al-Battānī is well known. He quotes him fairly often, especially—as does Peurbach—in the chapters dealing with the problems of solar motion and of precession.[75] Much more frequent references to him are found in Tycho Brahe's writings and in G. B. Riccioli's *New Almagest;*[76] in addition, Kepler and—only in his earliest writings—Galileo evidence their interest in al-Battānī's observations.

From the point of view of the history of astronomy, the names of two men are to be mentioned, although with a totally different weight. In 1819 Delambre published his *Histoire de l'astronomie du moyen âge.*[77] In chapter 2 he devotes fifty-three pages to a very thorough analysis of the *Zīj,* on the basis of the Bologna edition of Plato of Tivoli's translation. Even to the modern reader the chapter is of interest, in spite of the fact that a certain superciliousness, characteristic of all Delambre's historical works, is sometimes embarrassing. For it is, of course, not as interesting to learn how one problem or the other could have been solved in a less circumstantial way as it would be to get an insight into the historical situation in which al-Battānī's work came into being. This, however, was beyond Delambre, for even if he had possessed a sufficient knowledge of Arabic (he had none at all), the only extant manuscript would not have been within his reach. Thus he had to rely on Plato of Tivoli's version, whose errors and misunderstandings naturally led him astray in more than one case.

Eighty years after Delambre, in 1899, the young Italian orientalist C. A. Nallino published his model edition of the complete Arabic text of al-Battānī's *Zīj.*[78] The two other volumes, containing a Latin translation and exceedingly detailed and learned commentaries, followed during the next eight years. In a time like ours, characterized by the abuse of superlatives, it is hard to describe Nallino's work in appropriate terms. Al-Battānī's Arabic style, which at first sight looks simple and straightforward, but which reveals itself difficult and even obscure on many occasions, is rendered here in a Latin whose purity and clarity deserve the highest praise. In reading this book, which is Nallino's *magnum opus,* one understands that it was not due purely to a whim that he decided to compose it in Latin. As for the technical aspect, Nallino's work bears witness to a great familiarity with the mathematical and astronomical problems occurring in al-Battānī's *Zīj,* and no less with the historical facts that form its background. This third Latin translation, written eight centuries after the first two, will always stand as one of the masterpieces of the history of science.

Until recently it was believed that none of the three minor works (all of astrological content) listed in the *Fihrist* and in Ibn al-Qifṭī's *Ta'rīkh al-ḥukamā'*[79] had survived, since, on the one hand, the authenticity of a manuscript preserved in Berlin seemed dubious[80] and, on the other, the only extant manuscript expressly titled "Commentary on Ptolemy's *Tetrabiblos,*" which figures still in Casiri's catalog,[81] could no longer be found in the Escorial library, as stated by H. Derenbourg[82] in 1884 and confirmed by Nallino in 1894 and by Father Pedro Blanco Soto in 1901.[83] Fortunately, however, the lost manuscript seems to have been recovered: in H.-P.-J. Renaud's new catalog,[84] it is listed as no. 969, 2 (not 966, as in Casiri), under the title *Kitāb al-arba' maqālāt fī aḥkām 'ilm al-nujūm,* the copy dating from 939/1533 and comprising sixty folios. The word *sharḥ* ("commentary") does not appear in the title, but Renaud's and Casiri's descriptions read "Commentary on Ptolemy's *Quadripartitum*" (i.e., *Tetrabiblos*). It will require a special study to establish whether the Berlin and the Escorial manuscripts are identical in text. The fact that the latter also contains tables (which the Greek original does not have) suggests the existence in the text of rules and prescriptions for their use that might justify calling it a "commentary."

In this context,[85] Nallino mentions that the Egyptian 'Alī ibn Riḍwān (latinized as Haly Heben Rodan, *d.* 453/1061) states that he has never come across any paraphrase (*glossa*) of the *Tetrabiblos* at all, whereas Abu'l-Ḥasan 'Alī ibn Abi'l-Rijāl (Albohazen Haly filius Abenragel, *fl. ca.* 1050) counts al-Battānī among those who, like Ptolemy, attributed special importance to astrological prognostications made on the basis of eclipses that occur during the years of planetary conjunctions. Nallino evidently believes this refers to *Tetrabiblos* II, 6,[86] which deals with the same subject matter. The case, however, is different. In the Saib (Ismā'īl Sā'ib) Library at Ankara there is preserved a volume (no. 1/199) containing three different works, the second of which (fols. 27r–42v) bears the title *Kitāb [Muḥammad ibn] Jābir b. Sinān al-Ḥarrānī al-Battānī fī dalā'il al-qirānāt wa'l-kusūfāt* ("Jābir . . . al-Battānī's Book on the Significations of Conjunctions and Eclipses").[87] It is undoubtedly this book, not listed in any of the great oriental bibliographies, on which bears Albohazen's remark. Judging from a cursory inspection of a photostatic copy in the possession of the Institute for the History of Science of the University of Frankfurt, I see no reason to doubt its authenticity.

Another manuscript, entitled *Tajrīd uṣūl tarkīb al-juyūb*[88] ("Construction of the Principles of Establishing [Tables of] Sines"), also carries al-Battānī's name. From the fact that al-Battānī, at least in his *Zīj,* avoids using the term *jayb* (plural, *juyūb*) for "sine,"[89] it might be inferred that this manuscript is spurious.

For a number of other definitely spurious works existing only in Latin translations, see the list (with comprehensive discussions) found in Nallino.[90]

NOTES

1. The transliteration system used in this article is that of the *Encyclopaedia of Islam,* 2nd ed., with the following simplifications: *j* instead of *dj*; *q* instead of *k* (NB: *qu* is pronounced *ku*, not as English *qu*); no underlinings to indicate compound consonants: *kh* instead of *kh* for the Scottish *ch*-sound, *th* and *dh* for the English voiceless and voiced *th,* respectively.
2. Of two numbers separated by a slash, the first indicates the year according to the Muslim calendar and the second its beginning according to the Christian calendar. In quotations from Arabic texts, Muslim years are denoted by H. (Hegira), and the corresponding Christian years are added in brackets. Note that the Muslim year is 3 percent shorter than the Julian.
3. *Kitāb al-Fihrist* (composed *ca.* A.D. 987 by Ibn al-Nadīm), G. Flügel, ed. (Leipzig, 1871–1872), I, 279. See also C. A. Nallino, *Al-Battānī sive Albatenii Opus astronomicum, ad fidem codicis escurialensis arabice editum, latine versum, adnotationibus instructum,* I (Milan, 1903), viii ff. This *magnum opus* (Vol. II, 1907; Vol. III, 1899), cited hereafter as *O.A.,* will always remain the chief source of information in Arabic astronomy and on al-Battānī in particular.
4. See B. Carra de Vaux, "al-Ṣābi'a," in *Encyclopaedia of Islam,* 1st ed., IV; and, for comprehensive information (although obsolete in certain parts), D. Chwolsohn, *Die Ssabier und der Ssabismus,* Vols. I/II (St. Petersburg, 1856).
5. *Die Ssabier,* I, 611.
6. *O.A.,* I, xiii.
7. *Fihrist,* p. 285.
8. p. 280.
9. J. Lippert, ed. (Leipzig, 1903), p. 280. Ibn al-Qifṭī, the author of this "History of Learned Men," died in 646/1248. His chapter on al-Battānī (which I follow in my translation), according to his own words, relies on Ṣā'id al-Andalusī. It contains information not found in the *Fihrist.*
10. Owing to a scribal error, the *Fihrist* and Qifṭī have 269.
11. Instead of 299/911, read 267/880 (scribal error). The epoch of the catalog is actually 267/880.
12. The meaning, evidently, is "because unjust taxes had been requested of them." The text leaves open whether "them" includes al-Battānī. Cf. Nallino, *O.A.,* I, viii. As for the Banu'l-Zayyāt, Nallino (*ibid.,* pp. xvii f.) considers it almost certain that they are the descendants of the famous poet and vizier 'Abd al-Malik ibn Abān al-Zayyād (executed by Caliph Mutawakkil in 233/847). It was to his great-grandson's son, Abū Tālib Aḥmad al-Zayyād, that Ibn Waḥshiyya dictated, in 318/930, his alleged "translation from the Syriac" of his book on the Nabataean agriculture.
13. In Ibn Khallikān's (*d.* 681/1282) biographical dictionary (Eng. trans. by Mac Guckin de Slane, Paris-London, 1843–1871, IV, 317–320; Arabic original: *Ibn Challikan, Vitae illustrium virorum,* F. Wüstenfeld, Göttingen, 1835–1842, no. 719 [cited after *O.A.,* I, ix, n. 6]), the place of al-Battānī's death is called Qaṣr al-Ḥaḍr. Nallino has shown (*O.A.,* p. xviii) that Jiṣṣ (of which Ḥaḍr is nothing but a graphical corruption) is the correct form.
14. Ibn al-Nadīm and Ibn Khallikān add the words "a first and a second; the second is better."
15. Ibn al-Nadīm adds the words *fī mā bayna arbā' al-falak* ("in the spaces between the four cardinal points of the sphere"). The book gives mathematical solutions of the astrological problem of finding the direction of the *aphet* (*tasyīr al-dalīl*).
16. Not listed by Ibn al-Nadīm.
17. *O.A.,* I, xvii, n. 1.
18. Bologna, 1651, II, xxix.
19. *Histoire des mathématiques,* new ed. (Paris, 1797–1800), I, 363.
20. *Astronomie,* 3rd ed. (Paris, 1792), I, 123.
21. *Histoire de l'astronomie du moyen âge* (Paris, 1819; repr. New York–London, 1965), pp. 4, 10.
22. In this title, the author is called "Mahometus, filius Geber, filius Crueni, qui vocatur Albategni." The strange name Cruenus is obviously due to a misreading of Sinanus, which may have been found spelled Cinenus.
23. Ch. 30, *O.A.,* I, 56.
24. Thus Ibn Khallikān and Ḥājjī Khalīfa (1017/1609–1067/1657); see *Haji Khalfae Lexicon bibliographicum et encyclopaedicum,* ed. and trans., with commentary, by G. Flügel (Leipzig–London, 1835–1858), III, 564, no. 6946.
25. *O.A.,* I, xxxi, n. 3.
26. In Byzantine Greek, the word is found as ζῆσι and identified with σύνταξις; see *O.A.,* I, xxxi, n. 5.
27. Ch. 57, which treats the theory of trepidation, refuted by al-Battānī but accepted by Thābit. The reference to al-Battānī is found in Thābit's letter to Isḥāq ibn Ḥunayn, preserved by Ibn Yūnus. See *O.A.,* I, 298.
28. Originally no. 903 (M. Casiri, *Bibliotheca arabico-hispanica Escurialensis,* Madrid, 1760, I, 342–343), now no. 908. Unbelievable as it sounds, only this copy of one of the most important books written in the Middle Ages has survived in the Arabic original.
29. *O.A.,* I, xxxii.
30. Ch. 1, *O.A.,* I, 5.
31. *Almagest,* III, 1 (German trans. by Karl Manitius, *Des Claudius Ptolemäus Handbuch der Astronomie,* Leipzig, 1912, p. 141). The wording there is a little different and contains no such express "admonition" or "order" (*amr*).
32. Except for ch. 1, which deals with the various eras and their mutual conversions, practically identical with al-Battānī's ch. 32. Cf. J. Golius' ed. and Latin trans.: *Muhammedis fil. Ketiri Ferganensis, qui vulgo Alfraganus dicitur, Elementa astronomica* (Amsterdam, 1669).
33. See W. Hartner, "The Obliquity of the Ecliptic According to the Hou-Han Shu and Ptolemy," in *Silver Jubilee Volume of the Zinbun-Kagaku-Kenkyusyo* (Kyoto, 1954), pp. 177–183; repr. in Hartner's *Oriens-Occidens* (Hildesheim, 1968), pp. 208–214.
34. See n. 32.
35. See p. 508 and n. 15.
36. See the figure and the accompanying text, *O.A.,* III, 96 f. (Arabic) and *O.A.,* I, 64 f. (Latin), from which Figure 1 in the text is reproduced.
37. *O.A.,* I, 237 f. Figure 2 in the text is reproduced from Schiaparelli's.
38. Nallino, *O.A.,* I, lxii, states that the Arabic original, from which Plato of Tivoli translated, and the Escorial MS (written, according to Nallino, about 1100) must both have belonged to the same archetype.
39. "Mediaeval Views on Cosmic Dimensions and Ptolemy's *Kitāb al-Manshūrāt,*" in *Mélanges Alexandre Koyré,* I (Paris, 1964), 254–282; repr. in W. Hartner, *Oriens-Occidens* (Hildesheim, 1968), pp. 319–348.
40. Bibliothèque Nationale, MS Ar. 2495, p. 222 (cited after *O.A.,* I, 157).
41. For an exact verification and comparison with modern formulas (Newcomb, de Sitter), the effect of refraction and of solar parallax has to be taken into account; by this the values derived from observation are reduced by about 40″, which of course is of no interest here (see n. 33).
42. Mas'ūdic Canon, VI, chs. 7 and 8 (*al-Qānūnal-Mas'ūdī,* pub. by The Dā'irat al-Ma'ārif Oṣmānia, II (Hyderabad-Dn., 1374/1955), pp. 650–685. Cf. W. Hartner and M. Schramm, "Al-Bīrūnī and the Theory of the Solar Apogee: An Example of Originality in Arabic Science," in A. C. Crombie, ed., *Scientific Change* (London, 1963), pp. 206–218.

43. Observation of the sun's passage through the points 15° Taurus, 15° Leo, 15° Scorpio, and 15° Aquarius.
44. According to the *Kitāb fī sanat al-shams bi'l-arṣād,* MS London India Office no. 734, fol. 6r, ll. 13 ff.
45. Schiaparelli (*O.A.*, I, 215) gives the erroneous value 83°50′51″ for A.D. 884.
46. Cf. Hartner and Schramm (n. 42), pp. 216–218.
47. Cf. *O.A.*, I, 213 f. For comparing the ancient with the modern values (elliptic eccentricity), the former must of course be halved: $2^p4'45''/60 = 0.034653 = 2 \cdot 0.017326$.
48. Cf. *O.A.*, I, 225 f.
49. Cf. *ibid.*, 58, 236. He either is unaware or avoids mentioning that his own observations of the moon's apparent diameter at apogee ($d_1 = 29.5'$) and at perigee ($d_2 = 35.3'$) are in the ratio 5:6. According to Ptolemy's and his own theory, they ought to be in the ratio 17:33, or nearly 1:2.
50. Cf. *ibid.*, 99 f.
51. Arabic text, *O.A.*, III, 245–274; Latin, *O.A.*, II, 144–177.
52. Cf. *O.A.*, I, xli and 20 (end of ch. 4).
53. See W. Hartner, "Mediaeval Views on Cosmic Dimensions" (n. 39), and B. R. Goldstein, "The Arabic Version of Ptolemy's *Planetary Hypotheses,*" in *Transactions of the American Philosophical Society,* n.s. **57,** pt. 4 (1967).
54. Ch. 21, pp. 80–82; see n. 32.
55. *Procli Diadochi Hypotyposis astronomicarum positionum,* ed. and trans. into German by K. Manitius (Leipzig, 1909), ch. 7, 19 (p. 220). As I have shown in "Mediaeval Views . . ." (see n. 39), it can no longer be doubted that the idea of contiguous spheres was conceived by Ptolemy. The final proof for the correctness of my assertion has been furnished by Goldstein (see n. 53), who found that the extant Arabic and Hebrew versions of the *Hypotheses* contain the part missing from J. L. Heiberg's edition (*Claudii Ptolemaei opera,* II, *Opera astronomica minora,* Leipzig, 1907, 69–145) at the end of Book I. It has exactly the same parameters and ratios as indicated in my paper.
56. *O.A.*, I, 17–19.
57. *Ibid.*, 165–177.
58. Cf. *ibid.*, xlii f.
59. On the back of astrolabes, preference is given to the terms *ẓill mabsūṭ* for the shadow cast by a vertical gnomon on a horizontal plane, and *ẓill maᶜkūs* (sometimes *mankūs*) for the shadow of a horizontal gnomon on a vertical plane.
60. For further information, see *O.A.*, I, 242–246.
61. See *O.A.*, I, xlix f. There can be no doubt that the name means Robert of Chester, a friend of Hermannus Dalmata. He was the first to translate the Koran into Latin (1143) and also one of the first translators of Muḥammad ibn Mūsā al-Khwārizmī's *Algebra.* See L. C. Karpinski, "Robert of Chester's translation of al-Khowarizmi," in *Bibliotheca mathematica,* **11** (1911), 125–131. Robertus Retinensis is not identical with Robertus Anglicus, who lived in the thirteenth century.
62. Cf. the other edition of al-Farghānī's *Elements,* quoted in n. 32. The division into chapters is different in the two editions.
63. For C. A. Nallino's Latin translation and edition, see p. 513.
64. Described by Rico y Sinobas in *Libros del saber de astronomia del Rey D. Alfonso X de Castilla,* V, pt. 1 (Madrid, 1867), 19 f.
65. Cf. *O.A.*, I, xxxiv; and S. Gandz, trans., "The Code of Maimonides, Book III, Treatise 8, Sanctification of the New Moon: With Supplementation and an Introduction by J. Obermann and an Astronomical Commentary by Otto Neugebauer," in J. Obermann, ed., *Yale Judaica Series,* XI (New Haven, 1956), 47–56.
66. *O.A.*, II, 20, 22, 75, and 78 ff. Note that for the sun's mean motion, the values given in the tables on pp. 22 and 75 differ by 1″ and 2″ for the arguments 9^d and 10^d. The figures on p. 75 are the correct ones: 9^d, 8°52′*15*″; 10^d, 9°51′*23*″.
67. *Jalāʾ al-adhhān fī Zīj al-Battānī,* according to al-Bīrūnī's own bibliography, published in E. Sachau, ed., *Chronologie orientalischer Völker von Albêrûnî* (Leipzig, 1878), p. xxxxvi.
68. Cf. de Slane, trans., *Les prolégomènes d'Ibn Khaldūn* (Paris, 1863–1868), III, 148; cf. F. Rosenthal, trans., *Ibn Khaldûn, The Muqaddimah,* III (New York, 1958), 136.
69. Cod. Vat. Lat. 3098 (cited after *O.A.*, I, xxxvi).
70. Nuremberg, *ca.* 1473 (the exact year of this incunabulum cannot be established).
71. In the chapter "De motu octavae sphaerae." The folios carry no numbers.
72. "Albategni vero dicebat eas moveri uno gradu in sexaginta annis et quatuor mensibus semper versus orientem."
73. Cf. p. 510.
74. See p. 509.
75. See e.g., Copernicus, *De revolutionibus,* III, 13.
76. See n. 18.
77. See n. 21.
78. See n. 3.
79. See p. 508.
80. Staatsbibliothek, MS no. 5875; see W. Ahlwardt, *Verzeichniss der arabischen Handschriften der Kgl. Bibliothek zu Berlin,* V, 273 f. The MS, written *ca.* 800/1397 by Aḥmad ibn Tamīm and comprising 62 folios, lacks the title page and the first pages of the text. At the end is the grammatically incorrect phrase *tamma kitāb al-arbaᶜa* [*sic!*] *sharḥ al-Battānī* ("Here ends the Book of the Four [Maqālas] of al-Battānī's commentary"), which obviously alludes to Ptolemy's *Tetrabiblos.* According to Ahlwardt, no division into four *maqālas* and no sections marked as commentaries (*sharḥ*) are recognizable. As Nallino (I, xxi ff.) has shown, the subjects treated and their sequence are, with few exceptions, those of the *Tetrabiblos.*
81. See n. 28. I, 399: "Cod. CMLXVI, nr. 2°: Commentarius in Quadripartitum Ptolemaei de astrorum iudiciis: subiectis tabulis. Auctor est vir clarissimus Mohammad Ben Geber Albategnius."
82. *Les manuscrits arabes de l'Escurial* (Paris, 1884), I, xxiv.
83. *O.A.*, I, xx.
84. "Les manuscrits arabes de l'Escurial décrits d'après les notes de Hartwig Derenbourg," in *Publications de l'École Nationale des Langues Orientales Vivantes,* 6th ser., **5,** 2, fasc. 3 (1941), 116.
85. *O.A.*, I, xxiii.
86. Cited after the anonymous Latin translation *C. Ptolemaei de praedictionibus astronomicis, cui titulum fecerunt Quadripartitum, libri IV. Ed. posterior* (Frankfurt, 1622).
87. This important MS was discovered by Fuat Sezgin, Institut für Geschichte der Naturwissenschaften, University of Frankfurt. It dates from the sixth/thirteenth century.
88. Istanbul, Carullah 1499, fol. 81v, written in 677/1278, consisting of only one page. This MS was discovered by Fuat Sezgin.
89. See p. 511.
90. *O.A.*, I, xxiii–xxxi.

BIBLIOGRAPHY

Consult the following works by C. A. Nallino: *Al-Battānī . . . Opus astronomicum* (see note 3); "Al-Battānī," in *Encyclopaedia of Islam,* Vol. I, repr. with augmented bibliography, *ibid.*, 2nd ed., Vol. I; "Astronomy," *ibid.;* "Astrologia e astronomia presso i Musulmani," in his *Raccolta di scritti editi e inediti,* Maria Nallino, ed., V (Rome, 1944), 1–87, esp. 52; "Storia dell'astronomia presso gli Arabi nel Medio Evo," *ibid.*, pp. 88–329, trans. by Maria Nallino from the Arabic original, *ᶜIlm al-Falak . . .* (Rome, 1911–1912); and "Albatenio," in *Enciclopedia italiana,* repr. in his *Raccolta,* V, 334–336.

See also H. Suter, "Die astronomischen Tafeln des Muḥammad ibn Mūsā al-Khwārizmī," in *Det Kgl. Danske Videnskabernes Selskabs Skrifter,* 7. Række, Historisk og Filologisk Afdeling, **3,** no. 1 (1914); J. M. Millás-Vallicrosa,

Estudios sobre Azarquiel (Madrid–Granada, 1943–1950); E. Honigmann, "Bemerkungen zu den geographischen Tabellen al-Battānī's," in *Rivista degli studi orientali,* **11** (1927), 169–175; and E. S. Kennedy and Muhammad Agha, "Planetary Visibility Tables in Islamic Astronomy," in *Centaurus,* **7** (1960), 134–140.

WILLY HARTNER

BAYES, THOMAS (*b.* London, England, 1702; *d.* Tunbridge Wells, England, 17 April 1761)

Bayes was a member of the first secure generation of English religious Nonconformists. His father, Joshua Bayes, F.R.S., was a respected theologian of dissent; he was also one of the group of six ministers who were the first to be publicly ordained as Nonconformists. Privately educated, Bayes became his father's assistant at the presbytery in Holborn, London; his mature life was spent as minister at the chapel in Tunbridge Wells. Despite his provincial circumstances, he was a wealthy bachelor with many friends. The Royal Society of London elected him a fellow in 1742. He wrote little: *Divine Benevolence* (1731) and *Introduction to the Doctrine of Fluxions* (1736) are the only works known to have been published during his lifetime. The latter is a response to Bishop Berkeley's *Analyst,* a stinging attack on the logical foundations of Newton's calculus; Bayes's reply was perhaps the soundest retort to Berkeley then available.

Bayes is remembered for his brief "Essay Towards Solving a Problem in the Doctrine of Chances" (1763), the first attempt to establish foundations for statistical inference. Jacques Bernoulli's *Ars conjectandi* (1713) and Abraham de Moivre's *The Doctrine of Chances* (1718) already provided great textbooks of what we now call probability theory. Given the probability of one event, the logical principles for inferring the probabilities of related events were quite well understood. In his "Essay," Bayes set himself the "converse problem": "*Given* the number of times in which an unknown event has happened and failed: *Required* the chance that the probability of its happening in a single trial lies somewhere between any two degrees of probability that can be named." "By chance," he said, "I mean the same as probability."

In the light of Bernoulli's *Ars conjectandi,* and of a paper by John Arbuthnot (1710), there was some understanding of how to reject statistical hypotheses in the light of data; but no one had shown how to measure the probability of statistical hypotheses in the light of data. Bayes began his solution of the problem by noting that sometimes the probability of a statistical hypothesis is given before any particular events are observed; he then showed how to compute the probability of the hypothesis after some observations are made. In his own example:

> Postulate: 1. I suppose the square table or plane ABCD to be so made and levelled that if either of the balls O or W be thrown upon it, there shall be the same probability that it rests upon any one equal part of the plane as another, and that it must necessarily rest somewhere upon it.
>
> 2. I suppose that the ball W shall be first thrown, and through the point where it rests a line *os* shall be drawn parallel to AD, and meeting CD and AB in *s* and *o,* and that afterwards the ball O shall be thrown $p + q$ or n times, and that its resting between AD and *os* after a single throw be called the happening of the event M in a single trial.

For any fractions f and b (between zero and one), Bayes was concerned with the probability of assertions of the form

$$f \leq \text{probability of M} \leq b\,.$$

From his physical assumptions about the table ABCD, he inferred that the prior probability (i.e., the probability before any trials have been made) is $b - f$. He proved, as a theorem in direct probabilities, that the posterior probability (i.e., the probability, on the evidence, that M occurred p times and failed q times) is

$$\int_f^b x^p(1-x)^q\,dx \Big/ \int_0^1 x^p(1-x)^q\,dx.$$

A generalization on this deduction is often, anachronistically, called Bayes's theorem or Bayes's formula. In the case of only finitely many statistical hypotheses, $H_1, \cdots, H_n$, let there be prior data D and some new observed evidence E. Then the prior probability of H_i is Prob (H_i/D); the posterior probability is Prob $(H_i/D$ and $E)$; the theorem asserts:

$$\text{Prob}\,(H_i/D \text{ and } E) = \frac{\text{Prob}\,(H_i/D)\ \text{Prob}\,(E/H_i \text{ and } D)}{\sum_{j=1}^{j=n} \text{Prob}\,(H_j/D)\ \text{Prob}\,(E/H_j \text{ and } D)}.$$

A corresponding theorem holds in the continuum; Bayes's deduction essentially involves a special case of it.

The work so far described falls entirely within probability theory, and would now be regarded as a straightforward deduction from standard probability axioms. The striking feature of Bayes's work is an argument found in a *scholium* to the paper, which does not follow from any standard axioms. Suppose we have no information about the prior probability of a statistical hypothesis. Bayes argues by analogy that, in this case, our ignorance is neither more nor less than in his example where prior probabilities are known to be entirely uniform. He concludes, "I shall take for granted that the rule given concerning the event M . . . is also the rule to be used in relation to any event concerning the probability of which nothing at all is known antecedently to any trials made or observed concerning it."

If Bayes's conclusion is correct, we have a basis for the whole of statistical inference. Richard Price, who sent Bayes's paper to the Royal Society, seems to imply in a covering letter that Bayes was not satisfied with his argument by analogy and, hence, had declined to publish it. Whatever the case with Bayes, Laplace had no qualms about Bayes's argument; and from 1774 he regularly assumed uniform prior probability distributions. His enormous influence made Bayes's ideas almost unchallengeable until George Boole protested in his *Laws of Thought* (1854). Since then, Bayes's technique has been a constant subject of controversy.

Today there are two kinds of Bayesians. Sir Harold Jeffreys, in his *Theory of Probability,* maintains that, relative to any body of information, even virtual ignorance, there is an objective distribution of degrees of confidence appropriate to various hypotheses; he often rejects Bayes's actual postulate, but accepts the need for similar postulates. Leonard J. Savage, in his *Foundations of Statistics,* rejects objective probabilities, but interprets probability in a personal way, as reflecting a person's personal degree of belief; hence, a prior probability is a person's belief before he has made some observations, and his posterior probability is his belief after the observations are made. Many working statisticians who are Bayesians, in the sense of trying to argue from prior probabilities, try to be neutral between Jeffreys and Savage. In this respect they are perhaps close to Bayes himself. He defined the probability of an event as "the ratio between the value at which an expectation depending upon the happening of the event ought to be computed, and the value of the thing expected upon its happening." This definition can be interpreted in either a subjective or an objective way, but there is no evidence that Bayes had even reflected on which interpretation he might prefer.

BIBLIOGRAPHY

I. Original Works. Bayes's works published during his lifetime are *Divine Benevolence, or an Attempt to Prove That the Principal End of the Divine Providence and Government Is the Happiness of His Creatures* (London, 1731); and *An Introduction to the Doctrine of Fluxions, and a Defence of the Mathematicians Against the Objections of the Author of* The Analyst (London, 1736). "An Essay Towards Solving a Problem in the Doctrine of Chances" was published in *Philosophical Transactions of the Royal Society of London,* **53** (1763), 370–418, with a covering letter written by Richard Price; repr. in *Biometrika,* **45** (1958), 296–315, with a biographical note by G. A. Barnard. Also of interest is "A Letter on Asymptotic Series from Bayes to John Canton," in *Biometrika,* **45** (1958), 269–271; repr. with the paper from the *Philosophical Transactions* in *Facsimiles of Two Papers by Bayes* (Washington, D.C., n.d.), with a commentary on the first by Edward C. Molina and on the second by W. Edwards Deming.

II. Secondary Literature. Supplementary information may be found in John Arbuthnot, "An Argument for Divine Providence Taken From the Constant Regularity of the Births of Both Sexes," in *Philosophical Transactions of the Royal Society of London,* **23** (1710), 186–190; George Berkeley, *The Analyst* (London–Dublin, 1734); Jacques Bernoulli, *Ars conjectandi* (Basel, 1713); George Boole, *An Investigation of the Laws of Thought* (London, 1854); Harold Jeffreys, *Theory of Probability* (Oxford, 1939; 3rd ed., 1961); Pierre Simon Laplace, "Mémoire sur la probabilité des causes par les événements," in *Mémoires par divers savants,* **6** (1774), 621–656, and *Théorie analytique des probabilités* (Paris, 1812); Abraham de Moivre, *The Doctrine of Chances* (London, 1718; 3rd ed., 1756); and Leonard J. Savage, *The Foundations of Statistics* (New York–London, 1954).

Ian Hacking

BEAUGRAND, JEAN (*b.* Paris [?], France, *ca.* 1595 [?]; *d.* Paris [?], *ca.* 22 December 1640)

In spite of the important role he played in the mathematics of the 1630's, what little is known or surmised about Beaugrand has had to be pieced together from sources dealing with his friends and enemies, and only rarely with him directly. There are few manuscripts or letters, and no records. He may have been the son of Jean Beaugrand, author of *La paecilographie* (1602) and *Escritures* (1604), who was chosen to teach calligraphy to Louis XIII. He studied under Viète and became mathematician to Gaston of Orléans in 1630; in that year J. L. Vaulezard dedicated his *Cinq livres des zététiques de Fr. Viette* to Beaugrand, who had already achieved a certain notoriety from having published Viète's *In artem analyticam isagoge,* with scholia and a mathematical compendium, in 1631. Some of the scholia were incorporated in Schooten's edition of 1646.

Beaugrand was an early friend of Fermat[1] and Étienne Despagnet (the son of Jean Despagnet); later of Mersenne and his circle; and for a time, before their bitter break, of Desargues. He seems to have been an official Paris correspondent to Fermat and was replaced in that function by Carcavi.[2] In 1634 he was one of the scientists who officially examined Morin's method for determining longitudes.[3] The following year he assumed the functions of *sécrétaire du roi,* possibly under Pierre Séguier, who was appointed chancellor in the same year.

Sometime before 1630 Beaugrand visited England;[4] he met Hobbes in Paris, at the home of Mersenne, in 1634 and 1637.[5] He spent a year in Italy, from February 1635, as part of Bellièvre's entourage.[6] While there, he visited Castelli in Rome,[7] Cavalieri in Bologna,[8] and Galileo in Arcetri,[9] and communicated to them some of Fermat's results in a conversation alluded to in his *Géostatique.* All of them, especially Cavalieri, appear to have been impressed with Beaugrand as a mathematician, and he continued to correspond with them after his return to Paris in February 1636.[10] He conveyed results of the French mathematicians without always bothering about provenance, a habit that resulted in misunderstandings.

Although Beaugrand's *Géostatique* (1636) was well received by Castelli and Cavalieri, it was a disappointment in France; and his violent polemical exchanges with Desargues, his anonymous pamphlets against Descartes, and the disdain that characterizes Descartes's references to him, as well as the cooling of his relations with Fermat, seem to stem from the period of its publication. Its main thesis is that the weight of a body varies as its distance from the center of gravity. Fermat[11] had adopted this law, and sought to demonstrate it in a satisfactory manner by arguing from a thought-experiment in which Archimedean arguments were applied to a lever with its fulcrum at the earth's center. Thus he defended a law of gravity later taken up independently by Saccheri in his *Neo-Statica* (1703).

Fermat's proposition gave rise to a long debate involving Étienne Pascal, Roberval, and Descartes.[12] Desargues appended a text inspired by this controversy to his *Brouillon projet.* Beaugrand in turn claimed that the proposition which occupies most of the *Brouillon projet* is nothing but a corollary to Apollonius, *Conics* III, prop. 17.[13] This attack was preserved by Desargues's enemies and occasioned Poncelet's rediscovery of Desargues's work 150 years later. Beaugrand's attacks on Descartes[14] took a similar form, including a charge of plagiarism from Harriot,[15] and are to be found in three anonymous pamphlets and a letter to Mersenne claiming that Viète's methods were superior and that Descartes had derived his *Géométrie* from them.[16]

NOTES

D, F, and *M* below refer to the respective standard editions (see bibliography) of the correspondence of Descartes, Fermat, and Mersenne.

1. *M,* V, 466 f.
2. Cf. C. de Waard, in *Bulletin des sciences mathématiques,* 2nd ser., **17** (June 1918).
3. Bigourdan, "La conférence des longitudes de 1634," in *Comptes rendus de l'Académie des sciences,* **163** (1916), 229-233.
4. *M,* II, 514.
5. *D,* III, 342.
6. *M,* V, 271.
7. Paris, B.N., f. fr. 15913, 15914.
8. *M,* V, 429. Cf. C. de Waard, in *Bollettino di bibliografia di storia delle scienze matematiche* (1919), 1-12.
9. *M,* V, 454; Galileo, Edizione nazionale, XVI (1905), 335-337, 340-344.
10. *Lettres de Chapelain,* Tamizey de Larroque, ed., I (1880), 109.
11. *F,* V, 100-103.
12. Cf. Descartes to Mersenne, 13 July 1638.
13. R. Taton, *L'oeuvre mathématique de Desargues* (Paris, 1937), *passim.*
14. P. Tannéry, *Oeuvres scientifiques,* V, 503-512; VI, 206 ff.
15. *M,* VII, 201 f.
16. *Ibid.,* 87-104.

BIBLIOGRAPHY

References to Beaugrand are scattered throughout the standard eds. of the correspondence of Fermat (P. Tannéry and C. Henry, eds. [Paris, 1891-1912], supp. vol., N. de Waard, ed. [Paris, 1922]), Descartes (Adam and P. Tannéry, eds. [Paris, 1897-1913]), and Mersenne (Paris, 1933-).

The extant writings by Beaugrand, besides his ed. of Viète's *In artem analyticam isagoge* (Paris, 1631) and *Géostatique* (Paris, 1636), pub. in Latin as *Geostatica* (Paris, 1637), are a letter on tangents in Fermat's *Oeuvres,* supp. vol. (1922), pp. 102-113; a letter to Desargues, in R. Taton, *L'oeuvre mathématique de Desargues* (Paris, 1951), pp. 186-190; four writings against Descartes, "Lettre de M. de Beaugrand (10 Aug. 1640)," in Descartes, *Oeuvres,* V, 503-512; letter to Mersenne (Apr. [?] 1638), in Descartes, *Correspondance* (1903); three anonymous pamphlets, in P. Tannéry, *Mémoires scientifiques,* VI (Paris, 1896), 202-229 ("La correspondance de Descartes dans les inédits du fonds Libri"); and Mersenne, *Harmonie universelle,* II, *Livre I des instrumens,* props. 14, 15, 31, and his *Correspondance,* IV, 429-431.

See also Guy de Brosse, *Éclaircissement d'une partie des paralogismes* . . . (1637); P. Costabel, "Centre de gravité et équivalence dynamique," in *Les conférences du Palais de la Découverte,* ser. D, no. 34 (Paris, 1954); and P. Duhem, *Les origines de la statique* (Paris, 1906), pp. 178 ff. For the confused priority controversy over the cycloid, see Pascal, *Oeuvres,* L. Brunschvicq and E. Boutroux, eds., VIII (Paris, 1914), 181-223.

HENRY NATHAN

BELL, ERIC TEMPLE (*b.* Aberdeen, Scotland, 7 February 1883; *d.* Watsonville, California, 21 December 1960)

The younger son of James Bell, of a London commercial family, and Helen Lyndsay Lyall, whose family were classical scholars, he was tutored before entering the Bedford Modern School, where a remarkable teacher, E. M. Langley, inspired his lifelong interest in elliptic functions and number theory. Bell migrated to the United States in 1902 "to escape being shoved into Woolwich or the India Civil Service" (as he later explained) and was able to "cover all the mathematics offered" at Stanford and graduate Phi Beta Kappa in two years. A single year at the University of Washington netted an M.A. in 1908; another at Columbia sufficed for the Ph.D. in 1912. The years between he spent as a ranch hand, mule skinner, surveyor, school teacher, and partner in an unsuccessful telephone company. In 1910 he married Jessie L. Brown, who died in 1940. They had one son, Taine Temple Bell, who became a physician in Watsonville. Bell produced about 250 mathematical research papers, four learned books, eleven popularizations, and, as "John Taine," seventeen science fiction novels, many short stories, and some poetry. He was active in organizations of research mathematicians, teachers, and authors. In religion and politics he was an individualist and uncompromising iconoclast. He remained active in retirement and was writing his last book in the hospital when overtaken by a fatal heart attack.

At the University of Washington from 1912, Bell published a number of significant contributions on numerical functions, analytic number theory, multiply periodic functions, and Diophantine analysis. His "Arithmetical Paraphrases" (1921) won a Bôcher Prize. Other honors (e.g., the presidency of the Mathematical Association of America [1931–1933]), editorial duties, and invitations multiplied, but they did not reduce his output. After lecturing at Chicago and Harvard, he went, in 1926, to the California Institute of Technology, where he remained (emeritus after 1953) until hospitalized a year before his death. Bell will be longest known for his *Men of Mathematics* and other widely read books "on the less inhuman aspects of mathematics," and for *The Development of Mathematics,* whose insights and provocative style continue to influence and intrigue professional mathematicians—in spite of their historical inaccuracies and sometimes fanciful interpretations.

BIBLIOGRAPHY

I. Original Works. Typical are his first publication, "An Arithmetical Theory of Certain Numerical Functions," University of Washington Publication, no. 1 (1915); "Arithmetical Paraphrases, Part I," in *Transactions of the American Mathematical Society,* **22,** no. 1 (Jan. 1921), 1–30, and no. 3 (Oct. 1921), 273–275, which won a Bôcher Prize; *Algebraic Arithmetic,* American Mathematical Society Colloquium Publication, no. 7 (1927), which was based on his invited lectures at the Eleventh Colloquium of the American Mathematical Society in 1927; *Before the Dawn* (Baltimore, Md., 1934), which was his favorite science fiction novel, the only one published under his own name and inspired, he said, by boyhood views of models of dinosaurs in Croydon Park near London; *Men of Mathematics* (New York, 1937), awarded the gold medal of the Commonwealth Club of California; *The Development of Mathematics* (New York, 1940; 2nd ed., 1945); *Mathematics, Queen and Servant of Science* (New York, 1951), his most ambitious popularization based on two previous books, *Queen of the Sciences* and *The Handmaiden of the Sciences;* and *The Last Problem* (New York, 1961), a study of Fermat's conjecture, which was unfinished at the time of Bell's death.

II. Secondary Literature. There is no detailed biography. Only the following give more information than appears in *American Men of Science, Who's Who in America,* and *Who Was Who:* an autobiography in *Twentieth Century Authors,* supp. 1 (New York, 1955), 70–71, from which we have taken the quotations in the article; T. A. A. Broadbent, obituary in *Nature,* no. 4763 (11 Feb. 1961), 443; and a news release from the California Institute of Technology News Bureau (21 Dec. 1960).

Kenneth O. May

BELLAVITIS, GIUSTO (*b.* Bassano, Vicenza, Italy, 22 November 1803; *d.* Tezze, near Bassano, 6 November 1880)

Bellavitis was the son of Ernesto Bellavitis, an accountant with the municipal government of Bassano, and Giovanna Navarini; the family belonged to the nobility but was in modest circumstances. He did not pursue regular studies but was tutored under the guidance of his father, who directed his interest toward mathematics. Soon he surpassed his tutor and diligently pursued his studies on his own, occupying himself with the latest mathematical problems.

From 1822 to 1843 Bellavitis worked for the municipal government of Bassano—without pay for the first ten years—and conscientiously discharged his duties, occupying his free time with mathematical studies and research. During this period he published his first major works, including papers (1835, 1837) on the method of equipollencies, which were hailed as one of his major contributions. On 26 September 1840 Bellavitis became a fellow of the Istituto Veneto, and in 1843 he was appointed professor of mathematics and mechanics at the *liceo* of Vicenza. He then married Maria Tavelli, the woman who for fourteen years had comforted and encouraged him in his difficult career.

On 4 January 1845, through a competitive examination, Bellavitis was appointed full professor of descriptive geometry at the University of Padua. On 4 July 1846, the university awarded him an honorary doctorate in philosophy and mathematics. He transferred in 1867 to the professorship of complementary algebra and analytic geometry. On 15 March 1850, Bellavitis became a fellow of the Società Italiana dei Quaranta, and in 1879 a member of the Accademia dei Lincei. In 1866 he was named a senator of the Kingdom of Italy.

Bellavitis' method of equipollencies belongs to a special point of view in mathematical thought: geometric calculus. According to Peano, geometric calculus consists of a system of operations to be carried out on geometric entities; these operations are analogous to those executed on numbers in classical algebra. Such a calculus "enables us to express by means of formulae the results of geometric constructions, to represent geometric propositions by means of equations, and to replace a logical argument with the transformation of equations." This approach had been developed by Leibniz, who intended to go beyond the Cartesian analytic geometry, by performing calculations directly on the geometric elements, rather than on the coordinates (numbers). Moebius' barycentric calculus finds its expression within this context, but Bellavitis made special reference to Carnot's suggestion of 1803, when he wrote in 1854:

> This method complies with one of Carnot's wishes, i.e., he wanted to find an algorithm that could simultaneously represent both the magnitude and the position of the various components of a figure; with the immediate result of obtaining elegant and simple graphic solutions to geometrical problems ["Sposizione del metodo delle equipollenze," p. 226].

In order to indicate that two segments, AB and DC, are equipollent—i.e., equal, parallel, and pointing in the same direction—Bellavitis used the formula

$$AB \simeq DC.$$

Thus we are given a kind of algebra analogous to that of complex numbers with two units; it found its application in various problems of plane geometry and mechanics, and paved the way for W. R. Hamilton's theory of quaternions (1853), through which geometric calculus can be applied to space; it also led to Grassmann's "Ausdehnungslehre" (1844), and finally to the vector theory. With his barycentric calculus, Bellavitis created a calculus more general than Moebius' "baricentrische Calcul."

In 1834, in his formula expressing the area of polygons and the volume of polyhedra as a function of the distances between their vertexes, Bellavitis anticipated results that were later newly discovered by Staudt and published in 1842.

In algebraic geometry, Bellavitis introduced new criteria for the classification of curves, and then completed Newton's findings on plane cubic curves, adding six curves to the seventy-two already known; these six had not been mentioned by Euler and Cramer. He also began the classification of curves of class three. He offered a graphical solution of spherical triangles, based on the transformation—through reciprocal vector radia—of a spherical surface into a plane. This method finds application in the solution of crystallographic problems.

Bellavitis furthered the progress of descriptive geometry with his textbook on the subject. Considering mathematics to be based essentially upon physical facts and proved by sensible experience, Bellavitis looked down on geometry of more than three dimensions and on non-Euclidean geometry. He did, however, like Beltrami's research on the interpretation of Lobachevski's geometry of the pseudosphere, for he felt that this research would help to diminish the prestige of the new geometry, reducing it to geometry of the pseudosphere. He continued to pursue his research on geodetic triangles on such surfaces as the pseudosphere.

In algebra, Bellavitis thoroughly investigated and continued Paolo Ruffini's research on the numerical solution of an algebraic equation of any degree; he also studied the theory of numbers and of congruences. He furnished a geometric base for the theory of complex numbers. Several of Bellavitis' contributions deal with infinitesimal analysis. In this connection we should mention his papers on the Eulerian integrals and on elliptic integrals.

Bellavitis solved various mechanical problems by original methods, among them Hamilton's quaternions. He developed very personal critical observations about the calculus of probabilities and the theory of errors. He also explored physics, especially optics and electrology, and chemistry. As a young man, Bellavitis weighed the problem of a universal scientific language and published a paper on this subject in 1863. He also devoted time to the history of mathematics and, among other things, he vindicated Cataldi by attributing the invention of continuous fractions to him.

BIBLIOGRAPHY

I. Original Works. Bibliographies of Bellavitis' works are in A. Favaro, in *Zeitschrift für Mathematik und Physik,*

Historisch-literarische Abteilung, **26** (1881); and E. Nestore Legnazzi, *Commemorazione del Conte Giusto Bellavitis* (Padua, 1881), pp. 74–88, which gives the titles of 181 published works, together with numerous "Riviste di giornali," in which Bellavitis examines the results of other authors and uses his problem-solving methods, published in the *Atti dell'Istituto veneto* between 1859 and 1880.

Among his works are "Sopra alcune formule e serie infinite relative ai fattoriali ed agli integrali euleriani," in *Annali delle scienze del Regno Lombardo Veneto,* **4** (1834), 10–19; "Teoremi generali per determinare le aree dei poligoni ed i volumi dei poliedri col mezzo delle distanze dei loro vertici," in *Annali Fusinieri* (1834); "Saggio di applicazioni di un nuovo metodo di geometria analitica-calcolo delle equipollenze," *ibid.,* **5** (1835); "Memoria sul metodo delle equipollenze," in *Annali delle scienze del Regno Lombardo Veneto,* **7** (1837), 243–261; **8** (1838), 17–37, 85–121; "Sul movimento di un liquido che discende in modo perfettamente simmetrico rispetto a un asse verticale," in *Atti dell'Istituto veneto,* **3** (1844), 206–210, and *Memorie dell'Istituto veneto,* **2** (1845), 339–360; "Sul più facile modo di trovare le radici reali delle equazioni algebriche e sopra un nuovo metodo per la determinazione delle radici immaginarie," *ibid.,* **3** (1847), 109–220; "Considerazioni sulle nomenclature chimiche, sugli equivalenti chimici e su alcune proprietà, che con questi si collegano," *ibid.,* 221–267; *Lezioni di geometria descrittiva* (Padua, 1851, 1858); "Sulla classificazioni delle curve del terzo ordine," in *Memorie della Società italiana delle scienze* (*dei Quaranta*), ser. 1, **25** (1851), 1–50; "Classificazione delle curve della terza classe," in *Atti dell'Istituto veneto,* ser. 3, **4** (1853), 234–240; "Teoria delle lenti," in *Annali Tortolini,* **4** (1853), 26–269, and *Atti dell'Istituto veneto,* ser. 4, **2** (1872), 392–406; "Sposizione del metodo delle equipollenze," in *Memorie della Società italiana delle scienze,* ser. 1, **25** (1854), 225–309, trans. into French by C. A. Laisant, in *Nouvelles annales de mathématiques* (1874); "Calcolo dei quaternioni di W. R. Hamilton e sue relazioni col metodo delle equipollenze," in *Memorie della Società italiana delle scienze,* ser. 2, **1** (1858), 126–184, and *Atti dell'Istituto veneto,* ser. 3, **3** (1856–1857), 334–342; "Sulla misura delle azioni elettriche," *ibid.,* **9** (1863), 773–786, 807–818; "Pensieri sopra una lingua universale e sopra alcuni argomenti analoghi," in *Memorie dell'Istituto veneto,* **11** (1863), 33–74; and "Sopra alcuni processi di geometria analitica" in *Rivista periodica della R. Accademia di scienze lettere e arti di Padova,* **30** (1880), p. 73.

II. SECONDARY LITERATURE. Works on Bellavitis are G. Loria, *Storia delle matematiche,* III (Turin, 1933), 500–501; E. Nestore Legnazzi (see above); G. Peano, *Calcolo geometrico secondo l'Ausdehnungslehre di H. Grassmann* (Turin, 1888), p. v; D. Turazza, "Commemorazione di G. Bellavitis," in *Atti dell'Istituto veneto,* ser. 5., **8** (1881–1882), 395–422; and N. Virgopia, "Bellavitis, Giusto," in *Dizionario biografico degli italiani* (Rome, 1965), VII.

ETTORE CARRUCCIO

BELTRAMI, EUGENIO (*b.* Cremona, Italy, 16 November 1835; *d.* Rome, Italy, 18 February 1900)

Beltrami was born into an artistic family: his grandfather, Giovanni, was an engraver of precious stones, especially cameos; his father, Eugenio, painted miniatures. Young Eugenio studied mathematics from 1853 to 1856 at the University of Pavia, where Francesco Brioschi was his teacher. Financial difficulties forced Beltrami to become secretary to a railroad engineer, first in Verona and then in Milan. In Milan he continued his mathematical studies and in 1862 published his first mathematical papers, which deal with the differential geometry of curves.

After the establishment of the kingdom of Italy in 1861, Beltrami was offered the chair of complementary algebra and analytic geometry at Bologna, which he held from 1862 to 1864; from 1864 to 1866 he held the chair of geodesy in Pisa, where Enrico Betti was his friend and colleague. From 1866 to 1873 he was back in Bologna, where he occupied the chair of rational mechanics. After Rome had become the capital of Italy in 1870, Beltrami became professor of rational mechanics at the new University of Rome, but served there only from 1873 to 1876, after which he held the chair of mathematical physics at Pavia, where he also taught higher mechanics. In 1891 he returned to Rome, where he taught until his death. He became the president of the Accademia dei Lincei in 1898 and, the following year, a senator of the kingdom. A lover of music, Beltrami was interested in the relationship between mathematics and music.

Beltrami's works can be divided into two main groups: those before *ca.* 1872, which deal with differential geometry of curves and surfaces and were influenced by Gauss, Lamé, and Riemann, and the later ones, which are concerned with topics in applied mathematics that range from elasticity to electromagnetics. His most lasting work belongs to this first period, and the paper "Saggio di interpretazione della geometria non-euclidea" (1868) stands out. In a paper of 1865 Beltrami had shown that on surfaces of constant curvature, and only on them, the line element $ds^2 = Edu^2 + 2Fdudv + Gdv^2$ can be written in such a form that the geodesics, and only these, are represented by linear expressions in u and v. For positive curvature R^{-2} this form is

$$ds^2 = R^2[(v^2 + a^2)du^2 - 2uvdudv + (u^2 + a^2)dv^2] \times (u^2 + v^2 + a^2)^{-2}.$$

The geodesics in this case behave, locally speaking, like the great circles on a sphere. It now occurred to Beltrami that, by changing R to iR and a to ia ($i = \sqrt{-1}$), the line element thus obtained,

$$ds^2 = R^2[(a^2 - v^2)du^2 + 2uvdudv + (u^2 + a^2)dv^2] \times (a^2 - u^2 - v^2)^{-2},$$

which defines surfaces of constant curvature $-R^{-2}$, offers a new type of geometry for its geodesics inside the region $u^2 + v^2 < a^2$. This geometry is exactly that of the so-called non-Euclidean geometry of Lobachevski, if geodesics on such a surface are identified with the "straight lines" of non-Euclidean geometry.

This geometry, developed between 1826 and 1832, was known to Beltrami through some of Gauss's letters and some translations of the work of Lobachevski. Few mathematicians, however, had paid attention to it. Beltrami now offered a representation of this geometry in terms of the acceptable Euclidean geometry: "We have tried to find a real foundation [*substrato*] to this doctrine, instead of having to admit for it the necessity of a new order of entities and concepts." He showed that all the concepts and formulas of Lobachevski's geometry are realized for geodesics on surfaces of constant negative curvature and, in particular, that there are rotation surfaces of this kind. The simplest of this kind of "pseudospherical" surface (Beltrami's term) is the surface of rotation of the tractrix about its asymptote, now usually called the pseudosphere, which Beltrami analyzed more closely in a paper of 1872.

Thus Beltrami showed how possible contradictions in non-Euclidean geometry would reveal themselves in the Euclidean geometry of surfaces; and this removed for most, or probably all, mathematicians the feeling that non-Euclidean geometry might be wrong. Beltrami, by "mapping" one geometry upon another, made non-Euclidean geometry "respectable." His method was soon followed by others, including Felix Klein, a development that opened entirely new fields of mathematical thinking.

Beltrami pointed out that his representation of non-Euclidean geometry was valid for two dimensions only. In his "Saggio" he was hesitant to claim the possibility of a similar treatment of non-Euclidean geometry of space. After he had studied Riemann's *Über die Hypothesen welche der Geometrie zu Grunde liegen,* just published by Dedekind, he had no scruples about extending his representation of non-Euclidean geometry to manifolds of $n > 2$ dimensions in "Teoria fondamentale degli spazi di curvatura costante."

In a contribution to the history of non-Euclidean geometry, Beltrami rescued from oblivion the Jesuit mathematician and logician Giovanni Saccheri (1667–1733), author of *Euclides ab omni naevo vindicatus,* which foreshadowed non-Euclidean geometry but did not achieve it.

In his "Ricerche di analisi applicata alla geometria," Beltrami, following an idea of Lamé's, showed the power of using so-called differential parameters in surface theory. This can be considered the beginning of the use of invariant methods in differential geometry.

Much of Beltrami's work in applied mathematics shows his fundamental geometrical approach, even in his analytical investigations. This trait characterizes the extensive "Richerche sulle cinematica dei fluidi" (1871–1874) and his papers on elasticity. In these he recognized how Lamé's fundamental formulas depend on the Euclidean character of space, and he sketched a non-Euclidean approach (1880–1882). He studied potential theory, particularly that of ellipsoids and cylindrical discs; wave theory in connection with Huygens' principle; and further problems in thermodynamics, optics, and conduction of heat that led to linear partial differential equations. Some papers deal with Maxwell's theory and its mechanistic interpretation, suggesting a start from d'Alembert's principle rather than from that of Hamilton (1889).

BIBLIOGRAPHY

I. Original Works. Beltrami's works are collected in *Opere matematiche,* 4 vols. (Milan, 1902–1920). Important individual works are "Saggio di interpretazione della geometria non-euclidea," in *Giornale di matematiche,* **6** (1868), 284–312, and *Opere,* I, 374–405, also translated into French in *Annales scientifiques de l'École Normale Supérieure,* **6** (1869), 251–288; "Richerche di analisi applicata alla geometria," in *Giornale di matematiche,* **2** (1864) and **3** (1865), also in *Opere,* I, 107–206; a paper on surfaces of constant curvature, in *Opere,* I, 262–280; "Teoria fondamentale degli spazi di curvatura costante," in *Annali di matematica,* ser. 2 (1868–1869), 232–255, and *Opere,* I 406–429; "Richerche sulle cinematica dei fluidi," in *Opere,* II, 202–379; a paper on the pseudosphere, in *Opere,* II, 394–409; a non-Euclidean approach to space, in *Opere,* III, 383–407; "Sulla teoria della scala diatonica," in *Opere,* III, 408–412; an article on Saccheri, in *Rendiconti della Reale Accademia dei Lincei,* ser. 4, **5** (1889), 441–448, and *Opere,* IV, 348–355; and papers on Maxwell's theory, in *Opere,* IV, 356–361.

II. Secondary Literature. There is a biographical sketch by L. Cremona in *Opere,* I, ix–xxii. See also L. Bianchi, "Eugenio Beltrami," in *Enciclopedia italiana,* VI (1930), 581; G. H. Bryan, "Eugenio Beltrami," in *Proceedings of the London Mathematical Society,* **32** (1900), 436–439; and G. Loria, "Eugenio Beltrami e le sue opere matematiche," in *Bibliotheca mathematica,* ser. 3, **2** (1901), 392–440. On Beltrami's contribution to non-Euclidean geometry, consult, among others, R. Bonola, *Non-Euclidean Geometry* (Chicago, 1912; New York, 1955), pp. 130–139, 234–236.

D. J. Struik

BENEDETTI, GIOVANNI BATTISTA (*b.* Venice, Italy, 14 August 1530; *d.* Turin, Italy, 20 January 1590)

Benedetti is of special significance in the history of science as the most important immediate forerunner of Galileo. He was of patrician status, but has not been definitely connected with any of the older known families of that name resident at Venice. His father was described by Luca Guarico as a Spaniard, philosopher, and *physicus,* probably in the sense of "student of nature" but possibly meaning "doctor of medicine." It was to his father that Benedetti owed most of his education, which Guarico says made him a philosopher, musician, and mathematician by the age of eighteen. One of the few autobiographical records left by Benedetti asserts that he had no formal education beyond the age of seven, except that he studied the first four books of Euclid's *Elements* under Niccolò Tartaglia, probably about 1546–1548. Their relations appear to have been poor, for Tartaglia nowhere mentions Benedetti as a pupil; Benedetti named Tartaglia in 1553 only "to give him his due" and severely criticized his writings in later years.

Benedetti's originality of thought and mathematical skill are evident in his first book, the *Resolutio,* published at Venice when he was only twenty-two. The *Resolutio* concerns the general solution of all the problems in Euclid's *Elements* (and of some others) using only a compass of fixed opening. Benedetti's treatment was more comprehensive and elegant than that of Tartaglia or Ludovico Ferrara in the published polemics of 1546–1547, and was more systematic than Tartaglia's later attack on the same problem in his final work, the *Trattato generale di numeri e misure* of 1560, in which he ignored the work of his former pupil.

Benedetti had one daughter, who was born at Venice in 1554 and died at Turin in 1580, but there is no record of his marriage. In 1558 he went to Parma as court mathematician to Duke Ottavio Farnese, in whose service he remained about eight years. In the winter of 1559/60 he lectured at Rome on the science of Aristotle; Girolamo Mei, who heard him there, praised his acumen, independence of mind, fluency, and memory. At Parma, Benedetti gave instruction at the court, served as astrologer, and advised on the engineering of public works. He also carried out some astronomical observations and constructed sundials mentioned in a later book on that subject. It appears that his private means were considerable, so that he was not inconvenienced by long delays in the payment of his salary.

In 1567 he was invited to Turin by the duke of Savoy and remained there until his death. The duke, Emanuele Filiberto, had great plans for the rehabilitation of Piedmont through public works, military engineering, and the general elevation of culture. Benedetti's duties included the teaching of mathematics and science at court. Tradition places him successively at the universities of Mondovì and Turin, although supporting official records are lacking and Benedetti never styled himself a professor. He appears, however, to have served as the duke's adviser on university affairs; for instance, he secured the appointment of Antonio Berga to the chair of philosophy at the University of Turin in 1569. Benedetti later engaged in a polemic with Berga, and on the title page of his *Consideratione* (1579) he referred to Berga as professor at Turin, but to himself only as philosopher to the duke of Savoy.

While at Turin, Benedetti designed and constructed various public and private works, such as sundials and fountains. His learning and mathematical talents were frequently praised by the duke and were mentioned by the Venetian ambassador in 1570, when Benedetti was granted a patent of nobility. In 1585 he appears to have been married a second time or rejoined by the mother of his daughter. In the same year he published his chief work, the *Speculationum,* a collection of treatises and of letters written to various correspondents on mathematical and scientific topics.

Benedetti died early in 1590. He had forecast his death for 1592 in the final lines of his last published book. On his deathbed he recomputed his horoscope and declared that an error of four minutes must have been made in the original data (published in 1552 by Luca Guarico), thus evincing his lifelong faith in the doctrines of judiciary astrology.

Benedetti's first important contribution to the birth of modern physics was set forth in the letter of dedication to his *Resolutio.* The letter was addressed to Gabriel de Guzman, a Spanish Dominican priest with whom he had conversed at Venice in 1552. It appears that Guzman had shown interest in Benedetti's theory of the free fall of bodies, and had asked him to publish a demonstration in which the speeds of fall would be treated mathematically. In order to forestall the possible theft of his ideas, Benedetti published his demonstration in this letter despite its irrelevance to the purely geometrical content of the book. Benedetti held that bodies of the same material, regardless of weight, would fall through a given medium at the same speed, and not at speeds proportional to their weights, as maintained by Aristotle. His demonstration was based on the principle of Archimedes, which probably came to his attention through Tartaglia's publication at Venice in 1551 of a vernacular translation of the first book of the Archimedean treatise on the behavior of bodies in water. Benedetti's "buoyancy theory of fall" is in many respects identical with that which Galileo set forth in his first treatise *De motu*, composed at Pisa about 1590 but not published during his lifetime.

Although no mention of Benedetti's theory has been found in books or correspondence of the period, lively discussions appear to have taken place concerning it, some persons denying the conclusion and others asserting that it did not contradict Aristotle. In answer to those contentions, Benedetti promptly published a second book, the *Demonstratio* (1554), restating the argument and citing the particular texts of Aristotle that it contradicted. In the new preface, also addressed to Guzman, Benedetti mentioned opponents as far away as Rome who had declared that since Aristotle could not err, his own theory must be false. Such discussions may explain the otherwise remarkable coincidence that another book published in 1553 also contains a statement related to free fall. This was *Il vero modo di scrivere in cifra*, by Giovanni Battista Bellaso of Brescia, in which it was asked why a ball of iron and one of wood will fall to the ground at the same time.

Two editions of Benedetti's *Demonstratio*, which was by no means a mere republication of the *Resolutio*, appeared in rapid succession. The first edition maintained, as did the *Resolutio*, that unequal bodies of the same material would fall at equal speed through a given medium. The second edition stated that resistance of the medium is proportional to the surface rather than the volume of the falling body, implying that precise equality of speed for homogeneous bodies of the same material and different weight would be found only in a vacuum. This correction of the original statement was repeated in Benedetti's later treatment of the question in *Speculationum* (1585).

Benedetti's original publication of his thesis in 1553 was designed to prevent its theft; perhaps he had in mind the fate of Tartaglia's solution of the cubic equation a few years earlier. But even repeated publication failed to protect it, and indeed became the occasion of its theft. Jean Taisnier, who pirated the work of Petrus Peregrinus de Maricourt in his *Opusculum . . . de natura magnetis* (1562), included with it—as his own—Benedetti's *Demonstratio*. Taisnier's impudent plagiarism enjoyed wider circulation than Benedetti's original, and was translated into English by Richard Eden about 1578. Simon Stevin cited the proposition as Taisnier's when he published his own experimental verification of it in 1586. But since Taisnier had stolen the *Demonstratio* in its earlier form, he was criticized by Stevin for the very fault which Benedetti had long since corrected in the second *Demonstratio* of 1554. Taisnier's appropriation of his book ultimately became known to Benedetti, who complained of it in the preface to his *De gnomonum* (1573). The relatively small circulation of Benedetti's works is evidenced by the fact that it was not until 1741 that general attention was first called to the theft, by Pierre Bayle.

Benedetti's ultimate expansion of his discussion of falling bodies in the *Speculationum* is of particular interest because it includes an explanation of their acceleration in terms of increments of impetus successively impressed *ad infinitum*. That conception is found later in the writings of Beeckman and Gassendi, but it appears never to have occurred to Galileo. Despite this insight, however, Benedetti failed to arrive at (or to attempt) a mathematical formulation of the rate of acceleration. The difference between Galileo's treatment and Benedetti's is perhaps related to the fact that Benedetti neglected the medieval writers who had attempted a mathematical analysis of motion and did not adopt their terminology, which is conspicuous in Galileo's early writings. Benedetti was deeply imbued with the notion of impetus as a self-exhausting force, a concept that may have prevented his further progress toward the inertial idea implicit in the accretion of impetus.

Benedetti's next contribution to physics was made about 1563, the most probable date of two letters on music written to Cipriano da Rore and preserved in the *Speculationum*. Those letters, in the opinion of Claude Palisca, entitle Benedetti to be considered the true pioneer in the investigation of the mechanics of the production of musical consonances. Da Rore was choirmaster at the court of Parma in 1561–1562, when he returned to Venice. Benedetti's letters probably supplemented his discussions with da Rore at Parma. Departing from the prevailing numerical theories of harmony, Benedetti inquired into the relation of pitch, consonance, and rates of vibration. He attributed the generation of musical consonances to the concurrence or cotermination of waves of air. Such waves, resulting from the striking of air by vibrating strings, should either agree with or break in upon one another. Proceeding thus, and asserting that the frequencies of vibration of two strings under equal tension vary inversely with the string lengths, Benedetti proposed an index of agreement obtained by multiplication of the terms of the ratio of a given consonance; by this means he could express the degree of concordance in a mathematical scale. Benedetti's empirical approach to musical theory, as applied to the tuning of instruments, anticipated the later method of equal temperament and contrasted sharply with the rational numerical rules offered by Gioseffo Zarlino. It is of interest that Zarlino was the teacher of Galileo's father, who in 1578 attacked Zarlino's musical theories on somewhat similar empirical grounds. But since Benedetti's letters were not published until 1585, they were probably not known to Vincenzio Galilei when he launched his attack.

Benedetti's first publication after his move to Turin was a book on the theory and construction of sundials, *De gnomonum* (1573), the most comprehensive treatise on the subject to that time. It dealt with the construction of dials at various inclinations and also with dials on cylindrical and conical surfaces. This book was followed by *De temporum emendatione,* on the correction of the calendar (1578). In 1579 he published *Consideratione,* a polemic work in reply to Antonio Berga, concerning a dispute over the relative volumes of the elements earth and water. As with Galileo's polemic on floating bodies, the dispute had arisen at court as a result of the duke's custom of inviting learned men to debate topics of philosophical or scientific interest before him. Of all Benedetti's books, this appears to be the only one to have received notice in a contemporary publication, Agostino Michele's *Trattato della grandezza dell'acqua et della terra* (1583).

Benedetti's final work, containing the most important Italian contribution to physical thought prior to Galileo, was the *Diversarum speculationum* (1585). Its opening section includes a number of arithmetical propositions demonstrated geometrically. Other mathematical sections include a treatise on perspective, a commentary on the fifth book of Euclid's *Elements,* and many geometrical demonstrations—including a general solution of the problem of circumscribing a quadrilateral of given sides; the development of various properties of spherical triangles, circles, and conic sections; discussion of the angle of contact between circular arcs; and theorems on isoperimetric figures, regular polygons, and regular solids.

The section on mechanics is largely a critique of certain parts of the pseudo-Aristotelian *Questions of Mechanics* and of propositions in Tartaglia's *Quesiti, et inventioni diverse.* Benedetti disputed Tartaglia's assertion that no body may be simultaneously moved by natural and violent motions, although he did not enter into a discussion of projectile motion giving effect to composition. He did, however, assert clearly and for the first time that the impetus of a body freed from rapid circular motion is rectilinear and tangential in character, a conception of fundamental importance to his criticisms of Aristotle and to his attempted explanation of the slowing down of wheels and of spinning tops.

Following the section on mechanics is an attack on many of Aristotle's basic physical conceptions. This section restates the "buoyancy theory of fall" as it was set forth in the second edition of the *Demonstratio.* For equality of speed of different weights falling *in vacuo,* Benedetti proposed a thought experiment that is often said to be identical with Galileo's, although the difference is considerable. Benedetti supposes two bodies of the same weight connected by a line and falling *in vacuo* at the same speed as a single body having their combined weight; he appeals to intuition to show that whether connected or not, the two smaller bodies will continue to fall at the same speed. In Galileo's argument, two bodies of different weight—and therefore of different speeds, according to Aristotle—are tied together; by the Aristotelian assumption, the slower would impede the faster, resulting in an intermediate speed for the pair. But the pair being heavier than either of its parts, it should fall faster than either, under the Aristotelian rule. Thus Galileo's argument, unlike Benedetti's, imputes self-contradiction to Aristotle's view. Benedetti's discussion of the ratios of speeds of descent in different media is also essentially different from Galileo's in *De motu,* for it includes both buoyancy and the effect of resistance proportional to the surface; the latter effect was neglected by Galileo in his earlier writings.

Again, Benedetti correctly holds that natural rectilinear motion continually increases in speed because of the continual impression of downward impetus, whereas Galileo wrongly believed that acceleration was an accidental and temporary effect at the beginning of fall only, an error which vitiated much of the reasoning in *De motu* and was corrected only in his later works. These differences create historical perplexities described below.

Another of Benedetti's contributions to mechanics is the description of hydrostatic pressure and the idea of a hydraulic lift, prior to Stevin's discussion of the hydrostatic paradox (1586). Benedetti also attributed winds to changes in density of air, caused by alterations of heat. In opposition to the view that clouds are held in suspension by the sun, he applied the Archimedean principle and stated that clouds seek air of density equal to their own; he also observed that bodies are heated by the sun in relation to their degree of opacity.

Benedetti published no separate work on astronomy, but his letters in the *Speculationum* show that he was an admirer of Copernicus and that he was much concerned with accuracy of tables and precise observation. His astronomical interests appear to have been astrological rather than physical and systematic, as were those of Kepler, Galileo, and Stevin. Benedetti offered a correct explanation of the ruddy color of the moon under total eclipse, however, based on refraction of sunlight in the earth's atmosphere.

Benedetti's scientific originality and versatility leave little doubt that his work afforded a basis for the overthrow of Aristotelian physics. The extent of its actual influence on others, however, presents very difficult questions. Stevin was certainly unaware of Benedetti when he published his basic contributions to mechanics and hydrostatics. He had seen Benedetti's *Speculationum* before 1605, when he published on perspective, but in that work he built more on Guido Ubaldo del Monte than on any other writer. Kepler mentioned Benedetti but once, and only in the most general terms. Willebrord Snell's attention was called to Benedetti by Stevin. The case of Galileo is the most perplexing. It is widely held that he was directly indebted to Benedetti for the ideas underlying *De motu,* but the resemblances of those ideas are easily accounted for by the Archimedean principle and the medieval impetus theory, easily accessible to both men independently, while the differences, particularly with respect to acceleration and the accumulation of impressed motion, are hard to explain if the young Galileo had the work of Benedetti before him. The absence of Benedetti's name in Galileo's books and notes, where other kindred spirits such as Gilbert and Guido Ubaldo are praised, is suggestive; much more so is the fact that Benedetti is not mentioned to or by Galileo in the vast surviving correspondence of his time. Jacopo Mazzoni has been proposed as a positive link—he was a colleague and friend of Galileo's at Pisa about 1590, and certainly knew Benedetti's work by 1597; but since Galileo left Pisa for Padua in 1592, the connection is uncertain. Benedetti appears to have remained unknown to Galileo's teacher at Pisa, Francesco Buonamico, who in 1591 published a treatise, *De motu,* of over a thousand pages. On the whole, it appears that Benedetti's *Speculationum* was not widely read by his contemporaries, despite its outstanding achievements in extending the horizons of mathematics, physics, and astronomy beyond the Peripatetic boundaries.

BIBLIOGRAPHY

I. Original Works. No collection of Benedetti's work has been published. Because the original editions are very scarce, locations of known copies not listed in the Union Catalogue are indicated by the following abbreviations: BM—British Museum; BN—Bibliothèque Nationale; BNT—Biblioteca Nazionale di Torino; ULT—University of Toronto Library.

Resolutio omnium Euclidis problematum aliorumque ad hoc necessario inventorum una tantummodo circini data apertura, per Ioannem Baptistam de Benedictis inventa (Venice, 1553), BM, BN, BNT, ULT.

Demonstratio proportionum motuum localium contra Aristotelem et omnes philosophes (Venice, 1554), first ed. in Vatican Library, 2nd ed. in Biblioteca Universitaria, Padua. First edition pirated by Jean Taisnier, *Opusculum perpetua memoria dignissimum de natura magnetis . . . Item de motu continuo, demonstratio proportionum motuum localium contra Aristotelem etc.* (Cologne, 1562; facs. repr., London, 1966). English translation by Richard Eden is in *A very necessarie and profitable Booke concerning Navigation, compiled in Latin by Joannes Taisnierus . . .* (London, 1578?), BM, Brown University Library. Both eds. repr. in C. Maccagni, *Le speculazioni giovanili "de motu" di G. B. Benedetti* (Pisa, 1967).

De gnomonum umbrarumque solarium usu liber . . . nunc primum publicae utilitati, studiosorumque commoditati in lucem aeditus (Turin, 1573), BM, BN, BNT, ULT.

De temporum emendatione opinio . . . (Turin, 1578), BM, MSS copies in BNT and Archivio di Stato, Turin. Repr. in *Speculationum,* pp. 205–210.

Consideratione di Gio. Battista Benedetti . . . d'intorno al discorso della grandezza della terra, et dell'acqua, del Eccelent. Sig. Antonio Berga . . . (Turin, 1579), BN, BNT, ULT; a Latin trans. by F. M. Vialardi is reported to be contained in Antonio Berga, *Disputatio de magnitudine terrae et aquae* (Turin, 1580).

Lettera per modo di discorso all'Ill. Sig. Bernardo Trotto intorno ad alcune nuove riprensioni et emendationi contra alli calculatori delle effemeridi . . . (Turin, 1581), BNT, Latin trans. in *Speculationum,* pp. 228–248.

Diversarum speculationum mathematicarum, et physicarum, liber (Turin, 1585), BM, BN, BNT, ULT. Reissued as *Speculationum mathematicarum, et physicarum, fertilissimus, pariterque utilissimus tractatus . . .* (Venice, 1586) and as *Speculationum liber: in quo mira subtilitate haec tractata continentur . . .* (Venice, 1599), BM, Biblioteca Marciana, Venice.

De coelo et elementis . . . (Ferrara, 1591), sometimes reported as Benedetti's, was in fact written by Giovanni Benedetto of Tirna (Orsova).

Two volumes of manuscript letters and astronomical observations by Benedetti, formerly in the Biblioteca Nazionale, Turin, were lost in 1904 in a fire that also destroyed the only known portrait of Benedetti.

Manuscript volumes reported to be privately owned in Italy are "Descrittione, uso et ragioni del triconolometro. Al serenissimo Prencipe di Piemonte. Trattato di Giovan Battista Benedetti. MDLXXVII," 94 unnumbered pages including 21 blanks; "La generale et necessaria instruttione per l'intelligentia et compositione d'ogni sorte horologij solari," 46 folio pages, unnumbered, without the name of the author but in the hand of same scribe as the above MS; and "Dechiaratione delle parti et use dell'instromento chiamato isogonio," 24 folio pages in the same hand as the foregoing.

II. SECONDARY LITERATURE. The principal monograph is Giovanni Bordiga, "Giovanni Battista Benedetti, filosofo e matematico veneziano del secolo XVI," in *Atti del Reale Istituto veneto di scienze, lettere ed arti,* **85,** pt. 2 (1925–1926), 585–754.

Apart from histories of mathematics or physics, such as those of Guillaume Libri, Kurt Lasswitz, Moritz Cantor, Rafaello Caverni, and Ernst Mach, discussions of Benedetti's work (listed chronologically) are in Emil Wohlwill, "Die Entdeckung des Beharrungsgesetzes," in *Zeitschrift für Völkerpsychologie und Sprachwissenschaft,* **14** (1885), 391–401, and *Galileo Galilei und sein Kampf* . . . (Hamburg-Leipzig, 1909), I, 111 ff.; Giovanni Vailati, "Le speculazione di Giovanni Battista Benedetti sul moto dei gravi," in *Atti dell'Accademia delle scienze di Torino,* **33** (1897–1898), 559 ff., reprinted in *Scritti di G. Vailati* (Leipzig-Florence, 1911), pp. 161–178; Pierre Duhem, *Les origines de la statique* (Paris, 1905), I, 226–235; "De l'accélération produite par une force constante," Congrès International d'Histoire des Sciences, IIIe Session (Geneva, 1906), pp. 885 ff; and *Études sur Léonard de Vinci* (Paris, 1913), III, 214 ff.

See also E. J. Dijksterhuis, *Val en Worp* (Groningen, 1924), pp. 179–190, and *The Mechanization of the World Picture* (Oxford, 1961), pp. 269–271; Alexandre Koyré, *Études galiléennes* (Paris, 1939), I, 41–54, and "Jean-Baptiste Benedetti critique d'Aristote," in *Mélanges offerts à Étienne Gilson* (Toronto–Paris, 1959), pp. 351–372, reprinted in *Études d'histoire de la pensée scientifique* (Paris, 1966), pp. 122–146, an English trans. in *Galileo, Man of Science,* ed. E. McMullin (New York, 1967); Claude Palisca, "Scientific Empiricism in Musical Thought," in *Seventeenth Century Science and the Arts* (Princeton, 1961), pp. 104 ff.; I. E. Drabkin, "Two Versions of G. B. Benedetti's *Demonstratio,*" in *Isis,* **54** (June 1963), 259–262, and "G. B. Benedetti and Galileo's *De motu,*" in *Proceedings of the Tenth International Congress of the History of Science* (Paris, 1964), I, 627–630; and C. Maccagni, "G. B. Benedetti: *De motu,*" in *Atti del Symposium Internazionale di Storia, Metodologia, Logica e Filosofia della Scienza* (Florence, 1966), pp. 53–54; "Contributi alla biobibliografia di G. B. Benedetti," in *Physis,* **9** (1967), 337–364; and *Le speculazioni "de motu" di G. B. Benedetti* (Pisa, 1967). English translations of Benedetti's most important scientific writings by I. E. Drabkin are included in *Mechanics in Sixteenth-Century Italy* (Madison, Wis., 1968).

STILLMAN DRAKE

BERGMAN, STEFAN (*b.* Czestochowa, Poland, 5 May 1895; *d.* Palo Alto, California, 6 June 1977)

Stefan Bergman was the son of the Jewish merchant Bronislaw Bergman and his wife, Tekla. He graduated from the local gymnasium in 1913 and studied in the schools of engineering in Breslau and Vienna, receiving a degree as *Diplomingenieur* in 1920.

In 1921 Bergman entered the Institute for Applied Mathematics at the University of Berlin. Richard von Mises, the founder and director of the institute, was a leading theoretician in fluid dynamics and probability, and influenced Bergman during his whole career. Bergman worked on various problems of potential theory as applied to electrical engineering, elasticity, and fluid flow. To obtain a large number of harmonic functions in space, he applied and generalized the Whittaker method to create such functions by means of integrals over analytic functions. Using algebraic-logarithmic analytic functions as generators in the integral, he created harmonic functions that are multivalued in space and have closed branch lines. This led him further to a general theory of integral operators that map arbitrary analytic functions into solutions of various partial differential equations. He devoted many years of work to this topic, producing a monograph in 1969.

The decisive influence on Bergman's scientific development came from Erhard Schmidt, who, with David Hilbert, had developed an elegant and seminal approach to the theory of integral equations with symmetric kernel. The eigenfunctions $\phi_\nu(x)$ of such equations over an interval $\langle a, b\rangle$ form an orthonormal system, that is, one has

$$\int_a^b \phi_\nu(x)\phi_\mu(x)dx = \delta_{\nu\mu} = \begin{cases} 0 \text{ if } \nu \neq \mu \\ 1 \text{ if } \nu = \mu \end{cases}.$$

Bergman generalized this concept in a very original manner. Let D be a domain in the complex z-plane ($z = x + iy$) and consider analytic functions $f(z)$ in D such that

$$\iint_D |f(z)|^2 dxdy < \infty.$$

Consider a system $\{\phi_\nu(z)\}$ of the type such that

$$\iint_D \phi_\nu(z)\overline{\phi_\mu(z)}\,dxdy = \delta_{\nu\mu}$$

and such that every $f(z)$ can be written as

$$f(z) = \sum_{\nu=1}^{\infty} a_\nu\phi_\nu(z)$$

where the series converges uniformly in each closed subdomain of D. Such a system is called complete and orthonormal.

To a given domain D there exists an infinity of possible systems of this kind, but Bergman made the surprising discovery that the combination

$$K(z,\bar{\zeta}) = \sum_{\nu=1}^{\infty} \phi_\nu(z)\overline{\phi_\nu(\zeta)}$$

converges uniformly in each closed subdomain of D and is independent of the particular system used in its construction. For each $f(z)$ we have the identity

$$f(z) = \iint_D K(z,\bar{\zeta}) f(\zeta) d\xi d\eta.$$

Therefore, Bergman called $K(z,\bar{\zeta})$ the reproducing kernel of the domain; it is now called the Bergman kernel. It has a simple covariance behavior under conformal mapping and is a very useful tool in the theory of analytic functions. Bergman's thesis in 1922 summarized his researches and led to his doctor's degree.

He soon realized that his method worked equally well when applied to analytic functions $f(z_1, z_2, \cdots, z_n)$ of n-complex variables. In the early 1920's the theory of such functions was in its initial stages, and Bergman was forced to do much pioneering work in this field. He may be considered as one of the founders of this theory, which is today an important field of research. The kernel function plays a very useful role in the theory of "pseudo-conformal" mapping that carries a domain D in the space of $z_l, \cdots, z_n$ into a domain Δ in the space $w_l, \cdots, w_n$ by the relation $w_i = f_i(z_l, \cdots, z_n)$, $i = l, \cdots, n$. Again the kernel function has the same covariance behavior, and one can construct invariants from it and introduce a metric in D that is invariant under pseudo-conformal mapping. It is a special case of an important class, called "Kähler metrics," which was much later defined to deal with Riemannian manifolds.

Several important concepts in the theory of analytic functions of n-complex variables are due to Bergman. He discovered, for example, that for a large class of domains, an analytic function in it is completely determined by its values on a relatively small part of its boundary. He called it the "distinguished boundary" of D, and it now goes by the name "Bergman-Shilov boundary." Bergman used this concept to give a generalization of the Cauchy integral formula and to represent the value of a function at an interior point of D in terms of its values on the distinguished boundary.

In 1930 Bergman became a *Privatdozent* at the University of Berlin with a habilitation thesis on the behavior of the kernel function on the boundary of its domain. In 1933 the Nazi seizure of power forced him out of his position and out of Germany. From 1934 to 1937 Bergman taught in Russia (Tomsk, 1934–1936; Tbilisi, 1936–1937). From 1937 to 1939 he worked at the Institut Henri Poincaré in Paris, where he wrote a two-volume monograph on the kernel function and its applications in complex analysis.

Just before the outbreak of World War II, Bergman moved to the United States. He taught at MIT, Yeshiva College, and Brown University. In 1945 he joined his old teacher and friend von Mises at Harvard Graduate School of Engineering. He worked on various problems of fluid dynamics, using his methods on orthonormal developments, on integral operators, and on functions of several complex variables.

He settled into a more leisurely life. In 1950 he married Adele Adlersberg. He found time to summarize his results on the kernel function in a monograph. He started a collaboration with M. Schiffer, who has shown the close connection of the kernel function of a plane domain with its harmonic Green's function. They extended the kernel function concept to the case of elliptic partial differential equations. One orthonormalizes solutions of such equations in an appropriate metric, forms the kernel function in an analogous way, and constructs from it the fundamental solutions of the equation for the given domain. This was summarized in *Kernel Functions and Elliptic Differential Equations in Mathematical Physics* (1953). In 1952 Bergman accepted a position as professor at Stanford University, where he taught and did active research until his death.

BIBLIOGRAPHY

I. Original Works. Bergman's writings are given in *Poggendorff.* Important books are *Sur les fonctions orthogonales de plusieurs variables complexes avec les applications à la théorie des fonctions analytiques* (Paris, 1947); *Sur la fonction-noyau d'un domaine et ses applications dans la théorie des transformations pseudo-conformes* (Paris, 1948); *Kernel Functions and Elliptic Differential Equations in Mathematical Physics* (New York, 1953), with M. Schiffer; *Integral Operators in the Theory of Linear Partial Differential Equations*, 2nd rev. ed. (New York, 1969); and *The Kernel Function and Conformal Mapping*, 2nd rev. ed. (Providence, R.I., 1970).

II. Secondary Literature. Obituaries are in *Applicable Analysis*, **8**, no. 3 (1979), 195–199 (by Menahem Schiffer and Hans Samelson); and *Annales polonici mathematici*, **39** (1981), 5–9 (by M. M. Schiffer).

M. M. Schiffer

BERNAYS, PAUL ISAAC (*b.* London, England, 17 October 1888; *d.* Zurich, Switzerland, 18 September 1977)

Bernays came from a distinguished German-Jewish family of scholars and businessmen. His great-grandfather, Isaac ben Jacob Bernays, chief rabbi of Hamburg, was known for both strict Orthodox views and modern educational ideas. His grandfather, Louis Bernays, a merchant, traveled widely before helping to found the Jewish community in Zurich, while his great-uncle, Jacob Bernays, was a *Privatdozent* at the University of Bonn. In 1887 his father, Julius Bernays, a businessman, married Sara Brecher, who had likewise descended from Isaac Bernays. Their first child, Paul, born in London as a Swiss citizen and a *Bürger* of Zurich, was followed by a brother and three sisters.

After living in Paris for a time, the family settled in Berlin, where Paul Bernays had what he later described as a happy childhood. From 1895 to 1907 he attended the Köllnisches Gymnasium in Berlin. At an early age his talent as a pianist attracted attention, and he began to try his hand at composing. While at school, he added to his musical interests a growing attraction to ancient languages and mathematics. At eighteen, after hesitating between a career in music and one in mathematics, he opted for engineering (which his parents regarded as an eminently practical way to use his mathematical talent) and spent the summer semester of 1907 studying that subject at the Technische Hochschule in Charlottenburg. This experience made it clear to him that his future lay in pure mathematics rather than in its applications. Consequently, in the winter he transferred to the University of Berlin. For the next two years he studied there the three subjects of central interest to him: mathematics, mainly under Issai Schur, Edmund Landau (including lectures on set theory), Leo Frobenius, and Friedrich H. Schottky; philosophy under Alois Riehl, Carl Stumpf, and Ernst Cassirer; and physics under Max K. E. L. Planck. Then, from 1910 to 1912, he attended lectures at Göttingen, chiefly by David Hilbert, Landau, Hermann Weyl, and Felix Klein in mathematics; by Woldemar Voigt and Max Born in physics; and by Leonard Nelson in philosophy. Göttingen would always remain his spiritual home.

In 1912 he received his doctorate at Göttingen with a thesis, supervised by Landau, on the analytic number theory of binary quadratic forms. After his *Habilitationsschrift* on modular elliptic functions was accepted at the University of Zurich the following year, he served as assistant to Ernst F. F. Zermelo (who was then professor there) and as a *Privatdozent* until the spring of 1919. When Zermelo left the University of Zurich in 1916 (both for reasons of health and because of disagreements with the university), Bernays took over his courses. Although Bernays lectured primarily on topics in analysis, during his last year in Zurich (probably influenced by Hilbert), he gave courses on the foundations of geometry and on set theory. While at Zurich, he became both a friend and a colleague of Pólya, had conversations with Einstein, and was received socially at the home of Hermann Weyl.

When Hilbert came to Zurich to lecture on "Axiomatisches Denken" in the fall of 1917, he invited Bernays to come to Göttingen as his assistant and to help him to resume investigations of the foundations of arithmetic. During 1918 Bernays quickly wrote for Göttingen a second *Habilitationsschrift*, establishing in it the completeness of propositional logic. But he continued to teach at Zurich during both the summer semester and the winter semester of 1918. When he moved to Göttingen in 1919, Bernays received the *venia legendi*, which permitted him to lecture. He served as a *Privatdozent* until he was made untenured extraordinary professor in March 1922. As at Zurich, he lectured chiefly on topics in analysis, but, beginning in 1922, he also gave courses on the foundations of geometry and (jointly with Hilbert) on the foundations of arithmetic. During the winter semester of the year 1929–1930 he first lectured on mathematical logic, giving at the end a version of his axiomatization for set theory. Believing that he learned better orally than through reading, he attended lectures by Emmy Noether, van der Waerden, and Herglotz. During the academic holidays he traveled regularly to Berlin to visit his family. His father died in 1916.

On 28 April 1933 the dean at Göttingen ordered Bernays, as a "non-Aryan," to stop teaching pending a final decision on his official status by the minister of education. In August he was relieved of his position as an assistant at the Mathematical Institute, and a month later his right to teach was officially withdrawn by the minister. For six months during this period Hilbert employed Bernays privately as his assistant. Finally Bernays and his family, having remained Swiss citizens, returned to Zurich.

From time to time, beginning with the summer semester of 1934, Bernays held a temporary teaching position at the Eidgenössische Technische Hochschule (E.T.H.) in Zurich. Meanwhile, he visited the Institute for Advanced Study at Princeton during the academic year 1935–1936 (as he was to do again during the academic year 1959–1960). In October 1939 the E.T.H. granted him the *venia legendi* for four years, renewing it in 1943. At last, in October 1945, he received a half-time appointment as extraordinary professor at the E.T.H., a position that he continued to hold until 1959, when he became professor emeritus. During the spring semester of 1956, and again during 1961 and 1965, he was visiting professor at the University of Pennsylvania and gave lectures at several American universities. Although some mathematicians thought that the E.T.H. had not granted Bernays a position commensurate with his abilities, he himself always remained grateful to the E.T.H. for its support under difficult circumstances.

Bernays, who remained mathematically active until the end of his life, held a variety of positions: corresponding member in the Academy of Sciences of Brussels and in that of Norway, president of the International Academy of the Philosophy of Science, and honorary chairman of the German Society for Mathematical Logic and Foundational Research in the Exact Sciences. In addition he served on the editorial board of *Dialectica* and was a coeditor for both the *Journal of Symbolic Logic* and *Archiv für mathematische Logik und Grundlagenforschung*. In 1976 he received an honorary doctorate from the University of Munich for his work in proof theory and set theory. After a brief illness he died of a heart condition at the age of eighty-eight.

Bernays' earliest publications, beginning in 1910, were devoted to philosophy. They showed the direct influence of his teacher Leonard Nelson, head of the neo-Friesian school, which had revived the philosophy of Jacob Fries and extended it to ethics. Except for his doctoral thesis and his Zurich *Habilitationsschrift*, Bernays published no mathematical articles until 1918. His attempt during that period to extend the special theory of relativity was preempted when Einstein introduced general relativity.

Then, answering Hilbert's call to Göttingen to collaborate on foundational (especially proof-theoretic) questions, Bernays began the work in mathematical logic that molded his career. The first product was his 1918 *Habilitationsschrift*, "Beiträge zur axiomatischen Behandlung des Logik-Kalküls," which was devoted to the metamathematics of the propositional calculus (the heir of George Boole's logic) and was a contribution to Hilbert's program. In contrast to most earlier logicians, Bernays had a firm grasp of the difference between syntax and semantics, and he distinguished carefully between provable formulas and valid formulas. By establishing the completeness theorem for propositional logic, he showed these two notions to be equivalent in that context. Further, he gave a partial solution to Hilbert's decision problem (*Entscheidungsproblem*) by stating a decision procedure for validity in this part of logic. He also demonstrated that one of the axioms for propositional logic in *Principia Mathematics* was redundant while the four remaining axioms were independent. In these independence proofs, many-valued logic was utilized for the first time. Although in 1926 his *Habilitationsschrift* of 1918 was published in part, Post had independently published the same completeness result in 1921—with the effect that, outside the Hilbert school, Post was usually given credit for it.

The most enduring achievement of the collaboration between Hilbert and Bernays was their *Grundlagen der Mathematik*, published in two volumes in 1934 and 1939, which for decades remained the standard work on proof theory. It appears that, while the overall approach was due to Hilbert, the specific contents and the actual writing came from Bernays. There Bernays developed the ε-calculus and the ε-theorems for eliminating quantifiers so as to give a decision procedure for various theories. Moreover, he provided the first detailed proof of Gödel's second incompleteness theorem and supplied the first correct proof for Herbrand's theorem (Herbrand's proof was faulty). Finally, he demonstrated a proof-theoretic version of Gödel's completeness theorem for first-order logic.

In 1937, when Bernays published the first of his seven-part article on his axiomatization of set theory, he pointed out that his aim was to modify von Neumann's axiom system (based on function and argument rather than on set and membership) so as to make it resemble more closely Zermelo's original system, and thereby to use some of the set-theoretic concepts of Schröder and Whitehead-Russell, while expressing the theory in first-order logic. Bernays chose his groups of axioms in order to render them analogous, whenever possible, to Hilbert's (1899) groups of axioms for geometry. As Hilbert had done, Bernays explored (in 1941 and 1942) the consequences of various axioms within a group, and showed which of his axioms were needed to develop number theory on the one hand and analysis (up to Lebesgue measure) on the other. While doing so, he formulated the principle of dependent choices (the form of the axiom of choice sufficient for analysis), later independently rediscovered by Tarski. In the last two sections (published in 1948 and 1954) he investigated the independence of his axioms, mainly by using number-theoretic models in the spirit of Ackermann. Bernays' axiom system, slightly modified by Gödel, is now generally known as Bernays-Gödel set theory.

"In philosophy," Bernays wrote in his autobiography about his return to Zurich in 1934, "I came into closer contact with Ferdinand Gonseth. . . . Because of my interior dialogues on the philosophy of Kant, Fries, and Nelson, I had come very close to Gonseth's views, and so I joined his school of philosophy." Bernays was sympathetic, in particular, to Gonseth's "open philosophy," with its emphasis on dialogue between opposing viewpoints, and encouraged tolerance between diverse foundational positions (such as Platonism and intuitionism). In 1946 Bernays, Gonseth, and Karl Popper founded the Internationale Gesellschaft zur Pflege der Logik und Philosophie der Wissenschaft, which started the journal *Dialectica* the following year. Bernays' philosophical writings, so refreshingly undogmatic, are models of clarity.

Bernays directed a number of doctoral theses. At Göttingen he was involved with Haskell Curry's and Gerhard Gentzen's, and even supervised Saunders Mac Lane's (1934), though Weyl conducted Mac Lane's oral examination since the Nazis had already dismissed Bernays. At the E.T.H. in Zurich he directed theses by Martin Altwegg (1948), Hugh Ribeiro (1949), J. Richard Büchi (1950), Walter Strickler (1955), Erwin Engeler (1958), and Hersz Wermus (1961), as well as serving as *Korreferent* for six other dissertations.

Bernays' precise contributions are often difficult to ascertain because of his preference for collaboration (especially with Hilbert) and his modesty. Engeler, his former student, described him as a "great scholar and kind man." Yet Hilbert's 1922 letter recommending Bernays for an extraordinary professorship at Göttingen remains the most fitting tribute to his life's work:

> Bernays' publications extend over the most diverse fields of mathematics . . . [and] are all marked by thoroughness and reliability. . . . He is distinguished by a deep-seated love for science as well as a trustworthy character and nobility of thought, and is highly valued by everyone. In all matters concerning foundational questions in mathematics, he is the most knowledgeable expert and, especially for me, the most valuable and productive colleague.

BIBLIOGRAPHY

I. ORIGINAL WORKS. A bibliography of Bernays' publications up to 1976 can be found in Gert H. Müller, ed., *Sets and Classes: On the Work by Paul Bernays* (New York, 1976) and is supplemented in Müller's 1981 article mentioned below. The same book, which contains a photo of Bernays, reprints his seven-part article giving his axiom system for set theory and includes an English translation of his 1961 article on strong axioms of infinity. Fourteen of his philosophical essays (eight of them on logic or foundational questions) are reprinted in his *Abhandlungen zur Philosophie der Mathematik* (Darmstadt, 1976). He also edited the later editions of David Hilbert's *Grundlagen der Geometrie* (Stuttgart, 1977) and was an editor of Leonard Nelson's *Gesammelte Schriften*.

The *Wissenschaftshistorische Sammlungen* at the Eidgenössische Technische Hochschule in Zurich has a rich collection of material on Bernays, including many of his unpublished lectures and a voluminous correspondence, as well as his lecture notes for courses (generally in Gabelsberger shorthand). Some of Bernays' letters and manuscripts are located at the *Niedersächsische Staats- und Universitätsbibliotek* in Göttingen.

II. SECONDARY LITERATURE. Bernays wrote a brief autobiography for the Müller volume as well as the *Lebenslauf* at the end of his 1912 dissertation. Obituaries are by Ernst Specker and Erwin Engeler, in *Neue Zürcher Zeitung* (26 September 1977); and Gert H. Müller, in the *Mathematical Intelligencer*, **1** (1978), 27–28. More extensive discussions of his life and work can be found in Erwin Engeler, "Zum logischen Werk von Paul Bernays," in *Dialectica*, **32** (1978), 191–200; Abraham Fraenkel, "Paul Bernays and die Begründung der Mengenlehre," in *Dialectica*, **12** (1958), 274–279; Henri Lauener, "Wissenschaftstheorie in der Schweiz," and "Paul Bernays (1888–1977)," in *Zeitschrift für Allgemeine Wissenschaftstheorie*, **2**, no. 2 (1971), 294–299, and **9**, no. 1 (1978), 13–20 Gert H. Müller, "Framingham Mathematics," in *Epistemologia*, **4** (1981), 253–285; Andrés R. Raggio, "Die Rolle der Analogie in Bernays' Philosophie der Mathematik," in *Dialectica*, **32** (1978), 201–207; Ernst Specker, "Paul Bernays," in Maurice Boffa *et al.*, eds., *Logic Colloquium '78* (1979), 381–389; Gaisi Takeuti, "Work of Paul Bernays and Kurt Gödel," in L. Jonathan Cohen *et al.*, eds., *Logic, Methodology, and Philosophy of Science*, VI (1982), 77–85.

GREGORY H. MOORE

BERNOULLI, DANIEL (*b.* Groningen, Netherlands, 8 February 1700; *d.* Basel, Switzerland, 17 March 1782)

Life. Daniel Bernoulli was the second son of Johann I Bernoulli and Dorothea Falkner, daughter of the patrician Daniel Falkner. At the time of Bernoulli's birth his father was professor in Groningen, but he returned to Basel in 1705 to occupy the chair of Greek. Instead, he took over the chair of mathematics, which had been made vacant by the death of his brother Jakob (Jacques) I. In 1713 Daniel began to study philosophy and logic, passed his baccalaureate in 1715, and obtained his master's degree in 1716. During this period he was taught mathematics by his father and, especially, by his older brother Nikolaus II. An attempt to place young Daniel as a commercial apprentice failed, and he was allowed to study medicine—first in Basel, then in Heidelberg (1718) and Strasbourg (1719). In 1720 he returned to Basel, where he obtained his doctorate in 1721 with a dissertation entitled *De respiratione* (1). That same year he applied for the then vacant professorship in anatomy and botany (2), but the drawing of the lot went against him. Bad luck also cost him the chair of logic (3). In 1723 he journeyed to Venice, whence his brother Nikolaus had just departed and continued his studies in practical medicine under Pietro Antonio Michelotti. A severe illness prevented him from realizing his plan to work with G. B. Morgagni in Padua.

In 1724 Bernoulli published his *Exercitationes mathematicae* (4) in Venice, which attracted so much attention that he was called to the St. Petersburg Academy. He returned to Basel in 1725 and declared his readiness to go to the Russian capital with Nikolaus. That same year, he won the prize awarded by the Paris Academy, the first of the ten he was to gain. Bernoulli's stay in St. Petersburg was marred by the sudden death of his beloved brother and by the rigorous climate, and he applied three times for a professorship in Basel, but in vain. Finally, in 1732, he was able to obtain the chair of anatomy and botany there.

His Petersburg years (1725–1733 [after 1727 he worked with Euler]) appear to have been Bernoulli's most creative period. During these years he outlined the *Hydrodynamica* and completed his first important work on oscillations (23) and an original treatise on the theory of probability (22). In 1733 he returned to Basel in the company of his younger brother Johann II, after a long detour via Danzig, Hamburg, and Holland, combined with a stay of several weeks in Paris. Everywhere he went, scholars received him most cordially.

Although largely occupied with his lectures in medicine, Bernoulli continued to publish in mathematics and mechanics, which interested him much more intensely. His principal work, the *Hydrodynamica* (31), had been completed as early as 1734 but was not published until 1738. About the same time his father published *Hydraulica,* predated to 1732.[1] This unjustifiable attempt to insure priority for himself was one among many instances that exhibited Johann I Bernoulli's antagonism toward his second son.

In 1743 Daniel Bernoulli was able to exchange his lectures in botany for those in physiology, which were more to his liking. Finally, in 1750, he obtained the chair of physics, which was his by rights. For almost thirty years (until 1776) he delivered his lectures in physics, which were enlivened by impressive experiments and attended by numerous listeners. He was buried in the Peterskirche, not far from his apartment in the Kleine Engelhof.

Works. Daniel Bernoulli's works include writings on medicine, mathematics, and the natural sciences, especially mechanics. His works in these different areas were usually conceived independently of each other, even when simultaneous. As a consequence it is legitimate to distinguish them by subject matter and to consider them in chronological order within each subject.

Medicine. Bernoulli saw himself, against his inclination, limited to the field of medicine. Thus the future physicist promptly turned his interest to the mechanical aspects of physiology.[2] In his inaugural dissertation of 1721 (1), as a typical iatrophysicist under the decisive influence of Borelli and Johann Bernoulli, he furnished a comprehensive review of the mechanics of breathing. During the same year he applied for the then vacant chair of anatomy and botany, presenting pertinent theses (2) in support of his candidacy. In St. Petersburg in 1728 he published a strictly mechanical theory of muscular contraction (10), which disregarded the hypothesis of fermentation in the blood corpuscles assumed by Borelli and Johann Bernoulli. That same year he furnished a beautifully clear contribution to the determination of the shape and the location of the entrance of the optic nerve into the bulbus, or blind spot (11). Also of great importance is a lecture on the computation of the mechanical work done by the heart (*vis cordis*). Bernoulli gave this address in 1737 at the graduation exercises of two candidates in medicine, and it was thus that he first developed a correct method for such calculations. Because of its lasting significance, this lecture was published with its German translation in 1941 (75). Contributions to the physiology of work, more particularly to the determination of the maximum work that a man can perform, are found in *Hydrodynamica* (sec. 9) and the prize-winning treatise of 1753 (47). (In this context, Bernoulli meant by "maximum work" the quantity that a man could do over a sustained period of time, e.g., a working day.)

Mathematics. Medical research, however, did not divert Bernoulli from his primary interest, the mathematical sciences. This is evidenced by the publication in 1724 of his *Exercitationes mathematicae,* which he wrote during his medical studies in Italy. This treatise combined four separate works dealing, respectively, with the game of faro, the outflow of water from the openings of containers, Riccati's differential equation, and the lunulae (figures bounded by two circular arcs). Ultimately, Bernoulli's talent proved to lie primarily in physics, mechanics, and technology, but his mathematical treatises originated partly from external circumstances (Riccati's differential equation) and partly from applied mathematics (recurrent series, mathematics of probability).

The discussions on Jacopo Riccati's differential equation were initiated in 1724 by the problem presented by Riccati in the *Supplementa* to the *Acta eruditorum.* Immediately thereafter Daniel Bernoulli offered a solution in the form of an anagram (5). In the two following papers, published in the *Acta eruditorum* (6, 7), as well as in the *Exercitationes mathematicae,* Bernoulli demonstrated that Riccati's special differential equation $ax^n\,dx + u^2\,dx = b\,du$ could be integrated through separation of the variables for the values $n = -4c/(2c \pm 1)$, where c takes on all integral values—positive, negative, and zero.

In the first part of the *Exercitationes* (4), dealing with faro, Bernoulli furnished data on recurrent series that later proved to have no practical application. According to De Moivre, these series result from the generative fraction

$$\frac{a + bz + cz^2 + \cdots + rz^m}{1 - \alpha z - \beta z^2 - \cdots - \sigma z^n}.$$

Bernoulli made use of these series in (16) for the approximate calculation of the roots of algebraic equations. For this purpose, the fraction is broken up into partial fractions, which are then developed into power series yielding, in the case of simple roots $1/p$, $1/q$, and so on, the general term

$$P = (Ap^n + Bq^n + \cdots)z^n$$

and the following member

$$Q = (Ap^{n+1} + Bq^{n+1} \cdots)z^{n+1}.$$

If p is considerably larger than $q \cdots$, etc., then, for sufficiently large n, P is approximated by Ap^n, Q by Ap^{n+1}, and thus the smallest root, $1/p$, is approximated by P/Q. In treatise (20) this method is applied to infinite power series.

Divergent sine and cosine series are treated by Bernoulli in three papers (62, 64, 66). The starting point is the thesis formulated by Leibniz and Euler that the equation $1 - 1 + 1 - 1 \cdots = 1/2$ is valid, which they base on the equation $1/(1 + x) = 1 - x + x^2 \pm \cdots$ for $x = 1$ and by observing that the arithmetic mean of the two possible partial sums of the series equals $1/2$. In reality, however, this divergent series can be summed to many values, depending on the expression from which it is derived. On the other hand, it can be demonstrated that the mean-value method for the equations found by Euler,

$$\sum_{n=1}^{\infty} \cos nx = -\frac{1}{2}$$

and

$$\sum_{n=1}^{\infty} \sin nx = \frac{1}{2}\frac{\sin x}{1 - \cos x} = \frac{1}{2}\cot\frac{1}{2}x,$$

leads to a correct result. For if x is commensurable with π, but not a multiple of π, then the terms of these series for a definite p and for each n satisfy the conditions $a_{n+p} = a_n$ and $a_1 + a_2 + a_3 + \cdots + a_p = 0$. For this case, according to the Leibniz-Bernoulli rule, the sum of the series $\Sigma_1^\infty a_n$ becomes equal to the arithmetic mean of the values a_1, $a_1 + a_2$, $a_1 + a_2 + a_3$, $\cdots a_1 + a_2 + a_3 + \cdots + a_p$.

Interestingly, in (64) the integration of the above cosine series, with application of Leibniz' series for $\pi/2$, yields the convergent series:

$$\sin x + \frac{1}{2}\sin 2x + \frac{1}{3}\sin 3x + \cdots = \frac{\pi - x}{2}.$$

In (66) Bernoulli let the formulas derived by Bossut[3] for the sums of the finite sine and/or cosine series n extend to the infinite. He assigned the value zero to the corresponding $\cos \infty x$ and $\sin \infty x$ and thereby obtained the correct sums.

In his later years Bernoulli contributed two additional papers (70, 71) to the theory of the infinite continued fractions.

Rational mechanics. In order to appreciate Daniel Bernoulli's contributions to mechanics, one must consider the state of this branch of science in the first half of the eighteenth century. Newton's great work was already available but could be rendered fruitful only by means of Leibniz' calculus. Collaterally there appeared Jakob Hermann's *Phoronomia* (1716), a sort of textbook on the mechanics of solids and liquids that used only the formal geometrical method. Euler's excellent *Mechanica* (1736) dealt only with the mechanics of particles. The first theory on the movement of rigid bodies was published by Euler in 1765. The fields of oscillations of rigid bodies and the mechanics of flexible and elastic bodies were new areas that Daniel Bernoulli and Euler dominated for many years.

In his earliest publication in mechanics (9), Bernoulli attempted to prove the principle of the parallelogram of forces on the basis of certain cases, assumed to be self-evident, by means of a series of purely logical extensions; this was in contrast with Newton and Varignon, who attempted to derive this principle from the composition of velocities and accelerations. Like all attempts at logical derivation, Bernoulli's was circular, and today the principle of the parallelogram of forces is considered an axiom. This was one of the rare instances when Bernoulli discussed the basic principles of mechanics. Generally he took for granted the principles established by Newton; only in cosmology or astronomy (gravity) and magnetism was he unable to break away completely from a modified vortex theory of subtle matter propounded by Descartes and Huygens. The deduction of gravity from the rotation of the subtle matter can be found in (79) and (31, ch. 11) and the explanation of magnetism in (41).

Treatise (13), inspired by Johann I Bernoulli's reports, is a contribution to the theory of rotating bodies, which at that time, considering the state of the dynamics of rigid bodies, was no trivial subject. The starting point was the simple case of a system consisting of two rigidly connected bodies rotating around a fixed axis. By means of geometric-mechanical considerations based on Huygens, Bernoulli solved a number of pertinent problems. Let us mention here only a special case of König's theorem (1751), derived by formal geometrical means. Written analytically, it states that

$$m_1v_1^2 + m_2v_2^2 = (m_1 + m_2)V^2 + m_1v_1'^2 + m_2v_2'^2,$$

where v_1 and v_2 represent velocities in a fixed system, V the velocity of the center of gravity, and v_1' and v_2' the velocities around the center of gravity.

The determination of a movement imparted to a body by an eccentric thrust and the calculation of the center of instantaneous rotation were accomplished by Bernoulli in 1737 (27). At his invitation Euler took up the problem simultaneously, with similar results. In this problem, Bernoulli limited himself to the simplest case, that involving rigid, infinitely thin rods. The motion caused by an impact on elastic rods was dealt with only much later (61).

The principle of areas and an extended version of the principle concerning the conservation of live force, both of which furnished integrals of Newton's basic equations, were published by Bernoulli, probably with Euler's assistance, in the *Berlin Mémoires* in 1745 and 1748 (40, 43). The principle of areas (40) was used and clearly formulated almost simultaneously by Bernoulli and Euler in their treatments of the problem involving the movement of a tube rotating around a fixed point and containing freely moving bodies.

The principle of conservation of live force (43) was developed by Bernoulli not only—as had been done before him—for the movements within a field of uniform gravity or within a field of one or several fixed centers of force, but also for a system of mobile, mutually attracting mass points. For example, given three centers with the masses m_1, m_2, m_3, whose mutual distances change from initial a, b, c, to x, y, z, Bernoulli finds that if the gravity constant equals ρ^2/μ for the difference of live forces,

$$\sum_{i=1}^{3} (m_iv_i^2 - m_iv_{io}^2) = 2\rho^2/\mu[m_1m_2(1/x - 1/a) + m_1m_3(1/y - 1/b) + m_2m_3(1/z - 1/c)].$$

Most probably this is the first time that the double sum of m_hm_k/r_{hk} appears. However, the force function for conservative systems was first discovered by Lagrange.

Bernoulli also investigated problems of friction of solid bodies (36, 57, 60). In his first such paper (36) he studied the movement of a uniformly heavy sphere rolling down an inclined plane and calculated the inclination at which the pure rotation changes into a motion composed of a rotatory and a sliding part.

The main problem of (60) consists in determining the progressive and rotatory motion of a uniformly heavy rod pressing upon a rough surface while a force oblique to the axis of the rod acts upon the rod.

A group of papers (14, 18, 21) dealing with the movement of solid bodies in a resisting medium is based on the presentation given by Newton in the *Principia.* The first two papers (14) deal with a rectilinear motion, the three subsequent ones (18, 21) with movement along a curve (pendulum swing). Here Bernoulli started with the usual premise that the resistance is largely proportional to the square of the velocity. At the same time he denied Newton's affirmation of a partial linear relation between resistance and velocity, but considered as probable the assumption that part of the resistance, at least for viscous fluids, is proportional to time (i.e., independent of speed). The value of these five papers rests primarily on their consistent analytical presentation and on the treatment of certain special problems.

Hydrodynamics.[4] Traditionally, Bernoulli's fame rests on his *Hydrodynamica* (31)—a term he himself introduced. The first attempt at solving the problem of outflow as presented in the *Exercitationes mathematicae* was conceived in accordance with the concepts of the time, and did little to advance them.

Essentially it contained a controversy with Jacopo Riccati over Newton's two different views on the force of a liquid issuing from an opening. But as early as 1727 Bernoulli succeeded in breaking through to an accurate calculation of the problem (12). Further progress was represented by the published experiments on the pressure exerted on the walls of a tube by a fluid flowing through it (19). In 1733 Bernoulli left behind in St. Petersburg a draft of the *Hydrodynamica* that agrees extensively in substance although not in form with the final version. Only the thirteenth chapter of the definitive work is missing (82).

The treatise opens with an interesting history of hydraulics, followed by a brief presentation of hydrostatics. The following three chapters contain formulas for velocity, duration, and quantity of fluid flowing out of the opening of a container. The author treats both the case of a falling level of the residual fluid and that of a constant level in the reservoir, and takes into consideration the starting process (nonstationary flow) and radial contraction of the stream. Bernoulli based these deductions on the principle of the conservation of live force or, as he says, the equality of the *descensus actualis* (actual descent) and *ascensus potentialis* (potential ascent), whereby these physical magnitudes, which pertain to the center of gravity, are obtained from the former through division by the mass of water in the container. If we equate the changes in *ascensus potentialis* and *descensus actualis* resulting from the water outflow, we obtain, in the case of a dropping water level, a linear differential equation. The kinematic principle used was the hypothesis of the parallel cross sections, which states that all particles of the liquid in a plane vertical to the flow have the same velocity, and that this velocity is inversely proportional to the cross section (principle of continuity).

Chapter 7 deals with the oscillations of the water in a tube immersed in a water tank and considers mainly the energy loss. Many years later Borda resumed these investigations, but arrived at another formula for the loss.

Chapter 9 contains a theory of machinery, lifting devices, pumps, and such, and their performance, as well as an extensive theory of the screw of Archimedes. A spiral pump related to the latter was discussed by Bernoulli much later (65). A theory of windmill sails concludes the chapter.

Chapter 10 is devoted to the properties and motions of "elastic fluids" (i.e., gases), and its main importance lies in its sketch of a "kinetic gas theory," which enabled Bernoulli to explain the basic gas laws and to anticipate—in incomplete form—Van der Waals' equation of state, which was developed some hundred years later. Further on, Bernoulli examined the pressure conditions in the atmosphere, established a formula for relating pressure to altitude, provided a formula for the total refraction of light rays from various stellar heights, and was the first to derive a formula for the flow velocity of air streaming from a small opening.

Chapter 12 contains the somewhat questionable derivation of a rather unusual form of the so-called Bernoulli equation for stationary currents. For the wall pressure p in a horizontal tube, connected to an infinitely wide container filled with water to the level a and having the cross section n and an outlet with the cross section 1, he determined the expression $p = [(n^2 - 1)/n^2]a$. Since $a/n^2 \sim u^2$ represents the height from which a body must fall to obtain the velocity u at the point observed, that expression becomes the equation $p + u^2 = a =$ const. More generally, for a current in a tube of any shape and inclination, u^2 must equal A/n^2, A or a being the distances between water surface and discharge opening or any cross section n. We then obtain the equation $p + A/n^2 = a$, and—with $A - z = a$ ($z =$ distance between n and opening)—the term $p + z + u^2 = A =$ const. for the stationary current. Because of the system of measures used by Bernoulli, the constant factors have values other than those customarily used.

Chapter 13 is concerned with the calculation of the force of reaction of a laterally discharged fluid jet as well as with the determination of its pressure upon a facing plate. With the aid of the impulse theorem, Bernoulli proved that both pressures p are equal to the weight of the cylinder of water whose base equals the area n of the opening for the discharge and whose length is double the height a of the water. It is thus $p = 2\ gan = nu^2$. In contrast, Johann I Bernoulli advocated throughout his life the erroneous assumption of a cylinder length equal to the height of the water. A complicated calculation of the pressure of a water jet on an inclined plate is contained in (26). Toward the end of chapter 13 Daniel Bernoulli discusses the question of whether the traditional propelling forces of sail and oar could be replaced by such a force of reaction. This principle was converted to practice only many years later.

The weaknesses in the deduction of the so-called Bernoulli equation and Daniel's incomplete concepts of internal pressure can only be mentioned here. In this respect, Johann Bernoulli's *Hydraulica* represents a certain progress, which in turn inspired Euler in his work on hydrodynamics.

Vibrating systems. From 1728, Bernoulli and Euler dominated the mechanics of flexible and elastic bodies,[5] in that year deriving the equilibrium curves for these bodies. In the first part of (15) Bernoulli determined the shape that a perfectly flexible thread assumes when acted upon by forces of which one component is vertical to the curve and the other is parallel to a given direction. Thus, in one stroke he derived the entire series of such curves as the velaria, lintearia, catenaria, etc.

More original was the determination of the curvature of a horizontal elastic band fixed at one end—a problem simultaneously undertaken by Euler. Bernoulli showed that the total moment of a uniform band around point s, by virtue of the weight P at its free end and of its own weight p acting on the center of gravity, relates to the curvature radius R by means of the equation

$$Px + \frac{p}{l}\int s\,dx = \frac{m}{R},$$

whereby the arc length s and the abscissa x are to be taken starting from the free end, with m being the modulus of bending and l the length of the string. A case involving a variable density and an optionally directed final load is quite possible.

When he departed from St. Petersburg in 1733, Bernoulli left behind one of his finest works (23), ready for the printer. Here, for the first time, he defined the "simple modes" and the frequencies of oscillation of a system with more than one degree of freedom, the points of which pass their positions of equilibrium at the same time. The inspiration for this work must have been the reports made by Johann I, toward the end of 1727, on treatment of a similar problem. In the first part of the treatise, Daniel Bernoulli discussed an arrangement consisting of a hanging rope loaded with several bodies, determined their amplitude rates and frequencies, and found that the number of simple oscillations equals the number of bodies (i.e., the degrees of freedom).

For a uniform, free-hanging rope of length l he found the displacement, y, of the oscillations at distance x from the lower end by means of the equation

$$y = AJ_o\left(2\sqrt{\frac{x}{\alpha}}\right),$$

where α has to be determined from the equation $J_o\left(2\sqrt{\frac{l}{\alpha}}\right) = 0$ and J_o is the first appearance of Bessel's function. It shows that α is the length of the simple pendulum of equal frequency. The above equation has an infinite number of real roots. Thus the rope can perform an infinite number of small oscillations with the frequencies $\nu = \frac{1}{2\pi}\sqrt{g/\alpha}$. These theorems were demonstrated in (25) on the basis of a principle that is equivalent to that subsequently named after d'Alembert.

Immediately following Bernoulli's departure from St. Petersburg, there began between him and Euler one of the most interesting scientific correspondences of that time. In its course, Bernoulli communicated much important information from which Euler, through his analytical gifts and tremendous capacity for work, was able to profit within a short time.

The above results were corroborated by Bernoulli and Euler through additional examples. Thus Bernoulli, in extending paper (30), investigated small vibrations of a plate immersed in water (32) and those of a rod suspended from a flexible thread (34). Both works stress the difference between simple and composite vibrations. He investigated only the former, however, for composite vibrations ultimately change into the slower ones.

The following two papers (37, 38), dating from 1741–1743, deal with the transversal vibrations of elastic strings, with (37) discussing the motion of a horizontal rod of length l, fastened at one end to a vertical wall. In order to derive the vibration equation, whose form he had known since 1735 (35), Bernoulli used the relation between curvature and moment, as detailed in (15): $m/R = M$. The resulting differential equation is $f^4\,d^4y = y\,dx^4$, where y becomes the amplitude at distance x from the band end, and $f^4 = m^4L/g$, if L is the length of the simple pendulum isochronal with the band vibrations and g is the load per unit of length. Bernoulli used the solution $y = y(x/f)$ through infinite series as well as in closed expression by means of exponential and trigonometric functions. The series of the roots l/f is an example of nonharmonic oscillations. In (38) Bernoulli discusses the differential equation in the case of free ends.

Treatise (45), on vibrating strings, represented a reaction to the publications of d'Alembert and Euler, who calculated the form of the vibrating string from the partial differential equation

$$\partial^2y/\partial t^2 = c^2\partial^2y/\partial x^2.$$

They thus moved the inference from the finite to the infinite up into the hypothesis, whereas Bernoulli always made this transition without thinking about it in the final, completed formula.

His deliberations in (45) started from the assumption that the single vibrations of a string of length a were furnished by $y = \alpha_n \sin n\pi x/a$ (n = any inte-

BERNOULLI, D.

gral number). From this and from his previous deliberations he deduced that the most general motion could be represented by the superposition of these single vibrations, i.e., by a series of the form

$$y = \sum_{n=1}^{\infty} A_n \sin \frac{n\pi x}{a} \cos \frac{cn\pi t}{a}.$$

This equation appears nowhere explicitly, but it can be derived from a combination of various passages of this work and is valid only with the assumption of an initial velocity equaling zero.

In (46) Bernoulli determined the vibrations of a weightless cord loaded with n weights. He shows that in the case of $n = 2$, two simple vibrations, either commensurable or incommensurable, are possible, depending on the position and value of the two weights.

Treatise (53) is a beautiful treatment of the oscillations inside organ pipes, using only elementary mathematics. It is assumed that the movement of the particles parallel to the axis, the velocities, and the pressure are equal at all points of the same cross section and that the compression at the open end of the pipes equals zero. Among other things, this work contains the first theory of conical pipes and an arrangement consisting of two coaxial pipes of different cross sections as well as a series of new experiments.

In paper (54), on the vibrations of strings of uneven thickness, Bernoulli inquires about cases where oscillations assume the form $y = Aq \sin p \sin \nu t$, where p and q are functions of x only and ν is a constant. Here, for the first time, are solutions for the inverse problem, the determination of vibration curves from the distribution of density. In (63) he treats a special case in which the string consists of two parts of different thickness and length.

In treatise (67) Bernoulli compared the two possible oscillations of a body suspended from a flexible thread with the movement of a body bound with a rigid wire, and showed that one of the two oscillations of the first arrangement closely approximated the oscillation of the second arrangement. The method followed by Bernoulli is applicable only to infinitely small vibrations, and thus represents only a special case of the problem treated simultaneously by Euler by means of the Newtonian fundamental equations of mechanics.

In (68, 69) Bernoulli once more furnished a comprehensive presentation of his views on the superposition principle, which he clarified by means of the example of the frequently studied double pendulum. These last papers show that he had nothing new to add to the problem of vibrations.

Probability and statistics. A number of valuable papers were published by Bernoulli on probability theory and on population statistics.[6] True, his youthful work on faro within the framework of the *Exercitationes mathematicae* contributed hardly anything new, but it was evidence of his early interest in the work on the theory of probability done by his predecessors Montmort and De Moivre, which had been nourished by discussions with his cousin Nikolaus I. The most important treatise, and undoubtedly the most influential, was the *De mensura sortis* (22), conceived while he was in St. Petersburg, which contains an unusual evaluation of capital gains, and thus also contains the mathematical formulation of a new kind of value theory in political economy.[7]

The basic idea is that the larger a person's fortune is, the smaller is the moral value of a given increment in that fortune. If we assume, with Bernoulli, the special case, that a small increase of assets dx implies a moral value, dy, that is directly proportional to dx and inversely proportional to the fortune a—i.e., $dy = b\,dx/a$—then it follows that the moral value y of the gains $x - a$ complies with the formula $y = \log x/a$.

If a person has the chances $p_1, p_2, p_3 \cdots$, to make the gains $g_1, g_2, g_3 \cdots$, where $p_1 + p_2 + \cdots = 1$, which reflects one and only one gain, then the mean value of the moral values of the gains is equal to

$$bp_1 \log a\,(a + g_1) + bp_2 \log a\,(a + g_2) + \cdots - b \log a$$

and the moral expectation (hope)

$$H = (a + g_1)^{p_1}(a + g_2)^{p_2} \cdots - a.$$

If gains are very small in comparison with the assets, then the moral hope converts to the mathematical expectation $H = p_1 g_1 + p_2 g_2 + \cdots$. There follow some applications of the preceding to risk insurance and a discussion of the Petersburg paradox.

Only in 1760 did Bernoulli again treat a problem of this sort: medical statistics concerning the rate of mortality resulting from smallpox in the various age groups (51). If ξ is the number of survivors and s the number of those who at age x have not yet had smallpox, there results—given certain conditions—a differential equation containing three variables that defines the ratio s/ξ as a function of x. A table calculated on that basis contains the values of ξ, s, $\xi - s$, and so on valid for the first twenty-four years; ξ was taken from Halley's mortality table.[8] In (52) Bernoulli ardently advocated inoculation as a means of prolonging the average lifetime by three years.

In paper (55) Bernoulli treats, by means of urn

models, problems of probability theory as applied to his treatise on population statistics (56). Their main purpose was to determine for every age the expected average duration of a marriage. Here and in his subsequent papers (58, 59) Bernoulli preferred to make use of infinitesimal calculus in probability theory by assuming continuously changing states. The problem treated in (58) is as follows: Given several urns, each of which contains *n* slips of the same color, but of a different color for each urn, one slip is taken from each urn and deposited in the next one, with the slip taken from the last urn deposited in the first. The question is, How many slips of each color do the various urns contain after a number *r* of such "permutations"? The problem treated in (59) belongs in the field of the theory of errors, and concerns the determination of the probability with which (expressed in modern terms) a random variable subject to binomial distribution would assume values between two boundaries on either side of the mean value.

In paper (72) Bernoulli seeks to deal with the theory of errors in observation as a branch of probability theory. He challenges the assumption of Simpson and Lagrange that all observations are of equal importance. Rather, he maintains that small errors are more probable than large ones. Thus Bernoulli approximates the modern concept, except that he selects the semicircle instead of Gauss's probability curve.

Treatise (73) deals with errors to be considered in pendulum clocks, which are calculated partially by means of the method presented in (59).

Prizes of the Paris Academy. Bernoulli was highly esteemed for clarifying problems for a general public interested in the sciences. Of his essays entered in the competitions of the Paris Academy, ten were awarded prizes. Most of them concerned marine technology, navigation, and oceanology; but astronomy and magnetism were also represented.

His prize-winning paper of 1725 (8) dealt with the most appropriate shape for and the installation of hourglasses filled with sand or water. The subject of the 1728 contest was the cause and nature of gravity, on which Bernoulli prepared a manuscript, but the prize went to the Cartesian G. B. Bilfinger (79). In his entry for the 1729 competition Bernoulli indicated several methods for determining the height of the pole, particularly at sea, when only one unknown star is visible, or when one or more known stars are visible. The essay did not win a prize (80), but the manuscript is extant.

The prize of 1734 (24) was shared with his father, who begrudged Daniel his share of success. Here Daniel postulated an atmosphere resembling air and rotating around the solar axis, resulting in an increasing inclination of the planetary orbits toward the equator of the sun.

Bernoulli shared the 1737 prize for the best form of an anchor with Poleni (28). The 1740 prize on the tides was shared with Euler and several others. This important paper (33) on the relationship, recognized by Newton, between the tides and solar and lunar attraction, respectively, is still of interest, inasmuch as it furnishes a complete equilibrium theory of these phenomena.

The prize-winning papers of 1743 (39) and 1746 (41) deal with problems of magnetism. In the first paper Bernoulli considered all possibilities for reducing the sources of error in the inclination compass by improving construction. According to his instructions, the Basel mechanic Dietrich constructed such needles (49). The 1746 paper, written with his brother Johann II, contains an attempt to establish a theory of magnetism. Both authors believed that there is a subtle matter which moves in the direction of the magnetic meridian and forms a vortex around the magnet.

The next prize, for the best method of determining the time at sea with the horizon not visible, was offered in 1745 for the first time. It was offered for a second time in 1747, and Bernoulli won (42). Included in the wealth of information contained in this paper are the proposals for improving pendulum and spring clocks and the description of a mechanism for holding a rod equipped with diopter in a vertical position, even in a turbulent sea. A detailed account of the determination of the time, with the position of a given star known, concludes this paper (see 17).

The 1748 prize, for the irregular movements of Saturn and Jupiter (81), went to Euler. Bernoulli's manuscript has been preserved. The prize essay for 1749–1751 (44) discussed the question of the origin and nature of ocean currents, and added suggestions for measuring current velocities.

The problem treated by the prize essay of 1753 (47), the effect on ships of forces supplementary to that of the wind (e.g., rudder forces), was answered by Bernoulli, mainly by means of detailed data on the maximum work that could be performed by a man in a given unit of time. Among other things, he calculated the number of oarsmen required for attaining a given ship velocity.

The subject of the prize essay for 1757 (48), proposals for reducing the roll and pitch of ships, gave Bernoulli the opportunity to air his views on the pertinent works of Bouguer and Euler, published several years earlier. Whereas Euler had limited himself to the free vibrations of a ship, Bernoulli extended his views to the behavior of ships in turbulent seas, i.e., to forced vibrations. His findings prevailed for almost a century.

Evaluation and Appreciation. In order to appreciate both Bernoulli's importance in science, as indicated by the above summaries of his published works, and his private life, it is necessary to consider his extensive correspondence.[9] This includes his exchange of letters with Christian Goldbach (1723–1730), Euler (1726–1767, especially 1734–1750), and his nephew Johann III (1763–1774). Also important are his contemporaries' evaluations of Bernoulli and of his work. Unfortunately, his extremely popular lectures on experimental physics, in which he often introduced unproved hypotheses that have since been confirmed, apparently are not extant. Among them was his assertion of the validity of the relation later known as Coulomb's law in electrostatics. All of these achievements brought Bernoulli considerable fame in intellectual circles during his lifetime. He was a member of the leading learned societies and academies, including Bologna (1724), St. Petersburg (1730), Berlin (1747), Paris (1748), London (1750), Bern (1762), Turin (1764), Zurich (1764), and Mannheim (1767).

We can now assert that Bernoulli was the first to link Newton's ideas with Leibniz' calculus, which he had learned from his father and his brother Nikolaus. He did not, however, attempt to solve the problems that confronted him by means of the fundamental Newtonian equations; rather, he preferred to use the first integrals of these equations, especially Leibniz' principle of the conservation of living force, which his father had emphasized. Like Newton, whose battles he fought on the Continent, Bernoulli was first and foremost a physicist, using mathematics primarily as a means of exploring reality as it was revealed through experimentation. Thus he was interested in physical apparatus as well as the practical application of the results of physics and other sciences.

Bernoulli's active and imaginative mind dealt with the most varied scientific areas. Such wide interests, however, often prevented him from carrying some of his projects to completion. It is especially unfortunate that he could not follow the rapid growth of mathematics that began with the introduction of partial differential equations into mathematical physics. Nevertheless, he assured himself a permanent place in the history of science through his work and discoveries in hydrodynamics, his anticipation of the kinetic theory of gases, a novel method for calculating the value of an increase in assets, and the demonstration that the most common movement of a string in a musical instrument is composed of the superposition of an infinite number of harmonic vibrations (proper oscillations).

Otto Spiess instituted the publication of editions of the works and correspondence of the Bernoullis, a project that has continued since Spiess's death.

NOTES

1. *Johannis Bernoulli Hydraulica nunc primum detecta ac demonstrata directe ex fundamentis pure mechanicis,* in his *Opera omnia,* IV (Lausanne-Geneva, 1742), 387–488.
2. Friedrich Huber, *Daniel Bernoulli (1700–1782) als Physiologe und Statistiker,* Basler Veröffentlichungen zur Geschichte der Medizin und der Biologie, fasc. 8 (Basel, 1958).
3. Charles Bossut, "Manière de sommer les suites . . .," in *Mémoires de mathématiques et de physique de l'Académie royale des sciences, Paris,* 1769 (1772), 453–466.
4. For Daniel Bernoulli's hydrodynamic studies, see Clifford Truesdell, *Rational Fluid Mechanics,* intro. to Euler's *Opera omnia,* 2nd ser., XII, XIII (Zurich, 1954–1955).
5. Two excellent works are Clifford Truesdell, "The Rational Mechanics of Flexible or Elastic Bodies (1638–1788)"; his intro. to Euler's *Opera omnia,* 2nd ser., X, XI (Zurich, 1960); and H. Burkhardt, "Entwicklungen nach oscillierenden Functionen und Integration der Differentialgleichungen der mathematischen Physik," in *Jahresbericht der Deutschen Mathematiker-Vereinigung,* **10,** no. 2 (1908), 1–24.
6. I. Todhunter, *A History of the Mathematical Theory of Probability From the Time of Pascal to That of Laplace* (Cambridge-London, 1865; repr. New York, 1949), pp. 213–238.
7. An English trans. by Louise Sommer appeared in *Econometrica,* **22** (Jan. 1954). There is also a German trans. with extensive commentary by Alfred Pringsheim (Leipzig, 1896).
8. Edmund Halley, "An Estimate of the Degrees of the Mortality of Mankind," in *Philosophical Transactions of the Royal Society of London,* no. 196 (1694), 596–610.
9. Correspondence with Euler and Christian Goldbach—as far as available—appeared in *Correspondance mathématique et physique de quelques célèbres géomètres du XVIIIème siècle,* II (St. Petersburg, 1843). Letters exchanged by Bernoulli and his nephew Johann III have not yet been published.

BIBLIOGRAPHY

The following abbreviations of journal titles are used in the listing of Bernoulli's published works: *AE, Acta eruditorum; AP, Acta Academiae Scientiarum Imperialis Petropolitanae; CP* (or *NCP*), *Commentarii* (or *Norvi commentarii*) *Academiae Scientiarum Imperialis Petropolitanae; Prix, Pièces qui ont remporté les prix de l'Académie royale des sciences* (Paris); *Hist. Berlin, Histoire de l'Académie royale des sciences et belles lettres, Berlin; Mem. Berlin, Mémoires de l'Académie royale des sciences et belles lettres, Berlin; Mem. Paris, Mémoires de mathématiques et de physique de l'Académie royale des sciences, Paris.*

The first year following a journal title is the serial year; the second is the year of publication.

1. *Dissertatio inauguralis physico-medica de respiratione* (Basel, 1721).
2. *Positiones miscellaneae medico-anatomico-botanicae* (Basel, 1721).
3. *Theses logicae sistentes methodum examinandi syllogismorum validitatem* (Basel, 1722).
4. *Exercitationes quaedam mathematicae* (Venice, 1724).

5. "Notata in praecedens schediasma Ill. Co. Jacobi Riccati," in *AE*, supp. **8** (1724).

6. "Danielis Bernoulli explanatio notationum suarum, quae exstant Supplem. Tomo VIII Sect II," *ibid.*, 1725 (1725), also published in (4).

7. "Solutio problematis Riccatiani propositi in Act. Lips. Suppl. Tom. VIII p. 73," *ibid.*, 1725 (1725), also published in (4).

8. "Discours sur la manière la plus parfaite de conserver sur mer l'égalité du mouvement des clepsidres ou sabliers," in *Prix,* 1725 (1725).

9. "Examen principiorum mechanicae, et demonstrationes geometricae de compositione et resolutione virium," in *CP,* **1,** 1726 (1728).

10. "Tentamen novae de motu musculorum theoriae," *ibid.*

11. "Experimentum circa nervum opticum," *ibid.*

12. "Theoria nova de motu aquarum per canales quoscunque fluentium," *ibid.*, **2,** 1727 (1729).

13. "De mutua relatione centri virium, centri oscillationis et centri gravitatis," *ibid.*

14. "Dissertatio de actione fluidorum in corpora solida et motu solidorum in fluidis," *ibid.;* "Continuatio," *ibid.*, **3,** 1728 (1732).

15. "Methodus universalis determinandae curvaturae fili," *ibid.*

16. "Observationes de seriebus quae formantur ex additione vel subtractione quacunque terminorum se mutuo consequentium," *ibid.*

17. "Problema astronomicum inveniendi altitudinem poli una cum declinatione stellae ejusdemque culminatione," *ibid.*, **4,** 1729 (1735).

18. "Theorema de motu curvilineo corporum, quae resistentiam patiuntur velocitatis suae quadrato proportionalem," *ibid.;* "Additamentum," *ibid.*, **5,** 1730/1731 (1738).

19. "Experimenta coram societate instituta in confirmationem theoriae pressionum quas latera canalis ab aqua transfluente sustinent," *ibid.*, **4,** 1729 (1735).

20. "Notationes de aequationibus, quae progrediuntur in infinitum, earumque resolutione per methodum serierum recurrentium," *ibid.*, **5,** 1730/1731 (1738).

21. "Dissertatio brevis de motibus corporum reciprocis seu oscillatoriis, quae ubique resistentiam patiuntur quadrato velocitatis suae proportionalem," *ibid.*

22. "Specimen theoriae novae de mensura sortis," *ibid.*

23. "Theoremata de oscillationibus corporum filo flexili connexorum et catenae verticaliter suspensae," *ibid.*, **6,** 1732/1733 (1738).

24. "Quelle est la cause physique de l'inclinaison des plans des orbites des planètes par rapport au plan de l'équateur de la révolution du soleil autour de son axe," in *Prix,* 1734 (1735).

25. "Demonstrationes theorematum suorum de oscillationibus corporum filo flexili connexorum et catenae verticaliter suspensae," in *CP,* **7,** 1734/1735 (1740).

26. "De legibus quibusdam mechanicis, quas natura constanter affectat, nondum descriptis, earumque usu hydrodynamico, pro determinanda vi venae aqueae contra planum incurrentis," *ibid.*, **8,** 1736 (1741).

27. "De variatione motuum a percussione excentrica," *ibid.*, **9,** 1737 (1744).

28. "Réflexions sur la meilleure figure à donner aux ancres," in *Prix,* 1737 (1737).

29. "Commentationes de immutatione et extensione principii conservationis virium vivarum, quae pro motu corporum coelestium requiritur," in *CP,* **10,** 1738 (1747).

30. "Commentationes de statu aequilibrii corporum humido insidentium," *ibid.*

31. *Hydrodynamica, sive de viribus et motibus fluidorum commentarii* (Strasbourg, 1738). The following trans. exist: German, with extensive commentary by Karl Flierl, in the series Veröffentlichungen des Forschungsinstituts des Deutschen Museums für die Geschichte der Naturwissenschaften und der Technik, Reihe C: Quellentexte und Uebersetzungen, nos. 1a, 1b (Munich, 1965); English, *Hydrodynamics by Daniel Bernoulli,* trans. Thomas Carmody and Helmut Kobus (New York, 1968), bound with Johann I Bernoulli's *Hydraulics* (pp. 343–451); and Russian, *Daniel Bernoulli. Gidrodinamika ili zapiski o silakh i dvizheniakh zhidkostei,* trans. A. I. Nekrasov, K. K. Baumgart, and V. I. Smirnov (Moscow, 1959).

32. "De motibus oscillatoriis corporum humido insidentium," in *CP,* **11,** 1739 (1750).

33. "Traité sur le flux et reflux de la mer," in *Prix,* 1740 (1741).

34. "De oscillationibus compositis praesertim iis quae fiunt in corporibus ex filo flexili suspensis," in *CP,* **12,** 1740 (1750).

35. "Excerpta ex litteris ad Leonhardum Euler," *ibid.*, **13,** 1741–1743 (1751).

36. "De motu mixto, quo corpora sphaeroidica super plano inclinato descendunt," *ibid.*

37. "De vibrationibus et sono laminarum elasticarum," *ibid.*

38. "De sonis multifariis quos laminae elasticae diversimode edunt disquisitiones mechanico-geometricae experimentis acusticis illustratae et confirmatae," *ibid.*

39. "Mémoire sur la manière de construire les boussoles d'inclinaison," in *Prix,* 1743 (1748).

40. "Nouveau problème de mécanique," in *Mem. Berlin,* 1745 (1746), trans. into German in Ostwald's Klassiker der Exacten Wissenschaften, no. 191 (Leipzig, 1914), pp. 29–43.

41. "Nouveaux principes de mécanique et de physique, tendans à expliquer la nature & les propriétés de l'aiman," written with Johann II, in *Prix,* 1746 (1748).

42. "La meilleure manière de trouver l'heure en mer," *ibid.*, 1745 and 1747 (1750).

43. "Remarques sur le principe de la conservation des forces vives pris dans un sens général," in *Mem. Berlin,* 1748 (1750), trans. into German in Ostwald's Klassiker der Exacten Wissenschaften, no. 191 (Leipzig, 1914), pp. 67–75.

44. "Sur la nature et la cause des courans," in *Prix,* 1749 and 1751 (1769).

45. "Réflexions et éclaircissemens sur les nouvelles

vibrations des cordes," in *Mem. Berlin*, 1753 (1755).

46. "Sur le mélange de plusieurs espèces de vibrations simples isochrones, qui peuvent coexister dans un même système de corps," *ibid.*

47. "Recherches sur la manière la plus avantageuse de suppléer à l'action du vent sur les grands vaisseaux," in *Prix*, 1753 (1769).

48. "Quelle est la meilleure manière de diminuer le roulis & le tangage d'un navire," *ibid.*, 1757 (1771).

49. "Sur les nouvelles aiguilles d'inclinaison," in *Journal des sçavans*, 1757 (1757).

50. "Lettre de monsieur Daniel Bernoulli à M. Clairaut, au sujet des nouvelles découvertes faites sur les vibrations des cordes tendues," *ibid.*, 1758 (1758).

51. "Essai d'une nouvelle analyse de la mortalité causée par la petite vérole, & des avantages de l'inoculation pour la prevenir," in *Mem. Paris*, 1760 (1766).

52. "Réflexions sur les avantages de l'inoculation," in *Mercure de France* (June 1760).

53. "Sur le son & sur les tons des tuyaux d'orgues," in *Mem. Paris*, 1762 (1764).

54. "Mémoire sur les vibrations des cordes d'une épaisseur inégale," in *Mem. Berlin*, 1765 (1767).

55. "De usu algorithmi infinitesimalis in arte coniectandi specimen," in *NCP*, **12**, 1766/1767 (1768).

56. "De duratione media matrimoniorum, pro quacunque coniugum aetate," *ibid.*

57. "Commentatio de utilissima ac commodissima directione potentiarum frictionibus mechanicis adhibendarum," *ibid.*, **13**, 1768 (1769).

58. "Disquisitiones analyticae de novo problemate coniecturali," *ibid.*, **14**, 1769, pt. 1 (1770).

59. "Mensura sortis ad fortuitam successionem rerum naturaliter contingentium applicata," *ibid.*; "Continuatio," *ibid.*, **15**, 1770 (1771).

60. "Commentationes physico-mechanicae de frictionibus," *ibid.*, **14**, 1769, pt. 1 (1770).

61. "Examen physico-mechanicum de motu mixto qui laminis elasticis a percussione simul imprimitur," *ibid.*, **15**, 1770 (1771).

62. "De summationibus serierum quarundam incongrue veris," *ibid.*, **16**, 1771 (1772).

63. "De vibrationibus chordarum," *ibid.*

64. "De indole singulari serierum infinitarum quas sinus vel cosinus angulorum arithmetice progredientium formant, earumque summatione et usu," *ibid.*, **17**, 1772 (1773).

65. "Expositio theoretica singularis machinae hydraulicae," *ibid.*

66. "Theoria elementaria serierum, ex sinibus atque cosinibus arcuum arithmetice progredientium diversimode compositarum, dilucidata," *ibid.*, **18**, 1773 (1774).

67. "Vera determinatio centri oscillationis in corporibus qualibuscunque filo flexili suspensis eiusque ab regula communi discrepantia," *ibid.*

68. "Commentatio physico-mechanica generalior principii de coexistentia vibrationum simplicium haud perturbatarum in systemate composito," *ibid.*, **19**, 1774 (1775).

69. "Commentatio physico-mechanica specialior de motibus reciprocis compositis," *ibid.*

70. "Adversaria analytica miscellanea de fractionibus continuis," *ibid.*, **20**, 1775 (1776).

71. "Disquisitiones ulteriores de indole fractionum continuarum," *ibid.*

72. "Diiudicatio maxime probabilis plurium observationum discrepantium atque verisimillima inductio inde formanda," in *AP*, 1777, pt. 1 (1778).

73. "Specimen philosophicum de compensationibus horologicis, et veriori mensura temporis," *ibid.*, pt. 2 (1780).

74. "Sur la cause des vents," in Berlin Academy's *Recueil des prix* without Bernoulli's name. Also at University of Basel, LIa753E5.

75. "Oratio physiologica de vita," with German trans. and historical essays, ed. O. Spiess and F. Verzár, in *Verhandlungen der Naturforschenden Gesellschaft Basel*, **52** (1940/1941), 189-266. Also at University of Basel, LIa-753E18.

The library of the University of Basel has most of Bernoulli's original MSS, and photocopies of the rest.

76. "Methodus isoperimetricorum ad novam problematum classem promota," LIa751C3. From all curves of equal length lying between two fixed points, to find the ones for which $\int R^m ds$ is a minimum, where R^m is the mth power of the radius of curvature R and ds is the arc element. This was first satisfactorily solved by Euler.

77. "Solutio problematis inveniendi curvam, quae cum aliis data sit tatuochrona" (1729), LIa751C4. Solution to the problem of finding the curves in which the oscillations of a center of mass moving in a vacuum are isochronous regardless of starting point. Also treated by Euler.

78. "De legibus motus mixti variati, quo corpus sphaericum super plano aspero progredietur," LIaC19.

79. "Discours sur la cause et la nature de la pesantur," LIa752D2, submitted in the 1728 prize competition of the Paris Academy. The prize was awarded to Bilfinger.

80. "Quelle est la meilleure méthode d'observer les hauteurs sur mer par le soleil et par les étoiles," LIa752D3, submitted in the 1729 prize competition of the Paris Academy. The prize was awarded to Bouguer.

81. "Recherches mécaniques et astronomiques sur la théorie de Saturne et de Jupiter," LIa33, submitted in the 1748 prize competition of the Paris Academy. The prize was awarded to Euler.

82. An outline of the *Hydrodynamica* (1733) is in Archives of the Academy of Sciences, Leningrad; a photocopy is in Basel.

Biographical works on Bernoulli include Daniel II Bernoulli, "Vita Danielis Bernoulli," in *Acta Helvetica*, **9** (1787), 1-32, a memorial address with an almost complete bibliography of printed works; "Die Basler Mathematiker Bernoulli und Leonhard Euler. Vorträge von Fr. Burckhardt u.a.," in *Verhandlungen der Naturforschenden Gesellschaft Basel*, **7** (1884), appendix; Marquis de Condorcet, "Éloge de M. Bernoulli," in *Hist. Paris*, 1782 (1785), 82-107, and in *Oeuvres de Condorcet*, II (Paris, 1847), 545-585; *Gedenkbuch der Familie Bernoulli zum 300. Jahrestage ihrer Aufnahme in das Basler Bürgerrecht. 1622,*

1922 (Basel, 1922); Peter Merian, *Die Mathematiker Bernoulli. Jubelschrift zur 4. Säcularfeier der Universität Basel, 6 September 1860* (Basel, 1860); Otto Spiess, *Basel anno 1760* (Basel, 1936); "Daniel Bernoulli," in Eduard Fueter, ed., *Grosse Schweizer Forscher* (Zurich, 1939), pp. 110–112; "Johann Bernoulli und seine Soehne," in *Atlantis* (1940), 663–669; "Die Mathematikerfamilie Bernoulli," in Martin Huerlimann, ed., *Grosse Schweizer,* 2nd ed. (Zurich, 1942), pp. 112–119; and "Bernoulli, Basler Gelehrtenfamilie," in *Neue deutsche Biographie* (1955), pp. 128–131; and Rudolf Wolf, "Daniel Bernoulli von Basel, 1700–1782," in *Biographien zur Kulturgeschichte der Schweiz,* 3rd ser. (Zurich, 1860), pp. 151–202.

HANS STRAUB

BERNOULLI, JAKOB (JACQUES) I (*b.* Basel, Switzerland, 27 December 1654; *d.* Basel, 16 August 1705)

Bernoulli came from a line of merchants. His grandfather, Jakob Bernoulli, was a druggist from Amsterdam who became a citizen of Basel in 1622 through marriage. His father, Nikolaus Bernoulli, took over the thriving drug business and became a member of the town council and a magistrate; his mother, Margaretha Schönauer, was the daughter of a banker and town councillor. Jakob was married in 1684 to Judith Stupanus, the daughter of a wealthy pharmacist; their son Nikolaus became a town councillor and master of the artists' guild.

Bernoulli received his master of arts in philosophy in 1671, and a licentiate in theology in 1676; meanwhile, he studied mathematics and astronomy against the will of his father. In 1676 he went as a tutor to Geneva, where in 1677 he began his informative scientific diary, *Meditationes;* he then spent two years in France, familiarizing himself with the methodological and scientific opinions of Descartes and his followers, among whom was Nicolas Malebranche. Bernoulli's second educational journey, in 1681–1682, took him to the Netherlands, where he met mathematicians and scientists, especially Jan Hudde, and to England, where he met Robert Boyle and Robert Hooke. The scientific result of these journeys was his inadequate theory of comets (1682) and a theory of gravity that was highly regarded by his contemporaries (1683).

After returning to Basel, Bernoulli conducted experimental lectures, concerning the mechanics of solid and liquid bodies, from 1683 on. He sent reports on scientific problems of the day to the *Journal des sçavans* and the *Acta eruditorum,* and worked his way through the principal mathematical work of those days, *Geometria,* the Latin edition of Descartes's *Géométrie,* which had been edited and provided with notes and supplements by Frans van Schooten (2nd ed., Amsterdam, 1659–1661). As a result of this work, Bernoulli contributed articles on algebraic subjects to the *Acta eruditorum.* His outstanding achievement was the division of a triangle into four equal parts by means of two straight lines perpendicular to each other (1687). After these contributions had been extended and supplemented, they were published as an appendix to the *Geometria* (4th ed., 1695).

In four disputations published from 1684 to 1686, Bernoulli presented formal logical studies that tended toward the sophistical. His first publication on probability theory dates from 1685. By working with the pertinent writings of John Wallis (those of 1656, 1659, and 1670–1671) and Isaac Barrow (1669–1670), concerning mathematical, optical, and mechanical subjects, Bernoulli was led to problems in infinitesimal geometry.

In the meantime his younger brother Johann began attending the University of Basel after an unsuccessful apprenticeship as a salesman. As respondent to one of Jakob's scholarly logic debates, Johann earned his master of arts degree in 1685 and, by order of his father, studied medicine. Simultaneously, however, he secretly studied mathematics under his brother, becoming well versed in the fundamentals of the field. In 1687 Jakob became professor of mathematics at Basel, and with his brother he studied the publications of Leibniz and of Ehrenfried Walther von Tschirnhaus in *Acta eruditorum* (1682–1686), which had in essence been limited to examples and intimations of infinitesimal mathematics and its application to mechanics and dynamics. After much effort, Bernoulli was able to make himself master of these new methods, which he erroneously believed to be merely a computational formalism for Barrow's geometrical treatment of infinitesimals. His mathematical studies reached a first peak about 1689 with the beginnings of a theory of series, the law of large numbers in probability theory, and the special stress on complete induction.

Bernoulli showed his mastery of the Leibnizian calculus with his analysis (in May 1690) of the solutions given by Huygens in 1687 and by Leibniz in 1689 to the problem of the curve of constant descent in a gravitational field. (It was in that analysis that the term "integral" was first used in its present mathematical sense.) The determination of the curve of constant descent had been posed as a problem by Leibniz in 1687. As a counterproblem Bernoulli raised the determination of the shape of the catenary, to which he had, perhaps, been directed by Albert Girard's notes to the *Oeuvres* of Simon Stevin (1634);

Girard claimed that the catenary is a parabola. Leibniz promptly referred to the significance of this counterproblem, which he had spontaneously solved (1690) and which was later treated by Johann Bernoulli, Huygens, and himself in the *Acta eruditorum* (1691). Jakob, who found himself at that time in difficulties at the university because of his open criticism of university affairs and saw himself being overshadowed by his brother, did not take part directly, but proposed generalizations of the problem, allowing the links of the chain to be elastic or of unequal weight. He also announced a treatise on the *elastica*, the form of a bent elastic beam, which, under certain conditions, satisfies the differential equation $dy/dx = x^2/\sqrt{a^4-x^4}$. Later he investigated this thoroughly, supposing arbitrary functions of elasticity (1694). In two notable contributions to differential calculus (1691), he examined the parabolic spiral (in polar coordinates: $r = a - b\sqrt{\phi}$, the elliptical integral for the curve length with its characteristic feature of symmetry) and the logarithmic spiral.

In Johann Bernoulli's study concerning the focal line of incident parallel rays of light on a semicircular mirror (1692), there is reference to Jakob's general procedure for determination of evolutes. This procedure is based on the generation of an algebraic curve as the envelope of its circles of curvature, and this procedure is worked out fully in the case of the parabola. Here Bernoulli corrected a mistake made by Leibniz (1686)—the statement that the circle of curvature meets the curve at four coinciding points—but he himself made a mistake in his assertion that the radius of curvature becomes infinite at every point of inflection. This error, corrected in 1693 by G. F. A. de L'Hospital, was the occasion for Bernoulli's removing of the singularity $a^2x^3 = y^5$ in the origin (1697). Almost simultaneously, and independently of each other, the brothers recognized that the form of a sail inflated by the wind is described by $(dx/ds)^3 = ad^2y/dx^2$. Jakob made a preliminary report in 1692 and a thorough one in 1695.

Further investigations concerned evolutes and caustics, first of the logarithmic spiral (*spira mirabilis*) and the parabola (1692), and later of epicycloids (1692) and diacaustic surfaces (1693), this in connection with Johann's similar studies. These last were included in his private instruction to L'Hospital (1691-1692). Here, for the first time, public reference was made to the *theorema aureum,* which had been developed in the spring of 1692. The theorem, which gives the radius of curvature as $(ds/dx)^3 : (d^2y/dx^2)$, was published in 1694. Bernoulli's solution of the differential equation proposed by Johann Bernoulli (1693), $xdy - ydx/yds = a/b$, was completed by Huygens (1693). In treating the paracentric isochrone, a problem proposed by Leibniz (1689) that leads to the differential equation

$$(xdx + ydy)/\sqrt{y} = (xdy - ydx)/\sqrt{a},$$

Bernoulli separated the variables by substituting

$$x^2 + y^2 = r^2, \qquad ay = rt$$

and was able to relate the solution to the rectification of the *elastica;* later he found the reduction to the rectification of the lemniscate,

$$x^2 + y^2 = a\sqrt{x^2 - y^2}.$$

These and other studies—among which the kinetic-geometrical chord construction for the solution (1696) of $dy/dx = t(x)/a$ and the solution (1696) of the so-called Bernoullian differential equation $y' = p(x)y + q(x)y^n$ (1696) merit special attention—are proof of Bernoulli's careful and critical work on older as well as on contemporary contributions to infinitesimal mathematics and of his perseverance and analytical ability in dealing with special pertinent problems, even those of a mechanical-dynamic nature.

Sensitivity, irritability, a mutual passion for criticism, and an exaggerated need for recognition alienated the brothers, of whom Jakob had the slower but deeper intellect. Johann was more gifted in working with mathematical formulations and was blessed above all with a greater intuitive power and descriptive ability. Johann was appointed a professor at the University of Groningen in 1695, and in 1696 he proposed the problem to determine the curve of quickest descent between two given points, the brachistochrone. In connection with this he replied to the previous gibes of his brother with derisive insinuations. Jakob gave a solution (1697) that was closely related to that given by Leibniz (1697). It is based on the sufficient but not necessary condition that the extreme-value property of the curve in question (a common cycloid) is valid not only for the entire curve but also for all its parts. As a counterproblem Jakob set forth the so-called isoperimetric problem, the determination of that curve of given length between the points $A(-c; 0)$, $B(+c; 0)$ for which $\int_{-c}^{c} y^n dx$ takes a maximum value. Johann, in the *Histoire des ouvrages des savants* (1697), through a misunderstanding of the difficulty of the problem and of its nature (calculus of variations), gave a solution based on a differential equation of the second degree. A differential equation of the third degree is necessary, however. After showing that a third-degree equation is required (1701), Jakob was able also to furnish the proof, which Johann and Leibniz had been seeking in vain, that the inexpansible and homogeneous catenary is the curve of deepest center of gravity between the points of suspension.

Johann Bernoulli may have comprehended the justification for his brother's argument soon after publication of the dissertation of 1701 (*Analysis magni problematis isoperimetrici*), but he remained silent. Only after Brook Taylor had adopted Jakob's procedure (1715) was he induced to accept Jakob's point of view. In the 1718 series of the *Mémoires* of the Paris Académie des Sciences, of which the brothers had been corresponding members since 1699, Johann gave a presentation, based on Jakob's basic ideas but improved in style and organization. It was not superseded until Leonhard Euler's treatment of the problems of variations (1744).

The antagonism between the brothers soon led to ugly critical remarks. In 1695 Jakob failed to appreciate the significance of Johann's extraordinarily effective series expansion (1694), which is based on iterated integration by parts and leads to a remainder in integral form. On the other hand, Johann, who in 1697 had challenged the criterion for geodetic lines on convex surfaces, complained in the following year that his brother knew how to solve the problem "only" on rotation surfaces. Other items of disagreement were the determination of elementary quadrable segments of the common cycloid and related questions. The brothers argued over this in print in 1699 and 1700. The formulas for the multisection of angles are connected with these problems. In his ingenious use of Wallis' incomplete induction (1656), Jakob presented $2 \cdot \cos n\alpha$ and $2 \cdot \sin n\alpha$ as functions of $2 \cdot \sin \alpha$. This is related to his notes from the winter of 1690–1691, in which, furthermore, the exponential series was derived from the binomial series in a bold but formally unsatisfactory manner.

Jakob Bernoulli's decisive scientific achievement lay not in the formulation of extensive theories, but in the clever and preeminently analytical treatment of individual problems. Behind his particular accomplishments there were, of course, notions of which Bernoulli was deeply convinced, primarily concerning continuity of all processes of nature (*natura non facit saltum*). Although Bernoulli assigned great significance to experimental research, he limited himself—for example, in investigations of mechanics—to a few basic facts to which he tried to cling and on which he sought to base full theories. For this reason his final results were intellectually interesting, and as points of departure they were significant for further investigation by his contemporaries and subsequent generations. Naturally enough, they usually do not conform to more modern conclusions, which rest on far wider foundations. It is to be regretted, however, that Bernoulli's contributions to mechanics are hardly ever mentioned in the standard works.

The theory that seeks to explain natural phenomena by assuming collisions between particles of the ether, developed in the *Dissertatio de gravitate aetheris* (1683), of course does not mean much to a later generation. There are extensive discussions about the center point of oscillation, which had been determined correctly for the first time by Huygens in his *Horologium oscillatorium* (1673), but this was strongly debated by some of the members of the Cartesian school. On this subject Bernoulli expressed his opinions first in 1684, and then in more detail in 1686 and 1691; finally he succeeded in developing a proof from the properties of the lever (1703–1704). Important also is his last work, on the resistance of elastic bodies (1705). Supplementary material from his scientific diary is contained in the appendix to his *Opera*. Additional, but unpublished, material deals with the center of gravity of two uniformly moved bodies, the shape of a cord under the influence of several stretching forces, centrally accelerated motion (in connection with the statements of Newton in his *Principia* [1687]), and the line of action and the collective impulse of infinitely many shocks exerted on a rigid arc in the plane.

In the field of engineering belongs the 1695 treatment of the drawbridge problem (the curve of a sliding weight hanging on a cable that always holds the drawbridge in balance), stemming from Joseph Sauveur and investigated in the same year by L'Hospital and Johann Bernoulli. Leibniz was also interested in the problem. In Bernoulli's published remains, the contour is determined upon which a watch spring is to be developed so that the tension always remains the same for the movements of the watch.

The five dissertations in the *Theory of Series* (1682–1704) contain sixty consecutively numbered propositions. These dissertations show how Bernoulli (at first in close cooperation with his brother) had thoroughly familiarized himself with the appropriate formulations of questions to which he had been led by the conclusions of Leibniz in 1682 (series for $\pi/4$ and log 2) and 1683 (questions dealing with compound interest). Out of this there also came the treatise in which Bernoulli took into account short-term compound interest and was thus led to the exponential series. He thought that there had been nothing printed concerning the theory of series up until that time, but he was mistaken: most conclusions of the first two dissertations (1689, 1692) were already to be found in Pietro Mengoli (1650), as were the divergence of the harmonic series (Prop. 16) and the sum of the reciprocals of infinitely many figurate numbers

(Props. 17–20).

The so-called Bernoullian inequality (Prop. 4), $(1 + x)^n > 1 + nx$, is intended for $x > 0$, n as a whole number > 1. It is taken from Barrow's seventh lecture in the *Lectiones geometricae* (1670). Bernoulli would have been able to find algebraic iteration processes for the solution of equations (Props. 27–35) in James Gregory's *Vera . . . quadratura* (1667). The procedure of proof is still partially incomplete because of inadmissible use of divergent series. At the end of the first dissertation Bernoulli acknowledged that he could not yet sum up $\Sigma_{k=1}^{\infty} k^{-2}$ in closed form (Euler succeeded in doing so first in 1737); but he did know about the majorant $\Sigma_{k=1}^{\infty} 2k^{-1}(k + 1)^{-1}$, which can be summed in elementary terms. In Proposition 24 it is written that $\Sigma_{k=1}^{\infty} (2k - 1)^{-m}/\Sigma_{k=1}^{\infty} (2k)^{-m}$ equals $(2^m - 1)/1$ (m integer > 1), and that $\Sigma_{k=1}^{\infty} k^{-1/2}$ diverges more rapidly than $\Sigma_{k=1}^{\infty} k^{-1}$. Informative theses, based on Bernoulli's earlier studies, were added to the dissertations; and theses 2 and 3 of the second dissertation are based on the still incomplete classification of curves of the third degree according to their shapes into thirty-three different types.

The third dissertation was defended by Jakob Hermann, who wrote Bernoulli's obituary notice in *Acta eruditorum* (1706). In the introduction L'Hospital's *Analyse* is praised. After some introductory propositions, there appear the logarithmic series for the hyperbola quadrature (Prop. 42), the exponential series as the inverse of the logarithmic series (Prop. 43), the geometrical interpretation of

$$\sum_{k=1}^{\infty} k^{-2}x^k$$

(Prop. 44), and the series for the arc of the circle and the sector of conic sections (Props. 45, 46). All of these are carefully and completely presented with reference to the pertinent results of Leibniz (1682; 1691). In 1698 previous work was supplemented by Bernoulli's reflections on the catenary (Prop. 49) and related problems, on the rectification of the parabola (Prop. 41), and on the rectification of the logarithmic curve (Prop. 52).

The last dissertation (1704) was defended by Bernoulli's nephew, Nikolaus I, who helped in the publication of the *Ars conjectandi* (1713) and the reprint of the dissertation on series (1713) and became a prominent authority in the theory of series. In the dissertation Bernoulli first (Prop. 53) praises Wallis' interpolation through incomplete induction. In Proposition 54 the binomial theorem is presented, with examples of fractional exponents, as an already generally known theorem. Probably for this reason there is no reference to Newton's presentation in his letters to Leibniz of 23 June and 3 November 1676, which were made accessible to Bernoulli when they were published in Wallis' *Opera* (Vol. III, 1699). In proposition 55 the method of indeterminate coefficients appears, without reference to Leibniz (1693). Propositions 56–58 and 60 deal with questions related to the *elastica.*

In Proposition 59 it is stated that the series

$$\sum_{k=1}^{\infty} (-1)^{k+1}k^{-1}$$

for log 2 should be replaced by

$$\sum_{k=1}^{\infty} 2^{-k}\, k^{-1},$$

which converges more rapidly. From the letter to Leibniz of 2 August 1704, we know that in Proposition 59 Bernoulli used an idea of Jean-Christophe Fatio-de-Duillier (1656–1720), an engineer from Geneva, for the improvement of convergence. The procedure was expanded by Euler in the *Institutiones calculi differentialis* (1755) to his so-called series transformation. In the dissertations on series Bernoulli apparently wished to reproduce everything he knew about the subject. In this he was primarily concerned with the careful rendering of the results and not so much with originality.

The *Ars conjectandi* is Bernoulli's most original work, but unfortunately it is incomplete. The first part is basically a first-rate commentary on Huygens' *De ratiociniis in aleae ludo,* which was published as an appendix to van Schooten's *Exercitationes mathematicae* (1657). In the second part Bernoulli deals with the theory of combinations, based on the pertinent contributions of van Schooten (1657), Leibniz (1666), Wallis (1685), and Jean Prestet's *Élémens de mathématiques* (1675; 2nd ed., 1689). The chief result here is the rigid derivation of the exponential series through complete induction by means of the so-called Bernoullian numbers. In the third part Bernoulli gives twenty-four examples, some simple, some very complicated, on the expectation of profit in various games.

The fourth part contains the philosophical thoughts on probability that are especially characteristic of Bernoulli: probability as a measurable degree of certainty; necessity and chance; moral versus mathematical expectation; a priori and a posteriori probability; expectation of winning when the players are divided according to dexterity; regard of all available arguments, their valuation, and their calculable evaluation; law of large numbers, and reference to the *Art de penser* (*Logique de Port Royal,* Antoine Arnauld and Pierre Nicole, eds., 1662). The last section contains a penetrating discussion of *jeu de paume,* a complicated predecessor of tennis that was very popular. This part is Bernoulli's answer to the anonymous gibes occasioned by his debate of 1686 on scholarly logic.

Bernoulli's ideas on the theory of probability have contributed decisively to the further development of the field. They were incorporated in the second edition of Rémond de Montmort's *Essai* (1713) and were considered by Abraham de Moivre in his *Doctrine of Chances* (1718).

Bernoulli greatly advanced algebra, the infinitesimal calculus, the calculus of variations, mechanics, the theory of series, and the theory of probability. He was self-willed, obstinate, aggressive, vindictive, beset by feelings of inferiority, and yet firmly convinced of his own abilities. With these characteristics, he necessarily had to collide with his similarly disposed brother. He nevertheless exerted the most lasting influence on the latter.

Bernoulli was one of the most significant promoters of the formal methods of higher analysis. Astuteness and elegance are seldom found in his method of presentation and expression, but there is a maximum of integrity. The following lines taken from the *Ars conjectandi* (published posthumously in 1713) are not without a certain grace, however, and represent an early statement, made with wit and clarity, of the boundaries of an infinite series.

Ut non-finitam Seriem finita cöercet,
  Summula, & in nullo limite limes adest:
Sic modico immensi vestigia Numinis haerent
  Corpore, & angusto limite limes abest.
Cernere in immenso parvum, dic, quanta voluptas!
  In parvo immensum cernere, quanta, Deum!

Even as the finite encloses an infinite series
  And in the unlimited limits appear,
So the soul of immensity dwells in minutia
  And in narrowest limits no limits inhere.
What joy to discern the minute in infinity!
  The vast to perceive in the small, what divinity!

BIBLIOGRAPHY

I. ORIGINAL WORKS. Bernoulli's most famous single writing is *Ars conjectandi* (Basel, 1713; Brussels, 1968). His *Opera*, G. Cramer, ed. (Geneva, 1744; Brussels, 1968), contains all his scientific writings except the *Neuerfundene Anleitung, wie man den Lauff der Comet- oder Schwantzsternen in gewisse grundmässige Gesätze einrichten und ihre Erscheinung vorhersagen könne* (Basel, 1681), as well as a *Prognosticon.* Its contents were incorporated in the *Conamen novi systematis cometarum . . .* (Amsterdam, 1682), which is reproduced in the *Opera* as part 1.

Two collections of letters are printed: those to Leibniz in Leibniz' *Mathematische Schriften,* Vol. III, C. I. Gerhardt, ed. (Halle, 1855; Hildesheim, 1962); those to his brother Johann, in *Der Briefwechsel von Johann Bernoulli,* Vol. I, O. Spiess, ed. (Basel, 1955).

His MSS at the library of the University of Basel are *Reisebüchlein* (1676–1683); *Meditationes, annotationes, animadversiones* (1677–1705); *Stammbuch* (1678–1684); *Tabulae gnomicae. Typus locorum hypersolidorum,* which concerns classification of the curves of the third degree into thirty-three types; *Memorial über die Missbräuche an der Universität* (1691); and *De arte combinatoria* (1692) (all unpublished manuscripts); and "De historia cycloidis" (1701), in *Archiv für Geschichte der Mathematik und Naturwissenschaften,* **10** (1927–1928), 345 ff.

Bernoulli's unpublished manuscripts at the library of the University of Geneva are lectures on the mechanics of solid and liquid bodies, *Acta collegii experimentalis* (1683–1690), parts of which have been transcribed.

The collected works are in preparation. Included are Bernoulli's correspondence with Nicolas Fatio-de-Duillier (1700–1701) and with Otto Mencke (1686, 1689). The most important correspondence with L'Hospital and Pierre Varignon seems to have been lost.

Translations from the *Opera* are in the series Ostwald's Klassiker der Exacten Wissenschaften: *Unendliche Reihen* (1689–1704), translated into German by G. Kowalewski, no. 171 (Leipzig, 1909); and *Abhandlungen über das Gleichgewicht und die Schwingungen der ebenen elastischen Kurven von Jakob Bernoulli (1691, 1694, 1695) und Leonh. Euler (1744),* translated into German by H. Linsenbarth, no. 175 (Leipzig, 1910). Other translations are *Abhandlungen über Variations-Rechnung. Erster Theil: Abhandlungen von Joh. Bernoulli (1696), Jac. Bernoulli (1697) und Leonhard Euler,* translated into German by P. Stäckel, no. 46 (Leipzig, 1894; 2nd ed., 1914); and *Jakob Bernoulli: Wahrscheinlichkeitsrechnung,* translated into German by R. Haussner, nos. 107 and 108 (Leipzig, 1899). The latter was translated into English by Fr. Masères in his *Doctrine of Permutations and Combinations* (London, 1795) and in *Scriptores logarithmici,* Vol. III (London, 1796).

II. SECONDARY LITERATURE. Works concerning Bernoulli and his contributions to mathematics are P. Dietz, "The Origins of the Calculus of Variations in the Works of Jakob Bernoulli," in *Verhandlungen der Naturforschenden Gesellschaft in Basel,* **70** (1959), 81–146, a dissertation presented at the University of Mainz in 1958; J. O. Fleckenstein, *Johann und Jakob Bernoulli* (Basel, 1949), which is supp. 6 to the journal *Elemente der Mathematik;* J. E. Hofmann, *Uber Jakob Bernoullis Beiträge zur Infinitesimalmathematik* (Geneva, 1956), no. 3 in the series *Monographies de l'Enseignement Mathématique;* and O. Spiess, "Bernoulli," in *Neue deutsche Biographie,* II (Berlin, 1955), 128–129, and "Jakob Bernoulli," *ibid.*, pp. 130–131, which include supplementary bibliographical material.

The poem "On Infinite Series," Helen M. Walker, trans., appears in D. E. Smith, *A Source Book in Mathematics;* repr. by permission Harvard University Press.

J. E. HOFMANN

BERNOULLI, JAKOB (JACQUES) II (*b.* Basel, Switzerland, 17 October 1759; *d.* St. Petersburg, Russia, 15 August 1789)

Jakob II was Johann II's most gifted son. He graduated in jurisprudence in 1778 but successfully engaged in mathematics and physics. In 1782 he presented a paper (6) to support his candidacy for the chair of his uncle Daniel. The decision (made by drawing lots) was against him, however, and he traveled as secretary of the imperial envoy to Turin and Venice, where he received a call to St. Petersburg. There he married a granddaughter of Euler and published several treatises (2–4) at the Academy. When only thirty years old, he drowned while swimming in the Neva.

BIBLIOGRAPHY

Jakob's writings include (1) "Lettre sur l'élasticité," in *Journal de physique de Rozier,* **21** (1782), 463–467; (2) "Considérations hydrostatiques," in *Nova acta Helvetica,* **1**, 229–237; (3) "Dilucidationes in Comment. L. Euleri de ictu glandium contra tabulam explosarum," in *Nova acta Petropolitana,* **4** (1786), 148–157; (4) "De motu et reactione aquae per tubos mobiles transfluentis," *ibid.,* **6** (1788), 185–196; (5) "Sur l'usage et la théorie d'une machine, qu'on peut nommer instrument ballistique," in *Mém. Acad. Berl.* (1781), pp. 347–376; and (6) *Theses physicae et physico-mathematicae quas vacante cathedra physica die 28 Maii 1782 defendere conabitur Jacobus Bernoulli* (Basel, 1782).

J. O. FLECKENSTEIN

BERNOULLI, JOHANN (JEAN) I (*b.* Basel, Switzerland, 6 August 1667; *d.* Basel, 1 January 1748)

The tenth child in the family, Johann proved unsuited for a business career, much to his father's sorrow. He therefore received permission in 1683 to enroll at his native city's university, where his brother Jakob (or Jacques), who was twelve years older and who had recently returned from the Netherlands, lectured as *magister artium* on experimental physics. In 1685 Johann, respondent to his brother in a logical disputation, was promoted to *magister artium* and began the study of medicine. He temporarily halted his studies at the licentiate level in 1690, when his first publication appeared, a paper on fermentation processes.[1] (His doctoral dissertation of 1694[2] is a mathematical work despite its medical subject, and reflects the influence of the iatromathematician Borelli.)

Bernoulli privately studied mathematics with the gifted Jakob, who in 1687 had succeeded to the vacant chair of mathematics at the University of Basel. From about this time, both brothers were engrossed in infinitesimal mathematics and were the first to achieve a full understanding of Leibniz' abbreviated presentation of differential calculus.[3] The extraordinary solution[4] of the problem of *catenaria* posed by Jakob Bernoulli (*Acta eruditorum,* June 1691) was Johann's first independently published work, and placed him in the front rank with Huygens, Leibniz, and Newton. Johann spent the greater part of 1691 in Geneva. There he taught differential calculus to J. C. Fatio-de-Duillier (whose brother Nicolas later played a not very praiseworthy role in the Leibniz-Newton priority dispute) and worked on the deepening of his own mathematical knowledge.

In the autumn of 1691 Bernoulli was in Paris, where he won a good place in Malebranche's mathematical circle as a representative of the new Leibnizian calculus, and did so by virtue of a "golden theorem" (stemming actually from Jakob)—the spectacular determination of the radius of curvature of a curve by means of the equation $\rho = dx/ds : d^2y/ds^2$. During this period he also met L'Hospital, then probably France's most gifted mathematician. "Grandseigneur of the science of mathematics"—he corresponded also with Huygens—L'Hospital engaged Bernoulli to initiate him into the secrets of the new infinitesimal calculus. The lessons were given in Paris and sometimes in L'Hospital's country seat at Oucques, and Bernoulli was generously compensated. L'Hospital even induced Bernoulli to continue, for a considerable fee, these lessons by correspondence after the latter's return to Basel. This correspondence[5] subsequently became the basis for the first textbook in differential calculus,[6] which assured L'Hospital's place in the history of mathematics. (Bernoulli's authorship of this work, which was still doubted by Cantor,[7] has been substantiated by the Basel manuscript of the *Differential Calculus* discovered in 1921 by Schafheitlin,[8] as well as by Bernoulli's correspondence with L'Hospital.[9])

In 1692 Bernoulli met Pierre de Varignon, who later became his disciple and close friend. This tie also resulted in a voluminous correspondence.[10] In 1693 Bernoulli began his exchange of letters with Leibniz, which was to grow into the most extensive correspondence ever conducted by the latter.

Bernoulli's most significant results during these years were published in the form of numerous memoirs in *Acta eruditorum* (*AE*) and shorter papers in the *Journal des Sçavans* (*JS*). Bernoulli's two most important achievements were the investigations concerning the function $y = x^x$ and the discovery, in 1694, of a general development in series by means of repeated integration by parts, the series subsequently named after him:

$$\int_0^x y\,dx = xy - \frac{x^2}{2!}y' + \frac{x^3}{3!}y'' - + \cdots$$

(cf. *Addidamentum AE,* 1694, letter to Leibniz of 2 September 1694). This series—whose utility, incidentally, Jakob Bernoulli failed to recognize—is based on the general Leibnizian principle for the differentiation of a product:

$$d^m[f(x)g(x)] = (df + dg)^{(m)} = \sum_{\nu=0}^{m}\binom{m}{\nu} d^{m-\nu}fd^{\nu}g.$$

This formalism is characteristic of a large part of the Bernoulli-Leibniz correspondence between 1694 and 1696.

Integration being viewed as the inverse operation of differentiation, Bernoulli worked a great deal on the integration of differential equations. This view was generally accepted in the Leibniz circle. In Paris he had already demonstrated the efficacy of Leibniz' calculus by an anonymous solution of "Debeaune's problem" (*JS,* 1692), which had been put to Descartes as the first inverse tangent problem. Five years later he demonstrated that with the aid of the calculus much more complex differential equations could be solved. In connection with Debeaune's problem, Jakob Bernoulli had proposed the general differential equation since called by his name,

$$y' + P(x)y + Q(x)y^n = 0,$$

and had solved it in a rather cumbersome way. Johann, more flexible with regard to formalism, solved this equation by considering the desired final function as the product of two functions, $M(x)$ and $N(x)$. In the resulting equation,

$$\frac{dM}{M} + \frac{dN}{N} + P(x)\,dx + (MN)^{n-1}Q(x)\,dx = 0,$$

the arbitrariness of the functions M and N makes it possible to subject one of them (e.g., M) to the secondary condition

$$\frac{dM}{M} + P(x)\,dx = 0,$$

resulting in $M = \exp[-\int P(x)\,dx]$. This substitution promptly leads to a linear differential equation in N.

Bernoulli's "exponential calculus" is nothing other than the infinitesimal calculus of exponential functions. Nieuwentijt, in a paper criticizing the lack of logical foundations in Leibniz' calculus,[11] pointed out the inapplicability of Leibniz' published differentiation methods to the exponential function x^ν. Thereupon Bernoulli developed, in "Principia calculi exponentialium seu percurrentium" (*AE,* 1697), the "exponential calculus," which is based on the equation

$$d(x^\nu) = x^\nu \log x\,dy + yx^{\nu-1}\,dx.$$

Also in 1695 came Bernoulli's summation of the infinite harmonic series

$$\sum_{K=1}^{n}(-1)^{K-1}K^{-1}\binom{n}{K}$$

from the difference scheme, the development of the addition theorems of trigonometric and hyperbolic functions from their differential equations, and the geometric generation of pairs of curves, wherein the sum or difference of the arc lengths can be represented by circular arcs. Neither Johann nor Jacob Bernoulli succeeded in mastering the problem, originated by Mengoli, of the summation of reciprocal squares ($\Sigma_{k=1}^{\infty} 1 : k^2$). This problem was solved only by Johann's greatest pupil, Leonhard Euler.[12]

In 1695 Bernoulli was offered both a professorship at Halle, and, through the intervention of Huygens, the chair of mathematics at Groningen. He eagerly accepted the latter offer, particularly since his hopes of obtaining a chair in Basel were nil as long as his brother Jakob was alive. On 1 September 1695 he departed for Holland with his wife (the former Dorothea Falkner) and seven-month-old Nikolaus, his first son, not without resentment against Jakob, who had begun to retaliate for Johann's earlier boastfulness when he solved the differential equation of the velaria (*JS,* 1692): Jakob termed Johann his pupil, who after all could only repeat what he had learned from his teacher. This cutting injustice was promptly paid back by Johann, now his equal in rank.

In June 1696, Johann posed (in *AE*) the problem of the brachistochrone, i.e., the problem of determining the "curve of quickest descent." Since no solution could be expected before the end of the year, Bernoulli, at Leibniz' request, republished the problem in the form of a leaflet dedicated to *acutissimis qui in toto orbe florent mathematicis* ("the shrewdest mathematicians of all the world") and fixed a six-month limit for its solution. Leibniz solved the problem on the day he received Bernoulli's letter, and correctly predicted a total of only five solutions: from the two Bernoullis, Newton, Leibniz, and L'Hospital. (It should be noted that it was only through Johann's assistance—by correspondence—that L'Hospital had arrived at his solution.)

This problem publicly demonstrated the difference in the talents of the two brothers. Johann solved the

BERNOULLI, JOHANN I

problem by ingenious intuition, which enabled him to reduce the mechanical problem to the optical problem already resolved by means of Fermat's principle of least time. He deduced the differential equation of the cycloid from the law of refraction. Jakob, on the other hand, furnished a detailed but cumbersome analysis, and came upon the roots of a new mathematical discipline, the calculus of variations. Unlike Jakob, Johann failed to perceive that such extreme-value problems differed from the customary ones in that it was no longer the unknown extreme values of a function that were to be determined, but functions that made a certain integral an extreme.[13]

In connection with his solution of the brachistochrone problem, Jakob (*AE,* May 1697) posed a new variational problem, the isoperimetric problem.[14] Johann underestimated the complexity of this problem by failing to perceive its variational character; and he furnished an incomplete solution (wherein the resulting differential equation is one order too low) in *Histoire des ouvrages des savants* (VI, 1697), and thereby brought on himself the merciless criticism of his brother.[15] This was the beginning of alienation and open discord between the brothers—and also the birth of the calculus of variations. A comparison of Jakob's solution (Basel, 1701; *AE,* May 1701) with Johann's analysis of the problem (which he presented through Varignon to the Paris Academy on 1 February 1701) clearly shows Johann's to be inferior. Nevertheless, Jakob was not able to enjoy his triumph, since—for reasons that remain mysterious—the sealed envelope containing Johann's solution was not opened by the Academy until 17 April 1706, the year following Jakob's death.

Soon after publication of Jakob's *Analysis magni problematis isoperimetrici* (1701), Johann must have felt that his brother's judgment was valid, although he never said so. Only after having been stimulated by Taylor's *Methodus incrementorum* (1715) did he produce a precise and formally elegant solution of the isoperimetric problem along the lines of Jakob's ideas (*Mémoires de l'Académie des sciences,* 1718). The concepts set forth in this paper contain the nucleus of modern methods of the calculus of variations. Also in this connection Bernoulli made a discovery pertaining to the variational problem of geodetic lines on convex surfaces: in a letter addressed to Leibniz, dated 26 August 1698, he perceived the characteristic property of geodetic lines, i.e., three consecutive points determine a normal plane of the surface.

Bernoulli's studies on the determination of all rationally quadrable segments of the common cycloid —the "fateful curve of the seventeenth century" (*AE,* July 1699)—in connection with the cyclotomic equation (*AE,* April 1701; more detailed in his correspondence with Moivre[16])—resulted in a systematic treatment of the integrals of rational functions by means of resolution into partial fractions. The general advance in algebraic analysis under Bernoulli's influence is evident in the typical case of the relation

$$2i \arctan x = \log \frac{x - i}{x + i}.$$

Nevertheless, Bernoulli had not yet perceived that such logarithmic expressions may take on infinitely many values.

Immediately after Jakob's death, Johann succeeded him in Basel, although he would undoubtedly have preferred to accept the repeated invitations extended to him by the universities of Utrecht and Leiden (see correspondence of the rector of Utrecht University, Pieter Burman, with Bernoulli's father-in-law, Falkner[17]). Family circumstances, however, caused him to settle in Basel.

Bernoulli's criticism of Taylor's *Methodus incrementorum* was simultaneously an attack upon the method of fluxions, for in 1713 Bernoulli had become involved in the priority dispute between Leibniz and Newton. Following publication of the Royal Society's *Commercium epistolicum* in 1712, Leibniz had no choice but to present his case in public. He released —without naming names—a letter by Bernoulli (dated 7 June 1713) in which Newton was charged with errors stemming from a misinterpretation of the higher differential. Thereupon Newton's followers raised complicated analytical problems, such as the determination of trajectories and the problem of finding the ballistic curve, which Newton had solved only for the law of resistance $R = av$ (R = resistance, a = constant, v = velocity). Bernoulli solved this problem (*AE,* 1719) for the general case ($R = av^n$), thus demonstrating the superiority of Leibniz' differential calculus.

After Newton's death in 1727, Bernoulli was unchallenged as the leading mathematical preceptor to all Europe. Since his return to Basel in 1705, he had devoted himself—in the field of applied mathematics—to theoretical and applied mechanics. In 1714 he published his only book, *Théorie de la manoeuvre des vaisseaux.* Here Bernoulli (as Huygens had done before him) criticizes the navigational theories advanced in 1679 by the French naval officer Bernard Renau d'Eliçagaray (1652–1719), a friend of Varignon's. In this book Bernoulli exposed the confusion in Cartesian mechanics between force and *vis viva* (now kinetic energy). On 26 February 1715—and not 1717, as stated in the literature because of a printing error in Varignon's *Nouvelle mécanique* (1725)—Bernoulli communicated to Varignon the principle of virtual velocities for the first time in analytical form. In modern notation it is

$$\partial A = \sum_{i=1}^{n} \vec{K}_i \, \partial \vec{s}_i = 0.$$

Since this principle can be derived from the energy principle $A + mv^2/2 = \text{const.}$, which Bernoulli applied several times to conservative mechanical systems of central forces, he considered it a second general principle of mechanics—which, however, he had demonstrated only for the statical case. For central forces, Bernoulli applied the *vis viva* equation to the inverse two-body problem, which he for the first time expressed in the form used today for the equation of the orbit (*Mémoires de l'Académie des sciences,* 1710):

$$\varphi(r) = \varphi\left(\frac{1}{u}\right) = \vartheta(u) = \int \frac{c\,du}{\sqrt{2(u+h) - u^2c^2}}$$

For the corresponding problem of centrally accelerated motion in a resisting medium (*ibid.,* 1711), he solved the differential equation

$$\frac{a}{\rho}\frac{dv}{v}\frac{ds}{d\theta} \pm av^{n-2}\,ds + \frac{dv}{v} = 0$$

(ρ = radius of curvature of the orbit) on the premise that $v = M(r)N(r)$, and determined the central force, in accordance with Huygens' formula, from

$$\rho(r) = \frac{v^2}{\rho}\frac{ds}{rd\theta}.$$

Newton severely criticized the Cartesian vortex theory in Book II of the *Principia.* Bernoulli's advocacy of the theory delayed the acceptance of Newtonian physics on the Continent. In three prize-winning papers, Bernoulli treated the transmission of momentum (1727), the motions of the planets in aphelion (1730), and the cause of the inclination of the planetary orbits relative to the solar equator (1735). Bernoulli's 1732 work on hydraulics (*Opera,* IV) was generally considered a piece of plagiarism from the hydrodynamics of his son Daniel. Nevertheless, Bernoulli did try to manage without Daniel's formulation of the principle of *vis viva.*

Bernoulli also worked in experimental physics. In several papers (*Mémoires de l'Académie des sciences,* 1701; Basel, 1719), he investigated the phenomenon of the luminous barometer within the framework of contemporary Cartesian physics, although he was unable to furnish a sufficient explanation for the electrical phenomenon of triboluminescence discovered by Picard.

Bernoulli was a member of the royal academies of Paris and Berlin, of the Royal Society, of the St. Petersburg Academy, and the Institute of Bologna. As son-in-law of Alderman Falkner, he not only enjoyed social status in Basel, but also held honorary civic offices there. He became especially well known as a member of the school board through his efforts to reform the humanistic Gymnasium. His temperament might well have led him to a career in politics, but instead it only involved him in scientific polemics with his brother Jakob and in the Leibniz-Newton priority dispute. Even abroad he was unable to curb his "Flemish pugnacity." In 1702, as professor in Groningen, he became involved in quarrels with the theologians, who in turn, because of his views in natural philosophy, accused him of what was then the worst of heresies, Spinozism.

Bernoulli's quarrelsomeness was matched by his passion for communicating. His scientific correspondence comprised about 2,500 letters, exchanged with some 110 scholars.

NOTES

1. *De effervescentia et fermentatione.*
2. *De motu musculorum.*
3. Leibniz, *Nova methodus de maximis et minimis.*
4. J. E. Hofmann, "Vom öffentlichen Bekanntwerden der Leibniz'schen Infinitesimalmathematik."
5. O. Spiess, ed., *Der Briefwechsel von Johann Bernoulli.*
6. L'Hospital, *Analyse des infiniment petits.*
7. Cantor, *Vorlesungen über Geschichte der Mathematik.*
8. *Lectiones de calculo differentialium,* MS Universitätsbibliothek, Basel.
9. O. J. Rebel, *Der Briefwechsel zwischen Johann Bernoulli und dem Marquis de l'Hôpital.*
10. E. J. Fedel, *Johann Bernoullis Briefwechsel mit Varignon aus den Jahren 1692–1702.*
11. *Considerationes secundae circa calculi differentialis principia.*
12. O. Spiess, *Die Summe der reziproken Quadratzahlen.*
13. P. Dietz, *Die Ursprünge der Variationsrechnung bei Jakob Bernoulli;* J. E. Hofmann, *Ueber Jakob Bernoullis Beiträge zur Infinitesimalmathematik.*
14. J. O. Fleckenstein, *Johann und Jakob Bernoulli.*
15. Hofmann, *Ueber Jakob Bernoullis Beiträge zur Infinitesimalmathematik.*
16. K. Wollenschlaeger, *Der mathematische Briefwechsel zwischen Johann I Bernoulli und Abraham de Moivre.*
17. O. Spiess, ed., *Der Briefwechsel von Johann Bernoulli.*

BIBLIOGRAPHY

I. Original Works. Among Bernoulli's writings are *De effervescentia et fermentatione* (Basel, 1690); *De motu musculorum* (Basel, 1694), his doctoral dissertation; and *Lectiones de calculo differentialium,* MS in library of Univ. of Basel, also trans. and ed. by P. Schafheitlin as no. 211 in Ostwald's Klassiker der Exakten Wissenschaften (Leipzig, 1924). His works were collected as *Opera Johannis Bernoullii,* G. Cramer, ed., 4 vols. (Geneva, 1742). For his correspondence, see Bousquet, ed., *Commercium philosophicum et mathematicum G. Leibnitii et Joh. Bernoullii* (Geneva, 1745); his correspondence with Euler in *Bibliotheca mathematica,* 3rd ser., **4** (1903)–**6** (1905); E. J. Fedel, *Johann Bernoullis Briefwechsel mit Varignon aus den Jahren 1692–1702* (Heidelberg, 1934), dissertation; O. J. Rebel, *Der Briefwechsel zwischen Johann Bernoulli und dem Marquis de l'Hôpital* (Heidelberg, 1934), dissertation; O. Spiess, ed., *Der Briefwechsel von Johann Bernoulli,* I (Basel, 1955); and K. Wollenschlaeger, *Der mathematische Briefwechsel zwischen Johann I Bernoulli und Abraham de Moivre* (Basel, 1932), dissertation, publ. separately in *Verhandlungen der Naturforschenden Gesellschaft in Basel.* Handwritten material is in the library of the University of Basel.

II. SECONDARY LITERATURE. Writings on Bernoulli, on his work, or on background material are Jakob Bernoulli, *Analysis magni problematis isoperimetrici* (Basel, 1701); M. Cantor, *Vorlesungen über Geschichte der Mathematik,* 2nd ed., III (Leipzig, 1901), 207–233; C. Carathéodory, "Basel und der Beginn der Variationsrechnung," in *Festschrift zum 60. Geburtstag von Andreas Speiser* (Zurich, 1945), pp. 1–18; P. Dietz, *Die Ursprünge der Variationsrechnung bei Jakob Bernoulli* (Basel, 1959), dissertation, Univ. of Mainz; J. O. Fleckenstein, "Varignon und die mathematischen Wissenschaften im Zeitalter des Cartesianismus," in *Archives d'histoire des sciences* (1948); and *Johann und Jakob Bernoulli* (Basel, 1949), supp. no. 6 of *Elemente der Mathematik;* J. E. Hofmann, *Ueber Jakob Bernoullis Beiträge zur Infinitesimalmathematik,* no. 3 in the series Monographies de l'Enseignement Mathématique (Geneva, 1956); "Vom öffentlichen Bekanntwerden der Leibniz'schen Infinitesimalmathematik," in *Sitzungsberichte der Oesterreichischen Akademie der Wissenschaften,* no. 8/9 (1966), 237–241; and "Johann Bernoulli, Propagator der Infinitesimalmethoden," in *Praxis der Mathematik,* **9** (1967/1968), 209–212; Guillaume de L'Hospital, *Analyse des infiniment petits* (Paris, 1696); G. Leibniz, "Nova methodus de maximis et minimis," in *Acta eruditorum* (Oct. 1684); B. Nieuwentijt, *Considerationes secundae circa calculi differentialis principia* (Amsterdam, 1696); A. Speiser, "Die Basler Mathematiker," *Neujahrsblatt der G.G.G.,* no. 117 (Basel, 1939); O. Spiess, "Johann B. und seine Söhne," in *Atlantis* (1940), pp. 663 ff.; "Die Summe der reziproken Quadratzahlen," in *Festschrift zum 60. Geburtstag von Andreas Speiser* (Zurich, 1945), pp. 66 ff.; *Die Mathematiker Bernoulli* (Basel, 1948).

E. A. FELLMANN

J. O. FLECKENSTEIN

BERNOULLI, JOHANN (JEAN) II (*b.* Basel, Switzerland, 28 May 1710; *d.* Basel, 17 July 1790)

Johann II was perhaps the most successful of Johann I's sons, inasmuch as he succeeded his father in the chair of mathematics after having previously taught rhetoric. In 1727 he obtained the degree of doctor of jurisprudence (1). Subsequently he won the prize of the Paris Academy four times, either by himself or with his father (2-5)—undoubtedly sufficient qualification to make him Johann I's successor. But thereafter his mathematical production dwindled to occasional academic papers and a treatise (6), although he lived to be almost as old as his father. His shyness and frail constitution did not, however, prevent him from engaging in extensive scientific correspondence (about 900 items) and from furthering the publication, in four volumes, of his father's *Opera omnia.* He personified the mathematical genius of his native city in the second half of the eighteenth century. In 1756, after resigning as president of the Berlin Academy, Maupertuis found refuge with him in Basel, where he died in 1759.

BIBLIOGRAPHY

Bernoulli's writings include (1) *De compensationibus* (Basel, 1729), dissertation for the doctor of jurisprudence; (2) "Recherches physiques et géométriques sur la question: Comment se fait la propagation de la lumière," in *Recueil des pièces qui ont remporté les prix de l'Académie royale des sciences,* III (1736); (3) "Discours sur les ancres," *ibid.* (1737); (4) "Discours sur le cabestan," *ibid.*, V (1741); (5) "Nouveaux principes de mécanique et de physique tendans à expliquer la nature et les propriétés de l'Aiman," *ibid.*, V (1743); and (6) "Réponse à une lettre anonyme sur la figure de la terre," in *Journal Helvét.* (1740), pp. 219 *et seq.*

J. O. FLECKENSTEIN

BERNOULLI, JOHANN (JEAN) III (*b.* Basel, Switzerland, 4 November 1744; *d.* Berlin, Germany, 13 July 1807)

The most successful of the sons of Johann II—although his mathematical achievements were insignificant—Johann was a universally knowledgeable child prodigy. At fourteen he obtained the degree of master of jurisprudence, and at twenty he was invited by Frederick II to reorganize the astronomical observatory at the Berlin Academy. His frail health and his encyclopedic inclinations hampered him in his practical scientific activities, however. His treatises are of no particular interest. On the other hand, his travel accounts (1772–1776; 1777–1779; 1781) had a great cultural and historical impact. With Hindenburg he

BERNOULLI, NIKOLAUS I

published the *Leipziger Magazin für reine & angewandte Mathematik* from 1776–1789.

Johann was entrusted with the administration of the mathematical estate of the Bernoulli family. The major part of the correspondence was sold to the Stockholm Academy; and its existence there was overlooked until his letters were rediscovered by Gylden at the Stockholm Observatory in 1877. His correspondence, comprising about 2,800 items, exceeded that of Johann I.

BIBLIOGRAPHY

Johann's writings include various essays in *Mém. Acad. Berlin* (1766–1775), as well as astronomical observations and computations, 1767–1807, in *Neue Berliner Ephemeriden* and *Bodes astronomisches Jahrbuch.* Other works are *Recueil pour les astronomes,* 3 vols. (Berlin, 1772–1776); *Liste des astronomes connus actuellement* (Berlin, 1776); *Lettres écrites pendant la cours d'un voyage par l'Allemagne 1774/75,* 3 vols. (Berlin, 1777–1779); "Essai d'une nouvelle méthode de déterminer la diminution séculaire de l'obliquité de l'écliptique," in *Mém. Acad. Berlin* (1779), pp. 211–242; and *Lettres astronomiques* (Berlin, 1781).

J. O. FLECKENSTEIN

BERNOULLI, NIKOLAUS I (*b.* Basel, Switzerland, 21 October 1687; *d.* Basel, 29 November 1759)

The son of Nikolaus Bernoulli, a Basel alderman and painter, Nikolaus I studied with his two uncles, Jakob I and Johann I, and made rapid progress in mathematics. As early as 1704, studying under Jakob I, he obtained his master's degree by defending Jakob's last thesis on infinite series (1), in which quadratures and rectifications are determined by means of series expansions, arrived at by the method of undetermined coefficients or by interpolation, after Wallis, for binomial expansions. In 1709 he obtained the degree of doctor of jurisprudence (2) with a dissertation on the application of the calculus of probability to questions of law. In 1712 Nikolaus undertook a journey to Holland, England, and France, where he met Montmort, later his friend and collaborator. He became a member of the Berlin Academy in 1713, of the Royal Society in 1714, and of the Academy of Bologna in 1724. In 1716 he succeeded Hermann as professor of mathematics in Padua, but in 1722 he returned to Basel in order to accept the chair of logic, which he exchanged in 1731 for a professorship in law. He served four times as rector of the University of Basel.

Nikolaus was a gifted but not very productive mathematician. As a result, his most important achievements are hidden throughout his correspondence, which comprises about 560 items. The most important part of his correspondence with Montmort (1710–1712) was published in the latter's *Essai d'analyse sur les jeux de hazard* (2nd ed., Paris, 1713). Here Nikolaus formulated for the first time the problem of probability theory, later known as the St. Petersburg problem.

In his correspondence with Leibniz (1712–1716), Nikolaus discussed questions of convergence and found that the binomial expansion $(1 + x)^n$ diverges for $x > 1$. In his letters to Euler (1742–1743) he criticized Euler's indiscriminate use of divergent series. In this correspondence he also solved the problem of the sum of reciprocal squares $\Sigma_{\nu=1}^{\infty} 1/\nu^2 = \pi^2/6$, which had confounded Leibniz and Jakob I. His personal copy of the *Opera omnia* of his uncle Jakob, which he had published, contains the proof, which does not require the help of analytical methods.

To his edition of his uncle's *Opera,* he added as an appendix thirty-two articles from Jakob I's diary ("Annotationes et meditationes"). His concern with editing his uncle's works went back to at least 1713, when he published the *Ars conjectandi.*

In the priority quarrel with Newton, Nikolaus sided with his uncle Johann in defending the interests of Leibniz. It was he who pointed out Newton's misunderstanding of the higher-order derivatives (3), which had caused Newton's errors with the inverse problem of central force in a resisting medium (5). He also considered the problem of orthogonal trajectories (6) and Riccati's differential equation (6, 8, 10–12).

BIBLIOGRAPHY

Jakob I's last thesis on infinite series is (1) *De seriebus infinitis earumque usu in quadraturis spatiorum et rectificationibus curvarum* (Basel, 1704). Nikolaus' writings include (2) *De usu artis conjectandi in jure* (Basel, 1709); (3) "Addition au Mém. de Mr. Jean Bernoulli touchant la manière de trouver les forces centrales dans les milieux résistans . . . ," in *Mémoires de l'Académie des Sciences* (1711), pp. 53–56; (4) "Solutio generalis problematis 15 propositi a D. de Moivre in Transactiones de mensura sortis," in *Philosophical Transactions of the Royal Society,* **29** (1714), 133–144; (5) "Calculus pro invenienda linea curva, quam describit projectile in medio resistente," in *Acta eruditorum* (1719), 224–226; (6) "Modus inveniendi aequationem differentialem completam ex data aequatione differentiali incompleta . . . ," *ibid.,* supp. **7** (1719), pp. 310–859; (7) "Tentamen solutionis generalis problematis de construenda curva, quae alias ordinatim positione datas ad angulos rectos secat," *ibid.* (1719), pp. 295–304; (8) "Novum theorema pro integratione aequationum differentialium secundi gradus, quae nullam constantem differentialem supponunt," *ibid.*, supp. **9** (1720); (9) *Theses logicae de methodo analytica et synthetica* (Basel, 1722); (10) "Annotazioni sopra lo schediasma del Conte Jacopo Riccati etc. coll'annessa soluzione propria del problema inverso delle forze centrali . . . ," in *Giornale de letterati d'Italia,* **20,** 316–351; (11) "Dimostrazione analitica di un teorema, il qual serve per la soluzione del problema proposto nel T.XX. del Giorn. Lett. Ital. . . . ," *ibid.,* **29,** 163–171; and (12) "Òsservazione intorno al teorema proposto dal Conte Jacopo de Fagnano," *ibid.*, pp. 150–163. See also *Athenae Rauricae* (Basel, 1778), pp. 148–151.

J. O. FLECKENSTEIN

BERNOULLI, NIKOLAUS II (*b.* Basel, Switzerland, 6 February 1695; *d.* St. Petersburg, Russia, 31 July 1726)

Nikolaus was the favorite son of Johann I, whose mediation made it possible for him to enter the University of Basel at the age of thirteen. There he passed the master's examinations at sixteen, and in 1715 he became a licentiate in jurisprudence (1). Nikolaus assisted his father with his correspondence, particularly in the priority quarrel between Leibniz and Newton, during which he drafted the reply to Taylor (6) and supplied valuable contributions to the problem of trajectories (2–4). With his brother Daniel he traveled in France and Italy, where both received and accepted appointments to the St. Petersburg Academy. Within the year, however, he contracted and died of a hectic fever.

BIBLIOGRAPHY

Nikolaus' writings are (1) *Dissertatio de jure detractionis* (Basel, 1715); (2) "Solutio problematis invenire lineam, quae ad angulos rectos secet omnes hyperbolas ejusdem verticis et ejusdem centri," in *Acta eruditorum* (1716), pp. 226-230; (3) "Exercitatio geometrica de trajectoriis orthogonalibus . . . ," *ibid.* (1720), pp. 223-237; (4) "De trajectoriis curvas ordinatim positione datas ad angulos rectos vel alia lege secantibus," *ibid.* (1718), pp. 248–262; (5) "Animadversiones in Jac. Hermanni solutionem propriam duorum problematum geometricorum . . . ," *ibid.*, supp. **8** (1720), pp. 372-389; (6) "Responsio ad Taylori Angli querelas . . . ," *ibid.* (1720), pp. 279-285; (7) "Analysis aequationum quarundam differentialium," in *Comment. Acad. Petrop.*, **1** (1728), 198-207; and (8) "De motu corporum ex percussione," *ibid.*, pp. 121-126.

J. O. FLECKENSTEIN

BERNSTEIN, FELIX (*b.* Halle, Germany, 24 February 1878; *d.* Zurich, Switzerland, 3 December 1956)

Bernstein's father, Julius, who wrote on electrobiology, studied under DuBois Reymond. Felix studied in Halle with Georg Cantor, a friend of his father, then went to Göttingen to study with Hilbert and Klein. In 1896 he took his Abitur in Halle, then taught mathematics and studied physiology there. He received his Ph.D. at Göttingen in 1901 and his Habilitation in Halle in 1907. He returned to Göttingen in 1911 as associate professor of mathematical statistics. After military service in World War I, he headed the statistical branch of the Office of Rationing and in 1921 became commissioner of finance. Also in 1921 he became full professor and founded the Institute of Mathematical Statistics, where he was director until 1934. He emigrated to the United States, where he became a citizen in 1940. He taught at Columbia, New York, and Syracuse universities. In 1948 he returned to Göttingen.

It was in 1895 or 1896 while a student at the Gymnasium that Bernstein gave the first proof of the equivalence theorem of sets. If each of two sets, A and B, is equivalent to a subset of the other, then A is equivalent to B. This theorem establishes the notion of cardinality and is thus the central theorem in set theory. It bears some similarity to the Eudoxean definition of equal irrationals.

Cantor, who had been working on the equivalence problem, had left for a holiday and Bernstein had volunteered to correct proofs of his book on transcendental numbers. In that interval, the idea for a solution came to Bernstein one morning while shaving. Cantor then worked with the approach for several years before formulating it to his satisfaction. Cantor always gave full credit to Bernstein, who meanwhile had become a student of fine arts at Pisa. He was persuaded to return to mathematics by two professors there who had heard Cantor expound the equation at a mathematical congress. Bernstein retained this interest in the arts, particularly painting and sculpture, throughout his life.

Bernstein's subsequent work in pure and applied mathematics shows great versatility, and includes some of the earliest applications of set theory outside pure mathematics, contributions to isoperimetric problems, convex functions, the Laplace transform, and number theory, as well as set theory itself.

Toward the 1920's Bernstein became increasingly interested in the mathematical treatment of questions in genetics; he was to contribute decisively to the development of population genetics in the analysis of modes of inheritance. The discovery of human blood groups had made possible an entirely new approach to human genetics. In 1924 Bernstein was able to show that the A, B, and O blood groups are inherited on the basis of a set of triple alleles, and not on the basis of two pairs of genes, as had been thought. He compared a population genetic analysis of the frequencies of the four blood groups—numerous records of racially variant blood-group frequencies had been available since the discovery of this phenomenon by L. and H. Hirschfeld—with the expectations for the blood-group frequencies according to the expanded Hardy-Weinberg formula $p^2{:}2pq{:}q^2$, and found significant and consistent differences. When he applied the same technique to an expectation based on a triple-allelic system of a single locus, the agreement with observation was excellent.

Bernstein also applied the techniques of population genetics to such problems as linkage, to the measures of the degree of inbreeding for individuals and populations, to determination of the presence of recessive inheritance, to a method for deriving genetic ratios based on an a priori expectation, and to use of the development of presbyopia as an indicator of age. He also interpreted the direction of hair whorl and variations in singing voice, as found in different populations, in terms of allelic differences of single pairs of genes, but this interpretation has not withstood the test of time.

BIBLIOGRAPHY

Bernstein's writings are *Untersuchungen aus der Mengenlehre,* dissertation (Halle, 1901); "Ueber die Reihe der transfiniten Ordnungszahlen," in *Mathematische Annalen,* **60**, no. 2 (1905), 187-193; "Die Theorie der reellen Zahlen," in *Jahresbericht der Deutschen Mathematikervereinigung,* **14**, no. 8/9 (1905); "Zur Theorie der trigonometrischen Reihe," in *Bericht. Königliche Sächsische Gesellschaft der Wissenschaften zu Leipzig,* Math.-phys. Klasse, **60** (meeting of 7 Dec. 1908); "Ueber eine Anwendung der Mengenlehre auf ein aus der Theorie der säkularen Störungen herrührendes Problem," in *Mathematische Annalen,* **71** (1909), 417-439 (see also *ibid.*, **72** [1912], 295-296, written with P. Bohl and E. Borel); "Ueber den letzten Fermatschen Lehrsatz," in *Nachrichten von der Gesellschaft der Wissenschaften zu Göttingen,* Math.-phys. Klasse (1910); "Zur Theorie der konvexen Funktionen," in *Mathematische Annalen,* **76**, no. 4 (1915); "Die Mengenlehre Georg Cantors und der Finitismus," in *Jahresbericht der Deutschen Mathematikervereinigung,* **28**, no. 1/6 (1919), 63-78; "Die Theorie der gleichsinnigen Faktoren in der Mendelschen Erblichkeitslehre vom Standpunkt der mathematischen Statistik," in *Zeitschrift für induktive Abstammungs- und Vererbungslehre* (1922); "Probleme aus der Theorie der Wärmeleitung. I. Mitteilung. Eine neue Methode zur Integration partieller Differentialgleichungen. Der lineare Wärmeleiter mit verschwindender Anfangstemperatur," in *Mathematische Zeitschrift,* **22**, no. 3/4 (1925), written with Gustav Doetsch; "Zusammenfassende Betrachtungen über die erblichen Blutstrukturen des Menschen," in *Zeitschrift für induktive Abstammungs- und Vererbungslehre* (1925); "Ueber die numerische Ermittlung verborgener Periodizitäten," in *Zeitschrift für angewandte Mathematik und Mechanik,* **7** (1927), 441-444; "Fortgesetzte Untersuchungen aus der Theorie der Blutgruppen," in *Zeitschrift für induktive Abstammungs- und Vererbungslehre* (1928); "Ueber Mendelistische Anthropologie," in *Verhandlungen des V. internationalen Kongresses für Vererbungswissenschaft* (Berlin, 1927), repr. in *Zeitschrift für induktive Abstammungs- und Vererbungslehre* (1928); "Ueber die Anwendung der Steinerschen Fläche in der Erblichkeitslehre, insbesondere in der Theorie der Blutgruppen," in *Zeitschrift für angewandte Mathematik und Mechanik,* **9** (1929); "Ueber die Erblichkeit der Blutgruppen," in *Zeitschrift für induktive Abstammungs- und Vererbungslehre* (1930); "Berichtigung zur Arbeit: Zur Grundlegung der Chromosomentheorie der Vererbung beim Menschen mit bes. Berücksichtigung der Blutgruppen," *ibid.* (1931, 1932); "Principles of Probability in Natural Science," in *Journal of Mathematics and Physics,* **14** (Mar. 1935); "The Continuum Problem," in *Proceedings of the National Academy of Sciences,* **24**, no. 2 (Feb. 1938), 101-104; and "Law of Physiologic Aging as Derived from Long Range Data on Refraction of the Human Eye," in *Archives of Ophthalmology,* **34** (Nov.-Dec. 1945), written with Marianne Bernstein. See also Corrado Gini, "Felix Bernstein," in *Revue de l'Institut international de statistique,* **25** (1957), 1-3; English trans. in *Records of the Genetics Society of America,* **60** (1968), 522-523. Bernstein's correspondence with Einstein (1933-1952) is at the Institute for Advanced Study, Princeton, and Houghton Library, Harvard.

HENRY NATHAN

BERNSTEIN, SERGEY NATANOVICH (*b.* Odessa, Russia, 5 March 1880; *d.* Moscow, U.S.S.R., 26 October 1968)

Bernstein was the son of Natan Osipovich Bernstein, lecturer in anatomy and physiology at the Novorossysky University in Odessa. After graduating from high school in 1898, he studied at the Sorbonne and the École d'Électrotechnique Supérieure in Paris; in 1902-1903 he also studied at Göttingen. He defended his doctoral dissertation at the Sorbonne in 1904 and, after returning to Russia in 1905, defended his master's thesis (1908) and his doctoral dissertation at Kharkov (1913) because scientific degrees awarded abroad did not entitle one to a university post in Russia. From 1907 to 1933 Bernstein taught at Kharkov University, first as a lecturer and then as a professor after

1917, laying the foundations of a mathematical school that included N. I. Akhiezer and V. L. Goncharov. During this period Bernstein frequently gave series of lectures and presented reports abroad; in 1915 he participated in the Second All-Russian Congress of High School Teachers; and in 1930 he organized the First All-Union Mathematical Congress, held in Kharkov. He was director of the Mathematical Research Institute in 1928–1931 and was one of the leaders of the Kharkov Mathematical Society from 1911. In 1925 he was elected member of the Academy of Sciences of the Ukrainian S.S.R.

In 1933 Bernstein began lecturing at the University of Leningrad and the Polytechnical Institute, while he worked also in the Mathematical Institute of the U.S.S.R. Academy of Sciences, of which he had been elected corresponding member in 1924 and member in 1929. He moved to Moscow in 1943, continuing his work at the Mathematical Institute. He edited Chebyshev's *Polnoe sobranie sochineny* ("Complete Works"; 1944–1951) and in his later years prepared a four-volume edition of his own writings.

Bernstein was a member of the Paris Académie des Sciences (elected corresponding member in 1928 and foreign member in 1955), doctor *honoris causa* of the universities of Algiers (1944) and Paris (1945), and honorary member of the Moscow (1940) and Leningrad (1966) mathematical societies. In 1942 his scientific achievement was recognized with the State Award, first class; earlier he had received awards from the Belgian Academy of Sciences and from the Paris Academy of Sciences for the book based on his lectures at the Sorbonne in 1923.

In his work Bernstein united traditions of Chebyshev's St. Petersburg mathematical school with western European mathematical thought, particularly that of France (Picard, Vallée-Poussin) and Germany (Weierstrass, Hilbert). Three fields dominated his work: partial differential equations, theory of best approximation of functions, and probability theory.

Bernstein's doctoral dissertation at the Sorbonne held the solution of Hilbert's nineteenth problem (1900), particular cases of which had been treated shortly before by Picard and others. Bernstein's result read: If a solution $Z\ (x,y)$ of an analytical differential equation $F(x,y,z,p,q,r,s,t) = 0$ of elliptical type $4\frac{\delta F}{\delta r}\cdot\frac{\delta F}{\delta t}-\left(\frac{\delta F}{\delta s}\right)^2 > 0$, where $p=\frac{\delta z}{\delta x}$, $q=\frac{\delta z}{\delta y}$, $r=\frac{\delta^2 z}{\delta x^2}$, $s=\frac{\delta^2 z}{\delta x \delta y}$, $t=\frac{\delta^2 z}{\delta y^2}$ possesses continuous derivatives up to the third order (inclusive), the solution is analytical. In his master's thesis Bernstein solved Hilbert's twentieth problem, demonstrating the possibility of an analytical solution of Dirichlet's problem for a wide class of nonlinear elliptical equations. A number of theorems on the differential geometry of surfaces followed, particularly on the theory of minimal surfaces. The above-mentioned studies were further advanced by Bernstein and many others, and are still being developed.

Another area of Bernstein's work concerned the theory of the best approximation of functions, to which he contributed new ideas and that he called the constructive theory of functions (1938). In this theory, calculation and investigation of functions are carried out with the notion introduced by Chebyshev in 1854 of the best approximation of a given function $f(x)$ by means of a polynomial $g_n(x)$ of a given degree n or by means of some other relatively simple function $g(x)$ depending on the finite number of parameters. If parameters are selected so that on a segment (a,b) the value of max $|f(x) - g_n(x)| = E_n[f(x)]$ is minimal, the function $g_n(x)$ is called the best approximation of a function $f(x)$. Chebyshev and his immediate successors were more interested in finding the polynomial of best approximation $g_n(x)$ when n is given, than in exploring the general functional properties of the quantity $E_n[f(x)]$. In 1885 Weierstrass demonstrated that any function $f(x)$ continuous on a segment (a,b) can be expanded into a uniformly convergent series of polynomials so that $\lim_{n\to\infty} E_n[f(x)] = 0$, whatever the continuous function $f(x)$ is.

The point of departure for Bernstein was the problem of estimating the order of the quantity E_n for $f(x) \equiv |x|$ on a segment $(-1,+1)$, posed by Vallée-Poussin. In 1911 Bernstein demonstrated that the best approximation $E_{2n}(|x|)$ by means of a polynomial of degree $2n$ lay between $\frac{\sqrt{2}-1}{4(2n-1)}$ and $\frac{2}{\pi(2n+1)}$, and that there existed $\lim_{n\to\infty} 2n\, E_{2n}(|x|) = \lambda$, with $0.278 < \lambda < 0.286$, so that for sufficiently great values of n the inequality $\frac{0.278}{2n} < E_{2n} < \frac{0.286}{2n}$ holds. Bernstein also studied asymptotic values of the best approximation for various classes of functions and established the closest relations between the law of decrease of the quantity $E_n[f(x)]$ and the analytical and differential properties of the function $f(x)$. These relations were the subject of his report at the Fifth International Congress of Mathematicians, held at Cambridge in 1912. Bernstein later continued his studies in that area, solving problems relevant to the theory of interpolation, methods of mechanical quadratures, and the best approximation on an infinite axis. In 1914 he introduced an important new class of quasi-analytical functions.

Almost simultaneous with the theory of best approximation Bernstein approached probability theory. In 1917 he suggested the first system of axioms for probability theory; he later conducted a number of fundamental studies relevant to the generalization of the law of large numbers, the central limit theorem, Markov chains, the theory of stochastic processes, and applications of probability theory to genetics. All these works by Bernstein greatly influenced the advance of contemporary probability theory.

BIBLIOGRAPHY

I. Original Works. Bernstein's writings were collected as *Sobranie sochineny akademika S. N. Bernshteina* ("Collected Works . . ."), 4 vols. (Moscow, 1952–1964). They include "Sur la nature analytique des solutions des équations différentielles aux dérivées partielles du second ordre," in *Mathematische Annalen*, **59** (1904), 20–76, his doctoral diss. at the Sorbonne; "Issledovanie i integrirovanie differentsialnykh uravneny s chastnymi proizvodnymi vtorogo poryadka ellipticheskogo tipa" ("Research on the Elliptical Partial Differential Second-Order Equations and Their Integration"), in *Soobshcheniya i protokoly Kharkovskago matematicheskago obshchestva*, **11** (1910), 1–164, his master's thesis, also in *Sobranie sochineny*, III; *Teoria veroyatnostey* ("Probability Theory"; Kharkov, 1911; 4th ed., Moscow–Leningrad, 1946); *O nailuchshem priblizhenii nepreryvnykh funktsy posredstvom mnogochlenov dannoy stepeni* ("On the Best Approximation of Continuous Functions by Means of Polynomials of Given Degree"; Kharkov, 1912), his Russian doctoral diss., also in *Sobranie sochineny*, I, and in French as "Sur l'ordre de la meilleure approximation des fonctions continues par des polynomes de degré donné," in *Mémoires de l'Académie royale de Belgique. Classe des sciences. Collection*, 2nd ser., **4** (1912), 1–103; and *Leçons sur les propriétés extrémales et la meilleure approximation des fonctions analytiques d'une variable réelle* (Paris, 1926), based on lectures delivered at the Sorbonne in 1923.

II. Secondary Literature. See N. I. Akhiezer, *Akademik S. N. Bernshtein i ego raboty po konstruktivnoy teorii funktsy* ("Academician S. N. Bernstein and His Research on the Constructive Theory of Functions"; Kharkov, 1955); A. N. Kolmogorov, Y. V. Linnik, Y. V. Prokhorov, and O. V. Sarmanov, "Sergey Natanovich Bernshtein," in *Teoria veroyatnostei i ee primenenie*, **14**, no. 1 (1969), 113–121; A. N. Kolmogorov and O. V. Sarmanov, "O rabotakh S. N. Bernshteina po teorii veroiatnostey" ("S. N. Bernstein's Research on Probability Theory"), *ibid.*, **5**, no. 2 (1960), 215–221; *Matematika v SSSR za sorok let* ("Forty Years of Mathematics in the U.S.S.R."), 2 vols. (Moscow, 1959), see index; *Matematika v SSSR za tridtsat let* ("Thirty Years of Mathematics in the U.S.S.R."; Moscow-Leningrad, 1948), see index; I. Z. Shtokalo, ed., *Istoria otechestvennoy matematiki* ("History of Native Mathematics"), II and III (Kiev, 1967–1968), see index; and A. P. Youschkevitch, *Istoria matematiki v Rossii do 1917 goda* ("History of Mathematics in Russia Before 1917"; Moscow, 1968), see index.

A. P. Youschkevitch

BERTINI, EUGENIO (*b.* Forlì, Italy, 8 November 1846; *d.* Pisa, Italy, 24 February 1933)

In 1863 Bertini registered at the University of Bologna, intending to study engineering, but after taking the course taught by Luigi Cremona, he turned to pure mathematics. In 1866 he fought with Garibaldi in the third war for Italian independence. On the advice of Cremona, he resumed his studies and transferred to the University of Pisa, from which he received his degree in mathematics in 1867. During the academic year 1868–1869 he attended the course in Milan taught by L. Cremona, F. Brioschi, and F. Casorati. This course, dealing with Abel's integrals, exerted considerable influence on Bertini's own research.

In 1870 Bertini began his teaching career in the secondary schools of Milan, and in 1872 taught in Rome. There, on the recommendation of Cremona, he was appointed a special lecturer to teach descriptive and projective geometry. In 1875 he accepted the professorship of advanced geometry at the University of Pisa. From 1880 to 1892 he taught at the University of Pavia, and then returned to his former professorship at Pisa, a post he held until his retirement at the age of seventy-five. For the next ten years he taught an elective course in geometrical complements, which he had started as an introductory course to higher geometry.

Bertini's research deals particularly with algebraic geometry and constitutes definite progress in relation to the studies pursued by the school of Cremona. In this connection it is necessary to note that Cremona, having formulated the theory on plane and space transformations that bears his name, availed himself of the same transformations to change higher geometric figures into simpler figures and then apply to the higher figures the properties of the simpler ones. Bertini studied the geometric properties that remain constant during such transformations. He conceived the idea of exploring this field after studying the problem of the classification of plane involutions. In 1877 he succeeded in determining the various types, irreducible from each other, in which the planar involutions may be reduced through Cremona's transformations. His treatises are noteworthy for their order and clarity.

BIBLIOGRAPHY

I. Original Works. Bertini's works include "La geometria delle serie lineari sopra una curva piana, secondo il metodo algebrico," in *Annali di matematica pura ed applicata,* 2nd ser., **22** (1894), 1–40; *Introduzione alla geometria proiettiva degli iperspazi* (Pisa, 1906; Messina, 1923); and *Complementi di geometria proiettiva* (Bologna, 1927).

II. Secondary Literature. More information on Bertini may be found in G. Castelnuovo, "Commemorazione del socio Eugenio Bertini," in *Atti della Reale Accademia nazionale dei Lincei. Rendiconti,* Classe di scienze fisiche, matematiche e naturali, 6th ser., **17** (1933), 745–748; and F. Enriques, *Le matematiche nella storia e nella cultura* (Bologna, 1938), pp. 284, 286, 287, 292.

Ettore Carruccio

BERTRAND, JOSEPH LOUIS FRANÇOIS (*b.* Paris, France, 11 March 1822; *d.* Paris, 5 April 1900)

Bertrand's father was Alexandre Bertrand, a writer of popular scientific articles and books. Alexandre had attended the École Polytechnique in Paris with Auguste Comte and Jean Marie Constant Duhamel, and the latter married his sister. When his father died, young Bertrand went to live with the Duhamels. A well-known professor of mathematics at the École Polytechnique, Duhamel was the right man to guide his precocious nephew. At the age of eleven the boy was allowed to attend classes at the École Polytechnique. In 1838, at sixteen, Bertrand took the degrees of bachelor of arts and bachelor of science, and at seventeen he received the doctor of science degree with a thesis in thermomechanics. The same year (1839) he officially entered the École Polytechnique, and in 1841 he entered the École des Mines. Bertrand's first publications date from this period, the first being "Note sur quelques points de la théorie de l'électricité" (1839), which deals with Poisson's equation, $\Delta V = -4\pi\rho$, and the law of Coulomb.

In 1841 Bertrand became a professor of elementary mathematics at the Collège Saint-Louis, a position that he filled until 1848. In May 1842 he and his brother, returning to Paris from a visit to their friends the Aclocques at Versailles, were nearly killed in a railroad accident which left a scar on Bertrand's face. Bertrand married Mlle. Aclocque in 1844, in which year he also became *répétiteur d'analyse* at the École Polytechnique. Three years later he became *examinateur d'admission* at this school and *suppléant* of the physicist Jean-Baptiste Biot at the Collège de France. In 1848, during the revolution, Bertrand served as a captain in the national guard. He published much during these years—in mathematical physics, in mathematical analysis, and in differential geometry. The first of Bertrand's many textbooks, the *Traité d'arithmétique,* appeared in Paris in 1849 and was followed by the *Traité élémentaire d'algèbre* (1850); both were written for secondary schools. They were followed by textbooks for college instruction. Bertrand always knew how to fascinate his readers and his lecture audiences, and his books had a wide appeal because of content and style. In 1853 he edited and annotated the third edition of J. L. Lagrange's *Mécanique analytique.* From the many publications in this period, one, "Mémoire sur le nombre de valeurs . . .," introduces the so-called problem of Bertrand: to find the subgroups of the symmetric groups of lowest possible index. Another publication, "Mémoire sur la théorie des courbes à double courbure" (1850), discusses curves with the property that a linear relation exists between first and second curvature; these are known as curves of Bertrand.

In 1852 Bertrand became professor of special mathematics at the Lycée Henry IV (then Lycée Napoléon). He also taught at the École Normale Supérieure. In 1856 he replaced Jacques Charles François Sturm as professor of analysis at the École Polytechnique, where he became the colleague of Duhamel. He then left secondary education to pursue his academic career. In 1862 he succeeded Biot at the Collège de France. Bertrand held his position at the École Polytechnique until 1895, that at the Collège de France until his death.

In 1856 Bertrand was elected to the Académie des Sciences, where in 1874 he succeeded the geologist Élie de Beaumont as *secrétaire perpétuel.* In 1884 he replaced the chemist Jean-Baptiste Dumas in the Académie Française. These high academic positions, combined with his erudition, his eloquence, and his natural charm, gave him a position of national prominence in the cultural field.

During the Commune of 1871 Bertrand's Paris house was burned, and many of his manuscripts were lost, among them those of the third volume of his textbook on calculus and his book on thermodynamics. He was able to rewrite and publish the latter as *Thermodynamique.* Afterward he lived at Sèvres and then at Viroflay. At his home Bertrand enjoyed being the center of a lively intellectual circle. Many of his pupils became well-known scientists—for instance, Gaston Darboux, who succeeded him as *secrétaire perpétuel.* In his *Leçons sur la théorie générale des surfaces,* Darboux elaborated many results of Bertrand and his mathematical circle.

Bertrand's publications, apart from his textbooks, cover many fields of mathematics. Although his work lacks the fundamental character of that of the great mathematicians of his period, his often elegant studies on the theory of curves and surfaces, of differential equations and their application to analytical mechanics, of probability, and of the theory of errors were widely read. Many of his articles are devoted to subjects in theoretical physics, including capillarity, theory of sound, electricity, hydrodynamics, and even the flight of birds. In his *Calcul des probabilités,* written, like all his books, in an easy and pleasant style, there is a problem in continuous probabilities known as Bertrand's paradox. It deals with the probability that a stick of length $a > 2l$, placed blindly on a circle of radius l, will be cut by the circle in a chord of less than a given length $b < 2l$. It turns out that this probability is undetermined unless specific assumptions are made about what constitute equally likely cases (i.e., what is meant by "placed blindly").

From 1865 until his death Bertrand edited the *Journal des savants.* For this periodical, as for the *Revue des deux mondes,* he wrote articles of a popular nature, many dealing with the history of science. This interest in history of science appears also in the many *éloges* he wrote as *secrétaire perpétuel* of the Academy, among which are biographies of Poncelet, Élie de Beaumont, Lamé, Leverrier, Charles Dupin, Foucault, Poinsot, Chasles, Cauchy, and F. F. Tisserand. He also wrote papers on Viète, Fresnel, Lavoisier, and Comte, and books on d'Alembert and Pascal.

Bertrand spent the later part of his life in the midst of his large family, surrounded by his friends, who were many and distinguished. His son Marcel and his nephews Émile Picard and Paul Appell were his fellow members in the Académie des Sciences. In 1895 his pupils gave him a medal in commemoration of his fifty years of teaching at the École Polytechnique. The influence of Bertrand's work, however, is hardly comparable to that of several of his contemporaries and pupils. Lest it be judged ephemeral, it must be viewed in the context of nineteenth-century Paris and of Bertrand's brilliant academic career, his exalted social position, and the love and respect given him by his many pupils.

BIBLIOGRAPHY

I. ORIGINAL WORKS. Bertrand's works include "Note sur quelques points de la théorie de l'électricité," in *Journal de mathématiques pures et appliquées,* **4** (1839), 495–500; "Mémoire sur le nombre de valeurs que peut prendre une fonction quand on y permute les lettres qu'elle renferme," in *Journal de l'École polytechnique,* **30** (1845), 123–140; *Traité d'arithmétique* (Paris, 1849); "Mémoire sur la théorie des courbes à double courbure," in *Journal de mathématiques pures et appliquées,* **15** (1850), 332–350; *Traité élémentaire d'algèbre* (Paris, 1850); *Traité de calcul différentiel et de calcul intégral,* 2 vols. (Paris, 1864–1870); *Les fondateurs de l'astronomie moderne* (Paris, 1867); *Rapport sur les progrès les plus récents de l'analyse mathématique* (Paris, 1867); *L'Académie des sciences et les académiciens de 1666 à 1793* (Paris, 1869); "Considérations relatives à la théorie du vol des oiseaux," in *Comptes rendus de l'Académie des sciences,* **72** (1871), 588–591; *Thermodynamique* (Paris, 1887); *Calcul des probabilités* (Paris, 1889; 2nd ed., 1897); *D'Alembert* (Paris, 1889); *Éloges académiques* (Paris, 1889); *Leçons sur la théorie mathématique de l'électricité* (Paris, 1890); *Pascal* (Paris, 1891); *Éloges académiques, nouvelle série* (Paris, 1902), which has a complete bibliography of Bertrand's works on pp. 387–399.

II. SECONDARY LITERATURE. Gaston Darboux, "Éloge historique de J. L. F. Bertrand," in Bertrand's *Éloges académiques, nouvelle série,* pp. 8–51, and in Darboux's *Éloges académiques et discours* (Paris, 1912), pp. 1–60. Another source of information is *Comptes rendus de l'Académie,* **130** (1900), 961–978, addresses delivered in the Academy to honor Bertrand and used by G. H. Bryan for his article "Joseph Bertrand," in *Nature,* **61** (1899–1900), 614–616. The library of the Institut de France nos. 2029–2047 comprises correspondence and some papers of Bertrand; 2719 (5) contains "Notes autobiographiques" (information from Henry Nathan)—these are probably the notes used by Darboux in his *Éloge.* Discussion of Bertrand's problem may be found in H. Weber, *Lehrbuch der Algebra,* II (Brunswick, 1899), 154–160. The curves of Bertrand are dealt with in books on differential geometry, e.g., G. Darboux, *Leçons sur la théorie générale des surfaces,* I (Paris, 1887), 13–17, 44–46, and III (Paris, 1894), 313–314.

D. J. STRUIK

BERWICK, WILLIAM EDWARD HODGSON (*b.* Dudley Hill, England, 11 March 1888; *d.* Bangor, Wales, 13 May 1944)

Berwick's total output of original work is relatively small (thirteen papers and a monograph), due in part to ill health, and is concerned primarily with the theory of numbers and related topics, including the theory of equations. A penchant for problems involving numerical computation is reflected throughout his publications.

Much of Berwick's work is concerned with the following problem: Given a simple algebraic extension of the rational field, establish methods for computing its algebraic integers and the ideals they form. In the monograph *Integral Bases* (1927) Berwick made his most significant contribution to the resolution of this problem by developing methods for constructing an integral basis for the algebraic integers in such a field. The theoretical existence of integral bases is easily established but does not afford a practicable computational procedure. Methods for special cases—such as quadratic, cubic, and cyclotomic fields—had already been devised, but Berwick was the first to attack the much more formidable problem of developing methods that would apply to simple algebraic extensions in general. Although his method is not workable in certain exceptional cases, it possesses a wide range of applicability. Its strong numerical orientation, however, kept his work outside the mainstream of developments in algebraic number theory.

Berwick also obtained a necessary and sufficient condition that the general quintic equation be solvable by radicals in the field of its coefficients (1915), and was instrumental in bringing about the publication of tables of reduced ideals in quadratic fields by the British Association for the Advancement of Science (1934).

BIBLIOGRAPHY

Further information on Berwick is in H. Davenport, "W. E. H. Berwick," in *The Journal of the London Mathematical Society,* **21** (1946), 74–80, which contains references to all of Berwick's scientific work. See also the notes by Davenport and E. H. Neville in *Nature,* **154** (1944), 265, 465.

THOMAS HAWKINS

BESICOVITCH, ABRAM SAMOILOVITCH (*b.* Berdyansk, Russia, 24 January 1891; *d.* Cambridge, England, 2 November 1970)

Besicovitch was the fourth child in the family of four sons and two daughters of Samuel and Eva Besicovitch. The family had to live frugally. All the children were talented and studied at the University of St. Petersburg, the older ones in turn earning money to help support the younger. From an early age Besicovitch showed a remarkable aptitude for solving mathematical problems.

Besicovitch graduated in 1912 from the University of St. Petersburg, where one of his teachers was Andrei A. Markov. When, in 1917, he became professor in the School of Mathematics at the newly established University of Perm, his intention was to work in mathematical logic. He abandoned this idea because the library was inadequate, and as a result continued to work on fundamental problems in analysis. In order to obtain a counterexample to a plausible conjecture about repeated Riemann integrals in $\mathbb{R}^2$, he was led to construct a compact plane set F of zero Lebesque measure but containing unit line segments in every direction (1919–1920). Using a suggestion of J. Pál, Besicovitch later (1928) used F to show that zero is the lower bound of the area of plane sets in which a unit segment can be continuously turned through two right angles. The solution of this "Kakeya problem" was the subject of a lecture filmed by the Mathematical Association in 1958. The set F has turned out to be useful in many contexts. For example, R. O. Davies applied the Besicovitch method to a construction of Otton Nikodym to produce a plane set of full measure with continuum many lines of accessibility through each point. Charles Fefferman used F to obtain a negative solution to the multiplier problem for a ball, and C. R. Putnam obtained a characterization of the spectra of hyponormal operators using Davies' work.

In 1916 Besicovitch married Valentina Vietalievna, a mathematician older than himself. Three years later, during the civil war, the University of Perm was destroyed and partially reestablished at Tomsk. Besicovitch locked books in cellars and preserved much of the valuable property of the Faculty of Mathematics, then worked with A. A. Fridman to reestablish the university after the liberation of Perm. In 1920 he returned to Leningrad as professor in the Pedagogical Institute and lecturer in the university. The political powers forced him to teach classes of workers who lacked the background to understand the lectures, so there was little time for research.

Besicovitch was offered a Rockefeller fellowship to work abroad, but repeated requests for permission to leave the country were refused. In 1924 he escaped and made his way to Copenhagen, where the Rockefeller fellowship enabled him to work for a year with Harald Bohr, who was then developing the theory of almost periodic functions. This contact resulted in several papers, in the most important of which ("On Generalized Almost Periodic Functions") he showed that the analogue of the Riesz-Fischer theorem is false for Bohr's almost periodic functions and developed a new definition of "almost periodic" for which Riesz-Fischer is valid. His *Al-*

most Periodic Functions became the standard work on the classical theory of that subject.

In 1925 Besicovitch visited Oxford. Godfrey H. Hardy quickly recognized his analytical abilities, securing for him a position as lecturer at the University of Liverpool in 1926–1927. He moved to Cambridge in 1927 as a university lecturer and was elected a fellow of Trinity College in 1930. Besicovitch's wife remained in Russia, and the marriage was dissolved in 1926. While in Perm he had befriended a woman named Maria Denisova and her children. He brought them to England and in 1928 married the elder daughter, Valentina Alexandrovna, then aged sixteen.

At about the time of his arrival in England, Besicovitch started his deep analysis of plane sets of dimension 1 that has become the foundation of modern geometric measure theory as developed by Herbert Federer and his school. He obtained the fundamental structure theorems for linearly measurable plane sets—the regular sets are a subset of a countable union of rectifiable arcs and have a tangent almost everywhere ("On the Fundamental Geometrical Properties of Linearly Measurable Plane Sets of Points"), while the irregular sets intersect no rectifiable arc in a set of positive length, have a tangent almost nowhere, and project in almost all directions onto a set of zero linear Lebesque measure. Besicovitch also considered sets with non-integer dimension ("On Linear Sets of Points of Fractional Dimension," "On Lipschitz Numbers") and showed that these could not have nice geometric properties of regularity. These sets occur naturally in many physical situations where there is an element of randomness (for an extensive recent account see Mandelbrot, who calls such sets "fractals"). The basic Besicovitch contribution to geometric measure theory is carefully developed by Federer, and a simpler version is given by Falconer.

Besicovitch had shown that the study of local density was fundamental to an understanding of the geometric properties of small sets. John Manstrand, 1954, showed that a strict density cannot exist for any set of non-integer dimension. Claude Tricot developed a new packing measure and showed by considering density that only for surfacelike sets with integer dimension can Hausdorff and packing measures be equal and finite positive.

In 1950, on his fifty-ninth birthday, Besicovitch was elected to the House Ball chair of mathematics at Cambridge. Although he retired in 1958, he remained active in teaching and research and spent eight successive years as visiting professor at various universities in the United States. Besicovitch developed a new interest in the definition of area for a parametric surface in $\mathbb{R}^3$ starting about 1942. He produced a beautiful example of a topological disk with arbitrarily small Lebesque-Fréchet area (defined by approximating polyhedral) but arbitrarily large (three-dimensional) Lebesque measure. He concluded that the only satisfactory concept of area is a two-dimensional Hausdorff measure and undertook a program of solving anew many of the classical problems of surface area.

Besicovitch exhibited an open mind in all of his work. When solving a problem, most mathematicians make a commitment to the nature of the solution before that solution has been found, and this commitment interposes a barrier to the consideration of other possibilities. Besicovitch seems never to have been troubled in this way. He therefore obtained results that astounded his contemporaries and remain surprising today.

In recognition of his outstanding talent, Besicovitch received the Adams Prize of the University of Cambridge in 1930, was elected a fellow of the Royal Society in 1934, was awarded the Morgan Medal by the London Mathematics Society in 1950, and received the Sylvester Medal of the Royal Society in 1952. His many mathematical contributions remain a stimulus to research activity.

In the decade 1980–1989 there was an explosion of interest in fractals as a tool for modeling phenomena from a wide variety of different contexts. Dynamical systems involving the interation of a transformation produce fractals for a critical set—see the book by Heinz-Otto Peitgen and P. H. Richter *The Beauty of Fractals*. In physics there are many critical phenomena where fractals provide a helpful insight, and each year has seen international symposia focusing on this area. It is fair to say that the geometrical insights of Besicovitch's work laid the foundation for this development.

[The material in this biography is condensed from an obituary notice published in the Bulletin of the London Mathematical Society, with some comments about recent developments.]

BIBLIOGRAPHY

I. ORIGINAL WORKS. A complete list of Besicovitch's works is in J. C. Burkill, "Abram Semoilovich Besicovitch," in *Biographical Memoirs of Fellows of the Royal Society*, 17 (1971), 1–16. Papers by Besicovitch cited in the text are "Nouvelle forme des conditions d'intégrabilité des fonctions," in *Journal de la Société de physique et de mathématique* (Perm), **1** (1918–1919), 140–145; "On Generalized Almost Periodic Functions," in *Proceedings of the London Mathematical Society*, 2nd ser., **25** (1926), 495–512; "Fundamental Geometric Properties of Linearly Measurable Plane Sets of Points," in *Bulletin of the American Mathematical Society*, **33** (1927), 652; "On Kakeya's Problem and a Similar One," in *Mathematische Zeitschrift*, **27** (1928), 312–320; "On the Fundamental Geometrical Properties of Linearly Measurable Plane Sets of Points," in *Mathematische Annalen*, **98** (1928), 422–464; "On Linear Sets of Points of Fractional Dimension," *ibid.*, **101** (1929), 161–193; "On Lipschitz Numbers," in *Mathematische Zeitschrift*, **30** (1929), 514–519; *Almost Periodic Functions* (Cambridge, 1932; repr. New York, 1955); "On the Fundamental Geometrical Properties of Linearly Measurable Plane Sets of Points (III)," in *Mathematische Annalen*, **116** (1939), 349–357; "On the Definition and Value of The Area of a Surface," in *Quarterly Journal of Mathematics* (Oxford), 1st ser., **16** (1945), 88–102; "Parametric Surfaces, III. On Surfaces of Minimum Area," in *Journal of the London Mathematical Society*, **23** (1948), 241–246; "Parametric Surfaces, I. Compactness," in *Proceedings of the Cambridge Philosophical Society*, **45** (1949), 5–13; Parametric Surfaces, II. Lower Semicontinuity of the Area," *ibid.*, 14–23; "Parametric Surfaces, IV. The Integral Formula for the Area," in *Quarterly Journal of Mathematics* (Oxford) 1st ser., **20** (1949), 1–7; and "The Kakeya Problem," in *American Mathematical Monthly*, **70** (1963), 697–706.

II. SECONDARY LITERATURE. R. O. Davies, "On Accessibility of Plane Sets and Differentiation of Functions of Two Real Variables," in *Proceedings of the Cambridge Philosophical Society*, **48** (1952), 215–232; K. J. Falconer, *The Geometry of Fractal Sets* (Cambridge, 1985); Herbert Federer, *Geometric Measure Theory* (New York, 1969); Charles Fefferman, "The Multiplier Problem for the Ball," in *Annals of Mathematics*, 2nd ser., **94** (1971), 330–336; Benoit B. Mandelbrot, *The Fractal Geometry of Nature* (San Francisco, 1982); J. M. Marstrand, "Some fundamental geometrical properties of plane sets of fractional dimensions," Proceedings of the London Mathematical Society, **15** (1954), 257–302; Otton Nikodym, "Sur la mésure des ensembles plans dont tous les points sont rectilinéairement accessibles," in *Fundamenta mathematicae*, **10** (1927), 116–168; H.-O. Peitgen and P. H. Richter, *The beauty of fractals* (Berlin, 1986); Pietronera and Tosatti, eds., *Proceedings of Sixth International Symposium on Fractals in Physics* (North Holland, Amsterdam, 1986); C. R. Putnam, "The Role of Zero Sets in the Spectra of Hyponormal Operators," in *Proceedings of the American Mathematical Society*, **43** (1974), 137–140; S. J. Taylor and C. Tricot, Packing measure and its evaluation for a Brown path, Trans. Amer. Math Soc **288** (1985) 679–699.

S. JAMES TAYLOR

BESSEL, FRIEDRICH WILHELM (*b.* Minden, Germany, 22 July 1784; *d.* Königsberg, Germany [now Kaliningrad, U.S.S.R.], 17 March 1846)

Bessel's father was a civil servant in Minden; his mother was the daughter of a minister named Schrader from Rheme, Westphalia. Bessel had six sisters and two brothers, both of whom became judges of provincial courts. He attended the Gymnasium in Minden but left after four years, with the intention of becoming a merchant's apprentice. At school he had had difficulty with Latin, and apart from an inclination toward mathematics and physics, he showed no signs of extraordinary talent until he was fifteen. (Later, after studying on his own, Bessel wrote extensively in Latin, apparently without difficulty.)

On 1 January 1799 Bessel became an apprentice to the famous mercantile firm of Kulenkamp in Bremen, where he was to serve for seven years without pay. He rapidly became so proficient in calculation and commercial accounting that after his first year he received a small salary; this was gradually increased, so that he became financially independent of his parents.

Bessel was especially interested in foreign trade, so he devoted his nights to studying geography, Spanish, and English, learning to speak and write the latter language within three months. In order to qualify as cargo officer on a merchant ship, he studied books on ships and practical navigation. The problem of determining the position of a ship at sea with the aid of the sextant stimulated his interest in astronomy, but knowing how to navigate by the stars without deeper insight into the foundations of astronomy did not satisfy him. He therefore began to study astronomy and mathematics, and soon he felt qualified to determine time and longitude by himself.

Bessel made his first time determination with a clock and a sextant that had been built to his specifications. The determination of the longitude of Bremen and the observation of the eclipse of a star by the moon are among his first accurate astronomical exercises. He learned of observations and discoveries through the professional astronomical journals *Monatliche Correspondenz* and *Berliner astronomisches Jahrbuch,* and thus was able to judge the accuracy of his own observations.

In a supplementary volume of the *Berliner astronomisches Jahrbuch* Bessel found Harriot's 1607 observations of Halley's Comet, which he wanted to use to determine its orbit. He had equipped himself for this task by reading Lalande and then Olbers on the easiest and most convenient method of calculating a comet's orbit from several observations. The reduction of Harriot's observations and his own determination of the orbit were presented to Olbers in 1804. With surprise Olbers noted the close agreement of Bessel's results with Halley's calculation of the comet's elliptical elements. He immediately recognized the great achievement of the twenty-year-old apprentice and encouraged him to improve his determination of the comet's orbit by making additional observations. After Bessel had done so, this work was printed, upon Olbers' recommendation, in *Monatliche Correspondenz*. The article, which was on the level of a doctoral dissertation, attracted much attention because of the circumstances under which it had been written. It marks the turning point in Bessel's life; from then on he concentrated on astronomical investigations and celestial mechanics. Later, Olbers claimed that his greatest service to astronomy was having encouraged Bessel to become a professional astronomer.

At the beginning of 1806, before the expiration of his apprenticeship with Kulenkamp, Bessel accepted the position of assistant at Schröter's private observatory in Lilienthal, near Bremen, again on Olbers' recommendation. Schröter, a doctor of law and a wealthy civil servant, was renowned for his observations of the moon and the planets; and as a member of various learned societies, he was in close contact with many scientists. In Lilienthal, Bessel acquired practical experience in observations of comets and planets, with special attention to Saturn and its rings and satellites. At the same time, he studied celestial mechanics more intensively and made further contributions to the determination of cometary orbits. In 1807 Olbers encouraged him to do a reduction of Bradley's observations of the positions of 3,222 stars, which had been made from 1750 to 1762 at the Royal Greenwich Observatory. This task led to one of his greatest achievements.

When Friedrich Wilhelm III of Prussia ordered the construction of an observatory in Königsberg, Bessel was appointed its director and professor of astronomy (1809), on the recommendation of Humboldt. He had previously declined appointments in Leipzig and Greifswald. He took up his new post on 10 May 1810. The title of doctor, a prerequisite for a professorship, had been awarded to him without further formalities by the University of Göttingen after Gauss had proposed it. Gauss had met Bessel in 1807 at Bremen and had recognized his unusual ability.

While the observatory in Königsberg was being built (1810–1813), Bessel made considerable progress in the reduction of Bradley's observations. In 1811 he was awarded the Lalande Prize of the Institut de France for his tables of refraction derived from these observations, and the following year he became a member of the Berlin Academy of Sciences. In 1813 Bessel began observations in Königsberg, primarily of the positions of stars, with the Dollond transit instrument and the Cary circle. The observatory's modest equipment was markedly improved by the acquisition of a Reichenbach-Ertel meridian circle in 1819, a large Fraunhofer-Utzschneider heliometer in 1829, and a Repsold meridian circle in 1841. Bessel remained in Königsberg for the rest of his life, pursuing his research and teaching without interruption, although he often complained about the limited possibilities of observation because of the unfavorable climate. He declined the directorship of the Berlin observatory, fearing greater administrative and social responsibilities, and nominated Encke, who was appointed in his stead. Of Bessel's students, several became important astronomers; Argelander is perhaps the most famous.

Bessel married Johanna Hagen in 1812, and they had two sons and three daughters. The marriage was a happy one, but it was clouded by sickness and by the early death of both sons. Bessel found relaxation from his intensive work in daily walks and in hunting. He corresponded with Olbers, Schumacher (the founder of the *Astronomische Nachrichten*), and Gauss, and left Königsberg only occasionally.

From 1840 on, Bessel's health deteriorated. His last long trip, in 1842, was to England, where he participated in the Congress of the British Association in Manchester. His meeting with important English scientists, including Herschel, impressed him deeply and stimulated him to finish and publish, despite his weakened health, a series of works.

After two years of great suffering, Bessel died of cancer. He was buried near the observatory. Bessel was small and delicate, and in his later years he appeared prematurely aged because of his markedly pale and wrinkled face. This appearance altered, however, as soon as he began to talk; then the force of a strong mind was evidenced in brilliant, rapid speech, and his otherwise rigid expression revealed mildness and friendliness.

Newcomb, in his *Compendium of Spherical Astronomy* (1906), has called Bessel the founder of the German school of practical astronomy. This German school started with astrometry and, after Bessel's death, was expanded to astrophysics by Bunsen and Kirchhoff's discovery of spectral analysis. Foremost among the interests of this school were the construction of precision instruments, the study of all possible instrument errors, and the careful reduction of observations. Bessel's contributions to the theory of astronomical instruments are for the most part restricted to those instruments used for the most accurate measurement of the positions of the stars and planets. The principles he laid down for the determination of errors were later followed so painstakingly by less gifted astronomers that the goal to be achieved—the making of a great number of good observations—was relegated to the background in favor of important investigations relative to the instruments themselves. Such was never Bessel's intention; he was undoubtedly one of the most skillful and diligent observers of his century. His industry is well illustrated by the twenty-one volumes of *Beobachtungen der Königsberger Sternwarte.*

Bessel recognized that Bradley's observations gave a system of very accurate star positions for the epoch 1755 and that this could be utilized in two ways. First, a reference system for the measurement of positions of stars and planets was required. Second, the study of star motions necessitated the determination of accurate positions for the earliest possible epoch. Tobias Mayer had determined fundamental star positions from his own observations around the middle of the eighteenth century, but Bradley was never able to reduce his own numerous observations.

The observations of star positions had to be freed of instrumental errors, insofar as these could be determined from the measurements themselves, and of errors caused by the earth's atmosphere (refraction). The apparent star positions at the time of a particular observation (observation epoch) had to be reduced to a common point in time (mean epoch) so that they would be freed of the effects of the motion of the earth and of the site of observation. For this a knowledge of the precession, the nutation, and the aberration was necessary. Bessel determined the latitude of Greenwich for the mean epoch 1755 and the obliquity of the ecliptic, as well as the constants of precession, nutation, and aberration. To determine precession from proper motions, Bessel used both Bradley's and Piazzi's observations. Bessel's first published work on the constant of precession (1815) was awarded a prize by the Berlin Academy of Sciences.

The positions of Bradley's stars valid for 1755 were published by Bessel as *Fundamenta astronomiae pro anno 1755* (1818). This work also gives the proper motions of the stars, as derived from the observations of Bradley, of Piazzi, and of Bessel himself. It constitutes a milestone in the history of astronomical observations, for until then positions of stars could not be given with comparable accuracy: through Bessel's work, Bradley's observations were made to mark the beginning of modern astrometry. During this investigation Bessel became an admirer of the art of observation as practiced by Bradley; and because Bradley could not evaluate his own observations, Bessel followed and also taught the principle that immediately after an observation, the reduction had to be done by the observer himself. Further, he realized that the accurate determination of the motions of the planets and the stars required continuous observations of their positions until such motions could be used to predict "the positions of the stars . . . for all times with sufficient accuracy."

Later, when many unpublished observations of Bradley's were found and when, about 1860, Airy had made accurate observations of the same stars at the Royal Greenwich Observatory, Auwers improved Bessel's reductions and derived proper motions of better quality. Auwers' star catalog was published in three volumes (1882–1903).

Bessel's first and very important contribution to the improvement of the positions and proper motions of stars consisted of the observations of Maskelyne's thirty-six fundamental stars. As Bradley's successor, Maskelyne had chosen these stars to define the system of right ascensions. Bradley had been able to make differential measurements of positions with such accuracy that the star positions for 1755 and those determined by Airy for 1860 resulted in proper motions with the excellent internal accuracy of about one second of arc per century. Greater difficulties were experienced, however, with the measurement of positions with respect to the vernal equinox as zero point of the right ascensions. The continuously changing position of the vernal equinox had to be determined at the time of the equinoxes from the differences in time of the transits of bright stars and the sun through the meridian. In 1820 Bessel succeeded in determining the position of the vernal equinox with an accuracy of .01 second by observing both Maskelyne's stars and the sun. This can be verified by measurements made in the twentieth century.

In *Tabulae Regiomontanae* (1830), Bessel published the mean and the apparent positions of thirty-eight stars for the period 1750–1850. He added the two polar stars α and δ Ursae Minoris to Maskelyne's thirty-six fundamental stars. The foundations for the ephemerides were the mean positions for 1755 and the positions derived for 1820 from observations at Königsberg. The position of the vernal equinox for 1822, as determined by Bessel, served as the zero point for counting the right ascensions. Bessel derived the ephemerides of the *Tabulae Regiomontanae* without using a specific value of the constant of precession, for in order to find a third position from two given positions of a star, it is necessary to know only the annual variation of precession, not the value of precession itself. Therefore Bessel's ephemerides are correct (aside from errors in observation) up to and including the first magnitude for the proper motions and up to the second magnitude for precession. Only for the two polar stars did Bessel determine the proper motions and also give the values, since for these stars the terms of higher order in proper motion and precession could not be neglected. In calculating the data of the *Tabulae Regiomontanae* Bessel improved his 1815 determination of the precession by utilizing his Königsberg observations of Bradley's stars.

The star positions given for one century in the *Tabulae Regiomontanae* constitute the first modern reference system for the measurement of the positions of the sun, the moon, the planets, and the stars, and for many decades the Königsberg tables were used as ephemerides. With their aid, all observations of the sun, moon, and planets made since 1750 at the Royal Greenwich Observatory could be reduced; and thus these observations could be used for the theories of planetary orbits.

During observations of the stars α Canis Major (Sirius) and α Canis Minor (Procyon), which are among Maskelyne's fundamental stars, Bessel discovered the variation of their proper motions. He concluded that these stars must have dimmer companions whose masses, however, were large enough to make visible the motions of the brighter double-star components around the center of gravity. Arguing from the variation of the proper motion, more than a hundred years later astronomers discovered stars with extremely low luminosity, called dark companions.

Observing the positions of numerous stars with the Reichenbach meridian circle, Bessel pursued two aims: the determination of the motions of the stars in such a way that their positions could be predicted for all time, and the definition of a reference system for the positions of the stars. Between 1821 and 1833 he determined the positions of approximately 75,000 stars (brighter than ninth magnitude) in zones of declination between −15° and +45°. With these observations he also developed the methods for determining instrumental errors, including those of the division of the circle, and eliminated such errors from his observations. He published all measurements in detail, and thus they can be verified. These observations were continued by Argelander, who measured the positions of stars in zones of declination from +45° to +80° and from −16° to −32°. The work of Bessel and Argelander encouraged the establishment of two large-scale programs: Argelander's *Bonner Durchmusterung* and the first catalog of the Astronomische Gesellschaft (*AGK 1*) with the positions of the stars of the entire northern sky. The *Bonner Durchmusterung* is a map of the northern sky that contains all stars up to magnitude 9.5, and the catalog is the result of meridian circle observations made at many observatories.

One of Bessel's greatest achievements was the first accurate determination of the distance of a fixed star. At the beginning of the nineteenth century, the approximate radius of the earth's orbit (150,000,000 km.) was known, and there was some idea of the dimensions of the planetary system, although Neptune and Pluto were still unknown. The stars, however, were considered to be so far away that it would be hopeless to try to measure their distances. The triangulation procedure was already known, and for this the diameter of the earth's orbit could serve as the base line, since its length was known. It was also known that the motion of the earth around the sun must be mirrored in a periodic motion of the stars within the period of a year, in such a way that a star at the pole of the ecliptic would describe a circular orbit around the pole, stars at ecliptical latitudes between 0° and 90° would describe ellipses, and stars at the ecliptic would undergo periodic variations of their ecliptical longitudes. This change of position of the stars, as evidenced by the motion of the earth, was considered to be immeasurably small, however. The radius of the circle, of the ellipse, or of the ecliptical segment of arc—the so-called parallax figure—is the parallax of the star; the parallax π is the angle subtended by the radius of the earth's orbit at the position of the star. If this angle π can be measured, then the distance r of a star can be obtained from $\sin \pi = a/r$, where a represents the radius of the earth's orbit. An angle of $\pi = 1''$ corresponds to 206,265 radii of the earth's orbit (or $3.08 \cdot 10^{13}$ km., or 3.26 light-years).

In the first half of the eighteenth century Bradley had attempted to determine the parallaxes of the stars γ Draco and η Ursa Major by measurements of the angular distances of these stars from the zenith (zenith distances). Both stars culminate in the vicinity of the zenith of Greenwich and thus are particularly suitable for the accurate measurement of zenith distances. The "absolute" parallax of the stars—that is, the parallactic change of position with respect to a fixed direction on earth (direction of the plumb line at Greenwich)—should be determinable from the variation of the zenith distances. Bradley found an annual variation with an amplitude of twenty seconds of arc, but the phase was shifted by three months from the expected parallactic change of position. He correctly interpreted the phenomenon as a change in direction —arising from the motion of the earth in its orbit—of the stellar light that reaches the earth, and thus discovered the aberration of light. However, he could not detect parallaxes of the stars, but could only conclude that the parallaxes must be smaller than .50 second of arc for the stars he observed.

As a result of this knowledge of the small size of the parallaxes to be expected, the measuring procedures were changed in later experiments, for the accuracy of the measurements of zenith distances was obviously inadequate for the purpose. The angular distance between two stars very close together on the sphere could be determined much more accurately. If one star of a star pair is very far from the sun and the other is near the sun, then the parallax figure of the nearer star must become visible as a result of frequent measurements of the angular distances between the two stars. It was therefore suggested that astronomers measure "relative" parallaxes, that is, the parallactic changes in the position with reference to other stars that can be assumed to be very far away. Herschel's attempts to measure stellar parallaxes in this way led to the discovery of the physical double stars; he found that the components of most star pairs are near to each other in space, as is shown by their motion around the common center of gravity. Herschel's attempt to determine parallaxes failed, however.

This lack of success led to a search for signs that one of the stars would be especially near, with great brightness of an individual star regarded as an indication of its great nearness. (This assumption would be correct if all stars had the same luminosity and if there were no inhomogeneous interstellar absorption. Since both of these conditions are not fulfilled, the relation between apparent magnitude and distance holds only in the statistical mean.) In determining proper motions, Bessel found that individual stars are marked by especially great motions and that these stars are not among the brightest. He concluded that great proper motions are, in most cases, the result of small star distances. Therefore, in order to determine the parallax, he selected the star with the greatest proper motion known to him (5.2″ per year), a star of magnitude 5.6, which had been designated as 61 Cygni in Flamsteed's star catalog.

To determine the parallax Bessel used the Fraunhofer heliometer, an instrument intended primarily for the measurement of the angular diameter of the sun and the planets. The heliometer is a telescope with an objective that can be rotated around the optical axis. The objective is cut along a diameter; both halves can be shifted along the cutting line and the displacement can be measured very accurately. Each half of the objective acts optically as a complete objective would, so that upon moving the halves, two noncoincident images of one object arise. The distance of two stars, A and B, that are in the field of view is measured by sliding the halves so that the image of A coincides with the image of B produced in the second half; thus the two stars appear as one. In Bessel's day this procedure of coincidence determination permitted more accurate measurements than did the customary micrometer determinations with an ordinary telescope; the latter were used to determine the angular distances of the components of double stars. Further, with the heliometer one could measure greater angular distances than with the micrometer (up to nearly two degrees with Bessel's heliometer). For determining the parallax of 61 Cygni, Bessel selected two comparison stars of magnitude 9–10 at distances of roughly eight and twelve minutes of arc. 61 Cygni is a physical double star whose components differ in brightness by less than one magnitude. The distance of sixteen seconds of arc between the components favored the accuracy of the determination of the parallax because pointing could be carried out with two star images. After observing for eighteen months, by the fall of 1838 Bessel had enough measurements for the determination of a reliable parallax. He found that $\pi = 0.314''$ with a mean error of $\pm 0.020''$. This work was published in the *Astronomische Nachrichten* (1838), the first time the distance of a star became known. Bessel's value for the parallax shows excellent agreement with the results obtained by extensive modern photographical parallax determinations, which have yielded the value $\pi = 0.292''$, with a mean error of $\pm 0.0045''$. The distance of 61 Cygni thus amounts to $6.9 \cdot 10^5$ radii of the earth's orbit, or 10.9 light-years.

Bessel's conjecture that the stars with the greatest proper motions are among the nearest was later proved correct, and the amount of proper motion has remained a criterion for the choice of stars for parallax programs. Only one year after the completion of Bessel's work, two other successful determinations of parallaxes were made known. F. G. W. Struve in Dorpat determined the parallax of the bright star α Lyra (Vega) by means of micrometric measurements. The value he found, $\pi = 0.262'' \pm 0.037''$ (m.e.) nevertheless deviates considerably from the now reliably known value $\pi = 0.121'' \pm 0.006''$ (m.e.). In addition, Thomas Henderson had observed the bright star α Centaurus at the Cape Observatory and had found a parallax of approximately one second of arc. The reliable value for this today amounts to $\pi = 0.75''$. The pioneering work of Bessel, Henderson, and Struve not only opened up a new area of astronomical research but also laid the foundation for the investigation of the structure of our star system.

Bessel was also an outstanding mathematician

whose name became generally known through a special class of functions that have become an indispensable tool in applied mathematics, physics, and engineering. The interest in the functions, which represent a special form of the confluent hypergeometric function, arose in the treatment of the problem of perturbation in the planetary system. The perturbation of the elliptic motion of a planet caused by another planet consists of two components, the direct effect of the perturbing planet and its indirect effect, which arises from the motion of the sun caused by the perturbing planet. Bessel demonstrated that it is appropriate to treat the direct and the indirect perturbations separately, so that in the series development of the indirect perturbation, Bessel functions appear as coefficients. In studying indirect perturbation, Bessel made a systematic investigation of its functions and described its main characteristics. This work appeared in his Berlin treatise of 1824. Special cases of Bessel coefficients had been known for a long time; in a letter to Leibniz in 1703, Jakob Bernoulli mentioned a series that represented a Bessel function of the order 1/3. In addition, in a work on the oscillations of heavy chains (1732) Daniel Bernoulli used Bessel coefficients of the order zero, and in Euler's work on vibrations of a stretched circular membrane (1744) there was a series by means of which $J_n(z)$ was defined. Probably a work by Lagrange on elliptical motion (1769), in which such series appear, had led Bessel to make these investigations. The impulse, however, did not come from pure mathematical interests, but from the necessity of applying such series in the presentation of indirect perturbations. Bessel left few mathematical works that do not have some practical astronomical application.

Like nearly all great astronomers of his era, Bessel was obliged to spend part of his time surveying wherever the government wished. In 1824 he supervised the measurement of a 3,000-meter base line in the Frischen Haff because he liked to spend a day in the fresh air once in a while. In 1830 he was commissioned to carry out triangulation in East Prussia, after Struve had completed the triangulation of the Russian Baltic provinces. Bessel designed a new measuring apparatus for the determination of base lines that was constructed by Repsold; he also developed methods of triangulation by utilizing Gauss's method of least squares. Bessel's measuring apparatus and method of triangulation have been widely used. The triangulation in East Prussia and its junction with the Prussian-Russian chain of triangulation was described in a book written with J. J. Baeyer (1838). From his own triangulations and from those of others, Bessel made an outstanding determination of the shape and dimensions of the earth that won him international acclaim.

Among Bessel's works that contributed to geophysics were his investigations on the length of the simple seconds' pendulum (1826), the length of the seconds' pendulum for Berlin (1835), and the determination of the acceleration of gravity derived from observing the pendulum. Bessel achieved the standardization of the units of length then in use by introducing a standard measure in Prussia, the so-called Toise (1 Toise = 1.949063 meters). The necessity of a standard of length had become apparent to him during his work on triangulation in East Prussia, as did the necessity of an international organization to define the units of measures. This need led to the founding of the International Bureau of Weights and Measures.

BIBLIOGRAPHY

I. Original Works. A collection of Bessel's numerous papers is *Abhandlungen von Friedrich Wilhelm Bessel,* Rudolf Engelmann, ed., 3 vols. (Leipzig, 1875). Vol. I contains Bessel's account of his youth, "Kurze Erinnerungen an Momente meines Lebens," with a supp. by the ed., 23 papers on the motions of planets, and 28 papers on spherical astronomy. Vol. II contains 25 papers on the theory of astronomical instruments, 29 papers on stellar astronomy, and 19 papers on mathematics. Vol. III contains 11 papers on geodesy, 17 papers on physics (mostly geophysics), and 33 on other subjects. Engelmann's collection is not complete, however. *Beobachtungen der Königsberger Sternwarte,* 21 vols., presents Bessel's observations. Major separate publications are *Fundamenta astronomiae pro anno 1755 deducta ex observationibus viri incomparabilis James Bradley in specola astronomica Grenovicensi per anno 1750–1762 institutis* (Königsberg, 1818) and *Tabulae Regiomontanae reductionum observationum astronomicarum ab anno 1750 usque ad annum 1850 computatae* (Königsberg, 1830). A complete list of Bessel's publications, presented at the end of *Abhandlungen,* III, has 399 entries, including books and book reviews by Bessel.

II. Secondary Literature. A bibliography of sketches of Bessel's life and astronomical works is given in *Abhandlungen,* III, 504. Noteworthy are C. Bruhns, in *Allgemeine deutsche Biographie,* pt. 9 (Leipzig, 1875), 558–567; and Sir William Herschel's addresses delivered to Bessel on presenting honorary medals of the Royal Astronomical Society, in *Monthly Notices of the Royal Astronomical Society,* **1** (1829), 110–113, and **5** (1841), 89. A biography of Bessel in anecdotal style is J. A. Repsold, in *Astronomische Nachrichten,* **210** (1919), 161–214. An excellent review of the first determination of a stellar parallax is H. Strassl, "Die erste Bestimmung einer Fixsternentfernung," in *Naturwissenschaften,* 33rd year (1946), 65–71.

Walter Fricke

BETTI, ENRICO (*b.* near Pistoia, Italy, 21 October 1823; *d.* Pisa, Italy, 11 August 1892)

Since his father died when Betti was very young, the boy was educated by his mother. At the University of Pisa, from which he received a degree in physical and mathematical sciences, he was a disciple of O. F. Mossotti, under whose leadership he fought in the battle of Curtatone and Montanara during the first war for Italian independence.

After having taught mathematics at a Pistoia high school, in 1865 Betti was offered a professorship at the University of Pisa; he held this post for the rest of his life. He also was rector of the university and director of the teachers college in Pisa. In addition, he was a member of Parliament in 1862 and a senator from 1884. His principal aim, however, was always pure scientific research with a noble philosophical purpose.

In 1874 Betti served for a few months as under-secretary of state for public education. He longed, however, for the academic life, solitary meditation, and discussions with close friends. Among the latter was Riemann, whom Betti had met in Göttingen in 1858, and who subsequently visited him in Pisa.

In algebra, Betti penetrated the ideas of Galois by relating them to the previous research of Ruffini and Abel. He obtained fundamental results on the solubility of algebraic equations by means of radicorational operations. It should be noted that the most important results of Galois's theory are included—without demonstration and in a very concise form—in a letter written in 1832 by Galois to his friend Chevalier on the eve of the duel in which Galois was killed. The letter was published by Liouville in 1846. When Betti was able to demonstrate—on the basis of the theory of substitutions, which he stated anew—the necessary and sufficient conditions for the solution of any algebraic equation through radicorational operations, it was still believed in high mathematical circles that the questions related to Galois's results were obscure and sterile. Among the papers in which Betti sought to demonstrate Galois's statements are "Sulla risoluzione delle equazioni algebriche" (1852) and "Sopra la teorica delle sostituzioni" (1855). They constitute an essential contribution to the development from classical to abstract algebra.

Another area of mathematical thought developed by Betti is that of the theory of functions, particularly of elliptic functions. Betti illustrated—in an original way—the theory of elliptic functions, which is based on the principle of the construction of transcendental entire functions in relation to their zeros by means of infinite products.

Betti published these results in a paper entitled "La teorica delle funzioni ellitiche" (1860-1861). These ideas were further developed by Weierstrass some fifteen years later. However, Betti, who in the meantime had turned to another theory of elliptic functions—this one inspired by Riemann—did not wish to claim priority. These two methods are linked with the two basic aspects of Betti's mathematical thought: the algebraic mode of thought, which went deep into Galois's research, and the physicomathematical mode of thought, developed under Riemann's influence. Betti, an enthusiastic supporter of theoretical physics, had turned toward the procedures already started in electricity and subsequently applied to analysis.

Among Betti's physicomathematical researches inspired by Riemann are *Teorica della forze newtoniane* (1879) and "Sopra le equazioni di equilibrio dei corpi solidi elastici." A law of reciprocity in elasticity theory, known as Betti's theorem, was demonstrated in 1878. Having mastered the methods by which Green had opened the way to the integration of Laplace's equations, which constitute the basis for the theory of potentials, Betti applied these methods to the study of elasticity and then to the study of heat.

Of particular interest is Betti's research on "analysis situs" in hyperspace, which is discussed in "Sopra gli spazi di un numero qualunque di dimensioni" (1871). This research inspired Poincaré in his studies in this field and originated the term "Betti numbers," which subsequently became common usage for numbers characterizing the connection of a variety.

Betti played an important role in the rebirth of mathematics after the Risorgimento. He loved classical culture, and with Brioschi he championed the return to the teaching of Euclid in secondary schools, for he regarded Euclid's work as a model of discipline and beauty. This led to *Gli elementi d'Euclide* (1889).

His enthusiasm and brilliance made Betti an excellent teacher. At the University of Pisa and at the teachers college, he guided several generations of students toward scientific research, among them the mathematicians U. Dini, L. Bianchi, and V. Volterra.

BIBLIOGRAPHY

I. Original Works. Betti's collected writings are *Opere matematiche*, R. Accademia dei Lincei, ed., 2 vols. (Milan, 1903-1915). Among his works are "Sulla risoluzione delle equazioni algebriche," in *Annali di scienze matematiche e fisiche*, **3** (1852), 49-115; "Sopra la teorica delle sostituzioni," *ibid.*, **6** (1855), 5-34; "La teorica delle funzioni ellitiche," in *Annali di matematica pura e applicata*, **3** (1860), 65-159, 298-310; **4** (1861), 26-45, 57-70, 297-336; "Sopra gli spazi di un numero qualunque di dimensioni," *ibid.,* 2nd ser., **4** (1871), 140–158; "Sopra le equazioni di equilibrio dei corpi solidi elastici," *ibid.,* **6** (1874), 101–111; *Teorica della forze newtoniane* (Pisa, 1879); and *Gli elementi d'Euclide con note aggiunte ed esercizi ad uso dei ginnasi e dei licei* (Florence, 1889), written with Brioschi.

II. Secondary Literature. Works on Betti are F. Brioschi, "Enrico Betti," in *Annali di matematica pura e applicata,* 2nd ser., **20** (1892), 256, or his *Opere matematiche,* III (Milan, 1904), 41–42; F. Enriques, *Le matematiche nella storia e nella cultura* (Bologna, 1938), pp. 187, 203–204, 222, 224–226; and his article on Betti in *Enciclopedia italiana Treccani,* VI (1930), 834; G. Loria, *Storia delle matematiche,* III (Turin, 1933), 497, 541, 556–557; and V. Volterra, *Saggi scientifici* (Bologna, 1920), pp. 37, 40–41, 46-50, 52-54.

Ettore Carruccio

BEZOUT, ÉTIENNE (*b.* Nemours, France, 31 March 1739; *d.* Basses-Loges, near Fontainebleau, France, 27 September 1783)

Étienne Bezout, the second son of Pierre Bezout and Hélène-Jeanne Filz, belonged to an old family in the town of Nemours. Both his father and grandfather had held the office of magistrate (*procureur aux baillage et juridiction*) there. Although his father hoped Étienne would succeed him, the young man was strongly drawn to mathematics, particularly through reading the works of Leonhard Euler. His accomplishments were quickly recognized by the Académie des Sciences, which elected him *adjoint* in 1758, and both *associé* and *pensionnaire* in 1768. He married early and happily; although he was reserved and somewhat somber in society, those who knew him well spoke of his great kindness and warm heart.

In 1763, the duc de Choiseul offered Bezout a position as teacher and examiner in mathematical science for young would-be naval officers, the Gardes du Pavillon et de la Marine. By this time, Bezout had become a father and needed the money. In 1768 he added similar duties for the Corps d'Artillerie. Among his published works are the courses of lectures he gave to these students. The orientation of these books is practical, since they were intended to instruct people in the elementary mathematics and mechanics needed for navigation or ballistics. The experience of teaching nonmathematicians shaped the style of the works: Bezout treated geometry before algebra, observing that beginners were not yet familiar enough with mathematical reasoning to understand the force of algebraic demonstrations, although they did appreciate proofs in geometry. He eschewed the frightening terms "axiom," "theorem," "scholium," and tried to avoid arguments that were too close and detailed. Although criticized occasionally for their lack of rigor, his texts were widely used in France. In the early nineteenth century, they were translated into English for use in American schools; one translator, John Farrar, used them to teach the calculus at Harvard University. The obvious practical orientation, as well as the clarity of exposition, made the books especially attractive in America. These translations considerably influenced the form and content of American mathematical education in the nineteenth century.

A conscientious teacher and examiner, Bezout had little time for research and had to limit himself to what was, for his time, a very narrow subject—the theory of equations. His first two papers (1758–1760) were investigations of integration, but by 1762 he was devoting all his research time to algebra. In his mathematical papers, Bezout often followed a "method of simplifying assumptions," concentrating on those specific cases of general problems which could be solved. This approach is central to the conception of Bezout's first paper on algebra, "Sur plusieurs classes d'équations" (1762).

This paper provides a method of solution for certain *n*th-degree equations. Bezout related the problem of solving *n*th-degree equations in one unknown to the problem of solving simultaneous equations by elimination: "It is known that a determinate equation can always be viewed as the result of two equations in two unknowns, when one of the unknowns is eliminated."[1] Since an equation can be so formed, Bezout investigated what information could be gained by assuming that it actually was so formed. Such a procedure resembles the eighteenth-century study of the root-coefficient relations in an *n*th-degree equation by treating it as formed by the multiplication of *n* linear factors. Now, if one of the two composing equations had some very simple form—for instance, had only the *n*th-degree term and a constant—Bezout saw that he could determine the form of its solution. Conversely, if the coefficients of a given *n*th-degree equation in one unknown had the form built up from such a special solution, that *n*th-degree equation could be solved. Bezout's principal example considers

$$x^n + mx^{n-1} + px^{n-2} + \cdots + M = 0$$

as resulting from the equations

$$y^n + h = 0 \quad \text{and} \quad y = \frac{x+a}{x+b}.$$

The importance of this paper lay in drawing Bezout's attention from the problem of explicitly solving the *n*th-degree equation—an important concern of eighteenth-century algebraists—to the theory of elimination, the area of his most significant contributions. The central problem of elimination theory for Bezout was this: given n equations in n unknowns, to find and study what Bezout called the resultant equation in one of the unknowns. This equation contains all values of that unknown that occur in solutions of the n given equations. Bezout wanted to find a resultant equation of as small degree as possible, that is, with as few extraneous roots as possible. He wanted also to find its degree, or at least an upper bound on its degree.

In his 1764 paper, "Sur le degré des équations résultantes de l'évanouissement des inconnues," he discussed Euler's method for finding the equation resulting from two equations in two unknowns, and computed an upper bound on its degree.[2] He extended this method to N equations in N unknowns. But, although Euler's method yielded an upper bound on the degree of the resultant equation, Bezout observed that it was too clumsy to use for equations of high degree.

Another procedure, which gives a resultant equation of lower degree (now called the Bezoutiant) is given at the end of the 1764 paper. The equations to be solved are

$$(1) \qquad Ax^m + Bx^{m-1} + \cdots + V = 0$$
$$(2) \qquad A'x^{m'} + B'x^{m'-1} + \cdots + V' = 0$$

where $A, A', B, B', \cdots$ are functions of y, and where $m \geqslant m'$. From these, he obtained m polynomials in x, of degree less than or equal to m-1, which have among their common solutions the solutions of (1) and (2). For the case $m = m'$, these polynominals are

$$A'(Ax^m + Bx^{m-1} + \cdots + V) - A(A'x^{m'} + \cdots + V') = 0,$$
$$(A'x + B')(Ax^m + \cdots + V) - (Ax + B)(A'x^{m'} + \cdots + V') = 0, \text{etc.}$$

He considered these polynomial equations as m linear equations in the unknowns $x, x^2, \cdots, x^{m-1}$. And he observed that (1) and (2) have a common solution if these linear equations do. But when can the linear equations be solved?

At the beginning of this 1764 paper, Bezout had expressed what we would call a determinant by means of permutations of the coefficients, in what is sometimes called the Table of Bezout. He described the use of this table in solving simultaneous linear equations and, in particular, as a criterion for their solvability. This gave him a criterion for finding the resultant of (1) and (2). J. J. Sylvester, in 1853, explicitly gave the determinant of the coefficients of these m linear equations, and called it the Bezoutiant. The Bezoutiant, considered as a function of y, has as its zeros all the y's that are common solutions of equations (1) and (2).

It was not until 1779 that Bezout published his *Théorie des équations algébriques,* his major work on elimination theory. Its best-known achievement is the statement and proof of Bezout's theorem: "The degree of the final equation resulting from any number of complete equations in the same number of unknowns, and of any degrees, is equal to the product of the degrees of the equations."[3] Bezout, following Euler, defined a complete polynomial as one that contains each possible combination of the unknowns whose degree is no more than the degree of the polynomial. Bezout also computed that the degree of the resultant equation is less than the product of the degrees for various systems of incomplete equations. Here we shall consider only the complete case.

The proof makes one marvel at the ingenuity of Bezout, who, like Euler, not only could manipulate formulas but also had the ability to choose those manipulations that would be fruitful. He was compelled to justify his nth-order results by a naive "induction" from the observed truth of the statements for 1, 2, 3, $\cdots$. Also, numbered subscripts had not yet come into use, and the notations available were clumsy.

Here is Bezout's argument. Given n equations in n unknowns, of degrees $t, t', t'', \cdots$. Let us call the equations $P_1(u,x,y,\cdots)$, $P_2(u,x,y,\cdots)$, $\cdots$. (Bezout wrote them $(u\cdots n)^t$, $(u\cdots n)^{t'}$, $\cdots$). Suppose now that P_1 is multiplied by an indeterminate polynomial, which we shall designate as Q for definiteness, of degree T. If a Q can be found such that P_1Q involves only the unknown u, P_1Q will be the resultant; Bezout's problem then becomes to compute the smallest possible degree of such a P_1Q.

Bezout stated, and later[4] gave an argument to show, that he could solve the equations

$$P_2(u, x, y, \cdots) = 0, \cdots P_n(u, x, y, \cdots) = 0$$

to determine, respectively, $x^{t'}, y^{t''}, z^{t'''}, \cdots$ in terms of lower powers of the unknowns. Substituting the values for $x^{t'}$, $y^{t''}$, $\cdots$ in the product P_1Q would eliminate all the terms divisible by those powers of the unknowns.

The key to Bezout's proof was in counting the number of terms in the final polynomial, P_1Q. Bezout began his book with a derivation, by means of finite differences, of a complicated formula for the number of terms in a complete polynomial in several unknowns which are not divisible by the unknowns to particular powers; that is, for a complete polynomial in $u, x, y, z, \cdots$ of degree T, he gave an expression for the number of terms not divisible by $u^p, x^q, y^r, \cdots$, where $p + q + r + \cdots < T$. Bezout used this formula to compute the number of terms in the polynomials P_1Q and Q which remained after the elimination of $x^{t'}, y^{t''}, \cdots$.

Let us write N (instead of Bezout's complicated expression) for the number of terms remaining in P_1Q, M for those remaining in Q. If the degree of the resultant is to be D, then it will have $D + 1$ terms, since it is an equation in the single unknown u. Then the coefficients of Q must be such that $N - (D + 1)$ terms in the product P_1Q will be annihilated by them. But, since Q or any multiple of Q would have the same effect, one of the coefficients of Q may be taken arbitrarily. Thus, Bezout argued, there were $M - 1$ coefficients at his disposal to annihilate the number of terms beyond $D + 1$ remaining in the product P_1Q. In other words, Bezout had to solve $N - (D + 1)$ linear equations in $M - 1$ unknowns—these unknowns being the coefficients of Q. This can be done if the number of equations equals the number of unknowns, although Bezout did not explicitly state this. Equating $N - (D + 1)$ with $M - 1$, and using his formulas for N and M, Bezout was able to compute that $D = t, t', t'', t''', \cdots$.[5] Bezout briefly noted that his theorem has a geometric interpretation: "The surfaces of three bodies whose nature is expressible by algebraic equations cannot meet each other in more points than there are units in the product of the degrees of the equations."[6] We should note that Bezout did not show that the equations for the coefficients of Q form a consistent, independent set of linear equations, or that extraneous roots can never occur in the resultant equation. Further, the geometric statement must be modified to deal with special cases, since, for instance, three planes can have a straight line in common.

Later on in the work,[7] Bezout discussed another method of finding the resultant equation; this was by finding polynomials, which we may write $Q_1, \cdots, Q_n$, such that

$$P_1Q_1 + P_2Q_2 + \cdots + P_nQ_n = 0$$

is the resultant equation. Each Q_k has indeterminate coefficients, which Bezout explicitly determined for many systems of equations by comparing powers of the unknowns $x, y, z, \cdots$.

Bezout's work on resultants stimulated many investigations in the modern theory of elimination, including Cauchy's refinements of elimination procedure and Sylvester's work on resultants and inertia forms. Bezout's theorem is crucial to the study of the intersection of manifolds in algebraic geometry. In the preface to the *Théorie des équations,* Bezout had complained that algebra was becoming a neglected science. But his accomplishment showed that the fact that his contemporaries could not solve the general equation of *n*th degree did not mean that there were no fruitful areas of investigation remaining in algebra.

NOTES

1. "Sur plusieurs classes d'équations," 20.
2. For Euler's method, see *Introductio in analysin infinitorum* (Lausanne, 1748), 2, secs. 483 ff.
3. *Théorie des équations algébriques,* 32.
4. *Ibid.,* 206.
5. *Ibid.,* 32.
6. *Ibid.,* 33.
7. *Ibid.,* 187 ff.

BIBLIOGRAPHY

I. Original Works. Bezout's major works are the following: "Sur plusieurs classes d'équations de tous les degrés qui admettent une solution algébrique," in *Mémoires de l'Académie royale des sciences* (1762), 17–52; *Cours de mathématiques à l'usage des Gardes du Pavillon et de la Marine,* 6 vols. (Paris, 1764–1769), reprinted many times with slight variations in the title, often translated or revised in parts; "Sur le degré des équations résultantes de l'évanouissement des inconnues," in *Mémoires de l'Académie royale des sciences* (1764), 288–338; "Sur la resolution des équations de tous les degrés," *ibid.* (1765), 533–552; and *Théorie générale des équations algébriques* (Paris, 1779).

II. Secondary Works. Secondary works are Georges Bouligand, "À une étape décisive de l'algèbre. L'oeuvre scientifique d'Étienne Bezout," in *Revue générale des sciences,* **55** (1948), 121–123; Marquis de Condorcet, "Éloge de M. Bezout," in *Éloges des académiciens de l'Académie Royale des Sciences,* **3** (1799), 322–337; E. Netto and R. Le Vavasseur, "Les fonctions rationnelles," in *Encyclopédie des sciences mathématiques pures et appliquées,* I, pt. 2 (Paris–Leipzig, 1907), 1–232; and Henry S. White, "Bezout's Theory of Resultants and Its Influence on Geometry," in *Bulletin of the American Mathematical Society,* **15** (1909), 325–338.

Judith V. Grabiner

BHĀSKARA II (*b.* 1115)

Bhāskara II has been one of the most impressive Indian astronomers and mathematicians, not only to modern students of the history of science but also to his contemporaries and immediate successors. An important inscription discovered at Pāṭṇā, near Chalisgaon in East Khandesh, Mahārāṣṭra, by Bhāu Dājī, and reedited by F. Kielhorn (*Epigraphia Indica,* **1** [1892], 338–346), records the endowment, by Soïdeva the Nikumbha, on 9 August 1207, of an educational institution (*maṭha*) for the study of Bhāskara's works, beginning with the *Siddhāntaśiromaṇi.* There is further reference in this inscription to Soïdeva's brother and successor, Hemāḍideva, who was a feudatory of the Yādava king of Devagiri, Siṅghaṇa, whose rule began in 1209/1210. The following genealogy is given in the inscription.

Trivikrama belonged to the Śāṇḍilya *gotra*—which indicates that he and his descendants were Brāhmaṇas. His son was Bhāskarabhaṭṭa, who was given the title of Vidyāpati by Bhojarāja (the Paramāra king of Dhārā from *ca.* 995 to *ca.* 1056). The next four generations were respectively Govinda, Prabhākara, Manoratha, and Maheśvara; the last was the father of Bhāskara II. Bhāskara's son, Lakṣmīdhara, was made chief of the Paṇḍitas by Siṅghaṇa's predecessor, Jaitrapāla (1191–1209); and Laksmīdhara's son, Caṅgadeva, was the chief astrologer to Siṅghaṇa himself. It is confirmed in Bhāskara's works—e.g., in the concluding verses of the *Siddhāntaśiromaṇi*—that his father was Maheśvara of the Śāṇḍilya *gotra;* it is further added that he came from the city Vijjaḍaviḍa (Bījāpur in Mysore), which was probably named after the Kalacūri king Vijjaḷa II (1156–1175). If this identification is correct—since the *Siddhāntaśiromaṇi* was written in 1150—Bhāskara II must have been in Vijjaḷa's capital while the latter was still *daṇḍanāyaka* of the Cālukya kings, Jagadekamalla II (1138–1150) and Taila III (1150–1156). We further know from Trivikrama's *Damayantīkathā* that he was the son of Nemāditya (Devāditya?) and the grandson of Śrīdhara; and there exists a popular astrological work by Maheśvara, Bhāskara II's father, entitled *Vṛttaśataka.*

Bhāskara II is the author of at least six works, and possibly of a seventh as well:

1. *Līlāvatī* (see Essay XII).
2. *Bījagaṇita* (see Essay XII).
3. *Siddhāntaśiromaṇi* (see Essay IV).
4. *Vāsanābhāṣya* on the *Siddhāntaśiromaṇi* (see Essay IV).
5. *Karaṇakutūhala* (see Essay IV).
6. *Vivaraṇa* on the *Śiṣyadhīvṛddhidatantra* of Lalla (see Essay V).
7. *Bījopanaya* (see Essay IV).

The *Līlāvatī* and the *Bījagaṇita* are sometimes taken to be parts of the *Siddhāntaśiromaṇi;* the ascription of the *Bījopanaya* to Bhāskara II is questionable.

1. The *Līlāvatī* is a work on mathematics addressed by Bhāskara II to a lady (his daughter or wife?) named Līlāvatī. It contains thirteen chapters:

1. Definitions of terms.
2. Arithmetical operations.
3. Miscellaneous rules.
4. Interest and the like.
5. Arithmetical and geometrical progressions.
6. Plane geometry.

7–10. Solid geometry.

11. On the shadow of a gnomon.
12. Algebra: the pulverizer (*kuṭṭaka*). This is the same as chapter 5 of the *Bījagaṇita.*
13. Combinations of digits.

The *Līlāvatī* has been commented on many times:

1. *Karmapradīpikā* of Nārāyaṇa (*fl.* 1356).
2. *Vyākhyā* of Paraśurāma Miśra (1356).
3. *Vyākhyā* of Parameśvara (*fl.* 1400–1450).
4. *Gaṇitāmṛtasāgarī* of Gaṅgādhara (*ca.* 1420).
5. *Vyākhyā* of Lakṣmīdāsa (*fl.* 1501).
6. *Gaṇitāmṛtakūpikā* of Sūryadāsa (1541). See K. Madhava Krishna Sarma, *Siddha-Bhāratī,* part 2 (Hoshiarpur, 1950), 222–225.
7. *Buddhivilāsinī* of Gaṇeśa (1545). Published. See below, Sanskrit text of the *Līlāvatī* no. 14.
8. *Kriyākramakarī* of Śaṅkara (*fl.* 1556).
9. *Vivaraṇa* of Mahīdhara, alias Mahīdāsa (1587). Published. See below, Sanskrit text of the *Līlāvatī* no. 14.
10. *Mitabhāṣiṇī* of Raṅganātha (1630).
11. *Nisṛṣṭārthadūtī* of Munīśvara, alias Viśvarūpa (1635).
12. *Gaṇitāmṛtalaharī* of Rāmakṛṣṇa (1687). See P. K. Gode, "Date of Gaṇitāmṛtalaharī of Rāmakṛṣna," in *Annals of the Bhandarkar Oriental Research Institute,* **11** (1930), 94–95.
13. *Sarvabodhinī* of Śrīdhara (1717).
14. *Udāharaṇa* of Nīlāmbara Jhā (*fl.* 1823).
15. *Ṭīkā* in Kannada of Alasiṅgārya, alias Aliśiṅgarāja.
16. *Vyākhyā* of Bhaveśa.
17. *Udāharaṇa* of Candraśekhara Paṭanāyaka.
18. *Ṭīkā* of Dāmodara(?).
19. *Vilāsa* of Devīsahāya.
20. *Bhūṣaṇa* of Dhaneśvara. Refers to Sūryadāsa (1541).
21. *Ṭīkā* (in vernacular) of Giridhara.
22. *Vyākhyā* of Keśava.
23. *Ṭippaṇa* of Mukunda.
24. *Vṛtti* of Moṣadeva.
25. *Subodhinī* of Rāghava.
26. *Gaṇakabhūṣaṇa* of Rāmacandra, son of Ṣoṣaṇabhaṭṭa.
27. *Kautukalīlāvatī* of Rāmacandra, son of

Vidyādhara.

28. *Ṭippaṇa* of Rāmadatta (?).
29. *Manorañjana* of Rāmakṛṣṇadeva.
30. *Ṭīkā* of Rāmeśvara.
31. *Ṭīkā* of Śrīkaṇṭha.
32. *Gaṇitāmṛtavarṣiṇī* of Sūryamaṇi.
33. *Udāharaṇa* of Vīreśvara. Refers to Lakṣmīdāsa (1501).
34. *Udāharaṇa* of Viśveśvara.
35. *Ṭīkā* of Vṛndāvana (?).

In addition to these and a number of anonymous commentaries, there are others in Marāṭhī and Gujarāṭī. A modern Sanskrit commentary (aside from those which accompany some of the editions listed below) was published by Candra Śekhara Jhā under the title *Vyaktavilāsa* (Benares, 1924).

There are also numerous editions of the Sanskrit text of the *Līlāvatī:*

1. Calcutta, 1832.
2. Tārānātha Śarman, ed. (Calcutta, 1846).
3. Baptist Mission Press (Calcutta, 1846; 2nd ed., Calcutta, 1876).
4. With the *Vivaraṇa* of Mahīdhara and a Telugu commentary by Taḍakamalla Veñkaṭa Kṛṣṇarāva, Vāvilla Rāmasvāmin Śāstrin, ed. (Madras, 1863).
5. Jīvānanda Vidyāsāgara, ed. (Calcutta, 1876).
6. Sudhākara Dvivedin, ed. (Benares, 1878).
7. Edited, with his own Sanskrit commentary, by Bāpūdeva Śāstrin (Benares, 1883).
8. Bhuvanacandra Basak, ed. (Calcutta, 1885).
9. Edited as an appendix to Banerji's edition of Colebrooke's translation (Calcutta, 1892; 2nd ed., Calcutta, 1927).
10. Edited, with a Marāṭhī commentary, by Vināyaka Pāṇḍurañga Khānāpūrkar (Poona, 1897).
11. Sudhākara Dvivedin, ed., Benares Sanskrit Series, no. 153 (Benares, 1912).
12. Rādhāvallabha, ed. (Calcutta, 1914).
13. Edited, with his own Sanskrit commentary, by Muralīdhara Thākura, as Śrī Harikṛṣṇa Nibandha Maṇimālā Series, no. 3 (Benares, 1928; 2nd ed., Benares, 1938).
14. With *Buddhivilāsinī* of Gaṇeśa and *Vivaraṇa* of Mahīdhara, Dattātreya Āpṭe, ed., Ānandāśrama Sanskrit Series, no. 107, 2 vols. (Poona, 1937).
15. With Sanskrit commentary, edited by Dāmodara Miśra and Payanātha Jhā, as Prācīnācārya Granthāvalī Series, no. 8 (Durbhanga, 1959).
16. With Sanskrit and Hindī commentaries of Laṣaṇa Lāla Jhā, edited by Sureśa Śarman, as Vidyābhavana Saṃskṛta Granthamālā Series, no. 62 (Benares, 1961).

There are also many translations of the *Līlāvatī.* A Kaṇṇada version is supposed to have been made by Bhāskara II's contemporary Rājāditya, who flourished, apparently, under the Hoysala king Viṣṇuvardhana (1111-1141). There also exists a Hindī translation, and the various commentaries in Gujarāṭī, Marāṭhī, and Telugu have already been referred to. Three Persian translations are known. That made by Abū al-Fayḍ Fayḍī at the request of Akbar in 1587 was published at Calcutta in 1827; another was done by Dharma Narāyan ibn Kalyānmal Kāyath *ca.* 1663 (H. J. J. Winter and A. Mirza, in *Journal of the Asiatic Society of Science,* **18** [1952], 1-10); and the third was made in 1678 by Muḥammad Amīn ibn Shaykh Muḥammad Saʿīd. There are also two English translations. That by J. Taylor was published at Bombay in 1816, and that by H. T. Colebrooke in his *Algebra, With Arithmetic and Mensuration: From the Sanscrit of Brahmegupta and Bháscara* (London, 1817). The latter was republished by Haran Chandra Banerji as *Colebrooke's Translation of the Lílávati* (Calcutta, 1892; 2nd ed., Calcutta, 1927).

2. The *Bījagaṇita,* on algebra, contains twelve chapters:

1. On positive and negative numbers.
2. On zero.
3. On the unknown.
4. On surds.
5. On the pulverizer (*kuṭṭaka*).
6. On indeterminate quadratic equations.
7. On simple equations.
8. On quadratic equations.
9. On equations having more than one unknown.
10. On quadratic equations having more than one unknown.
11. On operations with products of several unknowns.
12. On the author and his work.

The commentaries on the *Bījagaṇita* are all relatively late, and they are far fewer in number than those on the *Līlāvatī.*

1. *Sūryaprakāśa* of Sūryadāsa (1538). See K. Madhava Krishna Sarma, in *Poona Orientalist,* **11** (1946), 54-66, and his article in *Siddha-Bhāratī,* part 2 (Hoshiarpur, 1950), 222-225.
2. *Navāñkura* (or *Bījapallava,* or *Bījāvataṃsa,* or *Kalpalatāvatāra*) of Kṛṣṇa (1602). See M. M. Patkar, in *Poona Orientalist,* **3** (1938), 169. Published. See below, Sanskrit texts nos. 13 and 16.
3. *Bījaprabodha* of Rāmakṛṣṇa (1687). See P. K. Gode in *Annals of the Bhandarkar Oriental Research Institute,* **10** (1929), 160-161, and **11** (1930), 94-95.

4. *Bālabodhinī* of Kṛpārāma (1792).
5. *Vāsanābhāṣya* of Haridāsa.
6. *Bījālavāla* of Nijānanda.
7. *Kalpalatā* of Paramaśukla (most likely Kṛṣṇa's work?).
8. *Bījavivaraṇa* of Vīreśvara (?).

The Sanskrit text has been frequently published:

1. Calcutta, 1834; rev. ed., Calcutta, 1834.
2. Calcutta, 1846.
3. Partial edition with a German translation by H. Brockhaus, "Über die Algebra des Bhāskara," in *Berichte über die Verhandlungen der Königlich Sächsischen Gesellschaft der Wissenschaften zu Leipzig, Philosophisch-historische Klasse,* **4** (Leipzig, 1852), 1-46.
4. Calcutta, 1853.
5. Gopinātha Pāṭhaka, ed. (Benares, 1864).
6. Bāpūdeva Śāstrin, ed., 2 parts (Calcutta [?], 1875).
7. Jīvānanda Vidyāsāgara, ed. (Calcutta, 1878).
8. Edited, with his own Sanskrit commentary, by Jīvanātha Śarman (Benares, 1885).
9. Edited, with his own Sanskrit commentary, by Sudhākara Dvivedin (Benares, 1888).
10. Edited, with a Marāṭhī translation and commentary, by Vināyaka Pāṇḍuraṅga Khānāpūrkar (Poona, 1913).
11. Edited, with his own Sanskrit commentary, by Rādhāvallabha (Calcutta, 1917).
12. Edited, with Sudhākara Dvivedin's Sanskrit commentary and one of his own, by Muralīdhara Jhā, as Benares Sanskrit Series, no. 154 (Benares, 1927).
13. Edited, with the *Navāṅkura* of Kṛṣṇa, by Dattātreya Āpṭe, as Ānandāśrama Sanskrit Series, no. 99 (Poona, 1930).
14. Edited, with his own Sanskrit and Hindī commentaries, by Durgāprasāda Dvivedin (3rd. ed., Lakṣmaṇapura, 1941; the preface is dated Jayapura, 1916).
15. Edited, with Jīvanātha Śarman's Sanskrit commentary and with his own in Sanskrit and Hindī, by Acyutānanda Jhā, as Kāśī Sanskrit Series, no. 148 (Benares, 1949).
16. Edited, with the *Bījapallava* of Kṛṣṇa, by T. V. Rādhākṛṣṇa Śāstrin, as Tanjore Sarasvati Mahal Series, no. 78 (Tanjore, 1958).

There are two Persian translations of the *Bījagaṇita,* one anonymous and the other by ʿAtā allāh Rashīdī ibn Aḥmad Nādir for Shah Jahan in 1634/1635. An English translation of the latter by E. Strachey, with notes by S. Davis, was published at London in 1813. It was also translated into English directly from the Sanskrit by H. T. Colebrooke in *Algebra, With Arithmetic and Mensuration* . . . (London, 1817).

3. The *Siddhāntaśiromaṇi,* which was written in 1150, consists of two parts—the *Grahagaṇitādhyāya* (or *Gaṇitādhyāya*) and the *Golādhyāya*—which are sometimes preserved singly in the manuscripts. The first part, on mathematical astronomy, contains twelve chapters:

1. On the mean longitudes of the planets.
2. On the true longitudes of the planets.
3. On the three problems involving diurnal motion.
4. On the syzygies.
5. On lunar eclipses.
6. On solar eclipses.
7. On planetary latitudes.
8. On the heliacal risings and settings of the planets.
9. On the lunar crescent.
10. On planetary conjunctions.
11. On conjunctions of the planets with the stars.
12. On the *pātas* of the sun and moon.

The second part, on the sphere, contains thirteen chapters:

1. Praise of (the study of) the sphere.
2. On the nature of the sphere.
3. On cosmography and geography.
4. Principles of planetary mean motion.
5. On the eccentric-epicyclic model of the planets.
6. On the construction of an armillary sphere.
7. Principles of spherical trigonometry.
8. Principles of eclipse calculations.
9. Principles of the calculation of the first and last visibilities of the planets.
10. Principles of the calculation of the lunar crescent.
11. On astronomical instruments.
12. Descriptions of the seasons.
13. On problems of astronomical computations.

The chapter on the sine function is placed differently in different editions. The *Golādhyāya,* then, is to a large extent an expansion and explanation of the *Gaṇitādhyāya.*

The following commentaries on the *Siddhāntaśiromaṇi* are known (besides various anonymous ones):

1. *Mitākṣarā* (or *Vāsanābhāṣya*) of Bhāskara II himself (see **4,** below). Published. See below, under Sanskrit texts.
2. *Gaṇitatattvacintāmaṇi* of Lakṣmīdāsa (1501).
3. *Śiromaṇiprakāśa* of Gaṇeśa (*b.* 1507). Published in part. See below, Sanskrit text of *Grahagaṇitādhyāya,* no. 4.

4. *Marīci* of Munīśvara, alias Viśvarūpa (*b.* 1603). Published. See below, under Sanskrit texts.
5. *Ṭīkā* of Rāmakṛṣṇa (*fl.* 1687).
6. *Ṭīkā* of Cakracūḍāmaṇi (?).
7. *Vyākhyā* of Dhaneśvara.
8. *Vyākhyā* of Harihara (?).
9. *Ṭīkā* of Jayalakṣmaṇa (?).
10. *Lakṣmīnāthī* of Lakṣmīnātha Miśra (?).
11. *Bhāṣya* of Maheśvara (?).
12. *Vāsanā* of Mohanadāsa (?).
13. *Vyākhyā* of Raṅganātha.
14. *Ṭīkā* of Vācaspati Miśra (?).

The *Ṭippaṇīvivaraṇa* of Buddhinātha Jhā was published at Benares in 1912.

The list of editions of the text is arranged under three headings: *Siddhāntaśiromaṇi, Grahagaṇitādhyāya,* and *Golādhyāya.*

Siddhāntaśiromaṇi.

1. *Siddhāntaśiromaṇiprakāśa* (of Gaṇeśa?), with a Marāṭhī translation (Bombay, 1837).
2. *Siddhāntaśiromaṇi,* with the *Prakāśa* (of Gaṇeśa?), Rāmacandra, ed. (Madras, 1837).
3. Edited, with the *Vāsanābhāṣya,* by Bāpūdeva Śāstrin (Benares, 1866); revised by Candradeva (Benares, 1891); revised by Gaṇapatideva Śāstrin, as Kāśī Sanskrit Series, no. 72 (Benares, 1929).
4. Edited, with the *Vāsanābhāṣya,* the *Vāsanāvārttika* of Nṛsiṃha, and the *Marīci* of Munīśvara, by Muralīdhara Jhā, in *The Pandit,* n.s. **30-38** (1908-1916)—incomplete; the first chapter of the *Grahagaṇitādhyāya* was reprinted at Benares in 1917.
5. Edited, with a Sanskrit commentary, by Girijāprasāda Dvivedin (Ahmadabad, 1936).

Grahagaṇitādhyāya.

1. Edited, with the *Mitākṣarā,* by L. Wilkinson (Calcutta, 1842).
2. Edited, with the *Mitākṣarā,* by Jīvānanda Vidyāsāgara (Calcutta, 1881).
3. Edited, with a Marāṭhī translation and commentary, by Vināyaka Pāṇḍuraṅga Khānāpūrkar (Poona, 1913).
4. Edited, with the *Vāsanābhāṣya* and the *Śiromaṇiprakāśa* of Gaṇeśa, by Dattātreya Āpṭe, as Ānandāśrama Sanskrit Series, no. 110, 2 vols. (Poona, 1939-1941).
5. Edited, with the *Vāsanābhāṣya* and his own Sanskrit commentary, by Muralīdhara Ṭhakkura, as Kāśī Sanskrit Series, no. 149 (Benares, 1950)—the first two chapters only.
6. Edited, with the *Vāsanābhāṣya,* the *Marīci* of Munīśvara, and his own Sanskrit and Hindī commentaries, by Kedāradatta Jośī, 3 vols. (Benares, 1961-1964); this edition does not include the *Marīci* on chapter 1.

Golādhyāya.

1. Edited, with the *Mitākṣarā,* by L. Wilkinson (Calcutta, 1842).
2. Calcutta, 1856.
3. Edited, with the *Vāsanābhāṣya,* by Jīvānanda Vidyāsāgara (Calcutta, 1880).
4. Edited, with the *Vāsanābhāṣya* and a Bengali translation, by Rasikamohana Chattopādhyāya (Calcutta, 1887).
5. Edited, with the *Vāsanābhāṣya* and a Bengali translation, in *Aruṇodaya,* **1** (1890), part 6.
6. Edited, with a Marāṭhī translation and commentary, by Vināyaka Pāṇḍuraṅga Khānāpūrkar (Bombay, 1911)—chapters 1-8 only.
7. Edited, with the *Vāsanābhāṣya* and a Hindī commentary, by Girijāprasāda Dvivedin (Lucknow, 1911).
8. Edited, with the *Vāsanābhāṣya* and a Bengali translation, by Rādhāvallabha (Calcutta, 1921).
9. Edited, with the *Vāsanābhāṣya* and the *Marīci* of Munīśvara, by Dattātreya Āpṭe, as Ānandāśrama Sanskrit Series, no. 122, 2 vols. (Poona, 1943-1952).

Aside from the translations into the vernacular mentioned above, I know only of the following two: a Latin translation of the *Grahagaṇitādhyāya* published by E. Roer in *Journal of the Royal Asiatic Society of Bengal,* **13** (1844), 53-66, and an English translation of the *Golādhyāya* by L. Wilkinson, revised by Bāpūdeva Śāstrin, as Bibliotheca Indica, no. 32 (Calcutta, 1861), with the Paṇḍit's translation of the *Sūryasiddhānta.* See also L. Wilkinson, "On the Use of the Siddhāntas in the Work of Native Education," in *Journal of the Royal Asiatic Society of Bengal,* **3** (1834), 504-519.

4. The *Vāsanābhāṣya* or *Mitākṣarā* is Bhāskara II's own commentary on the *Siddhāntaśiromaṇi.* A commentary on it, the *Vāsanāvārttika,* was written by Nṛsiṃha of Golagrāma in 1621. Editions of both these works have been listed in the preceding material on the *Siddhāntaśiromaṇi.*

5. The *Karaṇakutūhala,* which is also known as the *Brahmatulya,* the *Grahāgamakutūhala,* and the *Vidagdhabuddhivallabha,* was written in 1183; it gives simpler rules for solving astronomical problems than does the *Siddhāntaśiromaṇi.* There are ten sections:

1. On the mean longitudes of the planets.
2. On the true longitudes of the planets.
3. On the three problems involving diurnal motion.
4. On lunar eclipses.
5. On solar eclipses.
6. On heliacal risings and settings.

7. On the lunar crescent.
8. On planetary conjunctions.
9. On the *pātas* of the sun and moon.
10. On the syzygies.

There are, aside from the usual quantity of anonymous commentaries on the *Karaṇakutūhala,* eight whose authors' names are known:

1. *Bhāṣya* of Ekanātha (*ca.* 1370).
2. *Nārmadī* of Padmanābha (*ca.* 1575).
3. *Udāharaṇa* of Viśvanātha (1612).
4. *Gaṇakakumudakaumudī* of Sumatiharṣa Gaṇi (1622). Published. See below.
5. *Ṭīkā* of Caṇḍīdāsa.
6. *Brahmatulyasāra* of Keśavārka (?).
7. *Ṭīkā* of Saṅkara.
8. *Ṭīkā* of Soḍhala.

For a set of tables based on the *Karaṇakutūhala,* see David Pingree, "Sanskrit Astronomical Tables in the United States," in *Transactions of the American Philosophical Society,* n.s. **58,** no. 3 (1968), 36–37.

The *Karaṇakutūhala* has twice been edited: by Sudhākara Dvivedin, with his own Sanskrit commentary (Benares, 1881); and, with the *Gaṇakakumadakaumudī* of Sumatiharṣa Gaṇi, by Mādhava Śāstrī Purohita (Bombay, 1902).

6. Bhāskara II's *Vivaraṇa* on the *Śiṣyadhīvṛddhidatantra* of Lalla has not been studied or published. There are three manuscripts: in Benares, in Bikaner, and in Ujjain.

7. A short text of fifty-nine verses entitled *Bījopanaya* is attributed to Bhāskara II. The author claims to be that scholar and to have written this work in 1151. A *Tithinirṇayakārikā* published with it is the only other Sanskrit work to mention it; the author of this text claims to be Śrīnivāsa Yajvan, who flourished in Mysore in the second half of the thirteenth century and wrote a *Śuddhidīpikā* and a commentary on the *Karaṇaprakāśa* of Brahmadeva. Both works, despite their acceptance by Mukhopadhyaya and Sengupta, are evidently late forgeries.

Kuppanna Sastri has shown that the *Bījopanaya,* which gives rules for computing a correction to the moon's equation of the center and variation, was most probably forged in south India in the early 1870's to buttress the position of the partisans of the *dṛk* system against those of the *vākya* system. His argument is based on three main points:

(1) The first correction is astronomically invalid and would have appeared so to the author of the *Siddhāntaśiromaṇi.*

(2) The style is completely at variance with Bhāskara's normal method of exposition.

(3) There are oblique references in the *Vāsanābhāṣya,* a commentary accompanying the *Bījopanaya,* which is also alleged to be by Bhāskara II, to Raṅganātha's commentary on the *Sūryasiddhānta,* which was written in 1602 and was published in 1859.

These arguments seem to this writer quite convincing.

The *Bījopanaya* has been published twice: by Cintāmaṇi Raghunāthācārya and Taḍhakamalla Veṅkaṭakṛṣṇa Rāya at Madras in 1876; and by Ekendranāth Ghosh at Lahore in 1926.

BIBLIOGRAPHY

The following bibliography generally excludes articles that deal only in part with Bhāskara II. It is divided into five sections: General, *Līlāvatī, Bījagaṇita, Siddhāntaśiromaṇi,* and *Bījopanaya.* All entries are listed in chronological order.

I. GENERAL. The following deal with Bhāskara II and his works in general: Bhāu Dājī, "Brief Notes on the Age and Authenticity of the Works of Aryabhaṭa, Varāhamihira, Brahmagupta, Bhaṭṭotpala, and Bhāskarāchārya," in *Journal of the Royal Asiatic Society* (1865), 392–418, esp. 410–418; Janārdana Bāḷājī Moḍaka, *Bhāskara Āchārya and His Astronomical System* (n.p., 1887); Sudhākara Dvivedin, *Gaṇakataraṅgiṇī* (Benares, 1933; repr. from *The Pandit,* n.s. **14** [1892]), pp. 34–42; Bāpūdeva Śāstrin, "A Brief Account of Bhāskara, and of the Works Written, and Discoveries Made, by Him," in *Journal of the Asiatic Society of Bengal,* **62** (1893), 223–229; S. B. Dīkṣita, *Bhāratīya Jyotiḥśāstra* (Poona, 1931; repr. of Poona, 1896), pp. 246–254; G. Thibaut, *Astronomie, Astrologie und Mathematik, Grundriss der indo-arischen Philologie und Altertumskunde,* III, pt. 9 (Strasbourg, 1899), 60; S. K. Ganguly, "Bhāskarāchārya's References to Previous Teachers," in *Bulletin of the Calcutta Mathematical Society,* **18** (1927), 65–76; B. Datta, "The Two Bhāskaras," in *Indian Historical Quarterly,* **6** (1930), 727–736; and Brij Mohan, "The Terminology of Bhāskara," in *Journal of the Oriental Institute, Baroda,* **9** (1959/1960), 17–22.

II. LĪLĀVATĪ. The *Līlāvatī* is discussed in E. Strachey, *Observations on the Mathematical Science of the Hindoos, With Extracts From Persian Translations of the Leelawuttee and Beej Gunnit* (Calcutta, 1805); H. Suter, "Über die Vielecksformel in Bhāskara," in *Verhandlungen des 3. Mathematikerkongresses in Heidelberg* (Leipzig, 1905), pp. 556–561; Sarada Kanta Ganguly, "Bhāskarācārya and Simultaneous Indeterminate Equations of the First Degree," in *Bulletin of the Calcutta Mathematical Society,* **17** (1926), 89–98; M. G. Inamdar, "A Long Forgotten Method," in *Annals of the Bhandarkar Oriental Research Institute,* **9** (1927/1928), 304–308; A. A. Krishnaswami Ayyangar, "Bhaskara and Samclishta Kuttaka," in *Journal of the Indian Mathematical Society,* **18** (1929), 1–7; Saradakanta Ganguli, "Bhāskara and Simultaneous Indeterminate Equations of the First Degree," *ibid.,* **19** (1931/1932), 6–9; A. S. Bhandarkar, "'Method of False

Assumption' of Pacioli, an Italian Mathematician," in *Indian Culture,* **8** (1941/1942), 256–257; K. S. Nagarajan, "Bhaskara's Leelavathi," in *The Aryan Path* (1949), 310–314; D. A. Somayaji, "Bhaskara's Calculations of the Gnomon's Shadow," in *The Mathematics Student,* **18** (1950), 1–8; and Brij Mohan, "The Terminology of Līlāvatī," in *Journal of the Oriental Institute, Baroda,* **8** (1958/1959), 159–168.

III. BĪJAGAṆITA. The *Bījagaṇita* is dealt with in Reuben Burrow, "A Proof That the *Hindoos* Had the *Binomial Theorem,*" in *Asiatick Researches,* **2** (1790), 487–497; A. A. Krishnaswami Ayyangar, "New Light on Bhaskara's Chakravala or Cyclic Method of Solving Indeterminate Equations of the Second Degree in Two Variables," in *Journal of the Indian Mathematical Society,* **18** (1929), 225–248; K. J. Sanjana, "A Brief Analysis of Bhaskara's *Bījagaṇita* With Historical and Critical Notes," *ibid.,* 176–188; and D. H. Potts, "Solution of a Diophantine System Proposed by Bhaskara," in *Bulletin of the Calcutta Mathematical Society,* **38** (1946), 21–24.

IV. SIDDHĀNTAŚIROMAṆI. Works discussing the *Siddhāntaśiromaṇi* are Bapudeva Sastri, "Bhāskara's Knowledge of the Differential Calculus," in *Journal of the Asiatic Society of Bengal,* **27** (1858), 213–216; W. Spottiswoode, "Note on the Supposed Discovery of the Principle of the Differential Calculus by an Indian Astronomer," in *Journal of the Royal Asiatic Society* (1860), 221–222; H. Suter, "Eine indische Methode der Berechnung der Kugeloberfläche," in *Bibliotheca mathematica,* 3rd ser., **9** (1908/1909), 196–199; R. Sewell, "The Siddhanta-siromani," in *Epigraphia Indica,* **15** (1919/1920), 159–245; M. G. Inamdar, "A Formula of Bhaskara for the Chord of a Circle Leading to a Formula for Evaluating Sin $\alpha°$," in *The Mathematics Student,* **18** (1950), 9–11; and A. A. Krishnaswami Ayyangar, "Remarks on Bhaskara's Approximation to the Sine of an Angle," *ibid.,* 12.

V. BĪJOPANAYA. Further discussion of the *Bījopanaya* can be found in Dhirendranath Mukhopadhyaya, "The Evection and the Variation of the Moon in Hindu Astronomy," in *Bulletin of the Calcutta Mathematical Society,* **22** (1930), 121–132; P. C. Sengupta, "Hindu Luni-solar Astronomy," *ibid.,* **24** (1932), 1–18; and T. S. Kuppanna Sastri, "The Bījopanaya: Is It a Work of Bhāskarācārya?," in *Journal of the Oriental Institute, Baroda,* **8** (1958/1959), 399–409.

DAVID PINGREE

BIANCHI, LUIGI (*b.* Parma, Italy, 18 January 1856; *d.* Pisa, Italy, 6 June 1928)

The son of Francesco Saverio Bianchi, a jurist and senator of the kingdom of Italy, Bianchi entered the Scuola Normale Superiore of Pisa after passing a competitive examination in November 1873. He studied under Betti and Dini at the University of Pisa, from which he received his degree in mathematics on 30 November 1877. He remained in Pisa for two additional years, pursuing postgraduate studies. Later he attended the universities of Munich and Göttingen, where he studied chiefly under Klein.

Upon his return to Italy in 1881, Bianchi was appointed professor at the Scuola Normale Superiore of Pisa, and after having taught differential geometry at the University of Pisa, in 1886 he was appointed extraordinary professor of projective geometry on the basis of a competitive examination. During the same year he was also made professor of analytic geometry, a post he held for the rest of his life. By special appointment Bianchi also taught higher mathematics and analysis. After 1918 he was director of the Scuola Normale Superiore. He was a member of many Italian and foreign academies, and a senator of the kingdom of Italy.

Bianchi concentrated on studies and research in metric differential geometry. Among his major results was his discovery of all the geometries of Riemann that allow for a continuous group of movements, that is, those in which a figure may move continuously without undergoing any deformation. These results also found application in Einstein's studies on relativity. In addition, Bianchi devoted himself to the study of non-Euclidean geometries and demonstrated how the study of these geometries may lead to results in Euclidean geometry that, through other means, might have been obtained by more complex methods.

A writer of clear and genial treatises, Bianchi wrote many works on mathematics, among which are some dealing with functions of a variable complex, elliptic functions, and continuous groups of transformations.

BIBLIOGRAPHY

I. ORIGINAL WORKS. *Lezioni di geometria differenziale* (Pisa, 1886; 3rd ed., 1922–1923); *Lezioni sulla teoria dei gruppi di sostituzioni e delle equazioni algebriche secondo Galois* (Pisa, 1900); *Lezioni sulla teoria aritmetica delle forme quadratiche binarie e ternarie* (Pisa, 1912); *Lezioni di geometria analitica* (Pisa, 1915); *Lezioni sulla teoria delle funzioni di variabile complessa e delle funzioni ellittiche* (Pisa, 1916); *Lezioni sulla teoria dei gruppi continui finiti di trasformazioni* (Pisa, 1918); *Lezioni sulla teoria dei numeri algebrici e principii di geometria analitica* (Bologna, 1923). Bianchi's works were collected in *Opere,* Edizioni Cremonese, 11 vols. (Rome, 1952–1959); Vol. I, pt. 1 contains a bibliography and analyses of Bianchi's scientific work by G. Scorza, G. Fubini, A. M. Bedarida, and G. Ricci.

II. SECONDARY LITERATURE. Works on Bianchi are G. Fubini, "Luigi Bianchi e la sua opera scientifica," in *Annali di matematica,* 4th ser., **6** (1928–1929), 45–83, and "Commemorazione di Luigi Bianchi," in *Rendiconti della Accademia nazionale dei Lincei,* Classe di scienze fisiche matematiche e naturali, ser. 6a, **10** (1929), xxxiv–xliv (appendix).

ETTORE CARRUCCIO

BIENAYMÉ, IRÉNÉE-JULES (*b.* Paris, France, 28 August 1796; *d.* Paris, 19 October 1878)

Bienaymé's secondary education began at the *lycée* in Bruges and concluded at the Lycée Louis-le-Grand, Paris. He took part in the defense of Paris in 1814 and enrolled at the École Polytechnique the following year; the institution was closed briefly in his first year, however. Bienaymé became lecturer in mathematics at the military academy at St.-Cyr in 1818, leaving in 1820 to enter the Administration of Finances. He soon became inspector and, in 1834, inspector general. At about this time he became active in the affairs of the Société Philomatique de Paris. The revolution of 1848 led Bienaymé to retire from the civil service, and he received a temporary appointment as professor of the calculus of probabilities at the Sorbonne. Despite his retirement, he had considerable influence as a statistical expert in the government of Napoleon III; he was attached to the Ministry of Commerce for two years and was praised in a report to the Senate in 1864 for his actuarial work in connection with the creation of a retirement fund. At the Paris Academy, to which he was elected in 1852, he served for twenty-three years as a referee for the statistics prize of the Montyon Foundation, the highest French award in that field.

Bienaymé was a founding member of the Société Mathématique de France (president in 1875, life member thereafter), corresponding member of the St. Petersburg Academy of Sciences and of the Belgian Central Council of Statistics, and honorary member of the Association of Chemical Conferences of Naples. He became an officer of the Legion of Honor in 1844. Bienaymé had a considerable knowledge of languages; he translated a work by Chebyshev from Russian and at his death was preparing an annotated translation of Aristotle from classical Greek.

Laplace's *Théorie analytique des probabilités* (1812) was Bienaymé's guiding light; and some of his best work, particularly on least squares, elaborates, generalizes, or defends Laplacian positions. Bienaymé corresponded with Quetelet, was a friend of Cournot's, and was on cordial terms with Lamé and Chebyshev. His papers were descriptive, his mathematics laconic; and he had a penchant for controversies. No sooner was he elected to the Academy than he locked horns with Cauchy over linear least squares. In 1842 he had attempted to criticize Poisson's law of large numbers (pertaining to inhomogeneous trials); this invalid criticism was not published until 1855. He also sent a group of communications to the Academy criticizing the Metz Mutual Security Society. Bertrand was to take blistering exception to his style.

Bienaymé did not publish until he was in his thirties, and only twenty-two articles appeared. Almost half are in a now obscure source, the scientific newspaper-journal *L'Institut, Paris*, and were reprinted at the end of the year of their appearance in the compendium *Extraits des Procès-Verbaux de la Société philomatique de Paris*.

The early writings lean to demography; "De la durée de la vie en France" (1837) discusses the life tables of Antoine Deparcieux and E. E. Duvillard de Durand, both of which were widely used in France. Its major object is to present overwhelming evidence against the continued use of the Duvillard table, employment of which by insurance companies had been to their undoubted financial advantage, since the mortality rates that it predicted were much more rapid than was appropriate for France at that time. Apart from writings on the stability of insurance companies, Bienaymé's other direct contribution to the social sciences concerned the size of juries and the majority required for conviction of the accused. The jury system in France had been in a state of flux; its revision was based largely on interpretations of results obtained by Laplace, whose conclusions were later rejected by Poisson in *Recherches sur la probabilité des jugements* . . . (1837); Bienaymé naturally sided with Laplace. Some other papers by Bienaymé have demographic or sociological motivation but involve major methodological contributions to probability or mathematical statistics.

The stability and dispersion theory of statistical trials is concerned with independent binomial trials, the probability of success p_i in the ith trial in general depending on i. The subject forms the early essence of the "Continental direction" of statistics, which is typified by Lexis, Bortkiewicz, A. A. Chuprov, and Oskar Anderson. One of its major aims is to test for, and typify, any heterogeneity in the p_i's (the homogeneous, or Bernoulli, case is that of all p_i's being equal). Bienaymé introduced a physical principle of *durée des causes*, with which he showed that the proportion of successes exhibits more variability than in the homogeneous case (this fact might therefore explain such manifested variability). His reasoning here was not understood until much later. In the context of a set of Bernoulli trials in which there is a specified number of successes, divided into two successive blocks of trials, Bienaymé in 1840 showed an understanding of the important statistical concept of sufficiency, now attributed to Fisher (1920). These contributions established him, after Poisson, as a founder of the "Continental direction."

In linear least squares one is concerned with the estimation of (in modern notation) an $r \times 1$ vector, β, of unknowns from a number N of observations Y, related linearly to β but subject to error ϵ: $Y = A\beta + \epsilon$. Bienaymé extended Laplace's asymptotic treatment of the system as $N \rightarrow \infty$; but the only essential originality is in a largely unsuccessful attempt to find a simultaneous confidence region for all the coefficients β_i, $i = 1, \cdots, r$. Nevertheless, "Mémoire sur la probabilité des erreurs" contains a deduction of an almost final form of the continuous chi-squared density, with n degrees of freedom, for the sum of squares of n independent and identically distributed $N(0,1)$ random variables. The impassioned defense of least squares against Cauchy ("Considérations à l'appui de la découverte de Laplace," 1853) contains three important incidental results, the most startling of which is the Bienaymé-Chebyshev inequality,

$$P(|\bar{X} - EX| \geq \epsilon) \leq \text{var } X/(\epsilon^2 n),$$

proved by the simple argument still used. Chebyshev obtained it by a more difficult means in 1867 and published his results simultaneously in Russian and French. This was juxtaposed with a reprint of Bienaymé's paper and in 1874 Chebyshev himself credited Bienaymé with having arrived at the inequality via the "method of moments," the discovery of which he ascribed to Bienaymé.

Perhaps the most startling of Bienaymé's contributions to probability is a completely correct statement of the criticality theorem for simple branching processes. His "De la loi de la multiplication et de la durée des familles" (1845) anticipated the partly correct statement of Galton and Watson by some thirty years, and predated the completely correct one of Haldane (until recently thought to be the first) by over eighty years. This work may have been stimulated by L. F. Benoiston de Châteauneuf. Of only slightly less significance is a remarkably simple combinatorial test for randomness of observations on a continuously varying quantity. This method involves counting the number of local maxima and minima in the series; Bienaymé stated in 1874 that the number of intervals, complete and incomplete, between extrema in a sequence of N observations is (under assumption of randomness) approximately normally distributed about a mean of $(2N - 1)/3$ with variance $(16N - 29)/90$. This result, which is describable in modern terms as both a nonparametric test and a limit theorem, is technically complex to prove even by modern methods.

A sophisticated limit theorem proved (but not rigorously) by Bienaymé is the following: If the random variables Θ_i, $i = 1, \cdots, m$ satisfy $0 \leq \Theta_i \leq 1$, $\Sigma\Theta_i = 1$, and the joint probability density function of the first $(m - 1)$ is const. $\Theta_1^{x_1} \Theta_2^{x_2} \cdots \Theta_m^{x_m}$ where $x_i \geq 0$ is an integer, then if $V = \Sigma\gamma_i\Theta_i$, as $n \rightarrow \infty$

$$\sqrt{n}\,(V - \bar{\gamma})/\sqrt{\Sigma(\gamma_i - \bar{\gamma})^2 x_i/n} \rightarrow N(0,1),$$

where $\bar{\gamma} = \Sigma\gamma_i x_i/n$, $n = \Sigma x_i$, $r_i = x_i/n = \text{const.}_i > 0$. With a more general distribution for the Θ_i, this result was reobtained in 1919 by Von Mises, who regarded it as a *Fundamentalsatz.*

Finally, there is the algebraic result announced by Bienaymé in 1840: let $\{a_i\}$, $\{c_i\}$ be sets of positive numbers. Then

$$\left(\sum_{i=1}^{n} c_i a_i^m \Big/ \sum_{i=1}^{n} c_i\right)^{1/m}$$

is nondecreasing in $m \geq 0$. In a probabilistic setting this result is credited to Lyapounov, the mathematical attribution being to O. Schlömilch (1858). The result contains the Cauchy inequality and the earlier inequality between the arithmetic and geometric means, which it also complements by another consequence:

$$n^{-1}(a_1 + \cdots + a_n) < (a_1^{a_1} \cdots a_n^{a_n})^{(a_1 + \cdots + a_n)^{-1}}.$$

Bienaymé was far ahead of his time in the depth of his statistical ideas. Because of this and the other characteristics of his work, and his being overshadowed by the greatest figures of his time, his name and contributions are little known today.

BIBLIOGRAPHY

I. Original Works. Bienaymé's writings include "De la durée de la vie en France depuis le commencement du XIXe siècle," in *Annales d'hygiène publique et de médecine légale,* **18** (1837), 177–218; "De la loi de multiplication et de la durée des familles," in *Société philomatique de Paris. Extraits des procès-verbaux des séances,* 5th ser., **10** (1845), 37–39, also in *L'Institut, Paris,* no. 589 (1845), 131–132, and repr. by Kendall in 1975 (see below); *De la mise à l'alignement des maisons* (Paris, 1851), a satirical dialogue that demonstrates his abhorrence of the legal system; "Mémoire sur la probabilité des erreurs d'après la méthode des moindres carrés," in *Journal des mathématiques pures et appliquées,* **17** (1852), 33–78, repr. in *Mémoires presentés par savants étrangers à l'Académie des sciences,* **15** (1868), 615–663; *Notice sur les travaux scientifiques de M. I.-J. Bienaymé* (Paris, 1852), with a partial bibliography; and "Considérations à l'appui de le découverte de Laplace sur la loi de probabilité dans la méthode des moindres carrés," in *Comptes rendus . . . de l'Académie des sciences,* **37** (1853), 309–324, repr. in *Journal des* *mathématiques pures et appliquées*, 2nd ser., **12** (1867), 158–176.

II. SECONDARY LITERATURE. See A. Gatine, "Bienaymé," in *École polytechnique. Livre du centenaire 1794–1894*, III (Paris, 1897), 314–316; J. de la Gournerie, "Lecture de la note suivant, sur les travaux de M. Bienaymé," in *Comptes rendus . . . de l'Académie des sciences*, **87** (1878), 617–619; C. C. Heyde and E. Seneta, "The Simple Branching Process, a Turning Point Test and a Fundamental Inequality: A Historical Note on I.-J. Bienaymé," in *Biometrika*, **59**, no. 3 (1972), 680–683; and "Bienaymé," in *Proceedings of the 40th Session of the International Statistical Institute* (Warsaw, 1975); D. G. Kendall, "Branching Processes Since 1873," in *Journal of the London Mathematical Society*, **41** (1966), 385–406; and "The Genealogy of Genealogy: Branching Processes Before (and After) 1873," in *Bulletin of the London Mathematical Society*, **7** (1975), 225–253; M. G. Kendall and A. Doig, *Bibliography of Statistical Literature*, III (Edinburgh, 1968), the most extensive bibliography; H. O. Lancaster, "Forerunners of the Pearson χ^2," in *Australian Journal of Statistics*, **8** (1966), 117–126; R. von Mises, *Mathematical Theory of Probability and Statistics*, edited and complemented by Hilda Geiringer (New York, 1964), 352–357; and L. Sagnet, "Bienaymé (Irénée-Jules)," in *Grande encyclopédie, inventaire raisonné des sciences, des lettres et des arts*, VI (Paris, n.d. [1888]), 752.

C. C. HEYDE
E. SENETA

BILLY, JACQUES DE (*b.* Compiègne, France, 18 March 1602; *d.* Dijon, France, 14 January 1679)

A Jesuit, Billy spent his teaching career in the *collèges* of the society's administrative province of Champagne—Pont à Mousson, Rheims, and Dijon. He taught either theology or mathematics, depending on which was needed. In 1629–1630 he taught mathematics at Pont à Mousson while he was still a theology student and not yet ordained a priest. Billy taught mathematics at Rheims from 1631 to 1633. Around this time he became a close friend of Claude Gaspar Bachet de Méziriac, the commentator on Diophantus who introduced him to indeterminate analysis.

Billy became master of studies and professor of theology at the Collège de Dijon, where one of his students was Jacques Ozanam, whom he taught privately because there was no chair of mathematics at the *collège*, and in whom he instilled a profound love for calculus. Finally, a professorship having been created in mathematics, he taught his favorite subject from 1665 to 1668.

An active correspondence between Billy and Fermat began before 1659, of which one letter remains. Some of Billy's writings originated in this exchange, including parts of the *Doctrinae analyticae inventum novum*, through which his name is still known to number theorists. It is an elaborate study of the techniques of indeterminate analysis used by Fermat and, on the whole, it explains them correctly. From it one can guess at Fermat's general line of activity in a field in which there are few pertinent documents.

In astronomy Billy published numerical tables applicable to the three important theories (Ptolemy, Brahe, Copernicus) of the time. There are also a study on comets and several critiques against forensic astrology.

BIBLIOGRAPHY

I. ORIGINAL WORKS. Billy's works are *Abrégé des préceptes d'algèbre* (Rheims, 1637); *Le siège de Landrecy* (Paris, 1637); *Nova geometriae clavis algebra* (Paris, 1643); *Tabulae Lodoicae, seu eclipseon doctrina* (Dijon, 1656); *Tractatus de proportione harmonica* (Paris, 1658); *Diophantus geometria, sive opus contextum ex arithmetica et geometria simul. . . .* (Paris, 1660); *Opus astronomicum* (Dijon, 1661); *Discours de la comète qui a paru l'an 1665 au mois d'avril* (Paris, 1665); *Crisis astronomica de motu cometarum* (Dijon, 1666); *Diophanti redivivi pars prior . . . pars posterior* (Lyons, 1670); and "Doctrinae analyticae inventum novum, collectum a R. P. Jacobo de Billy . . . ex variis epistolis quas ad eum diversis temporibus misit D. P. de Fermat. . . .," a study in Samuel Fermat, *Diophanti Alexandrini arithmeticorum libri sex* (Toulouse, 1670), Latin text and German trans. by P. von Schaewen (Berlin, 1910), French trans. by Paul Tannery, in *Oeuvres de Fermat*, III (Paris, 1896).

The Dijon municipal library owns several of Billy's autograph manuscripts. Paul Tannery wished to publish the part of the correspondence concerned with indeterminate analysis, but he died before he could carry out the project.

II. SECONDARY LITERATURE. There is a notice on Billy in R. P. Niceron, *Mémoires pour servir à l'histoire des hommes illustres dans la république des lettres*, XL (Paris, 1739), 232-244.

JEAN ITARD

BIRKHOFF, GEORGE DAVID (*b.* Overisel, Michigan, 21 March 1884; *d.* Cambridge, Massachusetts, 12 November 1944)

The son of a physician, Birkhoff studied at the Lewis Institute (now Illinois Institute of Technology) in Chicago from 1896 to 1902. After a year at the University of Chicago he went to Harvard, where he received the A.B. in 1905. Returning to the University of Chicago, he was awarded the Ph.D., *summa cum laude*, in 1907. His graduate study at the University of Chicago was followed by two years as an instructor in the University of Wisconsin. In 1908 he was married to Margaret Elizabeth Grafius.

In 1909 Birkhoff went to Princeton as a preceptor and in 1911 was promoted to a full professorship in response to a call from Harvard. The following year he accepted an assistant professorship at Harvard, where he became professor in 1919, Perkins professor in 1932, and dean of the Faculty of Arts and Sciences from 1935 to 1939. As Perkins professor, the major part of his academic life was devoted to mathematical research and direction of graduate students.

Birkhoff was very generally regarded, both in the United States and abroad, as the leading American mathematician of his day. Honors came early in life and from all over the world. He was president of the American Mathematical Society in 1925 and of the American Association for the Advancement of Science in 1937.

Of Birkhoff's teachers, Maxime Bôcher of Harvard and E. H. Moore of the University of Chicago undoubtedly influenced him most. He was introduced by Bôcher to classical analysis and algebra. From Moore he learned of "general analysis." There are indications that Birkhoff preferred the approach of Bôcher to that of Moore. Through his reading, Birkhoff made Henri Poincaré his teacher and took over Poincaré's problems in differential equations and celestial mechanics. Like Moore, Birkhoff was a pioneer among those who felt that American mathematics had come of age.

He had many close friends among his colleagues in Europe. With Hadamard he shared a deep interest and understanding of Poincaré. Neils Nörlund and Birkhoff had common ground in their study of difference equations. Between Levi-Cività and Birkhoff there were deep ties of friendship cemented by their common interest in the problem of three bodies. The correspondence of Sir Edmund Whittaker and Birkhoff on the existence of periodic orbits in dynamics was intense, illuminating, and friendly.

Birkhoff's thesis was concerned with asymptotic expansions, boundary-value problems, and the Sturm-Liouville theory. Nonself-adjoint operators

$$L(z) = \frac{d^n z}{dx^n} + * + p_2(x)\frac{d^{n-2}z}{dx^{n-2}} + \cdots + p_n(x)z \qquad (a \leq x \leq b)$$

were introduced with continuous coefficients and n boundary conditions, $U_i(u) = 0$, $i = 1, \cdots, n$, linear and homogeneous in u and its first n-1 derivatives at $x = a$ and $x = b$. Birkhoff defined an operator $M(z)$ adjoint to $L(z)$, and boundary conditions $V_i(v) = 0$, $i = 1, \cdots, n$ adjoint to the conditions $U_i(u) = 0$. For $n > 2$ he introduced a parameter λ, as in the classical Sturm-Liouville equations, and, with suitable conditions on the matrix of coefficients in the boundary conditions, obtained an expansion of a prescribed real function $x \to f(x)$, "piecewise" of class C^1. This expansion was shown to converge essentially as does the classical Fourier expansion. This work of depth admitted extension both by Birkhoff and by such pupils as Rudolph Langer and Marshall Stone; he collaborated with Langer on "The Boundary Problems and Developments . . ." (1923).

Birkhoff next devoted his attention to linear differential equations, difference equations, and the generalized Riemann problem. With Gauss, Riemann, and Poincaré showing the way, second-order differential equations of the Fuchsian type with regular singular points have become central in conformal mapping, in the theory of automorphic functions, and in mathematical physics, including quantum mechanics. Linear differential systems with irregular singular points appeared as a challenging new field, and Birkhoff turned to it.

Thomé had used formal solutions; Poincaré and Jakob Horn, asymptotic expansions; Hilbert and Josef Plemelj, unknown to Birkhoff, had solved one of the relevant matrix problems; and Ebenezer Cunningham had generalized Poincaré's use of Laplace's transformation. It remained for Birkhoff to formulate a program of so vast a scope that it is still an object of study today.

Among analytic systems with a finite number of irregular singular points with prescribed ranks, Birkhoff defined a "canonical system" and a notion of the "equivalence" of singular points. Under the title "generalized Riemann problem," Birkhoff sought to construct a system of linear differential equations of the first order with prescribed singular points and a given monodromy group. That he carried his program as far as he did is remarkable. The total resources of modern function space analysis are now involved.

Carmichael's thesis, done under Birkhoff's supervision at Princeton in 1911, was perhaps the first significant contribution on difference equations in America. Birkhoff extended his notion of a "generalized Riemann problem" to systems of difference equations. In "Analytic Theory of Singular Difference Equations," he collaborated with Trjitzinsky in an extension and modification of earlier work.

Birkhoff's major interest in analysis was in dynamical systems. He wished to extend the work of Poincaré, particularly in celestial mechanics. One can divide his dynamics into formal and nonformal dynamics. The nonformal portion includes the metrical and topological aspects.

Birkhoff was concerned with a real, analytic Hamiltonian or Pfaffian system. A periodic orbit gives rise, after a simple transformation, to a "generalized equilibrium point" at which the "equations of variation" are independent of t. First-order formal stability at such a point requires that the characteristic multipliers at the point be purely imaginary. Formal trigonometric stability is then defined. It is a major result of Birkhoff's work that under the limitations on generality presupposed by Poincaré, first-order formal stability at a generalized equilibrium point implies formal trigonometric stability.

Possibly the most dramatic event in Birkhoff's mathematical life came when he proved Poincaré's "last geometric theorem." In "Sur un théorème de géométrie" (1912), Poincaré had enunciated a theorem of great importance for the restricted problem of three bodies, acknowledging his inability to prove this theorem except in special cases. The young Birkhoff formulated this theorem in "Proof of Poincaré's Geometric Theorem" (1913, p. 14):

> Let us suppose that a continuous one-to-one transformation T takes the ring R, formed by concentric circles C_a and C_b of radii a and b ($a > b > 0$), into itself in such a way as to advance the points of C_a in a positive sense, and the points of C_b in a negative sense, and at the same time preserve areas. *Then there are at least two invariant points.*

Birkhoff's proof of this theorem was one of the most exciting mathematical events of the era.

In 1912, in "Quelques théorèmes sur le mouvement des systèmes dynamiques," Birkhoff introduced his novel conceptions of minimal or recurrent sets of motions and established their existence under general conditions. This was the beginning of a new era in the theory of dynamical systems. Birkhoff continued by introducing the concepts of wandering, central, and transitive motions.

Metric transitivity, as defined by Birkhoff and Paul Smith in "Structure Analysis of Surface Transformations" (1928), requires that the only sets that are invariant under the "flow" in phase space be sets of measure zero or measure of the space. Metric transitivity implies topological transitivity (i.e., the existence of a transitive motion). Great problems abound and are today the object of research. On a compact regular analytic manifold it is not known, even today, whether topological transitivity implies metric transitivity.

From these concepts of Birkhoff's the main body of modern dynamics has emerged, together with such branches as symbolic dynamics and topological dynamics. Other concepts of Birkhoff's, his minimax principle and his theorem on the fixed points of surface transformations, have motivated some of the greatest advances in global analysis and topology.

One of Birkhoff's theorems of major current interest in his "ergodic theorem." Following an idea of Bernard Koopman, Von Neumann established his "mean ergodic theorem" in 1931. Stimulated by these ideas, Birkhoff presented his famous "pointwise ergodic theorem." As formulated by Khintchine, Birkhoff's theorem takes the form "The space M is assumed to have a finite measure m invariant under the flow. Let f be integrable over M and let P be a point of M. Then

$$\lim_{T\to\infty} \frac{\int_0^T f(P_t)\,dt}{T}$$

exists for almost all P on M."

Birkhoff thought critically for many years about the foundations of relativity and quantum mechanics. His philosophical and scientific ideas found vivid expression in "Electricity as a Fluid" (1938), where he described a "perfect fluid" that he proposed as a model from which to deduce the observed spectrum of hydrogen without postulating "energy levels." In "El concepto matemático . . ." (1944) he formulated a theory of gravitation in flat space-time, and deduced from it the three "crucial effects." Both of these models were consistent with special relativity; both avoided the general curvilinear coordinates basic to Einstein's general relativity but always considered by Birkhoff to be unnecessary and difficult to interpret experimentally.

Although Birkhoff's physical models may be controversial, his original critiques and interpretations are stimulating and illuminating.

Birkhoff wrote on many subjects besides those of his major works; for example, he devised a significant formula for the ways of coloring a map. At sixteen, he began a correspondence with H. S. Vandiver, who was eighteen, on number theory. A significant paper resulted in 1904.

Another paper, written in collaboration with his colleague Oliver Kellogg (1922), was one of the openers of the age of function spaces. Schauder and Leray acknowledged this paper as an inspiration for their later, more powerful theorem.

In 1929 Birkhoff and Ralph Beatley joined in writing a textbook on elementary geometry, which they called "basic geometry." After a period of revision and development, the pedagogical conceptions of this book have been widely adopted in current teaching of high school geometry.

Birkhoff's lifelong interest in music and the arts culminated in his book *Aesthetic Measure* (1933), in preparation for which he had spent a year traveling around the world, observing objects of art, ornaments, tiles, and vases, and recording impressions of music and poetry.

BIBLIOGRAPHY

I. ORIGINAL WORKS. Among Birkhoff's works are "On the Integral Divisors of $a^n - b^n$," in *Annals of Mathematics,* **5** (1904), 173–180, written with H. S. Vandiver; "On the Asymptotic Character of the Solutions of Certain Differential Equations Containing a Parameter," in *Transactions of the American Mathematical Society,* **9** (1908), 219–231; "Boundary Values and Expansion Problems of Ordinary Linear Differential Equations," *ibid.,* 373–395; "Quelques théorèmes sur le mouvement des systèmes dynamiques," in *Bulletin de la Société mathématique de France,* **40** (1912), 305–323; "Proof of Poincaré's Geometric Theorem," in *Transactions of the American Mathematical Society,* **14** (1913), 14–22; "Invariant Points in Function Space," *ibid.,* **23** (1922), 96–115, written with O. D. Kellogg; "The Boundary Problems and Developments Associated With a System of Ordinary Linear Differential Equations of First Order," in *Proceedings of the American Academy of Arts and Sciences,* **58** (1923), 49–128, written with R. E. Langer; "Structure Analysis of Surface Transformations," in *Journal de mathématiques pures et appliquées,* 9th ser., **7** (1928), 345–379, written with P. A. Smith; "On the Number of Ways of Coloring a Map," in *Proceedings of the Edinburgh Mathematical Society,* 2nd ser., **2** (1930), 83–91; *Aesthetic Measure* (Cambridge, Mass., 1933); "Analytic Theory of Singular Difference Equations," in *Acta mathematica,* **60** (1933), 1–89, written with W. J. Trjitzinsky; "Electricity as a Fluid," in *Journal of the Franklin Institute,* **226** (1938), 315–325; *Basic Geometry* (1940), written with Ralph Beatley; "El concepto matemático de tiempo y la gravitación," in *Boletín de la Sociedad matemática mexicana,* **1** (1944), 1–24; and *Dynamical Systems,* rev. ed. (Providence, R.I., 1966), with introduction, bibliography, and footnotes by Jürgen Moser.

His works have been brought together by the American Mathematical Society as *Collected Mathematical Works of George David Birkhoff,* 3 vols. (Providence, R.I., 1950).

II. SECONDARY LITERATURE. Works on Birkhoff are American Mathematical Society Semicentennial Publications, I, *History* (Providence, R.I., 1938), p. 212, a list of his honors up to 1938; P. Masani, "On a Result of G. D. Birkhoff on Linear Differential Systems," in *Proceedings of the American Mathematical Society,* **10** (1959), 696–698; and H. L. Turrittin, "Reduction of Ordinary Differential Equations to the Birkhoff Canonical Form," in *Transactions of the American Mathematical Society,* **107** (1963), 485–507.

MARSTON MORSE

AL-BĪRŪNĪ (or **Bērūnī**), **ABŪ RAYḤĀN** (or **Abu'l-Rayḥān**) **MUḤAMMAD IBN AḤMAD** (*b.* Khwārazm [now Kara-Kalpakskaya A.S.S.R.], 4 September 973; *d.* Ghazna [?] [now Ghazni, Afghanistan], after 1050)

Bīrūnī was born and grew up in the region south of the Aral Sea, known in ancient and medieval times as Khwārazm. The town of his birth now bears his name. The site was in the environs (*bīrūn,* hence his appellation) of Kāth, then one of the two principal cities of the region, located (in the modern Kara-Kalpakskaya A.S.S.R.) on the right bank of the Amu Dar'ya (the ancient Oxus) and northeast of Khīva. The second capital city of Khwārazm was Jurjāniyya (modern Kunya-Urgench, Turkmen S.S.R.), on the opposite side of the river and northwest of Khīva. There also Abū Rayḥān spent a good deal of time during the early part of his life. About his ancestry and childhood nothing is known. In verses ridiculing a certain poet (Yāqūt, p. 189; trans., *Beiträge,* LX, p. 62) he claims ignorance of his own father's identity, but the statement may have been rhetorical. He very early commenced scientific studies and was taught by the eminent Khwārazmian astronomer and mathematician Abū Naṣr Manṣūr. At the age of seventeen he used a ring graduated in halves of a degree to observe the meridian solar altitude at Kāth, thus inferring its terrestrial latitude (*Taḥdīd,* 249:7). Four years later he had made plans to carry out a series of such determinations and had prepared a ring fifteen cubits in diameter, together with supplementary equipment. There was, however, time only for an observation of the summer solstice of 995, made at a village south of Kāth and across the Oxus from it. At this time, civil war broke out. Bīrūnī went into hiding and shortly had to flee the country (*Taḥdīd,* 87:3, 109:6–110:11). "After I had barely settled down for a few years," he writes, "I was permitted by the Lord of Time to go back home, but I was compelled to participate in worldly affairs, which excited the envy of fools, but which made the wise pity me."

Since these "worldly affairs" essentially affected not only Bīrūnī's personal well-being but also his scientific work, it is necessary to introduce the names of six princely dynasties with which he became directly involved.

(1) The ancient title of Khwārazmshāh had long been held by the lord of Kāth, a member of the Banū ʿIrāq. Abū Naṣr was a prince of this house (Krause, p. 3). In 995, however, the emir of Jurjāniyya attacked his suzerain, captured and killed him, and seized the title for himself (*Chahār Maqāla,* p. 241). It was this disturbance that caused Bīrūnī's flight.

(2) For well over a century the Khwārazmshāhs

had been dominated by the Sāmānids, a royal house of Zoroastrian origin but early converted to Islam. The Sāmānid capital was in Bukhara, about two hundred miles southeast of Khīva, from whence the dynasty ruled in its heyday an area comprising roughly all of present Afghanistan, Transoxiana, and Iran. In Bīrūnī's youth this empire was rapidly breaking up. Nevertheless, in a poem written much later (Yāqūt, p. 187; trans., *Beiträge*, LX, p. 61) he names as his first patron Manṣūr II, almost the last of the Sāmānid line, who reigned from 997 to 999.

(3) Much farther to the west flourished the Buwayhid dynasty, which had originated in the highlands south of the Caspian and extended its domain south to the Persian Gulf and, by 945, west over Mesopotamia.

(4) Set precariously between the Sāmānids and the Buwayhids was the Ziyārid state, based in Gurgān, a city just back of the southeast corner of the Caspian shore.

(5) All these competing dynasties were menaced, and eventually absorbed, by the swift expansion of another kingdom, that of the Ghaznavids, named from Ghazna, their base in east-central Afghanistan. Sultan Maḥmūd, son of a Turkish slave and the second and greatest of the line, was two years older than Bīrūnī. By 1020 he had carved out a realm extending a thousand miles north and south, and twice as far east and west.

(6) Over these kaleidoscopic shifts there presided at Baghdad the spectral figure of the Abbasid caliph, retaining only the shadow of power over these fragments of his ancestors' empire. Playing a role somewhat analogous to that of the medieval popes, he was accorded a strange religious respect by the temporal princes of Islam. Upon them the successive caliphs conferred prestige by investing them with honorific titles and robes of honor.

To which or from which of these kingdoms Bīrūnī fled in 995 is now uncertain. It may have been then that he went to Rayy, near modern Teheran. In the *Chronology* (p. 338) he quotes a ribald poem on the tribulations of penury, and to illustrate it states that he was once in Rayy, bereft of a royal patron and in miserable circumstances. A local astrologer chose to ridicule his views on some technical matter because of his poverty. Later, when his circumstances improved, the same man became friendly.

At the command of the Buwayhid prince, Fakhr al-Dawla, the astronomer al-Khujandī built a large mural sextant on a mountain above Rayy. With this Fakhrī sextant, named for the ruler, he observed meridian transits during 994. Bīrūnī wrote a treatise describing this instrument (*Sextant*) and a detailed account of the observations (*Taḥdīd,* 101:20–108:19). Part of his information was obtained from al-Khujandī in person, and since the latter died about 1000 (Suter, p. 74), the conversation between the two cannot have been long after the observations.

There is some reason for thinking that Abū Rayḥān also was in the Caspian province of Gīlān about this time. He dedicated a book (*RG* 7) to the Ispahbad (Persian for "ruler," or "commander") of Gīlān, Marzubān ibn Rustam, who was connected with the Ziyārids. In the *Chronology,* completed about 1000 (trans., pp. 47, 191), he mentions having been in the presence of this individual, perhaps the same Ispahbad who sheltered Firdawsī, the epic poet of Iran, from the wrath of Sulṭān Maḥmūd (Browne, pp. 79, 135).

Regardless of where he had been, Bīrūnī was back in Kāth by 997, for on 24 May of that year he observed a lunar eclipse there (Oppolzer 3403), having previously arranged with Abu'l-Wafā' that the latter should simultaneously observe the same event from Baghdad (*Taḥdīd,* 250:11, gives only the year; but Oppolzer 3404, on 17 November 997, was invisible from both cities). The time difference so obtained enabled them to calculate the difference in longitude between the two stations.

This year saw the beginning of the short reign of the Sāmānid Manṣūr II. If Bīrūnī ever resided at his court in Bukhara (as Bīrūnī's poem mentioned above may imply), it probably was at this time. Meantime, the ruler of Gurgān, the Ziyārid Qābūs, had been expelled from his lands, and at Bukhara he sought support for a return to power. He succeeded in reestablishing himself at Gurgān, and Bīrūnī either accompanied him or followed almost immediately thereafter, for about 1000 Bīrūnī dedicated to Qābūs his earliest extant major work, the *Chronology* (text, p. xxiv). This was by no means his first book, for in it he refers incidentally to seven others already completed, none of which are extant. Their titles indicate that he had already broken ground in the fields he later continued to cultivate, for one (*RG* 34) is on decimal computation, one (*RG* 46) on the astrolabe, one (*RG* 146) on astronomical observations, three (*RG* 42, 99, 148) on astrology, and two (*RG* 161, 162) are histories. By this time he also had engaged in an acrimonious correspondence with the brilliant Bukharan philosopher and physician Avicenna on the nature and transmission of heat and light. Bīrūnī refers to him (*Chronology,* text, p. 257) as "the youth." The appellation, coming from an individual still in his twenties, may seem less condescending when it is realized that the precocious Avicenna was still in his teens.

In the *Taḥdīd* (214:15–215:3), after describing the measurement of a degree along a terrestrial meridian made at the direction of the Caliph Ma'mūn, Bīrūnī writes of his own abortive project to repeat the operation. A suitable tract of land was chosen between Gurgān and the land of the Oghuz Turks (in the deserts east of the Caspian?), but the patron, presumably Qābūs, lost interest.

The end of Abū Rayḥān's sojourn at the Ziyārid court can be fixed within precise limits, for in 1003 he observed two lunar eclipses from Gurgān, one on 19 February and the other on 14 August. On 4 June of the following year he observed a third lunar eclipse (*Canon,* pp. 740, 741), but this one from Jurjāniyya. Hence, sometime in the interim he had returned to his homeland, high in favor with the reigning Khwārazmshāh. This was now a certain Abu'l-'Abbās Ma'mūn, a son of the usurper to the title mentioned above. Both Ma'mun and a brother who preceded him on the throne had married sisters of the ever more powerful and truculent Sultan Maḥmūd of Ghazna.

The bounty of the shah enabled Bīrūnī to set up at Jurjāniyya an instrument, apparently a large ring fixed in the meridian plane, which in gratitude he called the Shāhiyya ring (*Canon,* 612:5). He reports in various places in the *Taḥdīd* and the *Canon* some fifteen solar meridian transit observations at Jurjāniyya, the first the summer solstice of 7 June 1016, the last on 7 December of the same year. It was probably during this interlude of prosperity and royal favor that he had a hemisphere constructed, ten cubits in diameter, to be used as a plotting device for the graphical solution of geodetic problems (*Taḥdīd,* 38:6).

Meanwhile, Khwārazmian political affairs, in which Bīrūnī was closely involved, had been building up to a climax. The Caliph Qādir conferred upon Ma'mūn an honorific title and dispatched an envoy bearing the insignia of the award. The shah was frightened lest Maḥmūd take offense at his accepting the honor conferred directly and not through Maḥmūd as implied overlord. Ma'mūn therefore sent Bīrūnī west into the desert to intercept the embassy, take delivery of the objects, and thus forestall a public investiture.

In 1014 Maḥmūd let it be understood to Ma'mūn that he wanted his own name inserted into the *khuṭba,* the Friday prayer for the faithful and for the reigning monarch. Ma'mūn convened an assembly of the notables, proposing that he accede to this demand, but the chiefs refused to allow him to do so, realizing that it meant the end of the region's autonomy. Ma'mūn then sent to them Bīrūnī, who, "with tongue of silver and of gold," convinced them that their liege was only testing them by his request and that the *khuṭba* would not be changed. At this, Maḥmūd dispatched an insulting ultimatum to the shah, demanding that he keep his nobles in line, or he, Maḥmūd, would do it himself. The hapless Ma'mūn introduced the sultan's name into the *khuṭba* in the provincial mosques, but not those of Jurjāniyya and Kāth. Thereupon the Khwārazmian army revolted and killed Ma'mūn. This was all Maḥmūd needed. He marched into Khwārazm with ample forces, obtained the delivery of his sister, the Khwārazmshāh's widow, took Kāth, on 3 July 1017, cruelly executed the insurgent leaders, and set one of his officers on the throne. The surviving princes of the local dynasty were carried off to imprisonment in various parts of his domain (Barthold, pp. 275–279).

Much of our knowledge of these events is from Bīrūnī's extensive history of his native land, a work that has been lost except for fragments incorporated into other histories. As for Abū Rayḥān himself, he also was led off by the conqueror, partly, no doubt, to grace the sultan's court but also to remove an active partisan of the native rulers from the scene. He is next heard of in a village near Kabul, depressed and in miserable circumstances, but hard at work on the *Taḥdīd* (119:1–12). On 14 October 1018 he wanted to take the solar altitude, but had no instrument. He therefore laid out a graduated arc on the back of a calculating board (*takht*) and, with a plumb line, used it as an improvised quadrant. On the basis of the results obtained, he calculated the latitude of the locality.

The next firm date at our disposal is 8 April 1019, when he observed a solar eclipse from Lamghān (modern Laghman?), north of Kabul. He uses this, and the lunar eclipse mentioned below, to comment sarcastically upon the ignorance of the local astronomers.

Sachau has shown (*India,* trans., I, xi) that Bīrūnī's relations with Maḥmūd were never good, although the stories in the *Chahār Maqāla* (text, pp. 57–59) alleging cruel and arbitrary treatment of the savant by the sultan are doubtless apocryphal. It is evident that Abū Rayḥān received some sort of official support for his work, for in the *Canon* (p. 609) he writes of having determined the latitude of Ghazna by a series of observations carried out between 1018 and 1020 with an instrument he calls the Yamīnī ring. A title bestowed upon Sultan Maḥmūd by the caliph was Yamīn al-Dawla ("Right Hand of the State"). No doubt this ring was a monumental installation named, as was the custom, for the ruler patron.

It is also clear that Bīrūnī's interests in Sanskrit and in Indian civilization are due to his having become an involuntary resident of an empire that had by then expanded well into the Indian subcontinent. Already in 1002 Maḥmūd had conquered the district of Waihand, on the Indus east of Ghazna. By 1010 he had subjugated Multan and Bhatinda, the latter 300 miles east of the Indus. Twice repulsed (in 1015 and 1021) from the borders of Kashmir, by 1022 he had penetrated and subdued the Ganges valley to a point not far west of Benares. In 1026 Maḥmūd led a raid due south from Ghazna all the way to the Indian Ocean. From Somnāth, at the tip of the Kathiawar Peninsula, he carried off immensely valuable booty, as well as fragments of the phallic idol in the temple. One of the pieces was laid at the entrance to the Ghazna mosque, to be used as a footscraper by the worshipers (*India,* trans., II, 103; Nāẓim, ch. 8).

Abū Rayḥān profited from these events by travel and residence in various parts of India. The names of many of the places he saw are known, but no dates can be given for his visits. They were confined to the Punjab and the borders of Kashmir. Sachau (*India,* text, p. xii) lists some eleven Indian towns whose latitudes Bīrūnī reports as personally determined by him. Bīrūnī himself writes that while living (in detention?) at Nandana Fort, he used a nearby mountain to estimate the earth's diameter (*Taḥdīd,* 222:10). The installation at Nandana, taken by Maḥmūd in 1014, commanded the route by which he, the Moghuls after him, and Alexander the Great long before, penetrated the Indus valley. Bīrūnī's temporary residence overlooked the site where, in the face of King Poros and his elephants, Alexander effected his famous crossing of the Jhelum River, the classical Hydaspes (Stein).

It is also clear that Bīrūnī spent a great deal of time at Ghazna. The cluster of recorded observations made by him there commences with a series of meridian solar transits covering the summer solstice of 1019, and includes the lunar eclipse on 16 September of the same year (*Taḥdīd,* 291:9). He continued to observe equinoxes and solstices at Ghazna, the last being the winter solstice of 1021. In fact, this is the latest of Bīrūnī's observations that has been preserved. At about this time, according to Barani (*Canon,* III, vii), he completed his treatise on *Shadows.*

In 1024 the ruler of the Volga Turks sent an embassy to Ghazna. These people had trade relations with inhabitants of the polar regions, and Bīrūnī questioned members of the mission to supplement his knowledge of these lands. One of the ambassadors asserted in the sultan's presence that in the far north the sun sometimes did not set for days on end. Maḥmūd at first angrily put this down as heresy, but Abū Rayḥān convinced him that the report was both credible and reasonable (*Commemoration Volume,* p. 235; Yāqūt).

By the late summer of 1027 the treatise on *Chords* was completed (according to the Patna MS). During the same year a Chinese and Uighur Turkish embassy came to Ghazna, and from this mission Bīrūnī obtained geographical information on the Far East which he later incorporated into the *Canon* (*Commemoration Volume,* p. 234).

In 1030 Sultan Maḥmūd died, and the succession was disputed between two of his sons for a short period. Bīrūnī finished the *India* during this interim and, perhaps because of the uncertain political situation, refrained from dedicating it to any particular patron. Within the year Masʿūd, the elder son, won the crown. His accession brought about a drastic improvement in the situation of his most famous scientist, and Bīrūnī named the *Canon* for the new ruler amid "a farrago of high-sounding words" in the preface (*India,* trans., I, xii).

Perhaps it was the change of regime that enabled him to revisit his native land. By whatever means, he made at least one trip back, for in the *Bibliography* he writes that for over forty years he had sought a certain Manichaean work, a copy of which he at length procured while in Khwārazm (*Chronology,* text, p. xxxvi). In the same source Bīrūnī relates that after he was fifty years old he suffered from a series of serious illnesses, and in his distress inquired of several astrologers concerning the length of his life. Their answers diverged wildly, and some were patently absurd. At the end of his sixty-first (lunar?) year he began improving, and had a dream in which he was seeking the new moon. As its crescent disappeared, a voice told him that he would behold 170 more of the same.

Masʿūd was murdered by his officers and succeeded by his son Mawdūd in 1040. During Mawdūd's eight-year reign, Bīrūnī wrote the *Dastūr* (*RG* 167) and the *Gems.* Of his subsequent activities we have no knowledge, save that in the *Pharmacology* (p. 7) he notes having passed his eightieth (lunar?) year; his eyesight and hearing are failing, but he is still hard at work with the assistance of a collaborator. Thus the date of his death given by Ghaḍanfar as 13 December 1048 is incorrect; Bīrūnī outlasted his third Ghaznavid patron and achieved the life-span foretold in his dream.

When he was sixty-three years old, Bīrūnī prepared a bibliography of the works of the physician Muḥammad ibn Zakariyya al-Rāzī, to which he appended a list of his own books. This runs to 113 titles (not counting twenty-five additional treatises written "in his name" by friends), partially arranged by subject matter and occasionally with a brief indication of the contents. Most of the entries also give the length of the particular manuscript in folios. The list is incomplete, for Abū Rayḥān lived at least fourteen years after this, working until he died. Moreover, seven additional works by him are extant and many more are named, some in his own writings and others in a variety of sources. All told, these come to 146. The reckoning is uncertain, for some titles counted separately may be synonyms, and additional items may well turn up in the future.

There is a wide range in size of the treatises. Several amount to only ten folios each, while, at the other extreme, three lost astronomical works run to 360, 550, and 600 folios respectively. Largest of all is the *India,* at 700 folios. The English translation of the latter, incidentally, takes up 654 pages of small type, so that one of Bīrūnī's folios is roughly equivalent to a modern printed page. The mean length of the seventy-nine books of known size is very nearly ninety folios. Assuming that the same holds for all 146 works, it follows that Bīrūnī's total output is on the order of 13,000 folios (or pages), consisting for the most part of highly technical material, including numerical tables, the results of involved computations, and analyses of materials from multifarious sources—a formidable accomplishment indeed.

The classification attempted in the table below is only approximate; for instance, a book placed in the geographical category could legitimately be classed as primarily geodetic, and so on. Practically nothing Bīrūnī wrote confines itself strictly to a single subject, and in many cases where the title alone survives, an informed guess is our only recourse. Nevertheless the table gives a reasonable breakdown of the man's activity. In the second column a "major work" has been taken arbitrarily as anything of 200 folios or more. The third and fourth columns show, respectively, the compositions known to exist in manuscript form and the numbers of these that have thus far been printed. Roughly four-fifths of Bīrūnī's work has vanished beyond hope of recovery. Of what has survived, about half has been published. Most of the latter (with the notable exception of the *Canon*) has been translated into other languages and has received some attention from modern scholars.

The table also clearly reveals both scope and areas of concentration. Bīrūnī's interests were very wide and deep, and he labored in almost all the branches of science known in his time. He was not ignorant of philosophy and the speculative disciplines, but his bent was strongly toward the study of observable phenomena, in nature and in man. Within the sciences themselves he was attracted by those fields then susceptible of mathematical analysis. He did serious work in mineralogy, pharmacology, and philology, subjects where numbers played little part; but about half his total output is in astronomy, astrology, and related subjects, the exact sciences par excellence of those days. Mathematics in its own right came next, but it was invariably applied mathematics.

CLASSIFICATION OF BĪRŪNĪ'S WORKS

	Works		Major Works	Extant	Published
Astronomy	35	62	8	4	3
On astrolabes	4			2	
Astrology	23		1	3	2
Chronology		5	1	1	1
Time measurement		2			
Geography	9	19	1	1	1
Geodesy and Mapping Theory	10			1	
Mathematics					
Arithmetic	8	15		1	1
Geometry	5			1	1
Trigonometry	2			1	
Mechanics		2		1	
Medicine and Pharmacology		2	1	1	
Meteorology		1			
Mineralogy and Gems		2		1	1
History		4			
India		2	1	1	1
Religion and Philosophy		3		1	1
Literary		16			
Magic		2		1	
Unclassified		9	1	1	1
Total		146	14	22	13

Below are brief descriptions of most of Bīrūnī's works that are still available. They are our best sources for estimating the extent and significance of his accomplishments.

The *Chronology.* The day, being the most apparent and fundamental chronological unit, is the subject of the first chapter. Bīrūnī discusses the advantages of various calendric epochs—sunset or sunrise (horizon-based), noon or midnight (meridian-based) —and names the systems that use each. Next the several varieties of year are defined—lunar, solar, lunisolar, Julian, and Persian—and the notion of intercalation is introduced. Chapter 3 defines and discusses the eras of the Creation, the Flood, Nabonassar, Philip Arrhidaeus, Alexander, Augustus, Antoninus, Diocletian, the Hegira, Yazdigird, the

Caliph Muʿtaḍid, the pre-Islamic Arabs, and Bīrūnī's native Khwārazm. Chapter 4 discusses the Alexander legend, giving sundry examples of pedigrees, forged and otherwise. Next are lists of the month names, with variants, used by the Persians, Soghdians, Khwārazmians, Egyptians, Westerners (Spaniards?), Greeks, Jews, Syrians, pre-Islamic Arabs, Muslims, Indians, and Turks. In this chapter, the fifth, Bīrūnī commences his very extensive description of the Jewish calendar. (Except for the work of al-Khwārizmī, another Muslim, his is the earliest extant scientific discussion of this calendar.)

Chapter 6 culminates with a table (trans., p. 133) giving the intervals in days between each pair of the eras named above. This is preceded, however, by chronological and regnal tables in years (sometimes with months and days) for the Jewish patriarchs and kings; the Assyrians, Babylonians and Persians; the Pharaohs, Ptolemies, Caesars, and Byzantine emperors; the mythical Iranian kings; and the Achaemenid, Parthian, and Sasanian dynasties. Where tables from different sources conflict, all are given in full, and there are digressions on the length of human life and the enumeration of chessboard moves.

Chapter 7 continues the exhaustive discussion of the Jewish calendar, but includes a derivation of the solar parameters, a table of planetary names, and the Mujarrad table giving the initial weekdays of the mean (thirty-year cycle) lunar year.

Chapter 8 is on the religions of various pseudo prophets, the most prominent being the Sabians (or Mandaeans, alleged to be followers of Būdhāsaf= Bodhisattva!), Zoroastrians, Manichaeans, and adherents of Mazdak.

The remaining half of the book (save the last chapter) describes the festivals and fasts of the following peoples: Chapter 9, the Persians; 10, the Soghdians; 11 and 12, the Khwārazmians; 13, the Greeks (including material from Sinān ibn Thābit ibn Qurra on the parapegmatists); 14, the Jews; 15, the Melchite Christians; 16, the Jewish Passover and Christian Lent; 17, the Nestorian Christians; 18, the Magians and Sabians; 19, the pre-Islamic Arabs; 20, the Muslims. The concluding chapter, 21, gives tables and descriptive matter on the lunar mansions, followed by explanations of stereographic projection and other plane mappings of the sphere.

The *Astrolabe.* Amid the plethora of medieval treatises on the astrolabe, this is one of the few of real value. It describes in detail not only the construction of the standard astrolabe but also special tools used in the process. Numerical tables are given for laying out the families of circles engraved on the plates fitting into the instrument. Descriptions are also given of the numerous unusual types of astrolabes that had already been developed in Bīrūnī's time. As for the underlying theory, not only are the techniques and properties of the standard stereographic projection presented, but also those of certain nonstereographic and nonorthogonal mappings of the sphere upon the plane.

The *Sextant.* This two-page treatise describes the giant mural instrument for observing meridian transits built by al-Khujandī at Rayy for Fakhr al-Dawla, and perhaps seen by al-Bīrūnī, although he does not say so.

The *Taḥdīd.* The central theme is the determination of geographical coordinates of localities. In particular, Bīrūnī sets out to calculate the longitudinal difference between Baghdad and Ghazna. Several preliminary problems present themselves: latitude determinations, inclination of the ecliptic, the distribution of land masses and their formation, length of a degree along the terrestrial meridian, and differences in terrestrial longitudes from eclipse observations. Techniques and observations used by Bīrūnī and by others are reported. Application is made of a theorem of Ptolemy's that gives the longitudinal difference between two places in terms of the latitude of each and the great circle distance between them. The latter was estimated from caravan routes and lengths of stages. Successive computations then yield the differences in longitude between Baghdad, Rayy, Jurjāniyya, Balkh, and Ghazna, and likewise along a southern traverse including Shiraz and Zaranj. The final result is in error by only eighteen minutes of arc.

The *Densities.* By means of an ingenious form of balance exploiting Archimedes' principle, Bīrūnī worked out a technique for ascertaining the specific gravity of a solid of irregular shape. He reports very precise specific gravity determinations for eight metals, fifteen other solids (mostly precious or semiprecious stones), and six liquids.

The *Shadows.* As its full title indicates, this is a comprehensive presentation of all topics known to Bīrūnī to be connected with shadows. Of the total of thirty chapters, the first three contain philosophical notions about the nature of light, shade, and reflection. There are many citations from the Arabic poets descriptive of kinds of shadows.

Chapter 4 shows that the plane path traced in a day by the end point of a gnomon shadow is a conic. The next two chapters discuss the properties of shadows cast in light emanating from celestial objects. Chapters 7 and 8 define the shadow functions (tangent and cotangent) and explain the origins of the gnomon divisions used in various cultures: the

AL-BĪRŪNĪ

Hellenistic 60, Indian 12, Muslim 7 or 6-1/2. The succeeding three chapters explain rules for converting between functions expressed in different gnomon lengths and for conversions into the other trigonometric functions (sine, secant, and their cofunctions, together with *their* various parameters), and vice versa. Chapter 12 gives tangent-cotangent tables for the four standard gnomon lengths and discusses interpolation. The next two chapters explain how to engrave the shadow functions on astrolabes. There follows, in Chapter 15, a discussion of gnomon shadows cast on planes other than horizontal, and on curved surfaces. Chapters 16 and 17 consider the effect of solar declination and local latitude on the meridian shadow length. A number of nontrigonometric approximate Indian rules are given. Chapters 18–21 list a variety of meridian-determination methods (including one from the lost *Analemma* of the first-century B.C. Diodorus). Chapter 22 is on daylight length and rising times of the signs as functions of the local latitude and the season. Here and in the next two chapters (on determining the time of day from shadows) rules are reproduced from numerous Indian, Sasanian, and early Islamic documents, many no longer extant. Some early Muslim rules are in Arabic doggerel written in imitation of Sanskrit *slokas.* Chapters 25 and 26 define the time of the Muslim daily prayers, some in terms of shadow lengths. Chapter 27 shows that in many situations on the celestial sphere, Menelaus' theorem gives relations between shadow functions. The concluding three chapters describe Indian and early Islamic techniques for calculating terrestrial and celestial distances by the use of shadows.

The *Chords.* The book begins by stating the following theorem: A, B, and C, three points on a circle, are so situated that $AB > BC$. From D, the midpoint of arc AC, drop a perpendicular, DE, to the chord AB. Then the foot of the perpendicular bisects the broken line ABC. There follow a number of proofs of this theorem, attributed to sundry Greek and Islamic mathematicians, some otherwise unknown to the literature. A second theorem, that in the configuration above, $\overline{AD}^2 = \overline{AB} \times \overline{BC} + \overline{BD}^2$, is also followed by a long series of proofs. The same thing is done for the expression $\triangle ADC - \triangle ABC = \overline{DE} \times \overline{EB}$. Then comes a set of metric relations between chords, based on the foregoing and leading up to propositions useful for calculating a table of chords (or sines).

The *Patañjali.* Cast in the form of a series of questions put by a hermit student and the answers given by a sage, this book deals with such philosophical and mystical topics as liberation of the soul and its detachment from the external world, the attributes of God, the power of spirit over the body, and the composition of the universe.

The *Tafhīm.* A manual of instruction in astrology, well over half of the book is taken up with preliminaries to the main subject. Persian and Arabic versions are extant, both apparently prepared by Bīrūnī himself. It is arranged in the form of questions and answers. There are five chapters in all, the first (thirty-three pages in the Persian edition) on geometry, ending with Menelaus' theorem on the sphere. The second (twenty-three pages) is on numbers, computation, and algebra. Chapter 3, the longest (229 pages), deals with geography, cosmology, and astronomy. From it a complete technical vocabulary may be obtained, as well as sets of numerical parameters, some of them uncommon. The next chapter (thirty-one pages) describes the astrolabe, its theory and application. Only the last chapter (223 pages) is on astrology as such, but it is complete and detailed.

The *India.* The book commences with a prefatory chapter in which the author states that the subject is difficult because Sanskrit is not easy; there are extreme differences between Indians and non-Indians; and Indian fear and distrust has been exacerbated by Muslim conquests. The book will not be polemical and, when appropriate, Indian customs and beliefs will be compared with cognate ones of the Greeks.

Chapters 2–8 are on religion and philosophy: the nature of God, the soul, matter, mysticism, paradise, and hell. Chapters 9, 10, and 11 describe, respectively, the Hindu castes, laws concerning marriage, and the construction of idols. Chapters 12, 13, and 14 are on categories of literature: sacred, grammatical, and astronomical. The latter gives a table of contents of the *Brāhmasphuṭasiddhānta.* Chapter 15 presents tables of metrological units and gives various approximations to the number π. The next two chapters are on Indian systems of writing, number names, chess rules, and superstitions. Chapter 18 is geographical; in particular, sixteen itineraries are given with the distances in *farsakhs* between successive stages. Chapters 19–30 present astronomical and cosmological nomenclature, legends, and theories. Chapter 31 cites the geodetic parameters used by various astronomers, and the latitudes (observed by Bīrūnī) of a number of Indian cities. Chapters 32–53 are on Indian notions of time, including detailed definitions of the hierarchies of enormous cycles—the *yugas, kalpas,* and so on—interspersed with accounts of sundry religious legends. Calendric procedures are given in great profusion. Chapters 54–59 are astronomical, dealing with the computation of mean planetary positions, the sizes and distances of the planets, heliacal risings, and eclipses. The remainder of the book is largely astrological, but includes chapters on rites, pilgrimages, diet, lawsuits, fasts, and festivals.

The *Ghurra.* This is an example of an Indian *karaṇa,* a handbook enabling the user to solve all the standard astronomical problems of his time, with the emphasis on actual computation rather than on theory. Hence it resembles an Islamic *zīj* (astronomical handbook). Topics include calendric rules; length of daylight; determination of the astrological lords of the year, month, day, and hour; mean and true positions of the sun, moon, and planets; time of day; local latitude; solar and lunar eclipses; and visibility conditions for the moon and the planets. Bīrūnī has added worked-out examples, in particular, conversions from the Šaka calendar into the Hegira, Yazdigird, and Greek (so-called era of Alexander) calendars. Otherwise, he states, in his translation he has made no changes.

In general, the methods are those common to medieval Indian astronomy, but the parameters are not identical with any extant Sanskrit document. For instance, the radius of the defining circle for the sine function is 200 minutes, and the increment of arc, the *kardaja,* is ten degrees.

The *Canon.* This most comprehensive of Bīrūnī's extant astronomical works contains detailed numerical tables for solving all the standard problems of the medieval astronomer-astrologer. But it also has much more in the way of observation reports and derivations than the typical *zīj.* It is organized in eleven treatises (*maqāla*) that are further subdivided into chapters and sections.

Treatises 1 and 2 set forth and discuss general cosmological principles (that the earth and heavens are spherical, that the earth is stationary, etc.), units of time measurement, calendars, and regnal and chronological tables. This covers much of the ground gone over in the *Chronology,* but the chapter on the Indian calendar is additional.

Treatises 3 and 4 are on plane and spherical trigonometry respectively. There are tables of all the standard trigonometric functions, more extensive and precise than preceding or contemporary tables. Methods of solving many problems of spherical astronomy appear, together with tables of ancillary functions: oblique ascensions, declinations, and so on.

Treatise 5, on geodesy and mathematical geography, reworks much of the subject matter of the *Taḥdīd.* A table gives the geographical coordinates of localities.

Treatises 6 and 7 are on the sun and moon, respectively. Here (and with planetary theory farther on) the abstract models are essentially Ptolemaic, but many parameters are independently derived on the basis of all available observations (including Bīrūnī's own).

Treatise 8 treats of eclipse computations and the first visibility of the lunar crescent.

Treatise 9, on the fixed stars, includes a star table with 1,029 entries (cf. Ptolemy's 1,022). Magnitudes according to Ptolemy and to al-Ṣūfī are given.

The next treatise is on the planets, with tables and text for calculating longitudes, latitudes, stations, visibility, distances, and apparent diameters.

The concluding treatise is on astrological operations, describing various doctrines for calculating the astrological mansions, projection of the rays, the *taysīr,* the sectors (*niṭāqāt*), transits, and the curious cycles apparently developed by Abū Maʿshar.

The *Transits.* This book describes the various categories of astrological phenomena to which the term *mamarr* (transit or passage) was attached. One planet was said to transit another if it passed the other planet in celestial longitude, or celestial latitude, or in its relative distance from the earth. The notion seems to have been developed by astrologers using non-Ptolemaic astronomical doctrines described in documents no longer extant. Hence the main interest of the work is the assistance it gives toward the reconstruction of these lost Indian, Sasanian, and early Islamic theories.

The *Gems.* The work is organized in two parts, the first being on precious and semiprecious stones, the second on metals. Bīrūnī brings together material from Hellenistic, Roman, Syriac, Indian, and Islamic sources, supplemented by his own observations. In addition to descriptions of the physical properties of the various substances, there are very extensive etymological discussions of the technical terminology in many languages and dialects, and numerous illustrative quotations from Arabic poetry. The principal mines and sources of supply are cited. Relative weights of the metals with respect to gold are given, and there are tables showing the prices of pearls and emeralds as functions of size.

The *Pharmacology.* The book commences with an introduction in five chapters. The first presents an etymology for the Arabic word for druggist. The second gives technical terminology for categories of drugs. The next chapter is on the general theory of medicaments. In the fourth and fifth chapters Bīrūnī states his preference for Arabic over Persian as a language of science, and he names polyglot dictionaries available to him.

The main body of the work is an alphabetical listing of drugs comprising about 720 articles. For a typical entry the name of the substance is given in Arabic,

Greek, Syriac, Persian, and an Indian language, and sometimes also in one or more less common languages or dialects: Hebrew, Khwārazmian, Tokharian, Zabuli, and so on. There follows a full presentation of the Arabic variants and synonyms, liberally illustrated with quotations from the Arabic poets. The substance is described, its place or places of origin named, and its therapeutic properties given, although Bīrūnī disclaims medical competence on his own part. Sources are fully and critically mentioned.

Abū Rayḥān's dominant trait was a passion for objective knowledge. In pursuit of this he early began studying languages. His mother tongue was Khwārazmian, an Iranian language in which, he wrote, it would be as strange to encounter a scientific concept as to see a camel on a roof gutter (*mīzāb*) or a giraffe among thoroughbred horses (*ʿirāb,* an example of rhymed prose). Therefore he acquired a deep knowledge of both Arabic and Persian. The former, in spite of the ambiguity of its written characters, he esteemed a proper vehicle for the conveyance of science, whereas the latter he deemed fit only for the recital of bedtime stories (*al-asmār al-layliyya*) and legends of the kings (*al-akhbār al-kisrawiyya,* more rhymed prose; *Pharmacology,* p. 40). Of Greek, Syriac, and Hebrew he attained at least sufficient knowledge to use dictionaries in these languages. His command of Sanskrit, on the other hand, reached the point where, with the aid of *pandits,* he was able to translate several Indian scientific works into Arabic, and vice versa. He took obvious delight in Arabic poetry, composed verses himself, and liberally interlarded his writings with quotations from the classics.

Thus equipped, he made full use of all the documents that came to his hand (many of which have since disappeared), exercising a critical faculty that extended from the minutiae of textual emendations to the analysis of scientific theories. A strong sense of history permeates all his writings, making them prime sources for studying the work of his predecessors, as well as his own and that of his contemporaries.

Bīrūnī's pursuit of the truth was not confined to the written or spoken word. He had a strong penchant for firsthand investigation of natural phenomena, exercised at times under very trying circumstances. Along with this went an ingenuity in the devising of instruments and a flair for precision in observations. Because of this feeling for accuracy, and because of a well-founded fear of losing precision in the course of calculations, he tended to prefer observational methods that yielded direct results, as against techniques requiring extensive reduction by computation.

Speculation played a small role in his thinking; he was in full command of the best scientific theories of his time, but he was not profoundly original or a constructor of new theories. His attitude toward astrology has been debated. He spent a great deal of time in serious study of the subject, but Krause (p. 10) has collected passages in which Bīrūnī not only heaps ridicule upon ignorant or unscrupulous astrological practitioners, but indicates disbelief in the basic tenets of this pseudo science. Krause also reminds us that there were many centuries when the casting of horoscopes was the only way by which an astronomer could support himself in the exercise of his profession.

As for religion, Bīrūnī was doubtless a sincere Muslim, but there is no firm evidence of his having been an adherent of any particular sect within the faith. In the *Chronology* (trans., pp. 79, 326), written at the court of Qābūs, are passages that have been interpreted as betraying a Shīʿi (hence anti-Arab and pro-Persian) bent. On the other hand, the *Pharmacology,* compiled under Ghaznavid patronage, represents the author as an orthodox Sunnī. Probably these two situations reflect no more than the fact that the two patrons were Shīʿi and Sunnī, respectively. From time to time Bīrūnī inveighs harshly against various groups, but the criticism is of particular acts or attitudes, not of the group as such. Thus his strictures against the Arab conquerors of Khwārazm were called forth, not because they were Arab, or alien, but because they destroyed ancient books. Concerning the Christian doctrine of forgiveness he writes, "Upon my life, this is a noble philosophy, but the people of this world are not all philosophers. . . . And indeed, ever since Constantine the Victorious became a Christian, both sword and whip have ever been employed" (*India,* trans., II, 161).

In these, and in most matters, Bīrūnī had a remarkably open mind, but his tolerance was not extended to the dilettante, the fool, or the bigot. Upon such he exercised a broad and often crude sarcasm. Upon his showing an instrument for setting the times of prayer to a certain religious legalist, the latter objected that it had engraved upon it the names of the Byzantine months, and this constituted an imitation of the infidels. "The Byzantines also eat food," stated Abū Rayḥān. "Then do not imitate them in this!" and he ejected the fellow forthwith (*Shadows,* 37:9).

Such were the life, labors, and character of a man known to his contemporaries as the Master (*al-Ustādh*). Unknown in the medieval West, except perhaps by the garbled name Maîtrę Aliboron, his name and fame have been secure in his own lands from his time until the present.

BIBLIOGRAPHY

The standard bibliographical work on Bīrūnī is D. J. Boilot, "L'oeuvre d'al-Beruni. Essai bibliographique," in *Mélanges de l'Institut dominicain d'études orientales,* **2** (1955), 161–256; and "Corrigenda et addenda," *ibid.,* **3** (1956), 391–396; no attempt has been made here to duplicate it. A good deal of material has, of course, appeared since it was published in 1955.

For points of view somewhat different from that expressed in the text, see Boilot's article on al-Bīrūnī in the new ed. of the *Encyclopaedia of Islam,* Krause's paper (cited below), and Sachau's prefaces to the text and to the translation of the *Chronology* and the *India. RG* stands for "Répertoire général," the numbered listing of Bīrūnī's works in Boilot.

I. Original Works. Following are Bīrūnī's extant major works, listed alphabetically.

Astrolabe (*RG* 46). The Arabic title is *Kitāb fī istīʿāb al-wujūh fī ṣanʿat al-asṭurlāb.* Several MSS exist (see Boilot), but the text has not been published. Sections of it have, however, been translated and studied.

Bibliography (*RG* 168). Bīrūnī calls this *Risāla fī fihrist kutub Muḥammad b. Zakariyyāʾ al-Rāzī.* The text was published by Paul Kraus as *Épître de Bērūnī contenant le répertoire des Ouvrages de Muḥammad b. Zakarīyā ar-Rāzī* (Paris, 1936). The text of the part giving Bīrūnī's own bibliography appears in the text edition of the *Chronology,* pp. xxxviii–xxxxviiii. It is translated into German in Wiedemann's "Beiträge," LX.

Canon (*RG* 104). The Arabic text has been published as *al-Qānūn al-Masʿūdī* (Canon Masudicus), 3 vols. (Hyderabad-Dn., 1954–1956). References in the article are to page and line of the printed text, pagination of which is continuous, not commencing anew with each volume. A Russian translation, in preparation by P. G. Bulgakov, M. M. Rozhanskaya, and B. A. Rozenfeld, will be Vol. V of the *Selected Works.*

Chords (*RG* 64). There are three MS versions of this work: (1) Leiden Or. 513(5) = CCO 1012; (2) Bankipore Arabic MS 2468/42 = Patna 2,336,2519/40; (3) Murat Molla (Istanbul) 1396. The Leiden version has been published in translation and with a commentary, both by H. Suter, as "Das Buch der Auffindung der Sehnen im Kreise . . . ," in *Bibliotheca mathematica,* **11** (1910), 11–78. The text of version (2) has been published as the first of the four *Rasāʾil* (Arabic for *treatises*). This contains, however, extraneous material, part of which is probably not by Bīrūnī, and part probably a fragment of *RG* 11. Many topics in (2) and (3) are missing from (1), and those parts that are in common are in drastically different orders. Two recensions by Bīrūnī himself are indicated. See H. Hermelink, in *Zentralblatt für Mathematik und ihre Grenzgebiete,* **54** (1956), 3; and A. S. Saidan, in *Islamic Culture,* **34** (1960), 173–175. Many of the additional sections in (2) and (3) are described by E. S. Kennedy and Ahmad Muruwwa in *Journal of Near Eastern Studies,* **17** (1958), 112–121. A composite Arabic text based on (2) and (3) was published by A. S. Demerdash as *Istikhrāj al-awtār fiʾl-dāʾira* (Cairo, 1965). There is a Russian translation by C. A. Krasnova and L. A. Karpova, with commentary by B. A. Rosenfeld and C. A. Krasnova: *Iz istorii nauki i texniki v stranax Vostoka,* III (Moscow, 1963).

Chronology (*RG* 105). In Arabic this is *al-Āthār al-bāqiya min al-qurūn al-khāliya.* It was edited by E. Sachau as *Chronologie orientalischer Voelker von Albērūnī* (Leipzig, 1878, 1923; repr. Baghdad, 1963). The parts missing from Sachau's text are given by K. Garbers and J. Fück in J. Fück, ed., *Documenta Islamica inedita* (Berlin, 1952), pp. 45–98. It was translated into English by Sachau as *The Chronology of Ancient Nations* (London, 1879). The Russian translation by M. A. Sal'e, *Pamyatniki minuvshikh pokolenii,* is Vol. I of the *Selected Works* (Tashkent, 1957).

Densities (*RG* 63). This work's Arabic title is *Maqāla fiʾl-nisab allatī bayn al-filizzāt waʾl-jawāhir fiʾl-ḥajm* ("Treatise on the Ratios Between the Volumes of Metals and Jewels"). The text has never been published, but portions of it have been taken over by other authors and have been studied in modern times.

Gems (*RG* 156). Known as the *Kitāb al-jamāhir fī maʿrifat al-jawāhir,* this text was edited by F. Krenkow (Hyderabad-Dn., 1936). Krenkow also translated the text, but only the chapter on pearls has been published (see Boilot). There is, however, a translation by A. M. Belenskii—*Mineralogiya* (Moscow, 1963).

Ghurra. The *Ghurrat al-zījāt* is Bīrūnī's Arabic translation of the Sanskrit astronomical handbook called *Karaṇatilaka* (forehead caste mark of the Karaṇas), by one Vijayanandin or Vijaya Nanda. The original text is not extant, but a MS of the translation is in the Dargah Library of Pir Muhammad Shah, Ahmadabad. Portions of the Arabic text, with English translation, and a commentary were published in installments by Sayyid Samad Husain Rizvi in *Islamic Culture,* **37** (1963), 112–130, 223–245, and **39** (1965), 1–26, 137–180. Another text, translation, and commentary, by M. F. Qureshi, exist in typescript but have not been published.

India (*RG* 93). Also known as *Kitāb fī taḥqīq ma liʾl-Hind . . .,* this was edited by E. Sachau (London, 1888). A later edition has been published by the Osmania Oriental Publications Bureau (Hyderabad-Dn., 1958). Translated by E. Sachau as *Al-Beruni's India,* 2 vols. (London, 1910). Translated into Russian by A. B. Khalidov and Y. N. Zavadovskii as Vol. II of *Selected Works* (Tashkent, 1963).

Patañjali (*RG* 98). Bīrūnī's Arabic translation of this Sanskrit work is extant only in an incomplete MS edited by H. Ritter as "Al-Bīrūnī's Übersetzung des Yoga-Sūtra des Patañjali," in *Oriens,* **9** (1956), 165–200. See Boilot.

Pharmacology (*RG* 158). The Arabic title of this is *Kitāb al-ṣaydala fi ʾl-ṭibb.* There is no edition of the entire work. M. Meyerhof translated it into German, but of this only the introduction has been published, together with the corresponding part of the Arabic text and an extremely valuable foreword and commentary: "Das Vorwort zur Drogenkunde des Bērūnī," in *Quellen und Studien zur Geschichte der Naturwissenschaften,* **3** (1932), 157–208. A Russian translation, in preparation by U. I. Kazimov, will be Vol. IV of *Selected Works.*

Rasā 'ilu-l-Bīrūnī. This is the Arabic text of *RG* 64, 15, 45, and 38, published by Osmania Oriental Publications Bureau (Hyderabad-Dn., 1948).

Selected Works (*Izbrannye proizvedeniya*). Bīrūnī's extant works are being published in Russian by the Academy of Sciences of the Uzbek S.S.R. Volumes in print or in preparation are listed by individual titles.

Sextant (*RG* 169). The *Ḥikāyat al-ālāt al-musammāt al-suds al-fakhrī* ("Account of the Instrument Known as the Fakhrī Sextant") is MS 223, pp. 10–11, of the Univ. of St. Joseph, Beirut. It was edited by L. Cheikho in *Al-Mashriq,* **11** (1908), 68–69. With minor changes, this small treatise was copied without acknowledgment by Abu'l-Ḥasan al-Marrākushī as part of a larger work. Text and French translation appear in L. A. Sédillot, "Les instruments astronomiques des arabes," in *Mémoires . . . à l'Académie royale des inscriptions . . .,* 1st ser., **1** (1844), 202–206.

Shadows (*RG* 15). The text has been published as the second of the *Rasā 'il* with the title *Kitāb fī ifrād al-maqāl fī amr al-ẓilāl* ("The Exhaustive Treatise on Shadows"). An English translation has been made by E. S. Kennedy, but publication awaits completion of the commentary. References to the *Shadows* made in the article are to page and line of the published text.

Tafhīm (*RG* 73). This is the *Kitāb al-tafhīm li-awā'il ṣinā'at al-tanjīm.* R. Ramsay Wright published an edition of the Arabic text with English translation as *The Book of Instruction in the Art of Astrology* (London, 1934). Bīrūnī's Persian version was published by Jalāl Humā'i (Teheran, 1940).

Taḥdīd (*RG* 19). The Arabic title is *Taḥdīd nihāyāt al-amākin li-taṣḥiḥ masāfāt al-masākin,* and the work is extant in the unique Istanbul MS Fatih 3386. The Arabic text was published by P. Bulgakov as a special number of the Arab League journal, *Majallat ma'had al-makhṭūṭāt al-'arabiyya* (Cairo, 1962). Translated into Russian by P. G. Bulgakov as *Geodeziya,* Vol. III of *Selected Works* (Tashkent, 1966). An English translation by Jamil Ali is *The Determination of the Coordinates of Cities, al-Bīrūnī's Taḥdīd al-Amākin* (Beirut, 1967). References in the article to the *Taḥdīd* are to page and line of the published text.

Transits (*RG* 45). In Arabic this is *Tamhīd al-mustaqarr li-taḥqīq ma'nā al-mamarr* ("Smoothing the Basis for an Investigation of the Meaning of Transits"). The text has been published as the third of the *Rasā'il.* A translation by Mohammad Saffouri and Adnan Ifran, with commentary by E. S. Kennedy, is *Al-Bīrūnī on Transits* (Beirut, 1959).

II. SECONDARY LITERATURE. Works referred to parenthetically in the text, by author and page, are W. Barthold, *Turkestan Down to the Mongol Invasion,* 2nd ed. (London, 1928); E. G. Browne, *A Literary History of Persia,* II (Cambridge, 1928); *Chahār Maqāla of Aḥmad ibn 'Ali an-Niẓāmī al-'Arūḍī as-Samarqandī,* Mirza Muḥammad ibn 'Abd'l-Wahhāb, ed. (Leiden–London, 1910); Iran Society, *Al-Bīrūnī Commemoration Volume, A. H. 362–A. H. 1362* (Calcutta, 1951); Max Krause, "Al-Biruni. Ein iranischer Forscher des Mittelalters," in *Der Islam,* **26** (1940), 1–15; Muḥammad Nāẓim, *The Life and Times of Sulṭān Muḥmūd of Ghazna* (Cambridge, 1931); Aurel Stein, "The Site of Alexander's Passing of the Hydaspes and the Battle With Poros," in *Geographical Journal,* **80** (1932), 31–46; Heinrich Suter, "Die Mathematiker und Astronomen der Araber . . .," in *Abhandlungen zur Geschichte der mathematischen Wissenschaften . . .,* X (Leipzig, 1900); Eilhard Wiedemann et al., "Beiträge zur Geschichte der Naturwissenschaften," in *Sitzungsberichte der Physikalisch-medizinischen Sozietät in Erlangen;* and Yāqūt al-Rūmī, Shihāb al-Dīn, Abū 'Abdallāh, *Mu'jam al-udabā'* (= *Irshād al-arīb ilā ma'rifat al-adīb*), XVII (Cairo, 1936–1938).

E. S. KENNEDY

BJERKNES, CARL ANTON (*b.* Christiania [later Kristiania, now Oslo], Norway, 24 October 1825; *d.* Kristiania, 20 March 1903)

Bjerknes was the son of Abraham Isaksen Bjerknes, a veterinarian, and Elen Birgitte Holmen. Both of his parents were of peasant stock, and throughout his life Bjerknes retained strong ties to his relatives in the country. The father, who as the youngest son did not inherit any land, died in 1838, leaving his widow and three children in straitened circumstances. In 1844 Bjerknes entered the University of Christiania and completed his undergraduate studies in 1848 with a degree in mining engineering. After several years at the Kongsberg silver mines (1848–1852) and as a mathematics teacher (1852–1854), he was awarded a fellowship that enabled him to study mathematics in Göttingen and Paris (1856–1857). The lectures of Dirichlet made a great impression on him and turned his interest to hydrodynamics, which later became the main subject of his research.

In 1859 Bjerknes married Aletta Koren, daughter of a minister. Two years later he was appointed lecturer in applied mathematics at the University of Christiania and was promoted to professor in 1866; in 1869 the professorship was converted to a chair of pure mathematics.

Bjerknes had a delightful personality and was an excellent teacher who was greatly respected by his students for his personal qualities and outstanding lectures. As the years passed, however, he showed an increasing tendency to professional isolation and a fear of publishing the results of his research, which was concerned mainly with hydrodynamic problems. Apart from the very close cooperation with his son Vilhelm, he lived for the most part in his own world. At one point Vilhelm had to extricate himself from this collaboration in order to avoid the danger of unproductive isolation. Nevertheless, in many fields he contributed to the elucidation and continuation of his father's theories.

Bjerknes had been particularly impressed by Dirichlet's demonstration that, according to the principles of hydrodynamics, a ball can move at a constant speed and without external force through ideal (frictionless) fluids, i.e., without the fluid's offering resistance to the ball's movement. Earlier, he had been greatly influenced by Leonhard Euler's *Lettres à une princesse d'Allemagne,* in which Euler opposed the concept of certain forces, such as Newtonian gravity, which are presumed to work at a distance rather than through an overall encompassing medium or ether. One of the strongest objections to the ether theory had always been the difficulty in understanding that according to the principle of inertia, a body not influenced by force should be able to move through such a medium without resistance, but in his lectures Dirichlet had proved that this was possible for movements in the frictionless fluids of hydrodynamics.

Slowly, Bjerknes developed the notion that it was possible, on the basis of hydrodynamics, to form a general theory of the forces active between the solid elements and the influence of the forces on the movements of those elements. First he studied the movement of a ball of variable volume through frictionless fluid according to the method of mathematical physics, and was thus led to further calculations of the simultaneous movements of two such balls. In this way he arrived at the historical conclusion, in 1875, that two harmoniously pulsating balls moving through frictionless fluid react as though they were electrically charged, i.e., they attract or repel one another with a force similar to that of Coulomb's law: they repulse one another when performing harmoniously pulsating oscillations in opposite phases (i.e., when one has maximum volume and the other's volume is minimal); conversely, they attract each other when oscillating in the same phase, thus attaining maximum or minimum volume at the same time.

This important discovery was followed by a number of tests that further stressed the analogy between the movement of bodies in frictionless fluids and the phenomena of electrodynamics. This research, which Bjerknes carried out in collaboration with his son, was substantiated by experiments that drew considerable attention at the electrical exhibition held in Paris in 1881.

Bjerknes' goal was now to develop this analogy to include Maxwell's general theory for electrodynamic phenomena, but despite his intensive efforts he did not attain this goal. His "hydrodynamic picture of the world" and his efforts to explain the electromagnetic forces through hydrodynamics are today more a fascinating analogy than a basic physical theory, yet through this research Bjerknes attained a great insight into hydrodynamic phenomena and thus anticipated later developments in several fields. It is especially noteworthy that through his efforts to describe the action of a magnetic field on an electric current he came to the conclusion that a cylinder rotating in a moving fluid is influenced by a force of the type that today is known as the hydrodynamic transverse force.

Shortly before his father's death Vilhelm Bjerknes published a work on long-range hydrodynamic forces as formulated in his father's theories. In it he explains and clarifies the important results of his father's research.

BIBLIOGRAPHY

I. Original Works. Among Bjerknes' writings are *Niels Henrik Abel, en skildring af hans liv og videnskabelige virksomhed* (Stockholm, 1880) and *Hydrodynamische Fernkräfte. Fünf Abhandlungen,* no. 195 in the series Ostwald's Klassiker der exakten Wissenschaften (Leipzig, 1915).

II. Secondary Literature. Works on Bjerknes are Vilhelm Bjerknes, *Vorlesungen über hydrodynamische Fernkräfte nach C. A. Bjerknes's Theorie,* 2 vols. (Leipzig, 1900–1902); "Til minde om professor Carl Anton Bjerknes," in *Forhandlinger i Videnskabs-selskabet i Kristiania,* no. 7 (1903), 7–24; *Fields of Force* (New York, 1906); *Die Kraftfelder* (Brunswick, 1909); and *C. A. Bjerknes. Hans liv og arbejde* (Oslo, 1925), translated as *Carl Anton Bjerknes. Sein Leben und seine Arbeit* (Berlin, 1933); Elling Holst, "C. A. Bjerknes som matematiker," in *Det Kongelige Frederika Universitet 1811–1911,* II (Kristiania, 1911); and Holtsmark, in *Norsk biografisk leksikon,* I, 581–583.

Mogens Pihl

BLASCHKE, WILHELM JOHANN EUGEN (*b.* Graz, Austria, 13 September 1885; *d.* Hamburg, Germany, 17 March 1962)

Blaschke's father, Josef Blaschke (1852–1917), was professor of descriptive geometry at the Landes-Oberrealschule at Graz. Wilhelm inherited his father's predilection for the geometry of Jakob Steiner and his love of concrete problems. Josef also imparted to the boy a feeling for history and an open-mindedness toward foreign cultures that remained with him throughout his life.

Blaschke began his studies at the Technische

Hochschule of Graz and earned his doctorate from the University of Vienna in 1908. For more than a decade afterward he traveled through Europe, seeking contact with many of the leading geometers of his day. He spent some months in Pisa with Luigi Bianchi and a semester in Göttingen, drawn there by Felix Klein, David Hilbert, and Carl Runge. He worked at Bonn with Eduard Study, whose main fields of research were geometry, kinematics, and the theory of invariants. Blaschke became *Privatdozent* at Bonn in 1910, but in the following year he went to the University of Greifswald to join Friedrich Engel, with whom he shared an admiration for the great Norwegian mathematician Sophus Lie.

In 1913 Blaschke accepted an extraordinary professorship at the Deutsche Technische Hochschule in Prague, and in 1915 he moved to Leipzig, where he became a close friend of Gustav Herglotz. Two years later he was made full professor at the University of Königsberg. After a short stay at Tübingen, Blaschke was called in 1919 to the full professorship of mathematics at the University of Hamburg, a position he retained until his retirement in 1953. He also held visiting professorships at Johns Hopkins University, at the University of Chicago, at the University of Istanbul, and at the Humboldt University in Berlin, and lectured at universities all over the world. He was married to Augusta Meta Röttger and had two children.

At Hamburg, Blaschke succeeded within a few years in gaining worldwide recognition for the department of mathematics of the newly founded university, for he was able to attract to Hamburg such well-known mathematicians as Erich Hecke, Emil Artin, and Helmut Hasse. Very soon Hamburg became a center of great mathematical activity and productivity, testimony to which is given by the *Abhandlungen aus dem mathematischen Seminar der Universität Hamburg* and the *Hamburger mathematische Einzelschriften,* both founded by Blaschke.

One of the leading geometers of his time, Blaschke centered most of his research on differential and integral geometry and kinematics. He combined an unusual power of geometrical imagination with a consistent and suggestive use of analytical tools; this gave his publications great conciseness and clarity and, with his charming personality, won him many students and collaborators.

Blaschke made "kinematic mapping" (discovered independently in 1911 by Josef Grünwald), which established a mapping between the group of isometries (motions) in the plane and the three-dimensional point space, a central tool in kinematics; and in an abstract turn given to it by Kurt Reidemeister, it proved very useful in the axiomatic foundation of several geometries. In *Kreis und Kugel* (1916), Blaschke investigated the isoperimetric properties of convex bodies, characterizing circles and spheres as figures of minimal properties. In this he was following methods suggested by Steiner, who had been criticized by Dirichlet for omitting an existence proof. This was first remedied by Weierstrass by means of the calculus of variation, but Blaschke supplied the necessary existence proofs in a fashion closer to the spirit of Steiner.

Blaschke's books on differential geometry soon gained worldwide recognition. The three-volume *Vorlesungen* (1921–1929) put into practice Felix Klein's "Erlangen Program" for differential geometry: Volume I was devoted to classical geometry, Volume II to affine differential geometry (a subject developed by Blaschke and his pupils), and Volume III to the differential geometry of circles and spheres, controlled by the transformation groups of Moebius, Laguerre, and Sophus Lie. (The treatment of projective differential geometry, however, was left to Blaschke's pupil Gerrit Bol.) Furthermore, Blaschke originated topological differential geometry, which studies invariants of differentiable mappings; he collected the results in his books *Geometrie der Gewebe* (1938) and *Einführung in die Geometrie der Waben* (1955). In 1950 Blaschke gave a new, concise exposition of differential geometry based on ideas of E. Cartan.

Inspired by Gustav Herglotz and by some classical problems of geometrical probability (Buffon's needle problem, Crofton's formulas), Blaschke began, about 1935, a series of papers on integral geometry. Because of its relations to convex bodies and kinematics, this field of research was especially to his liking; and many of his students continued his work in this area—Hadwiger, Wu, Chern, and Santaló.

Blaschke received honorary doctorates from the universities of Sofia, Padua, and Greifswald, and the Karlsruhe Technische Hochschule. He was elected corresponding or honorary member of about a dozen European scientific academies.

BIBLIOGRAPHY

I. Original Works. Blaschke's works include *Kreis und Kugel* (Leipzig, 1916; Berlin, 1956), trans. into Russian (Moscow, 1967); *Vorlesungen über Differentialgeometrie,* 3 vols., I (Berlin, 1921, 1924, 1930, 1945), trans. into Russian (Moscow, 1935); II, rev. by Kurt Reidemeister (Berlin, 1923); III, rev. by G. Thomsen (Berlin, 1929); *Vorlesungen über Integralgeometrie,* 2 vols., I (Leipzig-Berlin, 1935, 1936, 1955), trans. into Russian (Moscow, 1938); II (Leipzig-Berlin, 1937; 3rd ed., 1955—together with Vol. I); *Ebene

Kinematik (Leipzig–Berlin, 1938); *Geometrie der Gewebe,* written with Gerrit Bol (Berlin, 1938); *Einführung in die Differentialgeometrie* (Berlin, 1950; 2nd ed., 1960), written with Hans Reichardt, trans. into Russian (Moscow, 1957); *Einführung in die Geometrie der Waben* (Basel–Stuttgart, 1955), trans. into Russian (Moscow, 1959), trans. into Turkish (Istanbul, 1962); *Ebene Kinematik,* written with H. R. Müller (Munich, 1956); *Reden und Reisen eines Geometers* (Berlin, 1957, 1961); and *Kinematik und Quaternionen* (Berlin, 1960).

II. SECONDARY LITERATURE. The following obituary notices describe Blaschke's life and work in greater detail: Werner Burau, "Wilhelm Blaschkes Leben und Werk," in *Mitteilungen der Mathematischen Gesellschaft in Hamburg,* **9,** no. 2 (1963), 24–40; Otto Haupt, "Nachruf auf Wilhelm Blaschke," in *Jahrbuch 1962 der Akademie der Wissenschaften und der Literatur zu Mainz* (Mainz–Wiesbaden, 1962), pp. 44–51; Erwin Kruppa, "Wilhelm Blaschke," in *Almanach der Österreichischen Akademie der Wissenschaften,* **112** (for 1962) (Vienna, 1963), 419–429; Hans Reichardt, "Wilhelm Blaschke †," in *Jahresbericht der Deutschen Mathematiker-Vereinigung,* **69** (1966), 1–8; and Emanuel Sperner, "Zum Gedenken an Wilhelm Blaschke," in *Abhandlungen aus dem Mathematischen Seminar der Universität Hamburg,* **26** (1963), 111–128 (with a bibliography by W. Burau, to which Reichardt gives an addition).

CHRISTOPH J. SCRIBA

BLASIUS OF PARMA (*b.* Parma, Italy, *ca.* 1345; *d.* Parma, 1416)

Although presumably he was born in Parma, the first known reference to Blasius is found in the records for 1377 of the University of Pavia, where he took his doctorate, perhaps in 1374 (the latter date makes 1345 a plausible birth year). Listed as an examiner in March 1378, Blasius probably left Pavia by October of that year for the University of Bologna, where he remained at least until 1382 (for 1379–1380, he was officially described as a teacher of logic, philosophy, and astrology), and probably through 1383. On 20 May 1384, he agreed to teach at the University of Padua for four years; his name appears in the university records from February 1386 to 11 May 1387 and again on 16 December 1388 as the sponsor of a doctoral candidate who was represented by another scholar, probably because in 1387 Blasius had returned to Bologna as professor of philosophy and astrology for the period 1387–1388. On 29 July 1388, he was appointed a lecturer in natural philosophy at the University of Florence, where he remained until 1389.

During the next decade, when he reached the summit of his career, Blasius was again at Pavia as professor of "mathematical arts and both philosophies" (i.e., moral and natural). His whereabouts between 1400 and 1403 are unknown, but in subsequent years he taught at the University of Pavia (1403–1407) and the University of Padua (1407–1411). In October 1411 he was dismissed from the latter because he lacked students and was deemed no longer fit to teach, conditions that were probably caused by the infirmities of old age. He died five years later.

A sojourn in Paris, where he received his doctorate (so we are told in an explicit to his *Questio de tactu corporum duorum,* which was disputed at Bologna no later than 1388), is mentioned in his *Questiones super tractatum de ponderibus.*[1] It was probably while in Paris that he absorbed the new ideas of the Parisian Scholastics, ideas that he was to disseminate and popularize in Italy.

Blasius was not merely an Aristotelian commentator, but also wrote independent treatises on important scientific topics. Prior to 16 October 1396, when he was compelled to recant unspecified transgressions against the Church[2] (by this time he had probably written the bulk of his extant treatises), Blasius seems to have been a materialist and determinist, accepting as true certain articles condemned at Paris in 1277. In his *Questiones de anima* (Padua, 1385), he denied that the intellective soul was separable from the body, insisting that it was produced from transient matter. It was only by authority of the Church and faith—not by natural reason or evidence—that one ought to believe in its separability. Furthermore, he denied the immortality of the intellective soul while accepting the eternity of the world and a necessary determinism exerted by the celestial bodies and constellations on terrestrial and human events. Such opinions, characteristic of earlier Bolognese Averroists, were probably instrumental in provoking the ecclesiastical authorities. Blasius capitulated and complied swiftly. During 1396–1397, in lectures delivered at Pavia on the *Physics* of Aristotle, he repudiated all these views; and in 1405 he attacked astrological determinism (but not astrology) in his *Iudicium revolutionis anni 1405,* declaring that while the stars influenced men and events, the will of God and human free will could resist if they chose.

Of his numerous scientific treatises, only those on optics, statics, and intension and remission of forms have received more than cursory examinations, resulting in partial or complete modern editions. In addition to relevant discussions on optics in his *Questiones de anima* and *Meteorologica,* Blasius also wrote *Quaestiones perspectivae* (dated 1390 in one manuscript), a lengthy commentary on some of the propositions of John Peckham's enormously popular thirteenth-century optical treatise, *Communis perspectiva.*

Guided by an empiricist outlook derived ultimately from the optics of Ibn al-Haytham (Alhazen), and perhaps influenced by fourteenth-century nominalism, he made visual sensation the basis for human certitude and knowledge; consequently he placed heavy emphasis upon the psychology of perception. Traditional geometric optics was placed in the broader matrix of a theory of knowledge and cognitive perception based on vision.

Blasius composed at least two treatises on statics: one Scholastic, the other longer and non-Scholastic in form. The longer work, *Tractatus de ponderibus,* drew heavily on the thirteenth-century statical treatises associated with the name of Jordanus de Nemore. It was probably from the *Elementa Jordani super demonstrationem ponderum* that Blasius adopted the important concept of "positional gravity," which involved a resolution of forces where the effective "heaviness" or weight of a body in a constrained system is proportional to the directness of its descent as measured by the projection of an arbitrary segment of its path onto the vertical drawn through the fulcrum of a lever or balance. Ignoring straightforward and available definitions of positional gravity, Blasius presents the concept in Pt. I, Supps. 6 and 7, proving in the first of these that "in the case of equal arcs unequally distant from the line of equality (i.e., the line of horizontal balance) that which is a greater distance intercepts less of the vertical [through the axis]," and in the second that "one body is heavier than another by the amount that its movement toward the center [of the world] is straighter."[3] But the more of the vertical cut off by a projected arc, the straighter its descent and, therefore, the greater its positional gravity.

In Pt. II, Prop. 4 (probably based upon *Elementa Jordani,* Th. 2), Blasius misapplied the concept of positional gravity in demonstrating that "when the equal arms of a balance are not parallel with the horizon and equal weights are hung [on their ends], the beam assumes a horizontal position."[4] In Figure 1, let arms *AB* and *BC* be equal but not parallel to the horizon, *DF.* If equal weights are suspended at the ends of the equal arms, the latter would become parallel to the horizon, or *DF.* This will occur because, being heavy bodies, *a* and *c* will seek to descend, *c* to *F* and *a* to *G.* Assuming, quite improperly, that arcs *CF* and *AG* are equal, but unequally distant from *DF,* Blasius applies Pt. I, Supp. 6, to show that arc *CF* cuts off more of the vertical along *HG* than does arc *AG,* and concludes that *c*'s downward motion to *F* is more direct than *a*'s to *G.* Consequently (by Pt. I, Supp. 7, which is not cited but is clearly required), *c* is positionally heavier than *a* and will descend,

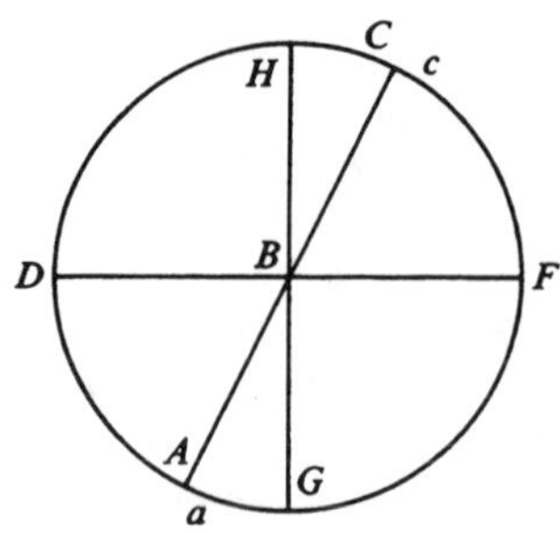

FIGURE 1

forcing *a* upward until horizontal equilibrium is attained. The basic error in all this lies in assuming a simultaneous descent for *c* and *a,* instead of comparing the descent of *c* with the ascent of *a* and the ascent of *c* with the descent of *a.* The equality of these two ratios would have yielded the desired proof.

Positional gravity was more felicitously applied in proving the law of the lever (Pt. II, Prop. 10) and in demonstrating that equilibrium is attained on a bent lever when equal weights are suspended on its unequal arms, which terminate equidistantly from the axis of support (Pt. II, Prop. 11). A brief third part concerned the specific gravities of fluids and solids. Dynamic considerations played a role, since Blasius says (Pt. III, Prop. 1) that of two solid bodies descending in water, the heavier will descend more quickly. For comparison of liquids, a hydrometer was used, and its principle was utilized in the comparison of two solid, similarly shaped floating bodies, when Blasius advocated that each be divided into twelve equally spaced parts.

In one of two treatises on intension and remission of forms, *Questiones de latitudinibus formarum,* Blasius included both the English (arithmetic) and French (geometric) fourteenth-century versions of the mean speed theorem[5] that demonstrated the equality of the distances traversed during the same time by one body moving with uniform acceleration and another moving with a uniform speed equal to the velocity acquired by the body in uniform acceleration at the middle instant of its period of acceleration (i.e., $S = V_0t + at^2/2$, where S is distance; V_0 initial velocity; a acceleration; and t time). Blasius may have introduced both versions into Italy.

Over a long career, Blasius discussed many traditional scientific concepts. Initially an apparent supporter of the impetus theory, he later denied, in his *Questiones super octo libros physicorum* (1397), that it could explain acceleration in free fall or the rebound of bodies.[6] He accepted "Bradwardine's function,"[7] which described the relationship between the speeds of two bodies as $F_2/R_2 = (F_1/R_1)^{V_2/V_1}$, where F is motive power; R, the resistive force of the body

BLASIUS OF PARMA

in motion; and *V*, velocity. He also reflects common Parisian arguments when he denies the natural existence of vacuum inside or outside the cosmos[8] and then allows (contrary to Aristotle) that if a separate vacuum did exist, bodies could undergo motion and change[9] (in his *Questio de tactu corporum duorum,* Blasius holds that if a vacuum actually existed, many difficulties and contradictions involving the physical contact of two bodies could be resolved).[10]

Although not an original thinker, Blasius sympathetically absorbed the scientific ideas current among the "moderns" at the University of Paris during the fourteenth century. He helped disseminate these in Italy, where they were widely discussed until the time of Galileo.

NOTES

1. Quoted by Marshall Clagett in Marshall Clagett and E. A. Moody, *The Medieval Science of Weights,* pp. 413–414.
2. The brief document has been translated by L. Thorndike in *University Records and Life in the Middle Ages,* pp. 258–259.
3. Clagett and Moody, *op. cit.,* p. 243.
4. *Ibid.,* p. 251. The figure appears on p. 250.
5. Marshall Clagett, *Science of Mechanics,* pp. 402–403.
6. A. Maier, *Zwei Grundprobleme der scholastischen Naturphilosophie,* pp. 271–273.
7. *Questiones super tractatu De proportionibus Thome Berduerdini,* questions 10, 11 (MS Vat. lat. 3012, 151r–153v).
8. *Questiones super octo libros physicorum,* MS Vat. lat. 2159, 120v, c. 1.
9. *Ibid.,* 124r, c. 2–124v, c. 1.
10. G. F. Vescovini, "Problemi di fisica aristotelica in un maestro del XIV secolo: Biagio Pelacani da Parma," in *Rivista di filosofia,* **51** (1960), 196.

BIBLIOGRAPHY

I. Original Works. All but a few of Blasius' works are unpublished. References to manuscripts of these treatises can be found in L. Thorndike and P. Kibre, "Blasius of Parma," in *A Catalogue of Incipits of Mediaeval Scientific Writings in Latin* (rev. and enl. ed., Cambridge, Mass., 1963), c. 1764; and, in an earlier but more conveniently arranged list, in L. Thorndike, *A History of Magic and Experimental Science,* IV (New York, 1934), app. 40, pp. 652–662.

Questions or commentaries on the following works of Aristotle are extant: *Questiones librorum de caelo et mundo* (Milan, Ambros. P. 120 Sup., 1–69; Bodleian Library, Canonicus Misc. 422, 1–52; Rome, Angelica 592 [F.6.4], 1–34; Rome, Angelica 595 [folio numbers unavailable]; Vienna, National Bibliothek, 2402, 1–63v); *Commentaria in Aristotelis de generatione et corruptione* (Vienna, National Bibliothek, 2402, 99r–123v); *Questiones de anima* (Vat. Chigi O IV 41, 112–217v; Vat. Urbinas lat. 1489, 74–[terminating folio number unavailable]; Bodleian Library, Canonicus Misc. 393, 1–78; Turin 1247 [folio numbers unavailable]); *Questiones in libros metheororum* (Vat. lat. 2160, 63–138v, which is immediately preceded by Blasius' *Conclusiones super libris methaurorum Aristotelis,* a work differing from the *Questiones;* Florence, Ashburnham 112, 1–60; Vat. Chigi O IV 41, 62–108v; University of Chicago 10, 39 ff.). On the *Physics* of Aristotle, Blasius left at least three versions: (1) *Expositio per conclusiones super octo libros physicorum Aristotelis* (Vat. lat. 2159, 1–98v); (2) *Questiones super octo libros physicorum,* preserved, with variant titles, in separate versions, one written in or before 1385 at Padua, of which only the first two books remain (Vat. Chigi O IV 41), and the other, copied in 1397 in Pavia, differing somewhat and embracing all eight books (Vat. lat. 2159, 61r–230r; despite an apparent overlap in pagination with the *Expositio,* it immediately follows the latter with independent pagination beginning with 61r); an incomplete and mutilated version of the Pavia copy is contained in Vat. lat. 3012, 2v–110v; and (3) an arrangement of Buridan's *Questiones super octo phisicorum libros Aristotelis* made around 1396 (Venice, S. Marco X, 103, 83–84).

The two works on statics are *Questiones super tractatum de ponderibus,* containing five questions and known only in a single manuscript (Milan, Ambros. F. 145 Sup., 18r–28r), edited and translated by Father Joseph Brown in a thesis, "The *Scientia de ponderibus* in the Later Middle Ages" (Univ. of Wis., 1967); and *Tractatus de ponderibus,* edited and translated by Marshall Clagett in Marshall Clagett and E. A. Moody, *The Medieval Science of Weights* (Madison, Wis., 1952), pp. 238–279. On intension and remission of forms, Blasius left two treatises, *De intensione et remissione formarum* and *Questiones super tractatu de latitudinibus formarum:* for manuscripts of both, see Marshall Clagett, *The Science of Mechanics in the Middle Ages* (Madison, Wis., 1959), pp. 404, 685–686; the second treatise was published in 1482 and 1486 at Padua and in 1505 at Venice, while part of the third and final question of the second treatise was edited and translated by Clagett in *Science of Mechanics,* pp. 402–408. On problems of motion, he wrote *Questiones super tractatu De proportionibus Thome Berduerdini* (i.e., Bradwardine); for manuscripts, see Marshall Clagett, *The Science of Mechanics in the Middle Ages,* p. 686; and *De motu iuxta mentem Aristotelis* (MS Vat. Barb. 357, 1–16v).

Of the three books and twenty-four questions of the *Quaestiones perspectivae,* Book I, quests. 1–10 were edited by F. Alessio as "Questioni inedite di ottica di Biagio Pelacani da Parma," in *Rivista critica di storia della filosofia,* **16** (1961), 79–110, 188–221; Book I, quests. 14 and 16, and Book III, quest. 3 (*ultima questio*), were edited by G. F. Vescovini as "Le questioni di 'Perspectiva' di Biagio Pelacani da Parma," in *Rinascimento,* **1** (1961), 207–243—the text is preceded by a lengthy discussion of the questions and their historical context on pp. 163–206. The 1505 edition of *Questiones super tractatu de latitudinibus formarum* includes Blasius' *Questio de tactu corporum duorum,* which is summarized by G. F. Vescovini in "Problemi di fisica aristotelica in un maestro del XIV secolo: Biagio Pelacani da Parma," in *Rivista di filosofia,* **51** (1960), 179–200.

On astronomy, Blasius wrote *Questiones super tractatum sperae Johannis de Sacrobosco* (MS Parma 984) and a *Theorice planetarum* (Vat. lat. 4082, 47r–60v; Venice, S. Marco VIII.69, 175r–216v). The Latin text of the titles of the problems discussed by Blasius in the latter treatise was published by L. Thorndike in *Isis,* **47** (1956), 398–400. Thorndike mentions that the Latin texts of the first three problems and the last were published by G. Boffito and U. Mazzia in *Bibliofilia,* **8** (1907), 372–383, where they are mistakenly ascribed to Peter of Modena. In the same article, Thorndike (*Isis,* **47** [1956], 401–402) cites another astronomical work by Blasius, *Demonstrationes geometrice in theorica planetarum,* printed anonymously by Octavianus Scotus (Venice, 1518), fols. 143r–152v (a possible manuscript version of this treatise is Vat. lat. 3379, 52r–61r, which bears the slightly variant title *Blasii Parmensis demonstrationes geometrie in theoricam planetarum*). An astrological prediction constitutes Blasius' *Iudicium revolutionis anni 1405* (Bibliothèque Nationale MS 7443, 11v–17r).

The diverse treatises cited below conclude the list of Blasius' scientific and philosophic works known thus far: *Questiones super tractatus loyce* [i.e., *logice*] *magistri Petri Hyspani* [i.e., Peter of Spain] (Bodleian Library, Canonicus Misc. 421, 92–222); *Questiones undecim de locis* (Venice, S. Marco X, 208, 82–92); *Queritur utrum spericum tangat planum* (Bodleian Library, Canonicus Misc. 177, 153–154); *Questiones viginti sex predicamentis* (Venice, S. Marco X, 208, 43–82 and perhaps also Vat. Barberini 357); *De motu* (Vat. Barberini 357, 1–16v); *Elenchus questionum Buridani* (i.e., *A Refutation of Questions of Buridan;* Venice, S. Marco X, 103, 83–84); and a *De terminis naturalibus* (Bodleian Library, Canonicus Misc. 393, 78–83), of uncertain attribution. A theological work, *De predestinatione,* has also been preserved (Venice, Bibl. de' Santi Giovanni e Paolo 163).

II. SECONDARY LITERATURE. There is relatively little literature on Blasius. To what has already been cited, we may add L. Thorndike, *A History of Magic and Experimental Science,* IV, ch. 39; G. F. Vescovini, *Studi sulla prospettiva medievale* (Turin, 1965), ch. 12; A. Maier, *Die Vorläufer Galileis im 14. Jahrhundert* (Rome, 1949; 2nd ed., 1966), pp. 279–299, and *Zwei Grundprobleme der scholastischen Naturphilosophie,* 2nd ed. (Rome, 1951), pp. 270–274; and F. Amodeo, "Appunti su Biagio Pelacani da Parma," in *Atti del IV Congresso Internazionale dei Matematici,* **3** (Rome, 1909), 549–553.

EDWARD GRANT

BLICHFELDT, HANS FREDERICK (*b.* Illar, Denmark, 9 January 1873; *d.* Palo Alto, California, 16 November 1945)

The son of Erhard Christoffer Laurentius Blichfeldt, a farmer who came from a long line of ministers, and Nielsine Maria Scholer, Blichfeldt showed unusual mathematical aptitude at an early age. He was assisted in his studies by his father, and in general he did well in all subjects. He passed the university entrance examinations with honors but did not attend because his parents were unable to afford it.

Fortunately for Hans, his family emigrated to the United States when he was fifteen. He spent four years as a laborer on farms and in sawmills in the Midwest and West and two years traveling about the country as a surveyor. His phenomenal ability to do all the surveying computations mentally so impressed his colleagues that they encouraged him to become a mathematician. He entered the recently founded Stanford University in 1894 and received his B.A. in 1896 and his M.A. in 1897. Not having enough money to go to Europe for a doctorate, as was the custom among the better-known mathematicians, he borrowed the money from a Stanford professor, Rufus L. Green, and enrolled in the University of Leipzig, where he studied under the famous mathematician Sophus Lie. In one year he received his doctorate *summa cum laude,* with the dissertation "On a Certain Class of Groups of Transformation in Three-dimensional Space."

During the year 1898 Blichfeldt was employed by Stanford as an instructor. He obtained the rank of full professor in 1913. He accepted the chairmanship of the mathematics department in 1927 and served in that capacity until his retirement in 1938. In addition, Blichfeldt served as a visiting professor at the University of Chicago in the summer of 1911 and at Columbia University during the summers of 1924 and 1925. He was professor emeritus at Stanford until his death.

Blichfeldt was extremely active in the American Mathematical Society and gave numerous talks in many parts of the country on his favorite topics, group theory and number theory. In 1912 he was elected vice-president of the Society.

Blichfeldt's contributions were primarily in the form of articles for the Society publications and European mathematics journals. His lifework was devoted to group theory and number theory. Some of the many topics that he covered were diophantine approximations, orders of linear homogeneous groups, theory of geometry of numbers, approximate solutions of the integers of a set of linear equations, low-velocity angle fire, finite collineation groups, and characteristic roots. In addition, he published the text *Finite Collineation Groups* and coauthored *Theory and Applications of Finite Groups* with G. A. Miller and L. E. Dickson.

During his life Blichfeldt received many honors. In 1920 he was elected to the National Academy of Sciences, which at the time was an achievement for a mathematician. From 1924 to 1927 he was a member of the National Research Council. After he retired from Stanford, the king of Denmark made him a Knight of the Order of the Dannebrog.

Blichfeldt's contributions in group theory and group characteristics are now of considerable importance because of recent applications of Lie groups in the sciences.

BIBLIOGRAPHY

Blichfeldt's works include "On a Certain Class of Groups of Transformation in Three-dimensional Space," in *American Journal of Mathematics,* **22** (1900), 113-120; "On the Determination of the Distance Between Two Points in *m* Dimensional Space," in *Transactions of the American Mathematical Society,* **3** (1902), 467-481; "On the Order of Linear Homogeneous Groups. I," *ibid.,* **4** (1903), 387-397; ". . . II," **5** (1904), 310-325; ". . . III," **7** (1906), 523-529; ". . . IV," **12** (1911), 39-42; "A Theorem Concerning the Invariants of Linear Homogeneous Groups With Some Applications to Substitution Groups," *ibid.,* **5** (1904), 461-466; "Theorems on Simple Groups," *ibid.,* **11** (1910), 1-14; "Finite Groups of Linear Homogeneous Transformations," Part II of *Theory and Applications of Finite Groups* (London-New York, 1916), pp. 17-390, written with G. A. Miller and L. E. Dickson; and *Finite Collineation Groups* (Chicago, 1917).

G. H. MILLER

BLISS, GILBERT AMES (*b.* Chicago, Illinois, 9 May 1876; *d.* Harvey, Illinois, 8 May 1961)

Gilbert Ames Bliss, the son of George Harrison Bliss and Mary Maria Gilbert, devoted his life to the study of mathematics. Although his scientific interests ranged broadly over the field of analysis, with special emphasis on the basic existence theorems, the focal point of much of his work was the calculus of variations. Prior to World War I he wrote, with Max Mason and A. L. Underhill, on the application of the methods of Weierstrass to a number of problems in the latter subject. He worked in the ballistic laboratory at Aberdeen, Maryland, during the war, and used his knowledge of the calculus of variations to construct new firing tables. In the 1920's his papers encompassed the transformation of Clebsch, proofs of the necessity of the Jacobi condition, multiple integrals, and boundary value problems in his field.

His elementary Carus Monograph on the calculus of variations (1925) was followed, after some twenty years, by his definitive book: *Lectures on the Calculus of Variations* (1946). In this publication Bliss employed the scattered results of mathematicians of past decades, many of whom were his former students, to establish firmly the theoretical foundations of the calculus of variations. He approached his subject from the viewpoint of analysis and covered the use of existence theorems for implicit functions, differential equations, and the analysis of singular points for the transformations of the plane. He improved upon and extended the theories of the problems of Lagrange, Mayer, and Bolza and simplified the proofs of the necessary and sufficient conditions of these problems. He clearly presented the theory of the calculus of variations for cases involving no side conditions. Overall he gave a greater comprehensiveness and generality to the field than had previously existed. As a result of his earlier work as summarized in this book, Bliss may be judged one of the chief architects of the edifice of the calculus of variations.

Bliss's work represents a turning point in American mathematics. With his generation, American mathematics came of age. Previously, most American mathematicians had received their training in, and inspiration from, Europe. From the beginning of his career, Bliss was identified with the University of Chicago. He enrolled there in 1893, one year after the university opened its doors. He received his bachelor's degree in 1897, his master's in 1898, and his doctorate in 1900. Although he began his studies in mathematical astronomy, under the guidance of F. R. Moulton, he soon turned to the study of pure mathematics. E. H. Moore, Oskar Bolza—who aroused his interest in the calculus of variations—and H. Maschke were his instructors.

Bliss spent his apprenticeship as a mathematics instructor at the universities of Minnesota (1900-1902) and Chicago (1903-1904). From 1902 to 1903 he did postgraduate work at the University of Göttingen. Bliss was assistant professor of mathematics at the University of Missouri (1904-1905) and at Princeton (1905-1908). In 1908 he returned to Chicago as an associate professor.

On 15 June 1912, Bliss married Helen Hurd (*d.* 1918). They had two children, Elizabeth and Gilbert, Jr. He married Olive Hunter 12 October 1920.

Bliss taught and worked at the University of Chicago from 1908 to 1941. He was associate professor until 1913, professor from 1913 to 1941, and professor emeritus from 1941. He succeeded Moore as chairman of the mathematics department in 1927 and was Martin A. Ryerson distinguished professor of mathematics from 1933 to 1941. Throughout his career at Chicago he was known for his lively sense of humor and for stressing the importance of a strong union between teaching and fundamental mathematical research.

From 1909 until his death, Bliss exerted a strong

influence on the American mathematical scene. He was an associate editor of the *Transactions of the American Mathematical Society* from 1909 to 1916, and from 1921 to 1922 was president of the society. He was elected to the National Academy of Sciences in 1916, and in 1924, with G. D. Birkhoff and Oswald Veblen, he became a member of the awards committee of the newly instituted National Research Fellowships in mathematics. Bliss served on this committee until 1936. In 1925 he received the first Chauvenet Prize awarded by the Mathematical Association of America for his paper "Algebraic Functions and Their Divisors." The following year Bliss was elected a member of the American Philosophical Society. In 1935 he was made a fellow of the American Academy of Arts and Sciences. For many years Bliss served as chairman of the editorial committee established by the Mathematical Association of America for its Carus Monographs, a series of short expository books on mathematics for the layman.

BIBLIOGRAPHY

I. Original Works. Bliss's books are *Fundamental Existence Theorems* (Princeton, 1913); *Calculus of Variations*, Carus Mathematical Monograph No. 1 (Chicago, 1925); *Algebraic Functions*, American Mathematical Society Colloquium Publications, XVI (New York, 1933); *Mathematics for Exterior Ballistics* (New York, 1944); *Lectures on the Calculus of Variations* (Chicago, 1946).

Bliss also wrote many articles: "The Geodesic Lines on the Anchor Ring" (doctoral dissertation), in *Annals of Mathematics*, **4** (1902), 1-21; "The Solutions of Differential Equations of the First Order as Functions of Their Initial Values," *ibid.*, **6** (1905), 49-68; "A Problem of the Calculus of Variations in Which the Integrand Is Discontinuous," in *Transactions of the American Mathematical Society*, **7** (1906), 325-336, written with Max Mason; "A New Proof of Weierstrass' Theorem Concerning the Factorization of a Power Series," in *Bulletin of the American Mathematical Society*, **9** (1910), 356-359; "Generalizations of Geodesic Curvatures and a Theorem of Gauss Concerning Geodesic Triangles," in *American Journal of Mathematics*, **37** (1914), 1-18; "A Note on the Problem of Lagrange in the Calculus of Variations," in *Bulletin of the American Mathematical Society*, **22** (1916), 220-225; "Integral of Lebesgue," *ibid.*, **24** (1917), 1-47; "Solutions of Differential Equations as Functions of the Constants of Integration," *ibid.*, **25** (1918), 15-26; "The Problem of Mayer With Variable End Points," in *Transactions of the American Mathematical Society*, **19** (1918), 305-314; "Functions of Lines in Ballistics," *ibid.*, **21** (1920), 93-106; "Algebraic Functions and Their Divisors," in *Annals of Mathematics*, **26** (1924), 95-124; "The Transformation of Clebsch in the Calculus of Variations," in *Proceedings of the International Congress of 1924 at Toronto*, **1** (1928), 589-603; "The Problem of Lagrange in the Calculus of Variations," in *American Journal of Mathematics*, **52** (1930), 673-744; "The Problem of Bolza in the Calculus of Variations," in *Annals of Mathematics*, **33** (1932), 261-274; "Mathematical Interpretations of Geometrical and Physical Phenomena," in *American Mathematical Monthly*, **40** (1933), 472-480; "The Calculus of Variations for Multiple Integrals," *ibid.*, **49** (1942), 77-89.

II. Secondary Literature. Articles on Bliss are L. M. Graves, "Gilbert Ames Bliss, 1876-1951," in *Bulletin of the American Mathematical Society*, **58** (1952), 251-264 (this article contains a bibliography of Bliss's publications); and Saunders MacLane, "Gilbert Ames Bliss (1876-1951)," in *Yearbook of the American Philosophical Society for 1951*, pp. 288-291.

Ronald S. Calinger

BOBILLIER, ÉTIENNE (*b.* Lons-le-Saulnier, France, 17 April 1798; *d.* Châlons-sur-Marne, France, 22 March 1840)

Étienne Bobillier was the second son of Ignace Bobillier, a merchant, who died when Étienne was seven years old. He and his brother Marie André were raised by their mother, a wallpaper merchant. Étienne attended the local secondary school and seemed inclined toward literary studies, in which he won awards. Until he was sixteen, he showed no interest in mathematics, but then his brother, a student at the *lycée* of Besançon, was accepted by the École Polytechnique. Étienne resolved to follow this example and, shutting himself up with the books left behind by his brother and aided from time to time by advice from him, he completed the course in special mathematics. He then presented himself for the competitive entrance examination in 1817. The examiner, well known for his severity, put Étienne first on his list. He was admitted to the École Polytechnique as fourth in rank.

Bobillier finished his first year eighth out of sixty-four students. Because of financial needs, he took a leave of absence from the École Polytechnique in October 1818, in order to become an instructor in mathematics at the École des Arts et Métiers at Châlons. The young instructor soon showed a remarkable gift for teaching; exhibiting a rapid judgment, lively mind, lucid language, and strength of character that impressed, captivated, and subdued his students.[1] He taught trigonometry, statics, analytic geometry, descriptive geometry, practical mechanics, physics, and chemistry.

In 1829 Bobillier, who saw no future where he was, applied for a university post and, upon Poisson's recommendation, he became professor of special mathematics at the Collège Royal of Amiens. The minister of commerce, however, who had authority over all Écoles des Arts et Métiers, named him director of studies at the École of Angers. He took up his post there on 1 January 1830. After the July Revolution, civil war broke out again in the west and Bobillier, a volunteer in the National Guard of Angers, fought in a rather hard month-long campaign against the Chouans.

In 1832 his post as director of studies was abolished, and Bobillier returned to Châlons as instructor-in-chief in mathematics. By 1834 he was full professor, a rank he retained until his death. He also held a professorship of special mathematics at the municipal high school. Bobillier was named Chevalier of the Legion of Honor in 1839.

In 1836 he became seriously ill; but the following year he married. In spite of a recurring illness, Bobillier refused to interrupt his work, even though he finally was confined to bed. Imprudently, he resumed his teaching and other activities too soon—a decision that hastened his death in 1840.

Bobillier became known to the scientific world particularly through his contributions to the *Annales de Gergonne.*[2] The first, in August 1826, was a modest solution of certain problems posed to the readers by the editor. In April 1830 he went on to demonstrate the principle of virtual velocities for machines in equilibrium. He also contributed to Quetelet's *Correspondance mathématique et physique,*[3] to the *Mémoires de l'Académie de Caen,*[4] and to a few provincial journals[5]—probably a total of some forty writings. He also edited for his students a book of elementary algebra and a complete course in geometry. His courses in mechanics and physics were written out in autograph.[6]

At the time of his death, Bobillier was working on a dissertation concerning the geometric laws of motion[7] that he meant to present as a report before the Académie des Sciences. Some of the passages in his course in geometry are probably an early outline for this.

Because of his isolation in the provinces, Bobillier had few direct contacts with the scientific world of his time. His premature departure from the École Polytechnique prevented him from forming the lasting friendships that are one of the principal hallmarks of that famous school.

He knew Poncelet, however, through correspondence and a close relationship that began in 1828–1829.[8] Unfortunately, their correspondence seems to have been lost. Bobillier never met J. D. Gergonne, the editor of the *Annales,* nor Adolphe Quetelet and Michel Chasles. In spite of the coincidence of their statements and interests, and of the fact that questions of priority arose between them, they do not seem to have corresponded directly. In fact, in the notice that Chasles wrote on Bobillier, he made a serious error as to the date of his death.[9]

There is even more reason to think that Bobillier had neither contact nor correspondence with Jakob Steiner and Julius Plücker, his emulators on the staff of the *Annales.* It should be noted that Gergonne often edited the articles of his collaborators to suit himself, which makes it difficult to judge them definitively.

Loyal to Gaspard Monge's ideas, Bobillier treated geometric problems in a way akin to both analytic geometry and projective geometry. He first set up a problem in the form of an equation in a particular case, simple enough so that the analytic geometry of his time could deal with it. Then, through a transformation by reciprocal polars, he obtained the dual. In this respect he was a disciple of Gergonne.

Such a method was hardly suitable for treating metric proportion. In 1824 Poncelet presented to the Académie des Sciences a report in which he solved the difficulty by taking the sphere as the quadric of reference.[10] Since his report had not been published, he then, at Gergonne's insistence, gave a somewhat sybilline sketch of it in the *Annales.*[11] Upon reading this, Chasles and Bobillier rediscovered Poncelet's method; and Bobillier was first to publish it.[12]

In his course in geometry Bobillier was the very first to use transformation by reciprocal polars relative to a circle in order to provide an elementary study of conic sections. For a more sophisticated point of view of the same field, his following proposition may be cited: The polar circles of a fixed point of a conic section, relative to all the triangles inscribed in the curve, meet at the same point.[13]

Bobillier is best known, however, for his studies of successive polars of curves or algebraic surfaces, and for his abridged notation. He stated, following Monge, that the tangents drawn from a point to a plane curve of order m have their points of contact on a curve of order $m - 1$, which he called the polar of the point. He made analogous statements concerning space.

In a series of studies[14] Bobillier showed that the polars of collinear points have $(m - 1)^2$ points in common. The polars of a point relative to a linear pencil (an expression that came into use after his time) of curves of order m form a pencil of order $(m - 1)$. If the point describes a straight line, the $(m - 1)^2$ points at the base of this pencil describe a curve of order $2(m - 1)$.

In considering the successive polars of the same points that are of order $(m - 1)$, $(m - 2)$ $\cdots$ 1, one is led to the following theorem: The polar of order n of a point P is the locus of all points whose polars of order $(m - n)$ pass through P. Plücker agreed with Bobillier in stating this theorem, which he had mentioned to Gergonne without any proof.

In May 1828 there appeared in the *Annales* Bobillier's essay on a new mode of research on the properties of space.[15] The method of research that he expounded was, he stated, susceptible to various applications, which he hoped to publish in successive issues.

With A a linear function of two coordinates and a a constant, $A = 0$ is the equation of a straight line. $ABC = 0$ is the equation of the extensions of the sides of a triangle, known as the equation of the triangle; and $aBC + bCA + cAB = 0$ is the general equation of a conic section circumscribed about the triangle. Its tangents at the vertices are $bC + cB = 0$; $cA + aC = 0$; $aB + bA = 0$. In fact, the straight line $bC + cB = 0$ meets the conic only at the point $B = 0$, $C = 0$. The triangle circumscribed about the conic, the points of contact being the vertices of the first triangle, has for its "equation" $(bC + cB)(cA + aC)(aB + bA) = 0$. The straight line passing through the three points of intersection of the tangents with the corresponding sides of the original triangle is $bcA + caB + abC = 0$. The lines of junction of the corresponding vertices of the two triangles—$cB - bC = 0$; $aC - cA = 0$; $bA - aB = 0$—are concurrent. It is then a trivial matter to show that this point and this line are pole and polar of each other in relation to the conic section in question.

Bobillier showed by a similar and clever process that, in space, if a tetrahedron is inscribed in a quadric, then another tetrahedron can be circumscribed about the same quadric so that the points of contact of its faces are the vertices of the original tetrahedron. The oppositely placed faces of the two tetrahedrons cut each other in four lines, and their oppositely placed vertices are joined by four other lines. The straight lines of each group belong to the same quadric.

Aware of the value of his method, Bobillier applied it in the 1 June 1828 number of the *Annales* to some elementary geometric propositions.[16] In particular, he obtained from it the known proposition concerning the chords common to a circle and a conic section, and the theorems of Pascal and C. J. Brianchon. The efficacy of the method may be judged by these simple examples.

In statics, in which Bobillier was particularly concerned with catenaries, his report "De l'équilibre de la chaînette sur une surface courbe"[17] should be mentioned. This problem was taken over by F. Minding in 1835, by C. Gudermann in 1834 and 1846, by P. Appell in 1885, and by A. G. Greenhill in 1897. In spite of a few minor errors in computation, the work remains most elegant.

Bobillier's demonstration of the principle of virtual velocities[18] consisted in substituting "for any ordinary machine, whose character can be changed in an infinite number of ways, the winch, whose conditions of equilibrium are so well known and that, at least for the infinitely small deviation that we can estimate in its equilibrium, remains exactly the same." His method is extremely clever.

In kinematics there seem to be no known traces of the work Bobillier was doing toward the end of his life, although the passages in his book on geometry that treat this subject are still extant.[19] Two theorems and one problem are particularly in evidence: All movement of a triangle on a plane can be produced by rolling a certain line over another fixed line, the triangle being invariably linked to the first line. If a triangle, *abc*, moves in such a fashion that the sides *ab* and *ac* constantly touch two circles, the envelope of the third side is also a circle; and the centers of the three envelopes determine a new circle that includes all the instantaneous centers of rotation. Bobillier then went on to pose the problem of how to determine the corresponding center of curvature in the path of the third vertex, *c*, when given the centers of curvature at points *a* and *b* of the paths described by vertices *a* and *b* of triangle *abc*. The construction he gave of this center is known as the Bobillier construction.

NOTES

1. Obituary, in *Almanach du département de la Marne* (1841), pp. 316–320.
2. In vols. **17–20.**
3. Vol. **4** (1828).
4. "De la courbe nommée chaînette," 1831.
5. E.g., *Recueil des travaux de la Société d'agriculture, commerce, sciences et arts de la Marne:* "Notes sur les puits à bascule" (1826) and "Note sur le principe de Roberval" (1834).
6. From the obituary of 1841.
7. From the obituary. However, Bobillier notes this memoir in the 10th ed. of the *Géométrie,* p. 208.
8. Poncelet, *Applications d'analyse et de géométrie,* II, 486. Poncelet calls Bobillier "an intelligent and singularly active mind."
9. *Rapport sur les progrès de la géométrie,* pp. 65–68. "We owe remarkable researches to Bobillier, a distinguished geometer who gave hopes of great achievements for mathematical sciences, from which he was snatched in 1832 at the age of thirty-five."
10. See, e.g., *Applications,* p. 529.
11. Vol. **17,** pp. 265–272; see also vol. **18,** pp. 125–149.
12. *Annales,* **18,** pp. 185–202, "Démonstration de divers théorèmes de géométrie." "In writing the above article we have used only the contents of M. Poncelet's letter" (the letter in vol. **17**). On

p. 269 of vol. **18**, Chasles said: "It was only yesterday evening that your number of January 1828 reached me. I have read M. Bobillier's report with considerable eagerness . . . but I must say that the special case in which a sphere is taken . . . has come to me only through the reading of the analysis in the report" (report by Poncelet, vol. **17**, p. 265).
13. "Mémoire sur l'hyperbole équilatère."
14. *Annales*, vol. **18**, pp. 89, 157, 253; vol. **19**, pp. 106, 138, 302.
15. Vol. **18**, pp. 321-339.
16. "Philosophie mathématique. Démonstration nouvelle de quelques propriétés des lignes du second ordre."
17. *Annales*, vol. **20**, pp. 153-175.
18. *Ibid.*, pp. 285-288.
19. *Cours de géometrie*, 10th ed., pp. 204-208.

BIBLIOGRAPHY

I. Original Works. Among Bobillier's writings are "Notes sur les puits à bascule," in *Recueil des travaux de la société d'agriculture, commerce, sciences et arts de la Marne* (1826); material in *Correspondance mathématique et physique*, **4** (1828); "De la courbe nommée chaînette," in *Mémoires de l'Académie de Caen* (1831); "Note sur le principe de Roberval," in *Recueil des travaux . . .* (1834); *Cours de géométrie* (10th ed., Paris, 1850); and *Principes d'algèbre* (6th ed., Paris, 1865).

Many of his articles were published in the *Annales de mathématiques pures et appliquées:* "Démonstration de divers théorèmes de géométrie," **18**, 185-202; "En rédigeant l'article qu'on vient de lire . . . ," *ibid.*, 269; an article on polars of collinear points, *ibid.*, 89, 159, 253, and **19**, 106, 138, 302; an article on new methods of research on the properties of space, **18**, 321-339; "Philosophie mathématique. Démonstration nouvelle de quelques propriétés des lignes du second ordre," *ibid.*, 359-367; "Mémoire sur l'hyperbole équilatère," **19**, 349-359; "De l'équilibre de la chaînette sur une surface courbe," **20**, 153-175; and an article on the principle of virtual velocity, *ibid.*, 285-288.

II. Secondary Literature. Works providing more information on Bobillier and his accomplishments are Michel Chasles, *Rapport sur les progrès de la géométrie* (Paris, 1870), pp. 65-68, excellent from a mathematical standpoint; J. L. Coolidge, *A History of Geometrical Methods* (Oxford, 1940; New York, 1963), p. 143, which perpetuates Chasles's error on the date of Bobillier's death; and Poncelet's *Applications d'analyse et de géométrie* (Paris, 1864), II, 486, 529; and an article on the sphere as the quadric of reference, in *Annales de mathématiques pures et appliquées*, **17**, 265-272, and **18**, 125-149. There is an obituary of Bobillier in *Almanach du département de la Marne* (1841), 316-320.

J. Itard

BÔCHER, MAXIME (*b.* Boston, Massachusetts, 28 August 1867; *d.* Cambridge, Massachusetts, 12 September 1918)

Maxime Bôcher was the son of Ferdinand Bôcher, the first professor of modern languages at the Massachusetts Institute of Technology, and Caroline Little, of Boston. He entered Harvard in 1883, specializing in mathematics and natural science under W. E. Byerly, B. O. Peirce, and J. M. Peirce. He was elected to Phi Beta Kappa upon his graduation in 1888. Bôcher then went to Göttingen as a traveling fellow to audit the lectures of Felix Klein, Schönflies, Schur, Schwarz, and Voigt. Encouraged by Klein, he wrote a tract that won the prize in a competition sponsored by the Philosophical Faculty at Göttingen in 1891. It also served as his doctoral dissertation (1891), and was published as a book (1894) with an introduction by Klein.

In 1891 Bôcher returned to Harvard as an instructor in mathematics, and rose through the ranks to a professorship in 1904. In 1913 he was an exchange professor at the Sorbonne for a three-month period beginning in November.

He served the mathematical community unstintingly as a member of the editorial staff of the *Annals of Mathematics* in 1896-1900, 1901-1907, and 1911-1914; as vice-president, in 1902, and as president, in 1909 and 1910, of the American Mathematical Society; and as editor of the Society's *Transactions* in 1908, 1909, and 1911-1913. Under Klein's leadership as president of the International Commission on the Teaching of Mathematics, Bôcher served as chairman of the American Committee on Graduate Work in Universities, which published the report "Graduate Work in Mathematics in Universities and in Other Institutions of Like Grade in the United States" in the *Bulletin of the U.S. Bureau of Education*, no. 6 (1911). He was an invited speaker at the St. Louis Congress of Mathematicians in 1904 and at the Fifth International Congress of Mathematicians, Cambridge, England, in 1912, where his paper dealt with boundary problems in one dimension.

Bôcher was a prolific contributor to mathematical journals on the theory of differential equations and related questions. His research topics included systems of linear differential equations of the first order, singular points of functions satisfying partial differential equations of the elliptic type, exposition of the work of Jacques Sturm on algebraic and differential equations, boundary problems, and George Green's functions for linear differential and difference equations, and the theorems of oscillation of Sturm and Klein.

He was a member of the National Academy of Sciences and the American Philosophical Society, and was a fellow of the American Academy of Arts and Sciences.

BIBLIOGRAPHY

I. ORIGINAL WORKS. Bôcher's books are *Über die Reihenentwickelungen der Potentialtheorie* (Leipzig, 1894), his doctoral thesis; *Introduction to Higher Algebra* (New York, 1907); *An Introduction to the Study of Integral Equations,* Cambridge Tracts in Mathematics and Mathematical Physics, no. 10 (Cambridge, 1909); *Plane Analytic Geometry With Introductory Chapters on the Differential Calculus* (New York, 1915); *Trigonometry With the Theory and Use of Logarithms* (New York, 1915), written with H. D. Gaylord; *Leçons sur les méthodes de Sturm dans la théorie des équations différentielles linéaires et leurs développements modernes,* delivered at the Sorbonne in 1913–1914, G. Julia, ed. (Paris, 1916), in the Borel series.

His numerous papers are listed in Poggendorff, V, 129. A more complete list is found in G. D. Birkhoff, "The Scientific Work of Maxime Bôcher," in *Bulletin of the American Mathematical Society,* **25,** no. 5 (1919), 197–216.

II. SECONDARY LITERATURE. Further biographical detail may be found in W. F. Osgood, "The Life and Services of Maxime Bôcher," in *Bulletin of the American Mathematical Society,* **25,** no. 8 (1919), 337–350; in "Maxime Bôcher," in *Science,* n.s. **48,** no. 1248 (29 Nov. 1918), 534–535, repr. by the National Academy of Sciences in its *Annual Report* for 1918, pp. 49–50, and also by *The Harvard University Gazette* (22 Oct. 1918), p. 14; in the *Lebenslauf* in his doctoral thesis (gift copy presented by Bôcher to Widener Library, Harvard University, 19 Sept. 1891); in *Who's Who in Science* (1912), p. 53; in *American Men of Science* (1910), p. 47; and in the "Reports of Meetings," in *Bulletin of the American Mathematical Society,* **17** (1910–1911), 77, 277, 507.

CAROLYN EISELE

BOCHNER, SALOMON (*b.* Cracow, Austria-Hungary [now Poland]), 20 August 1899; *d.* Houston, Texas, 2 May 1982)

Bochner, a mathematician noted for the breadth and originality of his work in analysis, was born in a highly orthodox Jewish community. His father, Joseph, a small businessman, and his mother, Rude Haber, were self-educated beyond grade school but were both assiduous readers—she especially of Shakespeare and Ibsen, and he especially of works of Hebrew scholarship. Bochner had a younger sister, Fanny.

When a Russian invasion threatened in 1914, the family fled to Berlin. Although they were poorer after this move, young Salomon had much greater educational opportunities in the more liberal atmosphere of Berlin. He attended an outstanding gymnasium, brilliantly passing his entrance examinations only a few months after arriving in the city. He was strongly drawn to history and the humanities, but his mathematical talents had long been evident and the limited financial resources of his family impelled him to pursue a surer career in mathematics. He earned a Ph.D. from the University of Berlin in 1921, with a dissertation on orthogonal systems of complex analytic functions.

Inflation was then devastating Germany, so to help his family Bochner abandoned mathematics for a few years and went into the import-export business, in which he was successful but quite unhappy. His real interest was still mathematics; and at the urging and with the full support of his family, he returned to that field.

Bochner's dissertation topic had been treated independently by S. Bergman, so Bochner moved on to other topics. At that time Harald Bohr was developing the theory of almost periodic functions, which he described in short notes published in 1923. Bochner read these and was inspired to work out much of the theory on his own, in the process developing a highly original method of summation quite different from, and in some ways better than, that used by Bohr. This so impressed Bohr that he promptly invited the younger mathematician to visit Copenhagen. Bochner also discovered an alternative characterization of almost periodic functions in terms of the compactness of the sets of translates of the functions; this was the basis for future generalizations of the notion of almost periodicity by Bochner and others. From 1924 to 1926 Bochner was a fellow of the International Education Board, and in addition to Copenhagen he visited Oxford to work with G. H. Hardy and Cambridge to work with J. E. Littlewood. That led to an interest in yet another area, the theory of zeta functions and their functional equations, to which he would return later.

Bochner spent the years from 1926 to 1933 as a lecturer at the University of Munich. This was a very productive period, during which he began the research on Fourier analysis that was perhaps his greatest achievement. The culmination of this work at Munich was the publication in 1932 of *Vorlesungen über Fouriersche Integrale*, an influential book that has become a mathematical classic. Among much else the book contains Bochner's most famous theorem, characterizing the Fourier-Stieltjes transforms of positive measures as positive-definite functions; this result was the cornerstone of the subsequent development of abstract harmonic analysis. The book contained the seeds of what developed in other hands into the theory of distributions, another major mathematical tool.

In 1937 Bochner published his generalization of the Lebesgue integral to functions with values in an infinite-dimensional normed linear space, the

Bochner integral. In a quite different area, during his earlier years at Munich he studied the continuation of Riemann surfaces; his paper on that subject (1928) contained, incidentally, a result about mathematical logic that was discovered independently some seven years later by Max Zorn and is usually called Zorn's lemma. Bochner was an influential figure in Munich, not just among the mathematicians but also among the physicists. He published papers on X-ray crystallography with H. Seyfarth.

The rise of Nazism in Germany impelled Bochner to move in 1933, when he accepted a position at Princeton University. He became a naturalized citizen of the United States in 1938. Except for a visiting professorship at Harvard in the spring of 1947 and one at the University of California at Berkeley in the spring of 1953, he was away from Princeton only for brief trips and summers during the thirty-five years before his retirement. Until World War II broke out, he returned to Europe every summer to visit his family, to whom he was devoted. He urged them to move to England; and when they did so, he helped to arrange for his sister Fanny's children to attend good schools there. During one of these trips he met Naomi Weinberg, whose father was a New York real estate entrepreneur and founder (and for fifty years publisher) of the Jewish newspaper *The Day*. He and Naomi were married on 1 November 1938, with John von Neumann as best man. They had a daughter, Deborah.

Bochner was a major figure at Princeton and influential in the world of mathematics. During the 1930's a number of National Research Council fellows came to Princeton to work with him: Ralph Boas, R. H. Cameron, Norman Levinson, William T. Martin, and Angus Taylor, among others; K. Chandrasekharan and Kentaro Yano followed later. He had thirty-five doctoral students in a wide variety of fields, almost a quarter of the Ph.D.s in mathematics produced during his years on the Princeton faculty. When he was awarded the Leroy P. Steele Prize of the American Mathematical Society in 1979, he was cited for the cumulative impact of his mathematical work and for his influence on mathematics through his students. He was elected to the National Academy of Sciences in 1950 and served as vice-president of the American Mathematical Society from 1957 to 1958.

Bochner's research continued unabated at Princeton, in part as an extension of the work on almost periodic functions and Fourier analysis he had begun in Germany. He undertook the first profound investigation of the summation of Fourier series in several variables, discovering that Riemann's localization theorem, a basic result for Fourier series in one variable, fails in the case of several variables. John von Neumann had extended the theory of almost periodic functions to functions on arbitrary groups, and he and Bochner jointly extended the theory still further to functions with values in complete normed linear spaces. Bochner also introduced various generalized notions of almost periodicity.

With characteristic originality and facility Bochner extended his research in a number of new directions. In the late 1930's he began investigations in the theory of functions of several complex variables by determining the envelopes of holomorphy of tube domains. He continued in the 1940's by developing extensions of the Cauchy integral formula, including the Bochner-Martinelli formula that has been basic in the subject, and by using these formulas to characterize the boundary values of complex analytic functions. In this work, in the guise of conglomerate functions and their saltuses, there appeared the germ of the theory of cohomology groups with coefficients in holomorphic vector bundles, a theory that was extensively developed by others over the next quarter of a century as a basic tool in complex analysis. Bochner's outlook in this field was summarized in *Several Complex Variables* (1948), written with W. T. Martin. Also in the late 1930's Bochner began to work in differential geometry, showing that Riemann surfaces admit real-analytic embeddings into Euclidean spaces.

This research continued in the 1940's in joint work with Deane Montgomery, in which they proved that the group of holomorphic automorphisms of a compact complex manifold is a complex Lie group. At the Princeton Bicentennial Conference in 1946, Bochner presented a proof showing that the additive Cousin problem always has a solution on a compact Kähler manifold with positive Ricci curvature, thus inaugurating the theory of curvature and Betti numbers that he developed further in the 1940's and 1950's. This theory has been of fundamental importance, with a wide variety of applications—for instance, in the magisterial work of Kunihiko Kodaira characterizing algebraic manifolds as those complex manifolds that admit a Hodge metric. During the 1940's and 1950's Bochner also embarked on investigations in mathematical probability, summarized in his 1955 book *Harmonic Analysis and the Theory of Probability*. In addition he wrote a number of papers on partial differential equations, on zeta functions, and on gamma factors, among other topics.

In the mid 1960's Bochner turned in an altogether new direction, devoting himself wholeheartedly to the history and philosophy of science, particularly of mathematics. His books *The Role of Mathematics in the Rise of Science* (1966) and *Eclosion and Synthesis* (1969), as well as papers of that period, contain fascinating, idiosyncratic, and often provocative observations. They fuse his lifelong interest in history, literature, and philosophy, along with his undoubted gift for languages, with an understanding of mathematical creativity. He participated in the seminars of the history of science program at Princeton during this period, and was the only scientist member of the editorial board that supervised the publication of the five-volume *Dictionary of the History of Ideas*.

In 1968 Bochner retired from the Henry Burchard Fine professorship of mathematics at Princeton, which he had held since 1959, and moved to Rice University as the first Edgar Odell Lovett professor of mathematics. He was as influential at Rice as he had been at Princeton, if not more so, for he also served as chairman of the mathematics department there from 1969 to 1976 and took a great interest in developing the department. In addition to teaching mathematics he participated in the history of science program, was responsible for the foundation of an interdisciplinary institute for the history of ideas, and gave university-wide public lectures on the history of science. He died after a brief illness.

BIBLIOGRAPHY

I. Original Works. Many of Bochner's writings were collected in *Selected Papers of Salomon Bochner* (New York, 1969). His books include *Several Complex Variables* (Princeton, 1948), written with William T. Martin; *Fourier Transforms* (Princeton, 1949), written with K. Chandrasekharan; *Curvature and Betti Numbers* (Princeton, 1953), written with Kentaro Yano; *Harmonic Analysis and the Theory of Probability* (Berkeley, 1955); *Lectures on Fourier Integrals*, Morris Tenenbaum and Harry Pollard, trans. (Princeton, 1959); *The Role of Mathematics in the Rise of Science* (Princeton, 1966); and *Eclosion and Synthesis* (New York, 1969).

II. Secondary Literature. On Bochner's role in the "prehistory" of the theory of distributions, see J. Lutzen, *The Prehistory of the Theory of Distributions* (New York, 1982).

R. C. Gunning

BOETHIUS, ANICIUS MANLIUS SEVERINUS

(*b.* Rome [?], *ca.* 480; *d.* near Pavia, Italy, 524/525)

Very little is known of Boethius' life before his downfall, imprisonment, and execution (522–525). He belonged to one of the more eminent families of the Roman aristocracy, the Anicii, to which two emperors and perhaps also Pope Gregory the Great belonged. Manlius Boethius, consul for 487, may have been his father, and a prefect of the *praetorium* for 454 may have been his grandfather. Indirect evidence suggests an approximate date for Boethius' birth: he was younger than the writer Ennodius (*b.* 475), his distant relative and friend; he considered himself not old in 523; and he achieved public eminence in 510. His appointment to the honorific title of consul in 510, while he was writing a commentary on Aristotle's *Categories;* his presence in Rome in 522, when he delivered a speech in the Senate before King Theodoric, who had just made Boethius' two sons consuls; his imprisonment in or near Pavia in 522/523; and his death there two years later are well documented. All other chronological data are hypothetical, including his appointment to one of the highest offices in the Roman Gothic kingdom, the *magisterium officiorum,* which gave him some measure of control over state affairs.

For a long time it was taken for granted that Boethius studied in Athens because of a statement made in Theodoric's name by Cassiodorus that in fact suggests a contrary conclusion: "You [Boethius] have penetrated *from a distance* the schools of Athens" (italics author's).[1] Many now accept the view that he studied under Ammonius in Alexandria; the hypothesis is based on a vague possibility that a prefect of Alexandria *ca.* 476 named Boetios was Boethius' father and on the close connection of many passages in the two philosophers' works.[2] But common doctrines most often derive from common sources, and books travel more easily than men. There is no reason to believe that Boethius ever left Italy.

When still young Boethius lost his father, but acquired the powerful and inspiring protection of Q. Aurelius Memmius Symmachus, a member of an eminent Roman family that combined public authority with great culture. Symmachus may well have provided Boethius with his first knowledge of fourth-century Greco-Latin learning and with the encouragement to bring it up to date. Symmachus' daughter, Rusticiana, became Boethius' wife and bore him two sons, Boethius and Symmachus. Theodoric flattered him for his learning, and asked his advice when the king of France wanted a harper and when the king of Burgundy wanted a water clock and a sundial. Whether Theodoric appointed him to high office because of his special abilities or in order to strengthen his hold on the Roman nobility we cannot know; but he certainly did not take into account Boethius' solidarity with other members of the Senate and his attachment to the idea of the Roman Empire and Roman "freedom," nor did he realize that collaboration does not necessarily mean submission and renunciation. In 522, when Boethius defended Albinus against the charge of betraying the Gothic king for the Roman emperor, Theodoric took his revenge: he ordered Boethius' imprisonment and death.

Boethius left no perceptible mark on politics and statesmanship. His death inspired many to consider him a martyr,[3] but hagiography does not lead to proper appreciation of a man's work. On the other hand, centuries after his death Boethius was responsible for what he probably achieved in a very small measure during his lifetime: the spread of encyclopedic learning. He became the broadcaster of much Greek knowledge to many generations who used Latin and, through them, to many others. Several factors converged to produce this result: basic among them are the body of works that he translated, elaborated, or adapted from the Greek and his own writings, in which he probably exercised somewhat more independent judgment.

Here again we must be cautious. Much has been made of Boethius' grand plan to leave behind, in Latin, the achievements of the Greek past, but he did not outline any such plan. His interests were varied; he had some acquaintance with the general scheme of the lay encyclopedia of knowledge dominating the Greek schools and cultural life of his time, and with the new developments of Christian doctrine. However, for two areas of knowledge he outlined a vague scheme. The first was the basic doctrines of philosophy: "I shall translate and comment upon as many works by Aristotle and Plato as I can get hold of, and I shall try to show that their philosophies agree."[4] This echoes a plan first suggested by Plotinus' forerunner Ammonius Saccas and partly carried out by Plotinus' faithful pupil Porphyry. It is particularly important because it can be shown more than once that Boethius is repeating his source almost literally, even where the translation is disguised; and Porphyry was often his source. It must also be noted that Boethius speaks of writings of which he can "get hold," thus hinting that he was not working where works of Aristotle and Plato were easily obtained.

Another partial plan is suggested by the introductory section of Boethius' *Arithmetic,* dedicated to his father-in-law.[5] There he says that he intends to produce a handbook for each of the four mathematical disciplines—arithmetic, music, geometry, astronomy—which he calls the *quadrivium,* probably the first time this word was used. This led, by analogy, to the term *trivium* for the disciplines dealing with words instead of with numbers or magnitudes. Here again one ought to be cautious and not interpret the intention as a definite plan: the four disciplines were linked in the Greek tradition from which Boethius drew his material.[6] Nor should one be drawn by the flattering letter of Theodoric/Cassiodorus (*ca.* 507–513) into believing that what is written there described works already composed rather than Boethius' knowledge and an ability to discuss matters contained in Greek works.

We know too little about schools and intellectual life when Boethius was young to be able to infer what he learned from whom, or how and where he learned it. We can only try to find out from his works what may have contributed to their composition. The two elements that seem to emerge from such an inquiry are the Roman intellectual life of the latter fourth century and the Greek scholastic tradition as it appeared in the fifth century.

A few books, possibly very few, written in fourth-century Rome had come into Boethius' hands: books of logic or on the line between logic and rhetoric. He may have learned more from his father-in-law, one of whose ancestors had been a member of the learned circles of *ca.* 360–380. Representing that period in Boethius' works are Marius Victorinus, African and pagan by birth, Roman and Christian by adoption; Vettius Agorius Praetextatus, the leader of the pagan revival; Albinus; and Themistius, the eminent Greek rhetorician, philosopher, and teacher of many Romans, including Agorius, in Constantinople. Cicero should be added, because he was the great Roman of that period, master and inspirer of these revivalists.

Boethius possessed, at least in part, Victorinus' Latin adaptation of Porphyry's *Isagoge* and used it for his shorter commentary, in dialogue form, on this work. Victorinus may even have encouraged him to present as his original work what he was actually adapting from the Greek: Victorinus had done this in the *Isagoge* and Boethius did it in several of his "original" works of logic and, perhaps, of theology. Victorinus may also have been the source for other writings by Boethius, if we accept as authentic one of the two basic versions of Cassiodorus' *Institutiones:* there[7] Victorinus is credited with a translation of Aristotle's *Categories* and *De interpretatione,* commentaries on the *Categories* and Cicero's *Topica,* and a *De syllogismis hypotheticis.* In any case, Victorinus provided an example of how to spread Greek culture among Latin-speaking people.

Boethius may have known one work by Agorius Praetextatus: his Latin version of Themistius' paraphrase of Aristotle's *Analytics,* but he is rather ambiguous: he may simply have known that such a version existed. Of Albinus, Boethius knew that he had written something on logic. It may be suspected that Albinus was in fact responsible for the Latin version of Themistius' exposition of the *Categories,* which, from *ca.* 780, was ascribed to St. Augustine;[8] but Boethius was not familiar with it. The connection with Themistius appears to be indirect. Apart from Agorius' (and Albinus'?) dependence on Themistius, this idea seems to be confirmed by the place that Themistius' doctrines concerning the "topics," or types of logical and rhetorical arguments, have in Boethius' work; Themistius' classification of topics is discussed by Boethius as a parallel to Cicero's classification and analysis of them.

Greece and the Greek world still had active and organized centers of higher studies and well-stocked libraries. Boethius may never have gone near them, but he could try to obtain some of the books used there, most probably in Athens, by students and teachers. There is no mention in his works[9] of contemporary Greek scholars or philosophers, nor of those of the two or three previous generations. The most modern man he mentions is Proclus' teacher Syrianus (first half of the fifth century). More than once mention is made of Iamblichus, a Neoplatonist of the first half of the fourth century, whose intellectual legacy passed, after three generations, to Proclus, a Constantinopolitan who headed the Athenian school in the decades immediately preceding Boethius' birth. Recent studies have strengthened the hypothesis that the few books from which Boethius derived his knowledge of Greek philosophy and science came from Athenian circles.

When it is maintained, with a great wealth of quotations and parallel passages, that Boethius was a pupil of Ammonius,[10] master in Alexandria, nothing more is shown than that what Ammonius had learned from his masters in Athens, especially from Proclus, had also reached Boethius. The detailed analysis of the Porphyrian and Aristotelian commentaries of Boethius made by J. Shiel leaves little doubt that his conclusions are right: Boethius possessed one volume of the Greek *Organon,* in which the logical texts of Porphyry and Aristotle were surrounded by a rich collection of passages extracted from the main commentaries of the third and fourth centuries. All the quotations from and references to Porphyry, Iamblichus, Themistius, and Alexander of Aphrodisias are secondhand. Wherever it is possible to check, they are also found in the corresponding extant Greek commentaries. Even quotations from other works of Aristotle, not commented upon by Boethius, come from these selections of Greek commentaries.

In general, considering the nature of most of Boethius' writings, one would do well to discount even internal references to "past" works: some of these references may come from the original Greek works[11] or—as happens with many writers—may be expressions based on the author's wishful thought that, by the time one work is finished, others will also be completed, so that the reader will be able to take the whole series of works in a definite systematic order linked by cross-references. Consequently, it is reasonable to consider as works surely written by Boethius those which are extant and cannot easily be denied as his. Doubts still remain regarding the actual "Boethian" form of several of these works: double recensions suggest that early editors took more freedom than we should like in reshaping the works of the man they intended to glorify. This might even lead us to suggest that Boethius' name was soon added to works not his own, as was done in later times.

The existing works include a considerable body of logical writings: translations, commentaries, and independent treatises.[12] We still have the translations of (1) Porphyry's *Isagoge* (*ca.* 507), in two slightly different versions; (2) Aristotle's *Categories* (before 510), in one uniform, quite polished recension and in a mixture of parts of this recension with parts of a rougher rendering (perhaps Boethius' own, incompletely preserved); (3) Aristotle's *De interpretatione* (before 513), in three slightly different forms; (4) Aristotle's *Prior Analytics* (before 520), like the *Categories,* in one polished recension and in a mixture of parts of this with parts of a more primitive (perhaps Boethius' original) rendering; (5) Aristotle's *Topics* (before 520), in a uniform, unpolished edition and one small section from a more finished text; (6) Aristotle's *Sophistical Refutations* (before 520), in one recension (another existing recension is probably the result of the mixture of the usual recension by Boethius with some elements of a twelfth-century translation or revision by James of Venice). The suggestion that a Latin collection of passages from Greek commentaries on *Prior Analytics* was also translated by Boethius may have to be discarded, and there is only scanty evidence that he translated the *Posterior Analytics.* The translations, especially if one considers only the less finished recensions as undoubtedly authentic, suggest that Boethius' knowledge of Greek was by no means excellent.

The logical works commented upon by Boethius are (1, 2) Porphyry's *Isagoge:* one commentary (*ca.* 505), in the form of a dialogue, is based on some sections of Victorinus' adaptation, and another (*ca.* 508), in five books, is based on Boethius' own translation; (3) Aristotle's *Categories* (509–511), on the basis of Boethius' translation, with a second commentary perhaps intended but probably never written;[13] (4, 5) Aristotle's *De interpretatione* (513–516), a shorter commentary in two books and a longer one in six, both based on Boethius' translation; (6) Cicero's *Topics* (*ca.* 522), preserved incomplete, in seven books. A commentary on Aristotle's *Topics* is mentioned by Boethius, but it is not known whether it was ever written.

The "independent" logical works are (1) *On Categorical Syllogism* (*ca.* 505–506), in two books; (2) *On Division* (*ca.* 507); (3) *On Hypothetical Syllogisms* (*ca.* 518), in three books; (4) *Prolegomena* (*ca.* 523), known in the Middle Ages as *Antepraedicamenta* and, from 1492 on, as *Introductio in syllogismos categoricos;* and (5) *De differentiis topicis* (*ca.* 523). (*On Definitions,* a treatise ascribed to Boethius from the twelfth to the nineteenth centuries, is the work of Marius Victorinus. Small rhetorical treatises published as independent works are extracts or adaptations from the *De differentiis topicis.*)[14]

Two works by Boethius on disciplines of the *quadrivium* still exist: the *Arithmetic,* in two books, and the *Music,* in five. No agreement has been reached by scholars on the status of the various recensions of a *Geometry* that bear Boethius' name in many manuscripts and editions and were quoted as his for several centuries; it is quite possible that they include at least some sections originally written by him as translations of and adaptations from Euclid. None of the texts on astronomy that have been tentatively connected with Boethius can be ascribed to him unless new evidence comes to light.

Boethius' writings on theology are confined to two short pamphlets, *On the Trinity* and *On the Two Natures and One Person of Christ,* and the briefly argued answers to two questions, *Are "Father," "Son," "Holy Spirit" Predicated Substantially of "God"* and *How Can Substances Be Good in Virtue of Their Existence, Without Being "Goods" qua Substances* (*Quomodo Substantiae . . .,* often known as *De hebdomadibus*).[15]

All these writings are obviously didactic or scholastic. The same character is shared, but veiled in a literary form, by Boethius' one personal, original, and attractive work, the *Consolation of Philosophy* (523–524), written in verse and prose while he was awaiting execution.

Among the books most frequently—and erroneously—ascribed to him are Dominic González' (or Gundissalinus') *De unitate et uno* (twelfth century) and Thomas of Erfurt's *De disciplina scholarium* (thirteenth century). Translations from Aristotle (*Metaphysics, Ethics,* etc.) made in the twelfth century were occasionally attributed to Boethius from the twelfth to the sixteenth centuries; more persistent was the attribution, from 1510 to the early twentieth century, of the translation by James of Venice of the *Posterior Analytics* (*ca.* 1140).

Originality is rare in Boethius' works. Even where the sources of the doctrines expounded cannot be traced back exactly to a particular author, it can easily be assumed that he was following a definite model. It is also clear, especially in advanced logic, mathematics, and theology, that his preparation, and possibly his linguistic knowledge, was not sufficient for him to pass on all the best that was available to him. But, considering the enormous influence that his works exerted on the revival of learning from the late eighth to the thirteenth centuries, it is important to delineate the doctrines he expounded. We shall not include, however, those contained in those works of Aristotle that he translated.

Two points from the commentaries on Porphyry—which go back mainly to the commentaries of the Porphyrian school itself as it continued, particularly in Athens—deserve special mention. One concerns the Aristotelian divisions of philosophy, and more especially the general plan of logic.[16] Boethius' texts contributed more than anything else to popularization of those divisions. Philosophy, as the encyclopedia of knowledge, is divided into two parts: the theoretical (speculative) sciences and the practical sciences. The first is tripartite: it contains the sciences of nature that consider things material and changeable (physical sciences in a wide sense); those that consider the same things abstracted from movement and matter (mathematical, or "intelligible," sciences); and those that consider things immaterial and unchangeable ("theology" or, later, metaphysics). The second part contains the sciences that deal with action, in relation either to the individual (ethics), or to the family ("economics"), or to social life (politics). Logic is the science of persuasive argument, composed of several propositions; it is the science of syllogism in its general form, or in its applications in common discussion, or in its application to demonstration. This main part of logic must be preceded by a study of individual propositions, and this, in its turn, by the study of individual terms or classes of terms.

The other point concerns what came to be known as the problem of universals.[17] Porphyry had only mentioned its difficulties; Boethius treated some of them and suggested solutions. Especially important are his distinction between "things as they are" and "things as they are conceived" and his mention of the theory of *indifferentia,* a half-way solution that simultaneously allows for and denies the presence of, in things outside the mind, the common element that characterizes universality. This became the doctrine of one of the main schools of thought of the early twelfth century.

In the commentary to the *Categories,* derived largely from the two commentaries by Porphyry, one finds such statements as "A sign of continuity in a body is this: if one part of it is put in motion, the whole body is put in motion, and, if a body which is a whole is moved, at least other parts near those which are set in motion will be moved; as if I push a stick touching one extreme, the other parts of the stick will be moved as that extreme."[18] The commentaries on *De interpretatione* contain interesting analyses of the meanings of necessity[19] and—a source of interminable meditation and discussion—the different aspects of the so-called problem of future contingents:[20] Is a future event, which is not foreseeable on the basis of a known law of nature, such that a proposition describing it is bound to be true or false?

The *De divisione,* covering one of the main sections of logic as detailed by Porphyry at the beginning of the *Isagoge* and possibly based on a similar treatise of the Roman or Athenian school of the fourth or fifth century, contains a classification and partial analysis of the kinds of distinctions that must be considered when inquiring into one's subject matter. It propounds the elements for a methodical approach to scientific inquiry. Four kinds of "division" are listed: (1) division of a genus according to fundamental, substantial, different features and according to species, which are determined by at least some of these differences—this is indispensable for achieving satisfactory definitions; (2) division of a whole into its constituent parts, so that precision in accounting for the nature and structure of the whole may be attained; (3) "division of words," i.e., classification of the different meanings or functions of individual words, in order to avoid confusion and sophistry; and (4) "division of accidents," i.e., classification of some feature that may belong, but not essentially, to many different things or kinds of things (the blue of the sea, the blue of a wall, etc.), which will aid in understanding the relationship between accidental features and the essential nature of things.

The *Prolegomena* (*Introductio ad syllogismos categoricos*), which may go back, directly or indirectly, to a similar introduction by Porphyry and is mentioned by Boethius in his first commentary on the *Isagoge,*[21] restates and expands Aristotelian doctrines on noun and verb, but concentrates mainly on the relationships between propositions that are quantified in the subject and either positive or negative in the subject and/or the predicate. This is a later and more extensive treatment of what had appeared as the first book of *De syllogismis categoricis,* the second book of which is a rather poor synthesis, with the addition of a few mechanically constructed combinations, of the first part of Aristotle's *Prior Analytics.* This work most probably also reflects an elementary textbook of Porphyrian origin.

In *De syllogismis hypotheticis* the basic formulation of the Theophrastian syllogism ("If A then B; if B then C; therefore, if A then C") is played upon through a multiplication of formulas resulting from the insertion of the negative at different places in the premise. The importance of this is limited because A, B, C, must stand for nouns; thus, we fall directly back into the nonhypothetical syllogism. The Stoic hypothetical syllogism had its role in this work, as well as in the commentary on the *Topics* of Cicero, but with no original contribution. The one element that may be useful for an analysis of scientific method is the distinction between accidental connection or coincidence ("Fire being warm, the heavens are spherical") and natural connection ("There being man, there is animal" and, more compelling, "If the Earth comes in between, there follows an eclipse of the moon"), technically termed by Boethius *consequentia secundum accidens* and *consequentia naturae* (the latter being either *non per positionem terminorum* or *per positionem terminorum*).

The commentary on Cicero's *Topics* and the *De differentiis topicis* deal with the kinds of arguments used to persuade, either in a purely theoretical context or in a practical one, i.e., in dialectical or rhetorical arguments. The second work includes most that is important, from a methodological point of view, in the first. It is a systematic exposition of the nature of individual propositions (categorical and hypothetical), questions, theses, and rhetorical "hypotheses," and of connected propositions (such as syllogisms); and then of the headings under which arguments can be classified according to Themistius and Cicero. The importance of such a work lies mainly in its provision of the tools for a critical evaluation of arguments used in discussion and exposition of theories and facts. Thus, distinctions are made between arguments based on definitions, on descriptions, on similarities, on different interpretations of words, on assertions valid for whole classes (and therefore for subclasses), on regular causality, on contradiction, on authority, and on parallelism of situations.

The theological treatises must be considered here because of their role in training several generations, from the ninth century to the thirteenth, to apply the concepts developed by philosophy as a basis for clear thinking to fields where acceptance of dogmatic statement would have appeared more apposite. In *On the Trinity* and, within narrower limits, in the question on the predication of the three Persons to the subject "God," Boethius tries to explain the apparently absurd equation "one = three" by using the distinctions of Porphyry's (and Aristotle's) classes of predicates (genus, species, difference, accident, property) and the ten Aristotelian categories (substance, quantity, quality, relation, etc.). He was, of course, not the inventor of rational theology: *On the Trinity,* which reflects one of the revolutionary trends in Greek theology, is perhaps no more than a disguised translation. But his exposition of the problem and the attempt to locate the absurdity, or possibly the validity, of a statement within the intellectual framework of his time give him an eminent position in the progress toward clarity and exercise of critical power.

The short work on goodness of beings (*Quomodo substantiae. . .*) also claims more than an antiquarian interest. In this writing Boethius set out to solve an eminently nonmathematical problem with something of a mathematical method, and thereby, through many centuries, trained students to organize their thoughts and apply their powers of deduction: "Just as is the custom in mathematics and other disciplines, I begin with a series of definitions and axioms or postulates, from which all the rest will be derived."[22] The *Quomodo* is also important for the neat distinction between essence (*esse*) and existence (*quod est*), which may have a distant echo in the distinction between hypothesis and verification.

The treatise *Two Natures and One Person in Christ* provides us with, among other things, an analysis of the meanings that *natura* has in different contexts. The four meanings are set forth in these formulas: "Nature is to be found in things that can somehow be grasped by our mind"; "Nature (of substances) is what can bring about or be the recipient of an effect"; "Nature (of bodily substances) is the principle of movement per se, not accidentally"; and "Nature is the specific difference giving a definite thing its form." With the definition of *persona*—which became traditional in theology and is at the basis of most of our usages of "person"—Boethius also contributed to the establishment of the technical distinction between *personalis* and *confusa* in the context of the development of the medieval and modern theory of "supposition." For this second purpose, Boethius' definition ("Person is the individual substance of a rational nature") lost the connotation "rational," preserving above all the element of individuality.

The mathematical works by Boethius reproduced Greek works. Although it is not as clear as it has been thought, partly on the basis of what Boethius himself says, exactly which Greek works were reproduced,[23] it is clear that the neo-Pythagorean theory of number as the very divine essence of the world is the view around which the four sciences of the quadrivium are developed. Number, qua multitude considered in itself, is the subject matter of arithmetic; qua multitude applied to something else (relations between numbers?), the subject matter of music; qua magnitude without movement, of geometry; and qua magnitude with movement, of astronomy. The *Arithmetic* develops here and there what was too concise in Nicomachus and abbreviates what was too diffuse. Further, it passes on to the Latin reader many of the basic terms and concepts of arithmetical theory: prime and composite numbers, proportionality, *numeri figurati* (linear, triangular, etc.; pyramidal and other solid numbers), and ten different kinds of *medietates* (arithmetical, geometrical, harmonic, counterharmonic, etc.). His interest in proportions is perhaps connected with the story according to which, while in prison, he thought out a game based on number relations. Here it is noticeable, however, that his understanding of arithmetic, and possibly of Greek, was limited: the more advanced propositions and proofs in Nicomachus, such as the proposition that cubic numbers can be expressed as the successive sums of odd numbers and the proposition expressing the relation between triangular numbers and the polygonal numbers of polygons with *n* sides, are missing from the *Arithmetic.* He does not, however, miss such elementary things as the multiplication table up to ten.

The *Music* is a continuation of the *Arithmetic,* which contains several elements and terms more appropriate for the treatment of speculative, purely arithmetical music. But, before he comes to this, the very essence of the second science of the quadrivium, Boethius reminds us of the Platonic view that, unlike the other "mathematical sciences," which have only a theoretical value, music has a moral value as well. He also distinguishes the three kinds of music in which number relationships express themselves: the music of the universe (each of the heavens has its special chord), the music of human nature (which harmonizes man's bodily and psychic activities), and the music of some instruments. The third is the only one that, although deteriorated because of its involvement in matter, can be heard. Most of the book is devoted to a lengthy catalog of somewhat classified number relations, most of them with their technical terms and with some description of the nature of the sounds corresponding to them. But, music being considered as science, most of what the musicologist, the artistic composer, and the practicing player would consider essential to the understanding of what music is, is beyond Boethius' grasp.

Boethius' *Geometry,* which is mentioned in Cassiodorus' *Institutiones,* may well have been very different from any of the texts, varied in extent and, in many cases, with different contents, that appeared under his name during the Middle Ages. There is very little more of a geometrical nature in the most ancient manuscripts ascribed to Boethius than Euclid's definitions (from Book I) and some propositions (from Books III and IV) without the proofs. But, as part of the *Geometry,* there is the description of the abacus, the elementary computer based on a decimal system with the individual numbers classified under the headings *numeri incompositi*—the *digiti* (1-9) and the *articuli* (10, 20, · · ·, 100, etc.)—and *compositi* (11-19, 21-29, · · ·, 101-109, etc.), and there are rules for multiplication and division.

One additional contribution to mathematics that reached the Middle Ages through Boethius is in his commentaries to Porphyry (a sign that his knowledge of such matters is secondhand): the formula $\frac{n(n-1)}{2}$ for the number of possible combinations of two elements in a class of n elements.[24]

The *De consolatione philosophiae,* considered from the doctrinal point of view, is on the whole a restatement of the eclectic Neoplatonic cosmology. Three aspects may be usefully emphasized, because this book contributed in large measure to impressing them into the minds of philosophers and scientists, and of the world at large. (1) Independently of any revelation, the mind can achieve certainty about the existence of God, his goodness, and his power of ruling over the universe. (2) The universe is ordered according to unbroken chains of causes and effects, where necessity, under supervision and determination by God, would be apparent to an all-knowing mind and where chance is nothing more than the coincidental intersection of distinct lines of causation. (3) The order of the universe includes a descent from the first cause to the lowest effects and a return from the lowest ends to the highest beginning. Causality, in the more restricted modern sense, and teleology have preserved a stronger hold on the minds of many generations because of the enormous popularity, until the sixteenth century, of the *Consolatio.* But Boethius' insistence on the possibility of combining freedom of the will with God's eternally present knowledge of the order he willed engaged scholars in theological subtleties more than in a scientific approach to research or organization of knowledge.

NOTES

1. Cassiodorus, *Variae* I.45.3.
2. P. Courcelle, *Les lettres grecques,* p. 299, n. 1.
3. E.g., Dante, *Divine Comedy, Paradiso* X.124–129.
4. *Second Commentary on De interpretatione,* Meiser, ed., pp. 79–80.
5. *Arithmetic,* Friedlein, ed., p. 3.
6. See esp. Iamblichus' *Commentary on Nicomachus' Arithmetic,* E. Pistelli, ed. (Leipzig, 1894), pp. 5–8.
7. Cassiodorus, *Institutiones* I.iii.18, R. A. B. Mynors, ed. (Oxford, 1937), p. 128.
8. *Categoriae,* in *Aristoteles Latinus* I.1-5 (Bruges, 1961), p. lxxviii.
9. There is no foundation for the view held by Courcelle in *Les lettres grecques* (p. 278) that *audivimus* in Boethius' *Second Commentary,* Meiser, ed., p. 361, line 9, should be read "Ammonius."
10. Courcelle, pp. 270–277.
11. See J. Shiel, "Boethius' Commentaries on Aristotle," *passim.*
12. For the dates of the logical works I follow De Rijk, "On the Chronology." Some of the views I express here on the question of second recensions are at variance with hypotheses I put forward in the past.
13. But see P. Hadot, in *Archives d'histoire doctrinale et littéraire du moyen âge.*
14. A. Mai "discovered" these texts in MS Vat. lat. 8591; they are part of a collection of Boethian logical texts made in Constantinople *ca.* 530, of which many copies exist.
15. Views have been expressed by competent scholars both for and against the authenticity of a fifth theological text, the *De fide Catholica,* which seems to have intruded itself, anonymously, at some later stage into the collection of the other four. The arguments in favor seem unsatisfactory.
16. G. Schepss and S. Brandt, eds., pp. 7-10.
17. *Ibid.,* pp. 23–32, 159–167.
18. *Patrologia Latina,* LXIV, cols. 204–205.
19. E.g., in the *Second Commentary on the De interpretatione,* Meiser, ed., pp. 241 ff.
20. *Ibid.,* pp. 190–230.
21. Schepss and Brandt, p. 15.
22. H. F. Stewart and E. K. Rand, eds., p. 40.
23. Very close similarities can be noticed between Boethius and Nicomachus' commentator Iamblichus.
24. Schepss and Brandt, pp. 118–120, 319–321.

BIBLIOGRAPHY

I. ORIGINAL WORKS. The first ed. meant to contain all the works of Boethius was brought out by Iohannes and Gregorius de Gregoriis, with the scholarly collaboration of Nicolaus Iudecus (Venice, 1491–1492; repr. 1498–1499); it did not include the translations of *Prior Analytics, Topics,* and *Sophistical Refutations* but did contain the pseudepigrapha *On Definition, De unitate et uno,* and *De disciplina scholarium.* A complete ed. (Basel, 1546, 1570), with the pseudepigrapha and the non-Boethian translation of *Posterior Analytics* includes the translations missing from the Venice collection reproduced from a text rev. by Jacques Lefèvre d'Étaples (Paris, 1503), which was based on the Greek, under the supervision and with the collaboration of Heinrich Lorit; for the logical works (except the uncommented translations) and for the theological treatises this ed. depends on Giulio Marziano Rota's ed. (Venice,

1537). J. P. Migne, ed., *Patrologia Latina,* LXIII and LXIV, contains all the works of the 1570 ed., some of them from more recently published texts, and some fragments wrongly thought to be new discoveries. Both the Corpus Scriptorum Ecclesiasticorum Latinorum and the Corpus Christianorum include complete editions of Boethius in their plans. In Vol. 48 of the former (Vienna, 1906), G. Schepss and S. Brandt edited the two *Commentaries on Porphyry,* and in Vol. 67 (Vienna, 1934), W. (Guillelmus) Weinberg edited the *Consolatio philosophiae;* in Vol. 94 of the latter (Turnhout, Belgium, 1957), L. Bieler edited the *Consolatio.*

Critical editions of the translations are being done by L. Minio-Paluello, partly with the collaboration of B. G. Dod, as part of the *Aristoteles Latinus,* a section of the Corpus Philosophorum Medii Aevi (Bruges-Brussels-Paris): I, pts. 1-2, *Categoriae* (1961); III, pts. 1-2, *Analytica priora* (1962); II, pt. 1, *De interpretatione* (1965); I, pt. 6, Porphyry's *Isagoge* (1966); V, pts. 1-2, *Topica* (1969); and VI, pt. 1, *Elenchi sophistici* (in preparation).

Among the earliest eds. are *Consolatio philosophiae* (Savigliano, *ca.* 1471)—at least sixty-two Latin eds. of the work were printed before 1501; *Analytica priora* (Louvain, 1475); *Second Commentary on Porphyry, Commentary on Categories,* text of *De interpretatione* (Naples, *ca.* 1476); all the translations (Augsburg, 1479); *De differentiis topicis* and *In Ciceronis Topica commentarium* (Rome, 1484); *De institutione arithmetica* (Augsburg, 1488); *De Trinitate, Utrum Pater . . ., Quomodo substantiae* (Venice, 1489); and the doubtful *De fide Catholica* (Leiden, 1656).

Among the recent eds. not mentioned above, the following are important: *In Ciceronis Topica commentarium,* I. G. Baiter, ed., in Cicero's *Opera,* I. C. Orelli and I. G. Baiter, eds., I (Zurich, 1833)—this ed. also contains the short section discovered and published by C. B. Hase in *Johannis Laurentii Lydi, De ostentis* (Paris, 1823), pp. 341-356; *De institutione arithmetica, De institutione musica, Geometria,* G. Friedlein, ed. (Leipzig, 1867); *Opera theologica,* R. Peiper, ed. (Leipzig, 1871); *Commentaries on the De interpretatione,* C. Meiser, ed. (Leipzig, 1877-1880); *De divisione,* in an appendix to L. Davidson, *The Logic of Definition* (London, 1885); *The Theological Tractates,* with English translation by H. F. Stewart and E. K. Rand, and *The Consolation of Philosophy,* with English translation by I. T. [John Thorpe?], rev. by H. F. Stewart (London-Cambridge, Mass., 1936). A fragment, believed by the ed. to come from Boethius' *Second Commentary to the Categories,* was published by P. Hadot in *Archives d'histoire doctrinale et littéraire du moyen âge,* **34** (1960), 10-27.

II. Secondary Literature. Extensive bibliographies on Boethius can be found in L. Bieler's ed. of the *Consolatio* (see above), pp. xvi-xxvi; P. Courcelle, *Les lettres grecques en occident de Macrobe à Cassiodore,* 2nd ed. (Paris, 1948), pp. 401-415, and *La consolation de philosophie dans la tradition littéraire* (Paris, 1967), pp. 383-402 and, for the commentaries on the *Consolatio,* pp. 403-438; M. Cappuyns, "Boèce," in *Dictionnaire d'histoire et de géographie ecclésiastique,* IX (1937), cols. 349-380; B. Geyer, *Die patristische und scholastische Philosophie,* Vol. II of Friedrich Ueberweg's *Grundriss der Geschichte der Philosophie,* 11th ed. (Berlin, 1928), pp. 133, 669-670; C. Leonardi, L. Minio-Paluello, U. Pizzani, and P. Courcelle, "Boezio," in *Dizionario biografico degli italiani,* XII (in press); and A. Momigliano, "Cassiodorus and Italian Culture of His Time," in *Proceedings of the British Academy,* **41** (1955), 227-245.

Besides the above-mentioned works by Cappuyns, Courcelle (*Les lettres . . .*), and Momigliano, see the following on Boethius' life and work in general: H. M. Barrett, *Boethius, Some Aspects of His Times and Works* (Cambridge, 1940); M. Grabmann, *Geschichte der scholastischen Methode,* I (Freiburg, 1909), 148-177; M. Manitius, *Geschichte der lateinischen Literatur des Mittelalters,* I (Munich, 1911), 22-36; A. Momigliano, "Gli Anicii e la storiografia latina del VI secolo," in *Rendiconti dell'Accademia nazionale dei Lincei, classe scienze morali,* 8th ser., **9** (1956), 279-297; B. G. Picotti, "Il Senato Romano e il processo di Boezio," in *Archivio storico italiano,* 7th ser., **15** (1931), 205-228; E. K. Rand, *Founders of the Middle Ages* (Cambridge, Mass., 1928), pp. 135-180; and H. Usener, *Anecdoton Holderi* (Bonn, 1877).

On the influence of Boethius see R. Murari, *Dante e Boezio* (Bologna, 1905); and H. R. Patch, *The Tradition of Boethius: A Study of His Importance in Mediaeval Culture* (New York-Oxford, 1935).

On Boethius' logical works (sources, chronology, translations, theories, influences) see L. Bidez, "Boèce et Porphyre," in *Revue belge de philologie et d'histoire,* **2** (1923), 189 ff.; I. M. Bocheński, *Formale Logik* (Freiburg-Munich, 1956), translated by I. Thomas (Notre Dame, Ind., 1961); L. M. De Rijk, "On the Chronology of Boethius's Works on Logic," in *Vivarium,* **2** (1964), 1-49, 125-162, which supersedes all previous studies on the subject; K. Dürr, *The Propositional Logic of Boethius* (Amsterdam, 1951); W. Kneale and M. Kneale, *The Development of Logic,* (Oxford, 1962), pp. 189-198; L. Minio-Paluello, "Iacobus Veneticus Grecus, Canonist and Translator of Aristotle," in *Traditio,* **8** (1952), 265-304, and "Les traductions et les commentaires aristotéliciens de Boèce," in *Texte und Untersuchungen zur Geschichte der altchristlichen Literatur,* Vol. 64 of Studia Patristica (1957), pp. 358-365; C. Prantl, *Geschichte der Logik im Abendlande,* I (Leipzig, 1855; repr. Graz, 1955), 679-721; A. N. Prior, "The Logic of Negative Terms in Boethius," in *Franciscan Studies,* **13** (1953), 1-6; J. Shiel, "Boethius' Commentaries on Aristotle," in *Mediaeval and Renaissance Studies,* **4** (1958), 217-244; and A. Van de Vyver, "Les étapes du développement philosophique du haut moyen âge," in *Revue belge de philologie et d'histoire,* **8** (1929), 425-452.

Also see the prefaces to Minio-Paluello's eds. of Boethius' works listed above; however, some of the views expressed in this article are new, and will be discussed in future writings. The previous literature on the authorship of the translations is discussed in full in these prefaces.

For the theological treatises see, besides Usener's *Anecdoton Holderi,* V. Schurr, *Die Trinitätslehre des Boethius im Lichte der skytischen Kontroversen* (Paderborn,

1935). The latest discussion of the authenticity of *De fide Catholica,* with references to the previous works on the subject, is W. Bark, "Boethius's Fourth Tractate: The So-called 'De Fide Catholica,'" in *Harvard Theological Review,* **59** (1946), 55–69. For the influence of the treatises in the Middle Ages, see M. Grabmann, *Die theologische Erkenntnis- und Einleitungslehre des heiligen Thomas auf Grund seiner Schrift In Boethium De Trinitate* (Fribourg, 1948); and N. M. Haring's editions of *A Commentary on Boethius' De hebdomadibus by Clarenbaldus of Arras* and *The Commentaries of Gilbert, Bishop of Poitiers on the Two Boethian Opuscula Sacra on the Holy Trinity,* in *Nine Mediaeval Texts,* Vol. I of Studies and Texts, published by the Pontifical Institute of Mediaeval Studies (Toronto, 1955), pp. 1-96.

On the mathematical works, including the *De musica,* see M. Cantor, *Vorlesungen über Geschichte der Mathematik,* 3rd ed., I (Leipzig, 1907), 573-585, which contains references to previous works, especially Friedlein's; J. L. Heiberg, in *Philologus,* **43,** 507–519; F. T. Koppen, "Notiz über die Zahlwörter im Abacus des Boethius," in *Bulletin de l'Académie des sciences de St. Pétersbourg,* **35** (1892), 31–48; O. Paul, *Boethius, fünf Bücher über die Musik aus dem lateinischen . . . übertiagen und . . . sachlich erklärt* (Leipzig, 1872); G. Pietzsch, *Die Klassifikation der Musik von Boetius bis Ugolino von Orvieto* (Halle, 1929); U. Pizzani, "Studi sulle fonti del *De institutione musica* di Boezio," in *Sacris erudiri,* **16** (1965), 5-164; H. Potiron, *Boèce théoricien de la musique grecque* (Paris, 1961); P. Tannery, "Notes sur la pseudo-géométrie de Boèce," in *Bibliotheca mathematica,* **3** (1900), 39-50; and R. Wagner, "Boethius," in *Die Musik in Geschichte und Gegenwart,* II (Kassel-Basel, 1952), cols. 49-57.

All the relevant bibliography for the *De consolatione,* its sources, doctrines, diffusion, and influence, is in the edition by Bieler and in Courcelle's *La consolation.*

A good source for recent bibliography is Menso Folkerts' critical edition of the two-book version of Boethius' *Geometry, Boethius Geometrie II: Ein mathematisches Lehrbuch des Mittelalters* (Göttingen, 1967), doctoral dissertation.

LORENZO MINIO-PALUELLO

BOHL, PIERS (*b.* Walka, Livonia [now Latvian S.S.R.], 23 October 1865; *d.* Riga, Latvia, 25 December 1921)

The son of George Bohl, a merchant, Piers Bohl first studied in his native city and then at a German Gymnasium in Viljandi, Estonia. In 1884 he entered the department of physics and mathematics at the University of Dorpat, Estonia, from which he graduated in 1887 with a candidate's degree in mathematics (equivalent to a master's degree in the United States), having won a gold medal for a competitive essay on the theory of invariants of linear differential equations (1886). Bohl defended dissertations in applied mathematics for his master's degree in 1893 (equivalent to a doctorate in the United States) and for his doctorate in 1900. (The doctorate, a degree that can be gained only after the candidate has done outstanding work in his chosen field, allows the holder to be called professor.) He received both of these advanced degrees from Dorpat. From 1895 Bohl taught at Riga Polytechnic Institute (from 1900 with the rank of professor); and when the institute was evacuated to Moscow at the beginning of World War I, he accompanied it. He returned to Riga in 1919 and was appointed professor at the University of Latvia, which had been founded that year. Two years later he died of a cerebral hemorrhage.

In his master's dissertation, Bohl was the first to introduce and to study that class of functions (more general than ordinary periodic functions) which in 1903 were named quasi-periodic by the French mathematician E. Esclangon, who discovered them later than, but independently of, Bohl. Finite sums of periodic functions with, generally speaking, incommensurable periods (of the type $\sin x + \sin \sqrt{2}x + \sin \sqrt{3}x$) are an example. Harald Bohr's concept of almost-periodic functions is the further generalization of this class.

In his doctoral dissertation, Bohl, following Henri Poincaré and A. Kneser, presented a new development of topological methods of systems of differential equations of the first order. To the investigation of the existence and properties of the integrals of these systems, he applied a series of theorems, which he developed and proved, concerning points that remain fixed for continuous mappings of n-dimensional sets of points. L. Brouwer's famous theorem on the existence of a fixed point under the condition of the mapping of a sphere onto itself is easily obtained as a consequence of one of the propositions completely demonstrated in Bohl's "Über die Bewegung. . . ." Bohl's topological theorems did not, however, attract the attention of contemporary mathematicians.

Studying one problem of the theory of secular perturbations (1909), Bohl encountered the question of the uniform distribution of the fractional parts of functions satisfying certain conditions. The theorem he developed was also developed independently by H. Weyl and W. Sierpinski; it was generalized by Weyl in 1916. Later the theory of the distribution of fractional parts of functions became a large part of number theory.

BIBLIOGRAPHY

I. ORIGINAL WORKS. For Bohl's early work, see *Theorie und Anwendung der Invarianten der linearen Differential-*

gleichungen (Dorpat, 1886), which manuscript is in the Historical Archive of the Estonian S. S. R., Tartu; and *Über die Darstellung von Funktionen einer Variablen durch trigonometrische Reihen mit mehreren einer Variablen proportionalen Argumenten* (Dorpat, 1893), his master's dissertation. His doctoral dissertation, "O Nekotorykh Differentsialnykh Uravneniakh Obshchego Kharaktera, Primenimykh v Mekhanike" ("On Some Differential Equations of a General Character, Applicable in Mechanics;" Yurev, 1900), is also available in French as "Sur certaines équations différentielles d'un type général utilisables en mécanique," in *Bulletin de la Société mathématique de France,* **38** (1910), 1-134. See also "Über die Bewegung eines mechanischen Systems in der Nähe einer Gleichgewichtslage," in *Journal für reine und angewandte Mathematik,* **127** (1904), 179-276; and "Über ein in der Theorie der säkularen Störungen vorkommendes Problem," *ibid.,* **135** (1909), 189-283.

II. SECONDARY LITERATURE. For further information on Bohl, see A. Kneser and A. Meder, "Piers Bohl zum Gedächtnis," in *Jahresbericht der Deutschen Mathematiker-vereinigung,* **33** (1925), 25-32. A complete bibliography of Bohl's work and of literature devoted to him appears in A. D. Myshkis and I. M. Rabinovich, eds., *P. G. Bohl. Izbrannye Trudy* ("P. G. Bohl, Selected Works"; Riga, 1961), biography and analysis of scientific activity, pp. 5-29.

A. P. YOUSCHKEVITCH

BOHR, HARALD (*b.* Copenhagen, Denmark, 22 April 1887; *d.* Copenhagen, 22 January 1951)

Bohr's father was the distinguished physiologist Christian Bohr; his mother, a daughter of the prominent financier, politician, and philanthropist D. B. Adler. In the home he and his elder brother Niels imbibed a deep love of science. At the age of seventeen Bohr entered the University of Copenhagen. Of his teachers, he felt the closest kinship to H. G. Zeuthen, but the most decisive factor in his development as a mathematician was his study of Jordan's *Cours d'analyse* and Dirichlet's *Vorlesungen über Zahlentheorie* with Dedekind's supplements. In his later student years, his interests centered on analysis. After his master's examination he went to study with Landau in Göttingen. This center of mathematics became like a second home to Bohr, and he returned there often. During the years before World War I, he also came into close contact with Hardy and Littlewood, and he often went to Cambridge and Oxford to study.

After obtaining his doctor's degree in 1910, Bohr joined the faculty of the University of Copenhagen. In 1915 he was appointed professor at the College of Technology, a position he retained until returning in 1930 to the University of Copenhagen, where he headed the newly founded Institute of Mathematics. Bohr was one of the leading analysts of his time, and he exerted an extraordinary influence both in international mathematical circles and in the academic life of his own country. As a teacher he was greatly admired and loved. When the rise of Nazism in Germany in 1933 endangered the academic community, among others, Bohr was among the first to offer help. His close personal relations with colleagues in many countries enabled him to help in finding new homes for those scientists who were either forced to leave Germany or who chose to do so, and he turned all his energies to this task. He himself did not escape exile in the latter part of World War II, when he was compelled to take refuge in Sweden.

Bohr's contribution to mathematics is one of great unity. His first comprehensive investigation, which formed the subject of his doctor's thesis, was concerned with the application of Cesàro summability to Dirichlet series. In a number of later papers he studied other aspects of the theory of Dirichlet series, in particular the distribution of the values of functions represented by such series. His method consists in a combination of arithmetic, geometric, and function-theoretic considerations. His collaboration with Landau was concentrated mainly on the theory of the Riemann zeta-function. It culminated in the so-called Bohr-Landau theorem (1914), concerning the distribution of its zeros. In later papers Bohr gave a detailed study of the distribution of its values in the half plane to the right of the critical line.

The problem of which functions may be represented by Dirichlet series led Bohr to his main achievement, the theory of almost periodic functions, on which the greater part of his later work is concentrated. If a Dirichlet series is considered on a vertical line in the complex plane, it reduces to a trigonometric series. It was therefore natural to consider more generally the problem of which functions of a real variable can be represented by such a series, i.e., can be formed by superposition of pure oscillations. In the special case where the frequencies of the oscillations are integers, the answer is given in the classical theory of Fourier series of periodic functions. Whereas hitherto in the theory of Dirichlet series one had always worked with frequencies forming a monotonic sequence, Bohr discovered that in order to obtain an answer to the problem one would have to consider series with quite arbitrary frequencies. The answer was obtained by introducing the notion of almost periodicity. The theory was published in three papers in *Acta mathematica* (1924-1926), and numerous mathematicians joined in the work on its simplification and extension. Thus Weyl and Wiener connected it with the classical theories of integral equations and Fourier integrals, and Bochner developed a summation method for Bohr-Fourier series generalizing Fejér's theorem. Stepanoff, Wiener, and Besicovitch studied generalizations depending on the Lebesgue integral. Other aspects of the theory were studied by Favard, Wintner, and many others. In the 1930's Von Neumann succeeded in extending the theory to functions on arbitrary groups, and it thus found a central place in contemporary mathematics.

BIBLIOGRAPHY

Bohr's *Collected Mathematical Works,* 3 vols. (Copenhagen, 1952), contain all his mathematical writings, with the exception of elementary articles and textbooks in Danish. An English translation of an autobiographical lecture appears as a preface to this edition.

Obituaries of Bohr include those by S. Bochner, in *Bulletin of the American Mathematical Society,* **58** (1952), 72–75; B. Jessen, in *Acta mathematica,* **86** (1951), i–xxiii, repr. as supp. S. 25 in Bohr's *Collected Mathematical Works,* III, supp. 163–176; O. Neugebauer, in *Year Book 1952 of the American Philosophical Society* (1953), pp. 307–311; N. E. Nørlund, in *Oversigt over det Kongelige Danske Videnskabernes Selskabs Virksomhed, 1950–1951* (1951), pp. 61–67, in Danish; O. Perron, in *Jahresbericht der Deutschen Mathematiker-vereinigung,* **55** (1952), pt. 1, 77–88; and E. C. Titchmarsh, in *Journal of the London Mathematical Society,* **28** (1953), 113–115.

BØRGE JESSEN

BOLYAI, FARKAS (WOLFGANG) (*b.* 9 February 1775, Bolya [German, Bell], near Nagyszeven [German, Hermannstadt], Transylvania, Hungary [now Sibiu, Rumania]; *d.* 20 November 1856, Marosvásárhely, Transylvania, Hungary [now Târgu-Mureş, Rumania])

Farkas Bolyai was the son of Gáspár (Kasper) Bolyai and Christina Vajna (von Páva) Bolyai. Bolya was the hereditary estate of the noble family of Bolyai de Bolya, which was mentioned as early as the thirteenth and fourteenth centuries. By the time of Gáspár it had been reduced to a small holding, but Gáspár added another holding (which belonged to his wife's family) in Domáld, near Marosvásárhely. He enjoyed a reputation as an industrious and intelligent landholder of strong character.

Young Farkas received an education at the Evangelical-Reformed College in Nagyszeven, where he stayed from 1781 to 1796. He excelled in many fields, especially in mathematics, and showed interest in theology, painting, and the stage. In 1796, he traveled to Germany, going first to Jena and then, with a fellow student at Nagyszeven, Baron Simon Kemény, entered the University of Göttingen, where he studied until 1799. Among his teachers were the astronomer Felix Seyffer and the mathematician Abraham Gotthelf Kästner. It was at this time that Bolyai began his lifelong friendship with Carl Friedrich Gauss, also a student at Göttingen, who already was intensely engaged in mathematical research. From this period dates Bolyai's interest in the foundations of geometry, especially in the so-called Euclidean or parallel axiom, to which Kästner and Seyffer, as well as Gauss, were devoting attention. Bolyai maintained a correspondence with Gauss that, with interruptions, lasted all their lives.

After his return to Transylvania, Bolyai became a superintendent in the house of the Keménys in Koloszvár (German, Klausenburg; now Cluj, Rumania). In 1801 he married Susanna von Árkos, the daughter of a surgeon. His wife was talented but sickly and nervous, and the marriage was not a happy one. The couple settled in Domáld, where Bolyai farmed from 1801 to 1804. In 1802 their son, János, was born, at the von Árkos home in Koloszvár.

In 1804, Farkas accepted the position of professor of mathematics, physics, and chemistry at the Evangelical-Reformed College at Marosvásárhely, where he taught until his retirement in 1853. During this half century he was known as a patient and kind teacher, but one who lacked the faculty of easily transmitting to others his own scientific enthusiasm, despite the emphasis he placed on correct mathematical education. Meanwhile, he continued his research, concentrating on the theory of parallels. He sent a manuscript on this subject, *Theoria parallelarum,* with an attempt to prove the Euclidean axiom, to Gauss in 1804. The reasoning, however, satisfied neither Gauss nor himself; and Bolyai continued to work on it and on the foundations of mathematics in general.

The Euclidean axiom, which appears as the fifth postulate in Book I of Euclid's *Elements,* is equivalent to the statement that through a given point outside a given line only one parallel can be drawn to the line. It is also equivalent to the statement that there exists a triangle in which the sum of the three angles is equal to two right angles and, hence, that all triangles have this property. Attempts to prove this axiom—that is, to deduce it from other, more obvious, assumptions—began in antiquity. These attempts were always unsatisfactory, however, and the nature of the axiom had remained a challenge to mathematicians. Bolyai, working in almost total scientific isolation, often despaired while trying to understand it.

During such moments of discouragement, he sought consolation in poetry, music, and writing for the stage. In 1817, his *Ot Szomorujátek, Irta egy Hazafi* ("Five Tragedies, Written by a Patriot") was entered in a contest. The following year, another play, *A Párisi Par* ("The Paris Process"), appeared. Bolyai's wife died in 1821, and in 1824 he married Theresia Nagy, the daughter of an iron merchant in Marosvásárhely. They had one son, Gregor.

Farkas began to interest himself in mathematics again when his son János evinced unusual mathematical talent. In 1829 Bolyai finished his principal work, but because of technical and financial problems it was not published until 1832–1833. It appeared in two volumes, with the title *Tentamen juventutem studiosam in elementa matheseos purae, elementaris ac sublimioris, methodo intuitiva, evidentiaque huic propria, introducendi, cum appendice triplici* ("An Attempt to Introduce Studious Youth Into the Elements of Pure Mathematics, by an Intuitive Method and Appropriate Evidence, With a Threefold Appendix"). While writing the *Tentamen,* Bolyai had his first difficulties with his son János. In spite of warnings from his father to avoid any preoccupation with Euclid's axiom, János not only insisted on studying the theory of parallels, but also developed an entirely unorthodox system of geometry based on the rejection of the parallel axiom, something with which his father could not agree. However, despite misgivings, Bolyai added his son's paper to the first volume and thus, unwittingly, gave it immortality. In 1834, a Hungarian version of Volume I was published.

The *Tentamen* itself, the fundamental ideas of which may date back to Bolyai's Göttingen days, is an attempt at a rigorous and systematic foundation of geometry (Volume I) and of arithmetic, algebra, and analysis (Volume II). The huge work shows the critical spirit of a man who recognized, as did few of his contemporaries, many weaknesses in the mathematics of his day, but was not able to reach a fully satisfactory solution of them. Nevertheless, when it is remembered that Bolyai worked in almost total isolation, the *Tentamen* is a most remarkable witness to the sharpness of his mind and to his perseverance. In many respects, he can be taken as a precursor of Gottlob Frege, Pasch, and Georg Cantor; but, as with many pioneers, he did not enjoy the credit that accrued to those who followed him.

The *Tentamen* was almost totally unappreciated by Bolyai's contemporaries, although Gauss expressed his pleasure at finding "everywhere thoroughness and independence." Disappointed and again a widower, the sensitive man found little consolation in the equally disappointed János, who after his retirement from military service had come to live in Marosvásárhely. The two men often clashed. In 1837 both entered a contest on complex numbers sponsored by the Jablonow Society in Leipzig. The elder Bolyai's contribution was taken essentially from his *Tentamen.* When no prize was awarded to either of them, their disillusionment grew; but whereas the son sank more and more into melancholy, the father—poetic, musical, and venerable—remained an outstanding, although somewhat eccentric, citizen of the provincial town, who was often consulted on technical questions. Both men also wrote much on a theory of salvation for mankind, and both returned occasionally to mathematics. Besides some elementary books, Bolyai published a summary of his *Tentamen* in German as *Kurzer Grundriss eines Versuches* (1851); after retiring from college teaching, and after having heard of Gauss's death, he wrote *Abschied von der Erde.* He died after suffering several strokes.

BIBLIOGRAPHY

I. Original Works. Among Bolyai's works are *Az arithmetica Eleje* ("Elements of Arithmetic," Marosvásárhely, 1830); *Ürtan elemei kerdóknek* ("Elements of the Theory of Space for Beginners," Marosvásárhely, 1850–1851); and *Kurzer Grundriss eines Versuches* (Marosvásárhely, 1851). His major work, the *Tentamen,* was published in Latin in 2 vols. (Marosvásárhely, 1832–1833); 2nd ed., Vol. I (Budapest, 1897), Vol. II (Budapest, 1904), with an additional volume of figures.

II. Secondary Literature. For information on Bolyai, see P. Stäckel, *W. und J. Bolyai, Geometrische Untersuchungen,* 2 vols. (Leipzig, 1913): the first volume is biographical; the second contains German translations of the theory of parallels of 1804, parts of the *Tentamen,* and the *Kurzer . . . Versuches.* The correspondence between Bolyai and Gauss is found in *Briefwechsel zwischen C. F. Gauss und W. Bolyai* (Leipzig, 1899). Further biographical material may be found in L. David, *A két Bólyai élete és munkássága* ("Life and Work of the Two Bolyais," Budapest, 1923) and "Die beiden Bolyai," supp. to *Elemente der Mathematik,* no. 11 (1951). A memorial work, *Bolyai Farkas 1856–1956,* was published in Târgu-Mureş in 1957. A stage play by Lászlo Németh, "A két Bólyai" ("The Two Bolyais") was first produced in 1962, and is collected in the author's *Változatok egy témara* (Budapest, 1961). See also K. R. Biermann, "Ein Brief von Wolfgang Bolyai," in *Mathematische Nachrichten,* **32** (1966), 341–346.

D. Struik

BOLYAI, JÁNOS (JOHANN) (*b.* 15 December 1802, Koloszvár [German, Klausenburg], Transylvania, Hungary [now Cluj, Rumania]; *d.* 27 January 1860, Marosvásárhely, Hungary [now Târgu-Mureş, Rumania])

The son of Farkas (Wolfgang) Bolyai and Susanna von Árkos Bolyai, János Bolyai received his early education in Marosvásárhely, where his father was professor of mathematics, physics, and chemistry at Evangelical-Reformed College. The precocious lad was first taught by his father and showed early proficiency not only in mathematics but also in other fields, such as music. He mastered the violin at an early age. From 1815 to 1818, he studied at the college where his father taught. The elder Bolyai had hopes that the son would go on to Göttingen to study with his friend Gauss, but he did not. In 1818 János entered the imperial engineering academy in Vienna, where he received a military education; he remained there until 1822.

From his father, János had inherited an interest in the theory of parallels; but in 1820 his father warned him against trying to prove the Euclidean axiom that there can be only one parallel to a line through a point outside of it:

> You should not tempt the parallels in this way, I know this way until its end—I also have measured this bottomless night, I have lost in it every light, every joy of my life— . . . You should shy away from it as if from lewd intercourse, it can deprive you of all your leisure, your health, your peace of mind and your entire happiness.—This infinite darkness might perhaps absorb a thousand giant Newtonian towers, it will never be light on earth, and the miserable human race will never have something absolutely pure, not even geometry . . . [Stäckel, pp. 76–77].

In the same year, however, János began to think in a direction that led him ultimately to a non-Euclidean geometry. He profited by conversations with Karl Szász, governor in the house of Count Alexis Teleki. In 1823, after vain attempts to prove the Euclidean axiom, he found his way by assuming that a geometry can be constructed without the parallel axiom; and he began to construct such a geometry. "From nothing I have created another entirely new world," he jubilantly wrote his father in a letter of 3 November 1823. By this time János had finished his courses at the academy and had entered upon a military career, beginning as a sublieutenant. His duties took him first to Temesvár (now Timişoara, Rumania), in 1823–1826, then to Arad (Rumania), in 1826–1830, and finally to Lemberg (now Lvov, W. Ukraine), where in 1832 he was promoted to lieutenant second class. During his military service, he was often plagued with intermittent fever, but he built up a reputation as a dashing officer who dueled readily. In 1833 he was pensioned off as a semi-invalid, and he returned to his father's home in Marosvásárhely.

While visiting his father in February 1825, János had shown him a manuscript that contained his theory of absolute space, that is, a space in which, in a plane through a point P and a line l not through P there exists a pencil of lines through P which does not intersect l. When this pencil reduces to one line, the space satisfies the Euclidean axiom. Farkas Bolyai could not accept this geometry, mainly because it depended on an arbitrary constant, but he finally decided to send his son's manuscript to Gauss. The first letter (20 June 1831) went unanswered, but Gauss did answer a second letter (16 January 1832). In this famous reply, dated 6 March 1832 and directed to his "old, unforgettable friend," Gauss said:

> Now something about the work of your son. You will probably be shocked for a moment when I begin by saying *that I cannot praise it,* but I cannot do anything else, since to praise it would be to praise myself. The whole content of the paper, the path that your son has taken, and the results to which he has been led, agree almost everywhere with my own meditations, which have occupied me in part already for 30–35 years. Indeed, I am extremely astonished. . . .

Further on, after mentioning that there had been a time when he had been inclined to write such a paper himself, Gauss continued, "Hence I am quite amazed, that now I have been saved the trouble, and I am very glad indeed that it is exactly the son of my ancient friend who has preceded me in such a remarkable way." Gauss ended with some minor remarks, among them a challenge to János to determine, in his geometry, the volume of a tetrahedron, and a critique of Kant's theory of space.

It is now known from Gauss's diaries and from some of his letters that he was not exaggerating; but for János the letter was a terrible blow, since it robbed him of the priority. Even after he became convinced that Gauss spoke the truth, he felt that Gauss had done wrong in remaining silent about his discovery. Nevertheless, he allowed his father to publish his manuscript, which appeared as an appendix to the elder Bolyai's *Tentamen* (1832), under the title "Appendix scientiam spatii absolute veram exhibens" ("Appendix Explaining the Absolutely True Science of Space"). This classic essay of twenty-four pages, which contains János' system of non-Euclidean geometry, is the only work of his published in his lifetime. Gauss's letters had such a discouraging influence on him that he withdrew into himself more and more, and for long periods he did hardly any mathematics. Disappointment grew when his essay evoked no response from other mathematicians.

After his retirement from the army, János lived with his father, who was then a widower. This arrangement lasted only a short time, however. Tension grew between father and son, who were both disappointed at the poor reception given their work, and János withdrew to the small family estate at Domáld, visiting Marosvásárhely only occasionally. In 1834 he contracted an irregular marriage with Rosalie von Orbán. The couple had three children, the first born in 1837.

In an attempt to reestablish themselves in mathematics, both father and son participated in the Jablonow Society prize contest in 1837. The subject was the rigorous geometric construction of imaginary quantities, at that time a subject to which many mathematicians (for example, Augustin Cauchy, W. R. Hamilton, and Gauss) were paying attention. The Bolyais' solutions were too involved to gain a prize, but János' solution resembled that of Hamilton, which was published about the same time, although in simpler terms, and which considered complex numbers as ordered pairs of real numbers. Again the Bolyais had failed to obtain due recognition. János continued to do mathematical work, however, some of it strong and some, because of his isolation, very weak. His best work was that on his absolute geometry, on the relation between absolute trigonometry and spherical trigonometry, and on the volume of the tetrahedron in absolute space. On the last subject, there are notes written as late as 1856. Nikolai Lobachevski's *Geometrische Untersuchungen zur Theorie der Parallellinien* (1840), which reached him through his father in 1848, worked as a powerful challenge, for it established independently the same type of geometry that he had discovered. In his later days he occasionally worried about the possibility of contradictions in his absolute geometry—a real difficulty that was not overcome until Beltrami did so later in the nineteenth century. János also worked on a salvation theory, which stressed that no individual happiness can exist without a universal happiness and that no virtue is possible without knowledge.

János' father died in 1856 and his relationship with Rosalie ended at about the same time, thus depriving him of two of his few intimate contacts. However, in the four years left to him, he did have his good moments. He could write enthusiastically about the ballet performances of the Vienna Opera and compose some beautiful lines to the memory of his mother. He died after a protracted illness, and was buried in the Evangelical-Reformed Cemetery in Marosvásárhely.

The "Appendix" was practically forgotten until Richard Baltzer discussed the work of Bolyai and Lobachevski in the second edition of his *Elemente der Mathematik* (1867). Jules Houel, a correspondent of Baltzer's, then translated Lobachevski's book into French (1867) and did the same with Bolyai's "Appendix" (1868). Full recognition came with the work of Eugenio Beltrami (1868) and Felix Klein (1871).

BIBLIOGRAPHY

In addition to the works cited in the article on Farkas Bolyai, see the English translation of the "Appendix," with an introduction, by G. B. Halsted (Austin, Texas, 1891; new ed., Chicago–London, 1914), reprinted in R. Bonola, *Non-Euclidean Geometry* (reprinted New York, 1955). There are accounts of Bolyai's geometry in the many books on non-Euclidean geometry. See D. M. Y. Sommerville, *Bibliography of Non-Euclidean Geometry* (London, 1911). Further material may be found in I. Tóth, *Bolyai János élete és müve* ("Life and Work of Johann Bolyai," Bucharest, 1953); *János Bolyai Appendix* (Bucharest, 1954), in Rumanian.

E. Sarlóska, "János Bolyai, the Soldier," in *Magyar tudományos akadémia Matematikai eś fizikai osztályanak közleményei,* **15** (1965), 341–387, contains a documentary study of Bolyai's army life.

D. J. STRUIK

BOLZA, OSKAR (*b.* Bergzabern, Germany, 12 May 1857; *d.* Freiberg im Breisgau, Germany, 5 July 1942)

Bolza's principal mathematical investigations covered three topics: the reduction of hyperelliptic integrals to elliptic integrals, elliptic and hyperelliptic functions, and the calculus of variations. On the first two topics Bolza proved an able follower of his teachers Karl Weierstrass and Felix Klein. In the realm of reduction problems he worked chiefly on third-degree and fourth-degree transformations. He stressed elliptic theory and often reformulated it as a special case of the hyperelliptic theory in his papers on hyperelliptic θ, σ, and ζ functions. On the third topic his book *Lectures on the Calculus of Variations* (1904) presented the most recent contributions of Weierstrass, Adolf Kneser, and David Hilbert, as well as his own comments. In this book and other writings he added to the theory in the plane and the problem of Lagrange with fixed end points. He extended and applied existence theorems for implicit functions and for solutions to differential equations. Bolza's most significant single contribution was the unification of the problems of Lagrange and Mayer into his more general problem of Bolza. This problem was the fifth, classical necessary condition for a minimum to appear. Leonhard Euler, Adrien-Marie Legendre, Karl Jacobi, and Karl Weierstrass had formulated the previous four. The problem of Bolza in parametric form is to find in a class of arcs $y_i(x)$, where $(i = 1, \cdots, n; x_0 < x < x_1)$ which satisfy equations of the form

$$\phi_\beta(y, y') = 0 \qquad (\beta = 1, \cdots, p)$$
$$\psi_\mu(y) = 0 \qquad (\mu = 1, \cdots, q)$$

and end conditions of the form

$$J_\gamma[y(x_0), y(x_1)] = 0 \qquad (\gamma = 1, \cdots, r),$$

one that minimizes a sum of the form

$$I = G[y(x_0), y(x_1)] + \int_{x_0}^{x_1} f(y, y')\, dx.$$

In this formulation the problem of Mayer with variable end points is the problem of Bolza with its integrand function f identically zero, while the problem of Lagrange with variable end points is the case when G is absent from I.

The son of Emil Bolza and Luise König, Bolza displayed a variety of interests during his youth. At the Gymnasium in Freiburg, he eagerly studied languages and comparative philology, but when he entered the University of Berlin in 1875, he decided to study physics under Kirchhoff and Helmholtz. After tiring of experimental work, in 1878 Bolza switched to the study of pure mathematics. The chief mentor for his mathematical studies at Berlin was Weierstrass, who was particularly interested in the calculus of variations and strongly influenced the course of Bolza's research. From 1878 to 1880 Bolza's studies led him from Berlin to Strasbourg, back to Berlin, and then to Göttingen. After deciding that he wanted to teach, either in a Gymnasium or a university, he interrupted his mathematical studies from 1880 to 1883 in order to prepare for and pass the Staatsexamen, a prerequisite for Gymnasium teaching. From 1883 to 1885 Bolza returned to his mathematical studies, working privately on his doctoral dissertation at the University of Freiburg. After Felix Klein accepted his dissertation on hyperelliptic integrals, he received his doctorate from Göttingen in June 1886. He followed this with a year's private seminar with Klein in Göttingen.

After completing his studies, two reasons prompted Bolza to abandon his teaching plans and go to the United States. Friends complained of the lack of time allowed for research in German schools; second, he was not robust and feared that Gymnasium teaching would be too strenuous for him. He had been rejected for military service in 1887. Bolza arrived in the United States in 1888, and in January 1889 he became reader in mathematics at Johns Hopkins University. In October of that same year he advanced to associate professor in mathematics at Clark University. On 1 January 1893, Bolza became associate professor of mathematics at the newly founded University at Chicago. He advanced to full professor in the following year.

After 1898 Bolza felt a growing desire to return to Germany. In 1908 the death of Heinrich Maschke, an old college friend and a colleague at Chicago, severed perhaps the strongest bond that kept him in America. In addition, he felt that America had made great strides in the training of scholars and believed that he should step aside for the increasing number of young American-trained teachers. In 1910, when he left the University of Chicago, he was given the title of nonresident professor of mathematics.

Upon his return to Germany, Bolza studied various subjects. He accepted the position of honorary professor of mathematics at the University of Freiburg, but in a few years World War I turned his prime interest from mathematics to religious psychology and languages, especially Sanskrit. He had grown up in a pre-World War I Europe in which people believed no major war could occur again: all problems would be resolved by reason. The trauma of World War I shook the foundations of thought for many, including Bolza; he turned to religious psychology and Sanskrit in search of answers on how to establish a better society. Bolza studied Sanskrit so that he could read firsthand the literature concerning the religious systems of India. His new interests prompted him to interrupt his mathematical research in 1922 and his class lectures in 1926. Bolza became more and more engrossed in psychological research, and he devoted full time to it from 1926 until 1929. The result of this work was *Glaubenlose Religion,* which he published in 1931 under the pseudonym F. H. Marneck.

In his final years Bolza remained an active academician. He returned to lecturing on mathematics at the University of Freiburg from 1929 to 1933, when he retired. After his retirement he continued to publish papers on mathematics and religious psychology. At the request of friends he wrote a brief autobiography, *Aus meinen Leben.* As late as 1939 Bolza wrote to friends of his interest in studying the foundations of geometry.

BIBLIOGRAPHY

I. Original Works. Books by Bolza include *Lectures on the Calculus of Variations* (Chicago, 1904); *Vorlesungen über Variationsrechnung, Umgearbeitete und stark Ver-*

mehrte deutsche Ausgabe der "Lectures on the Calculus of Variations" (Leipzig, 1908); "Gauss und die Variationsrechnung," in Gauss's *Werke,* X, pt. 2, 5 (Göttingen, 1922); *Aus meinen Leben* (privately published, 1936); *Glaubenlose Religion* (Munich, 1931), published under the pseudonym F. H. Marneck; *Meister Eckehart als Mystiker, eine religions-psychologische Studie* (Munich, 1938). See also "Elliptic Functions," a handwritten record of a course given at the University of Chicago, probably in the winter quarter, 1901; and "Lectures on Integral Equations," in W. V. Lovitt, *Linear Integral Equations* (New York, 1924).

For articles by Bolza see "Über die Reduction hyperelliptischen Integrale erste Ordnung und erster Gattung auf elliptische durch eine Transformation vierten Grades," in *Mathematical Annals,* **28** (1887), 447–456; "On Binary Sextics With Linear Transformations Into Themselves," in *American Journal of Mathematics,* **10** (1888), 47–70; "The Elliptic Function Considered as a Special Case of the Hyperelliptic Function," in *Transactions of the American Mathematical Society,* **1** (1900), 53–65; "Weierstrass' Theorem and Kneser's Theorem on Transversals for the Most General Case of an Extremum of a Simple Definite Integral," *ibid.,* **7** (1906), 459–488; "Die Lagrangeschen Multiplikatorenregel in die Variationsrechnung für den Fall von gemischten Bedingung bei variabeln Endpunkten," in *Mathematical Annals,* **64** (1907), 370–387; "Heinrich Maschke, His Life and Work," in *Bulletin of the American Mathematical Society,* **15** (1908), 85–95; "Über den Hilbertischen Unabhangigkeitssatz beim Lagrangeschen Variationsproblem," in *Rendiconti del Circolo matematico di Palermo,* **31** (1911), 257–272; "Über zwei Eulersche Aufgaben aus der Variationsrechnung," in *Annali di matematica pura ed applicata,* **20** (1913), 245–255; "Einführung in E. H. Moore's *General Analysis* und deren Anwendung auf die Verallgemeinerung der Theorie der linearen Integralgleichungen," in *Jahrbuch Deutschen Mathematische Verein,* **23** (1914), 248–303; "Der singuläre Fall der Reduction hyperelliptische Integrale erster Ordnung auf elliptische durch Transformation dritten Grades," in *Mathematical Annals,* **111** (1935), 477–500.

II. SECONDARY LITERATURE. An article on Bolza is G. A. Bliss, "Oskar Bolza—In Memoriam," in *Bulletin of the American Mathematical Society,* **50** (1944), 478–489, which contains a chronological list of Bolza's writings.

RONALD S. CALINGER

BOLZANO, BERNARD (*b.* Prague, Czechoslovakia, 5 October 1781; *d.* Prague, 18 December 1848)

Bolzano was born in one of the oldest quarters of Prague and was baptized Bernardus Placidus Johann Nepomuk. His mother, Caecilia Maurer, daughter of a hardware tradesman in Prague, was a pious woman with an inclination to the religious life. At the age of twenty-two she married the elder Bernard Bolzano, an Italian immigrant who earned a modest living as an art dealer. The father was a widely read man with an active social conscience, and felt responsible for the well-being of his fellow men. He put his ideas into practice and took an active part in founding an orphanage in Prague.

Bernard was the fourth of twelve children, ten of whom died before reaching adulthood. Of delicate health, he had a quiet disposition, although he was easily irritated and very sensitive to injustice.

From 1791 to 1796 he was a pupil in the Piarist Gymnasium, and in 1796 he entered the philosophical faculty of the University of Prague, where he followed courses in philosophy, physics, and mathematics. His interest in mathematics was stimulated by reading A. G. Kästner's *Anfangsgründe der Mathematik,* because Kästner took care to prove statements which were commonly understood as evident in order to make clear the assumptions on which they depended.

The benevolence of the environment in which Bernard Bolzano was reared, both at home and in school, influenced his entire life. In fact, he raised to the supreme principle of moral conduct the precept always to choose that action, of all possible actions, which best furthers the commonweal.

After having finished his studies in philosophy in 1800, Bolzano entered the theological faculty. These studies did not strengthen his belief or resolve his doubts concerning the truth and divinity of Christian religion, but he found a solution in his professor's statement that a doctrine may be considered justified if one is able to show that faith in it yields moral profit. This made it possible for Bolzano to reconcile religion with his ethical views and to consider Catholicism the perfect religion.

In 1805 Emperor Franz I of Austria, of which Czechoslovakia was then a part, decided that a chair in the philosophy of religion would be established in each university. The reasons for this were mainly political. The emperor feared the fruits of enlightenment embodied in the French Revolution, and therefore was sympathetic to the Catholic restoration that joined issue with the spirit of freethinking which had spread over Bohemia. Bolzano, who had taken orders in 1804, was called to the new chair at the University of Prague in 1805.

Spiritually, Bolzano belonged to the Enlightenment. Both his religious and social views made him quite unsuitable for the intended task, and difficulties were inevitable. His appointment was received in Vienna with suspicion, and it was not approved until 1807.

Bolzano's lectures, in which he expounded his own views on religion, were enthusiastically received by his students; in particular, his edifying Sunday speeches (*Erbauungsreden,* in *Gesammelte Schriften,* I) to the students were warmly applauded. He was respected by his colleagues, and in 1815 became a member of the Königlichen Böhmischen Gesellschaft der Wissenschaften and, in 1818, dean of the Prague philosophical faculty.

In the struggle between the Catholic restoration and the Enlightenment action against Bolzano was postponed until 1816, when a charge was brought against him at the court in Vienna; his dismissal was issued on 24 December 1819. He was forbidden to publish and was put under police supervision. Bolzano repeatedly refused to recant the heresies of which he was accused, and in 1825 the action came to an end through the intervention of the influential nationalist leader J. Dobrovsky.

From 1823 on, Bolzano spent summers on the estate of his friend J. Hoffmann, near the village of Těchobuz in southern Bohemia. He lived there permanently from 1831 until the death of Mrs. Hoffmann in 1842. Then he returned to Prague, where he continued his mathematical and philosophical studies until his death.

Though Bolzano's career was concerned mainly with social, ethical, and religious questions, he was irresistibly attracted by philosophy, methodology of science, and especially mathematics and logic. His philosophical education—which acquainted him with the Greeks and with Wolff, Leibniz, and Descartes—convinced him of the necessity of forming clear concepts and of sound reasoning, starting from irreducible first principles and using only intrinsic properties of defined concepts. Such methods could not take into account properties alien to their definition, such as geometrical evidence (see *Beyträge*). On occasion he applied these principles with remarkable results; on other occasions, however, his philosophical approach, particularly to mathematics, led him to introduce insufficiently founded and incorrect assumptions. Such was the case in *Die drey Probleme,* which was explicitly intended to lead to a completely new theory of space—which, of course, it failed to do. In the domain of mathematical analysis, however, Bolzano's struggle for clear concepts did lead to profound results that, unfortunately, did not attract the attention of the mathematical world or influence the development of mathematics.

Around the turn of the nineteenth century, mathematicians in Europe were concerned with two major problems. The first was the status of Euclid's parallel postulate, and the second was the problem of providing a solid foundation for mathematical analysis, so as to remove the so-called scandal of the infinitesimals. Bolzano tried his hand at both problems, with varying success.

In 1804 he published his *Betrachtungen über einige Gegenstände der Elementargeometrie,* in which he tried to base the theory of triangles and parallels on a theory of lines, without having recourse to theorems of the plane. The full development of this theory of lines was postponed—and although Bolzano often returned to the theory of parallels (without success), his linear theory was never completed.

In the course of the following years, Bolzano became acquainted with the extensive work done in the theory of parallels, such as that of A. M. Legendre and F. K. Schweikart. There are no indications that he ever knew of the final breakthrough to non-Euclidean geometry by Nikolai Lobachevski and János Bolyai, although the latter's work was published in 1832 in Hungary. Bolzano's own manuscript "Anti-Euklid" follows a different line of thought and is devoted mainly to methodological criticism of Euclid's *Elements.* In fact, in his methodological principles he went so far as to require definitions of such geometrical notions as those of (simple closed) curve, surface, and dimension (see *Die drey Probleme; Ueber Haltung;* "Geometrische Begriffe"; and E. Winter, *Die historische Bedeutung*), and to require proofs of such seemingly evident statements as "A simple closed curve divides the plane into two parts," which is now known as the Jordan curve theorem. Indeed, the discussion in "Anti-Euklid" confirms the opinion held by H. Hornich that Bolzano was the first to state this as a theorem (requiring proof). The problems raised in this connection by Bolzano found their final solution at the end of the nineteenth century and the beginning of the twentieth in that branch of mathematics called topology (for a discussion of these matters, see Berg, *Bolzano's Logic*).

It should be emphasized that Bolzano was not the only one, or even the first, to be concerned with the problem of rigorous proofs in mathematics. A curious fact, however, is that although many of the mathematicians actively interested in the problem of the foundation of mathematical analysis surpassed him in mathematical skill, Bolzano overcame them decisively in the foundation of analysis, in which as early as 1817 (see *Rein analytischer Beweis*) he obtained fundamental results, which were completed in 1832–1835 in his theory of real numbers (see Rychlík, *Theorie der reellen Zahlen*).

The introduction of infinitesimals by Newton and Leibniz in the seventeenth century met with violent resistance from philosophers and mathematicians, and vivid discussions on infinitesimal quantities went on throughout the eighteenth century. Bishop Berkeley's attack in *The Analyst* (1734) is well known.

Although Leibniz himself did not consider the existence of infinitesimals to be well founded, and held that their use could be avoided, he admitted them as ideal quantities, which could be handled in calculations like ordinary quantities (except that they equal their finite multiples). These arithmetical properties, however, formed the weak point in the theory of infinitesimals because of the lack of an exhaustive description of the real number system, which was accomplished only in the second half of the nineteenth century. How badly the general laws of arithmetic were understood may be illustrated by the problem of division by zero. This problem kept Bolzano busy from 1815 on, and he never fully got to the bottom of it, as can be seen, for instance, in §34 of his *Paradoxien des Unendlichen,* where he admits identities of the form $A/0 = A/0$, despite his knowledge of Ohm's solution.

To overcome the difficulties presented by infinitesimals, Lagrange proposed to base analysis on the existence of Taylor's expansion for functions, and this attitude was widely accepted for a time. Bolzano did not escape its influence, and made extensive studies on Taylor's theorem (see *Der binomische Lehrsatz* and "Miscellanea mathematica").

A different position was held by d'Alembert, who proposed to found differential calculus on the notion of limit and contended that differential calculus does not treat of infinitely small quantities, but of limits of finite quantities.

Certainly d'Alembert's opinion impressed his contemporaries, and many attempts, such as Lagrange's, were made to free differential calculus from infinitesimals. The first successful attempt was made by Bolzano in his *Rein analytischer Beweis* (1817), which is devoted to a proof of the important theorem which states that if for two continuous functions f and ϕ we have $f(\alpha) < \phi(\alpha)$ and $f(\beta) > \phi(\beta)$, then there is an x between α and β such that $f(x) = \phi(x)$.

Bolzano argues that a sound proof of this theorem presupposes a sound definition of continuous function. In his introduction he gives such a definition, which is important because it is the first that does not involve infinitesimals, and is, essentially, the one used up to now. In the more accurate formulation of Volume I of the *Functionenlehre,* it reads: If $F(x + \Delta x) - Fx$ in absolute value becomes less than an arbitrary given fraction $1/N$, if one takes Δx small enough, and remains so, the smaller one takes Δx, the function Fx is said to be continuous (in x). Bolzano also distinguishes between right and left continuity.

It should be noted that in 1821 Cauchy, in his *Cours d'analyse,* adopted a different definition: $f(x + \alpha) - f(x)$ infinitely small for all infinitely small α. Because of its elegance, this definition was generally accepted.

In his proof of the theorem in the *Rein analytischer Beweis,* Bolzano uses a lemma that later proved to be the cornerstone of the theory of real numbers. He was fully aware of the paramount importance of this theorem, and he formulated it with great generality, as follows: If a property M does not hold for all values of a variable x, but does hold for all x less than a certain u, then there is a quantity U, which is the greatest of all those for which it holds that all x less than it have property M.

In modern terminology, U is the greatest lower bound of the (nonempty) set of x for which M does not hold.

Though the two theorems mentioned above already bear witness to the outstanding content of the *Rein analytischer Beweis,* it contains another theorem of equal importance, which is known as Cauchy's condition of convergence. Bolzano devotes a whole section to it and proves that if a sequence $F_1(x)$, $F_2(x)$, $F_3(x)$, $\cdots$, $F_n(x)$, $\cdots$, $F_{n+r}(x)$ is such that the difference between the nth term $F_n(x)$ and every later one $F_{n+r}(x)$ remains less than any given quantity if only n has been taken large enough, then there is a fixed quantity, and only one, to which the terms approach—as near as one likes, if one continues the sequence far enough.

The proofs of these theorems are incomplete, and were bound to be so, because complete proofs would require a precise notion of quantity (real number), which Bolzano did not have at that time. He was aware of at least some of the difficulties involved, because his methodology, as expounded in the *Beyträge,* demanded the systematic development of a theory of real numbers that should logically precede his theory of real functions.

A fairly complete theory of real functions is contained in Bolzano's *Functionenlehre,* including many of the fundamental results that were rediscovered in the second half of the nineteenth century through the work of K. Th. Weierstrass and many others.

In the first part, concerning continuous functions, it is shown that a function Fx which is unbounded on the closed interval $[a, b]$ cannot be continuous on $[a, b]$. The proof uses the so-called Bolzano-Weierstrass theorem that a bounded infinite point set has an accumulation point. For this theorem Bolzano refers to his own work, in which up to now it has not been found.

Functions continuous on a closed interval attain there a maximal and a minimal value. Bolzano sharply distinguishes between continuity and the property of assuming intermediate values, and proves that continuous functions assume all values intermediate between any two function values, while the converse is shown not to be true.

In §13 Bolzano notices a property of continuous functions which is rather close to uniform continuity, a notion which is due to E. Heine (1870, 1872). In connection with the function

$$Fx = \frac{1}{1-x},$$

which is continuous on (0, 1), he observes that though a function may be continuous on the open interval (a, b), it does not follow that a real number e, independent of x in (a, b), exists, such that one need not choose $\Delta x < e$ in order that $F(x + \Delta x) - Fx < 1/N$. Indeed, if in the example x approaches 1, the Δx has to be taken increasingly smaller in order that $F(x + \Delta x) - Fx < 1/N$.

As K. Rychlík has pointed out in his commentary in Volume I of the *Schriften,* the said property is weaker than uniform continuity. One may be tempted, however, to assume that Bolzano intended uniform continuity and that only the formulation is defective. The more so, when in "Verbesserungen und Zusätze" we find the correct theorem: If the function Fx is continuous on the closed interval $[a, b]$, then there exists a (real) number e such that for all x in $[a, b]$ the Δx need not be chosen $<e$ in order that $F(x + \Delta x) - Fx <$ a given number $1/N$. Further reading reveals, however, that Bolzano had no clear notion of uniform continuity after all.

Careful attention is paid to the connection between monotonicity and continuity. Thereby the following correction to §79 of the *Functionenlehre* in "Verbesserungen und Zusätze" should not remain unnoticed: If the (real) function Fx increases (or decreases) steadily on the closed interval $[a, b]$, then Fx is continuous on $[a, b]$, with the exception of a set of isolated values of x which may be infinite or finite.

The most remarkable result of the *Functionenlehre,* however, is the construction in §75 of the so-called Bolzano function. There Bolzano constructs a function as the limit of a sequence of continuous functions which is continuous on the closed interval [0, 1] such that it is in no subinterval monotone. The importance of this function, however, derives from another property—its nondifferentiability.

The second part of the *Functionenlehre* is devoted to derivatives. Particular emphasis is laid on the distinction between continuity and differentiability. Bolzano shows that the above-mentioned function, though continuous in [0, 1]—which is not proved—fails to be differentiable on an everywhere dense subset of [0, 1]. In fact, the function is nowhere differentiable on [0, 1]. This example preceded by some forty years that of Weierstrass, who in 1875 published a different example of a nowhere differentiable continuous function which roused wide interest and even indignation.

Bolzano erroneously believed that his function was continuous because it was the limit of continuous functions; in explanation it may be remarked that Cauchy made the same error. Apparently Bolzano was not aware of a counterexample given by N. H. Abel in 1826.

Though the second part of the *Functionenlehre* contains many interesting results, it contains as many errors, such as the statement that the derivative of an infinite series is the sum of the derivatives of its terms, and the conclusion that the limit of a sequence of continuous functions again is a continuous function. Both errors tie up with the notion of uniformity and therefore are explainable; the following error is less easy to understand. In 1829 Cauchy put forward the function

$$C(x) = e^{-1/x^2} \text{ (to be completed by } C[0] = 0)$$

as an example of a function, different from zero for all $x \neq 0$, having all its derivatives zero for $x = 0$ and, hence, not admitting a Taylor expansion in the neighborhood of $x = 0$. Bolzano knew of this example in 1831 (see "Miscellanea mathematica," p. 1999), yet in the *Functionenlehre,* §89, we find the following theorem:

If $F^{n+r}a = 0$ for $r > 0$, then

$$F(a + h) = Fa + h \cdot F'a + \frac{h^2}{2} F''a + \cdots + \frac{h^n}{2.3 \cdots n} F^n a,$$

which is clearly refuted by Cauchy's example.

The firm base on which the theory of functions was to rest, according to Bolzano's methodology—the theory of quantities (real numbers)—was completed in 1832–1835. Like most of Bolzano's mathematical work, it remained in manuscript and was published for the first time only in 1962 (see Rychlík, *Theorie der reellen Zahlen*). As a result, this bold enterprise failed to exercise any influence on the development of mathematics, which in the second half of the nineteenth century independently took the same course.

Real numbers occur in Bolzano's writings under the name of measurable infinite number-expressions. They make their appearance in "Miscellanea mathematica," pt. 22, p. 2000–2001 (1832), in connection with the geometric progression, which has inspired many interesting ideas. The representation of the sum S of an infinite geometric progression as given in the footnote to §18 of the *Paradoxien des Unendlichen* is paradigmatic.

Bolzano's idea is that descriptions of (real) numbers make sense only if they permit determination of the numbers described with an arbitrarily high degree of precision by means of rational numbers. In general, these descriptions require an infinite number of arithmetical operations to be carried out—for instance, the sum S of a geometric progression. These are the infinite number expressions with which Bolzano is concerned. If the results obtained by carrying out only a finite number of operations is always positive, the number expression is called positive.

An infinite number expression S is called measurable (or determinable by approximation) if to any natural number q there is an integer p, such that

$$S = \frac{p}{q} + P_1 = \frac{p+1}{q} - P_2,$$

where P_1 and P_2 are positive (infinite) number expressions.

Infinitely small numbers are those for which all $p = 0$, i.e., those S for which

$$S = P_1 = \frac{1}{q} - P_2,$$

as well as their opposites.

An essential requirement is that measurable numbers differing in an infinitesimal number have to be considered as equal. Therefore, equality is defined by equality of p for all q in the above representation of infinite number expressions. On the basis of these definitions, Bolzano completed his systematic exposition of the theory of real numbers and, thereby, of mathematical analysis.

The elaboration is not quite satisfactory because of many errors due to his insufficient mathematical skill (for interpretations and evaluation of Bolzano's theory, see Laugwitz, "Bemerkungen"; van Rootselaar, "Bolzano's Theory of Real Numbers"; Rychlík, *Theorie der reellen Zahlen*).

The essential differences between Bolzano's incomplete theory of real numbers and those of, for instance, Weierstrass and Georg Cantor are marked by the shift from intensional meaning, in Bolzano's work, toward a general tendency to extensionality, and, above all, by the possibility of creating new mathematical objects by means of definition by abstraction, based on equivalence relations, of which Bolzano was unaware. These differences also appear clearly in his *Paradoxien des Unendlichen,* which contains many interesting fragments of general set theory.

The existence of infinite sets is proved in a way similar to that followed by Richard Dedekind in his memoir *Was sind und was sollen die Zahlen* (1887). Most noteworthy, however, is that in §20 of *Paradoxien des Unendlichen* Bolzano is at the border of cardinal arithmetic, a border which he is unable to cross. There he notices a property of infinite sets: that they may be brought into one-to-one correspondence with a proper subset. In fact, he observes that this will always be the case with infinite sets. That two sets may be brought into one-to-one correspondence is no reason for him to consider them to be composed of the same number of elements (*Paradoxien des Unendlichen,* §21), however, and he sees no reason to consider such sets as equal. On the contrary, in order for two sets to be considered as equal, he argues, they must be defined on the same basis (*gleiche Bestimmungsgründe haben*). Needless to say, this is too vague to be dealt with mathematically. Here again, we see that Bolzano halts at a point where application of the method of definition by abstraction would have opened entirely new fields of knowledge.

Precisely that property of infinite sets noticed by Bolzano was afterward used by Dedekind as a definition of the infinite (1882). The introduction of equivalence classes of sets under one-to-one correspondence was fully exploited by Cantor in his theory of cardinals, a very important chapter of general set theory.

Bolzano planned to elaborate the methodology begun in his *Beyträge* and to develop it into a complete theory of science, of which a treatise on logic was to form the cornerstone. From 1820 on, he worked steadily on it, and his four-volume treatise *Wissenschaftslehre* appeared in 1837. The plan of the *Wissenschaftslehre* appears clearly from the following subdivision (see Kambartel, *Bernard Bolzano's Grundlegung der Logik,* pp. 14–17):

(1) Fundamental theory: proof of the existence of abstract truths and of the human ability to judge.

(2) Elementary theory: theory of abstract ideas, propositions, true propositions, and deductions.

(3) Theory of knowledge: condition of the human faculty of judgment.

(4) Heuristics: rules to be observed in human thought in the search for truths.

(5) Proper theory of science: rules to be observed in the division of the set of truths into separate sciences and in their exposition in truly scientific treatises.

The work did not induce a complete revision of science, as Bolzano hoped, but, on the contrary,

BOLZANO

remained unnoticed and did not exercise perceptible influence on the development of logic. Some of the innovations in logic contained in the first two volumes did attract attention, as well as excessive praise—notably from Edmund Husserl and Heinrich Scholz (see Berg, *op. cit.*; Kambartel, *op. cit.*; and the literature cited in them).

The rise of logical semantics, initiated by Alfred Tarski in the 1930's, has led to a revival of the study of Bolzano's logic in the light of modern logic (see Berg, *op. cit.*) and of his theory of an ideal language.

The heart of Bolzano's logic is formed by his concepts of (abstract) proposition (*Satz an sich*), abstract idea (*Vorstellung an sich*), truth, and the notions of derivability (*Ableitbarkeit*) and entailment (*Abfolge*).

These notions may be explained with the help of Bolzano's example:

(*a*) Cajus is a human being.

(*b*) All human beings have immortal souls.

(*c*) Cajus has an immortal soul.

First of all, (*a*) expresses an abstract proposition, which in itself has no real existence, but is something to which (*a*) refers and which is either true or false. An abstract proposition may be expressed in many ways linguistically, and it is said to be true if it asserts something as it actually is (*"so wie es ist," Wissenschaftslehre,* §25).

Bolzano argues that any proposition may be expressed in the normal form "*A* has *b*." For instance,

(*a'*) Cajus has human existence

is the normal form of the proposition expressed by (*a*).

Parts of propositions which are not themselves propositions are (abstract) ideas; for example, in (*a'*) the expression "human existence" refers to an abstract idea.

Between abstract propositions there exist relations, among which those of consistency and derivability are of paramount importance. Propositions $A, B, C, \cdots$ are called consistent with respect to the common ideas $i, j, \cdots$ if there are ideas $i', j', \cdots$ which, after substitution for $i, j, \cdots$ turn the propositions $A, B, C, \cdots$ into simultaneously true propositions A', B', C', $\cdots$. Propositions A', B', C', $\cdots$ are called derivable from $A, B, C, \cdots$ with respect to the ideas $i, j, \cdots$ whenever $A, B, C, \cdots, A', B', C', \cdots$ are consistent with respect to $i, j, \cdots$ and if any substitution $i', j', \cdots$ for $i, j, \cdots$ that turns $A, B, C, \cdots$ into true propositions also turns $A', B', C', \cdots$ into true propositions. According to Bolzano, (*c*) is derivable from (*a*) and (*b*).

The relation of entailment (*Abfolge*) may subsist between true propositions, and refers to the situation that A is true because $A_1, A_2, \cdots$ are true. The treatment of this notion, however, is rather unsatisfactory (see Berg, *op. cit.;* Buhl, *Ableitbarkeit und Abfolge;* Kambartel, *op. cit.* for details).

The resemblance that many of the concepts introduced by Bolzano bear to modern logic has led to the opinion that Bolzano may be considered a true precursor of modern logic. (For a detailed account, consult Berg, *op. cit.;* and Kambartel, *op. cit.;* for Bolzano's philosophy, Fujita, *Borutsāno no tetsugaku* ["Bolzano's Philosophy"]).

BIBLIOGRAPHY

I. Original Works. Bolzano's published works include the following: *Betrachtungen über einige Gegenstände der Elementargeometrie* (Prague, 1804; repr. *Schriften,* V); *Beyträge zu einer begründeteren Darstellung der Mathematik* (Prague, 1810; new ed. by H. Fels, Paderborn, 1926); *Der binomische Lehrsatz und als Folgerung aus ihm der polynomische und die Reihen, die zur Berechnung der Logarithmen und Exponentialgrössen dienen, genauer als bisher erwiesen* (Prague, 1816); *Die drey Probleme der Rectification, der Complanation und der Cubirung, ohne Betrachtung des unendlich Kleinen, ohne die Annahmen des Archimedes, und ohne irgend eine nicht streng erweisliche Voraussetzung gelöst; zugleich als Probe einer gänzlichen Umstaltung der Raumwissenschaft, allen Mathematikern zur Prüfung vorgelegt* (Leipzig, 1817; repr. *Schriften,* V); *Rein analytischer Beweis des Lehrsatzes, dass zwischen je zwey Werthen, die ein entgegengesetztes Resultat gewähren, wenigstens eine reelle Wurzel der Gleichung liege* (Prague, 1817; new ed. in Ostwald's Klassiker der exakten Wissenschaften, no. 153 [Leipzig, 1905]; also in Kolman, *Bernard Bolzano*).

Also *Lebensbeschreibung des Dr. Bernard Bolzano mit einigen seiner ungedruckten Aufsätze und dem Bildnisse des Verfassers,* ed. M. J. Fesl (Sulzbach, 1836; repr. Vienna, 1875), an autobiography; *Wissenschaftslehre, Versuch einer ausführlichen und grösstentheils neuen Darstellung der Logik mit steter Rücksicht auf deren bisherigen Bearbeiter,* 4 vols. (Sulzbach, 1837; new ed. by A. Höfler and W. Schultz, 4 vols. [Leipzig, 1914–1931]; also in *Gesammelte Schriften*); *Paradoxien des Unendlichen,* ed. F. Přihonsky (Leipzig, 1851; English ed. by D. A. Steele, *Paradoxes of the Infinite* [New Haven, 1950]); *Ueber Haltung, Richtung, Krümmung und Schnörkelung bei Linien sowohl als Flächen sammt einigen verwandten Begriffen* (ed. in *Schriften,* V).

There are two collections of Bolzano's works. One is *Gesammelte Schriften,* 12 vols. (Vienna, 1882); the contents are as follows: I: *Erbauungsreden;* II: *Athanasia oder Gründe für die Unsterblichkeit der Seele;* III–VI: *Lehrbuch der Religionswissenschaft;* VII–X: *Wissenschaftslehre;* XI: *Dr. Bolzano und seine Gegner;* XII: *Bolzano's Wissenschaftslehre und Religionswissenschaft in beurteilender Übersicht.* The other is *Bernard Bolzano's Schriften,* 5 vols., ed. Königlichen Böhmischen Gesellschaft der Wissenschaften (Prague, 1930–1948), which contains the following: I: *Functionenlehre,* ed. K. Rychlik (1930); II: *Zahlentheorie,* ed. K. Rychlik (1931); III: *Von dem besten Staate,* ed. A. Kowalewski (1932); IV: *Der Briefwechsel B. Bolzano's mit F. Exner,* ed. E. Winter (1935); V: *Mémoires géometriques,* ed. J. Vojtech (1948).

Additional works are in manuscript: "Anti-Euklid" (fragment), in Österreichische Nationalbibliothek, Vienna, Handschriftensammlung, Series Nova, 3459, section 5 (also edited in Večerka, "Bernard Bolzano's Anti-Euklid"); "Geometrische Begriffe, die jeder kennt und nicht kennt," in Österreichische Nationalbibliothek, Vienna, Handschriftensammlung, Series Nova, 3459, sections 3b and 3c; "Miscellanea mathematica," 1-24, in Österreichische Nationalbibliothek, Vienna, Handschriftensammlung, Series Nova, 3453-3455; and "Verbesserungen und Zusätze zu dem Abschnitt von der Differenzialrechnung," in Österreichische Nationalbibliothek, Vienna, Handschriftensammlung, Series Nova, 3472, section 7.

II. SECONDARY LITERATURE. Works on Bolzano include J. Berg, *Bolzano's Logic* (Stockholm, 1962), which has an extensive bibliography; and "Bolzano's Theory of an Ideal Language," in R. E. Olson, ed., *Contemporary Philosophy in Scandinavia* (Baltimore, in press); G. Buhl, "Ableitbarkeit und Abfolge in der Wissenschaftstheorie Bolzanos," in *Kantstudien,* **83** (1961); H. Fels, *Bernard Bolzano, sein Leben und sein Werk* (Leipzig, 1929), which includes a Bolzano bibliography; I. Fujita, *Borutsāno no tetsugaku* ("Bolzano's Philosophy") (Tokyo, 1963); H. Hornich, "Ueber eine Handschrift aus dem Nachlass von B. Bolzano," in *Anzeiger. Osterreichische Akademie der Wissenschaften,* mathematische-naturwissenschaftliche Klasse, no. 2 (1961); F. Kambartel, *Bernard Bolzano's Grundlegung der Logik* (Hamburg, 1963), which includes selections from Wissenschaftslehre I and II and an excellent introduction; A. Kolman, *Bernard Bolzano* (Berlin, 1963), which has an extensive bibliography; D. Laugwitz, "Bemerkungen zu Bolzanos Grössenlehre," in *Archive for History of Exact Sciences,* **2** (1964), 398–409; B. van Rootselaar, "Bolzano's Theory of Real Numbers," in *Archive for History of Exact Sciences,* **2** (1964), 168–180; K. Rychlik, *Theorie der reellen Zahlen im Bolzanos handschriftlichen Nachlasse* (Prague, 1962); K. Večerka, "Bernard Bolzano's Anti-Euklid," in *Sbornik pro dějiny přirodnich věd a teckniky* (*Acta historiae rerum naturalium nec non technicarum,* Prague), **11** (1967), 203–216; E. Winter, *Leben und geistige Entwicklung des Sozialethikers und Mathematikers B. Bolzano 1781–1848,* Hallische Monographien, no. 14 (Halle, 1949), which has a Bolzano bibliography; *Die historische Bedeutung der Frühbegriffe B. Bolzano's* (Berlin, 1964); and *Wissenschaft und Religion im Vormärz. Der Briefwechsel Bernard Bolzanos mit Michael Josef Fesl 1822–1848* (Berlin, 1965); and E. Winter, P. Funk, J. Berg, *Bernard Bolzano, Ein Denker und Erzieher in Österreichischen Vormärz* (Vienna, 1967).

B. VAN ROOTSELAAR

BOMBELLI, RAFAEL (*b.* Bologna, Italy, January 1526; *d.* 1572)

Rafael Bombelli's family came from Borgo Panigale, a suburb three miles north of Bologna. The original family name was Mazzoli. The Mazzolis, who seem to have been small landowners, adopted the name Bombelli early in the sixteenth century. Some of them were supporters of the Bentivoglio faction. An unsuccessful conspiracy to restore the Bentivoglio *signoria* in 1508 resulted in the execution of seven men, among whom was Giovanni Mazzoli, Rafael Bombelli's great-grandfather. Giovanni Mazzoli's property was confiscated but was later restored to his grandchildren. One of them was Antonio Mazzoli, alias Bombelli, who later became a wool merchant and moved to Bologna. There he married Diamante Scudieri, the daughter of a tailor. Six children were born to this marriage, of whom the eldest son was Rafael Bombelli.

All that is known about Bombelli's education is that his teacher (*precettore*) was Pier Francesco Clementi of Corinaldo, an engineer-architect. It has been suggested that Bombelli might have studied at the University of Bologna, but this seems unlikely when one considers his family background and the nature of his profession. He spent the greater part of his working life as an engineer-architect in the service of his patron, Monsignor Alessandro Rufini, a Roman nobleman. Rufini was *cameriere* and favorite of Pope Paul III, and later was bishop of Melfi. The major engineering project on which Bombelli was employed was the reclamation of the marshes of the Val di Chiana. It was at a time when the reclamation work had been suspended that he wrote his treatise on algebra in the peaceful atmosphere of his patron's villa in Rome. His professional engagements seem to have delayed the completion of the book, but the more important part of it was published in 1572. His death soon afterward prevented the publishing of the remainder of the work. It was not published until 1929.

Bombelli's teacher, Pier Francesco Clementi, was employed by the Apostolic Camera (*ca.* 1548) in draining the marshes of the Topino River at Foligno (100 miles from Rome). It is not known whether Bombelli himself worked in Foligno; but by 1551 he had begun to work for Rufini in the reclamation of the Val di Chiana marshes. Rufini began to take an interest in this project in 1549, when the rights of reclamation of that part of the marshes which belonged to the Papal States were obtained by his nominee. Evidence of Bombelli's activity is found in the record relating to the marking out and settlement of the boundaries of the reclaimed land. The work of reclamation was interrupted sometime between 1555 and 1560. By 1560 Bombelli had returned to the Val di Chiana, and his work there ended in that year. In 1561 he was in Rome, where he took part in the unsuccessful attempt to repair the Ponte Santa Maria, one of the bridges over the Tiber.

Bombelli's work in the Val di Chiana earned him a reputation as an engineer, and led to his being one of the consultants on a proposed project for draining a part of the Pontine Marshes during the reign of Pius IV (1559–1565). The historian Nicolai, in his *De' bonificamenti delle Terre Pontine* (1800), says that the work was to have been directed by Rafael Bombelli, "famous among hydraulic engineers for having successfully drained the marshes of the Val di Chiana." The project was not realized, however.

Rafael Bombelli grew up in an Italy that was active in the production of works on practical arithmetic. Luca Pacioli, author of the *Summa di arithmetica, geometria, . . .* (1494), had lectured at Bologna at the beginning of the century. So had Scipione dal Ferro, a citizen of Bologna and one of the foremost mathematicians of the time. Their successors, Cardano, Tartaglia, and Ferrari, who were attempting the solution of the cubic and biquadratic equations, lived and worked in the neighboring cities of northern Italy. Cardano's *Practica arithmeticae* was published in 1539 and was followed in 1545 by his great treatise on algebra, the *Ars magna,* which gave the methods of dal Ferro and Ferrari for solving the cubic and biquadratic equations, respectively. In 1546 the controversy between Cardano and Tartaglia became public with the appearance of the latter's *Quesiti et inventioni diverse.* Copies of the *Cartelli di matematica disfida* (1547–1548), exchanged between Ferrari and Tartaglia, were circulated in the principal cities of Italy. Such was the climate in which Bombelli conceived the idea of writing a treatise on algebra. He felt that none of his predecessors except Cardano had explored the subject in depth; but Cardano, he thought, had not been clear in his exposition. He therefore decided to write a book that would enable anyone to master the subject without the aid of any other text. The work, written between 1557 and 1560, was a systematic and logical exposition of the subject in five parts, or books. In Book I, Bombelli dealt with the definitions of the elementary concepts (powers, roots, binomials, trinomials) and applications of the fundamental operations. In Book II he introduced algebraic powers and notation, and then went on to deal with the solution of equations of the first, second, third, and fourth degrees. Bombelli considered only equations with positive coefficients, thus adhering to the practice of his contemporaries. He was therefore obliged to deal with a large number of cases: five types of quadratic equations, seven cubic, and forty-two biquadratic. For each type of equation, he gave the rule for solution and illustrated the rule with examples. Bombelli feared that the examples given in Book II would not be sufficient for a beginner who wished to master the subject, so he decided to include in Book III a series of problems by which the student would be taken, in stages, through the various operations of algebra. For this purpose he chose problems that were common to books on practical arithmetic of his day. Many of them were "applied problems"—that is, problems that had denominate numbers—and not mere exercises in manipulating symbols. They were often woven into incidents that could have occurred in the marketplace or tavern. Books IV and V formed the geometrical portion of the work. Book IV contained the application of geometrical methods to algebra, *algebra linearia,* and Book V was devoted to the application of algebraic methods to the solution of geometrical problems. Unfortunately, Bombelli was unable to complete the work as he had originally planned, in particular Books IV and V.

He had the opportunity, however, of studying a codex of Diophantus' *Arithmetic* in the Vatican Library during a visit to Rome. It was shown to him by Antonio Maria Pazzi, *lector ad mathematicam* at the University of Rome. They set out to translate the manuscript, but circumstances prevented them from completing the work. The changes that Bombelli made in the first three books of his *Algebra* show evidence of the influence of Diophantus. At the end of Book III, Bombelli said that the geometrical part, Books IV and V, was not yet ready for the publisher, but that it would follow shortly. His death prevented his keeping the promise. It was only in 1923 that the manuscript of the *Algebra* was rediscovered by Ettore Bortolotti in the Biblioteca Comunale dell'Archiginnasio in Bologna.

In his *Algebra,* Bombelli gave a comprehensive account of the existing knowledge of the subject, enriching it with his own contributions. Cardano had observed that the general rule given by dal Ferro could not be applied in solving the so-called irreducible case of the cubic equation, but Bombelli's skill in operating with "imaginary numbers" enabled him to demonstrate the applicability of the rule even in this case. Because of the special nature and importance of these imaginary quantities, he took great care to make the reader familiar with them by introducing them early in his work—at the end of Book I. He said he had found "un altra sorte di radice cuba legata" ("another kind of cube root of an aggregate") different from the others. This was the cube root of a complex number occurring in the solution of the irreducible case of the cubic equation. He called the square roots of a negative quantity *più di meno* and *meno di meno* (that is, *p. di m.* 10, *m. di m.* 10 for $+\sqrt{-10}$, $-\sqrt{-10}$). Having pointed out that the complex root is always accompanied by its conjugate, he set out the rules for operating with complex numbers and gave examples showing their application. Here he showed himself to be far ahead of his time, for his treatment was almost that followed today. Bombelli also pointed out that the problem of trisecting an angle could be reduced to that of solving the irreducible case of the cubic equation (this was illustrated in Book V). Although he made no significant contribution to the solution of the biquadratic equation, he showed the application of Ferrari's rule to every possible case.

In Book III of the printed version of the *Algebra* one finds no trace of the influence that practical arithmetics originally had on Bombelli. He said in the preface that he had deviated from the custom of those authors of arithmetics who stated their problems in the guise of human actions; his intention was to teach the "higher arithmetic." The problems of applied arithmetic that were originally included in Book III were left out of the published work; by doing so, Bombelli helped to raise algebra to the status of an independent discipline. In place of these applied problems he introduced a number of abstract problems, of which 143 were taken from the *Arithmetic* of Diophantus. Although Bombelli did not distinguish Diophantus' problems from his own, he acknowledged that he had borrowed freely from the *Arithmetic.* He was in fact the first to popularize the work of Diophantus in the West.

Apart from the solution of the irreducible case of the cubic equation, the most significant contribution Bombelli made to algebra was in the notation he adopted. He represented the powers of the unknown quantity by a semicircle inside which the exponent was placed: $\underset{\smile}{1}$ for the modern x, $\underset{\smile}{2}$ for x^2, and $5\underset{\smile}{1}$ or $\overset{\underset{\smile}{1}}{5}$ for $5x$. In the printed work the semicircle was reduced to an arc: $\underset{\smile}{1}$, $\underset{\smile}{2}$, $\overset{\underset{\smile}{1}}{5}$. The zero exponent, $\underset{\smile}{0}$, was used in the manuscript, 48 $\underset{\smile}{0}$ for 48, but was omitted from the published work. The notation ℞$\lfloor\quad\rfloor$ was used in the manuscript in applying the radical to the aggregate of two or more terms: ℞$\lfloor$4p℞6$\rfloor$ for $\sqrt{4+\sqrt{6}}$. He even used the radical sign as a double bracket: ℞$^3\lfloor 2p$℞$\lfloor 0m121\rfloor\,\rfloor$ for $\sqrt[3]{2+\sqrt{0-121}}$. In the printed work the horizontal line was broken, and ℞, ℞^{3} became *Rq. Rc:* for example, $Rc\lfloor 2pRq\lfloor 0m121\rfloor\,\rfloor$.

Although incomplete, Books IV and V of the *Algebra* reveal Bombelli's versatility as a geometer. He had reduced some of the arithmetical problems of Book III to an abstract form and had interpreted them geometrically. He did not feel obliged to give geometrical proofs for the correctness of the results that he had obtained by algebraic methods. In doing so, he had broken away from a long-established tradition. The linear representation of powers, the use of the unit segment, and the representation of a point by "orthogonal coordinates" are some of the noteworthy features of this part of the work.

Bombelli was the last of the algebraists of Renaissance Italy. The influence that his *Algebra* had in the Low Countries is attested to by Simon Stevin and Adrien Romain. In the course of a short historical survey of the solution of equations, in his *Arithmetique,* Stevin referred to Bombelli as "great arithmetician of our time." He used a slightly modified form of Bombelli's notation for the powers of the unknown. While giving Bombelli due credit, he stressed the superiority of his notation to that of the Cossists. About a century later Leibniz, while teaching himself mathematics, used Bombelli's *Algebra* as a guide to the study of cubic equations. His correspondence with Huygens shows the keen interest these two men took in the work of the Italian mathematicians of the Renaissance. In the words of Leibniz, Bombelli was an "outstanding master of the analytical art."

BIBLIOGRAPHY

I. Original Works. Versions of the *Algebra* are *L'algebra di Rafaello Bombello, cittadino bolognese,* in Biblioteca Comunale dell'Archiginnasio in Bologna, Codex B.1569; *L'algebra* (Bologna, 1572); and Ettore Bortolotti, ed., *L'algebra, opera di Rafael Bombelli da Bologna, Libri IV e V* (Bologna, 1929).

II. Secondary Literature. For references to earlier literature, see S. A. Jayawardene, "Unpublished Documents Relating to Rafael Bombelli in the Archives of Bologna," in *Isis,* **54** (1963), 391–395, and "Rafael Bombelli, Engineer-Architect: Some Unpublished Documents of the Apostolic Camera," *ibid.,* **56** (1965), 298–306.

S. A. Jayawardene

BONNET, PIERRE-OSSIAN (*b.* Montpellier, France, 22 December 1819; *d.* Paris, France, 22 June 1892)

Bonnet was the son of Pierre Bonnet, *commis banquier,* and Magdelaine Messac. After attending the College of Montpellier, he in 1838 entered the

École Polytechnique in Paris, where he studied at the École des Ponts et des Chaussées. After graduation, however, he declined an engineering position, preferring teaching and research. In 1844 he became *répétiteur* at the École Polytechnique, augmenting his income by private tutoring. In a paper of 1843 he published convergence criteria of series with positive terms, among them logarithmic criteria. Another paper on series was honored by the Brussels Academy of Sciences and was published in 1849. By that time Bonnet had, starting in 1844 with the paper "Sur quelques propriétés générales des surfaces," begun to publish that series of papers on differential geometry on which his fame is based. The merit of this work was recognized by the Académie des Sciences when it elected Bonnet to membership in 1862 to replace Biot.

In 1868 Bonnet became Michel Chasles's *suppléant* at the École Polytechnique in the latter's course on higher geometry, and in 1871 he became director of studies there. He also taught at the École Normale Supérieure. In 1878 he obtained a chair at the Sorbonne, succeeding the astronomer Leverrier, and in 1883 he succeeded Liouville as a member of the Bureau des Longitudes. Married and the father of three sons, he always lived the quiet and unpretentious life of a scholar.

Bonnet's favorite field was the differential geometry of curves and surfaces, a field opened by Euler, Monge, and Gauss, but at that time lacking systematic treatment and offering wide fields of research. Between 1840 and 1850 this challenge was taken up by Bonnet and a group of younger French mathematicians—Serret, Frenet, Bertrand, and Puiseux—but it was Bonnet who most consistently continued in this field. In the "Mémoire sur la théorie générale des surfaces," presented in 1844 to the Académie, Bonnet introduced the concepts of geodesic curvature and torsion, and proved a series of theorems concerning them. One of these is the formula for the line integral of the geodesic curvature along a closed curve on a surface, known as the Gauss-Bonnet theorem (Gauss had published only a special case). Bonnet also showed the invariance of the geodesic curvature under bending of the surface.

From 1844 to 1867 Bonnet wrote a series of papers on differential geometry of surfaces. Special attention should be given to the "Mémoire sur la théorie des surfaces applicables sur une surface donnée" (1865–1867), written as a solution for a prize contest announced by the Académie in 1859: i.e., to find all surfaces of a given linear element. The problem is sometimes associated with Edouard Bour, who wrote a competing memoir (1862). The third entrant was Delfino Codazzi. Bonnet, in his contribution, showed the importance of certain formulas introduced in 1859 by Codazzi, formulas now taken as part of the so-called Gauss-Codazzi relations. He also showed the role these formulas play in the existence theorem for surfaces, if first and second fundamental forms are given. Bour, in his paper, came to similar conclusions.

In these and other papers Bonnet stressed the usefulness of special coordinate systems on a surface, such as isothermic and tangential coordinates; studied special curves, such as lines of curvature with constant geodesic curvature (1867); and investigated the conditions under which geodesic lines are the shortest connection between two points on a surface. He also paid much attention to minimal surfaces—for instance, those applicable on each other—and surfaces of constant total and constant mean curvature (1853).

Bonnet also published works on geodesy and cartography, theory of series (convergence criteria), algebra, rational mechanics, and mathematical physics. In 1871 he gave a definition of the limit for functions of a real variable.

BIBLIOGRAPHY

I. ORIGINAL WORKS. Among Bonnet's papers are "Note sur la convergence et divergence des séries," in *Journal de mathématiques pures et appliquées,* **8** (1843), 73–109; "Sur quelques propriétés générales des surfaces et des lignes tracées sur les surfaces," in *Comptes rendus de l'Académie des Sciences,* **14** (1844); "Mémoire sur la théorie générale des surfaces," in *Journal de l'École Polytechnique,* **32** (1848), 1–46; "Sur la théorie des séries," in *Mémoires courronnés de l'Académie de Bruxelles,* **22** (1849); "Mémoire sur l'emploi d'un nouveau système de variables dans l'étude des propriétés des surfaces courbes," in *Journal de mathématiques pures et appliquées,* ser. 2, **5** (1860), 153–266; and "Mémoire sur la théorie des surfaces applicables sur une surface donnée," in *Journal de l'École Polytechnique,* **41** (1865), 201–230, and **42** (1867), 1–151.

Bonnet's most important papers are mainly in the *Journal de l'École Polytechnique,* the *Journal de mathématiques pures et appliquées,* and the *Comptes rendus de l'Académie des Sciences.* He also wrote a *Mécanique élémentaire* (Paris, 1858). Bonnet's papers have never been collected, but the essence of his work on the theory of surfaces can be found in Gaston Darboux's *Leçons sur la théorie générale des surfaces,* 4 vols. (Paris, 1887–1896), *passim.*

II. SECONDARY LITERATURE. Works on Bonnet are P. Appell, "Notice sur la vie et les travaux de Pierre Ossian Bonnet," in *Comptes rendus de l'Académie des Sciences,* **117** (1893), 1013–1024; Michel Chasles, *Rapport sur les progrès de la géometrie en France* (Paris, 1870), pp. 199–214; and

A. Franceschini, "Bonnet," in *Dictionnaire de biographie française,* Vol. VI (Paris, 1954).

D. J. STRUIK

BOOLE, GEORGE (*b.* Lincoln, England, 1815; *d.* Cork, Ireland, 1864)

George Boole was the son of John Boole, a cobbler whose chief interests lay in mathematics and the making of optical instruments, in which his son learned to assist at an early age. The father was not a good businessman, however, and the decline in his business had a serious effect on his son's future. The boy went to an elementary school and for a short time to a commercial school, but beyond this he educated himself, encouraged in mathematics by his father and helped in learning Latin by William Brooke, the proprietor of a large and scholarly circulating library. He acquired a knowledge of Greek, French, and German by his own efforts, and showed some promise as a classical scholar; a translation in verse of Meleager's "Ode to the Spring" was printed in a local paper and drew comments on the precocity of a boy of fourteen. He seems to have thought of taking holy orders, but at the age of fifteen he began teaching, soon setting up a school of his own in Lincoln.

In 1834 the Mechanics Institution was founded in Lincoln, and the president, a local squire, passed Royal Society publications on to the institution's reading room, of which John Boole became curator. George, who now devoted his scanty leisure to the study of mathematics, had access to the reading room, and grappled, almost unaided, with Newton's *Principia* and Lagrange's *Mécanique analytique,* gaining such a local reputation that at the age of nineteen he was asked to give an address on Newton to mark the presentation of a bust of Newton, also a Lincolnshire man, to the Institution. This address, printed in 1835, was Boole's first scientific publication. In 1840 he began to contribute to the recently founded *Cambridge Mathematical Journal* and also to the Royal Society, which awarded him a Royal Medal in 1844 for his papers on operators in analysis; he was elected a fellow of the Royal Society in 1857.

In 1849, Boole, on the advice of friends, applied for the professorship of mathematics in the newly established Queen's College, Cork, and was appointed in spite of his not holding any university degree. At Cork, although his teaching load was heavy, he found more time and facilities for research. In 1855 he married Mary Everest, the niece of a professor of Greek in Queen's College and of Sir George Everest, after whom Mount Everest was named.

Boole was a clear and conscientious teacher, as his textbooks show. In 1864 his health began to fail, and his concern for his students may have hastened his death, since he walked through rain to a class and lectured in wet clothes, which led to a fatal illness.

Boole's scientific writings consist of some fifty papers, two textbooks, and two volumes dealing with mathematical logic. The two textbooks, on differential equations (1859) and finite differences (1860), remained in use in the United Kingdom until the end of the century. They contain much of Boole's original work, reproducing and extending material published in his research papers. In the former book, so much use is made of the differential operator D that the method is often referred to as Boole's, although it is in fact much older than Boole. Both books exhibit a great technical skill in the handling of operators: in the volume on finite differences, an account is given of the operators π and ρ, first introduced in Boole's Royal Society papers. The basic operators of this calculus, Δ and E, are defined by the equations

$$\Delta u_x = u_{x+1} - u_x,\ E\ u_x = u_{x+1};$$

Boole then defines his new operators by the operational equations

$$\pi = x\Delta,\ \rho = xE,$$

and shows how they can be used to solve certain types of linear difference equations with coefficients depending on the independent variable. These operators have since been generalized by L. M. Milne-Thomson.

In papers in the *Cambridge Mathematical Journal* in 1841 and 1843, Boole dealt with linear transformations. He showed that if the linear transformation

$$x = pX + qY, y = rX + sY$$

is applied to the binary quadratic form

$$ax^2 + 2hxy + by^2$$

to yield the binary quadratic form

$$AX^2 + 2HXY + BY^2,$$

then $$AB - H^2 = (ps - qr)^2\,(ab - h^2).$$

The algebraic fact had been partly perceived by Lagrange and by Gauss, but Boole's argument drew attention to the (relative) invariance of the discriminant $ab - h^2$, and also to the absolute invariants of the transformation. This was the starting point of the theory of invariants, so rapidly and extensively developed in the second half of the nineteenth century;

Boole himself, however, took no part in this development.

Other papers dealt with differential equations, and the majority of those published after 1850 studied the theory of probability, closely connected with Boole's work on mathematical logic. In all his writings, Boole exhibited considerable technical skill, but his facility in dealing with symbolic operators did not delude him into an undue reliance on analogy, a fault of the contemporary British school of symbolic analysis. E. H. Neville has remarked that mathematicians of that school treated operators with the most reckless disrespect, and in consequence could solve problems beyond the power not merely of their predecessors at the beginning of the century but of their inhibited successors at the end of the century, obtaining many remarkable and frequently correct formulas but ignoring conditions of validity.

Boole greatly increased the power of the operational calculus, but seldom allowed himself to be carried away by technical success: at a time when the need for precise and unambiguous definitions was often ignored, he was striving, although perhaps not always with complete success, to make his foundations secure. There is a clear and explicit, although later, statement of his position in his *Investigation of the Laws of Thought;* there are, he says, two indispensable conditions for the employment of symbolic operators: "First, that from the sense once conventionally established, we never, in the same process of reasoning, depart; secondly, that the laws by which the process is conducted be founded exclusively upon the above fixed sense or meaning of the symbols employed." With the technical skill and the desire for logical precision there is also the beginning of the recognition of the nonnumerical variable as a genuine part of mathematics. The development of this notion in Boole's later and most important work appears to have been stimulated almost accidentally by a logical controversy.

Sir William Hamilton, the Scottish philosopher (not to be confused with the Irish mathematician Sir William Rowan Hamilton), picked a logical quarrel with Boole's friend Augustus De Morgan, the acute and high-minded professor of mathematics at University College, London. De Morgan's serious, significant contributions to logic were derided by Hamilton, on the grounds that the study of mathematics was both dangerous and useless—no mathematician could contribute anything of importance to the superior domain of logic. Boole, in the preface to his *Mathematical Analysis of Logic* (1847), demonstrated that, on Hamilton's own principles, logic would form no part of philosophy. He asserted that in a true classification, logic should not be associated with metaphysics, but with mathematics. He then offered his essay as a construction, in symbolic terms, of logic as a doctrine, like geometry, resting upon a groundwork of acceptable axioms.

The reduction of Aristotelian logic to an algebraic calculus had been more than once attempted; Leibniz had produced a scheme of some promise. If the proposition "All A is B" is written in the form A/B, and "All B is C" in the form B/C, then it is tempting to remove the common factor B from numerator and denominator and arrive at A/C, to be correctly interpreted as the conclusion "All A is C." Any attempt to extend this triviality encountered difficulties: Boole's predecessors had tried to force the algebra of real numbers onto logic, and since they had not envisaged a plurality of algebras, it was believed that only if the elementary properties of the symbols implied formal rules identical with those of the algebra of real numbers could the subject be regarded as a valid part of mathematics. Boole recognized that he had created a new branch of mathematics, but it is not clear whether he appreciated that he had devised a new algebra. He appears not to have known that geometries other than Euclidean could be constructed; but he knew of Rowan Hamilton's quaternions, an algebra of quadruplets in which products are noncommutative, for one of his minor papers (1848) deals with some quaternion matters. Grassmann's similar, if more general, work in the *Ausdehnungslehre* (1844) seems to have been unknown. Boole, then, knew of an algebra similar to, but not identical with, the algebra of real numbers.

If we consider a set U, the universal set or the universe of discourse, often denoted by 1 in Boole's work, subsets can be specified by elective operators $x, y, \cdots$, so that xU is the subset of U whose elements have the property defining the operator x. Thus, if U is the set of inhabitants of New York, we can select those who are, say, male by an elective operator x and denote the set of male inhabitants of New York by xU. Similarly, the left-handed inhabitants of New York may be denoted by yU, and blue-eyed inhabitants by zU, and so on. The elective operators may be applied successively. Thus we may first select all the males and from these all the left-handers by the symbolism $y(xU)$; if we first select all the left-handers and from these all the males, we have the symbolism $x(yU)$. Since in each case the final set is the same, that of all left-handed males, we can write $y(xU) = x(yU)$, or, since the universe of discourse U is understood throughout, simply write $yx = xy$. The analogy with the commutative algebraic product is clear. The associative law for products, $x(yz) = (xy)z$, can be verified at once in this interpretation, since each side denotes the set of those who are at once male, left-handed, and blue-eyed; Boole uses this without bothering to give any explicit justification. He was careful, however, to remark that although an analogy exists, the evidence on which the laws are based in his work is not related to the evidence on which the laws of the algebra of real numbers are based. To select the set of males from the set of males is merely to arrive at the set of males; thus the definition of the operator x leads to the idempotent law $x(xU) = xU$, or $x^2 = x$, the first break with ordinary algebra.

The product or intersection operation can also be regarded as a symbolic expression of the logical concept of conjunction by means of the conjunctive "and," since xy will denote the set of those inhabitants of New York who are at once male *and* left-handed.

If xU is the subset of males in the universal set U, it is natural to write the set of nonmales, that which remains when the set of males is subtracted from U, as $U - xU$, or, briefly, $1 - x$. This set, the complement of x relative to U, which Boole for brevity denoted by $\bar{x}$, can be regarded as arising from the application of the logical negation "not" to the set x. Addition has not yet been defined, but Boole did not hesitate to rewrite the equation $\bar{x} = 1 - x$ in the form $x + \bar{x} = 1$, implying that the universal set is made up of the elements of the subset x or of the subset not-x; this suggests that the sign $+$ is the symbol for the connective "or." But the word "or" in English usage has an inclusive and an exclusive sense: "either . . . or . . . and possibly both" and "either . . . or . . . but not both." Boole chose the exclusive sense, and so did not allow the symbolism $x + y$ unless the sets x, y were mutually exclusive.

Modern usage takes $x + y$ for the union or logical sum, the set of elements belonging to at least one of x,y: this union Boole included in his symbolism as $x + \bar{x}y$. Kneale suggests that Boole's choice of the exclusive sense for the symbol $+$ was caused by a desire to use the minus sign $(-)$ as the inverse of the plus sign $(+)$. If y is contained in x, $x - y$ can consistently denote those elements of x which are not elements of y—the complement of y relative to x—but if $+$ is used in the inclusive sense, then the equations $x = y + z$, $x = y + w$ do not imply $z = w$, so that $x - y$ is essentially indeterminate. Alternately, a use of the idempotent law implies that

$$(x - y)^2 = x - y,$$

and a further application of this law suggests that from

$$x^2 - 2xy + y^2 = x - y$$

it follows that

$$x - 2xy + y = x - y$$

and, hence, that $y = xy$; this is a symbolic statement that y is a subset of x. Boole was thus led to the use of the sign $+$ in the exclusive sense, with the sign $-$ as its inverse.

The idempotent law $x^2 = x$ is expressed in the form $x(1 - x) = 0$, but it is not altogether clear whether Boole regarded this as a deduction or as a formulation of the fundamental Aristotelian principle that a proposition cannot be simultaneously true and false. Some of the obscurity is due to the fact that Boole does not always make clear whether he is dealing with sets, or with propositions, or with an abstract calculus of which sets and propositions are representations.

Much of the 1847 tract on the mathematical analysis of logic is devoted to symbolic expressions for the forms of the classical Aristotelian propositions and the moods of the syllogism. The universal propositions "All X's are Y's," "No X's are Y's" take the forms $x(1 - y) = 0$, $xy = 0$. The particular propositions "Some X's are Y's," "Some X's are not Y's" do not take what might appear to be the natural forms $xy \neq 0$, $x(1 - y) \neq 0$, possibly because Boole wished to avoid inequalities and to work entirely in terms of equations. He therefore introduced an elective symbol, v; any elements common to x and y constitute a subset v; which, he says, is "indefinite in every respect but this"—that it has some members. The two particular propositions he wrote in the forms $xy = v$, $x(1 - y) = v$. This ill-defined symbol needs careful handling when the moods and figures of the syllogism are discussed. Thus the premises "All Y's are X's," "No Z's are Y's" give the equations $y = vx$, $0 = zy$, with the inference $0 = vzx$ to be interpreted as "Some X's are not Z's." Boole explains that it would be incorrect to interpret $0 = vzx$ as "Some Z's are not X's" because the equation $y = vx$ fixes the interpretation of vx as "Some X's" and "v is regarded as the representation of 'Some' only with respect to the class X."

A similar obscurity is encountered when an attempt is made to define division. If $z = xy$, what inferences can be drawn about x, in the hope of defining the quotient z/y? Since z is the intersection of x and y, and thus is contained in y, $yz = z$; thus x, which contains z, contains yz. Any other element of x that is not in z cannot be in y, and hence x is made up of yz and an indeterminate set of which all that can be said is that its elements belong neither to y nor to z, and thus belong to the intersection of $1 - y$ and $1 - z$. Thus

$$z/y = yz + \text{an indefinite portion of } (1 - y)(1 - z).$$

Boole gave this result as a special case of his general expansion formula, and his argument is typical of that used to establish the general theorem. From $y + \bar{y} = 1$, $z + \bar{z} = 1$, it follows that $yz + y\bar{z} + \bar{y}z + \bar{y}\bar{z} = 1$, that is, the universe of discourse is the sum of the subsets $yz, y\bar{z}, \bar{y}z, \bar{y}\bar{z}$. Hence, any subset whatsoever will be at most a sum of elements from each of these four subsets; thus

$$z/y = Ayz + By\bar{z} + C\bar{y}z + D\bar{y}\bar{z},$$

with coefficients A, B, C, D to be determined. First, set $y = 1, z = 1$, so that $\bar{y} = \bar{z} = 0$; then $A = 1$. Next, set $y = 1$, $z = 0$, so that $\bar{y} = 0$, $\bar{z} = 1$; then $B = 0$. Third, set $y = 0$, $z = 1$, so that $\bar{y} = 1$, $\bar{z} = 0$; if the term in $\bar{y}z$ were present, then C would have to be infinite; hence, the term in $\bar{y}z$ cannot appear. Finally, if $y = z = 0$, the coefficient D is of the form $0/0$, which is indeterminate. This asserts the possible presence of an indefinite portion of the set $\bar{y}\bar{z}$. Thus, as before,

$$z/y = yz + \text{an indefinite portion of } \bar{y}\bar{z},$$

or, as Boole frequently wrote it,

$$\frac{z}{y} = yz + \frac{0}{0}(1 - y)(1 - z).$$

Schröder showed that the introduction of division is unnecessary. But the concept of the "development" of a function of the elective symbols is fundamental to Boole's logical operations and occupies a prominent place in his great work on mathematical logic, the *Investigation of the Laws of Thought.* If $f(x)$ involves x and the algebraic signs, then it must denote a subset of the universe of discourse and must therefore be made up of elements from x and $\bar{x}$. Thus

$$f(x) = Ax + B\bar{x},$$

where the coefficients A and B are determined by giving x the values of 0 and 1. Thus

$$f(x) = f(1)x + f(0)(1 - x),$$

which in the *Mathematical Analysis of Logic* Boole regards as a special case of MacLaurin's theorem, although he dropped this analogy in the *Investigation of the Laws of Thought.* A repeated application of this method to an expression $f(x,y)$ containing two elective symbols yields

$$f(x,y) = f(1,1)\,xy + f(1,0)\,x(1 - y) + f(0,1)(1 - x)y + f(0,0)(1 - x)(1 - y),$$

and more general formulas can be written down by induction. Logical problems which can be expressed in terms of elective symbols may then be reduced to standard forms expediting their solution.

Boole's logical calculus is not a two-valued algebra, although the distinction is not always clearly drawn in his own work. The principles of his calculus, as a calculus of sets, are nowhere set out by him in a formal table, but are assumed, sometimes implicitly, and are, save one, analogous to the algebraic rules governing real numbers:

$$xy = yx$$
$$x + y = y + x$$
$$x(y + z) = xy + xz$$
$$x(y - z) = xy - xz.$$

If $x = y$, then

$$xz = yz$$
$$x + z = y + z$$
$$x - z = y - z.$$

$$x(1 - x) = 0.$$

Of these, only the last has no analogue in the algebra of real numbers. These principles suffice for the calculus of sets. But Boole observes that in algebra the last principle is an equation whose only roots are $x = 0$, $x = 1$. In the calculus of sets this would assert that any set is either the null set or the universal set. Boole added this numerical interpretation in order to establish a two-valued algebra, of which one representation would be a calculus of propositions in which the truth of a proposition X is denoted by $x = 1$ and its falsehood by $x = 0$: the truth-value of a conjunction "X and Y" will be given by xy, and of an exclusive disjunction "X or Y" by $x + y$. The distinction between propositions and propositional functions, not drawn by Boole, was made later by C. S. Peirce and Schröder.

The use of $x + y$ to denote the exclusive sense of "or" led to difficulties, such as the impossibility of interpreting $1 + x$ and $x + x$, which Boole surmounted with considerable ingenuity. But Jevons, in his *Pure Logic* (1864), used the plus sign in its inclusive (and/or) sense, a use followed by Venn and C. S. Peirce and since then generally adopted. Peirce and Schröder emphasized that the inclusive interpretation permits a duality between sum and product, and they also showed that the concepts of subtraction and division are superfluous and can be discarded. With the use of $x + y$ to denote "either x or y or both," the expression $x + x$ presents no difficulty, being just

x, while $1 + x$ is the universal set 1. The duality of the two operations of sum and product exemplified by the equations $xx = x$, $x + x = x$ can now be carried further: the formulas

$$xy + xz = x(y + z), \qquad (x + y)(x + z) = x + yz$$

are duals, since one can be derived from the other by an interchange of sum with product. This duality is clearer if these operations are denoted by the special symbols $\cap$, $\cup$ now in general use for product and sum, that is, for intersection and union. In this notation, the preceding equations are written

$$(x \cup y) \cap (x \cup z) = x \cup (y \cap z),$$
$$(x \cap y) \cup (x \cap z) = x \cap (y \cup z).$$

With the inclusive interpretation, the system can now be shown to obey the dual rules of De Morgan:

$$\overline{xy} = \bar{x} + \bar{y}, \qquad \overline{x + y} = \bar{x}\bar{y}.$$

In the *Investigation of the Laws of Thought,* the calculus is applied to the theory of probability. If $P(X) = x$ is the probability of an event X, then if events X, Y are independent, $P(X \text{ and } Y) = xy$, while if X and Y are mutually exclusive, $P(X \text{ or } Y) = x + y$. The principles laid down above are satisfied, except for the additional numerical principle in which the allowable values of x are 0 and 1, which is not satisfied. A clear and precise symbolism enabled Boole to detect and correct flaws in earlier work on probability theory.

E. V. Huntington in 1904 gave a set of independent axioms on which Boole's apparatus can be constructed, and various equivalent sets have been exhibited. One formulation postulates two binary operations $\cup$, $\cap$ (union and intersection) which have the commutative and distributive properties:

$$x \cup y = y \cup x, \qquad x \cap y = y \cap x,$$
$$x \cup (y \cap z) = (x \cup y) \cap (x \cup z),$$
$$x \cap (y \cup z) = (x \cap y) \cup (x \cap z);$$

further, there are two distinct elements, 0 and 1, such that for all x

$$x \cup 0 = x, \qquad x \cap 1 = x;$$

also, for any x, there is an element $\bar{x}$ (the complement) for which

$$x \cup \bar{x} = 1, \qquad x \cap \bar{x} = 0.$$

The system so defined is self-dual, since the set of axioms remains unchanged if $\cup$ and $\cap$ are interchanged when 0, 1 are also interchanged. The associative laws for union and intersection are not required as axioms, since they can be deduced from the given set.

If intersection and complement are taken as the basic operations, with the associative law $x \cap (y \cap z) = (x \cap y) \cap z$ now an axiom and the relation between the basic operations given by the statements

$$\text{if } x \cap \bar{y} = z \cap \bar{z} \text{ for some } z, \text{ then } x \cap y = x,$$
$$\text{if } x \cap y = x, \text{ then } x \cap \bar{y} = z \cap \bar{z} \text{ for any } z,$$

then union can now be defined in terms of intersection and complement by the equation

$$x \cup y = \overline{\bar{x} \cap \bar{y}},$$

0 can be defined as $x \cap \bar{x}$, and 1 as the complement of 0. The two systems are then equivalent.

The theory of lattices may be regarded as a generalization. A lattice is a system with operations $\cup$, $\cap$ having the commutative, distributive, and associative properties. Thus every Boolean algebra is a lattice; the converse is not true. The lattice concept is wider than the Boolean, and embraces interpretations for which Boolean algebra is not appropriate.

Boole's two-valued algebra has recently been applied to the design of electric circuits containing simple switches, relays, and control elements. In particular, it has a wide field of application in the design of high-speed computers using the binary system of digital numeration.

BIBLIOGRAPHY

I. Original Works. Boole's papers include "Researches on the Theory of Analytical Transformations, With a Special Application to the Reduction of the General Equation of the Second Order," in *Cambridge Mathematical Journal,* **2** (1841), 64–73; "On a General Method in Analysis," in *Philosophical Transactions of the Royal Society of London,* **134** (1844), 225–282. *An Address on the Genius and Discoveries of Sir Isaac Newton* was published in Lincoln in 1835.

His textbooks are *Treatise on Differential Equations* (Cambridge, 1859, and later editions); a posthumous *Supplementary Volume* (Cambridge, 1865), compiled from Boole's notes by Isaac Todhunter, and containing a list of Boole's publications; *Treatise on the Calculus of Finite Differences* (Cambridge, 1860, and later editions).

On mathematical logic: *The Mathematical Analysis of Logic, Being an Essay Towards a Calculus of Deductive Reasoning* (Cambridge, 1847; repr. Oxford, 1948, and in Boole's *Collected Logical Works,* I, Chicago–London, 1916); *An Investigation of the Laws of Thought, on Which Are Founded the Mathematical Theories of Logic and Probability* (London, 1854; repr. New York, 1951, and in Boole's *Collected Logical Works,* II, Chicago–London, 1916).

II. Secondary Literature. E. V. Huntington, "Sets of Independent Postulates for the Algebra of Logic," in *Transactions of the American Mathematical Society,* **5**

(1904), 208–309; E. V. Huntington, "Postulates for the Algebra of Logic," in *Transactions of the American Mathematical Society,* **35** (1933), 274–304; W. Kneale, "Boole and the Revival of Logic," in *Mind,* **57** (1948), 149–175, which contains a useful bibliography; W. Kneale, "Boole and the Algebra of Logic," in *Notes and Records of the Royal Society of London,* **12** (1956), 53–63; Sir Geoffrey Taylor, "George Boole, 1815–1864," *ibid.,* 44–52, which gives an account of Boole's life by his grandson.

T. A. A. BROADBENT

BORCHARDT, CARL WILHELM (*b.* Berlin, Germany, 22 February 1817; *d.* Rudersdorf, near Berlin, 27 June 1880)

The son of Moritz Borchardt, a wealthy and respected Jewish merchant, and Emma Heilborn, Borchardt had among his private tutors the mathematicians J. Plücker and J. Steiner. From 1836 he studied at the University of Berlin with Dirichlet, and from 1839 at the University of Königsberg with Bessel, F. Neumann, and Jacobi. In his doctoral thesis (1843; unpublished and now lost), written under the supervision of Jacobi, he dealt with certain systems of nonlinear differential equations. In 1846–1847 he was in Paris, where he met Chasles, Hermite, and Liouville. Borchardt became a *Privatdozent* at the University of Berlin in 1848, and a member of the Berliner Akademie der Wissenschaften in 1855. He married Rosa Oppenheim. Very poor health interrupted his teaching for years; nevertheless, from 1856 to 1880 he edited, as Crelle's successor, Volumes **57–90** of the celebrated *Crelle's Journal für die reine und angewandte Mathematik,* upholding its high standard of mathematical scholarship.

Borchardt became known as a mathematician through his first publication (1846), in which he generalized a result obtained by Kummer concerning the equation that determines the secular disturbances of the planets (characteristic equation, or secular equation). By means of determinants Borchardt proved that in this case Sturm's functions can be represented as a sum of squares. From this it follows that the roots of the characteristic equation are real. In several further papers Borchardt applied the theory of determinants to algebraic questions, mostly in connection with symmetric functions, the theory of elimination, and interpolation. Another group of his papers dealt with the arithmetic-geometric mean (AGM). Gauss and Lagrange had established its connection with the complete elliptic integral of the first class. Borchardt, starting from the functional equation for the limit value of the AGM, derived a linear differential equation of the second order, the differential equation of the complete, first-class elliptic integral. He also studied a variant process of the AGM connected with the circular functions, and the generalization of the AGM to four elements and its relation to hyperelliptic integrals. Other papers dealt with problems of maxima and the theory of elasticity.

BIBLIOGRAPHY

I. ORIGINAL WORKS. Borchardt's *Gesammelte Werke,* G. Hettner, ed. (Berlin, 1888), contains 25 papers and some short communications. His works are listed in Poggendorff, I, 238; III, 162; IV, 158.

II. SECONDARY LITERATURE. Works on Borchardt are Maurice d'Ocagne, "C. W. Borchardt et son oeuvre," in *Revue des questions scientifiques* (Jan. 1890), also repr. separately (Brussels, 1890); and Max Steck, in *Neue deutsche Biographie,* II (Berlin, 1955), 456.

CHRISTOPH J. SCRIBA

BORDA, JEAN-CHARLES (*b.* Dax, France, 4 May 1733; *d.* Paris, France, 19 February 1799)

Borda was the tenth child and the sixth son of the sixteen children of Jean-Antoine de Borda and Jeanne-Marie-Thérèse de Lacroix. His parents were both of the nobility, and his parental ancestors had been in the military since the early seventeenth century. Borda began his studies at the Collège des Barnabites at Dax, then continued at the Jesuit Collège de la Flèche. He entered the École du Génie de Mézières in 1758 and finished the two-year course in one year. Borda scorned religion, at least in his youth, and he never married. While commanding a flotilla of six ships in the Antilles in 1782, Borda was taken prisoner by the English. After this misfortune, his health declined steadily. He was elected a member of the Paris Académie des Sciences in 1756 (and of its successor, the Institut de France), the Académie de Bordeaux in 1767, the Académie de Marine in 1769, and the Bureau des Longitudes in 1795. Borda is a major figure in the history of the French navy. He attained the rank of *capitaine de vaisseau,* participated in several scientific voyages and in the American Revolution, and in 1784 was named *inspecteur des constructions et de l'École des Ingénieurs de vaisseau.*

Borda's most important contributions are his work in fluid mechanics and his development and use of instruments for navigation, geodesy, and the determination of weights and measures. In a series of theoretical and experimental memoirs he studied fluid flow reactions and fluid resistance as applied to artillery, ships, scientific instruments, and hydraulic wheels and pumps. Specifically, he demonstrated that Newton's theory of fluid resistance was untenable and that the resistance is proportional to the square of the fluid velocity and to the sine of the angle of incidence. He introduced the Borda mouthpiece and calculated the coefficient of fluid contraction from an orifice. Borda's use of the principle of conservation of *vis viva* was important as a precursor of Lazare Carnot's work in mechanics.

Borda's development of a surveying instrument, the *cercle de réflexion,* contributed to the French success in measuring the length of the meridional arc. He participated in the work on a standard system of weights and measures, and designed the platinum standard meter and the standard seconds pendulum. He contributed memoirs on the calculus of variations and, in connection with his *cercle de réflexion,* developed a series of trigonometric tables. Borda's importance to science lies in his skillful use of calculus and experiment, unifying them in diverse areas of physics. This led Biot to state that one owes to Borda and Coulomb the renaissance of exact physics in eighteenth-century France.

BIBLIOGRAPHY

I. Original Works. A complete bibliography of Borda's memoirs is contained in Mascart (see below). His various papers on fluid mechanics are contained in the *Mémoires de l'Académie des sciences* for the years 1763 and 1766–1769. For a description of his *cercle de réflexion,* see *Description et usage du cercle de réflexion avec différentes méthodes pour calculer les observations nautiques, par le Chevalier de Borda* (Paris, 1787; 4th ed., 1816).

II. Secondary Literature. The most important treatment of Borda's work is the massive 800-page study by Jean Mascart, *La vie et les travaux du Chevalier Jean-Charles de Borda,* published as a volume of the *Annales de l'Université de Lyon,* n.s., **2**, Droit, Lettres, fasc. 33 (Lyons-Paris, 1919). The best contemporary essay is S. F. Lacroix, *Éloge historique de Jean-Charles Borda* (Paris, *ca.* 1800). For a recent summary of Borda's work in fluid mechanics, see R. Dugas, *Histoire de la mécanique* (Paris, 1950), pp. 292–300.

C. Stewart Gillmor

BOREL, ÉMILE (FÉLIX-ÉDOUARD-JUSTIN) (*b.* Saint-Affrique, Aveyron, France, 7 January 1871; *d.* Paris, France, 3 February 1956)

Borel's father, Honoré, son of an artisan, was a Protestant village pastor. His mother, Émilie Teissié-Solier, came of a local merchant family. In 1882, already known as a prodigy, he left his father's school for the *lycée* at nearby Montauban. In Paris as a scholarship student preparing for the university, he entered the family circle of G. Darboux through friendship with his son, saw the "good life" of a leading mathematician, and set his heart on it. In 1889, after winning first place in the École Polytechnique, the École Normale Supérieure, and the general competitions, Borel chose the gateway to teaching and research, in spite of the blandishments of a special representative of the École Polytechnique.

Fifty years later Borel's colleagues celebrated the jubilee of his entrance to the École Normale, rightly considering that as the beginning of his scientific career. Indeed, he published two papers during his first year and appears to have established there his lifetime pattern of intensely serious and well-organized activity. He embraced an agnostic, scientific, and rational outlook that implied a responsible interest in all aspects of human affairs, and the extensive friendships of his undergraduate days helped make possible his broad cultural and political influence in later life. First in the class of 1893, he was promptly invited to teach at the University of Lille, where he wrote his thesis and twenty-two papers in three years before being called back to the École Normale, where publications, honors, and responsibilities piled up rapidly.

In 1901 Borel married Paul Appell's eldest daughter, Marguerite, who had interested him for some time but had only then turned seventeen. She wrote more than thirty novels (as Camille Marbo), was president of the Société des Gens de Lettres, and both assisted and complemented her husband's many-sided activity. They had no children but adopted Fernand Lebeau, son of the older of Borel's two sisters, after the early death of his parents. In 1906 they used money from one of Émile's prizes to launch *La revue du mois,* which appealed successfully to a very broad circle until the war and economic crisis killed it in 1920. During this period Borel's publications and activities showed a progressive broadening of interest from pure mathematics to applications and public affairs. Without seeming to diminish his mathematical creativity, he wrote texts and popularizations, edited several distinguished series of books, contributed to popular magazines and the daily press, played leading roles in professional and university affairs, and maintained acquaintances ranging from poets to industrialists.

Such an implausible level of activity was possible because Borel's uncommon intelligence and vigor were accompanied by efficient organization and self-discipline. He could be kind and generous of his time and energy in meeting his official or self-imposed obligations. He was even ready to risk his status for a good cause. But he had no time for "small talk" or trivial activity, seemed formidable and even rude to outsiders, and with increasing age grew more impatient with would-be wasters of his time. His lectures displayed his mind at work rather than a finished exposition, and his teaching consisted primarily in directing his students' efforts.

In 1909 Borel occupied the chair of theory of functions, newly created for him at the Sorbonne, and began thirty-two years on the University Council, representing the Faculty of Science. In 1910 he entered what he called the happiest time of his life as vice-director of the École Normale in charge of science students, but World War I cut it short. His service in sound location at the front (while Marguerite headed a hospital), and in organizing research and development in the War Office under his old friend Paul Painlevé, turned his interests more than ever toward applications. After the war he could not be happy again at the École Normale. There were "too many ghosts in the hallways," including that of his adopted son. At his request he moved to the chair of probability and mathematical physics at the Sorbonne and maintained only honorary connections with the École Normale. The era was closed by the longest of his many trips abroad, including five months in China with Painlevé, and by his election to the Academy in 1921.

While continuing his flow of publications and his lectures in mathematics, Borel now moved rapidly into politics as mayor of Saint-Affrique (with Marguerite presiding over the Jury Femina), councillor of the Aveyron district, Radical and Radical-Socialist member of the Chamber of Deputies (1924–1936), and minister of the navy (1925). Important scientific legislation, the founding of the Centre National de la Recherche Scientifique, and several ships named after mathematicians are traceable to his initiative. He helped plan and raise funds for the Institut Henri Poincaré and served as director from its founding in 1928 until his death.

Retired from politics in 1936 and from the Sorbonne in 1940, Borel still had the vigor to produce more than fifty additional books and papers, to participate in the Resistance in his native village, to which he returned after a brief imprisonment by the Germans in 1940, and to travel extensively. The breadth of his services was recognized by such honors as the presidency of the Academy (1934), the Grand Cross of the Legion of Honor (1950), the first gold medal of the Centre Nationale de la Recherche Scientifique (1955), the Croix de Guerre (1918), and the Resistance Medal (1945). A fall on the boat while returning from giving a paper at a meeting of the International Institute of Statistics in Brazil in 1955 hastened his death the following year at eighty-five.

Borel's undergraduate publications showed virtuosity in solving his elders' problems rather than great originality, but a "big idea" was incubating. Already in 1891 he was "extrêmement séduit" by Georg Cantor, whose "romantic spirit" mixed explosively with Borel's rigorous training in classical analysis and geometry. By sensing both the power and danger of set concepts, Borel anticipated the unifying themes of his lifework and of much mathematics in the twentieth century. In his thesis of 1894, which Collingwood rightly calls "an important mathematical event," can be found the ideas with which he initiated the modern theories of functions of a real variable, measure, divergent series, nonanalytic continuation, denumerable probability, Diophantine approximation, and the metrical distribution theory of values of analytical functions. All are related to Cantorian ideas, especially to the notion of a denumerable set. This is obvious for the two most famous results in the thesis, the Heine-Borel covering theorem (misnamed later by Schoenflies) and the proof that a denumerable set is of measure zero. The first asserted that if a denumerable set of open intervals covers a bounded set of points on a line, then a finite subset of the intervals is sufficient to cover. The second involves implicitly the extension of measure from finite sets of intervals to a very large class of point sets, now known as Borel-measurable sets.

Borel exploited his first insights in many directions. His *Leçons* of 1898 and other works laid the basis of measure theory so solidly that in that field the letter *B* means Borel. In 1905 he noticed that probability language was convenient for talking about measure of point sets, and in 1909 he introduced probability on a denumerable set of events, thus filling the gap between traditional finite and "geometrical" (continuous) probability. In the same paper he proved a special case of his strong law of large numbers. But Borel remained skeptical of the actual infinite beyond the denumerable and of nonconstructive definitions. Much of his work was motivated by finitistic ideas, and his last book (1952) discussed his observation that most real numbers must be "inaccessible," since with a finite alphabet we can name at most a denumerable subset. By this caution he avoided some of the pitfalls into which others fell, but he also was barred from the fruits of greater daring. It was Lebesgue, Baire, Fréchet, and others who pushed set and measure theoretic ideas more boldly and so opened the way to the abstract analysis of the mid-twentieth century.

Other motivations are visible in Borel's work: the challenge of unsolved classical problems and visible gaps, an early and increasing admiration for Cauchy, an interest in physical and social problems, all tinged strongly with French patriotism. Often his solutions opened whole fields for exploitation by others. His "elementary" proof of Picard's theorem in 1896 not only created a sensation because the problem had resisted all attacks for eighteen years, but also established methods and posed problems that set the theme of complex function theory for a generation. Borel's work on divergent series in 1899 filled the gap between convergent and divergent series. His work on monogenic functions (summed up in his monograph of 1917) showed the primacy of Cauchy's idea of the existence of the derivative over the Weierstrassian notion of series expansion and filled the gap between analytic and very discontinuous functions.

Before World War I, Borel had worked out most of his original ideas, and thereafter his scientific publications were largely the development and application of earlier ideas and the solution of minor problems. A major exception is the series of papers on game theory (1921-1927) in which he was the first to define games of strategy and to consider best strategies, mixed strategies, symmetric games, infinite games, and applications to war and economics. He proved the minimax theorem for three players, after some doubts for five and seven, and finally (1927) conjectured its truth a year before John von Neumann independently first took up the subject and proved the general theorem. Although Borel's papers were overlooked until after von Neumann's work was well known, he must be considered the inventor, if not the founder, of game theory.

Borel's innovations are essential in twentieth-century analysis and probability, but his research methods belong rather to the nineteenth. He abjured generalization except when it was forced on him. He was motivated by specific problems and applications. He disliked formalism ("pure symbolism turning about itself"), logicism, and intuitionism (both too removed from the physical reality that he thought should guide mathematics). Borel was the most successful mathematician of his generation in using specific problems and results as scientific parables pointing the way to broad theories that still remain fertile.

BIBLIOGRAPHY

I. Original Works. A complete scientific bibliography to 1939 appears in *Selecta. Jubilé scientifique de M. Émile Borel* (Paris, 1940), and is extended to 1956 in the biographies by Collingwood and Fréchet, which also analyze Borel's work in detail. The papers in the *Selecta* are in part more representative of the commentators' interests than of Borel's most significant work, but a complete collected works is in preparation. His writings on philosophical questions, pedagogy, and social problems are well covered in *Émile Borel, philosophe et homme d'action. Pages choisies et presentées par Maurice Fréchet* (Paris, 1967). Borel's own analysis of his work appears in his *Notice sur les travaux scientifiques* (Paris, 1912) and his *Supplément (1921) à la Notice (1912)*, in the *Selecta.* Very revealing also are his "Documents autobiographiques," in *Organon* (Warsaw), **1** (1936), 34-42, repr. in *Selecta,* and "Allocution," in *Notices et discours de l'Académie des Sciences,* **2** (1949), 350-359.

Of more than 300 scientific publications the most notable are his thesis, "Sur quelques points de la théorie des fonctions," in *Annales de l'École Normale,* 3rd ser., **12** (1895), 9-55; "Démonstration élémentaire d'un théorème de M. Picard sur les fonctions entières," in *Comptes rendus de l'Académie des Sciences,* **122** (1896), 1045-1048; "Fondements de la théorie des séries divergentes sommables," in *Journal de mathématique,* 5th ser., **2** (1896), 103-122; "Sur les zéros des fonctions entières," in *Acta mathematica,* **20** (1897), 357-396; *Leçons sur la théorie des fonctions* (Paris, 1898; 4th ed., 1950), his most influential book; "Mémoire sur les séries divergentes," in *Annales de l'École Normale,* 3rd ser., **16** (1899), 9-131, which won a grand prize of the Academy and led to over 200 papers by others during the following two decades; *Leçons sur les fonctions entières* (Paris, 1900; 2nd ed., 1921), an exposition of the work growing out of his paper on the Picard theorem; *Leçons sur les séries divergentes* (Paris, 1901; 2nd ed., 1928); *Leçons sur les fonctions de variables réeles et les développements en séries de polynomes* (Paris, 1905; 2nd ed., 1928); "Les probabilités dénombrables et leurs applications arithmétiques," in *Rendiconti del Circolo Matematico di Palermo,* **27** (1909), 247-270; *Le hasard* (Paris, 1914), probably his best popularization; "I. Aggregates of Zero Measure. II. Monogenic Uniform Non-analytic Functions," in *Rice Institute Pamphlet,* 4th ser., **1** (1917), 1-52; *Leçons sur les fonctions monogènes uniformes d'un variable complexe* (Paris, 1917), the definitive exposition of his work in this area; "La théorie du jeu et les équational intégrales à noyau symétrique," in *Comptes rendus de l'Académie des Sciences,* **173** (1921), 1302-1308—this and two later notes (1924, 1927) on game theory appear in translation with commentary by Fréchet and von Neumann in *Econometrica,* **21** (1953), 95-125; *Méthodes et problèmes de la théorie des fonctions* (Paris, 1922), a collection winding up his work in that area; *La politique républicaine* (Paris, 1924), his most substantial political work; *Principes et formules classiques du calcul des probabilités* (Paris, 1925), the first fascicle of the Traité; *Valeur pratique et philosophique des probabilités* (Paris, 1939), the last fascicle of the Traité; *Théorie mathématique du bridge à la portée de tous* (Paris, 1940), written with A. Cheron; *Le jeu, la chance et les théories scientifiques modernes* (Paris,

1941); "Sur l'emploie du théorème de Bernoulli pour faciliter le calcul d'une infinité de coefficients—Application au problème de l'attente à un quichet," in *Comptes rendus de l'Académie des Sciences,* **214** (1942), 425–456, his last original contribution to probability theory; *Les probabilités et la vie* (Paris, 1943), another fine popularization with later editions and translations; *Éléments de la théorie des ensembles* (Paris, 1949), a summation containing some new results; and *Les nombres inaccessibles* (Paris, 1952), his last book.

Series that he edited (always contributing substantially also) include Collection de Monographies sur la Théorie de Fonctions (Paris, 1898–1952)—sometimes called the Borel tracts, this totaled over fifty volumes, ten by Borel himself—and Cours de Mathématiques (Paris, 1903–1912), a series of elementary texts designed to cover various curricula, usually written with collaborators. Other series include La Nouvelle Collection Scientifique (1910–1922), thirty-five popularizations; Bibliothèque d'Éducation par la Science (Paris, 1924–1946), high-level popularizations for the educated layman; Traité de Calcul des Probabilités et de Ses Applications (Paris, 1925–1938), eighteen fascicles in four volumes, intended to cover the whole field as it had developed since 1875; Collection de Physique Mathématique (Paris, 1928–1950); and Collection de Monographies des Probabilités et de Leurs Applications (Paris, 1937–1950), seven volumes intended to supplement the Traité by current research.

II. SECONDARY LITERATURE. Along with the material in the *Selecta* and Borel's autobiographical writings cited above, the best sources are "Jubilé scientifique de M. Émile Borel . . . 14 janvier 1940," in *Notices et discours de l'Académie des Sciences,* **2** (1949), 324–359; L. de Broglie, *ibid.,* **4** (1957), 1–24; E. F. Collingwood, in *Journal of the London Mathematical Society,* **34** (1959), 488–512, and **35** (1960), 384; M. Fréchet, "La vie et l'oeuvre d'Émile Borel," in *Enseignement mathématique,* 2nd ser., **11** (1965), 1–95; M. Loève, "Integration and Measure," in *Encyclopaedia Britannica* (1965); and P. Montel, in *Comptes rendus de l'Académie des Sciences,* **242** (1965), 848–850.

KENNETH O. MAY

BORELLI, GIOVANNI ALFONSO (*b.* Naples, Italy, January 1608; *d.* Rome, Italy, 31 December 1679)

Borelli is not as widely known or appreciated as perhaps he should be. What reputation he has is based upon his mechanics, including celestial mechanics, and his physiology or iatromechanics. The former, unfortunately, was quickly and completely overshadowed by the work of Isaac Newton; and his iatromechanics, although important and influential, was too much informed by what proved to be a relatively sterile systematic bias to bear much immediate fruit. Accordingly historians have undervalued his place in the development of the sciences in the seventeenth century, and they have paid little attention to his career or his personality. (There has been no lengthy treatment of his life since the eighteenth century, and important and elementary biographical information is still hard to come by.) But he was highly respected by his contemporaries. He read widely, and he drew his scientific inspiration from a broad spectrum of the heroes and near-heroes of the early seventeenth century: such men as Galileo Galilei, William Harvey, Johannes Kepler, and Santorio Santorio. He worked on many problems, contributed significantly to all the topics he touched, and in fact played an important part in establishing and extending the new experimental-mathematical philosophy. He was brilliant enough scientifically to be very much ahead of his time, even if he was not quite brilliant enough nor free enough from other commitments to produce general synthetic solutions in his fields of interest which would be either successful or entirely convincing.

During the century prior to Borelli's birth, Italians had been in the forefront of the late Renaissance effort to translate and master the Alexandrian astronomers, mathematicians, and physiologists. By the end of that century many had learned all they could from the past and had begun to strike out on their own. Galileo's telescopic discoveries only dramatically underscored the fact that major innovations were underway in all fields of natural philosophy. And they also indicated that the Italians could be expected to continue playing a leading role in these new enterprises. But during Borelli's lifetime the world saw Galileo condemned for his innovations, the Lincei persecuted, the Cimento disbanded, and the Investiganti of Naples suspended. It also saw the death, in the decade of the 1640's, of many of Galileo's most talented disciples: Benedetto Castelli, Bonaventura Cavalieri, Vincenzo Renieri, and Evangelista Torricelli. Borelli's Italy rejoiced over the conversion of Queen Christina of Sweden and perhaps was as much interested in the fact of Nicholas Steno's conversion as in his scientific accomplishments. Moreover, it was a politically fragmented Italy, portions of which were absorbed in struggles to throw off oppressive foreign domination. And later on its best investigators, for example, Marcello Malpighi and Gian Domenico Cassini, had to find recognition and support north of the Alps. In sum, the new philosophy faced distracting competition and even open hostility from several quarters, and in the long run the Italians could find neither the wherewithal nor the enthusiasm to support science in the ways it was beginning to be supported elsewhere. Borelli's career, then, is an illuminating record of an original scientist who was also politically active in Counter-Reformation Italy. Borelli himself ended his life in political exile in Rome—poverty stricken, teaching elementary mathematics.

Borelli's birth was not auspicious. As part of their rule of southern Italy at the turn of the century, the Spanish maintained military garrisons in the three principal fortresses of Naples. On 28 January 1608, a Spanish infantryman, Miguel Alonso, stationed at Castel Nuovo, witnessed the baptism of his first son, Giovanni Francesco Antonio. The mother was a local woman by the name of Laura Porrello (variously spelled in the records as *porrello, porrella, borrella, borriello, borrelli*). The couple went on to have one daughter and four more sons, including a Filippo baptized 9 March 1614. In later years both Giovanni and Filippo used Borelli as a family name; Giovanni dropped two of his baptismal names but retained an Italianized version of his father's name in their place. Why they did this perhaps can be guessed from the circumstances of their early years.

In November 1614 Tommaso Campanella was returned to Castel St. Elmo, where he had previously been confined. Meanwhile Miguel Alonso had been ordered to Castel St. Elmo. Just after Campanella's return, Miguel became implicated in some serious offense and was arrested along with several other persons. Although it is not known for certain what the alleged crime was, responsible sources suggest that there may have been a conspiracy to free Campanella. In any case the interrogations and trial took place in secret, and during the summer of 1615 Miguel was found guilty and sentenced to the galleys. Upon his certification that he was unable to serve in the galleys the sentence was commuted to exile. Miguel seems to have gone to Rome, and it has usually been supposed that this was the occasion for young Borelli's presence there and eventual contact with Benedetto Castelli. But now we know that Miguel did not remain in exile. He appealed his case and was exonerated. In April 1617 he returned to duty at Castel St. Elmo, where he stayed until he died in 1624. Laura Porrello possibly remained attached to Castel St. Elmo in some capacity, for at her death in 1640 she was buried, as Miguel had been, at the church serving the fortress.

We can guess that sometime before 1626 young Borelli came to the attention of Campanella; there was no lack of opportunity. In 1616 the latter was given a few months of at-large detention in Castel Nuovo (he may have written his *Defense of Galileo* at this time), but he was back in the dungeon of Castel St. Elmo when Miguel returned from exile. In May 1618 he was again sent to Castel Nuovo, where he had a relatively easy imprisonment; he was able to write, see friends, and even have students. It is possible that Borelli was among these, and it is also possible that Borelli received some medical training at the University of Naples in this period, although we have no published records to that effect. In 1626 Campanella was taken to Rome, where he was fully liberated in 1628. Five years later a disciple, under duress, implicated Campanella in a plot to assassinate the Spanish viceroy in Naples. Under great pressures Campanella fled Italy for Paris, in 1634, taking Filippo Borelli with him. There Filippo helped to edit and publish various of Campanella's works, and in at least one he appears as *nipote ed amanuense dello autore*. What happened to Filippo later is not known, but a letter of another of Campanella's disciples in 1657 connects Giovanni Alfonso with information concerning several hundred copies of Campanella's books left at the Dominican convent of Santa Maria Sopra Minerva and also indicates that Giovanni had a brother, a "P. Tomaso filosofo." It has been suggested that on Campanella's death, in 1639, Filippo entered orders and took the name Tommaso.

We do not know when Borelli himself went to Rome. Anytime after 1628 he could have resumed whatever relationship he had established in Naples with Campanella; and it is quite possible that Campanella in turn introduced him to Castelli. In any case he became a student of Castelli along with Torricelli. He must have been in Rome through the period of the publication of Galileo's *Dialogo* and the subsequent trial. Although he did not meet Galileo, he probably had access to all the ins and outs of the affair through both his mentors. And possibly it was during this period that he acquired a copy of calculations or tables made by Galileo concerning the Medici planets (the moons of Jupiter), calculations which were not among the papers inherited by Vincenzo Viviani at Galileo's death and which Viviani requested a copy of in 1643. After Campanella left Rome, Borelli continued for a while with Castelli. In 1635, or shortly thereafter, Castelli's recommendation obtained for Borelli the public lectureship in mathematics in Messina, Sicily. And Castelli continued to look after Borelli's welfare. In 1640, when the mathematics chair at the University of Pisa became vacant, he wrote two letters to Galileo praising Borelli very highly, calling him in one *huomo di grandissimo ingegno e sapere, versatissimo nelle dottrine di V.S. molto Ill.re e tutto tutto* NOSTRI ORDINIS. Galileo's choice, however, was Vincenzo Renieri who then held the position until his death in 1647. Borelli would eventually obtain the post, but not until 1656.

Meanwhile Borelli made his way in Messina. The

city had had little to boast of since the death of Francesco Maurolico in 1575. In the 1630's, however, there was an effort toward a political and intellectual revival which included an attempt to improve substantially the city's university. The people backing these moves were among the same who formed the Accademia della Fucina in 1639, a group of the young, enlightened nobility and merchant class, jealous of its political rights and beginning to grow restless under the restrictions of Spanish rule. The Fucina itself became a forum for both political and intellectual discussion, and in 1642 it came under the direct protection of the Messinese senate. It is not clear when Borelli became a member, but his talents as a public lecturer of mathematics were already highly appreciated. In 1642 the senate provided him with ample funds and sent him on a mission to leading universities to hire away good teachers, especially in law and medicine. We can guess that on this trip Borelli stopped in Naples to see Marco Aurelio Severino, perhaps renewing an old association. He must have visited Castelli in Rome. We know that he visited Tuscany, but unfortunately too late to see Galileo. But he did spend some time in Florence, and while there he met both Viviani and Prince Leopold, the youngest brother of the grand duke. After Florence he went on to Bologna where he very favorably impressed Bonaventura Cavalieri. Then he was off to Padua and eventually Venice where he planned to catch a ship back to Messina. Among the topics of discussion in Florence must have been the work of Santorio, for in Venice he bought a copy of *De statica medicina* and mailed it back to Viviani along with other items of scientific interest. By 1643, then, even though he had not yet published, he was beginning to be known in Italy, and what evidence we have indicates that he had already exposed himself to the studies that were to concern him for the rest of his life: mathematics, physiology, and planetary astronomy.

From 1643 to 1656 Borelli remained in Sicily, so far as we know; he published two works and possibly had a hand in a third. The first developed out of a dispute that may have had some polemic roots in the political and intellectual rivalry between Messina and Palermo. In 1644 a Pietro Emmanuele of Palermo published a *Lettera intorno alla soluzione di un problema geometrico.* This was attacked, so he followed it a year later with a *Lettera in difesa di un problema geometrico.* In the second, at least, Borelli's reputation was impugned, and Borelli replied in the *Discorso del Signor Gio: Alfonso Borelli, accademico della Fucina e professore delle scienze matematiche nello Studio della nobile città di Messina, nel quale si manifestano le falsità, e gli errori, contenuti nella difesa del Problema Geometrico, risoluto dal R. D. Pietro Emmanuele* (Messina, 1646). The Fucina also reacted to protect both itself and Borelli by encouraging the publication of several pamphlets. In one of them, Daniele Spinola's *Il Crivello* (Macerata, 1647), the resolution of the original problem was provided by Giovanni Ventimiglia, a student and a friend of Borelli.

As this controversy died down, Sicily was invaded by an epidemic of fevers. Messina was especially hard hit and the senate encouraged its local *dotti* to try to discern its causes. One study that resulted was Borelli's *On the causes of the malignant fevers of Sicily in the years 1647 and 1648 . . .*; to which he added a section entitled *And at the end the digestion of food is treated by a new method* (Cosenza, 1649). During his investigation of the epidemic Borelli had visited other cities, observed autopsies, and noted in detail the circumstances under which the disease was prevalent. He concluded that in no way were the fevers caused by meteorological conditions or astrological influences, but were probably caused by something getting into the body from the outside. Since this thing seemed to be chemical, Borelli prescribed a chemical remedy, sulfur, and for this recommendation he acknowledged the counsel of his friend and colleague Pietro Castelli (*d.* 1661). In the addendum he again disclosed a chemical approach; he characterized digestion as the action of a *succo acido corrosivo* turning food into a liquid form. Borelli would repeat and expand this particular inquiry during his stay in Pisa.

In 1650 Borelli was considered for the chair of mathematics at Bologna. Cavalieri had died in 1647 and the authorities there wished to fill the post with someone equally able. Accordingly they made inquiries concerning Borelli and received strong endorsements for him as the best mathematician in Italy after Cavalieri. They also learned that Borelli was a trifle capricious and had a leaning toward the "moderns," Copernicus and Galileo (*il Gubernico et il Galileo*). Whether or not this latter was a factor, Borelli was passed over and the chair went to Gian Domenico Cassini. So Borelli remained in Messina and was there when Maurolico's *Emendatio et restitutio conicorum Apollonii Pergaei* was finally published in 1654. The original of the *Conics* of Apollonius had contained eight books, but the sixteenth century possessed only the texts of the first four. Maurolico had attempted to reconstruct Books V and VI. The extent of Borelli's connection with this project is not certain. We do know that he had composed a digest of the first four books before he left Messina. On this account alone he would have been prepared for an opportunity that presented itself when he later arrived in Pisa. Sometime previously the Medici had acquired an Arabic manuscript which seemed to contain all the original eight books. As early as 1645 Michelangelo Ricci had corresponded with Torricelli about the possibility of translating and publishing it, but with no results. Somehow Borelli had learned of it, however, for just a month after his inaugural lecture at Pisa, in the spring of 1656, he wrote to Leopold suggesting that with the aid of someone who knew Arabic he could edit these "most eagerly awaited" last four books. This led, in 1658, to a long summer's collaboration in Rome with the Maronite scholar Abraham Ecchellensis during which the two substantially completed an edition of Books V, VI, and VII. (It turned out that Book VIII was missing from the manuscript.) After many frustrating delays the work finally saw print in 1661 along with an appended Archimedean *Liber assumptorum* taken from another manuscript.

We must presume that in the years before Borelli left Messina he was already in touch with what would become a very important group in Naples. Tommaso Cornelio and Leonardo Di Capoa had both studied with Marco Aurelio Severino. On Severino's urging Cornelio had traveled for several years and had studied with such leading innovators of northern Italy as Ricci, Torricelli, and Cavalieri. When he came back to Naples in 1649 he brought with him the works of Galileo, Descartes, Gassendi, Bacon, Harvey, and Boyle, among others; and he and a lawyer named Francesco d'Andrea started an informal gathering which met to hear the results of its members' investigations. As it gained notoriety, the group faced various pressures, among them political, and in 1663 expediency compelled it to organize formally as the Accademia degli Investiganti under the protection of Andrea Concublet, the marchese d'Arena. All the while it pursued its physical, chemical, and physiological inquiries; corresponded with individuals and groups in other cities; and from time to time received distinguished visitors. Marcello Malpighi, for instance, had been at Pisa from 1656 to 1659 and then went to Bologna. In 1662 Borelli recommended him for the chair that had become vacant with the death of Pietro Castelli in Messina, and on his way south in the fall of that year Malpighi was warmly entertained by Cornelio and Di Capoa. From at least the time of his return to Naples, Cornelio had devoted himself to physiological experimentation in the new mathematical-mechanical manner. He became a professor of mathematics at the University of Naples in 1653. By 1656 his old teacher Severino had persuaded Cornelio to publish his investigations and speculations; delays occurred, unfortunately, but when his *Progymnasmata physica* appeared in 1663 one section of it carried a dedication to Borelli. For Borelli's part, almost immediately upon his arrival in Pisa he established a flourishing anatomical laboratory in his own house. Here he collaborated with and taught many talented students of the various disciplines of anatomy from Marcello Malpighi, at the beginning of his stay, to Lorenzo Bellini and Carlo Fracassati, in his last few years. Here also he nurtured his great iatromechanical project, a work on the movements of animals. He probably had had such an endeavor in mind before he came; in 1659 he could already complain of having to put it aside because of the work on Apollonius. By 1659, of course, Borelli had become involved in many things, not the least of them the experimental investigations of the Accademia del Cimento.

One year after Borelli arrived in Tuscany the Accademia del Cimento held its first session; the year Borelli left, the Cimento quietly died. Indeed, Borelli seems to have been the principal animus of the academy, but lest he appear the sole mover, we should recall the documentation, especially for the extensive experimental work performed during this Galilean epoch, in Giovanni Targioni Tozzetti's *Atti e memorie inedite dell'Accademia del Cimento e notizie aneddote dei progresse delle scienze in Toscana.* In fact the Tuscan court had been thoroughly infected by Galileo's ideas and those of his pupils. Grand Duke Ferdinand II, from the time of his accession to power in 1628 until his death in 1670, maintained a personal laboratory as did Prince Leopold. From the time of the death of the Master, Galileo, informal gatherings met at the court and presented and discussed experiments. At first Torricelli was the most prominent figure; after his death in 1647 Viviani presided over the activities.

Then, possibly under the crystallizing influence of Borelli, Leopold asked for and received permission from Ferdinand to organize formally an academy for purely experimental research. Under Leopold's aegis it met for the first time in June of 1657. Among its more distinguished members, besides Borelli and Viviani, were Antonio Oliva (*d.* 1668), Carlo Rinaldini (*d.* 1698), and Francesco Redi (*d.* 1697). Nicholas Steno arrived in Florence in 1666 and soon thereafter joined the group. Lorenzo Magalotti, after attending the University of Pisa as a student, was appointed secretary in 1660. The Cimento had adopted a policy of submerging the identities of its members and presenting itself as a group. Accordingly, when Magalotti brought out the *Saggi di naturali esperienzi fatte nell'Accademia del Cimento* in 1666–1667, it appeared anonymously and refrained from identifying the individual contributions of the members. Actually the *Saggi* presented only part of the work performed; it tended to emphasize the identification and description of physical phenomena and the perfecting of measuring techniques. It failed to present other interesting investigations, including some potentially controversial observations and discussions of comets.

During the life of the Cimento dissension appeared among the membership; Borelli may have originated some of it. He seems to have chafed under the requirement of anonymity, and by all accounts he was a touchy person to get along with under any circumstances. In any case, toward the end of 1666 and just after the publication of his important work on the theory of the motions of the moons of Jupiter, Borelli made his decision to leave Tuscany and return to Messina. In 1667 Leopold was created a cardinal and thus had some of his energies diverted. Rinaldini moved on to the University of Padua, and Antonio Oliva went to Rome where he came under the suspicion of the Inquisition and died by throwing himself from a window of one of its prisons. In December of 1667 Steno converted to Catholicism and shortly thereafter set out on a series of journeys. How or whether any of these events may have been connected is not known with any degree of certainty. But at this point the Cimento effectively ceased to function, even though it apparently was not formally dissolved, and even though Prince, now Cardinal, Leopold continued to direct some experimental work until he died in 1675. As far as Borelli was concerned, he had been, and afterward remained, on excellent terms with Leopold; and Leopold maintained his high regard for Borelli.

Besides his involvement with the Cimento and his own laboratory, Borelli had had other things to keep him busy during these years in Tuscany, among them his teaching duties. He was by no means the usual sort of professor. Nor did he bother to cultivate the finer graces of that calling. His first lectures at Pisa, for instance, were something of a disaster. He lacked any particular eloquence and was long-winded and dull. The students reacted with catcalls and agitation, once forcing him to stop before finishing his lesson. Very quickly, however, he demonstrated his capabilities, and his lack of Tuscan oratorical polish probably became less of a barrier. Then, in connection with his post, he prepared for publication of his *Euclides restitutus.* Not one to be overawed by canonical texts, he frankly stated that although Euclid had done an excellent job in compiling his *Elements,* these nevertheless could be repetitive and prolix, and it was time to put the material together in a clearer and more concise package. While he was about it, Borelli took the opportunity not only to reexamine the parallel postulate and propose his own version but also to try to establish the theory of proportions on firmer grounds. The Latin edition of this work appeared in 1658. Five years later his student Domenico Magni undertook the task of providing a "Euclid for the layman" by editing out most of Borelli's technical commentary and shortening and translating the remainder into Italian. Both works apparently were very well received. In subsequent editions of the Latin version, Borelli's short summary of Apollonius and other brief analyses appeared.

One of the more notable events during Borelli's stay in Pisa had been the appearance of a comet in late 1664. Borelli immediately took up the vigil and kept very close track of it throughout December and until the beginning of February 1665. Out of this came a small paper, which he published in the form of a letter addressed to Stefano degli Angeli, a mathematician at the University of Padua. Borelli showed that, no matter which interpretation one preferred, Ptolemaic, Tychonic, or Keplerian, one had to admit that the comet changed in its absolute distance from the earth. This fact raised obvious difficulties for the first two systems, and Borelli argued that it presented difficulties for the Keplerian also. He went on to show that his parallax measurements proved the comet to be above the moon, at least toward the end of the observations presented here. This was touchy material, and Borelli published under the pseudonym of Pier Maria Mutoli. His interest in comets continued into the spring. In early May he wrote Leopold that he believed that the true motion of a comet *then* visible could in no ways be accounted for by means of a straight line but rather by a curve very similar to a parabola. And he proposed to demonstrate it, not only by calculation, but also with some kind of mechanical device. Borelli apparently built this instrument; unfortunately, neither it nor any description of it remains.

During the summer of 1665 Borelli established an astronomical observatory in the fortress of San Miniato, a pleasant site on a hill a short distance from Florence. Here he used an excellent Campani telescope and some instruments of his own design to try to determine with extreme accuracy the motions of Jupiter's satellites. From this work came his *Theoricae mediceorum planetarum ex causis physicis deductae* (1666), in which, among other things, he explained how the elliptical orbits of planetary bodies could be understood in terms of three types of action. In the first place, a planetary body has a tendency toward a central body and would move toward that central body if no other factors intervened. Then, a central body, such as the sun, sends out rays and as that body rotates the rays also rotate. The cumulative effect of the impacts of these seemingly corporeal rays is to impart to the planet a motion around the central body. This motion in revolution thus produces a centrifugal tendency which balances the original centripetal one and thereby establishes the planet in a given mean orbit. Small self-correcting fluctuations account qualitatively for the observed ellipses. There are some obvious difficulties in accommodating these proposals to the satellites of the major planets, and it is clear that Borelli had much more in mind than just explaining the motions of the moons of Jupiter. The Copernican implications of his scheme, however, could be masked by seeming to focus attention on Jupiter.

Meanwhile, as time allowed, Borelli continued his anatomical research. He collaborated with Lorenzo Bellini in an investigation of the structure of the kidney, and in 1664 this resulted in a short piece entitled *De renum usu judicum.* And he also produced two major studies which were not only exercises in pure mechanics but also, in the eyes of Borelli himself, necessary introductions to what he would consider to be his most important work, the *De motu animalium.* Respectively, these were *De vi percussionis* (1667) and *De motionibus naturalibus a gravitate pendentibus* (1670). Both cover considerably more subject matter than their titles indicate. In the first, for instance, Borelli discusses percussion in detail, some general problems of motion, gravity, magnetism, the motion of fluids, the vibrations of bodies, and pendular motion, to cite just a few items. Likewise, in the second, he argues against positive levity, discusses the Torricellian experiment, takes up siphons, pumps, and the nature of fluidity, tries to understand the expansion of water while freezing, and deals with fermentation and other chemical processes. When we consider that all this was the product of years of experimental and theoretical investigation, we should not wonder that he objected to giving it over to be brought out anonymously by the Cimento just because he happened to present a good deal of it before that society. To the apparent displeasure of Leopold, Borelli published *De vi percussionis* in Bologna. And in the early summer of 1667 he set out once more to Messina.

On the way he passed through Rome and stopped for the summer in Naples. While there he was the guest of the Investiganti for whom he repeated many of the experiments he had performed at the Cimento. And he also repeated for his own edification some work that the Investiganti had accomplished independently. As a result of this visit, Concublet provided for the publication of *De motionibus naturalibus,* for which Borelli reciprocated by writing a warm dedication to him. Back in Messina, Borelli resumed his chair in mathematics. Stefano degli Angeli had raised some objections to parts of *De vi percussionis,* so in 1668 Borelli wrote the short *Risposta;* one of the problems concerned the deviation toward the east of a body dropped from a tower. In 1669 there occurred a major eruption of Etna and Borelli took the occasion to observe it closely, making notes on the topography of the mountain, the locations of the flows, and the nature of the various materials ejected, and offering some reasoned speculations of the sources of the heat powering the display. These he published in the *Historia et meteorologia incendii Aetnaei anni 1669.* Meanwhile he tried to return to his long delayed *De motu animalium.*

Borelli did not confine himself only to the sciences. He had always taken a great interest in the public affairs of Messina. For example, while he was in Tuscany he helped to procure a copy of a manuscript the Messinese wished to publish. The work in question was the *Storia della guerra di Troja* by Guido Giudici delle Collone. A Latin version had been found among the papers of Maurolico, but it was known that the Accademia della Crusca had cited an Italian translation in Florence. At the request of the Messinese senate and with the aid of Borelli a copy was made in 1659. The Fucina published it in 1665 with a dedication to the senate. When Borelli returned from Pisa, then, he was coming home. And even though he was nearing sixty, he seems to have taken up an active political role. Agitation had been growing between the local citizens and their Spanish overlords. This led in 1674 to an open revolt. With some assistance from the French the struggle continued until 1678 when the French decided to leave the city, taking with them many of the city's leaders and (among other things) ensuring the closing of the Fucina. But trouble had brewed even before 1674. Borelli himself was thought to have provided the ideological inspiration for a party of republicans. In 1672 the Spanish Conservatore del Regno managed to stir up riots against the party, during which the home of Carlo Di Gregorio, which served as the meeting place for the Fucina, was burned. Borelli was declared a rebel and a price was placed on his head. He left very quickly and seems to have gone directly to Rome. One of his current projects also became a casualty. He had been into the papers of Maurolico and was publishing the latter's edition of the works of Archimedes when in 1672 the Spanish confiscated the nearly completed printing.

When Borelli arrived in Rome he was by no means

unknown to that city. Besides his years of study there and several visits during the intervening period, he also knew and had corresponded frequently with Michelangelo Ricci and from its beginning the *Giornale de' Letterati* had published news of his scientific accomplishments: abstracts of his longer works and complete versions of a few shorter pieces. It is not surprising, then, that he would come to the attention of Queen Christina and come under her somewhat erratic patronage. Christina had been the only legal offspring of Gustavus Adolphus of Sweden. She had received an excellent education and undertook many projects, among them the creation of a learned academy in Stockholm. One of her first acts after her spectacular conversion to Catholicism was to attempt to start an academy in Rome, this in early 1656. Unfortunately, political and financial problems occupied her attention for many years. Finally, in 1674, she launched her Accademia Reale. Borelli appeared twice before it in 1675—in February when he spoke on the construction of the triremes of the ancients and again in April when he discussed Etna, this time including considerations resulting from a climb to the rim of the volcano in 1671. Christina also patronized another, more scientific group, known variously as the Accademia dell'Esperienza or the Accademia Fisica-matematica. It was organized in July of 1677 under the leadership of Giovanni Giustino Ciampini, who was also connected with the *Giornale de' Letterati.* Its membership included Borelli and an old friend and disciple, Lucantonio Porzio. But recognition apparently did not entail too much tangible support, and Borelli began to look farther afield for that. Cassini had been in Paris for several years and had become a member of the Royal Academy of Sciences. In 1676 Borelli wrote him complaining of the extreme circumstances to which he had been reduced by his enemies and the lack of quiet which was interfering with the completion of his works; he hinted that he too would like to serve the Most Christian King. By February 1677, negotiations were under way. A year later he had hopeful news, but he wrote that he was too old to travel to Paris. Instead he would send his work on the motion of animals to be printed there with a dedication to the king. In May of 1678 he still hoped for his election to the Royal Academy, but since he did not wish to trust his only copy of *De motu animalium* to the mails, he wrote that he needed time to have another made. Actually it is unlikely that he ever was elected to the Academy. A short time previously he had been robbed of all his possessions by a servant. Lacking adequate means, he had accepted the hospitality of the fathers of the Casa di S. Pantaleo and had entered their house on 13 September 1677. For the last two years of his life he taught mathematics at its Scuole Pie. Apparently he never sent a copy of his manuscript to Paris. Then in late 1679 Queen Christina agreed to bear the printing costs and Borelli dedicated the *De motu animalium* to her. He died in December, however, and his benefactor at the convent, P. Giovanni di Gesù, accepted the responsibility of seeing this last and most important work through the press. Volume I, treating of external motions, or the motions produced by the muscles, appeared in 1680. Volume II, dealing with internal motions, such as the movements of the muscles themselves, circulation, respiration, the secretion of fluids; and nervous activity, appeared in late 1681. A simple stone in the wall of the Church of S. Pantaleo recalls: *Joh. Alphonso Borellio, neapolitano, philosopho medico et matematico, clarissimo, . . .*

BIBLIOGRAPHY

I. ORIGINAL WORKS. Borelli's major writings are *Discorso . . . nel quale si manifestano le falsità e gli errori contenuti nella difesa del problema geometrico risoluto dal R. D. Pietro Emmanuele* (Messina, 1646); *Delle cagioni delle febbri maligne di Sicilia negli anni 1647 e 1648, . . . Ed in fine si tratta della digestione di cibi con nuovo metodo* (Cosenza, 1649); *Euclides restitutus* (Pisa, 1658); *Apollonius Pergaeus Conicorum lib. v. vi. vii. paraphraste Abalphato Asphahanensi nunc primum editi. Additus in calce Archimedis assumptorum liber, ex codicibus Arabicis m. ss. . . . Abrahamus Eccellensis . . . latinos reddidit* (Florence, 1661); *Euclide rinnovato* (Bologna, 1663); *Del movimento della cometa apparsa il mese di Dicembre 1664* (Pisa, 1665); *Theoricae mediceorum planetarum ex causis physicis deductae* (Florence, 1666); *De vi percussioni liber* (Bologna, 1667); *Risposta . . . alle considerazioni fatte sopra alcuni luoghi del suo libro della forza della percossa del R. P. F. Stefano de gl' Angeli* (Messina, 1668); *De motionibus naturalibus a gravitate pendentibus, liber* (Regio Iulio [Reggio di Calabria], Bologna, 1670); *Istoria et meteorologia incendii Aetnaei anni 1669 . . . accessit. Responsio ad censuras Rev. P. Honorati Fabri contra librum auctoris De vi percussionis* (Regio Iulio [Reggio di Calabria], 1670); *Elementa conica Apollonii Pergaei, et Archimedis opera, nova et breviori methodo demonstrata* (Rome, 1679); *De motu animalium . . . Opum Posthumum. Pars prima* (Rome, 1680), *Pars altera* (Rome, 1681); and "Discorso sopra la laguna di Venezia. Relazione sopra lo stagno di Pisa. Supplemento da aggiungersi alla proposizione seconda del secondo libro del P. Castelli, ecc.," in *Raccolta d'autori che trattano del moto dell'acque,* IV (Florence, 1765), 15-63.

Shorter tracts and less important works appeared in various issues of *Giornale de' Letterati;* Borelli, et al., *Tetras anatomicarum epistolarum de lingua, et cerebro* (Bologna, 1665); Marcello Malpighi, *Opera posthuma* (London,

1697); and Giovanni Targione Tozzetti, *Atti e memorie inedite dell' Accademia del Cimento,* 3 vols. (Florence, 1780).

The collections of the libraries of Florence, especially the Galileiana of the Biblioteca Nazionale, contain a great deal of unpublished correspondence to, from, and relating to Borelli. Other Italian libraries, and perhaps French and English ones, must still have a great deal of unrecognized and unpublished Borelli materials. The following have made many Borelli letters available: Howard B. Adelmann, *Marcello Malpighi and the Evolution of Embryology,* 5 vols. (Ithaca, N. Y., 1966); Giovanni Arenaprimo di Montechiaro, "Gio: Alfonso Borelli a Marcello Malpighi," in *Studi di medicina legale e varii . . . in onore di Giuseppe Ziino ecc.* (Messina, 1907), pp. 467–475; Vincenzo Busacchi and Giordano Muratori, "Giovanni Alfonso Borelli e lo Studio di Bologna," in *Bollettino delle scienze mediche* [Società di Bologna], **136** (1964), 86–90; Modestino Del Gaizo, *Alcune lettere di Giovanni Alfonso Borrelli, dirette una al Malpighi, le altre al Magliabechi* (Naples, 1886); "Contributo allo studio della vita e delle opere di Giovanni Alfonso Borrelli," *Atti dell'Accademia Pontaniana, Napoli,* **20** (1890), 1–48; "Una lettera di G. A. Borelli ed alcune indagini di pneumatica da lui compiute," in *Memorie della Pontificia Accademia Romana dei Nuovi Lincei,* **21** (1903), 61–78; "Note di storia della vulcanologia," *Memoria* no. 5 in *Atti dell'Accademia Pontaniana, Napoli,* **36** (1906); "Evangelista Torricelli e Giovanni Alfonso Borrelli. Appunti raccolti nel compiersi il terzo secolo dalla loro nascita," in *Rivista di fisica, matematica e scienze naturali* (Pavia), **17** (1908), 385–402; "L'opera scientifica di G. A. Borelli e la Scuola di Roma nel secolo XVII," in *Memorie della Pontificia Accademia Romana dei Nuovi Lincei,* **27** (1909), 275–307; and "Di una lettera inedita di G. A. Borelli diretta a M. Malpighi," in *Atti dell'Accademia Pontaniana, Napoli,* **49** (1919), 29–40; Tullio Derenzini, "Alcune lettere di Giovanni Alfonso Borelli ad Alessandro Marchetti," in *Physis,* **1** (1959), 224–243; and "Alcune lettere di Giovanni Alfonso Borelli a Gian Domenico Cassini," *ibid.,* **2** (1960), 235–241; Angelo Fabroni, *Lettere inedite di uomini illustri,* 2 vols. (Florence, 1773–1775); Giovanni Giovannozzi, "La versione borelliana dei *Conici* di Apollonio," in *Memorie della Pontificia Accademia Romana dei Nuovi Lincei,* 2nd ser., **2** (1916), 1–32; *Lettere inedite di Giovanni Alfonso Borelli al P. Angelo* [*Morelli*] *di S. Domenico sulla versione di Apollonio* (Florence, 1916); "Carte Borelliane nell' Archivio Generale delle Scuole Pie a Roma," in *Atti della Pontificia Accademia Romana dei Nuovi Lincei,* **72** (1918–1919), 81–86; and "Una lettera di Famiano Michelini a Giovanni Alfonso Borelli," *ibid.,* **80** (1926–1927), 315–319; Ugo Morini and Luigi Ferrari, *Autografi e codici di lettori dell'Ateneo Pisano esposti in occasione dell' XI congresso di medicina interna* (Pisa, 1902), pp. 19–23; Giuseppe Mosca, *Vita di Lucantonio Porzio pubblico primario cattedratico di Notomia* (Naples, 1765); Luigi Tenca, "Le relazioni fra Giovanni Alfonso Borelli e Vincenzio Viviani," in *Rendiconti dell'Istituto Lombardo di scienze e lettere, Milano,* **90** (1956), 107–121; and Giambatista Tondini, *Delle lettere di uomini illustri* (Macerata, 1782).

Among the translations of portions of the *De motu animalium* are Max Mengeringhausen, *Die Bewegung der Tiere,* no. 221 in *Ostwald's Klassiker der exakten Wissenschaften* (Leipzig, 1927); and T. O'B. Hubbard and J. H. Ledoboer, *The Flight of Birds,* Royal Aeronautical Society of London, Aeronautical Classics, no. 6 (London, 1911).

II. Secondary Literature. The most extensive treatment of Borelli's life is in Angelo Fabroni, *Vitae italorum doctrina excellentium,* II (Pisa, 1778), 222–324. More recently, Gustavo Barbensi, *Borelli* (Trieste, 1947), and Tullio Derenzini, "Giovanni Alfonso Borelli, fisico," in *Celebrazione dell'Accademia del Cimento nel tricentenario della fondazione* (Pisa, 1958), pp. 35–52, offer useful shorter treatments. Luigi Amabile, in his *Fra Tommaso Campanella ne' castelli di Napoli, in Roma ed in Parigi,* 2 vols. (Naples, 1887), published the documents pertaining to Borelli's birth and family and possible connections with Campanella, II, 361–369. Both Max H. Fisch, "The Academy of the Investigators," in E. A. Underwood, ed., *Science, Medicine and History: Essays . . . in Honor of Charles Singer,* I (Oxford, 1953), 521–563; and Nicola Badaloni, *Introduzione a G. B. Vico* (Milan, 1961), provide much information about the Investiganti and Borelli's relation to it. Howard B. Adelmann's work on Malpighi (cited above) is indispensable for Borelli's life and work after he came to Pisa. For the Fucina and Borelli's connection with the Messina revolt one can begin with Giacomo Nigido-Dionisi, *L'Accademia della Fucina di Messina* (*1639–1678*) *ne' suoi rapporti con la storia della cultura in Sicilia* (Catania, 1903), and Giuseppe Olivà, "Abolizione e rinacimento della Università di Messina," in *CCCL Anniversario della Università di Messina* (Messina, 1900), Parte Prima, 209–365.

Borelli's celestial mechanics have been studied in Angus Armitage, "'Borell's Hypothesis' and the Rise of Celestial Mechanics," in *Annals of Science,* **6** (1950), 268–282; Alexandre Koyré, "La mécanique céleste de J. A. Borelli," in *Revue d'histoire des sciences et de leurs applications,* **5** (1952), 101–138; "La gravitation universelle de Kepler à Newton," in *Archives internationales d'histoire des sciences,* **4** (1954), 638–653; "A Documentary History of the Problem of Fall from Kepler to Newton," in *Transactions of the American Philosophical Society,* n.s. **45** (1955), 327–395; and *La révolution astronomique: Copernique, Kepler, Borelli* (Paris, 1961); and Charles Serrus, "La mécanique de J.-A. Borelli et la notion d'attraction," in *Revue d'histoire des sciences et de leur applications,* **1** (1947), 9–25. His physics have been examined in particular in Pierre Varignon, *Projet d'une nouvelle mechanique, avec Un Examen de l'opinion de M. Borelli, sur les propriétez des poids suspendus par des cordes* (Paris, 1687); Giovanni Antonio Amedeo Plana, "Mémoire sur la découverte de la loi du choc direct des corps durs publiée en 1667 par Alphonse Borelli . . .," in *Memorie della Reale Accademia delle scienze di Torino,* 2nd ser., **6** (1844), esp. 1–37; and J. MacLean, "De historische ontwikkeling der stootwetten van Aristoteles tot Huygens," a dissertation (Amsterdam, 1959).

Various particular aspects of Borelli's life and work, as well as additional bibliographical sources, are given in the following: Gustavo Barbensi, "Di una diversa soluzione di un problema di meccanica muscolare da parte di due medici matematici," in *Rivista di storia delle scienze mediche e naturali, Siena,* **29** (1938), 168–180; Pietro Capparoni, "Sulla patria di Giovanni Alfonso Borelli," *ibid.,* **22** (1931), 53–63; Modestino Del Gaizo, *Studii di Giovanni Alfonso Borrelli sulla pressione atmosferica, con note illustrative intorno alla vita ed alle opere di lui* (Naples, 1886); "Di un' antica indagine sul calore animale," in *Atti della R. Accademia medico-chirurgica di Napoli,* **49** (1895), 378–394; "Di un' opera di G. A. Borelli sulla eruzione dell' Etna del 1669 e di Adriano Auzout corrispondente, in Roma, del Borelli," in *Atti della Pontificia Accademia Romana dei Nuovi Lincei,* **60** (1906–1907), 111–117; "Qualche ricordo di Giovanni Alfonso Borelli in Firenze," in *Studium: Rivista universitaria mensile,* **2** (1907), 234–238; "Giovanni Alfonso Borrelli e la sua opera *De motu animalium,* discorso," in *Atti della R. Accademia medico-chirurgica di Napoli,* **62** (1908), 147–169; "Il *De motu animalium* di G. A. Borelli studiato in rapporto del *De motu cordis et sanguinis* di G. Harvey," *ibid.,* **67** (1914), 195–227; and "Ipotesi di antiche fisiologi e specialmente di Giovanni Alfonso Borelli sulla esistenza del succo nervoso," *ibid.,* **69** (1916), 85–108; Giovanni Battista De Toni, "Per la conoscenza delle opinioni sulla ascesa dei liquidi nelle piante," in *Rivista di fisica, matematica e scienze naturali,* **3** (1901), 199–203; Pietro Franceschini, "L'apparato motore nello studio di Borelli e di Stenone," in *Rivista di storia delle scienze mediche e naturali,* **42** (1951), 1–15; Giovanni Giovanozzi, "La patria di Gio. Alfonso Borelli," in *Atti della Pontificia Accademia Romana dei Nuovi Lincei,* **79** (1925–1926), 61–66; Raymond Hierons and Alfred Meyer, "Willis's Place in the History of Muscle Physiology," in *Proceedings of the Royal Society of Medicine,* **57** (1964), 687–692; Michelangelo Macri, "Lettere d'illustre autori de' secoli XVII e XVIII," in *Nuova Biblioteca Analitica di scienze, lettere ed arti,* **14** (1819), letters 1 and 1 *bis,* 349–353; and Giuseppe Ziino, "G. A. Borelli medico e igienista," in *CCCL Anniversario della Università di Messina* (Messina, 1900), Parte Seconda, 3–40.

THOMAS B. SETTLE

BORSUK, KAROL (*b.* Warsaw, Poland, 8 May 1905; *d.* Warsaw, Poland, 24 January 1982)

Borsuk was the son of Marian Borsuk and Zofia Maciejewska. His father was a well-known surgeon in Warsaw. After receiving a master's degree in 1927 and a doctorate in 1930, both from the University of Warsaw, he became *Privatdozent* there in 1934. Borsuk married Zofia Paczkowska on 26 April 1936; they had two daughters.

After joining the faculty at Warsaw in 1929, Borsuk advanced to professor of mathematics in 1946 and director of the Mathematical Institute from 1952 to 1964. He was at the Institute for Advanced Study at Princeton from 1946 to 1947, and later visiting professor at the University of California at Berkeley (1959–1960) and at the University of Wisconsin at Madison (1963–1964).

Borsuk was vice director of the Institute of Mathematics of the Polish Academy of Sciences in 1956. He was corresponding member of the Polish and Bulgarian academies of sciences.

Borsuk worked primarily in the area of geometric topology. Although he is known for widespread contributions in topology, a particularly important discovery was the distillation of a central topological feature of polyhedra and its generalization to a larger class of spaces. This concept, that of absolute neighborhood retract, was introduced in Borsuk's doctoral dissertation at the University of Warsaw under S. Mazurkiewicz, "Sur les rétractes" (published in 1931), and permeated a great deal of his work. It has greatly influenced the direction of research in topology throughout the world.

It will be helpful to define an absolute neighborhood retract. Let X be a metric space and A a subset of X. A continuous function r from X to A is said to be a retraction provided it has the property that $r(x) = x$ for all x in A. If X has the property that whenever X is embedded as a closed subset of a metric space Y, there is a retraction of Y onto X, then X is said to be an absolute retract (AR). The unit interval and the real line are examples of AR's. If whenever X is embedded in Y as a closed subset, there is a retraction of a neighborhood of X in Y onto X, then X is said to be an absolute neighborhood retract (ANR). Prime examples of ANR's are metric polyhedra and manifolds. If the polyhedron or manifold is contractible, then it is in fact an AR. The abstracting of this property of polyhedra is one of the most remarkable accomplishments of geometric topology. Although the concept was due to Borsuk, the entire community of topologists contributed to its full development.

John H. C. Whitehead showed in 1950 that an ANR is homotopy equivalent to a polyhedron. Thus this property virtually characterizes spaces that are homotopy equivalent to polyhedra. Borsuk asked in 1954 whether a compact ANR is homotopy equivalent to a compact polyhedron. This query was answered in the affirmative by J. E. West. In 1974 Robert Edwards was able to bring together the results of many researchers in topology to show that the product of a compact ANR with the Hilbert cube is a Hilbert cube manifold and the product of a compact AR with the Hilbert cube is the Hilbert cube. Complete proofs of these results, together with references, are given in Thomas Chapman's

Lectures on Hilbert Cube Manifolds (1976). Borsuk had been intrigued by the Hilbert cube at an early stage in his career. In *The Scottish Book* in 1938 he posed the following questions: Is it true that the product of a triod with the Hilbert cube is homeomorphic to the Hilbert cube? Is it also true that the infinite product of triods is homeomorphic to the Hilbert cube? An affirmative answer to these questions was given by Richard D. Anderson in 1964. A published proof of this result, together with the fact that the product of any compact polyhedron with the Hilbert cube is a Hilbert cube manifold, was given by Anderson's student J. E. West. The remarkable theorem by Edwards would not have been possible without a thorough investigation into infinite dimensional topology, of which the Anderson-West result was the preliminary essential step. Borsuk showed exceptional insight in conceiving of this conjecture so early in his career.

For most of his career Borsuk was connected with the University of Warsaw. During the Nazi occupation of Poland, he labored at keeping intellectual life in Poland alive through the "underground university." This and other "illegal" activities led to his imprisonment, escape, and hiding until the end of the war.

When Poland began to rebuild, Borsuk and Kazimierz Kuratowski began the work of restoring mathematics in Warsaw, and Borsuk's disrupted career came back into focus. He continued his studies in topology. In the mid 1960's he came across another fundamental concept in topology, the notion of shape. An ANR is a very nice space with many convenient local properties. Unfortunately, there are many mathematical spaces that do not have nice local properties. It was Borsuk's idea that such spaces could be "smoothed" by embedding them in AR's, in particular by embedding them in the Hilbert cube. One could then study the original space by studying the system of neighborhoods of the space in the Hilbert cube. Since these neighborhoods are ANR's, one is thus studying an arbitrary compact metric space by approximating it by a system of ANR's. Borsuk's first publication in shape theory was in 1968 in *Fundamenta mathematicae*. At about the same time he gave several talks in Europe and the United States disseminating his ideas.

Shape theory has had tremendous influence in topology. There are, however, complications in giving credit to Borsuk for its discovery because it has been shown that it is equivalent to several earlier theories and constructions. In particular, etale homotopy theory and the Kan and Čech extension of the homotopy functor on the category of polyhedra are equivalent to Borsuk's theory of shape. Several mathematicians discovered these equivalences independently at about the same time. Although these constructions are in a technical sense the same, it can certainly be said that Borsuk was the first to use these ideas as he did. His motivation was always to understand the geometry of separable metric spaces, and he showed how shape theory could be an effective tool for this purpose.

In recent times many different areas of topology have begun to merge. The theory of manifolds, the theory of CW-complexes and polyhedra, the theory of ANR's, combinatorial topology, homotopy theory, algebraic topology, shape theory, infinite-dimensional topology, and geometric topology have had considerable interaction. Borsuk played a significant role in developing several of these areas and in making them fit coherently into the whole.

Borsuk was much honored by Poland, receiving many decorations to honor his contributions to mathematics, education, and political life. He was also widely honored in the mathematical community. He participated in some twenty conferences and delivered major addresses at many of them. He gave numerous talks on his work at centers of learning. In 1978 Borsuk organized the International Conference on Geometric Topology, held in Warsaw. This conference demonstrated his widespread and profound influence on topology and the high regard in which he was held.

BIBLIOGRAPHY

I. Original Works. Many of Borsuk's writings are brought together in *Karol Borsuk: Collected Papers*, 2 vols. (Warsaw, 1983). Among his books are *Foundations of Geometry* (Amsterdam and New York, 1960), written with Wanda Szmielew, rev. trans. by Erwin Marquit; *Theory of Retracts* (Warsaw, 1967); *Multidimensional Analytic Geometry*, trans. Halina Spalinska (Warsaw, 1969); and *Theory of Shape* (Warsaw, 1975). With A. Krikor, Borsuk edited *Proceedings of the International Conference on Geometric Topology* (Warsaw, 1980).

II. Secondary Literature. Writings related to Borsuk's work are Thomas A. Chapman, *Lecture Notes on Hilbert Cube Manifolds*, Conference Board of the Mathematical Society, Regional Conference Series in Mathematics, no. 28 (Providence, R.I., 1976); Jerzy Dydak and Jack Segal, *Shape Theory: An Introduction*, Lecture Notes in Mathematics no. 688 (Berlin and New York, 1978); Sibe Mardešić and Jack Segal, eds., *Shape Theory and Geometric Topology*, Lecture Notes in Mathematics no. 870 (Amsterdam and New York, 1982); D. Mauldin, ed., *The Scottish Book* (Stuttgart and Boston, 1981). (*The Scottish Book* was originally a notebook of mathematical problems started by a group of Polish mathematicians in Lwow in 1935. This edition is an English translation, together with a commentary on the problems.) See also J. E. West, "Infinite Products Which Are Hilbert Cubes," in *Transactions of the American Mathematical Society*, **150** (1970), 1–25, and "Mapping Hilbert Cube Manifolds ANR's: A Solution of a Conjecture of Borsuk," in *Annals of Mathematics*, **106** (1977), 1–8.

JAMES KEESLING

BORTKIEWICZ (or **Bortkewitsch**), **LADISLAUS** (or **Vladislav**) **JOSEPHOWITSCH** (*b.* St. Petersburg, Russia, 7 August 1868; *d.* Berlin, Germany, 15 July 1931)

Bortkiewicz's mother was Helene von Rokicka; his father was Joseph Ivanowitsch Bortkewitsch, a member of the gentry from the Kovno [now Kaunas] province of Russia who was a colonel, an instructor in artillery and mathematics, a notary, and an author of several textbooks on elementary mathematics and works in economics and finance.

Bortkiewicz graduated from the Faculty of Law of the University of St. Petersburg in 1890 and took a postgraduate course in political economy and statistics. He also studied at Strasbourg (1891–1892) under G. F. Knapp, at Göttingen (1892) under W. Lexis, and at Vienna and Leipzig. In 1893 he defended his doctoral dissertation in philosophy at Göttingen. Bortkiewicz was a *Privatdozent* in Strasbourg and lectured in actuarial science and theoretical statistics in 1895–1897; in 1897–1901 he was a clerk in the general office of the Railway Pension Committee in St. Petersburg. Simultaneously, from 1899 to December 1900, he taught statistics at the prestigious Alexandrowsky Lyceum. In 1901 he became extraordinary professor of statistics at the University of Berlin, where he spent the rest of his life, becoming ordinary professor of statistics and political economy in 1920. He was a member of the Swedish Academy of Sciences, the Royal Statistical Society, the American Statistical Association, and the International Statistical Institute.

Bortkiewicz's publications concern population and statistical theory; mathematical statistics; and application of the latter and of probabilities to statistics, to actuarial science, and to political economy. Following Lexis' reasoning, Bortkiewicz was a proponent (almost the only one) of connecting statistics with the theory of probabilities and mathematical statistics. This idea was featured in an empirical "law of small numbers" (law of rare events, which formerly, beginning with Jakob I Bernoulli, were considered "morally" impossible and were discarded as such): The small numbers of events in large series of trials are stable in time; oscillations of the numbers of such events are accounted for by the Lexis criterion (*Q* quotient). The most important feature of this law, contrary to Bortkiewicz's opinion, appeared to be its connection with the Poisson law of large numbers and the popularization of the Poisson distribution. The *Q* quotient was regularly used by Bortkiewicz (who, moreover, deduced its expectation and standard deviation) in the same way that the x^2 criterion is used now. His other works in the theory of probabilities and mathematical statistics pertain to radioactivity, the theory of runs, and order statistics (he was a pioneer in the latter).

Noting the concrete and social nature of statistical deductions, Bortkiewicz recommended that legislation be based on them. His works are distinguished by independent opinions (dissenting with V. J. Buniakowsky, G. F. Knapp, M. E. L. Walras, and others), rigorous deductions, and voluminous references of international scope. At the same time, being comprehensive and not accompanied by a summary, they make hard reading.

Bortkiewicz was one of the main representatives of the "Continental direction" in mathematical statistics and its application to statistics, but he left no monographs, and the German scientists were only marginally interested in his works. He did not create a school but was closely associated with A. A. Tschuprow.

His last days were marred by a heated argument with Gini, an Italian statistician, who accused Bortkiewicz of plagiarism. Original correspondence on this alleged plagiarism is appended to Andersson's obituary (see bibliography).

BIBLIOGRAPHY

I. ORIGINAL WORKS. The only more or less comprehensive enumeration of approximately 100 of Bortkiewicz's works is in the obituary by T. Andersson (see below). These works include a few books, papers (including rather lengthy ones in various journals), and reviews. Seven of his papers (1889–1910) are in Russian; the other works are almost exclusively in German. Among his writings are *Das Gesetz der kleinen Zahlen* (Leipzig, 1898); *Die radioaktive Strahlung als Gegenstand wahrscheinlichkeitstheoretischer Untersuchungen* (Berlin, 1913); *Die Iterationen* (Berlin, 1917); "Die Variabilitätsbreite beim Gauschen Fehlergesetz," in *Nordisk statistisk tidskrift,* **1** (1922), 11–38, 193–220; and "Variationsbreite und mittlerer Fehler," in *Sitzungsberichte der Berliner mathematischen Gesellschaft,* **21** (1922), 3–11.

Three of his papers are available in English trans. by the W.P.A., published in the early 1940's together with trans. of related works, notably those of W. Lexis: "Kritische Betrachtungen zur theoretischen Statistik" (1894–1896), trans. as "Critical Comments on the Theory of Statistics"; "Homogeneität und Stabilität in der Statistik" (1918), trans. as "Homogeneity and Stability in Statistics"; and "Das Helmertsche Verteilungsgesetz für die Quadratsumme zufälliger Beobachtungsfehler" (1918), trans. as "Helmert's Law of Distribution for the Sum of Squares of Random Errors of Observation." The W.P.A. trans. are accompanied by a short bibliography of Bortkiewicz's works. At least two of his works in economics are also available in English.

Information about the St. Petersburg period of Bortkiewicz's life and about his father is in the U.S.S.R. State Historical Archives, Leningrad. Information about his life in Berlin is in the archives of the Humboldt University, Berlin.

II. SECONDARY LITERATURE. Information on the life and works of Bortkiewicz (with reference to his obituaries) is in *Kürschners deutscher Gelehrten-Kalender* (Berlin–Leipzig, 1931), 274; *Reichshandbuch der deutschen Gesellschaft,* I, *Handbuch der Persönlichkeiten in Wort und Bild* (Berlin, 1930), 188, with portrait; *Neue deutsche Biographie,* II (Berlin, 1955), 478; and Poggendorff, VI, pt. 1. The most comprehensive obituary is T. Andersson, in *Nordisk statistik tidskrift,* **10** (1931), 1–16, published simultaneously in English in *Nordic Statistical Journal,* **3** (1931), 9-26. The latest published biography is E. J. Gumbel, in *International Encyclopedia of the Social Sciences* (New York, 1968).

O. B. SHEYNIN

BORTOLOTTI, ETTORE (*b.* Bologna, Italy, 6 March 1866; *d.* Bologna, 17 February 1947)

A disciple of Salvatore Pincherle, Bortolotti received his degree in mathematics *summa cum laude* from the University of Bologna in 1889. He was a university assistant until 1891, when he was appointed professor at the lyceum of Modica, Sicily. After completing postgraduate studies in Paris in 1892–1893, he taught in Rome from 1893 to 1900. In the latter year Bortolotti was appointed professor of infinitesimal calculus at the University of Modena, where he taught analysis and rational mechanics. He was dean of the Faculty of Science from 1913 to 1919, the year in which he assumed the professorship of analytical geometry at the University of Bologna. He retired in 1936.

Bortolotti's early studies were devoted to topology, whereas his later works in pure mathematics dealt largely with analysis: calculus of finite differences, the general theory of distributive operations, the algorithm of continuous fractions and its generalizations, the order of infinity of functions, the convergence of infinite algorithms, summation and asymptotic behavior of series and of improper integrals.

Bortolotti's interest in the history of mathematics was clear in his early works on topology; it increased during his stay in Rome, when he was an associate of the physicist and mathematician Valentino Cerruti; and it was fully developed in Modena, when he made deep studies of Paolo Ruffini's manuscripts. His first published historical work was "Influenza dell'opera matematica di Paolo Ruffini sullo svolgimento delle teorie algebriche" (1902). He later edited Ruffini's *Opere matematiche* (1953–1954). Bortolotti gradually widened the scope of his studies to include more remote times. The period in the seventeenth century during which infinitesimal analysis was developed was the subject of profound studies by Bortolotti, who revealed the importance of Torricelli's infinitesimal results while vindicating Cataldi's claim to the discovery of continuous fractions.

Bortolotti also studied the work of Leonardo Fibonacci and of Scipione Dal Ferro, Nicolò Tartaglia, Girolamo Cardano, Ludovico Ferrari, and Rafael Bombelli. He found and published (1929), with an introduction and notes, the manuscript of books IV and V of Bombelli's *L'algebra.* Among his other contributions is the objective reconstruction of the argumentations of the Sumerian, Assyrian, Babylonian, and Egyptian mathematicians.

BIBLIOGRAPHY

I. ORIGINAL WORKS. Bortolotti's works total more than 220, and lists of them may be found in the appendixes to the articles by Bompiani and Segre (see below). Among his works are "Influenza dell'opera matematica di Paolo Ruffini sullo svolgimento delle teorie algebriche," in *Annuario della R. Università di Modena, 1902–1903,* pp. 21–77; *Lezioni di geometrica analitica,* 2 vols. (Bologna, 1923); *Studi e ricerche sulla storia della matematica in Italia nei secoli XVI e XVII* (Bologna, 1928); *I cartelli di matematica disfida e la personalità psichica e morale di Girolamo Cardano* (Imola, 1933); and *La storia della matematica nella Università di Bologna* (Bologna, 1947). He also edited Books IV and V of *L'algebra, opera di Rafael Bombelli da Bologna* (Bologna, 1929) and Ruffini's *Opere matematiche,* 3 vols. (Rome, 1953–1954).

II. SECONDARY LITERATURE. Works on Bortolotti are E. Bompiani, "In ricordo di Ettore Bortolotti," in *Atti e memorie dell'Accademia di scienze, lettere e arti di Modena,* 5th ser., **7** (1947); E. Carruccio, "Ettore Bortolotti," in *Periodico di matematiche,* 4th ser., **26** (1948), and "Commemorazione di Ettore Bortolotti," in *Atti della Società* *italiana di scienze fisiche e matematiche "Mathesis"* (1952); and B. Segre, "Ettore Bortolotti—commemorazione," in *Rendiconti dell'Accademia delle scienze dell'Istituto di Bologna, classe di scienze fisiche,* n.s. **52** (1949), 47–86.

ETTORE CARRUCCIO

BOŠKOVIĆ, RUDJER J. (*b.* Dubrovnik, Yugoslavia, 18 May 1711; *d.* Milan, Italy, 13 February 1787)

Bošković was perhaps the last polymath to figure in an important way in the history of science, and his career was in consequence something of an anachronism and presents something of an enigma. He stands between the natural philosophy of Newton and Leibniz at one extreme and Faraday and field theory at the other, but too far from both for the connection either forward or backward to appear a coherent one. A somewhat isolated figure, he belonged to no definite eighteenth-century tradition. Croatian by birth, he became a Jesuit; and like many intellectuals from the Dalmatian cities, he was drawn to Italy and lived the first part of his career in Rome. A man of the Enlightenment, he sometimes gives the effect of a Renaissance scholar moving about Europe from place to place for reasons of circumstance and patronage and departing on great journeys at critical junctures. As will appear from consulting his bibliography, he published in the mode of an earlier time. He wrote treatises on whole sciences, and at certain periods in his life composed several such works in the course of a year. Nevertheless, his reputation has been rather that of a forerunner than a survival. His doctrine of atomism which modified the massy corpuscles of Newtonian natural philosophy into immaterial centers of force appeared to foretell, and there are historical reasons to believe that it actually influenced, the basic position of nineteenth-century field physics in regard to the relations between space and matter.

Life. Bošković was the son of Nikola Bošković, a merchant of Dubrovnik, and Paula Bettera, the daughter of Bartolomeo Bettera, a merchant originally from Bergamo, Italy. The family was of average means and was noted for its literary interests and accomplishments. Bošković began his education in the Jesuit college of Dubrovnik and continued it in Rome, first at the novitiate of Sant'Andrea, which he entered in 1725 at the age of fourteen, and later at the Collegium Romanum. He was extraordinarily sharp of mind, comprehensive in intelligence, and tireless in application—in short, an outstanding student. He learned science in a way characteristic of his later career, through independent study of mathematics, physics, astronomy, and geodesy. In 1735 he began studying Newton's *Opticks* and the *Principia* at the Collegium Romanum, where he made himself an enthusiastic propagator of the new natural philosophy. The exact sciences were what always appealed to him—in the first instance mathematics. In 1740, although he had not yet completed his theological studies, he was appointed professor of mathematics at the Collegium Romanum. That event largely determined the course of his career. Teaching interested him in its methods as well as for its content. In this respect, as in others, his spirit was progressive. He published a textbook of his teaching in 1754—*Elementa universae matheseos*—of which the third and final volûme contains an original theory of conic sections.

During this period of his life Bošković undertook, as was customary among qualified clergymen of his time, several practical and diplomatic commissions for lay or ecclesiastical authorities. The cupola of St. Peter's having developed alarming fissures, a commission was appointed consisting of Bošković and two fellow "mathematicians," F. Jacquier and Th. Le Seur, to investigate the causes and make recommendations. Bošković drafted the report which, analyzing the problem in theoretical terms, achieved—despite certain errors—the reputation of a minor classic in architectural statics. Thereafter the papal government entrusted the planning for draining of the Pontine marshes to Bošković. He composed a series of memoirs on the practice of hydraulic engineering, on regulation of the flow of the Tiber and other streams, and on harborworks. He did a plan for the harbor at Rimini in 1764 and for that at Savona in 1771.

Archaeology also interested Bošković. In 1743 he discovered and excavated an ancient Roman villa above Frascati in Tusculum, and in 1746 published a description of a sundial that had been among the finds. In 1750 he also published a critical study of the Augustan obelisk in the Campo Marzio. In 1757 Bošković undertook the most important of his several diplomatic missions, representing the interests of the Republic of Lucca before the Hapsburg court in Vienna in a dispute with Tuscany over water rights. He won the case, and in the intervals of tending to its ramifications, he also while in Vienna completed his major work in the field of natural philosophy, *Philosophiae naturalis theoria,* which appeared in the autumn of 1758.

As the years went by, Bošković fell out of sympathy with certain policies of his ecclesiastical superiors. He resented their rejection of proposals he had advanced looking to the modernization of education both in method and in subject matter. He disliked the

Vatican's reaction to the persecution of his order in Portugal. He was disappointed by the negative attitude that a number of Jesuit philosophers—Peripatetics he thought them to be—adopted toward his own system of natural philosophy. It seemed time for a move. The Academy of Sciences in Paris had long since elected him to corresponding membership—he was correspondent of Dortous de Mairan—on the publication in 1738 of his discourse on the aurora borealis. His superiors gave him permission, and in 1759 Bošković set off on his travels, going first to Paris.

There he remained for six months, well received in aristocratic, scientific, and literary circles. He came to know members of the Academy of Sciences at first hand. A diplomatic intervention on behalf of his native city of Dubrovnik took him to the court at Versailles. He decided not to remain in Paris, however, and in 1760 crossed over to London, where again his reputation had preceded him among literary and scientific people. He had discussions with representatives of the Church of England; met Benjamin Franklin, who showed him electrical experiments; and visited Oxford and Cambridge. On 15 January 1761 the Royal Society elected him a fellow, and in recognition of the honor, he dedicated to it a poem on eclipses of the sun and moon. He then lent his weight to efforts to persuade the Society to organize an expedition for the purpose of observing the transit of Venus in June 1761.

Bošković had planned to make such observations himself in Istanbul but, dependent in his plans on a companion, Correr, the new Venetian ambassador to Istanbul, Bošković arrived too late for observation. He made a trip through Flanders, Holland, the court of Stanislas in Nancy, and various centers in Germany. Once in Istanbul, he fell dangerously ill and had to remain there for seven months of recuperation. Partially recovered he set off again, this time in the company of the British ambassador, and traveled through Bulgaria and Moldavia, and went on alone from there to Poland. In Warsaw he was received in ecclesiastical and diplomatic circles. The Czartoryski and the Poniatowski connections took him up. His *Diary* of the trips he made through Bulgaria and Moldavia amounts to a systematic description of the country. It was published in Italian in 1784, having already been translated into French and German. From Poland, finally, he returned to Rome—by way of Silesia, Austria, and Venice—arriving there in November 1763 after an absence of over four years which marked a stage in his life.

Back in Italy, Bošković found a situation in Pavia, where at the end of the year he won election as professor of mathematics at the university, revived under Austrian administration. He organized both his own lectures and his department realistically, with an emphasis upon applied mathematics. At Pavia he concentrated his own efforts mainly in the field of optics and the improvement of telescopic lenses, and played a leading role in the organization of the Jesuit observatory at Brera near Milan in 1764. Had his program been carried out and the instruments he advocated installed, the observatory would have been one of the most elaborate in Europe. Remembering his interest in the transits of Venus, the Royal Society invited him to lead an expedition to California for the purpose of observing the second of the famous pair of transits, that of 1769. Unfortunately political conditions prevented that trip. In 1770 he moved his work to the department of optics and astronomy at the Scuole Palatine in Milan. As time went on, he provoked opposition among his colleagues at the observatory. In 1772 the court in Vienna yielded to the demands of the majority and relieved Bošković of "concern" for the observatory. In despair he resigned his professorship also. All his world was dissolving: the next year, 1773, the pope suppressed the Jesuit order.

By now Bošković was in his sixty-third year. Influential friends urged him to repair to Paris. There a post was arranged for him as director of optics for the navy, and he even became a subject of the French crown. In Paris during this, the last productive period of his life, he worked mainly on problems of optics and astronomy. It may be that his nature was a little contentious, for there too disputes attended him, one with the young Laplace over Bošković's early method (1746) of determining the path of a comet, another with the Abbé Alexis de Rochon over priorities in the invention of a type of micrometer and megameter consisting of pairs of rotating prisms. The device became important in the design of geodetic telemeters. In search of health and tranquillity, Bošković spent the greater part of each year in the country residing at the estates of one or another of his friends.

In 1782 Bošković received leave to return again to Italy in order to ready his French and Latin manuscripts for the press. He settled in Bassano, and there in 1785 the printing firm of the brothers Remondini brought out his five-volume *Opera.* The preparation of those writings and the strain of proofreading told on Bošković's health. Once again he set out to travel, although only in Italy, in order to visit old friends. He found a cordial welcome in Milan, where former opponents were inclined to let bygones be bygones, and settled down in the Brera observatory, which he had founded, to work on the notes for the third volume of Benedict Stay's poem *Philosophiae recentioris versibus traditae libri X,* on Newtonian natural philosophy. His mental powers were leaving him, however. Forgetfulness, anxiety, fear for his scientific reputation grew upon him, and it was clear that his mind was failing. He mercifully died of a lung ailment before the decline reached an extreme and was buried in the church of Santa Maria Podone in Milan, where, however, all trace of his tomb has been lost.

Bošković's interests were more manifold than was at all normal, even in the eighteenth century, for one who participated deeply in the actual work of science. For purposes of clarity, they may be grouped under the headings of the instrumental sciences of astronomy, optics, and geodesy, and the abstract subjects of mathematics, mechanics, and natural philosophy. It must be appreciated, however, that such a classification is a mere convenience. Bošković's work in the former trio exhibited a consistent penchant for the invention or improvement of instruments of observation as well as for recognition and compensation of procedural errors. In the second, theoretical set of sciences, his writings develop a highly individual point of view. All his work, finally, may be read as physical essays in the working out of an epistemology and metaphysic that styled his career in a way, again, not at all characteristic of his century.

Instrumental Sciences. Bošković's earliest (1736) publication was a description of methods for the determination of the elements of the rotation of the sun on its axis from three observations of a single sunspot. In 1737 there followed an exposition of a graphical method for the resolution on a plane of problems in spherical trigonometry and the treatment of an actual problem in the transit of Mercury. In 1739, two years after the treatise on the aurora borealis, Bošković published an account of the principle of the circular micrometer based on the idea that the circular aperture of the objective may serve for determination of the times at which a celestial body enters and leaves the field of vision of a telescope; these values, when compared with those of a known star, give the relative positions of the two bodies.

From these specific matters, Bošković turned his attention in astronomy to a comprehensive survey of the theoretical foundations and instrumental practice and resources of practical, observational astronomy, and in the years 1742 through 1744 he published a series of works that deal with these matters in a spirit of *severioris critices leges.*

Thereafter, Bošković took up the study of comets. A widely read work of 1746 offered his opinions on a number of questions concerning the nature of comets. In it he proposed his first method—that much later criticized adversely by Laplace—for the determination of parabolic orbits. The procedure was essentially similar to that afterward introduced by J. H. Lambert (1761). Bošković's method, developed in Volume III of his *Opera pertinenta ad opticam et astronomiam* (1785), comes close to the classic method of H. W. Olbers (1797). An interesting treatise of 1749 concerns the determination of an elliptical orbit by means of a construction previously employed for resolving the reflection of a light ray from a spherical mirror. Bošković employed this method again in 1756, in a treatise discussing the reciprocal perturbations of Jupiter and Saturn, which he entered in a competition on the subject set by the Academy of Sciences in Paris. The winner was Leonhard Euler; Bošković received an honorable mention.

Bošković's interest in optics seems to have developed in the first instance out of his astronomical concerns. As early as 1747 he was discussing the tenuity, or rarity, of sunlight, apparently with the old question in mind of the hypothetical materiality of light, and at the same time attempted to estimate the density of a solar atmosphere, supposing it to reach as far as the earth. Having reflected on the problems of light, Bošković published in 1748 a treatise (in two parts) of a broadly critical nature. The central Newtonian positions in optics did not at all appear to him to be securely established. It is perhaps the most interesting feature of his critical attitude that he regarded rectilinear propagation as an unproved hypothesis, a question on which he dwelt in detail. Some other aspects of optical phenomena he thought hidden or unclear even after Newton's discoveries. Discussing phenomena of parallax, he drew attention to the distance of fixed stars in dimensions of light-years. He formulated, and was the first to do so, a general photometric law of illumination and enounced the law of emission of light known under Lambert's name. He was critical of Newton's account of colors arising from the passage of light through thin plates involving the ether and periodicity, and he provided an alternative interpretation in the spirit of his own theory of natural forces, of which more below.

In his later years at Pavia and at the observatory in Brera, he concentrated his attention on the improvement of lenses and optical devices. A series of five discourses on dioptrics (1767) treats of achromatic lenses and offers an impressive example of Bošković's experimental dexterity and accuracy, most notably in respect of measurements of the reflection and dispersion of light by means of his vitrometer. Having confirmed that two-lens arrangements will recombine

BOŠKOVIĆ

only two spectral colors, he recommended a composition involving three or more lenses. He also stressed the importance of the eyepiece in achromatic telescopes. In the actual fabrication of lenses he worked with Stephen Conti of Lucca, who manufactured them according to his specifications and assisted in performing the optical experiments.

At Brera he worked intensively on methods for verifying and rectifying astronomical instruments and improved or invented a number of them, of which accounts later appeared in Volume IV of his *Opera.* Perhaps the most ingenious were a leveler that determined the plane of the edge of a quadrant and a micrometric wedge. To ensure that the border of an astronomical quadrant would be on the same level as the plane passing through the center, Bošković made use of a sort of surveying device. In a canal filled with water leading around the border of the quadrant and along one of its radii floated a small boat with a wire mast hooked at the top. Its point nearly touched the border of the instrument, permitting the measurement of small distances between the point and the water level, thus revealing the true form of the so-called plane of the quadrant. Bošković's micrometric wedge is a metallic wedge truncated on the thin side, which he used to measure the distance between two planes by inserting it into the opening between them and noting the corresponding number on the scale engraved on its side. He also thought that it ought to be possible to decide between Newton's emission theory of light and the wave theory by observations of aberration of light from the fixed stars, first through an ordinary telescope and then through a telescope filled with water. It was his further prediction that observation would detect an aberration of light from terrestrial sources: in these matters research in the nineteenth century failed to confirm his expectations.

Bošković's work in meteorology and geophysics was closely related to astronomical concerns. In 1753 he advanced the idea that the moon was probably enveloped not by an atmosphere like that of the earth, but rather by a concentric layer of some homogeneous, extremely transparent fluid. As to our own atmosphere and its behavior, or misbehavior, he investigated a tornado that devastated Rome in June 1749 and attempted to interpret its effects in terms of Stephen Hales's theory of "fixed air"—it was ever his way to try connecting phenomena in one domain with famous developments in the science of another; his mind ranged over the whole of physical science with more or less cogency, but never without imagination.

It was his idea that mountains had originated from the undulation of rock strata under the influence of subterranean fires, and developing this notion in 1742 led him to the concept of compensation of strata, which could be taken as basis of the later theory of isostasy. He also conceived the idea of a kind of gravimeter for measuring gravitation even in the ocean. At the same time, he proposed a method for determining the mean density of the earth by measuring the incremental attraction of masses of water at high tide by the deviation of a pendulum situated in the proximity.

Early in his career his interest was drawn to the problem of the size and shape of the earth, an issue intensively discussed in the first half of the eighteenth century, since its resolution was thought to be crucial in an eventual choice between a Cartesian cosmology of vortices, which predicted an earth slightly elongated at the poles, and a Newtonian one of inertial motion under attractive forces, in which case the globe should be slightly flattened. In 1739 Bošković initiated a critical investigation of existing measurements of the length of a degree along the meridian. It appeared to him that in addition to cosmological effects, superficial inequalities and irregularities of structure and density beneath the surface might well affect and distort measurements of distance along a meridian, modify the length of the second pendulum at a given locality, and bias the apparent direction of the vertical.

Bošković always promoted international cooperation in geodesy. On his initiative, meridians were measured in Austria, Piedmont, and Pennsylvania, and he himself readily collaborated with an English colleague, Christopher Maire, rector of the English Jesuit College in Rome, in surveying the length of two degrees of the meridian between Rome and Rimini. The onerous work took three years. Its results confirmed, among other things, the geodetic consequences of unevenness in the earth's strata, the possibility of determining surface irregularities by such measurements, as well as the deviation of meridians and parallels from a properly spherical shape. The report on these measurements came out in Rome at the end of 1755. Bošković employed novel methods for measuring the base line in his surveys, and he developed an exact theory of errors and learned to employ his instruments to the most accurate effect. The earliest device for verifying the points of division on the edge of such an instrument originated with Bošković, who determined from the inequalities of their chords that the circular arcs on the border of the instrument, although theoretically equal, were not in fact so. Having determined errors of division corresponding to 60° by comparing the chord with the radius of the instrument, he proceeded by bisecting to angles of 30°, 15°, and finally 5°. The method of compensating errors being applicable to astronomical as well as geodetic observations, he took an important step toward the newer practical astronomy, which for most astronomers begins with Friedrich Bessel. In the French edition of his report on measurements of the meridian, Bošković included the first theory of the combination of observations based on a minimum principle for determining their most suitable values, making use of absolute values instead of their squares, as Gauss later did in his classical method of least squares.

Abstract Sciences. Science in general took its lead in physics from Newton and in mathematical analysis from Leibniz, and it was at the root of Bošković's idiosyncrasy that, whether deliberately or not, he took the opposite tack in both respects. Mathematics had always attracted him. Instead of the calculus as developed by the great analysts among his own contemporaries—d'Alembert, the Bernoullis, and Euler—he preferred the geometric method of infinitely small magnitudes "which Newton almost always used," as he said, and which embodied the "power of geometry." He particularly applied it to problems of differential geometry, terrestrial and celestial mechanics, and practical astronomy. In 1740 he studied the properties of osculatory circles, and in 1741 devoted an entire treatise to the nature of the infinitely great and small magnitudes employed in that method. He relied upon it also in a few problems of classical mechanics: in 1740 he studied the motion of a material point and in 1743 was the first to solve the problem of the body of greatest attraction.

In mechanics (as in optics), however, his allegiance to Newton was qualified. True, he annotated Stay's elegant Latin verses on Newtonian natural philosophy, the *Philosophiae,* published in Rome in three volumes, the first in 1755. Nevertheless, his heterodoxy in mechanics began to be apparent at least as early as 1745, when he published an important discourse on the subject of living force (*vis viva*). He there put forward the view that the speed of a movement is to be computed from the *actio momentanea* of the force that generates it. Attacking the problem of the generation (*generatio*) of velocity in a new way, by distinguishing between actual and potential velocity and by introducing subtle conceptions in connection with the notion of force, he reduced the famous debate over the true measure of force, whether it be momentum (mv) or *vis viva* (mv^2), to the status of a mere argument "over titles." This discourse contained the first statement of Bošković's universal force law.

That law was inspired partly by Leibniz' law of continuity and partly by the famous thirty-first query with which Newton concluded the fourth and final edition of his *Opticks.* There Newton raised speculatively the question whether there might not exist both attractive and repulsive forces alternately operative between the particles of matter. From this idea Bošković proceeded by way of an analysis of collision of bodies to the enunciation of a "universal law of forces" between elements of matter, the force being alternately attractive or repulsive, depending upon the distance by which they are separated. As that distance diminishes toward zero, repulsion predominates and grows infinite so as to render direct contact between particles impossible. A fundamental role is played by the points of equilibrium between the attractive and repulsive forces. Bošković called such points "boundaries" (*limes,* the Latin singular). Some of them are points of stable equilibrium for the particles in them and others are points of unstable equilibrium. The behavior of these boundaries and the areas between them enabled Bošković to interpret cohesion, impenetrability, extension, and many physical and chemical properties of matter, including its emission of light.

It was because of its consequences for the constitution of matter that the law of forces was particularly important. In Bošković's natural philosophy the "first elements" of matter became mere points—real, homogeneous, simple, indivisible, without extension, and distinguished from geometric points only by their possession of inertia and their mutual interaction. Extended matter then becomes the dynamic configuration of a finite number of centers of interaction. Many historians have seen in Bošković's derivation of matter from forces an anticipation of the concept of the field, an anticipation still more clearly formulated very much later by Faraday in 1844. Matter, then, is not a continuum, but a discontinuum. Mass is the number of points in the volume, and drops out of consideration as an independent entity. In the special case of high-speed particles, Bošković even envisaged the penetrability of matter.

The principle of inertia itself did not escape his criticism. It was impossible in his view to prove it or indeed to prove any metaphysical principle to be true of physical reality a priori. But neither could it be proved a posteriori as Newtonians were wont to do from "the phenomenon of movement." Bošković emphasized the necessity of defining the space to which the principle relates. Since he held it to be impossible to distinguish absolute from relative motion by direct observation and without invoking "unproven physical hypotheses," he introduced the notion that inertia as it is observed is relative to a space chosen to include all the bodies in the universe that are within range of our senses, i.e., all the subjects of all our experiments and observations. The translation of that space as a whole can have no effect on the motion of a body within it, on its rotation at a given angle, or on its contraction or dilation if there is a simultaneous and equivalent contraction or dilation of the scale of forces. From these considerations Bošković concluded that experiment and observation could never decide whether inertia is relative or absolute.

It must not be supposed, however, that his natural philosophy represents a reversion to a Leibnizian metaphysic. He was in fact as skeptical and critical of the principle of sufficient reason or final causes as of that of inertia. In general Bošković was convinced that we know nothing so far as the absolute is concerned and just as little of what is relative. He often emphasized the impotence of the human mind, and spoke more than once of the imaginability of beings with a geometry different from ours. He had a clear understanding of the hypothetical-deductive nature of geometry, especially of the Euclidean fifth postulate about parallels. In his view our universe is no more than a grain of sand in a horde of other universes. There might well be other spaces quite unconnected to our own and other times that run some different course.

Sharp in thought, bold in spirit, independent in judgment, zealous to be exact, Bošković was a man of eighteenth-century European science in some respects and far ahead of his time in others. Among his works are writings that still repay study, and not only from a historical point of view.

BIBLIOGRAPHY

I. Original Works. Bošković's more important treatises and works include *De maculis solaribus* (Rome, 1736); *De Mercurii novissimo infra solem transitu* (Rome, 1737); *Trigonometriae sphaericae constructio* (Rome, 1737); *De aurora boreali* (Rome, 1738); *De novo telescopii usu ad objecta caelestia determinanda* (Rome, 1739); *Dissertatio de telluris figura* (Rome, 1739); *De circulis osculatoribus* (Rome, 1740); *De motu corporum projectorum in spatio non resistente* (Rome, 1740); *De inaequalitate gravitatis in diversis terrae locis* (Rome, 1741); *De natura, & usu infinitorum & infinite parvorum* (Rome, 1741); *De annuis fixarum aberrationibus* (Rome, 1742); *De observationibus astronomicis, et quo pertingat earundem certitudo* (Rome, 1742); *Disquisitio in universam astronomiam* (Rome, 1742); *Parere di tre mattematici sopra i danni, che si sono trovati nella cupola di S. Pietro sul fine dell'anno MDCCXLII, dato per ordine di Nostro Signore Papa Benedetto XIV* (Rome, 1742).

Later works are *De motu corporis attracti in centrum immobile viribus decrescentibus in ratione distantiarum reciproca duplicata in spatiis non resistentibus* (Rome, 1743); "Problema mecanicum de solido maximae attractionis solutum a P. Rogerio Josepho Boscovich," in *Memorie sopra la fisica e istoria naturale di diversi valentuomini*, **1** (Lucca, 1743), 63–88; *Nova methodus adhibendi phasium observationes in eclipsibus lunaribus ad exercendam geometriam, et promovendam astronomiam* (Rome, 1744); *De viribus vivis* (Rome, 1745); *De cometis* (Rome, 1746); *Dissertatio de maris aestu* (Rome, 1747); *Dissertazione della tenuità della luce solare* (Rome, 1747); *Dissertationis de lumine pars prima* (Rome, 1748); *Dissertationis de lumine pars secunda* (Rome, 1748); *De determinanda orbita planetae ope catoptricae ex datis vi, celeritate et directione motus in dato puncto* (Rome, 1749); *Sopra il turbine, che la notte tra gli 11 e 12 di giugno del 1749 daneggiò una gran parte di Roma* (Rome, 1749).

During the 1750's Bošković wrote *De lunae atmosphaera* (Rome, 1753); *De continuitatis lege et ejus consectariis pertinentibus ad prima materiae elementa eorumque vires* (Rome, 1754); *Elementa universae matheseos*, 3 vols. (Rome, 1754); *De lege virium in natura existentium* (Rome, 1755); *De litteraria expeditione per Pontificiam ditionem ad dimetiendos duos meridiani gradus et corrigendam mappam geographicam jussu, et auspiciis Benedicti XIV. Pont. Max. suscepto a Patribus Societ. Jesu Christophoro Maire et Rogerio Josepho Boscovich* (Rome, 1755), trans. into French as *Voyage astronomique et géographique dans l'état de l'Église, entrepris par l'ordre et sous les auspices du Pape Benoît XIV, pour mesurer deux degrés du méridien et corriger la carte dans l'état ecclésiastique par les PP. Maire et Boscovich, traduit du latin* (Paris, 1770); *De inaequalitatibus, quas Saturnus et Jupiter sibi mutuo videntur inducere, praesertim circa tempus conjunctionis* (Rome, 1756); "De materiae divisibilitate, et principiis corporum" (1748), in *Memorie sopra la fisica . . .*, IV (Lucca, 1757); *Philosophiae naturalis theoria redacta ad unicam legem virium in natura existentium* (Vienna, 1758).

Bošković's works in his last quarter-century include *De solis ac lunae defectibus libri V* (London, 1760); *Dissertationes quinque ad dioptricam pertinentes* (Vienna, 1767); *Les éclipses* (Paris, 1779); *Giornale di un viaggio da Constantinopoli in Polonia, dell'Abate R. G. Boscovich* (Bassano, 1784); and *Rogerii Josephi Boscovich Opera pertinentia ad opticam et astronomiam maxima ex parte nova et omnia hucusque inedita in V tomos distributa* (Bassano, 1785).

II. Secondary Literature. The earlier works are F. Ricca, *Elogio storico dell'abate Ruggiero Giuseppe Boscovich* (Milan, 1789); M. Oster, *Roger Joseph Boscovich als Naturphilosoph*, dissertation (Cologne, 1909); V. Varićak, "L'oeuvre mathématique de Bošković," in *Rad* (Zagreb), **181, 185, 190, 193** (1910–1912), condensed by Ž. Marković, in *Bulletin des travaux de la classe des sciences mathématiques et naturelles de l'Académie yougoslave de Zagreb*, **1** (1914), 1–24.

See also D. Nedelkovitch, *La philosophie naturelle et relativiste de R. J. Boscovich* (Paris, 1922); *A Theory of Natural Philosophy, Put Forward and Explained by Roger Joseph Boscovich, S. J.*, Lat.-Eng. ed. with trans. by J. M. Child from 1st Venetian ed. (1763), with a short life of Bošković

(Chicago-London, 1922); V. Varićak, "Latin-English Edition of Bošković's Work *Theoria philosophiae naturalis,*" in *Bulletin des travaux de la classe des sciences mathématiques naturelles de l'Académie de Zagreb,* **19-20** (1923-1924), 45-102; L. Čermelj, "Roger Joseph Boscovich als Relativist," in *Archiv für Geschichte der Mathematik, der Naturwissenschaft und der Technik,* **2,** no. 4 (1929), 424-444; and H. V. Gill, *Roger Boscovich, Forerunner in Modern Physical Theories* (Dublin, 1941).

A bibliography of publications on Bošković in English, French, German, and Italian up to 1961 is in L. L. Whyte, ed., *Roger Joseph Boscovich, S.J., F.R.S., 1711-1787, Studies of His Life and Work on the 250th Anniversary of His Birth* (London, 1961), which contains articles on Bošković by E. Hill, L. L. Whyte, Ž. Marković, L. P. Williams, R. E. Schofield, Z. Kopal, J. F. Scott, C. A. Ronan, and Churchill Eisenhart. G. Arrighi has published newly found correspondence between Bošković and G. A. Arnolfini of Lucca in *Quaderni della rivista "La provincia di Lucca,"* **3** (1963), **5** (1965), *Studi scientifici;* and correspondence between Bošković and G. A. Slop, the Pisan astronomer, in *Studi trentini di scienze storiche,* **43,** no. 3 (1964), 209-242; he also published a study on Bošković's good friend Conti, "Scienziati lucchesi del settecento: Giovan Stefano Conti," in *La provincia di Lucca,* **2,** no. 3 (July-Sept. 1962), 31-44. R. Hahn, "The Boscovich Archives at Berkeley," in *Isis,* **56,** no. 183 (Spring 1965), 70-78, reports on the literary legacy of Bošković that has been at the University of California since 1962. Of the recent articles, we should mention P. Costabel's "Le *De viribus vivis* de R. Boscovic ou de la vertu des querelles de mots," in *Archives internationales d'histoire des sciences,* **14,** nos. 54-55 (Jan.-June 1961), 3-12.

The literature on Bošković in Yugoslavia is abundant. On the occasion of the centenary of his death, the Yugoslav Academy of Arts and Sciences in Zagreb issued a collection of works on Bošković in its publication *Rad,* **87, 88,** and **90** (1887-1888), including his correspondence from the archives of the observatory at Brera as transcribed by G. V. Schiaparelli. The latter correspondence was reprinted in *Publicazioni del R. Osservatorio astronomico di Milano-Merate,* n.s. no. 2 (1938). *Gradja za život i rad Rudjera Boškovića* ("Material Concerning the Life and Work of Rudjer Bošković"), 2 vols. (Zagreb, 1950-1957), is a separate publication of the Yugoslav Academy of Arts and Sciences.

Other publications on Bošković in languages other than Serbo-Croatian are in *Actes du symposium international R. J. Bošković 1958* (Belgrade-Zagreb-Ljubljana, 1959); *Actes du symposium international R. J. Bošković 1961* (Belgrade-Zagreb-Ljubljana, 1962); and *Atti del convegno internazionale celebrativo del 250° anniversario della nascita di R. G. Boscovich e del 200° anniversario della fondazione dell' Osservatorio di Brera* (Milan, 1963).

Studies on Bošković have made considerable advances in Yugoslavia, as shown by the works of V. Varićak, in the Yugoslav Academy's *Rad;* B. Truhelka, in various reviews, based on unpublished material on Bošković, especially correspondence with his brothers; S. Hondl, in *Almanah Bošković* ("The Bošković Almanac") of the Croatian Society of Natural Science; J. Majcen; Ž. Marković; Ž. Dadić; D. M. Grmek; and others. Mention should also be made of D. Nedeljković's numerous articles in reviews, as well as in the publications of the Serbian Academy of Arts and Sciences in Belgrade; and of the works of S. Ristić, D. Nikolić, and others. A comprehensive general bibliography up to 1956 can be found in "Bošković," in *Enciklopedija Jugoslavije* ("The Encyclopedia of Yugoslavia"), II (Zagreb, 1956).

ŽELJKO MARKOVIĆ

BOSSE, ABRAHAM (*b.* Tours, France, 1602; *d.* Paris, France, 14 February 1676)

The son of Louis Bosse, a tailor, and Marie Martinet, Bosse settled in Paris around 1625 and worked as a draftsman and engraver. In 1632 he married Catherine Sarrabat; four of their children lived to adulthood.

His drafting technique was obviously derived from the *méthode universelle* of perspective, presented by Girard Desargues as early as 1636. Bosse became Desargues's most ardent propagandist, and it was through his efforts that Desargues's methods achieved some success among artists of the seventeenth century and spread to foreign countries.

The art world of the seventeenth century was split into vigorously warring factions. Bosse sided with Desargues, who was conducting violent polemics, and in 1643 published two treatises, *La pratique du trait à preuves de Mr. Desargues . . . pour la coupe des pierres en l'architecture* and *Manière universelle de Mr. Desargues . . . pour poser l'essieu & placer les heures et autres choses aux cadrans au soleil,* which were complex expositions of two essays that Desargues had written in 1640 on the cutting of stone and on gnomonics.

In 1648 Bosse published a third tract, *Manière universelle de Mr. Desargues pour pratiquer la perspective,* which included several texts by Desargues himself, some of which had not been published before. Among them was the famous theorem on perspective triangles. In 1653 the work was amplified by a demonstration of the application of perspective to curvilinear surfaces. Bosse followed this work with several others dealing with particular applications, and became involved in controversies that eventually cost him his membership in the Académie Royale de Peinture et de Sculpture.

Bosse also illustrated books, particularly works on science. These included such various works as Glaser's *Traité de la chymie,* M. Cureau de La Chambre's *Traité de la lumière,* Moyse Charas's *Pharmacopée royale,* and a series of botanical plates for Dodart's *Mémoires pour servir à l'histoire des plantes.*

BIBLIOGRAPHY

I. ORIGINAL WORKS. Bosse's writings include *La pratique du trait à preuves de Mr. Desargues, Lyonnois, pour la coupe des pierres en l'architecture* (Paris, 1643), also translated into German (Nuremberg, 1699); *La manière universelle de Mr. Desargues, Lyonnois, pour poser l'essieu & placer les heures et autres choses aux cadrans au soleil* (Paris, 1643), also translated into English (London, 1659); *Traité des manières de graver en taille douce sur l'airin par le moyen des eaux fortes et des vernix durs et mols* (Paris, 1645), often reissued and translated; *Manière universelle de Mr. Desargues pour pratiquer la perspective par petit-pied, comme le géometral. Ensemble les places et proportions des fortes et foibles touches, teintes et couleurs* (Paris, 1648), also translated into Dutch (Amsterdam, 1664, 1686); *Moyen universel pour pratiquer la perspective sur les tableaux ou surfaces irrégulières. Ensemble quelques particularitez concernant cet art & celuy de la gravure en taille douce* (Paris, 1653), also translated into Dutch (Amsterdam, 1664, 1686); *Représentations géométrales de plusieurs parties de bastiments faites par les reigles de l'architecture antique* (Paris, 1659); *Traité des manières de dessiner les ordres de l'architecture antique en toutes leurs parties* (Paris, 1664); *Traité des pratiques géométrales et perspectives enseignées dans l'Académie Royale de la Peinture et Sculpture* (Paris, 1665); *Le peintre converty aux précises et universelles regles de son art* (Paris, 1667); *Regle universelle pour décrire toutes sortes d'arcs rampans sur des points donnez de sujetion* (Paris, 1672); *Catalogue des traitez que le Sieur Bosse a mis au jour* (Paris, 1674); and *Recueil des plantes gravées par ordre du roi Louis XIV,* 3 vols. (Paris, n.d.), with N. Robert and L. Chatillon.

A more complete bibliography is in J. C. Brunet (see below) and especially in A. Blum, *Abraham Bosse et la société française du dix-septième siècle,* pp. 217-227, which also reproduces numerous documents relating to the polemic between Bosse and the Académie Royale de Peinture et de Sculpture.

II. SECONDARY LITERATURE. Bosse or his work is discussed in the following (listed chronologically): J. and L. G. Michaud, *Biographie universelle,* new ed., V (Paris, 1843), 124–125; J. M. B. Renouvier, *Des types et des manières des maîtres-graveurs,* XVI–XVII, pt. 2 (Montpellier, 1856), 117–123; P. J. Mariette, *Abecedario,* P. de Chennevières and A. de Montaiglon, eds., II (Paris, 1851–1853), 159–161; G. Duplessis, *Catalogue de l'oeuvre d'A. Bosse* (Paris, 1859); J. C. Brunet, *Manuel du libraire,* I (Paris, 1860), cols. 1126–1129; F. Hoefer, *Nouvelle biographie générale,* IV (1862), cols. 786–787; G. Poudra, *Oeuvres de Desargues,* 2 vols. (Paris, 1864), I, 352–493, II, 1–113, and *Histoire de la perspective* (Paris, 1864); A. Jal, *Dictionnaire critique de biographie et d'histoire,* 2nd ed. (Paris, 1872), pp. 348-352; A. de Montaiglon, *Procès-verbaux de l'Académie Royale de Peinture et de Sculpture, 1648-1792,* I (Paris, 1875), *passim;* E. Haag and E. Haag, *La France protestante,* 2nd ed., II (Paris, 1879), cols. 922–928; A. Valabrègue, *Abraham Bosse* (Paris, 1892); G. C. Williamson, *Bryan's Dictionary of Painters and Engravers,* new ed., I (London, 1903), 174; U. Thieme and F. Becker, *Allgemeines Lexikon der bildenden Künstler,* IV (Leipzig, 1910), 402–403; A. Fontaine, *L'art dans l'ancienne France. Académiciens d'autrefois* (Paris, 1914), pp. 67–114; F. Amodeo, "Lo sviluppo della prospettiva in Francia nel secolo XVII," in *Atti dell'Accademia Pontaniana,* **63** (Naples, 1933); A. Blum, *Abraham Bosse et la société française du dix-septième siècle* (Paris, 1924), and *L'oeuvre gravé d'Abraham Bosse* (Paris, 1925); R. Taton, *L'oeuvre mathématique de Desargues* (Paris, 1951), see Index H, and "La première oeuvre géométrique de Philippe de La Hire," in *Revue d'histoire des sciences,* **6** (1953), 93–111; M. L. Blumer, in *Dictionnaire de biographie française,* VI (Paris, 1954), cols. 1146–1147; F. Bénézit, *Dictionnaire des peintres, sculpteurs, dessinateurs et graveurs,* new ed., II (Paris, 1961), 33–34; and A. Kondo, "Abraham Bosse et Poussin devant les problèmes de l'espace et du temps," in *Annales,* 23rd year (1968), 127–135.

A more complete bibliography relating to the artistic aspect of Bosse's work is given by A. Blum in *Abraham Bosse et la société française du dix-septième siècle,* pp. 213–221; more precise references to the geometrical aspect of the problems are in R. Taton, *L'oeuvre mathématique de Desargues,* pp. 70–71.

RENÉ TATON

BOSSUT, CHARLES (*b.* Tartaras, Rhône-et-Loire, France, 11 August 1730; *d.* Paris, France, 14 January 1814)

Bossut was the son of Barthélemy Bossut and Jeanne Thonnerine. His father died when Charles was six months of age, and the boy was raised by a paternal uncle. He entered the Jesuit Collège de Lyon at fourteen and was a student of Père Béraud, a mathematician whose pupils included Jean Étienne Montucla and Joseph Jérome Lalande. Bossut took minor ecclesiastical orders and was an *abbé* until 1792. He was aided in his professional formation by d'Alembert, Clairaut, and the Abbé Charles Étienne Louis Camus. Bossut never married, was without family, and, according to some, lived his last years as a misanthrope.

Bossut's importance for the history of science lies in his role as a major contributor to European scientific education. His career began in 1752, when he was appointed as professor of mathematics at the École du Génie at Mézières. He remained as professor until 1768, then continued as examiner of students until 1794. His other teaching post was from 1775 to 1780, in the chair of hydrodynamics established by Turgot at the Louvre. For a time he was also examiner of students at the École Polytechnique. Bossut wrote a series of textbooks that appeared in several French and foreign-language editions and won wide acceptance from the 1770's until the early years of the Empire. The texts of Bossut and Étienne Bézout best represent the emergence in the eighteenth century of a standardized, rigorous system of engineering physics textbooks. In France, for example, Bossut's course was used at the Benedictine Collège de Sorèze, the Collège de France, the École du Génie, the École des Ponts et Chaussées, and the École des Mines. He also wrote a history of mathematics that achieved popularity, but never the scholarly recognition of Montucla's history. He edited the works of Pascal, contributed to the *Encyclopédie méthodique,* and aided d'Alembert in editing contributions to Diderot's *Encyclopédie.*

Bossut was one of a very few whom d'Alembert took as students, and as such he was admitted as a *correspondant* to the Académie des Sciences on 12 May 1753; subsequently, he rose to *géomètre, mécanicien,* and *mathématicien.* In 1761, 1762, and 1765 he won or shared prizes given by the Academy for memoirs on mechanics applied to the operation of ships and on the resistance of the ether in planetary motions. He won additional prizes for his mechanics memoirs from the academies of Lyons and Toulouse, and was elected to the scientific academies of Bologna, Turin, and St. Petersburg. In 1775 he participated with d'Alembert and Condorcet in a well-known series of experiments on fluid resistance. Never more than a minor mathematician or physicist, Bossut is nevertheless one of the important figures in the history of physics and engineering education.

BIBLIOGRAPHY

I. Original Works. Most of Bossut's memoirs appeared in the *Mémoires* and publications of the Académie des Sciences, Paris. Some of these were reissued in the collection *Mémoires de mathématiques, concernant la navigation, l'astronomie physique, l'histoire . . . par Charles Bossut* (Paris, 1812). His first textbook, a volume that does not figure in the catalogs of most major libraries, is *Traité élémentaire de méchanique et de dinamique appliqué principalement aux mouvemens des machines* (Charleville, 1763). The various editions of his textbooks (*Cours de mathématiques, Traité élémentaire d'arithmétique,* and others) are cited in the general catalogs of the Bibliothèque Nationale and the British Museum. The first edition of his history of mathematics is *Essai sur l'histoire générale des mathématiques,* 2 vols. (Paris, 1802). For Bossut's edition of Pascal's works see Blaise Pascal, *Oeuvres complètes,* 5 vols. (The Hague, 1779).

II. Secondary Literature. For a short biography, see M. E. Doublet, "L'abbé Bossut," in *Bulletin des sciences mathématiques,* 2nd ser., **38** (1914), 93–96, 121–125, 158–160, 186–190, 220–224. See also the *éloge* by J. B. J. Delambre in *Mémoires de l'Académie Royale des Sciences de l'Institut de France—Année 1816,* **1** (1818), xci–cii. For Bossut's career at Mézières and for his general influence on education, see René Taton, ed., *Enseignement et diffusion des sciences en France au XVIIIe siècle* (Paris, 1964); Vol. XI of the series Histoire de la Pensée. Bossut's appointment to the chair of hydrodynamics is discussed in Roger Hahn, "The Chair of Hydrodynamics in Paris, 1775–1791: A Creation of Turgot," in *Acts of the Xth International Congress of the History of Science (Ithaca)* (Paris, 1964), pp. 751–754. A convenient summary of Bossut's work in fluid resistance is in René Dugas, *A History of Mechanics,* J. R. Maddox, trans. (Neuchâtel, 1955), pp. 313–316. On the question of whether Bossut was a Jesuit, see Thomas F. Mulcrone, S.J., "A Note on the Mathematician Abbé Charles Bossut," in *Bulletin—American Association of Jesuit Scientists,* **42** (1965), 16–19.

C. Stewart Gillmor

BOUGAINVILLE, LOUIS ANTOINE DE (*b.* Paris, France, 11 November 1729; *d.* Paris, 31 August 1811)

Bougainville was the son of a notary, Pierre-Yves de Bougainville. To escape his father's profession he joined the army, saw service with Montcalm in Canada, and, on his own initiative, founded a French colony in the Falkland Islands in 1764. Two years later he was commissioned to sail around the world. On his return he received many honors and was promoted in both the army and the navy. He saw further service in North America. He married into a naval family in 1780 and had four children. Despite his royalist sympathies, he survived the Terror. He escaped the massacre of Paris and lived quietly for the rest of his life. He was an associate of the Académie des Sciences, a member of the Legion of Honor, a count of the empire under Napoleon, and a senator. He was buried with full honors in the Panthéon.

Bougainville's contributions to science were twofold: he began a career in mathematics but achieved his greatest fame as an explorer. At the completion of his schooling he came under the influence of d'Alembert, and as a result he wrote the *Traité du calcul-intégral* during 1752. L'Hospital had written the first textbook on calculus in 1696. Bougainville's contribution was to extend L'Hospital's treatise to cover the integral calculus and to bring the differential calculus up to date. He brought such clarity and order to the subject, as well as incorporating new work, that he achieved immediate recognition. The Académie des Sciences noticed the work in January 1753. It was published the following year, and at the beginning of 1756, it brought Bougainville election to the Royal Society of London. A further volume was published in 1756, and this was the end of his career as a mathematician.

At the end of 1766 Bougainville left Nantes in the frigate *La Boudeuse.* After handing over the Falkland Island colony to Spain in 1767, he called at Rio de Janeiro to meet his supply ship. On board was the botanist Commerson. Among the plants Commerson collected around Rio de Janeiro was a climbing shrub with large purple-red bracts which he named bougainvillea.

The two ships left the Falkland Islands in July 1767 and sailed through the Strait of Magellan. By the end of March 1768, Bougainville was discovering new islands in the Pacific archipelago of Tuamotu. He sailed on to Tahiti, only to find that La Nouvelle Cythère, as he named it, had been discovered eight months earlier by Samuel Wallis. Sailing west, he almost reached the Great Barrier Reef but turned north without exploring further. Bougainville sailed through an archipelago that he named the Louisiade, and discovered two of the Treasury Islands before reaching the Solomons. On 1 July he left the west coast of Choiseul Island and for three days sailed along "a new coast which is of an astonishing height." This is now Bougainville Island, and the strait between it and Choiseul is Bougainville Strait.

Putting into the Moluccas, Bougainville found a "species of wild cat that carries her young in a pocket below her belly," and thus confirmed what Buffon had doubted, that pouched mammals exist in the East Indies. In 1771 Bougainville published the best-selling *Voyage autour du monde.*

It has been said by Frenchmen that, in spite of his mathematical abilities, Bougainville was no great navigator. But he was the first Frenchman to sail around the world. His voyage took three years and, in an age when the death rate for sailors was high, he lost only seven men. He named new islands in the Solomons and the Tuamotu Archipelago; and he was the first to make systematic astronomical observations of longitude, providing valuable charts for future sailors in the Pacific.

Bougainville's attitude toward exploration can be summed up in his own words: "But geography is a science of facts; one cannot speculate from an armchair without the risk of making mistakes which are often corrected only at the expense of the sailors" (*Voyage autour du monde,* p. 210).

BIBLIOGRAPHY

I. Original Works. Bougainville's works include *Traité du calcul-intégral, pour servir de suite à l'analyse des infiniment-petits du Marquis de l'Hôpital,* 2 vols. (Paris, 1754–1756); *Voyage autour du monde* (Paris, 1771); "Journal de l'expédition d'Amérique . . .," in *Rapport de l'archiviste de la province de Québec* (1923/1924), pp. 204–393, trans. and ed. by E. P. Hamilton as *Adventure in the Wilderness, the American Journals 1756–60* (Norman, Okla., 1964). MSS are in the Archives Nationales, Paris.

II. Secondary Literature. Works on Bougainville are J. Dorsenne, *La vie de Bougainville* (Paris, 1930); and J. Lefranc, *Bougainville et ses compagnons* (Paris, 1929).

Wilma George

BOULLIAU, ISMAEL (*b.* Loudun, France, 28 September 1605; *d.* Paris, France, 25 November 1694)

Boulliau was born of Calvinist parents, but he became a Roman Catholic at the age of twenty-one. About four years later, he was ordained a priest. His early studies had been in law and the humanities, but upon settling in Paris in 1633, he resumed an early interest in astronomical observation, a taste he had shared with his father. Thereafter, he pursued a predominantly scientific career, becoming known as Clarissimus Bullialdus. In addition to the usual French and Latin spellings of his name, there were such variants as Bouillaud, Boulliaud, and Bulliald.

The Galilean storm broke during the very year that Boulliau joined the Parisian scientific circle. A recent convert both to Catholicism and to science, he nevertheless joined his friend Gassendi in support of Galileo. Boulliau's publication of the *Philolaus* in 1639 placed him squarely in the Copernican camp, although not yet as a Keplerian. In assuming that the sun stood still, so that he could retain uniform circular motions, Copernicus had been right for the wrong reason. So it was with Boulliau. In the *Philolaus,* Boulliau went further than Copernicus in suggesting the resolution of rectilinear accelerated motion in free fall into two uniform circular components. His law of fall (equivalent to $s = k$ vers t) is in close agreement with the definitive Galilean formulation for small intervals of time only.

In 1645 Boulliau published his most significant scientific work, a more accomplished heliocentric treatise entitled *Astronomia philolaica.* He had now become one of the very few astronomers to accept the ellipticity of orbits, but he categorically rejected all those suggestions of variation in celestial forces which had made Kepler's *Astronomia nova* of 1609 more revolutionary, in a sense, than the work of Copernicus. As against Kepler's astrophysics, Boulliau preferred a geometrical astronomy which saved uniformity of circular motion. He asserted, however, that *if* a planetary moving force did in fact exist, then it should vary inversely as the square of the distance—and not, as Kepler had held, inversely as the first power. The inverse-square hypothesis, which Boulliau published in his *Astronomia philolaica,* evidently had been carried over from his *De natura lucis* of 1638, in which the inverse-square law for intensity of illumination, used earlier by Kepler, had appeared. Rejecting all dynamic hypotheses, including the inverse-square hypothesis in astronomy, Boulliau proposed instead a kinematic representation of planetary motion in which a planet moved along a linear element of an oblique cone while the element in turn revolved uniformly about the axis of the cone. In this way, he reconciled ellipticity of orbits with uniformity of circular motion. Seth Ward modified the scheme shortly afterward in a hypothesis by which the motion of the planet is uniform as seen from the "blind" focus of the ellipse.

The *Astronomia philolaica* was one of the most important treatises written in the period between Kepler and Newton. In his *Principia,* Newton referred to Boulliau's inverse-square hypothesis and praised the accuracy of his tables (Bk. 3, Phen. 4). Boulliau was also highly regarded as a mathematician. Before he was thirty, he had prepared the first printed edition (1644) of the *Arithmetica* of Theon of Smyrna; in his fifties, he published (besides several minor works) the *De lineis spiralibus* (1657), a work inspired by Archimedes; and when he was more than seventy-five years of age, he published a ponderous *Opus novum ad arithmeticam infinitorum* (1682), purporting to clarify the *Arithmetica infinitorum* of Wallis. The mathematical works of Boulliau had little influence on the development of the subject, however, because they were old-fashioned. He evidently failed to see the significance of the Cartesian contributions, whether to mathematics or to science, and seems pointedly to have avoided mentioning Descartes's name. Boulliau's astronomical observations at Paris covered over half a century, but it has been ungenerously said that Boulliau's only permanent contribution to science is the word "evection" in astronomy. Nevertheless, it was Boulliau who, in his *Ad astronomos monita duo* of 1667, first established the periodicity of a variable star, Mira Ceti. His explanation of the phenomenon as a rotating semiluminous body or "half sun" was incorrect, but his estimate of the period as 333 days was accurate, exceeding by less than two days that determined since then.

Boulliau was one of the last reputable scholars to maintain confidence in astrology. Among the works he edited were the *Astronomicon* of Marcus Manilius (1655) and the *De judicandi facultate* of Ptolemy (1667). Despite all his publications, Boulliau's contribution to science should perhaps be measured less by his treatises and ideas than by his scientific activity. He rivaled Mersenne as a correspondent. He served as librarian, first to the brothers du Puy, then to de Thou, French ambassador in Holland, and ultimately to the Bibliothèque Royale in Paris. There he joined the groups which gave rise to the Académie des Sciences. Although never elected to the Academy, in 1663 he was among the first foreign associates elected to the Royal Society of London. It was to Boulliau that Huygens first entrusted his secret of the rings of Saturn and to him that he sent his earliest pendulum clocks. The distribution in Paris of Huygens' *Systema saturnium* (1658) was entrusted to Boulliau; and it was through Boulliau that Pascal's *Lettres d'Amos Dettonville* (1658–1659) went to English and Dutch mathematicians. Prince Leopold in Italy and Hevelius in Danzig depended upon Boulliau to keep them informed of scientific news from Paris, although at times Boulliau was himself traveling to England or Poland or the Levant, seeking out manuscripts, books, and information.

BIBLIOGRAPHY

I. Original Works. Thirty-nine volumes containing Boulliau's unedited papers and correspondence are to be found in Paris (Bibliothèque Nationale, fonds franc. 13019–13058). His published works include *De natura lucis* (Paris, 1638); *Philolaus* (Amsterdam, 1639); *Astronomia philolaica* (Paris, 1645); *De lineis spiralibus* (Paris, 1657); *Ad astronomos monita duo* (Paris, 1667); *Opus novum ad arithmeticam infinitorum* (Paris, 1682). He also edited works of Theon of Smyrna (Paris, 1644), Ptolemy, and Marcus Manilius, as noted in the text.

II. Secondary Literature. There is no biography of Boulliau. Some information on his life and work may be found in G. Bigourdan, *Histoire de l'astronomie d'observation et des observatoires en France,* pt. 1 (Paris, 1918), and in J. P. Niceron, *Mémoires pour servir à l'histoire des hommes illustres dans la république des lettres* (Paris, 1727–1745), Vols. I, X.

Carl B. Boyer

BOUQUET, JEAN-CLAUDE (*b.* Morteau, Doubs, France, 7 September 1819; *d.* Paris, France, 9 September 1885)

After entering the École Normale Supérieure in 1839, Bouquet became a professor at the lycée of Marseilles. He received the *doctorat ès sciences* in 1842, presenting a thesis on the variation of double integrals, and was appointed professor at the Faculté des Sciences of Lyons. There he found his school friend Charles Briot, with whom he collaborated throughout his career.

Bouquet taught special mathematics at the Lycée Bonaparte (now the Lycée Condorcet) from 1852 to 1858, then at the Lycée Louis-le-Grand until 1867. After serving as *maître de conférence* at the École Normale Supérieure and *répétiteur* at the École Polytechnique, Bouquet succeeded J. A. Serret in the chair of differential and integral calculus at the Sorbonne (1874–1884). He was elected to the Académie des Sciences in 1875.

After his thesis Bouquet took up differential geometry, writing a memoir on the systems of straight lines of space and one on orthogonal surfaces that was basic to the important research carried on successively by Ossian Bonnet, Gaston Darboux, Maurice Levy, and Arthur Cayley.

From 1853 on, Bouquet's name is generally associated with that of his friend Briot. Their joint scientific work was a profound study and clarification of the analytic work of Augustin Cauchy. In a memoir that has remained famous since 1853, they proposed to establish precisely the conditions that a function must fulfill in order to be developable into an entire series. They also perfected the analysis by which Cauchy had, for the first time, established the existence of the integral of a differential equation. They opened the way to research on singular points and showed their importance for knowledge of the integral. Their works of 1859 and 1875 on elliptic functions finally brought out the great force of Cauchy's analytic methods.

The mathematical activity of Bouquet and Briot was equaled by remarkable teaching activity. Bouquet, who was as fond of teaching as of science, taught Jules Tannery. Collaborating with Briot, he produced several textbooks that went into numerous printings.

BIBLIOGRAPHY

I. Original Works. Bouquet's works include "Sur la variation des intégrales doubles," doctoral thesis (Faculté des Sciences, Paris, 1842); "Remarques sur les systèmes de droites dans l'espace," in *Journal des mathématiques pures et appliquées,* 1st ser., **11** (1846), 125 ff.; "Note sur les surfaces orthogonales," *ibid.*, 446 ff.; *Mémoire sur les propriétés d'un système de droites* (Lyons, 1848); "Sur la courbure des surfaces," a note in Cournot's *Traité de la théorie des fonctions* (Paris, 1857), along with other, lesser notes by Bouquet and Briot; "Mémoire sur la théorie des intégrales ultra-elliptiques," in a shorter version in *Comptes rendus des séances de l'Académie des sciences* (1868), which led to a report by J. A. Serret on 4 July 1870, in *Recueil des savants étrangers,* pp. 417–470; *Notice sur les travaux mathématiques de M. Bouquet* (Paris, 1870); "Sur l'intégration d'un système d'équations différentielles totales simultanées du Ier ordre," in *Bulletin des sciences mathématiques et astronomiques,* **3** (1872), 265 ff.; "Note sur le calcul des accélérations des divers ordres dans le mouvement d'un point sur une courbe gauche," in *Annales scientifiques de l'École normale supérieure,* 2nd ser., **3** (1874).

Works written in collaboration with Charles Briot are "Note sur le développement des fonctions en séries convergentes, ordonnées suivant les puissances croissantes de la variable," in *Comptes rendus des séances de l'Académie des sciences,* **36** (1853), 334; "Recherches sur les séries ordonnées suivant les puissances croissantes d'une variable imaginaire," *ibid.,* 264 ff.; "Recherches sur les propriétés des fonctions définies par des équations différentielles," *ibid.,* **39** (1854), *séance* of 21 August; "Additions au mémoire précédent," *ibid.*—Cauchy's report on this memoir, *ibid.,* **40** (1855), 567 ff.; "Recherches sur les fonctions doublement périodiques," *ibid.,* **40** (1855), 342 ff.; "Mémoire sur l'intégration des équations différentielles au moyen des fonctions elliptiques," *ibid.,* **41** (1855), 1229, with Cauchy's report in **43** (1856), 27, *séance* of 7 July 1856. All these memoirs, divided into three distinct parts, form, "with certain modifications," the *Journal de l'École polytechnique,* **36** (1856).

Other works are *Théorie des fonctions doublement périodiques et en particulier des fonctions elliptiques* (Paris, 1859), also translated into German (Halle, 1862); *Leçons de géométrie analytique* (Paris, 1875); *Leçons nouvelles de trigonométrie* (Paris, 1875); and *Théorie des fonctions elliptiques* (Paris, 1875).

II. Secondary Literature. Works on Bouquet are Michel Chasles, *Rapport sur les progrès de la géométrie* (Paris, 1870), pp. 214–215; G. H. Halphen, "Notice nécrologique sur Bouquet," in *Comptes rendus des séances de l'Académie des sciences,* **102,** no. 23 (7 June 1886); and Jules Tannery, "Notice nécrologique sur Bouquet," in *Mémorial de l'Association des anciens élèves de l'École normale* (Paris, 1885).

Jean Itard

BOUR, EDMOND (*b.* Gray, Haute-Saône, France, 19 May 1832; *d.* Paris, France, 9 March 1866)

Bour, the son of Joseph Bour and Gabrielle Jeunet, came from a rather modest provincial family. After receiving his secondary education in Gray and

Dijon, he was admitted in 1850 to the École Polytechnique, from which he graduated first in his class in 1852; he then continued his studies at the École des Mines in Paris. At this time he worked on the paper "Sur l'intégration des équations différentielles de la mécanique analytique," which he read before the Académie des Sciences of Paris on 5 March 1855. He also wrote two theses in celestial mechanics, one on the three-body problem and the other on the theory of attraction, which he set forth brilliantly before the Faculté des Sciences in Paris on 3 December 1855.

In July 1855 Bour became both a mining engineer and professor of mechanics and mining at the École des Mines of Saint-Étienne, but he returned to Paris at the end of 1859 as lecturer in descriptive geometry at the École Polytechnique. The following year he was appointed professor at the École des Mines, and professor of mechanics at the École Polytechnique in 1861. Also in 1861 he received the grand prize in mathematics awarded by the Académie des Sciences for his paper "Théorie de la déformation des surfaces." In April 1862 Bour was a candidate for membership in the Académie des Sciences but was defeated by Ossian Bonnet. Disappointed by this failure, he concentrated entirely on his course in mechanics at the École Polytechnique.

Although Bour died of an incurable disease at the age of thirty-four, he left valuable works in mathematical analysis, algebra, infinitesimal geometry, theoretical and applied mechanics, and celestial mechanics. In mechanics his essential contributions dealt with differential equations in dynamics, the theme of his first memoir and of another published in 1862; the analytical study of the composition of movements (1865); and the reduction of the three-body problem to the plane case. In infinitesimal geometry his memoir on the deformation of surfaces, in line with the analogous studies of Bonnet and Codazzi, contained several theorems on ruled surfaces and minimal surfaces; but in its printed version this work does not include the test for the integration of the problem's equations in the case of surfaces of revolution, which had enabled Bour to surpass the other competitors for the Academy's grand prize.

BIBLIOGRAPHY

I. ORIGINAL WORKS. A nearly complete list of Bour's published works is given in Poggendorff and the *Catalogue of Scientific Papers* (see below). Among his works are "Sur l'intégration des équations différentielles de la mécanique analytique," in *Journal de mathématiques pures et appliquées,* **20** (1855), 185–202; his theses for the *docteur-ès-sciences* were published separately (Paris, 1855) as *Thèses présentées à la Faculté des Sciences à Paris pour obtenir le grade de docteur-ès-sciences. . . .* and reproduced in *Journal de l'École polytechnique,* **21**, cahier 36 (1856), 35–84; "Théorie de la déformation des surfaces," *ibid.,* **22**, cahier 39 (1862), 1–148; *Cours de mathématiques et machines,* 3 vols. (Paris, 1865–1874); and *Lettres choisies,* Joseph Bertin and Charles Godard, eds. (Gray, 1905).

II. SECONDARY LITERATURE. Works on Bour are M. Chasles, *Rapport sur les progrès de la géométrie* (Paris, 1870), pp. 211, 295, 325–327; M. D'Ocagne, *Histoire abrégée des sciences mathématiques* (Paris, 1955), p. 300; A. Franceschini, in *Dictionnaire de biographie française,* VI (1954), col. 1383; A. de Lapparent, in *École Polytechnique. Livre du centenaire,* I (Paris, 1895), 143–145; "Notice biographique sur Edmond Bour," in *Nouvelles annales de mathématiques,* 2nd ser., **6** (1867), 145–157; Poggendorff, III, 172–173; and Royal Society of London, *Catalogue of Scientific Papers, 1800–1863,* I (1867), 532.

RENÉ TATON

BOURBAKI, NICOLAS. Bourbaki is the collective pseudonym of an influential group of mathematicians, almost all French, who since the late 1930's have been engaged in writing what is intended to be a definitive survey of all of mathematics, or at least of all those parts of the subject which Bourbaki considers worthy of the name. The work appears in installments that are usually from 100 to 300 pages long. The first appeared in 1939 and the thirty-third in 1967; many intervening installments have been extensively revised and reissued. The selection of topics is very different from that in a traditional introduction to mathematics. In Bourbaki's arrangement, mathematics begins with set theory, which is followed, in order, by (abstract) algebra, general topology, functions of a real variable (including ordinary calculus), topological vector spaces, and the general theory of integration. To some extent the order is forced by the logical dependence of each topic on its predecessors. Bourbaki has not yet reached the other parts of mathematics. Although the work as a whole is called *Elements of Mathematics,* no one could read it without at least two years of college mathematics as preparation, and further mathematical study would be an advantage.

The exact composition of the Bourbaki group varies from year to year and has been deliberately kept mysterious. The project was begun by a number of brilliant young mathematicians who had made important contributions to mathematics in their own right. At the beginning they made no particular attempt at secrecy. With the passage of time, however, they seem to have become more and more enamored of their joke, and have often tried to persuade people that there is indeed an individual named N. Bourbaki, who writes the books. Indeed, Bourbaki once applied for membership in the American Mathematical Society, but was rejected on the ground that he was not an individual. The original group included H. Cartan, C. Chevalley, J. Dieudonné, and A. Weil (all of whom are among the most eminent mathematicians of their generation). Many younger French mathematicians have joined the group, which is understood to have ten to twenty members at any one time and has included two or three Americans. The founding members are said to have agreed to retire at the age of fifty, and are believed to have done so, although with some reluctance.

The origin of the name Nicolas Bourbaki is obscure. The use of a collective pseudonym was presumably intended to obviate title pages with long and changing lists of names and to provide a simple way of referring to the project. The family name appears to be that of General Charles-Denis-Sauter Bourbaki (1816–1897), a statue of whom stands in Nancy, where several members of the group once taught. Possibly the Christian name was supposed to suggest St. Nicholas bringing presents to the mathematical world.

In the early days Bourbaki published articles in mathematical journals, as any mathematician would. He soon gave that up, however, and his reputation rests on his books. People who are unsympathetic to the "new mathematics" introduced into the schools since 1960 accuse Bourbaki of having inspired that movement. The accusation is probably unjustified, although aspects of his work bear a superficial resemblance to less attractive aspects of new mathematics. Bourbaki himself does not intend his approach to be used even in college teaching. Rather, it is meant to improve a mathematician's understanding of his subject after he has learned the fundamentals and to serve as a guide to research.

The most obvious aspects of Bourbaki's work are his insistence on a strict adherence to the axiomatic approach to mathematics and his use of an individual and (originally) unconventional terminology (much of which has since become widely accepted). The former is the more important. Any mathematical theory starts, in principle, from a set of axioms and deduces consequences from them (although many subjects, such as elementary algebra, are rarely presented to students in this way). In classical axiomatic theories, such as Euclidean geometry or Peano's theory of the integers, one attempts to find a set of axioms that precisely characterize the theory. Such an axiomatization is valuable in showing the logical arrangement of the subject, but the clarification so achieved is confined to the one subject, and often seems like quibbling.

A good deal of the new mathematics consists of introducing such axiomatizations of elementary parts of mathematics at an early stage of the curriculum, in the hope of facilitating understanding. Bourbaki's axiomatization is in a different spirit. His axioms are for parts of mathematics with the widest possible scope, which he calls structures. A mathematical structure consists, in principle, of a set of objects of unspecified nature, and of certain relationships among them. For example, the structure called a group consists of a set of elements such that any two can be combined to give a third. The way in which this is done must be subject to suitable axioms. The structure called an order consists of a set of elements with a relationship between any two of them, corresponding abstractly to the statement (for numbers) that one is greater than the other.

Having studied a structure, one may add axioms to make it more special (finite group or commutative group, for example). One can combine two structures, assuming that the objects considered satisfy the axioms of both (obtaining, for example, the theory of ordered groups). By proceeding in this way, one obtains more and more complicated structures, and often more and more interesting mathematics. Bourbaki, then, organizes mathematics as an arrangement of structures, the more complex growing out of the simpler.

There are great advantages in dealing with mathematics in this way. A theorem, once proved for an abstract structure, is immediately applicable to any realization of the structure, that is, to any mathematical system that satisfies the axioms. Thus, for example, a theorem about abstract groups will yield results (which superficially may look quite different) about groups of numbers, groups of matrices, or groups of permutations. Again, once it is recognized that the theory of measure and the theory of probability are realizations of a common set of axioms, all results in either theory can be reinterpreted in the other. Historically, in fact, these two theories were developed independently of each other for many years before their equivalence was recognized. Bourbaki tries to make each part of mathematics as general as possible in order to obtain the widest possible domain of applicability. His detractors object that he loses contact with the actual content of the subject, so that students who have studied only his approach are likely to know only general theorems without specific instances. Of course, the choice of an axiom system is never arbitrary. Bourbaki's collaborators are well aware of the concrete theories they are generalizing, and select their axioms accordingly.

Bourbaki has been influential for a number of reasons. For one thing, he gave the first systematic account of some topics that previously had been available only in scattered articles. His orderly and very general approach, his insistence on precision of terminology and of argument, his advocacy of the axiomatic method, all had a strong appeal to pure mathematicians, who in any case were proceeding in the same direction. Since mathematicians had to learn Bourbaki's terminology in order to read his work, that terminology has become widely known and has changed much of the vocabulary of research. The effect of the work in the development of mathematics has been fully commensurate with the great effort that has gone into it.

BIBLIOGRAPHY

I. Original Works. Works by Bourbaki include "The Architecture of Mathematics," in *American Mathematical Monthly,* **57** (1950), 221–232; and *Éléments de mathématique,* many numbers in the series Actualités Scientifiques et Industrielles (Paris, 1939–).

II. Secondary Literature. André Delachet, "L'école Bourbaki," in *L'analyse mathématique* (Paris, 1949), pp. 113–116; Paul R. Halmos, "Nicolas Bourbaki," in *Scientific American,* **196,** no. 5 (May 1957), 88–99.

R. P. Boas, Jr.

BOUSSINESQ, JOSEPH VALENTIN (*b.* St.-André-de-Sangonis, Hérault, France, 15 March 1842; *d.* Paris, France, 19 February 1929)

Boussinesq came from a family of small farmers, and his first lessons were given by the village schoolteacher and by his uncle, a priest. He then attended the small seminary at Montpellier. After receiving the *baccalauréat,* he became an assistant master in a private school but was not responsible for teaching the children. When he obtained his *licence ès sciences* in 1851, Boussinesq went on to teach at the Collège d'Agde, then at Le Vigan, and later at Gap. Self-taught in scientific matters, he nevertheless was able, in 1865, to present a report on capillarity to the Académie des Sciences. In 1867 his thesis on the spreading of heat won him his *docteur ès sciences* as well as the goodwill of the academician and mathematician Barré de Saint-Venant. Boussinesq then became a professor at the Faculté des Sciences in Lille in 1873, and later he was assigned the chair of physical and experimental mechanics in Paris, followed by those of mathematical physics and of the calculus of probabilities. He was elected to the Académie des Sciences in January 1866 and eventually became its dean; at his death he was its oldest member.

Boussinesq led a simple, secluded life dedicated entirely to science and meditation on philosophical and religious problems, particularly on the conciliation of determinism and free will. He humbly admitted "the smallness of the ensemble of our unclouded knowledge lost in an ocean of darkness."

Faithful to mechanistic thought, which seeks kinematic representations, Boussinesq started with the principle of the conservation of energy and the principle that the accelerations of the points in an isolated system depend solely upon its static state and not on the velocities. He combined a great imaginative boldness with submission to experimental results. One of his conclusions was that simplicity is indispensable in scientific organization and that intuition is a valuable guide. Boussinesq loathed the introduction of such monsters as continuous functions without derivatives and of non-Euclidean space. Hostile to relativist innovations, he remained loyal to classical mechanics and sure of the reality of the ether. He did, however, make important contributions to all branches of mathematical physics except that of electromagnetism.

Boussinesq brought the theoretical study of ether closer to the study of experimental hydrodynamics in his researches on light waves and the theory of heat. His work on hydraulics was considerable; and with extraordinary insight he was able to use a method of legitimate approximation that made it possible to carry out intricate calculations concerning the study of whirlpools, liquid waves, the flow of fluids, the mechanics of pulverulent masses, the resistance of a fluid against a solid body, and the cooling effect of a liquid flow.

Although Boussinesq approached mathematics only in order to apply it practically, he was led to some interesting analyses in seeking the solution of particular problems. In the field of elasticity he obtained some intuitive results when considering certain potentials (logarithmic potentials with three variables, spherical potentials with four variables). In 1880 Boussinesq came upon nonanalytic integrals of hydrodynamic equations. He also found some asymptotic solutions of differential equations corresponding to cases of physical indetermination.

Boussinesq left a considerable amount of work. Besides the hundred or more papers he submitted to learned societies, he published several scholarly and abstruse books, full of original ideas but unorganized and often obscure. By virtue of the spirit of his research he can be considered one of the last figures of classical science in the nineteenth century.

BIBLIOGRAPHY

Among Boussinesq's works are *Étude dynamique d'un effect de capillarité* (Paris, 1865); "Fropagation de la chaleur (Ellipsoïde des conductibilités linéaires)," his thesis (1867); "Essai sur la théorie des eaux courantes, précédé d'un rapport sur le mémoire, suivi d'additions et d'éclaircissements," in *Mémoires présentés par divers savants à l'Académie des Sciences de l'Institut National de France,* XXIII, no. 7 (1872) and XXIV, no. 2 (1875); *Essai théorique sur l'équilibre des massifs pulverulents comparé à celui des massifs solides et sur la poussée des terres sans cohésion* (Brussels, 1876; 1885); *Leçons synthétiques de mécanique générale, introduction au cours de mécanique physique* (Paris, 1883); "Applications des potentiels à l'étude de l'équilibre et du mouvement des solides élastiques," in *Annales de l'École Normale Supérieure* (1885); and *Cours de physique mathématique,* 4 vols. (Paris, 1901–1929). The correspondence between Boussinesq and Saint-Venant is in the archives of the Academy of Sciences, Paris.

LUCIENNE FÉLIX

BOUTROUX, PIERRE LÉON (*b.* Paris, France, 6 December 1880; *d.* France, August 1922)

Pierre Boutroux came from a distinguished family. The only son of the celebrated French philosopher Émile Boutroux and Aline Catherine Eugénie Boutroux, he was also the nephew of the statesman Raymond Poincaré and the physicist Lucien Poincaré and a cousin of the noted mathematician Henri Poincaré.

Boutroux's serious academic life began with his studies at the École Normale Supérieure in Paris. In 1900, when he was but nineteen, the University of Paris published his thesis of *licence, L'imagination et les mathématiques selon Descartes.* After lecturing in mathematics at the University of Montpellier, Boutroux served as professor of integral calculus at the University of Poitiers from 1908 until 1920. During this period he traveled widely. In 1909 he was a visiting professor at the University of Nancy. Shortly thereafter he lectured at the Collège de France on mathematical functions defined by first-order differential equations. Then he departed for the United States and Princeton University, where he occupied the chair of higher mathematics from 1913 through 1914. At Princeton he also assumed the chairmanship of the graduate department of mathematics.

With the advent of World War I, Boutroux took a leave of absence from Princeton in order to join the French army. After serving with distinction, he remained in France. In 1920 he returned to the Collège de France, where he accepted the professorial chair of the general history of science, which Auguste Comte had first sought to have created in 1832. Although it was finally established in 1892, Boutroux was the first historian of science to occupy it. Had it not been for his untimely death at the age of forty-one, Boutroux, with his extensive erudition, might have made famous the chair of Comte. After his death in 1922, the chair was discontinued.

The writings of Boutroux reflect a wide-ranging scientific interest. In the area of pure mathematics, his chief contribution was his study of multiform functions and the singularities of differential equations.

In the nineteenth century, Augustin Cauchy, Karl Weierstrass, and Henri Poincaré had made significant advances in the theory of differential equations in the complex domain. Late in the century the French mathematician Paul Painlevé undertook the study of the singularities of analytic functions. After 1887, in a series of brilliant articles, he established a firm foundation for the analytic theory of differential equations and specifically introduced new equations not integrable in terms of elliptic functions or any of their degenerate cases. These equations defined new transcendents. Early in the twentieth century Boutroux not only continued Painlevé's work on these new transcendents, but also helped develop Henri Poincaré's and Charles Picard's study in the complex field, around a zero point, of the differential system

$$\frac{dx^1}{X_1} = \frac{dx^2}{X_2} = \cdots = \frac{dx^n}{X_n}$$

where the X's are all zero in o and holomorphic in its neighborhood.

Boutroux's principal pure mathematical publication is *Leçons sur les fonctions définies par les équations différentielles du premier ordre.* After reading this text and several of his articles, one can see that his main contributions to mathematics arose from the extension and clarification of extant ideas rather than from his formulation of new ones.

Boutroux's contributions to the history and philosophy of science are, however, more original and more extensive. The two-volume *Les principes de l'analyse mathématique* is a transitional work encompassing both pure mathematics and the history and philosophy of mathematics. These volumes contain a comprehensive view of the whole field of mathematics in the second decade of the twentieth century, both as a body of knowledge and as a mode of thought. Boutroux's topics range from rational numbers to an analysis of the notion of function. In light of the historical method used by the author, he might better have entitled this book "An Analysis of the Progress of Mathematical Thought." Some of his historical sections are open to criticism. In one instance, for example, his underrating of the accomplishments of Isaac Barrow and Gottfried Leibniz detract from his analysis of the development of the infinitesimal calculus.

Boutroux clearly presented his view of the nature of mathematical analysis in *Les principes.* He saw analysis as the combination or reconciliation of two often opposing approaches to explaining the world's phenomena: empiricism and rationalism. His summary of historical developments strikingly shows that modern analysis now envelops these two approaches.

Les principes is a substantial contribution to mathematical literature. Its lucid presentation of some of the most important topics in the field has proved to be a valuable guide for graduate students and teachers of mathematics. In addition, this book is a useful source of information for historians of mathematics.

Probably Boutroux's foremost work is *L'idéal scientifique des mathématiciens dans l'antiquité et dans les temps modernes.* In this volume he asserts that the synthetic conception of Cartesian algebra represents a median period in the evolution of mathematics between the aesthetic, contemplative Greek attitude and the apparently groping and incoherent researches of contemporary mathematicians. Throughout these three different ages runs the unity of a search for progress, the attainment of a higher reality. This progress depends neither solely upon mathematicians nor upon the abstract systems of rational or conventional construction. Progress involves many varied rational and practical advances.

The main purpose of Boutroux in writing this book, however, was not to investigate the constituent elements of progress. He had two didactic goals in mind. After showing that the different sciences do not progress independently, he first asserted that the history of science should be a study of the continuous interactions between the various sciences. He opposed the view of the history of science as consisting only of narrow, technical studies. Second, he told teachers and researchers that no one type of solution exists for all problems. He felt that the nature of the problem best dictated the methods needed for its solution.

Boutroux's contributions to the literature of the history of science extend beyond the general surveys mentioned above. His edition of the works of Blaise Pascal provided the source material needed for the study of seventeenth-century mathematics. He also improved upon some of Pierre Duhem's studies of mechanics and carefully analyzed the writings of the French historian Paul Tannery. Judging from his writings, Boutroux fits into the group of historical thinkers consisting of Auguste Comte, Paul Tannery, Pierre Duhem, and George Sarton.

BIBLIOGRAPHY

I. ORIGINAL WORKS. Books by Boutroux are the following: *L'imagination et les mathématiques selon Descartes* (Paris, 1900); *Leçons sur les fonctions définies par les équations différentielles du premier ordre* (Paris, 1908), with notes by Paul Painlevé; *Oeuvres de Blaise Pascal, pub. suivant l'ordre chronologique avec documents complémentaires* (Paris, 1908– ; 2nd ed., 1929), with introduction and notes by Léon Brunschvicg and Boutroux; *Henri Poincaré: L'oeuvre scientifique, l'oeuvre philosophique* (Paris, 1914), written with Vito Volterra, Jacques Hadamard, and Paul Langevin; *Les principes de l'analyse mathématique. Exposé historique et critique,* 2 vols. (Paris, 1914–1919); and *L'idéal scientifique des mathématiciens dans l'antiquité et dans les temps modernes* (Paris, 1920).

Boutroux's articles include "Les origines du calcul des probabilités," in *Revue du mois,* **5** (1908), 641–654; "Le calcul combinatoire et la science universelle," in *Revue du mois,* **9** (1910), 50–62; "Fonctions analytiques: Exposé d'après l'article allemand de W. F. Osgood," in *Encyclopédie des sciences mathématiques* (Paris, 1904–1913), Tome 2, Vol. II, written with Jean Chazy; "Remarques sur les singularités transcendantes des fonctions de deux variables," in *Comptes rendus de l'Académie royale des sciences,* **39,** nos. 2–3 (1911), 296–304; "L'edifice géométrique et la démonstration," in *L'enseignement mathématique,* **14,** no. 6 (1912), 281–305; "Les étapes de la philosophie mathématique," in *Revue de métaphysique et de morale,* **21,** nos. 3–5 (1913), 307–328; "Recherches sur les transcendantes de M. Painlevé et l'étude asymptotique des équations différentielles du second ordre," in *Annales scientifiques de l'École Normale Supérieure,* 3rd ser., **30,** nos. 6–12 (1914), 255–375, and **31,** nos. 2–6 (1914), 99–159; "L'histoire des sciences et les grands courants de la pensée mathématique," in *Revue du mois,* **20** (1915), 604–621; "Sur une mode de définition d'une classe de fonctions multiformes dans tout le domaine d'existence de ces fonctions," in *Comptes rendus de l'Académie royale des sciences,* **163** (1919), 1150–1152; "Sur une famille de fonctions multiformes définies par des équations différentielles du premier ordre," *ibid.,* **170** (1920), 15–26; "L'enseignement de la mécanique en France au XVIIe siècle," in *Isis,* **4** (1921), 276–295; "L'histoire des principes de la dynamique avant Newton," in *Revue de métaphysique et de morale,* **28** (1921), 656–688; "On Multiform Functions Defined by Differential Equations of the First Order," in *Annals of Mathematics,* **22** (1922), 1–29; "Sur les fonctions associées à un groupe autogène de substitution," in *Comptes rendus de l'Académie royale des sciences,* **173** (1922), 821–832; and "L'oeuvre de Paul Tannery," in *Osiris,* nos. 4–5 (1938), 690–705.

II. SECONDARY LITERATURE. A book containing material on Boutroux is Doyen Roissonnade, *Histoire de l'Université de Poitiers passé et présent (1432–1932)* (Poitiers, 1932). An article dealing with Boutroux is Léon Brunschvicg, "L'oeuvre de Pierre Boutroux," in *Revue de métaphysique et de morale,* **29–30** (1922), 285–289.

RONALD S. CALINGER

BOUVELLES, CHARLES (*b.* Saucourt, Picardy, France, *ca.* 1470; *d.* Noyon, France, *ca.* 1553)

The most important mathematical work of Bouvelles, who was also known as Charles de Bouelles, was published in three languages: in Latin as *Geometricae introductionis* (1503); in French as *Livre singulier et utile* (1542, with several later editions); and in Dutch as *Boeck aenghaende de Conste en de Practycke van Geometrie* (1547). According to H. Bosmans (*Bibliotheca mathematica,* **7** [1906], 384) this translation is a bit abbreviated. The *Geometricae* includes chapters on stellated polygons, which had been discussed in Bradwardine's *De geometria speculativa* (1495). It is very likely that Bouvelles knew this tract, for he refers to Bradwardine in his introduction to the section on the quadrature of the circle, which also was discussed in the *Geometria.* Extending the sides of a regular convex polygon results in a stellated polygon of the first order; in the same way the latter can be transformed into a stellated polygon of the second order, and so on. Bouvelles started with the stellated pentagon, the first stellated polygon of the first order, and showed that the sum of its angles equals two right angles. For this he used the regularity of the polygon and showed that every angle is 36°, so the sum is 180°. After having shown that the sum of the angles of a stellated hexagon equals four right angles, he went on to the first stellated polygon of the second order, the heptagon; and, referring to his proof for the pentagon, he said that the sum of the angles of the heptagon also equals two right angles.

Bouvelles made several attempts to solve the old problem of the quadrature of the circle. In the Middle Ages there had been several treatises on that subject: the *De quadratura circuli* of Franco of Liège (eleventh century), the *De triangulis* of Jordanus de Nemore and the *De quadratura et triangulatura circuli* of Ramón Lull (thirteenth century), the *De geometria speculativa* of Bradwardine (according to Bouvelles, his quadrature is not right), and the *Quaestio de quadratura circuli* of Albert of Saxony (fourteenth century); the *De circuli quadratura* of Nicholas of Cusa (fifteenth century) was refuted by Regiomontanus, but Bouvelles agreed with it, remarking that Nicholas used infinite dimensions unknown to any geometer who would never confess that they were possible.

In the age of Bouvelles, too, there were treatises: Oronce Fine's *De quadratura circuli* (1544), Jean Buteo's *De quadratura circuli* (1559), and Joseph Scaliger's *Cyclometrica elementa* (1594), which was refuted by Vieta in his *Munimen adversus nova Cyclometrica* (1594) and in his *Pseudo-mesolabium* (1595). In the solution given in the *Livre singulier,* Bouvelles considered a circle rolling along a straight line. After a quarter of a revolution, the point on the circle at which the distance from the line is equal to the radius of the circle has touched the line and has described an arc of a circle, the center of which lies $5/4\ r$ (radius) beneath the starting point of the center of the given circle. His construction agrees with the Hindu value of $\pi = \sqrt{10}$. Günther has seen in this the first genetic construction of the cycloid, but this is very unlikely.

In his *Liber de XII numeris* (1510) Bouvelles wrote on perfect numbers, i.e., numbers that are equal to the sum of all their possible factors, such as 6, 28, and 496. He asserted, without proof, that a perfect number (except 6) is always a multiple of 9, plus 1, but that the inverse is not true. This rule was given, also without proof, by Tartaglia in his *General trattato di numeri et misure* (1556).

In 1511 Bouvelles published the *Géométrie en françoys,* probably the first geometrical treatise printed in French.

BIBLIOGRAPHY

I. ORIGINAL WORKS. Bouvelles' major work appeared in three versions: in Latin, as *Geometricae introductionis libri sex, breviusculis annotationibus explanati, quibus annectuntur libelli de circuli quadratura, et de cubicatione spherae et introductione in perspectivam* (Paris, 1503); in French, as *Livre singulier et utile touchant l'art et pratique de géométrie, composé nouvellement en françoys, par Maistre Charles de Bouvelles, chanoyne de Noyon* (Paris, 1542); in Dutch, as *Boeck aenghaende de Conste en de Practycke van Geometrie* (Antwerp, 1547). His other works are *Liber de XII numeris* (Paris, 1510) and *Géométrie en françoys* (Paris, 1511).

II. SECONDARY LITERATURE. Works on Bouvelles are Marshall Clagett, *Archimedes in the Middle Ages* (Madison, Wis., 1964), pp. 33–36; J. Dippel, *Versuch einer systematischen Darstellung der Philosophie des Carolus Bovillus* (Würzburg, 1865); J. Fontès, "Sur le *Liber de numeris perfectis* de Charles de Bouëlles," in *Mémoires de l'Académie des Sciences, Inscriptions et Belles-Lettres de Toulouse,* **6** (1894), 155–167; S. Günther, "Lo sviluppo storico della teoria dei poligoni stellati nell' antichità e nel medio evo," in *Bollettino di bibliografia e di storia,* **6** (1873), 313–340; S. Günther, "War die Zykloide bereits im XVI. Jahrhunderte bekannt?," in *Bibliotheca mathematica,* **1** (1887), 8–14;

D. Mahnke, *Unendliche Sphäre und Allmittelpunkt* (Halle, 1937), pp. 108–117.

H. L. L. BUSARD

BOWEN, RUFUS (ROBERT) (*b*. Vallejo, California, 23 February 1947; *d*. Santa Rosa, California, 30 July 1978)

The son of Marie De Winter Bowen, a schoolteacher, and Emery Bowen, a budget officer at Travis Air Base in California, Robert Bowen attended public schools in the small city of Fairfield. He published his first mathematical paper at the age of seventeen, and four more before he was twenty-one. The University of California at Berkeley awarded him a bachelor's degree, with prizes for scholarship, in 1967, and the doctorate in 1970. He was appointed assistant professor of mathematics at Berkeley in 1970 and was promoted to professor in 1977. On 6 March 1968 Bowen married Carol Twito of Hayward, California; they had no children. Deeply concerned with social problems, as were many of his generation, he was active in organizations devoted to preventing nuclear war. Bowen belonged to Phi Beta Kappa and the American Mathematical Society. In 1970 he changed his first name to Rufus. He died of a cerebral aneurysm.

The subject of Bowen's doctoral dissertation, and of all his later work, was dynamical systems theory. Originated by Henri Poincaré in the 1880's, this field was developed intensively in the 1960's, largely under the leadership of Bowen's dissertation supervisor, Stephen Smale. The latter's seminal paper, "Differentiable Dynamical Systems" (*Bulletin of the American Mathematical Society*, **73** [1967], 747–817), was much admired by Bowen and strongly influenced the direction of his work.

As studied by Smale, a dynamical system comprises a manifold M and a smooth mapping $f: M \rightarrow M$ (usually a diffeomorphism); the goal is to describe the limiting behavior of the trajectories $f^n(x)$ of points $x \in M$ as n goes to infinity. As Poincaré emphasized, there is no general procedure for this, and therefore one must resort to describing average, typical, or most probable behavior. Bowen's work is an important part of the program of expressing these vague ideas in mathematically precise and useful ways.

Smale singled out what he called "axiom A systems" as being simple enough to study and complex enough to include many interesting examples. His "spectral decomposition theorem" states that there is a finite number of indecomposable subsystems, called "basic sets," to which all trajectories tend, and that the dynamics of the basic sets is not too wild. Most of Bowen's work is concerned with the dynamics in a basic set of an axiom A system.

Bowen's early papers give useful estimates for the topological entropy $h(f)$ of a dynamical system. This topological invariant, which had recently been discovered by others, measures the complexity of the system. For axiom A systems Bowen proved that

$$h(f) = \limsup_{n \rightarrow \infty} n^{-1} \log N_n(f),$$

where $N_n(f)$ is the number of fixed points of f^n. Other results give lower bounds for $h(f)$ in terms of the automorphisms induced by f on the fundamental and homology groups of M.

Most of Bowen's subsequent work concerns invariant measures associated to dynamical systems. First used by Poincaré and J. Willard Gibbs, these measures are intimately related to statistical mechanics and other branches of mathematical physics. A major achievement was Bowen's construction of an invariant, ergodic probability measure μ_X for any basic set X, for which periodic points are uniformly distributed.

In this work Bowen developed new methods in the symbolic dynamics pioneered by Jacques Hadamard and Marston Morse. He constructed a certain covering of X by closed sets $R_1, \cdots, R_n$, called a Markov partition. To any x in M one associates a doubly infinite sequence $y = (y_i)$ such that $y_i \in \{1, \cdots, n\}$, and $f^i x \in R_j$ if $y_i = j$. The Markov partition has the property that each x corresponds to at most n^2 sequences, and most x to exactly one sequence. The space Σ of all such sequences is readily described; it carries the "shift" homeomorphism $Ty = z$ defined by $z_i = y_{i+1}$. There is a continuous map P from Σ onto X such that $P(Ty) = f(Py)$. This means that T and f have practically the same dynamics. Bowen was able to infer much about f from the easily analyzed dynamics of T. In particular he showed that (f, X), considered as an automorphism of the measure space (X, μ_X), is a Markov chain. This means that most points of X have trajectories that are randomly distributed over X.

Bowen then turned to analogous but much more subtle problems for continuous-time systems, called flows: here one has a one-parameter group of maps indexed by the real numbers. An important technical achievement was the description of suitable analogues, for flows, of symbolic dynamics. An important theorem (proved with David Ruelle) states that every attracting basic set Z of a twice-differentiable, axiom A flow on M carries an invariant probability measure μ_0 with the following property: For any continuous function g on M and almost every point x in a neighborhood of Z (in the sense of Lebesgue measure), the time average of g over the forward orbit of x equals the μ_0 average of g over Z. This measure is now called the Bowen-Ruelle measure. Bowen applied his results to the geodesic flow on the unit tangent bundle of a compact manifold of constant negative curvature, showing that periodic geodesics are equidistributed in the Riemannian measure as the periods tend to infinity.

In his last, posthumous paper, Bowen applied his measure-theoretic methods in a novel way to classical problems in the geometry of Fuchsian groups. Besides its considerable intrinsic interest, this paper demonstrates that Bowen's methods have application far beyond the axiom A systems for which they were invented. The Bowen-Ruelle measure, for example, has already proved significant in other dynamical settings. His papers, models of clarity, simplicity, and originality, have a permanent importance in dynamical systems theory.

BIBLIOGRAPHY

The best sources for an overview of much of Bowen's work are the following surveys written by him: "Symbolic Dynamics for Hyperbolic Flows," in *Proceedings of the International Congress of Mathematicians* (Vancouver, 1974), 299–302; *Equilibrium States and the Ergodic Theory of Anosov Diffeomorphisms*, Lecture Notes in Mathematics no. 470 (New York, 1975); and *On Axiom A Diffeomorphisms* (Providence, R.I., 1978). His work with David Ruelle is "The Ergodic Theory of Axiom A Flows," in *Inventiones Mathematicae*, **29** (1975), 181–202. His last paper is "Hausdorff Dimension of Quasi-circles," in *Publications mathématiques de l'Institut des hautes études scientifiques*, no. 50 (1978), 259–273. Papers covering other aspects of his work are "Entropy for Maps of the Interval," in *Topology*, **16** (1977), 465–467; and "A Model for Couette Flow-data," in P. Bernard and T. Ratin, eds., *Turbulence Seminar, Proceedings 1976/77* (New York, 1977), 117–133.

MORRIS HIRSCH

BRADWARDINE, THOMAS (*b.* England, *ca.* 1290–1300; *d.* Lambeth, England, 26 August 1349)

Both the date and place of Bradwardine's birth are uncertain, although record of his early connection with Hartfield, Sussex, has often been taken as suggestive. His own reference (*De causa Dei,* p. 559) to his father's present residence in Chichester is too late to be relevant.

Our knowledge of Bradwardine's academic career begins with the notice of his inscription as fellow of Balliol College in August 1321. Two years later we find him as fellow of Merton College, a position he presumably held until 1335. We also have evidence of a number of other university positions during this period. The succession of his Oxford degrees would seem to be the following: B.A. by August 1321; M.A. by about 1323; B.Th. by 1333; D.Th. by 1348.

Bradwardine's ecclesiastical involvement appears to have begun with his papal appointment as canon of Lincoln in September 1333, although his less official entry about 1335 into the coterie of Richard de Bury, then bishop of Durham, was probably of greater importance in determining the remainder of his career. For not only did this latter move place Bradwardine in more intimate contact with some of the more engaging theologians in England, but it also may well have proved to be of some effect in introducing him to the court of Edward III. Indeed, shortly after his appointment as chancellor of St. Paul's, London (19 September 1337), we find him as chaplain, and perhaps confessor, to the king (about 1338/1339). We know that he accompanied Edward's retinue, perhaps to Flanders, but certainly to France during the campaign of 1346. In point of fact, it was late in that year, in France, that Bradwardine delivered his (still extant) *Sermo epinicius* in the presence of the king, the occasion being the commemoration of the battles of Crécy and Neville's Cross. The closeness of his ties with Edward might also be inferred from the fact that the king annulled Bradwardine's first election to the archbishopric of Canterbury (31 August 1348). He was, however, elected a second time (4 June 1349), apparently without Edward's opposition, and consecrated at Avignon approximately a month later (10 July 1349). Bradwardine immediately returned to England, where, after scarcely more than a month as archbishop, he fell before the then raging plague and died at the residence of the bishop of Rochester in Lambeth, 26 August 1349.

Although our evidence is not absolutely conclusive, it seems highly probable that Bradwardine composed all of his philosophical and mathematical works between the onset of his regency in arts at Oxford and approximately 1335.

Early Logical Works. In spite of the lack of any direct testimony, it is nevertheless a reasonable assumption that the early logical works were the result of a youthful Bradwardine first trying his hand at a kind of activity common, even expected, among recent arts graduates in the earlier fourteenth century. A number of these logical treatises ascribed to Bradwardine are undoubtedly spurious, but at least two seem, to judge in terms of present evidence, to be most probably genuine: *De insolubilibus* and *De incipit et desinit.* Neither of these works has been edited or studied, yet the likelihood is not great that they will eventually reveal themselves to be much more than expositions of the *opinio communis* concerning their subjects. Both treatises are of course relevant to the history of medieval logic, but the *De incipit et desinit,* like the many other fourteenth-century tracts dealing with the same topic, had a direct bearing upon current problems in natural philosophy as well. For the medieval works grouped under this title (or under the alternative *De primo et ultimo instanti*) address themselves to the problem of ascribing what we would call intrinsic or extrinsic boundaries to physical changes or processes occurring within the continuum of time. Thus, to cite the fundamental assumption of Bradwardine's *De incipit* (an assumption shared by almost all his contemporaries), the duration of the existence of a permanent entity (*res permanens*) that lasts through some temporal interval is marked by the fact that it possesses a first instant of being (*primum instans in esse*) but no last instant of being (*ultimum instans in esse*); its termination is signified, rather, by an extrinsic boundary, a first instant of nonbeing (*primum instans in non esse*).

Tractatus de proportionibus velocitatum in motibus. It is this work, composed in 1328, that has firmly established Bradwardine's position within the history of science. As its title indicates, it treats of the "ratios of speeds in motions," a description of the contents of the *Tractatus* that becomes more properly revealing once one identifies the basic problem Bradwardine set out to resolve: How can one correctly relate a variation in the speeds of a mobile (expressed, as in the work's title, as a "ratio of speeds") to a variation in the causes, which is to say the forces and resistances, determining these speeds? The proper answer to this question is, without doubt, the fundamental concern of the *Tractatus de proportionibus.* In Bradwardine's own words, to find the correct solution is to come upon the *vera sententia de proportione velocitatum in motibus, in comparatione ad moventium et motorum potentias* (Crosby ed., p. 64).

Answers to this question were, Bradwardine points out, already at hand. Yet they failed, he argues, to resolve the problem satisfactorily. Basically, their failure lay in that they would generate results which were inconsistent with the "postulate" of Scholastic-Aristotelian natural philosophy which stipulated that motion could ensue only when the motive power exceeded the power of resistance: when, to use modern symbols, $F > R$. Thus, for example, one unsatisfactory answer was that implied by Aristotle. For, although Aristotle was certainly not conscious of Bradwardine's problem as such and, it can be argued, never had as a goal the firm establishment of any mathematical relation as obtaining for the variables involved, the medieval natural philosopher took much of what he had to say in the *De caelo* and the *Physics* (especially in bk. VII, ch. 5) to entail what is now most frequently represented by $V \propto F/R$. But this will not do. For, if one begins with a given $F_1 > R_1$, and if one continually doubles the resistance (i.e., $R_2 = 2R_1$, $R_3 = 2R_2$, etc.), then F_1 as a randomly given mover will be of infinite capacity (*quelibet potentia motiva localiter esset infinita* [*ibid.,* p. 98]). In our terms, what Bradwardine intends by his argument is that, under the continual doubling of the resistance, if we hold F_1 constant, then at some point one will reach $R_n > F_1$, which, on grounds of the suggested resolution represented by $V \propto F/R$, implies that some "value" would still obtain for V; this in turn violates the "motion only when $F > R$" postulate. Therefore, $V \propto F/R$ is an unacceptable answer to his problem. Bradwardine also sets forth related arguments against other possible answers, which are usually symbolized by $V \propto F - R$ and $V \propto (F - R)/R$.

The correct solution, in Bradwardine's estimation, is that "the ratio of the speeds of motions follows the ratio of the motive powers to the resistive powers and vice versa, or, to put the same thing in other words: the ratios of the moving powers to the resistive powers are respectively proportional to the speeds of the motions, and vice versa. And," he concludes, "geometric proportionality is that meant here" (*Proportio velocitatum in motibus sequitur proportionem potentiarum moventium ad potentias resistivas, et etiam econtrario. Vel sic sub aliis verbis, eadem sententia remanente: Proportiones potentiarum moventium ad potentias resistivas, et velocitates in motibus, eodem ordine proportionales existunt, et similiter econtrario. Et hoc de geometrica proportionalitate intelligas* [*ibid.,* p. 112]).

Given just this much, it is not at all immediately clear what Bradwardine had in mind. His intentions reveal themselves only when one begins to examine his succeeding conclusions and, especially, the examples he uses to support them. If we generalize what we then discover, we can, in modern terms, say that his solution to his problem of the corresponding "ratios" of speeds, forces, and resistances is that speeds vary arithmetically while the ratios of forces to resistances determining these speeds vary geometrically. That is, to use symbols, for the series $V/n, \cdots V/3, V/2, V, 2V, 3V, \cdots nV$, we have the corresponding series $(F/R)^{1/n}, \cdots (F/R)^{1/3}, (F/R)^{1/2}, F/R, (F/R)^2, (F/R)^3, \cdots (F/R)^n$. Or, straying an even

BRADWARDINE

greater distance from Bradwardine himself, we can arrive at the now fairly traditional formulations of his so-called "dynamical law":

$$(F_1/R_1)^{V_2/V_1} = F_2/R_2 \text{ or } V = \log_a F/R, \quad \text{where } a = F_1/R_1.$$

Furthermore, if we continue our modern way of putting Bradwardine's solution to his problem, we can more easily express the advantage it had over the medieval alternatives cited above. In essence, this advantage lay in the fact that Bradwardine's "function" allowed one to continue deriving "values" for V, since such values—the repeated halving of V, for example—never correspond to a case of $R>F$ (as was the case with $V \propto F/R$); they correspond, rather, to the repeated taking of roots of F/R, and if the initial $F_1>R_1$ (as is always assumed), then for any such root $F_n/R_n = (F_1/R_1)^{1/n}$, F_n is always greater than R_n. With this in view, it would seem that Bradwardine's most notable accomplishment lay in discovering a mathematical relation governing speeds, forces, and resistances that fit more adequately than others the Aristotelian-Scholastic postulates of motion involved in the problem he set out to resolve.

It is of the utmost importance to note, however, that almost all we have said in expounding Bradwardine's function goes well beyond what one finds in the text of the *Tractatus de proportionibus* itself. Notions of arithmetic versus geometric increase or of the exponential character of his "function" may well translate his intentions into our way of thinking, but they also simultaneously tend to mislead. Thus, to speak of exponents at once implies or suggests a mathematical sophistication that is not in Bradwardine, and also obscures the relative simplicity of his manner of expressing (by example, to be sure) his "function." This simplicity derives from the symmetrical use of the relevant terminology: If one *doubles* a speed, he would say, then one *doubles* the ratio of force to resistance, and if one *halves* the speed, then one *halves* the ratio. Although we feel constrained to note that doubling or halving a *ratio* amounts, in our terms, to squaring or taking a square root, such an addendum was unnecessary for Bradwardine, since for him the effect of applying such operations as doubling or halving to ratios was unambiguous. To double A/B always gave—again in our terms—$(A/B)^2$, and never $2(A/B)$. What is more, the examples Bradwardine utilizes to express his function deal *merely* with doubling and halving, a factor which makes it evident that he was still at a considerable remove from the general exponential function so often invoked in explaining the crux of the *Tractatus de proportionibus.*

This limitation not only derived from the fact that the relevant material in Aristotle so often spoke of doubles and halves, but may also be related to the possible origin of Bradwardine's function itself. The locale of this origin is medieval pharmacology, where we find discussion of a problem similar to Bradwardine's; in place of investigating the corresponding variations between the variables of motion, we have instead to do with an inquiry into the connection of variables within a compound medicine and its effects. Given any such medicine, how is a variation in the strength (*gradus*) of its effect related to the variation of the relative strengths (*virtutes*) of the opposing qualities (such as hot-cold or bitter-sweet) within the medicine which determine that effect? As early as the ninth century, the Arab philosopher al-Kindī replied to this question by stipulating that while the *gradus* of the effect increases arithmetically, the ratio of the opposing *virtutes* increases geometrically (where this geometric increase follows the progression of successive "doubling," that is, squaring). Now, not only was the pertinent text of al-Kindī translated into Latin, but the essence of his answer to this pharmacological puzzle was analyzed, developed, and, in a way, even popularized by the late thirteenth-century physician and alchemist Arnald of Villanova. From Arnald's work al-Kindī's "function" found its way into early fourteenth-century pharmacological works, even into the *Trifolium* of Simon Bredon, fellow Mertonian of Bradwardine in the 1330's.

Now it is certainly possible, indeed even probable, that Bradwardine may have appropriated his function from the al-Kindian tradition (a borrowing that may also have occurred in the case of the use of "exponential" relations within certain fourteenth-century alchemical tracts as well). But even admitting this, Bradwardine did a good deal more than simply transfer the function from the realm of compound medicines to the context of his problem of motion. For, quite unlike his pharmacological forerunners, he developed the mathematics behind his function by axiomatically connecting it with the whole medieval mathematics of ratios as he knew it. Thus, the entire first chapter (there are but four) of his *Tractatus* is devoted to setting forth the mathematical framework required for his function. A beginning exposition of the standard Boethian division of particular numerical ratios (e.g., *sesquialtera, superpartiens,* etc.) furnishes him with the terminology with which he was to operate. Second, and of far greater insight and importance, he axiomatically tabulated the substance of the medieval notion of composed ratios. That is, to use our terms, A/C is composed of (*componitur ex*) $A/B \cdot B/C$. Furthermore (and here lies the specific connection with Bradwardine's function), when $A/B = B/C$, then $A/C = (A/B)^2$. Or, as Bradwardine stated in general, if $a_1/a_2 = a_2/a_3 = \cdots a_{n-1}/a_n$, then $a_1/a_n = a_1/a_2 \cdot a_2/a_3 \cdot \cdots a_{n-1}/a_n$ and $a_1/a_n = (a_1/a_2)^{n-1}$. In point of fact, the insertion of geometric means and the addition of continuous proportionals that are here manipulated were Bradwardine's, and the standard medieval, way of dealing with what are (for us), respectively, the roots and powers involved in his function.

The fact that Bradwardine was thus able to state in its general form the medieval mathematics behind his function suggests that, although his expression of the function itself in mathematical terms was never general, this was due to his inability to formulate such a general mathematical statement. The best he could do was, perhaps, to give his function in the rather opaque, and certainly mathematically ambiguous, form we have quoted *in extenso* above, and then merely to express the mathematics of it all by way of example.

Proper generalization of Bradwardine's function had to await, it seems, his successors. Hence, John Dumbleton, like Bradwardine a Mertonian, gave a more general interpretation of the function through a more systematic investigation of its connections with the composition of ratios (see his *Summa de logicis et naturalibus,* pt. III, chs. 6–7). He also extended Bradwardine by translating him, as it were, into the then current language of the latitude of forms (that is, equal latitudes of motion [V] always correspond to equal latitudes of ratio [F/R], where the corresponding "scales" of such latitudes are, respectively, what we would term arithmetic and geometric).

A further development of Bradwardine, in many ways the most brilliant, occurred in the *Liber calculationum* of Richard Swineshead, yet another Mertonian successor. In *Tractatus* XIV (entitled *De motu locali*) of this work, Swineshead elaborates his predecessor's function by setting forth some fifty-odd rules that, assuming Bradwardine to be correct, specify which different *kinds* of change (uniform, difform, uniformly difform, and so on) in F/R obtain relative to corresponding variations in V. Swineshead also extended Bradwardine in *Tractatus* XI (*De loco elementi*) of his *Liber calculationum,* where, in what is something of a fourteenth-century mathematical tour de force, he applies his function to the problem of the motion of a long, thin, heavy body (*corpus columare*) near the center of the universe.

Another significant medieval development of Bradwardine's function was effected by Nicole Oresme in his *De proportionibus proportionum.* Here one observes an extension of the mathematics implicit in the function into a whole new "calculus of ratios" in which rules are prescribed for dealing with what are, for us, rational and irrational exponents. Moreover, Oresme then applies this calculus to the problem of the possible incommensurability of heavenly motions and the consequences of such a possibility for astrological prediction.

Many other Scholastic legatees of the Bradwardinian tradition could be cited as well, but, unlike the three we have mentioned above, most appear to have concerned themselves chiefly with rather belabored expositions of what Bradwardine meant, although a few, such as Blasius of Parma and Giovanni Marliani, produced somewhat unimpressive dissents from his opinion.

One should not close an account of the *Tractatus de proportionibus* without some mention of its final chapter. Here, in effect, Bradwardine attacks the question of the appropriate measure of a body in uniform motion, a matter that becomes problematic when rotational movement is considered. Again investigating, and rejecting, proposed alternative solutions to his question, he argues that the proper measure must be determined by the fastest-moving point of the mobile at issue. Once more his decision bore fruit, especially in his English successors. The resulting "fastest moving point rule" gave birth to an extensive literature treating of the sophisms that arise when one attempts to apply the rule to bodies undergoing condensation and rarefaction or generation and corruption. (The work of the Mertonian William Heytesbury furnishes the best example of this literature.)

Tractatus de continuo. In book VI of the *Physics,* Aristotle had formulated a battery of arguments designed to refute, once and for all, the possible composition of any continuum out of indivisibles. Like all Aristotelian positions, this received ample confirmation and elaboration in the works of his Scholastic commentators. Yet two features of the medieval involvement with this particular segment of *Physics* VI are especially important as background to Bradwardine's entry, with his *Tractatus de continuo,* into what was soon to become a heated controversy among natural philosophers. To begin with, from the end of the thirteenth century on, Scholastic support and refortification of Aristotle's anti-indivisibilist position almost always included a series of mathematical arguments that did not appear in the *Physics* itself or in the standard commentary on it afforded by Averroës. Considerable impetus and authority were given to the inclusion of such arguments by the fact that Duns Scotus had seen fit to feature them, as it were, in his own pro-Aristotelian treatment of the "continuum composition" problem in book II of his *Commentary on the Sentences.* The second important medieval move in the history of this problem occurred in the early years of the fourteenth century, when we witness the eruption of anti-Aristotelian, proindivisibilist sentiments. These two factors alone do much to explain the nature and purpose of Bradwardine's treatise, for he wrote it (sometime after 1328, since it refers to his *Tractatus de proportionibus*) to combat the rising tide of atomism, or indivisibilism, as personified by its two earliest adherents: Henry of Harclay (chancellor of Oxford in 1312) and Walter Chatton (an English Franciscan, *fl. ca.* 1323). Furthermore, in attacking the atomistic views of his two adversaries, Bradwardine used as his most lethal ammunition the appeal to mathematical arguments that, as we have noted, were by now standard Scholastic fare. But he developed this application of mathematics to the problem at issue far beyond that of his predecessors.

The *Tractatus de continuo* was, first of all, mathematical in form as well as content, for it was modeled on the axiomatic pattern of Euclid's *Elements,* beginning with twenty-four "Definitions" and ten "Suppositions," and continuing with 151 "Conclusions" or "Propositions," each of them directly critical of the atomist position. These "Conclusions" purport to reveal the absurdity of atomism in all branches of knowledge (to wit: arithmetic, geometry, music, astronomy, optics, medicine, natural philosophy, metaphysics, logic, grammar, rhetoric, and ethics), but the nucleus of it all lies in the geometrical arguments Bradwardine brought to bear upon his opponents.

To understand, even in outline, the substance and success of what Bradwardine here accomplished, one should note at the outset that the atomism he was combating was, at bottom, mathematical. The position of the fourteenth-century atomistic thinker consisted in maintaining that extended continua were composed of nonextended indivisibles, of points. Given this, Bradwardine astutely saw fit to expand the mathematical arguments that were already popular weapons in opposing those of atomist persuasion. Such arguments can be characterized as attempts to reveal contradictions between geometry and atomism, in which the revelation takes place when assorted techniques of radial and parallel projection are applied to the most rudimentary of geometrical figures. For example, parallels drawn between all the "point-atoms" in opposite sides of a square will destroy the incommensurability of the diagonal, while the construction of all the radii of two concentric circles will, if both are composed of extensionless indivisibles, entail the absurdity that they have equal circumferences. In applying these and related arguments, Bradwardine effectively demolished the atomist contentions of his opponents, at least when they maintained that the atoms composing geometrical lines, surfaces, and solids were finite in number or, if not that, were in immediate contact with one another. His success (and that of others who employed similar arguments against atomism) was not as notable, however, in the case of an opponent who held that continua were composed of an infinity of indivisibles between any two of which there is always another. Here the argument by geometrical projection faltered due to a failure—which Bradwardine shared—to comprehend the one-to-one correspondence among infinite sets and their proper subsets (although this property was properly appreciated, it seems, by Gregory of Rimini in the 1340's).

The major accomplishment of Bradwardine's *Tractatus de continuo* lay, however, in yet another mathematical refutation of his atomist antagonist. To realize the substance of what he here intended, we should initially note that Aristotle's own arguments in *Physics* VI against indivisibilism made it abundantly clear that the major problem for any prospective mathematical atomist was to account for the connection or contact of the indivisibles he maintained could compose continua. As if to grant his opponent all benefit of the doubt, Bradwardine suggests that this problematic contact of point-atoms might appropriately be interpreted in terms of the eminently respectable geometrical notion of superposition (*superpositio*), a respectability guaranteed for the medieval geometer in the application of this notion within Euclid's proof of his fundamental theorems of congruence (*Elements* I, 4 and 8; III, 24). However, immediately after this concession to the opposing view, Bradwardine strikes back and, in a sequence of propositions, conclusively reveals that the superposition of any two geometrical entities systematically excludes their forming a single continuum. Consequently, the urgently needed contact of atoms is geometrically inadmissible.

Finally, as if to reveal his awareness of the mathematical basis of his whole *Tractatus,* toward its conclusion Bradwardine puts himself the question of whether, in using geometry as the base of his refutation of atomism, he had perhaps not begged the very question at issue; does not geometry *assume* the denial of atomism from the outset? He replies by carefully pointing out that while some kinds of atomism are, by assumption, denied in geometry, others are not. And he explains why and how. In our terms, he has attempted to point out just which

BRADWARDINE

continuity assumptions are independent of the axioms and postulates, both expressed and tacit, of Euclid's *Elements* and which are not. That he realized the pertinence of such an issue to the substance of the medieval continuum controversy is certainly much to his credit.

Geometria speculativa and *Arithmetica speculativa.* These two mathematical works, about which we lack information concerning the date of composition, are both elementary compendia of their subjects and were intended, it seems plausible to claim, for arts students who may have wished to learn something of the quadrivium, but with a minimal exposure to mathematical niceties. The *Arithmetica* is the briefer of the two and appears to be little more than the extraction of the barest essentials of Boethian arithmetic. More interesting, both to us and to the medievals themselves, to judge from the far greater number of extant manuscripts, is the *Geometria speculativa.* From the mathematical point of view, it contains little of startling interest, although it does include elementary materials not developed in Euclid's *Elements* (e.g., stellar polygons, isoperimetry, the filling of space by touching polyhedra [*impletio loci*], and so on). Of greater significance would seem to be Bradwardine's concern with relating the mathematics being expounded to philosophy, even to selecting his mathematical material on the basis of its potential philosophical relevance. Such a guiding principle was surely in Bradwardine's mind when he saw fit to have his compendium treat of such philosophically pregnant matters as the horn angle, the incommensurability of the diagonal of a square, and the puzzle of the possible inequality of infinites. Indeed, it is precisely to passages of the *Geometria* dealing with such questions that we find reference in numerous later authors, such as Luis Coronel and John Major. Such authors were fundamentally philosophers—philosophers, moreover, with little mathematical expertise—and it would seem fair to conclude that Bradwardine had just this type of audience in view when he composed his *Geometria.*

Theological Works. Bradwardine's earliest venture into theology is perhaps represented by his treatment of the problem of predestination, extant in a *questio* entitled *De futuris contingentibus.* His major theological work, indeed the *magnum opus* of his whole career, is the massive *De causa Dei contra Pelagium et de virtute causarum ad suos Mertonenses,* completed about 1344. Its primary burden was to overturn the contemporary emphasis upon free will, found in the writings of those with marked nominalist tendencies (the "Pelagians" of the title), and to reestablish the primacy of the Divine Will. Although this reaffirmation of a determinist solution to the problem of free will is not of much direct concern to the history of science, brief excursions into sections of the *De causa Dei* have revealed that it is not without interest for the development of late medieval natural philosophy. Thus, to cite but two instances, Bradwardine discusses the problem of an extramundane void space and, within the context of rejecting the possible eternity of the world, again struggles with the issue of unequal infinites. One is tempted to suggest that closer study of the *De causa Dei* will reveal that Bradwardine's theological efforts contain yet other matters of importance for the history of science.

BIBLIOGRAPHY

I. LIFE. The fundamental point of departure is A. B. Emden, *A Bibliographical Register of the University of Oxford to A.D. 1500,* I (Oxford, 1957), 244–246. One may also profitably consult H. A. Obermann, *Archbishop Thomas Bradwardine, a Fourteenth Century Augustinian* (Utrecht, 1958), pp. 10–22. The *Sermo epinicius* has been edited with a brief introduction by H. A. Obermann and J. A. Weisheipl, in *Archives d'histoire doctrinale et littéraire du moyen age,* **25** (1958), 295–329.

II. WRITINGS AND DOCTRINE. The most complete bibliography of the editions and MSS of Bradwardine's works is to be found in the unpublished thesis of J. A. Weisheipl, "Early Fourteenth-Century Physics and the Merton 'School'" (Oxford, 1957), Bodl. Libr. MS D. Phil. d.1776.

Logical Works. The unedited *De insolubilibus* is extant in at least twelve MSS, including Erfurt, Amplon. 8° 76, 6r–21v and Vat. lat. 2154, 13r–24r. For the equally unedited *De incipit et desinit:* Vat. lat. 3066, 49v–52r and Vat. lat. 2154, 24r–29v. Although Bradwardine's treatises are not considered, the kinds of problems they bear upon are dealt with (for the *De insolubilibus*) in I. M. Bochenski, *A History of Formal Logic* (Notre Dame, Ind., 1961), pp. 237-251; and (for the *De incipit*) in Curtis Wilson, *William Heytesbury. Medieval Logic and the Rise of Mathematical Physics* (Madison, Wis., 1956), pp. 29–56. A variety of other logical writings, although often ascribed to Bradwardine in MSS, are most likely spurious; they are too numerous to mention here.

Tractatus de proportionibus velocitatum in motibus. This has been edited and translated, together with an introduction, by H. Lamar Crosby as *Thomas of Bradwardine. His Tractatus de Proportionibus. Its Significance for the Development of Mathematical Physics* (Madison, Wis., 1955). Corrections to some of Crosby's views can be found in Edward Grant, ed., *Nicole Oresme. De proportionibus proportionum and Ad pauca respicientes* (Madison, Wis., 1966), pp. 14–24, a volume that also contains a text, translation, and analysis of Oresme's extension of the mathematics of Bradwardine's "function." For the problem and doctrine of Bradwardine's *Tractatus* one should also note Marshall Clagett, *The Science of Mechanics in the Middle Ages* (Madison, Wis.,

1959), pp. 215–216, 220–222, 421–503; and Anneliese Maier, *Die Vorläufer Galileis im 14. Jahrhundert,* 2nd ed. (Rome, 1966), pp. 81–110. Discussion of some of the factors of the above-cited application of Bradwardine's function in the *Liber calculationum* of Richard Swineshead can be found in John E. Murdoch, *"Mathesis in philosophiam scholasticam introducta:* The Rise and Development of the Application of Mathematics in Fourteenth Century Philosophy and Theology," in *Acts of the IVth International Congress of Medieval Philosophy, Montreal, 1967* (in press); and M. A. Hoskin and A. G. Molland, "Swineshead on Falling Bodies: An Example of Fourteenth Century Physics," in *British Journal for the History of Science,* **3** (1966), 150–182, which contains an edition of the text of Swineshead's *De loco elementi* (*Tractatus* XI of his *Liber calculationum*). For a new interpretation of how Bradwardine's function should be understood, see A. G. Molland, "The Geometrical Background to the 'Merton School': An Exploration Into the Application of Mathematics to Natural Philosophy in the Fourteenth Century," in *British Journal for the History of Science,* **4** (1968), 108–125. A brief discussion and citation of the relevant texts in Dumbleton that treat of Bradwardine will appear in an article by John Murdoch in a forthcoming volume of the *Boston University Studies in the Philosophy of Science.* Finally, the issue of the probable pharmacological origin of Bradwardine's function is treated in Michael McVaugh, "Arnald of Villanova and Bradwardine's Law," in *Isis,* **58** (1967), 56–64.

Tractatus de continuo. The as yet unpublished text of this treatise was first indicated, and extracts given, in Maximilian Curtze, "Über die Handschrift R. 4° 2: Problematum Euclidis Explicatio, des Königl. Gymnasial Bibliothek zu Thorn," in *Zeitschrift für Mathematik und Physik,* **13** (1868), Hist.-lit. Abt., 85–91. A second article giving a partial analysis of the contents of the *Tractatus* is Edward Stamm, "Tractatus de Continuo von Thomas Bradwardina," in *Isis,* **26** (1936), 13–32, while V. P. Zoubov gives a transcription of the enunciations of the definitions, suppositions, and propositions of the *Tractatus,* with an accompanying analysis of the whole, in "Traktat Bradvardina 'O Kontinuume,'" in *Istoriko-matematicheskiie Issledovaniia,* **13** (1960), 385–440. A critical edition of the text has been made from the two extant MSS (Torun, Gymn. Bibl. R. 4° 2, pp. 153–192; Erfurt, Amplon. 4° 385, 17r–48r) by John Murdoch and will appear in a forthcoming volume on mathematics and the continuum problem in the later Middle Ages. Some indication of the issues dealt with in the *De continuo* can be found in Anneliese Maier, *Die Vorläufer Galileis im 14. Jahrhundert,* 2nd ed. (Rome, 1966), pp. 155–179; and John Murdoch, *"Rationes mathematice." Un aspect du rapport des mathématiques et de la philosophie au moyen age,* Conférence, Palais de la Découverte (Paris, 1961), pp. 22–35; "Superposition, Congruence and Continuity in the Middle Ages," in *Mélanges Koyré,* I (Paris, 1964), 416–441; and "Two Questions on the Continuum: Walter Chatton (?), O.F.M. and Adam Wodeham, O.F.M.," in *Franciscan Studies,* **26** (1966), 212–288, written with E. A. Synan.

Mathematical Compendia. The *Arithmetica speculativa* was first printed in Paris, 1495, and reprinted many times during the fifteenth and sixteenth centuries. The *Geometria speculativa* (Paris, 1495) was also republished, and has recently been edited by A. G. Molland in his unpublished doctoral thesis, *"Geometria speculativa* of Thomas Bradwardine: Text with Critical Discussion" (Cambridge, 1967); cf. Molland's "The Geometrical Background to the 'Merton School,'" cited above. Brief consideration of the *Geometria* can also be found in Moritz Cantor, *Vorlesungen über Geschichte der Mathematik,* 2nd ed., II (Leipzig, 1913), 114–118. One might note that a good deal of Bradwardine's *Geometria* was repeated in a fifteenth-century *Geometria* by one Wigandus Durnheimer (MS Vienna, Nat. Bib. 5257, lr–89v). The *Rithmomachia* ascribed to Bradwardine (MSS Erfurt, Amplon. 4° 2, 38r–63r; Vat. Pal. lat. 1380, 189r–230v) is most probably spurious.

The *Questio de futuris contingentibus* was edited by B. Xiberta as "Fragments d'una qüestió inèdita de Tomas Bradwardine," in *Beiträge zur Geschichte der Philosophie des Mittelalters,* Supp. **3**, 1169–1180. The *editio princeps* of the *De causa Dei* at the hand of Henry Savile (London, 1618) has recently been reprinted (Frankfurt, 1964). The basic works dealing with Bradwardine's theology are Gordon Leff, *Bradwardine and the Pelagians* (Cambridge, 1957), and H. A. Obermann, *Archbishop Thomas Bradwardine. A Fourteenth Century Augustinian* (Utrecht, 1958), whose bibliographies give almost all other relevant literature. For the discussion of void space and infinity in the *De causa Dei,* see Alexandre Koyré, "Le vide et l'espace infini au XIVe siècle," in *Archives d'histoire doctrinale et littéraire du moyen age,* **17** (1949), 45–91; and John Murdoch, *"Rationes mathematice"* (see above), pp. 15–22. Also of value are A. Combes and F. Ruello, "Jean de Ripa I Sent. Dist. XXXVII: De modo inexistendi divine essentie in omnibus creaturis," in *Traditio,* **23** (1967), 191–267; and Edward Grant, "Medieval and Seventeenth-Century Conceptions of an Infinite Void Space Beyond the Cosmos," in *Isis* (in press).

If one disregards the various epitomes of the *De causa Dei,* it would appear that the only remaining work which may well be genuine is a *Tractatus de meditatione* ascribed to Bradwardine (MSS Vienna, Nat. Bibl. 4487, 305r–315r; Vienna, Schottenkloster 321, 122r–131v). Of the numerous other works that are in all probability spurious, it will suffice to mention the *Sentence Commentary* in MS Troyes 505 and the *Questiones physice* in MS Vat. Pal. lat. 1049, which is not by Bradwardine but, apparently, by one Thomas of Prague.

JOHN E. MURDOCH

BRAIKENRIDGE (BRAKENRIDGE), WILLIAM
(*b. ca.* 1700; *d.* 30 July 1762)

The precise date and the place of Braikenridge's birth are not known. He lived in a period of intense mathematical activity, one that abounded in illustrious mathematicians: the Bernoullis, Maclaurin, and Brook Taylor, to name but a few. Newton was still in his prime, but his interest in mathematics had begun to wane (no doubt as a result of his important duties as master of the Mint).

The main lines of development in mathematics at this time were the extension and systematization of the calculus, the further study of the theory of equations, and a revival of interest in geometry. It was in the last of these that Braikenridge excelled, and it is upon his *Exercitatio geometrica de descriptione linearum curvarum* (1733) that his reputation mainly rests.

This work is divided into three parts, and its scope is indicated by their titles: "De descriptione curvarum primi generis seu linearum ordinis secundi," "De descriptione linearum cujuscunque ordinis ope linearum ordinis inferioris," and "Ubi describuntur sectiones conicae ope plurium rectarum circa polos moventium."

The study of the properties of curves has always been an inexhaustible subject of speculation and research among geometers. Colin Maclaurin had already published his *Geometria organica* (1720), which contained an elegant investigation of curves of the second order by regarding them as generated by the intersection of lines and angles turning about fixed points, or poles. Many of Maclaurin's theorems were discovered independently by Braikenridge, notably the Braikenridge-Maclaurin theorem: If the sides of a polygon are restricted so that they pass through fixed points while all the vertices except one lie on fixed straight lines, the free vertex will describe a conic or a straight line. A general statement of this appeared in 1735 in the *Philosophical Transactions* (no. 436), and a dispute at once arose regarding priority. Braikenridge, in the Preface to the *Exercitatio,* maintained that as early as 1726, when he was living in Edinburgh, he had discovered many of the propositions contained in that work and had actually discussed some of them with his contemporaries, including Maclaurin. There followed a lively correspondence between the two men which, however, it would be profitless to discuss here.

About the middle of the century, interest in the geometry of curves began to languish. It was revived, however, when a group of French mathematicians—Monge, Carnot, Poncelet—by employing projective methods, gave the study a fresh impetus.

Braikenridge was a noted theologian, and for many years he was rector of St. Michael's, Bassishaw, London. On 6 February 1752 he was elected fellow of the Royal Society of Antiquaries, and on 9 November of the same year he became a fellow of the Royal Society.

Braikenridge contributed a number of papers to the *Philosophical Transactions.* Their titles reflect the wide range of his interests: "A General Method of Describing Curves, by the Intersection of Right Lines, Moving About Points in a Given Plane"; "A Letter . . . Concerning the Number of Inhabitants Within the London Bills of Mortality"; "A Letter . . . Concerning the Method of Constructing a Table for the Probabilities of Life in London"; "A Letter . . . Concerning the Number of People in England"; "A Letter . . . Concerning the Present Increase of the People in Britain and Ireland"; "A Letter . . . Containing an Answer to the Account of the Numbers and Increase of the People of England by the Rev. Mr. Forster"; "A Letter Containing the Sections of a Solid, Hitherto not Considered by Geometers."

BIBLIOGRAPHY

Works concerning Braikenridge are Moritz Cantor, *Vorlesungen über Geschichte der Mathematik,* III (Leipzig, 1894–1898), 761–766, 773; and J. F. Montucla, *Histoire des mathématiques,* III (Paris, 1799–1802), 87.

J. F. SCOTT

BRAMER, BENJAMIN (*b.* Felsberg, Germany, *ca.* February 1588; *d.* Ziegenhain, Germany, 17 March 1652)

After the death of his father in 1591, Bramer was taken as a foster son into the home of his sister and her husband, the court clockmaker Joost Bürgi, in Kassel. His brother-in-law tutored Bramer and awakened his passion for mathematics, which was later combined with his architectural abilities. When Bürgi left Kassel in 1604, Bramer accompanied him to the imperial court at Prague; he returned to Kassel in 1609. In 1612 Landgrave Moritz of Hesse-Kassel appointed Bramer the master builder of the court in Marburg, and he was naturalized there on 16 February 1625. (Since 1620 he had been directing the construction of fortifications at the castle and in the town.) In the same year he was consultant to the count of Solms at the fortress of Rheinfels. From 1630 to 1634, Bramer was in charge of the fortifications in Kassel, and in November 1635 he was appointed princely master builder and treasurer of the important Hessian fortress of Ziegenhain.

In his first publication on the calculation of sines (1614), Bramer's talents are evident. In a work on the vacuum (1617), we can see his wide-ranging interests, but no particular field of concentration. The problem of empty space, which had been under active investigation since classical times, was of special topical interest in the seventeenth century. On this matter Bramer held the views of Tommaso Campanella, the contemporary and follower of Galileo.

The problem of central perspective obtained by means of instruments, which had been taken up by Leone Battista Alberti in 1435 and for which instruments had been designed by Albrecht Dürer in 1525 and by Bürgi in 1604, was further developed by Bramer in 1630 by means of a device that enabled one to draw accurate geometrical perspectives true to nature. He described his method in his *Trigonometria planorum* (1617). In 1651 Bramer contributed to the completion of the instruments for triangulation with the semicirculus: he used an inclined ruler, in order to determine simultaneously the sighted point and its inclination; the instrument, however, differed little from a similar one described by Leonhard Zubler in 1607. Another form of this instrument was mounted on a calibrated plate to determine angulation; Bramer used this for the solution of planar triangles.

We know very little of Bramer's architectural achievements. From advice he gave in 1618 to Count Christian von Waldeck, we know of a plan for construction of a new church for the city of Wildungen. Although the project was not undertaken because of the Thirty Years' War, it is of special importance because it is one of the earliest plans to introduce central church construction into Protestant German church architecture.

BIBLIOGRAPHY

I. ORIGINAL WORKS. *Problema, wie aus bekannt gegebenem sinu eines Grades, Minuten oder Sekunden alle folgenden sinus aufs leichteste zu finden und der canon sinuum zu absolvieren sei* (Marburg, 1614); *Beschreibung und Unterricht, wie allerlei Teilungen zu den mathematischen Instrumenten zu verfertigen, neben dem Gebrauch eines neuen Proportional-Instrumentes* (Marburg, 1615); *Bericht und Gebrauch eines Proportional-Lineals, neben kurzem Unterricht eines Parallel-Instrumentes* (Marburg, 1617); *Kurze Meldung vom Vacuo oder leerem Orte, neben anderen wunderbaren und subtilen Quaestionen, desgleichen Nic. Cusani Dialogus von Waag und Gewicht* (Marburg, 1617); *Trigonometria planorum mechanica oder Unterricht und Beschreibung eines neuen und sehr bequemen geometrischen Instrumentes zu allerhand Abmessung* (Marburg, 1617); *Etliche geometrische Quaestiones, so mehrerteils bisher nicht üblich gewesen. Solviert und beschrieben* (Marburg, 1618); *Beschreibung eines sehr leichten Perspektiv- und Grundreissenden Instrumentes auf einem Stande: auf Joh. Faulhabers, Ingenieurs zu Ulm, weitere Continuation seines mathematischen Kunstspiegels geordnet* (Kassel, 1630); *Appollonius Cattus oder Kern der ganzen Geometrie,* 3 vols. (Kassel, 1634–1684); *Benjamin Brameri Bericht zu Meister Jobsten seligen geometrischen Triangularinstrument* (Kassel, 1648); *Kurzer Bericht zu einem Semicirculo, damit in allen Triangeln in einer Observation nicht allein die drei latera, sondern auch die drei Winkel eines Triangels zu finden* (Augsburg, 1651); *Von Wasserwerken* (unpub. MS Math. 4°27), National Library, Kassel.

II. SECONDARY LITERATURE. Johann Heinrich Zedler, *Universal-Lexikon,* IV (Halle-Leipzig, 1733), 997; Christian Gottlieb Jöcher, *Allgemeines Gelehrten-Lexikon,* I (Leipzig, 1750), 1328; Friedrich Wilhelm Strieder, *Grundlage zu einer hessischen Gelehrten- und Schriftstellergeschichte,* I (Göttingen, 1781), 521 ff.; *Nouvelles annalès de mathématiques* (*Bulletin de bibliographie*) (Paris, 1858), 75 ff.; Wolfgang Medding, "Das Projekt einer Zentralkirche des hessischen Hofbaumeisters Benjamin Bramer", in *Hessenland, Heimatzeitschrift für Kurhessen,* **49** (Marburg, 1938), 82 ff.; Karl Justi, "Das Marburger Schloss," *Veröffentlichungen der Historischen Kommission für Hessen und Waldeck,* XXI (Marburg, 1942), 94, 98, 105.

PAUL A. KIRCHVOGEL

BRASHMAN, NIKOLAI DMITRIEVICH (*b.* Rassnova, near Brno, Czechoslovakia, 14 June 1796; *d.* Moscow, Russia, 13 May 1866)

Although Brashman's family was of limited means, he was able to study at the University of Vienna and the Vienna Polytechnical Institute by working as a tutor. In 1824 he went to Russia, and after a short stay in St. Petersburg he obtained the post of assistant professor of physicomathematical sciences at the University of Kazan, where he taught mathematics and mechanics.

In 1834 Brashman accepted a professorship of applied mathematics (mechanics) at the University of Moscow. Here he became known as a gifted scientist and teacher, and laid the foundations of instruction in both theoretical and practical mechanics.

In his lectures on mechanics and in his articles Brashman not only tried to show the achievements of this science, but also worked out its most difficult sections. He also prepared textbooks for Russian institutions of higher education. His texts on mathematics and mechanics reflect the state of science at that time, and his proofs of important theorems show originality, clarity, and comprehensiveness. Brashman wrote one of the best analytical geometry texts of his time, for which the Academy of Sciences awarded him the entire Demidov Prize in 1836.

In 1837 Brashman published the textbook on mechanics, *Teoria ravnovesia tel tverdykh i zhidkikh,* which contains an original presentation of problems of statics and hydrostatics. Upon the recommendation of Ostrogradski, this work also brought Brashman the full Demidov Prize.

In 1859 Brashman published a textbook, *Teoreticheskaya mekhanika* ("Theoretical Mechanics"), dealing with the theories of equilibrium and the motion of a point and of a system of points.

In addition to texts, Brashman wrote articles on various problems in mathematics and mechanics. Brashman's memoirs on mathematics were intended for those interested in the progress of the mathematical sciences, and dealt with the latest results of Russian and foreign scientists.

More important are Brashman's memoranda on mechanics. "O prilozhenii printsipa naimenshego deystvia k opredeleniu obema vody na Vodoslive" ("On the Application of the Principle of Minimum Action to the Determination of Water Volume in a Spillway," 1861), which was published in both Russian and foreign periodicals, drew much favorable attention.

Also in 1861 Brashman published "Note concernant la pression des wagons sur les rails droits et des courants d'eau sur la rive droite du mouvement en vertu de la rotation de la terre" (*Comptes rendus de l'Académie des sciences,* **53,** [1861], 370–376). With the aid of general equations, he tried to prove in this article that the rotation of the earth invariably imposes a pressure on the right rail of a railroad track as a train travels over it and on the right bank of a river as the current moves along it, no matter in what direction the train is moving or the river is flowing, provided this force is a single one (i.e., the motion must be rectilinear and uniform).

Another article of considerable interest is his "Printsip naimenshego deystvia" ("Principle of Minimum Action") that appeared in *Mélanges mathématiques et astronomiques* (**1** [1859], 26–31).

Brashman was not only an important scientist but also an excellent teacher. His students included such prominent scientists as P. L. Chebyshev, I. I. Somov, and other talented specialists in mathematics and mechanics. He founded the Moscow Mathematical Society and its journal, *Matematicheskiy sbornik* ("Mathematical Symposium"), the first issue of which appeared in the year of his death. This journal was equal to the best European publications in its scientific value and wide range of contents.

For his distinguished services to science, Brashman was elected a corresponding member of the Petersburg Academy of Sciences in 1855.

BIBLIOGRAPHY

I. Original Works. Brashman's writings include *Kurs analiticheskoy geometrii* ("Course in Analytical Geometry"; Moscow, 1836); *Teoria ravnovesia tel tverdykh i zhidkikh. Statika i gidrostatika* ("Theory of Equilibrium of Solid and Liquid Bodies. Statics and Hydrostatics"; Moscow, 1837); and *Teoreticheskaya mekhanika* ("Theoretical Mechanics"; Moscow, 1859).

II. Secondary Literature. Works on Brashman are A. Davidov, *Biograficheskiy slovar professorov i prepodovateley Moskvskogo Universiteta* ("Biographical Dictionary of Professors and Teachers at Moscow University"), I (Moscow, 1855), 206; *Matematicheskiy sbornik,* **1** (1866); A. T. Grigorian, *Ocherki istorii mekaniki v Rossii* ("Essays on the History of Mechanics in Russia"; Moscow, 1961), pp. 96–107; I. I. Liholetov and S. H. Yanovskaja, "Iz istorii prepodavaniya mehaniki v Moskovskom Universitete" ("From History of Teaching Mechanics at Moscow University"), in *Istoriko-matematicheskie issledovaniya,* **8,** 294–368; M. Viyodski, "Matematika i eyo deyateli v Moskovskom Universitete vo vtoroy polovine XIX V." ("Mathematics and Its Representatives at Moscow University in the Second Half of the Nineteenth Century"), *ibid.,* **1,** 141–149.

A. T. Grigorian

BRAUER, RICHARD DAGOBERT (*b.* Berlin, Germany, 10 February 1901; *d.* Boston, Massachusetts, 17 April 1977)

Brauer was the youngest of three children of Max Brauer, an influential and wealthy businessman in the wholesale leather trade, and his wife, Lilly Caroline Jacob. He attended the Kaiser-Friedrich-Schule in Berlin-Charlottenburg and had an interest in science and mathematics as a young boy, an interest that owed much to the influence of his gifted brother Alfred, who was seven years older.

In February 1919 Brauer enrolled in the Technische Hochschule in Berlin but soon realized that, in his own words, his interests were "more theoretical than practical." He transferred to the University of Berlin after one term. He took his Ph.D. there in 1925, under the guidance of the algebraist Issai Schur.

On 17 September 1925 Brauer married Ilse Karger, a fellow student and the daughter of a Berlin physician. They had two sons, George Ulrich and Fred Günther, both of whom became research mathematicians.

Brauer's first academic post was at the University of Königsberg (now Kaliningrad), where he remained until dismissed by Hitler's 1933 decree banning Jews from university teaching. He spent 1933 and 1934 at the University of Kentucky at Lexington, and 1934 and 1935 at the Institute for Advanced Study at Princeton, where he was assistant to Hermann Weyl. After this Brauer held professorships at the University of Toronto (1935–1948), the University of Michigan at Ann Arbor (1948–1952), and Harvard (1952–1971). He lived near Boston for the rest of his life. Weakened by aplastic anemia, he died of a generalized infection.

Brauer was an elected member of the Royal Society of Canada, the American Academy of Arts and Sciences, the National Academy of Sciences, the London Mathematical Society, the Akademie der Wissenschaften (Göttingen), and the American Philosophical Society. He was president of the Canadian Mathematical Congress (1957–1958) and of the American Mathematical Society (1959–1960). He received the Guggenheim Memorial Fellowship (1941–1942), the Cole Prize of the American Mathematical Society (1949), and the National Medal for Scientific Merit (1971).

Brauer was one of the most influential algebraists of the twentieth century. He built on the foundations of the representation theory of groups that were laid by Georg Frobenius, William Burnside, and Issai Schur in the years 1895–1910; and over his long career he brought the representation theory of finite groups, in particular, to a remarkable depth and sophistication. His first important research, however, was concerned with the representations of a continuous (topological) group.

By a representation of a given linear group Γ is meant a homomorphism $H:\Gamma \rightarrow GL(N,\mathbf{C})$, whereby each element s of Γ is represented by a nonsingular complex matrix or linear transformation $H(s)$ of some finite degree N. If Γ is a topological group, it is assumed that H is continuous, that is, that each matrix coefficient of $H(s)$ is a continuous function of s. Among topological groups the most important are the classical linear groups, such as the group $O(n)$ of all real orthogonal transformations of n variables, or its subgroup $SO(n)$ (often called the rotation group) consisting of the orthogonal transformations of determinant 1.

In 1897 Adolf Hurwitz introduced a new and fundamental idea into the study of such groups, that of an invariant integral. He defined such an integral for $SO(n)$ and used it to calculate polynomial invariants for this group. Schur realized that his own treatment of Frobenius' character theory of a finite group Γ could be extended to a continuous linear group Γ on which an invariant integral could be defined. In a series of papers published in 1924, he used Hurwitz's integral to find the irreducible characters of $O(n)$. Brauer was attending Schur's seminar at this time, and Schur suggested to him that it might be possible to find a purely algebraic treatment of this work, that is, one that did not rely on the analytic notion of an integral. Brauer found such a treatment, and with it calculated the irreducible characters of the groups $O(n)$ and $SO(n)$; this became his dissertation, for which he was awarded the Ph.D. summa cum laude in 1926.

While Brauer was writing his dissertation, Hermann Weyl was working on his papers on the representations of semisimple Lie groups (these include the classical linear groups). This work of Weyl's has claim to be the finest single mathematical achievement of the twentieth century. It is based on Schur's methods with the invariant integral and Élie Cartan's construction of representations of a semisimple Lie group Γ by means of representations of its Lie algebra $\mathfrak{g}$; Schur's and Brauer's results on $O(n)$ and $SO(n)$ come out as special cases. Weyl's results and methods have been the starting point of a huge amount of research in pure mathematics and in quantum physics. By contrast Brauer's algebraic treatment for the orthogonal groups is little known—it uses difficult and (now) unfashionable techniques from the theories of determinants and invariants, and was published only as his Ph.D. dissertation.

Brauer greatly admired Weyl, and during his year as Weyl's assistant at the Institute for Advanced Study, he briefly returned to the classical linear groups. From this period date a joint paper with Weyl on spinors and a paper in which Brauer calculates, by purely algebraic means, the Poincaré polynomials of the classical groups (unitary, symplectic, and orthogonal). Brauer's last paper on continuous groups, published in 1937, hints at a general representation theory for continuous groups, strictly algebraic in nature and based on invariant theory. A promised sequel never appeared.

Much of Brauer's work while he was in Königsberg (1925–1933) was concerned with simple algebras and rooted in Schur's theory of splitting fields. Suppose k is a given field, K an algebraically closed field that contains k, and that $H:\Gamma \rightarrow GL(f,K)$ is an irreducible representation of some group Γ. Then each element s of Γ is represented by a nonsingular $f \times f$ matrix $H(s)$ whose coefficients lie in K; the condition that H be irreducible means that the set of all K-linear combinations of the $H(s)$, $s \in \Gamma$, is the full matrix algebra K_f of *all* $f \times f$ matrices over K. We shall assume that the trace $\chi(s)$ of each matrix $H(s)$ lies in the ground field k. Then a field L ($k \subseteq L \subseteq K$) is a splitting field for H (or for its character X) if L is a finite extension of k and there exists a matrix $P \in GL(f,K)$ such that all the coefficients of all the matrices $P^{-1}H(s)P$, $s \in \Gamma$, lie in L. The least degree $m_k(H) = m_k(X)$ over k, among all such splitting fields L, is called the Schur index of H or X over k; Schur had initiated the study of splitting fields (in the case where k is an algebraic number field and $k = \mathbb{C}$) in the early 1900's, and had proved a number of facts about the Schur index.

Brauer and Emmy Noether (who was then at Göttingen) showed, in a paper published in 1927, how the splitting fields of H are determined by the algebra A of all k-linear combinations of the matrices $H(s)$, $s \in \Gamma$. A is a finite dimensional simple algebra over k that is central; its center consists only of the scalar multiples of the identity. A given field L of finite degree $(L:k)$ is a splitting field for H if and only if $L \otimes_k A$ is isomorphic to the full matrix algebra L_f over L. This last condition depends only on the algebra A, and a field L that satisfies it is called a splitting field for A. Brauer and Noether's main result (proved under certain restrictions on the ground field k, which were later shown by Noether to be unnecessary) was that the splitting fields of a given central, simple k-algebra A are (up to isomorphism) the same as the maximal subfields of the algebras B in the same algebra class as A. The algebra class $[A]$ of A is defined as follows. By Joseph Wedderburn's structure theorem (1907), A is isomorphic to the algebra D_t of all $t \times t$ matrices over a certain central division algebra D and for a certain positive integer t; the class $[A]$ then consists of all central simple algebras over k that are isomorphic to D_s, for any positive integer s. The set of all such algebra classes, with given ground field k, forms a group $B(k)$, now known as the Brauer group of k; the product of classes $[A]$, $[B]$ is defined to be the class $[A \otimes_k B]$, and the identity element of $B(k)$ is the class $[k]$. It has turned out that $B(k)$ is a fundamentally important invariant of the field k. Brauer studied it with the help of a technique of factor sets, and from this beginning has grown the theory of Galois cohomology and its many uses in number theory. In another direction, M. Auslander and O. Goldman showed in 1960 how to define $B(R)$ for an arbitrary commutative ring R, thereby beginning a new chapter in commutative algebra.

Brauer's work with Emmy Noether brought him into contact not only with this influential algebraist and her school in Göttingen but also with the famous conjecture of L. E. Dickson that every central simple algebra A over an algebraic number field k contains a maximal subfield L that is a Galois extension of k with cyclic Galois group. This conjecture was proved in 1931 in a joint paper by Brauer, Noether, and H. Hasse that is the culmination of a long development in the theory of algebras. Brauer's association with this work secured his reputation as one of the best mathematicians of the rising generation in Germany.

Brauer was abruptly dismissed in 1933, along with all other Jewish university teachers in Germany. The disadvantages and disruptions of a forced emigration at the age of thirty-two were offset to some extent by the new contacts Brauer made, not only with American mathematicians but also with other German scientists who found refuge in America in the 1930's. The year 1934–1935, when Brauer was Weyl's assistant at the Institute for Advanced Study, saw an extraordinary gathering of mathematicians and physicists of the first rank: J. W. Alexander, Albert Einstein, John von Neumann, Oswald Veblen, and Weyl were permanent professors at the Institute; and the mathematics faculty at Princeton University included Salomon Bochner, S. Lefschetz, and Joseph H. M. Wedderburn. Among the visiting members of the Institute that year were, besides Brauer, W. Magnus, C. L. Siegel, and Oscar Zariski.

In 1935 Brauer took up a post as assistant professor at the University of Toronto, where he remained until 1948, becoming in due course associate and then full professor. Here he developed his modular representation theory of finite groups, which will probably continue to be regarded as his most original and characteristic contribution to mathematics.

Representation theory began with Frobenius' paper "Über Gruppencharaktere," published in 1896. In Frobenius' theorem the irreducible characters of a group were defined in terms of what can now be described as the representations of the center of the group algebra $\mathbb{C}G$ ($\mathbb{C}G$ is the linear algebra over the complex field $\mathbb{C}$ having the elements of G as basis). Schur (who had been Frobenius' pupil) reformulated Frobenius' character theory in a beautiful paper published in 1905 that became the basis of all subsequent expositions of the subject. Schur defined the character X_H of an arbitrary representation $H:G \rightarrow GL(n,\mathbb{C})$ of G to be the complex-valued function $X_H:G \rightarrow \mathbb{C}$ given by $X_H(s)$, = trace $H(s)$, $s \in G$. If H is an irreducible representation, then X_H is said to be a simple, or irreducible, character. Schur rederived Frobenius' orthogonality relations for the irreducible characters, from which follows the fundamental theorem: Two representations H, H' of the group G are equivalent if, and only if, their characters are equal, $X_H = X_{H'}$.

It was recognized very soon that Frobenius' arguments do not hold when $\mathbb{C}$ is replaced by an algebraically closed field k of finite characteristic p, although L. E. Dickson proved in 1902 that the orthogonality relations for the characters are still true, provided p does not divide the order $|G|$ of G. In two later papers Dickson considered the case where p divides $|G|$. In this case the group algebra kG is not semisimple. A representation $F:G \rightarrow GL(n,k)$ is no longer determined up to equivalence by the natural character X_F = trace F. After Dickson's papers were published in 1907, little more was done on representations over fields of finite characteristic until the mid 1930's, when Brauer laid the foundations of his modular representation theory in three fundamental papers, the last two of which were written with C. Nesbitt, who took his Ph.D. at Toronto under Brauer's supervision.

Let G_0 denote the set of all p'-elements (or p-regular elements) of G; these are the elements whose order is prime to p. Let $|G| = p^a m$, where $a \geq 0$ and p does not divide m. Then each element g of G_0 satisfies the equation $g^m = 1$, so if $F:G \rightarrow GL(n,k)$ is a representation, the eigenvalues $\alpha_1, \ldots, \alpha_n$ of $F(g)$ are mth roots of unity in the field k. The set $U_m(k)$ of all mth roots of unity in k forms a cyclic group of order m, the group operation being multiplication in k. But the multiplicative group $U_m(\mathbb{C})$ of all complex mth roots of unity is also cyclic of order m. Therefore one can find a multiplicative isomorphism $\mathbf{c}:U_m(k) \rightarrow U_m(\mathbb{C})$; in general this can be done in many ways. Choose any such isomorphism $\mathbf{c}$. Brauer defines the modular character (later known as the Brauer character) of the representation F to be the function $\beta_F:G_0 \rightarrow \mathbb{C}$ given by

$$\beta_F(g) = \mathbf{c}(\alpha_1) + \cdots + \mathbf{c}(\alpha_n), g \in G_0. \tag{1}$$

This gives a complex valued function in place of the k-valued natural character X_F, for which

$$X_F(g) = \text{trace}\, F(g) = \alpha_1 + \cdots + \alpha_n, \tag{2}$$

by the daring—almost impudent—device of complexifying the eigenvalues $\alpha_1, \ldots, \alpha_n$. That definition (1), and not the natural definition (2), is the correct basis for a modular character theory soon becomes clear. If $F_1, \cdots, F_l$ is a full set of irreducible representations of G over k, then their Brauer characters $\beta_1, \cdots, \beta_l$ are linearly independent functions on G_0. For any representation $F:G \rightarrow GL(n,k)$ one has $\beta_F = \Sigma n_i(F)\beta_i$, where $n_i(F)$ is the multiplicity with which F_i appears as a composition factor in F. Brauer characters (like natural characters) are class functions, that is, $\beta_F(g) = \beta_F(g')$ whenever g,g' belong to the same conjugacy class of G. Frobenius had shown that the number of irreducible ordinary characters of G is equal to the number of conjugacy classes of G; Brauer showed that the number l of irreducible modular characters is equal to the number of p-regular classes, that is, to the number of conjugacy classes lying in G_0.

From the beginning, Brauer saw the modular character theory—which is based on representations of G over a field k of finite characteristic p—as a source of information on the ordinary characters—which is based on representations on $\mathbb{C}$ or some other field of characteristic zero. If $X_1, \cdots, X_s$ are the irreducible ordinary characters of G, and $\beta_1, \cdots, \beta_l$ are the irreducible modular characters, there exist nonnegative integers $d_{\sigma i}$ such that the equations

$$X_\sigma(g) = \sum_{i=1}^{l} d_{\sigma i}\beta_i(g) \tag{3}$$

hold for all elements g in G_0. To explain these equations, we need some technical preliminaries. Let L be a field of characteristic zero that is a splitting field for G; this means that for each $\sigma = 1, \cdots, s$, the character X_σ can be obtained from a matrix representation X_σ, such that all the coefficients of the matrices $X_\sigma(g)$ lie in L. This is to say that L is a splitting field for all the X_σ, in the sense we used earlier. We assume that L has a subring R that is a principal ideal domain, such that L is the field of quotients of R; moreover, R should have a prime ideal $\mathfrak{p}$ containing the integer p. We identify $\overline{R} = R/\mathfrak{p}$ (which is a field of characteristic p) with a subfield of the field k. The matrix representations X_σ can be chosen so that the matrix coefficients of $X_\sigma(g)$ all lie in R.

Taking these mod $\mathfrak{p}$, we get a modular representation $\overline{X}_\sigma:g \rightarrow \overline{X_\sigma(g)}$ of G, that is, a representation over the field k. The Brauer character of $\overline{X}_\sigma$ is (suitably identifying a part of L with a part of $\mathbb{C}$, so that the character values $X_\sigma[g]$ can be regarded as elements of $\mathbb{C}$) identical with the restriction of X_σ to G_0. Equations (3) therefore say that $d_{\sigma i}$ is the multiplicity of F_i as composition factor of $\overline{X}_\sigma$; Brauer called the $d_{\sigma i}$ decomposition numbers; they record the decomposition that the ordinary irreducible representations X_σ of G undergo when they are reduced mod $\mathfrak{p}$. But these numbers have another, quite separate interpretation. Brauer found that the modular irreducibles $F_1, \cdots, F_l$ are in natural correspondence with the indecomposable direct summands $U_1, \cdots, U_l$ of the regular representation of the group algebra $A = kG$. (He showed, in fact, in joint work with Nesbitt, that this holds for any finite-dimensional k-algebra A. U_i is what is now called the projective cover of F_i. Brauer's ideas from this period—the late 1930's—pervade much modern research on algebras and their representations.) If splitting field L is taken to be complete with respect to a suitable discrete valuation, with R as the ring of valuation integers, then each U_i can be lifted to a representation $\tilde{U}_i$ of G over R, that is, to a representation in characteristic zero, which therefore has an ordinary character η_i, say.

There hold then the remarkable equations

$$\eta_i = \sum_{\sigma=1}^{s} d_{\sigma i} X_\sigma, \quad i = 1, \cdots, l \qquad (4)$$

that are in some sense dual to (3). From (3) and (4) one deduces equations

$$c_{ij} = \sum_{\sigma=1}^{s} d_{\sigma i} d_{\sigma j}, \quad i, j = 1, \cdots, l, \qquad (5)$$

where the c_{ij} are the Cartan invariants of the algebra $A = kG$; c_{ij} may be defined as the multiplicity (as composition factor) of F_j in U_i. Cartan invariants exist for any algebra A, but equations (5) show that for a group algebra $A = kG$, the $l \times l$ matrix $C = (c_{ij})$ has special properties: it is symmetric and positive definite. Brauer also discovered the deep theorem that det C is a power of the characteristic p of k. This was published in the first of a remarkable series of papers appearing in 1941 and 1942. In these Brauer introduced new and sophisticated methods for the study of group characters, and began to give applications of his theory to the structure theory of finite groups.

Fundamental to this work was the idea of a block. Blocks are most easily defined by taking a decomposition $1 = e_1 + \cdots + e_t$ of 1 as sum of orthogonal primitive idempotents of e_τ of the center $Z(kG)$ of kG. This can be lifted to a corresponding decomposition $1 = \hat{e}_1 + \cdots + \hat{e}_t$ in $Z(RG)$. An ordinary (or modular) irreducible character ψ of G is said to belong to the block B_τ of G if $\hat{e}_\tau$ (or e_τ) is represented by the identity matrix in a representation corresponding to ψ. In this way both sets $\{X_1, \cdots, X_s\}$ and $\{\beta_1, \cdots, \beta_l\}$ are partitioned among the t blocks $B_1, \cdots, B_t$ of G. Block theory aims to give information about the ordinary characters of a given block B_τ of G, in terms of information available for a block b in some p-local subgroup H of G (H is usually the normalizer or centralizer in G of some p-subgroup of G).

In the most favorable cases, Brauer's methods show that a part of the character table for H is almost identical with a part of the character table for G; this is now much used in the computation of character tables for known finite groups. Brauer saw in his theory a potential tool for studying finite simple groups. (We shall return to this later.)

The main facts about blocks of a group G and their relation to blocks of subgroups H of G, as well as the important refinement to equations (3) involving coefficients called the generalized decomposition numbers, had been published (sometimes without proofs, which appeared years later) by 1947. In that year Brauer also published a solution to Emil Artin's conjecture that the sums of the Artin L-series are entire functions. Brauer had held a Guggenheim fellowship in 1941 and 1942 and spent a part of this time visiting Artin in Bloomington, Indiana. They both knew that the solution of Artin's conjecture rested on the validity of a certain statement about group characters; and at some point in the next few years Brauer realized that this statement could be proved, using methods he had developed for his modular character theory.

By 1953 he embodied the essential idea from these methods in a theorem—perhaps his most widely known—that if Θ is a complex valued class function on a finite group G, then Θ is a generalized character of G, if its restriction $\Theta|_E$ is a generalized character of E, for every elementary subgroup E of G. (If $X_1, \cdots, X_s$ are the irreducible ordinary characters of a group G, then functions of form $z_1X_1 + \cdots + z_sX_s$ with the z_i integers—not necessarily positive—are called generalized characters of G. A group E is elementary if, for some prime p, E is the direct product of a p-group and a cyclic group.) From this theorem Brauer also obtained a new proof of a much older conjecture (which he had first solved a few years earlier): that if ε is a primitive gth root of unity, where g is the order of G, then $\mathbf{Q}(\varepsilon)$ is a splitting field for G (that is, for all the irreducible characters of G).

In 1948 Brauer moved from Toronto to the University of Michigan at Ann Arbor, and four years later to Harvard. From this period can be dated the first systematic attack on the problem of describing (or classifying) all finite simple groups. In a paper written with his pupil K. A. Fowler, Brauer proved by very elementary means a striking fact: Let G be a simple group of even order, and let x be an involution in G (that is, an element satisfying the conditions $x^2 = 1$, $x \neq 1$). Let $H = C_G(x)$ be the centralizer of x and let n be the order of H. Then G has a proper subgroup of index less than $\frac{1}{2}n(n + 1)$. This gives hope to a general program announced by Brauer in 1954: Given an abstract group H with an involution x in its center, to find all simple groups G containing H as a subgroup in such a way that $H = C_G(x)$. For the theorem above shows that (with H and x given) the number of isomorphism types of such groups G is finite—although it does not provide practical means of constructing them. It is natural to take for H the centralizer of an involution in some known simple group G_0. It may happen that G_0 is—up to isomorphism—the only simple group having an involution x such that $C_G(x) \cong H$; we have then a characterization of G_0 by an internal property.

By 1954 Brauer (and independently M. Suzuki and G. E. Wall) had found characterizations of this kind for groups of type $PSL(2,q)$. The method in such problems is to build up knowledge of the ordinary character table of G from what is given about H. This is exactly the kind of work for which Brauer's modular methods were designed, and he used these methods successfully on many simple group characterizations during the next twenty-five years, constantly refining and developing his modular theory. But now new actors began to appear in the drama of the simple groups. Suzuki and Wall used only ordinary character theory in their work on $PSL(2,q)$, and their methods—still following Brauer's program—led eventually to the discovery of new simple groups. Around 1960 J. G. Thompson began a powerful attack on the internal structure of simple groups, using new group-theoretical methods. In 1963 he and W. Feit verified the long-standing conjecture that every simple (noncyclic) group G has even order—which showed that G must possess involutions, so that Brauer's general program will always apply. The Feit-Thompson paper, remarkable for its length and difficulty, again used only ordinary character theory, based on an old theorem of Frobenius.

In the period 1960–1980 dozens of people joined the common effort to find all finite simple groups. Many new simple groups were found, some by application of Brauer's program and others from quite different sources. Brauer was deeply involved in this effort right up to the end of his life but did not see its final success, of which he must be counted one of the chief architects.

BIBLIOGRAPHY

I. ORIGINAL WORKS. Facsimile reprints of most of Brauer's mathematical publications are in *Richard Brauer: Collected Papers*, Paul Fong and Warren J. Wong, eds., 3 vols. (Cambridge, Mass., and London, 1980), which includes an autobiographical preface by Brauer, a complete bibliography, and a reprint of Green's biographical article (see below).

II. SECONDARY LITERATURE. Articles on Brauer are W. Feit, "Richard D. Brauer," in *Bulletin of the American Mathematical Society*, n.s. **1** (1979), 1–20; and J. A. Green, "Richard Dagobert Brauer," in *Bulletin of the London Mathematical Society*, **10** (1978), 317–342.

J. A. GREEN

BRAUNMÜHL, ANTON VON (*b.* Tiflis, Russia, 12 December 1853; *d.* Munich, Germany, 7 March 1908)

Braunmühl, descended from the old Bavarian nobility, was the son of the famous architect Anton von Braunmühl (1820–1858), who had studied with Fr. Gärtner, and Anna Maria Schlenz (1823–1892). In 1879 he married Franziska Stölzl (1853–1917), who bore him two daughters.

After the sudden death of his father, Braunmühl grew up in Munich and enrolled in its university in 1873. There he attended lectures on astronomy by Johann Lamont, on physics by Philipp Jolly, on the history of literature by Michael Bernays, and on cultural history by Wilhelm Riehl; he also studied mathematics under Ludwig Seidel, Gustav Bauer, and Friedrich Narr. At the Munich Technical University, Braunmühl studied further under Alexander Brill, Felix Klein, and Johann Bischoff. In 1888 he was appointed extraordinary professor of mathematics at the Technical University and was promoted to ordinary professor of mathematics in 1892. He was recognized as a scientist and was held in extraordinary esteem as a teacher. Braunmühl's lectures on the history of mathematics, given regularly after 1893, were unique in that they were offered without credit, as were the seminars on the history of mathematics that were given right after the lectures. These lectures and seminars stimulated Wilhelm Kutta, Axel Bjoernbo, and Carl Wallner, among others, to undertake independent work in the history of mathematics.

At the turn of the century Braunmühl, Moritz Cantor, Maximilian Curtze, and Sigmund Günther were leading authorities on the history of mathematics in Germany. Braunmühl's contributions, pertaining especially to the history of trigonometry, surpass those of many of his contemporaries in thorough study of sources, complete reflection of previous literature, and precise presentation of specific details, as well as in their critical evaluation.

BIBLIOGRAPHY

I. ORIGINAL WORKS. Braunmühl's writings include *Chr. Scheiner als Mathematiker, Physiker und Astronom* (Bamberg, 1891); "Beiträge zur Geschichte der Trigonometrie," in *Nova acta Leopoldina*, **71** (1897), 1–30; and *Vorlesungen über Geschichte der Trigonometrie*, 2 vols. (Leipzig, 1900–1903).

Preliminary studies by Braunmühl were utilized after his death by H. Wieleitner in *Geschichte der Mathematik,* II, pt. 1 (Leipzig, 1911).

II. SECONDARY LITERATURE. Works on Braunmühl are S. Günther, "Anton von Braunmühl," in *Mitteilungen zur Geschichte der Medizin und der Naturwissenschaften,* **7** (1908), 362–367; J. E. Hofmann, "Anton von Braunmühl," in *Neue deutsche Biographie,* II (1955), 560; and H. Wieleitner, "Zum Gedächtnis Anton von Braunmühls," in *Bibliotheca mathematica,* 3rd ser., **11** (1910), 316–330, with a portrait and a bibliography.

JOSEPH E. HOFMANN

BREDON, SIMON (*b.* Winchcomb, England, *ca.* 1300; *d. ca.* 1372)

Originally a fellow of Balliol College, Oxford, Bredon moved to Merton College and was a fellow there in 1330, becoming junior proctor of the university in 1337 and keeper of the Langton chest about 1339. In 1348 he left Merton to become vicar of Rustington, Sussex, and thereafter held a succession of church appointments. His will, probated in 1372, listed the contents of his library, which covered theology, law, medicine, mathematics, and astronomy, as well as grammar and dialectic.

Bredon's earliest writings were concerned with philosophy, but he soon turned to mathematics and produced an explanation of Boethius' *Arithmetic.* This he split up into two parts, the first dealing with numbers, including multiplication, the second concerned with geometrical figures—triangles, squares, pentagons, hexagons, etc. In his copy of William Rede's astronomical tables for 1341–1344 he jotted down five conclusions on square numbers, which he considered useful for the squaring of the circle. These were followed by two criticisms of statements made by Vitello in his book on perspective, which Bredon dubbed "marvellous but false." His possession of Richard of Wallingford's book on sines and John Maudith's table of chords shows him to have taken an interest in trigonometry, but his own writings on these subjects have not survived except for a few brief notes; therefore it is not possible to assess his contribution in this field.

Bredon's works on astronomy are better attested. He wrote a treatise on the use of the astrolabe, giving detailed instructions how to find the altitude, degree, and declination of the sun; the latitude of any region; the degree of eclipse; and so on. The opening paragraph, entitled "Nomina instrumentorum," is not his work, but a borrowing from Messehallach. His *Theorica planetarum,* sometimes attributed to Walter Brytte, a contemporary at Merton, sometimes to Gerardo da Sabbionetta, is largely a paraphrase of the latter's treatise, although it lacks the two final sections on the latitude of the planets and the invection of the aspects of the planets. The text *De equationibus planetarum* formerly ascribed to Bredon has been shown to belong to Chaucer.

Bredon wrote a commentary on the first three books of Ptolemy's *Almagest.* No complete copy survives, but the work can be reconstructed from two incomplete manuscripts, both of which were annotated by Thomas Allen and John Dee. According to a marginal note in MS Digby 179, Bredon also made a new translation of Ptolemy's *Quadrepartitum,* probably to be identified with the *Astronomia judiciaria* mentioned in John Bale's *Index Britanniae scriptorum.* This translation is inserted into the lower margins of the version done by Egidius de Thebaldis of Parma, a copy of which was in Bredon's library. He drew up tables for the declination of the sun and the ascension of the signs and gave the longitude of Oxford as 14°56′. Bale ascribes three other works to him—*Super introductorio Alcabitii, Astronomia calculatoria,* and *Astronomia judiciaria*—without giving incipits.

Bredon's most ambitious work was the *Trifolium,* a medical compilation modeled on Avicenna's *Canon.* Only one-twelfth of it survives, dealing with the prognostication of disease from feces and urine, and with the composition of medicines. He was physician to Richard, Earl of Arundel, in 1355 and treated Joanna, Queen of Scots, in 1358.

BIBLIOGRAPHY

I. ORIGINAL WORKS. Bredon's writings are *Questiones in X libros Ethicorum Aristotelis:* Vienna, Bibl. Monast. B.V.M. ad Scotos MS 278.

De arithmetica: Oxford, Digby MS 98, fols. 109–117; Digby MS 147, fols. 92–103; Corpus Christi Coll. MS 118, fols. 101–118; Cambridge, Univ. Lib. MS Ee.iii, 61, fols. 92–101; Univ. of Alabama, MS 1, fols. 1–16; Boston Public Lib. MS 1531. On the last, see Margaret Munsterberg, "An Unpublished Mathematical Treatise by Simon Bredon," in *More Books, The Bulletin of the Boston Public Library,* **19** (1944), 411.

Conclusiones quinque de numero quadrato: Digby MS 178, fols. 11v–14.

Massa compoti (of Alexandre de Ville Dieu, not of Grosseteste, as ascribed by Bale): Digby MS 98, fols. 11–21, "bene correctus secundum sententiam Bredone."

Theorica planetarum: London, British Museum Egerton MS 847, fols. 104–122; Egerton MS 889; Oxford, Digby MS 48; Digby MS 93; Digby MS 98. The following MSS listed by Lynn Thorndike do not contain Bredon's work, but the treatise by Gerardo da Sabbionetta: London, B.M.

Royal 12 C.ix; Royal 12 C.xvii; Royal 12 E.xxv; Oxford, Digby MS 47; Digby MS 168; Digby MS 207.

Commentum . . . Almagesti: Oxford, Digby MS 168, fols. 21-39; Digby MS 178, fols. 42-87; Cambridge, Univ. Lib. Ee.iii, 61, art. 8.

Astrolabii usus et declaracio: London, B.M. Harl. 321, fols. 24v-28.

Liber Quadrepartiti Ptolemei: Digby MS 179. See Axel Anthon Björnbo, "Die Mittelalterlichen lateinischen Übersetzungen aus dem Griechischen auf dem Gebiete der mathematischen Wissenschaften," in *Archiv für Geschichte der Naturwissenschaften und der Technik,* **1** (1909), 391 ff.

Trifolium: Oxford, Digby MS 160, fols. 102-223.

Bredon is quoted in Thomas Werkworth, *Tractatus de motu octavae spherae* (1396): Digby MS 97, fol. 143.

Two letters addressed to him are in London, B.M. Royal 12 D.xi, fols. 25r, 35r. His longitude for Oxford is in Royal 12 D.v, fol. 50r.

II. SECONDARY LITERATURE. Full biographical details are in A. B. Emden, *A Biographical Register of the University of Oxford to A.D. 1500,* I (Oxford, 1957), 257-258; R. T. Gunther, *Early Science in Oxford,* II (Oxford, 1923), 52-55; and Lynn Thorndike, *A History of Magic and Experimental Science,* III (New York, 1934), 521-522. See also C. H. Talbot, "Simon Bredon (*c.* 1300-1372), Physician, Mathematician and Astronomer," in *British Journal of the History of Science,* **1** (1962-1963), 19-30; and J. A. Weisheipl, "Early 14th Century Physics and the Merton School," Bodl. Lib. MS D.Phil. d.1776. A list of the contents of Bredon's library is in F. M. Powicke, *The Mediaeval Books of Merton College* (Oxford, 1931), pp. 82-86, 138-142.

C. H. TALBOT

BRET, JEAN JACQUES (*b.* Mercuriol, Drôme, France, 25 September 1781; *d.* Grenoble, France, 29 January 1819)

He was the son of Jacques Bret, a notary. After passing the entrance examinations given at Lyons, Bret entered the École Polytechnique on 22 November 1800 and was admitted to the course of preparation for civil engineering (Service des Ponts et Chaussées). Unfortunately, because of poor health, he did not complete his studies, but was forced to take a leave of absence from October 1802 to November 1803. The school administration offered to let him stay a fourth year on condition that he take the examinations. He was definitely removed from the rolls in December 1803.

In 1804 Bret became professor of transcendental mathematics at the lycée in Grenoble, and from 8 October 1811 until his death, he was professor at the Faculté des Sciences in the same city, having became *docteur ès sciences* on 10 March 1812.

There are some twenty publications by Bret in the *Annales de mathématiques de Gergonne,* a note in the *Correspondance* of the École Polytechnique, and a memoir in the latter's journal. Most of his articles deal with analytical geometry on plane surfaces and in space, notably with the theory of conics and quadrics. He sets forth, for example, the third-degree equation that determines the length of the axes of a central quadric.

In this research the cumbersome techniques of the time are unpleasantly obvious. By way of exception, a study on the squares of the distance between a point in space and fixed points is remarkable for its simplicity, elegance, and generality.

Other works have a bearing on the theory of algebraic equations, particularly upon the limitation of real roots, a subject in style at the time. Bret also worked on the theory of elimination, where he used the greatest common divisor of polynomials in order to establish Bézout's theorem on the degree of the polynomial resultant.

Bret became involved in a long polemic with J. B. E. Dubourguet in the *Annales de Gergonne.* This had to do with the demonstration of the fundamental theorem that an algebraic equation admits a number of roots equal to its degree.

BIBLIOGRAPHY

Among Bret's works are "Sur la méthode du plus grand commun diviseur appliquée à l'élimination," in *Journal de l'École polytechnique,* **15** (1809), 162-197; and "Sur les équations du quatrième degré," in *Correspondance de l'École polytechnique,* **2** (1811), 217-219.

Of particular note, all in *Annales de mathématiques,* are "Recherche des longueurs des axes principaux dans les surfaces du second ordre qui ont un centre," **2** (1812), 33-38; "Recherche de la position des axes principaux dans les surfaces du second ordre," *ibid.,* 144-152; "Discussion de l'équation du second degré entre deux variables," *ibid.,* 218-223; "Démonstration de quelques théorèmes relatifs au quadrilatère," *ibid.,* 310-318; "Théorie de l'élimination entre deux équations de degrés quelconques, fondée sur la théorie du plus grand commun diviseur," **3** (1812), 13-18; "Démonstration du principe qui sert de fondement au calcul des fonctions symétriques et de la formule binomiale de Newton," **4** (1813), 25-28; "Théorèmes nouveaux sur les limites des racines des équations numériques," **6** (1815), 112-122; and "Théorie générale des fractions continues," **11** (1818), 37-51.

An article on Bret is Niels Nielsen, "Bret," in *Géomètres français sous la Révolution* (Copenhagen, 1929), pp. 31-37.

JEAN ITARD

BRIANCHON, CHARLES-JULIEN (*b.* Sèvres, France, 19 December 1783; *d.* Versailles, France, 29 April 1864)

There appears to be no record of Brianchon's early years. He entered the École Polytechnique in 1804 and was a pupil of the noted geometer Gaspard Monge. While a student there, he published his first paper, "Sur les surfaces courbes du second degré" (1806), which contained the famous theorem named after him.

Brianchon graduated first in his class in 1808 and became a lieutenant in artillery in the armies of Napoleon. He took part in the Peninsular campaigns, serving in Spain and Portugal, and is said to have distinguished himself both in bravery and ability. The rigors of his army service affected his health, and after the cessation of hostilities in 1813, Brianchon applied for a teaching position. He was finally appointed professor at the Artillery School of the Royal Guard in 1818.

By this time he had published several works in geometry, including "Sur les surfaces courbes du second degré" (1816), *Mémoire sur les lignes du second ordre* (1817), *Application de la théorie des transversales* (1818), and "Solution de plusieurs problèmes de géométrie" (1818).

Brianchon's teaching duties apparently affected both his output and his interests. In 1820 there appeared "Recherches sur la détermination d'une hyperbole équilatère, au moyen de quatres conditions données," written with Poncelet. It is notable for containing the nine-point circle theorem and is an instance of the many times this theorem has been rediscovered by independent investigators. At any rate, this paper contains the first complete proof of the theorem and the first use of the term "nine-point circle."

Brianchon's next publication, "Description du laboratoire de chimie de l'École d'Artillerie de la Garde Royale" (1822), indicates his change of interests. Two works appeared in 1823: "Des courbes de raccordement" and *Mémoire sur la poudre à tirer.* His last known work, *Essai chimique sur les réactions foudroyantes,* appeared in 1825. Brianchon ceased writing after 1825 and devoted all his time to teaching. Details of his personal life are singularly scarce.

Brianchon's fame rests ultimately on one theorem. In 1639 Pascal had proved that "If all the vertices of a hexagon lie on a circle, and if the opposite sides intersect, then the points of intersection lie on a line." He then boldly extended this result to a hexagon inscribed in any conic, since he recognized that his theorem was projective in nature. Oddly enough, it took 167 years before someone else—Brianchon—realized that since the theorem is projective in nature, its dual should also be true. Simply stated, Brianchon's theorem is "If all the sides of a hexagon are tangent to a conic, then the diagonals joining opposite vertices are concurrent." The theorem is useful in the study of the properties of conics and—if the hexagon is specialized in various ways—for the study of properties of pentagons, quadrilaterals, and triangles.

BIBLIOGRAPHY

Brianchon's writings are "Sur les surfaces courbes du second degré," in *Journal de l'École Polytechnique* (1806); "Sur les surfaces courbes du second degré," *ibid.* (1816); *Mémoire sur les lignes du second ordre* (Paris, 1817); *Application de la théorie des transversales* (Paris, 1818); "Solutions de plusieurs problèmes de géométrie," in *Journal de l'École Polytechnique,* **4** (1818); "Recherches sur la détermination d'une hyperbole équilatère, au moyen de quatres conditions données," *ibid.* (1820); "Description du laboratoire de chimie de l'École d'Artillerie de la Garde Royale," in *Annales de l'industrie nationale* (1822); "Des courbes de raccordement," in *Journal de l'École Polytechnique,* **12** (1823); *Mémoire sur la poudre à tirer* (Paris, 1823); and *Essai chimique sur les réactions foudroyantes* (Paris, 1825).

S. L. GREITZER

BRIGGS, HENRY (*b.* Warleywood, Yorkshire, England, February 1561; *d.* Oxford, England, 26 January 1630)

Although J. Mede of Christ's College, Cambridge, wrote on 6 February 1630, "Mr. Henry Briggs of Oxford, the great mathematician, is lately dead, at 74 years of age," implying thereby that Briggs was born about 1556, it seems that he was in error. The Halifax parish register gives the 1561 date.

After a local grammar schooling in Greek and Latin, Briggs went to St. John's College, Cambridge, about 1577, and was admitted as a scholar on 5 November 1579. He received the B.A. in 1581 and the M.A. in 1585, became examiner and lecturer in mathematics in 1592, and soon afterward was appointed Dr. Linacre's reader of the physic (medicine) lecture. He had been elected fellow of his college in 1589.

Early in 1596 Briggs became the first professor of geometry at the newly founded Gresham College in London. He first worked on navigation and composed a table for the finding of the height of the pole, the magnetic declination being given. By 1609 he was in correspondence with James Ussher, later the famous archbishop of Armagh; from one of Briggs's letters we learn that he was studying eclipses in 1610. By 10 March 1615, however, he was entirely engaged in the study of logarithms, the subject for which he is renowned: "Neper, lord of Markinston, hath set my head and hands a work with his new and admirable logarithms. I hope to see him this summer, if it please God, for I never saw book, which pleased me better, and made me more wonder."

Briggs at once applied his energies to the advancement of logarithms and to lecturing on them at Gresham College. He soon proposed a modification of the scale of logarithms from Napier's hyperbolic form, a change that Napier discussed with Briggs, who went to Edinburgh for a month's visit after completing his lectures in the summer of 1616. One result of these exchanges was that Briggs saw E. Wright's translation of Napier's *Canon mirificus* through the press, Wright having died. To the work Briggs added a preface and some material of his own—"A description of an instrument table to find the part proportional, devised by Mr. Edward Wright" (1616).

Briggs's *Logarithmorum chilias prima* is dated 1617; in the preface, which mentions the recent death of Napier, the change from the hyperbolic form of logarithms is justified and the publication of Napier's *Rhabdologia* foretold. That work duly appeared in 1619, with comments by Briggs himself on the new form of logarithms and on the solution of spherical triangles.

The parts taken by Napier and Briggs in developing logarithms were described by the latter in his *Arithmetica logarithmica* (1624). The proposals there recorded do not yield common logarithms: for if R is the radius, Briggs suggested that $\log R = 0$ and $\log R/10 = 10^{10}$. Napier, having abandoned the hyperbolic form in which

$$\text{Nap. } \log y = 10^7 \log_e \frac{10^7}{y},$$

proposed an improvement whereby $\log 1 = 0$ and $\log R = 10^{10}$. Later, Briggs replaced $\log R = 10^{10}$ with $\log 10 = 1$. Brigg's key words are:

> I myself, when expounding this doctrine publicly in London to my auditors in Gresham College, remarked that it would be much more convenient that 0 should be kept for the logarithm of the whole sine (as in the *Canon Mirificus*), but that the logarithm of the tenth part of the same whole sine, that is to say 5 degrees 44 minutes and 21 seconds should be 10,000,000,000. And concerning that matter I wrote immediately to the author himself.

Later, however, in Edinburgh, Napier suggested to Briggs "that 0 should be the logarithm of unity and 10,000,000,000 that of the whole sine; which I could not but admit," says Briggs, "was by far the most convenient."

Briggs's edition of Euclid's *Elements* (Books I–VI), printed without the editor's name, was published in London in 1620. In the previous year Sir Henry Saville had invited Briggs to become professor of geometry at Oxford, where he took up his duties at Merton College in January 1620. In his last lecture, Saville introduced Briggs with the words, "Trado lampadem successori meo, doctissimo viro, qui vos ad intima geometriae mysteria perducet." Tactfully Briggs began his lecture course where Saville had left off, at the ninth proposition of Euclid.

His next achievement was the *Arithmetica logarithmica,* which included thirty thousand logarithms, those from 1 to 20,000 and those from 90,000 to 100,000. The work contains a dissertation on the nature and use of logarithms and proposes a scheme for dividing among several hands the calculation of the intermediate numbers from 20,000 to 90,000. Briggs even offered to supply paper specially divided into columns for the purpose. Chapters 12 and 13 of the introduction explain the principles of the method of constructing logarithms by interpolation from differences, an interesting forerunner of the *Canonotechnia* of Roger Cotes. A second edition of the *Arithmetica,* completed by Adrian Vlacq (or Flack), contained the intermediate seventy chiliads and appeared in 1628.

Vlacq also printed Briggs's tables of logarithmic sines and tangents. The responsibility for seeing this work through the press was entrusted by Briggs, when dying, to his friend Henry Gellibrand, then professor of astronomy at Gresham College, who added a preface explaining the application of logarithms to plane and spherical trigonometry. The work was published in 1633 as *Trigonometria Britannica sive de doctrina triangulorum.*

Briggs was an amiable man, much liked by his contemporaries. Unlike Napier, he scorned astrology, thinking it to be "a system of groundless conceits." His last years were spent at Merton College, Oxford, where he died. Some Greek elegiacs were written for him by his Merton colleague Henry Jacob; they end with the statement that not even death has put a stop to his skill, for his soul still astronomizes while his body measures the earth. Oughtred called him "the mirrour of the age for excellent skill in geometry," and Isaac Barrow expressed in his inaugural lecture at Gresham College the sincere gratitude of mathematical contemporaries to Briggs for his outstanding work on logarithms. The interest of this brilliant man extended to the problem of a northwest passage to the South Seas, on which he wrote a treatise (1622), and to the relative merits of the ancients and moderns.

BIBLIOGRAPHY

I. Original Works. Briggs's contributions, and the rest of Napier's *Canon mirificus,* were published at London in 1616 and reprinted in 1618; his own *Logarithmorum chilias prima* soon followed the original edition of the *Canon* (London, 1617). Briggs also added comments to Napier's *Rhabdologia* (Edinburgh, 1619) and edited a version of Euclid's *Elements,* Books I–VI (London, 1620), although his name did not appear as editor. His interest in a northwest passage to the South Seas was expressed in a treatise on the subject (London, 1622). A major work by Briggs was *Arithmetica logarithmica* (London, 1624); a second edition, completed by Adrian Vlacq (Gouda, 1628), contained the intermediate seventy chiliads. The relative merits of the ancients and moderns were discussed in *Mathematica ab antiquis minus cognita,* published in the second edition of G. Hakewill's *Apologie* (1630). Briggs's last work was *Trigonometria Britannica sive de doctrina triangulorum* (Gouda, 1633).

II. Secondary Literature. Works concerning Briggs are D. M. Hallowes, "Henry Briggs, Mathematician," in *Transactions of the Halifax Antiquarian Society* (1962), 79–92; Christopher Hill, *Intellectual Origins of the English Revolution* (Oxford, 1965), p. 38, where it is claimed that "significant though Briggs was as a mathematician in his own right, his greatest importance was as a contact and public relations man"; C. Hutton, *Mathematical Tables,* 5th ed. (London, 1811), pp. 33–37, and *A Philosophical and Mathematical Dictionary,* I (London, 1815), 254–255; F. Maseres, ed., *Scriptores logarithmici,* I (London, 1791), lxxvi ff. (on Briggs's abacus ΠΑΓΧΡΗΣΤΟΣ and binomials, see especially p. lxviii); Thomas Smith, biography of Briggs, in his *Vitae quorundam eruditissimorum et illustrium virorum* (1707), translated into English by J. T. Foxell in A. J. Thompson, *Logarithmetica Britannica,* I (Cambridge, 1952), lxvii–lxxvii; H. W. Turnbull, a study of Briggs's work on finite differences, in *Proceedings of the Edinburgh Mathematical Society,* 2nd ser., **3** (1933), 164–170; J. Ward, biography of Briggs, in *The Lives of the Professors of Gresham College* (London, 1740), pp. 120–129, which includes a list of Briggs's writings, both published and unpublished; D. T. Whiteside, "Patterns of Mathematical Thought in the Later Seventeenth Century," in *Archive for the History of the Exact Sciences,* **1** (1961), 232–236.

G. Huxley

BRILL, ALEXANDER WILHELM VON (*b.* Darmstadt, Germany, 20 September 1842; *d.* Tübingen, Germany, 8 June 1935)

Brill, the nephew of the geometer Christian Wiener, was a student of Alfred Clebsch at both the Politechnikum in Karlsruhe and at the University of Giessen. He graduated in 1864 and passed his *Habilitation* in 1867. From then until 1869 he was a *Dozent* at Giessen; from 1869 to 1875, a professor at the Politechnikum in Darmstadt; and from 1875 to 1884, a professor at the Politechnikum in Munich, where he worked with Felix Klein and was influenced by him. From 1884 to 1918, when he retired, Brill was a professor at the University of Tübingen. He worked primarily on the theory of algebraic functions and algebraic geometry, characteristically using algebraic methods, striving to avoid transcendental methods and aiming at "Weierstrassian strictness" of exposition. The systematic study of those properties of algebraic functions which are invariant under birational transformations is contained in his fundamental work, written with Max Noether (1874). In it many of the results obtained by Riemann and by Clebsch and Gordan, using transcendental means, are substantiated by algebraic-geometrical methods. Also noteworthy are his papers on three-dimensional algebraic curves (1907) and on pseudospherical three-dimensional space (1885), where the impossibility of putting such a space into a Euclidean four-dimensional space and the possibility of its being placed in a Euclidean five-dimensional space are proved.

At the end of the last century, Brill published a series of articles on methodology of mathematics, participated—following Klein—in the movement to reform its teaching, and was an initiator of the use of models of geometrical figures in teaching; many such models were prepared under his guidance.

Brill also wrote on the theory of determinants, on the theory of elimination, on the theory of elliptic functions, on some special curves and surfaces, and on the singularities of planar and spatial algebraic curves. He was also concerned with theoretical mechanics. In *Vorlesungen über allgemeine Mechanik* (1928) and *Vorlesungen über algebraische Kurven und algebraische Functionen* (1925) Brill, who was then retired, summed up his scientific and pedagogical career.

Brill's survey of the development of the theory of algebraic functions ("Die Entwicklung der Theorie der algebraischen Functionen in älterer und neurer Zeit," 1894), which was written with Noether, has significance for the history of mathematics. His last work, published when he was eighty-seven, dealt with Kepler's *New Astronomy.*

BIBLIOGRAPHY

I. ORIGINAL WORKS. Among Brill's writings are "Ueber die algebraische Functionen und ihre Anwendung in der Geometrie," in *Mathematische Annalen,* **7** (1874), 269–370, written with Max Noether; "Bemerkungen ueber pseudophärischen Mannigfaltigkeiten," *ibid.,* **26** (1885), 300-303; "Die Entwicklung der Theorie der algebraischen Functionen in älterer und neurer Zeit," in *Jahresbericht der Deutschen Mathematiker-Vereinigung,* **3** (1894), 107-566, written with Max Noether; "Ueber algebraische Raumkurven," in *Mathematische Annalen,* **64** (1907), 289-324; *Vorlesungen über algebraische Kurven und algebraische Functionen* (Brunswick, 1925); and *Vorlesungen über allgemeine Mechanik* (Munich-Berlin, 1928). For a more complete list see Poggendorff.

II. SECONDARY LITERATURE. See S. Finsterwalder, "Alexander von Brill. Ein Lebensbild," in *Mathematische Annalen,* **112** (1936), 653-663; and F. Severi, "Alexander von Brill," in *Jahresbericht der Deutschen Mathematiker-Vereinigung,* **31** (1922), 89-96

J. B. POGREBYSSKY

BRILLOUIN, MARCEL LOUIS (*b.* Melle, Deux-Sèvres, France, 19 December 1854; *d.* Paris, France, 16 June 1948)

Brillouin came from a middle-class family. His father was a painter, and the family lived in Paris, where Marcel studied at the Lycée Condorcet. They moved back to Melle during the Franco-Prussian War, and he spent the years 1870 and 1871 reading all the books on philosophy he could find in his grandfather's big library. Back in Paris in 1872, he brilliantly passed his baccalaureate the following year and became a student at the École Normale Supérieure (1874–1878). He then was an assistant, at the Collège de France, to the well-known physicist Mascart, whose daughter he later married. In 1881 Brillouin obtained doctorates in both mathematics and physics. He spent the next several years, as assistant professor of physics, at the universities of Nancy, Dijon, and Toulouse. Brillouin returned to the École Normale Supérieure in 1888, when he married Charlotte Mascart. From 1900 on, he was professor of mathematical physics at the Collège de France until his retirement in 1931. He became a member of the Académie des Sciences de Paris in 1921.

Brillouin was a prominent theoretical physicist, but he was also a very skillful experimenter. He always had a laboratory and a large library nearby. In his teaching he always outlined the history of the subject and organized a seminar on the history and philosophy of physics for all his students. He had a great influence on the formation and careers of such students as Perrin, Langevin, Villat, Pérès, A. Foch, his son Léon, and J. Coulomb. He also maintained friendly personal relations with many foreign scientists, including Kelvin, Lorentz, Planck, and Sommerfeld.

In his long career Brillouin published more than 200 papers and books. He was a great admirer of Kelvin's lectures and wrote a preface and notes for their translation (1893); he also provided notes for a book of translations of original papers on meteorology (1900), a subject in which he was always highly interested. His interest in the kinetic theory of gases, liquids, and solids is reflected in his contribution of a preface and many notes to the French translation of Boltzmann's book (1902). This was followed by a book on viscosity (1906–1907) and a number of papers on kinetic theory and thermodynamics of liquids (isotropic or anisotropic) and solids, plasticity, and melting conditions. A book on the propagation of electricity (1904) included a complete calculation of proper vibrations for a metallic ellipsoid, a problem that became later of great importance for ultrashort wavelengths.

About 1900 Brillouin spent considerable time building a new model of the Eötvös balance and testing it in the Simplon Tunnel, which was opened in 1906. This is described in a long paper published by the Académie des Sciences in 1908. The Brillouin balance was later used for oil prospecting.

There followed a series of important papers on Helmholtz' flow and surfaces of discontinuity, with applications to hydrodynamics and hydraulic problems, and a long paper on the stability of airplanes.

From 1918 to 1922, and later, Brillouin tried to find an explanation of Bohr's condition of stable atom trajectories and their *n, l, m* quantum numbers. He attempted to use retarded actions of unknown nature (rather similar to de Broglie waves) and obtained stability conditions containing some sort of quantum numbers. Similar conditions were used later by de Broglie and modified by Schrödinger.

A few papers on the problem of an electromagnetic source in uniaxial or biaxial crystals are of interest for crystal optics. From 1925 on, most of Brillouin's research centered on physics of the earth, especially tides, and was published in the Academy's *Comptes rendus.* He also lectured on these subjects at the Collège de France and the Institut Poincaré (1930). His lectures on tides were edited by J. Coulomb, but most of them remained unpublished. Brillouin discussed a variety of mathematical problems in connection with tides, especially problems of varying boundary conditions, and transformations of spherical harmonics from one polar axis to another, the idea being to use, for tides, an axis of coordinates running through continental regions.

The interests of this wide-ranging, open-minded scientist extended from the history of science to the physics of the earth and the atom.

BIBLIOGRAPHY

I. Original Works. Books that Brillouin wrote or contributed to are *Conférences de Lord Kelvin,* Lugol, trans. (Paris, 1893), ed., preface, and notes by Brillouin; *Mémoires originaux sur la théorie de la circulation de l'atmosphere* (Paris, 1900), notes by Brillouin; *Théorie cinétique des gaz de Boltzmann* (Paris, 1902), notes and preface by Brillouin; pt. 2, *Sur la condition de l'état permanent. Sur la tendance apparente à l'irréversibilité d'après Gibbs* (Paris, 1905); *Propagation de l'électricité, histoire et théorie* (Paris, 1904); and *Leçons sur la viscosité des liquides et des gaz,* 2 vols. (Paris, 1906–1907).

Papers of special importance are "Vents contigus et nuages," in *Mémoires du Bureau central météorologique* (1897), also in *Annales de chimie et physique,* **12** (1897), 145 ff.; "L'ellipticité du geoïde dans le tunnel du Simplon," in *Mémoires présentés par divers savants à l'Académie des sciences de l'Institut de France,* **23** (1908); "Stabilité des aéroplanes, surface métacentrique, planeurs, etc.," in *Revue de mécanique* (1909–1910); "Surfaces de glissement d'Helmholtz et resistance des fluides," in *Annales de chimie et physique,* **23** (1911); "Structure des cristaux et anisotropie des molécules," Solvay Congress, 1913; "Milieux biaxes," in *Comptes rendus de l'Académie des sciences,* **165** (1917) and **166** (1918); "Sources électromagnétiques dans les milieux uniaxes," in *Bulletin des sciences mathématiques,* **42** (1918); "Actions mécaniques à hérédité discontinue, essai de l'atome à quanta," in *Comptes rendus de l'Académie des sciences,* **168** (1919), **171** (1920), **173** (1921), and **174** (1922); and "Atome de Bohr, fonction de Lagrange circumnucléaire," in *Journal de physique,* **3** (1922).

II. Secondary Literature. Works on Brillouin are H. Villat, ed., *Jubilé de M. Brillouin pour son 80ème anniversaire,* 2 vols. (Paris, 1935); and H. Villat, *Titres et travaux scientifiques* (Paris, 1930), pp. 8, 10, 19–21, 25–26, and "Notice nécrologique sur Marcel Brillouin," in *Comptes rendus de l'Académie des sciences,* **226**, no. 25 (1948), 2029.

L. Brillouin

BRING, ERLAND SAMUEL (*b.* Ausås, Kristianstad, Sweden, 19 August 1736; *d.* Lund, Sweden, 20 May 1798)

The son of Iöns Bring, a clergyman, and Christina Elisabeth Lagerlöf, Erland Bring studied jurisprudence at Lund University from 1750 to 1757. Beginning in 1762 he was a reader at Lund and from 1779 a professor. He taught history at the university, although his favorite field was mathematics. In the university library are preserved eight volumes of his manuscript compositions on various questions of algebra, geometry, mathematical analysis, and astronomy, and commentaries on the work of L'Hospital, Christian von Wolf, Leonhard Euler, and other scholars.

In 1786 Bring's *Meletemata* was published. Like many eighteenth-century mathematicians, he attempted to solve equations of higher than fourth degree in radicals by means of reduction into binomial form, employing the transformation of the unknown quantity first proposed by Tschirnhaus (1683). Bring succeeded in reducing a general fifth-degree equation to the trinomial form $x^5 + px + q = 0$, using a transformation whose coefficients are defined by equations of not higher than the third degree. This remarkable result received practically no attention at the time and was obtained independently by George Birch Jerrard in his *Mathematical Researches* (1832–1835). Shortly thereafter, Sir William R. Hamilton demonstrated (1836) that with the aid of this operation a general fifth-degree equation reduces to any of four trinomial forms. It is not known whether Bring hoped to solve the fifth-degree equation in radicals with the aid of his transformation; Jerrard retained this hope, even though Niels Abel proved (1824–1826) that such a solution is impossible for a general fifth-degree equation.

In 1837 Bring's nephew, the historian Ebbe Samuel Bring, tried unsuccessfully to attract the attention of mathematicians to the algebraic investigations of his uncle. The deep significance of the Bring-Jerrard transformation was ascertained only after Charles Hermite (1858) used the above-mentioned trinomial form for the solution of fifth-degree equations with the aid of elliptic modular functions, thereby laying the foundations for new methods of studying and solving equations of higher degrees with the aid of transcendental functions.

Hermite cited only Jerrard, calling his result the most important event in the theory of fifth-degree equations since Abel. Shortly thereafter, in 1861, the scholarly world also recognized Bring's merits, mainly through the efforts of Carl J. D. Hill, professor of mathematics at Lund University.

BIBLIOGRAPHY

Bring's major work is *Meletemata quaedam mathematica circa transformationem aequationum algebraicarum* (Lund, 1786).

Writings on Bring include Moritz Cantor, *Vorlesungen über Geschichte der Matematik,* IV (Leipzig, 1908), 130–132;

C. J. D. Hill, "Nagra ord om Erland Sam. Brings reduktion af 5te gradens equation," in *Öfversigt af Kongelige vetenskapsakademiens förhandlingar* (1861), pp. 317–355; Felix Klein, *Vorlesungen über die Ikosaeder* (Leipzig, 1884), pp. 143–144, 207–209, 244; and *Svenska män och kvinnor biografisk uppslagsbok,* I (Stockholm, 1942), 466.

A. P. YOUSCHKEVITCH

BRINKLEY, JOHN (*b.* Woodbridge, England, 1763; *d.* Dublin, Ireland, 14 September 1835)

Brinkley, whose greatest contribution was his researches into stellar parallaxes, received his early education at Woodbridge Grammar School and with a Mr. Tilney of Harleston. He went on to Caius College, Cambridge, and received his B.A. as senior wrangler and first Smith's Prizeman in 1788. During his senior year he was assistant to N. Maskelyne at Greenwich and was fellow of his college from 1788 to 1792. Upon Maskelyne's personal recommendation he was appointed Andrews professor of astronomy at Dublin University, 11 December 1790. The following year Brinkley was ordained a priest at Lincoln and received his M.A. at Cambridge. In 1792 he was incorporated at Dublin and elected first astronomer royal for Ireland. He proceeded D.D. (Dublin) 1806. Between 1790 and 1808 he prepared the excellent textbook *Elements of Plane Astronomy,* published in 1808, and ten mathematical papers, some with direct application to celestial astronomy.

Upon acquiring a splendid eight-foot meridian circle in 1808, Brinkley attempted to determine the long-sought parallax of the fixed stars, with a view to determining their distances. Two years later he announced the detection of an annual (double) parallax for α Lyrae of 2″.52, and in 1814 similarly large values of 2″.0, 5″.5, 2″.2, and 2″.1 for the stars α Lyrae, α Aquilae, Arcturus, and α Cygni, respectively. The validity of these measurements was disputed in the literature for fourteen years by Pond, who was unable to deduce analogous results with Greenwich instruments. This controversy, by necessitating repeated tests of the observations, was of great value in stimulating the study of previously unappreciated factors affecting the measurements. Brinkley's results, although now themselves discredited, thus led to the later successful detection of stellar parallaxes.

Among Brinkley's other major work was the publication of a new theory of astronomical refractions (1815), estimation of the obliquity of the ecliptic (1819), determination of north polar distances of the principal fixed stars (1815, 1824), and determination of the precession of the equinoxes (1828). He also used the south polar distances of certain fixed stars observed by Sir Thomas Brisbane at Paramatta, New South Wales, to investigate the accuracy of separate determinations by himself and by Bessel of their north polar distances (1826). His astronomical career ended with his elevation, after numerous ecclesiastical preferments, as bishop of Cloyne, 28 September 1826.

Brinkley's honors were many. Fellowship of the Royal Society (1803) was followed by the Conyngham Medal of the Royal Irish Academy, for his essay on investigations relating to the mean motion of the lunar perigee (1817). He was also awarded the Copley Medal of the Royal Society (1824) for his scientific achievements and his approximations to the solution of the parallax problem. He was president of the Royal Irish Academy from 1822 to 1835, vice-president of the Astronomical Society from 1825 to 1827, and its president from 1831 to 1833.

BIBLIOGRAPHY

I. ORIGINAL WORKS. Brinkley's various observations at Greenwich (1787–1788) are distributed through Maskelyne's *Astronomical Observations Made at the Royal Observatory, Greenwich,* **3** (1799), starting with an entry for 23 Sept. 1787. Maskelyne appends the letters *JB* to Brinkley's observations; those by Brinkley's contemporary John Bumpstead appear under Bumpstead's full name.

His elementary astronomical textbook was compiled from lectures given between 1799 and 1808 to undergraduates at Dublin University. The earliest record of the course is *Synopsis of Astronomical Lectures to Commence October 29, 1799 at Philosophical School, Trinity College, Dublin* (Dublin, 1799). The finished book, *Elements of Plane Astronomy* (Dublin, 1808), was prepared at the request of the board of the college when the acquisition of a meridian circle diverted Brinkley's efforts to practical astronomy. The book went through five editions subject to his revision during his lifetime; a sixth edition was edited and revised by Thomas Luby (Dublin, 1845), and two further editions were revised and partly rewritten by J. W. Stubbs and F. Brünnow (London, 1874, 1886).

Ten mathematical papers of considerable elegance were published between 1800 and 1818, nine in the *Transactions of the Royal Irish Academy* (see its Index) and one in *Philosophical Transactions of the Royal Society,* **97** (1807), 114–132.

Eighteen significant astronomical papers on various subjects appeared between 1810 and 1828, eight in *Transactions of the Royal Irish Academy,* eight in *Philosophical Transactions of the Royal Society,* and two in *Memoirs of the Astronomical Society* (see Royal Society's *Catalogue of Scientific Papers,* I [1867], 627–629). Those relating to the parallax question include the following: Brinkley's original announcement of his detection of the annual (double) parallax of α Lyrae, communicated to the Royal Society by Maskelyne, in *Philosophical Transactions,* **100** (1810), 204. The 1814 report of similar and even larger results for other stars, in *Transactions of the Royal Irish Academy,* **12** (1815), 33–75. Discordance with Pond's results suggested to be due to uncertainty of elements used in reduction of Greenwich observations, in *Philosophical Transactions,* **108** (1818), 275–302. Results of further observations introducing a determination of the constant of aberration and of that of lunar nutation, *ibid.,* **109** (1819), 241–248, and **111** (1821), 327–360. An instrumental investigation of the effect of solar nutation cited to exhibit the competence of his equipment to detect the larger quantity of parallax, first reported to the Royal Irish Academy in 1822, in *Transactions of the Royal Irish Academy,* **14** (1825), 3–37. Disengagement from Greenwich results of a parallax for α Lyrae not differing sensibly from that measured at Dublin, in *Memoirs of the Royal Astronomical Society,* **1,** pt. 2 (1822), 329–340. Reassertion of parallax of α Lyrae and attempt to form a correct estimate of the absolute and relative degrees of accuracy of the Dublin and Greenwich instruments, in *Philosophical Transactions,* **114** (1824), 471–498.

Among the ten remaining catalogued papers, see *Transactions of the Royal Irish Academy,* **13** (1818), 25–51, containing an essay on investigations relative to the mean motion of the lunar perigee, which was awarded the Conyngham Medal of the Academy; and *Memoirs of the Astronomical Society,* **2,** pt. 1 (1826), 105–123, containing Brisbane's Paramatta observations. There are several minor references in the *Quarterly Journal of Science, Literature and the Arts,* **9** (1820), 164–167; **11** (1821), 364–370, 370–372; and **12** (1822), 151–154; and in *Astronomische Nachrichten,* **3** (1825), cols. 105–106; **4** (1826), cols. 101–104; and **5** (1827), cols. 131–138.

II. Secondary Literature. An excellent discussion of Brinkley's life and work is contained in *Dictionary of National Biography,* VI (1886); a more general account is in Sir Robert Ball, *Great Astronomers* (London, 1895), pp. 233–246. A synopsis of the contents of his Royal Society papers is in *Proceedings of the Royal Society,* **3** (1835), 354–355. An account of the oration by Sir Humphry Davy upon the award to Brinkley of the Copley Medal may be found in *Philosophical Magazine,* **64** (1824), 459–462.

Obituaries are Henry Cotton, *Fasti ecclesiae Hibernicae,* I (Dublin, 1851), 307–309; *Gentlemen's Magazine,* **11** (1835), 547; Rev. J. B. Leslie, *Clogher Clergy and Parishes* (Enniskillen, 1929), p. 47; and *Memoirs of the Royal Astronomical Society,* **9** (1836), 281–282.

Susan M. P. McKenna

BRIOSCHI, FRANCESCO (*b.* Milan, Italy, 22 December 1824; *d.* Milan, 14 December 1897)

Brioschi graduated in 1845 from the University of Pavia, where he was a student of Antonio Bordoni. From 1852 to 1861 he was a professor of applied mathematics there, teaching theoretical mechanics, civil architecture, and hydraulics. He was the general secretary of the Ministry of Education in 1861–1862, a senator from 1865, and, from 1870 until 1882, a member of the Executive Council of the Ministry of Education. In 1863 Brioschi organized the Istituto Tecnico Superiore in Milan, serving as director and professor of mathematics and hydraulics until his death. From 1884 he was president of the Accademia Nazionale dei Lincei.

From the beginning of his career, Brioschi strove to overcome the backwardness of Italian mathematics, to popularize new scientific trends, and to raise the quality of the teaching of mathematics in secondary schools and universities. He published many essays and reviews, and participated in the organization of the journal *Annali di matematica pura ed applicata,* heading its editorial staff from 1867 until his death (until 1877 in conjunction with Cremona). He also helped to organize the journal *Politecnico.*

In his original papers Brioschi appears as a virtuoso in computation, as an analyst, and as an algebraist. In the works of his most fruitful decade (1851–1860) he widely applied and developed the still new theory of determinants. His *Teoria dei determinanti* (1854) was the first nonelementary statement of the theory and its basic applications. Brioschi devoted several important papers, following Caley, Sylvester, and Hermite, to the then developing theory of forms of two or more variables, which Hermite termed ". . . one of the major mathematical achievements of our time." He applied exclusively algebraic means of solution to such questions as the deduction of equations in partial derivatives for the discriminant of a binary form and for the resultant of two such forms. A significant part of his results in this area was included in a monograph published in the first four volumes of *Annali di matematica.*

In these same years Brioschi added new results to the theory of the transformation of elliptic and Abelian functions. In his greatest achievement, following Hermite and simultaneously with Kronecker, he applied elliptical modular functions to the solution of fifth-degree equations. At the same time, Brioschi popularized Gauss's theory of surfaces in Italy and brought forth, in connection with this, geometric papers.

During the 1860's and 1870's Brioschi continued his work in algebra and analysis in traditional directions, using the Weierstrass theory of elliptic functions. From these viewpoints, he addressed himself to the theory of differential equations and, in the 1880's, to the theory of hyperelliptic functions. His second great achievement relates to this latter period:

the solution of sixth-degree equations with the aid of hyperelliptic functions.

Brioschi did not propound any strikingly new ideas in mathematics, nor did he discover any new fields. "I am only a calculator," he humbly characterized himself. However, he was a brilliant analyst with algebraic propensities and possessed a rare mobility of thought that responded to new ideas from their very inception. This enabled him to enrich science with new results for half a century.

Along with Betti, Brioschi began a new epoch in the history of Italian mathematics, leading it out of its provincial backwardness. He was the teacher of its most outstanding representatives in the next generation, among them Casorati, Cremona, and Beltrami.

In mechanics Brioschi dealt with problems of statics, proving Moebius' results by analytic means; with the integration of equations in dynamics, according to Jacobi's method; with hydrostatics; and with hydrodynamics. His work as a hydraulic engineer was significant, although it is reflected comparatively little in his publications. Brioschi used the findings of a series of major projects or participated in the projects' development—for example, in the regulation of the Po and Tiber (which goals remained unaccomplished). Two more of Brioschi's works should be mentioned: with Betti he brought out a treatment of the first six books of Euclid's *Elements* for secondary schools, and he edited Leonardo da Vinci's *Codice Atlantico,* an important source for the history of science and technology.

An adherent of pure mathematics, Brioschi highly valued its significance in application and allotted to it a significant place in technical education, emphasizing the great role of the latter in the development of national industry. At the same time he insisted on the value of the humanities and, simultaneously with his founding of the Politechnicum, he organized the Accademia Scientifica-Litteraria in Milan.

In addition to the publication of the *Codice Atlantico,* Brioschi produced several important articles on contemporary mathematicians.

BIBLIOGRAPHY

I. Original Works. Many of Brioschi's writings have been brought together in Ascoli *et al.*, eds., *Opere,* 5 vols. (Milan, 1901–1908). Among individual works of note are *Teoria dei determinanti* (Pavia, 1854) and "La teoria dei covarianti e degli invarianti delle forme binarie, e le sue principali applicazioni," in *Annali di matematica,* **1** (1858), 269–309, 549–561; **2** (1859), 82–85, 265–277; **3** (1860), 160–168; **4** (1861), 186–194.

II. Secondary Literature. The fullest characterization of Brioschi's scientific work is in M. Noether, "Francesco Brioschi," in *Mathematische Annalen,* **50** (1898), 477–491. On Brioschi as an engineer, see E. Paladini, "Commemorazione di F. Brioschi," in *Atti del Collegio degli ingegneri ed architetti* (Milan), **30** (1898). See also E. Beltrami's obituary notice of Brioschi in *Annali di matematica,* 2nd ser., **26** (1897), 340–342; Charles Hermite, "Notice sur M. F. Brioschi," in *Comptes rendus de l'Académie des sciences,* **125** (1897), 1139–1141; and the speeches given at Brioschi's funeral, in *Reale Istituto tecnico superiore, programma 1891–1898* (Milan, 1898).

Joseph Pogrebyssky

BRIOT, CHARLES AUGUSTE (*b.* St.-Hippolyte, France, 19 July 1817; *d.* Bourg-d'Ault, France, 20 September 1882)

Briot's father, Auguste, a merchant at St.-Hippolyte, had a considerable reputation in the tanning trade. Charles, the eldest of a large family, became a teacher after an accident that left him with a stiff arm. He was sent to Paris and in only five years attained a remarkable level of scholarship. When he entered the École Normale Supérieure in 1838, he was ranked second. Three years later he completed the course and received his *agrégation* in mathematics with the highest rank. In March 1842 he received his doctorate of science, having presented his thesis on the movement of a solid body round a fixed point. This brilliant success lit the way for a group of young men from his native Franche-Comté: Claude Bouquet, L. E. Bertin, and Louis Pasteur.

Briot devoted himself to teaching, first as a professor at the Orléans Lycée and afterward at the University of Lyons, where he reencountered his friend Claude Bouquet. In 1851 he moved to Paris, where he taught the course in *mathématiques speciales* (preparation for the École Normale Supérieure and the École Polytechnique) at the Lycée Bonaparte and later at the Lycée Saint-Louis, as well as acting as substitute at both the École Polytechnique and the Faculté des Sciences for the courses in mechanical engineering and surveying (1850), calculus (1853), and mechanics and astronomy (1855). From 1864 on, he was a professor at the Sorbonne and at the École Normale Supérieure. In his courses he particularly stressed the relation between thermodynamics and rational mechanics.

Briot's studies on heat, light, and electricity were based on the hypothesis of the existence in the ether of imponderable molecules acting upon each other, as well as upon the ponderable molecules of matter. Particularly in his study of the crystalline medium, he linked his findings to Pasteur's experimental work on the dissymmetry of crystals. These studies, which were conducted from a mathematical point of view, led to the simplification of methods for integral calculus and the advance of the theories of elliptic and Abelian functions. To honor him for this work, the Göttingen Academy named him a corresponding member.

A large part of Briot's activity was devoted to the writing of textbooks for students, so that he and Bouquet could provide them with a library of basic books on arithmetic, algebra, calculus, geometry, analytical geometry, and mechanics. These books were published in numerous editions and for many years contributed to establishing the level of mathematics teaching in France. Briot also published, with Bouquet, an important work on elliptic functions (1875) and, alone, a treatise on Abelian functions (1879). The Académie des Sciences awarded Briot the Poncelet Prize in 1882 for his work in mathematics.

BIBLIOGRAPHY

Briot's works include "Recherches sur la théorie des fonctions," in *Journal de l'École Polytechnique* (1859), also published as an independent work (Paris, 1859); *Théorie des fonctions doublement périodiques,* written with Bouquet, 2 vols. (Paris, 1859; 2nd ed., 1875); *Essai sur la théorie mathématique de la lumière* (Paris, 1864); *Théorie mécanique de la chaleur* (Paris, 1869); *Théorie des fonctions elliptiques,* written with Bouquet (Paris, 1875); and *Théorie des fonctions abéliennes* (Paris, 1879).

LUCIENNE FÉLIX

BRISSON, BARNABÉ (*b.* Lyons, France, 11 October 1777; *d.* Nevers, France, 25 September 1828)

The son of Antoine-François Brisson, inspector of commerce and manufacture for the financial district of Lyons, Brisson studied at the Collège Oratorien de Juilly and was admitted to the École des Ponts et Chaussées in December 1793. A year later, at the newly founded École Centrale des Travaux Publics (the future École Polytechnique), he became one of the brilliant team of aspiring instructors and was highly thought of by Gaspard Monge. In December 1796, upon graduation from this school, he was admitted to the Corps des Ponts et Chaussées, where he remained for the rest of his career.

After completing his professional training at the École des Ponts et Chaussées in May 1798, Brisson specialized in the design and construction of ship canals. In 1802 he and his colleague Pierre-Louis Dupuis-Torcy presented a brilliant memoir based on applying methods of descriptive geometry to the determination of crest lines and of thalwegs, as well as establishing the course of the canals. After having been the civil engineer for the department of Doubs, he collaborated from 1802 to 1809 in the construction of the Canal de St.-Quentin, and then in the extension of the dikes and canals of the department of l'Escaut (until 1814). Appointed professor of stereometry and construction at the École des Ponts et Chaussées in 1820, he later assumed the additional duties of inspector for the school (from 1821) and secretary of the Conseil Royal des Ponts et Chaussées (from 1824).

Brisson remained one of Monge's favorite disciples, and his marriage in 1808 to Anne-Constance Huart, the latter's niece, strengthened his admiration and affection for the famous geometer. In 1820 he edited the fourth edition of Monge's *Géométrie descriptive* and finished off the work with two previously unpublished chapters on the theory of shadows and on perspective, which he revised with great care. But his favorite field of study was the theory of partial differential equations. Brisson drew up two important reports on this subject. One was read before the Académie des Sciences by Biot, his fellow student at the École Polytechnique and his brother-in-law. This paper was published in 1808. The other was read in 1823 and was not published. The main idea in these reports was the application of functional calculus, through symbols, to the solution of certain kinds of linear differential equations and of linear equations with finite differences.

The 1823 report was the object of lively discussion in 1825 before the Academy and was approved of by Cauchy, who, although he had some reservations about the validity of some of the symbols used and the equations obtained, emphasized the elegance of the method and the importance of the objects to which they were applied. Cauchy followed the way opened by Brisson, who thus became one of those who developed the methods of functional calculus.

BIBLIOGRAPHY

I. ORIGINAL WORKS. Brisson's writings include "Essai sur l'art de projeter les canaux de navigation," in *Journal de l'École polytechnique,* **7**, no. 14 (Apr. 1808), 262–288; "Mémoire sur l'intégration des équations différentielles partielles," *ibid.,* 191–261; *Notice historique sur Gaspard Monge* (Paris, 1818); *Nouvelle collection de 530 dessins ou feuilles de textes relatifs à l'art de l'ingénieur et lithographiés . . . sous la direction de M. Brisson,* 2 vols. (Paris, 1821–1825); and *Essai sur le système général de navigation intérieure* *de la France* (Paris, 1829).

II. SECONDARY LITERATURE. Biographical sketches of Brisson are A. Debauve, *Les travaux publics et les ingénieurs des ponts et chaussées depuis le XVIIe siècle* (Paris, 1893), pp. 381–382; *École polytechnique—Livre du centenaire,* III (Paris, 1895), 62–64, *passim.;* F. Hoefer, in *Nouvelle biographie générale,* VII (1863), cols. 436–437; H. Massiani, in *Dictionnaire de biographie française,* VII (1956), col. 364; J. and L. G. Michaud, *Biographie universelle,* new ed., V (1843), 565–567; *Le moniteur* (19 Oct. 1828); N. Nielsen, *Géomètres français sous la Révolution* (Paris, 1937), pp. 37–38, 83–84; J. Petot, *Histoire de l'Administration des ponts et chaussées (1599–1815)* (Paris, 1955); S. Pincherle, "Opérations fonctionnelles," in *Encyclopédie des sciences mathématiques,* II, fasc. 26, 10; Poggendorff, III (1898), col. 196; and *Procès verbaux de l'Académie des sciences,* VIII (Hendaye, 1918), 223–226.

RENÉ TATON

BROCARD, PIERRE RENÉ JEAN-BAPTISTE HENRI (*b.* Vignot, France, 12 May 1845; *d.* Bar-le-Duc, France, 16 January 1922)

Henri Brocard, born in a small, unpretentious town in northeastern France, was the son of Jean Sebastien and Elizabeth Auguste Liouville Brocard. No record has been found of brothers, sisters, or other close relatives, and Brocard never married. He is now known chiefly for his work in the geometry of the triangle, but he is also remembered as a French army officer and a meteorologist.

For some time, knowledge of Brocard's life fell far short of knowledge about the Brocard configuration, on which his renown rests. This was remedied by an autobiographical account published in 1894 at Bar-le-Duc. It covers the first fifty years of Brocard's life and tells of his mathematical and scientific publications and activities. He sent a copy of this pamphlet to the Smithsonian Institution shortly after its publication.

Brocard received his early education at the *lycée* of Marseilles, and the *lycée* and academy of Strasbourg. He attended the École Polytechnique from 1865 to 1867, and then joined the Corps of Engineers of the French army. It is known that he was a prisoner of war at Sedan in 1870, but for the most part his army career was devoted to teaching and research rather than to active combat. He became a life member of the newly organized Société Mathématique de France in 1873, and in 1875 he was made a life member of the Association Française pour l'Avancement des Sciences and of the Société Météorologique de France. For several years after 1874 he was assigned to service in north Africa, chiefly in Algiers and Oran. He was a co-founder of the Meteorological Institute at Algiers.

As a member of the local committee for the tenth session of the Association Française pour l'Avancement des Sciences, which met in Algiers in 1881, he presented a paper entitled "Étude d'un nouveau cercle du plan du triangle." It was in this paper that he announced the discovery of the circle that is now known by his name. In 1884 he returned to Montpellier, where he had taught for a short time after his graduation from the École Polytechnique.

There followed appointments to many government commissions and many scientific honors. Brocard served with the Meteorological Commission at Montpellier, Grenoble, and Bar-le-Duc. In 1894 he became a member of the Society of Letters, Sciences, and Arts of Bar-le-Duc; and it is through the publications of this society that one can follow the activities of the last twenty-six years of his life. His scientific and mathematical publications began when he was about twenty-three, and over the years showed him to be an indefatigable correspondent with the editors of mathematical and scientific journals. Brocard contributed to *Nouvelles annales de mathématiques, Bulletin de la Société mathématique de France, Mathesis, Zeitschrift für mathematischen und naturwissenschaftlichen Unterricht, Educational Times, El progreso matemático, L'intermédiaire des mathématiciens,* and many others. In his autobiography, a brief descriptive paragraph of about three or four lines is devoted to each journal, giving the names of the editors, the dates of publication, etc. These paragraphs provide a succinct and handy source of information, particularly for journals that later ceased publication.

Brocard's most extensive publication was a large, two-part work entitled *Notes de bibliographie des courbes géométriques,* followed by *Courbes géométriques remarquables,* which appeared under the joint authorship of Brocard and T. Lemoyne. The first part of the earlier work appeared in 1897, and the second in 1899. Probably no more than about fifty copies of this work were prepared, lithographed in the printscript of the author, and privately distributed. The *Notes* may be regarded as a source book of geometric curves, with a painstakingly prepared index containing more than a thousand named curves. The text consists of brief descriptive paragraphs, with diagrams and equations of these curves. About twenty years later, Volume I of the projected three-volume work *Courbes géométriques remarquables* was published in Paris. In 1967 both Volume II and a new edition of Volume I were published in Paris. *Courbes géométriques remarquables* is described as an outgrowth of *Notes de bibliographie des courbes géométriques.*

During the latter part of his life, Brocard made his home in Bar-le-Duc. He lived completely alone and rarely had visitors. He obviously enjoyed his membership in, and his work as librarian of, the Society of Letters, Sciences, and Arts of Bar-le-Duc, although he had declined the honor of becoming president. Largely through his efforts, one of the streets of Bar-le-Duc was named for Louis Joblot, a native Barisian who was an acknowledged but almost forgotten pioneer in the field of microscopy. When he retired from the army in 1910, Brocard was a lieutenant colonel and an officer in the Legion of Honor. In his retirement he spent much of his time making astronomical observations with a small telescope in the garden behind his house. Every fourth year he took a long trip to the meetings of the International Congress of Mathematicians.

The unit of mathematical theory identified as the Brocard configuration is founded upon two points, O and O', in a triangle ABC such that the angles OAB, OBC, and OCA, and the angles $O'BA$, $O'CB$, and $O'AC$ are equal. Brocard readily admitted that he had no claim to priority in the discovery of the existence of these points. Yet his influence upon his contemporaries was so great that the points O and O' are now universally recognized as the Brocard points of a triangle.

Of the several solutions available for the construction of the Brocard points of a triangle, the most striking and familiar is one in which circles are drawn as follows: A circle tangent to side AB of triangle ABC at A and passing through C; a second circle tangent to BC at B and passing through A; and a third circle tangent to CA at C and passing through B. It is easily proved that these three circles are concurrent at a point O which satisfies the above conditions (see Figure 1). Point O' is obtained in a similar manner, after a slight modification in procedure. The angle OAB (angle W) is called the Brocard angle of triangle ABC, and it is a simple matter to prove that

$$\cot W = \cot A + \cot B + \cot C.$$

Obviously a similar relation holds for angle $O'BA$ (angle W'). Brocard's truly original contribution to the theory of the geometry of the triangle was his discovery of the circle drawn on the line segment PK as diameter, where P is the circumcenter of the triangle and K is its symmedian point. This circle, called the Brocard circle of a triangle, passes through the points O and O' and has many additional interesting geometric properties.

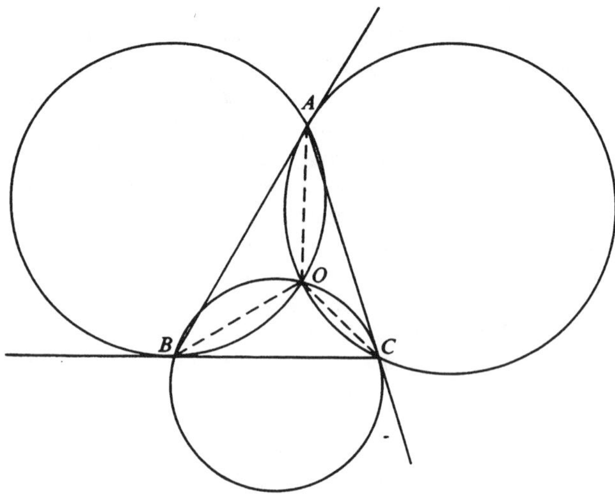

FIGURE 1

During the last decade of the nineteenth century several books were published about the Brocard configuration. The subject, which stirred the imagination and aroused the enthusiasm of many mathematicians in different parts of the world, has remained a pleasant and fruitful topic for discussion.

On 16 January 1922, Brocard was found dead at his desk. In accordance with his specific request, he was buried in the small cemetery at Vignot, next to his father and mother.

BIBLIOGRAPHY

I. ORIGINAL WORKS. Brocard's works are *Notice sur les titres et travaux scientifiques* (Bar-le-Duc, 1895); *Notes de bibliographie des courbes géométriques,* 2 vols. (Bar-le-Duc, 1897–1899); and *Courbes géométriques remarquables,* 2 vols. (I, Paris, 1920; new ed., 1967; II, Paris, 1967), written with T. Lemoyne.

II. SECONDARY LITERATURE. Works dealing with Brocard are Lucien Braye, "De New York à Bar-le-Duc sur les traces d'un théorème," in *L'est républicain,* Bar-le-Duc sec. (16 Sept. 1951); A. Emmerich, *Die Brocard'schen Gebilde* (Berlin, 1891); Laura Guggenbuhl, *Concerning Notes de bibliographie des courbes géométriques* (New York, 1951), and "Henri Brocard and the Geometry of the Triangle," in *Mathematical Gazette,* **32,** no. 322 (Dec. 1953), 241–243, also in *Proceedings of the International Congress of Mathematicians,* II (Amsterdam, 1954), 420–421; and Roger A. Johnson, *Modern Geometry* (Boston, 1929), chs. 12, 16, 17, 18; repr. in paperback as *Advanced Euclidean Geometry* (New York, 1960). Illustration courtesy of *Mathematical Gazette.*

LAURA GUGGENBUHL

BROMWICH, THOMAS JOHN I'ANSON (*b.* Wolverhampton, England, 8 February 1875; *d.* Northhampton, England, 26 August 1929)

Bromwich, whose father was a woolen draper, received his early education in Wolverhampton and in Durban, South Africa, where the family immigrated. He entered Cambridge in October 1892 as a pensioner of Saint John's College and graduated three years later as senior wrangler in a class that included E. T. Whittaker and J. H. Grace. He obtained a fellowship in 1897 but left Cambridge in 1902 to become professor of mathematics at Queen's College, Galway. Bromwich returned in 1907 as permanent lecturer in mathematics at Saint John's College and received the Sc.D. in 1909. He was elected to the Royal Society in 1906 and was active in the London Mathematical Society, serving as its secretary (1911–1919) and vice-president (1919, 1920). The first two decades of Bromwich's career were distinguished by numerous publications and vigorous teaching, but mental affliction led to diminished productivity in his later years and eventually to suicide.

Described by G. H. Hardy as the "best pure mathematician among the applied mathematicians at Cambridge, and the best applied mathematician among the pure mathematicians," Bromwich was well known for his precision, mastery of technique, and skill in algebraic manipulation. But Hardy also described Bromwich as lacking the power of "thinking vaguely" and Bromwich's work as "a little wanting in imagination."

The author of two books, two pamphlets, and some eighty papers, Bromwich is best known for his encyclopedic *Introduction to the Theory of Infinite Series* (1908). Although this book has been praised for its richness of detail and its abundance of examples, it has also been criticized for defects in its general structure—for example, its frequent failure to set off and to emphasize fundamental ideas. The book, based on Bromwich's lectures at Galway, incorporates many of his own researches separately published between 1903 and 1908.

Another series of researches culminated in Bromwich's Cambridge Tract, *Quadratic Forms and Their Classification by Means of Invariant Factors* (1906). In these publications Bromwich's creative powers are most fully evident, for in them he both introduced English readers to Kronecker's ideas and methods in the theory of quadratic and bilinear forms and advanced the knowledge of these forms.

Bromwich's first publication, as well as many later papers, was in applied mathematics. Especially under the influence of George Stokes, Bromwich did significant work in the mathematics of electromagnetism and of other subjects as well (including lawn tennis). Most memorable is a series of papers that began in 1916 with "Normal Coordinates in Dynamical Systems." In this paper Bromwich indicated how Oliver Heaviside's much criticized calculus of symbolic operators could be developed in a manner acceptable to pure mathematicians by treating his operators as contour integrals.

BIBLIOGRAPHY

I. Original Works. Bromwich's two books are *Quadratic Forms and Their Classification by Means of Invariant Factors* (Cambridge, 1906); and *An Introduction to the Theory of Infinite Series* (London, 1908, 1926). For a bibliography of his papers, see below.

II. Secondary Literature. Articles on Bromwich are G. H. Hardy, "Thomas John I'Anson Bromwich," in *Journal of the London Mathematical Society,* **5** (1930), 209–220; and Harold Jeffreys, "Bromwich's Work on Operational Methods," *ibid.,* 220–223. See also G. H. Hardy, *Proceedings of the Royal Society of London* (Section A), **129** (1930), i–x. All three of the above articles include bibliographies; the last includes a portrait. See also "Bromwich," in *Alumni Cantabrigienses,* Part II, Vol. I (Cambridge, 1940), 392.

Michael J. Crowe

BROUNCKER, WILLIAM (*b.* 1620; *d.* Westminster, London, England, 5 April 1684)

Brouncker's father was Sir William Brouncker, who was created viscount of Castle Lyons, Ireland, in September 1645; the father died the same November, and was succeeded by the son. The title passed to William's brother Henry in 1684, and since both were unmarried, became extinct when Henry died in 1687. William's mother was Winefrid, daughter of William Leigh of Newenham, Warwickshire.

Brouncker entered Oxford University at the age of sixteen and showed proficiency in mathematics, languages, and medicine. He received the degree of Doctor of Physick in 1647, and for the next few years devoted himself mainly to mathematics.

He held several offices of prominence: Member of Parliament for Westbury in 1660, president of Gresham College from 1664 to 1667, commissioner for the navy from 1664 to 1668, comptroller of the treasurer's accounts from 1668 to 1679, and master of St. Catherine's Hospital near the Tower from 1681 to 1684.

Brouncker was the king's nominee for president of the Royal Society, and he was appointed without opposition—at a time when there were many talented scientists. He was reappointed annually, and he guarded his position zealously, possibly holding on to it for too long. He resigned in 1677, in effect at the suggestion of an election, and was succeeded by Sir Joseph Williamson. He was an enthusiastic supporter of the society's bias toward experimentation and was very energetic in suggesting and assessing experimental work until Hooke took over that job. Sprat's history records two experiments performed by Brouncker, one on the increase of weight in metals due to burning and the other on the recoil of guns.

His major scientific work was undoubtedly in mathematics. Much of his work was done in correspondence with John Wallis and was published in the latter's books.

One of Wallis' major achievements was an expression for π in the form of an infinite product, recorded in his *Arithmetica infinitorum.* This book states that Brouncker was asked to give an alternative expression, which he did in terms of continued fractions, first used by Cataldi in 1613, as

$$\frac{4}{\pi} = 1 + \frac{1^2}{2+}\frac{3^2}{2+}\frac{5^2}{2+}\cdots,$$

from which he calculated π correct to ten decimal places.

In an exchange of letters between Fermat and Wallis, the French mathematician had proposed for general solution the Diophantine equation $ax^2 + 1 = y^2$. Brouncker was able to supply an answer equivalent to $x = 2r/r^2 - a, y = r^2 + a/r^2 - a$, where r is any integer, as well as another answer in terms of continued fractions.

A paper in the *Philosophical Transactions* (**3** [1668], 753–764) gives a solution by Brouncker of the quadrature of a rectangular hyperbola. He arrived at a result equivalent to

$$\int_0^1 \frac{dx}{1+x} = \frac{1}{1\cdot 2} + \frac{1}{3\cdot 4} + \frac{1}{5\cdot 6} + \cdots$$

or

$$1 - \frac{1}{2} + \frac{1}{3} - \frac{1}{4} + \cdots,$$

and found similar infinite series related to this problem. In order to calculate the sum, he discussed the convergence of the series and was able to compute it as 0.69314709, recognizing this number as proportional to log 2. By varying the problem slightly, he was able to show that 2.302585 was proportional to log 10.

Brouncker also improved Neile's method for rectifying the semicubical parabola $ay^2 = x^3$ and made at least three attempts to prove Huygen's assertion that the cycloidal pendulum was isochronous. A letter from Collins to James Gregory indicates that Brouncker knew how to "turn the square root into an infinite series," possibly an allusion to the binomial series.

Brouncker was a close associate of Samuel Pepys, socially and professionally, and is mentioned many times in the *Diary.* Pepys valued his friendship highly, but sometimes doubted his professional ability. Brouncker shared with Pepys an interest in music, and his only published book is a translation (1653) of Descartes's *Musicae compendium* with notes as long as the work itself, including a mathematical attempt to divide the diapason into seventeen equal semitones.

His fame as a mathematician rests largely on an ability to solve problems set by others. If he had devoted himself more fully to his own studies, he would undoubtedly have been one of the best mathematicians during a period in which talent abounded.

A portrait by Sir Peter Lely is in the possession of the Royal Society.

BIBLIOGRAPHY

Works concerning Brouncker or his work are E. S. de Beer, ed., *The Diary of John Evelyn,* III (Oxford, 1955), 285–286, 332, 353; T. Birch, *History of the Royal Society,* Vol. I (London, 1756–1757); Lord Braybrooke, ed., *Diary and Correspondence of Samuel Pepys* (London, 1865); Sir B. Burke, *Extinct Peerages* (London, 1883), p. 78; M. H. Nicolson, *Pepys' Diary and the New Science* (Charlottesville, Va., 1965), pp. 11, 28–29, 109, 135; H. W. Robinson and W. Adams, *The Diary of Robert Hooke* (London, 1935); J. F. Scott and Sir Harold Hartley, "William Viscount Brouncker," in *Notes and Records of the Royal Society,* **15** (1960–1961), 147–156; T. Sprat, *History of the Royal Society* (London, 1667), pp. 57, 136, 228–229; J. Wallis, *Arithmetica infinitorum* (Oxford, 1656), p. 181; *Tractatus duo* (Oxford, 1659), p. 92; *A Treatise of Algebra* (Oxford, 1685), p. 363; D. T. Whiteside, "Brouncker's Mathematical Papers," in *Notes and Records of the Royal Society,* **15** (1960–1961), 157; A. à Wood, *Athenae oxonienses,* P. Bliss, ed. (London, 1820), p. 98.

JOHN DUBBEY

BROUWER, LUITZEN EGBERTUS JAN (*b.* Overschie, Netherlands, 27 February 1881; *d.* Blaricum, Netherlands, 2 December 1966)

Brouwer first showed his unusual intellectual abilities by finishing high school in the North Holland town of Hoorn at the age of fourteen. In the next two years he mastered the Greek and Latin required for admission to the university, and passed the entrance examination at the municipal Gymnasium in Haarlem, where the family had moved in the meantime. In the same year, 1897, he entered the University of Amsterdam, where he studied mathematics until 1904. He quickly mastered the current mathematics, and, to the admiration of his professor, D. J. Korteweg, he obtained some results on continuous motions in four-dimensional space that were published in the reports of the Royal Academy of Science in Amsterdam in 1904. Through his own reading, as well as through the stimulating lectures of Gerrit Mannoury, he became acquainted with topology and the foundations of mathematics. His great interest in philosophy, especially in mysticism, led him to develop a personal view of human activity and society that he expounded in *Leven, Kunst, en Mystiek* ("Life, Art, and Mysticism"; 1905), where he considers as one of the important moving principles in human activity the transition from goal to means, which after some repetitions may result in activities opposed to the original goal.

Brouwer reacted vigorously to the debate between Russell and Poincaré on the logical foundations of mathematics. These reactions were expressed in his doctoral thesis, *Over de Grondslagen der Wiskunde* ("On the Foundations of Mathematics"; 1907). In general he sided with Poincaré in his opposition to Russell's and Hilbert's ideas about the foundations of mathematics. He strongly disagreed with Poincaré, however, in his opinion on mathematical existence. To Brouwer, mathematical existence did not mean freedom from contradiction, as Poincaré maintained, but intuitive constructibility.

Brouwer conceived of mathematics as a free activity of the mind constructing mathematical objects, starting from self-evident primitive notions (primordial intuition). Formal logic had its *raison d'être* as a means of describing regularities in the systems thus constructed. It had no value whatsoever for the foundation of mathematics, and the postulation of absolute validity of logical principles was questionable. This held in particular for the principle of the excluded third, briefly expressed by $A \vee \neg A$—that is, A or not A—which he identified with Hilbert's statement of the solvability of every mathematical problem. The axiomatic foundation of mathematics, whether or not supplemented by a consistency proof as envisaged by Hilbert, was mercilessly rejected; and he argued that Hilbert would not be able to prove the consistency of arithmetic while keeping to his finitary program. But even if Hilbert succeeded, Brouwer continued, this would not ensure the existence (in Brouwer's sense) of a mathematical system described by the axioms.

In 1908 Brouwer returned to the question in *Over de Onbetrouwbaarheid der logische Principes* ("On the Untrustworthiness of the Logical Principles") and—probably under the influence of Mannoury's review of his thesis—rejected the principle of the excluded third, even for his constructive conception of mathematics (afterward called intuitionistic mathematics).

Brouwer's mathematical activity was influenced by Hilbert's address on mathematical problems at the Second International Congress of Mathematicians in Paris (1900) and by Schoenflies' report on the development of set theory. From 1907 to 1912 Brouwer engaged in a great deal of research, much of it yielding fundamental results. In 1907 he attacked Hilbert's formidable fifth problem, to treat the theory of continuous groups independently of assumptions on differentiability, but with fragmentary results. Definitive results for compact groups were obtained much later by John von Neumann in 1934 and for locally compact groups in 1952 by A. M. Gleason and D. Montgomery and L. Zippin.

In connection with this problem—a natural consequence of Klein's Erlanger program—Brouwer discovered the plane translation theorem, which gives a homotopic characterization of the topological mappings of the Cartesian plane, and his first fixed point theorem, which states that any orientation preserving one-to-one continuous (topological) mapping of the two-dimensional sphere into itself leaves invariant at least one point (fixed point). He generalized this theorem to spheres of higher dimension. In particular, the theorem that any continuous mapping of the n-dimensional ball into itself has a fixed point, generalized by J. Schauder in 1930 to continuous operators on Banach spaces, has proved to be of great importance in numerical mathematics.

The existence of one-to-one correspondences between numerical spaces R_n for different n, shown by Cantor, together with Peano's subsequent example (1890) of a continuous mapping of the unit segment onto the square, had induced mathematicians to conjecture that topological mappings of numerical spaces R_n would preserve the number n (dimension). In 1910 Brouwer proved this conjecture for arbitrary n.

His method of simplicial approximation of continuous mappings (that is, approximation by piecewise linear mappings) and the notion of degree of a mapping, a number depending on the equivalence class of continuous deformations of a topological mapping (homotopy class), proved to be powerful enough to solve the most important invariance problems, such as that of the notion of n-dimensional domain (solved by Brouwer) and that of the invariance of Betti numbers (solved by J. W. Alexander).

Finally, mention may be made of his discovery of indecomposable continua in the plane (1910) as common boundary of denumerably many, simply connected domains; of his proof of the generalization to n-dimensional space of the Jordan curve theorem (1912); and of his definition of dimension of topological spaces (1913).

In 1912 Brouwer was appointed a professor of mathematics at the University of Amsterdam, and in the same year he was elected a member of the Royal Netherlands Academy of Science. His inaugural address was not on topology, as one might have expected, but on intuitionism and formalism.

He again took up the question of the foundations of mathematics. There was no progress, however, in the reconstruction of mathematics according to intuitionistic principles, the stumbling block apparently being a satisfactory notion of the constructive continuum. The first appearance of such a notion was in his review (1914) of the Schoenflies-Hahn report on the development of set theory. In the following years he scrutinized the problem of a constructive foundation of set theory and came fully to realize the role of the principle of the excluded third. In 1918 he published a set theory independent of this logical principle; it was followed in 1919 by a constructive theory of measure and in 1923 by a theory of functions. The difficulty involved in a constructive theory of sets is that in contrast with axiomatic set theory, the notion of set cannot be taken as primitive, but must be explained. In Brouwer's theory this is accomplished by the introduction of the notion of free-choice sequence, that is, an infinitely proceeding sequence of choices from a set of objects (e.g., natural numbers) for which the set of all possible choices is specified by a law. Moreover, after every choice, restrictions may be added for future possible choices. The specifying law is called a spread, and the ever-unfinished free-choice sequences it allows are called its elements. The spread is called finitary if it allows only choices from a finite number of possibilities. In particular, the intuitionistic continuum can be looked upon as given by a finitary spread. By interpreting the statement "All elements of a spread have property p" to mean "I have a construction that enables me to decide, after a finite number of choices of the choice sequence α, that it has property p," and by reflection on the nature of such a construction, Brouwer derived his so-called fundamental theorem on finitary spreads (the fan theorem). This theorem asserts that if an integer-valued function, f, has been defined on a finitary spread, S, then a natural number, n, can be computed such that, for any two free-choice sequences, α and β, of S that coincide in their first n choices, we have $f(\alpha) = f(\beta)$.

This theorem, whose proof is still not quite accepted, enabled Brouwer to derive results that diverge strongly from what is known from ordinary mathematics, e.g., the indecomposability of the intuitionistic continuum and the uniform continuity of real functions defined on it.

From 1923 on, Brouwer repeatedly elucidated the role of the principle of the excluded third in mathematics and tried to convince mathematicians that it must be rejected as a valid means of proof. In this connection, that the principle is noncontradictory, that is, that $\neg\neg(A \vee \neg A)$ holds, is a serious disadvantage. Using the fan theorem, however, he succeeded in showing that what he called the general principle of the excluded third is contradictory, that is, there are properties for which it is contradictory that for all elements of a finitary spread, the property either holds or does not hold—briefly, $\neg(\forall\alpha)(P(\alpha) \vee \neg P(\alpha))$ holds.

In the late 1920's the attention of logicians was drawn to Brouwer's logic, and its relation to classical logic was investigated. The breakdown of Hilbert's foundational program through the decisive work of Kurt Gödel and the rise of the theory of recursive functions has ultimately led to a revival of the study of intuitionistic foundations of mathematics, mainly through the pioneering work of S. C. Kleene after World War II. It centers on a formal description of intuitionistic analysis, a major problem in today's foundational research.

Although Brouwer did not succeed in converting mathematicians, his work received international recognition. He held honorary degrees from various universities, including Oslo (1929) and Cambridge (1955). He was elected to membership in many scientific societies, such as the German Academy of Science, Berlin (1919); the American Philosophical Society, Philadelphia (1943); and the Royal Society of London (1948).

BIBLIOGRAPHY

I. Original Works. "Over een splitsing van de continue beweging om een vast punt 0 van R_4 in twee continue bewegingen om 0 van R_3's," in *Verslagen. Koninklijke akademie van wetenschappen te Amsterdam,* **12** (1904), 819–839; *Leven, Kunst en Mystiek* (Delft, 1905); *Over de Grondslagen der Wiskunde* (Amsterdam, 1907); "Over de onbetrouwbaarheid der logische principes," in *Tijdschrift voor wijsbegeerte,* **2** (1908), 152–158; "Die Theorie der endlichen Kontinuierlichen Gruppen, unabhängig von den Axiomen von Lie (erste Mitteilung)," in *Mathematische Annalen,* **67** (1909), 246–267, and "... (zweite Mitteilung)," *ibid.,* **69** (1910), 181–203; "Zur Analysis Situs," *ibid.,* **68**

(1910), 422–434; "Beweis des Jordanschen Kurvensatzes," *ibid.,* **69** (1910), 169–175; "Beweis des Jordanschen Satzes für den n-dimensionalen Raum," *ibid.,* **71** (1912), 314–319; "Über eineindeutige, stetige Transformationen von Flächen in sich," *ibid.,* **69** (1910), 176–180; "Beweis der Invarianz der Dimensionenzahl," *ibid.,* **70** (1911), 161–165; "Über Abbildung von Mannigfaltigkeiten," *ibid.,* **71** (1912), 97–115, 598; "Beweis der Invarianz des n-dimensionalen Gebietes," *ibid.,* **71** (1912), 305–313; "Zur Invarianz des n-dimensionalen Gebiets," *ibid.,* **72** (1912), 55–56; "Beweis des ebenen Translationssatzes," *ibid.,* **72** (1912), 37–54; "Beweis der Invarianz der geschlossene Kurve," *ibid.,* **72** (1912), 422–425; "Über den natürlichen Dimensionsbegriff," in *Journal für die reine und angewandte Mathematik,* **142** (1913), 146–152; "Intuitionism and Formalism," in *Bulletin of the American Mathematical Society,* **20** (1913), 81–96; review of A. Schoenflies and H. Hahn, *Die Entwicklung der Mengenlehre und ihrer Anwendungen. Erste Hälfte. Allgemeine Theorie der unendlichen Mengen und Theorie der Punktmengen* (Leipzig–Berlin, 1913), in *Jahresbericht der Deutschen Mathematikervereinigung,* **23** (1914), 78–83; "Begründung der Mengenlehre unabhängig vom logischen Satz vom ausgeschlossenen Dritten. Erster Teil: Allgemeine Mengenlehre," in *Verhandelingen Koninklijke akademie van wetenschappen te Amsterdam,* **12,** no. 5 (1918), 1–43, and ". . . II. Theorie der Punktmengen," *ibid.,* **12,** no. 7 (1919), 1–33; "Begründung der Funktionenlehre unabhängig vom logischen Satz vom ausgeschlossenen Dritten. Erster Teil: Stetigkeit, Messbarkeit, Derivierbarkeit," *ibid.,* **13,** no. 2 (1923), 1–24; "Intuitionistische Einführung des Dimensionsbegriffes," in *Proceedings. Koninklijke akademie van wetenschappen te Amsterdam,* **29** (1926), 855–863; "Über Definitionsbereiche von Funktionen," in *Mathematische Annalen,* **97** (1927), 60–75; "Essentially Negative Properties," in *Proceedings. Koninklijke akademie van wetenschappen te Amsterdam,* **51** (1948), 963–964; "Consciousness, Philosophy and Mathematics," in *Proceedings of the Tenth International Congress of Philosophy,* I (Amsterdam, 1949), 1235–1249. For Brouwer's topological work, consult the book by Alexandroff and Hopf listed below. Extensive bibliographies of his foundational work may be found in the books by Heyting and Van Heijenoort (see below). A complete edition of Brouwer's work is planned by the Dutch Mathematical Society.

II. SECONDARY LITERATURE. Brouwer or his work is discussed in P. Alexandroff and H. Hopf, *Topologie* (Berlin, 1935), *passim;* P. Benacerraf and H. Putnam, *Philosophy of Mathematics* (Englewood Cliffs, N.J., 1964), pp. 66–84; J. van Heijenoort, *From Frege to Gödel, a Source Book in Mathematical Logic, 1879–1931* (Cambridge, Mass., 1967), pp. 334–345, 446–463, 490–492; A. Heyting, *Intuitionism, An Introduction* (Amsterdam, 1965), *passim;* S. Lefschetz, *Introduction to Topology* (Princeton, N.J., 1949), pp. 1–26, 117–131; S. C. Kleene and R. E. Vesley, *The Foundations of Intuitionistic Mathematics* (Amsterdam, 1965); G. Kreisel, "Functions, Ordinals, Species," in *Logic, Methodology and Philosophy of Science,* III, ed. B. van Rootselaar and J. F. Staal (Amsterdam, 1968), pp. 145–159; J. Myhill, "Formal Systems of Intuitionistic Analysis I," *ibid.,* pp. 161–178; A. S. Troelstra, "The Theory of Choice Sequences," *ibid.,* pp. 201–223.

B. VAN ROOTSELAAR

BROŻEK (or **Broscius**), **JAN** (*b.* Kurzelow, near Sieradz, Poland, November 1585; *d.* Krakow, Poland, 21 November 1652)

Brożek's father, Jakub, was an educated landowner who taught his son the art of writing and the principles of geometry. Jan went to primary school in Kurzelow and then to the University of Krakow, where he passed his baccalaureate in March 1605. Among his professors were Stanislaw Jacobeius and Walenty Fontanus. In March 1610 Brożek won the rank of *magister,* and in 1611 he was ordained a priest. His contacts with Adriaan Van Roomen (Romanus), an eminent Belgian mathematician then in Krakow, greatly influenced his studies.

Early in 1614 Brożek became a professor at the Collegium Minus of the University of Krakow, where he was assigned the chair of astrology, and in 1619 at the Collegium Maius. In 1618 he traveled to Torun, Danzig, and Frombork to gather material on Copernicus. In 1620, at Innsbruck, he met the astronomer Christoph Scheiner. From June 1620 to June 1624 Brożek studied medicine in Padua, receiving his doctorate in medicine in 1624, and was physician to the bishop of Krakow until the autumn of 1625. In 1625 the University of Krakow elected him professor of rhetoric, and in 1629 he gave up his chair in astrology because he had received higher ecclesiastical orders and had become canon of St. Anne's church. He then passed his baccalaureate in theology and became professor of that discipline.

In 1630 Brożek gave up his chair of rhetoric, and from April 1631 to December 1638 he was director of the library of the Collegium Maius. He became active in organizing the teaching of "practical geometry," which was entrusted to his favorite pupil, Pawel Herka, with some supervision on his part during 1635 and 1636. In 1639 Brozek presented his library to the University of Krakow, along with a substantial sum for the purchase of additional books and instruments. He gave up his professorship and the apartment at the Collegium Maius, as well as the canonry of the church of St. Florent, and moved to Międzyrzecze. In 1648, however, he returned to Krakow, where he received the master of theology. In February 1650 he became doctor of theology, and rector of his university in 1652.

Brożek's loyalty to the University of Krakow, one of his strongest characteristics, even surpassed his attachment to the Catholic Church. On the side of the university he took part in the fight against the Jesuit domination of schools, sending reports to Rome and making ten trips to Warsaw (1627–1635) in order to defend the university's rights. In the course of his struggle he answered a letter from a priest, Nicolas Łęczycki, by publishing (1626) a satirical dialogue, *Gratis,* which was soon burned in the public square of Krakow. It provoked a long answer from a priest, Frédéric Szembek, entitled *Gratis plebański gratis wyćwiczony* ("The Priests' *Gratis* Gratuitously Beaten," Poznan, 1627).

It was Brożek's hope to write the history of the University of Krakow, showing its role in the general development of science and education in Poland, but fragments of manuscripts are all that remain. The most important are "De antiquitate litterarum in Polonia" and an excellent biography of Stanislaw Grzepski, Polish geometer and philologist of the sixteenth century. In spite of his being enlightened and erudite, a partisan of progress who was active in reforming the teaching of mathematics, Brożek was not free from astrological prejudices or belief in the magical properties of numbers and their relation to medicine.

Brożek was the author of more than thirty publications. The ones concerning Copernicus, and particularly those dealing with mathematics, which won him the reputation of being the greatest Polish mathematician of his time, are of considerable interest. Among the first are the poem *Septem sidera* (of doubtful authenticity) and many Copernican documents but, unfortunately, not the letters by and about Copernicus that Brożek collected but did not publish that are now lost. In the second group are his purely mathematical works and opuscules, the most important being *Arithmetica integrorum* (1620), a new didactic manual, in which logarithms, then recently discovered, were introduced in schools; *Aristoteles et Euclides defensus contra Petrum Ramum* (1638), reissued in 1652 and 1699 under the title *Apologia pro Aristotele . . .*; a dissertation containing original research on the star-shaped polygons; and two treatises entitled *De numeris perfectis* (1637, 1638), which brought new results, at the time, on perfect numbers and amicable numbers. There one finds the basic theorem of the elementary theory of numbers, better known as Fermat's theorem, which was published in 1670 (also without its proof).

Jan Brożek should not be confused with Nicolas Brożek, nephew or grandson of his sister (*b.* Kurzelow, *ca.* 1635; *d.* Krakow, 1676). His scientific and ecclesiastic career was very similar to Jan Brożek's, but with only slight results, even for his epoch.

BIBLIOGRAPHY

I. Original Works. Among Brożek's more than thirty writings are *Arithmetica integrorum* (Krakow, 1620); *Gratis* (Krakow, 1626); *De numeris perfectis* (Krakow, 1637, 1638); and *Aristoteles et Euclides defensus contra Petrum Ramum* (Krakow, 1638), reissued as *Apologia pro Aristotele . . .* (Krakow, 1652, 1699). Available in manuscript are parts of "De antiquitate litterarum in Polonia" and the "Biography of Stanislaw Grzepski," and Brożek's diary for 1636–1643, with gaps, in the form of notes written in the margins of the "Ephemerides" edited by L. Eichstadt, MS Bibl. Jagellone, Krakow, sign. Mathesis 513 R.X.VI.12.

II. Secondary Literature. Works dealing with Brożek are M. A. Baraniecki, *Arytmetyka,* 2nd ed. (Warsaw, 1894), pp. 43–49; H. Barycz, *Wstęp i przypisy do nowego wydania Gratisa* ("Introduction and Commentaries on the New Edition of *Gratis*"), Vol. LXXXII of Biblioteka Pisarzy Polskich (Krakow, 1929); and "Pierwszy historyk nauki i kultury w Polsce" ("First Historian of Science and Culture in Poland"), in *Księga pamiątkowa ku czci W. Sobieskiego* ("Commemorative Volume in Honor of W. Sobieski"; Krakow, 1932); A. Birkenmajer, "Brożek (Broscius), Jan," in *Polski słownik biograficzny* ("Dictionary of Polish Biography"), II (Krakow, 1937), 1–3; L. A. Birkenmajer, *Mikołaj Kopernik,* I (Krakow, 1900); A. Favaro, *Tito-Livio Burattini* (Venice, 1896), p. 74; W. Konczyńska, *Zarys historii Biblioteki Jagiellońskiej* ("Sketch of the History of the Jagellone Library"; Krakow, 1923); J. Krókowski, *De septem sideribus, quae Nicolao Copernico vulgo tribuuntur* (Krakow, 1926); a monograph on Brożek, with portrait; Z. Mysłakowski, *Walerian Magni,* Vol. LI A of *Rozprawy Wydziału matematyczno-przyrodniczego PAU* (Krakow, 1911); K. Piekarski, *Ex libris Jana Brożka,* Vol. III of *Silva rerum* (Krakow, 1927); E. Stamm, "Z historii matematyki XVII wieku w Polsce" ("History of Mathematics in the Seventeenth Century in Poland"), in *Wiadomości matematyczne,* **40** (1935); and S. Temberski, *Roczniki* (Krakow, 1897). A long monograph on Brożek, containing a reproduction of his portrait at the University of Krakow, was published by J. N. Franke (Krakow, 1884).

B. Knaster

BRYSON OF HERACLEA

The name Bryson occurs several times in Aristotle's writings. A "sophist" Bryson is mentioned as the son of Herodorus of Heraclea (*Historia animalium* VI, 5, 563a7; IX, 11, 615a10); is blamed for his "sophistic" (in fact, probably proto-Stoic) assertion that there is no such thing as "indecent" language (*Rhetoric* III, 2, 1405b9); and is blamed for his "eristic" and "sophistic" method of squaring the circle (*Posterior Analytics* I, 9, 75b40; *De sophisticis elenchis* 11, 171b16–172a4). A Bryson is named in Plato's *Epistles* XIII, where Polyxenus, teacher of Helicon, is designated as his ἑταῖρος. Theopompus, in Athen XI, 508d (*Fragmenta graecorum historicorum,* F. Jacoby, ed., 115F259), accuses Plato of having plagiarized Bryson's *Diatribes.* It seems preferable (in agreement with Natorp rather than Zeller) to assume that all the above passages refer to one and the same person, although it must be admitted that other biographical information preserved in Diogenes Laertius and Suda, particularly concerning his relations with Socrates, Euclid of Megara, Cleinomachus, Plato, Pyrrho, and Theodorus the Atheist, contain some chronological contradictions.

With the help of ancient commentators Bryson's method of squaring the circle, criticized by Aristotle, can tentatively be reconstructed as follows. We start with two squares, one inscribed in a circle, the other circumscribed. Then we construct successively regular circumscribed and inscribed polygons the perimeters of which approach as closely as we like to the circumference of the circle. Thus, exhausting the area by which one square is larger and the other is smaller than the circle, we eventually make the areas of the larger and the smaller polygon coincide, which means that their areas at that time equal the area of the circle, since the polygon and the circle are both smaller than the circumscribed polygons and greater than all the inscribed figures. Since we can always construct a square equal in area to a polygon, the problem of how to square the circle is solved.

Aristotle criticizes this method because it is based on a principle that is too general and not peculiar to the matter at hand. By this he probably means a principle like this: If two quantities, one larger and one smaller than a third, become equal, they also become equal to that third quantity. It seems that Bryson's method can, however, be defended against Aristotle and can be considered another anticipation of the principles underlying the method of exhaustion.

No other opinions of Bryson have survived. But since his name is linked with that of Polyxenus, who has been credited with having been the first to put forward the so-called third-man argument, and since Plato was accused of plagiarizing Bryson, it could be that there were similarities between Bryson's *Diatribes* and Plato's *Parmenides,* in which the third-man argument is indeed discussed.

BIBLIOGRAPHY

In addition to the sources listed in the text, see John Philoponus, *In Analytica posteriora,* XIII, pt. 3 of *Commentaria in Aristotelem Graeca* (1909), 111-115, 149; Pseudo-Alexander of Aphrodisias, *In Sophisticos elenchos,* III, pt. 3 of *Commentaria* . . . (1898), 76, 90, 92; and Themistius, *Analytica posteriora paraphrasis,* V, pt. 1 of *Commentaria* . . . (1900), 19-20.

Literature that deals with Bryson includes T. L. Heath, *A History of Greek Mathematics,* I (Oxford, 1921), 223-225; Paul Natorp, "Bryson 2," in Pauly-Wissowa, *Real-Encyclopädie,* III, pt. 1 (1897); W. D. Ross, *Aristotle's Prior and Posterior Analytics* (Oxford, 1949), 536 f.; and E. Zeller, *Die Philosophie der Griechen,* 5th ed., II, pt. 1 (1922), esp. 250, n. 4.

A different interpretation of Bryson's attempt to square the circle, according to which he proposed establishing some kind of proportion between the circumscribed and the inscribed circles as extremes, the middle term being the square in question, is in A. Wasserstein, "Some Early Greek Attempts to Square the Circlē," in *Phronesis,* **4** (1959), 92-100, esp. 95-100.

PHILIP MERLAN

BUDAN DE BOISLAURENT, FERDINAND FRANÇOIS DÉSIRÉ (worked Paris, France, *ca.* 1800–at least 1853)

Almost nothing is known of Budan's life except for the information he provided on the title pages of his published works. He was a doctor of medicine and an amateur mathematician. He was educated in the classics and occasionally quoted Virgil and Horace in his works. A royalist, he published a Latin ode on the birth of the posthumous son of the duke of Burgundy. Budan was named *chevalier* of the Legion of Honor in 1814. He held the post of inspector general of studies at the University of Paris for over twenty years; this post may have been responsible for his interest in finding mathematical methods that would be easy for beginning students to use.

Budan is known in the theory of equations as one of the independent discoverers of the rule of Budan and Fourier, which gives necessary conditions for a polynomial equation to have n real roots between two given real numbers. He announced his discovery of the rule and described its use in a paper read to the Institut de France in 1803 and published the paper, with explanatory notes, as *Nouvelle méthode pour la résolution des équations numériques d'un degré quelconque,* in 1807.

Budan's definitive formulation of his rule was the following: "If an equation in x has n roots between zero and some positive number p, the transformed equation in $(x - p)$ must have at least n fewer variations [in sign] than the original" ("Appendice," p. 89). The "transformed equation in $(x - p)$" is the original polynomial equation developed in powers of $(x - p)$. In modern notation: let $P(x) = 0$ be the given polynomial equation, and let $G(x - p) = P(x)$. Then $G(x - p) = 0$ is what Budan called the "transformed equation in $(x - p)$." The term "variation in sign" is borrowed from Descartes's rule of signs: No polynomial can have more positive roots than there are variations in sign in the successive terms of that polynomial. Indeed, Budan appears to have been led to his rule by Descartes's rule of signs.

Budan's first formulation of his rule assumed that all the roots of the original equation were real. In this case, Budan's rule tells exactly how many roots there are between zero and p, just as Descartes's rule gives the exact number of positive roots in the same case. Budan stated that, for the case of all real roots, his rule could be derived from Descartes's rule. It is not difficult to reconstruct such a derivation, even though Budan did not give it, once one has observed that when x is between zero and p, $(x - p)$ is negative.

The need for a rule such as his was suggested to Budan by Lagrange's *Traité de la résolution des équations numériques* (1767). This seems to have been almost the only nonelementary work Budan had read, and it influenced him greatly. He quoted Lagrange to show that it would be useful to give the rules for solving numerical equations entirely by means of arithmetic, referring to algebra only if absolutely necessary. Budan's goal was to solve Lagrange's problem—between which real numbers do real roots lie? —purely by methods of elementary arithmetic. Accordingly, the chief concern of Budan's *Nouvelle méthode* was to give the reader a mechanical process for calculating the coefficients of the transformed equation in $(x - p)$. He did not appeal to the theory of finite differences or to the calculus for these coefficients, preferring to give them "by means of simple additions and subtractions."[1] His *Nouvelle méthode* includes many specific numerical examples in which the coefficients are calculated and the number of sign changes in the polynomials P and G are compared; he intended this to be a simple and practical procedure.

In 1811 Budan presented a proof for his rule to the Institute; he published the proof, along with a reprint of his original article, as *Appendice à la nouvelle méthode,* in 1822. A. M. Legendre, reporting to the Institute in 1811 on Budan's rule and its proof, recognized the utility of being able to know that there could be no real roots between two given real numbers. Apparently unaware of the prior work of Joseph Fourier, he stated that the result was new.[2] Legendre added that the proof given by Budan was valid only after certain gaps were filled, notably the assumption without proof of Segner's theorem (1756): If $P(x)$ is multiplied by $(x - a)$, the number of variations in sign in the product polynomial is at least one greater than that in $P(x)$. Budan himself did not appreciate the force of this objection; he protested that there was nothing wrong with using a known result, although in fact he assumed it without stating it and, until Legendre's remark, did not seem to realize that the proof needed it.

Budan's success in discovering a correct rule and giving a reasonably satisfactory proof of it shows that, at the beginning of the nineteenth century, it was still possible for one without systematic training in mathematics to contribute to its progress; but mathematics was giving increasing attention to rigor and precision of statement, qualities slighted in Budan's work. The professionals were about to take over. Fourier's simultaneous and independent discovery, using derivatives, exemplifies the powerful methods available to one thoroughly schooled in mathematics. J. C. F. Sturm (1836) gave a necessary *and sufficient* condition for a root to lie between two bounds, thus completely solving the theoretical problem of how many roots lie between given limits. Yet Budan's rule remains the most convenient for computation, although finding bounds on roots is no longer the major business of the algebraist.

NOTES

1. This method is fairly efficient. It is equivalent to the use of successive synthetic divisions, a method often discussed in works on the theory of equations. See, e.g., W. S. Burnside and A. W. Panton, *The Theory of Equations* (Dublin-London, 1928), I, 10 ff., 64 ff.
2. Fourier taught his version of the rule before 1797, although it was not published until after his death, in 1831. Fourier's version is: If $f(x)$ is a polynomial of degree n, the number of real roots of $f(x) = 0$ lying between a and b cannot exceed the difference in the number of changes in sign in the sequence $f(b), f'(b), f''(b), \cdots, f^n(b)$ and that of the sequence $f(a), f'(a), f''(a), \cdots, f^n(a)$. See J. Fourier, *Analyse des équations déterminées,* pp. 98–100; on his priority, see the "Avertissement" to that work by C. L. M. H. Navier, p. xxi. Although the formulations of Budan and Fourier are equivalent, the great difference in conception argues for independence of discovery.

BIBLIOGRAPHY

I. Original Works. Budan's writings are *Nouvelle méthode pour la résolution des équations numériques d'un degré quelconque* (Paris, 1807), and "Appendice à la nouvelle méthode," in *Nouvelle méthode pour la résolution des équations numériques d'un degré quelconque, revue, augmentée d'un appendice, et suivie d'un aperçu concernant les suites syntagmatiques* (Paris, 1822).

II. Secondary Literature. Additional information may be found in J. Fourier, *Analyse des équations déterminées* (Paris, 1830 [*sic*]), which includes C. L. M. H. Navier, "Avertissement de l'éditeur," pp. i-xxiv, dated 1 July 1831; and F. N. W. Moigno, "Note sur la détermination du nombre des racines réelles ou imaginaires d'une équation numérique, comprises entre des limites données. Theorèmes de Rolle, de Budan ou de Fourier, de Descartes, de Sturm et de Cauchy," in *Journal de mathématiques pures et appliquées,* 5 (1840), 75-94.

JUDITH V. GRABINER

BUGAEV, NICOLAY VASILIEVICH (*b.* Dusheti, near Tiflis [now Tbilisi], Russia, 14 September 1837; *d.* Moscow, Russia, 11 June 1903)

The son of a military physician, Bugaev was educated in Moscow, where he was sent at the age of ten and where, while a student, he had to work as a tutor. In 1855 he entered the Physical-Mathematical Faculty of Moscow University. After graduating in 1859, he studied at the Engineering Academy in St. Petersburg but returned to Moscow in 1861 and from then on devoted himself to mathematics. In 1863 Bugaev defended his master's thesis, on constructing a general theory of the convergence of infinite series, then for two and a half years continued his education abroad, studying at Berlin under Kummer and Weierstrass and at Paris under Liouville.

In 1866 Bugaev defended his doctoral dissertation, which dealt with numerical identities related to the properties of the symbol *e*. The following year he became professor at Moscow University, serving as dean of the Physical-Mathematical Faculty from 1886 until 1903.

Many of Bugaev's pupils, including N. Y. Sonin and D. F. Egorov, became prominent scholars. In the last quarter of the nineteenth century he exerted considerable influence upon the work of his faculty and the Moscow Mathematical Society, of which he was cofounder, vice-president (1886), and president (1891). Bugaev was one of the most regular contributors to *Matematicheskii sbornik*, the society's journal, founded in 1866. Bugaev's proposal, that contributions to this journal by Russian authors always be published in Russian, led to the development of Russian mathematical terminology. As a proponent of the dissemination of mathematical knowledge and of the application of mathematics to technology, Bugaev was founder of the Society for Dissemination of Technological Knowledge in the late 1860's and headed its educational branch. He was elected a corresponding member of the St. Petersburg Academy of Sciences in 1898, and was an honorary member of numerous Russian and West European societies.

Bugaev's research was concerned mainly with mathematical analysis and number theory. In number theory Bugaev deduced many identities important in various problems of applied mathematics. Using elliptic functions, he proved formulas of number theory that had been given without proof by Liouville. He also published articles on algebra, the theory of algebraic functions, and the theory of ordinary differential equations.

BIBLIOGRAPHY

I. ORIGINAL WORKS. Bugaev's 76 books, articles, and reviews are listed in *Matematicheskii sbornik*, **25**, no. 2 (1905), 370–373. Works published before 1890 are also listed in F. A. Brockhaus and I. A. Efron, eds., *Entsiklopedichesky slovar*, IVa (St. Petersburg, 1891), 827–829. A synopsis of Bugaev's writings published before 1892 is in F. Y. Shevelev, ed., "Kratkoe obozrenie uchenykh trudov professora N. V. Bugaeva (sostavlennoe im samim)" ("A Short Review of Scientific Works by Professor N. V. Bugaev [Compiled by Bugaev Himself]"), in *Istoriko-matematicheskie issledovaniya* (1959), no. 12, 525–558.

II. SECONDARY LITERATURE. Various aspects of Bugaev's work are treated in a group of articles in *Matematicheskii sbornik*, **25**, nos. 1–2 (1904–1905). Of especial interest are L. K. Lakhtin, "Nicolay Vasilievich Bugaev (biografichesky ocherk)" (". . . Bugaev [a Biographical Essay]"), in no. 2, 251–269; and "Trudy N. V. Bugaeva v oblasti analiza" ("Bugaev's Works in the Area of Analysis"), *ibid.*, 322–330; and A. P. Minin, "O trudakh N. V. Bugaeva po teorii chisel" ("On Bugaev's Works in Number Theory"), *ibid.*, 293–321.

Bugaev's work is also described in general histories of mathematics: L. E. Dickson, *History of the Theory of Numbers*, 2nd ed., 3 vols. (Washington, D.C., 1934), see index; *Istoria otechestvennoy matematiki* ("National History of Mathematics"), II (Kiev, 1967), 297–299; A. A. Kiselev and E. P. Ozhigova, "K istorii elementarnogo metoda v teorii chisel" ("On the History of the Elementary Method in the Theory of Numbers"), in *Actes du XIe Congrès international d'histoire des sciences*, III (Wrocław-Warsaw-Cracow, 1968), 244–249; and A. P. Youschkevitch, *Istoria matematiki v Rossii do 1917 goda* ("History of Mathematics in Russia Before 1917"; Moscow, 1968), 483–489.

ALEKSANDR VOLODARSKY

BUNYAKOVSKY, VIKTOR YAKOVLEVICH (*b.* Bar, Podolskaya gubernia [now Vinnitsa oblast], Russia, 16 December 1804; *d.* St. Petersburg, Russia, 12 December 1889)

Bunyakovsky was the son of Colonel Yakov Vasilievich Bunyakovsky. After a basic education at home, he completed his studies abroad, receiving the doctorate in mathematical sciences at Paris in 1825. He returned the following year to St. Petersburg, where he subsequently began his scientific research and teaching. For many years Bunyakovsky lectured on mathematics and mechanics at the First Cadet Corps (later the Naval Academy) and at the Communications Institute. From 1846 to 1880 he was a professor at St. Petersburg University.

Bunyakovsky's scientific work was done at the St. Petersburg Academy of Sciences, of which he was named adjunct in mathematics (1828), extraordinary academician (1830), and ordinary academician (1841). He was elected vice-president in 1864 and retained the post for twenty-five years.

Of Bunyakovsky's approximately 150 published works in mathematics and mechanics, a monograph on inequalities relating to integrals in finite intervals (1859) is particularly well known. In this work he first stated the important integral inequality named for him:

$$\left[\int_a^b f(x)\,\phi(x)\,dx\right]^2 \leq \int_a^b f^2(x)\,dx \int_a^b \phi^2(x)\,dx.$$

Rediscovered and published by Hermann Schwarz in 1884, it is now often known as the Schwarz inequality. Bunyakovsky produced many works on number theory and in particular solved a series of specific equations and gave a new proof for the law of quadratic reciprocity.

Some of Bunyakovsky's results were included in P. Bachmann's *Niedere Zahlentheorie*, and about forty references to his original results appear in L. E. Dickson's *History of the Theory of Numbers*. His contributions to number theory include a work (1846) in which he gave an original exposition of this science and of its application to insurance and demography.

Bunyakovsky's works also deal with geometry. In 1853 he critically examined previous attempts to prove Euclid's fifth postulate concerning parallel lines and attempted a proof himself—unaware of the significance of Lobachevsky's non-Euclidean geometry. Active in disseminating mathematical knowledge in Russia, he also contributed substantially to the enrichment of Russian mathematical terminology.

Bunyakovsky's works on applied mechanics and hydrostatics are also of interest. To commemorate fifty years of his research and teaching, the St. Petersburg Academy in 1875 issued a medal and established a prize bearing his name for outstanding work in mathematics.

BIBLIOGRAPHY

I. ORIGINAL WORKS. Bunyakovsky's major writings are "Du mouvement dans la machine d'Atwood, en ayant égard à l'élasticité du fil," in *Mémoires de l'Académie impériale des sciences de St.-Pétersbourg*, 6th ser., **2** (1833), 179–186; *Leksikon chistoy i prikladnoy matematiki* ("Lexicon of Pure and Applied Mathematics"; St. Petersburg, 1837); *Osnovania matematicheskoy teorii veroyatnostey* ("Foundations of the Mathematical Theory of Probability"; St.-Petersburg, 1846); "Note sur le maximum du nombre des positions d'équilibre d'un prisme triangulaire homogène plongé dans un fluide," in *Bulletin de la classe physico-mathématique de l'Académie impériale des sciences de St-Pétersbourg*, **10**, no. 4 (1852), 49–58; *Parallelnye linii* ("Parallel Lines"; St. Petersburg, 1853); *O nekotorykh neravenstvakh, otnosyashchikhsya k opredelennym integralam ili integralam v konechnykh raznostyakh* ("On Certain Inequalities Relating to Definite Integrals or Integrals in Finite Intervals"; St. Petersburg, 1859); "Sur les planimètres libres," in *Bulletin de l'Académie des sciences de St.-Pétersbourg*, 3rd ser., **11** (1860), 567–573; and *O samoschetakh i o novom ikh primenenii* ("On Computing Machines and New Uses for Them"; St. Petersburg, 1876).

II. SECONDARY LITERATURE. See K. A. Andreev, *V. Y. Bunyakovsky* (Kharkov, 1890); L. E. Dickson, *History of the Theory of Numbers*, 3 vols. (Washington, D.C., 1919–1923), see index; I. G. Melnikov, "O rabotakh V. Y. Bunyakovskogo po teorii chisel" ("Bunyakovsky's Works on Number Theory"), in *Trudy Instituta istorii estestvoznaniya i tekhniki. Akademiya nauk SSSR*, **17** (1957), 270–286; *Opisanie prazdnovania doktorskogo yubileya vitse-prezidenta Akademii nauk akademika V. Y. Bunyakovskogo 19 maya 1875 g.* ("Description of the Celebration of the Doctoral Jubilee of the Vice-President of the Academy of Sciences, Academician Bunyakovsky, 19 May 1875"; St. Petersburg, 1876); V. E. Prudnikov, *V. Y. Bunyakovsky, ucheny i pedagog* (". . . Scientist and Teacher"; Moscow, 1954); and A. P. Youschkevitch, *Istoria matematiki v Rossii do 1917 goda* ("History of Mathematics in Russia Before 1917"; Moscow, 1968), esp. 296–302.

A. T. GRIGORIAN

BUOT, JACQUES (*d. ca.* 1675)

Buot was a member of the Académie des Sciences of Paris from the time it was founded in 1666; as such he received an annual stipend of 1,200 livres.

Buot probably was present on 16 July 1667 when Huygens observed the exact hour at which the diameter of the ring of Saturn seemed to be parallel to the horizon. From this observation, Huygens calculated the inclination of the ring to the equator as 8°58′ and to the ecliptic as 31°22′; Buot found a value of 31°38′35″ for the latter. (As early as 1659, in his *Systema Saturnium*, Huygens had attempted to determine these values as precisely as possible.) On 15 August 1667 Huygens, Jean Picard, Jean Richer, and Buot repeated the experiment and obtained values of 9°32′50″ and 32°0′.

Buot made a further contribution to astronomy by inventing the *équerre azimutale*, an instrument for finding the intersection of the meridian with a horizontal plane. He was also active as a physicist, once again drawing upon Huygens' work. In 1667 Huygens and members of the Accademia del Cimento in Florence had made experiments to determine the forces that cause water to expand on congelation. In 1670 Buot repeated these experiments for water and oils and observed that the congealing of water differs from that of oils. In 1669 Buot joined Huygens and others in the discussions on the causes of gravitation that were held by the Academy; in his *mémoire* of 21 August 1669, he showed himself opposed to the action-at-a-distance theory.

Condorcet wrote that Buot died in 1675. A letter from Olaus Römer to Huygens, dated 30 December 1677, states, however, *Dominus Buot post aliquot mensium morbum fato appropinquare creditur*—"After an illness of some months Mr. Buot seems to feel that his end is drawing near." The *Comptes des bâtiments* gives the date of his last stipend as 10 June 1676.

BIBLIOGRAPHY

I. Original Works. Buot's writings include *Usage de la rouë de proportion, avec un traité d'arithmétique* (Paris, 1647); and "Équerre azimutale," in Gallon, ed., *Machines et inventions approuvées par l'Académie royale des sciences depuis 1666 jusqu'en 1701*, I (Paris, 1735), 67–70.

II. Secondary Literature. Works dealing with Buot are Condorcet, *Éloges des Académiens de l'Académie royale des sciences, morts depuis 1666 jusqu'en 1699* (Paris, 1773), p. 157; J. Guiffrey, *Comptes des bâtiments du roi, sous le règne de Louis XIV*, I (Paris, 1881), 163, 227, 299, 378, 449, 565, 650, 782, 856; Panckoucke, ed., *Histoire de l'Académie royale des sciences 1666 à 1698*, I (Paris, 1777), 121; and *Oeuvres complètes de Christiaan Huygens*, VI (The Hague, 1895), 58–66, 139–142, 143–147; VIII (The Hague, 1899), 54; XV (The Hague, 1925), 43, 93, 94, 478; XIX (The Hague, 1937), 182, 183, 344, 630; E. Maindron, *L'Académie des sciences* (Paris, 1888), p. 98; and D. Shapeley, "Pre-Huygenian Observations of Saturn's Rings," in *Isis*, **40** (1949), 12–17.

H. L. L. Busard

BURALI-FORTI, CESARE (*b.* Arezzo, Italy, 13 August 1861; *d.* Turin, Italy, 21 January 1931)

After obtaining his degree from the University of Pisa in December 1884, Burali-Forti taught at the Scuola Tecnica in Augusta, Sicily. In 1887 he moved to Turin after winning a competition for extraordinary professor at the Accademia Militare di Artiglieria e Genio. In Turin he also taught at the Scuola Tecnica Sommeiller until 1914. He remained at the Accademia Militare, teaching analytical projective geometry, until his death. He was named ordinary professor in 1906 and held a prominent position on the faculty; in 1927 he was the only ordinary among twenty-five civilian professors.

After an early attempt to obtain the *libera docenza* failed because of the antagonism to the new methods of vector analysis on the part of some members of the examining committee, he never again attempted to obtain it and thus never held a permanent university position. (The *libera docenza* gave official permission to teach at a university and was required before entering a competition for a university chair.) He was assistant to Giuseppe Peano at the University of Turin during the years 1894–1896, but he had come under Peano's influence earlier, however, and had given a series of informal lectures at the university on mathematical logic (1893–1894). These were published in 1894. Many of Burali-Forti's publications were highly polemical, but to his family and his friends he was kind and gentle. He loved music; Bach and Beethoven were his favorite composers. He was not a member of any academy. Always an independent thinker, he asked that he not be given a religious funeral.

The name Burali-Forti has remained famous for the antinomy he discovered in 1897 in his critique of Georg Cantor's theory of transfinite ordinal numbers. The critique begins: "The principal purpose of this note is to show that there exist *transfinite numbers* (or *ordinal types*) a, b, such that a is neither equal to, nor less than, nor greater than b." Essentially, the antinomy may be formulated as follows: To every class of ordinal numbers there corresponds an ordinal number which is greater than any element of the class. Consider the class of all ordinal numbers. It follows that it possesses an ordinal number that is greater than every ordinal number. This result went almost unnoticed until Bertrand Russell published a similar antinomy in 1903. It should be noted, however, that Cantor was already aware of the Burali-Forti antinomy in 1895 and had written of it to David Hilbert in 1896.

Burali-Forti was one of the earliest popularizers of Peano's discoveries in mathematical logic. In 1919 he published a greatly enlarged edition of the *Logica mathematica,* which contained many original contributions. He also contributed much to Peano's famous *Formulaire de mathématiques* project, especially with his study of the foundations of mathematics (1893).

Burali-Forti's most valuable mathematical contributions were his studies devoted to the foundations of vector analysis and to linear transformations and their various applications, especially in differential geometry. A long collaboration with Roberto Marcolongo was very productive. They published a series of articles in the *Rendiconti del Circolo matematico di Palermo* on the unification of vectorial notation that included a full analysis, along critical and historical lines, of all the notations that had been proposed for a minimal system. There followed a book treating the fundamentals of vector analysis (1909), which was almost immediately translated into French. Their proposals for a unified system of vectorial notation, published in *L'enseignement mathématique* in 1909, gave rise to a polemic with various followers of Josiah Gibbs and Sir William Hamilton that lasted into the following year and consisted of letters, responses, and opinions contributed by Burali-Forti and Marcolongo, Peano, G. Comberiac, H. C. F. Timerding, Felix Klèin, E. B. Wilson, C. G. Knott, Alexander Macfarlane, E. Carvallo, and E. Jahnke. The differences in notation continued, however, and the Italian school, while quite productive, tended to remain somewhat isolated from developments elsewhere. Also in 1909 Burali-Forti and Marcolongo began their collaboration in the study of linear transformations of vectors.

Burali-Forti's introduction of the notion of the derivative of a vector with respect to a point allowed him to unify and greatly simplify the foundations of vector analysis. The use of one simple linear operator led to new applications of the theory of vector analysis, as well as to improved treatment of operators previously introduced, such as Lorentz transformations, gradients, and rotors, and resulted in the publication (1912–1913) of two volumes treating linear transformations and their applications. Burali-Forti was able to apply the theory to the mechanics of continuous bodies, optics, hydrodynamics, statics, and various problems of mechanics, always refining methods, simplifying proofs, and discovering new and useful properties. He did not live to see the completion of his dream, a small encyclopedia of vector analysis and its applications. The part dealing with differential projective geometry (1930) was Burali-Forti's last work.

The long collaboration with Marcolongo—their friends called them "the vectorial binomial"—was partly broken by their divergent views on the theory of relativity, the importance of which Burali-Forti never understood. With Tommaso Boggio he published a critique (1924) in which he meant "to consider Relativity under its mathematical aspect, wishing to point out how arbitrary and irrational are its foundations." "We wish," he wrote in the preface, "to shake Relativity in all its apparent foundations, and we have reason for hoping that we have succeeded in doing it." At the end he stated: "Here then is our conclusion. Philosophy may be able to justify the space-time of Relativity, but mathematics, experimental science, and common sense can justify it NOT AT ALL."

Burali-Forti had a strong dislike for coordinates. In 1929, in the second edition of the *Analisi vettoriale generale,* written with Marcolongo, we find: "The criteria of this work . . . are not different from those with which we began our study in 1909, namely, an absolute treatment of all physical, mechanical, and geometrical problems, independent of any system of coordinates whatsoever."

BIBLIOGRAPHY

Besides his scientific publications, Burali-Forti wrote many school texts. In all, his publications total more than two hundred.

No complete list of the works of Burali-Forti has been published, but the following may be considered representative: *Teoria delle grandezze* (Turin, 1893); *Logica matematica* (Milan, 1894; 2nd ed., rev., Milan, 1919); "Una questione sui numeri transfiniti," in *Rendiconti del Circolo matematico di Palermo,* **11** (1897), 154–164; *Lezioni di geometria metrico-proiettiva* (Turin, 1904); *Elementi di calcolo vettoriale, con numerose applicazioni alla geometria, alla meccanica e alla fisica-matematica,* written with R. Marcolongo (Turin, 1909), translated into French by S. Lattès as *Éléments de calcul vectoriel, avec de nombreuses applications à la géometrie, à la mécanique et à la physique mathématique* (Paris, 1910); "Notations rationelles pour le système vectoriel minimum," in *L'enseignement mathématique,* **11** (1909), 41–45, written with Marcolongo; *Omografie vettoriali con applicazioni alle derivate rispetto ad un punto ed alla fisica-matematica* (Turin, 1909), written with Marcolongo; *Analyse vectorielle générale,* 2 vols. (Pavia, 1912–1913), written with Marcolongo; *Espaces courbes. Critique de la relativité* (Turin, 1924), written with Tommaso Boggio; and *Analisi vettoriale generale e applicazioni,* Vol. II, *Geometria differenziale* (Bologna, 1930), written with P. Burgatti and Tommaso Boggio.

A work dealing with Burali-Forti is Roberto Marcolongo, "Cesare Burali-Forti," in *Bollettino dell'Unione matematica italiana,* **10** (1931), 182–185.

HUBERT C. KENNEDY

BÜRGI, JOOST (*b.* Liechtenstein, 28 February 1552; *d.* Kassel, Germany, 31 January 1632)

There is no precise account of Bürgi's youth. Most likely he received no systematic education, for he did not even know Latin, the scientific language of his time. From 1579 he was the court watchmaker to Duke Wilhelm IV, and he probably completed his education while working in the duke's observatory at Kassel. There he worked on the construction of several instruments, especially astronomical ones, and made astronomical observations, developing his skill, inventiveness, and accuracy. Bürgi also improved instruments for use in practical geometry. His proportional compasses competed with those of Galileo for priority, although both were probably no more than an improvement of devices already in use.

The fame of Bürgi's instruments, which made possible more accurate astronomical observations in the observatory at Kassel, drew the attention of scientists assembled at the court of Emperor Rudolf II, who tried to establish a science center in Prague and to enlist prominent European scientists. After the death of Wilhelm IV, Bürgi entered the service of Rudolf and became his court watchmaker, also holding this position under Rudolf's successors Matthias and Ferdinand II. He lived in Prague from about 1603 and became assistant to and computer for Kepler, who was working on the results of astronomical observations made by Tycho Brahe. Even after the imperial court moved to Vienna and the leading foreign scientists left Prague, and the Bohemian anti-Hapsburg revolt was defeated (1620), Bürgi remained in Prague. Here he became scientifically isolated, which lessened the favorable response to his results. Shortly before his death (probably as late as 1631) Bürgi returned to Kassel.

In mathematics Bürgi was by no means a theoretician, but an indefatigable and inventive computer whose help Kepler appreciated. Bürgi's manuscript "Arithmetics" was taken to Pulkovo with Kepler's unpublished papers. In this manuscript Bürgi uses (probably independently of Stevin) the decimal point and sometimes substitutes a small arc for it. Starting from the method known as *regula falsi,* Bürgi also elaborated the method of approximate calculation of the roots of algebraic equations of higher degree. The need to make the tables of sines more precise led him to undertake this problem. His tables of sines, which have the difference 2″, were never published, and not even the manuscript exists.

The computation of the tables of sines and the elaboration of astronomical data led Bürgi to an easier method of multiplying large numbers. From about 1584 he was engaged, like several other astronomers and computers in the sixteenth century, in the improvement of "prosthaphairesis," the method of converting multiplication into addition by means of trigonometrical formulas—for example, $\sin\alpha \cdot \sin\beta = 1/2[\cos(\alpha - \beta) - \cos(\alpha + \beta)]$. Later, possibly at the end of the 1580's, the idea of logarithms occurred to him. Although he did not know Stifel's *Arithmetica integra,* in which the idea of comparing arithmetic and geometric progression is outlined, Bürgi learned of it from other sources. He had computed the tables of logarithms before his arrival in Prague, but he did not publish them until 1620, under the title *Arithmetische und geometrische Progress-Tabulen, sambt gründlichem Unterricht, wie solche nützlich in allerley Rechnungen zu gebrauchen, und verstanden werden sol;* however, the instruction promised in the title remained in manuscript.

The geometrical progression begins with the value 100,000,000 and has the quotient 1.0001. A term of the arithmetical progression 0, 10, 20, 30, 40, $\cdots$ corresponds to each term of the geometrical series. The tables extend to the value 1,000,000,000 in the geometrical progression, with the corresponding value 230,270,022 in the arithmetic progression. Consequently, Bürgi's logarithms correspond to our so-called natural logarithms with the base *e.* By their arrangement they are in fact antilogarithmic, for the basic progressions are logarithms. This circumstance could have made the use and spread of the tables more difficult, but the fate of Bürgi's work was influenced much more by the disintegration of the scientific and cultural center in Prague after 1620. The Prague edition of the tables remained almost unnoticed, and only a few copies were saved; probably the only complete copy is kept, together with the handwritten "instruction," in the library at Danzig. Thus, Bürgi's greatest discovery had no apparent influence on the development of science.

BIBLIOGRAPHY

Bürgi's only published work is *Arithmetische und geometrische Progress-Tabulen, sambt gründlichem Unterricht, wie solche nützlich in allerley Rechnungen zu gebrauchen, und verstanden werden sol* (Prague, 1620), repr. in H. R. Gieswald, *Justus Byrg als Mathematiker und dessen Einleitung zu seinen Logarithmen* (Danzig, 1856).

There is neither a detailed biography nor an analysis of Bürgi's scientific work. Basic bibliographic data in the following works can be of use: G. Vetter, "Dějiny matematických věd v českých zemích od založení university v r. 1348 až do r. 1620" ("History of Mathematics in the Bohemian Lands From the Foundation of the University in 1348 until 1620"), in *Sborník pro dějiny přírodních věd a techniky* (Prague), **4** (1958), 87–88; and "Kratkiĭ obzor razvitija matematiki v cheshtskikh zemliakh do Belogorskoi bitvy," in *Istoriko-matematicheskie issledovaniya*, **11** (Moscow, 1958), 49, 512; E. Voellmy, "Jost Bürgi und die Logarithmen," in *Beihefte zur Zeitschrift für Elemente der Mathematik*, no. 5 (1948); and E. Zinner, *Deutsche und niederländische astronomische Instrumente des 11.–18. Jahrhunderts* (Munich, 1956), pp. 268–276.

LUBOŠ NOVÝ

BURNSIDE, WILLIAM (*b.* London, England, 2 July 1852; *d.* West Wickham, England, 21 August 1927)

Burnside's research was in such diverse fields as mathematical physics, complex function theory, geometry, group theory, and the theory of probability. On the basis of his work in the first two fields, he was elected a fellow of the Royal Society in 1893. It was to the theory of groups, however, that he made his most significant contributions. The beginnings of an interest in groups can be detected in papers of 1891 and 1892, in which groups of linear fractional transformations of a complex variable are involved. By 1894 the theory of groups of finite order had become the central concern of much of his research, and for the next twenty years Burnside remained one of the most active contributors to its development. A number of his results have become an integral part of the modern theory of groups and their representations.

With the hope of stirring up interest in group theory in England, Burnside published his *Theory of Groups* in 1897. It was the first treatise on groups in English and also the first to develop the theory from the modern standpoint of abstract groups vis à vis permutation groups, although this approach had already been pioneered by H. Weber in his *Lehrbuch der Algebra* (1896). One topic Burnside excluded from his book was that of linear groups, because it did not seem that any result could be obtained most directly by considering linear transformations. This opinion soon became outdated, however, with G. Frobenius' development of the theory of group representations and characters (1896–1899), and Burnside was one of the first to recognize the importance of Frobenius' ideas and to contribute to their development, simplification, and application.

Using group characters, Burnside was able to prove, for example, that every transitive group of prime degree is either solvable or doubly transitive (1901) and that every group of order $p^a q^b$ (p and q prime) is solvable (1904). The latter result greatly extended results of Sylow ($b = 0$, 1872), Frobenius ($b = 1$, 1895), and Jordan ($b = 2$, 1898). It was also Burnside who discovered that groups of odd order admit no nontrivial real irreducible representations, and he was led by its consequences to suspect that every group of odd order is solvable. W. Feit and J. G. Thompson finally established this in 1962 with a proof that involves, among other things, frequent applications of Burnside's discovery.

Because he was convinced of the important role that representation theory was destined to play in the future advancement of group theory, Burnside devoted considerable space to its systematic presentation in the second edition of *Theory of Groups* (1911). This edition was widely read and is now considered a classic.

BIBLIOGRAPHY

I. ORIGINAL WORKS. Besides *Theory of Groups of Finite Order* (Cambridge, 1897, 1911), Burnside also composed a treatise on probability, *Theory of Probability* (Cambridge, 1928), which was published posthumously.

II. SECONDARY LITERATURE. The only article dealing with Burnside's life and work in any detail is A. R. Forsyth's obituary notice in *Proceedings of the Royal Society*, **117A** (1928), xi–xxv; the emphasis is upon Burnside's early work, and insufficient attention is paid to his role in the development of the theory of groups. Some idea of the latter can be obtained from the historical and survey articles scattered throughout *The Collected Works of George Abram Miller*, 5 vols. (Urbana, Illinois, 1935–1959), esp. II, 1–18 and III, 1–15. See also H. Burkhardt and H. Vogt, "Sur les groupes discontinus," in *Encyclopédie des sciences mathématiques*, I, 1, fasc. 4 (Paris–Leipzig, 1909), 532–616.

THOMAS HAWKINS

BURRAU, CARL JENSEN (*b.* Elsinore, Denmark, 29 July 1867; *d.* Gentofte, Denmark, 8 October 1944)

Burrau studied mathematics at Copenhagen University and was an assistant astronomer at the university observatory from 1893 to 1898. He subsequently worked as an actuary. From 1906 to 1912 he lectured at Copenhagen University on practical mathematics. In his researches as an astronomer and as an actuary he was a disciple of T. N. Thiele.

In 1892 the Royal Danish Academy, at Thiele's suggestion, presented an astronomical prize problem concerning librations in the *problème restreint* with two equal masses in circular movement round their common center of gravity. In his solution, Burrau was the first to point out that a series of periodic orbits, into which the third (massless) body moves, develops into a limiting orbit of ejection from (or collision with) one of the masses. It was a pioneer achievement, the first step taken in the systematic search for periodic orbits in the three-body problem that was later carried out by E. Strömgren and his pupils (in its early years, in collaboration with Burrau).

Burrau's dissertation (1895) deals with the derivation of the constants of a measuring machine for photographic determination of star positions. He suggested a development of Bessel's classic method and discussed previously proposed simplifications.

The "distance" from these studies to actuarial work is short. In an obituary, Kristensen, who audited Burrau's lectures on practical mathematics, mentions "his ability to combine scientific points of view with instructions for using them in practice." Burrau's little book on actuarial mathematics, *Forsikringsstatistikens Grundlag,* which was originally written as a series of lectures and appeared in Danish, German, and Italian, is a similar attempt to use his mathematical knowledge in the domain in which he worked for most of his life. Later, he and B. Strömgren published a paper on dividing a frequency curve into its components.

BIBLIOGRAPHY

I. Original Works. Burrau's writings include "Recherches numériques concernant des solutions périodiques d'un cas spécial du problème des trois corps," in *Astronomische Nachrichten,* **135** (1894), 233-240; **136** (1894), 161-174; "Undersøgelser over Instrumentkonstanter ved Kjøbenhavns Universitets Astronomiske Observatoriums Maaleapparat for fotografiske Plader," his dissertation, Univ. of Copenhagen (1895); a review of Darwin's *Periodic Orbits* (1897), in *Vierteljahrsschrift der Astronomischen Gesellschaft,* **33** (1898), 21-33, containing information on the early development of the three-body problem; "Über einige in Aussicht genommene Berechnungen betreffend einen Spezialfall des Dreikörper-Problems," *ibid.,* **41** (1906), 261-266; and *Forsikringsstatistikens Grundlag* (Copenhagen, 1925), originally published in German in *Wirtschaft und Recht der Versicherung,* **56** (1924). Papers are in *Publikationer og mindre Meddelelser fra Københavns Observatorium* (1913-1934).

II. Secondary Literature. Articles on Burrau are *Dansk Biografisk Leksikon,* IV (1934), 365-366; and S. Kristensen, in *Skandinavisk Aktuarietidskrift,* **28** (1945), 128-130.

Axel V. Nielsen

BUTEO, JOHANNES (*b.* Charpey, Dauphine, France, *ca.* 1492; *d.* Romans-sur-Isère, Dauphine, *ca.* 1564-1572)

Buteo's father, François, seigneur d'Espenel, is said to have had twenty children. Because he did not wish to be a burden to his parents, Buteo entered the Abbaye de St.-Antoine about 1508. He had so much feeling for languages and mathematics, we are told, that he soon could comprehend Euclid in the original Greek. In 1522 he was sent to Paris, where he studied under Oronce Fine. By 1528 he longed for his monastic life and returned to St.-Antoine; he was abbot during two of his years there. In 1562, during the first of the Wars of Religion, he had to leave the monastery and take refuge with one of his brothers in Romans-sur-Isère. He died there of grief and boredom. His original French name was Jean Borrel (*bourreau* means "executioner," but is also a popular name for the buzzard, and in this last sense is translated as *Buteo*). There were such variants as Boteo, Butéon, and Bateon.

Buteo published his works only after he was sixty years old. The *Opera geometrica* contains fifteen articles on different subjects, the last six showing his interest in law through treatment of such mathematical aspects of jurisprudence as division of land and inheritances. The first nine articles treat mechanical, arithmetical, and geometrical problems. The most original is *Ad problema cubi duplicandi,* in which he refutes Michael Stifel's claim of an exact solution to this problem and gives an approximate one.

This is also the main theme of *De quadratura circuli,* in which Buteo refutes the pretensions of those who claimed to have found the solution of the quadrature, most notably those of his master, Oronce Fine. By contrast, he discusses appreciatively the approximations found by Bryson, Archimedes, and Ptolemy. He also mentions two approximate values for π: 3-17/120 (from Ptolemy) and $\sqrt{10}$ (Indian, although he believed it to be Arab).

In the second part of this work, Buteo criticizes errors of many of his contemporaries, particularly in terminological questions. An interesting point is his proof that the author of the proofs of Euclid's *Elements* was not Theon, as was the current opinion, but Euclid himself. Here, too, are the beginnings of the famous dispute involving Peletier, Clavius, and many others on the angle of contact. In the *Apologia* (1562) Buteo pursued his refutation of Peletier's theories.

Buteo's most important work, the *Logistica,* was divided into five books, of which the first two deal with arithmetic, the third deals with algebra, and the last two present many problems in both fields. Terms such as "million" and "zero," and symbols such as

p and m for $+$ and $-$ show Italian influence. There is a good treatment of simultaneous linear equations, with notations borrowed from Stifel; and there are approximations to $\sqrt{a}$ and $\sqrt[3]{a}$ influenced by Chucquet through Estienne de la Roche. The work was not practical enough to be reprinted, however.

Buteo's fame rests only on his books. He has been a solitary figure in his love of mathematics and mechanics, and he wanted to be so. As far as we know, he had no pupils; and his criticism, often excessively sharp, must have estranged other mathematicians.

BIBLIOGRAPHY

I. ORIGINAL WORKS. Buteo's works are *Opera geometrica* (Lyons, 1554; reissued 1559. See *British Museum, General Catalogue of Printed Books* for information on reprinted articles.); *Logistica, quae et arithmetica vulgo dicitur in libros quinque digesta . . . eiusdem ad locum Vitruvij corruptum restitutio* (Lyons, 1559, 1560); *Ad locum Vitruvij corruptum restitutio* was reprinted in J. Polenus, *Exercitationes Vitruvianae primae* (Padua, 1739), and M. Vitruvius, *Architectura,* IV, part 2 (Utini, 1825–1830), 37–43; *De quadratura circuli libri duo . . . Eiusdem annotationum opuscula in errores Campani, Zamberti, Orontij, Peletarij, Io. Penae interpretum Euclidis* (Lyons, 1559); and *Apologia adversus epistolam Jacobi Peletarii depravatoris Elementorum Euclidis* (Lyons, 1562).

II. SECONDARY LITERATURE. There is no biography of Buteo. The best sources for information on his life are J. A. de Thou, *Histoire universelle . . . depuis 1543 jusqu'en 1610* (The Hague, 1740), III, 493; and L. Moréri, *Le grand dictionnaire historique* (Paris, 1759; this edition only). G. Wertheim wrote on *Logistica* in *Bibliotheca mathematica,* **2** (1901), 213–219. On *Opera geometrica* and *De quadratura,* see Moritz Cantor, *Vorlesungen über Geschichte der Mathematik,* II (Leipzig, 1913), 561–563, but with the emendations by G. Eneström, in *Bibliotheca mathematica,* **12** (1912), 253.

J. J. VERDONK

CABEO, NICCOLO (*b.* Ferrara, Italy, 26 February 1586; *d.* Genoa, Italy, 30 June 1650)

A Jesuit, Cabeo taught moral theology and mathematics in Parma, then was a preacher in various Italian cities until he settled in Genoa, where he taught mathematics. He published two major works, *Philosophia magnetica* and *In quatuor libros meteorologicorum Aristotelis commentaria.*

Cabeo is remembered mainly because in Genoa he became acquainted with Giovanni Battista Baliani, who at the fortress of Savona had experimented with falling weights, which, although of different heaviness, took almost the same length of time to reach the ground. Cabeo interpreted these experiments perhaps too broadly and was therefore the indirect cause of other experiments conducted by Vincenzo Renieri, who refers to them in a letter of 13 March 1641 to Galileo. These experiments, however, showed considerable differences in time of descent because of air resistance. Renieri wrote that he had undertaken them "because a certain Jesuit writes that [two different weights] fall in the same length of time." Galileo wrote in the *Discorsi e dimostrazioni matematiche intorno a due nuove scienze* (*Edizione Nazionale delle Opere,* VIII, 128) that to conduct such experiments "involves some difficulties" and referred to descent along an inclined plane and to the oscillations of a pendulum. Thus Vincenzo Viviani's account of the results of Galileo's experiments that involved dropping different weights from the top of the bell tower in Pisa seems to be completely unfounded.

BIBLIOGRAPHY

I. ORIGINAL WORKS. Cabeo's books are *Philosophia magnetica in qua magnetis natura penitus explicatur, et omnium quae hoc lapide cernuntur, causae propriae afferuntur . . .* (Ferrara, 1629); and *In quatuor libros meteorologicorum Aristotelis commentaria . . .* (Rome, 1646).

II. SECONDARY LITERATURE. Galileo Galilei, *Discorsi e dimostrazioni matematiche intorno a due nuove scienze,* Adriano Carugo and Ludovico Geymonat, eds. (Turin, 1958), p. 689, note; and see Charles Sommerfeld, *Bibliothèque de la Compagnie de Jésus,* II, pt. 1 (Brussels–Paris, 1891).

ATTILIO FRAJESE

CALANDRELLI, IGNAZIO (*b.* Rome, Italy, 27 October 1792; *d.* Rome, 12 February 1866)

A nephew of Giuseppe Calandrelli, the astronomer, Ignazio was professor of astronomy and director of the observatory of the University of Bologna from 1845 to 1848. Before and after this he held a similar position at the Pontifical University and at the Observatory of the Campidoglio in Rome. The latter was founded by Pope Leo XII (through the bull *Quod divina sapientia*), which provided for the establishment of a good astronomical observatory for the compilation of a calendar computed for Rome. The observatory, which the pontiff conceived of as constituting the "first true Roman observatory," was completed in 1827, on the eastern tower of the Senatorial Palace of the Campidoglio.

Calandrelli's scientific work was confined almost exclusively to positional astronomy. In 1853 he provided the observatory with Ertel's meridian circle, with which he made observations on the determination of latitude; prepared a catalog of stars; and carried out studies on refraction. He also performed numerous calculations of the orbits of small planets and comets.

In 1858 Calandrelli published a memoir on the proper motion of Sirius and his observations on the solar eclipse of 15 March of that year. He observed the occultation of Saturn on 8 May 1859. Calandrelli was a member of the Accademia dei Nuovi Lincei in Rome.

BIBLIOGRAPHY

Calandrelli's works are listed in Poggendorff, III, 226. Among them is *Lezioni elementari di astronomia teorico-pratica ad uso dei giovani studenti nelle due Università dello Stato Pontificio* (Bologna, 1848).

Further information may be found in G. Abetti, *Storia dell'astronomia* (Florence, 1963), pp. 381, 388, 389; and *Osservatori astrofisici e astronomici italiani* (Rome, 1956).

GIORGIO ABETTI

CALLIPPUS (*b.* Cyzicus, Turkey, *ca.* 370 B.C.)

One of the great astronomers of ancient Greece, Callippus belonged to the distinguished line of mathematicians and astronomers who, with Eudoxus at their head, were associated with the Academy and the Lyceum. References to him, although rare, clearly establish the magnitude of his achievements. He continued the work of Eudoxus on the motion of the planets, made accurate determinations of the lengths of the seasons, and constructed a seventy-six-year cycle to harmonize the solar and lunar years. This "Callippic period" was used by all later astronomers to record and date observations of heavenly phenomena.

The main biographical information on Callippus is found in Simplicius' commentary on Aristotle's *De caelo*. It states: "Callippus of Cyzicus, having studied with Polemarchus, Eudoxus' pupil, following him to Athens dwelt with Aristotle, correcting and completing, with Aristotle's help, the discoveries of Eudoxus" (Heiberg, ed., p. 49). It seems Callippus was in Athens in the decade before the death of Alexander in 323 B.C. Ptolemy says in the *Almagest* (Heiberg, ed., I, p. 206) that the year 50 of the first Callippic period was forty-four years after the death of Alexander, thus placing the beginning of the period in 330/329 B.C.

The discoveries of Eudoxus that Callippus corrected and completed are described by Aristotle in *Metaphysics*, Λ. In order to "save the appearances," as Plato had proposed, Eudoxus fixed each planet on a sphere that rotated on poles attached inside another sphere rotating in a different direction at a different rate, and this sphere in another until enough concentric spheres were so arranged and moving as to account by their combined uniform motions for the observed irregularities of the planet's motion. Aristotle tells us that Callippus found it necessary to add two spheres each for the sun and moon, and one for each of the other planets except Jupiter and Saturn. These changes in Eudoxus' system are perhaps testimony to Callippus' careful observations.

A papyrus, the so-called *Ars Eudoxi,* states that Callippus had determined the lengths of the seasons more accurately than Meton, giving them as ninety-four, ninety-two, eighty-nine, and ninety days, respectively, from the vernal equinox. The error is much less than that in Meton's determinations, made a century earlier.

From such calculations Callippus was led to see that Meton's nineteen-year cycle was a trifle too long. He therefore combined four nineteen-year periods into one cycle of seventy-six years and dropped one day from the period. Thus he brought the measure of the year closer to its true value, and his period became the standard for later astronomers. Many of the observations cited by Ptolemy are given in reference to the Callippic period. Hipparchus, in Ptolemy's references, seems to have used that period regularly.

Although the system of concentric spheres gave way to epicycles and eccentrics, Callippus' period became the standard for correlating observations accurately over many centuries, and thus contributed to the accuracy of later astronomical theories.

BIBLIOGRAPHY

Ancient sources are Aristotle, *Metaphysics,* Sir David Ross, ed. (Oxford, 1924), ref. in text to 1073b32–38; Simplicius, *Commentary on Aristotle's De caelo,* J. L. Heiberg, ed. (Berlin, 1894), vol. VII of *Commentaria in Aristotelem Graeca,* which gives details from Eudemus' history of the work of Eudoxus and Callippus; Theon of Smyrna, *Expositio rerum mathematicarum ad legendum Platonem utilium,* E. Hiller, ed. (Leipzig, 1878), which covers much the same ground as Simplicius in his section on the planets; Geminus, *Elementa astronomiae,* or *Isagoge,* C. Manitius, ed. (Leipzig, 1898), pp. 120–122, an account of the period of Callippus, with number of months, including intercalary, and days in the cycle; *Ars Eudoxi,* Blass, ed. (Kiel, 1887), which gives lengths of seasons as determined by Callippus; and Ptolemy, *Almagest,* J. L. Heiberg, ed. (Leipzig, 1898),

CAMPANUS OF NOVARA

and Taliaferro, tr., Great Books of the Western World, vol. XVI, which frequently mentions the Callippic period.

Modern works are Sir Thomas Heath, *Aristarchus of Samos* (Oxford, 1913), which contains the best English-language appreciation of Callippus and refers to the relevant modern literature on him; and Pauly-Wissowa, X, pt. 2, cols. 1662 f., which gives an exhaustive account of the seventy-six-year cycle, with full references to ancient sources and modern discussions.

JOHN S. KIEFFER

CAMPANUS OF NOVARA (*b.* [probably] Novara, Italy, first quarter of thirteenth century; *d.* Viterbo, Italy, 1296)

Our scanty information on the life of Campanus is derived from a few references in contemporary documents and writers supplemented by inferences from his own works. His full style is Magister Campanus Nouariensis (there is no authority for the forename Iohannes occasionally applied to him from the sixteenth century on). He refers to himself as Campanus Nouariensis.[1] This presumably indicates that Novara was his birthplace. Contemporary documents usually refer to him as Magister Campanus. The title Magister would in this period usually mean that the holder was a member of a faculty at a university; but we have no other evidence connecting Campanus with any university. His birthdate can be only approximately inferred from the fact that he was holding ecclesiastical office and writing major works in the late 1250's and early 1260's.

The earliest piece of biographical evidence is contained in one manuscript of Campanus' edition of Euclid, which seems to connect the work with Jacques Pantaléon, patriarch of Jerusalem. This would date it between 1255 and 1261,[2] the years of Pantaléon's tenure of that position. The connection is a likely one, since when Pantaléon was elected to the papacy in 1261, becoming Urban IV, he took Campanus as one of his chaplains, as we learn from the latter's preface to his *Theorica planetarum,* which he dedicated to Urban. The letters of Urban reveal that he conferred other benefices on Campanus, including the rectorship of the Church of Savines in the diocese of Arles (reconferred 1263) and a canonicate in the cathedral of Toledo (1264). Urban died in 1264, but Campanus had another powerful patron in the person of Ottobono Fieschi, cardinal deacon of St. Adrian's and papal legate to England (later Pope Adrian V). Campanus was Ottobono's chaplain in 1263–1264, and it was probably through the influence of the cardinal that he became parson of Felmersham in Bedfordshire, England (he is attested as holding this benefice by a document of 1270).

Campanus' scientific reputation was already great enough by 1267 for Roger Bacon to name him as one of the four best contemporary mathematicians (although not one of the two "perfect").[3] Benjamin has suggested that Campanus may have accompanied Cardinal Ottobono when the latter was in England from 1265 to 1268, and there made Bacon's acquaintance. This hypothesis, although attractive, remains unproven, and indeed Campanus may never have left Italy, since the holding of benefices in absence was a common practice.

Later documents show that Campanus held a canonicate of Paris and was chaplain to popes Nicholas IV (1288–1292) and Boniface VIII (1294–1303). It is probable that he spent his later years at the convent of the Augustinian Friars at Viterbo. A letter of Boniface VIII, dated 17 September 1296, informs us that Campanus had just died at Viterbo; and in his will Campanus gave instructions for the construction of a chapel to St. Anne in the Church of the Holy Trinity there. The general impression one gets from these scattered pieces of information is of a life spent tranquilly cultivating the mathematical sciences under the patronage of powerful ecclesiastical figures, assisted by the income from a plurality of benefices that had made him a comparatively wealthy man at his death.

Of Campanus' numerous surviving works only one (the *Theorica planetarum*) exists in a modern critical edition. The unsatisfactory printed editions of others belong to the fifteenth and early sixteenth centuries; some exist only in manuscript. Much scholarly work remains to be done on these. Therefore the present survey, which is based mostly on arbitrarily selected manuscripts of the works in question, can be no more than an interim report on Campanus' output. It is not yet possible to set up even a relative system of dating of his writings as a preliminary to tracing his mathematical development. Certain individual works, however, can be quite closely dated. We have already seen that the Euclid can probably be dated to 1255–1259 and that the *Theorica* certainly belongs to the period of Urban IV's papacy (1261–1264). The planetary tables predate 1261, since they are cited in that year by Petrus Peregrinus of Maricourt. The *Computus maior* is dated to 1268 from a computation occurring in it. The *Sphere* is later than 1268, since it cites the *Computus.* An introductory letter to Simon of Genoa's *Clavis sanationis* belongs to the papacy of Nicholas IV (1288–1292), and the letter to Raner of Todi is datable to about the same period on internal evidence. But I am unable to draw any significant conclusions from the above dates, and therefore restrict myself to a description of the content of the surviving works.

The work by which Campanus is best known is his (Latin) edition of Euclid's *Elements* (in fifteen books, including the non-Euclidean books XIV and XV). This is the text of the *editio princeps* of Euclid, and it was reprinted at least thirteen more times in the fifteenth and sixteenth centuries. There are also very many manuscripts. It was undoubtedly the version in which Euclid was usually studied in the later Middle Ages. Yet surprisingly little is known of its general characteristics, and many false or misleading statements about it can be found in reference works. Thus it is frequently referred to as his "translation" of Euclid, and sometimes as his "commentary" on Euclid. Neither is accurate. We can state with confidence that Campanus did not possess the linguistic competence to translate from either Arabic or Greek: in none of his other works does he display any knowledge of either language (despite the fact that as chaplain of Urban IV he almost certainly came into close contact with the most competent Grecist of the time, William of Moerbeke, who was attached to the papal court as *poenitentiarius minor*). Campanus' edition is in fact a free reworking of an earlier translation or translations, at least one of which was made from the Arabic, as is evidenced by his retention of such terms as *(h)elmuhaym* (= Arabic *al-muʿayyan*) for "rhombus" and *(h)elmu(r)arife* (= Arabic *al-munḥarif*) for "trapezium." He may also have used existing translations from the Greek. Determination of the exact relationship of Campanus' edition to its antecedents must await publication and examination of the numerous versions of Euclid that were current in the Middle Ages. But it already seems certain that he was heavily dependent on one or more of the versions attributed to Adelard of Bath (early twelfth century).

If one compares Campanus' edition with the standard edition of the original Greek by Heiberg, one finds that the content (although not the wording) is much the same, except for some rearrangement of material and numerous additions, both small and large, in the Campanus text. Some of these additions can be found in other Greek or Arabic versions, but a number appear to stem from Campanus himself, and indeed in some manuscripts some are explicitly headed *commentum Campani*. They are, however, a commentary only in the medieval sense of "proof of an enunciated theorem," since they consist of alternative proofs, corollaries, and additional theorems. These additions are not necessarily original contributions of Campanus.

Clagett has pointed out that two demonstrations added to book I, prop. 1, are taken from the commentary of al-Nairīzī (Anaritius, translated from the Arabic by Gerard of Cremona),[4] and has printed *in extenso* a theorem on the trisection of an angle, added to book IV in some manuscripts, that seems to be related to a solution of the problem in the *De triangulis* of Jordanus de Nemore.[5] Murdoch has noted Campanus' dependence on the same author's *Arithmetica*, particularly in book VII.[6] The whole question of Campanus' originality in the *Elements* has still to be answered. But at the very least he produced from existing materials a textbook of elementary geometry and arithmetic that was written in a readily comprehensible form and language (unlike many versions of Euclid then current). Its popularity for the next 300 years is attested by the large number of manuscripts and printed copies still extant.

No other work of pure mathematics can be definitely attributed to Campanus. Most of his other writings are concerned with astronomy. Of these the most influential was the *Theorica planetarum*. It is a description of the structure and dimensions of the universe according to the Ptolemaic theory, together with instructions for the construction of an instrument for finding the positions of the heavenly bodies at any given moment (such an instrument was later known as an equatorium). Campanus' main source was the *Almagest* of Ptolemy, which he must have studied closely (probably in Gerard of Cremona's translation from the Arabic). He reproduces accurately the geometrical models evolved by Ptolemy for the explanation of the apparent motions of the heavenly bodies but refers the reader to Ptolemy's own writings for their justification (i.e., the groundwork of theory and observation).

In the *Almagest* Ptolemy had given no absolute dimensions, except for the distances of sun and moon: for the other five planets he had given only relative parameters, i.e., the size of epicycle and eccentricity in terms of a standard deferent circle with a radius of sixty units. Campanus, however, gives in addition the absolute dimensions of the whole system (in both earth radii and "miles," where one "mile" = 4,000 cubits). The mathematical basis for this lies in the assumptions that the order of the planetary spheres is known and that there is no space wasted in the universe. Then the farthest distance from the central earth reached by a planet is equal to the nearest distance to the earth reached by the planet next in order above it. Given an absolute distance of the lowest body, the moon (which Campanus takes from the *Almagest*), one can then compute all the other absolute distances. The author of this ingenious idea is also Ptolemy, in his *Planetary Hypotheses*. Campanus derived it from the work of the ninth-century Arabic author al-Farghānī (Alfraganus), which he knew in the Latin translation of John of Seville. From

CAMPANUS OF NOVARA

the latter he also took other data, such as his figure for the size of the earth and the relative sizes of the bodies of the planets. But the computations are all his own and are carried out with meticulous (indeed absurd) accuracy. Campanus obviously delighted in long arithmetical calculations, and went so far as to determine the area of the sphere of the fixed stars in square "miles."

Among the most interesting features of the work are the parts describing the construction of an equatorium. This is the first such description known in Latin Europe. It seems improbable, however, that Campanus conceived the idea independently. Descriptions of equatoria were written nearly 200 years earlier in Islamic Spain by Ibn al-Samḥ and al-Zarqāl.[7] It seems likely that Campanus got the idea, if not the particular form, of his equatorium from some (as yet unknown) Latin translation of an Arabic work. The instrument he describes is the simplest possible, being merely a scale model of the Ptolemaic system for each planet (motion in latitude is neglected, and hence a two-dimensional model suffices). Thus in Figure 1, which depicts the model for an outer planet, the outer graduated circle represents the ecliptic, the next smaller the equant, and the smallest the planet's epicycle. The double and dotted lines represent parts of the instrument that can be freely rotated. The user arranges the instrument to imitate exactly the positions of the various parts of the planet's mechanism at the given moment according to Ptolemaic theory, and then stretches a thread attached to *D*, which represents the observer (earth), through the point representing the planet and reads off its position on the outer circle.

The disadvantage of such an instrument is that it would be extremely laborious to construct, bulky to transport, and clumsy to use. The earliest treatise on the equatorium after Campanus, that of John of Lignières (early fourteenth century), is an explicit attempt to improve on Campanus' instrument.[8] This and later works on the subject describe much more compact and sophisticated instruments, and preserved examples of equatoria from the Middle Ages are far superior to Campanus' crude model.[9] But we cannot doubt that Campanus' description was a major (although not the sole) influence toward the subsequent development of the equatorium.

The *Theorica,* although it omits Ptolemy's proofs, is nevertheless a highly technical work; and its influence seems to have been confined mostly to professional astronomers. Campanus later produced a more popular work on the *Sphere* (*Tractatus de spera*). This is a description of the universe in language intelligible to the layman, requiring no great geometrical skill, and with none of the precise details of the *Theorica.*

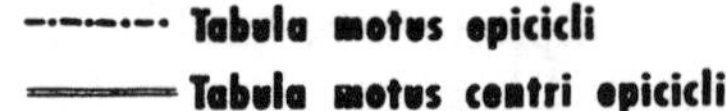

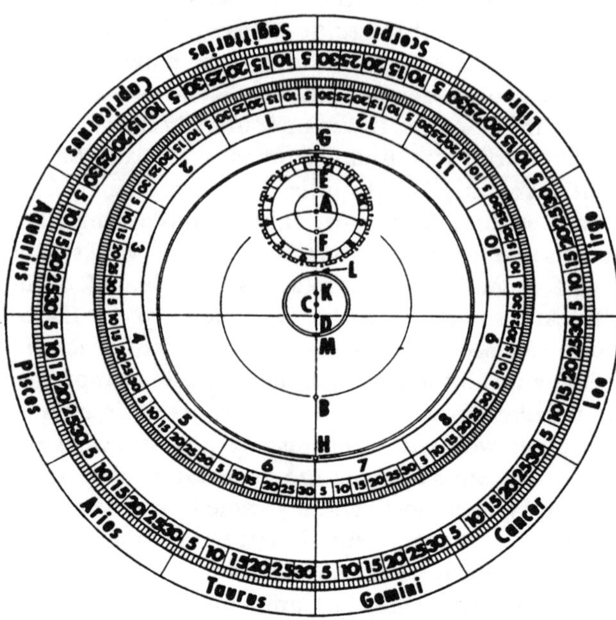

INSTRVMENTVM EQVATIONIS
SATVRNI IOVIS MARTIS ET VENERIS

FIGURE 1

It is similar in plan to the earlier works of the same name by Johannes de Sacrobosco and Robert Grosseteste, and shows no originality.[10]

Although the equatorium of the *Theorica* is explicitly intended for those who find operating with conventional astronomical tables too wearisome or difficult,[11] Campanus also describes in detail in that work how to use such tables. It is obvious that his examples are drawn from the Toledan Tables, an incongruous hodgepodge of tables carelessly extracted from the works of al-Khwārizmī, al-Battānī, and al-Zarqāl, probably translated by Gerard of Cremona and widely used in western Europe from the twelfth to the fourteenth centuries. This use of the Toledan Tables is not surprising, since Campanus had already produced an adaptation of them to Julian years, the Christian era, and the meridian of Novara (the originals are constructed for Arabic years, era of the Hegira, and the meridian of Toledo). The result is, naturally, no more satisfactory than the original, but the conversion is carried out fairly accurately. As we should also conclude from reading the relevant passages of the *Theorica,* Campanus was not merely able to use astronomical tables but understood the underlying structure of most of them, an uncommon accomplishment in his time.

CAMPANUS OF NOVARA

Campanus' third major work besides the Euclid and the *Theorica* is his *Computus maior*. The "computus" or "compotus" is a form of literature of which literally hundreds of examples were composed in the Middle Ages. Its origins lie in the difficulties of early Christians in computing the date of Easter. Works were written explaining the rather complicated rules governing such computation (on which different doctrines were held at different times by various branches of the Church). Since the computation involved both a lunar and a solar calendar, it was natural for dissertations on the calendar to be included in such works and for a sketch of the astronomical basis to be added. Bede's *De temporum ratione* (written in 725) gave the computus a form that was to be widely imitated and is essentially that adopted by Campanus.

After giving a definition of "time," Campanus discusses the various subdivisions of time: day, hour, week, month, and year. This naturally involves a good deal of astronomical discussion, and it is this portion that distinguishes Campanus' treatise from other such works, since he is able to introduce the most "modern" astronomical doctrine. The lengthy chapter 10 ("On the Solar Year") is especially notable. It contains an extended (and slightly erroneous) description of the theory of trepidation (oscillation of the equinoxes with respect to the fixed stars) of Thābit ibn Qurra, and criticisms of Ptolemy and Robert Grosseteste. From chapter 13 on, the treatise is more strictly calendrical, leading up to the computation of Easter by various methods, including the use of tables. The work concludes with a calendar giving, besides the main feast days, the tables necessary for the calculations described in the text. This part, although providing little scope for originality, is written in Campanus' usual clear and orderly way, and the work as a whole is one of the most successful examples of its genre. Since Campanus himself refers to it as "my greater computus,"[12] it is probable that he is the author of the shortened version that is found in some manuscripts.

The interest in astronomical instruments that is apparent in the *Theorica* led Campanus to compose two other short works, on the quadrant and on the astrolabe. The first is an instrument for measuring angles at a distance, and its principal use was to measure the elevation of the sun, although it could be applied in many other ways, e.g., to find the angular elevation of the top of a tower in order to compute its height. The second is a schematic representation of the celestial sphere on a plane by means of stereographic projection, and was used for the solution of problems involving the rising, setting, and transits of stars or parts of the celestial sphere that would otherwise have required spherical trigonometry. Campanus' *De quadrante* does little more than explain how to solve certain types of astronomical and mensurational problems by means of the quadrant, and is very similar to other medieval works on the subject, such as that attributed to Robert the Englishman (dated 1276). The slight work on the astrolabe, however, is unusual in that it is neither a description of the construction of the astrolabe nor of its use, but rather a series of theoretical geometrical problems connected with the astrolabe as an example of stereographic projection. I am not convinced that its attribution to Campanus is correct.

In later times Campanus had a considerable reputation as an astrologer.[13] Although the details of his prowess may be legendary, there is no doubt that like every highly educated man of his time he was well versed in astrological doctrine (this is obvious from, e.g., the *Computus* or the *Quadrant*). It seems that Campanus also wrote specifically astrological works, for a method of his for dividing the heavens into the twelve "houses" is mentioned by Regiomontanus and others, but no such work survives that can definitely be assigned to him. A long anonymous work on astrology that is found in three manuscripts is attributed to Campanus in the margin of one, but its authorship still awaits investigation.

A number of other mathematical and astronomical treatises and commentaries are occasionally attributed to Campanus in manuscripts or early printed editions. Of these the only one that is certainly his is a letter addressed to the Dominican friar Raner of Todi in response to a query of the latter on a point in Campanus' *Computus*. Others are certainly not his, e.g., a work on the instrument known as the solid sphere, and the so-called "Quadrature of the Circle."[14] A verdict on the others must await detailed examination of their contents, vocabulary, and style.

Whatever the result of such an examination, it is unlikely to have much effect on our judgment on Campanus as a man of science. He was a highly competent mathematician for his time and was thoroughly acquainted with the most up-to-date works on the subject, including the available translations from the Arabic. Thus he had read and understood Ptolemy's *Almagest,* and was able in his *Theorica* not only to summarize its conclusions but even on occasion to apply one of its techniques in another context.[15] Similarly, he was able to produce from the often obscure earlier translations of and commentaries on Euclid a version embodying their mathematical content in a more acceptable form. He had a gift for clear and plain exposition. But although he had a good understanding of his material and made few errors, he can hardly be called an original or creative scientist. His

CAMPANUS OF NOVARA

philosophical position was an unreflective Aristotelianism; his mathematics and cosmology were equally conventional for his time. His talent was for presenting the work of others in a generally intelligible form.

As such, Campanus was a writer of considerable influence. His Euclid was almost the canonical version until the sixteenth century, when it was gradually superseded by translations made directly from the Greek.[16] The continuing popularity of his *Computus* and *Sphere* is attested by their being printed several times in the sixteenth century. The *Theorica* was never printed, probably because, unlike the others, it was not a popular work but a technical one that would appeal only to those with a professional interest. It was nonetheless influential: this is shown both by the large number of surviving manuscripts and by the references to it in astronomical works of the fourteenth and fifteenth centuries. By the sixteenth century, however, it seems to have been little read (one may suspect that its role as a summary of the *Almagest* had been taken over by the Peurbach-Regiomontanus epitome of Ptolemy's work). Perhaps its greatest single contribution was the popularization of the idea of the planetary equatorium (the introduction of this is also Campanus' strongest claim to originality, but, as stated above, I believe that he owes the idea to some hitherto undiscovered Arabo-Latin source). The history of that instrument after Campanus is a good illustration of the technical ingenuity of the astronomy of the later Middle Ages and early Renaissance.

NOTES

1. E.g., *Theorica planetarum,* §1.
2. The earliest known manuscript of the work is dated 11 May 1259 (Murdoch, *Revue de synthèse,* 3rd ser., **89** [1968], 73, n. 18).
3. Bacon, *Opus tertium,* XI, 35.
4. *Isis,* **44** (1953), 29, n. 31 (4).
5. Clagett, *Archimedes,* I, 678–681.
6. *Revue de synthèse,* **89** (1968), 80, n. 41; 82, n. 53; 89, n. 84; 92, n. 100.
7. See Price, *Equatorie,* pp. 120–123.
8. *Ibid.,* p. 188.
9. See, e.g., the photograph of the equatorium at Merton College, Oxford, *ibid.,* frontispiece.
10. For a detailed outline of the contents, see Thorndike, *Sphere,* pp. 26–28.
11. *Theorica,* §§59–61.
12. "In compoto nostro maiori," MS Bibl. Naz., Conv. Soppr. J X 40, f. 47v.
13. See especially the work of Symon de Phares (late fifteenth century) on famous astrologers, Wickersheimer, ed., pp. 167–168.
14. A text of the "Quadratura circuli" has been published by Clagett, in *Archimedes,* I, 581–609, with an introduction in which the editor gives his reasons for doubting the authorship of Campanus.
15. See my note on §1280 of the *Theorica.*
16. The first version from the Greek to be printed was that of Zambertus (Venice, 1505); but Campanus' version continued to be printed for another fifty years.

BIBLIOGRAPHY

On Campanus' life, the unsatisfactory biographies in standard reference works are superseded by Benjamin's account in the Benjamin and Toomer ed. of the *Theorica planetarum,* intro., ch. 1. This contains references to all known sources. My summary is drawn from it. Roger Bacon mentions Campanus in *Fr. Rogeri Bacon opera quaedam hactenus inedita,* J. S. Brewer, ed., I (*Opus tertium*), in the "Rolls Series" (London, 1859), cap. 11, 35. The muddled account of Campanus by Symon de Phares is published in *Recueil des plus célèbres astrologues et quelques hommes faict par Symon de Phares du temps de Charles VIIIe,* E. Wickersheimer, ed. (Paris, 1929), pp. 167–168.

A full bibliography of works by or attributed to Campanus is given by Benjamin in the Benjamin and Toomer ed. of the *Theorica,* intro., ch. 2, with details of all printed eds. of such works in ch. 2, app. 1 (the evidence for the dates of writing is in ch. 1). The version of Euclid's *Elements* was first printed at Venice in 1482 by Erhardus Ratdolt. For later eds. see, besides Benjamin, Charles Thomas-Stanford, *Early Editions of Euclid's Elements* (London, 1926). The standard ed. of the Greek text is by J. L. Heiberg, *Euclidis opera omnia,* I–V (Leipzig, 1883–1888). No adequate study has been made of the relationship of Campanus' version to earlier medieval translations, but John E. Murdoch, "The Medieval Euclid: Salient Aspects of the Translations of the ELEMENTS by Adelard of Bath and Campanus of Novara," in *Revue de synthèse,* 3rd ser., **89** (1968), 67–94, is valuable, particularly for his demonstration of the didactic intent of many of the changes and additions made by Campanus. Much relevant material will also be found in Marshall Clagett, "The Medieval Latin Translations from the Arabic of the Elements of Euclid, with Special Emphasis on the Versions of Adelard of Bath," in *Isis,* **44** (1953), 16–41, and some in the same author's *Archimedes in the Middle Ages,* I, *The Arabo-Latin Tradition* (Madison, Wis., 1964); see general index under "Campanus of Novara."

The *Theorica planetarum* has been critically edited on the basis of almost all known manuscripts, with translation, commentary, and introduction, by Francis S. Benjamin, Jr., and G. J. Toomer (Madison, Wis., in press). For an account of the Ptolemaic system, see the intro. to that ed., ch. 4. The Greek text of the *Almagest* was edited by J. L. Heiberg, *Claudii Ptolemaei opera quae exstant omnia,* I, *Syntaxis mathematica,* 2 vols. (Leipzig, 1898–1903). Gerard of Cremona's translation from the Arabic was printed at Venice by Petrus Liechtenstein in 1515 as *Almagestum Cl. Ptolemaei Pheludiensis Alexandrini . . . opus ingens ac nobile.* Ptolemy's *Planetary Hypotheses* are printed in J. L. Heiberg, ed., *Claudii Ptolemaei opera quae exstant omnia,*

II, *Opera astronomica minora* (Leipzig, 1907), 70–145; but the most important passage in connection with Campanus is found only in Bernard R. Goldstein, "The Arabic Version of Ptolemy's Planetary Hypotheses," in *Transactions of the American Philosophical Society,* n.s. **57**, pt. 4 (1967). The translation of al-Farghānī used by Campanus was published in multigraph by Francis J. Carmody, *Alfragani differentie in quibusdam collectis scientie astrorum* (Berkeley, 1943). The origin and history of the system described above for determining the absolute dimensions of the universe are studied by Noel Swerdlow, *Ptolemy's Theory of the Distances and Sizes of the Planets,* Ph.D. diss. (Yale, 1968). On the history of the equatorium see D. J. Price, *The Equatorie of the Planetis* (Cambridge, 1955), esp. pp. 119–133; for the later Middle Ages and the Renaissance, Emmanuel Poulle, "L'équatoire de la Renaissance," in *Le soleil à la Renaissance, science et mythes, colloque de Bruxelles, avril 1963* (Brussels, 1965), pp. 129–148; and, for further bibliography, Poulle's "L'équatoire de Guillaume Gilliszoon de Wissekerke," in *Physis,* **3** (1961), 223–251, and "Un équatoire de Franciscus Sarzosius," *ibid.,* **5** (1963), 43–64, written with Francis Maddison.

Campanus' *Sphere* was printed by L. A. de Giunta at Venice in 1518, and three more times up to 1557 (see *Theorica,* intro., ch. 2, app. 1). Similar works by Sacrobosco and others can be found in the modern ed. of Lynn Thorndike, *The Sphere of Sacrobosco and Its Commentators* (Chicago, 1949). Grosseteste's *Sphere* is printed in *Die philosophischen Werke des Robert Grosseteste, Bischofs von Lincoln,* Ludwig Baur, ed., *Beiträge zur Geschichte der Philosophie des Mittelalters,* IX (Münster, 1912), 10–32. There is no printed ed. of Campanus' astronomical tables, nor of their parent Toledan Tables. An extensive analysis of the latter is given by G. J. Toomer in *Osiris,* **15** (1968), 5–174. The *Computus maior* was printed twice at Venice in 1518, by L. A. de Giunta and by Octavianus Scotus. On the technical content of the medieval computus, the best treatment is W. E. van Wijk, *Le nombre d'or* (The Hague, 1936). Bede's *De temporum ratione,* edited by Charles W. Jones as *Bedae opera de temporibus* (Cambridge, Mass., 1943), contains on pp. 3 ff. a useful account of the historical development of the computus. Campanus' works on the quadrant and astrolabe have never been printed. For the former, compare "Le traité du quadrant de Maître Robert Anglès . . . texte latin et ancienne traduction grecque publié par M. Paul Tannéry," in *Notices et extraits des manuscrits de la Bibliothèque nationale,* **35** (1897), 561–640, reprinted in Tannéry's *Mémoires scientifiques* (Paris, 1922), pp. 118–197. The work on astrology is attributed to Campanus only in MS Vat. Pal. 1363, where it is found on ff. 66r–88r. The letter to Raner of Todi is in only one MS: Florence, Biblioteca Nazionale Centrale J X 40, ff. 46v–56r. For other works that may or may not be by Campanus, see Benjamin in the Benjamin and Toomer ed. of the *Theorica,* intro., ch. 2.

No detailed study of the influence of Campanus' work exists. Some information will be found in the Benjamin and Toomer ed. of the *Theorica,* intro., ch. 8. The Peurbach-Regiomontanus epitome of the *Almagest* was printed at Venice in 1496 (colophon "Explicit Magne Compositionis Astronomicon Epitoma Johannis de Regio monte"), and several times subsequently.

G. J. Toomer

CAMUS, CHARLES-ÉTIENNE-LOUIS (*b.* Crécy-en-Brie, France, 25 August 1699; *d.* Paris, France, 4 May 1768)

Camus was the son of Marguerite Maillard and Étienne Camus, a surgeon. He early evidenced mathematical and mechanical abilities that induced his parents to send him to the Collège de Navarre. He subsequently continued to study mathematics (with Varignon) and also undertook work in civil and military architecture, mechanics, and astronomy.

In 1727 Camus entered the Academy of Sciences' prize competition for the best manner of masting vessels. His memoir on this subject won half the prize money and was published by the Academy; more important, it was mainly responsible for bringing him election to that body as an assistant mechanician on 13 August 1727.

During the next forty years Camus served the Academy as administrator (he was its director in 1750 and 1761), as frequent commissioner for diverse examinations, and as active scientist. In the last capacity he presented some purely mathematical memoirs, although the greatest number of his contributions dealt with problems of mechanics. These included treatments of toothed wheels and their use in clocks, studies of the raising of water from wells by buckets and pumps, an evaluation of an alleged solution to the problem of perpetual motion, and works on devices and standards of measurement. His most important scientific service was with Maupertuis, Clairaut, and Lemonnier on the Academy's 1736 expedition to Lapland to determine the shape of the earth. He subsequently served with the same people to determine the amplitude of the arc of Picard's earlier measure and, several years later, with Bouguer, Pingré, and Cassini de Thury in closely related operations. He was also involved in Cassini de Thury's famous cartographical venture, which produced the *Carte de la France* published by the Academy in 1744–1787.

In 1730 Camus was named to the Academy of Architecture and became its secretary shortly thereafter. There he gave public lessons to aspiring architects as the Academy's professor of geometry. These lessons later served as the basis of a *Cours de mathématiques* that he drew up for the use of engineering students, a task he assumed in 1748 in conjunction with the creation of the École du Génie at Mézières. A standard examination procedure was also established, and Camus was named the examiner of engineering students.

According to his instructions, Camus's course was to consist of four parts—arithmetic, geometry, mechanics, and hydraulics; the *Cours,* published in three parts from 1749–1751, covered all but the last. (Among the large number of manuscripts left at his death were a work on hydraulics, apparently intended to complete the *Cours,* and a treatise on practical geometry differing from what he had published.) In 1755, when Camus was also named the examiner for artillery schools, this *Cours* became the standard work for artillery students. Its great success was, therefore, due more to Camus's monopoly on examinations than to its intrinsic merit. In point of fact, the *Cours* came under increasing attack in the 1760's as inappropriate for artillery students and too elementary for those at Mézières.

BIBLIOGRAPHY

I. Original Works. Although published separately in 1728, Camus's prize-winning "De la mâture des vaisseaux" is most conveniently found in *Pièces qui ont remporté les prix de l'Académie royale des sciences,* II (Paris, 1732). His subsequent contributions to the *Mémoires de l'Académie royale des sciences* include the mathematical notices "Solution d'un problème de géométrie, proposé par M. Cramer, Professeur de mathématiques à Genève" (1732), 446–451; and "Sur les tangentes des points communs à plusieurs branches d'une même courbe" (1747), 272–286; the notices on mechanics "Sur la figure des dents des rouës, et des ailes des pignons, pour rendre les horloges plus parfaites" (1733), 117–140; "Sur l'action d'une balle de mousquet, qui perce une pièce de bois d'une épaisseur considerable sans lui communiquer de vitesse sensible" (1738), 147–158; "De la meilleure manière d'employer les séaux pour élever de l'eau" (1739), 157–188; "Sur les meilleures proportions des pompes, et des parties qui les composent" (1739), 297–332; "Sur un problème de statique, qui a rapport au mouvement perpétuel" (1740), 201–209; "Sur un instrument propre à jauger les tonneaux et les autres vaisseaux qui servent à contenir des liqueurs" (1741), 382–402; and, with Hellot, "Sur l'étalon de l'aune du Bureau des Marchands Mercier de la ville de Paris" (1746), 607–617; and the geodetic report, with P. Bouguer, C. F. Cassini de Thury, and A. G. Pingré, "Opérations faites par l'ordre de l'Académie pour mesurer l'intervalle entre les centres des pyramides de Villejuive et de Juvisy, en conclurre la distance de la tour de Montlhéri au clocher de Brie-Comte-Robert, et distinguer entre les différentes déterminations que nous avons du degré du méridien aux environs de Paris, celle qui doit être préférée" (1754), 172–186.

The *Cours de mathématiques* appeared as *Élémens d'arithmétique* (Paris, 1749), *Élémens de géométrie théorique et pratique* (Paris, 1750), and *Élémens de méchanique statique,* 2 vols. (Paris, 1750–1751).

II. Secondary Literature. The standard biographical sources on Camus are the *éloge* by Grandjean de Fouchy in *Histoire de l'Académie royale des sciences* (Paris, 1768), pp. 144–154; and Théophile Lhuillier, "Essai biographique sur le mathématicien Camus, né à Crécy-en-Brie," in *Almanach historique de Seine-et-Marne pour 1863* (Meaux, 1863). A brief evaluation of his work, but with several errors, is available in Niels Nielsen, *Géomètres français du dix-huitième siècle* (Paris, 1935), pp. 81–83. For more important considerations of his *Cours* and his role as examiner, see Roger Hahn, "L'enseignement scientifique aux écoles militaires et d'artillerie," in *Enseignement et diffusion des sciences en France au XVIIIe siècle,* René Taton, ed. (Paris, 1964), pp. 513–545; and René Taton, "L'École royale du Génie de Mézières," *ibid.,* pp. 559–615.

Seymour L. Chapin

CANTOR, GEORG (*b.* St. Petersburg, Russia, 3 March 1845; *d.* Halle, Germany, 6 January 1918)

Cantor's father, Georg Waldemar Cantor, was a successful and cosmopolitan merchant. His extant letters to his son attest to a cheerfulness of spirit and deep appreciation of art and religion. His mother, Marie Böhm, was from a family of musicians. Her forebears included renowned violin virtuosi; and Cantor described himself also as "rather artistically inclined," occasionally voicing regrets that his father had not let him become a violinist.

Like his father, Cantor was a Protestant; his mother was Catholic. The link with Catholicism may have made it easier for him to seek, later on, support for his philosophical ideas among Catholic thinkers.

Cantor attended the Gymnasium in Wiesbaden, and later the Grossherzoglich-Hessische Realschule in Darmstadt. It was there that he first became interested in mathematics. In 1862 he began his university studies in Zurich, resuming them in Berlin in 1863, after the sudden death of his father. At that time Karl Weierstrass, famed as a teacher and as a researcher, was attracting many talented students to the University of Berlin. His lectures gave analysis a firm and precise foundation, and later many of his pupils proudly proclaimed themselves members of the "Berlin school" and built on the ideas of their teacher.

Cantor's own early research on series and real numbers attests to Weierstrass' influence, although in Berlin he also learned much from Kummer and Kronecker. His dissertation, *De aequationibus secundi gradus indeterminatis,* dealt with a problem in number theory and was presented to the department by

Kummer. In those days it was still the custom for a doctoral candidate to have to defend his scholarly theses against some of his fellow students. Worthy of note is Cantor's third thesis, presented on receiving his doctor's degree in 1867: *In re mathematica ars proponendi pluris facienda est quam solvendi.* And indeed his later achievements did not always consist in *solving* problems. His unique contribution to mathematics was that his special way of asking questions opened up vast new areas of inquiry, in which the problems were solved partly by him and partly by successors.

In Berlin, Cantor was a member (and from 1864 to 1865 president) of the Mathematical Society, which sought to bring mathematicians together and to further their scientific work. In his later years he actively worked for an international union of mathematicians, and there can have been few other scholars who did as much as he to generate and promote the exchange of ideas among scientists. He conceived a plan to establish an Association of German Mathematicians and succeeded in overcoming the resistance to it. In 1890 the association was founded, and Cantor served as its first president until 1893. He also pressed for international congresses of mathematicians and was responsible for bringing about the first ever held, in Zurich in 1897.

Thus Cantor was no hermit living within his own narrow science. When, later, he did sever ties with many of his early friends—as with H. A. Schwarz in the 1880's—the reasons lay in the nature of his work rather than in his character. During the Berlin years a special friendship had grown up between him and Schwarz, who was two years his senior. Both revered their teacher, Weierstrass; and both were concerned to gain the good opinion of Kronecker, who frequently criticized the deductions of Weierstrass and his pupils as unsound. These first years of Cantor's early research were probably the happiest of his life. His letters from that period radiate a contentment seldom granted him in later times, when he was struggling to gain acceptance for his theory of sets.

In 1869 Cantor qualified for a teaching position at the University of Halle, soon becoming associate professor and, in 1879, full professor. He carried on his work there until his death. His marriage in 1874 to Vally Guttmann was born of deep affection, and the sunny personality of the artistically inclined "Frau Vally" was a happy counter to the serious, often melancholy, temperament of the great scholar. They had five children, and an inheritance from his father enabled Cantor to build his family a house. In those days a professor at Halle was so poorly paid that without other income he would have been in financial straits. It was Cantor's hope to obtain a better-endowed, more prestigious professorship in Berlin, but in Berlin the almost omnipotent Kronecker blocked the way. Completely disagreeing with Cantor's views on "transfinite numbers," he thwarted Cantor's every attempt to improve his standing through an appointment to the capital.

Recognition from abroad came early, however. Cantor's friend Mittag-Leffler accepted his writings for publication in his then new *Acta mathematica.* He became an honorary member of the London Mathematical Society (1901) and of other scientific societies, receiving honorary doctor's degrees from Christiania (1902) and St. Andrews (1911).

The closing decades of Cantor's life were spent in the shadow of mental illness. Since 1884 he had suffered sporadically from deep depression and was often in a sanatorium. He died in 1918 in Halle University's psychiatric clinic. Schoenfliess was of the opinion that his health was adversely affected by his exhausting efforts to solve various problems, particularly the continuum problem, and by the rejection of his pioneering work by other eminent mathematicians.

Cantor has gone down in history as the founder of set theory, but the science of mathematics is equally indebted to him for important contributions in classical analysis. We mention here his work on real numbers and on representation through number systems. In his treatise on trigonometric series, which appeared in 1872,[1] he introduced real numbers with the aid of "fundamental series." (Today we call them fundamental sequences or Cauchy sequences.) They are sequences of rational numbers $\{a_n\}$ for which, given an arbitrarily assumed (positive, rational) ϵ, we have an integer n_1 such that

$$|a_{n+m} - a_n| < \epsilon$$

if $n \geqq n_1$ and m is an arbitrary positive integer. To series having this property Cantor assigned a "limit" b. If $\{a'_n\}$ is a second sequence of the same kind and if $|a_n - a'_n| < \epsilon$ for sufficiently large n, then the same limit b is assigned to this second sequence. We say today that the real number b is defined as an equivalence class of fundamental sequences.

Cantor further showed[2] that any positive real number r can be represented through a series of the type

$$r = c_1 + \frac{c_2}{2!} + \frac{c_3}{3!} + \frac{c_4}{4!} + \cdots \qquad (1)$$

with coefficients c_γ that satisfy the inequality

$$0 \leqq c_\gamma \leqq \gamma - 1.$$

Series such as (1) are known today as Cantor series. The work also contains a generalization of representation (1) and representations of real numbers in terms of infinite products. With these writings (and with several remarkable studies on the theory of Fourier series) Cantor established himself as a gifted pupil of the Weierstrass school. His results extended the work of Weierstrass and others by "conventional" means.

In November 1873, in an exchange of letters with his colleague Dedekind in Brunswick, a question arose that would channel all of Cantor's subsequent scientific labor in a new direction. He knew that it was possible to "count" the set of rational numbers, i.e., to put them into a one-to-one correspondence with the set of natural numbers, but he wondered whether such one-to-one mapping were not also possible for the set of real numbers. He believed that it was not, but he "could not come up with any reason." A short time later, on 2 December, he confessed that he "had never seriously concerned himself with the problem, since it seemed to have no practical value," adding, "I fully agree with you when you say that it is therefore not worth very much trouble."[3] Nevertheless, Cantor did further busy himself with the mapping of sets, and by 7 December 1873 he was able to write Dedekind that he had succeeded in proving that the "aggregate" of real numbers was uncountable. That date can probably be regarded as the day on which set theory was born.[4] Dedekind congratulated Cantor on his success. The significance of the proof had meanwhile become clear, for in the interim Cantor (and probably Dedekind, independently) had succeeded in proving that the set of real algebraic numbers is countable. Here, then, was a new proof of Liouville's theorem that transcendental numbers do exist. The first published writing on set theory is found in *Crelle's Journal* (1874).[5] That work, "Über eine Eigenschaft des Inbegriffes aller reellen algebraischen Zahlen," contained more than the title indicated, including not only the theorem on algebraic numbers but also the one on real numbers, in Dedekind's simplified version, which differs from the present version in that today we use the "diagonal process," then unknown.[6]

Following his initial successes, Cantor tackled new and bolder problems. In a letter to Dedekind dated 5 January 1874, he posed the following question:

> Can a surface (say, a square that includes the boundaries) be uniquely referred to a line (say, a straight-line segment that includes the end points) so that for every point of the surface there is a corresponding point of the line and, conversely, for every point of the line there is a corresponding point of the surface? Methinks that answering this question would be no easy job, despite the fact that the answer seems so clearly to be "no" that proof appears almost unnecessary.[7]

The proof that Cantor had in mind was obviously a precise justification for answering "no" to the question, yet he considered that proof "almost unnecessary." Not until three years later, on 20 June 1877, do we find in his correspondence with Dedekind another allusion to his question of January 1874. This time, though, he gives his friend reasons for answering "yes." He confesses that although for years he had believed the opposite, he now presents Dedekind a line of argument proving that the answer to the following (more general) question was indeed "yes":

> We let $x_1, x_2, \cdots, x_\rho$ be ρ independent variable real quantities, each capable of assuming all values $\geqq 0$ and $\leqq 1$. We let y be a $\sqrt{(\rho + 1)}$ st variable real quantity with the same free range $\left(y \begin{matrix} \geqq 0 \\ \leqq 1 \end{matrix}\right)$. Does it then become possible to map the ρ quantities $x_1, x_2, \cdots, x_\rho$ onto the one y so that for every defined value system $(x_1, x_2, \cdots, x_\rho)$ there is a corresponding defined value y and, conversely, for every defined value y one and only one defined value system $(x_1, x_2, \ldots, x_\rho)$?[8]

Thus for $\rho \doteq 2$ we again have the old problem: Can the set of points of a square (having, say, the coordinates x_1 and x_2, $0 \leqq x_\gamma \leqq 1$) be mapped in a one-to-one correspondence onto the points of a line segment (having, say, the coordinates y, $0 \leqq y \leqq 1$)?

Today we are in a position to answer this question affirmatively with a very brief proof.[9] Cantor's original deduction[10] was still somewhat complicated, but it was correct; and with it he had arrived at a result bound to seem paradoxical to the mathematicians of his day. Indeed, it looked as if his mapping had rendered the concept of dimension meaningless. But Dedekind recognized immediately that Cantor's map of a square onto a line segment was discontinuous, suspecting that a continuous one-to-one correspondence between sets of points of different dimensions was not possible. Cantor attempted to prove this, but his deduction[11] did not stand up. It was Brouwer, in 1910, who finally furnished a complete proof of Dedekind's supposition.

Cantor's next works, dealing with the theory of point sets, contain numerous definitions, theorems, and examples that are cited again and again in modern textbooks on topology. The basic work on the subject by Kuratowski[12] contains in its footnotes many historical references, and it is interesting to note how many of the now generally standard basic concepts in topology can be traced to Cantor. We mention only the "derivation of a point set," the idea of "closure," and the concepts "dense" and "dense in itself." A set that was closed and dense in itself Cantor called "perfect," and he gave a remarkable example of a perfect discontinuous set. This "Cantor set" can be defined as the set of all points of the interval] 0; 1 ["which are contained in the formula

$$z = \frac{c_1}{3} + \frac{c_2}{3^2} + \frac{c_3}{3^3} + \cdots$$

where the coefficients c_γ must arbitrarily assume the values 0 or 2, and the series may consist of both a finite and an infinite number of terms."[13] It was Cantor, too, who provided the first satisfactory definition of the term "continuum," which had appeared as early as the writings of the Scholastics. A continuous perfect set he called a continuum, thereby turning that concept, until then very vague, into a useful mathematical tool. It should be noted that today a continuum is usually introduced as a compact continuous set, a definition no longer matching Cantor's. The point is, though, that it was he who provided the first definition that was at all usable.

With his first fundamental work, in 1874,[14] Cantor showed that, with the aid of the one-to-one correspondence, it becomes possible to distinguish differences in the infinite: There are *countable* sets and there are sets having the power of a *continuum.* Of root importance for the development of general set theory was the realization that for every set there is a set of higher power. Cantor substantiated this initially through his theory of ordinal numbers. It can be seen much more simply, though, through his subset theorem, which appears in his published writings in only one place,[15] and there for only one special case. But in a letter to Dedekind dated 31 August 1899,[16] we find a remark to the effect that the so-called "diagonal process," which Cantor had been using, could be applied to prove the general subset theorem. The essence of his proof was the observation that there can be no one-to-one correspondence between a set L and the set M of its subsets. To substantiate this, Cantor introduced functions $f(x)$ that assign to the elements x of a set L the image values 0 or 1. Each such function defines a subset of L—the set, say, for which $f(x) = 0$—and to each subset $L' \subset L$ there belongs a function $f(x)$, which becomes 0 precisely when x belongs to L'.

Now, if there were a one-to-one correspondence between L and M, the set of functions in question could be written in the form $\varphi\,(x,z)$

> . . . so that through each specialization of z an element $f(x) = \varphi(x,z)$ is obtained and, conversely, each element $f(x)$ of M is obtained from $\varphi(x,z)$ through a particular specialization of z. But this leads to a contradiction, because, if we take $g(x)$ as the single-valued function of x which assumes only the values 0 or 1 and is different from $\varphi(x,x)$ for each value of x, then $g(x)$ is an element of M on the one hand, while, on the other, $g(x)$ cannot be obtained through any specialization $z = z_0$, because $\varphi(z_0,z_0)$ is different from $g(z_0)$.[17]

According to the subset theorem, for each set there is a set of higher power: the set of subsets or the power set $P(M)$. The question of a general "set theory" thus became acute. Cantor regarded his theory as an expansion of classical number theory. He introduced "transfinite" numbers (cardinal numbers, ordinal numbers) and developed an arithmetic for them. With these numbers, explained in terms of transfinite sets, he had, as Gutzmer remarked on the occasion of Cantor's seventieth birthday in 1915, opened up "a new province" for mathematics.

Understandably, the first probing steps taken in this new territory were shaky. Hence, the definition of the basic concept has undergone some noteworthy modifications. In Cantor's great synoptic work in the *Mathematische Annalen* of 1895 we read:

> We call a power or cardinal number that general concept which with the aid of our active intelligence is obtained from the set M by abstracting from the nature of its different elements m and from the order in which they are given. Since every individual element m, if we disregard its nature, becomes a 1, the cardinal number M itself is a definite set made up merely of ones.[18]

Modern mathematics long ago dropped this definition, and with good reason. Today two sets are called "equal" if they contain the same elements, however often they are named in the description of the set. So if between the braces customarily used in defining these sets we place several 1's, we then have the set with the single element 1: e.g., $\{1,1,1,1,1\} = \{1\}$.

Cantor himself may have sensed the inadequacy of his first definition. In discussing a book in 1884, and later in 1899 in a letter to Dedekind, he called a power "that general concept that befits it and all its equivalent sets." Today we would say, more simply, that "a cardinal number is a set of equivalent sets." But this second definition turns out to be inadequate, too. We know, of course, that the concept of a "set of all sets" leads to contradictions. From this, though, it follows that the concept of a "set of all sets equivalent to a given set M" is also inconsistent. We let M, for example, be a given infinite set and

$$M^* = M \cup \{\mathfrak{M}\},$$

where $\mathfrak{M}$ encompasses the set of all sets. The set $\{\mathfrak{M}\}$ then naturally has the power 1, and the sets M^* (which contain only one element more than M) are all equivalent to M. Accordingly, the system of the sets M is a genuine subset of the "set of all sets equivalent to M." But since we can map this system into the elements of the "set of all sets," we thus have a concept that must lead to antinomies.

In short, in all of Cantor's works we find no usable definition of the concept of the cardinal number. The same is true of the ordinal number.

But the story does not end there. A third Cantor definition of a cardinal number appears in a report by Gerhard Kowalewski, included in his biography, *Bestand und Wandel,* of meetings that he had had with Georg Cantor. The eighty-year-old Kowalewski wrote the book shortly before his death, around 1950. With graphic vividness he tells of events and meetings that had occurred a half century before. Around 1900, Kowalewski was a *Privatdozent* in Leipzig. In those days the mathematicians from Halle and Leipzig used to meet about twice a month, first in one city, then in the other. On these occasions they would discuss their work. Although by then Cantor was no longer publishing, he often, according to the report of a young colleague, impressively held forth at the meetings on his theory of manifolds. This included his studies on the "number classes," the set of ordinal numbers that belong to equivalent sets. The numbers of the second number class were, for example, the ordinal numbers of the countable sets. Kowalewski then discusses powers (which were called "alephs"):

> This "power" can also be represented, as was Cantor's wont, by the smallest or initial number of that number class, and the alephs can be identified with these initial numbers so that such and such would be the case if we wished to use those designations for the initial terms of the second and third number class from the Schoenfliess report on set theory.[19]

In a modern book on set theory we find the following definition of a cardinal number: "A cardinal number is an ordinal number which is not similar to any smaller ordinal number."[20] So modern mathematics has adopted Cantor's belated definition, which is not to be found anywhere in his published writings. It is unlikely that Stoll, author of the above book, ever read Kowalewski's biography. The modern view of the cardinal-number concept lay dormant for a time, to be embraced by younger scholars. One should mention, though, that even Cantor himself finally did arrive at the definition of a cardinal number considered "valid" today. True, this modern version of the concept does presuppose the availability of an ordinal-number concept. Here again we cannot accept Cantor's classical definition, for roughly the same reasons that prevent our accepting the early versions of the cardinal-number concept. Today, according to John von Neumann, an ordinal number is described as a well-ordered set w in which every element $v \in w$ is equal to the segment generated by v:

$$v = A_v.$$

To sum up, we are not indebted to Cantor only for his initiative in developing a theory of transfinite sets. He proved the most important theorems of the new theory himself and laid the groundwork for the present-day definitions of the concept. It would be silly to hold against him the fact that his initial formulations did not fully meet modern precision requirements. One who breaks new ground in mathematics needs a creative imagination, and his initial primitive definitions cannot be expected to stand up indefinitely. When Leibniz and Newton founded infinitesimal calculus, their definitions were crude indeed compared with the elegant versions of centuries later, refined by Weierstrass and his pupils. The same is true of the beginnings of set theory, and it is worthy of note that Cantor himself was inching ever closer to the definitions that the present generation accepts as "valid."

By his bold advance into the realm of the infinite, Cantor ignited twentieth-century research on the fundamentals. Hilbert refused to be driven out of the "paradise" that Cantor had created. But Cantor himself was not an axiomaticist. His way of thinking belonged more to the classical epoch. In the annotations to his *Grundlagen einer allgemeinen Mannigfaltigkeitslehre* (1883) he expressly acknowledged his adherence to the "principles of the Platonic system," although he also drew upon Spinoza, Leibniz, and Thomas Aquinas.

For Cantor the theory of sets was not only a mathematical discipline. He also integrated it into metaphysics, which he respected as a science. He sought, too, to tie it in with theology, which used metaphysics as its "scientific tool."[21] Cantor was convinced that the actually infinite really existed "both concretely and abstractly." Concerning it he wrote: "This view, which I consider to be the sole correct one, is held by only a few. While possibly I am the very first in history to take this position so explicitly, with all of its logical consequences, I know for sure that I shall not be the last!"[22]

Mathematicians and philosophers oriented toward Platonic thought accepted actual infinity abstractly, but not concretely. In a remarkable letter to Mittag-Leffler, Cantor wrote that he believed the atoms of

CANTOR

the universe to be countable, and that the atoms of the "universal ether" could serve as an example of a set having the power of a continuum. Present-day physicists are not likely to be much interested in these quaint opinions. Today his philosophical views also appear antiquated. When we now ask what is left of Cantor's work, we can answer very simply: Everything formalizable is left. His statements in the realm of pure mathematics have been confirmed and extended by subsequent generations, but his ideas and conceptions in that of physics would not be acceptable to most of the present generation.

To the end Cantor believed that the basis of mathematics was metaphysical, even in those years when Hilbert's formalism was beginning to take hold. Found among his papers after his death was a shakily written penciled note (probably from 1913) in which he reaffirms his view that "without some grain of metaphysics" mathematics is unexplainable. By metaphysics he meant "the theory of being." There are several important theorems in set theory that were first stated by Cantor but were proved by others. Among these is the Cantor-Bernstein equivalence theorem: "If a set A is equivalent to a subset $B' \subset B$ and B to a subset $A' \subset A$, then A and B are equivalent." A simple proof of this, first demonstrated by Cantor's pupil Bernstein, is found in a letter from Dedekind to Cantor.[23] That every set can be well ordered was first proved by Zermelo with the aid of the axiom of choice. This deduction provoked many disagreements because a number of constructivists objected to pure "existence theorems" and were critical of the paradoxical consequences of the axiom of choice.

More fundamental, though, were the discussions about the antinomies in set theory. According to a theorem proved by Cantor, for every set of ordinal numbers there is one ordinal number larger than all the ordinal numbers of the set. One encounters a contradiction when one considers the set of all ordinal numbers. Cantor mentioned this antinomy in a letter to Hilbert as early as 1895. A much greater stir was caused later by the Russell antinomy, involved in the "set of all sets which do not contain themselves as an element." It was chiefly Hilbert who was looking for a way out of the impasse, and he proposed a strict "formalization" of set theory and of all mathematics. He hoped thereby to save the "paradise" that Cantor had created. We do not have time or space here to dwell upon the arguments that raged around Hilbert's formalism. Suffice it to say that today's generally recognized structural edifice of mathematics is formalistic in the Hilbertian sense. The concept of the set is preeminent throughout.

When we pick up a modern book on probability theory or on algebra or geometry, we always read something about "sets." The author may start with a chapter on formal logic, usually followed by a section on set theory. And this specialized discipline is described as the theory of certain classes of sets. An algebraic structure, say, is a set in which certain relations and connections are defined. Other sets, defined by axioms concerning "neighborhoods," are called spaces. In probability theory we are concerned with sets of events and such.

In Klaua's *Allgemeine Mengenlehre* there is a simple definition of mathematics: "Mathematics is set theory." Actually, we can regard all mathematical disciplines as the theory of special classes of sets. True, a high price (in Cantor's eyes) was paid for this development. Modern mathematics deals with formal systems; and Cantor, probably the last great Platonist among mathematicians, never cottoned to the then nascent formalism. For him the problem of the continuum was a question in metaphysics. He spent many years attempting to show that there can be no power between that of the countable sets and the continuum. In recent time it has been shown (by Gödel and Cohen) that the continuum hypothesis is independent of the fundamental axioms of the Zermelo-Fraenkel system. That solution of the problem would not have been at all to Cantor's taste. Yet had he not defended, against his antagonist Kronecker, the thesis that the essence of mathematics consists in its freedom?[24] Does this not include the freedom for a theory created by Cantor to be interpreted in a way not in conformity with his original ideas? The fact that his set theory has influenced the thinking of the twentieth century in a manner not in harmony with his own outlook is but another proof of the objective significance of his work.

NOTES

1. *Gesammelte Abhandlungen,* pp. 92 ff.
2. *Ibid.,* pp. 35 ff.
3. E. Noether and J. Cavaillès, *Briefwechsel Cantor–Dedekind,* pp. 115–118.
4. The first version of Cantor's proof (in his letter to Dedekind) was published in E. Noether and J. Cavaillès, *Briefwechsel Cantor–Dedekind,* pp. 29–34, and by Meschkowski, in *Probleme des Unendlichen,* pp. 30 ff.
5. *Gesammelte Abhandlungen,* pp. 115 ff.
6. See, for instance, Meschkowski, *Wandlungen des mathematischen Denkens,* pp. 31 ff.
7. E. Noether and J. Cavaillès, *Briefwechsel Cantor–Dedekind,* pp. 20–21.
8. *Ibid.,* pp. 25–26.
9. Meschkowski, *Wandlungen des mathematischen Denkens,* pp. 32 ff.
10. *Crelle's Journal,* **84** (1878), 242–258; *Gesammelte Abhandlungen,* pp. 119 ff.

11. *Gesammelte Abhandlungen,* pp. 134 ff.
12. K. Kuratowski, *Topologie I, II* (Warsaw, 1952).
13. *Gesammelte Abhandlungen,* p. 193.
14. "Über eine Eigenschaft des Inbegriffes aller reellen algebraischen Zahlen," in *Crelle's Journal,* **77** (1874), 258–262; also in *Gesammelte Abhandlungen,* pp. 115 ff.
15. *Gesammelte Abhandlungen,* pp. 278 ff.; *Jahresbericht der Deutschen Mathematikervereinigung,* **1** (1890–1891), 75–78.
16. *Gesammelte Abhandlungen,* p. 448.
17. *Ibid.,* p. 280.
18. *Mathematische Annalen,* **46** (1895), 481
19. G. Kowalewski, *Bestand und Wandel,* p. 202.
20. R. Stoll, *Introduction to Set Theory and Logic* (San Francisco, 1961), p. 317.
21. See Meschkowski, *Probleme des Unendlichen,* ch. 8.
22. *Gesammelte Abhandlungen,* p. 371.
23. *Ibid.,* p. 449.
24. *Ibid.,* p. 182.

BIBLIOGRAPHY

I. Original Works. Cantor's important mathematical and philosophical works are contained in *Gesammelte Abhandlungen mathematischen und philosophischen Inhalts,* E. Zermelo, ed. (Berlin, 1930; repr. Hildesheim, 1962), with a biography of Cantor by A. Fraenkel.

There are several other publications on mathematical and theological questions and on the Shakespeare-Bacon problem, which greatly interested Cantor for a time: "Vérification jusqu'à 1000 du théorème empirique de Goldbach," in Association Française pour l'Avancement des Sciences, *Comptes rendus de la 23me session (Caen 1894),* pt. 2 (1895), 117–134; "Sui numeri transfiniti. Estratto d'una lettera di Georg Cantor a G. Vivanti, 13 dicembre 1893," in *Rivista di matematica,* **5** (1895), 104–108 (in German); "Lettera di Georg Cantor a G. Peano," *ibid.,* 108–109 (in German); "Brief von Carl Weierstrass über das Dreikörperproblem," in *Rendiconti del Circolo matematico di Palermo,* **19** (1905), 305–308; *Resurrectio Divi Quirini Francisci Baconi Baronis de Verulam Vicecomitis Sancti Albani CCLXX annis post obitum eius IX die aprilis anni MDCXXVI* (Halle, 1896), with an English preface by Cantor; *Confessio fidei Francisci Baconi Baronis de Verulam . . . cum versione Latina a. G. Rawley . . . nunc denuo typis excusa cura et impensis G. C.* (Halle, 1896), with a preface in Latin by Cantor; *Ein Zeugnis zugunsten der Bacon-Shakespeare-Theorie mit einem Vorwort herausgegeben von Georg Cantor* (Halle, 1897); *Ex oriente lux* (Halle, 1905), conversations of a teacher with his pupil on important points of documented Christianity; and *Contributions to the Founding of the Theory of Transfinite Numbers* (Chicago–London, 1915).

Cantor's letters have been published in a number of works listed below. A fairly large number of letters and a complete list of all the published letters appear in Meschkowski's *Probleme des Unendlichen* (see below).

II. Secondary Literature. On Cantor or his work see J. Bendiek, "Ein Brief Georg Cantors an P. Ignatius Jeiler OFM," in *Franziskanische Studien,* **47** (1965), 65–73; A. Fraenkel, "Georg Cantor," in *Jahresberichte der Deutschen Mathematikervereinigung,* **39** (1930), 189–266; H. Gericke, "Aus der Chronik der Deutschen Mathematikervereinigung," *ibid.,* **68** (1966), 46–70; G. Kowalewski, *Bestand und Wandel* (Munich, 1950), 106–109, 198–203, 207–210; *Lied eines Lebens: 1875–1954* (n.p., n.d.), pp. 1–10, an anonymous, privately printed biography of Else Cantor; W. Lorey, "Der 70. Geburtstag des Mathematikers Georg Cantor," in *Zeitschrift für mathematischen und naturwissenschaftlichen Unterricht,* **46** (1915), 269–274; H. Meschkowski, *Denkweisen grosser Mathematiker* (Brunswick, 1961), pp. 80–91; "Aus den Briefbüchern Georg Cantor," in *Archive for the History of Exact Sciences,* **6** (1965), 503–519; and *Probleme des Unendlichen. Werk und Leben Georg Cantors* (Brunswick, 1968); E. Noether and J. Cavaillès, *Briefwechsel Cantor–Dedekind* (Paris, 1937); B. Russell, *Portraits From Memory and Other Essays* (London, 1956), pp. 24–25; and *The Autobiography of Bertrand Russell 1872–1914* (London, 1967), pp. 217–220; A. Schoenfliess, "Zur Erinnerung an Georg Cantor," in *Jahresberichte der Deutschen Mathematikervereinigung,* **31** (1922), 97–106; and "Die Krisis in Cantors mathematischen Schaffen," in *Acta mathematica,* **50** (1927), 1–23; J. Ternus, "Zur Philosophie der Mathematik," in *Philosophisches Jahrbuch der Görres-Gesellschaft,* **39** (1926), 217–231; and "Ein Brief Georg Cantors an P. Joseph Hontheim S.J.," in *Scholastik,* **4** (1929), 561–571; A. Wangerin, "Georg Cantor," in *Leopoldina,* **54** (1918), 10–13, 32; and W. H. Young, "The Progress of Mathematical Analysis in the Twentieth Century," in *Proceedings of the London Mathematical Society,* **24** (1926), 412–426.

H. Meschkowski

CANTOR, MORITZ BENEDIKT (*b.* Mannheim, Germany, 23 August 1829; *d.* Heidelberg, Germany, 9 April 1920)

Cantor's father, Isaac Benedikt Cantor, was from Amsterdam; his mother, Nelly Schnapper, was the daughter of a money changer. Cantor married Tilly Gerothwohl, from Frankfurt am Main.

Cantor was first taught by private tutors and completed his secondary education at the Gymnasium in Mannheim. In 1848 he began studying at Heidelberg under Franz Schweins and Arthur Arneth, and from 1849 to 1851 he worked at Göttingen under Gauss and Moritz Stern. He took his degree at Heidelberg in 1851 with the thesis *Ein wenig gebräuchliches Coordinatensystem.* During the summer semester of 1852 he studied in Berlin under Dirichlet and Jakob Steiner and qualified for inauguration at Heidelberg in 1853 with *Grundzüge einer Elementar-Arithmetik.*

Cantor was greatly influenced by Arneth's *Geschichte der reinen Mathematik in ihrer Beziehung zur Entwicklung des menschlichen Geistes* and was encouraged in his work by Stern and the cultural philosopher E. M. Roeth. During a stay in Paris he became a close friend of Chasles and of Joseph

Bertrand. From 1860 he lectured on the history of mathematics. In 1863, as a result of his *Mathematischen Beiträge zum Culturleben der Völker,* Cantor was appointed extraordinary professor. The *Römischen Agrimensoren und ihre Stellung in der Geschichte der Feldmesskunst* (1875) led to his appointment as honorary professor; in 1908 he became full professor, and in 1913 he became emeritus.

From 1856 to 1860 Cantor was coeditor of *Kritischen Zeitschrift für Chemie, Physik und Mathematik,* and from 1860 of *Zeitschrift für Mathematik und Physik;* from 1877 to 1899 he edited *Abhandlungen zur Geschichte der Mathematik.* He published many short papers and reviews in periodicals devoted to pure mathematics and the history of science and, from 1875, wrote most of the biographies of mathematicians in *Allgemeine Deutsche Biographie.*

Together with Curtze and Günther, Cantor was one of the leading historians of mathematics in Germany at the turn of the century. He is best known for the once highly praised *Vorlesungen über Geschichte der Mathematik,* which, despite many contemporary emendations (such as those of Braunmühl, Gustaf Eneström, and Wieleitner), has not been equaled in content and extent. Although the *Vorlesungen* is now dated, it gave a definite impetus to the development of the history of mathematics as a scholarly discipline.

BIBLIOGRAPHY

I. ORIGINAL WORKS. Cantor's best-known work is *Vorlesungen über Geschichte der Mathematik,* 4 vols. (Leipzig, 1880–1908). His other writings include *Ein wenig gebräuchliches Coordinatensystem* (Frankfurt, 1851); *Grundzüge einer Elementar-Arithmetik* (Heidelberg, 1855); *Mathematischen Beiträge zum Culturleben der Völker* (Halle, 1863); and *Römischen Agrimensoren und ihre Stellung in der Geschichte der Feldmesskunst* (Leipzig, 1875).

II. SECONDARY LITERATURE. Writings on Cantor or his work are Karl Bopp, "M. Cantor †, Gedächtnisrede, gehalten im Mathematischen Verein zu Heidelberg am 19.VI.1920," in *Sitzungsberichte der Heidelberger Akademie der Wissenschaften,* Math.-nat. Kl., Abt. A (1920); and "Cantor, M.," in *Deutsches biographisches Jahrbuch,* II (Stuttgart–Berlin–Leipzig, 1928), 509–513, with complete bibliography; M. Curtze, "Verzeichnis der mathematischen Werke, Abhandlungen und Recensionen von M. Cantor," in *Zeitschrift für Mathematik und Physik,* **44,** supp. (1899), 625–650, with portrait; and "Zum 70. Geburtstage M. Cantors," in *Bibliotheca mathematica,* 3rd ser., **1** (1900), 227–231; and J. E. Hofmann, "Cantor, M. B.," in *Neue Deutsche Biographie,* III (Berlin, 1957), 129.

J. E. HOFMANN

CARAMUEL Y LOBKOWITZ, JUAN (*b.* Madrid, Spain, 23 May 1606; *d.* Milan, Italy, 7 September 1682)

The son of Lorenzo Caramuel y Lobkowitz, a Bohemian engineer in Spain, and Catalina de Frisia, Caramuel became a member of the Cistercian Order and studied at Alcalá and Salamanca, the principal Spanish universities of the time. He received the doctorate in theology at Louvain. He held various important posts within the Cistercian Order and spent most of his life in Flanders, Bohemia, and Italy. Caramuel was in the service of Emperor Ferdinand III and then of Pope Alexander VII, who appointed him bishop of Campagna (near Amalfi). He died while serving in that post.

Caramuel's some seventy works treat many subjects. One of the more important is *Mathesis biceps: Vetus et nova* (Campagna, 1670), which, although it contains no sensational discovery, presents some original contributions to the field of mathematics. In it he expounded the general principle of the numbering systems of base n (illustrated by the values 2, 3, . . ., 10, 12, and 60), pointing out that some of these might be of greater use than the decimal. He also proposed a new method of approximation (although he did not say so) for trisecting an angle. Caramuel developed a system of logarithms of which the base is 10^9, the logarithm of 10^{10} is 0, and the logarithm of 1 is 10. Thus, his logarithms are the complements of the Briggsian logarithms to the base 10 and therefore do not have to use negative characteristics in trigonometric calculations. In these particulars Caramuel's logarithms prefigure cologarithms, but he was not understood by his contemporaries; some, such as P. Zaragoza, raised strenuous objections.

A man of encyclopedic knowledge, Caramuel tried to apply a mechanical formulation to astronomy, relegating astrology to the domain of superstition and criticizing some of the statements of Tycho Brahe. In addition, he made meteorological observations, investigated the globe's physical properties, and theorized about the possibility of aerial navigation.

BIBLIOGRAPHY

Writings on Caramuel are enumerated in Ramón Ceñal, S. J., "Juan Caramuel. Su epistolario con Atanasio Kircher S. I.," in *Revista de filosofía,* **12,** no. 44 (1953), 101–147; David Fernández Diéguez, "Juan Caramuel," in *Revista matemática hispano-americana,* **1** (1919), 121–127, 178–189, 203–212; and Patricio Peñalver y Bachiller, *Bosquejo de la matemática española en los siglos de la decadencia* (Seville, 1930), pp. 29–33.

JUAN VERNET

CARATHÉODORY CONSTANTIN (*b.* Berlin, Germany, 13 September 1873; *d.* Munich, Germany, 2 February 1950)

Carathéodory was descended from an old Greek family that had lived for several generations in Adrianople (now Edirne), Turkey. His grandfather had been a professor at the Academy of Medicine in Constantinople and attending physician to two Turkish sultans. His father, who had been a diplomat in the Turkish embassies in St. Petersburg and Berlin, was the Turkish ambassador in Brussels from 1875 on.

Carathéodory won prizes in mathematics while still in secondary school. From 1891 to 1895 he attended the École Militaire de Belgique. After completing his education, he went to Egypt in the employ of the British government as assistant engineer at the Asyut dam. In 1900, however, Carathéodory suddenly decided to go to Berlin and study mathematics. There he was stimulated by the students of Hermann Amandus Schwarz. In 1902 he followed his friend Erhard Schmidt to Göttingen, where, under Hermann Minkowski, he received the doctorate in 1904. Encouraged by Klein and Hilbert, who had recognized his genius, he qualified as a university lecturer a year later.

After having taught in Bonn, Hannover, Breslau, Göttingen, and Berlin, Carathéodory was called to Smyrna by the Greek government in 1920, to direct the completion of its university. In 1922, when Smyrna was burned by the Turks, Carathéodory was able to rescue the university library and take it to Athens. He then taught for two years at Athens University, and in 1924 accepted an invitation to the University of Munich as the successor of C. L. F. Lindemann. He remained there for the rest of his life.

For many years, Carathéodory was the editor of *Mathematische Annalen.* He was a member of scientific societies and academies in many countries; his membership in the Papal Academy was particularly noteworthy.

Carathéodory married a distant cousin, Euphrosyne Carathéodory. The marriage produced one son and one daughter.

Carathéodory was the most notable Greek mathematician of recent times, and the only one who does not suffer by comparison with the famous names of Greek antiquity. He made significant contributions to several branches of mathematics, and during the period of his activity he worked in all of them more or less simultaneously.

The first field was the calculus of variations, the theory of maxima and minima in curves. In his dissertation and in his habilitation thesis, Carathéodory drew up a comprehensive theory of discontinuous solutions (curves with corners). Previously, only the so-called Erdmann corner condition was known, but Carathéodory showed that all of the theory known for smooth curves can also be applied to curves with corners. He was also concerned with the fields of solution curves, which play a central part in the theory. Thoroughly familiar with the history of the subject, he drew upon many ideas of such mathematicians as Christiaan Huygens and Johann I Bernoulli. Inspired by these ideas, he restudied the relationship between the calculus of variations and first-order partial differential equations. The result of this was *Variationsrechnung und partielle Differentialgleichungen erster Ordnung,* which includes a quite surprising new "entry" to the theory.

By means of this method, Carathéodory was able to make significant progress in solving the so-called problem of Lagrange, i.e., variation problems with differential side conditions. He also wrote fundamental papers on the variation problems of m-dimensional surfaces in an n-dimensional space. Except for the case $m = 1$ of the curves, far-reaching results had until then been available only for the case $m = n - 1$. Carathéodory was the first to tackle the general case successfully. Here again, the consideration of fields played a decisive part.

Carathéodory was particularly interested in the application of the calculus of variations to geometrical optics. This interest is best shown in his "Elementare Theorie des Spiegelteleskops von B. Schmidt," for which he carried out complete numerical calculations.

In the second main field, the theory of functions, Carathéodory's achievements are in many areas: the problems concerning Picard's theorem, coefficient problems in expansions in a power series, and problems arising from Schwarz's lemma; he also significantly advanced the theory of the functions of several variables. His most important contributions, however, are in the field of conformal representation. The so-called main theorem of conformal representation of simply connected regions on the circle of unit radius had been proved rigorously for the first time shortly before World War I, and Carathéodory was able to simplify the proof greatly. His main achievement in this area was his theory of boundary correspondence, in which he investigated the geometrical-set theoretic properties of these boundaries in a completely new way.

The third main field consists of the so-called theory of real functions and the theory of the measure of point sets and of the integral. Carathéodory's book on this subject, *Vorlesungen über reelle Funktionen* (1918), represents both a completion of the development begun around 1900 by Borel and Lebesgue and the beginning of the modern axiomatization of this field. He returned to it in the last decade of his life, when he carried the axiomatization or, as he called it, the algebraization, of the concepts one step further.

In applied mathematics Carathéodory produced papers on thermodynamics and on Einstein's special theory of relativity.

BIBLIOGRAPHY

Carathéodory's articles were collected in *Gesammelte mathematische Schriften*, 5 vols. (Munich, 1954–1957); vol. V has autobiographical notes up to 1908 (pp. 387–408) and an obituary by Erhard Schmidt (pp. 409–419). Carathéodory's books are *Vorlesungen über reelle Funktionen* (Leipzig–Berlin, 1918; 2nd ed., 1928); *Conformal Representation*, Cambridge Tracts in Mathematics and Mathematical Physics, no. 28 (Cambridge, 1932); *Variationsrechnung und partielle Differentialgleichungen erster Ordnung* (Leipzig–Berlin, 1935; 2nd. ed., 1956); *Geometrische Optik*, IV, pt. 5 of the series Ergebnisse der Mathematik und ihrer Grenzgebiete (Berlin, 1937); *Reelle Funktionen*, I (Leipzig–Berlin, 1939); *Funktionentheorie*, 2 vols. (Basel, 1950); and *Mass und Integral und ihre Algebraisierung* (Basel, 1956).

An article on Carathéodory is Oskar Perron, "Constantin Carathéodory," in *Jahresbericht der Deutschen Mathematikervereinigung*, **55** (1952), 39–51.

H. BOERNER

CARCAVI, PIERRE DE (*b.* Lyons, France, *ca.* 1600; *d.* Paris, France, April 1684)

The son of a banker named Trapezita, he was made a member of the *parlement* of Toulouse on 20 July 1632, and in 1636 left for Paris after having bought the office of member of the *grand conseil* there. In 1645 he entered the renewed dispute over the quadrature of the circle. John Pell was involved in a controversy with the Danish astronomer Longomontanus, who claimed to have effected the quadrature of the circle; Carcavi sent Pell a refutation in which he claimed that this was impossible. About 1648 he was forced to sell his office as member of the *grand conseil*, in order to be able to pay his father's debts, and entered the service of the Duke of Liancourt. A protégé of the duke, Amable de Bourzeis, presented Carcavi to Colbert, who in 1663 charged him with the classification of his library and made him custodian of the Royal Library (later the site of the meetings of the French Academy of Sciences). At the Academy's first official meeting there, 22 December 1666, Carcavi announced the king's decision to protect the new institution. On 30 May 1668 Colbert charged Huygens, Roberval, Carcavi, Auzout, Picard, and Gallois with research on the method of determining longitude at sea that had been proposed by R. de Neystt. On 6 June 1668 the commission rejected the method. After the death of Colbert in 1683 Carcavi was replaced by Gallois at the Academy and the Royal Library.

Carcavi rendered great services to science. His polite and engaging manner brought him many friends, including Huygens, Fermat, and Pascal. He carried on an extensive correspondence and thus was a medium for the communication of scientific intelligence. His friendship with Fermat dates from his time at Toulouse, when both were members of the *parlement*. He was probably the first to recognize Fermat's extraordinary scientific abilities. After Carcavi went to Paris, Fermat corresponded with him and sent him many treatises; for instance, in the autumn of 1637 Carcavi received the text of Fermat's *Isagoge ad locos planos et solidos*, a short introduction into analytical geometry written in 1636, a year before Descartes published his *Géométrie*.

After the death of Mersenne in 1648, Carcavi offered Mersenne's correspondence to Descartes. In his letter of 11 June 1649 the philosopher thanked Carcavi and asked him about the experiment of Pascal, who had had a barometer carried to the top of the Puy de Dôme. This experiment showed that the greater the altitude, the lower the air pressure. Descartes claimed that he had given Pascal the idea two years before. In his answer of 9 July 1649, Carcavi said that the report of the experiment had been printed some months previously. At the same time he informed Descartes of Roberval's objections to his *Géométrie*. On 17 August 1649 Descartes replied with a refutation of Roberval's assertions. After Carcavi's answer of 24 September 1649, in which he defended Roberval, Descartes broke with him.

In the spring of 1650 Fermat sent Carcavi a treatise entitled *Novus secundarum et ulterioris ordinis radicum in analyticis usus*, in which he corrected the process given by Viète in his *De aequationum recognitione et emendatione* (written 1591) by treating the method of elimination of one or more unknowns in several equations. This is the first known method of elimination. When Fermat began to fear that his discoveries might be lost, he tried to find collaborators and asked Pascal and Carcavi to publish his papers. This attempt failed (letter of 27 October 1654 from Pascal to Fermat), as did the second attempt by Carcavi, who on 22 June 1656 proposed to Huygens that the papers be published by Elsevier in Amsterdam. Carcavi made a new attempt in his letter of 14 August 1659 to Huygens. He informed him that he had a collection of Fermat's papers, corrected by the author himself, ready for publication. He also enclosed a paper by Fermat on his discoveries concerning the theory of numbers. In his answer of 4 September 1659 Huygens promised that he would deal with the publisher. In the years 1659–1662 Carcavi sent Huygens more treatises by Fermat that mentioned Huygens' new results; Huygens was not pleased with them. This may be one reason why the papers were not published. It was not until 1679 that Samuel de Fermat succeeded in publishing the *Varia opera mathematica,* which did not contain all Fermat's discoveries.

Carcavi was also a friend of Pascal, who gave him his calculating machine. When in 1658 Pascal sent all mathematicians a challenge offering prizes for the first two solutions of some problems concerning the cycloid, he lodged the prizes and his own solutions with Carcavi, who, with Roberval, was to act as a judge.

BIBLIOGRAPHY

Carcavi's letters can be found in collections of the correspondence of Galileo, Mersenne, Torricelli, Descartes, Fermat, Pascal, and Huygens.

Some information on Carcavi's life and work is in Charles Henry, "Pierre de Carcavy, intermédiaire de Fermat, de Pascal, et de Huygens," in *Bollettino di bibliografia e storia delle scienze matematiche e fisiche,* **17** (1884), 317–391.

H. L. L. BUSARD

CARDANO, GIROLAMO (*b.* Pavia, Italy, 24 September 1501; *d.* Rome, Italy, 21 September 1576)

Cardano was the illegitimate son of Fazio Cardano and Chiara Micheri, a widow of uncertain age who was both ignorant and irascible. The early years of his life were characterized by illness and mistreatment. Encouraged to study the classics, mathematics, and astrology by his father, a jurist of encyclopedic learning and a friend of Leonardo da Vinci, Cardano began his university studies in 1520 at Pavia and completed them at Padua in 1526 with the doctorate in medicine. Almost immediately he began to practice his profession in Saccolongo, a small town near Padua, where he spent nearly six years; he later recalled this period as the happiest of his life. Having been cured of impotence, which had afflicted him throughout his youth, he married Lucia Bandareni in 1531; they had two sons and a daughter.

In 1534, sponsored by noblemen who were friends of his father, Cardano became a teacher of mathematics in the "piattine" schools of Milan. (These schools, founded by a bequest of Tommaso Piatti [*d.* 1502], taught Greek, dialectics, astronomy, and mathematics.) He simultaneously practiced medicine, achieving such success that his colleagues became envious. His first work, *De malo recentiorum medicorum usu libellus* (Venice, 1536), was directed against them. Within a few years Cardano became the most famous physician in Milan, and among the doctors of Europe he was second only to Vesalius. Among his famous patients was John Hamilton, archbishop of Edinburgh, who suffered from asthma. Cardano remained in Scotland for most of 1552 in order to treat the archbishop and a number of other English noblemen.

In 1539, while awaiting the publication of *Practica arithmetice,* his first book on mathematics, Cardano learned that Nicolò Tartaglia knew the procedure for solving third-degree equations. He succeeded in obtaining this information by promising, possibly under oath, not to reveal it. After having kept the promise for six years, he considered himself released from it when he learned that the credit for the discovery actually belonged to Scipione dal Ferro. He therefore published the method in his *Artis magnae sive de regulis algebraicis liber unus* (1545), commonly called *Ars magna,* his greatest work in mathematics. Its publication angered Tartaglia, who in his *Quesiti et inventioni diverse* (1546) accused Cardano of perjury and wrote of him in offensive terms that he repeated in *General trattato di numeri et misure* (1556–1560). The latter work was well known among mathematicians and thus contributed greatly to posterity's low opinion of Cardano.

In 1543 Cardano accepted the chair of medicine at the University of Pavia, where he taught until 1560, with an interruption from 1552 to 1559 (when the stipend was not paid). In 1560 his elder son, his favorite, was executed for having poisoned his wife. Shaken by this blow, still suffering public condemnation aroused by the hatred of his many enemies, and embittered by the dissolute life of his younger son, Cardano sought and obtained the chair of medicine at the University of Bologna, to which he went in 1562.

In 1570 Cardano was imprisoned by the Inquisition. He was accused of heresy, particularly for having cast the horoscope of Christ and having attributed the events of His life to the influence of the stars. After a few months in prison, having been forced to recant and to abandon teaching, Cardano went in 1571 to Rome, where he succeeded in obtaining the favor of Pope Pius V, who gave him a lifetime annuity. In Rome, in the last year of his life, he wrote *De propria vita,* an autobiography—or better, an *apologia pro vita sua*—that did not shrink from the most shameful revelations. The *De propria vita* and the *De libris propriis* are the principal sources for his biography.

Cardano wrote more than 200 works on medicine, mathematics, physics, philosophy, religion, and music. Although he was insensitive to the plastic arts, his was the universal mentality to which no branch of learning was inaccessible. Even his earliest works show the characteristics of his highly unstable personality: encyclopedic learning, powerful intellect combined with childlike credulity, unconquerable fears, and delusions of grandeur.

Cardano's fame rests on his contributions to mathematics. As early as the *Practica arithmetice,* which is devoted to numerical calculation, he revealed uncommon mathematical ability in the exposition of many original methods of mnemonic calculation and in the confidence with which he transformed algebraic expressions and equations. One must remember that he could not use modern notation because the contemporary algebra was still verbal. His mastery of calculation also enabled him to solve equations above the second degree, which contemporary algebra was unable to do. For example, taking the equation that in modern notation is written $6x^3 - 4x^2 = 34x + 24$, he added $6x^3 + 20x^2$ to each member and obtained, after other transformations,

$$4x^2(3x + 4) = (2x^2 + 4x + 6)(3x + 4),$$

divided both members by $3x + 4$, and from the resulting second-degree equation obtained the solution $x = 3$.

His major work, though, was the *Ars magna,* in which many new ideas in algebra were systematically presented. Among them are the rule, today called "Cardano's rule," for solving reduced third-degree equations (i.e., they lack the second-degree term); the linear transformations that eliminate the second-degree term in a complete cubic equation (which Tartaglia did not know how to solve); the observation that an equation of a degree higher than the first admits more than a single root; the lowering of the degree of an equation when one of its roots is known; and the solution, applied to many problems, of the quartic equation, attributed by Cardano to his disciple and son-in-law, Ludovico Ferrari. Notable also was Cardano's research into approximate solutions of a numerical equation by the method of proportional parts and the observation that, with repeated operations, one could obtain roots always closer to the true ones. Before Cardano, only the solution of an equation was sought. Cardano, however, also observed the relations between the roots and the coefficients of the equation and between the succession of the signs of the terms and the signs of the roots; thus he is justly considered the originator of the theory of algebraic equations. Although in some cases he used imaginary numbers, overcoming the reluctance of contemporary mathematicians to use them, it was only in 1570, in a new edition of the *Ars magna,* that he added a section entitled "De aliza regula" (the meaning of *aliza* is unknown; some say it means "difficult"), devoted to the "irreducible case" of the cubic equation, in which Cardano's rule is extended to imaginary numbers. This was a recondite work that did not give solutions to the irreducible case, but it was still important for the algebraic transformations which it employed and for the presentation of the solutions of at least three important problems.

His passion for games (dice, chess, cards) inspired Cardano to write the *Liber de ludo aleae,* which he completed in his old age, perhaps during his stay at Bologna; it was published posthumously in the *Opera omnia.* The book represents the first attempt at a theory of probability based on the philosophical premise that, beyond mere luck, laws and rules govern any given case. The concept of probability was introduced, expressed as the ratio of favorable to possible cases; the law of large numbers was enunciated; the so-called "power law" (if p is the probability of an event, the probability that the event will be repeated n times is p^n) was presented; and numerous problems relating to games of dice, cards, and knucklebones were solved. The book was published, however, subsequent to the first research into the theory of games developed in the correspondence between Fermat and Pascal in 1654; it had no influence on the later development of the field.

Cardano published two encyclopedias of natural science: *De subtilitate libri XXI* (1550) and *De rerum varietate* (1557), a supplement to *De subtilitate.* The two works, written in an elliptical and often obscure Latin, contain a little of everything: from cosmology to the construction of machines; from the usefulness of natural sciences to the evil influence of demons; from the laws of mechanics to cryptology. It is a mine of facts, both real and imaginary; of notes on the state of the sciences; of superstition, technology, alchemy, and various branches of the occult. The similarities between the scientific opinions expressed by Cardano in these two works and those of Leonardo da Vinci, at that time unpublished, has led some historians, particularly Pierre Duhem, to suppose that Cardano has used Leonardo's manuscript notes; others insist that the similarity is entirely coincidental. Be that as it may, Cardano must always be credited with having introduced new ideas that inspired new investigations. In the sixteenth century there were five editions of *De rerum varietate* and eight of *De subtilitate,* as well as seven editions of the French translation of the latter.

Cardano reduced the elements to three (air, earth, water), eliminating fire, which he considered a mode of existence of matter; and he reduced the four qualities to two (hot and moist). His magic was, above all, an attempt to interpret natural phenomena in terms of sympathy and antipathy.

In mechanics, Cardano was a fervent admirer of Archimedes. He studied the lever and the inclined plane in new ways and described many mechanical devices, among them "Cardano's suspension," known in classical antiquity, which he attributed to a certain Jannello Turriano of Cremona. Cardano followed a middle road between the partisans of the theory of impetus and the supporters of the Aristotelian theory, who attributed the movement of projectiles to pushing by the air: he favored the idea that at the beginning of its trajectory the projectile was moved by the impetus of the firing mechanism but subsequently was accelerated by the movement of the air. Notable is his observation that the trajectory described by a projectile is not rectilinear at the center, but is a line "which imitates the form of a parabola." Cardano's chief claim to fame, however, was his affirmation of the impossibility of perpetual motion, except in heavenly bodies.

Cardano's contributions to hydrodynamics are important: counter to contemporary belief, he observed that in a conduit of running water, the water does not rise to the level from which it started, but to a lower level that becomes lower as the length of the conduit increases. He also refuted the Aristotelian "abhorrence of a vacuum," holding that the phenomena attributed to this abhorrence can be explained by the force of rarefaction. Cardano investigated the measurement of the capacity of streams and stated that the capacity is proportional to the area of the cross section and the velocity. He observed that a stream presses against its banks and, counter to contemporary opinion, he held that the upper levels of moving water move faster than the lower levels.

In his *Opus novum de proportionibus,* Cardano turned to problems of mechanics, with the principal aim of applying quantitative methods to the study of physics. His use of the concept of moment of a force in his study of the conditions of equilibrium in balance and his attempt to determine experimentally the relation between the densities of air and water are noteworthy. The value that he obtained, 1 : 50, is rough; but it is the first deduction to be based on the experimental method and on the hypothesis that the ratio of the distances traveled by bullets shot from the same ballistic instrument, through air and through water, is the inverse of the ratio between the densities of air and water.

Geology is indebted to Cardano for several theories: that the formation of mountains is often due to erosion by running water; that rise of the ocean floor is indicated by the presence of marine fossils in land that was once submerged; and the idea—then novel—that streams originate from rainwater, which runs back to the sea and evaporates from it, to fall back to earth as rain, in a perpetual cycle.

The many editions of Cardano's works and the citations of them by writers of the second half of the sixteenth century demonstrate their influence, especially as a stimulus to the study of the particular and the concrete.

BIBLIOGRAPHY

I. Original Works. Nearly all of Cardano's writings are collected in the *Opera omnia,* Charles Sponi, ed., 10 vols. (Leiden, 1663). The published works to which scholars most often refer are *Practica arithmetice et mensurandi singularis* (Milan, 1539); *Artis magnae, sive de regulis algebraicis liber unus* (Nuremberg, 1545); *De subtilitate liber XXI* (Nuremberg, 1550; 6th ed., 1560), trans. by Richard Le Blanc as *De la subtilité . . .* (Paris, 1556; 9th ed., 1611), and bk. 1, trans., with intro. and notes, by Myrtle Marguerite Cass (Williamsport, Pa., 1934); *Liber de libris propriis* (Leiden, 1557); *De rerum varietate libri XVII* (Basel, 1557; 5th ed., 1581); *De subtilitate . . . cum additionibus. Addita insuper Apologia adversus calumniatorem* (Basel, 1560; 4th ed., 1611); and *Opus novum de proportionibus numerorum, motuum, ponderum, sonorum, aliarumque rerum mensurandarum. . . . Item de aliza regula liber* (Basel, 1570). The autobiography was published by Gabriel Naudé as *De propria vita liber . . .* (Paris, 1643; 2nd ed., Amsterdam, 1654); it was translated into Italian (Milan, 1821, 1922; Turin, 1945); German (Jena, 1914); and English (New York, 1930). The French translation by Jean Dayre (Paris, 1936) includes the Latin text with the variants of a 17th-century MS preserved in the Biblioteca Ambrosiana in Milan. The *Liber de ludo aleae* was first published in the *Opera omnia* and translated into English by Sidney Henry Gould as *The Book on Games of Chance* (New York, 1961).

II. Secondary Literature. On Cardano himself, the following works contain many bibliographic references: Angelo Bellini, *Girolamo Cardano e il suo tempo* (Milan, 1947); and Henry Morley, *The Life of Girolamo Cardano of Milan, Physician,* 2 vols. (London, 1854). His mathematical work is analyzed in Ettore Bortolotti, *I contributi del Tartaglia, del Cardano, del Ferrari e della scuola matematica bolognese alla teoria algebrica delle equazioni cubiche,* no. 9 in the series Studi e Memorie per la Storia dell'Università di Bologna (Bologna, 1926), pp. 55–108, and *I cartelli di matematica disfida*, no. 12 in the series Studi e Memorie per la Storia dell'Università di Bologna (Bologna, 1935), pp. 3–79; Moritz Cantor, *Vorlesungen über Geschichte der Mathematik*, 2nd ed. (Leipzig, 1899), II, 484–510, 532–541; and Pietro Cossali, *Origine e trasporto in Italia dell'algebra*, II (Parma, 1797), 159–166, 337–384. The most profound study of Cardano's contribution to the theory of games is Oystein Ore, *Cardano the Gambling Scholar* (Princeton, 1953), which concludes with Gould's translation of the *Liber de ludo aleae*.

Cardano's physics is presented in Raffaello Caverni, *Storia del metodo sperimentale in Italia*, I (Florence, 1891), 47–50, and IV (Florence, 1895), 94–95, 197–198, 385–386 (entire work repr. Bologna, 1969). The hypothesis of his intellectual debt to Leonardo is defended by Pierre Duhem in *Les origines de la statique*, I (Paris, 1895), 237–238, 242; and *Études sur Léonard de Vinci*, I (Paris, 1906), 223–245. On Cardano's work in magic, alchemy, and the arts of divination, see Lynn Thorndike, *A History of Magic and Experimental Science*, V (New York, 1951), 563–579; on his contributions to cryptology, see David Kahn, *The Codebreakers* (London, 1967).

MARIO GLIOZZI

CARNOT, LAZARE-NICOLAS-MARGUERITE (*b.* Nolay, Côte-d'Or, France, 13 May 1753; *d.* Magdeburg, Germany, 2 August 1823)

Known to French history as the "Organizer of Victory" in the wars of the Revolution and to engineering mechanics for the principle of continuity in the transmission of power, Carnot remains one of the very few men of science and of politics whose career in each domain deserves serious attention on its own merits. His father, Claude, lawyer and notary, was among the considerable bourgeois of the small Burgundian town of Nolay in the vicinity of Beaune though on the wrong side of the ridge for the vineyards. The family still owns the ancestral house. His most notable descendants have been his elder son Sadi, famous in thermodynamics, and a grandson, the latter's nephew, also called Sadi, president of the French Republic from 1887 until his assassination in 1894.

Carnot had his early education in the Oratorian *collège* at Autun. Thereafter, his father enrolled him in a tutoring school in Paris which specialized in preparing candidates for the entrance examinations to the service schools that trained cadets for the navy, the artillery, and the Royal Corps of Engineers. Strong in technique and weak in prestige, the Corps of Engineers was the only branch of military service in which a commoner might still hold a commission. Carnot graduated from its school at Mézières after the normal course of two years.

Promotion was slower for engineers than for line officers. After routine assignments at Calais, Cherbourg, and Béthune, he was posted to Arras, where society was livelier. There in 1787 he became acquainted with Maximilien de Robespierre, a fellow member of the literary and philosophic society of the Rosati. During these years of garrison duty, Carnot sought reputation by writing of mechanics, mathematics, and military strategy in essays prepared for competitions of the kind regularly set by learned societies in the eighteenth century.

It was, indeed, only through his writings on military strategy that Carnot won a certain minor recognition prior to the Revolution. In 1784 the Academy of Dijon set as subject for its annual prize the career of the founder of the Royal Corps of Engineers, the Maréchal de Vauban (like Carnot a Burgundian), whose theory and practice of fortification and siege-craft had guided the strategy of Louis XIV and become standard doctrine in the limited warfare of the Enlightenment. Carnot's *Éloge de Vauban* carried off that award. Its publication brought him into the crossfire of a skirmish of the books that had broken out among members of the French armed forces wherein the political interests and social prestige of the several arms and services were entangled with opposing theories of warfare. Writing out of the specialist tradition of the engineering corps, Carnot upheld the purportedly humane view of warfare that made its purpose the defense of civilization in the wise employment of prepared positions rather than the barbarous destruction of an enemy in conflict to the death. His argument criticized the emphasis of the combat arms on gallantry, movement, and command under fire, aspects recommended anew to elements among the line officers by the recent example of Frederick the Great and the resurgence of aristocratic pretensions in French society.

Carnot entered politics in 1791 when he was elected a deputy to the Legislative Assembly from the Pas-de-Calais. As the monarchy proved its untrustworthiness in 1791 and 1792, he became a republican out of a kind of civic commitment natural to his class and family background. Following the outbreak of war in April 1792, the services of a patriotic deputy competent in military matters were at a premium. Carnot combined integrity with the engineer's ability to improvise arrangements and organize procedures. His mission to the Army of the Rhine immediately after the overthrow of the monarchy in August 1792 imposed the sovereign authority of the Republic upon the officers and local agents whose allegiance had been to the Crown. Amid the military disasters in Belgium in the spring of 1793, it was Carnot who, as representative of the people incarnating its revolutionary will, had to override the demoralized generals and organize first the defense and then the attack to his own prescription. Never an ideologist, never really a democrat, he had the reputation of a tough and reliable patriot when, in August 1793, he was called by the more politically minded men already constituting the emergency Committee of Public Safety to serve among its membership of twelve men who, ruling France throughout the Jacobin Terror, converted anarchy into authority and defeat into victory.

His main responsibility was for the war, and he alone of his erstwhile colleagues continued in office after the fall of Robespierre in July 1794 through the ensuing reaction and on into the regime of the Directory that followed in 1795. For two more years Carnot was the leading member of that body, in which office he, together with four incompatible colleagues, exercised the executive power of the French Republic. In 1797 the leftist coup d'état of 18 Fructidor (4 September) displaced Carnot from government. He took refuge in Switzerland and Germany, returning in 1800 soon after Napoleon's seizure of power.

Carnot had given Napoleon command of the Army of Italy in 1797, and now Napoleon named his sometime patron minister of war. The Bonapartist dispensation proved uncongenial to an independent spirit, however, and after a few months Carnot resigned.

Thereupon he devoted his older years to the technical and scientific interests of his younger days, having qualified for membership in the Institut de France in 1796 by virtue of his prominence if not of any wide comprehension of his youthful work in mechanics, his only scientific work then in print. Throughout the Napoleonic period he served on numerous commissions appointed by the Institute to examine the merits of many of the mechanical inventions that testify to the fertility of French technical imagination in those years of conquest and warfare. He was never too old for patriotism, however. Amid the crumbling of the Napoleonic system, he offered his services when the retreat from Moscow reached the Rhine. In those desperate circumstances Napoleon appointed him governor of Antwerp. Carnot commanded the defense. He rallied to the emperor again during the Hundred Days and served as his last minister of the interior. That act bespoke the consistency of the old revolutionary yet more decisively than Carnot's having voted death to Louis XVI some twenty-two years before. He was not forgiven by a monarchy that had had to be restored twice, and he fled into exile once again, leaving in France his elder son, Sadi, an 1814 graduate of the École Polytechnique, and taking the younger, Hippolyte, to bring up in Magdeburg, in which tranquil city he lived out his days corresponding with old associates and publishing occasional verse.

Scientists often become public figures, but public figures seldom produce science, and a glance at the Bibliography below will suggest that the range and originality of his published work in mechanics, geometry, and the foundations of the calculus in the ten years following his fall from power in 1797 must be unique in the annals of statesmen in political eclipse. The phenomenon is the more interesting in that its beginnings go back to his days as a young engineering officer who had failed to win a hearing for the approach that began to be appreciated only in the days of his later prominence. The *Essai sur les machines en général* of 1783 contains all the elements of his engineering mechanics, in which subject it was the first truly theoretical treatise. It attracted no detectable attention prior to the revision he published in 1803 under the title *Principes fondamentaux de l'équilibre et du mouvement.* Even the analysis given the problem of machine motion in the latter work began to affect the actual treatment of problems only in the 1820's through the theoretical practice of his son Sadi and his contemporary polytechnicians, notably Navier, Coriolis, and Poncelet. The lag is not to be explained on the grounds either of some mathematical sophistication in the analysis or of the unexpectedness of some signal discoveries. On the contrary, the style and argument seem naïve and literal compared to the mathematical mode of treatment that Lagrange set as the standard of elegance for rational mechanics in *Mécanique analytique* (1788), a work to which Carnot never aspired to compare his own. The unfamiliarity of Carnot's approach derived from his purpose, not his content, from what he thought to do with the science of mechanics rather than what he added to it.

His purpose was to specify in a completely general way the optimal conditions for the operation of machines of every sort. Instead of adapting the laws of statics and dynamics to the properties of the standard classes of simple machine—i.e., the lever, the wedge, the pulley, the screw, and so forth—as did conventional manuals of applied mechanics, he began with a completely abstract definition. A machine is an intermediary body serving to transmit motion between two or more primary bodies that do not act directly on one another. The problem of a truly general mechanics of machines could then be stated:

> Given the virtual motion of any system of bodies (i.e., that which each of the bodies would describe if it were free), find the real motion that will ensue in the next instant in consequence of the mutual interactions of the bodies considered as they exist in nature, i.e., endowed with the inertia that is common to all the parts of matter.

In developing the reasoning, Carnot gave important impetus to what was to become the physics of energy, not by building out from the mathematical frontier of analytical mechanics, but by starting behind those front lines with the elementary principles of mechanics itself. From among them he selected the conservation of live force or *vis viva*, the quantity MV^2 or the product of the mass of a body multiplied by the square of its velocity, as the basis from which propositions adaptable to the problem of machine motion might most naturally be derived. The principal explicit finding of the *Essai sur les machines en général* was that it is a condition of maximum efficiency in the operation of machines that power be transmitted without percussion or turbulence (in the case of hydraulic machines). That principle of continuity was usually known as Carnot's until after the middle of the nineteenth century, when its parentage became obscured in the generality of conservation of energy, of which felt but unstated law it was one of many early partial instances.

In the course of deriving his own principle of continuity from that of live force, Carnot recognized its equivalent, the product of the dimensions of force multiplied by distance—*MGH* in the gravitational case, for he usually preferred to reason on the example of weights serving as loads or motive forces—to be the quantity that mechanics might most conveniently employ to estimate the efficacy of machines. In 1829 Coriolis proposed to designate by the word "work" any quantity thus involving force times distance. Carnot had called it "moment of activity." Although he did not explicitly state the measure of power to be the quantity of live force (energy) expended or moment of activity (work) produced in a given time, that usage is implicit in the argument, of which the central thrust in effect transformed the discussion of force and motion into an analysis of the transmission of power. Dimensionally, of course, there was nothing new about it: the equivalence of $MV^2/2$ to *MGH* derived from Galileo's law of fall as the means of equating the velocity that a body would generate in falling a certain height with the force required to carry it back on rebound.

It was the engineer in Carnot that saw the advantage of winning from that trivial dimensional equivalence an application of the science of mechanics to analysis of the operation of machines. In the ideal case, live force reappears as moment of activity; or, in much later words, input equals output. It was simply a condition of perfect conversion that nothing be lost in impacts and that motion be communicated smoothly—hence his principle. His approach carried over the employment of live-force conservation from hydrodynamics into engineering mechanics generally. Following publication in 1738 of Daniel Bernoulli's *Hydrodynamica,* that subject had been the only one that regularly invoked the principle of live force in the solution of engineering problems; and except for certain areas of celestial mechanics, it was the only sector of the science in which it had survived the discredit of the metaphysical disputes between partisans of the Newtonian and Leibnizian definitions of force early in the century. The evidence runs through all of Carnot's writings on mechanics and into those of his son Sadi that the hydraulic application of principles and findings, although ostensibly a special case, actually occupied a major if not a primary place in their thinking.

Carnot did not reach his conclusions so easily as this, however, and certain features of his reasoning point much further than its mere results, namely in the direction of dimensional and vector analysis and also toward the concept of reversible processes. Wishing to attribute to machines no properties except those common to all parts of matter, Carnot envisaged them as intrinsically nothing more than systems composed of corpuscles. He began his analysis with the action of one corpuscle upon another in machine motions, and obtained an equation stating that in such a system of "hard" (inelastic) bodies, the net effect of mutual interaction among the corpuscles constituting the system is zero:

$$\int mVU \cos Z = 0,$$

where the integral sign means summation; m is the mass of each corpuscle; V its actual velocity; U the velocity that it "loses", i.e., the resultant of V and its virtual velocity; and Z the angle between the directions of V and U. The notion of balancing the forces and motions "lost" and "gained" from the constraints of the system was central to his analysis of the manner in which he imagined forces transmitted by shafts, cords, and pulleys constraining and moving points within systems composed of rigid members. In his way of seeing the problem, he had necessarily to find constructs that would incorporate the direction as well as the intensity of forces in expressions of their quantity; and in combining and resolving such quantities, he habitually adopted simple trigonometric relations in a kind of proto-vector analysis that permitted him to represent the projection of the quantity of a force or velocity upon a direction other than its own. In the *Principes fondamentaux de l'équilibre et du mouvement,* he proposed that the projection $\overline{Aa'}$ of one force or velocity $\overline{Aa}$ upon an intersecting straight line $\overline{AB}$ be represented by the notation

$$\overline{Aa'} = \overline{Aa} \cos \overline{Aa} \wedge \overline{AB},$$

where the last term represents the angle, a convention that would have been obvious although cumbersome had it been much adopted (Fig. 1). Not that Carnot had given his reader the assistance of such a diagram in the *Essai sur les machines,* but adapting it to the equation above makes it easier to see at a glance what was then in his mind, and also to appreciate his strategy: since

$$U \cos Z = V,$$

the relation reduces to

$$\int MV^2 = 0,$$

which is to say the principle of live-force conservation.

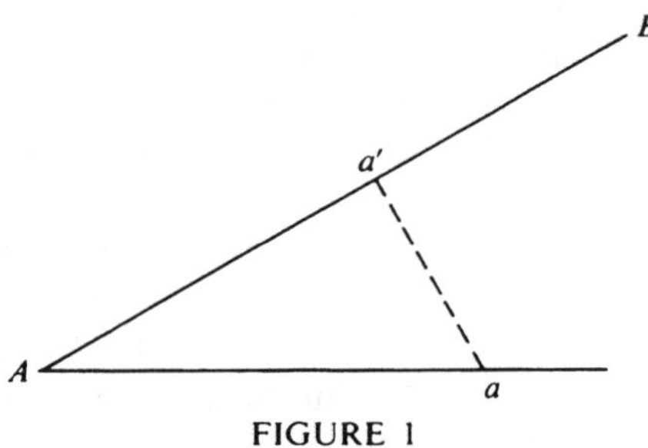

FIGURE 1

Given the generality of his statement of the problem of machine motion, Carnot could not simply proceed to a direct application of that principle, for along with the legacy of eighteenth-century matter theory he inherited that of seventeenth-century collision theory. According to the former, solid matter consists in impenetrable, indeformable corpuscles connected by rods and shafts: rigid ones in "hard" or inelastic bodies and springs in elastic bodies. Micromachines Carnot imagined the former to be, and took them for the term of comparison to which real machines ideally reduced in nature. As for the other states of matter, liquids were fluids congruent with hardness in mechanical properties since they were incompressible although deformable (a circumstance reinforcing the primacy of hydrodynamics in his thought) and gases were fluids mechanically congruent with elasticity. His difficulty was that in classical collision theory live force was conserved only in the interaction of elastic bodies; in the supposedly more fundamental case of "hard" body, live force was conserved only when motion was communicated smoothly—by "insensible degrees" in his favorite phrase, to which processes was restricted the application of the fundamental equation stated above.

He had, therefore, to convert that equation into an expression applicable to all interactions in which motion was communicated, whatever the nature of the body or the contact. To that end Carnot introduced the notion that he always regarded as his most significant contribution to mathematics and to mechanics: the idea of geometric motions, which he defined as displacements depending for their possibility only on the geometry of a system quite independently of the rules of dynamics. The concept was that which in later mechanics was called virtual displacement. In the *Principes fondamentaux de l'équilibre et du mouvement* of 1803, Carnot simplified his definition so that it amounted to specifying geometric motions as those that involve no work done on or by the system. But historically his first elucidation is the more interesting for it exhibits that what suggested to Sadi the idea of a reversible process must almost certainly have been his father's concept of geometric motion.

Imagine, Carnot charged the reader of the *Essai sur les machines en général,* that any system of hard bodies be struck by an impact, and further that its actual motion be stilled at just this instant, and it be made instead to describe two successive movements, arbitrary in character, but subject to the condition that they be equal in velocity and opposite in direction. Such an effect could be accomplished in infinitely many ways and (this was the essential matter) by purely geometric operations. An important, though not exhaustive class of such motions would be those that involved the constituent bodies of a system in no displacement relative to one another. In such a generalized system, the velocities of the neighboring corpuscles relative to each other would be zero, and Carnot could derive the further fundamental equation

$$\int muU \cos z = 0,$$

which differs from the former in that the actual physical velocity V has been replaced by an idealized, geometric velocity u. It would apply, therefore, to interactions of elastic or of inelastic bodies whether gradual or sudden since by definition such motions were independent of the dynamical considerations that excluded inelastic collision. In later terms, what Carnot had done was to derive conservation of moment of momentum or torque from conservation of energy or work by considering the ideal system within which no energy or work was lost. What he himself claimed to have done was to derive a generalized indeterminate solution to the problem of machines from which could be deduced such established though partial principles as d'Alembert's and Maupertuis's least action. In actual cases, among all the motions of which a system was geometrically capable, that which would physically occur would be the geometric motion for which sum of the products of each of the masses by the square of the velocity "lost" was a minimum, i.e., for which

$$d\int mU^2 = 0.$$

His conception of the science of machines as a subject, however, rather than his somewhat jejune solution to its generalized problem, was what made Carnot an important influence upon the science of mechanics. Through that and similar influence it became in fact and not just in precept the basis of the profession of mechanical engineering. His analysis, which balanced accounts between "moment of activity produced" (work done on) and "moment of activity consumed" (work done by) the system, was the kind that the physics of work and energy have found useful ever since those topics became explicit in the 1820's, 1830's, and 1840's. Its most recognizable offspring was the heat cycle of Sadi Carnot, which considered a system in view of what had been done to it or by it in shifting from an initial to a final state. The family resemblance was marked in the abstractedness of the systems imagined; in the discussion of force in terms of what it can do, taken usually over distance when it was a question of its measure, and over time when it was a question of its realization in mechanical processes; in the notion that process consisted in the transition between successive "states" of a system; in the requirement that for purposes of theory this transition occur in infinitesimal and reversible changes (which for Lazare Carnot was to say that all motions be geometric); in the indifference (given these conditions) to the details of rate, route, or order of displacements; in the restrictive mode of reasoning by which, perpetual motion being excluded as physically unthinkable, the maximum possibilities in operations were thereby determined in the ideal case; in the relevance of this extreme schematization to the actuality of tools, engines, and machinery operating discontinuously and irreversibly in physical fact; and, finally, in thus making theoretical physics out of the engineering practice and industrial reality of the age.

The operationalism of the engineer distinguishes Carnot's mathematical writings in a similar manner. They may be summarized more briefly because, although more voluminous and evidently more important to him in his middle years, his work in mathematics did not enter into the texture of the subject as it did in mechanics. Not that it lacked for a public: his *Réflexions sur la métaphysique du calcul infinitésimal,* first published in 1797 while he was still in political office as director, was quickly translated into Portuguese, German, English, Italian, and Russian. Carnot revised and enlarged a second edition for publication in 1813; and that version was republished from time to time in Paris, most recently in 1921. His book frankly acknowledged the difficulties that infinitesimal analysis raises for common sense, and although it was reserved to the reforms initiated by Cauchy, Bolzano, and Gauss to put the calculus on a rigorous footing, Carnot's justification evidently answered for well over a century to the needs of a public that wished to understand its own use of the calculus.

The genius of the infinitesimal calculus, in Carnot's account, lay in its capacity to compensate in its own procedures for errors that it deliberately admitted into the process of computation for the purpose of facilitating a solution. The sort of error in question is that which arises from supposing that a curve can be considered equivalent to a polygon composed of a very large number of very short sides, but the compensation of error that justified the calculus meant neither the approximation of rectilinear elements to a curve by a method of exhaustion nor the cancellation of error through some balancing of excess against defect. Such procedures would merely reduce error to the tolerable or insignificant, whereas what Carnot meant by compensation actually eliminated error and made the procedures of analysis as rigorous as those of synthetic demonstration. What the calculus really involved, properly understood, was the auxiliary use of infinitesimal quantities in order to find relations between given quantities, and its results contained no errors at all, not even infinitesimal errors.

In explaining what he meant, Carnot proposed substituting for the conventional division of quantities into determinate and indeterminate a tripartite classification into quantities (1) that were invariant and given by the conditions of the problem, (2) that although variable by nature acquired determinate values because of the conditions of the problem, and (3) that were always indeterminate. To the last class belonged all infinitely great or small quantities, and also all those involving the addition of a finite and an infinitesimal quantity. Quantities of the first two classes Carnot called designated and those of the third nondesignated. What characterized these last was not that they were minute or negligible, but that they could be made arbitrarily small at the will of the calculator. Yet at the same time they were not merely arbitrary. On the contrary, they were related to quantities of the second class by one system of equations just as the latter were to quantities of the first class by another, not unrelated, system of equations. The systems containing only designated quantities Carnot called complete or perfect. Those containing terms in nondesignated quantities he called incomplete or imperfect. The art of the infinitesimal calculus, therefore, consisted in transforming insoluble or difficult complete equations into manageable incomplete equations and then managing the calculation so as to eliminate all nondesignated quantities from the result. Their absence proved its correctness.

The congruence between Carnot's point of view in calculus and in mechanics appears to excellent advantage in his development of these comparisons. Consider, he asked the reader, any general system of quantities, some constant and some variable, and suppose the problem is to find the relations between them. Let any specified state of the general system be taken for datum. Its quantities and the variables depending exclusively on them would be the designated ones. If now the system were to be considered in some different state invoked for the purpose of determining more readily the relations between the designated quantities of the fixed system, this latter state would serve an auxiliary role and its quantities would be auxiliary quantities. If further the auxiliary state be approached to the fixed state so that all the auxiliary quantities approach more and more closely to their designated analogues, and if it is in our power to reduce these remaining differences as far as we please, then the differences would be what is meant by infinitesimal quantities. Since they were merely auxiliary, these arbitrary quantities might not figure in the solution to the problem, which was to determine the relation between the designated quantities. Reciprocally, that no arbitrary quantities occur in the result was a proof of its validity. Thus had the error willfully introduced in order to solve the problem been eliminated. If it did persist, it could only be infinitesimal. But that was impossible since the result contains no infinitesimals. Hence the procedures of the calculus had eliminated it, and that was the secret of their success.

In effect, as Carnot made clear in a historical excursion, his doctrine of compensation of errors was an attempt to combine the analytical advantages of the Leibnizian method of infinitesimals with the rigor of the Newtonian method of limits or first and last ratios of vanishing quantities.

Carnot's main geometric writings were also motivated largely by the attempt to make reasonable the employment of unreasonable quantity in analysis, although with the focus on negative rather than infinitesimal quantity. Indeed, it is clear from the manuscript remains of his mature years that he regarded the unthinking manipulation of quantities that could have no literal physical meaning as an impropriety, not to say a scandal, in mathematics that made the obscurity attending infinitesimal quantity relatively venial. There was no doubt that infinitesimals existed. The problem was only how to understand and manage them. On the other hand the difficulty with negative and imaginary numbers concerned finite analysis, went deeper, and occurred in almost every algebraic operation. In Carnot's own view his resolution of that anomaly in *De la corrélation des figures de géométrie* of 1801 and its extension, the *Géométrie de position* of 1803, constituted his most significant clarification of the procedures of mathematics.

Carnot found absurd the notion that a quantity itself could be less than zero. "Every quantity is a real object such that the mind can be seized of it, or at least its representation in calculation, in an absolute manner," he held robustly in *Géométrie de position* (p. 7), and insisted in *Corrélation des figures* on distinguishing between a quantity properly speaking and the algebraic value of a function. It was equally unacceptable to interpret the minus sign as meaning simply that a quantity was to be taken in a direction opposite to a positive one. A secant to the arc of a circle in the third quadrant was indistinguishable from one in the first in magnitude and direction. According to this latter interpretation, it should be positive in sign. In fact it is negative. Neither could this view explain why it is impossible to take the square root of a negative quantity: There is no difficulty in taking the square root of a left ordinate, after all. In short, none of the usual conventions could stand scrutiny.

There were only two senses, in Carnot's view, in which negative quantity could be rightly understood. One was the trivial sense in which it was the magnitude of a value governed by a minus sign, and this usage could be correct only when it was preceded by a positive value of greater magnitude. The deeper and more revealing sense was that a negative quantity was a magnitude governed by a sign that was wrong. Consider, for example, the formula

$$\cos(a + b) = \cos a \cdot \cos b - \sin a \cdot \sin b. \quad (1)$$

Now, in the first or literal sense, the last term here is negative. In the second sense it is positive, however, so long as a, b, and $(a + b)$ are each less than 90°, because since the equation is exact in the first quadrant, the sign is correct. But if $(a + b)$ were greater than 90°, the equation would be incorrect. For then it would turn out that

$$\cos(a + b) = \sin a \cdot \sin b - \cos a \cdot \cos b. \quad (2)$$

If formula (1) were to apply to this case, the first term, $\cos(a + b)$, would have to be regarded as governed by a sign contrary to what it ought to have been. For changing the sign would give

$$-\cos(a+b) = \cos a \cdot \cos b - \sin a \cdot \sin b, \quad (3)$$

which reduces to equation (2). In effect, therefore, applying equation (1) to the case in which $(a + b)$ was greater than 90° subjected the term, $\cos(a + b)$, to the wrong sign and made it a negative quantity in the second sense.

For quantities of this sort Carnot proposed the term "inverse" in contradistinction to "direct quantities" that bear their proper sign. How, then, did these inversions get into the process of calculation? Carnot said by error, but not quite the kind of error that introduced infinitesimals into the calculus. The occasion of error in finite analysis was rather a mistaken assumption about the basic conditions of the problem. A credit might be mistaken for a debt in actuarial work. The algebraic expression of what was to be paid or received would then be reversed, and we would recognize the error in the solution through knowledge of whether money was owed or owing. But the question was not merely one of correcting trivial misapprehensions. Often it was necessary to introduce quantities governed by a false sign into a calculation in order to formulate a problem at all. The ordinate of a curve might be required without the geometer's knowing in which quadrant it lay. Making an assumption would permit him to get an absolute value, and if he had been wrong about the sign, the error would show up as an absurdity in the result, which he could correct without redoing the computation. Indeed, what distinguished analysis from synthesis in Carnot's view was uniquely its capacity to employ negative and imaginary forms and to eliminate the unreal entities in the course of calculation after they had served their purpose of auxiliaries. In the end whatever was unintelligible was made to disappear, and there remained a result that in principle could have been discovered synthetically. But it had been obtained more easily and directly, almost mechanically. The difference between infinitesimal and finite analysis is that errors in the calculus are eliminated through the very process of computation, whereas in algebra they remain in the solution, where we recognize them by comparison with a rational or metrical reality, and that is where geometry comes in.

The service that geometry might render to analysis lay mainly through the study of the correlation of figures, and that in turn exhibits a certain congruence with his point of view in the mechanics of machine processes. Its subject matter is the comparison of geometric systems in various states that can evolve into each other. The state taken for term of comparison he called the primitive system and any other state a transformed system. An elementary example from the 1801 treatise *Corrélation des figures* will exhibit the nature of the problems and their relevance to resolving the anomaly of inverse quantity. In the triangle ABC (Fig. 2), the foot of the perpendicular AD falls between B and C in the primitive system.

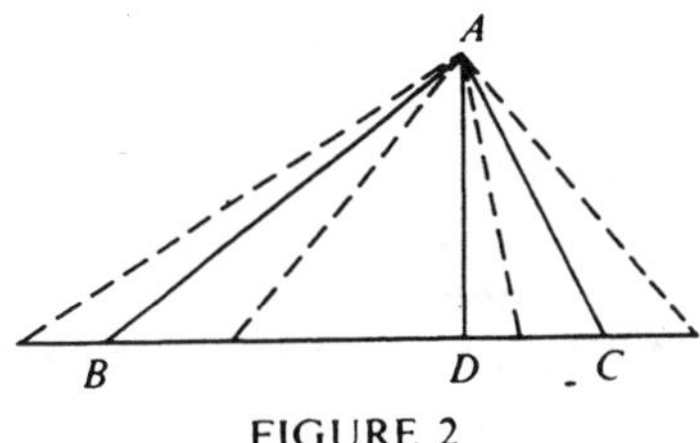

FIGURE 2

It is possible to transform the system by moving C to the left, however. In effect, the figure constitutes a system in which $\overline{CD}$ is a variable and $\overline{BD}$ a constant. In both primitive and transformed states, $\overline{BC} > \overline{BD}$ until C has passed to the left of D. Their difference, $\overline{CD}$, is a direct quantity, and $\overline{BC}$ and $\overline{BD}$ are in "direct order" in the two systems of which, therefore, the correlation was direct. Let the point C pass to the left of D, however, and then in the transformed system $\overline{BD} > \overline{BC}$, their difference $\overline{CD}$ is inverse, and the quantities $\overline{BC}$ and $\overline{BD}$ are in inverse order in the two systems, the correlation of which thereby becomes indirect.

By correlative systems Carnot meant all those that could be considered as different states of a single variable system undergoing gradual transformation. It was not necessary that all correlative systems should actually have been evolved out of the primitive system. It sufficed that they might be assimilated to it by changes involving no discontinuous mutations. The whole topic may be taken as the geometric operation of Carnot's favorite reasoning device—a comparison of systems between which the nexus of change is a continuum. When the correlation was direct, any train of reasoning that was valid for the primitive system would hold for the correlative system. When it was indirect, the formulas of the primitive system were applicable to the other by changing the signs of all the variables that had become inverted. Reciprocally, the procedure might be used in solving problems. Suppose, in the example it was given that the three sides were in the proportion

$$\overline{AC} = \overline{BC} = \frac{2}{3}\overline{AB},$$

and the segment $\overline{CD}$ was to be found. Trying the hypothesis that D was between B and C, we would have

$$\overline{AB}^2 - \overline{AC}^2 = \overline{BD}^2 - \overline{CD}^2,$$

which works out to give a negative value

$$\overline{CD} = -\frac{1}{12}\overline{AB}.$$

The minus sign signals that the hypothesis had been wrong, and that in fact C fell between B and D, for which assumption the problem yields a positive value in the solution.

In *Géométrie de position* Carnot developed what he had at first intended as a somewhat fuller edition of the *Corrélation des figures* into a vastly more extensive exploration of the problem-solving reaches of geometry. The method bore a marked resemblance to the porisms of Euclid, an affinity that Carnot recognized, for he was well versed in the history of geometry. He frequently expressed appreciation for eighteenth-century British geometry, and particularly the work of Colin Maclaurin, Robert Simson, John Landen, and Matthew Stewart—the last three names now largely forgotten in the history of mathematics. He no longer limited the scope of his work to correlations of particular geometric systems, but proposed to associate in a single treatment relations of magnitude as studied by the ancients with relations of position as studied more characteristically by the moderns, and thus to compare and unify the two main types of geometric relation. The *Géométrie de position* wears the appearance of a sort of engineering handbook of geometric systems that, were it ever to be completed, would permit resolving problems by considering unknown systems as correlatives of the set of primitive systems of which the properties were known. The formulas were to contain only real and intelligible expressions—no imaginary and no inverse quantities.

The entire subject Carnot imagined as preliminary to that which was closest to his heart and on which he promised a further book: the science of geometric motion. He redeemed the promise that same year by publishing the *Principes fondamentaux de l'équilibre et du mouvement,* which treats the science of machines in terms of geometric motions. For it is extremely interesting that it was in this that he thought to unify his geometric and mechanical interests. In *Géométrie de position,* he defines such motions as he had in the *Essai sur les machines en général,* motions depending on the geometry and not the dynamics of a system such that "the contrary motion is always possible." Such a science would be intermediary between geometry and mechanics and would rid mechanics and hydrodynamics of their analytical difficulties because it would then be possible to base both sciences entirely on the most general principle in the communication of motion, the equality and opposition of action and reaction.

BIBLIOGRAPHY

I. Original Works. Carnot's scientific works are as follows:

(1) *Essai sur les machines en général, par un officier du Corps Royal du Génie* (Dijon, 1783). Although absent from the first edition, the name of the author did appear on the second, otherwise identical printing (Dijon–Paris, 1786).

(2) *Réflexions sur la métaphysique du calcul infinitésimal* (Paris, 1797). The identical text was also published, together with (1) above, in *Oeuvres mathématiques du citoyen Carnot* (Basel, 1797). In 1813 Carnot published a revised and enlarged edition, which has been reprinted without change in all later French editions.

(3) *Lettre du citoyen Carnot au citoyen Bossut, contenant quelques vues nouvelles sur la trigonométrie,* in Charles Bossut, *Cours de mathématiques,* new ed., vol. II (Paris, 1800).

(4) *De la corrélation des figures de géométrie* (Paris, 1801).

(5) *Géométrie de position* (Paris, 1803).

(6) *Principes fondamentaux de l'équilibre et du mouvement* (Paris, 1803).

(7) *Mémoire sur la relation qui existe entre les distances respectives de cinq points quelconques pris dans l'espace, suivi d'un essai sur la théorie des transversales* (Paris, 1806), to which is appended a summary of the theory of negative quantity, "Digression sur la nature des quantités dites négatives."

Between 1800 and 1815 Carnot served on many commissions of the Institute to which numerous mechanical inventions and mathematical writings were submitted. His reports on these subjects will be found in Institut de France, Académie des Sciences, *Procès-verbaux des séances de l'Académie tenues depuis la fondation de l'Institut jusqu'au mois d'août 1835,* vols. I–V (Paris, 1910–1914). Each volume contains a full index of its contents. Carnot's most important reports were those on the Niepce and the Cagniard engines, III, 465–467, and IV, 200–202. The archives of the Academy in Paris contain the text of an unpublished "Lettre sur les aerostats" that Carnot submitted to the Academy on 17 January 1784 following the flight engineered by the brothers Montgolfier on 5 June 1783. The problem was that of propulsion.

II. Secondary Literature. There is a recent and largely reliable political biography, Marcel Reinhard, *Le grand Carnot,* 2 vols. (Paris, 1950–1952).

The memoir by Carnot's younger son, Hippolyte Carnot, *Mémoires sur Carnot,* 2 vols. (Paris, 1861–1863), is a work of anecdote animated by family piety but remains indispensable.

Carnot's scientific work forms the subject of a monograph, *Lazare Carnot savant,* by the undersigned (in press—scheduled for publication by Princeton University Press in 1971). The appendix of this work reprints in facsimile the theoretical portions of the two manuscripts on mechanics that Carnot submitted to the *Académie des sciences* in 1778 and 1780, and the entire text of the "Dissertation" on the infinitesimal calculus that he submitted to the Académie Royale des Sciences, Arts et Belles-Lettres de Berlin in 1785. The originals are contained in the archives of the respective academies. The forthcoming work also contains a commentary on this latter manuscript by A. P. Youschkevitch, who published an extensive introduction and commentary to the Russian translation of the *Réflexions sur la métaphysique du calcul infinitésimal: Lazar Karno, Razmyshlenia o metafizike ischislenia beskonechnomalykh,* N. M. Solovev, trans., with a critical introduction by A. P. Youschkevitch and a biographical sketch by M. E. Podgorny (Moscow, 1933).

Persons who consult accounts of Carnot's work in mechanics in the secondary literature—e.g., René Dugas, *Histoire de la mécanique* (Neuchâtel, 1950), or Émile Jouguet, *Lectures de mécanique,* 2 vols. (Paris, 1908–1909), should be warned that their authors have sometimes confused item I, 6, with item I, 1, above, and attributed passages from the later, more widely read work to the earlier one. There is a brief notice of Carnot's geometric work in Michel Chasles, *Aperçu historique sur l'origine et le développement des méthodes en géométrie* (2nd ed., Paris, 1875), and Felix Klein, *Vorlesungen über die Entwicklung der Mathematik im 19. Jahrhundert,* 2 vols. (Berlin, 1926) I, 79–80.

CHARLES C. GILLISPIE

CARTAN, ÉLIE (*b.* Dolomieu, France, 9 April 1869; *d.* Paris, France, 6 May 1951)

Cartan was one of the most profound mathematicians of the last hundred years, and his influence is still one of the most decisive in the development of modern mathematics. He was born in a village in the French Alps. His father was a blacksmith, and at that time children of poor families had almost no opportunity to reach the university. Fortunately, while he was still in elementary school, his intelligence impressed the young politician Antonin Dubost, who was then an inspector of primary schools (and was later president of the French Senate); Dubost secured for Cartan a state stipend enabling him to attend the *lycée* in Lyons and later to enter the École Normale Supérieure in Paris. After graduation he started his research with his now famous thesis on Lie groups, a topic then still in its very early stages. He held teaching positions at the universities of Montpellier, Lyons, Nancy, and finally Paris, where he became a professor in 1912 and taught until his retirement in 1940. In 1931 he was elected a member of the French Academy of Sciences, and in his later years he received many honorary degrees and was elected a foreign member of several scientific societies.

Cartan's mathematical work can be described as the development of analysis on differentiable manifolds, which many now consider the central and most vital part of modern mathematics and which he was foremost in shaping and advancing. This field centers on Lie groups, partial differential systems, and differential geometry; these, chiefly through Cartan's contributions, are now closely interwoven and constitute a unified and powerful tool.

Cartan was practically alone in the field of Lie groups for the thirty years after his dissertation. Lie had considered these groups chiefly as systems of analytic transformations of an analytic manifold, depending analytically on a finite number of parameters. A very fruitful approach to the study of these groups was opened in 1888 when Wilhelm Killing systematically started to study the group in itself, independent of its possible actions on other manifolds. At that time (and until 1920) only local properties were considered, so the main object of study for Killing was the Lie algebra of the group, which exactly reflects the local properties in purely algebraic terms. Killing's great achievement was the determination of all simple complex Lie algebras; his proofs, however, were often defective, and Cartan's thesis was devoted mainly to giving a rigorous foundation to the "local" theory and to proving the existence of the "exceptional" Lie algebras belonging to each of the types of simple complex Lie algebras Killing had shown to be possible. Later Cartan completed the "local" theory by explicitly solving two fundamental problems, for which he had to develop entirely new methods: the classification of simple real Lie algebras and the determination of all irreducible linear representations of simple Lie algebras, by means of the notion of weight of a representation, which he introduced for that purpose. It was in the process of determining the linear representations of the orthogonal groups that Cartan discovered in 1913 the spinors, which later played such an important role in quantum mechanics.

After 1925 Cartan grew more and more interested in topological questions. Spurred by Weyl's brilliant results on compact groups, he developed new methods for the study of global properties of Lie groups; in particular he showed that topologically a connected Lie group is a product of a Euclidean space and a compact group, and for compact Lie groups he discovered that the possible fundamental groups of the underlying manifold can be read from the structure of the Lie algebra of the group. Finally, he outlined a method of determining the Betti numbers of compact Lie groups, again reducing the problem to an algebraic question on their Lie algebras, which has since been completely solved.

Cartan's methods in the theory of differential systems are perhaps his most profound achievement. Breaking with tradition, he sought from the start to formulate and solve the problems in a completely invariant fashion, independent of any particular choice of variables and unknown functions. He thus was able for the first time to give a precise definition of what is a "general" solution of an arbitrary differential system. His next step was to try to determine all "singular" solutions as well, by a method of "prolongation" that consists in adjoining new unknowns and new equations to the given system in such a way that any singular solution of the original system becomes a general solution of the new system. Although Cartan showed that in every example which he treated his method led to the complete determination of all singular solutions, he did not succeed in proving in general that this would always be the case for an arbitrary system; such a proof was obtained in 1955 by Kuranishi.

Cartan's chief tool was the calculus of exterior differential forms, which he helped to create and develop in the ten years following his thesis, and then proceeded to apply with extraordinary virtuosity to the most varied problems in differential geometry, Lie groups, analytical dynamics, and general relativity. He discussed a large number of examples, treating them in an extremely elliptic style that was made possible only by his uncanny algebraic and geometric insight and that has baffled two generations of mathematicians. Even now, some twenty years after his death, students of his results find that a sizable number of them are still in need of clarification; chief among these are his theory of "equivalence" of differential systems and his results on "infinite Lie groups" (which are not groups in the usual sense of the word).

Cartan's contributions to differential geometry are no less impressive, and it may be said that he revitalized the whole subject, for the initial work of Riemann and Darboux was being lost in dreary computations and minor results, much as had happened to elementary geometry and invariant theory a generation earlier. His guiding principle was a considerable extension of the method of "moving frames" of Darboux and Ribaucour, to which he gave a tremendous flexibility and power, far beyond anything that had been done in classical differential geometry. In modern terms, the method consists in associating to a fiber bundle E the principal fiber bundle having the same base and having at each point of the base a fiber equal to the group that acts on the fiber of E at the same point. If E is the tangent bundle over the base (which since Lie was essentially known as the manifold of "contact elements"), the corresponding group is the general linear group (or the orthogonal group in classical Euclidean or Riemannian geometry). Cartan's ability to handle many other types of fibers and groups allows one to credit him with the first general idea of a fiber bundle, although he never defined it explicitly. This concept has become one of the most important in all fields of modern mathematics, chiefly in global differential geometry and in algebraic and differential topology. Cartan used it to formulate his definition of a connection, which is now used universally and has superseded previous attempts by several geometers, made after 1917, to find a type of "geometry" more general than the Riemannian model and perhaps better adapted to a description of the universe along the lines of general relativity.

Cartan showed how to use his concept of connection to obtain a much more elegant and simple presentation of Riemannian geometry. His chief contribution to the latter, however, was the discovery and study of the symmetric Riemann spaces, one of the few instances in which the initiator of a mathematical theory was also the one who brought it to its completion. Symmetric Riemann spaces may be defined in various ways, the simplest of which postulates the existence around each point of the space of a "symmetry" that is involutive, leaves the point fixed, and preserves distances. The unexpected fact discovered by Cartan is that it is possible to give a complete description of these spaces by means of the classification of the simple Lie groups; it should therefore not be surprising that in various areas of mathematics, such as automorphic functions and analytic number theory (apparently far removed from differential geometry), these spaces are playing a part that is becoming increasingly important.

Cartan's recognition as a first-rate mathematician came to him only in his old age; before 1930 Poincaré and Weyl were probably the only prominent mathematicians who correctly assessed his uncommon powers and depth. This was due partly to his extreme modesty and partly to the fact that in France the main trend of mathematical research after 1900 was in the field of function theory, but chiefly to his extraordinary originality. It was only after 1930 that a younger generation started to explore the rich treasure of ideas and results that lay buried in his papers. Since then his influence has been steadily increasing, and with the exception of Poincaré and Hilbert, probably no one else has done so much to give the mathematics of our day its present shape and viewpoints.

BIBLIOGRAPHY

I. ORIGINAL WORKS. Cartan's papers have been collected in his *Oeuvres complètes,* 6 vols. (Paris, 1952–1955). He published the following books: *Leçons sur les invariants intégraux* (Paris, 1922); *La géométrie des espaces de Riemann,* fasc. 9 of Mémorial des Sciences Mathématiques (Paris, 1925); *Leçons sur la géométrie des espaces de Riemann* (Paris, 1928, 1946); *Leçons sur la géométrie projective complexe* (Paris, 1931); *Les espaces métriques fondés sur la notion d'aire,* no. 1 of Exposés de Géométrie (Paris, 1933); *Les espaces de Finsler,* no. 2 of Exposés de Géométrie (Paris, 1934); *La théorie des groupes finis et continus et la géométrie différentielle* (Paris, 1937); *Leçons sur la théorie des spineurs,* 2 vols., no. 11 of Exposés de Géométrie (Paris, 1938); and *Les systèmes différentiels extérieurs et leurs applications géométriques,* no. 994 of Actualités Scientifiques et Industrielles (Paris, 1945).

II. SECONDARY LITERATURE. Two excellent obituary notices are S. S. Chern and C. Chevalley, in *Bulletin of the American Mathematical Society,* **58** (1952); and J. H. C. Whitehead, in *Obituary Notices of the Royal Society* (1952).

JEAN DIEUDONNÉ

CASTEL, LOUIS-BERTRAND (*b.* Montpellier, France, 15 November 1688; *d.* Paris, France, 11 January 1757)

Castel was probably the most vociferous opponent of Newtonian science during the second quarter of the eighteenth century in France. He failed to block the gradual acceptance of Newton's ideas because the Cartesian rationalism that he tried to establish found diminishing favor with French scientists, more and more influenced by the merits of the experimental approach.

The second son of Guillaume Castel, a physician, Louis-Bertrand received his early education at the Jesuit school of Toulouse and entered the Jesuit order at the age of fifteen. His obituary in the Jesuit periodical *Journal de Trévoux* states that Castel's early writings came to the attention of Fontenelle, the eminent Cartesian philosopher and scientist, who is credited with influencing Castel to leave Toulouse for the more intellectual climate of Paris in 1720. His being immediately chosen an associate editor of the *Journal de Trévoux* clearly indicates that Castel had already shown promise as a scholar. While working on the monthly, Castel was associated with the faculty of the Jesuit school in the rue Saint-Jacques, the present Lycée Louis-le-Grand, where he taught physics, mathematics, specialized courses in infinitesimal calculus, and mechanics. Once installed at Louis-le-Grand, he never left Paris except for one trip to southern France toward the end of his life. The political philosopher Montesquieu honored him with his friendship, did not hesitate to submit his manuscripts to him before publication, and even chose him to be his son's tutor for a time, a post that made Castel inordinately proud.

Upon his arrival in Paris, Castel's first article was published in the *Mercure de France.* The "Lettre à M. de ***" stressed that truth was one, and that therefore astronomy and religion could never come into conflict because both are true. In 1724 his *Traité de la pesanteur* attracted a great deal of attention, particularly because it was hostile to Newton. In 1730, through his friendship with the English oculist J. T. Woolhouse, Castel was elected to the Royal Society of London. He entered the Bordeaux Academy in 1746, and in 1748 he was elected to the academies of Rouen and Lyons.

Although Castel published a creditable anti-Newtonian scientific theory that succeeded in delaying the acceptance of Newton's ideas in France, he is remembered as the spokesman of French scientists who saw in Newton a threat to the prestige of their national hero, Descartes, and a threat to their religious faith. While Descartes's metaphysical system had generally been abandoned by the thinkers of the Enlightenment, Newton's growing prestige brought about a gradual rally to the physics and astronomy of Descartes. Even as late as 1738 most French scholars still supported Descartes; with the exception of Maupertuis and Clairaut, the Academy of Sciences was composed entirely of Cartesians. Even though Castel felt competent to refute Cartesian science, he never abandoned Descartes's a priori, rationalistic approach to science—hence his impatience with a science based on experimentation rather than on a logical process. Pascal's fundamental objection to Cartesian physics, almost a century before Castel's system, was that Descartes had reasoned a priori in physics instead of observing and experimenting. It was the latter approach to science that so many physicists and astronomers of the eighteenth century, with Castel at their head, found repugnant. As a consequence of this attitude, Cartesian physicists had rendered the French scientists indolent; they preferred an attractively reasoned system, with daring ideas based on the logical process, to seeking scientific truth painfully and laboriously. The net result of the Cartesian approach was the relative stagnation of research in France.

This leads one to appreciate Castel's reaction to Newton: he complained about the numerous experiments that formed the basis of Newton's theories because they were not within the reach of the common man, and he reproached Newton with wanting to reduce man to "using only his eyes." Physics, for Castel, must be based on reason instead of observations. Hence his contempt for the "complicated laboratories" of the disciples of Newton. Castel's second brief against Newton was that his system of the world was suspect to the religious man because it smacked of materialism. Castel's accusation was clearly expressed in *Journal de Trévoux* (July 1721, pp. 1233, 1236): influenced by Democritus and Epicurus, Newton sought to give a philosophical basis to materialism by substituting the void for divine intelligence. On the other hand, Voltaire was genuinely persuaded that Newton's discoveries of nature's secrets conclusively proved the existence of God.

There is little point in presenting an outline of the system Castel proposed to replace Newton's. It was an attempt to harmonize philosophy, scientific curiosity, and religious dogma by means of rationalism. Newton gradually secured a foothold in France, and Voltaire was not the last of the propagandists on his behalf.

Castel's ocular harpsichord helped to spread his fame much more than his scientific reputation did. The best sources available for an explanation of his invention are two articles in the *Journal de Trévoux* (1735): "Nouvelles expériences d'optique et d'acoustique" and "L'optique des couleurs fondée sur les simples observations." It was a scheme for making colors and musical tones correspond. By 1742 the fame of Castel and of his invention had reached as far as St. Petersburg and had been brought to the attention of the empress. The instrument was completed in July 1754, and on 21 December of the same year Castel gave a private demonstration of it before fifty guests. The spectators were enthusiastic and applauded several times (*Mercure de France* [July 1755], p. 145). The idea of the color organ did not die with him, since several varieties of it have appeared in Europe and in the United States at various times.

BIBLIOGRAPHY

Castel's writings include *Lettre philosophique pour rassurer l'univers contre les bruits populaires d'un dérangement dans le cours du soleil* (Paris, 1736); *Traité de physique sur la pesanteur universelle des corps,* 2 vols. (Paris, 1724); his 1735 art. in *Journal de Trévoux* cited above repr. as *L'optique des couleurs, fondée sur les simples observations, et tournée surtout à la pratique de la peinture* (Paris, 1740); *Dissertation philosophique et littéraire où, par les vrais principes de la physique et de la géométrie, on recherche si les règles des arts sont fixes ou arbitraires* (Amsterdam, 1741); and *Le vrai système de physique générale de M. Isaac Newton exposé et analysé en parallèle avec celui de Descartes, à la portée des physiciens* (Paris, 1743).

Castel and his work are discussed in Jean Ehrard, *L'idée de nature en France dans la première moitié du XVIIIe siècle* (Paris, 1963), pp. 117–121; 155–156.

A. R. DESAUTELS

CASTELNUOVO, GUIDO (*b.* Venice, Italy, 14 August 1865; *d.* Rome, Italy, 27 April 1952)

Castelnuovo studied mathematics at the University of Padua under Veronese and was graduated in 1886. He then spent a year in Rome on a postgraduate scholarship and subsequently became assistant to E. D'Ovidio at the University of Turin, where he had important exchanges of ideas with Segre. From 1891 until 1935 he taught projective and analytical geometry at the University of Rome. After the death of Cremona, Castelnuovo also taught advanced geometry and, later, courses in the calculus of probability. When Jewish students were barred from state universities, Castelnuovo organized courses for them.

After the liberation Castelnuovo was special commissioner of the Consiglio Nazionale delle Ricerche and then president of the Accademia Nazionale dei Lincei until his death. He was also a member of many other academies. On 5 December 1949 he was named senator of the Italian republic for life.

Castelnuovo's scientific activity was principally in algebraic geometry and was important in the Italian school of geometry, which included Cremona, Segre, Enriques, and Severi. His mathematical results particularly concerned algebraic surfaces and the theories constituting their background.

In connection with these results is the theorem of Kronecker-Castelnuovo: "If the sections of an irreducible algebraic surface with a doubly infinite system of planes turn out to be reducible curves, then the above surface is either ruled or the Roman surface of Steiner" (*Memorie scelte,* pp. 223–227). The origin of this theorem was explained by Castelnuovo as follows: Kronecker, during a meeting of the Accademia dei Lincei in 1886, had communicated verbally one of his theorems on irreducible algebraic surfaces having infinite plane sections that are split into two curves. But the written note was not sent by Kronecker to the Accademia dei Lincei, nor was it published elsewhere. Further, Castelnuovo held that perhaps Kronecker had not finished the final draft. On the basis of information furnished to him by Cremona and Cerruti, Castelnuovo reconstructed the demonstration of the theorem. He also developed the theorem that every unruled irreducible algebraic surface whose plane sections are elliptical curves (or are of genus 1) is rational (*Memorie scelte,* pp. 229–232).

Besides writing on algebraic geometry, the calculus of probability, and the theory of relativity, Castelnuovo also delved into the history of mathematics, producing *Le origini del calcolo infinitesimale nell'era moderna* (1938), which contains a quick and effective summary of the evolution of infinitesimal methods from the Renaissance to Newton and Leibniz.

BIBLIOGRAPHY

I. ORIGINAL WORKS. Castelnuovo's writings include *Lezioni di geometria analitica* (Milan–Rome–Naples, 1903; 7th ed., 1931); *Calcolo della probabilità* (Rome, 1919; 3rd ed., Bologna, 1948); *Spazio e tempo secondo le vedute di A. Einstein* (Bologna, 1923); *Memorie scelte* (Bologna, 1937), with a list of publications on pp. 581–584, to which should be added those in the obituary by A. Terracini (see below); *La probabilité dans les différentes branches de la science* (Paris, 1937); and *Le origini del calcolo infinitesimale nell'era moderna* (Bologna, 1938; 2nd ed., Milan, 1962). A picture of Castelnuovo's results in the geometry of surfaces may be obtained from the two articles he wrote in collaboration with Federigo Enriques: "Grundeigenschaften der algebraischen Flächen" and "Die algebraischen Flächen vom Gesichtspunkte der birationalen Transformationen aus," both in *Encycklopädie der mathematischen Wissenschaften* (Leipzig, 1903–1915), III, pt. 2.

II. SECONDARY LITERATURE. Obituaries include F. Conforto, in *Rendiconti di matematica e delle sue applicazioni,* 5th ser., **11** (1952), i–iii; and A. Terracini, "Guido Castelnuovo," in *Atti della Accademia delle scienze* (Turin), **86** (1951–1952), 366–377. Castelnuovo's numerous results in algebraic geometry are discussed in F. Conforto, *Le superficie razionali* (Bologna, 1939), index; and F. Enriques and O. Chisini, *Lezioni sulla teoria geometrica delle equazioni e delle funzioni algebriche,* 4 vols. (Bologna, 1915–1934), see indexes of the various volumes under "Castelnuovo."

ETTORE CARRUCCIO

CASTILLON, JOHANN (Giovanni Francesco Melchiore Salvemini) (*b.* Castiglione, Tuscany, Italy, 15 January 1704; *d.* Berlin, Germany, 11 October 1791)

The son of Giuseppe Salvemini and Maria Maddalena Lucia Braccesi, Castillon studied mathematics and law at the University of Pisa, where he received a doctorate in jurisprudence in 1729. Shortly afterward he went to Switzerland, where for some unknown reason he changed his name to Johann Castillon, after his birthplace. In 1737 he became the director of a humanistic school in Vevey, and in 1745 he took a teaching position in Lausanne. In that year he married Elisabeth du Frèsne, who died in 1757. He married Madeleine Ravène in 1759. From 1749 to 1751 Castillon taught in both Lausanne and Bern. In the summer of 1751 he received offers of positions in St. Petersburg and Utrecht; in December 1751, after much thought, he accepted the invitation of the prince of Orange to lecture on mathematics and astronomy at the University of Utrecht, where he acquired a doctorate in philosophy in 1754 and rose to professor of philosophy in 1755 and rector in 1758. In 1764 he traveled to Berlin to accept a position in the Mathematics Section of the Academy of Sciences there. In the following year he became the royal astronomer at the Berlin Observatory.

During his lifetime Castillon was known as an able geometer and a general philosopher. His work in mathematics, however, did not go far beyond elementary considerations. His first two mathematical papers dealt with the cardioid curve, which he named. He also studied conic sections, cubic equations, and artillery problems. After publishing the letters of Leibniz and Johann I Bernoulli in 1745, he edited Euler's *Introductio in analysin infinitorum* in 1748. In 1761 he published his useful commentary on Newton's *Arithmetica universalis.* Throughout his mathematical work there is a preference for synthetic, as opposed to analytic, geometry, which is perhaps a reflection of his preoccupation with Newton's mathematics. In addition to this mathematical research, Castillon delved into the study of philosophy. In general he opposed Rousseau and his supporters and leaned toward the thinkers of the English Enlightenment. He translated Locke's *Elements of Natural Philosophy* into French.

Castillon became a member of the Royal Society of London and the Göttingen Academy in 1753 and a foreign member of the Berlin Academy of Sciences in 1755; he was elected to full membership in the Berlin Academy in 1764, upon the personal recommendation of Frederick the Great. In 1787 he succeeded Lagrange as director of the Mathematics Section of the Berlin Academy, a post he held until his death.

BIBLIOGRAPHY

Castillon wrote *Discours sur l'origine de l'inégalité parmi les hommes . . .* (Amsterdam, 1756); and *Observations sur le livre intitulé Système de la nature* (Berlin, 1771). He edited the following: *Isaaci Newtoni, equitis aurati, opuscula mathematica, philosophica & philologica,* 3 vols. (Lausanne, 1744); *Virorum celeberr. Got. Gul. Leibnitii & Johan. Bernoullii commercium philosophicum & mathematicum* (Lausanne, 1745); and Euler's *Introductio in analysin infinitorum* (Lausanne, 1748). He translated Locke's *Elements of Natural Philosophy* as *Abrégé de physique* (Amsterdam, 1761); George Campbell's *A Dissertation on Miracles: Containing an Examination of the Principles Advanced by David Hume, Esq; in an Essay on Miracles* as *Dissertation sur les miracles, contenant l'examen des principes posés par M. David Hume dans son Essai sur les miracles* (Utrecht, 1765); and Francesco Algarotti's *Opere varie del Conte Francesco Algarotti* as *Mémoires concernant la vie & les écrits du comte François Algarotti* (Berlin, 1772).

Castillon's articles include "De curva cardiode," in *Philosophical Transactions of the Royal Society,* **41,** no. 461 (1741), 778–781; "De polynomia," *ibid.,* **42,** no. 464 (1742), 91–98; "Deux descriptions de cette espèce d'hommes, qu'on appelle negres-blans," in *Histoire de l'Académie royale des sciences et des belles lettres de Berlin (avec mémoires),* **18** (1762), 99–105; "Descartes et Locke conciliés," *ibid.* (1770), 277–282; "Mémoire sur les équations résolues par M. de Moivre, avec quelques réflexions sur ces équations et sur les cas irréductibles," *ibid.* (1771), 254–272; "Sur une nouvelle propriété des sections coniques," *ibid.* (1776), 284–311; "Sur un globe mouvant qui représente les mouvements de la Terre," *ibid.* (1779), 301–306; "Sur la division des instruments de géométrie et d'astronomie," *ibid.* (1780), 310–348; "Rapport sur une lettre italienne de M. le Professeur Moscati, concernant une végétation électrique nouvellement découverte," *ibid.* (1781), 22–23; "Mémoire sur la règle de Cardan, et sur les équations cubiques, avec quelques remarques sur les équations en général," *ibid.* (1783), 244–265; "Premier mémoire sur les parallèles d'Euclide," *ibid.,* **43** (1786–1787) and "Second mémoire . . .," **44** (1788–1789), 171–203; "Recherches sur la liberté de l'homme," *ibid.,* **43** (1786–1787), 517–533; "Examen philosophique de quelques principes de l'algèbre" (two memoirs), *ibid.,* **45** (1790–1791), 331–363; and "Essai d'une théorie métaphysico-mathématique de l'expérience," *ibid.,* 364–390.

An obituary is Friedrich von Castillon, "Éloge de M. de Castillon, père," in *Histoire de l'Académie royale des sciences et des belles lettres de Berlin (avec mémoires),* **46** (1792–1793), 38–60.

RONALD S. CALINGER

CATALDI, PIETRO ANTONIO (*b.* Bologna, Italy, 15 April 1552; *d.* Bologna, 11 February 1626)

Cataldi was the son of Paolo Cataldi, also of Bologna. Little else is known of his life. His first teaching position (1569–1570) was at the Florentine Academy of Design. He then went to Perugia to teach mathematics at the university; his first lecture was given on 12 May 1572. He also taught at the Academy of Design in Perugia and was a lecturer in mathematics at the Studio di Bologna from 1584 until his death. Cataldi showed his benevolence by giving the superiors of various Franciscan monasteries the task of distributing free copies of his *Pratica aritmetica* to monasteries, seminaries, and poor children.

In the history of mathematics Cataldi is particularly remembered for the *Trattato del modo brevissimo di trovar la radice quadra delli numeri,* finished in 1597 and published in 1613. In this work the square root of a number is found through the use of infinite series and unlimited continued fractions. It represents a notable contribution to the development of infinite algorithms.

In the orientation of mathematical thinking of the late Renaissance and the seventeenth century toward infinitesimal questions, along with geometric methods (such as Cavalieri's principle of indivisibles), in the field of arithmetic, the passage from the finite to the infinite appears in processes of iteration in calculus. In this area Cataldi started with the practical rules furnished by ancient treatises on arithmetic for finding the square root of any natural number N that is not a perfect square. These treatises gave first the basic rule for finding the natural number a such that

$$a^2 < N < (a+1)^2.$$

Then rules were given for finding approximate rational values of $\sqrt{N}$, expressed respectively by the formulas

$$a + \frac{N - a^2}{2a},$$

$$a + \frac{N - a^2}{2a + 1}.$$

The first of these formulas, which goes back at least as far as Hero of Alexandria (and probably to the Babylonians), coincides with the arithmetic mean $1/2\ (a + N/a)$ of the two values a and N/a (which have as their geometric mean $\sqrt{N}$, which is being sought). The second formula is obtained by a process of linear interpolation:

$$x_1 = a^2 \qquad x_2 = (a+1)^2 \qquad x = a^2 + r$$

$$y_1 = a \qquad y_2 = a + 1.$$

The y corresponding to x is determined by means of the equation

$$\frac{x - x_1}{x_2 - x_1} = \frac{y - y_1}{y_2 - y_1},$$

from which one obtains

$$y = a + \frac{r}{2a + 1}.$$

That is, setting $x = N = a^2 + r$, the result is

$$y = a + \frac{N - a^2}{2a + 1}.$$

Returning to the rounded maximum value (already considered), we write

$$a_1 = a + \frac{N - a^2}{2a}.$$

Starting with a_1, by an analogous procedure we obtain a new value, a_2, a closer approximation than a_1:

$$a_2 = a_1 - \frac{a_1^2 - N}{2a_1} = a + \frac{N - a^2}{2a} - \frac{a_1^2 - N}{2a_1}.$$

Setting $r_1 = a_1^2 - N \cdots r_{n-1} = a_{n-1}^2 - N$, one obtains

$$a_2 = a + \frac{r}{2a} - \frac{r_1}{2a_1}.$$

By iteration of the indicated procedure we obtain

$$a_n = a + \frac{r}{2a} - \frac{r_1}{2a_1} - \frac{r_2}{2a_2} - \cdots - \frac{r_{n-1}}{2a_{n-1}}.$$

As Cataldi established, r_n may be rendered as small as one wishes, provided that n is large enough. The formula

$$a_1 = \frac{1}{2a}(a^2 + N)$$

results in

$$r_1 = a_1^2 - N = \frac{1}{4a^2}[(a^2 + N)^2 - 4a^2 N]$$

$$= \frac{(a^2 - N)^2}{4a^2} = \left(\frac{r}{2a}\right)^2.$$

Analogously, in general

$$r_n = \left(\frac{r_{n-1}}{2a_{n-1}}\right)^2,$$

from which one obtains

$$\frac{r_n}{r_{n-1}} = \frac{r_{n-1}}{4a_{n-1}^2}.$$

Given $r_{n-1} < a_{n-1}^2$, one will have

$$\frac{r_n}{r_{n-1}} < \frac{1}{4},$$

which guarantees the rapid convergence of the series representing $\sqrt{N}$:

$$a + \frac{r}{2a} - \frac{r_1}{2a_1} - \frac{r_2}{2a_2} - \cdots - \frac{r_{n-1}}{2a_{n-1}} - \cdots.$$

Cataldi presents analogous considerations in relation to the other series, which is obtained from the rounded minimum values of $\sqrt{N}$:

$$a + \frac{r}{2a+1} + \frac{r_1}{2a_1+1} + \frac{r_2}{2a_2+1} + \cdots$$

$$+ \frac{r_{n-1}}{2a_{n-1}+1} + \cdots.$$

We shall now see how, starting with the rounded maximum value (already considered) of $\sqrt{N}$,

$$a_1 = a + \frac{r}{2a},$$

Cataldi arrives at continued fractions. With the aim of obtaining a better approximation than that reached with a_1, Cataldi adds to the denominator a value x, and then considers the expression

$$a + \frac{r}{2a + x}.$$

He observes that this expression has a rounded minimum value of $\sqrt{N}$ when (and only when) $a + x$ has a rounded maximum value of $\sqrt{N}$. That is (as can be verified by simple calculation),

$$\left(a + \frac{r}{2a + x}\right)^2 < a^2 + r$$

when and only when $(a + x)^2 > a^2 + r$. Therefore, given

$$\left(a + \frac{r}{2a}\right)^2 > a^2 + r,$$

one will have

$$\left(a + \frac{r}{2a + \frac{r}{2a}}\right)^2 < a^2 + r.$$

That is,

$$a_2 = a + \frac{r}{2a + \frac{r}{2a}}$$

has a rounded minimum value of $\sqrt{N}$, while, for reasons analogous to those already given, the rounded maximum value of the same root will be

$$a_3 = a + \frac{r}{2a + r/(2a + r/2a)},$$

and so on, indefinitely. If we write

$$a_1 = \frac{p_1}{q_1},\ a_2 = \frac{p_2}{q_2} \cdots a_n = \frac{p_n}{q_n},$$

we will see that the result p_n/q_n for order n can be expressed in terms of the result for order $n - 1$ by means of the formula

$$\frac{p_n}{q_n} = \frac{r}{2a + (p_{n-1}/q_{n-1})}.$$

From it are derived the recurrent formulas habitually used by Cataldi:

$$p_n = rq_{n-1}, \; q_n = 2aq_{n-1} + p_{n-1}.$$

Moreover, Cataldi finds the fundamental relation,

$$p_n q_{n-1} - p_{n-1} q_n = (-1)^n r^n,$$

from which can be obtained the expression of the difference between two consecutive results:

$$\frac{p_n}{q_n} - \frac{p_{n-1}}{q_{n-1}} = (-1)^n \frac{r^n}{q_n q_{n-1}}.$$

In sum, Cataldi compares the results of the series just studied with the results of the continued fraction, considering the same $\sqrt{N}$, and establishes that the results of the series obtained by starting with the rounded minimum values reproduce the results of even orders of the continued fraction (a_2, a_4, $\cdots$); the results of the series obtained by starting with the maximum values reproduce the results of order

$$(2^n - 1) \; (n = 1, 2, 3, \cdots).$$

Having examined Cataldi's contribution to the theory of continued fractions, clearly explained in various writings by E. Bortolotti, it remains for us to consider the place of these contributions in the history of mathematical thought. The question is complex and has given rise to many discussions and polemics. Given the great number of questions that can lead to consideration of continued fractions, hints of the theory of continued fractions are presented many times and in presumably independent ways in the course of mathematical history. It is not our task to reconstruct the history of continued fractions; we shall limit ourselves to indicating some elements of it in order to clarify Cataldi's position. We are led to consideration of this question when we come to Euclid's procedures for determining the greatest common divisor of two natural numbers (bk. VII, prop. 2), which lead to consideration of a limited continued fraction, while the Euclidean criterion for establishing whether two homogeneous magnitudes are commensurable or incommensurable leads in the latter case to an unlimited continued fraction (*Elements*, bk. X, prop. 2); in neither case is the algorithm presented explicitly.

The successive reductions of the continued fraction that is expressed by $\sqrt{2}$ appear in the work of the Neoplatonic philosopher Theon of Smyrna (second century A.D.), *Expositio rerum mathematicarum ad legendum Platonem utilium.* An examination of this text, however, leads one to conclude that such values were calculated with an aim different from that indicated above. For the sake of brevity we shall omit mention of other appearances of the continued fractions, which can be found in Greek, Indian, and Arabic writings.

In the Renaissance, Rafael Bombelli gave a procedure for the extraction of the square root of a number that is not a square, such that the successive steps in the procedure lead to the calculation of the successive results of a continued fraction. However, Bombelli, who refers to numerical cases, performs the calculations that have been considered, in such a way that the final result retains no traces of the algorithm implicitly defined by the procedure of iteration that is applied (see Bombelli's *L'algebra,* E. Bortolotti, ed. [Bologna, 1929], pp. 26–27).

The use of limited continued fractions in the expression of relationships between large numbers is found in the *Geometria practica* of Daniel Schwenter (1627), published soon after Cataldi's death.

The term "continued fraction" was introduced by John Wallis, who gave a systematic treatment of it in his *Arithmetica universalis* (1655). It contains an example of the development of a transcendental number, under the form that originated with William Brouncker:

$$\frac{4}{\pi} = 1 + \cfrac{1^2}{2 + \cfrac{3^2}{2 + \cfrac{5^2}{2 + \cfrac{7^2}{2 + \cdots}}}}.$$

A theory of continued fractions was devised by Euler, and Lagrange formulated the theorem concerning the periodic character of continued fractions that represent square roots.

Continued fractions have been of great use to mathematicians in the investigation of the nature of numbers—for instance, Liouville's work on the existence of transcendental numbers (1844) was based on the use of the algorithm considered above.

Cataldi also has a place in the history of the criticism of Euclid's fifth postulate, which led to construction of a non-Euclidean geometry. In his *Operetta delle linee rette equidistanti et non equidistanti,* he attempted to demonstrate the fifth postulate on the basis of remainders. The defect of his argument is found in his definition of equidistant straight lines: "A given straight line is said to be equidistant from another straight line in the same plane when the two shortest lines that are drawn from any two different points on the first line to the second line are equal." Cataldi did not realize that two conditions are imposed on the first, given line, which are not stated as compatible: (1) that it is a locus of points at a constant distance from the second line and (2) that it is a straight line. The admission of such a compatibility constitutes a postulate equivalent to Euclid's fifth postulate.

Cataldi's other works, which are mainly didactic, are concerned with theoretical and practical arithmetic, algebra, geometry, and astronomy, and furnish good documentation of the mathematical knowledge of his time.

BIBLIOGRAPHY

I. ORIGINAL WORKS. Cataldi's writings are *Prima lettione fatta pubblicamente nello studio di Perugia il 12 maggio 1572* (Bologna, 1572); *Due lettioni fatte nell'Accademia del disegno di Perugia* (Bologna, 1577); *Pratica aritmetica*, 4 pts. (Bologna, 1602–1617); *Operetta delle linee rette equidistanti et non equidistanti* (Bologna, 1603); *Trattato dei numeri perfetti* (Bologna, 1603); *Aggiunta all'operetta delle linee rette equidistanti et non equidistanti* (Bologna, 1604); *Trattato dell'algebra proportionale* (Bologna, 1610); *Trasformatione geometrica* (Bologna, 1611); *Trattato della quadratura del cerchio* (Bologna, 1612); *Due lettioni di Pietro Antonio Cataldi date nella Accademia erigenda; dove si mostra come si trovi la grandezza delle superficie rettilinee* (Bologna, 1613); *I primi sei libri de gl'Elementi d'Euclide ridotti alla prattica* (Bologna, 1613); *Tavola del levar del sole et mezo di per la città di Bologna* (Bologna, 1613); *Trattato del modo brevissimo di trovar la radice quadra delli numeri* (Bologna, 1613); *Aritmetica universale* (Bologna, 1617); *Algebra discorsiva numerale et lineale* (Bologna, 1618); *Operetta di ordinanze quadre di terreno et di gente* (Bologna, 1618); *Regola della quantità, o cosa di cosa* (Bologna, 1618); *Nuova algebra proportionale* (Bologna, 1619); *Diffesa d'Archimede, trattato del misurare o trovare la grandezza del cerchio* (Bologna, 1620); *Elementi delle quantità irrazionali, o inesplicabili necessarij alle operazioni geometriche et algebraiche* (Bologna, 1620); *I tre libri settimo ottavo et nono de gli Elementi aritmetici d'Euclide ridotti alla pratica* (Bologna, 1620); *Trattato geometrico . . . dove si esamina il modo di formare il pentagono sopra una linea retta, descritto da Alberto Durero. Et si mostra come si formino molte figure equilatere, et equiangole sopra ad una proposta linea retta* (Bologna, 1620); *Algebra applicata, dove si mostra la utilissima applicazione d'essa alla inventione delle cose recondite nelle diverse scienze* (Bologna, 1622); *Decimo libro degli Elementi d'Euclide ridotto alla pratica* (Bologna, 1625); and *Difesa d'Euclide* (Bologna, 1626).

II. SECONDARY LITERATURE. On Cataldi or his work see the following by E. Bortolotti: "Le antiche regole empiriche del calcolo approssimato dei radicali quadratici e le prime serie infinite," in *Bollettino della mathesis*, **11** (1919), 14–29; "La scoperta delle frazioni continue," *ibid.*, 101–123; "La storia dei presunti scopritori delle frazioni continue," *ibid.*, 157–188; "Ancora su la storia delle frazioni continue," *ibid.*, **12** (1920), 152–162; "La scoperta dell'irrazionale e le frazioni continue," in *Periodico di matematiche*, 4th ser., **11**, no. 3 (1931); "Cataldi, P. A.," in *Enciclopedia Italiana Treccani*, IX (1931), 403; "Frazione," *ibid.*, XVI (1932), 45–47; and "I primi algoritmi infiniti nelle opere dei matematici italiani del secolo XVI," in *Bollettino dell'Unione matematica italiana*, 2nd ser., **1**, no. 4 (1939), 22.

Works by other authors are G. Fantuzzi, *Notizie degli scrittori Bolognesi*, III (Bologna, 1733), 152–157; A. Favaro, "Notizie storiche su le frazioni continue," in *Bullettino Boncompagni*, **7** (1874), 451-502, 533-589; S. Gunther, "Storia dello sviluppo della teoria delle frazioni continue fino all'Euler," *ibid.*, 213-254; G. Libri, *Histoire des sciences mathématiques en Italie* (Paris, 1838–1841), IV, 87; and P. Riccardi, *Biblioteca matematica italiana*, I (Modena, 1893), 302-310.

ETTORE CARRUCCIO

CAUCHY, AUGUSTIN-LOUIS (*b.* Paris, France, 21 August 1789; *d.* Sceaux [near Paris], France, 22 May 1857)

Life. Cauchy's father, Louis-François Cauchy, was born in Rouen in 1760. A brilliant student of classics at Paris University, after graduating he established himself as a barrister at the *parlement* of Normandy. At the age of twenty-three he became secretary general to Thiroux de Crosnes, the *intendant* of Haute Normandie. Two years later he followed Thiroux to Paris, where the latter had been appointed to the high office of *lieutenant de police*.

Louis-François gradually advanced to high administrative positions, such as that of first secretary to the Senate. He died in 1848. In 1787 he married Marie-Madeleine Desestre, who bore him four sons and two daughters. She died in 1839. Of their daughters, Thérèse died young and Adèle married her cousin G. de Neuburg. She died in 1863. The youngest son, Amédée, died in 1831, at the age of twenty-five; Alexandre (1792–1857) held high judicial posts; and Eugène (1802–1877) held administrative posts and became known as a scholar in the history of law. Augustin was the eldest child.

Cauchy enjoyed an excellent education; his father was his first teacher. During the Terror the family escaped to the village of Arcueil, where they were neighbors of Laplace and Berthollet, the founders of the celebrated Société d'Arcueil. Thus, as a young boy Augustin became acquainted with famous scientists. Lagrange is said to have forecast his scientific genius while warning his father against showing him a mathematical text before the age of seventeen.

After having completed his elementary education at home, Augustin attended the École Centrale du

Panthéon. At the age of fifteen he completed his classical studies with distinction. After eight to ten months of preparation he was admitted in 1805 to the École Polytechnique (at the age of sixteen). In 1807 he entered the École des Ponts et Chaussées, which he left (1809?) to become an engineer, first at the works of the Ourcq Canal, then the Saint-Cloud bridge, and finally, in 1810, at the harbor of Cherbourg, where Napoleon had started building a naval base for his intended operations against England. When he departed for Cherbourg, his biographer says, Cauchy carried in his baggage Laplace's *Mécanique céleste,* Lagrange's *Traité des fonctions analytiques,* Vergil, and Thomas à Kempis' *Imitatio.* Cauchy returned to Paris in 1813, allegedly for reasons of health, although nothing is known about any illness he suffered during his life.

Cauchy had started his mathematical career in 1811 by solving a problem set to him by Lagrange: whether the angles of a convex polyhedron are determined by its faces. His solution, which surprised his contemporaries, is still considered a clever and beautiful piece of work and a classic of mathematics. In 1812 he solved Fermat's classic problem on polygonal numbers: whether any number is a sum of *n n*gonal numbers. He also proved a theorem in what later was called Galois theory, generalizing a theorem of Ruffini's. In 1814 he submitted to the French Academy the treatise on definite integrals that was to become the basis of the theory of complex functions. In 1816 he won a prize contest of the French Academy on the propagation of waves at the surface of a liquid; his results are now classics in hydrodynamics. He invented the method of characteristics, which is crucial for the theory of partial differential equations, in 1819; and in 1822 he accomplished what to the heterodox opinion of the author is his greatest achievement and would suffice to assure him a place among the greatest scientists: the founding of elasticity theory.

When in 1816 the republican and Bonapartist Gaspard Monge and the "regicide" Lazare Carnot were expelled from the Académie des Sciences, Cauchy was appointed (not elected) a member. (Even his main biographer feels uneasy about his hero's agreeing to succeed the highly esteemed and harshly treated Monge.) Meanwhile Cauchy had been appointed *répétiteur,* adjoint professor (1815), and full professor (1816) at the École Polytechnique [11]; [1] at some time before 1830 he must also have been appointed to chairs at the Faculté des Sciences and at the Collège de France.[2] His famous textbooks, which date from this period, display an exactness unheard of until then and contain his fundamental work in analysis, which has become a classic. These works have been translated several times.

In 1818 Cauchy married Aloïse de Bure, daughter (or granddaughter) of a publisher who was to publish most of Cauchy's work. She bore him two daughters, one of whom married the viscount de l'Escalopier and the other the count of Saint-Pol. The Cauchys lived on the rue Serpente in Paris and in the nearby town of Sceaux.

Cauchy's quiet life was suddenly changed by the July Revolution of 1830, which replaced the Bourbon king, Charles X, with the Orléans king of the bourgeoisie, Louis-Philippe. Cauchy refused to take the oath of allegiance, which meant that he would lose his chairs. But this was not enough: Cauchy exiled himself. It is not clear why he did so: whether he feared a new Terror and new religious persecutions, whether he meant it as a demonstration of his feelings against the new authority, or whether he simply thought he could not live honestly under a usurper.

Leaving his family, Cauchy went first to Fribourg, where he lived with the Jesuits. They recommended him to the king of Sardinia, who offered him a chair at the University of Turin.[3] Cauchy accepted. In 1833, however, he was called to Prague, where Charles X had settled, to assist in the education of the crown prince (later the duke of Chambord). Cauchy accepted the offer with the aim of emulating Bossuet and Fénelon as princely educators. In due time it pleased the ex-king to make him a baron. In 1834 Mme. Cauchy joined her husband in Prague—the biographer does not tell us for how long.

The life at court and journeys with the court took much of Cauchy's time, and the steady flow of his publications slowed a bit. In 1838 his work in Prague was finished, and he went back to Paris. He resumed his activity at the Academy, which meant attending the Monday meeting and presenting one or more communications to be printed in the weekly *Comptes rendus;* it is said that soon the Academy had to put a restriction on the size of such publications. In the course of less than twenty years the *Comptes rendus* published 589 notes by Cauchy—and many more were submitted but not printed. As an academician Cauchy was exempted from the oath of allegiance. An effort to procure him a chair at the Collège de France foundered on his intransigence, however. In 1839 a vacancy opened at the Bureau des Longitudes which legally completed itself by cooption. Cauchy was unanimously elected a member, but the government tied the confirmation to conditions that Cauchy again refused to accept. Biot [7] tells us that two subsequent ministers of education vainly tried to build golden bridges for Cauchy. Bertrand [11] more specifically says that the only thing they asked of him was to keep silent about the fact that he had not been administered the oath. But, according to Biot [7, p. 152], "even such an appearance terrified Cauchy, and he tried to make it impossible by all diplomatic finesses he could imagine, finesses which were those of a child."

When the February Revolution of 1848 established the Second Republic, one of the first measures of the government was the repeal of the act requiring the oath of allegiance. Cauchy resumed his chair at the Sorbonne (the only one that was vacant). He retained this chair even when Napoleon III reestablished the oath in 1852, for Napoleon generously exempted the republican Arago and the royalist Cauchy.

A steady stream of mathematical papers traces Cauchy's life. His last communication to the Academy closes with the words "C'est ce que j'expliquerai plus au long dans un prochain mémoire." Eighteen days later he was dead. He also produced French and Latin poetry, which, however, is better forgotten. More than a third of his biography deals with Cauchy as a devout Catholic who took a leading part in such charities as that of François Régis for unwed mothers, aid for starving Ireland, rescue work for criminals, aid to the Petit Savoyards, and important activity in the Society of Saint Vincent de Paul. Cauchy was one of the founders of the Institut Catholique, an institution of higher education; he served on a committee to promote the observance of the sabbath; and he supported works to benefit schools in the Levant. Biot [7] tells us that he served as a social worker in the town of Sceaux and that he spent his entire salary for the poor of that town, about which behavior he reassured the mayor: "Do not worry, it is only my salary; it is not my money, it is the emperor's."

Cauchy's life has been reported mainly according to Valson's work [8], which, to tell the truth, is more hagiography than biography. It is too often too vague about facts which at that time could easily have been ascertained; it is a huge collection of commonplaces; and it tends to present its hero as a saint with all virtues and no vices. The facts reported are probably true, but the many gaps in the story will arouse the suspicion of the attentive reader. The style reminds one of certain saccharine pictures of saints. Contrary to his intention Valson describes a bigoted, selfish, narrow-minded fanatic. This impression seems to be confirmed by a few contemporary anecdotal accounts. N. H. Abel [10] called Cauchy mad, infinitely Catholic, and bigoted. Posthumous accounts may be less trustworthy, perhaps owing their origin or form to a reaction to Valson's book.

A story that is hardly believable is told by Bertrand [9] in a review of Valson. Bertrand, who deeply admired Cauchy's scientific genius, recalled that in 1849, when Cauchy resumed his chair of celestial mechanics at the Sorbonne,

> . . . his first lessons completely deceived the expectation of a selected audience, which was surprised rather than charmed by the somewhat confused variety of subjects dealt with. The third lesson, I remember, was almost wholly dedicated to the extraction of the square root, where the number 17 was taken as an example and the computations were carried out up to the tenth decimal by methods familiar to all auditors but believed new by Cauchy, perhaps because he had hit upon them the night before. I did not return; but this was a mistake, since the next lectures would have introduced me ten years earlier to some of the most brilliant discoveries of the famous master.

This story was a vehement reaction to Valson's statement that Cauchy was an excellent teacher who ". . . never left a subject until he had completely exhausted and elucidated it so he could satisfy the demands of the most exacting spirits" [8, I, 64]. Clearly, this is no more than another of Valson's many cliché epithets dutifully conferred upon his subject. In fact Cauchy's manner of working was just the contrary of what is here described, as will be seen.

According to Valson, when Mme. Cauchy joined her husband in Prague [8, I, 90], he complained that he was still separated from his father and mother and did not mention his daughters. Yet according to Biot [7] his wife brought their daughters with her and the family stayed in Prague and left there together. It is characteristic of Valson that after the report of their birth he never mentions Cauchy's daughters, except for the report that one of them was at his bedside when he died. His wife is not mentioned much more. The result of such neglect is that despite the many works of charity one feels a disturbing lack of human relationships in Cauchy's life. Possibly this was less Cauchy's fault than that of his biographer. But even Bertrand [11], who was more competent than Valson, more broad-minded, and a master of the *éloge,* felt uneasy when he had to speak about Cauchy's human qualities. Biot [7] was more successful. It is reassuring to learn from him that Cauchy befriended democrats, nonbelievers, and odd fellows such as Laurent. And it is refreshing to hear Biot call Cauchy's odd behavior "childish."

A prime example of his odd behavior is his exile. One can understand his refusal to take the oath, but sharing exile with the depraved king is another matter. It could have been a heroic feat; unfortunately it was not. The lone faithful paladin who followed his king into exile while all France was gratified at the smooth solution of a dangerous crisis looks rather like the Knight of the Rueful Countenance. Yet his quixotic behavior is so unbelievable that one is readily inclined to judge him as being badly melodramatic. Stendhal did so as early as 1826, when he said in *New Monthly Magazine* (see [13], p. 192) about a meeting of the Académie des Sciences:

> After the lecture of a naturalist, Cauchy rose and protested the applause. "Even if these things would be as true as I think they are wrong"—he said—"it would not be convenient to disclose them to the public . . . this can only prejudice our holy religion." People burst out laughing at this talk of Cauchy, who . . . seems to seek the role of a martyr to contempt.

Probably Stendhal was wrong. Biot knew better: Cauchy was a child who was as naïve as he looked. Among his writings one finds two pieces in defense of the Jesuits [8, pp. 108–121] that center on the thesis that Jesuits are hated and persecuted because of their virtue. It would not be plausible that the man who wrote this was really so naïve if the author were not Cauchy.

Another story about Cauchy that is well confirmed comes from the diary of the king of Sardinia, 16 January 1831 [13, p. 160]. In an audience that the king granted Cauchy, five times Cauchy answered a question by saying, "I expected Your Majesty would ask me this, so I have prepared to answer it." And then he took a memoir out of his pocket and read it.

Cauchy's habit of reading memoirs is confirmed by General d'Hautpoul [12; 13, p. 172], whose memoirs of Prague shed an unfavorable light on Cauchy as an educator and a courtier.

Sometimes, in the steady flow of his Academy publications, Cauchy suddenly turned or returned to a different subject; after a few weeks or months it would become clear why he did so. He would then submit to the Academy a report on a paper of a *savant étranger* (i.e., a nonmember of the Academy), which had been sent to him for examination. Meanwhile he had proved anew the author's results, broadened, deepened, and generalized them. And in the report he never failed to recall all his previous investigations related to the subject of the paper under consideration. This looks like extremely unfair behavior, and in any other case it would be—but not with Cauchy. Cauchy did not master mathematics; he was mastered by it. If he hit on an idea—and this happened often—he could not wait a moment to publish it. Before the weekly *Comptes rendus* came into being this was not easy, so in 1826 he founded a private journal, *Exercices de mathématiques*. Its twelve issues a year were filled by Cauchy himself with the most improbable choice of subjects in the most improbable order. Five volumes of the *Exercices* appeared before he left Paris. In Turin he renewed this undertaking—and even published in the local newspaper—and continued it in Prague and again in Paris, finally reaching a total of ten volumes. He published in other journals, too; and there are at least eighteen memoirs by him published separately, in no periodical or collection, as well as many textbooks. Sometimes his activity seems explosive even by his own standards. At the meetings of the Academy of 14, 21, and 28 August 1848 he submitted five notes and five memoirs—probably to cover the holiday he would take until 9 October. Then in nine meetings, until 18 December, he submitted nineteen notes and ten memoirs. He always presented many more memoirs than the Academy could publish.

On 1 March 1847 Lamé presented to the Academy a proof of Fermat's last theorem. Liouville pointed out that the proof rested on unproved assumptions in the arithmetic of circle division fields. Cauchy immediately returned to this problem, which he had considered earlier. For many weeks he informed the Academy of all his abortive attempts to solve the problem (which is still unsolved) by proving Lamé's assumption. On 24 May, Liouville read a letter from Ernst Kummer, who had disproved Lamé's assumption. Even such an incident would not silence Cauchy, however, and a fortnight later he presented investigations generalizing those of Kummer.

The story that Abel's Paris memoir went astray [10] through Cauchy's neglect rests on gossip. It has been refuted by D. E. Smith, who discovered Legendre and Cauchy's 1829 report on Abel's work [10a; 10b]. In general it would be wrong to think that Cauchy did not recognize the merits of others. When he had examined a paper, he honestly reported its merits, even if it overlapped his own work. Of all the mathematicians of his period he is the most careful in quoting others. His reports on his own discoveries have a remarkably naïve freshness because he never forgot to sum up what he owed to others. If Cauchy were found in error, he candidly admitted his mistake.

Most of his work is hastily, but not sloppily, written. He was unlike Gauss, who published *pauca sed matura* only—that is, much less than he was able to, and many things never. His works still charm by their freshness, whereas Gauss's works were and still are turgid. Cauchy's work stimulated new investigations much earlier than Gauss's did and in range of subject matter competes with Gauss's. His publishing methods earned for Gauss an image of an almost demonic intelligence who knew all the secrets better and more deeply than ordinary men. There is no such mystery around Cauchy, who published lavishly—although nothing that in maturity could be compared with Gauss's publications. He sometimes published the same thing twice, and sometimes it is evident that he was unfamiliar with something he had brought out earlier. He published at least seven books and more than 800 papers.

More concepts and theorems have been named for Cauchy than for any other mathematician (in elasticity alone [35] there are sixteen concepts and theorems named for Cauchy). All of them are absolutely simple and fundamental. This, however, is an objective assessment and does not consider the subjective value they had for Cauchy. In the form that Cauchy discovered and understood them, they often were not so simple; and from the way that he used or did not use them, it often appears that he did not know that they were fundamental. In nearly all cases he left the final form of his discoveries to the next generation. In all that Cauchy achieved there is an unusual lack of profundity. He was one of the greatest mathematicians—and surely the most universal—and also contributed greatly to mathematical physics. Yet he was the most superficial of the great mathematicians, the one who had a sure feeling for what was simple and fundamental without realizing it.

Writings. Cauchy's writings appeared in the publications of the Academy, in a few scientific journals, separately as books, or in such collections as the *Exercices.* Some of his courses were published by others [3; 4]. There were, according to Valson, eighteen *mémoires détachés.* A Father Jullien (a Jesuit), under the guidance of Cauchy, once catalogued his work. The catalog has not been published. Valson's list was based on it, but he was not sure whether it was complete;[4] and it is not clear whether Valson ever personally saw all of the *mémoires détachés* or whether all of them really existed. Some of them, which have been lithographed, are rare.[5] Cauchy must have left an enormous quantity of anecdota, but nothing is known of what happened to them. What the Academy possesses seems to be insignificant.

In 1882 the Academy began a complete edition of Cauchy's work [1]. Volume XV of the second series is still lacking. In the second of the second series, which appeared as late as 1957, the commissioners of the Academy declared their decision to cease publication after still another volume. They did not say whether the edition would be stopped because it is finished or whether it will remain unfinished. The missing volume seems to have been reserved for the *mémoires détachés,* among which are some of Cauchy's most important papers. Fortunately, one of them has been reprinted separately [2; 2a; 2b].

The Academy edition of Cauchy's works contains no anecdota. Cauchy's papers have been arranged according to the place of original publication. The first series contains the Academy publications; the second, the remainder. This makes use of the edition highly inconvenient. Everything has been published without comment: there is no account of how the text was established and no statement whether printing errors and evident mistakes were corrected (sometimes it seems that they were not). Sometimes works have been printed twice (such as [1, 1st ser., V, 180–198], which is a textual extract of [1, 2nd ser., XI, 331–353]). In other cases such duplications have been avoided, but such avoidances of duplication have not regularly been accounted for. Since Cauchy and his contemporaries quote the *Exercices* according to numbers of issues it is troublesome that this subdivision has not been indicated. This criticism, however, is not to belittle the tremendous value of the Academy edition.

Important bibliographic work on Cauchy was done by B. Boncompagni [5].

Since Valson's biography [8] and the two biographic sketches by Biot and Bertrand [7; 11], no independent biographical research on Cauchy has been undertaken except for that by Terracini [13]. (It would be troublesome but certainly worthwhile to establish a faithful picture of Cauchy from contemporary sources. He was one of the best-known people of his time and must have been often mentioned in newspapers, letters, and memoirs.[6]) Valson's analysis of Cauchy's work is unsatisfactory because sometimes he did not understand Cauchy's mathematics; for instance, he mistook his definition of residue. Lamentably no total appreciation of Cauchy's work has been undertaken since. There are, however, a few historical investigations of mathematical fields that devote some space to Cauchy. See Casorati [19] on complex functions (not accessible to the present reporter); Verdet [20] on optics; Studnicka [21] on determinants (not accessible); Todhunter [21a] on elasticity; Brill and Noether [22] on complex functions (excellent); Stäckel and Jourdain [23, 24, 25] on complex functions; the *Encyclopädie der mathematischen Wissenschaften* [26] on mathematical physics and astronomy; Burkhardt [27] on several topics (chaotic, with unconnected textual quotations, but useful as a source); Miller [28] on group theory; Jourdain [29] on calculus (not accessible); Love [30] on elasticity (fair); Lamb [31] on hydrodynamics (excellent); Whittaker [32] on optics (excellent); Carruccio [33] on complex functions; Courant and Hilbert [34] on differential equations (fair); Truesdell and Toupin [35] on elasticity (excellent).

Because of the great variety of fields in which Cauchy worked it is extremely difficult to analyze his work and properly evaluate it unless one is equally experienced in all the fields. One may overlook important work of Cauchy and commit serious errors of evaluation. The present author is not equally experienced in all the fields: in number theory less than in analysis, in mathematical physics less than in mathematics, and entirely inexperienced in celestial mechanics.

Calculus. The classic French *Cours d'analyse* (1821), descended from Cauchy's books on calculus [1, 2nd ser., III; IV; IX, 9-184], forcefully impressed his contemporaries. N. H. Abel [17] called the work [1, 2nd ser., III] "an excellent work which should be read by every analyst who loves mathematical rigor." In the introduction Cauchy himself said, "As to the methods, I tried to fill them with all the rigor one requires in geometry, and never to revert to arguments taken from the generality of algebra." Cauchy needed no metaphysics of calculus. The "generality of algebra," which he rejected, assumed that what is true for real numbers is true for complex numbers; that what is true for finite magnitudes is true for infinitesimals; that what is true for convergent series is true for divergent ones. Such a remark that looks trivial today was a new, if not revolutionary, idea at the time.

Cauchy refused to speak about the sum of an infinite series unless it was convergent, and he first defined convergence and absolute convergence of series, and limits of sequences and functions [1, 2nd ser., III, 17-19]. He discovered and formulated *convergence criteria:* the Cauchy principle of $s_{m+n} - s_n$ becoming small[7] [1, 2nd ser., VII, 269], the root criterion using the lowest upper limit of $\sqrt[n]{|a_n|}$ [1, 2nd ser., III, 121], the quotient criterion using that of $|a_{n+1}|/|a_n|$ [1, 2nd ser., III, 123], their relation, the integral criterion [1, 2nd ser., VII, 267-269]. He defined upper and lower limits [1, 2nd ser., III, 121], was first to prove the convergence of $(1 + 1/n)^n$, and was the first to use the limit sign [1, 2nd ser., IV, 13 f.]. Cauchy studied convergence of series under such operations as addition and multiplication [1, 2nd ser., III, 127-130] and under rearrangement [1, 1st ser., X, 69; 1st ser., IX, 5-32]. To avoid pitfalls he defined convergence of double series too cautiously [1, 2nd ser., III, 441; X, 66]. Explicit estimations of convergence radii of power series are not rare in his work. By his famous example $\exp(-x^{-2})$ he warned against rashness in the use of Taylor's series [1, 2nd ser., II, 276-282]. He proved Lagrange's and his own remainder theorem, first by integral calculus [1, 2nd ser., IV, 214] and later by means of his own generalized mean-value theorem [1, 2nd ser., IV, 243, 364; VI, 38-42], which made it possible to sidestep integral calculus. In the first proof he used the integral form of the remainder that is closely connected to his famous formula [1, 2nd ser., IV, 208-213],

$$(1)\quad \int^t \underset{n}{\cdots} \int^t f(t)\,dt = \frac{1}{(n-1)!}\int^t (t-\tau)^{n-1} f(\tau)\,d\tau.$$

An important method in power series arising from multiplication, inversion, substitution, and solving differential equations was Cauchy's celebrated *calcul des limites* (1831-1832), which in a standard way reduces the convergence questions to those of geometrical series [1, 2nd ser., II, 158-172; XI, 331-353; XII, 48-112].

Cauchy invented our notion of continuity[8] and proved that a continuous function has a zero between arguments where its signs are different [1, 2nd ser., III, 43, 378], a theorem also proved by Bolzano. He also did away with multivalued functions. Against Lagrange he again and again stressed the limit origin of the differential quotient. He gave the first adequate definition of the definite integral as a limit of sums [1, 2nd ser., IV, 122-127] and defined improper integrals [1, 2nd ser., IV, 140-144], the well-known Cauchy principal value of an integral with a singular integrand [1, 1st ser., I, 288-303, 402-406], and closely connected, singular integrals (i.e., integrals of infinitely large functions over infinitely small paths [δ functions]) [1, 1st ser., I, 135, 288-303, 402-406; 2nd ser., I, 335-339; IV, 145-150; XII, 409-469]. Cauchy made much use of discontinuous factors [1, 1st ser., XII, 79-94] and of the Fourier transform (see under Differential Equations). Cauchy also invented what is now called the Jacobian, although his definition was restricted to two and three dimensions [1, 1st ser., I, 12].

In addition, Cauchy gave the proof of the fundamental theorem of algebra that uses the device of lowering the absolute value of an analytic function as long as it does not vanish [1, 2nd ser., I, 258-263; III, 274-301; IV, 264; IX, 121-126]. His investigations (1813, published in 1815) on the number of real roots [1, 2nd ser., I, 170-257] were surpassed by Sturm's (1829). In 1831 he expressed the number of complex roots of $f(z)$ in a domain by the logarithmic residue formula, noticing that the same expression gives the number of times $\operatorname{Re} f(z)/\operatorname{Im} f(z)$ changes from $-\infty$ to ∞ along a closed curve—in other words how often the f-image of the curve turns around 0—which led to a new proof of the fundamental theorem that was akin to Gauss's first, third, and fourth (reconstructed from [8, II, 85-88]—see also [1, 1st ser., IV, 81-83], since the 1831 *mémoire détaché* has not yet been republished). In [1, 2nd ser., I, 416-466] the proof has been fashioned in such a way that it applies to mappings of the plane into itself by pairs of functions.

With unsurpassed skill and staggering productivity he calculated and transformed integrals and series developments.

In mathematics Cauchy was no dogmatist. Despite his insistence on the limit origin of the differential quotient, he never rejected the formal approach, which he called symbolic [1, 2nd ser., VII, 198–254; VIII, 28–38] and often justified by Fourier transformation. On a large scale he used the formal approach in differential and difference equations. Cauchy admitted semiconvergent series, called "limited" [1, 1st ser., VIII, 18–25; XI, 387–406], and was the first to state their meaning and use clearly. By means of semiconvergent series in 1842 he computed all the classic integrals such as $\int_v^\infty \cos 1/2\pi v^2\, dv$ [1, 1st ser., VII, 149–157] and, in 1829 [1, 1st ser., II, 29–58], asymptotics of integrals of the form $\int u^n v\, dx$, particularly those such as $\int (1 - x)^m x^n f(x)\, dx$, where beta functions are involved if $f(x)$ is duly developed in a series [1, 1st ser., IX, 75–121; II, 29–58]; he used rearrangements of conditionally convergent series [1, 1st ser., IX, 5–14] in the same way.

In a more profound sense Cauchy was rather more flexible than dogmatic, for more often than not he sinned against his own precepts. He operated on series, Fourier transforms, and improper and multiple integrals as if the problems of rigor that he had raised did not exist, although certainly he knew about them and would have been able to solve them. Although he had been first to define continuity, it seems that Cauchy never proved the continuity of any particular function. For instance, it is well known that he asserted the continuity of the sum of a convergent series of continuous functions [1, 2nd ser., III, 120]; Abel gave a counterexample, and it is clear that Cauchy himself knew scores of them. It is less known that later Cauchy correctly formulated and applied the uniform convergence that is needed here [1, 1st ser., XII, 33]. He proved

$$\lim \left(1 + \frac{1}{n}\right)^n = \sum \frac{1}{n!}$$

by a popular but unjustified interchange of limit processes [1, 2nd ser., III, 147], although he was well acquainted with such pitfalls; it is less well-known that he also gave a correct proof [1, 2nd ser., XIV, 269–273]. Terms like "infinitesimally small" prevail in Cauchy's limit arguments and epsilontics still looks far away, but there is one exception. His proof [1, 2nd ser., III, 54–55] of the well-known theorem

$$\text{If } \lim_{x\to\infty} (f(x + 1) - f(x)) = \alpha, \quad \text{then } \lim_{x\to\infty} x^{-1} f(x) = \alpha$$

is a paragon, and the first example, of epsilontics—the character ϵ even occurs there. It is quite probable that this was the beginning of a method that, after Cauchy, found general acceptance. It is the weakest point in Cauchy's reform of calculus that he never grasped the importance of uniform continuity.

Complex Functions. The discoveries with which Cauchy's name is most firmly associated in the minds of both pure and applied mathematicians are without doubt his fundamental theorems on complex functions.

Particular complex functions had been studied by Euler, if not earlier. In hydrodynamics d'Alembert had developed what are now called the Cauchy-Riemann differential equations and had solved them by complex functions. Yet even at the beginning of the nineteenth century complex numbers were not yet unanimously accepted; functions like the multivalued logarithm aroused long-winded discussions. The geometrical interpretation of complex numbers, although familiar to quite a few people, was made explicit by Gauss as late as 1830 and became popular under his name. It is, however, quite silly to doubt whether, earlier, people who interpreted complex functions as pairs of real functions knew the geometric interpretation of complex numbers. Gauss's proofs of the fundamental theorem of algebra, although reinterpreted in the real domain, implicitly presupposed some facts from complex function theory. The most courageous ventures in complex functions up to that time were the rash ideas of Euler and Laplace of shifting real integration paths in the complex domain (for instance, that of e^{-x^2} from $-\infty$ to ∞) to get new formulas for definite integrals [24], then an entirely unjustified procedure. People sometimes ask why Newton or Leibniz or the Bernoullis did not discover Cauchy's integral theorem and integral formula. Historically, however, such a discovery should depend first on some geometrical idea on complex numbers and second on some more sophisticated ideas on definite integrals. As long as these conditions were not fulfilled, it was hardly possible to imagine integration along complex paths and theorems about such kinds of integrals. Even Cauchy moved slowly from his initial hostility toward complex integration to the apprehension of the theorems that now bear his name. It should be mentioned that Gauss knew most of the fundamental facts on complex functions, although he never published anything on them [22, pp. 155–160].

The first comprehensive theory of complex numbers is found in Cauchy's *Cours d'analyse* of 1821 [1, 2nd ser., III, 153–256]. There he justified the algebraic and limit operations on complex numbers, considered absolute values, and defined continuity for complex functions. He did not teach complex integration, although in a sense it had been the subject of his *mémoire* submitted to the French Academy in 1814 and published in 1825 [1, 1st ser., I, 329-506]. It is clear from its introduction that this *mémoire* was written in order to justify such rash but fruitful procedures as those of Euler and Laplace mentioned above. But Cauchy still felt uneasy in the complex domain. He interpreted complex functions as pairs of real functions of two variables to which the Cauchy-Riemann differential equations apply. This meant bypassing rather than justifying the complex method. Thanks to Legendre's criticism Cauchy restored the complex view in footnotes added to the 1825 publication, although he did not go so far as to admit complex integration paths. The problem Cauchy actually dealt with in this *mémoire* seems strange today. He considered a differentiable function $f = u + iv$ of the complex variable $z = x + iy$ and, using one of the Cauchy-Riemann differential equations, formed the double integral

$$\text{(2)} \qquad \iint u_x \, dx \, dy = \iint v_y \, dx \, dy$$

over a rectangle $x_0 \leqslant x \leqslant x_1, y_0 \leqslant y \leqslant y_1$. Performing the integrations, he obtained the fundamental equality

$$\text{(3)} \qquad \int_{y_0}^{y_1} (u(x_1,y) - u(x_0,y)) \, dy = \int_{x_0}^{x_1} (v(x,y_1) - v(x,y_0)) \, dx.$$

Using the other Cauchy-Riemann differential equation, he obtained a second equality; and together they yielded

$$\text{(4)} \qquad i\int_{y_0}^{y_1} (f(x_1,y) - f(x_0,y)) \, dy = \int_{x_0}^{x_1} (f(x,y_1) - f(x,y_0)) \, dx,$$

the Cauchy integral theorem for a rectangular circuit, as soon as one puts the i between the d and the y.

Of course regularity is supposed in this proof. Cauchy had noticed, however, that (3) and (4) may cease to hold as soon as there is a singularity within the rectangle; this observation had even been his point of departure. He argued that when drawing conclusions from (2), one had interchanged integrations; and he decided that this was not generally allowed. He tried to compute the difference between the two members of (4), but his exposition is quite confused and what he means is elucidated elsewhere [1, 2nd ser., VI, 113-123].

Let $a + ib$ be the (simple polar) singularity. Then the integrals in (3) and (4) have to be understood as their principal values, e.g.,

$$\int_{y_0}^{y_1} = \lim_{\varepsilon=0} \left(\int_{y_0}^{b-\varepsilon} + \int_{b+\varepsilon}^{y_1} \right).$$

This means that the first member of (3) is the limit of the sum of the double integrals over the rectangles

$$x_0 \leqslant x \leqslant x_1, y_0 \leqslant y \leqslant b - \varepsilon;$$
$$x_0 \leqslant x \leqslant x_1, b + \varepsilon \leqslant y \leqslant y_1;$$

and the difference between both members of (3) and (4) is the limit of the integral over

$$x_0 \leqslant x \leqslant x_1, b - \varepsilon \leqslant y \leqslant b + \varepsilon.$$

In other words,

$$\lim_{\varepsilon=0} \int_{x_0}^{x_1} (f(x, b + \varepsilon) - f(x, b - \varepsilon)) \, dx,$$

where x_0, x_1 may still be replaced by arbitrary abscissae around a. This expression is just what Cauchy calls a singular integral. In his 1814 paper he allows the singularity to lie on the boundary of the rectangle, and even in a corner. (To make the last step conclusive, one should define principal values in a more sophisticated way.)

Of course if there is one singularity $a + ib$ within the rectangle, then according to the residue theorem the difference of both members of (4) should be $2\pi i$ times the coefficient of $(z - (a + ib))^{-1}$ in the Laurent series of $f(z)$. This knowledge is still lacking in Cauchy's 1814 paper. He deals with simple polar singularities only, taking $f(z)$ as a fraction $g(z)/h(z)$ and proving that the difference equals

$$\text{(5)} \qquad 2\pi i \frac{g(a + ib)}{h'(a + ib)}.$$

In the 1825 footnotes he adds the expression

$$\text{(6)} \qquad 2\pi i \lim_{\varepsilon=0} \varepsilon f((a + ib) + \varepsilon),$$

which had already appeared in 1823 [1, 2nd ser., I, 337].

Cauchy's most important general result here is the computation of

$$\int_{-\infty}^{\infty} f(z) \, dz$$

(over the real axis) as a sum of expressions (5) from the upper half-plane; singularities on the real axis are half accounted for in such sums. The conditions under which he believes one is entitled to pass from the rectangle as an integration path to the real axis are not clearly formulated. It seems that he requires vanishing of $f(z)$ at infinity, which of course is too much; in any case, he applies the result to functions with an infinity of poles, where this requirement does not hold. In 1826 he stated more sophisticated but still too rigid conditions [1, 2nd ser., VI, 124–145]; strangely enough, at the end of this paper he returned to the useless older ones. In 1827 [1, 2nd ser., VII, 291–323] he discovered the "good conditions": $zf(z)$ staying bounded on an appropriate sequence of circles with fixed centers and with radii tending to infinity.

Even in the crude form of the 1814 *mémoire,* Cauchy's integral theorem proved to be a powerful instrument; a host of old and new definite integrals could be verified by this method. The approach by double integrals looks strange, but at that time it must have been quite natural; in fact, in his third proof of the fundamental theorem of algebra (1816), Gauss used the same kind of double integrals to deal with singularities [22, pp. 155–160].

Genuine complex integration is still lacking in the 1814 *mémoire,* and even in 1823 Poisson's reflections on complex integration [23] were bluntly rejected by Cauchy [1, 2nd ser., I, 354]. But they were a thorn in his side; and while Poisson did not work out this idea, Cauchy soon did. In a *mémoire détaché* of 1825 [2], he took a long step toward what is now called Cauchy's integral theorem. He defined integrals over arbitrary paths in the complex domain; and through the Cauchy-Riemann differential equations he derived, by variation calculus, the fact that in a domain of regularity of $f(z)$ such an integral depended on the end points of the path only. Curiously enough he did not introduce closed paths. Further, he allowed the changing path to cross a simple polar singularity γ, in which case the integral had to be interpreted by its principal value. Of course, the variation then would differ from zero; its value, equal toward both sides, would be

$$\lim_{\varepsilon=0} \varepsilon f(\gamma + \varepsilon)\pi i.$$

In the case of an $m$tuple polar singularity γ the integrals over paths on both sides of γ would differ by

$$(6)\qquad \frac{1}{(m-1)!}\lim_{\varepsilon=0}\frac{d^{m-1}\varepsilon^m f(\gamma+\varepsilon)}{d\varepsilon^{m-1}}2\pi i,$$

a formula that goes back at least as far as 1823 [1, 2nd ser., I, 337 n.]. (Notice that at this stage Cauchy did not know about power series development for analytic functions.) The foregoing yields the residue theorem with respect to poles; it was extended to general isolated singularities by P. A. Laurent in 1843 [22].

(It is a bewildering historical fact that by allowing for simple singularities upon the integration path, Cauchy handled his residue theorem as a much more powerful tool than the one provided by modern textbooks, with their overly narrow formulation.)

The important 1825 *mémoire* was neither used nor quoted until 1851 [1, 1st ser., XI, 328], a circumstance utterly strange and hard to explain. Did Cauchy not trust the variational method of proof? Was he bothered by the (unnecessary) condition he had imposed on the paths, staying within a fixed rectangle? Did he not notice that the statement could be transformed into the one about closed paths that he most needed? Or had he simply forgotten about that *mémoire détaché?* In any case, for more than twenty-five years he restricted himself to rectangular paths or circular-annular ones (derived from the rectangular kind by mapping), thus relying on the outdated 1814 *mémoire* rather than on that of 1825.

The circle as an integration path and Cauchy's integral formula for this special case had in a sense already been used in 1822 and 1823 [1, 2nd ser., II, 293–294; I, 338, 343, 348], perhaps even as early as 1819 [1, 2nd ser., II, 293 n.]. The well-known integral expression for the nth derivative also appeared, although of course in the form

$$(7)\qquad f^{(n)}(0) = \frac{n!}{2\pi}\int_0^{2\pi}(re^{i\phi})^{-n}f(re^{i\phi})\,d\phi,$$

since complex integration paths were still avoided. In 1840 (perhaps as early as 1831) such an expression would be called an average (over the unit circle) and, indeed, constructed as the limit of averages over regular polygons [1, 2nd ser., XI, 337].

Indirect applications of Cauchy's definition of integrals were manifold in the next few years. In the *Exercices* of 1826–1827 [1, 2nd ser., V–VI] many papers were devoted to a rather strange formal calculus of residues. The residue of $f(z)$ at γ is defined as the coefficient of πi in (6); the residue in a certain domain, as the sum of those at the different points of the domain. A great many theorems on residues are proved without recurring to the integral expressions, and it often seems that Cauchy had forgotten about that formula.

By means of residues Cauchy arrived at the partial fractions development of a function $f(z)$ with simple poles,

$$f(z) = \sum \frac{\alpha_\nu}{z-\gamma_\nu}.$$

The trouble with this series is the same as that with the residue theorem. Originally the asymptotic assumption under which this would hold, reads: vanishing at infinity. This is much too strong and surely is not what Cauchy meant when he applied the partial fractions development under much broader conditions. The condition in [1, 2nd ser., VII, 324–362] is still too strong. It is strange that in this case Cauchy did not arrive at the "good condition"; and it is stranger still that in 1843 he again required continuity at infinity, which is much too strong [1, 1st ser., VIII, 55–64].

From the partial fractions development of meromorphic functions it was a small step to the product representation of integral functions; it was taken by Cauchy in 1829–1830 [1, 2nd ser., IX, 210–253]. In special cases Cauchy also noticed the exponential factor, needed in addition to the product of linear factors; the general problem, however, was not solved until Weierstrass. Poles and roots in such investigations used to be simple; Cauchy tried multiple ones as well [1, 2nd ser., IX, 223], but this work does not testify for a clear view.

Cauchy skillfully used residues for many purposes. He expressed the number of roots of a function in a domain by logarithmic residues [1, 2nd ser., VII, 345–362] and, more generally, established a formula for sums over the roots z_i of $F(z)$,

$$(8) \qquad \Sigma\phi(z_i) = \text{sum of residues of} \frac{\phi(z)F'(z)}{F(z)},$$

which had many applications. He was well aware of the part played by arrangement in such infinite sums. In 1827 he derived the Fourier inversion formula in this context [1, 2nd ser., VI, 144; VII, 146–159, 177–209].

In 1827 Cauchy devised a method to check the convergence of a special power series for implicit functions, the so-called Lagrange series of celestial mechanics [1, 1st ser., II, 29–66]. It is the method that in the general case leads to the power series development: a function in the complex domain with a continuous derivative can be developed into a power series converging in a circle that on its boundary contains the next singularity. It seems to have been proved in the Turin *mémoires détachés* of 1831–1832; a summary of these papers was published in 1837 as *Comptes rendus* notes [1, 2nd ser., IV, 48–80] and the papers themselves, or a substantial part of them, were republished in 1840–1841 [1, 2nd ser., XI, 331–353; XII, 48–112; see also XI, 43–50]. Here Cauchy first derives in a remarkable way his integral formula from his integral theorem by means of

$$\oint \frac{f(\zeta) - f(z)}{\zeta - z} d\zeta = 0,$$

which is formulated for circular paths only, although it also applies to arbitrary circuits. The development of the integrand of

$$\frac{1}{2\pi i} \oint \frac{f(\zeta)}{\zeta - z} d\zeta = f(z)$$

according to powers of z yields the power series development of $f(z)$. Cauchy also finds an integral expression of the remainder if the development is terminated and the power series coefficients theorem

$$|a_n| \leqslant \max_{|z|=r} |f(z)| \cdot r^{-n}$$

(see also [1, 1st ser., VIII, 287–292]), which was to become the cornerstone of the powerful *calcul des limites*.

The results were applied to implicitly given functions. Using (8) a simple zero w of $F(z,w) = 0$ or a sum of simple roots or a sum $\Sigma\phi(w_i)$ over simple roots, w_i is developed into a power series according to z. Cauchy also noticed that the power series for a simple root will converge up to the first branching point, which is obtained by $\partial F(z,w)/\partial w = 0$—of course it should be one of the same sheet, but this was not clear at the time. In one of his 1837 notes [1, 1st ser., IV, 55–56] Cauchy had gone so far as to state that in all points developments according to fractional powers were available; in 1840–1841, however, he did not come back to this point.

The foregoing summarizes some of Cauchy's tremendous production in this one area of his work. It is awe-inspiring and yet, in a sense, disappointing. One feels that Cauchy had no clear overall view on his own work. Proofs are usually unnecessarily involved and older papers, superseded by newer results, are repeatedly used and quoted. Often he seems to be blindfolded; for example, he did not notice such a consequence of his work as that a bounded regular function must be constant [1, 1st ser., VIII, 366–385] until Liouville discovered this theorem in the special case of doubly periodic functions—this is why it is now (incorrectly) called Liouville's theorem. One can imagine that Cauchy felt ashamed and confused, so confused, indeed, that he missed the point to which he should have connected Liouville's theorem. Instead of using the power series coefficients theorem he handled it with partial fractions development, which does not work properly because of the asymptotic conditions.

Cauchy also failed to discover Laurent's theorem and the simple theorem about a function with an accumulating set of roots in a regularity domain, which he knew only in crude forms [1, 1st ser., VIII, 5–10]. He would have missed much more if others had cared about matters so general and so simple as those which occupied Cauchy. Most disappointing of all is, of course, the fact that he still did not grasp the fundamental importance of his 1825 *mémoire*. He confined himself to rectangular and circular integration paths and to a special case of his integral formula.

A sequence of *Comptes rendus* notes of 1846 [1, 1st ser., X, 70-74, 133-196] marks long-overdue progress. Cauchy finally introduced arbitrary closed integration paths, although not as an immediate consequence of his 1825 *mémoire*, which he did not remember until 1851 [1, 1st ser., XI, 328]; instead, he proved his integral theorem anew by means of what is now called Green's formula—a formula dating from 1828 but possibly rediscovered by Cauchy. A still more important step was his understanding of multivalued analytic functions. The history of this notion is paradigmatic of what often happens in mathematics: an intuitive notion that is fruitful but does not match the requirements of mathematical rigor is first used in a naïve uncritical fashion; in the next phase it is ignored, and the results to which it led are, if needed, derived by cumbersome circumvention; finally, it is reinterpreted to save both the intuitive appeal and the mathematical rigor. In multivalued functions Cauchy embodied the critical phase. From 1821 he treated multivalued functions with a kill-or-cure remedy: if branched at the origin, they would be admitted in the upper half-plane only [1, 2nd ser., III, 267]. Fortunately, he more often than not forgot this gross prescription, which if followed would lead him into great trouble, as happened in 1844 [1, 1st ser., VIII, 264] —strangely enough, he wrote this confused paper just after he had taken the first step away from this dogmatism. Indeed [1, 1st ser., VIII, 156-160], he had already allowed for a plane slit by the positive axis as the definition domain of functions branched at the origin; and he had even undertaken integrations over paths pieced together from $|z| = r$ in the positive sense, $r \leqslant z \leqslant R$ in the positive sense, $|z| = R$ in the negative sense, $r \leqslant z \leqslant R$ in the negative sense, where the two rectilinear pieces are combined into one over the jump function. Such paths had long since been obtained in a natural way by a mapping of rectangular paths.

The progress Cauchy achieved in 1846 consisted in restoring the intuitive concept of a multivalued function. Such a function may now freely be followed along rather arbitrary integration paths, which are considered closed only if both the argument and the function return to the values with which they started (of course this was not yet fully correct). Integration over such closed paths produces the *indices de périodicité* that are no longer due to residues.

This is a revival of the old idea of the multivalued function, with all its difficulties. In 1851—the year of Riemann's celebrated thesis—after Puiseux's investigations on branchings, which again depended on Cauchy's work, Cauchy came back with some refinements [1, 1st ser., XI, 292-314]. He slit the plane by rectilinear *lignes d'arrêt* joining singularities and, as in the 1844 paper, proposed to compute the *indices de périodicité* by means of the integrals of the jump functions along such slits. This is too crude, and it gave Cauchy wrong ideas about the number of linearly independent periods. The correct reinterpretation of multivalued functions is by means of Riemann surfaces, with their *Querschnitte;* Cauchy's *lignes d'arrêt* are drawn in the plane, which means that they may be too numerous.

Nevertheless, the progress made in Cauchy's 1846 notes was momentous. The periodicity of elliptic and hyperelliptic functions had previously been understood as an algebraic miracle rather than by topological reasons. Cauchy's crude approach was just fine enough for elliptic and hyperelliptic integrals, and his notes shed a clear light of understanding upon those functions. Notwithstanding Riemann's work, this seemed sufficient for the near future. Thus, Briot and Boucquet [18], when preparing the second edition of their classic work, saw no advantage in using Riemann surfaces and still presented Cauchy's theory in its old form.

Cauchy's work on complex functions has to be pieced together from numerous papers; he could have written a synthetic book on this subject but never did. The first to undertake such a project were Briot and Boucquet [18]. Nevertheless, complex function theory up to Riemann surfaces, with the sole exceptions of Laurent's theorem and the theorem on accumulating zeros, had been Cauchy's work. Of course he also did less fundamental work in complex function theory, such as generalizing Abel's theorem [1, 1st ser., VI, 149-175, 187-201], investigating "geometrical factorials" [1, 1st ser., VIII, 42-115] and so on.

Error Theory. Cauchy also made three studies of error theory, which he presented as logically connected; this, however, is misleading since to understand them one has to consider them as not connected at all.

The first seems to date from 1814, although it was not published until 1824 and 1831 [1, 2nd ser., II, 312-324; I, 358-402]. Laplace [14, II, 147-180] had tried to fit a set of n observational data $\ulcorner x_i, y_i \urcorner$ to a linear relation $y = ax + b$. Before Laplace, calculators proceeded by first shifting the average

$$\ulcorner \frac{1}{n} \Sigma x_i, \frac{1}{n} \Sigma y_i \urcorner$$

to the origin to make the problem homogeneous, and then estimating a by

$$\Sigma\delta_i y_i/\Sigma\delta_i x_i,\ \text{where}\ \delta_i = x_i/|x_i|.$$

Laplace proposed a choice of a and b that would make the maximal error $|y_i - ax_i - b|$ (or, alternatively, the sum of the absolute errors minimal). To do so Laplace developed a beautiful method, the first specimen of linear programming. Cauchy, following a suggestion of Laplace, extended his method to fitting triples of observational data $\ulcorner x_i, y_i, z_i \urcorner$ to a relation $z = ax + by + c$; where Laplace had reasoned by pure analysis, Cauchy presented his results in a geometrical frame, which shows him to be, as often, motivated by considerations of geometry.

At the time when Cauchy took up Laplace's problem, fitting by least squares had superseded such methods. Nevertheless, in 1837 [1, 1st ser., II, 5–17] Cauchy attempted to advocate the pre-Laplacian method. He postulated the maximal error (among the $|y_i - ax_i|$) to be "minimal under the worst conditions." It does not become clear what this means, although it is a principle vague enough to justify the older methods. Actually Cauchy now dealt with a somewhat different problem: fitting systems of observational data to polynomials (algebraic, Fourier, or some other kind)

$$u = ax + by + cz + \cdots$$

where the number of terms should depend on the goodness of fit, reached during the course of the computation. What Cauchy prescribes is no more than a systematic elimination of a, b, c, $\cdots$. In 1853, when Cauchy again drew attention to this method [1, 1st ser., XII, 36–46], he was attacked by Bienaymé [16], a supporter of "least squares." Cauchy [1, 1st ser., XII, 63–124] stressed the advantage of the indeterminate number of terms in his own method, obviously not noticing that "least squares" could easily be adapted to yield the same advantage; it is, however, possible that it was the first time he had heard of "least squares."

In this discussion with Bienaymé, Cauchy took a strange turn. What looks like an argument in favor of his second method is actually a third attempt in no way related to the first and second. Cauchy assumes the errors

$$\varepsilon_i = u_i - ax_i - by_i - cz_i - \cdots$$

to have a probability frequency f. The coefficients k_i by which a has to be eliminated from $\Sigma k_i\varepsilon_i = 0$ should be chosen to maximize the probability of $\Sigma k_i\varepsilon_i$ falling within a given interval $(-\eta,\eta)$. This is an unhealthy postulate, since generally the resulting k_i will depend on the choice of η. Cauchy's remedy is to postulate that f should be so well adapted that k_i would not depend on η. This is quite a strange assumption, since f is not an instrument of the observer but of nature; but it does produce a nice result: the only f that obey these requirements are those with a Fourier transform ϕ such that

$$\phi(\xi) = \exp(-\alpha\xi^N),$$

where α and N are constants. For $N = 1$ these are the celebrated Cauchy stochastics with the probability frequency

$$f(\xi) = \frac{\gamma}{\pi}\frac{1}{1 + \gamma^2\xi^2}.$$

Their paradoxical behavior of not being improved by averaging was noticed by Bienaymé and forged into an argument against Cauchy. In the course of these investigations Cauchy proved the central limit theorem by means of Fourier transforms in a much more general setting than Laplace had done. The present author adheres to the heterodox view that Cauchy's proof was rigorous, even by modern standards.

This was a muddy chapter of Cauchy's work, which shows him coining gold out of the mud.

Algebra. Cauchy published (1812) the first comprehensive treatise on determinants [1, 2nd ser., I, 64–169]; it contains the product theorem, simultaneously discovered by J. Binet; the inverse of a matrix; and theorems on determinants formed by subdeterminants. He knew "Jacobians" of dimension 3 [1, 1st ser., I, 12]; generally defined "Vandermonde determinants"; and in 1829, simultaneously with Jacobi, published the orthogonal transformation of a quadratic form onto principal axes [1, 2nd ser., IX, 172–195], although he must have discovered it much earlier in his work on elasticity. Through his treatise the term "determinant" became popular, and it is strange that he himself later switched to "resultant." A more abstract approach to determinants, like that of Grassmann's algebra, is found in [1, 2nd ser., XIV, 417–466].

Cauchy gave the first systematic theory of complex numbers [1, 2nd ser., III, 153–301]. Later he confronted the "geometric" approach with the abstract algebraic one of polynomials in x mod $x^2 + 1$ [1, 2nd ser., XIV, 93–120, 175–202].

One of Cauchy's first papers [1, 2nd ser., I, 64–169] generalized a theorem of Ruffini's; he proved that if under permutations of its n variables a polynomial assumes more than two values, it assumes at least p values, where p is the largest prime in n—in other words, that there are no subgroups of the symmetric group of n permutands with an index i such that $2 < i < p$. Bertrand here replaced the p with n itself for $n > 4$, although to prove it he had to rely on a hypothetical theorem of number theory (Bertrand's postulate) that was later verified by P. L. Chebyshev. Cauchy afterward proved Bertrand's result without this assumption [1, 1st ser., IX, 408-417]. His method in [1, 2nd ser., I, 64-169], further developed in [1, 2nd ser., XIII, 171-182; 1st ser., IX, 277-505; X, 1-68], was the *calcul des substitutions,* the method of permutation groups. Fundamentals of group theory, such as the order of an element, the notion of subgroup, and conjugateness are found in these papers. They also contain "Cauchy's theorem" for finite groups: For any prime p dividing the order there is an element of order p. This theorem has been notably reenforced by L. Sylow.

In 1812 Cauchy attacked the Fermat theorem on polygonal numbers, stating that every positive integer should be a sum of n $n$gonal numbers. At that time proofs for $n = 3,4$ were known. Cauchy proved it generally, with the addendum that all but four of the summands may be taken as 0 or 1 [1, 2nd ser., VI, 320-353]. Cauchy's proof is based on an investigation into the simultaneous solutions of

$$\Sigma x_i^2 = n, \ \Sigma x_i = m.$$

Cauchy contributed many details to number theory and attempted to prove Fermat's last theorem. A large treatise on number theory is found in [1, 1st ser., III].

Geometry. Cauchy's most important contribution to geometry is his proof of the statement that up to congruency a convex polyhedron is determined by its faces [1, 1st ser., II, 7-38]. His elementary differential geometry of 1826-1827 [1, 2nd ser., V] strongly influenced higher instruction in mathematics. Of course his elasticity theory contains much differential geometry of mappings and of vector and tensor fields, and the notions of grad, div, rot, and their orthogonal invariance.

Differential Equations. What is fundamentally new in Cauchy's approach to differential equations can be expressed in two ideas: (1) that the existence of solutions is not self-evident but has to be proved even if they cannot be made available in an algorithmic form and (2) that uniqueness has to be enforced by specifying initial (or boundary) data rather than by unimportant integration constants. The latter has become famous as the Cauchy problem in partial differential equations. It may have occurred to Cauchy in his first great investigation (1815), on waves in liquids [1, 1st ser., I, 5-318]. Indeed, the difficulty of this problem—and the reason why it had not been solved earlier—was that to be meaningful it had to be framed into a differential equation with initial and boundary data.

To solve ordinary differential equations Cauchy very early knew the so-called Cauchy-Lipschitz method of approximation by difference equations, although its proof was not published until 1840 [1, 2nd ser., XI, 399-404]. Several instances show that he was also acquainted with the principle of iteration [1, 1st ser., V, 236-260; 2nd ser., XI, 300-415 f.; 3, II, 702]. With analytic data the celebrated *calcul des limites* led to analytic solutions of ordinary differential equations [1, 1st ser., VI, 461-470; VII, 5-17; 3, II, 747].

Cauchy discovered (1819), simultaneously with J. F. Pfaff, the characteristics method for first-order partial differential equations [1, 2nd ser., II, 238-252; see also XII, 272-309; 1st ser., VI, 423-461]. His method was superior to Pfaff's and simpler, but it still appears artificial. The geometrical language in which it is taught today stems from Lie. Of course Cauchy also applied the *calcul des limites* to partial differential equations [1, 1st ser., VII, 17-68]. It is not quite clear which class of equations Cauchy had in mind. In 1875 Sonja (Sophia) Kowalewska precisely formulated and solved the problem by an existence theorem that usually bears the names of Cauchy and Kowalewska.

Another way to solve a system

$$\frac{dx_i}{dt} = X_i(x_1, \cdots, x_n)$$

was by means of exp tZ, with

$$Z = \Sigma X_i(x)\frac{\partial}{\partial x_i},$$

and by an analogous expression if X_i depended on t as well [1, 2nd ser., XI, 399-465; 1st ser., V, 236-250, 391-409]; the convergence of such series was again obtained by *calcul des limites.*

The greater part of Cauchy's work in differential equations was concerned with linear partial equations with constant coefficients, which he encountered in hydrodynamics, elasticity, and optics. The outstanding device of this research was the Fourier transform. It occurs in Cauchy's work as early as 1815, in his work on waves in liquids [1, 1st ser., I, 5-318], as well as in 1817 [1, 2nd ser., I, 223-232] and 1818 [1, 2nd ser., II, 278-279]. Fourier's discovery, while dating from 1807 and 1811, was published as late as 1824-1826 [27], so Cauchy's claim that he found the inversion formula independently is quite acceptable. It is remarkable that he nevertheless recognized Fourier's priority by calling the inversion formula Fourier's formula. Cauchy put the Fourier transform to greater use and used it with greater skill than anybody at that time and for long after—Fourier and Poisson included; and he was the first to formulate the inversion theorem correctly. He also stressed the importance of principal values, of convergence-producing factors with limit 1, and of singular factors (δ functions) under the integral sign [1, 2nd ser., I, 275-355]. His use of the Fourier transform was essentially sound—bold but not rash—but to imitate it in the pre-epsilontic age one had to be another Cauchy. After Weierstrass, Fourier transforms moved into limbo, perhaps because other methods conquered differential equations. Fourier transforms did not become popular until recently, when the fundamentals of Fourier integrals were proved with all desirable rigor; but so much time had elapsed that Cauchy's pioneering work had been forgotten.

From 1821 on, Cauchy considered linear partial differential equations in the operational form

$$F\left(\frac{\partial}{\partial x_1}, \cdots, \frac{\partial}{\partial x_n}, \frac{\partial}{\partial t}\right)\omega = 0, \tag{9}$$

with F as a polynomial function in $u_1, \cdots, u_n, s$. Such a differential equation has the exponential solutions

$$\exp(\Sigma u_i x_i + st),$$

which are functions of x_i, t for every system of u_i, s fulfilling

$$F(u_1, \cdots, u_n, s) = 0. \tag{10}$$

The Fourier transform method aims at obtaining the general solution by continuously superposing such exponential solutions, with imaginary $u_1, \cdots, u_n, s$. For wave equations this means wave solutions by superposition of plane harmonic waves. In the 1821 and 1823 papers [1, 2nd ser., II, 253-275; I, 275-333] a kind of interpolation procedure served to satisfy the initial conditions for $t = 0$. Another approach would be solutions arising from local disturbances (spherical waves under special conditions); they may be obtained from plane waves by superposition and in turn may give rise to general solutions by superposition. This idea is present in the 1815 papers on waves; it is neglected but not absent in the 1821 and 1823 papers.

In 1826 the residue calculus is introduced as a new device, first for solving linear ordinary differential equations with constant coefficients [1, 2nd ser., VI, 252-255; VII, 40-54, 255-266]. The general solution

$$F\left(\frac{d}{dt}\right)\omega = 0$$

is obtained as the integral

$$\frac{1}{2\pi i}\oint \frac{\phi(\zeta)e^{\zeta t}}{F(\zeta)}\,d\zeta$$

performed around the roots of F, with an arbitrary polynomial $\phi(\zeta)$. Several times Cauchy stressed that this formula avoids casuistic distinctions with respect to multiple roots of F [1, 1st ser., IV, 370].

In 1830, when Cauchy went into optics, this formula was applied to partial differential equations, which meant (10) and (9) explicitly and elegantly solved with respect to s and t, whereas with respect to $x_1, \cdots, x_n$ the Fourier transform method prevailed. Again due care was bestowed on the initial conditions at $t = 0$. The formula, obtained in polar coordinates, is involved and not quite clear; its proof is not available because the *mémoire* of which the 1830 paper is a brief extract seems never to have been published and possibly is lost. The construction of wave fronts rested upon intuitive arguments, in fact upon Huygens' principle, although he did not say so and never proved it. According to the same principle Cauchy constructed ray solutions as a superposition of planar disturbances in planes that should be slightly inclined toward each other, as Cauchy says.

From June 1839 to March 1842 Cauchy, again drawing on optics, tried new approaches to linear partial differential equations with constant coefficients. This work was instigated by P. H. Blanchet's intervention (see [1: 1st ser. IV, 369–426; V, 5–20; VI, 202–277, 288–341, 375–401, 404–420; 2nd ser., XI, 75–133, 277–264; XII, 113–124]). It now starts with a system of first-order linear ordinary differential equations, in modern notation

$$\frac{dx}{dt} = Ax, \tag{11}$$

where x is an n-vector and A a linear mapping. One considers

$$S(s) = \det(A - s)$$

and defines the *fonction principale* Θ as the solution of

$$S\left(\frac{d}{dt}\right)\Theta = 0,\ \Theta^{(i)}(0) = 0 \text{ for } i \leqslant n-2,$$

$$\Theta^{(n-1)}(0) = 1,$$

which is obtained as an integral

$$\frac{1}{2\pi i}\oint \frac{\phi(s)e^{st}}{S(s)}\,ds$$

around the roots of S. From Θ the solution of (11) with the initial vector $\ulcorner\alpha_1, \cdots, \alpha_n\urcorner$ is elegantly obtained by using

$$Q(s) = \det(A - s) \cdot (A - s)^{-1}$$

and applying $Q(d/dt)$ to the vector

$$(-1)^{n-1} \ulcorner \alpha_1 \Theta, \cdots, \alpha_n \Theta \urcorner.$$

This method is extended to partial differential equations, where it again suffices to solve (9) under the initial conditions

$$\left(\frac{d}{dt}\right)^i \omega = 0 \text{ for } 0 \leqslant i \leqslant n-2, \left(\frac{d}{dt}\right)^{n-1} \omega.$$

The formula obtained is much simpler than that of 1830, particularly if F is homogeneous. (See the quite readable presentation in [1, 1st ser., VI, 244–420].) If, moreover, the initial value of $(d/dt)^{n-1}\omega$ prescribed is a function Π of

$$\sigma = \Sigma\, u_i x_i,$$

one obtains, by first assuming Π to be linear and then using the homogeneity of F,

$$(12) \quad \omega(x,t) = \left(\frac{d}{dt}\right)^{1-n} \frac{1}{2\pi i} \oint \frac{s^{n-1}}{F(u,s)} \Pi(\sigma + st)\, ds,$$

where $(d/dt)^{-1}$ means the integration over t from 0. An analogous formula is obtained if the initial datum is assumed as a function of a quadratic function of x, say of $r = (\Sigma x_i^2)^{1/2}$.

The direct method of 1830 is again applied to the study of local disturbances and wave fronts, with Huygens' principle on the background. Cauchy apparently believed that disturbances of infinitesimal width stay infinitesimal, although this belief is disproved by $(d/dt)^{1-n}$ in (12) and by the physical argument of two or even three forward wave fronts in elasticity. It was only after Blanchet's intervention that Cauchy admitted his error.

It is doubtful whether Cauchy's investigations on this subject exerted strong immediate influence; perhaps the generations of Kirchhoff, Volterra, and Orazio Tedone were terrified by his use of Fourier transforms. Solutions arising from local disturbances, substituted into Green's formula, seemed more trustworthy. But even after Hadamard's masterwork in this field Cauchy's attempts should not be forgotten. The only modern book in which they are mentioned and used, although in an unsatisfactory and somewhat misleading fashion, is Courant and Hilbert [34].

It should be mentioned that Cauchy also grasped the notions of adjointedness of differential operators in special cases and that he attacked simple boundary problems by means of Green's function [1, 1st ser., VII, 283–325; 2nd. ser., XII, 378–408].

Mechanics. Cauchy can be credited with some minor contributions to mechanics of rigid bodies, such as the momental ellipsoid and its principal axes [1, 2nd ser., VII, 124–136]; the surfaces of the momentaneous axes of rigid motion [1, 2nd ser., VII, 119], discovered simultaneously with Poinsot; and the first rigorous proof that an infinitesimal motion is a screw motion [1, 2nd ser., VII, 116]. His proper domain, however, was elasticity. He created the fundamental mathematical apparatus of elasticity theory.

> The present investigations have been suggested by a paper of M. Navier, 14 August 1820. To establish the equation of equilibrium of the elastic plane, the author had considered two kinds of forces, the ones produced by dilatation or contraction, the others by flection of that plane. Further, in his computations he had supposed both perpendicular to the lines or faces upon which they act. It came into my mind that these two kinds could be reduced to one, still called tension or pressure, of the same nature as the hydrodynamic pressure exerted by a fluid against the surface of a solid. Yet the new pressure should not be perpendicular upon the faces which undergo it, nor be the same in all directions at a given point. . . . Further, the pressure or tension exerted against an arbitrary plane is easily derived as to magnitude and direction from the pressures or tensions exerted against three rectangular planes. I had reached that point when M. Fresnel happened to speak to me about his work on light, which he had only partially presented to the Academy, and told me that concerning the laws according to which elasticity varies in the different directions through one point, he had obtained a theorem like mine. However, this theorem was far from sufficient for the purpose I had in mind at that time, that is, to form the general equation of equilibrium and internal motion of a body, and it is only recently that I have succeeded in establishing new principles, suited to lead to this goal and the object of my communication. . . .

These lines, written by Cauchy in the fall of 1822 [1, 2nd ser., II, 300–304], announced the birth of modern elasticity theory. Rarely has a broad mathematical theory been as fully explained in as few words with as striking a lack of mathematical symbols. Never had Cauchy given the world a work as mature from the outset as this.

From Hooke's law in 1660 up to 1821, elasticity theory was essentially one-dimensional. Euler's theory of the vibrating membrane was one of the few exceptions. Another was the physical idea of internal shear stress, which welled up and died twice (Parent, 1713; Coulomb, 1773) with no impact upon the mathematical theory. Even in this one-dimensional setting, elasticity was a marvelous proving ground for Euler's analysis of partial derivatives and partial differential equations (see [36]). In 1821 Navier's paper on equilibrium and vibration of elastic solids was read to the Academy (published in 1827) [30, 32]. Navier's approach constituted analytic mechanics as applied to an isotropic molecular medium that should obey Hooke's law in molecular dimensions: any change in distance between two molecules causes a proportional force between them, the proportionality factor rapidly decreasing with increasing distance. Cauchy was one of the examiners of Navier's paper. It was not, however, this paper of Navier's to which Cauchy alluded in the above quotation. Cauchy's first approach was independent of Navier's; it was nonmolecular but rather geometrically axiomatic.

Still another advance had taken place in 1821. Thomas Young's investigations on interference in 1801 had made it clear that light should be an undulation of a hypothetical gaseous fluid, the ether. Consequently light waves were thought of as longitudinal, like those of sound in air, although the phenomena of polarization pointed to transverse vibrations. In 1821 Fresnel took the bold step of imagining an ether with resistance to distortion, like a solid rather than a fluid; and marvelously enough he found transmission by transverse waves (although longitudinal ones would subsist as well [32]). Fresnel's results encouraged Cauchy to pursue his investigations.

The short communication from which the above extract was taken was followed by detailed treatises in 1827–1829 [1, 2nd ser., VII, 60–93, 141–145; VIII, 158–179, 195–226, 228–287; IX, 342–369], but nearly all fundamental notions of the mechanics of continuous media were already clear in the 1822 note: the stress tensor (and the concept of tensor at all), the strain tensor, the symmetry of both tensors, their principal axes, the principle of obtaining equilibrium and motion equations by cutting out and freezing an infinitesimal piece of the medium, and the striking idea of requiring Hooke's law for the principal stresses and strains. For homogeneous media this led to Navier's equations, with one elastic constant, but independently of Navier's molecular substructure. Soon Cauchy introduced the second elastic constant, which arose from an independent relation between volume stress and volume strain. It led to the now generally accepted elasticity theory of isotropic media. For anisotropic media Cauchy was induced by Poisson's intervention to admit a general linear dependence between stress and strain, involving thirty-six parameters. The only fundamental notion then lacking was the elastic potential, which allows one to reduce the number of parameters to twenty-one; it is due to G. Green (1837) [30; 32].

Meanwhile, in 1828–1829 Cauchy had pursued Navier's molecular ideas and had arrived at a fifteen-parameter theory for anisotropic media [1, 2nd ser., VIII, 227–277; IX, 162–173].[9] The nineteenth-century discussions are long-since closed in favor of the axiomatic "multi-constant" theory and against the molecular "rari-constant" theory, if not against any molecular theory of elasticity at all.

Cauchy applied the general theory to several special problems: to lamellae [1, 2nd ser., VIII, 288–380], to the rectangular beam [1, 2nd ser., IX, 61–86] (definitively dealt with by Saint Venant), and to plane plates [1, 2nd ser., VIII, 381–426; IX, 9–60], in which Kirchhoff finally succeeded. The application on which Cauchy bestowed more pains than on any other subject was elastic light theory. The mathematical context of this theory was partial differential equations with constant coefficients. In the history of physics it was one of the great pre-Maxwellian efforts necessary before physicists became convinced of the impossibility of any elastic light theory.

Cauchy developed three different theories of reflection and refraction (1830, 1837, 1839) [1, 1st ser., II, 91–110; 2nd ser., II, 118–133; 1st ser., IV, 11–38; V, 20–39]. The problems were to explain double refraction (in which he succeeded fairly well), to adjust the elastic constants to the observational data on the velocity of light under different conditions in order to obtain Fresnel's sine and tangent laws of polarization by suitable boundary conditions, and to eliminate the spurious longitudinal vibrations. Whether he assumed the transverse vibrations to be parallel or orthogonal to the polarization plane (as he did in his first and second theories, respectively), he obtained strange relations between the elastic constants and was forced to admit unmotivated and improbable boundary conditions. His third theory, apparently influenced by Green's work, was based upon the curious assumption of an ether with negative compressibility—later called labile by Lord Kelvin—which does away with longitudinal waves. In 1835 Cauchy also attempted dispersion [1, 2nd ser., X, 195–464]; the problem was to explain the dependence of the velocity of light upon the wavelength by a more refined evaluation of the molecular substructure.

Celestial Mechanics. One not acquainted with the computational methods of astronomers before the advent of electronic apparatus can hardly evaluate Cauchy's numerous and lengthy contributions to celestial mechanics. In handbooks of astronomy he is most often quoted because of his general contributions to mathematics. Indeed, it must have been a relief for astronomers to know that the infinite series they used in computations could be proved by Cauchy to converge. But he also did much detailed work on series, particularly for the solution of the Kepler

CAUCHY

equation [1, 1st ser., VI, 16–48] and developments of the perturbative function [1, 1st ser., V, 288–321; VII, 86–126]; textbooks still mention the Cauchy coefficients. Cauchy's best-known contribution to astronomy (1845) is his checking of Leverrier's cumbersome computation of the large inequality in the mean motion of Pallas by a much simpler method [1, 1st ser., IX, 74–220; see also XI, 385–403]. His tools consisted of formulas for the transition from the eccentric to the mean anomaly [1, 1st ser., VI, 21]; the Cauchy "mixed method" [1, 1st ser., VIII, 168–188, 348–359], combining numerical and rational integrations when computing negative powers of the perturbative function; and asymptotic estimations of distant terms in the development of the perturbative function according to multiples of the mean anomaly—such asymptotics had interested Cauchy as early as 1827 [1, 1st ser., II, 32–58; see also IX, 5–19, 54–74; XI, 134–143].

NOTES

1. All references in brackets are to numbered works in the bibliography.
2. The data on his career in [7; 8; 9; 11] are incomplete and contradictory, even self-contradictory; but it still would not be too difficult to check them. According to Cauchy's own account [1, 2nd ser., II, 283] he taught in 1817 as Biot's *suppléant* at the Collège de France. However, on the title pages of his books published until 1830 he never mentions a chair at the Collège de France.
3. Turin was the capital of Piedmont; the dukes of Piedmont and Savoy had become kings of Sardinia.
4. In the library of the University of Utrecht I came across an unknown print of a work by Cauchy that must have appeared in a periodical. I noticed several quotations from papers missing from Valson's list and the Academy edition (e.g. [1, 2nd ser., II, 293, note]).
5. I know only two of them.
6. [1, 1st ser., IX, 186–190] shows him quarreling with the press.
7. Of course he did not prove it; he simply applied it. It had been discovered by Bolzano in 1817.
8. His own account of this invention [1, 1st ser., VIII, 145], although often repeated, is incorrect. With Euler and Lagrange, he said, "continuous" meant "defined by one single law." Actually, there was no serious definition of continuity before Cauchy.
9. I do not understand on what grounds Müller and Timpe [26, IV, 23] and Love [30] claim that Cauchy mistook his fifteen-parameter theory for the twenty-one-parameter theory. The common source of this criticism seems to be Clausius (1849). Although Cauchy was sometimes less outspoken on this point, the charge is at least refuted by [1, 2nd ser., IX, 348].

BIBLIOGRAPHY

1. Cauchy, *Oeuvres complètes,* 1st ser., 12 vols., 2nd ser., 14 vols. (Paris, 1882–). The final volume, 2nd ser., XV, is due to appear in 1970.

2. Cauchy, *Mémoire sur les intégrales définies prises entre des limites imaginaires* (Paris, 1825). To be republished in [1, 2nd ser., XV].

2a. Reprint of [2] in *Bulletin des sciences mathématiques,* **7** (1874), 265–304; **8** (1875), 43–55, 148–159.

2b. Cauchy, *Abhandlung über bestimmte Integrale zwischen imaginären Grenzen,* trans. of [2] by P. Stäckel, no. 112 in Ostwald's Klassiker der exacten Wissenschaften (Leipzig, 1900).

3. F. N. M. Moigno and M. Lindelöf, eds., *Leçons du calcul différentiel et de calcul intégral, rédigées d'après les méthodes et les oeuvres publiés ou inédits d'A.-L. Cauchy,* 4 vols. (Paris, 1840–1861).

4. F. N. M. Moigno, *Leçons de mécanique analytique, rédigées principalement d'après les méthodes d'Augustin Cauchy. . . . Statique* (Paris, 1868).

5. B. Boncompagni, "La vie et les travaux du baron Cauchy," in *Bollettino di bibliografia e di storia delle scienze matematiche e fisiche,* **2** (1869), 1–102. Review of [8].

6. K. Rychlik, "Un manuscrit de Cauchy aux Archives de l'Académie tchécoslovaque des sciences," in *Czechoslovak Mathematical Journal,* **7** **[82]** (1957), 479–481.

7. J. B. Biot, *Mélanges scientifiques et littéraires,* III (Paris, 1858), 143–160.

8. C. A. Valson, *La vie et les travaux du baron Cauchy,* 2 vols. (Paris, 1868).

9. J. Bertrand, "La vie et les travaux du baron Cauchy par C. A. Valson," in *Journal des savants* (1869), 205–215, and *Bulletin des sciences mathématiques,* **1** (1870), 105–116. Review of [8].

10. C. A. Bjerknes, *Niels-Henrik Abel, tableau de sa vie et de son action scientifique* (Paris, 1885), pp. 268–322, 342–347.

10a. D. E. Smith, "Among My Autographs, 29. Legendre and Cauchy Sponsor Abel," in *American Mathematical Monthly,* **29** (1922), 394–395.

10b. F. Lange-Nielsen, "Zur Geschichte des Abelschen Theorems. Das Schicksal der Pariser Abhandlung," in *Norsk matematisk tidsskrift,* **9** (1927), 55–73.

11. J. Bertrand, *Éloges académiques,* new ed. (Paris, 1902), pp. 101–120.

12. A. d'Hautpoul, *Quatre mois à la cour de Prague* (Paris, 1912). Not accessible to the present reporter.

13. A. Terracini, "Cauchy a Torino," in *Rendiconti del Seminario matematico* (Turin), **16** (1956–1957), 159–205.

14. P. S. Laplace, *Traité de la mécanique céleste,* II (Paris, 1804).

15. C. Sturm, "Analyse d'un mémoire sur la résolution des équations numériques," in *Bulletin universel des sciences et de l'industrie,* **11** (1829), 419–422.

16. J. Bienaymé, "Considerations . . ., Remarques . . .," in *Comptes rendus de l'Académie des sciences,* **37** (1853), 5–13, 68–69, 309–324.

17. N. H. Abel, "Untersuchungen über die Reihe . . .," in *Journal für reine und angewandte Mathematik,* **1** (1826), 311–359, also published as no. 71 in Ostwald's Klassiker der exacten Wissenschaften (1895).

18. S.-H. Briot and J. C. Boucquet, *Théorie des fonctions doublement périodiques et, en particulier, des fonctions elliptiques* (Paris, 1859); 2nd ed., *Théorie des fonctions elliptiques* (Paris, 1873–1875).

19. F. Casorati, *Teorica delle funzioni di variabili complesse* (Pavia, 1868). Not accessible to the present reporter.

20. E. Verdet, *Leçons d'optique physique,* vols. V–VI of

Verdet's *Oeuvres* (Paris, 1869–1872).

21. F. Studnicka, *A. L. Cauchy als formaler Begründer der Determinantentheorie* (Prague, 1876). Not accessible to the present reporter.

21a. I. Todhunter, *A History of the Theory of Elasticity and of the Strength of Materials from Galilei to the Present Time,* vol. I (Cambridge, 1886).

22. A. Brill and M. Noether, "Die Entwicklung der Theorie der algebraischen Funktionen in älterer und neuerer Zeit," in *Jahresbericht der Deutschen Mathematiker-Vereinigung,* **3** (1894), esp. 155–197.

23. P. Stäckel, "Integration durch das imaginäre Gebiet," in *Bibliotheca mathematica,* 3rd ser., **1** (1900), 109–128.

24. P. Stäckel, "Beitrag zur Geschichte der Funktionentheorie im 18. Jahrhundert," in *Bibliotheca mathematica,* 3rd ser., **2** (1901), 111–121.

25. P. Jourdain, "The Theory of Functions With Cauchy and Gauss," in *Bibliotheca mathematica,* 3rd ser., **6** (1905), 190–207.

26. The following articles in the *Encyklopädie der mathematischen Wissenschaften:* C. H. Müller and A. Timpe, "Grundgleichungen der mathematischen Elastizitätstheorie," IV (1907), 1; A. Wangerin, "Optik, ältere Theorie," V (1909), 21; K. F. Sundman, "Theorie der Planeten," VI, pt. 2 (1912), 15; H. von Zeipel, "Entwicklung der Störungsfunktion," VI, pt. 2 (1912), 557–665.

27. H. Burkhardt, "Entwicklungen nach oscillierenden Funktionen und Integration der Differentialgleichungen der mathematischen Physik," in *Jahresbericht der Deutschen Mathematiker-Vereinigung,* **10** (1904–1908).

28. E. A. Miller, "Historical Sketch of the Development of the Theory of Groups of Finite Order," in *Bibliotheca mathematica,* 3rd ser., **10** (1909), 317–329.

29. P. Jourdain, "The Origin of Cauchy's Conception of a Definite Integral and of the Continuity of a Function," in *Isis,* **1** (1913–1914), 661–703. Not accessible to the author.

30. A. E. H. Love, *A Treatise on the Mathematical Theory of Elasticity* (Oxford, 1927), esp. the introduction.

31. H. Lamb, *Hydrodynamics* (Cambridge, 1932), pp. 384 f.

32. E. T. Whittaker, *A History of the Theories of Aether and Electricity* (Edinburgh, 1951), esp. pp. 128–169.

33. E. Carruccio, "I fondamenti delle analisi matematica nel pensiero di Agostino Cauchy," in *Rendiconti del Seminario matematico* (Turin), **16** (1956–1957), 205–216.

34. R. Courant and D. Hilbert, *Methods of Mathematical Physics,* II (1962), esp. pp. 210–221.

35. C. Truesdell-R. Toupin, "The Classical Field Theories," in *Handbuch der Physik,* III (Berlin-Göttingen-Heidelberg, 1960), pp. 226–793, esp. 259–261, 270–271, 306–308, 353–356, 536–556.

36. C. Truesdell, "The Rational Mechanics of Flexible and Elastic Bodies, 1638–1788," in *Leonhardi Euleri Opera Omnia,* 2nd ser., XI, sec. 2 (Zurich, 1960), 7–435.

HANS FREUDENTHAL

CAVALIERI, BONAVENTURA (*b.* Milan, Italy, probably 1598; *d.* Bologna, Italy, 30 November 1647)

Cavalieri's date of birth is uncertain; the date given above is the one cited by Urbano d'Aviso, a disciple and biographer of Cavalieri. The name Bonaventura was not his baptismal name but rather that of his father. It is the name the mathematician adopted when, as a boy, he entered the Jesuati religious order, adherents of the rule of St. Augustine. Cavalieri was received in the minor orders in Milan in 1615 and in 1616 transferred to the Jesuati monastery in Pisa, where he had the good fortune of meeting the Benedictine monk Benedetto Castelli, who had studied with Galileo at Padua and was at the time a lecturer in mathematics at Pisa. Through him Cavalieri was initiated into the study of geometry. He quickly absorbed the classical works of Euclid, Archimedes, Apollonius, and Pappus, demonstrating such exceptional aptitude that he sometimes substituted for his teacher at the University of Pisa. He was introduced by Castelli to Galileo, whose disciple he always considered himself. He wrote Galileo at least 112 letters, which are included in the national edition of the *Opere di Galileo;* only two of Galileo's letters to Cavalieri have come down to us, however.

In 1620 Cavalieri returned to Rome under orders of his superiors, and in 1621 he was ordained a deacon to Cardinal Federigo Borromeo, who held Fra' Bonaventura in great esteem and gladly discussed mathematics with him; the cardinal subsequently wrote a letter commending him to Galileo. Cavalieri was hardly twenty-one when he taught theology at the monastery of San Girolamo in Milan, attracting attention by his profound knowledge of the subject.

During his Milan period (1620–1623) Cavalieri developed his first ideas on the method of indivisibles, his major contribution to mathematics. From 1623 to 1626 he was the prior of St. Peter's at Lodi. Later he was a guest in Rome of Monsignor Ciampoli, to whom he later dedicated his *Geometria.* From 1626 to 1629 he was the prior of the monastery of the Jesuati in Parma, hoping in vain to be appointed lecturer in mathematics at the university there. In the autumn of 1626, during a trip from Parma to Milan, he fell ill with the gout, from which he had suffered since childhood and which was to plague him to the end of his life. This illness kept him at Milan for a number of months. On 16 December 1627 he announced to Galileo and Cardinal Borromeo that he had completed his *Geometria.* In 1628, learning that a post of lecturer at Bologna had become vacant through the death of the astronomer G. A. Magini, he wrote Galileo for assistance in securing the appointment. Galileo, in 1629, wrote to Cesare Marsili, a gentleman of Bologna and member of the Accademia dei Lincei, who had been commissioned to find a new lecturer in mathematics. In his letter, Galileo said of Cavalieri, "few, if any, since Archimedes, have delved as far and as deep into the science of geometry." In support of his application to the Bologna position, Cavalieri sent Marsili his geometry manuscript and a small treatise on conic sections and their applications in optics. Galileo's testimonial, as Marsili wrote him, induced the "Gentlemen of the Regiment" to entrust the first chair in mathematics to Cavalieri, who held it continuously from 1629 to his death.

At the same time he was appointed prior of a convent of his own order in Bologna, specifically, at the Church of Santa Maria della Mascarella, enabling him to pursue without any impediment both his work in mathematics and his university teaching. During the period in which Cavalieri taught at Bologna, he published eleven books in that city, including the *Geometria* (1635).

Cavalieri's theory, as developed in this work and in others subsequently published, relates to an inquiry in infinitesimals, stemming from revived interest in Archimedes' works, which during the Renaissance were translated from Greek into Latin, with commentaries. The translations of Tartaglia, Maurolico, and Commandino are cited since they served as a point of departure for new mathematical developments.

The only writings of Archimedes known to seventeenth-century mathematicians were those based upon the strict method of exhaustion, by which the ancient mathematicians dealt with questions of an infinitesimal character without recourse to the infinite or to the actual infinitesimal. Nevertheless, the great mathematicians of the seventeeth century were so thoroughly pervaded with the spirit of Archimedes as to appreciate that in addition to the "method of exhaustion" the ancient geometricians must have known a more manageable and effective method for research. On this point Torricelli wrote:

> I should not dare affirm that this geometry of indivisibles is actually a new discovery. I should rather believe that the ancient geometricians availed themselves of this method in order to discover the more difficult theorems, although in their demonstration they may have preferred another way, either to conceal the secret of their art or to afford no occasion for criticism by invidious detractors. Whatever it was, it is certain that this geometry represents a marvelous economy of labor in the demonstrations and establishes innumerable, almost inscrutable, theorems by means of brief, direct, and affirmative demonstrations, which the doctrine of the ancients was incapable of. The geometry of indivisibles was indeed, in the mathematical briar bush, the so-called royal road, and one that Cavalieri first opened and laid out for the public as a device of marvelous invention [*Opere*, I, pt. I, 139–140].

In 1906 J. L. Heiberg found, in a palimpsest belonging to a Constantinople library, a small work by Archimedes in the form of a letter to Eratosthenes, which explained a method by which areas, volumes, and centers of gravity could be determined. This method, which in turn was related to the procedures of Democritus of Abdera, considered a plane surface as made up of chords parallel to a given straight line, and solids as made up of plane sections parallel to one another. In addition, according to Archimedes, principles of statics were applied, whereby the figures, thought of as heavy bodies, were weighed in an ideal scale. "I do believe," said Archimedes, "that men of my time and of the future, and through this method, might find still other theorems which have not yet come to my mind" (Rufini, *Il "Metodo" di Archimede e le origini del calcolo infinitesimale nell'antichità* [Milan, 1961], p. 103). The challenge that Archimedes extended was not taken up, as we know, by his contemporaries and fell into oblivion for many centuries.

The concept of indivisibles does sometimes show up fleetingly in the history of human thought: for example, in a passage by the eleventh-century Hebrew philosopher and mathematician Abraham bar Ḥiyya (Savasorda); in occasional speculations—more philosophical than mathematical—by the medieval Scholastics; in a passage by Leonardo da Vinci; in Kepler's *Nova stereometria doliorum* (Linz, 1615). By a conception differing from Cavalieri's, indivisibles are treated by Galileo in his *Discorsi e dimostrazioni matematiche intorno a due nuove scienze*.

In Cavalieri we come to a rational systematization of the method of indivisibles, a method that not only is deemed useful in the search for new results but also, contrary to what Archimedes assumed, is regarded as valid, when appropriately modified, for purposes of demonstrating theorems.

At this point a primary question arises: What significance did Cavalieri attribute to his indivisibles? This mathematician, while perfectly familiar with the subtle philosophical questions connected with the problem of the possibility of constituting continuous magnitudes by indivisibles, seeks to establish a method independent of the subject's hypotheses, which would be valid whatever the concept formed in this regard. While Galileo asserted, "The highest and the ultimate, although primary components of the continuous, are infinite indivisibles" (*Opere*, VII, 745–750), Cavalieri did not dare to assert that the continuous is composed of indivisible elements, about which he did not give an explicit definition, nor did he clarify whether they were actual or potential infinitesimals. It is also probable that Cavalieri's conception of his indivisibles underwent a change and that these were born as actual infinitesimals (like those of Galileo) and grew to become potential infinitesimals (see G. Cellini). It must be further pointed out, according to L. Lombardo Radice, that the Cavalieri view of the indivisibles has given us a deeper conception of the sets: it is not necessary that the elements of the set be assigned or assignable; rather it suffices that a precise criterion exist for determining whether or not an element belongs to the set.

Quite aside from any philosophical considerations on the nature of indivisibles, the determinations of area and volumes made by Cavalieri are based on the principle bearing his name, which may be formulated as follows:

> If two plane figures cut by a set of parallel straight lines intersect, on each of these straight lines, equal chords, the two figures are equivalent; if the chords pertaining to a single straight line of the set have a constant ratio, the same ratio obtains between the two figures.
>
> Similarly, in space: if the sections of two solids obtained by means of planes that are parallel to each other are equivalent two by two, the two solids are equivalent; if the two sections obtained with a given plane have a constant ratio when the plane is varied, the two solids have a ratio that is equal to that of two of their sections obtained with one same plane.

From the viewpoint of modern infinitesimal analysis, the Cavalieri principle affirms in substance that two integrals are equal if the integrands are equal and the integration limits are also equal. Furthermore, a constant that appears as a multiplier in the integrand may be carried out of the sign of integration without causing the value of the integral to vary.

However, the concept of the integral, according to the definition of A. Cauchy, was not precisely in the mathematical thought of Cavalieri, but rather was looked into by P. Mengoli, his disciple and successor in the chair at Bologna. Cavalieri pursued many paths to demonstrate his principle, and they are to be found in Book VII of his *Geometry*.

Let us consider the case in plane geometry, where, on the hypotheses of the stated principle, the corresponding chords of the given figures are equal in pairs (see Fig. 1). Cavalieri then, through a translation in the direction of the parallel straight lines in question, superimposes two equal chords. The parts of the figure which thus are superimposed are therefore equivalent

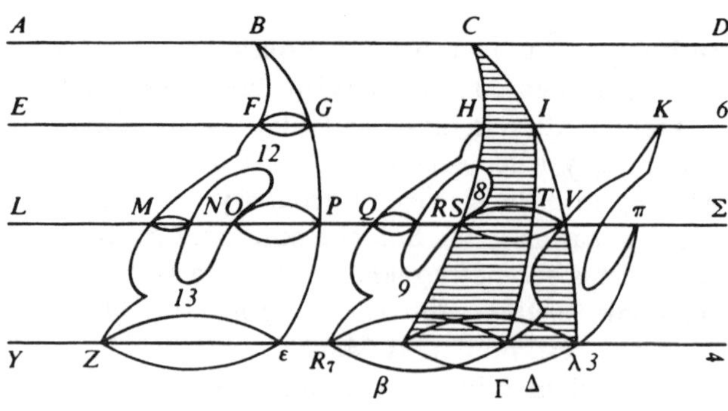

FIGURE 1

or, rather, equal, because they are congruent. The remaining parts, or residuals, which are not superimposed, will still satisfy the conditions relative to the chords that were satisfied in the original figure. In this way, one can proceed with successive superpositions by translation, and it is impossible at a given point in the successive operations that one figure be exhausted unless the other is also. Cavalieri concludes

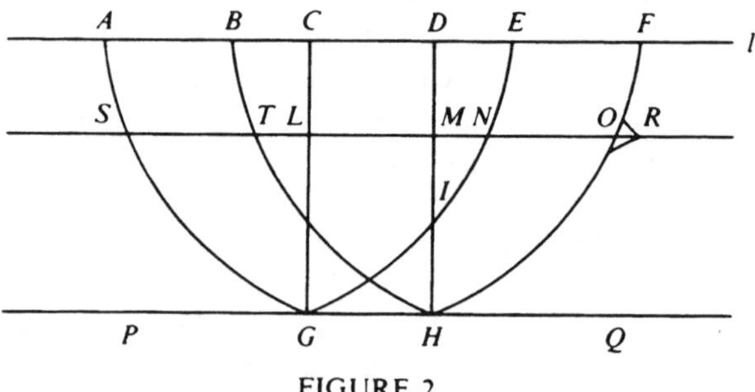

FIGURE 2

that the given figures are therefore equivalent. The argument is ingenious and intuitive, but it contains a weak point in that it is not proved that the residuals, in the described operations, become exhausted; nor is it established that the sum of such residuals can be made less than a given surface. Nevertheless, Cavalieri, in replying to the objections raised by Guldin, claims that elimination of the residuals in one of the figures, hence in the other, can be performed by means of infinite operations. The other demonstration

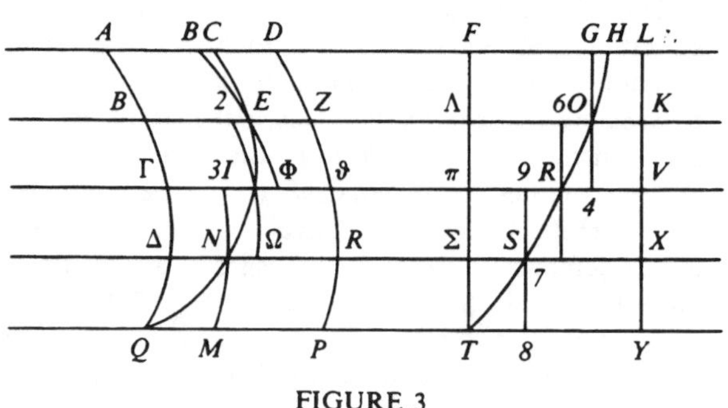

FIGURE 3

CAVALIERI

of the Cavalieri principle is made by the ancients' method of exhaustion and is a rigorous one for the figures that satisfy certain conditions: that is, the demonstration is valid for figures which, in addition to satisfying the hypothesis of the principle, fall into one of the following classes:

(1) Generalized parallelograms, namely, figures included between straight parallel lines p and l which intersect chords of constant length on straight lines running in the same direction as p and l (see Fig. 2).

(2) The *figurae in alteram partem deficientes* ("figures deficient in another part") are included between two parallel lines p and l and, in addition, the chords intercepted by a transverse line parallel to p diminish as the distance of the transverse from straight line p increases (see Fig. 3).

(3) Figures capable of being broken down into a finite number of parts belonging to either of the aforementioned two classes (see Fig. 4).

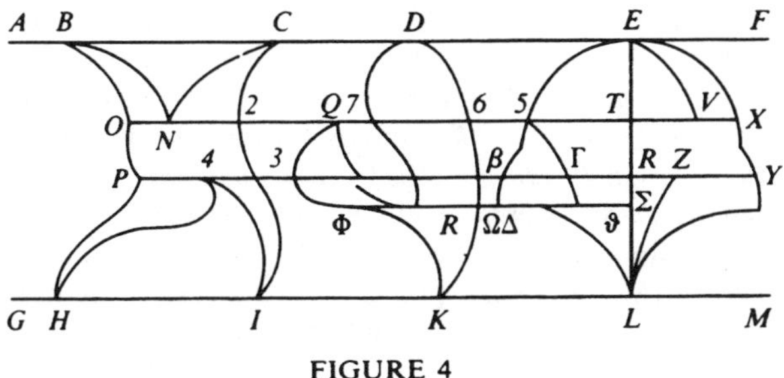

FIGURE 4

Notwithstanding the demonstrations mentioned and the success of the method of indivisibles, contemporary mathematicians, who were more attached to the traditions of classical mathematics, entered into a polemic with Cavalieri, unaware that Archimedes himself had already used methods similar to those that they were opposing. Such is the case of Guldin, who had an interesting discussion with Cavalieri that is summed up in exercise III of the *Exercitationes geometricae sex.*

Many results that were laboriously obtained by the method of exhaustion were obtained simply and rapidly through the Cavalieri principle: for example, the area of an ellipse and the volume of a sphere. Through his methods, Cavalieri had found the result which in today's symbols would be expressed as:

$$\int_0^a x^n \, dx = \frac{a^{n+1}}{n+1}$$

for any natural number $n(n = 1, 2, 3, \cdots)$. Cavalieri was unaware that this result, which appears in the *Centuria di varii problemi* (1639), had already been found as early as 1636 by Fermat and Roberval, who had arrived at it by other means.

By means of the method of indivisibles and based upon a lemma established by his pupil G. A. Rocca, Cavalieri proved the Guldin theorem on the area of a surface and the volume of rotating solids. This theorem, which also appears in certain editions of Pappus' works, although held to be an interpolation, was enunciated in the *Centrobaryca* of Guldin, who proved its correctness in certain particular cases, without, however, providing the general proof.

The most significant progress in the field of infinitesimal analysis along the lines set forth by Cavalieri was made by Evangelista Torricelli. In his *Arithmetica infinitorum* (1655), John Wallis also makes use of indivisibles.

Especially interesting is the opinion of the Cavalieri method expressed by Pascal in his *Lettres de Dettonville* (1658): "Everything that is demonstrated by the true rules of indivisibles will also and necessarily be demonstrated in the manner of the ancients. For which reason, in what follows, I shall not hesitate to use the very language of indivisibles." Although in the following years in the field of analysis of the infinitesimal, new ideas replaced the old on the indivisibles, the methods of Cavalieri and Torricelli exerted a profound influence, as Leibniz acknowledged in a letter to G. Manfredi: ". . . in the sublimest of geometry, the initiators and promotors who performed a yeoman's task in that field were Cavalieri and Torricelli; later, others progressed even further by availing themselves of the work of Cavalieri and Torricelli." Moreover, Newton, while assuming in his *Principia* a critical attitude in the matter of indivisibles, did nevertheless in his *Tractatus de quadratura curvarum,* use the term *fluens* to indicate a variable magnitude—a term previously used by Cavalieri in his *Exercitationes geometricae sex.*

In proposition I of Book I of the *Geometria,* we find in geometric form the theorem of mean value, also known as the Cavalieri theorem. The theorem is presented as the solution of the following problem: Given a plane curve, provided with a tangent at every point and passing through two points A and B, to find a straight line parallel to AB and tangent to the curve at some point on the curve between A and B. Analytically we have: If the real function $f(x)$ of the real variable x is continuous in the interval (a, b) and at every point within this interval it is differentiable, at least one point ζ exists such that $a < \zeta < b$, so that

$$\frac{f(b) - f(a)}{b - a} = f'(\zeta).$$

Logarithms were introduced into mathematics in the work of Napier in 1614. In Italy such valuable auxiliaries to numerical calculation were introduced by Cavalieri, together with noteworthy developments in trigonometry and applications to astronomy. In this connection we might mention *Directorium generale uranometricum* (1632), *Compendio delle regole dei triangoli* (1638), *Centuria di varii problemi* (1639), *Nuova pratica astrologica* (1639), and *Trigonometria plana, et sphaerica, linearis et logarithmica* (1643). The *Directorium*, the *Pratica*, and the *Trigonometria* contain, moreover, excellent logarithmic-trigonometric tables.

In the *Centuria*, Cavalieri dealt with such topics as the general definition of cylindrical and conical surfaces, formulas to determine the volume of a barrel and the capacity of a vault with pointed arches, and the means of obtaining from the logarithms of two numbers the logarithm of the sum or of the difference, a problem that was subsequently taken up by various mathematicians, Gauss among others. *Lo specchio ustorio* ("The Burning Glass") contains some interesting historical data on the origin of the theory of the conics among the Greeks; according to Cavalieri, the origins are to be found in the gnomonic requirements. In this work, we find a theory of conics with applications to optics and acoustics. Among the former, we note the idea of the reflecting telescope, of which—according to Piola and Favaro—Cavalieri was the first inventor, preceding Gregory and Newton; determination of the focal length of a lens of uneven sphericity; and explications of the burning glass of Archimedes. In the field of acoustics, Cavalieri attempted the archaeological reconstruction of the resonant vases mentioned by Vitruvius and used in theaters for amplifying sound.

In this work, various pointwise constructions of conics appear. More interesting still are the constructions given in the *Geometria* and in the *Exercitationes*, obtained by means of projective pencils which antedated the work of Steiner.

A delicate question relates to the astrological activities that Cavalieri engaged in by virtue of his office, but, as pointed out by D'Aviso, he was opposed to predictions based upon the position of the stars and states so at the end of his *Pratica astrologica*.

BIBLIOGRAPHY

I. ORIGINAL WORKS. Cavalieri's works include *Directorium generale uranometricum* (Bologna, 1632); *Geometria indivisibilibus continuorum nova quadam ratione promota* (Bologna, 1635; 2nd ed., 1653). Translated into Russian by S. J. Lure (Moscow-Leningrad, 1940). Translated into Italian, by Lucio Lombardo-Radice, as *Geometria degli indivisibili di Bonaventura Cavalieri*, with introduction and notes (Turin, 1966). *Compendio delle regole dei triangoli con le loro dimostrationi* (Bologna, 1638); *Centuria di varii problemi* (Bologna, 1639); *Nuova pratica astrologica* (Bologna, 1639); *Tavola prima logaritmica. Tavola seconda logaritmica. Annotationi nell'opera, e correttioni de gli errori più notabili* (Bologna, n. d.); *Appendice della nuova pratica astrologica* (Bologna, 1640); *Trigonometria plana, et sphaerica, linearis et logarithmica* (Bologna, 1643); *Trattato della ruota planetaria perpetua* (Bologna, 1646); *Exercitationes geometricae sex* (Bologna, 1647).

II. SECONDARY LITERATURE. See U. D'Aviso, "Vita del P. Buonaventura [sic] Cavalieri," in *Trattato della Sfera* (Rome 1682); G. Piola, *Elogio di Bonaventura Cavalieri* (Milan, 1844); A. Favaro, *Bonaventura Cavalieri nello studio di Bologna* (Bologna, 1885); E. Bortolotti, "I progressi del metodo infinitesimale nell'opera geometrica di Torricelli," in *Periodico di matematiche*, 4th ser., **8** (1928), 19-59; "La Scoperta e le successive generalizzazioni di un teorema fondamentale di calcolo integrale," in *Archivio di Storia della scienza* (1924), pp. 205-227; F. Conforto, "L'opera scientifica di Bonaventura Cavalieri e di Evangelista Torricelli," in *Atti del Convegno di Pisa* (23-27 Sept. 1948), pp. 35-56; A. Masotti, "Commemorazione di Bonaventura Cavalieri," in *Rendiconti dell'Istituto Lombardo di scienze e lettere, parte generale e atti ufficiali*, **81** (1948), 43-86; G. Castelnuovo, *Le origini del calcolo infinitesimale nell'era moderna* (Milan, 1962), pp. 43-53; G. Cellini, "Gli indivisibili nel pensiero matematico e filosofico di Bonaventura Cavalieri," in *Periodico di matematiche*, 4th ser., **44** (1966), 1-21; "Le dimostrazioni di Cavalieri del suo principio," *ibid.*, pp. 85-105.

ETTORE CARRUCCIO

CAYLEY, ARTHUR (*b.* Richmond, Surrey, England, 16 August 1821; *d.* Cambridge, England, 26 January 1895)

Cayley was the second son of Henry Cayley, a merchant living in St. Petersburg, and Maria Antonia Doughty. He was born during a short visit by his parents to England, and most of his first eight years were spent in Russia. From a small private school in London he moved, at fourteen, to King's College School there. At seventeen he entered Trinity College, Cambridge, as a pensioner, becoming a scholar in 1840. In 1842 Cayley graduated as senior wrangler and took the first Smith's prize. In October 1842 he was elected a fellow of his college at the earliest age of any man of that century. He was tutor there for three years, spending most of his time in research. Rather than wait for his fellowship to expire (1852) unless he entered holy orders or took a vacant teaching post, he entered the law, studying at Lincoln's Inn. He was called to the bar in 1849.

During the fourteen years Cayley was at the bar he wrote something approaching 300 mathematical papers, incorporating some of his best and most original work. It was during this period that he first met the mathematician J. J. Sylvester, who from 1846 read for the bar and, like Cayley, divided his time between law and mathematics. In 1852 Sylvester said of Cayley that he "habitually discourses pearls and rubies," and after 1851 each often expressed gratitude to the other in print for a point made in conversation. That the two men profited greatly by their acquaintance is only too obvious when one considers the algebraic theory of invariants, of which they may not unreasonably be considered joint founders. They drifted apart professionally when Cayley left London to take up the Sadlerian professorship but drew together again when, in 1881–1882, Cayley accepted Sylvester's invitation to lecture at Johns Hopkins University.

In 1863 Cayley was elected to the new Sadlerian chair of pure mathematics at Cambridge, which he held until his death. In September 1863 he married Susan Moline, of Greenwich; he was survived by his wife, son, and daughter. During his life he was given an unusually large number of academic honors, including the Royal Medal (1859) and the Copley Medal (1881) of the Royal Society. As professor at Cambridge his legal knowledge and administrative ability were in great demand in such matters as the drafting of college and university statutes.

For most of his life Cayley worked incessantly at mathematics, theoretical dynamics, and mathematical astronomy. He published only one full-length book, *Treatise on Elliptic Functions* (1876); but his output of papers and memoirs was prodigious, numbering nearly a thousand, the bulk of them since republished in thirteen large quarto volumes. His work was greatly appreciated from the time of its publication, and he did not have to wait for mathematical fame. Hermite compared him with Cauchy because of his immense capacity for work and the clarity and elegance of his analysis. Bertrand, Darboux, and Glaisher all compared him with Euler for his range, his analytical power, and the great extent of his writings.

Cayley was the sort of courteous and unassuming person about whom few personal anecdotes are told; but he was not so narrow in outlook as his prolific mathematical output might suggest. He was a good linguist; was very widely read in the more romantic literature of his century; traveled extensively, especially on walking tours; mountaineered; painted in watercolors throughout his life; and took a great interest in architecture and architectural drawing.

Characteristically, as explained in the bibliography of his writings, Cayley frequently gave abundant assistance to other authors (F. Galton, C. Taylor, R. G. Tait, G. Salmon, and others), even writing whole chapters for them—always without ostentation. Salmon, who corresponded with him for many years, gave *Esse quam videri* as Cayley's motto. Although Cayley disagreed strongly with Tait over quaternions (see below), their relations were always amicable; and the sixth chapter of the third edition of Tait's *Quaternions* was contributed by Cayley, much of it coming verbatim from letters to Tait. Cayley was above all a pure mathematician, taking little if any inspiration from the physical sciences when at his most original. "Whose soul too large for vulgar space, in *n* dimensions flourished," wrote Clerk Maxwell of Cayley. So far as can be seen, this was a more astute characterization than that of Tait, by whom Cayley was seen in a more pragmatic light, "forging the weapons for future generations of physicists." However true Tait's remark, it was not an indication of Cayley's attitude toward his own work.

A photograph of Cayley is prefixed to the eleventh volume of the *Collected Papers*. A portrait by Lowes Dickenson (1874, Volume VI) and a bust by Henry Wiles (1888) are in the possession of Trinity College, Cambridge. A pencil sketch by Lowes Dickenson (1893) is to be found in Volume VII.

Cayley's mathematical style was terse and even severe, in contrast with that of most of his contemporaries. He was rarely obscure, and yet in the absence of peripheral explanation it is often impossible to deduce his original path of discovery. His habit was to write out his findings and publish without delay and consequently without the advantage of second thoughts or minor revision. There were very few occasions on which he had cause to regret his haste. (References below to the *Collected Mathematical Papers*, abbreviated *C.M.P.*, contain the volume number, followed by the number of the paper, the year of original publication, and the page numbers of the reprint.)

Cayley is remembered above all else for his contributions to invariant theory. Following Meyer (1890–1891), the theory may be taken to begin with a paper by Boole, published in 1841, hints of the central idea being found earlier in Lagrange's investigation of binary quadratic forms (1773) and Gauss's similar considerations of binary and ternary forms (1801). Lagrange and Gauss were aware of special cases in which a linear homogeneous transformation turned a (homogeneous) quadratic into a second quadratic whose discriminant is equal to that of the original quadratic multiplied by a factor which was a function only of the coefficients of the transformation. Cauchy, Jacobi, and Eisenstein all have a claim to be mentioned in a general history of the concept of invariance, but in none of their writings is the idea explicit. Boole, on the other hand, found that the property of invariance belonged to all discriminants, and he also provided rules for finding functions of "covariants" of both the coefficients and the variables with the property of invariance under linear transformation.

In 1843 Cayley was moved by Boole's paper to calculate the invariants of *n*th-order forms. Later he published a revised version of two papers he had written. The first, with the title "On the Theory of Linear Transformations" (*C.M.P.,* I, no. 13 [1845], 80–94), dealt only with invariants; the second, "On Linear Transformations" (*C.M.P.,* I, no. 14 [1846], 95–112), introduced the idea of covariance. In this second paper Cayley set out "to find all the derivatives of any number of functions, which have the property of preserving their form unaltered after any linear transformations of the variables." He added that by "derivative" he meant a function "deduced in any manner whatever from the given functions." He also attempted to discover the relations between independent invariants—or "hyperdeterminants," as he called them at first, looking upon algebraic invariance as a generalized form of the multiplication of determinants. When writing the notes to his *Collected Papers,* he remarked that what he had done in this paper was to be distinguished from Gordan's "Ueberschiebung," or derivational theory. Cayley may be regarded as the first mathematician to have stated the problem of algebraic invariance in general terms.

Cayley's work soon drew the attention of many mathematicians, particularly Boole, Salmon, and Sylvester in England and Aronhold, Clebsch, and, later, Gordan in Germany. (Jordan and Hermite followed in France; and Brioschi in Italy was to carry the new ideas into the realm of differential invariants, in the study of which his compatriots later excelled.) Salmon's many excellent textbooks (in particular, see his *Modern Higher Algebra,* 1859, dedicated to Cayley and Sylvester), which were translated into several languages, diffused Cayley's results, to which Cayley himself constantly added. Sylvester was, among other things, largely responsible for the theory's luxuriant vocabulary; and in due course Aronhold related the theory to Hesse's applications of determinants to analytical geometry. The vocabulary of the subject is today one of the greatest obstacles to a discussion of invariant theory, since following Gordan's theorem of 1868 and Hilbert's generalizations of it, the tendency has been away from developing techniques for generating and manipulating a multiplicity of special invariants, each with its own name. Notice, however, that Cayley's "quantic" is synonymous with the "form" of later algebraists. As a typical source of terminological confusion we may take the contravariant (or the curve represented by the contravariant equation), called by Cayley the "Pippian" and known elsewhere (following Cremona) as the "Cayleyan."

Beginning with an introductory memoir in 1854, Cayley composed a series of ten "Memoirs on Quantics," the last published in 1878, which for mathematicians at large constituted a brilliant and influential account of the theory as he and others were developing it. The results Cayley was obtaining impressed mathematicians by their unexpectedness and elegance. To take three simple examples, he found that every invariant vanishes, for a binary p-ic which has a linear factor raised to the rth power, if $2r > p$; that a binary p-ic has a single or no p-ic covariant of the second degree in the coefficients according as p is or is not a multiple of 4; and that all the invariants of a binary p-ic are functions of the discriminant and $p-3$ anharmonic ratios, each formed from three of the roots together with one of the remaining $p-3$ roots. A more renowned theorem concerned the number of linearly independent seminvariants (or invariants) of degree i and weight w of a binary p-ic. Cayley found an expression giving a number which he proved could not be less than that required; and for a long time he treated this as the required number although admitting his inability to prove as much. Sylvester eventually gave the required proof.

An irreducible invariant (covariant) is one that cannot be expressed rationally and integrally in terms of invariants (covariants and invariants) of degree lower in the coefficients than its own, all invariants belonging to the same quantic or quantics. At an early stage Cayley appreciated that there are many cases in which the number of irreducible invariants and covariants is limited. Thus in his "Second Memoir on Quantics" (*C.M.P.,* II, no. 141 [1856], 250–275) he determined the number (with their degrees) of "asyzygetic" invariants for binary forms of orders 2 to 6, and he gave similar results for asyzygetic systems of irreducible covariants. Cayley made the mistake, however, of thinking that with invariants of forms of order higher than 4, the fundamental system is infinite. The error (which arose from his wrongly taking certain syzygies to be independent, thus increasing the number of invariants and covariants allowed for) stood for thirteen years, until Gordan (*Crelle's Journal,* **69** [1869], 323–354) proved that the complete system for a binary quantic of any order has a finite number of members. Hilbert, in 1888 and later, simplified and greatly generalized Gordan's findings.

Perhaps the best known of Cayley's "Memoirs on Quantics" was the sixth (*C.M.P.*, II, no. 158 [1859], 561–592; see also the note on 604–606, where he compares his work with that of Klein, which followed), in which Cayley gave a new meaning to the metrical properties of figures. Hitherto, affine and projective geometry had been regarded as special cases of metric geometry. Cayley showed how it was possible to interpret all as special cases of projective geometry. We recall some of the more important results of earlier geometrical studies. Poncelet (*ca.* 1822) had evolved the idea of the absolute involution determined by the orthogonal lines of a pencil on the line at infinity and having the "circular points" (so called because they are common to all circles in the plane) as double points. Beginning with the idea that perpendicularity could be expressed in terms of the formation of a harmonic range with the circular points, Laguerre (*ca.* 1853) showed that the numerical value of the angle of two lines of the Euclidean plane expressed in radian measure is $1/2i$ times the natural logarithm of the cross ratio which they form with the lines of their pencil through the circular points. Cayley now found that if P and Q are two points, and A and B are two further points in which the line PQ cuts a conic, then (if A and B are a real point pair; otherwise, where they are conjugate imaginaries we multiply by i) their separation could be expressed as a rather involved arc cosine function involving the coordinates, which space does not permit to be detailed here (see *C.M.P.*, II, no. 158 [1859], 589). A clear idea of the importance of his paper is obtained if we consider Klein's substitution of a logarithmic function for the arc cosine (which Cayley later admitted to be preferable), in which case

$$2c \log\left(\frac{AP \cdot BQ}{AQ \cdot BP}\right),$$

where c is a constant for all lines, may be taken as the generalized distance (which we may here call $\delta[P,Q]$) between P and Q, in the sense that the following fundamental requirements are met by the function: $\delta(P,Q) = 0$ if and only if P and Q are identical; $\delta(P,Q) = \delta(Q,P)$; $\delta(P,Q) + \delta(Q,R) \geq \delta(P,R)$, the equality holding when P, Q, and R are collinear. Cayley referred to the arbitrarily assumed conic as the "Absolute."

In his definition of distance Cayley has frequently been accused of circularity (recently, for example, by Max Jammer, in *Concepts of Space* [Cambridge, Mass., 1954], p. 156). Cayley anticipated such criticism, however, explaining in his note to the *Collected Papers* that he looked upon the coordinates of points as quantities defining only the ordering of points, without regard to distance. (This note shows that Klein drew his attention to Staudt's work in the same vein, of which he was ignorant when writing the sixth memoir.) Thus if x_a and x_b are coordinates belonging respectively to the points A and B, the corresponding coordinate of P may be written $\lambda_1 x_a + \lambda_2 x_b$, and similarly for the remaining points and coordinates. The function $\delta(P,Q)$ then reduces to one in which no trace of the ordinary (Euclidean) metric distance remains.

The full significance of Cayley's ideas was not appreciated until 1871, when Klein (*Mathematische Annalen*, **4** [1871], 573–625) showed how it was possible to identify Cayley's generalized theory of metrical geometry with the non-Euclidean geometries of Lobachevski, Bolyai, and Riemann. When Cayley's Absolute is real, his distance function is that of the "hyperbolic" geometry; when imaginary, the formulas reduce to those of Riemann's "elliptic" geometry. (The designations "hyperbolic" and "elliptic" are Klein's.) A degenerate conic gives rise to the familiar Euclidean geometry. Whereas during the first half of the century geometry had seemed to be becoming increasingly fragmented, Cayley and Klein, through the medium of these ideas, apparently succeeded for a time in providing geometers with a unified view of their subject. Thus, although the so-called Cayley-Klein metric is now seldom taught, to their contemporaries it was of great importance.

Cayley is responsible for another branch of algebra over and above invariant theory, the algebra of matrices. The use of determinants in the theory of equations had by his time become a part of established practice, although the familiar square notation was Cayley's (*C.M.P.*, I, no. 1 [1841], 1–4) and although their use in geometry, such as was provided by Cayley from the first, was then uncommon. (They later suggested to him the analytical geometry of n dimensions.) Determinants suggested the matrix notation; and yet to those concerned with the history of the "theory of multiple quantity" this notational innovation, even with its derived rules, takes second place to the algebra of rotations and extensions in space (such as was initiated by Gauss, Hamilton, and Grassmann), for which determinant theory provided no more than a convenient language.

Cayley's originality consisted in his creation of a theory of matrices that did not require repeated reference to the equations from which their elements were taken. In his first systematic memoir on the subject (*C.M.P.*, II, no. 152 [1858], 475–496), he established the associative and distributive laws, the special conditions under which a commutative law holds, and the principles for forming general algebraic functions of matrices. He later derived many important theorems of matrix theory. Thus, for example, he derived many theorems of varying generality in the theory of those linear transformations that leave invariant a quadratic or bilinear form. Notice that since it may be proved that there are $n(n + 1)/2$ relations between them, Cayley expressed the n^2 coefficients of the *n*ary orthogonal transformation in terms of $n(n - 1)/2$ parameters. His formulas, however, do not include all orthogonal transformations except as limiting cases (see E. Pascal's *Die Determinanten* [1919], paras. 47 ff.).

The theory of matrices was developed in two quite different ways: the one of abstract algebraic structure, favored by Cayley and Sylvester; the other, in the geometrical tradition of Hamilton and Grassmann. Benjamin Peirce (whose study of linear associative algebras, published in 1881 but evolved by him much earlier, was a strong influence on Cayley) and Cayley himself were notable for their ability to produce original work in both traditions. (It is on the strength of his work on linear associative algebras that Peirce is often regarded as cofounder of the theory of matrices.) In his many informal comments on the relation between matrices and quaternions (see, for example, his long report to the British Association, reprinted in *C.M.P.*, IV, no. 298 [1862], 513–593; and excerpts from his controversial correspondence with his friend P. G. Tait, printed in C. G. Knott's *Life and Scientific Work of P. G. Tait* [Cambridge, 1911], pp. 149–166) Cayley showed a clearer grasp of their respective merits than most of his contemporaries, but like most of them he found it necessary to favor one side rather than the other (coordinates rather than quaternions in his case) in a heated controversy in which practical expediency was the only generally accepted criterion. He had no significant part in the controversy between Tait and J. W. Gibbs, author of the much simpler vector analysis. In passing, we notice Cayley's statement of the origins of his matrices (Knott, *op. cit.*, p. 164, written 1894): "I certainly did not get the notion of a matrix in any way through quaternions: it was either directly from that of a determinant; or as a convenient mode of expression of the equations [of linear transformation]. . . ."

That Cayley found geometrical analogy of great assistance in his algebraic and analytical work—and conversely—is evident throughout his writings; and this, together with his studied avoidance of the highly physical interpretation of geometry more typical of his day, resulted in his developing the idea of a geometry of *n* dimensions. It is not difficult to find instances of the suggested addition of a fourth dimension to the usual trio of spatial dimensions in the work of earlier writers—Lagrange, d'Alembert, and Moebius are perhaps best known. (But only Moebius made his fourth dimension spatial, as opposed to temporal.) Grassmann's theory of extended magnitude, as explained in *Ausdehnungslehre* (1844), may be interpreted in terms of *n*-dimensional geometry; and yet by 1843 Cayley had considered the properties of determinants formed around coordinates in *n*-space. His "Chapter in the Analytical Geometry of (*n*) Dimensions" (*C.M.P.*, I, no. 11 [1843], 55–62) might have been considered at the time to have a misleading title, for it contained little that would then have been construed as geometry. It concerns the nonzero solutions of homogeneous linear equations in any number of variables.

By 1846 Cayley had made use of four dimensions in the enunciation of specifically synthetic geometrical theorems, suggesting methods later developed by Veronese (*C.M.P.*, I, no. 50 [1846], 317–328). Long afterward Cayley laid down in general terms, without symbolism, the elements of the subject of "hyperspace" (*cf.* his use of the terms "hyperelliptic theta functions," "hyperdeterminant," and so on) in his "Memoir on Abstract Geometry" (*C.M.P.*, VI, no. 413 [1870], 456–469), showing that he was conscious of the metaphysical issues raised by his ideas in the minds of his followers but that as a mathematician he was no more their slave then than when remarking in his paper of 1846 (published in French): "We may in effect argue as follows, *without having recourse to any metaphysical idea as to the possibility of space of four dimensions* (all this may be translated into purely analytic language). . . ."

As an example of Cayley's hypergeometry, we might take the result that a point of $(m - n)$-space given by a set of linear equations is conjugate, with respect to a hyperquadric, to every point whose coordinates satisfy the equations formed by equating to zero a certain simple set of determinants (involving the partial differential coefficients of the hyperquadric function). Cayley and Sylvester subsequently developed these ideas.

In 1860 Cayley devised the system of six homogeneous coordinates of a line, now usually known as Plücker's line coordinates. Plücker, who published his ideas in 1865 (*Philosophical Transactions of the Royal Society*, **155** [1865], 725–791), was working quite independently of Cayley (*C.M.P.*, IV, no. 284 [1860], 446–455, and no. 294 [1862], 490–494), who neglected to elaborate upon his own work. Influenced not by Cayley but by Plücker, Klein (Plücker's assistant at the time of the latter's death in 1868) exploited the subject most fully.

Cayley wrote copiously on analytical geometry, touching on almost every topic then under discussion. Although, as explained elsewhere, he never wrote a textbook on the subject, substantial parts of Salmon's *Higher Plane Curves* are due to him; and without his work many texts of the period, such as those by Clebsch and Frost, would have been considerably reduced in size. One of Cayley's earliest papers contains evidence of his great talent for the analytical geometry of curves and surfaces, in the form of what was often known as Cayley's intersection theorem (*C.M.P.*, I, no. 5 [1843], 25–27). There Cayley gave an almost complete proof (to be supplemented by Bacharach, in *Mathematische Annalen,* **26** [1886], 275–299) that when a plane curve of degree r is drawn through the mn points common to two curves of degrees m and n (both less than r), these do not count for mn conditions in the determination of the curve but for mn reduced by

$$(m + n - r - 1)\,(m + n - r - 2).$$

(The Cayley-Bacharach theorem was subsequently generalized by Noether. See Severi and Löffler, *Vorlesungen über algebraische Geometrie,* ch. 5.) He found a number of important theorems "on the higher singularities of a plane curve" (the title of an influential memoir; *C.M.P.*, V, no. 374 [1866], 520–528), in which they were analyzed in terms of simple singularities (node, cusp, double tangent, inflectional tangent); yet the methods used here did not find permanent favor with mathematicians. A chapter of geometry which he closed, rather than opened, concerns the two classifications of cubic curves: that due to Newton, Stirling, and Cramer and that due to Plücker. Cayley systematically showed the relations between the two schemes (*C.M.P.*, V, no. 350 [1866], 354–400).

It is possible only to hint at that set of interrelated theorems in algebraic geometry which Cayley did so much to clarify, including those on the twenty-eight bitangents of a nonsingular quartic plane curve and the theorem (first announced in 1849) on the twenty-seven lines that lie on a cubic surface in three dimensions (*C.M.P.,* I, no. 76 [1849], 445–456). (Strictly speaking, Cayley established the existence of the lines and Salmon, in a correspondence prior to the paper, established their number. See the last page of the memoir and G. Salmon, *The Geometry of Three Dimensions,* 2nd ed. [Dublin, 1865], p. 422.) Although no longer in vogue this branch of geometry, in association with Galois theory, invariant algebra, group theory, and hyperelliptic functions, reached a degree of intrinsic difficulty and beauty rarely equaled in the history of mathematics. The Cayley-Salmon theorem is reminiscent of Pascal's mystic hexagram, and indeed Cremona subsequently found a relation between the two (see B. Segre, *The Nonsingular Cubic Surface* [Oxford, 1942] for a survey of the whole subject). Cayley's twenty-seven lines were the basis of Schläfli's division of cubic surfaces into species; and in his lengthy "Memoir on Cubic Surfaces" Cayley discussed the complete classification with masterly clarity, adding further investigations of his own (*C.M.P.*, VI, no. 412 [1869], 359–455).

As might have been expected from his contributions to the theory of invariants, Cayley made an important contribution to the theory of rational transformation and general rational correspondence. The fundamental theorem of the theory of correspondence is difficult to assign to a particular author, for it was used in special cases by several writers; but Chasles (*Comptes rendus,* **58** [1864], 175) presented the theorem that a rational correspondence $F(x,y) = 0$ of degree m in x and n in y (x and y being, if necessary, parameters of the coordinates of two points) between spaces or loci in spaces gives in the general case $m + n$ correspondences. (For a history of the subject see C. Segre, "Intorno alla storia del principio di corrispondenza," in *Bibliotheca mathematica,* 2nd ser., **6** [1892], 33–47; Brill and Noether, "Bericht über die Entwicklung der Theorie der algebraischen Funktionen in älterer und neuerer Zeit," in *Jahresbericht der Deutschen Mathematiker-Vereinigung,* **3** [1894], secs. 6, 10.) Soon after this, Cayley generalized Chasles's theorem to curves of any genus (*C.M.P.*, V, no. 377 [1866], 542–545), but his proof was not rigorous and was subsequently amended by A. Brill. The Chasles-Cayley-Brill theorem states that an (m,n) correspondence on a curve of genus p will have $m + n + 2p\gamma$ coincidences, where γ is known as the "value of the correspondence." (The points corresponding to a point P, together with P taken γ times, is to be a group of a so-called linear point system.)

Cayley's many additions to the subject of rational correspondences have for the most part passed into anonymity, although the name "Cayley-Plücker equations" is a reminder to geometers of how early appreciated were the connections between the order, the rank, the number of chords through an arbitrary point, the number of points in a plane through which two tangents pass, and the number of cusps of a curve in space and corresponding quantities (class, rank, and so on) of its osculating developable. These equations are all due to Cayley but were deduced from Plücker's equations connecting the ordinary singularities of plane curves.

Cayley devoted a great deal of his time to the projective characteristics of curves and surfaces. Apart from his intricate treatment of the theory of scrolls (where many of his methods and his vocabulary still survive), the Cayley-Zeuthen equations are still a conspicuous reminder of the permanent value of his work. Given an irreducible surface in three-dimensional space, with normal singularities and known elementary projective characters, many other important characteristics may be deduced from these equations, which were first found empirically by Salmon and later proved by Cayley and Zeuthen. For further details of Cayley's very extensive work in algebraic geometry, an ordered if unintentional history of his thought is to be found almost as a supporting framework for Salmon's *Treatise on the Analytic Geometry of Three Dimensions* (of the several editions the third, of 1882, with its preface, is historically the most illuminating). (For a more general history of algebraic geometry see "Selected Topics in Algebraic Geometry," which constitutes *Bulletin of the National Research Council* [Washington, D.C.], **63** [1929] and supp. **96** (1934), written by committees of six and three, respectively.)

Cayley's wide mathematical range made it almost inevitable that he should write on the theory of groups. Galois's use of substitution groups to decide the algebraic solvability of equations, and the continuation of his work by Abel and Cauchy, had provided a strong incentive to many other mathematicians to develop group theory further. (Thus Cayley wrote "Note on the Theory of Permutations," *C.M.P.*, I, no. 72 [1849], 423–424.) Cayley's second paper on the theory (1854), in which he applied it to quaternions, contained a number of invaluable insights and provided mathematicians with what is now the accepted procedure for defining a group. In the abstract theory of groups, where nothing is said of the nature of the elements, the group is completely specified if all possible products are known or determinable. In Cayley's words: "A set of symbols, 1, α, β, . . . all of them different, and such that the product of any two of them (no matter in what order), or the product of any one of them into itself, belongs to the set, is said to be a *group.*" From the first Cayley suggested listing the elements in the form of a multiplication table ("On the Theory of Groups, as Depending on the Symbolic Equation $\theta^n = 1$," *C.M.P.*, II, no. 125 [1854], 123–130; second and third parts followed, for which see *C.M.P.*, II, no. 126 [1854], 131–132, and IV, no. 243 [1859], 88–91). This formulation differed from those of earlier writers to the extent that he spoke only of symbols and multiplication without further defining either. He is sometimes said to have failed to appreciate the step he had taken, but this seems unlikely when we consider his footnote to the effect that "The idea of a group *as applied to* permutations or substitutions is due to Galois . . ." (italics added). He went on to give what has since been taken as the first set of axioms for a group, somewhat tacitly postulating associativity, a unit element, and closure with respect to multiplication. The axioms are sufficient for finite, but not infinite, groups.

There is some doubt as to whether Cayley ever intended his statements in the 1854 paper to constitute a definition, for he not only failed to use them subsequently as axioms but later used a different and unsatisfactory definition. (See, for instance, an article for the *English Cyclopaedia,* in *C.M.P.*, IV, no. 299 [1860], 594–608; *cf.* the first two of a series of four papers in *C.M.P.*, X, no. 694 [1878], 401–403.) In a number of historical articles G. A. Miller (see volume I of his *Collected Works* [Urbana, Ill., 1935]) has drawn attention to the unsatisfactory form of a later definition and indeed has criticized other mathematicians for accepting it; but there are few signs that mathematicians were prepared for the postulational definition until well into the present century. In 1870 Kronecker explicitly gave sets of postulates applied to an abstract finite Abelian group; but even Lie and Klein did most of their work oblivious to the desirability of such sets of axioms, as a result occasionally using the term "group" in what would now be reckoned inadmissible cases.

In addition to his part in founding the theory of abstract groups, Cayley has a number of important theorems to his credit: perhaps the best known is that every finite group whatsoever is isomorphic with a suitable group of permutations (see the first paper of 1854). This is often reckoned to be one of the three most important theorems of the subject, the others being the theorems of Lagrange and Sylow. But perhaps still more significant was his early appreciation of the way in which the theory of groups was capable of drawing together many different domains of mathematics: his own illustrations, for instance, were drawn from the theories of elliptic functions, matrices, quantics, quaternions, homographic transformations, and the theory of equations. If Cayley failed to pursue his abstract approach, this fact is perhaps best explained in terms of the enormous progress he was making in these subjects taken individually.

In 1845 Cayley published his "Mémoire sur les fonctions doublement périodiques," treating Abel's doubly infinite products (*C.M.P.*, I, no. 25 [1845], 156–182; see his note on p. 586 of the same volume). Weierstrass subsequently (1876, 1886) simplified the initial form and in doing so made much of Cayley's work unnecessary (see Cayley's later note, *loc. cit.*). His work on elliptic functions, pursued at length and recurred to at intervals throughout his life, nevertheless contains ample evidence of Cayley's ability to simplify the work of others, an early instance being his establishment of some results concerning theta functions obtained by Jacobi in his *Fundamenta nova theoriae functionum ellipticarum* of 1829 (*C.M.P.*, I, no. 45 [1847], 290–300). Cayley's only full-length book was on elliptic functions, and he made a notable application of the subject to geometry when he investigated analytically the property of two conics such that polygons may be inscribed by one and circumscribed about the other. The property was appreciated by Poncelet and was discussed analytically by Jacobi (using elliptic functions) when the conics were circles. Using his first paper of 1853 and gradually generalizing his own findings, by 1871 Cayley was discussing the problem of the number of polygons which are such that their vertices lie on a given curve or curves of any order and that their sides touch another given curve or curves of any class. That he was able to give a complete solution even where the polygons were only triangles is an indication of his great analytical skill.

Cayley wrote little on topology, although he wrote on the combinatorial aspect, renewed the discussion of the four-color-map problem, and corresponded with Tait on the topological problems associated with knots. He wrote briefly on a number of topics for which alone a lesser mathematician might have been remembered. He has to his credit an extremely useful system of coordinates in plane geometry which he labeled "circular coordinates" (*C.M.P.*, VI, no. 414 [1868], 498) and which later writers refer to as "minimal coordinates." There is also his generalization of Euler's theorem relating to the numbers of faces, vertices, and edges of the non-Platonic solids. He wrote to great effect on the theory of the numbers of partitions, originated by Euler. (His interest in this arose from his need to apply it to invariant theory and is first evident in his second memoir on quantics, *C.M.P.*, II, no. 141 [1856], 250–281.) His short paper "On the Theory of the Singular Solutions of Differential Equations of the First Order" (*C.M.P.*, VIII, no. 545 [1873], 529–534) advanced the subject considerably and was part of the foundation on which G. Chrystal's first satisfactory treatment of the p-discriminant was based (*Transactions of the Royal Society of Edinburgh*, **138** [1896], 803 ff.).

Cayley long exploited the theory of linear differential operators (previously used by Boole to generate invariants and covariants), as when he factored the differential equation $(D^2 + pD + q)y = 0$ as $(D + \alpha[x])(D + \beta[x])y' = 0$, with $\alpha + \beta = p$ and $\alpha\beta + \beta' = q$ both being theoretically soluble (*C.M.P.*, XII, no. 851 [1886], 403). This technique is linked to that of characterizing invariants and covariants of binary quantics as the polynomial solutions of linear partial differential equations. (The differential operators were in this context known as annihilators, following Sylvester.) He wrote occasionally on dynamics, but his writings suggest that he looked upon it as a source of problems in pure mathematics rather than as a practical subject. Thus in five articles he considered that favorite problem of the time, the attraction of ellipsoids; and in a paper of 1875 he extended a certain problem in potential theory to hyperspace (*C.M.P.*, IX, no. 607 [1875], 318–423). That he kept himself informed of the work of others in dynamics is evident from two long reports on recent progress in the subject which he wrote for the British Association (*C.M.P.*, III, no. 195 [1857], 156–204; IV, no. 298 [1862], 513–593).

Cayley wrote extensively on physical astronomy, especially on the disturbing function in lunar and planetary theory; but the impact of what he wrote on the subject was not great, and Simon Newcomb, who spoke of Cayley's mathematical talents with extraordinary deference, did not allude to them in his *Reminiscences of an Astronomer* (London–New York, 1903, p. 280). (It is interesting to note that when he met Cayley at an Astronomical Society Club dinner, Newcomb mistook Cayley's garb for that of an attendant.) Cayley nevertheless performed a great service to his countryman John Couch Adams, who in 1853, taking into account the varying eccentricity of the earth's orbit, had obtained a new value for the secular acceleration of the moon's mean motion. Adams' figure, differing from Laplace's, was contested by several French astronomers, including Pontécoulant. Cayley looked into the matter independently, found a new and simpler method for introducing the variation of the eccentricity, and confirmed the value Adams had previously found (*C.M.P.*, III, no. 221 [1862], 522–561). Here was yet another instance of the truth of the remark made about Cayley by Sylvester: ". . . whether the matter he takes in hand be great or small, 'nihil tetigit quod non ornavit'" (*Philosophical Transactions*, **17** [1864], 605). And yet Cayley deserves to be remembered above all not for those parts of mathematics which he embellished, but for those which he created.

BIBLIOGRAPHY

I. ORIGINAL WORKS. The great majority of Cayley's mathematical writings (966 papers in all, with some short notes subsequently written about them) are in *The Collected Mathematical Papers of Arthur Cayley,* 13 vols. indexed in a 14th (Cambridge, 1889–1898). The printing of the first seven vols. and part of the eighth was supervised by Cayley himself. The editorial task was assumed by A. R. Forsyth when Cayley died. His excellent biography of Cayley is in vol. VIII, which also contains a complete list of the lectures Cayley gave in Cambridge as Sadlerian professor. The list of writings in vol. XIV includes the titles of several articles which Cayley contributed to the *Encyclopaedia Britannica.* See, e.g., in the 11th ed., "Curve" (in part), "Determinant," "Equation," "Gauss," "Monge," "Numbers, Partition of," and "Surface" (in part). A work in which Cayley's part was not negligible is G. Salmon, *A Treatise on the Higher Plane Curves,* 2nd and 3rd (1879) eds. Upward of twenty sections and the whole of ch. 1 were written by Cayley for the 2nd ed., and further additions were made in the 3rd ed. See Salmon's prefaces for further details. Cayley frequently gave advice and assistance to other authors. Thus he contributed ch. 6 of P. G. Tait's *An Elementary Treatise on Quaternions* (Cambridge, 1890), as well as making improvements. There is no systematic record as such of Cayley's less conspicuous work. He composed a six-penny booklet, *The Principles of Book-Keeping by Double Entry* (Cambridge, 1894). His *An Elementary Treatise on Elliptic Functions* (London, 1876) was issued in a 2nd ed. which, owing to his death, was only partly revised.

II. SECONDARY LITERATURE. There are few works dealing historically with Cayley's mathematics alone. General histories of mathematics are not listed here, nor are mathematical works in which historical asides are made. The best biographical notice is by A. R. Forsyth, reprinted with minor alterations in *The Collected Mathematical Papers of Arthur Cayley,* VIII (1895), ix–xliv, from the "Obituary Notices" in *Proceedings of the Royal Society,* **58** (1895), 1–43. Forsyth also wrote the article in the *Dictionary of National Biography,* XXII (supp.), 401–402. Another admirable and long obituary notice is by M. Noether, in *Mathematische Annalen,* **46** (1895), 462–480. Written during Cayley's lifetime was G. Salmon's "Science Worthies no. xxii.—Arthur Cayley," in *Nature,* **28** (1883), 481–485. Of general value are Franz Meyer, "Bericht über den gegenwärtigen Stand der Invariantentheorie," in *Jahresbericht der Deutschen Mathematiker-Vereinigung,* **1** (1890–1891), 79–288; and A. Brill and M. Noether, "Bericht über die Entwicklung der Theorie der algebraischen Functionen in älterer and neuerer Zeit," *ibid.,* **3** (1894), 107–566. The best specifically historical studies of aspects of Cayley's mathematics are Luboš Nový, "Arthur Cayley et sa définition des groupes abstraits-finis," in *Acta historiae rerum naturalium necnon technicarum* (Czechoslovak Studies in the History of Science, Prague), spec. issue no. 2 (1966), 105–151; and "Anglická algebraická školá," in *Dějiny věd a techniky,* **1,** no. 2 (1968), 88–105.

J. D. NORTH

ČECH, EDUARD (*b.* Stračov, Bohemia, 29 June 1893; *d.* Prague, Czechoslovakia, 15 March 1960)

Eduard Čech was the fourth child of Čeněk Čech, a policeman, and Anna Kleplová. After studying at the Gymnasium in Hradec Kralove, he attended lectures on mathematics at the Charles University of Prague from 1912 to 1914. In 1920 Čech took his degree in mathematics at the University of Prague. Even his first works showed his mathematical talent. He began to study differential projective properties of geometrical figures and became interested in the work of Guido Fubini. He obtained a scholarship for the school year 1921–1922 that enabled him to study with Fubini in Turin. Later they wrote *Geometria proiettiva differenziale* (1926–1927) and *Introduction à la géométrie projective différentielle des surfaces* (1931). In 1922 Čech was appointed associate professor of mathematics at the University of Prague; on this occasion he presented a study on differential geometry. From 1923 he was professor of mathematics at the Faculty of Natural Sciences of the University of Brno, lecturing on mathematical analysis and algebra.

From 1928 on, Čech was interested in topology, inspired by the works of mathematicians who contributed to the Polish journal *Fundamenta mathematicae.* His work from 1932 on, devoted to the general theory of homology in arbitrary spaces, the general theory of varieties, and theorems of duality, showed him to be one of the foremost experts in combinatorial topology. In September 1935 he was invited to lecture at the Institute for Advanced Study at Princeton. Čech returned to Brno in 1936 and founded a topology seminar among the young mathematicians there. During the three years the seminar was in existence, the works of P. S. Alexandrov and Pavel Uryson were studied and twenty-six papers were written. The group disbanded at the closing of Czech universities following the German occupation in 1939.

In his paper "On Bicompact Spaces" Čech stated precisely the possibilities of utilizing a new type of topological space (defined by Tichonow in 1930), which later came to be known as Čech's bicompact envelope (βS of a completely regular space S) or as Stone and Čech's compact envelope. Čech's interpretation became a very important tool of general topology and also of some branches of functional analysis.

Čech was also concerned with the improvement of the teaching of mathematics in secondary schools. He organized courses for secondary school teachers in Brno in 1938–1939; the results are shown in a series of mathematics textbooks for secondary schools that were written under his guidance after World War II.

In 1945 Čech went to the faculty of Natural Sciences of Charles University in Prague. There he was instrumental in founding two research centers: the Mathematical Institute of the Czechoslovak Academy of Science (1952) and the Mathematical Institute of Charles University.

In topology, in addition to the theory of topological spaces, Čech worked on the theories of dimension and continuous spaces. In combinatory topology he was concerned primarily with the theory of homology and general varieties. He was most active in differential geometry from 1921 to 1930, when he became one of the founders of systematic projective differential geometry; he dedicated himself chiefly to problems of the connection of varieties, to the study of correspondences, and to systematic utilization of duality in projective spaces. After 1945 he returned to problems of differential geometry and developed a systematic theory of correspondences between projective spaces. His attention was then drawn to the problems of congruences of straight lines that play a significant role in the theory of correspondences. Somewhat different is his work on the relations between the differential classes of points of a curve and the object attached to it. A number of his ideas were elaborated in the works of his students. They can also be found in some of his manuscripts that have been preserved, published in part in 1968.

BIBLIOGRAPHY

I. Original Works. The bibliography of Čech's scientific works compiled by Katětov, Novák, and Švec lacks only the rev. and enl. ed. of *Topological Spaces* and a number of articles on education. His papers include "O křivkovém a plošném elementu třetího řádu" ("On the Curve and Surface Element of the Third Order"), his thesis at the University of Prague, in *Časopis pro pěstování matematiky a fysiky*, **50** (1921), 219-249, 305-306; and "On Bicompact Spaces," in *Annals of Mathematics*, **38** (1937), 823-844. With Guido Fubini he wrote *Geometria proiettiva differenziale*, 2 vols. (Bologna, 1926-1927); and *Introduction à la géométrie projective différentielle des surfaces* (Paris, 1931). His *Topological Spaces* (Prague, 1959) was revised by Zdeněk Frolík and Miroslav Katětov (Prague, 1966).

II. Secondary Literature. M. Katětov, J. Novák, and A. Švec, "Akademik Eduard Čech," in *Časopis pro pěstování matematiky*, **85** (1966), 477-491, includes an almost complete bibliography on 488-491; it also appears in Russian in *Chekhoslovatsky matematichesky zhurnal* ("Czechoslovak Mathematical Journal"), **10** (1960), 614-630, with bibliography on 627-630. Two articles by K. Koutský discuss Čech's work: "Čechuv topologický seminář v Brně z let 1936-1939" ("Čech's Topological Seminar at Brno in 1936-1939"), in *Pokroky matematiky, fyziky a astronomie* (1964), 307-316; and "O Čechových snahách ve středoškolské matematice" ("Čech's Endeavors for the Reform of Secondary School Mathematics"), in *Sbornik pro dějiny přirodnich věd a techniky*, **11** (1967), 217-230. See also P. S. Aleksandrov, in *Uspekhi matematicheskikh nauk*, **15**, no. 2 (1960), 25-95; and J. Kelley, *General Topology* (New York-Toronto-London, 1955), p. 298.

LUBOŠ NOVÝ
JAROSLAV FOLTA

CESÀRO, ERNESTO (*b.* Naples, Italy, 12 March 1859; *d.* Torre Annunziata, Italy, 12 September 1906)

Cesàro was the son of Luigi Cesàro and Fortunata Nunziante, his second wife. The elder Cesàro owned a farm and shop in Torre Annunziata; he was one of the first farmers in Italy to introduce agricultural machinery, a supporter of Italian unification, and a backer of Garibaldi's revolution of 1860—all of which led him into financial difficulties.

Ernesto Cesàro completed the first class of the Gymnasium in Naples, studied in the seminary of Nola for two years, then returned to Naples to finish the fourth class of the Gymnasium in 1872. In 1873 his father sent him to Liège to join his older brother Giuseppe, who had gone there in 1867. Cesàro stayed for a year with his brother, who in the meantime had become lecturer in mineralogy and crystallography at the École des Mines, and then entered the École himself on a scholarship. He matriculated there, then applied unsuccessfully for admission to an Italian university, following which he was forced to enter the École des Mines of Liège. He studied mathematics with Eugène Catalan, who noticed Cesàro's talent and helped him publish his first mathematical paper in *Nouvelle correspondance de mathématiques*, of which Catalan was editor.

In 1879 Cesàro's father died, the family's financial troubles increased, and Cesàro was forced to return for some time to Torre Annunziata. Nevertheless, he finished the fourth form at Liège in 1881, and at the same time prepared his first major mathematical work, "Sur diverses questions d'arithmétique," which was published in 1883 in *Mémoires de l'Académie de Liège*. This paper brought Cesàro to the attention of the mathematical public.

In 1882 Cesàro returned once more to Belgium, having won another scholarship to continue his studies at Liège. Shortly thereafter he returned to Italy, where he married his stepbrother's daughter Angelina. At this period he also accompanied a friend, the son of the Prince de Soissons, to Paris, where he spent several months. He attended the lectures of Hermite,

Darboux, Serret, Briot, Bouquet, and Chasles at the Sorbonne; he attracted the attention of Hermite in particular. In 1883 the latter cited Cesàro's results. Darboux's lectures led Cesàro to formulate his "intrinsic geometry."

Cesàro did not finish his studies at Liège, perhaps because of a personal quarrel with a professor Deschamps. He returned to Torre Annunziata and once again sought to continue his work in Italy. His mathematical works and the recommendations of Cremona, Battaglini, and Dino secured him a scholarship to the University of Rome, which he entered in 1884 in the fourth form in pure mathematics. Here, in addition to attending a great many lectures, he wrote some eighty works—on infinite arithmetics, isobaric problems, holomorphic functions, theory of probability, and, particularly, intrinsic geometry—in the two years 1884–1886. Despite his intensive activity, he did not earn an advanced degree at this time. (The University of Rome gave him a doctorate, with honors, in February 1887.)

In 1886 Cesàro won a competition for the position of professor of mathematics at the Lycée Terenzio Mamiani in Rome; in similar competitions at the universities of Messina and Naples he placed first and second, respectively. On Cremona's advice, Cesàro left the Lycée Mamiani after a month to fill the vacant chair of higher algebra at the University of Palermo. He stayed at Palermo until 1891, when he accepted the chair of mathematical analysis at Naples. He held this chair until his death, never realizing his intention of going over to the chair of theoretical mechanics.

Cesàro's bibliography is extensive; indeed, the author of the most complete bibliography available, A. Perna, mentions 259 works and expresses doubt whether his list is complete. Cesàro's topics are varied. In 1878, when he was nineteen, he attempted to master certain topological problems in a non-traditional way in his *Forme poliedrichi regolari e semi-regolari in tutti gli spazii* (published in Lisbon in 1888). The most prominent of his early works, however, deal with the sums of divergent series, for Cesàro, Borel, Fejér, and Voronoj were together creating the techniques for the elaboration of such problems. One of Cesàro's first published works, *Sur diverses questions d'arithmétique* (Liège, 1882), and, more importantly, his series of nine articles published in *Annali di mathematica pura ed applicata* (**13** [1885], 235–351) are related to the theory of numbers. He was here concerned with such problems as the determination of the number of common divisors of two numerals, determination of the values of the sum totals of their squares, the probability of incommensurability of three arbitrary numbers, and so on; to these he attempted to apply obtained results in the theory of Fourier series. Later he occupied himself with prime numbers of a certain type and tried to make Chebyshev's formulas more precise ("Sulla distributione dei numeri primi," in *Rendiconti dell'Accademia delle scienze fisiche e matemetiche* (Naples), **2** [1896], 297–304).

Despite the generally sophisticated level of his mathematics, Cesàro reverted to such elementary problems as, for example, his work on constructions using limited geometrical means (1899) which repeats results already known. His textbooks, on the other hand, are rather exacting. They were successful and influential in their time; *Corso di analisi algebrica con introduzione al calculo infinitesimale* was published in Turin in 1894 and *Elementa di calcolo infinitesimale* appeared in Naples in 1899. Both texts were the outgrowth of Cesàro's lectures in Palermo and Naples and both were distinguished by the pertinent and novel exercises that they contained.

The two textbooks also reveal Cesàro's interest in the problems of mathematical physics. In addition, his textbook *Introduzione alla teoria matematica della elasticità* (Turin, 1894) had dealt with the theory of elasticity in an elementary way; there is no doubt that he planned to investigate mathematical physics in more detail, since he prepared two works on this subject, "Teoria matematica dels calore" and "Lezione sull'idrodinamica"; he died before he could publish these, however, and they remain unpublished to this day.

Cesàro's most important contribution remains his intrinsic geometry. It has been noted that he began to develop it while he was in Paris in 1883; it occupied him, with interruptions, from that time on. His earlier work on the subject is summed up in his monograph *Lezione di geometria intrinseca* (Naples, 1896), in which he proceeds from a utilization of Darboux's method of a mobile coordinate trihedral—formed by the tangent, the principal normal, and the binormal at a variable point of a curve—and used it to simplify the analytic expression and make it independent of extrinsic coordinate systems. By this means, Cesàro stressed the intrinsic qualities of the objects examined. This method proved fertile for him, and he systematically elaborated and propagated it, while at the same time pointing out further applications. The *Lezione* also describes the curves that bear Cesàro's name; Cesàro later expanded his method to the curves devised by H. von Koch, which are continuous but so constructed as to have no tangent at any point.

The last part of *Lezione* deals with the theory of surfaces and multidimensional spaces in general. Cesàro returned to this subject in the last years of his life and emphasized the independence of his geometry from the axiom of parallels. The special selection of the square of the linear element enabled him to extend the results to multidimensional spaces with constant curvature. He further established other bases on which to build non-Euclidean geometry, which he described in *Rendiconti della R. Accademia dei Lincei* ("Sui fondamenti della interseca non-euclidea," **13** [1904], 438–446) and more especially in "Fondamento intrinseco della pangeometria," in *Memorie della R. Accademia dei Lincei* (**5** [1904], 155–183).

Throughout his life, the variety of Cesàro's interests was always remarkable, ranging from elementary geometrical problems to the application of mathematical analysis; from the theory of numbers to symbolic algebra; from the theory of probability to differential geometry. Moreover, his admiration for Maxwell, whose faithful interpreter in theoretical physics he became, is worthy of note.

In recognition of his work he was named an honorary member of many learned and scientific societies.

Cesàro died of injuries sustained while coming to the aid of his seventeen-year-old son who was drowning in the rough sea near Torre Annunziata.

BIBLIOGRAPHY

I. ORIGINAL WORKS. In addition to the individual works cited in the text, extensive lists of Cesàro's writings may be found in A. Perna and P. del Pezzo, below, and in Poggendorff.

II. SECONDARY LITERATURE. Works on Cesàro include C. Alasia, "Ernesto Cesàro, 1859–1906," published simultaneously in French and Italian in *Rivista di fisica, matematica e scienze naturali,* **15** (1907), 23–46, and *Enseignement mathématique,* **9** (1907), 76–82; V. Cerruti, "Ernesto Cesàro, Commemorazione," in *Rendiconti della R. Accademia dei Lincei,* **16** (1907), 76–82; A. Perna, "Ernesto Cesàro," in *Giornale di matematiche di Battaglini,* **45** (1907), 299–319, which includes a bibliography of 259 items as well as a presentation of some of Cesàro's problems and a review of his solutions; and P. del Pezzo, "Ernesto Cesàro," in *Rendiconti dell'Accademia delle Scienze fisiche e matematiche,* 3rd ser., **12** (1906), 358–375, which includes a list of 254 of Cesàro's works.

LUBOŠ NOVÝ
JAROSLAV FOLTA

CEULEN, LUDOLPH VAN (*b.* Hildesheim, Germany, 28 January 1540; *d.* Leiden, Netherlands, 31 December 1610)

Van Ceulen's name may originally have been Ackerman, latinized as Colonus and gradually modified to Van Ceulen. He was the son of a merchant; and after traveling widely, he settled in Holland, first, perhaps, in Breda and Amsterdam. In 1580 he was in Delft, where he became a fencing master and mathematics instructor. During 1589 he spent some time in Arnhem, and in 1594 Van Ceulen received permission to open a fencing school in Leiden. In 1600 he was appointed teacher of arithmetic, surveying, and fortification at the engineering school founded in Leiden by Prince Maurice of Nassau. He held this position until his death. His second wife, Adriana Symons, whom he married in 1590, brought out Latin versions of two of his works posthumously, with the aid of Van Ceulen's pupil Willebrord Snell.

Van Ceulen was an indefatigable computer and concentrated on the computation of π, sometimes called Ludolph's number. This brought him into controversy with the master reckoner Simon Van der Eycke, who had published an incorrect quadrature of the circle (1584–1586). Then he became acquainted with Archimedes' *The Measurement of the Circle,* which his friend Jan Cornets de Groot, a mayor of Delft and father of Hugo Grotius, translated for him from the Greek. Now Van Ceulen began to work in the spirit of Archimedes, computing the sides of more regular polygons inscribed within and circumscribed about a circle than Archimedes had and inventing a special short division for such computation. In his principal work, *Van den Circkel* (1596), he published π to twenty decimal places by computing the sides of a regular polygon of 15×2^{31} sides. He continued to work on this subject; and in his *Arithmetische en geometrische fondamenten* (1615), published by his widow, he reached thirty-three decimal places, always enclosing π between an upper and a lower limit. Finally, Willebrord Snell, in his *Cyclometricus* (1621), published Van Ceulen's final triumph: π to thirty-five decimal places. This was inscribed on his tombstone in the Pieterskerk in Leiden.

The *Van den Circkel* consists of four sections. The first contains the computation of π. The second shows how to compute the sides of regular polygons of any number of sides, which in modern terms amounts to the expression of sin nA in terms of sin A (n is an integer). The third section contains tables of sines up to a radius of 10^7 (not an original achievement), and the fourth has tables of interest.

The first and second sections are the most original; they contain not only the best approximation of π reached at that time but also show Van Ceulen to be as expert in trigonometry as his contemporary Viète. In 1595 the two men competed in the solution of a forty-fifth degree equation proposed by Van Roomen in his *Ideae mathematicae* (1593) and recognized its relation to the expression of sin 45*A* in terms of sin *A*.

Van Ceulen's tables of interest were not the first to be published. He was anticipated by others, including his friend Simon Stevin (1583). Van Ceulen probably had computed his tables before he knew of Stevin's work.

BIBLIOGRAPHY

I. ORIGINAL WORKS. Two of Van Ceulen's books are *Van den Circkel* (Delft, 1596); and *Arithmetische en geometrische fondamenten* (Leiden, 1615). For the titles of Van Ceulen's early polemical writings and the full titles of his books, see Bierens de Haan and Bosmans (below). Snell's Latin versions are *Fundamenta arithmetica et geometrica* (Leiden, 1615; Amsterdam, 1619), a translation; and *L. à Ceulen De circulo et adscriptis liber* (Leiden, 1619), a modified version of the original. Van Ceulen also wrote a manuscript entitled "Algebra," which seems to have been lost.

II. SECONDARY LITERATURE. On Van Ceulen or his work, see D. Bierens de Haan, *Bouwstoffen voor de Geschiedenis der Wis-en Natuurkundige Wetenschappen in de Nederlanden,* 2 vols. (Amsterdam, 1876–1878), nos. 8, 9, 17 (repr. from *Verslagen en mededeelingen der Koninklijke Akademie van Wetenschappen Amsterdam*); H. Bosmans, "Un émule de Viète," in *Annales de la Société scientifique de Bruxelles,* **34**, pt. 2 (1910), 88–139, with an analysis of *Van den Circkel;* and "Ludolphe van Ceulen," in *Mathésis. Recueil mathématique à l'usage des écoles spéciales* (Ghent), **39** (1925), 352–360, with a portrait; and C. de Waard, "Ceulen," in *Nieuw Nederlandsch Biographisch Woordenboek,* VII (1927), cols. 291–295. See also P. Beydals, in *Nieuwe Rotterdamsche courant* (1 Oct. 1936). On his tables of interest, see Simon C. Stevin, *Tafelen van Interest* (Antwerp, 1583), repr. with English translation in *The Principal Works of S. Stevin,* IIa, Dirk J. Struik, ed. (Amsterdam, 1958), 13–24; and C. Waller Zeeper, *De oudste interesttafels* (Amsterdam, 1927). The fate of the tombstone is discussed by C. de Jong and W. Hope-Jones in *Mathematical Gazette,* **22** (1938), 281–282.

DIRK J. STRUIK

CEVA, GIOVANNI (*b.* Milan, Italy, 1647 or 1648; *d.* Mantua, Italy, 1734)

Ceva's dates must be inferred from incomplete information; he died sometime in 1734 at the age of eighty-six years and six months and therefore must have been born in 1647 or 1648. In his correspondence with Antonio Magliabecchi, the librarian of the grand duke of Tuscany, Ceva states that he studied in Pisa, and in the preface to one of his books he gives particular praise to Donato Rossetti, who was a professor of logic there until he moved to Turin in 1674. He further mentions Alessandro Marchetti (1633–1714) and his son Angiolo Marchetti (1674–1753), both professors of mathematics at Pisa. Ceva was married and a daughter was born to him on 28 October 1685. His father was still living with him in Mantua in 1686. His brother was the poet, philosopher, and mathematician Tommaso Ceva. The bishop of Tortona, Carlo Francesco Ceva, was his cousin.

Ceva described his youth as saddened by "many kinds of misfortune" and his later work as distracted by "serious cares and affairs of his friends and family." At the time of his death his name was carried in a register of the salaried employees of the royal court as "Commissario dell'arciducale Camera et Matematico cesareo." He was buried in the church of St. Teresa de' Carmelitani Scalzi.

Ceva's efforts concerning the problem of diverting the river Reno into the Po deserve special attention; his opposition to this plan of the Bolognese led to the abandonment of the project.

Ceva's most important mathematical work is *De lineis rectis* (Milan, 1678), dedicated to Ferdinando Carlo. Chasles mentions it with praise in his *Aperçu historique.* In this work Ceva used the properties of the center of gravity of a system of points to obtain the relation of the segments which are produced by straight lines drawn through their intersections. He further utilized these properties in many theorems of the theory of transverse lines—for example, in placing at the points of intersection of the straight lines weights that are inversely proportional to the segments. From the relations of the weights, which are determined by the law of the lever, the relation of the segments is then derived. Ceva first applied his method, which is a combination of geometry and mechanics, to five basic figures, which he called "elements." He then used these in special problems, in which given relations are used to calculate others. The theorem of Menelaus concerning the segments produced by a transverse line of a triangle is proved, as is the transversal theorem concerning the concurrency of the transverse lines through the vertices of a triangle, which is named after Ceva. This theorem was established again by Johann I Bernoulli. Ceva worked with proportions and proved their expansion; he calculated many examples in detail and for all possible cases. (Occasionally he treated examples in a purely geometrical manner to demonstrate the advantage of his method.)

In the second book of the *De lineis,* Ceva went on to more complex examples and applied his method to cylindrical sections, ellipses in the triangle, and conic sections and their tangents.

In a geometrical supplement, not related to either

of the first two books, Ceva dealt with classical geometrical theorems. He solved problems on plane figures bounded by arcs of circles and then calculated the volumes and centers of gravity of solid bodies, such as the paraboloid and the two hyperboloids of rotation. Cavalieri's indivisibles are used successfully in this case.

Ceva's mastery of all the other geometrical problems of his time is shown by other works which are dedicated to the mathematician Cardinal Ricci. Among these, the *Opuscula mathematica* (Milan, 1682) met with particular acclaim.

The *Opuscula* is in four parts. In the first part Ceva investigated forces and formed the parallelogram of forces and the resultants of many different forces. Geometrical proofs accompany the mechanical considerations. "Geometrical proofs can themselves provide a verification for that which we have determined mechanically," Ceva wrote in the scholium to the sixth proposition. He then considered levers at greater length and obtained proportions for the quadrangle by means of lever laws. He further discussed centers of gravity for surfaces and bodies. In all the problems he showed how geometry can be used profitably in statics.

In the second part of the book, Ceva investigated pendulum laws—here he refers to Galileo. In the third proposition of this section, Ceva arrived at the erroneous conclusion (which he later corrected) that the periods of oscillation of two pendulums are in the ratio of their lengths.

Solid bodies and perforated vessels are observed in flowing water in the last part of the work. Flow velocity is measured by means of the motion of pendulums suspended in the flow. Finally the amount of water is measured by means of flow cross sections. In the last pages, Ceva again added a geometrical appendix. He examined a ring with a semicircular cross section and proved that certain sections cannot be elliptical. He then calculated the center of gravity of the surface of a hemisphere by using Cavalieri's indivisibles and indicated that it is not necessary to work with parallel sections in this method. Central sections, "small cones," could also be used in the calculation. Ceva's infinitesimal method is sketched in this section with clear and detailed demonstrations.

A third work, *Geometria motus* (Bologna, 1692), is also of great interest. Here Ceva attempted to determine the nature of motions geometrically, stating that he has always been "interested without restraint" in such studies. His further prefatory remark—that geometry brings unadulterated truth—again indicated his interest in pure geometry. Ceva worked with coordinate systems

$$s = f(v);\ s = f(t), \text{ etc.}$$

The areas defined by the curves are determined by the Cavalieri method. Although he preferred the geometrical method, he did not hesitate to use indivisibles and he considered the points of curves to be quantities "smaller than any of those specified." After he had examined individual motions, he went on to a comparison of motions. This brought him to parabolas and hyperbolas, and he made particular reference to the work of Stephano de Angelis (*Miscellaneum hyperbolicum et parabolam,* Venice, 1659). Ceva assumed that, over an "infinitely short distance," motion can be considered uniform. He gave no more precise substantiation of this view, however.

Ceva treated composite motions in the second book of the *Geometria motus.* Here he also discussed the laws of pendulums and (in the scholium on the fifteenth proposition, theorem XI) corrected his error in the *Opuscula mathematica.* In considering motions of points along curves, Ceva was led to a comparison between parabolas and spirals with equal arcs. He considered the lines as "flows of points." He also investigated bodies formed by the rotation of certain figures and considered the falling of bodies along inclined planes, the subject of a great deal of his previous work. The final part of the *Geometria* consists of studies on the stretching and motion of ropes in which weights suspended by ropes are experimentally raised and dropped.

Although Ceva used archaic and complicated formulations, the *Geometria* anticipates or at least suggests elements of infinitesimal calculus.

Ceva's interest in a variety of problems led him to produce *De re numeraria* (Mantua, 1711), a work praised by Cinelli for its great accuracy.

Ceva frequently became involved in controversies on physical problems. In particular he criticized Paster Vanni's erroneous conception of the distribution of forces on an inclined plane.

BIBLIOGRAPHY

I. Original Works. Ceva's extant writings include *De lineis rectis se invicem secantibus statica constructio* (Milan, 1678); *Opuscula mathematica* (Milan, 1682); *Geometria motus* (Bologna, 1692); *Tria problemata geometrice proposita* (Mantua, 1710); *De re numeraria, quod fieri potuit, geometrice tractata* (Mantua, 1711); *De mundi fabrica, una gravitatis principio innixo* (Mantua, 1715); his polemical works concerning the diversion of the Reno into the Po, *Le conseguenze del Reno, se con l'aderire al progretto de' Signori Bolognesi si permetesse in Po grande* (Mantua, 1716; Bologna, 1716), *Replica de Giovanni Ceva indifesa delle sue dimostrazioni, e ragioni, per quali non debassi introdurre Reno in Po, contro la riposta data dal Sig. Eustachio Manfredi* (Mantua, 1721), and *Riposta de Giovanni Ceva alle osservazioni dal Signor dottor Eustachio Manfredi contro la di lui replica in proposito dell'immissione de Reno in Po grande pretesa da' Signori Bolognesi* (Mantua, 1721); *Hydrostatica* (Mantua, 1728); and two letters, one addressed to Vincenzo Viviani and the other to Antonio Magliabecchi, in the Royal Library in Florence.

II. SECONDARY LITERATURE. See Gino Loria, "Per la biografia de Giovanni Ceva," in *Rendiconti dell'istituto lombardo di scienze e lettere,* **48** (1915), 450–452.

HERBERT OETTEL

CEVA, TOMASSO (*b.* Milan, Italy, 20 December 1648; *d.* Milan, 3 February 1737)

Tomasso Ceva came from a rich and famous Italian family; he was the brother of Giovanni Ceva. In 1663 he entered the Society of Jesus and at an early age became professor of mathematics at Brera College in Milan.

Ceva's first scientific work, *De natura gravium* (1669), deals with physical subjects—such as gravity, the attraction of masses for each other, free fall, and the pendulum—in a philosophical and even theological way. (For example, several pages are devoted to the concept of the *spatium imaginarum.*) Ceva wrote the treatise in two months of steady work; in his "Conclusion," he asks his readers for emendations.

Ceva's only truly mathematical work is the *Opuscula mathematica* (1699; parts were published separately in the same year as *De ratione aequilibri, De sectione geometrico-harmonia et arithmetica,* and *De cycloide; de lineis phantasticis; de flexibilibus*). The book is discussed in *Acta eruditorum* (1707); its particular importance is that it is the summation of all of Ceva's mathematical work. It is concerned with gravity, arithmetic, geometric-harmonic means, the cycloid, division of angles, and higher-order conic sections and curves. It also contains a report on an instrument designed to divide a right angle into a specified number of equal parts; this same instrument was described in 1704 by L'Hospital—who makes no mention, however, of Ceva.

Higher-order curves are also the primary subject of an extensive correspondence between Ceva and Guido Grandi. Ceva proposed the problem; Grandi reported that such curves had well-defined properties. Grandi replied to Ceva's questions not only in letters, but also in a work on the logarithmic curve published in 1701 with an appended letter by Ceva.

Ceva's contribution to mathematics was modest; he is perhaps better remembered as a poet. Although some of his verse is mathematical and philosophical, he is best known for his religious poem *Jesus Puer,* which went through many printings and was translated into several languages. The German poet Lessing called Ceva a great mathematician as well as a great poet, while Schubart, writing in 1781, considered him the greatest Jesuit poet-genius.

BIBLIOGRAPHY

Ceva's mathematical and scientific works are *De natura gravium libri duo Thomae Cevae* (Milan, 1669); *Instrumentum pro sectione cujuscunque anguli rectilinei in partes quotcunque aequales* (Milan, 1695; repr. in *Acta eruditorum* [1695], p. 290); and *Opuscula mathematica Thomae Cevae e Soc. Jesu* (Milan, 1699), discussed in *Acta eruditorum* (1707), pp. 149–153.

Other works are *Jesus Puer, Poema* (Milan, 1690, 1699, 1704, 1718, 1732, 1733), translated into German (Augsburg, 1844), French, and Italian; *Sylvae. Carmina Thomae Cevae* (Milan, 1699, 1704, 1733); and *Carmina videlicet philosophia novo-antiqua* (Milan, 1704; Venice, 1732).

Ceva's correspondence with Grandi is in the Braidense Library (eight letters) and the Domus Galilaeana, Pisa (485 letters).

An important secondary source is Guido Grandi, *Geometrica demonstratio theorematum Hugenianorum circa logisticam, seu logarithmicam lineam, addita epistola geometrica ad P. Thomam Cevam* (Florence, 1701).

HERBERT OETTEL

CHAPLYGIN, SERGEI ALEKSEEVICH (*b.* Ranenburg [now Chaplygin], Russia, 5 April 1869; *d.* Moscow, U.S.S.R., 8 October 1942)

Chaplygin was born into the family of a shop assistant. His father, Aleksei Timofeevich Chaplygin, died suddenly of cholera in 1871, when his son was two. In 1886 Chaplygin graduated from the Voronezh Gymnasium and immediately enrolled at Moscow University, from which he graduated with a brilliant record in 1890; at the request of N. E. Zhukovsky he was retained there to prepare for a teaching career. He became an assistant professor at Moscow University in 1894. From 1896 until 1906 he taught mechanics at Moscow Technical College and from 1901 was professor of mechanics at Moscow Women's College, which he headed from 1905 until 1918.

Chaplygin's first scientific papers, which were written under Zhukovsky's influence, were devoted to hydromechanics. In 1893 he wrote a long article, "O nekotorykh sluchayakh dvizhenia tverdogo tela v zhidkosti" ("On Certain Cases of Movement of a Solid Body in a Liquid"), which was awarded the Brashman Prize. In 1897 there appeared a second article with the same title; this was his master's dissertation. In these papers Chaplygin gave a geometric interpretation of those cases of the movement of a body in a liquid that had earlier been studied from a purely analytic standpoint by the German scientists Clebsch and Kirchhoff, as well as by the Russian scientist Steklov. In this regard Zhukovsky has written that Chaplygin "demonstrated in his two excellent papers what strength the cleverly conceived geometrical methods of investigation can possess."

Even at the beginning of his scientific career Chaplygin devoted much attention to the development of the general methods of classical mechanics. A whole series of his papers, which appeared at the turn of the century, has among its topics the problem of a body's motion in the presence of nonintegrable relationships and the motion of a solid body around a fixed point. In the article of 1897, "O dvizhenii tverdogo tela vrashchenia na gorizontalnoy ploskosti" ("On the Motion of a Solid Body of Revolution in a Horizontal Plane"), general equations for the motion of nonholonomic systems were first obtained; these equations are a generalization of the Lagrangian equation. The Petersburg Academy of Sciences awarded Chaplygin a gold medal in 1899 for his investigations of the movement of a solid body.

Among Chaplygin's papers a special place is occupied by his investigation of the mechanics of liquids and gases. Even in the 1890's he had shown a great interest in the study of jet streams. At that time jet flow theory was the basis for study of the laws of motion of bodies in a fluid. In 1899 Chaplygin, using Zhukovsky's investigations as a base, solved somewhat differently the problem of a stream of incompressible fluid passing around a plate ("K voprosu o struyakh v neszhimaemoy zhidkosti" ["To the Problem of Currents in an Incompressible Fluid"]). The problem of gas passing around bodies was especially interesting to him.

In the nineteenth century Russian scientists as well as others had published a number of papers on the theory of a high-speed stream of gas. For example, in 1839 St. Venant had investigated the phenomenon of the escape of gas through an opening at a great rate of flow. In 1858 N. V. Maievsky established the influence of the compressibility of air on the resistance to the motion of a shell for a flight velocity close to the speed of sound.

In 1902 Chaplygin published his famous paper "O gazovykh struyakh" ("On Gas Streams"), in which he developed a method permitting the solution, in many cases, of the problem of the noncontinuous flow of a compressible gas. With this paper he opened the field of high-velocity aeromechanics. The method devised by Chaplygin made it possible to solve the problem of the flow of a gas stream if, under the limiting conditions, the solution to the corresponding problem of an incompressible liquid is known. The equations derived by Chaplygin for the motion of a compressible fluid are valid for the case in which the velocity of the current never exceeds the speed of sound. He applied this theory to the solution of two problems concerning the stream flow of a compressible fluid: escape from a vessel and flow around a plate that is perpendicular to the direction of flow at infinity.

Chaplygin found precise solutions to the problems he examined; they are still the only instances of precise solutions to problems in gas dynamics. He compared the results of his theoretical investigations on the escape of a gas and on the flow around a plate with experimental data and obtained qualitative confirmation of his theory.

Chaplygin also developed a method of approximation for the solution of problems in gas dynamics that was noteworthy for its simplicity; however, it is possible to apply this method only when the velocity of the gas flow does not exceed approximately half the speed of sound.

"O gazovykh struyakh" was Chaplygin's doctoral dissertation. At the time it did not receive wide recognition, partly because at the velocities then obtaining in aviation there was no need to consider the influence of the compressibility of air; on the other hand, in artillery great interest was centered on investigations at velocities greater than the speed of sound.

The significance of this paper for solving problems in aviation came to light at the beginning of the 1930's, when it became necessary to create a new science about the motion of bodies at velocities equal to and greater than the speed of sound, and for the flow patterns past them. The bases of this new science, gas dynamics, had been laid down by Chaplygin, who thus was more than thirty years ahead of the necessary technology.

In 1910 Chaplygin began his important investigations into the theory of the wing. That February he reported to the Moscow Mathematical Society on the aerodynamic forces acting on an airplane wing. He stated the results of these investigations in his paper "O davlenii plosko-parallelnogo potoka na pregrazhdayushchie tela (k teorii aeroplana)" ("On the Pressure Exerted by a Plane-parallel Stream on an Impeding Body [Toward a Theory of the Airplane]"), which was published that same year. The postulate concerning the determination of the rate of circulation around a wing was first precisely stated in this paper. This postulate—the so-called Chaplygin-Zhukovsky postulate—gives a complete solution to the problem of the forces exerted by a stream on a body passing through it. This article includes the fundamentals of plane aerodynamics, particularly Chaplygin's celebrated formulas for calculating the pressures exerted by the stream of a fluid on an impeding body. These formulas were applied by Chaplygin to the calculation of the stream pressure on various wing profiles for which he gives the construction.

In "O davlenii plosko-parallelnogo . . ." Chaplygin obtained a number of other remarkable results. He was the first to study thoroughly the question of the longitudinal moment acting on a wing, considering this question an essential element of the theory of the wing. On the basis of a study of the general formula for the moment of the lifting force he established a simple relationship between the longitudinal moment and the angle of attack; this relationship was not obtained experimentally until several years later and subsequently proved to be one of the fundamental aerodynamic characteristics of a wing.

After the October Revolution, Chaplygin immediately sided with the Soviet government and, with Zhukovsky, actively participated in the organization (1918) of the Central Aerohydrodynamic Institute; after the death of his friend and teacher, Chaplygin became the director of this prominent scientific center. In 1924 he was elected a corresponding member, and in 1929 a full member, of the Academy of Sciences of the U.S.S.R. In 1929 the title Honored Scientist of the R.S.F.S.R. was conferred on him. His scientific, technological, and organizational services were recognized in 1941, when he was awarded the title Hero of Socialist Labor.

Chaplygin's subsequent scientific papers were devoted to the development of aerohydrodynamics. His fundamental investigations of wing cross sections, wing profiles, a wing's irregular motion, and the theory of structural framework had great significance for the development of aerodynamics throughout the world.

Chaplygin's works also enriched mathematics: his studies of methods of approximation for solving differential equations are achievements of mathematical thought.

BIBLIOGRAPHY

Chaplygin's works have been brought together in *Sobranie sochineny* ("Collected Works"), 4 vols. (Moscow-Leningrad, 1948–1950).

On Chaplygin or his work, see V. V. Golubev, *Sergei Alekseevich Chaplygin (1869–1942)* (Moscow, 1951), in Russian, which includes a bibliography of Chaplygin's published works and critico-biographical literature about him; A. T. Grigorian, *Die Entwicklung der Hydrodynamik und Aerodynamik in der Arbeiten von N. E. Shukowski und S. A. Tschaplygin*, no. 5 in the series Naturwissenschaften, Technik und Medizin (Leipzig, 1965), pp. 39–62; and A. A. Kosmodemyansky, "Sergei Alekseevich Chaplygin," in *Lyudi russkoy nauki* ("People of Russian Science"), I (Moscow, 1961), 294–302.

A. T. GRIGORIAN

CHASLES, MICHEL (*b*. Épernon, France, 15 November 1793; *d*. Paris, France, 18 December 1880)

Chasles was born into an upper-middle-class Catholic family, settled in the region of Chartres. He was given the name Floréal, but it was changed to Michel by court order, 22 November 1809. His father, Charles-Henri, was a lumber merchant and contractor who became president of the *chambre de commerce* of Chartres. Chasles received his early education at the Lycée Impérial and entered the École Polytechnique in 1812. In 1814 he was mobilized and took part in the defense of Paris. After the war he returned to the École Polytechnique and was accepted into the engineering corps, but he gave up the appointment in favor of a poor fellow student. After spending some time at home, he obeyed his father's wishes and entered a stock brokerage firm in Paris. However, he was not successful and retired to his native region, where he devoted himself to historical and mathematical studies. His first major work, the *Aperçu historique*, published in 1837, established his reputation both as a geometer and a historian of mathematics. In 1841 he accepted a position at the École Polytechnique, where he taught geodesy, astronomy, and applied mechanics until 1851. In 1846 a chair of higher geometry was created for him at the Sorbonne, and he remained there until his death.

Chasles was elected a corresponding member of the Academy of Sciences in 1839 and a full member in 1851. His international reputation is attested to by the following partial list of his affiliations: member of the Royal Society of London; honorary member of the Royal Academy of Ireland; foreign associate of the royal academies of Brussels, Copenhagen, Naples, and Stockholm; correspondent of the Imperial Academy of Sciences at St. Petersburg; and foreign associate of the National Academy of the United States. In 1865 Chasles was awarded the Copley Medal by the Royal Society of London for his original researches in pure geometry.

Chasles published highly original work until his very last years. He never married, and his few interests outside of his research, teaching, and the Academy, which he served on many commissions, seem to have been in charitable organizations.

Chasles's work was marked by its unity of purpose and method. The purpose was to show not only that geometry, by which he meant synthetic geometry, had methods as powerful and fertile for the discovery and demonstration of mathematical truths as those of algebraic analysis, but that these methods had an important advantage, in that they showed more clearly the origin and connections of these truths. The methods were those introduced by Lazare Carnot, Gaspard Monge, and Victor Poncelet and included a systematic use of sensed magnitudes, imaginary elements, the principle of duality, and transformations of figures.

The *Aperçu historique* was inspired by the question posed by the Royal Academy of Brussels in 1829: a philosophical examination of the different methods in modern geometry, particularly the method of reciprocal polars. Chasles submitted a memoir on the principles of duality and homography. He argued that the principle of duality, like that of homography, is based on the general theory of transformations of figures, particularly transformations in which the cross ratio is preserved, of which the reciprocal polar transformation is an example. The work was crowned in 1830, and the Academy ordered it published. Chasles requested permission to expand the historical introduction and to add a series of mathematical and historical notes, giving the result of recent researches. His books and almost all of his many memoirs are elaborations of points originally discussed in these notes. One of his weaknesses—that he did not know German—is apparent here too, and as will be seen below, many of the results claimed as new had been wholly or partly anticipated. It was this expanded work which was published.

Chasles wrote two textbooks for his course at the Sorbonne. The first of these, the *Traité de géométrie supérieure* (1852), is based on the elementary theories of the cross ratio, homographic ranges and pencils, and involution, all of which were originally defined and discussed in the *Aperçu historique;* the cross ratio in note 9, involution in note 10. In the case of the cross ratio, which Chasles called the anharmonic ratio, he was anticipated by August Moebius, in his *Barycentrische Calcul* (1827). However, it was Chasles who developed the theory and showed its scope and power. This book, Chasles felt, showed that the use of sensed magnitudes and imaginary elements gives to geometry the freedom and power of analysis.

The second text, the *Traité sur des sections coniques* (1865), applied these methods to the study of the conic sections. This was a subject in which Chasles was interested throughout his life, and he incorporated many results of his own into the book. For example, he discussed the consequences of the projective characterization of a conic as the locus of points of intersection of corresponding lines in two homographic pencils with no invariant line, or dually as the envelope of lines joining corresponding points of two homographic ranges with no invariant point. Chasles had originally given this in notes 15 and 16 of the *Aperçu historique,* but here also he must share credit with a mathematician writing in German, the Swiss geometer Jacob Steiner.

The book also contains many of Chasles's results in what came to be called enumerative geometry. This subject concerns itself with the problem of determining how many figures of a certain type satisfy certain algebraic or geometric conditions. Chasles considered first the question of systems of conics satisfying four conditions and five conditions (1864). He developed the theory of characteristics and of geometric substitution. The characteristics of a system of conics were defined as the number of conics passing through an arbitrary point and as the number of conics tangent to a given line. Chasles expressed many properties of his system in formulas involving these two numbers and then generalized his results by substituting polynomials in the characteristics for the original values. There are many difficulties in this type of approach, and although Chasles generalized his results to more general curves and to surfaces, and the subject was developed by Hermann Schubert and Hieronymus Zeuthen, it is considered as lacking in any sound foundation.

Chasles did noteworthy work in analysis as well. In particular, his work on the attraction of ellipsoids led him to the introduction and use of level surfaces of partial differential equations in three variables (1837). He also studied the general theory of attraction (1845), and though many of the results in this paper had been anticipated by George Green and Carl Gauss, it remains worthy of study.

Chasles wrote two historical works elaborating points in the *Aperçu historique* (notes 12 and 3 respectively) which had given rise to controversy. The *Histoire d'arithmétique* (1843) argued for a Pythagorean rather than a Hindu origin for our numeral system. Chasles based his claim on the description of a certain type of abacus, which he found in the writings of Boethius and Gerbert. The second work was a reconstruction of the lost book of *Porisms* of Euclid (1860). Chasles felt that the porisms were essentially the equations of curves and that many of the results utilized the concept of the cross ratio. Neither of these works is accepted by contemporary scholars.

In 1867 Chasles was requested by the minister of public education to prepare a *Rapport sur le progrès de la géométrie* (1870). Although the work of foreign geometers is treated in less detail than that of the French, the *Rapport* is still a very valuable source for the history of geometry from 1800 to 1866 and for Chasles's own work in particular.

Chasles was a collector of autographs and manuscripts, and this interest allied with his credulity to cause him serious embarrassment. From 1861 to 1869 he was the victim of one of the most clever and prolific of literary forgers, Denis Vrain-Lucas. Chasles bought thousands of manuscripts, including a correspondence between Isaac Newton, Blaise Pascal, and Robert Boyle which established that Pascal had anticipated Newton in the discovery of the law of universal gravitation. Chasles presented these letters to the Academy in 1867 and took an active part in the furor that ensued (1867–1869), vigorously defending the genuineness of the letters. In 1869 Vrain-Lucas was brought to trial and convicted. Chasles was forced to testify and had to admit to having purchased letters allegedly written by Galileo, Cleopatra, and Lazarus, all in French.

But this misadventure should not be allowed to obscure his many positive contributions. He saw clearly the basic concepts and their ramifications in what is now known as projective geometry, and his texts were influential in the teaching of that subject in Germany and Great Britain as well as in France. Finally, with all its faults, the *Aperçu historique* remains a classic example of a good history of mathematics written by a mathematician.

BIBLIOGRAPHY

I. ORIGINAL WORKS. The first edition of the *Aperçu historique sur l'origine et le développement des méthodes en géométrie, particulièrement de celles qui se rapportent à la géométrie moderne, suivi d'un mémoire de géométrie sur deux principes généraux de la science, la dualité et l'homographie* appeared in *Mémoires couronnés par l'Académie de Bruxelles,* vol. **11** (1837) and is very rare; but it was reprinted, without change, in Paris in 1875 and again in 1888. A German translation, *Geschichte der Geometrie, hauptsächlich mit Bezug auf die neueren Methoden,* L. Sohncke, trans. (Halle, 1839), omits the last section.

The *Traité de géométrie supérieure* (Paris, 1852), reprinted in 1880, was freely translated into German under the title *Die Grundlehren der neueren Geometrie. Erster Theil: Die Theorie des anharmonischen Verhältnisses, der homographischen Theilung und der Involution, und deren Anwendung auf die geradlinigen und Kreis-Figuren,* C. H. Schnuse, trans. (Brunswick, 1856). Principal parts of the work also appear in Benjamin Witzchel, *Grundlinien der neueren Geometrie mit besonderer Berücksichtigung der metrischen Verhältnisse an Systemen von Punkten in einer Geraden und einer Ebene* (Leipzig, 1858), and in Richard Townsend, *Chapters on the Modern Geometry,* vol. II (Dublin, 1865). The second part of the *Traité des sections coniques faisant suite au traité de géométrie supérieure* (first part, Paris, 1865) never appeared.

The major results in enumerative geometry are summarized in "Considérations sur la méthode générale exposée dans la séance du 15 février. Différences entre cette méthode et la méthode analytique. Procédés généraux de démonstration," in *Comptes rendus hebdomadaires des séances de l'Académie des sciences,* **58** (1864), 1167–1176. The most important papers in analysis are "Mémoire sur l'attraction des ellipsoïdes," in *Journal de l'École polytechnique,* **25** (1837), 244–265; "Sur l'attraction d'une couche ellipsoïdale infiniment mince; Des rapports qui ont lieu entre cette attraction et les lois de la chaleur, dans un corps en équilibre de température," *ibid.,* pp. 266–316; and "Théorèmes généraux sur l'attraction des corps," in *Connaissance des temps ou des mouvements célestes pour l'année (1845),* pp. 18–33.

The historical works are *L'histoire d'arithmétique* (Paris, 1843); *Les trois livres de Porismes d'Euclide, rétablis pour la première fois, d'après la notice et les lemmes de Pappus, et conformément au sentiments de R. Simson sur la forme des énoncés de ces propositions* (Paris, 1860); and *Le rapport sur le progrès de la géométrie* (Paris, 1870). Chasles's contributions to the Pascal-Newton controversy are scattered throughout the *Comptes rendus:* **65** (1867); **66** (1868); **67** (1868); **68** (1869); and **69** (1869).

The *Rendiconti delle sessioni dell'Accademia delle scienze dell'Istituto di Bologna* (1881), pp. 51–70; the *Catalogue of Scientific Papers,* Royal Society of London, I (1867), 880–884; VII (1877), 375–377; IX (1891), 495–496; and Poggendorff, I (1863), 423, and III (1898), 261–264 all contain extensive lists of Chasles's works. The first named is the most complete, although it omits all works that appeared in the *Nouvelles annales de mathématique.*

II. SECONDARY LITERATURE. There are many biographical sketches of Chasles. Among the more valuable are Joseph Bertrand, *Éloges académiques* (Paris, 1902), pp. 27–58; Eduarde Merlieux, *Nouvelle biographie générale* (Paris, 1863), VIII, 38; and Claude Pichois, *Dictionnaire de biographie française* (Paris, 1959), X, 694, which contains a short bibliography.

Chasles's works are discussed in "Commemorazione di Michele Chasles" by Pietro Riccardi, in *Rendiconti* (1881), 37–51; Edward Sabine, "Presidential Address," in *Proceedings of the Royal Society,* London, **14** (1865), 493–496; and Gino Loria, "Michel Chasles e la teoria delle sezioni coniche," in *Osiris,* **1** (1936), 421–441.

Details of the Vrain-Lucas affair can be found in J. A. Farrar, *Literary Forgeries* (London, 1907), pp. 202–214.

ELAINE KOPPELMAN

CHEBOTARYOV, NIKOLAI GRIGORIEVICH (*b.* Kamenets-Podolsk [now Ukrainian S.S.R.], 15 June 1894; *d.* Moscow, U.S.S.R., 2 July 1947)

Chebotaryov became fascinated by mathematics while still in the lower grades of the Gymnasium. In 1912 he entered the department of physics and mathematics at Kiev University. Beginning in his second year at Kiev, Chebotaryov participated in a seminar given by D. A. Grave which included O. Y. Schmidt, B. N. Delaunay, A. M. Ostrowski and others. Chebotaryov's scientific interests took definite shape in this group. After graduating from the university in 1916, he taught and did research.

From 1921 to 1927 Chebotaryov taught at Odessa, where he prepared a paper on Frobenius' problem; he defended this paper as a doctoral dissertation in Kiev in 1927. In that year he was appointed a professor at Kazan University. In January 1928, he assumed his post at the university, where he spent the rest of his life and where he founded his own school of algebra. In 1929 Chebotaryov was elected a corresponding member of the Academy of Sciences of the Union of Soviet Socialist Republics, and in 1943 the title Honored Scientist of the Russian Soviet Federated Socialist Republic was conferred upon him. For his work on the theory of resolvents he was posthumously awarded the State Prize in 1948.

Chebotaryov's main works deal with the algebra of polynomials and fields (Galois's theory); the problem of resolvents (first raised by Felix Klein and David Hilbert)—that is, the problem of the transformation of a given algebraic equation with variable coefficients to an equation whose coefficients depend on the least possible number of parameters (1931 and later); the distribution of the roots of an equation on the plane (1923 and later); and the theory of algebraic numbers. In 1923 he published a complete solution to Frobenius' problem concerning the existence of an infinite set of prime numbers belonging to a given class of substitutions of Galois's group of a given normal algebraic field. This problem generalized Dirichlet's famous theorem concerning primes among natural numbers in arithmetic progressions. The method applied was utilized by E. Artin in 1927 in proving his generalized law of reciprocity. In 1934 Chebotaryov, applying the methods of Galois's theory and *p*-adic series, made significant advances toward a solution of the question—first posed by the ancient Greeks—of the possible number of lunes that are bounded by two circular arcs so chosen that the ratio of their angular measures is a rational number and that can be squared using only a compass and a straightedge. One of Chebotaryov's disciples, A. V. Dorodnov, completed the investigation of this famous problem in 1947. Chebotaryov also did work on the theory of Lie groups, in geometry (translation surfaces), and in the history of mathematics.

BIBLIOGRAPHY

I. Original Works. Chebotaryov's works may be found in the three-volume *Sobranie sochineny* ("Collected Works"; Moscow and Leningrad, 1949–1950).

II. Secondary Literature. More on Chebotaryov and his work is in *Nauka v SSSR za pyatnadtsat let. Matematika* ("Fifteen Years of Science in the U.S.S.R.: Mathematics"; Moscow-Leningrad, 1932), see index; and *Matematika v SSSR za tridtsat let* ("Thirty Years of Mathematics in the U.S.S.R."; Moscow-Leningrad, 1948), see index. *Matematika v SSSR za sorok let* ("Forty Years of Mathematics in the U.S.S.R."; Moscow-Leningrad, 1959), II, 747–750, contains a bibliography of Chebotaryov's works. An obituary of Chebotaryov is in *Uspekhi matematicheskikh nauk,* **2,** no. 6 (1947), 68–71. See also V. V. Morozov, A. P. Norden, and B. M. Gagaev, "Kazanskaya matematicheskaya shkola za 30 let" ("Thirty Years of the Kazan School of Mathematics"), *ibid.,* pp. 3–20; B. L. Laptev, "Matematika v Kazanskom universitete za 40 let (1917–1957)" ("Forty Years of Mathematics at Kazan University"), in *Istoriko-matematicheskie issledovania,* **12** (1959), 11–58; and *Istoria otechestvennoi matematiki* ("History of Native [Russian] Mathematics"), vols. II–III (Kiev, 1967–1968), see index.

A. P. Youschkevitch

CHEBYSHEV, PAFNUTY LVOVICH (*b.* Okatovo, Kaluga region, Russia, 16 May 1821; *d.* St. Petersburg, Russia, 8 December 1894)

Chebyshev's family belonged to the gentry. He was born on a small estate of his parents, Lev Pavlovich Chebyshev, a retired army officer who had participated in the war against Napoleon, and Agrafena Ivanovna Pozniakova Chebysheva. There were nine children, of whom, besides Pafnuty, his younger brother, Vladimir Lvovich, a general and professor at the Petersburg Artillery Academy, was also well known. Vladimir paid part of the cost of publishing the first collection of Pafnuty's works (1, 1a).

In 1832 the Chebyshevs moved to Moscow, where Pafnuty completed his secondary education at home. He was taught mathematics by P. N. Pogorelski, one of the best tutors in Moscow and author of popular textbooks in elementary mathematics.

In 1837 Chebyshev enrolled in the department of physics and mathematics (then the second section of the department of philosophy) of Moscow University. Mathematical disciplines were then taught brilliantly by N. D. Brashman and N. E. Zernov. Brashman, who always directed his pupils toward the most essential problems of science and technology (such as the theory of integration of algebraic functions or the calculus of probability, as well as recent inventions in mechanical engineering and hydraulics), was especially important to Chebyshev's scientific development. Chebyshev always expressed great respect for and gratitude to him. In a letter to Brashman, discussing expansion of functions into a series by means of continued fractions, Chebyshev said: "What I said illustrates quite sufficiently how interesting is the topic toward which you directed me in your lectures and your always precious personal talks with me" (2, II, 415). The letter was read publicly at a meeting of the Moscow Mathematical Society on 30 September 1865 and printed in the first issue of *Matematichesky sbornik* ("Mathematical Collection"), published by the society in 1866. Chebyshev was one of the first members of the society (of which Brashman was the principal founder and the first president).

As a student Chebyshev wrote a paper, "Vychislenie korney uravneny" ("Calculation of the Roots of Equations"), in which he suggested an original iteration method for the approximate calculation of real roots of equations $y = f(x) = 0$ founded on the expansion into a series of an inverse function $x = F(y)$. The first terms of Chebyshev's general formula are

$$x = \alpha - \frac{f(\alpha)}{f'(\alpha)} - \left[\frac{f(\alpha)}{f'(\alpha)}\right]^2 \frac{f''(\alpha)}{2f'(\alpha)} - \cdots,$$

where α is an approximate value of the root x of the equation $f(x) = 0$ differing from the exact value by sufficiently little. Choosing a certain number of terms of the formula and successively calculating from the chosen value α further approximations $\alpha_1, \alpha_2, \cdots$, it is possible to obtain iterations of different orders. Iteration of the first order is congruent with the widely known Newton-Raphson method: $\alpha_{n+1} = \alpha_n - f(\alpha_n)/f'(\alpha_n)$. Chebyshev gives an estimation of error for his formula. This paper, written by Chebyshev for a competition on the subject announced by the department of physics and mathematics for the year 1840–1841, was awarded a silver medal, although it undoubtedly deserved a gold one. It was published only recently (2, V).

In the spring of 1841 Chebyshev graduated from Moscow University with a candidate (bachelor) of mathematics degree. Proceeding with his scientific work under Brashman's supervision, he passed his master's examinations in 1843, simultaneously publishing an article on the theory of multiple integrals in Liouville's *Journal des mathématiques pures et appliquées* and in 1844 an article on the convergence of Taylor series in Crelle's *Journal für die reine und angewandte Mathematik* (see 1*a*, I; 2, II). Shortly afterward he submitted as his master's thesis, *Opyt elementarnogo analiza teorii veroyatnostey* ("An Essay on an Elementary Analysis of the Theory of Probability"; (see 2, V). The thesis was defended in the summer of 1846 and was accompanied by "Démonstration élémentaire d'une proposition générale de la théorie des probabilités" (*Journal für die reine und angewandte Mathematik*, 1846; see 1*a*, I; 2, II), which was devoted to Poisson's law of large numbers. These works aimed at a strict but elementary deduction of the principal propositions of the theory of probability; of the wealth of mathematical analysis Chebyshev used only the expansion of $ln(1 + x)$ into a power series. In the article on Poisson's theorem we find an estimation of the number of tests by which it is possible to guarantee a definite proximity to unit probability of the assumption that the frequency of an event differs from the arithmetic mean of its probabilities solely within the given limits. Thus, even in Chebyshev's earliest publications one of the peculiar aspects of his work is manifest: he aspires to establish by the simplest means the most precise numerical evaluations of the limits within which the examined value lies.

It was almost impossible to find an appropriate teaching job in Moscow, so Chebyshev willingly accepted the offer of an assistant professorship at Petersburg University. As a thesis *pro venia legendi* he submitted "Ob integrirovanii pomoshchyu logarifmov" ("On Integration by Means of Logarithms"), written, at least in the first draft, as early as the end of 1843. The thesis, defended in the spring of 1847, incidentally solved a problem of integration of algebraic irrational functions in the final form that had been posed shortly before by Ostrogradski. The thesis was published posthumously, as late as 1930 (see 2, V), but Chebyshev included its principal results in his first publication on the subject in 1853.

In September 1847, at Petersburg University, Chebyshev began lecturing on higher algebra and the theory of numbers. Later he lectured on numerous other subjects, including integral calculus, elliptic functions, and calculus of finite differences; but he taught the theory of numbers as long as he was at the university (until 1882). From 1860 he regularly lectured on the theory of probability, which had previously been taught for a long time by V. Y. Bunyakovski. A. M. Lyapunov, who attended Chebyshev's lectures in the late 1870's, thus characterized them:

> His courses were not voluminous, and he did not consider the quantity of knowledge delivered; rather, he

> aspired to elucidate some of the most important aspects of the problems he spoke on. These were lively, absorbing lectures; curious remarks on the significance and importance of certain problems and scientific methods were always abundant. Sometimes he made a remark in passing, in connection with some concrete case they had considered, but those who attended always kept it in mind. Consequently, his lectures were highly stimulating; students received something new and essential at each lecture; he taught broader views and unusual standpoints [4, p. 18].

Soon after Chebyshev moved to St. Petersburg, he was hired by Bunyakovski to work on the new edition of Euler's works on the theory of numbers that had been undertaken by the Academy of Sciences. This edition (*L. Euleri Commentationes arithmeticae collectae,* 2 vols. [St. Petersburg, 1849]) comprised not only all of Euler's previously published papers on the subject but also numerous manuscripts from the Academy's archives; in addition Bunyakovski and Chebyshev contributed a valuable systematic review of Euler's arithmetical works. Probably this work partly inspired Chebyshev's own studies on the theory of numbers; these studies and the investigations of Chebyshev's disciples advanced the theory of numbers in Russia to a level as high as that reached a century before by Euler. Some problems of the theory of numbers had been challenged by Chebyshev earlier, however, in his thesis *pro venia legendi.* He devoted to the theory of numbers his monograph *Teoria sravneny* ("Theory of Congruences"; 7), which he submitted for a doctorate in mathematics. He defended it at Petersburg University on 27 May 1849 and a few days later was awarded a prize for it by the Academy of Sciences. Chebyshev's systematic analysis of the subject was quite independent and contained his own discoveries; it was long used as a textbook in Russian universities. It also contained the first of his two memoirs on the problem of distribution of prime numbers and other relevant problems; the second memoir, submitted to the Academy of Sciences in 1850, appeared in 1852. Through these two works, classics in their field, Chebyshev's name became widely known in the scientific world. Later Chebyshev returned only seldom to the theory of numbers.

In 1850 Chebyshev was elected extraordinary professor of mathematics at Petersburg University; in 1860 he became a full professor. This was a decade of very intensive work by Chebyshev in various fields. First of all, during this period he began his remarkable studies on the theory of mechanisms, which resulted in the theory of the best approximation of functions. From his early years Chebyshev showed a bent for construction of mechanisms; and his studies at Moscow University stimulated his interest in technology, especially mechanical engineering. In 1849–1851 he undertook a course of lectures on practical (applied) mechanics in the department of practical knowledge of Petersburg University (this quasi-engineering department existed for only a few years); he gave a similar course in 1852–1856 at the Alexander Lyceum in Tsarskoe Selo (now Pushkin), near St. Petersburg. Chebyshev's mission abroad, from July to November 1852, was another stimulus to his technological and mathematical work. In the evenings he talked with the best mathematicians of Paris, London, and Berlin or proceeded with his scientific work; morning hours were devoted to the survey of factories, workshops, and museums of technology. He paid special attention to steam engines and hinge-lever driving gears. He began to elaborate a general theory of mechanisms and in doing so met, according to his own words, certain problems of analysis that were scarcely known before (2, V, 249). These were problems of the theory of the best approximation of functions, which proved to be his outstanding contribution; in this theory his technological and mathematical inclinations were synthesized.

Back in St. Petersburg, Chebyshev soon submitted to the Academy of Sciences his first work on the problem of the best approximation of functions, prepared mainly during his journey and published in 1854. This was followed by another work on the subject, submitted in 1857 and published in 1859. These two papers marked the beginning of a great cycle of work in which Chebyshev was engaged for forty years. While in Europe, Chebyshev continued his studies on the integration of algebraic functions. His first published work on the problem, far surpassing the results at which he had arrived in the thesis *pro venia legendi,* appeared in 1853. Chebyshev published papers on this type of problem up to 1867, the object of them being to determine conditions for integration in the final form of different classes of irrational functions. Here, as in other cases, research was associated with university teaching; Chebyshev lectured on elliptic functions for ten years, until 1860.

In 1853 Chebyshev was voted an adjunct (i.e., junior academician) of the Petersburg Academy of Sciences with the chair of applied mathematics. Speaking for his nomination, Bunyakovski, Jacobi, Struve, and the permanent secretary of the Academy, P. N. Fuss, emphasized that Chebyshev's merits were not restricted to mathematics; he had also done notable work in practical mechanics. In 1856 Chebyshev was elected an extraordinary academician and in 1859 ordinary academician (the highest academic rank), again with the chair of applied mathematics.

From 1856 Chebyshev was a member of the Artillery Committee, which was charged with the task of introducing artillery innovations into the Russian army. In close cooperation with the most eminent Russian specialists in ballistics, such as N. V. Maievski, Chebyshev elaborated mathematical devices for solving artillery problems. He suggested (1867) a formula for the range of spherical missiles with initial velocities within a certain limit; this formula was in close agreement with experiments. Some of Chebyshev's works on the theory of interpolation were the result of the calculation of a table of fire effect based on experimental data. Generally, he contributed significantly to ballistics.

Simultaneously Chebyshev began his work with the Scientific Committee of the Ministry of Education. Like Lobachevski, Ostrogradski, and a number of other Russian scientists, Chebyshev was active in working for the improvement of the teaching of mathematics, physics, and astronomy in secondary schools. For seventeen years, up to 1873, he participated in the elaboration of syllabi for secondary schools. His concise but solid reviews were of great value to the authors of textbooks that the Scientific Committee was supposed, as one of its principal functions, to approve or reject.

From the middle of the 1850's, the theory of the best approximation of functions and the construction of mechanisms became dominant in Chebyshev's work. Studies on the theory of functions embraced a very great diversity of relevant problems: the theory of orthogonal polynomials, the doctrine of limiting values of integrals, the theory of moments, interpolation, methods of approximating quadratures, etc. In these studies the apparatus of continued fractions, brilliantly employed by Chebyshev in many studies, was further improved.

From 1861 to 1888 Chebyshev devoted over a dozen articles to his technological inventions, mostly in the field of hinge-lever gears. Examples of these devices are preserved in the Mathematical Institute of the Soviet Academy of Sciences in Moscow and in the Conservatoire des Arts et Métiers in Paris.

In the 1860's Chebyshev returned to the theory of probability. One of the reasons for this new interest was, perhaps, his course of lectures on the subject started in 1860. He devoted only two articles to the theory of probability, but they are of great value and designate the beginning of a new period in the development of this field. In the article of 1866 Chebyshev suggested a very wide generalization of the law of large numbers. In 1887 he published (without extensive demonstration) a corresponding generalization of the central limit theorem of Moivre and Laplace.

Besides the above-mentioned mathematical and technological fields, which were of primary importance in Chebyshev's life and work, he showed lively interest in other problems of pure and applied mathematics. (His studies in cartography will be mentioned later.) His paper of 1878, "Sur la coupe des vêtements" (1a, II; 2, V), provided the basis for a new branch of the theory of surfaces. Chebyshev investigated a problem of binding a surface with cloth that is formed in the initial flat position with two systems of nonextensible rectilinear threads normal to one another. When the surface is bound with cloth the "Chebyshev net," whose two systems of lines form curvilinear quadrangles with equal opposite sides, appears. Wrapping a surface in cloth is a more general geometrical transformation than is deformation of a surface, which preserves the lengths of all the curved lines; distances between the points of the wrapped cloth that are situated on different threads are, generally speaking, changed in wrapping. In recent decades Chebyshev's theory of nets has become the object of numerous studies.

Theoretical mechanics also drew Chebyshev's attention. Thus, in 1884 he told Lyapunov of his studies on the problem of the ring-shaped form of equilibrium of a rotating liquid mass the particles of which are mutually attracted according to Newton's law. It is hard to know how far Chebyshev advanced in this field, for he published nothing on the subject. Still, the very problem of the form of equilibrium of a rotating liquid mass, which he proposed to Lyapunov, was profoundly investigated by the latter, who, along with Markov, was Chebyshev's most prominent disciple.

Among Chebyshev's technological inventions was a calculating machine built in the late 1870's. In 1882 he gave a brief description of his machine in the article "Une machine arithmétique à mouvement continu" (Ia, II; 2, IV). The first model (*ca.* 1876) was intended for addition and subtraction; he supplemented it with an apparatus enabling one to multiply and divide as well. Examples of the machine are preserved in the Museum of History in Moscow and in the Conservatoire des Arts et Métiers in Paris.

During this period Chebyshev was active in the work of various scientific societies and congresses. Between 1868 and 1880 he read twelve reports at the congresses of Russian naturalists and physicians, and sixteen at the sessions of the Association Française pour l'Avancement des Sciences between 1873 and 1882; it was at these sessions that he read "Sur la coupe des vêtements" and reported on the calculating machine. He gave numerous demonstrations of his technological inventions both at home and abroad.

Chebyshev was in contact with the Moscow and St. Petersburg mathematical societies and with the Moscow Technological College (now Bauman Higher Technological College).

In the summer of 1882, after thirty-five years of teaching at Petersburg University, Chebyshev retired from his professorship, although he continued his work at the Academy of Sciences. Nonetheless, he was constantly in touch with his disciples and young scientists. He held open house once a week, and K. A. Posse states that "hardly anybody left these meetings without new ideas and encouragement for further endeavor" (2, V, 210); it was sufficient only that the problem be relevant to the fields in which Chebyshev had been interested. When Chebyshev was over sixty, he could not work at his former pace; nevertheless, he published some fifteen scientific papers, including a fundamental article on the central limit theorem. He submitted his last work to the Academy of Sciences only a few months before his death at the age of seventy-three.

Besides being a member of the Petersburg Academy of Sciences, Chebyshev was elected a corresponding (1860) and—the first Russian scientist to be so honored—a foreign member (1874) of the Academy of Sciences of the Institut de France, a corresponding member of the Berlin Academy of Sciences (1871), a member of the Bologna Academy (1873), and a foreign member of the Royal Society of London (1877), of the Italian Royal Academy (1880), and of the Swedish Academy of Sciences (1893). He was also an honorary member of all Russian universities and of the Petersburg Artillery Academy. He was awarded numerous Russian orders and the French Legion of Honor.

Petersburg Mathematical School. Chebyshev's importance in the history of science consists not only in his discoveries but also in his founding of a great scientific school. It is sometimes called the Chebyshev school, but more frequently the Petersburg school because its best-known representatives were almost all educated at Petersburg University and worked either there or at the Academy of Sciences. The Petersburg mathematical school owes its existence partly to the activity of Chebyshev's elder contemporaries, such as Bunyakovski and Ostrogradski; nevertheless, it was Chebyshev who founded the school, directed and inspired it for many years, and influenced the trend of mathematics teaching at Petersburg University. For over half a century mathematical chairs there were occupied by Chebyshev's best disciples or their own disciples. Thus the mathematics department of Petersburg University achieved a very high academic level. Some disciples of Chebyshev took his ideas to other Russian universities.

Chebyshev was highly endowed with the ability to attract beginners to creative work, setting them tasks demanding profound theoretical investigation to solve and promising brilliant results. The Petersburg school included A. N. Korkin, Y. V. Sohotski, E. I. Zolotarev, A. A. Markov, A. M. Lyapunov, K. A. Posse, D. A. Grave, G. F. Voronoi, A. V. Vassiliev, V. A. Steklov, and A. N. Krylov. Chebyshev, however, was such a singular individual that he also influenced scientists who did not belong to his school, both in Russia (e.g., N. Y. Sonin) and abroad. During the latter half of the nineteenth and the beginning of the twentieth centuries the Petersburg mathematical school was one of the most prominent schools in the world and the dominant one in Russia. Its ideas and methods formed an essential component of many divisions of pure and applied mathematics and still influence their progress.

Although a great variety of scientific trends were represented in the Petersburg mathematical school, the work of Chebyshev and his followers bore some important common characteristics. Half seriously, Chebyshev shortly before his death said to A. V. Vassiliev that previously mathematics knew two periods: during the first the problems were set by gods (the Delos problem of the duplication of a cube) and during the second by demigods, such as Fermat and Pascal. "We now entered the third period, when the problems were set by necessity" (16, p. 59). Chebyshev thought that the more difficult a problem set by scientific or technological practice, the more fruitful the methods suggested to solve it would be and the more profound a theory arising in the process of solution might be expected to be.

The unity of theory and practice was, in Chebyshev's view, the moving force of mathematical progress. He said in a speech entitled "Cherchenie geograficheskikh kart" ("Drawing Geographical Maps"), delivered at a ceremonial meeting of Petersburg University in 1856:

> Mathematical sciences have attracted especial attention since the greatest antiquity; they are attracting still more interest at present because of their influence on industry and arts. The agreement of theory and practice brings most beneficial results; and it is not exclusively the practical side that gains; the sciences are advancing under its influence as it discovers new objects of study for them, new aspects to exploit in subjects long familiar. In spite of the great advance of the mathematical sciences due to works of outstanding geometers of the last three centuries, practice clearly reveals their imperfection in many respects; it suggests problems essentially new for science and thus challenges one to seek quite new methods. And if theory gains much when new

> applications or new developments of old methods occur, the gain is still greater when new methods are discovered; and here science finds a reliable guide in practice [2, V, 150].

Among scientific methods important for practical activity Chebyshev especially valued those necessary to solve the same general problem:

> How shall we employ the means we possess to achieve the maximum possible advantage? Solutions of problems of this kind form the subject of the so-called theory of the greatest and least values. These problems, which are purely practical, also prove especially important for theory: all the laws governing the movement of ponderable and imponderable matter are solutions of this kind of problem. It is impossible to ignore their special influence upon the advance of mathematical sciences [*ibid.*].

These statements (reminding one somewhat of Euler's ideas on the universal meaning of the principle of least action) are illustrated by Chebyshev with examples from the history of mathematics and from his own works on the theory of mechanisms and the theory of functions. The speech quoted above is specially devoted to solution of the problem of searching for such conformal projections upon a plane of a given portion of the earth's surface under which change in the scale of image (different in various parts of a map) is the least, so that the image as a whole is the most advantageous. The projection sought bears a characteristic particularity: on the border of the image the scale preserves the same value. Demonstration of this theorem of Chebyshev's was first published by Grave in 1894.

Chebyshev's general approach to mathematics quite naturally resulted in his aspiration toward the effective solution of problems and the discovery of algorithms giving either an exact numerical answer or, if this proved impossible, an approximation ready for scientific and practical applications. He interpreted the strictness of the theory in the event of approximate evaluations as a possibility of precise definition of limits not trespassed by the error of approximation. Chebyshev was a notable representative of the "mathematics of inequalities" of the latter half of the nineteenth century. His successors held similar views.

Lastly, not the least characteristic feature of Chebyshev's works from the early period on was his inclination toward possibly elementary mathematical apparatus, particularly his almost exclusive use of functions in the real domain. He was especially adept at using continued fractions. Many other scholars of his school made wider use of contemporary analysis, especially of the theory of functions of complex variables.

The Petersburg school was concerned with quite a number of subjects. It dealt primarily with the domains of pure and applied mathematics investigated by Chebyshev himself and developed by his disciples. However, Chebyshev's followers worked in other areas of mathematical sciences that were far from the center of Chebyshev's own interests. Growing in numbers and ability, the Petersburg school gradually became an aggregate of scientific schools brought together by similar principles of study and closely connected both on the level of ideas and on the personal level; they differed mainly in their predominant mathematical subjects: the theory of numbers, the theory of the best approximation of functions, the theory of probability, the theory of differential equations, and mathematical physics.

Although the work of Chebyshev and his school was independent in the formulation of numerous problems and in the elaboration of methods to solve them and discovered large new domains of mathematical study, it was closely related to mathematics of the eighteenth and the first half of the nineteenth centuries. In Russia the school developed the tradition leading back to Euler, whose works were thoroughly studied and highly valued. Much as they differed as individuals (the difference in mathematics of their respective epoches was no less great), Chebyshev and Euler had much in common. Both were interested in a great variety of problems, from the theory of numbers to mechanical engineering. Both were aware of the profound connection of mathematical theory with its applications and tended to set themselves concrete problems as a source of theoretical conclusions that were later generalized; both, on the other hand, understood the vital necessity of developing mathematics in its entirety, including problems the solution of which did not promise any immediate practical gain. Finally, both were always seeking most effective solutions that approached computing algorithms.

It is important to note that at the beginning of the present century younger representatives of the Chebyshev school started to bring about its contact with other trends in mathematics, which soon led to great progress.

Theory of Numbers. It had been proved in ancient Greece that there exist infinitely many prime numbers 2, 3, 5, 7, $\cdots$. This principal result in the doctrine of the distribution of prime numbers remained an isolated result until the end of the eighteenth century, when the first step in investigation of the frequency of prime numbers in the natural number series 1, 2, 3, 4, $\cdots$ was made: Legendre suggested in 1798–1808 the approximate formula

$$\pi(x) \approx \frac{x}{\ln x - 1.08366}$$

to express the number of prime numbers not exceeding a given number x, e.g., for the function designated $\pi(x)$. This formula accorded well with the table of prime numbers from 10,000 to 1,000,000. In his article "Sur la fonction qui détermine la totalité des nombres premiers inférieurs à une limite donnée" (1849; see 1a, I; 2, I) Chebyshev, making use of the properties of Euler's zeta function in the real domain, proved the principal inaccuracy of Legendre's approximate formula and made a considerable advance in the study of the properties of the function $\pi(x)$. According to Legendre's formula, the difference $x/\pi(x) - \ln x$ for $x \to \infty$ has the limit -1.08366. Chebyshev demonstrated that this difference cannot have a limit differing from -1. With sufficiently great x the integral $\int_2^x dx/\ln x$ gives better approximations to $\pi(x)$ than Legendre's and similar formulas; besides, the difference

$$\frac{x}{\ln x - 1.08366} - \int_2^x \frac{dx}{\ln x},$$

inconsiderable within the limits of the tables used by Legendre, reaches the minimum for $x \approx 1{,}247{,}689$ and then increases without limit with the increase of x.

It also followed from Chebyshev's theorems that the ratio of the function $\pi(x)$ to $\int_2^x dx/\ln x$ or to $x/\ln x$ cannot, for $x \to \infty$, have a limit differing from unity.

Chebyshev later continued the study of the properties of $\pi(x)$. In his "Mémoire sur les nombres premiers" (1850, pub. 1852; see 1a, I; 2, II) he demonstrated that $\pi(x)$ can differ from $x/\ln x$ by no more than approximately 10 percent—more exactly, that

$$0.92129x/\ln x < \pi(x) < 1.10555x/\ln x$$

(although he stated this result in a slightly different form).

Other remarkable discoveries were described in these two articles. The second article demonstrates Bertrand's conjecture (1845) that for $n > 3$, between n and $2n - 2$ there is always at least one prime number. In it Chebyshev also proved some theorems on convergence and on the approximate calculation of the sums of infinite series the members of which are functions of successive prime numbers (the first series of this kind were studied by Euler). In a letter to P. N. Fuss published in 1853 (1a, I; 2, II) Chebyshev set a problem of estimating the number of prime numbers in arithmetical progressions and gave some results concerning progressions with general members of the form $4n + 1$ and $4n + 3$.

Chebyshev's studies on the distribution of prime numbers were developed by numerous scientists in Russia and abroad. Important advances were made in 1896 by Hadamard and Vallée-Poussin, who, employing analytical functions of a complex variable, proved independently the asymptotic law of distribution of prime numbers:

$$\lim_{x \to \infty} \frac{\pi(x)}{x/\ln x} = 1.$$

Studies in this field of the theory of numbers are being intensively conducted.

Among Chebyshev's other works on the theory of numbers worthy of special attention is his article "Ob odnom arifmeticheskom voprose" ("On One Arithmetical Problem"; 1866; 1a, I; 2, II), which served as a point of departure for a series of studies devoted to a linear heterogeneous problem of the theory of diophantine approximations. The problem, in which Hermite, Minkowski, Remak, and others were later interested, was completely solved in 1935 by A. Y. Khintchine.

Integration of Algebraic Functions. Chebyshev's studies on the integration of algebraic functions were closely connected with the work of Abel, Liouville, and, in part, Ostrogradski. In the article "Sur l'intégration des différentielles irrationelles" (1853; see 1a, I; 2, II) Chebyshev succeeded in giving a complete solution of the problem of defining the logarithmic part of the integral

$$\int \frac{f(x)\,dx}{F(x)\sqrt[m]{\theta(x)}}$$

for the case when it is expressed in final form—here the functions $f(x)$, $F(x)$, $\theta(x)$ are integral and rational, and m is any positive integer. But the article is known mostly for the final solution of the problem of the integration of the binomial differential $x^m(a + bx^n)^p\,dx$ it contains; here m, n, p are rational numbers. Generalizing Newton's result, Goldbach and Euler showed that this type of integral is expressible in elementary functions in any of the three cases when p is an integer; $(m + 1)/n$ is an integer; and $(m + 1)/n + p$ is an integer. Chebyshev demonstrated that the three cases are the only cases when the integral mentioned is taken in the final form. This theorem is included in all textbooks on integral calculus.

In the theory of elliptic integrals Chebyshev substantially supplemented Abel's results. Integration of any elliptic differential in the final form is reduced to integration of a fraction that has a linear function $x + A$ in the numerator and a square root of a polynomial of the fourth degree in the denominator.

Chebyshev considered the problem in the article "Sur l'intégration de la différentielle

$$\frac{(x + A)\,dx}{\sqrt{x^4 + \alpha x^3 + \beta x^2 + \gamma x + \delta}}\text{''}$$

(1861; see 1a, I; 2, II). It is supposed that the polynomial in the denominator has no multiple roots (in the case of multiple roots the differential is integrated quite easily). The elliptic differential in question either is not integrable in elementary functions or is integrable for one definite value of the constant A. Abel had shown that the latter case occurred if a continued fraction formed by expansion of

$$\sqrt{x^4 + \alpha x^3 + \beta x^2 + \gamma x + \delta}$$

is periodic. However, Abel could offer no final criterion enabling one to ascertain nonperiodicity of such an expansion. Chebyshev gave a complete and efficient solution of the problem with rational numbers $\alpha, \beta, \gamma, \delta$: he found a method enabling one to ascertain nonperiodicity of such an expansion by means of the finite number of operations, which in turn depends on the finite number of integer solutions of a system of two equations with three unknowns; he also determined the limit of the number of operations necessary in case of integrability. He did not publish any complete demonstration of his algorithm; this was done by Zolotarev in 1872. Soon Zolotarev suggested a solution of the same problem for any real coefficients α, β, γ, δ, for which purpose he devised his own variant of the theory of ideals.

Chebyshev also studied the problem of integrability in the final form of some differentials containing a cube root of a polynomial. In Russia this direction of study was followed by I. L. Ptashitski and I. P. Dolbnia, among others.

Theory of the Best Approximation of Functions. It was said that Chebyshev had approached the theory of best approximation of functions from the problems of the theory of hinge mechanisms, particularly from the study of the so-called Watt parallelogram employed in steam engines and other machines for the transformation of rotating movement into rectilinear movement. In fact, it is impossible to obtain strictly rectilinear movement by this means, which produces a destructive effect. Attempting somehow to reduce the deviation of the resultant movement from the rectilinear, engineers searched empirically for suitable correlation between the parts of mechanisms. Chebyshev set the task of elaborating a sound theory of the problem, which was lacking; he also devised a number of curious mechanisms that, although they could not strictly secure rectilinear movement, could compete with "strict" mechanisms because the deviation was very small. Thus, the virtually exact seven-part rectifying device suggested by Charles Peaucellier and independently by L. I. Lipkin is, in view of the complexity of construction, less useful in practice than Chebyshev's four-part device described in the article "Ob odnom mekhanizme" ("On One Mechanism"; 1868; see 1a, II; 2, IV).

Chebyshev made a profound investigation of the elements of a hinge mechanism, setting out to achieve the smallest deviation possible of the trajectory of any points from the straight line for the whole interval studied. A corresponding mathematical problem demanded that one choose, from among the functions of the given class taken for approximation of the given function, that function with which the greatest modulo error is the smallest under all considered values of the argument. Some special problems of this kind had previously been solved by Laplace, Fourier, and Poncelet. Chebyshev laid foundations for a general theory proceeding from the approximation of functions by means of polynomials. The problem of approximation of the given function by means of polynomials might be formulated differently. Thus, in an expansion of the given function $f(x)$ into a Taylor series of powers of the difference $x - a$, the sum of the first $n + 1$ members of the series is a polynomial of nth degree that in the neighborhood of the value $x = a$ gives the best approximation among all polynomials of the same degree. Chebyshev set the task of achieving not a local best approximation but the uniform best approximation throughout the interval; his object was to find among all polynomials $P_n(x)$ of nth degree such a polynomial that the maximum $|f(x) - P_n(x)|$ for this interval is the smallest.

In the memoir "Théorie des mécanismes connus sous le nom de parallélogrammes" (1854; see 1a, I; 2, II), which was the first in a series of works in this area, Chebyshev considered the problem of the best approximation of the function $f(x) = x^n$ by means of polynomials of degree $n - 1$; that is, he considered the problem of the determination of the polynomial of the nth degree, $x^n + p_1x^{n-1} + \cdots + p_n$ with the leading coefficient equal to unity, deviating least from zero. This formulation of the problem engendered the frequently used term "theory of polynomials deviating least from zero" (the term was used by Chebyshev himself). In the case of the interval $(-1, +1)$ this polynomial is

$$\frac{1}{2^{n-1}}\,T_n(x) = \frac{1}{2^{n-1}}\cos\,(n \text{ arcos } x)$$

$$= x^n - \frac{n}{1\,!}\,\frac{x^{n-2}}{2^2}$$

$$+\frac{n(n-3)}{2!}\frac{x^{n-4}}{2^4}-\frac{n(n-4)(n-5)}{3!}\frac{x^{n-6}}{2^6}+\cdots,$$

and its maximum deviation from zero is $1/2^{n-1}$. Polynomials $T_n(x)$, named for Chebyshev, form an orthogonal system with respect to a weight function

$$\frac{1}{\sqrt{1-x^2}}.$$

In his next long memoir, "Sur les questions de minima qui se rattachent à la représentation approximative des fonctions" (1859; see 1a, I; 2, II), Chebyshev extended the problem to all kind of functions $F(x, p_1, p_2, \cdots, p_n)$ depending on n parameters, expressed general views concerning the method of solution, and gave a complete analysis of two cases when F is a rational function; in this work some curious theorems on the limits of real roots of algebraic equations were obtained. Varying restrictions might be imposed upon the function of the best approximation that is to be determined; Chebyshev also solved several problems of this type.

Gradually considering various problems either directly relevant to the theory of the best approximation of functions or connected with it, Chebyshev obtained important results in numerous areas.

(*a*) The theory of interpolation and, especially, interpolation on the method of least squares (1855–1875).

(*b*) The theory of orthogonal polynomials. Besides polynomials $T_n(x)$ deviating least from zero, Chebyshev in 1859 proceeded from consideration of different problems to the study of other orthogonal systems, such as Hermite and Laguerre polynomials. However, he did not take up the determination of polynomials under the condition of orthogonality in the given interval with respect to the given weight function; he introduced polynomials by means of an expansion in continued fractions of certain integrals of the

$$\int_a^b \frac{p(x)\,dx}{z-x}$$

type, where $p(x)$ is the weight function.

(*c*) The theory of moments was first treated by Chebyshev in his article "Sur les valeurs limites des intégrales" (1874; see 1a, I; 2, III). Here the following problem is considered: given the values of moments of different orders of an unknown function $f(x)$, e.g., of the integrals

$$\int_A^B f(x)\,dx = C_0,\ \int_A^B xf(x)\,dx = C_1, \cdots,$$

$$\int_A^B x^m f(x)\,dx = C_m$$

in an interval (A,B) where $f(x) > 0$, one is required to find the limits within which the value of the integral

$$\int_a^b f(x)\,dx$$

lies ($A < a < b < B$). Chebyshev once more connected the investigation of the problem with expansion of the integral

$$\int_A^B \frac{f(x)\,dx}{z-x}$$

in continued fraction; in conclusion he gave a detailed solution of the problem for a special case $m = 2$ formulated in mechanical interpretation: "Given length, weight, site of the center of gravity, and the moment of inertia of a material straight line with an unknown density that changes from one point to another, one is required to find the closest limits with respect to the weight of a certain segment of this straight line" (2, III, 65). Chebyshev's work on estimations of integrals received important application in his studies on the theory of probability.

(*d*) Approximate calculus of definite integrals. In his article "Sur les quadratures" (1874; 1a, II; 2, III) Chebyshev, proceeding from work by Hermite, suggested new general formulas of approximate quadratures in which all the values of the integrand are introduced under the same coefficient or, at least, under coefficients differing only in sign. The aforementioned characteristic of the coefficients renders Chebyshev's quadrature formulas very suitable for the calculus in many cases; A. N. Krylov used them in his studies on the theory of ships. One of the formulas is

$$\int_{-1}^{1} f(x)\,dx \approx k[f(x_1) + f(x_2) + \cdots + f(x_n)];$$

the values $x_1, x_2, x_3, \cdots$ are obtained from an equation of the nth degree: $k = \frac{2}{n}$. Chebyshev himself calculated these values for $n = 2, 3, 4, 5, 6, 7$; for $n = 8$ the equation has no real roots and the formula is unusable; for $n = 9$ the roots are real again but, as S. N. Bernstein demonstrated in 1937, beginning at $n = 10$ the formula is again unusable.

This large cycle of Chebyshev's works was carried further by Zolotarev, Markov, Sonin, Posse, Steklov, Stieltjes, Riesz, and many others; work in these and new fields is being continued. It is worth special mention that at the beginning of the twentieth century the theory of the best approximation acquired essentially new features through the connections between Chebyshev's ideas and methods, on the one hand, and those developed in western Europe, on the other. Works of S. N. Bernstein and his disciples were of primary importance here.

Theory of Probability. In his article "O srednikh velichinakh" ("On Mean Values"; 1866; see 1a, I; 2, II) Chebyshev, using an inequality previously deduced by J. Bienaymé, gave a precise and very simple demonstration of the generalized law of large numbers that might be thus expressed in modern terms: If $x_1, x_2, x_3, \cdots$ are mutually independent in pairs of random quantities, with expectation values $a_1, a_2, a_3, \cdots$ and dispersions $b_1, b_2, b_3, \cdots$, the latter being uniformly limited—e.g., all $b_n \leq C$—then for any $\varepsilon > 0$ the probability P of an inequality

$$\left|\frac{x_1 + x_2 + \cdots + x_n}{n} - \frac{a_1 + a_2 + \cdots + a_n}{n}\right| < \varepsilon$$

is $\geqslant 1 - (C/n\varepsilon^2)$. From this it follows immediately that

$$\lim_{n\to\infty} P\left(\left|\frac{x_1 + x_2 + \cdots + x_n}{n} - \frac{a_1 + a_2 + \cdots + a_n}{n}\right| < \varepsilon\right) = 1.$$

The theorems of Poisson and Jakob Bernoulli are only special cases of Chebyshev's law of large numbers for sequences of random quantities.

Developing his method of moments and of estimation of the limit values of integrals, Chebyshev also managed to extend to sequences of independent random quantities the central limit theorem of Moivre and Laplace: within the framework of former suppositions, supplemented with the condition that there exist expectation values (moments) of any order and that they all are uniformly limited,

$$\lim_{n\to\infty} P\left(t_1 < \frac{x_1 + x_2 + \cdots + x_n - a_1 - a_2 - \cdots - a_n}{\sqrt{2(b_1 + b_2 + \cdots + b_n)}} < t_2\right) = \frac{1}{\sqrt{\pi}} \int_{t_1}^{t_2} e^{-t^2}\, dt.$$

This theorem and the draft of its demonstration were published by Chebyshev in the article "O dvukh teoremakh otnositelno veroyatnostey" ("On Two Theorems Concerning Probability"; 1887; see 1a, II; 2, III); the first theorem mentioned in the title is the law of large numbers. Chebyshev's second theorem enabled one to apply, on a larger scale, the theory of probability to mathematical statistics and natural sciences; both regard the phenomenon under study as resulting from common action of a great number of random factors, each factor displaying considerably smaller influence independently in comparison with their influence as a set. According to this theorem, such common action closely follows the normal distribution law. Chebyshev's demonstration was supplemented a decade later by Markov.

Chebyshev's studies on limit theorems were successfully developed by his disciples and successors, first by Markov, Lyapunov, and Bernstein and later by numerous scientists. A. N. Kolmogorov, a foremost authority in the field, says:

> From the standpoint of methodology, the principal meaning of the radical change brought about by Chebyshev is not exclusively that he was the first mathematician to insist on absolute accuracy in demonstration of limit theorems (the proofs of Moivre, Laplace, and Poisson were not wholly consistent on the formal logical grounds in which they differ from those of Bernoulli, who demonstrated his limit theorem with exhaustive arithmetical accuracy). The principal meaning of Chebyshev's work is that through it he always aspired to estimate exactly in the form of inequalities absolutely valid under any number of tests the possible deviations from limit regularities. Further, Chebyshev was the first to estimate clearly and make use of the value of such notions as "random quantity" and its "expectation (mean) value." These notions were known before him; they are derived from fundamental notions of the "event" and "probability." But random quantities and their expectation values are subject to a much more suitable and flexible algorithm [21, p. 56].

BIBLIOGRAPHY

I. Original Works. During his lifetime Chebyshev's works appeared mainly in publications of the Petersburg Academy of Sciences—*Mémoires* or *Bulletin de l'Académie des sciences de St. Pétersbourg*—in Liouville's *Journal de mathématiques pures et appliquées,* in *Matematichesky sbornik,* and others; some are in Russian and some in French. A complete bibliography of Chebyshev's works, except some minor articles published in (8), is in (2), V, 467–471.

Chebyshev's works are the following:

(1) *Sochinenia,* A. A. Markov and N. Y. Sonin, eds., 2 vols. (St. Petersburg, 1899–1907). This Russian ed. is nearly complete but does not contain his master's thesis (6) and doctor's thesis (7) and some articles included in (2).

(1a) *Oeuvres de P. L. Tchebychef,* A. A. Markov and N. Y. Sonin, eds., 2 vols. (St. Petersburg, 1899–1907), a French version of (1). Both (1a) and (1) contain a biographical note based entirely on (9).

(2) *Polnoe sobranie sochineny,* 5 vols. (Moscow–Leningrad, 1944–1951): I, *Teoria chisel;* II–III, *Matematichesky analiz;* IV, *Teoria mekhanizmov;* V, *Prochie sochinenia. Biograficheskie materialy.* This ed. contains very valuable scientific commentaries that are largely completed and developed in (3).

(3) *Nauchnoe nasledie P. L. Chebysheva,* 2 vols. (Moscow-Leningrad, 1945): I, *Matematika;* II, *Teoria mekhanizmov.* This contains important articles by N. I. Akhiezer, S. N. Bernstein, I. M. Vinogradov and B. N. Delaunay, V. V. Golubev, V. L. Goncharov, I. I. Artobolevsky and N. I. Levitsky, Z. S. Blokh, and V. V. Dobrovolsky.

(4) *Izbrannye matematicheskie trudy* (Moscow-Leningrad, 1946).

(5) *Izbrannye trudy* (Moscow, 1955).

(6) *Opyt elementarnogo analiza teorii veroyatnostey* ("An Essay on an Elementary Analysis of the Theory of Probability"; Moscow, 1845; also [2], V), his master's thesis.

(7) *Teoria sravneny* ("Theory of Congruences"; · St. Petersburg, 1849, 1879, 1901; also [2], I), his doctoral thesis. Trans. into German as *Theorie der Congruenzen* (Berlin, 1888) and into Italian as *Teoria delle congruenze* (Rome, 1895).

(8) V. E. Prudnikov, "O statyakh P. L. Chebysheva, M. V. Ostrogradskogo, V. Y. Bunyakovskogo i I. I. Somova v Entsiklopedicheskom slovare, sostavlennom russkimi uchenymi i literatorami,'" in *Istoriko-matematicheskie issledovania,* no. 6 (1953).

II. Secondary Literature. On Chebyshev or his work, see the following:

(9) K. A. Posse, "P. L. Chebyshev," in S. A. Vengerov, *Kritiko-bibliografichesky slovar russkikh pisateley i uchenykh,* VI (St. Petersburg, 1897-1904; see also [1], II; [1a], II; [2], I).

(10) A. M. Lyapunov, *Pafnuty Lvovich Chebyshev* (Kharkov, 1895; see also [4], pp. 9-21).

(11) A. Wassiliev, "P. Tchébychef et son oeuvre scientifique," in *Bollettino di bibliografia e storia delle scienze matematiche,* I (Turin, 1898). Trans. into German as *P. L. Tchebychef und seine wissenschaftliche Leistungen* (Leipzig, 1900).

(12) N. Delaunay, *Die Tschebyschefschen Arbeiten in der Theorie der Gelenkmechanizmen* (Leipzig, 1900).

(13) V. G. Bool, *Pribory i mashiny dlya mekhanicheskogo proizvodstva matematicheskikh deystvy* (Moscow, 1896).

(14) L. E. Dickson, *History of the Theory of Numbers,* 3 vols. (Washington, D.C., 1919-1927).

(15) V. A. Steklov, *Teoria i praktika v issledovaniakh P. L. Chebysheva* (Petrograd, 1921), also in *Uspekhi matematicheskikh nauk,* **1,** no. 2 (1946), 4-11.

(16) A. V. Vassiliev, *Matematika,* pt. 1 (Petrograd, 1921), 43-61.

(17) L. Bianchi, *Lezzioni di geometria differenziale,* I, pt. 1 (Bologna, 1922), 153-192.

(18) A. N. Krylov, *Pafnuty Lvovich Chebyshev. Biografichesky ocherk* (Moscow-Leningrad, 1944).

(19) N. I. Akhiezer, "Kratky obzor matematicheskikh trudov P. L. Chebysheva," in (4), pp. 171-188.

(20) S. N. Bernstein, "Chebyshev, yego vlianie na razvitie matematiki," in *Uchenye zapiski Moskovskogo gosudarstvennogo universiteta,* no. 91 (1947), 35-45.

(21) A. N. Kolmogorov, "Rol russkoy nauki v razvitii teorii veroyatnostey," *ibid.,* 53-64.

(22) B. N. Delone, *Peterburgskaya shkola teorii chisel* (Moscow-Leningrad, 1947), pp. 5-42.

(23) B. V. Gnedenko, *Razvitie teorii veroyatnostey v Rossii.* Trudy Instituta istorii yestestvoznania, II (Moscow-Leningrad, 1948), 394-400.

(24) Y. L. Geronimus, *Teoria ortogonalnykh mnogochlenov. Obzor dostizheny otechestvennoy matematiki* (Moscow-Leningrad, 1950), *passim.*

(25) L. Y. Sadovsky, "Iz istorii razvitia mashinnoy matematiki v Rossii," in *Uspekhi matematicheskikh nauk,* **5,** no. 2 (1950), 57-71.

(26) M. G. Kreyn, "Idei P. L. Chebysheva i A. A. Markova v teorii predelnykh velichin integralov i ikh dalneyshee razvitie," *ibid.,* **6,** no. 4 (1951), 3-24.

(27) S. A. Yanovskaya, *Dva dokumenta iz istorii Moskovskogo universiteta,* Vestnik Moskovskogo Universiteta, no. 8 (1952).

(28) N. I. Akhiezer, "P. L. Chebyshev i yego nauchnoe nasledie," in (5), pp. 843-887.

(29) K. R. Biermann, *Vorschläge zur Wahl von Mathematikern in die Berliner Akademie* (Berlin, 1960), pp. 41-43.

(30) I. Y. Depman, "S.-Peterburgskoe matematicheskoe obshchestvo," in *Istoriko-matematicheskie issledovania,* no. 13 (1960), 11-106.

(31) *Istoria yestestvoznania v Rossii,* N. A. Figurovsky, ed. II (Moscow, 1961).

(32) A. A. Gusak, "Predystoria i nachalo razvitia teorii priblizhenia funktsy," in *Istoriko-matematicheskie issledovania,* no. 14 (1961), 289-348.

(33) L. Y. Maystrov, "Pervy arifmometr v Rossii," *ibid.,* 349-354.

(34) A. A. Kiselev and E. P. Ozhigova, "P. L. Chebyshev na siezdakh russkikh yestestvoispytateley i vrachey," *ibid.,* no. 15 (1963), 291-317.

(35) *Istoria Akademii nauk SSSR,* II (Moscow-Leningrad, 1964).

(36) V. E. Prudnikov, *P. L. Chebyshev, ucheny i pedagog,* 2nd ed. (Moscow, 1964).

(37) A. N. Bogolyubov, *Istoria mekhaniki mashin* (Kiev, 1964).

(38) V. P. Bychkov, "O razvitii geometricheskikh idey P. L. Chebysheva," in *Istoriko-matematicheskie issledovania,* no. 17 (1966), 353-359.

(39) A. P. Youschkevitch, "P. L. Chebyshev i Frantsuzskaya Akademia nauk," in *Voprosy istorii yestestvoznania i tekhniki,* no. 18 (1965), 107-108.

(40) *Istoria otechestvennoy matematiki,* I. Z. Shtokalo, ed. II (Kiev, 1967).

(41) A. P. Youschkevitch, *Istoria matematiki v Rossii do 1917 g.* (Moscow, 1968).

A. P. Youschkevitch

CHEYNE, GEORGE (*b.* Aberdeenshire, Scotland, 1671; *d.* Bath, England, 12 April 1743)

At first educated for the ministry, Cheyne was influenced by the Scottish iatromechanist Archibald Pitcairn to take up medicine instead. He studied with

Pitcairn in Edinburgh and then, in 1702, moved to London, where he joined the Royal Society and established a medical practice. Cheyne was soon an at least peripheral member of a prominent circle of medical and scientific writers that included the astronomers David Gregory and Edmund Halley and the physicians Richard Mead and John Arbuthnot. He spent several active years in London, winning a major reputation also as a wit and drinking companion in the tavern and coffeehouse set. Some years later, probably by 1720, he renounced his earlier life and moved permanently to Bath as a sober and dedicated medical practitioner. Cheyne spent the major part of his last decades advising his patients and correspondents (the novelist Samuel Richardson, for one) to lives of sober and pious moderation, while conveying his general precepts to the public in a series of popular medical tracts. Through these later works he became one of England's most widely read medical writers.

Cheyne's intellectual career was divided into two phases. During the first, which coincided with his association with Pitcairn in Scotland and his early years in London, he was a principal representative of British "Newtonianism" in its many cultural facets. His first book, *A New Theory of Fevers* (1702), was an elaborate, quasi-mathematical explication of febrile phenomena in terms of Pitcairn's supposedly "mathematical" and "Newtonian" variety of iatromechanism. Cheyne followed Pitcairn in positing a theory of the "animal oeconomy" based on a view of the body as a system of pipes and fluids, and, in fact, he called for the composition of a *Principia medicinae theoreticae mathematica,* which would treat such topics as the hydraulics of circulation and the elastic behavior of vascular walls with the same mathematical rigor that Newton applied to celestial mechanics.

In 1703 Cheyne followed his call for medical mathematicization with a treatise of his own on Newton-style mathematics, the *Fluxionum methodus inversa.* A work on the calculus of dubious mathematical validity (David Gregory counted 429 errors), the *Fluxionum* brought Cheyne more anguish than positive reputation. Abraham de Moivre responded with a thorough refutation, and the great Newton himself—so Gregory claimed—was sufficiently provoked to publish his work on "quadratures" in the 1704 edition of the *Opticks.*

Cheyne pressed ahead nevertheless, in 1705 turning his attention to the theological significance of Newtonian science. In *Philosophical Principles of Natural Religion,* along with several other arguments for the existence and continued superintendence of the Deity, he claimed that the observed phenomena of attraction in the universe argued for a Supreme Being. Since attraction was not a property essential to the mere being of brute and passive matter, its very occurrence, whether in planetary gravitation or in the simple cohesion of terrestrial materials, therefore gave immediate testimony to the hand of God in designing and maintaining the universe. Cheyne's argument proved very popular with his contemporaries, perhaps somewhat impressing even Newton. Sir Isaac included a discussion of the phenomena of attraction in the new and lengthy twenty-third "Query" to the 1706 edition of his *Opticks* (famous as the thirty-first "Query" of later editions) that seems to reflect some of Cheyne's examples and vocabulary. Cheyne at least thought so, for according to an entry in Gregory's *Memoranda,* "Dr. Cheyne uses to say among his Chronys that all the additions (made by S[r] Isaac to his book of Light and Colours in the latin version) were stolen from him."

In the second phase of his intellectual career, which coincided with his residence at Bath, Cheyne repudiated his youthful mathematical brashness and excessive Newtonian enthusiasm. Although he never gave up his intense interest in philosophical and theological speculations or even in Newtonian science, in the works composed while practicing at Bath, Cheyne turned his attention largely to medical subjects. In 1720 he published *An Essay on the Gout,* in 1724 *An Essay of Health and Long Life,* in 1740 *An Essay on Regimen,* and in 1742 *The Natural Method of Cureing the Diseases of the Body and the Disorders of the Mind Depending on the Body.* All these treatises were essentially practical guides that placed considerable emphasis on the medical wisdom of moderation in diet and drink. But Cheyne also devoted some space in each of these books to philosophical and theological issues. In medical theory, for example, he was much committed to directing attention from the body's fluids to its fibrous solids, his uncited guide in this matter almost certainly being the influential Leiden professor Hermann Boerhaave.

Cheyne's most elaborate development of his views on the bodily fibers was contained in the treatise *De natura fibrae* (1725). He was simultaneously concerned with the relationship between the immaterial, musician-like soul and the material, instrument-like body. Although opinions on this subject can be found in all his later writings, the most extensive account of his views was contained in *The English Malady* (1733). Through his later medical works generally, and especially through these last two, Cheyne seems to have aroused much interest in Britain in further investigation of the bodily fibers and in exploration of the metaphysical relationship of mind and body.

BIBLIOGRAPHY

Cheyne's principal writings have been mentioned above; no complete edition of his works exists. For useful biographical and bibliographical summaries that emphasize the later medical writings, see "George Cheyne," in *Dictionary of National Biography* and Charles F. Mullet, Introduction to *The Letters of Dr. George Cheyne to the Countess of Huntingdon* (San Marino, Calif., 1940). The best source for Cheyne's early activities as a "Newtonian" is W. G. Hiscock's edition of Gregory's *Memoranda,* published as *David Gregory, Isaac Newton and Their Circle* (Oxford, 1937). For an interesting summary of Cheyne's theological views, see Hélène Metzger, *Attraction universelle et religion naturelle chez quelques commentateurs anglais de Newton* (Paris, 1938). General summaries of some of Cheyne's medical theories can be found in Albrecht von Haller, *Bibliotheca medicinae practicae,* IV (Basel, 1788), 435–438; Kurt Sprengel, *Histoire de la médecine,* V (Paris, 1815), 167–170; and Charles Daremberg, *Histoire des sciences médicales,* II (Paris, 1870), 1207–1214.

THEODORE M. BROWN

CH'IN CHIU-SHAO (*b.* Szechuan, China, *ca.* 1202; *d.* Kwangtung, China, *ca.* 1261)

Ch'in Chiu-shao (literary name Tao-ku) has been described by George Sarton as "one of the greatest mathematicians of his race, of his time, and indeed of all times." A genius in mathematics and accomplished in poetry, archery, fencing, riding, music, and architecture, Ch'in has often been judged an intriguing and unprincipled character, reminding one of the sixteenth-century mathematician Girolamo Cardano. In love affairs he had a reputation similar to Ibn Sīnā's. Liu K'e-chuang, in a petition to the emperor, described him as a person "as violent as a tiger or a wolf, and as poisonous as a viper or a scorpion." He was also described as an ill-disciplined youth. During a banquet given by his father, a commotion was created when a stone suddenly landed among the guests; investigation disclosed that the missile had come from the direction of Ch'in, who was showing a *fille de joie* how to use a bow as a sling to hurl projectiles. Chou Mi, in his supplementary volume to the *Kuei-yu tsa-chih,* tells us how Ch'in deceived his friend Wu Ch'ien in order to acquire a plot of his land, how he punished a female member of his household by confinement and starvation, and how he became notorious for being inclined to poison those he found disagreeable. We are also told that on his dismissal from the governorship of Ch'iung-chou in 1258 he returned home with immense wealth—after having been in office for just over a hundred days.

According to a recent study by Ch'ien Pao-tsung and others Ch'in was born in the city of P'u-chou (now An-yüeh) in Szechuan province. Ch'in called himself a native of Lu-chün, in Shantung province; but he was simply referring to the place his ancestors came from rather than to his place of birth. His father, Ch'in Chi-yu (literary name Hung-fu), was a civil servant. In 1219 Ch'in joined the army as the head of a unit of territorial volunteers and participated in curbing a rebellion staged by Chang Fu and Mo Chien. In 1224–1225 he followed his father when the latter was transferred to the Sung capital, Chung-tu (now Hangchow). There he had the opportunity to study astronomy at the astronomical bureau under the guidance of the official astronomers. Shortly afterward, however, his father was sent to the prefecture of T'ung-ch'üan (now San-t'ai in Szechuan province), and Ch'in had to leave the capital. About 1233 he served as a sheriff in one of the subprefectures in Szechuan.

The Mongols invaded Szechuan in 1236, and Ch'in fled to the east, where he first became a vice-administrator (*t'ung-p'an*) in Ch'i-chou prefecture (now Ch'i-ch'un in Hupeh province) and then governor of Ho-chou (now Ho-hsien in Anhwei province). In the latter part of 1244 Ch'in was appointed one of the vice-administrators of the superior prefecture of Chien-k'ang-fu (now Nanking), but some three months later he relinquished this post because of his mother's death. He returned to Hu-chou (now Wu-hsing in Chekiang province), and it was probably there that he wrote his celebrated mathematical treatise *Shu-shu chiu-chang* ("Mathematical Treatise in Nine Sections"), which appeared in 1247. In the preface of this book Ch'in mentions that he learned mathematics from a certain recluse scholar, but he does not give his identity.

In 1254 Ch'in returned to Chung-tu to reenter civil service, but for some unknown reason he soon resigned and went back to his native home. He paid a visit to Chia Shih-tao, an influential minister at that time, and was appointed governor of Ch'iung-chou (in modern Hainan) in 1258. A few months later, however, Ch'in was dismissed because of charges of bribery and corruption. Nevertheless, he managed to find another job as a civil aide to an intimate friend of his, Wu Ch'ien (literary name Li-chai), who was then in charge of marine affairs in the district of Yin (near modern Ningpo in Chekiang province). Wu Ch'ien eventually became a minister, but in 1260 he lost favor and was given a lesser assignment in south China. Ch'in followed his friend to Kwangtung province and received an appointment in Mei-chou (now Mei-hsien), where he died shortly afterward. The year of Ch'in's death has been estimated as 1261, for there was an edict in the following year banning Wu Ch'ien and his associates from the civil service.

The title of Ch'in's *Shu-shu chiu-chang* has given rise to some confusion. According to Ch'en Chen-sun, a contemporary of Ch'in Chiu-shao's and owner of a copy of the work, the original title was *Shu shu* ("Mathematical Treatise"). However, in his *Chih chai shu lu chieh ti* he gives the title as *Shu-shu ta lüeh* ("Outline of Mathematical Methods"). During the thirteenth century this treatise was referred to as the *Shu-shu ta-lüeh* or the *Shu-hsüeh ta-lüeh* ("Outline of Mathematics"), while during the Ming period (1368–1644) it was known under the names *Shu-shu chiu-chang* and *Shu-hsüeh chiu-chang*. This has led Sarton to conclude that the *Shu-shu chiu-chang* and the *Shu-hsüeh ta-lüeh* were separate works. The treatise is now popularly known as the *Shu-shu chiu-chang*.

It appears that the *Shu-shu chiu-chang* existed only in manuscript form for several centuries. It was copied and included in the great early fifteenth-century encyclopedia *Yung-lo ta-tien* under the title *Shu-hsüeh chiu-chang*. This version was revised and included in the seventeenth-century imperial collection *Ssu-k'u ch'üan-shu*, and later a commentary was added to it by the Ch'ing mathematician Li Jui. There was also a handwritten copy of the *Shu-shu chiu-chang* during the early seventeenth century. A copy from the text belonging to the Wen-yüan k'o library was first made by Wang Ying-lin. And in 1616 Chao Ch'i-mei wrote that he had made a copy of the text that he borrowed from Wang Ying-lin and had added a new table of contents to it. Toward the beginning of the nineteenth century this handwritten copy came into the possession of the mathematician Chang Tun-jen and attracted much attention during the time when interest in traditional Chinese mathematics was revived. Many copies were reproduced from the text owned by Chang Tun-jen. It seems that blocks were also made for the printing of the book, but it is not certain whether it was actually printed. Also in the early nineteenth century Shen Ch'in-p'ei began to make a textual collation of the *Shu-shu chiu-chang*, but he died before his work was finished. One of his disciples, Sung Ching-ch'ang, completed it; and the result appeared in the *Shu-shu chiu-chang cha-chi* ("Notes on the Mathematical Treatise in Nine Sections"). In 1842 both the *Shu-shu chiu-chang* and the *Shu-shu chiu-chang cha-chi* were published and included in the *I-chia-t'ang ts'ung shu* collection. Later editions of both these books, such as those included in the *Ku-chin suan-hsüeh ts'ung shu*, the *Kuo-hsüeh chi-pen ts'ung shu*, and the *Ts'ung shu chi-ch'eng* collections, are based on the version in the *I-chia-t'ang ts'ung-shu* collection.

Each of the nine sections in the *Shu-shu chiu-chang* includes two chapters made up of nine problems. These sections do not correspond in any way to the nine sections of the *Chiu-chang suan-shu* of Liu Hui. They consist of (1) *ta yen ch'iu i shu*, or indeterminate analysis; (2) *t'ien shih*, which involves astronomical, calendrical, and meteorological calculations; (3) *t'ien yü*, or land measurement; (4) *ts'e wang*, referring to surveying by the method of triangulation; (5) *fu i*, or land tax and state service; (6) *ch'ien ku*, or money and grains; (7) *ying chien*, or structural works; (8) *chün lü*, or military matters; and (9) *shih wu*, dealing with barter and purchase. The complete text has not yet been translated or investigated in full, although some individual problems have been studied.

With Ch'in's *Shu-shu chiu-chang* the study of indeterminate analysis in China reached its height. It had first appeared in Chinese mathematical texts about the fourth century in a problem in the *Sun-tzu suan ching*:

> There is an unknown number of things. When counted in threes, they leave a remainder of two; when counted by fives, they leave a remainder of three; and when counted by sevens, they leave a remainder of two. Find the number of things.

The problem can be expressed in the modern form

$$N \equiv 2 \pmod 3) \equiv 3 \pmod 5) \equiv 2 \pmod 7),$$

where the least integer for N is required. The *Sun-tzu suan ching* gives the following solution:

$$N = 2 \times 70 + 3 \times 21 + 2 \times 15 - 2 \times 105 = 23.$$

There is no explanation of the mathematical method in general, but the algorithmical procedure is given as follows:

> If you count by threes and have the remainder 2, put 140.
>
> If you count by fives and have the remainder 3, put 63.
>
> If you count by sevens and have the remainder 2, put 30.
>
> Add these numbers, and you get 233.
>
> From this subtract 210, and you have the result.

A brief explanation of the procedure follows:

> For each 1 as a remainder, when counting by threes, put 70.
>
> For each 1 as a remainder, when counting by fives, put 21.
>
> For each 1 as a remainder, when counting by sevens, put 15.
>
> If the sum is 106 or more, subtract 105 from it, and you have the result.

(The number 105 to be subtracted is, of course, de-

CH'IN CHIU-SHAO

rived from the product of 3, 5, and 7.)

The next example of indeterminate problem appeared in that of the "hundred fowls," found in the fifth-century mathematical manual *Chang Ch'iu-chien suan ching.* It gives three different possible answers but no general solution. Since it is in the form of two simultaneous linear equations of three unknowns, i.e.,

$$ax + by + cz = 100$$
$$a'x + b'y + c'z = 100,$$

this problem is not of the same nature as that given in the *Sun-tzu suan ching.*

As early as the middle of the third century, Chinese calendar experts had taken as their starting point a certain date and time in the past known as the Grand Cycle (*Shang yuan*), which was the last time that the winter solstice fell exactly at midnight on the first day of the eleventh month, which also happened to be the first day (*chia-tzu,* cyclical day) of a sixty-day cycle. If a denotes the tropical year, R_1 the cyclical-day number of the winter solstice (i.e., the number of days in the sixty-day cycle between winter solstice and the last *chia-tzu* preceding it), b the synodic month, and R_2 the number of days between the first day of the eleventh month and the winter solstice, then N, the number of years since the Grand Cycle, can be found from the expression

$$aN \equiv R_1 \pmod{60} \equiv R_2 \pmod{b}.$$

For several hundred years, calendar experts in China had been working out the Grand Cycle from new astronomical data as it became available. None, however, has passed on the method of computation. The earliest elucidation of the method available to us comes from Ch'in Chiu-shao. Problem 12 in his *Shu-shu chiu-chang* deals exactly with the above and may be stated in the modern form

$$6{,}172{,}608\, N \equiv 193{,}440 \pmod{60 \times 16{,}900}$$
$$\equiv 16{,}377 \pmod{499{,}067},$$

taking $a = 365\frac{4{,}108}{16{,}900}$ days

$$b = 29\frac{8{,}967}{16{,}900} \text{ days.}$$

Ch'in's method of solving indeterminate analysis may be explained in the modern form as follows: Given $N \equiv R_1 \pmod{a_1} \equiv R_2 \pmod{a_2} \equiv R_3 \pmod{a_3} \equiv \cdots \equiv R_n \pmod{a_n}$ where $a_1, a_2, a_3, \cdots, a_n$ have no common factors.

If $k_1, k_2, k_3, \cdots k_n$ are factors such that

$$k_1 a_2 a_3 \cdots a_n \equiv 1 \pmod{a_1}$$
$$k_2 a_3 \cdots a_n a_1 \equiv 1 \pmod{a_2}$$
$$k_3 a_1 a_2 a_4 \cdots a_n \equiv 1 \pmod{a_3}, \text{ and}$$
$$k_n a_1 a_2 a_3 \cdots a_{n-1} \equiv 1 \pmod{a_n},$$

then $N \equiv (R_1 k_1 a_2 a_3 \cdots a_n) + (R_2 k_2 a_3 \cdots a_n a_1) + (R_3 k_3 a_1 a_2 a_4 \cdots a_n) + \cdots + (R_n k_n a_1 a_2 a_3 \cdots a_{n-1}) \pmod{a_1 a_2 a_3 \cdots a_n}$,

or, putting it more generally,

$$N \equiv \sum_1^n R_i k_i \frac{M}{a_i} - pM$$

where $M = a_1 a_2 a_3 \cdots a_i$, i.e., the least common multiple and p is the integer that yields the lowest value for N.

The rule is given in a German manuscript from Göttingen (*ca.* 1550), but it was not rediscovered in Europe before Lebesque (1859) and Stieltjes (1890). The identity of the Chinese rule with Gauss's formula has also been pointed out by Matthiessen in the last century, after Ch'in's study of indeterminate analysis was first brought to the attention of the West by Alexander Wylie.

The *Shu-shu chiu-chang* also deals with numbers which have common factors among them, in other words the more general form

$$N \equiv R_i \pmod{A_i}$$

where $i = 1, 2, 3, \cdots, n$ and where A_i has common factors with A_j, A_k, and so on.

The method involves choosing $A_1, A_2, \cdots, A_n$, which are relative primes in pairs such that each A_i divides the corresponding a_i and that further the *LCM* of $A_1, A_2, \cdots, A_n$ equals that of $a_1 a_2 \cdots a_n$. Then every solution of

$$N \equiv R_1 \pmod{A_1} \equiv R_2 \pmod{A_2}$$
$$\equiv \cdots \equiv R_n \pmod{A_n}$$

also satisfies

$$N \equiv R_1 \pmod{a_1} \equiv R_2 \pmod{a_2}$$
$$\equiv \cdots \equiv R_n \pmod{a_n}.$$

The above is valid only under the condition that each difference $R_i - R_j$ is divisible by d, the *GCD* of the corresponding moduli Ai and Aj, i.e., $R_i - R_j = 0 \pmod{d}$. The Chinese text does not mention this condition, but it is fulfilled in all the examples given by Ch'in Chiu-shao. Ch'in would go about searching for the least integral value of a multiple k_i such that

$$k_i \frac{M}{a_i} \equiv 1 \pmod{a_i}.$$

This is an important intermediate stage in the process of solving problems of indeterminate analysis; hence

CH'IN CHIU-SHAO

the Chinese term *ch'iu i shu* ("method of searching for unity") for indeterminate analysis. Over time the process became known as the *ta yen ch'iu i shu* ("the Great Extension method of searching for unity"). The term *ta yen* ("Great Extension") came from an obscure statement in the *Book of Changes.* In an ancient method of divination, fifty yarrow stalks were taken, and one was set aside before the remaining forty-nine were divided into two random heaps. The *Book of Changes* then says:

> The numbers of the Great Extension [multiplied together] make fifty, of which [only] forty-nine are used [in divination]. [The stalks representing these] are divided into two heaps to represent the two [emblematic lines, or heaven and earth] and placed [between the little finger and ring finger of the left hand], that there may thus be symbolized the three [powers of heaven, earth, and man]. [The heaps on both sides] are manipulated by fours to represent the four seasons. . . .

Ch'in sought to explain the term *ta yen ch'iu i shu* in the first problem of his book by introducing the so-called "Great Extension number" 50 and the number 49 and showing how they could be arrived at from the numbers 1, 2, 3, and 4—as mentioned above.

Since Ch'in also introduced many technical terms used in conjunction with indeterminate analysis, it will be worthwhile to follow, step by step, the actual process he used in working out the problem that may be expressed as $N \equiv 1 \pmod 1) \equiv 1 \pmod 2) \equiv 1 \pmod{3} \equiv 1 \pmod 4$.

Ch'in first arranged the given numbers 1, 2, 3, and 4, known as *yuan-shu* ("original number"), in a vertical column. He placed the number 1 to the left of each of these numbers, as in Fig. 1.

Celestial Monads	Original Numbers	Operation Numbers	Original Numbers
1	1	24	1
1	2	12	2
1	3	8	3
1	4	6	4

FIGURE 1 FIGURE 2

This he called the *t'ien-yuan* ("celestial monad" or "celestial element"). Next, he cross-multiplied each celestial monad by the original numbers not pertaining to it, thus obtaining the *yen-shu* ("operation numbers"), which were then placed to the left of the corresponding original numbers, as in Fig. 2.

He next removed all the common factors in the original numbers, retaining only one of each. Thus the original numbers became prime to one another and were known by the term *ting-mu* ("definite base numbers"), as in Fig. 3. Each celestial monad was cross-multiplied by the definite base numbers not pertaining to it, giving another set of operation numbers, which were then placed to the left of the corresponding definite base numbers as in Fig. 4.

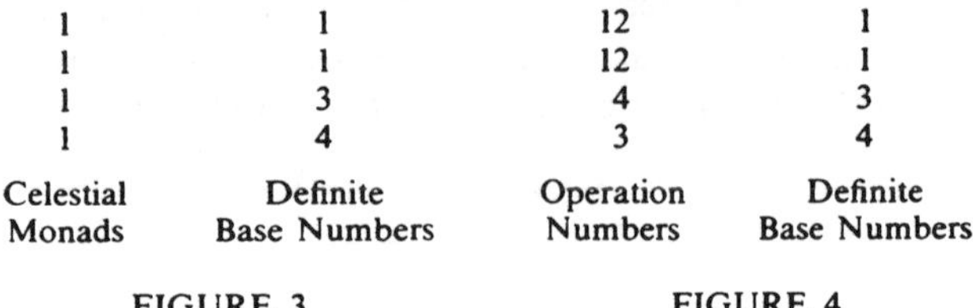

Celestial Monads	Definite Base Numbers	Operation Numbers	Definite Base Numbers
1	1	12	1
1	1	12	1
1	3	4	3
1	4	3	4

FIGURE 3 FIGURE 4

Ch'in then took the definite base numbers as moduli and formed the congruences with their respective operation numbers:

$$12 \equiv 1 \pmod 1$$
$$12 \equiv 1 \pmod 1$$
$$4 \equiv 1 \pmod 3$$
$$3 \equiv 3 \pmod 4.$$

For the residues (*ch'i shu*) that were unity, the corresponding multipliers (*ch'eng lü*) were taken as unity. A residue that was not unity was placed in the upper-right space on the counting board, with the corresponding definite base number below it. To the left of this residue Ch'in placed unity as the celestial monad, as in Fig. 5.

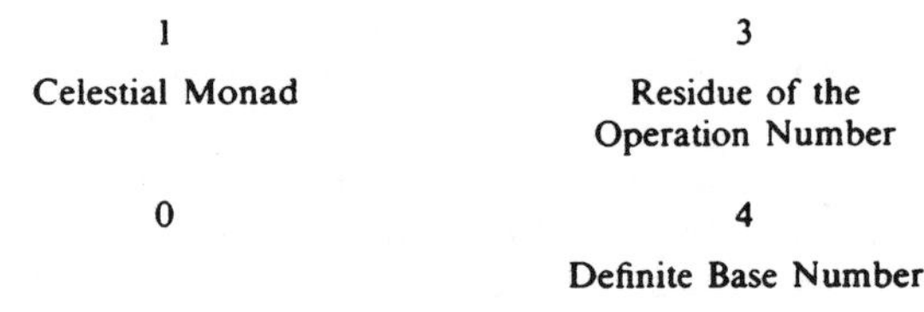

FIGURE 5

Dividing the definite base number by the residue yielded unity in this case. Ch'in next multiplied the celestial monad by unity and placed the result (in this case, also unity) at the bottom left. This he called the *kuei-shu* ("reduced number"). The space for the definite base number was then filled by the residue of the base number, as shown in Fig. 6.

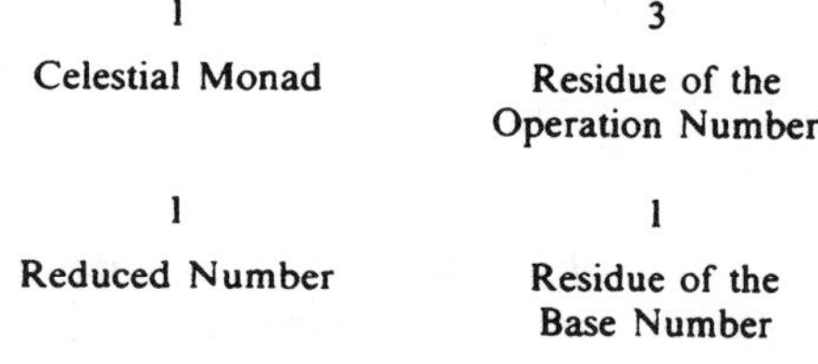

FIGURE 6

Next the residue of the operation number in the upper right-hand corner was divided by the residue of the base number so that a quotient could be found

CH'IN CHIU-SHAO

to give a remainder of unity. If a quotient could not be found, then the process had to be repeated, taking the number in the lower right-hand corner and that in the upper right-hand corner alternately until such a quotient was found. In this case, however, a quotient of 2 would give a remainder of unity, as in Fig. 7.

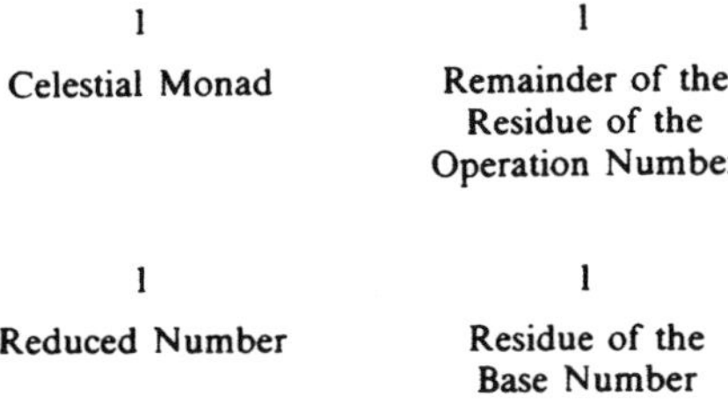

FIGURE 7

Multiplying the quotient of 2 by the reduced number and adding the result to the celestial monad gave 3, the corresponding multiplier, as in Fig. 8.

3	1
Multiplier	Remainder of the Residue of the Operation Number
1	1
Reduced Number	Residue of the Base Number

FIGURE 8

Having found all the multipliers, Ch'in then arranged them side by side with their operation numbers and definite base numbers, as in Fig. 9.

Multipliers	Operation Numbers	Definite Base Numbers
1	12	1
1	12	1
1	4	3
3	3	4

FIGURE 9

Then he multiplied the operation numbers by their corresponding multipliers and found the so-called "reduced use numbers" (*fan-yung-shu*). These were placed to the left of the corresponding definite base numbers, as in Fig. 10.

Reduced Use Numbers	Definite Base Numbers
12	1
12	1
4	3
9	4

FIGURE 10

The operation modulus (*yen-mu*), or the least common multiple, was obtained by multiplying all the definite base numbers together. If common factors had been removed, they had to be restored at this stage. The products of these factors and the corresponding definite base numbers and the reduced use numbers were restored to their original numbers, and the reduced use numbers became the definite use numbers (*ting-yung-shu*), as shown in Fig. 11.

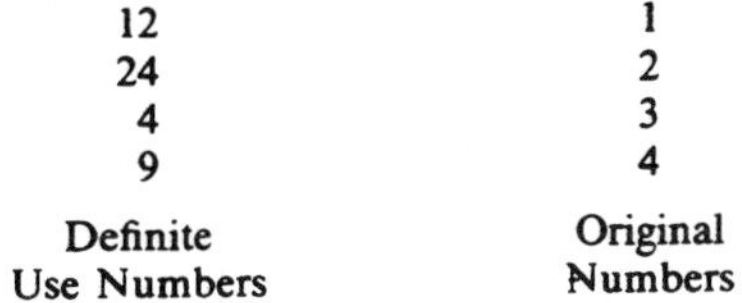

Definite Use Numbers	Original Numbers
12	1
24	2
4	3
9	4

FIGURE 11

In this particular problem Ch'in tried to explain that the sum of the operation numbers amounted to 50, while that of the definite use numbers came to 49. The former is the *ta yen* number, and the latter is the number that was put into use as stated in the *Book of Changes.* To obtain N, the definite use numbers were multiplied by the respective remainders given in the problem. Their sum, after it had been diminished repeatedly by the least common factor, would ultimately give the required answer.

A list of the technical terms used by Ch'in for indeterminate analysis is given in Fig. 12.

It should be pointed out that Ch'in's use of the celestial monad or celestial element (*t'ien-yuan*) differs from the method of celestial element (*t'ien-yuan-shu*) that was employed by his contemporary Li Chih and that later was known in Japan as the *tengen jutsu.* In the former, the celestial element denotes a known number, while in the latter it represents an unknown algebraic quantity.

Ch'in represented algebraic equations by placing calculating rods on the countingboard so that the absolute term appeared on the top in a vertical column; immediately below it was the unknown quantity, followed by increasing powers of the unknown quantity. Originally, Ch'in used red and black counting rods to denote positive and negative quantities, respectively; but in the text, negative quantities are denoted by an extra rod placed obliquely over the first figure of the number concerned. The *Shu-shu chiu-chang* also is the oldest extant Chinese mathematical text to contain the zero symbol. For example, the equation $-x^4 + 763{,}200x^2 - 40{,}642{,}560{,}000 = 0$ is represented by calculating rods placed on a countingboard as in Fig. 13, and can be expressed in Arabic numerals as in Fig. 14.

No.	Chinese Term	Translation		Modern Equivalent
		After Mikami	After Needham	
1.	*wen shu* *yuan-shu*	original number		A_i
2.	*ting-mu*	definite base number	fixed denominator	a_i
3.	*yen-mu*	operation modulus	multiple denominator	M
4.	*yen-shu*	operation number	multiple number	$\frac{M}{a_i}$
5.	*ch'eng lü*	multiplier	multiplying term	k_i
6.	*yu shu*			R_i
7.	*fan-yung-shu*	reduced use number		$\frac{k_iM}{a_i}$
8.	*ting-yung-shu*	definite use number		$\frac{k_iM}{a_i}\frac{A_i}{a_i}$
9.	*yung shu*		use number	either (7) or (8), depending on context
10.	*tsung teng*			$\frac{k_iM}{a_i} \cdot R_i$
11.	*tsung shu*			$\Sigma k_i \frac{M}{a_i} R_i$
12.	*ch'i shu*			$\frac{M}{a_i} - q_i a_i$
13.	*kuei shu*	reduced number		
14.	*t'ien-yuan*	celestial monad		

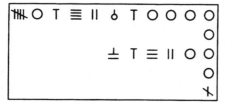

FIGURE 12

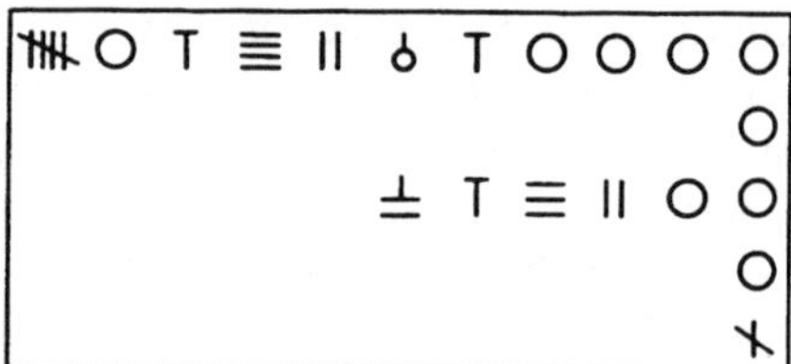

FIGURE 13

```
– 4 0 6 4 2 5 6 0 0 0 0
                      0
            7 6 3 2 0 0
                      0
                    – 1
```

FIGURE 14

More than twenty problems in the *Shu-shu chiu-chang* involve the setting up of numerical equations. Some examples are given below.

$$4.608x^3 - 3{,}000{,}000{,}000 \times 30 \times 800 = 0$$

$$-x^4 + 15{,}245x^2 - 6{,}262{,}506.25 = 0$$

$$-x^4 + 1{,}534{,}464x^2 - 526{,}727{,}577{,}600 = 0$$

$$400x^4 - 2{,}930{,}000 = 0$$

$$x^{10} + 15x^8 + 72x^6 - 864x^4 - 11{,}664x^2 - 34{,}992 = 0$$

Ch'in always arranged his equations so that the absolute term was negative. Sarton has pointed out that this is equivalent to Thomas Harriot's practice (1631) of writing algebraic equations so that the absolute term would stand alone in one member. Ch'in used a method called the *ling lung k'ai fang,* generally known by the translation "harmoniously alternating evolution," by which he could solve numerical equations of any degree. The method is identical to that rediscovered by Paolo Ruffini about 1805 and by William George Horner in 1819. It is doubtful that Ch'in was the originator of this method of solving numerical equations of higher degrees, since his contemporary Li Chih was also capable of solving similar equations, and some two decades later Yang Hui also described a similar method without mentioning Ch'in or Li, referring instead to several Chinese mathematicians of the twelfth century. Wang Ling and Joseph Needham have indicated that if the text of the *Chiu-chang suan-ching* (first century) is very carefully followed, the essentials of the method are there.

In the *Shu-shu chiu-chang* various values for π are used. In one place we find the old value $\pi = 3$, in another we come across what Ch'in called the "accurate value" $\pi = 22/7$, and in yet another instance

CH'IN CHIU-SHAO

the value $\pi = \sqrt{10}$ is given. This last value was first mentioned by Chang Heng in the second century.

Formulas giving the areas of various types of geometrical figures are also mentioned in the *Shu-shu chiu-chang*, although some of them are not very accurate. The area, A, of a scalene triangle with sides a, b, and c is obtained from the expression

$$A^4 - \frac{1}{4}\left\{a^2c^2 - \left(\frac{c^2 + a^2 - b^2}{2}\right)^2\right\} = 0.$$

That is,

$$A = \sqrt[4]{\frac{1}{4}\left\{a^2c^2 - \left(\frac{c^2 + a^2 - b^2}{2}\right)^2\right\}} = \sqrt{s(s-a)(s-b)(s-c)},$$

where $$s = \frac{1}{2}(a + b + c).$$

The area, A, of a quadrangle with two pairs of equal sides, a and b, with c the diagonal dividing the figure into two isosceles triangles (see Fig. 15) is given by

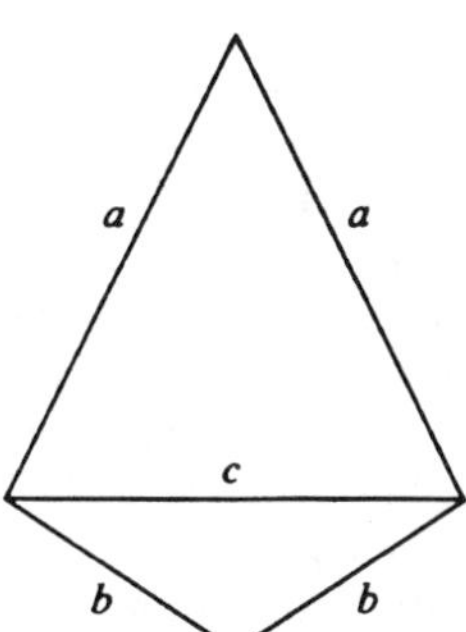

FIGURE 15

the expression

$$-A^4 + 2(X + Y)A^2 - (Y - X)^2 = 0,$$

where $$X = \left\{b^2 - \left(\frac{c}{2}\right)^2\right\}\left(\frac{c}{2}\right)^2$$

and $$Y = \left\{a^2 - \left(\frac{c}{2}\right)^2\right\}\left(\frac{c}{2}\right)^2.$$

The area, A, of a so-called "banana-leaf-shaped" farm (see Fig. 16) formed by two equal circular arcs with

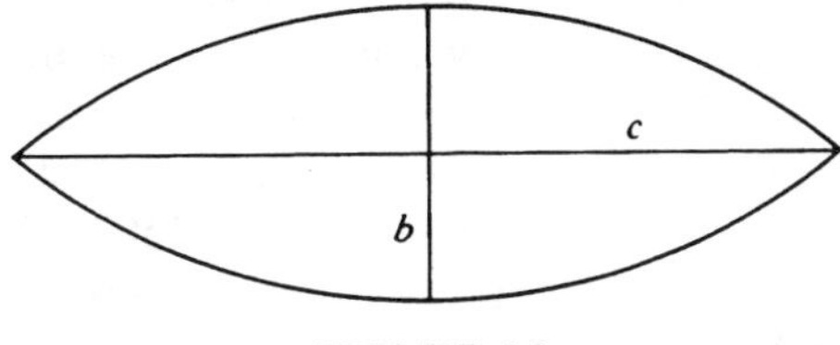

FIGURE 16

a common chord, c, and a common sagitta, b, is incorrectly given by the expression

$$(2A)^2 + 2A\left\{\left(\frac{c}{2}\right)^2 - \left(\frac{b}{2}\right)^2\right\} - 10(c + b)^3 = 0.$$

This formula is put in another form by Mikami but has been wrongly represented by Li Yen. An earlier expression for the area of a segment (Fig. 17) given

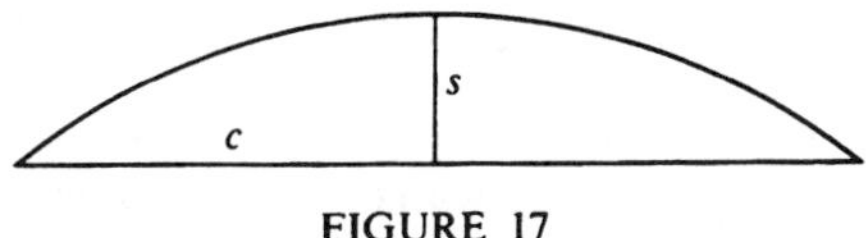

FIGURE 17

the chord, c, and the arc sagitta, s, is given in the *Chiu-chang suan-shu* in the form

$$A = \frac{1}{2}s(s + c).$$

This has been in use in China for 1,000 years. Ch'in's formula is a departure from the above, but it is not known how he arrived at it. In 1261 another formula was given by Yang Hui in the form

$$-(2A)^2 + 4Ab^2 + 4db^3 - 5b^4 = 0,$$

where d is the diameter of the circle.

Sometimes Ch'in made his process unusually complicated. For example, a problem in chapter 8 says:

> Given a circular walled city of unknown diameter with four gates, one at each of the four cardinal points. A tree lies three *li* north of the northern gate. If one turns and walks eastward for nine *li* immediately leaving the southern gate, the tree becomes just visible. Find the circumference and the diameter of the city wall.

If x is the diameter of the circular wall, c the distance of the tree from the northern gate, and b the distance to be traveled eastward from the southern gate before the tree becomes visible (as shown in Fig.

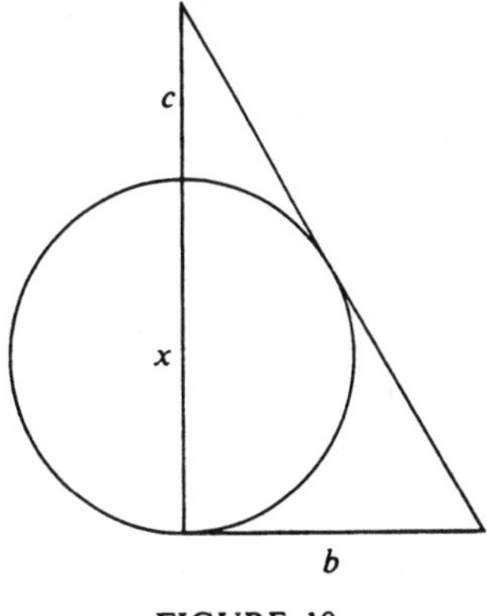

FIGURE 18

18), then Ch'in obtains the diameter from the following equation of the tenth degree:

$$y^{10} + 5cy^8 + 8c^2y^6 - 4c(b^2 - c^2)y^4 - 16c^2b^2y^2 - 16c^3b^3 = 0,$$

where $x = y^2$.

It is interesting to compare this with an equivalent but simpler expression given by Ch'in's contemporary Li Chih in the form

$$x^3 + cx^2 - 4cb^2 = 0.$$

In one of the problems in chapter 4, Ch'in intends to find the height of rainwater that would be collected on the level ground when the rain gauge is a basin with a larger diameter at the opening than at the base. The diameters of the opening and the base, a and b; the height, h, of rainwater collected in the basin; and the height, H, of the basin are given. The height of rain collected on level ground, h', is given by the formula $h' =$

$$\frac{h\{Hb[Hb + (a - b)h] + H^2b^2 + [Hb + (a - b)h]^2\}}{3(aH)^2}.$$

The *Shu-shu chiu-chang* also concerns itself with series, such as

$$\sum_1^n (a + \overline{n - 1}\, b) = na + \frac{n(n + 1)}{2}b$$

and

$$\sum_1^n n = \frac{(2m - 1)2m}{2},$$

where

$$m = \frac{n + 1}{2}.$$

One of the problems in chapter 13 deals with finite difference, a subject that had attracted considerable attention from Chinese mathematicians and calendar makers.

Linear simultaneous equations are also discussed in Ch'in's book. The numbers are set up in vertical columns. For example, the simultaneous equations

(1) $140x + 88y + 15z = 58{,}800$
(2) $792x + 568y + 815z = 392{,}000$
(3) $64x + 30y + 75z = 29{,}400$

are set up on the countingboard as follows:

29,400	392,000	58,800
64	792	140
30	568	88
75	815	15

These equations are solved by first eliminating z in equations (1) and (3), and then in (2) and (3). From these x and y are obtained. Finally z is found by substituting the values of x and y in equation (3).

Ch'ien Pao-tsung has pointed out that from the *Shu-shu chiu-chang* one can gather much information on the sociological problems in thirteenth-century China, from finance and commerce to the levy of taxes. The book gives information not only on the merchandise imported from overseas but also on the use of the rain gauge by the Sung government, which was greatly concerned with rainfall because of the importance of agriculture.

BIBLIOGRAPHY

Further information on Ch'in Chiu-shao and his work may be found in Ch'ien Pao-tsung, *Ku-suan kao-yüan* ("Origin of Ancient Chinese Mathematics") (Shanghai, 1935) pp. 7, 43–66; and *Chung-kuo shu-hsüeh-shih* ("History of Chinese Mathematics") (Peking, 1964) pp. 157–167, 206–209; Ch'ien Pao-tsung *et al., Sung Yuan shu-hsüeh-shih lun-wên-chi* ("Collected Essays on Sung and Yuan Chinese Mathematics") (Peking, 1966) pp. 60–103; Hsü Shun-fang, *Chung-suan-chia ti tai-shu-hsüeh yen-chiu* ("Study of Algebra by Chinese Mathematicians") (Peking, 1951) pp. 16–21; Li Yen, *Chung-kuo shu-hsüeh ta-kang* ("Outline of Chinese Mathematics") I (Shanghai, 1931) 117–136, and *Chung-kuo suan-hsüeh-shih* ("History of Chinese Mathematics") (Shanghai, 1937; repr. 1955) pp. 98-99, 128–132; Li Yen and Tu Shih-jan, *Chung-kuo ku-tai shu-hsüeh chien-shih* ("A Short History of Ancient Chinese Mathematics") I (Peking, 1963) II (Peking, 1964) 49–151, 210–216; Yoshio Mikami, *The Development of Mathematics in China and Japan* (Leipzig, 1913; repr. New York) pp. 63–78; Joseph Needham, *Science and Civilisation in China,* III (Cambridge, 1959) 40–45, 119–122, 472, 577–578; George Sarton, *Introduction to the History of Science,* III (Baltimore, 1947) 626–627; D. E. Smith and Yoshio Mikami, *A History of Japanese Mathematics* (Chicago, 1914) pp. 48–50, 63; and Alexander Wylie, *Chinese Researches* (Shanghai, 1897; repr. Peking, 1936; Taipei, 1966) pp. 175–180.

HO PENG-YOKE

CHRISTMANN, JACOB (*b.* Johannesberg, Rheingau, Germany, November 1554; *d.* Heidelberg, Germany, 16 June 1613)

Christmann studied oriental subjects at Heidelberg and became a teacher there in 1580. Shortly thereafter, however, he had to leave that university because he, as a Calvinist, could not subscribe to the concordat-formulary set down by the Lutheran Elector Ludwig VI. Christmann traveled for some time, then settled down to teach in a Reformed school in Neustadt, Pfalz. He was a teacher there in 1582. The death of Ludwig (12 October 1583) enabled him to return to Heidelberg, where he was appointed professor of Hebrew on 18 June 1584. From 1591 on he taught Aristotelian logic. He was made rector of the university in 1602.

In 1608 Frederick IV appointed Christmann professor of Arabic. Christmann thus became the second teacher of that subject in Europe, the first having been Guillaume Postel at Paris in 1538. This appointment must have given great satisfaction to its recipient, since in 1590, in the preface of his *Alfragani chronologica et astronomica elementa,* Christmann had advocated the establishment of a chair of Arabic "to open possibilities for teaching philosophy and medicine from the [original] sources." Indeed, Christmann had demonstrated his scholarly interest in the Arabic language as early as 1582, with the publication of his *Alphabeticum Arabicum,* a small book of rules for reading and writing Arabic. Besides Arabic, he is said to have known Syrian, Chaldaic, Greek, Latin, French, Italian, and Spanish. He was an extremely modest man despite his learning, with a passion for work that may well have hastened his death of jaundice.

On the death of Valentine Otho, Christmann inherited the entire library of G. J. Rhäticus, which had been in Otho's keeping. This collection contained trigonometric tables more extensive than those that Rhäticus had published in the *Opus Palatinum* of 1596 (adapted by B. Pitiscus as the basis for his *Thesaurus mathematicus* of 1613) as well as the original manuscript of Copernicus' *De revolutionibus orbium coelestium.* The inclusion of instruments in the bequest stimulated Christmann to begin making astronomical observations. In 1604 he proposed to Kepler that they should exchange the results of their researches. Christmann was the first to use the telescope in conjunction with such instruments as the sextant or Jacob's staff (1611), with the results reported in his *Theoria lunae* and *Nodus gordius.* These last works also show him to be a competent astronomical theorist. He gave a good treatment of prosthaphaeresis, the best method of calculating trigonometric tables to be developed before the invention of logarithms, which he based on such formulas as

$$2 \sin \alpha \sin \beta = \cos (\alpha - \beta) - \cos (\alpha + \beta);$$

he then went on to prove that this method had been devised by Johann Werner.

In his *Tractatio geometrica de quadratura circuli,* Christmann defended against J. J. Scaliger the thesis that the quadrature of the circle could be solved only approximately. In his books on chronology—a topic of great concern at a time of radical calendar reform—he disputed the work of not only Scaliger but also J. J. Lipsius. He further criticized Copernicus, Tycho Brahe, and Clavius—some such criticisms may be found in some detail in manuscript annotations of his own copy of *Alfragani chronologica et astronomica elementa,* which is now in the library of the University of Utrecht.

BIBLIOGRAPHY

I. Original Works. Christmann's works are *Alphabetum Arabicum cum isagoge scribendi legendique Arabice* (Neustadt, 1582); *Epistola chronologica ad Iustum Lipsium, qua constans annorum Hebraeorum connexio demonstratur* (Heidelberg, 1591; Frankfurt, 1593); *Disputatio de anno, mense, et die passionis Dominicae* (Frankfurt, 1593, combined with the 2nd ed. of *Epistola*); *Tractatio geometrica, de quadratura circuli* (Frankfurt, 1595); *Observationum solarium libri tres* (Basel, 1601); *Theŏriae lunae ex novis hypothesibus et observationibus demonstrata* (Heidelberg, 1611); and *Nodus gordius ex doctrina sinuum explicatus, accedit appendix observationum* (Heidelberg, 1612).

He translated from a Hebrew translation and commented on *Muhamedis Alfragani Arabis chronologica et astronomica elementa, additus est commentarius, qui rationem calendarii Romani . . . explicat* (Frankfurt, 1590, 1618) and translated and commented on *Uri ben Simeon, calendarium Palaestinorum* (Frankfurt, 1594). He edited, with translation and comments, *Is. Argyri computus Graecorum de solennitate Paschatis celebranda* (Heidelberg, *ca.* 1612).

II. Secondary Literature. On Christmann's life, see Melchior Adam, *Vitae Germanorum philosophorum* (Heidelberg, 1615), pp. 518–522; on his Arabic studies, Johann Fück, *Die arabischen Studien in Europa* (Leipzig, 1955), pp. 44–46; on his instruments, H. Ludendorff, "Über die erste Verbindung des Fernrohres mit astronomischen Messinstrumenten," in *Astronomische Nachrichten,* **213** (1921), cols. 385–390; on the prosthaphaeresis, A. von Braunmühl, *Vorlesungen über Geschichte der Trigonometrie,* I (Leipzig, 1900), see index. See also Daniël Miverius, *Apologia pro Philippo Lansbergio ad Jacobum Christmannum* (Middelburg, 1602); and J. Kepler, *Gesammelte Werke* (Munich, 1949–1954), esp. II (1939), 14–16—XV (1951), 41 f., gives a letter from Christmann to Kepler, dated 11 April 1604 (old style).

J. J. Verdonk

CHRISTOFFEL, ELWIN BRUNO (*b.* Montjoie [now Monschau], near Aachen, Germany, 10 November 1829; *d.* Strasbourg, France [then Germany], 15 March 1900)

Christoffel studied at the University of Berlin, where he received his doctorate in 1856 with a dissertation on the motion of electricity in homogeneous bodies. He continued his studies in Montjoie. In 1859 he became lecturer at the University of Berlin, in 1862 professor at the Polytechnicum in Zurich, and in 1869 professor at the Gewerbsakademie in Berlin. In 1872 he accepted the position of professor at the University of Strasbourg, newly founded after its acquisition by the Germans. Here he lectured until 1892, when his health began to deteriorate.

Christoffel has been praised not only as a very conscientious mathematician but also as a conscientious teacher. Politically he represented the traditional Prussian academician loyal to emperor and army. This may have contributed to his choice of Strasbourg and his endeavor to create a great German university in that city.

Scientifically, Christoffel was primarily a follower of Dirichlet, his teacher, and of Riemann, especially of the latter. Their ideas inspired his early publications (1867, 1870) on the conformal mapping of a simply connected area bounded by polygons on the area of a circle, as well as the paper of 1880 in which he showed algebraically that the number of linearly independent integrals of the first kind on a Riemann surface is equal to the genus p. The posthumous "Vollständige Theorie der Riemannschen θ-Function" also shows how, rethinking Riemann's work, Christoffel came to an independent approach characteristic of his own way of thinking. Also in the spirit of Riemann is Christoffel's paper of 1877 on the propagation of plane waves in media with a surface of discontinuity, an early contribution to the theory of shock waves.

Another interest of Christoffel's was the theory of invariants. After a first attempt in 1868, he succeeded in 1882 in giving necessary and sufficient conditions for two algebraic forms of order p in n variables to be equivalent. Christoffel transferred these investigations to the problem of the equivalence of two quadratic differential forms, again entering the Riemannian orbit. In what well may be his best-known paper, "Über die Transformation der homogenen Differentialausdrücke zweiten Grades," he introduced the three index symbols

$$\begin{bmatrix} g\,h \\ k \end{bmatrix} \text{ and } \begin{Bmatrix} g\,h \\ k \end{Bmatrix}, k, g, h = 1, 2, \cdots, n,$$

now called Christoffel symbols of the first and second order, and a series of symbols of more than three indices, of which the four index symbols, already introduced by Riemann, are now known as the Riemann-Christoffel symbols, or coordinates of the Riemann-Christoffel curvature tensor. The symbols of an order higher than four are obtained from those of a lower order by a process now known as covariant differentiation. Christoffel's reduction theorem states (in modern terminology) that the differential invariants of order $m \geq 2$ of a quadratic differential form

$$\Sigma a_{ij}(x)\, dx^i\, dx^j$$

are the projective invariants of the tensors a_{ij}, its Riemann-Christoffel tensor, and its covariant derivatives up to order $(m - 2)$. The results of this paper, together with two papers by R. Lipschitz, were later incorporated into the tensor calculus by G. Ricci and T. Levi-Cività.

Christoffel also contributed to the differential geometry of surfaces. In his "Allgemeine Theorie der geodätischen Dreiecke" he presented a trigonometry of triangles formed by geodesics on an arbitrary surface, using the concept of reduced length of a geodesic arc. When the linear element of the surface is $ds^2 = dr^2 + m^2\, dx^2$, m is the reduced length of arc r. In this paper Christoffel already uses the symbols $\begin{Bmatrix} g\,h \\ k \end{Bmatrix}$, but only for the case $n = 2$.

BIBLIOGRAPHY

I. Original Works. Christoffel's writings were brought together as *Gesammelte mathematische Abhandlungen,* L. Maurer, ed., 2 vols. (Leipzig–Berlin, 1910). Among his papers are "Ueber einige allgemeine Eigenschaften der Minimumsflächen," in *Journal für die reine und angewandte Mathematik,* **67** (1867), also in *Gesammelte Abhandlungen,* I, 259–269; "Allgemeine Theorie der geodätischen Dreiecke," in *Abhandlungen der Königlichen Akademie der Wissenschaften zu Berlin* (1868), 119–176, also in *Gesammelte Abhandlungen,* I, 297–346; "Über die Transformation der homogenen Differentialausdrücke zweiten Grades," in *Journal für die reine und angewandte Mathematik,* **70** (1869), 46–70, 241–245, also in *Gesammelte Abhandlungen,* I, 352–377, 378–382; "Ueber die Abbildung einer einblättrigen, einfach zusammenhängenden, ebenen Fläche auf einem Kreise," in *Nachrichten der Königlichen Gesellschaft der Wissenschaften zu Göttingen* (1870), 283–298, see also 359–369, also in *Gesammelte Abhandlungen,* II, 9–18, see also 19–25; "Ueber die Fortpflanzung von Stössen durch elastische feste Körper," in *Annali di matematica,* 2nd ser., **8** (1877), 193–243, also in *Gesammelte Abhandlungen,* II, 81–126; "Algebraischer Beweis des Satzes von der Anzahl der linearunabhangigen Integrale erster Gattung," *ibid.,* **10** (1883), also in *Gesammelte Abhandlungen,* II, 185–203; and "Vollständige Theorie der Riemannschen θ-Function," in *Mathematische Annalen,* **54** (1901), 347–399, also *Gesammelte Abhandlungen,* II, 271–324.

II. Secondary Literature. Christoffel and his work are discussed in C. F. Geiser and L. Maurer, "E. B. Christoffel," in *Mathematische Annalen,* **54** (1901), 328–341; and W. Windelband, *ibid.,* 341–344; there is a bibliography on 344–346. These articles are excerpted in *Gesammelte Abhandlungen,* I, v–xv. The papers by Lipschitz that were incorporated into the tensor calculus are "Untersuchungen in Betreff der ganzen homogenen Functionen von *n* Differentialen," in *Journal für die reine und angewandte Mathematik,* **70** (1869), 71–102; **72** (1870), 1–56; and "Entwickelung einiger Eigenschaften der quadratischen Formen von *n* Differentialen," *ibid.,* **71** (1870), 274–287, 288–295. Beltrami's comment on Christoffel's "Allgemeine Theorie der geodätischen Dreiecke" is in his *Opere matematiche,* 4 vols. (Milan, 1904), II, 63–73.

Mlle. L. Greiner of the Bibliothèque Nationale et Universitaire, Strasbourg, informs me that the *Handschriftlicher Nachlass* mentioned in the *Verzeichniss der hinterlassenen Büchersammlung des Herrn Dr. E. B. Christoffel* (n.p., 1900) is not in this library, contrary to what might be expected from a statement in the Geiser-Maurer article.

D. J. STRUIK

CHRYSTAL, GEORGE (*b.* Mill of Kingoodie, near Old Meldrum, Aberdeenshire, Scotland, 8 March 1851; *d.* Edinburgh, Scotland, 3 November 1911)

Chrystal's father, William, a self-made man, was successively a grain merchant, a farmer, and a landed proprietor. His mother was the daughter of James Burr of Mains of Glack, Aberdeenshire. Chrystal attended the local parish school and later Aberdeen Grammar School, from which he won a scholarship to Aberdeen University in 1867. By the time he graduated in 1871, he had won all the available mathematical distinctions and an open scholarship to Peterhouse, Cambridge. Entering Peterhouse in 1872, Chrystal came under the influence of Clerk Maxwell, and when the Cavendish Laboratory was opened in 1874 he carried out experimental work there. In the mathematical tripos examination of 1875 he was bracketed (with William Burnside) second wrangler and Smith's prizeman and was immediately elected to a fellowship at Corpus Christi College, Cambridge. In 1877 he was appointed to the Regius chair of mathematics in the University of St. Andrews and in 1879 to the chair of mathematics at Edinburgh University; in the same year he married a childhood friend, Margaret Ann Balfour.

Chrystal's thirty-two-year tenure of the Edinburgh chair saw a progressive and substantial rise in the standard of the mathematical syllabus and teaching at the university, especially after the institution of specialized honors degrees by the Universities (Scotland) Act of 1899. The main burden of formulating policies and drafting regulations under the act fell on Chrystal as dean of the Faculty of Arts, an office he held from 1890 until his death. He was an outstanding administrator, with an exceptionally quick grasp of detail, tactful, fair-minded, and forward-looking. He also contributed much to preuniversity education throughout Scotland, acting as inspector of secondary schools, initiating a scheme for a standard school-leaving-certificate examination, and negotiating the transfer of the teacher-training colleges from control by the Presbyterian churches to a new provincial committee, of which he was the first chairman.

Notwithstanding his administrative and teaching burdens, Chrystal found time for scientific work. His wide-ranging textbook on algebra, with its clear, rigorous, and original treatment of such topics as inequalities, limits, convergence, and the use of the complex variable, profoundly influenced mathematical education throughout Great Britain and beyond its borders. He published some seventy articles, about equally divided between scientific biography, mathematics, and physics. Many of the biographies, written for the *Encyclopaedia Britannica,* are still of considerable value. In the mathematical papers his strength lay particularly in lucid exposition and consolidation. Of the physics papers the most important are two long survey articles, "Electricity" and "Magnetism," in the ninth edition of the encyclopaedia, and his later hydrodynamic and experimental investigations of the free oscillations (known as seiches) in lakes, particularly the Scottish lochs, using the results of a recent bathymetric survey.

Chrystal held honorary doctorates from Aberdeen and Glasgow and was awarded a Royal Medal of the Royal Society of London just before his death. He was buried at Foveran, Aberdeenshire, and was survived by four sons and two daughters.

BIBLIOGRAPHY

I. ORIGINAL WORKS. A full list of Chrystal's publications is appended to the obituary notice in *Proceedings of the Royal Society of Edinburgh,* **32** (1911–1912), 477. The following items are important: *Algebra. An Elementary Textbook for the Higher Classes of Secondary Schools and for Colleges,* I (Edinburgh, 1886; 5th ed., London, 1904), II (Edinburgh, 1889; 2nd ed., London, 1900); *Introduction to Algebra for the Use of Secondary Schools and Technical Colleges* (London, 1898; 4th ed., London, 1920); the contributions (mentioned in the text) to the ninth edition of the *Encyclopaedia Britannica;* and the papers on seiches, in *Proceedings of the Royal Society of Edinburgh,* **25** (1904–1905), and *Transactions of the Royal Society of Edinburgh,* **41** (1905), **45** (1906), and **46** (1909).

II. SECONDARY LITERATURE. Besides the obituary notice referred to above, there is an excellent notice in *The Scotsman* (4 Nov. 1911), p. 9. See also A. Logan Turner, ed., *History of the University of Edinburgh 1883–1933* (Edinburgh, 1933), *passim.*

ROBERT SCHLAPP

CHU SHIH-CHIEH (*fl.* China, 1280–1303)

Chu Shih-chieh (literary name, Han-ch'ing; appellation, Sung-t'ing) lived in Yen-shan (near modern Peking). George Sarton describes him, along with Ch'in Chiu-shao, as "one of the greatest mathematicians of his race, of his time, and indeed of all times." However, except for the preface of his mathematical work, the *Ssu-yüan yü-chien* ("Precious Mirror of the Four Elements"), there is no record of his personal life. The preface says that for over twenty years he traveled extensively in China as a renowned mathematician; thereafter he also visited Kuang-ling, where pupils flocked to study under him. We can deduce from this that Chu Shih-chieh flourished as a mathematician and teacher of mathematics during the last two decades of the thirteenth century, a situation possible only after the reunification of China through the Mongol conquest of the Sung dynasty in 1279.

Chu Shih-chieh wrote the *Suan-hsüeh ch'i-meng* ("Introduction to Mathematical Studies") in 1299 and the *Ssu-yüan yü-chien* in 1303. The former was meant essentially as a textbook for beginners, and the latter contained the so-called "method of the four elements" invented by Chu. In the *Ssu-yüan yü-chien,* Chinese algebra reached its peak of development, but this work also marked the end of the golden age of Chinese mathematics, which began with the works of Liu I, Chia Hsien, and others in the eleventh and the twelfth centuries, and continued in the following century with the writings of Ch'in Chiu-shao, Li Chih, Yang Hui, and Chu Shih-chieh himself.

It appears that the *Suan-hsüeh ch'i-meng* was lost for some time in China. However, it and the works of Yang Hui were adopted as textbooks in Korea during the fifteenth century. An edition now preserved in Tokyo is believed to have been printed in 1433 in Korea, during the reign of King Sejo. In Japan a punctuated edition of the book (Chinese texts were then not punctuated), under the title *Sangaku keimo kunten,* appeared in 1658; and an edition annotated by Sanenori Hoshino, entitled *Sangaku keimo chūkai,* was printed in 1672. In 1690 there was an extensive commentary by Katahiro Takebe, entitled *Sangaku keimō genkai,* that ran to seven volumes. Several abridged versions of Takebe's commentary also appeared. The *Suan-hsüeh ch'i-meng* reappeared in China in the nineteenth century, when Lo Shih-lin discovered a 1660 Korean edition of the text in Peking. The book was reprinted in 1839 at Yangchow with a preface by Juan Yuan and a colophon by Lo Shih-lin. Other editions appeared in 1882 and in 1895. It was also included in the *ts'e-hai-shan-fang chung-hsi suan-hsüeh ts'ung-shu* collection. Wang Chien wrote a commentary entitled *Suan-hsüeh ch'i-meng shu i* in 1884 and Hsu Feng-k'ao produced another, *Suan-hsüeh ch'i-meng t'ung-shih,* in 1887.

The *Ssu-yüan yü-chien* also disappeared from China for some time, probably during the later part of the eighteenth century. It was last quoted by Mei Ku-ch'eng in 1761, but it did not appear in the vast imperial library collection, the *Ssu-k'u ch'üan shu,* of 1772; and it was not found by Juan Yuan when he compiled the *Ch'ou-jen chuan* in 1799. In the early part of the nineteenth century, however, Juan Yuan found a copy of the text in Chekiang province and was instrumental in having the book made part of the *Ssu-k'u ch'üan-shu.* He sent a handwritten copy to Li Jui for editing, but Li Jui died before the task was completed. This handwritten copy was subsequently printed by Ho Yüan-shih. The rediscovery of the *Ssu-yüan yü-chien* attracted the attention of many Chinese mathematicians besides Li Jui, Hsü Yu-jen, Lo Shih-lin, and Tai Hsü. A preface to the *Ssu-yüan yü-chien* was written by Shen Ch'in-p'ei in 1829. In his work entitled *Ssu-yüan yü-chien hsi ts'ao* (1834), Lo Shih-lin included the methods of solving the problems after making many changes. Shen Ch'in-p'ei also wrote a so-called *hsi ts'ao* ("detailed workings") for this text, but his work has not been printed and is not as well known as that by Lo Shih-lin. Ting Ch'ü-chung included Lo's *Ssu-yüan yü-chien hsi ts'ao* in his *Pai-fu-t'ang suan hsüeh ts'ung shu* (1876). According to Tu Shih-jan, Li Yen had a complete handwritten copy of Shen's version, which in many respects is far superior to Lo's.

Following the publication of Lo Shih-lin's *Ssu-yüan yü-chien hsi-ts'ao,* the "method of the four elements" began to receive much attention from Chinese mathematicians. I Chih-han wrote the *K'ai-fang shih-li* ("Illustrations of the Method of Root Extraction"), which has since been appended to Lo's work. Li Shan-lan wrote the *Ssu-yüan chieh* ("Explanation of the Four Elements") and included it in his anthology of mathematical texts, the *Tse-ku-shih-chai suan-hsüeh,* first published in Peking in 1867. Wu Chia-shan wrote the *Ssu-yüan ming-shih shih-li* ("Examples Illustrating the Terms and Forms in the Four Elements Method"), the *Ssu-yüan ts'ao* ("Workings in the Four Elements Method"), and the *Ssu-yüan ch'ien-shih* ("Simplified Explanations of the Four Elements Method"), and incorporated them in his *Pai-fu-t'ang suan-hsüeh ch'u chi* (1862). In his *Hsüeh-suan pi-t'an* ("Jottings in the Study of Mathematics"), Hua Heng-fang also discussed the "method of the four elements" in great detail.

A French translation of the *Ssu-yüan yü-chien* was made by L. van Hée. Both George Sarton and Joseph

Needham refer to an English translation of the text by Ch'en Tsai-hsin. Tu Shih-jan reported in 1966 that the manuscript of this work was still in the Institute of the History of the Natural Sciences, Academia Sinica, Peking.

In the *Ssu-yüan yü-chien* the "method of the celestial element" (*t'ien-yuan shu*) was extended for the first time to express four unknown quantities in the same algebraic equation. Thus used, the method became known as the "method of the four elements" (*ssu-yüan shu*)—these four elements were *t'ien* (heaven), *ti* (earth), *jen* (man), and *wu* (things or matter). An epilogue written by Tsu I says that the "method of the celestial element" was first mentioned in Chiang Chou's *I-ku-chi,* Li Wen-i's *Chao-tan,* Shih Hsin-tao's *Ch'ien-ching,* and Liu Yu-chieh's *Ju-chi shih-so,* and that a detailed explanation of the solutions was given by Yuan Hao-wen. Tsu I goes on to say that the "earth element" was first used by Li Te-tsai in his *Liang-i ch'un-ying chi-chen,* while the "man element" was introduced by Liu Ta-chien (literary name, Liu Jun-fu), the author of the *Ch'ien-k'un kua-nang;* it was his friend Chu Shih-chieh, however, who invented the "method of the four elements." Except for Chu Shih-chieh and Yüan Hao-wen, a close friend of Li Chih, we know nothing else about Tsu I and all the mathematicians he lists. None of the books he mentions has survived. It is also significant that none of the three great Chinese mathematicians of the thirteenth century—Ch'in Chiu-shao, Li Chih, and Yang Hui—is mentioned in Chu Shih-chieh's works. It is thought that the "method of the celestial element" was known in China before their time and that Li Chih's *I-ku yen-tuan* was a later but expanded version of Chiang Chou's *I-ku-chi.*

Tsu I also explains the "method of the four elements," as does Mo Jo in his preface to the *Ssu-yüan yü-chien.* Each of the "four elements" represents an unknown quantity—u, v, w, and x, respectively. Heaven (u) is placed below the constant, which is denoted by *t'ai,* so that the power of u increases as it moves downward; earth (v) is placed to the left of the constant so that the power of v increases as it moves toward the left; man (w) is placed to the right of the constant so that the power of w increases as it moves toward the right; and matter (x) is placed above the constant so that the power of x increases as it moves upward. For example, $u + v + w + x = 0$ is represented in Fig. 1.

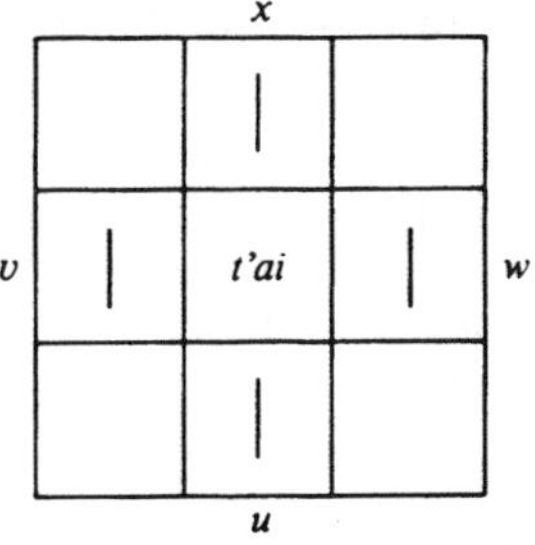

FIGURE 1

Chu Shih-chieh could also represent the products of any two of these unknowns by using the space (on the countingboard) between them rather as it is used in Cartesian geometry. For example, the square of

$$(u + v + w + x) = 0,$$

i.e.,

$$u^2 + v^2 + w^2 + x^2 + 2ux + 2vw + 2vx + 2wx = 0,$$

can be represented as shown in Fig. 2 (below). Obviously, this was as far as Chu Shih-chieh could go, for he was limited by the two-dimensional space of the countingboard. The method cannot be used to represent more than four unknowns or the cross product of more than two unknowns.

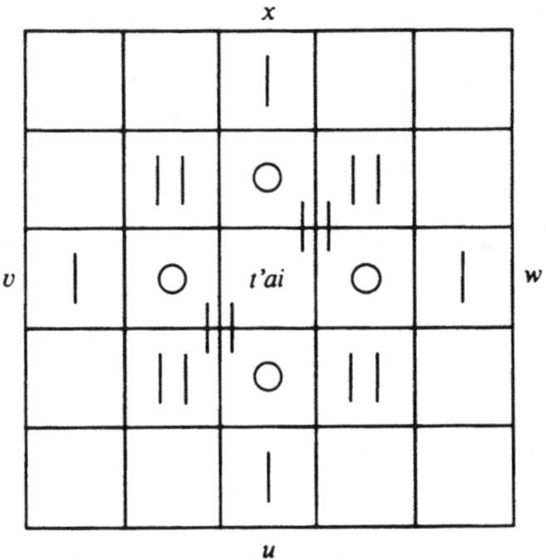

FIGURE 2

Numerical equations of higher degree, even up to the power fourteen, are dealt with in the *Suan-hsüeh ch'i-meng* as well as the *Ssu-yüan yü-chien.* Sometimes a transformation method (*fan fa*) is employed. Although there is no description of this transformation method, Chu Shih-chieh could arrive at the transformation only after having used a method similar to that independently rediscovered in the early nineteenth century by Horner and Ruffini for the solution of cubic equations. Using his method of *fan fa,* Chu Shih-chieh changed the quartic equation

$$x^4 - 1496x^2 - x + 558236 = 0$$

to the form

$$y^4 + 80y^3 + 904y^2 - 27841y - 119816 = 0.$$

Employing Horner's method in finding the first approximate figure, 20, for the root, one can derive the coefficients of the second equation as follows:

1	0	−1496	−1	+558236	20
	20	400	−21920	−438420	
	20	−1096	−21921	119816	
	20	800	−5920		
	40	−296	−27841		
	20	1200			
	60	904			
	20				
	80				

Either Chu Shih-chieh was not very particular about the signs for the coefficients shown in the above example, or there are printer's errors. This can be seen in another example, where the equation $x^2 - 17x - 3120 = 0$ became $y^2 + 103y + 540 = 0$ by the *fan fa* method. In other cases, however, all the signs in the second equations are correct. For example,

$$109x^2 - 2288x - 348432 = 0$$

gives rise to

$$109y^2 + 10792y - 93312 = 0$$

and

$$9x^4 - 2736x^2 - 48x + 207936 = 0$$

gives rise to

$$9y^4 + 360y^3 + 2664y^2 - 18768y + 23856.= 0.$$

Where the root of an equation was not a whole number, Chu Shih-chieh sometimes found the next approximation by using the coefficients obtained after applying Horner's method to find the root. For example, for the equation $x^2 + 252x - 5292 = 0$, the approximate value $x_1 = 19$ was obtained; and, by the method of *fan fa,* the equation $y^2 + 290y - 143 = 0$. Chu Shih-chieh then gave the root as $x = 19(143/1 + 290)$. In the case of the cubic equation $x^3 - 574 = 0$, the equation obtained by the *fan fa* method after finding the first approximate root, $x_1 = 8$, becomes $y^3 + 24y^2 + 192y - 62 = 0$. In this case the root is given as $x = 8(62/1 + 24 + 192) = 8\ 2/7$. The above was not the only method adopted by Chu Shih-chieh in cases where exact roots were not found. Sometimes he would find the next decimal place for the root by continuing the process of root extraction. For example, the answer $x = 19.2$ was obtained in this fashion in the case of the equation

$$135x^2 + 4608x - 138240 = 0.$$

For finding square roots, there are the following examples in the *Ssu-yüan yü-chien:*

$$\sqrt{265} = 16\frac{9}{2 \times 16 + 1} = 16\frac{9}{33}$$

$$\sqrt{74} = 8.6\frac{4}{2 \times 8.6 + 1} = 8.6\frac{4}{17.3}$$

Like Ch'in Chiu-shao, Chu Shih-chieh also employed a method of substitution to give the next approximate number. For example, in solving the equation $-8x^2 + 578x - 3419 = 0$, he let $x = y/8$. Through substitution, the equation became $-y^2 + 578y - 3419 \times 8 = 0$. Hence, $y = 526$ and $x = 526/8 = 65\text{-}3/4$. In another example, $24649x^2 - 1562500 = 0$, letting $x = y/157$, leads to $y^2 - 1562500 = 0$, from which $y = 1250$ and $x = 1250/157 = 7\ 151/157$. Sometimes there is a combination of two of the above-mentioned methods. For example, in the equation $63x^2 - 740x - 432000 = 0$, the root to the nearest whole number, 88, is found by using Horner's method. The equation $63y^2 + 10348y - 9248 = 0$ results when the *fan fa* method is applied. Then, using the substitution method, $y = z/63$ and the equation becomes $z^2 + 10348z - 582624 = 0$, giving $z = 56$ and $y = 56/63 = 7/8$. Hence, $x = 88\ 7/8$.

The *Ssu-yüan yü-chien* begins with a diagram showing the so-called Pascal triangle (shown in modern form in Fig. 3), in which

$$(x + 1)^4 = x^4 + 4x^3 + 6x^2 + 4x + 1.$$

Although the Pascal triangle was used by Yang Hui in the thirteenth century and by Chia Hsien in the twelfth, the diagram drawn by Chu Shih-chieh differs

1
1 1
1 2 1
1 3 3 1
1 4 6 4 1
1 5 10 10 5 1

FIGURE 3

from those of his predecessors by having parallel oblique lines drawn across the numbers. On top of the triangle are the words *pen chi* ("the absolute term"). Along the left side of the triangle are the values of the absolute terms for $(x + 1)^n$ from $n = 1$

CHU SHIH-CHIEH

to $n = 8$, while along the right side of the triangle are the values of the coefficient of the highest power of x. To the left, away from the top of the triangle, is the explanation that the numbers in the triangle should be used horizontally when $(x + 1)$ is to be raised to the power n. Opposite this is an explanation that the numbers inside the triangle give the *lien,* i.e., all coefficients of x from x^2 to x^{n-1}. Below the triangle are the technical terms of all the coefficients in the polynomial. It is interesting that Chu Shih-chieh refers to this diagram as the *ku-fa* ("old method").

The interest of Chinese mathematicians in problems involving series and progressions is indicated in the earliest Chinese mathematical texts extant, the *Chou-pei suan-ching* (*ca.* fourth century B.C.) and Liu Hui's commentary on the *Chiu-chang suan-shu.* Although arithmetical and geometrical series were subsequently handled by a number of Chinese mathematicians, it was not until the time of Chu Shih-chieh that the study of higher series was raised to a more advanced level. In his *Ssu-yüan yü-chien* Chu Shih-chieh dealt with bundles of arrows of various cross sections, such as circular or square, and with piles of balls arranged so that they formed a triangle, a pyramid, a cone, and so on. Although no theoretical proofs are given, among the series found in the *Ssu-yüan yü-chien* are the following:

$$(1)\ 1 + 2 + 3 + 4 + \cdots + n = \frac{n(n+1)}{2!}$$

$$(2)\ 1 + 3 + 6 + 10 + \cdots + \frac{n(n+1)}{2!} = \frac{n(n+1)(n+2)}{3!}$$

$$(3)\ 1 + 4 + 10 + 20 + \cdots + \frac{n(n+1)(n+2)}{3!} = \frac{n(n+1)(n+2)(n+3)}{4!}$$

$$(4)\ 1 + 5 + 15 + 35 + \cdots + \frac{n(n+1)(n+2)(n+3)}{4!} = \frac{n(n+1)(n+2)(n+3)(n+4)}{5!}$$

$$(5)\ 1 + 6 + 21 + 56 + \cdots + \frac{n(n+1)(n+2)(n+3)(n+4)}{5!} = \frac{n(n+1)(n+2)(n+3)(n+4)(n+5)}{6!}$$

$$(6)\ 1^2 + 2^2 + 3^2 + \cdots + n^2 = \frac{n(n+1)}{2!} \cdot \frac{(2n+1)}{3}$$

$$(7)\ 1 + 5 + 14 + \cdots + \frac{n(n+1)}{2!} \cdot \frac{(2n+1)}{3} = \frac{n(n+1)(n+2)}{3!} \cdot \frac{(2n+2)}{4}$$

$$(8)\ 1 + 6 + 18 + 40 + \cdots + \frac{n(n+1)}{2!} \cdot \frac{(3n+0)}{3} = \frac{n(n+1)(n+2)}{3!} \cdot \frac{(3n+1)}{4}$$

$$(9)\ 1 + 8 + 30 + 80 + \cdots + \frac{n(n+1)(n+2)}{3!} \cdot \frac{(4n+0)}{4} = \frac{n(n+1)(n+2)(n+3)}{4!} \cdot \frac{(4n+1)}{5}$$

After Chu Shih-chieh, Chinese mathematicians made almost no progress in the study of higher series. It was only after the arrival of the Jesuits that interest in his work was revived. Wang Lai, for example, showed in his *Heng-chai suan-hsüeh* that the first five series above can be represented in the generalized form

$$1 + (r+1) + \frac{(r+1)(r+2)}{2!} + \cdots + \frac{n(n+1)(n+2)\cdots(n+\overline{r-2})(n+\overline{r-1})}{r!} = \frac{n(n+1)(n+2)\cdots(n+\overline{r-1})(n+r)}{(r+1)!}$$

where r is a positive integer.

Further contributions to the study of finite integral series were made during the nineteenth century by such Chinese mathematicians as Tung Yu-ch'eng, Li Shan-lan, and Lo Shih-lin. They attempted to express Chu Shih-chieh's series in more generalized and modern forms. Tu Shih-jan has recently stated that the following relationships, often erroneously attributed to Chu Shih-chieh, can be traced only as far as the work of Li Shan-lan.

If $U_r = \frac{r^{|p|}}{1^{|p|}}$, where r and p are positive integers, then

$$(a)\ \sum_{r=1}^{n} \frac{r^{|p|}}{1^{|p|}}(n + 1 - r) = \sum_{r=1}^{n} \frac{r^{|p+1|}}{1^{|p+1|}},$$

with the examples

$$\sum_{r=1}^{n} r(n + 1 - r) = \sum_{r=1}^{n} \frac{r(r+1)}{2},$$

CHU SHIH-CHIEH

$$\sum_{r=1}^{n} \frac{r(r+1)(r+2)}{1\cdot 2\cdot 3}$$

$$= \sum_{r=1}^{n} \frac{(n+1-r)(n+2-r)(n+3-r)}{1\cdot 2\cdot 3},$$

and

$$(b)\quad \sum_{r=1}^{n} \frac{r^{|p|}}{1^{|p|}} \cdot \frac{(n+1-r)^{|q|}}{1^{|q|}} = \sum_{r=1}^{n} \frac{r^{|p+q|}}{1^{|p+q|}},$$

where q is any other positive integer.

Another significant contribution by Chu Shih-chieh is his study of the method of *chao ch'a* ("finite differences"). Quadratic expressions had been used by Chinese astronomers in the process of finding arbitrary constants in formulas for celestial motions. We know that this method was used by Li Shun-feng when he computed the Lin Te calendar in A.D. 665. It is believed that Liu Ch'uo invented the *chao ch'a* method when he made the Huang Chi calendar in A.D. 604, for he established the earliest terms used to denote the differences in the expression

$$S = U_1 + U_2 + U_3 + \cdots + U_n,$$

calling $\Delta = U_1$ *shang ch'a* ("upper difference"),

$\Delta^2 = U_2 - U_1$ *erh ch'a* ("second difference"),

$\Delta^3 = U_3 - (2\Delta^2 + \Delta)$ *san ch'a* ("third difference"),

$\Delta^4 = U_4 - [3(\Delta^3 + \Delta^2) + \Delta]$ *hsia ch'a* ("lower difference").

Chu Shih-chieh illustrated how the method of finite differences could be applied in the last five problems on the subject in chapter 2 of *Ssu-yüan yü-chien:*

> If the cube law is applied to [the rate of] recruiting soldiers, [it is found that on the first day] the *ch'u chao* [Δ] is equal to the number given by a cube with a side of three feet and the *tz'u chao* [$U_2 - U_1$] is a cube with a side one foot longer, such that on each succeeding day the difference is given by a cube with a side one foot longer than that of the preceding day. Find the total recruitment after fifteen days.

Writing down Δ, Δ^2, Δ^3, and Δ^4 for the given numbers, we have what is shown in Fig. 4. Employing the conventions of Liu Ch'uo, Chu Shih-chieh gave *shang ch'a* (Δ) = 27; *erh ch'a* (Δ^2) = 37; *san ch'a* (Δ^3) = 24;

Number of days	Total recruitment	Δ	Δ^2	Δ^3	Δ^4
1st day	27	$3^3 = 27$			
			37		
2nd day	91	$4^3 = 64$		24	
			61		6
3rd day	216	$5^3 = 125$		30	
			91		6
4th day	432	$6^3 = 216$		36	
			127		—
5th day	775	$7^3 = 343$		—	
			—		
———	—	———			

FIGURE 4

and *hsia ch'a* (Δ^4) = 6. He then proceeded to find the number of recruits on the *n*th day, as follows:

> Take the number of days [n] as the *shang chi*. Subtracting unity from the *shang chi* [$n - 1$], one gets the last term of a *chiao ts'ao to* [a pile of balls of triangular cross section, or $S = 1 + 2 + 3 + \cdots + (n-1)$]. The sum [of the series] is taken as the *erh chi*. Subtracting two from the *shang chi* [$n - 2$], one gets the last term of a *san chiao to* [a pile of balls of pyramidal cross section, or $S = 1 + 3 + 6 + \cdots + n(n-1)/2$]. The sum [of this series] is taken as the *san chi*. Subtracting three from the *shang chi* [$n - 3$], one gets the last term of a *san chio lo i to* series
>
> $$\left[S = 1 + 4 + 10 + \cdots + \frac{n(n-1)(n-2)}{3!}\right].$$
>
> The sum [of this series] is taken as the *hsia chi*. By multiplying the differences [*ch'a*] by their respective sums [*chi*] and adding the four results, the total recruitment is obtained.

From the above we have:

$$Shang\ chi = n$$

$$erh\ chi = 1 + 2 + 3 + \cdots + (n-1) = \frac{1}{2!}n(n-1)$$

$$san\ chi = 1 + 3 + 6 + \cdots + \frac{1}{2}n(n-1)$$

$$= \frac{1}{3!}n(n-1)(n-2)$$

$$hsia\ chi = 1 + 4 + 10 + \cdots + \frac{n}{3!}(n-1)(n-2)$$

$$= \frac{1}{4!}n(n-1)(n-2)(n-3).$$

Multiplying these by the *shang ch'a, erh ch'a, san ch'a,* and *hsia ch'a,* respectively, and adding the four terms, we get

$$f(n) = n\Delta + \frac{1}{2!}n(n-1)\Delta^2 + \frac{1}{3!}n(n-1)(n-2)\Delta^3 + \frac{1}{4!}n(n-1)(n-2)(n-3)\Delta^4.$$

The following results are given in the same section of the *Ssu-yüan yü-chien:*

$$\sum_{n=1}^{n} f(r) = \frac{1}{2!}n(n+1)\Delta + \frac{1}{3!}(n-1)n(n+1)\Delta^2$$

$$+ \frac{1}{4!}(n-2)(n-1)n(n+1)\Delta^3$$

$$+ \frac{1}{5!}(n-3)(n-2)(n-1)n(n+1)\Delta^4$$

$$\sum \frac{1}{3!}r(r+1)(2r+1) = \frac{1}{12}n(n+1)(n+1)(n+2)$$

$$\sum \frac{1}{2!}r(r+1)\cdot r = \frac{1}{4!}n(n+1)(n+2)(3n+1)$$

$$\sum \frac{1}{3!}r(r+1)(r+2)\cdot r$$

$$= \frac{1}{5!}n(n+1)(n+2)(n+3)(4n+1)$$

$$\sum r\{a+(r-1)b\} = \frac{1}{3!}n(n+1)\{2bn+(3a-2b)\}$$

$$\sum r(a+\overline{n-r}\cdot b) = \frac{1}{3!}n(n+1)\{bn+(3a-b)\}$$

$$\sum \frac{1}{2!}r(r+1)\cdot(a+\overline{r-1}\cdot b)$$

$$= \frac{1}{4!}n(n+1)(n+2)\{3bn+(4a-3b)\}$$

$$\sum r^2\cdot(a+\overline{n-r}\cdot b)$$

$$= \frac{1}{3!}n(n+1)(2n+1)a + \frac{2n}{4!}(n-1)n(n+1)b$$

The *chao ch'a* method was also employed by Chu's contemporary, the great Yuan astronomer, mathematician, and hydraulic engineer Kuo Shou-ching, for the summation of power progressions. After them the *chao ch'a* method was not taken up seriously again in China until the eighteenth century, when Mei Wen-ting fully expounded the theory. Known as *shōsa* in Japan, the study of finite differences also received considerable attention from Japanese mathematicians, such as Seki Takakazu (or Seki Kōwa) in the seventeenth century.

BIBLIOGRAPHY

For further information on Chu Shih-chieh and his work, consult Ch'ien Pao-tsung, *Ku-suan k'ao-yüan* ("Origin of Ancient Chinese Mathematics") (Shanghai, 1935), pp. 67–80; and *Chung-kuo shu-hsüeh-shih* ("History of Chinese Mathematics") (Peking, 1964), 179–205; Ch'ien Pao-tsung *et al., Sung Yuan shu-hsüeh-shih lun-wen-chi* ("Collected Essays on Sung and Yuan Chinese Mathematics") (Peking, 1966), pp. 166–209; L. van Hée, "Le précieux miroir des quatre éléments," in *Asia Major,* **7** (1932), 242; Hsü Shun-fang, *Chung-suan-chia ti tai-shu-hsüeh yen-chiu* ("Study of Algebra by Chinese Mathematicians") (Peking, 1952), pp. 34–55; E. L. Konantz, "The Precious Mirror of the Four Elements," in *China Journal of Science and Arts,* **2** (1924), 304; Li Yen, *Chung-kuo shu-hsüeh ta-kang* ("Outline of Chinese Mathematics"), I (Shanghai, 1931), 184–211; *"Chiu-chang suan-shu pu-chu" Chung-suan-shih lun-ts'ung* (German trans.), in *Gesammelte Abhandlungen über die Geschichte der chinesischen Mathematik,* III (Shanghai, 1935), 1–9; *Chung-kuo suan-hsüeh-shih* ("History of Chinese Mathematics") (Shanghai, 1937; repr. 1955), pp. 105–109, 121–128, 132–133; and *Chung Suan-chia ti nei-ch'a fa yen-chiu* ("Investigation of the Interpolation Formulas in Chinese Mathematics") (Peking, 1957), of which an English trans. and abridgement is "The Interpolation Formulas of Early Chinese Mathematicians," in *Proceedings of the Eighth International Congress of the History of Science* (Florence, 1956), pp. 70–72; Li Yen and Tu Shih-jan, *Chung-kuo ku-tai shu-hsüeh chien-shih* ("A Short History of Ancient Chinese Mathematics"), II (Peking, 1964), 183–193, 203–216; Lo Shih-lin, *Supplement to the Ch'ou-jen chuan* (1840, repr. Shanghai, 1935), pp. 614–620; Yoshio Mikami, *The Development of Mathematics in China and Japan* (Leipzig, 1913; repr. New York), 89–98; Joseph Needham, *Science and Civilisation in China,* III (Cambridge, 1959), 41, 46–47, 125, 129–133, 134–139; George Sarton, *Introduction to the History of Science,* III (Baltimore, 1947), 701–703; and Alexander Wylie, *Chinese Researches* (Shanghai, 1897; repr. Peking, 1936; Taipei, 1966), pp. 186–188.

HO PENG-YOKE

CHUQUET, NICOLAS (*b.* Paris [?], France; *fl.* second half fifteenth century)

Nicolas Chuquet is known only through his book, which as an entity has remained in manuscript; one part, the "Triparty," on the science of numbers, was published by Aristide Marre in 1880. The following year Marre published the statement of, and replies to, a set of 156 problems that follow the "Triparty" in the manuscript. The analysis of these problems remains unpublished, as do an application to practical geometry and a treatise on commercial arithmetic.

The conclusion of the "Triparty" indicates that it was composed by one Nicolas Chuquet of Paris, holder of the baccalaureate in medicine, at Lyons, in 1484. (Marre believes that he can date the work precisely: one problem in the treatise on business arithmetic permits fixing the work no later than May 1484.)

Only one copy of the book (the work of a firm of copyists) is known to exist; although it remained in manuscript until 1880, several passages from it were copied slavishly by "Master Étienne de la Roche, also called Villefranche, native of Lyons on the Rhone," in his arithmetic text of 1520, of which there was a second edition in 1538.

We owe confirmation of the existence and importance of Nicolas Chuquet to this unscrupulous Master Étienne, who appears to have been well established in Lyons, where his name was included on the tax rolls of 1493. He cites Chuquet and his "Triparty" at the beginning of his text—without, however, adding that he is plagiarizing outrageously.

Chuquet called himself a Parisian. He spent his youth in that city, where he was probably born and where the name is yet known. There he pursued his extensive studies, up to the baccalaureate in medicine (which implies a master of arts as well). It is difficult to say more about his life. He was living in Lyons in 1484, perhaps practicing medicine but more probably teaching arithmetic there as "master of algorithms." The significant place given to questions of simple and compound interest, the repayment of debts, and such in his work leads one to suppose this. However, he used these questions only as pretexts for exercises in algebra.

Chuquet's mathematical learning was solid. He cites by name Boethius—whom everyone knew at that time—Euclid, and Campanus of Novara. He knew the propositions of Archimedes, Ptolemy, and Eutocius, which he stated without indicating his sources (referring to Archimedes only as "a certain wise man"). In geometry his language seems to be that of a translator, transposing terms taken from Greek or Latin into French. By contrast, in the parts devoted solely to arithmetic or algebra there is no borrowing of learned terminology. Everything is written in simple, direct language, with certain French neologisms that have not been preserved elsewhere. The only exception is the ponderous nomenclature for the various proportions encumbering the first pages of the "Triparty," for Chuquet was respecting a style that goes back to Nicomachus and his translator Boethius and that still infested the teaching of mathematics in the seventeenth century.

On the whole Chuquet wrote a beautiful French that is still quite readable. His simple, very mathematical style does not lack elegance, although occasional affectation led to the use of three or four synonyms in order to avoid monotonous repetition. Marre purports to find many Italianisms in Chuquet's French. He attributes this peculiarity to the close relations between Lyons and the cities of northern Italy and to its large and prosperous Italian colony. Upon examination, many of these so-called Italianisms appear to be nothing more than Latinisms, however, and the French used by Chuquet seems as pure as that of his contemporaries.

As for his mathematical work, in order to judge it fairly, we must compare it with the work of such contemporaries as Regiomontanus, whose *De triangulis omnimodis* was written twenty years earlier, in 1464 (although it was not printed until 1533), and most notably with that of Luca Pacioli, whose *Summa de arithmetica, geometria proportioni et proportionalita* was published ten years later, in 1494.

Chuquet made few claims of priority. The only thing that he prided himself on as his personal discovery was his "règle des nombres moyens." On one further occasion he seemed also to be claiming for himself the "règle des premiers." ("What I call first numbers the ancients called 'things.'") But he says no more on this point—where, as far as we know, his originality is obvious.

Chuquet engaged in very little controversy, contenting himself with twice criticizing a certain Master Berthelemy de Romans, also cited by a contemporary French arithmetician, Jehan Adam (whose arithmetic manuscript is dated 1475). "Master Berthelemy de Romans, formerly of the Order of Preaching Friars [Dominicans] at Valence and Doctor of Theology" may well have been one of the mathematics professors of Chuquet and Adam. Nothing definite is known of this matter, however.

The "Triparty" is a treatise on algebra, although the word appears nowhere in the manuscript. This algebra deals only with numbers, but in a very broad sense of the term. The first part concerns rational numbers. Chuquet's originality in his rules for decimal numeration, both spoken and written, is immediately obvious. He introduced the practice of division into groups of six figures and used, besides the already familiar million, the words billion (10^{12}), trillion (10^{18}), quadrillion (10^{24}), etc. Here is an example of his notation:

$$745324^{3}804300^{2}700023^{1}654321.$$

In this example Chuquet's exponents are simply commas, but he points out that one can use ^{1} in place of the first comma, ^{2} in place of the second, ^{3} in place of the third, and so on.

Fractions, which Chuquet called "nombres routz" (*sic*), or broken numbers, were studied clearly and without complicated rules. Like all his contemporaries, however, he always used a numerator smaller than the denominator (and hence mixed numbers instead of improper fractions), a practice that led to unnecessary complications in his calculations.

CHUQUET

Chuquet's study of the rules of three and of simple and double false position, clear but commonplace, served as pretext for a collection of remarkable linear problems, expounded in a chapter entitled "Seconde partie d'une position." Here he did not reveal his methods but reserved their exposition for a later part of the work, where he then said that after having solved a problem by the usual methods—double position or algebra (his "règle des premiers")—one must vary the known numerical quantities and carefully analyze the sequence of computations in order to extract a canon (formula). This analysis generally led him to a correct formula, although at times he was mistaken and gave methods applicable only for particular values.

Another original concept occurred in this group of problems. In a problem with five unknowns, Chuquet concluded: "I find 30, 20, 10, 0, and minus 10, which are the five numbers I wished to have." He then pointed out that zero added to or subtracted from a number does not change the number and reviewed the rules for addition and subtraction of negative numbers. In the thirteenth century Leonardo Fibonacci had made a similar statement but had not carried it as far as Chuquet in the remainder of his work.

The first part of the "Triparty" ends with the "règle des nombres moyens," the only discovery to which Chuquet laid claim. According to him—and he was right—this rule allows the solution of many problems that are unapproachable by the classic rule of three or the rules of simple or double false position. It consisted of establishing that between any two given fractions a third can always be interpolated that has for numerator the sum of the numerators of the other two fractions, and for denominator the sum of their denominators. It has been demonstrated in modern times that by repeating this procedure it is possible to arrive at all the rational numbers included between the two given fractions. It is obvious, therefore, that this rule, together with a lot of patience, makes it possible to solve any problem allowing of a rational solution. Further on, Chuquet utilizes it in order to approach indeterminately the square roots, cube roots, and so on, of numbers that do not have exact roots. But here he used it to solve the equation

$$x^2 + x = 39\tfrac{13}{81}.$$

Successively interpolating five fractions between 5 and 6, he found the exact root, $5\frac{7}{9}$. Since he was, moreover, little concerned about rapid methods of approximation, Chuquet throughout his work used nothing but this one rule and only rarely at that.

The second part of the "Triparty" deals with roots and "compound numbers." There is no trace of Euclidean nomenclature, of "binomials," or of "apostomes." The language has become simpler: there is no question of square roots or cube roots, but of second, third, fourth roots, "and so on, continuing endlessly." The number itself is its own first root. Moreover, everything is called a "number"—whole numbers, rational numbers, roots, sums, and differences of roots—which, in the fifteenth century, was audacious indeed. The notation itself was original. Here are several examples:

Chuquet's Notation	*Modern Notation*
℞^{1} 12	12
3 $\bar{p}$ ℞^{2} 5	$3 + \sqrt{5}$
℞^{2} 2 $\bar{p}$ ℞^{2} 5	$\sqrt{2} + \sqrt{5}$
℞^{2} $\underline{14\ \bar{p}\ \text{℞}^2\ 180}$	$\sqrt{(14 + \sqrt{180})}$
℞^{2} $\underline{14\ \bar{m}\ \text{℞}^2\ 180}$	$\sqrt{(14 - \sqrt{180})}$

Unfortunately, Chuquet, a man of his times after all, occasionally became involved in computations that to us might seem inextricable. For example, he wrote the product of $\sqrt[6]{7} \times 2$ as ℞^{6} 448, whereas after Descartes it would be written $2\sqrt[6]{7}$.

The third part is by far the most original. It deals with the "règle des premiers," a "truly excellent" rule that "does everything that other rules do and, in addition, solves a great many more difficult problems." It is "the gateway and the threshold to the mysteries that are in the science of numbers." Such were the enthusiastic terms in which Chuquet announced the algebraic method. First, he explained his notation and his computational rules. The unknown, called the "first number" (*nombre premier*), is written as 1^1. Therefore, where Chuquet wrote 4^0, we should read 4; if he wrote 5^1, we should read $5x$; and if he wrote 7^3, we should read $7x^3$.

By a daring use of negative numbers, he wrote our $-12x$ as $\bar{m}12^1$, our $-\sqrt[3]{12} \cdot x^3$ as $\bar{m}$ ℞^{3} 12^3. For $12x^{-1}$ or $12/x$, he wrote $12^{1\bar{m}}$; for $-12x^{-1}$, he wrote $\bar{m}12^{1\bar{m}}$. In order to justify his rules of algebraic computation, and particularly those touching the product of the powers of a variable, he called upon analogy. He considered the sequence of the powers of 2 and showed, for example, that $2^2 \times 2^3 = 2^5$. He wished only to make clear, by an example that he considered commonplace and that goes back almost to Archimedes, the algebraic rule that if squares are multiplied by cubes the result is the fifth power.

For division he announced that the quotient of

$$\begin{array}{llllll} 36^3 & \text{by } 6^1 & \text{is } 6^2 & 36x^3 & \div\, 6x & = 6x^2 \\ 72^0 & \text{by } 8^3 & \text{is } 9^{3\bar{m}} & 72 & \div\, 8x^3 & = 9x^{-3} \\ 84^{2\bar{m}} & \text{by } 7^{3\bar{m}} & \text{is } 12^1 & 84x^{-2} & \div\, 7x^{-3} & = 12x. \end{array}$$

Further on—but only once in the entire work—he wrote down a rational function:

$$\frac{30\ m\ 1^1}{1^2\,p\ 1^1}\ \text{, i.e., } \left(\frac{30 - x}{x^2 + x}\right).$$

In accordance with the custom of Chuquet's time, all these rules of computation were simply set forth, illustrated by a few examples, and at times justified by analogy with more elementary arithmetic, but never "demonstrated" in the modern sense of the term. Having set down these preliminaries, Chuquet dealt with the theory of equations, which he called the "method of equaling."

In setting up an equation, he specified that 1^1 should be taken as the unknown and that this "premier" should be operated on "as required in 'la raison,'" that is, the problem under study.

One can, moreover, take 2^1, 3^1, etc., as the unknowns in place of 1^1. One should end with two expressions equal or similar to each other. These are the two "parts" of the equation. This is followed by the classic rules for solving binomial equations of the type $ax^m = b$.

These rules include procedures for reducing equations to the binomial form. Chuquet emphasized the importance of recognizing "equipollent numbers," i.e., expressions of the same power as $\sqrt{x^2}$ and x or $\sqrt[5]{x^{10}}$ and x^2. He notes that when the two parts of the equation are "similar" it may either have infinitely many solutions ($ax^m = ax^m$) or be impossible of solution ($ax^m = bx^m$; $a \neq b$). Several of the many numerical problems that follow—certain of them having several unknowns—come to one of these results. When the two parts are not similar, the equation has for Chuquet at most one solution. He is, however, of two minds regarding negative solutions; sometimes he accepts them, sometimes not.

Subsequently Chuquet solved problems that led to equations of the form

$$ax^{2m} + bx^m + c = 0.$$

Like all his contemporaries he distinguished three cases (a, b, c positive):

$$\begin{aligned} c + bx^m &= ax^{2m} \\ bx^m + ax^{2m} &= c \\ c + ax^{2m} &= bx^m. \end{aligned}$$

While he knew and stated that in the last case the equation might be insoluble, and admitted two solutions when it was soluble, he found only one solution in the other two cases. In this regard he did not show any progress over his predecessors.

On the subject of division into mean and extreme ratio, he showed, in fact, a profound ignorance of the theory of numbers.

Indeed, having to solve $144 + x^2 = 36x$, Chuquet obtained the answer $x = 18 - \sqrt{180}$, and, in effect, declared: "Campanus, in the ninth book of Euclid, at the end of Proposition 16, affirms that such a problem is impossible of solution in numbers, while in fact, as we have just seen, it is perfectly capable of solution."

Now in fact Campanus demonstrated, very elegantly, that the solution cannot be rational. Chuquet, who had a very broad concept of numbers, did not grasp the subtlety. In several other cases he also showed a lack of understanding, particularly regarding the problems that he included in his "rule of apposition and separation." These problems derive from Diophantine analysis of the first order, the exact theory of which had to await Bachet de Méziriac and the seventeenth century.

The "Triparty" ends with an admission of inadequacy: there remains the task of studying equations of a more general type, wrote the author, but he would leave them for those who might wish to go further with the subject. This attitude was common among the majority of the algebraists of the fifteenth century, who would have liked to go beyond the second degree but were not sure how to go about it.

Summarizing the "Triparty," we may say that it is a very abstract treatise on algebra, without any concrete applications, in which one can see a great extension of the concept of number—zero, negative numbers, and roots and combinations of roots all being included. There appear in it excellent notations that prefigure, in particular, those of Bombelli. But weak points remain. In linear algebra the cases of indetermination and insolubility were poorly set forth. In the theory of equations the importance of degree was not realized, and for equations of the second degree the old errors persisted. Moreover, Chuquet's taste for needlessly complicated computations—and beyond that the way in which the necessity for these computations arose in the shortcomings of numerical algebra—is painfully evident. At the end of a problem one may, for example, find

$$R^3\ \underline{13\frac{865}{1728}\,p\ R^2\ 182\frac{699841}{2985984}},$$

"which, if abbreviated by extraction of the second and third roots, comes to 3." Such an answer required a certain courage in the person making the calculation!

The "Triparty" has become well known since its publication in 1880. The same is not true of the sequel to the 1484 manuscript. It is true that Marre gave, in 1881, the statement of the 156 problems that follow the "Triparty," accompanied by answers and some remarks that Chuquet added to them. But this incomplete publication let several important points go by.

By contrast with the problems of the "Triparty," the greater part of those treated in this appendix appear to be concrete. But this is merely an appearance, and one can imagine the author coldly cutting an heir into several pieces if a problem concerning a will fails to come out even. Moreover, the questions dealt with were not all original; many were part of a long tradition going back at least as far as Metrodorus' anthology.

Marre indicated those problems that were taken over—almost word for word—by the plagiarist Étienne de la Roche and those that may be found in an almost contemporary treatise written in the Languedoc dialect of the region of Pamiers. One can find many other such duplications. Chuquet's originality lay not in his choice of topics but in his way of treating them. Indeed, he very often made use of his "règle des premiers," that is, of algebra.

A very important fact seems to have gone unnoticed by historians, no doubt because of the incomplete publication of this part of the work. It is known that, in his *Summa* of 1494, Luca Pacioli made use in certain cases of not one unknown but two: the *cosa* and the *quantita*. Now, what has passed unnoticed is that Chuquet employed the same device in 1484, and on at least five occasions. The first time was in the following problem:

> Three men have some coins. If the first man took 12 coins from the two others, he would have twice the amount remaining to them, plus 6 coins. If the second man took 13 coins from the first and the third, he would have four times as many as remained to them, plus 2 coins. If the third man took 11 coins from the two others, he would have three times what remained to them, plus 3 coins. How many coins does each man have?

Chuquet solved the problem by a mixed method, a combination of the rule of two false positions and his "règle des premiers." Someone (it must be Étienne de la Roche) has written in the margin "by the rule of two positions and by the rule of the 'thing' together." This annotator, perhaps under the influence of Pacioli, used the language of the Italian algebraists.

Chuquet posited 6 as the holdings of the first man, and with the first datum of the problem deduced that the three men have 24 coins among them. Assigning to the third the value 1^1 and basing himself on the third condition, he found, using the "règle des premiers," that the third man has $7\frac{3}{4}$ coins and therefore the second has $10\frac{1}{4}$.

By following the then classic method of false position, he established that the use of 6 for the first man's holdings gives, for the second condition, an excess of $18\frac{1}{4}$. He started again with 12, and by applying the classic rule, obtained the answer: the holdings are 8, 9, and 10.

But, a bit further on, he announced "another way of solving it, using only the 'règle des premiers.'" The annotator has written in the margin, "This rule is called the rule of quantity." Here it is plain that the annotator was familiar with Pacioli's *Summa.*

As we have already said, Chuquet liked to vary the numerical data of his problems. This was a necessity for him, and it mitigated to a degree the absence of literal computation. Thus he could better analyze the sequence of computations and draw from them the rules to follow for solving automatically problems of the same kind. Thus, he presented the following problem:

> If the first of three men took 7 coins from the others, he would have five times what remained to them, plus 1. If the second took 9 coins from the others, he would have six times what remained to them, plus 2, and if the third took 11 coins from the first two, he would have seven times as many as remained to them, plus 3.

Chuquet then posited 1^1—i.e., x—for the holdings of the first, and for the first datum found that they have, in all,

$$1^1\frac{1}{5}\ \bar{p}\ 8\frac{1}{5}\ ,\ \text{i.e.,}\left(\frac{6}{5}x + \frac{41}{5}\right).$$

"To find the portion belonging to the second man, I assign to him 1^2." This symbol no longer represents the square, x^2, of the unknown x but another unknown, y. Then, making use of the second condition of the problem, he found that

$$y = 1^1\frac{1}{35}\bar{m}\ 1\frac{24}{35}\ ,\ \text{i.e.,}\left(\frac{36}{35}x - \frac{59}{35}\right).$$

Finally, to find the third man's portion, he used the third condition and took 1^2 for the third unknown. This unknown is not the y of the preceding computation but a new unknown, z. He found

$$z = 1^1\frac{1}{20}\bar{m}\ 3\frac{9}{20}\ ,\ \text{i.e.,}\left(\frac{21}{20}x - \frac{69}{20}\right).$$

Writing

$$x + y + z = 1^1\frac{1}{5}\ \bar{p}\ 8\frac{1}{5},$$

he arrived at the final equation:

$$3^1\frac{11}{140}\ \bar{m}\ 5\frac{19}{140} \text{ equals } 1^1\frac{1}{5}\ \bar{p}\ 8\frac{1}{5},$$

which remains only to be solved.

Several problems on geometric progressions and compound interest were not completely solved until the introduction of logarithms. Chuquet was aware of the difficulty without finding a way to solve it.

> A vessel with an open spout loses one-tenth of its contents each day. In how many days will the vessel be half-empty?

After having answered that it will be $6\frac{31441}{531441}$ days, he adds, "Many people are satisfied with this answer. However, it seems that between six days and seven, one should search for a certain proportional number that, for the present, is unknown to us."

Among the numerous problems studied is a question of inheritance that is found in Bachet de Méziriac (1612) and again in Euler's *Algebra* (1769) and that, by its nature, demands a whole number as the answer.

> The oldest son takes 1 coin and one-tenth of the rest, the second takes 2 coins and one-tenth of the new remainder, and so on. Each of the children receives the same sum. How many heirs are there?

After having varied the numerical data, Chuquet gave a general rule for the solution of the problem, then treated eleven other numerical cases—in which the answers include fractions of an heir. One detects here not a number theorist, but a pure algebraist.

Many of Bachet de Méziriac's *Problèmes plaisans et délectables* can be found in Chuquet, especially in the chapter entitled "Jeux et esbatemens qui par la science des nombres se font." But they formed part of a thousand-year-old tradition, and a manuscript by Luca Pacioli, *De viribus quantitatis,* also dealt with them.

The geometric part of Chuquet's work is entitled "Comment la science des nombres se peut appliquer aux mesures de géométrie." It formed part of a tradition that goes back to the Babylonians and that developed over the centuries, in which figured notably Hero of Alexandria and, in the thirteenth century, Leonardo Fibonacci. It comprised, first of all, the measurement of length, area, and volume. Then it became more scientific and, in certain respects, a veritable application of algebra to geometry.

Rectilinear measure was either direct or effected by means of the quadrant, which was represented in practice by a figure on the back of the astrolabe that utilized a direct and inverse projection or shadow. No recourse was made to trigonometry, nor did any measurement of angles appear. In this we are removed from the astronomic tradition so brilliantly represented by Regiomontanus. The quadrant was used for measuring horizontal distances, depths, and heights. Other elementary techniques were also indicated, such as those of the vertical rod and the horizontal mirror.

As for curves, "the circular line is measured in a way that will be described in connection with the measuring of circular surfaces. Other curved lines are reduced as much as possible to a straight line or a circular line." For the circle the approximations $3\frac{1}{7}$ for π and $\frac{11}{14}$ for $\pi/4$ were the only ones indicated.

Chuquet separated triangles into equilateral and nonequilateral triangles. Each triangle consisted of one base and two hypotenuses. The "cathète" descends perpendicular to the base. This terminology was quite unusual and certainly different from classical terminology.

Chuquet knew Euclid's *Elements* very well, however. For him the following proposition was the fundamental one: "If the square of the perpendicular is subtracted from the square of the hypotenuse, the square root of the remainder will be the length of the part of the base that corresponds to the hypotenuse." He gave no demonstration. The first part of this practical geometry was completed by a few notes on the "measurement of hilly surfaces" and the volumes of spheres, pyramids, and cubes. These are scarcely developed. This work does not have the amplitude of Pacioli's treatment of the same topic in the *Summa* and is scarcely more than a brief summary of what can be found in the pages of Leonardo Fibonacci. But "the application of the aforesaid rules" brought forth a new spirit, and here the algebraist reappeared. For example, Chuquet applied Hero's rule on the expression of the area of a triangle as a function of its three sides to the triangle 11, 13, 24. He found the area to be zero, and from this concluded the nonexistence of the triangle.

Again, two vertical lines of lengths 4 and 5 are horizontally distant by 12. Chuquet sought a point on the horizontal that was equidistant from the two apexes. This led him to the equation

$$169m\ 24^1\ \bar{p}\ 1^2 \text{ equals } 1^2\ \bar{p}\ 16\ \cdots.$$

There are still other, similar algebraic exercises. Two of them are important.

In the first it is proposed to find the diameter of the circle circumscribed about a triangle whose base is 14 and whose sides are 13 and 15. To do this it was first necessary to compute the projections x and y of the sides on the base, using the relation $x^2 - y^2 = 15^2 - 13^2$. The perpendicular then follows directly. Now, taking as the unknown the distance from the center to the base and expressing the center as equidistant from the vertices, one is led to the equation

$$148m\ 24^1\ \bar{p}\ 1^2 \text{ equals } 49\ \bar{p}\ 1^2.$$

In the second exercise Chuquet proposed to compute the diameter of a circle circumscribed about a regular pentagon with sides of length 4. He first took as the unknown the diagonal of the pentagon. Ptolemy's theorem on inscribed quadrilaterals then leads to the equation

$$4^1\ \bar{p}\ 16 \text{ equals } 1^2,$$

which permitted him to make his computations. By this method he concluded that Euclid's proposition is correct: the square of the side of the hexagon added to that of the decagon gives that of the pentagon inscribed in the same circle.

Two analogous applications of algebra to geometry are in the *De triangulis* of Regiomontanus. Others are to be found in the geometrical part of Pacioli's *Summa*. Thus, it appears that this tradition was strongly implanted in the algebraists of the fifteenth century.

Without any vain display of erudition Chuquet showed his extensive learning in borrowings from Eutocius for the graphic extraction of cube roots. He also gave constructions with straight-edge and compasses and devoted a rather weak chapter to research on the squaring of the circle. Ramón Lull's quadrature was recalled here. Chuquet showed that it was equivalent to taking the value $2 + \sqrt{2}$ for π. As for the approximation 22/7, it is given by "a wise man. . . . But this is a thing that cannot be proved by any demonstration."

If Étienne de la Roche had been more insensitive—especially if he had plagiarized the "règle des premiers" and its applications—mathematics would perhaps be grateful to him for his larcenies. He was unfortunately too timid, and in his arithmetic text he returned to the classical errors of his time, and thus the most original part of Chuquet's work remained unknown. One cannot, however, assert that the innovations that Chuquet introduced were entirely lost. His notation can be found again, for example, in Bombelli. Was it rediscovered by the Italian algebraist? Was there a connection between the two, direct or indirect? Or did both derive from a more ancient source? These are the questions that remain open.

BIBLIOGRAPHY

The MS of Chuquet's book is in the Bibliothèque Nationale, Fonds Français, no. 1346. Aristide Marre's ed. of the "Triparty" is "Le Triparty en la science des nombres par Maistre Nicolas Chuquet, parisien, d'après le manuscrit fonds français, nº. 1346 de la Bibliothèque nationale de Paris," in *Bullettino di bibliografia e di storia delle scienze matematiche e fisiche,* **13** (1880), 593–659, 693–814, preceded by Marre's "Notice sur Nicolas Chuquet et son Triparty en la science des nombres," pp. 555–592; the appendix to the "Triparty" is *ibid.,* **14** (1881), 413–416, with extracts from the MS on pp. 417–460. Numerous passages from Chuquet are plagiarized in *Larismethique novellement composée par Maistre Estienne de la Roche dict Villefranche natif de Lyon sur le Rosne . . .* (Lyons, 1520, 1538).

Works comparable in certain ways to that of Chuquet are Bibliothèque Nationale, Fonds Français, nouvelles acquisitions no. 4140, a fifteenth-century arithmetic treatise in the Romance dialect of the Foix region; and Bibliothèque Ste. Geneviève, Paris, MS fr. no. 3143. On the latter, see Lynn Thorndike, "The Arithmetic of Jehan Adam, 1475 A.D.," in *The American Mathematical Monthly,* **33** (1926), 24–28; and *Isis,* **9**, no. 29 (Feb. 1927), 155. Chuquet's notations are discussed in Florian Cajori, *A History of Mathematical Notations,* 2 vols. (Chicago, 1928–1929). Studies on Chuquet are Moritz Cantor, *Vorlesungen über Geschichte der Mathematik,* II (Leipzig, 1892), pt. 1, ch. 58; and Charles Lambo, "Une algèbre française de 1484, Nicolas Chuquet," in *Revue des questions scientifiques,* **2** (1902), 442–472.

JEAN ITARD

CIRUELO, PEDRO, *also known as* **Pedro Sánchez Ciruelo** (*b.* Daroca, Spain, 1470; *d.* Salamanca [?], Spain, 1554)

Ciruelo learned logic and arts at Salamanca during the latter part of the fifteenth century, then proceeded to the University of Paris to complete his education. He studied theology there from 1492 to 1502, supporting himself by "the profession of the mathematical arts." In 1495 he published at Paris a treatise on practical arithmetic, *Tractatus arithmeticae practicae,* that went through many subsequent printings; in the same year he also published revised and corrected editions of Bradwardine's *Arithmetica speculativa* and *Geometria speculativa* that enjoyed a similar success. Dating from this same period are Ciruelo's editions of the *Sphere* of Sacrobosco, including the questions of Pierre d'Ailly (Élie cites editions of 1494, 1498, and 1515; Villoslada mentions others of 1499, 1505, and 1508 under a modified title). By 1502 Ciruelo was teaching mathematics at Paris; presumably he continued this career until about 1515, when he returned to Spain, attracted to the newly founded University of Alcalá.

At Alcalá, Ciruelo taught the theology of Aquinas; among his students was the young Domingo de Soto. Ciruelo maintained an interest in mathematics and philosophy, however, and in 1516 published his *Cursus quatuor mathematicarum artium liberalium;* this included a paraphrase of Boethius' *Arithmetica,* "more clearly and carefully edited than that of Thomas Bradwardine"; a brief compendium of Bradwardine's geometry, "with some additions"; another short compendium of John Peckham's *Perspectiva communis,* "to which also have been added a few glosses"; a treatise on music; and two short pieces on squaring the circle, both of which he recognized as defective. The *Cursus* appeared at both Paris and Alcalá, being reprinted at Alcalá in 1518 and in both places in 1523, 1526, and 1528. At Alcalá, Ciruelo also published his edition of the *Apotelesmata astrologiae christianae* in 1521 and a new edition of the *Sphere* in 1526. He transferred to the University of Salamanca some time after this; his first work to be published there was a *Summulae* (1537) that is a more mature treatment of logic than his *Prima pars logices* (Alcalá, 1519). Also published at Salamanca was his *Paradoxae quaestiones* (1538), two questions on logic, three on physics, and five on metaphysics and theology; these contain his somewhat singular views on gravity and impetus and his criticisms of the Jewish cabala, particularly as evaluated by Giovanni Pico della Mirandola.

BIBLIOGRAPHY

Ciruelo's works are listed and appraised in fragmentary fashion in the following: Vicente Muñoz Delgado, O.M., "La lógica en Salamanca durante la primera mitad del siglo XVI," in *Salmanticensis,* **14** (1967), 171-207, esp. 196–198 (logic); Hubert Élie, "Quelques maîtres de l'université de Paris vers l'an 1500," in *Archives d'histoire doctrinale et littéraire du moyen âge,* **18** (1950–1951). 193–243, esp. 236–237 (general); J. Rey Pastor, *Los matemáticos españoles del siglo XVI* (Toledo, 1926), pp. 54–61 (mathematics); David E. Smith, *Rara arithmetica* (Boston–London, 1908), see index; Lynn Thorndike, *The Sphere of Sacrobosco and Its Commentators* (Chicago, 1949), see index; and R. G. Villoslada, S. J., *La universidad de Paris durante los estudios de Francisco de Vitoria (1507–1522),* Analecta Gregoriana, no. 14 (Rome, 1938), pp. 402–404, *passim* (general).

WILLIAM A. WALLACE, O.P.

CLAIRAUT, ALEXIS-CLAUDE (*b.* Paris, France, 7 May 1713; *d.* Paris, 17 May 1765)

Clairaut's father, Jean-Baptiste Clairaut, was a mathematics teacher in Paris and a corresponding member of the Berlin Academy. His mother, Catherine Petit, bore some twenty children, few of whom survived. Of those who did, two boys were educated entirely within the confines of the family and showed themselves to be notably precocious children. The younger died around 1732 at the age of sixteen, however.

Alexis-Claude would probably have learned the alphabet from the figures in Euclid's *Elements.* When he was nine years old his father had him study Guisnée's *Application de l'algèbre à la géométrie.* Guisnée, who had studied under Varignon, taught mathematics to several important people, notably Pierre-Rémond de Montmort, Réaumur, and Maupertuis. His work, which was subsidized by Montmort, is a good introduction to the pioneering mathematics of that era: analytical geometry and infinitesimal calculus.

At the age of ten Clairaut delved into L'Hospital's posthumous *Traité analytique des sections coniques* and his *Analyse des infiniment petits,* which was based on Johann Bernoulli's lessons. Clairaut was barely twelve when he read before the Académie des Sciences "Quatre problèmes sur de nouvelles courbes," later published in the *Miscellanea Berolinensia.*

Around 1726 the young Clairaut, together with Jean Paul de Gua de Malves, who was barely fourteen years old; Jean Paul Grandjean de Fouchy, nineteen; Charles Marie de la Condamine, twenty-five; Jean-Antoine Nollet, twenty-six; and others founded the Société des Arts. Even though this learned society survived for only a few years, it was nonetheless a training ground for future members of the Académie des Sciences.

Around this time also Clairaut began his research on gauche curves. This work culminated in 1729 in a treatise (published in 1731) that led to his election to the Academy. The Academy proposed his election to the Crown on 4 September 1729, but it was not confirmed by the king until 11 July 1731, at which time he was still only eighteen.

In the Academy, Clairaut became interested in geodesy through Cassini's work on the measurement of the meridian. He allied himself with Maupertuis and the small but youthful and pugnacious group supporting Newton. It is difficult, however, to specify the moment at which he turned toward this new area of physics, for which his mathematical studies had so well prepared him.

He became a close friend of Maupertuis and was much in the company of the marquise du Châtelet and Voltaire. During the fall of 1734 Maupertuis and Clairaut spent a few months with Johann Bernoulli in Basel, and in 1735 they retired to Mont Valérien, near Paris, to concentrate on their studies in a calm atmosphere.

On 20 April 1736 Clairaut left Paris for Lapland, where he was to measure a meridian arc of one degree inside the arctic circle. Maupertuis was director of the expedition, which included Le Monnier, Camus, the Abbé Outhier, and Celsius. This enthusiastic group accomplished its mission quickly and precisely, in an atmosphere of youthful gaiety for which some reproached them. On 20 August 1737 Clairaut was back in Paris.

His work turned increasingly toward celestial mechanics, and he published several studies annually in *Mémoires de l'Académie des sciences.* From 1734 until his death, he also contributed to the *Journal des sçavans.* Clairaut guided the marquise du Châtelet in her studies, especially in her translation of Newton's *Principia* and in preparing the accompanying explanations. Even though the work was so sufficiently advanced in 1745 that a grant could be applied for and awarded, it did not appear until 1756, seven years after the marquise's death.

This translation of the *Principia* is elegant and, on the whole, very faithful to the original. It is, furthermore, most valuable because of its second volume, in which an abridged explanation of the system of the world is found. It illustrates, summarizes, and completes, on certain points, the results found in the *Principia,* all in about 100 pages. There is also an "analytical solution of the principal problems concerning the system of the world." Clairaut's contribution to this volume is a fundamental one, even greater than that to the translation. Many of his works are used in it. For example, in the section devoted to an explanation of light refraction there is a condensed version of his "Sur les explications cartésienne et newtonienne de la réfraction de la lumière," and the approximately sixty pages devoted to the shape of the earth constitute a very clear résumé of the *Figure de la terre.*

Clairaut's contribution to science, however, lies mainly in his own works: *Théorie de la figure de la terre* (1743), *Théorie de la lune* (1752), *Tables de la lune* (1754), *Théorie du mouvement des comètes* (1760 [?]), and *Recherches sur la comète* (1762). When we add to these works on celestial mechanics the two didactic works *Élémens de géométrie* (1741) and *Élémens d'algèbre* (1746) and the controversies that arose around these works, we have an idea of the intensity of Clairaut's effort.

Vivacious by nature, attractive, of average height but well built, Clairaut was successful in society and, it appears, with women. He remained unmarried. He was a member of the Royal Society and the academies of Berlin, St. Petersburg, Bologna, and Uppsala. Clairaut maintained an almost continuous correspondence with Gabriel Cramer and Euler and with six corresponding members of the Académie des Sciences: Samuel Koenig, whom he had met in Basel during his visit to Johann Bernoulli; François Jacquier and Thomas Le Seur, publishers of and commentators on the *Principia;* Samuel Klingenstierna, whom he had met during his trip to Lapland; Robert-Xavier Ansart du Petit Vendin; and the astronomer Augustin d'Arquier de Pellepoix.

In 1765 Clairaut wrote, concerning his theory of the moon: "A few years ago I began the tedious job of redoing all the calculations with more uniformity and rigor, and perhaps some day I shall have the courage to complete it. . . ." He was lacking not in courage, but in time; he died that year, at fifty-two, following a brief illness.

Although the expression "double-curvature curve" (gauche curve) is attributed to Henri Pitot (1724), Clairaut's treatise on this type of figure is no less original, representing the first serious analytical study of it. The curve is determined by two equations among the three orthogonal coordinates of its "point courant" (locus). Assimilation of the infinitesimal arc to a segment of a straight line permits determination of the tangent and the perpendiculars. It also permits rectification of the curve. This work also includes quadratures and the generation of some special gauche curves. "Sur les courbes que l'on forme en coupant une surface courbe quelconque par un plan donné de position" (1731) deals with plane sections of surfaces. The essential implement in this is a change in the reference point of the coordinates. Clairaut used this device mainly for explaining Newton's enumeration of curves of the third degree and the generation of all plane cubics through the central projection of one of the five divergent parabolas.

Clairaut's "Sur quelques questions de maximis et minimis" (1733) was noteworthy in the history of the calculus of variations. It was written, as were all his similar works, in the style of the Bernoulli brothers, by likening the infinitesimal arc of the curve of three elementary rectilinear segments. In the same vein was the memoir "Détermination géométrique . . . à la méridienne . . ." (1733), in which Clairaut made an elegant study of the geodesics of quadrics of rotation. It includes the property already pointed out by Johann Bernoulli: the osculating plane of the geodesic is normal to the surface.

What we call "Clairaut's differential equations" first appeared in the *Mémoires de l'Académie des sciences* for 1734. They are solved by differentiation and, in addition to the general integral, also allow for a singular solution. Brook Taylor had made this discovery in 1715.

In his research on integral calculus (1739–1740) Clairaut showed that for partial derivatives of the mixed second order, the order of differentiation is unimportant; and he established the existence of an integrating factor for linear differential equations of the first order. This factor had appeared in 1687, in the work of Fatio de Duillier. A lesson given by Johann Bernoulli to L'Hospital on this subject was summarized by Reyneau, in 1708. Euler also dealt with this subject at the same time as Clairaut.

As a result of the experiments of Dortous de Mairan, Clairaut proved in 1735 that slight pendulum oscillations remain isochronous, even if they do not occur in the same plane. His most significant paper on mechanics, however, is probably "Sur quelques principes . . . de dynamique" (1742), on the relative movement and the dynamics of a body in motion. Even though he did not clarify Coriolis's concept of acceleration, he did at least indicate a method of attacking the problem.

In 1743 the *Théorie de la figure de la terre* appeared. It was to some degree the theoretical epilogue to the Lapland expedition and to the series of polemics on the earth's shape—an oblate ellipsoid, according to Newton and Huygens, and a prolate ellipsoid, according to the Cassinis. Newton had merely outlined a proof; and Maclaurin, in his work on tides, which was awarded a prize by the Académie des Sciences in 1740, had set forth a general principle of hydrostatics that allowed this proof to be improved upon. Clairaut gave this principle an aspect that he felt was more general but that d'Alembert later showed to be the same as Maclaurin's. He drew from it an analytical theory that since George Green (1828) has been called the theory of potential. It allowed him to study the shape of the stars in more general cases than those examined by his predecessors. Clairaut no longer assumed that the fluid composing a star was homogeneous, and he considered various possible laws of gravitation. It was also in this work, considered a scientific classic, that the formula named for Clairaut, expressing the earth's gravity as a function of latitude, is found.

It was through the various works submitted for the 1740 competition on the theory of tides, and this work of Clairaut's, that Newton's theory of gravitation finally won acceptance in French scientific circles.

In 1743 Clairaut read before the Academy a paper entitled "L'orbite de la lune dans le système de M. Newton." Newton was not fully aware of the movement of the moon's apogee, and therefore the problem had to be reexamined in greater detail. However, Clairaut—and d'Alembert, and Euler, who were also working on this question—found only half of the observed movement in their calculations.

It was then that Clairaut suggested completing Newton's law of attraction by adding a term inversely proportional to the fourth power of the distance. This correction of the law elicited a spirited reaction from Buffon, who opposed this modification with metaphysical considerations on the simplicity of the laws of nature. Clairaut, more positive and more a pure mathematician, wanted to stick to calculations and observations. The controversy that arose between these two academicians appears in the *Mémoires* of the Academy for 1745 (published long afterward). Nevertheless, the minimal value of the term added soon made Clairaut think that the correction—all things considered—could apply to the calculations but not to the law. While the latter-day Cartesians were delighted to see Newtonianism at bay, Clairaut found toward the end of 1748, through a consideration that was difficult to hold in suspicion, given the state of mathematical analysis at the time, that in Newton's theory the apogee of the moon moved over a time period very close to that called for by observations. This is what he declared to the Academy on 17 May 1749.

He wrote to Cramer around that time:

> Messrs. d'Alembert and Euler had no inkling of the strategem that led me to my new results. The latter twice wrote to tell me that he had made fruitless efforts to find the same thing as I, and that he begged me to tell him how I arrived at them. I told him, more or less, what it was all about [Speziali, in *Revue d'histoire des science et de leurs applications,* p. 227, letter of 26 July 1749].

This first approximate resolution of the three-body problem in celestial mechanics culminated in the publication of the *Théorie de la lune* in 1752 and the *Tables de la lune* in 1754.

The controversies arose anew when Clairaut, strengthened by his first success, turned to the movement of comets.

In 1705 Edmund Halley had announced that the comet observed in 1552, 1607, and 1682 would reappear in 1758 or 1759. He attributed the disparity in its period of appearance to perturbations caused by Jupiter and Saturn. The attention of astronomers was therefore drawn toward this new passage, and Clairaut found in it a new field of activity. The conditions favorable, in the case of the moon, to solving the three-body problem did not exist here. The analysis had to be much more precise. It was essentially a question of calculating the perturbations brought about by the attractions of Jupiter and Saturn, in the movement of the comet. Clairaut thus began a race against time, attempting to calculate as accurately as possible the comet's passage to perihelion before it occurred. For purely astronomical calculations such as those of the positions of the two main planets, he enlisted the services of Lalande, who was assisted by a remarkable woman, Nicole-Reine Étable de Labrière Lepaute.

These feverishly completed calculations resulted in Clairaut's announcement, at the opening session of the Academy in November 1758, that passage to perihelion would occur about 15 April 1759. "You can see," he said, "the caution with which I make such an announcement, since so many small quantities that must be neglected in methods of approximation can change the time by a month."

The actual passage to perihelion took place on 13 March. By reducing his approximations even more, Clairaut calculated the date as 4 April. Then, in a paper awarded a prize by the Academy of St. Petersburg in 1762, and through use of a different method, he arrived at the last day of March as the date of passage. It was difficult to do any better. Nevertheless, there were arguments, particularly from d'Alembert.

Several anonymous articles appeared in 1759 in the *Observateur littéraire,* the *Mercure,* and the *Journal encyclopédique.* The latter, which Clairaut attributed to d'Alembert, was actually by Le Monnier. Clairaut offered a general reply in the November issue of the *Journal des sçavans.* "If," he stated, "one wishes to establish that Messrs. d'Alembert et al. can solve the three-body problem in the case of comets as well as I did, I would be delighted to let him do so. But this is a problem that has not been solved before, in either theory or practice."

In the fourteenth memoir of his *Opuscules mathématiques* (1761), d'Alembert attacked Clairaut ruthlessly. In December of that year Clairaut replied in the *Journal des sçavans:* "Since M. d'Alembert does not have the patience to calculate accurate tables, he should let alone those who have undertaken to do so." D'Alembert replied in the February 1762 issue of the *Journal encyclopédique,* and Clairaut put an end to the debate in the June issue of the *Journal des sçavans* by congratulating his adversary for his research on the comet "since its return."

In 1727 James Bradley made public his discovery of the aberration of light, and the Lapland expedition scrupulously took this phenomenon into consideration in the determination of latitudes. Bradley had not given any theoretical proof, however; and in a paper written in 1737, immediately following his return from the expedition, Clairaut offered the neglected proofs. He dealt with this question several times again; and in 1746 he indicated how to make corrections for the aberration of planets, comets, and satellites.

In 1739 Clairaut became interested in the problem of refraction in Newton's corpuscular theory of light. The theory had just been presented in France by Voltaire (probably inspired by Clairaut) in his *Élémens de philosophie de Newton.* It was the first time that Newton's theory of light had been presented in its entirety by a member of the Académie des Sciences.

The unequal refrangibility of light rays made the astronomical (refracting) telescope imperfect, and Newton had therefore preferred the reflecting telescope. In 1747 Euler suggested making up two-component glass object lenses with water enclosed between them. On the strength of Newton's experiments the English optician John Dollond rejected that solution, and Clairaut supported him. But in 1755 Klingenstierna sent a report to Dollond that led the latter to redo the Newtonian experiments and to go back to his original opinion. Thus, he used object lenses made up of two glasses having different optical qualities. His technique, however, still remained mysterious. Clairaut, thinking that it would be expedient to provide a complete theory on the question, undertook precise experiments in which he was assisted by the optician George and his colleague Tournière. In April 1761 and June 1762 Clairaut presented to the Académie des Sciences three mémoires under the title "Sur les moyens de perfectionner les lunettes d'approche par l'usage d'objectifs composés de plusieurs matières différemment réfringentes."

Clairaut's intention to publish a technical work on this subject for craftsmen was interrupted by his death. Shortly afterward d'Alembert published three extensive studies on the achromatic telescope. The Academy of St. Petersburg had made this question the subject of a competition in 1762, and the prize was won by Klingenstierna. Clairaut translated Klingenstierna's paper into French and had it published in the *Journal des sçavans* in October and November of that year.

Clairaut's mathematical education, conforming so little to university traditions, influenced his ideas on pedagogy. The parallel with Blaise Pascal is obvious. However, we know Pascal's ideas only through a few pages preserved by Leibniz and through what survives in the Port Royal *Géométrie.* As for Clairaut, he left us two remarkable didactic works.

In geometry Euclid's authority had undergone its first serious attack in France in the sixteenth century by Petrus Ramus. The influence of this reformer, however, was felt most in the Rhineland universities. Criticism of Euclid's geometric concepts reappeared in the following century in the Port Royal *Logique* and gave rise to the Port Royal *Géométrie*. At that point one could observe the appearance in mathematical teaching of a more liberal and intuitionist school (alongside a dogmatic school and in contrast with it) represented especially by the teachings of the Oratorians.

Clairaut's *Élémens de géométrie* is linked to the more liberal school. He wanted geometry to be rediscovered by beginners and therefore put together, for himself and for them, a very optimistic history of mathematical thought that reflected the concepts of his contemporaries Diderot and Rousseau.

> I intended to go back to what might have given rise to geometry; and I attempted to develop its principles by a method natural enough so that one might assume it to be the same as that of geometry's first inventors, attempting only to avoid any false steps that they might have had to take [*Élémens de géométrie,* preface].

He found that the measurement of land would have been the most suitable area to give rise to the first propositions. Through analogy, he went from there to more advanced and more abstract research, all the while resolving problems without setting forth theorems and admitting as obvious all truths that showed themselves to be self-evident.

This work is pleasant and has definite pedagogical value, but it remains on a very elementary level. The subject matter corresponds to books 1–4, 6, 11, and 12 of Euclid.

The *Élémens d'algèbre* was conceived in the same spirit. Clairaut again endeavored to follow a pseudo-historical path, or at least a "natural" one. First he deals with elementary problems and appeals to common sense alone. Then, gradually increasing the difficulty, he brings forth the necessity of an algebraic symbolism and technique. Much more scholarly than his geometry, his algebra extends all the way to the solution of fourth-degree equations.

The *Élémens d'algèbre* influenced the instructional technique of the *écoles centrales* of the Revolution. S. F. Lacroix, who republished and commented upon it, considered Clairaut to be the "first who, in blazing a philosophical path, shed a bright light on the principles of algebra."

However, the algebra of Bézout, which represented the dogmatic tendency in this field, frequently was victorious over Clairaut's. Euler's *Algebra* (1769) was in no way inferior to Clairaut's from the pedagogical point of view and greatly surpassed it from the scientific point of view. For example, it is very rich in material concerning the theory of numbers, an aspect of mathematics completely foreign to Clairaut's research and mathematical concepts.

As he says in the preface to the *Élémens d'algèbre,* Clairaut wanted to complete his didactic works with an application of algebra to geometry in which, among other things, he would have been able to study conic sections. Nothing more of this work seems to exist, and it may not have been undertaken. However, there is a manuscript entitled "Premières notions sur les mathématiques à l'usage des enfants," sent by Diderot to Catherine II of Russia as a work by Clairaut.

BIBLIOGRAPHY

I. Original Works. Clairaut's books are *Recherches sur les courbes à double courbure* (Paris, 1731); *Élémens de géométrie* (Paris, 1741; 5th ed., 1830; 11th ed., 2 vols., 1920), trans. into Swedish (Stockholm, 1744–1760), German (Hamburg, 1790), and English (London, 1881); *Théorie de la figure de la terre tirée des principes de l'hydrostatique* (Paris, 1743, 1808), trans. into German as Ostwald's Klassiker no. 189 (Leipzig, 1903), Italian (Bologna, 1928), and Russian (Leningrad, 1947); *Élémens d'algèbre* (Paris, 1746; 4th ed., 1768; 2 vols., 1797, 1801), trans. into German (Berlin, 1752) and Dutch (Amsterdam, 1760); *Théorie de la lune déduite du seul principe de l'attraction réciproquement proportionnelle aux quarrés des distances* (St. Petersburg, 1752), which won the prize offered by the Royal Academy of St. Petersburg in 1750, 2nd ed. (Paris, 1765) includes "Tables de la lune construites sur une nouvelle révision de toutes les espèces de calculs dont leurs équations dépendent"; *Tables de la lune, calculées suivant la théorie de la gravitation universelle* (Paris, 1754); *Réponse de Mr Clairaut à quelques pièces, la plupart anonymes, dans lesquelles on a attaqué le Mémoire sur la comète de 1682, lu le 14 novembre 1758* (Paris, 1759); *Théorie du mouvement des comètes, dans laquelle on a égard aux altérations que leurs orbites éprouvent par l'action des planètes . . .* (Paris, 1760 [?]); and *Recherches sur la comète des années 1531, 1607, 1682 et 1759, pour servir de supplément à la théorie, par laquelle on avait annoncé en 1758 le temps de retour de cette comète . . .* (St. Petersburg, 1762).

An exhaustive account of Clairaut's papers in the publications of learned societies is in the bibliography added by René Taton to Pierre Brunet's study on Clairaut (see below). This bibliography was taken up again and completed by Taton in *Revue d'histoire des sciences et des techniques,* **6**, no. 2 (April–June 1953), 161–168. Among Clairaut's papers are "Sur les courbes que l'on forme en coupant une surface courbe quelconque par un plan donné de position," in *Mémoires de l'Académie des sciences* (1731), 483–493: "Détermination géométrique de la perpendiculaire à la méridienne, tracée par M. Cassini, avec plusieurs méthodes d'en tirer la grandeur et la figure de la terre," *ibid.* (1733), 406–416; "Sur quelques questions de maximis et minimis," *ibid.,* 186–194; "Quatre problèmes sur de nouvelles courbes," in *Miscellanea Berolinensia,* **4** (1734),

143–152; "Solution de plusieurs problèmes où il s'agit de trouver des courbes dont la propriété consiste dans une certaine relation entre leurs branches, exprimée par une équation donnée," in *Mémoires de l'Académie des sciences* (1734), 196–215; "Examen des différentes oscillations qu'un corps suspendu par un fil peut faire lorsqu'on lui donne une impulsion quelconque," *ibid.* (1735), 281–298; "De l'aberration apparente des étoiles causée par le mouvement progressif de la lumière," *ibid.* (1737), 205–227; "Investigationes aliquot, ex quibus probetur terrae figuram secundam leges attractionibus in ratione inversa quadrati distanciarum maxime ad ellipsin accedere debere," in *Philosophical Transactions of the Royal Society* (1737), 19–25; "Recherches sur la figure des sphéroïdes qui tournent autour de leur axe, comme la Terre, Jupiter et le Soleil, en supposant que leur densité varie du centre à la périphérie," *ibid.* (1738); "Sur les explications cartésienne et newtonienne de la réfraction de la lumière," in *Mémoires de l'Académie des sciences* (1739), 258–275; "Sur la manière la plus simple d'examiner si les étoiles ont une parallaxe et de la déterminer exactement," *ibid.*, 358–369; "Recherches générales sur le calcul intégral," *ibid.*, 425–436; "Sur l'intégration ou la construction des équations différentielles du premier ordre," *ibid.* (1740), 293–323; "Sur quelques principes qui donnent la solution d'un grand nombre de problèmes de dynamique," *ibid.* (1742), 1–52; "De l'orbite de la lune dans le système de M. Newton," *ibid.* (1743), 17–32; "De l'aberration de la lumière des planètes, des comètes et des satellites," *ibid.* (1746), 539–568; "De l'orbite de la lune en ne négligeant pas les quarrés des quantités de même ordre que les perturbations," *ibid.* (1748); "Construction des tables du mouvement horaire de la lune," *ibid.* (1752), 593–622; "Construction des tables de la parallaxe horizontale de la lune," *ibid.*, 142–160; "Sur l'orbite apparente du soleil autour de la terre, en ayant égard aux perturbations produites par les actions de la lune et des planètes principales," *ibid.* (1754), 521–564; "Sur les moyens de perfectionner les lunettes d'approche, par l'usage d'objectifs composés de plusieurs matières différemment réfringentes," *ibid.* (1756), 380–437; (1757), 524–550; (1762), 578–631; and "Mémoire sur la comète de 1759, dans lequel on donne les périodes qu'il est le plus à propos d'employer, en faisant usage des observations faites sur cette comète dans les quatre premières apparitions," *ibid.* (1759), 115–120.

Also of note are *Principes mathématiques de la philosophie naturelle,* 2 vols. (Paris, 1756; new printing, 1966), which he helped the marquise du Châtelet to translate and explain; and "Premières notions sur les mathématiques à l'usage des enfants," Paris, Bibliothèque de l'Institut, MS 2102, a copy of the MS sent to Catherine II by Diderot.

Some of Clairaut's correspondence has been published. That with Lesage is in P. Prevost, *Notice sur la vie et les écrits de G. L. Lesage* (Geneva, 1805), pp. 362–372; with d'Alembert, in Charles Henry, "Correspondance inédite de d'Alembert avec Cramer, Lesage, Clairaut, Turgot, Castillon, Beguelin," in *Bollettino di bibliografia e di storia delle scienze matematiche e fisiche,* **18** (1886), 3–112; with Cramer, in Pierre Speziali, "Une correspondance inédite entre Clairaut et Cramer," in *Revue d'histoire des sciences et de leurs applications,* **8,** no. 3 (1955), 193–237. His correspondence with Euler is included in Euler's complete works (in press).

II. SECONDARY LITERATURE. On Clairaut or his work, see Jean Sylvestre Bailly, *Histoire de l'astronomie moderne,* III (Paris, 1785); Joseph Bertrand, "Clairaut, sa vie et ses travaux," in *Éloges académiques,* 2nd ser. (1902), 231–261; Charles Bossut, *Histoire générale des mathématiques depuis leur origine jusqu'à l'année 1808* (Paris, 1810), II, 346–350, 383–386, 418–433; Pierre Brunet, *La vie et l'oeuvre de Clairaut* (Paris, 1952); Moritz Cantor, *Vorlesungen über Geschichte der Mathematik,* III (Leipzig, 1901), 778–786; J. L. Coolidge, *A History of Geometrical Methods* (Oxford, 1940), pp. 135, 172, 321; René Dugas, *Histoire de la mécanique* (Paris-Neuchâtel, 1950), pp. 268–273, 354–357; "Éloge de Clairaut," in *Journal des sçavans* (1765); Jean Grandjean de Fouchy, "Éloge de Clairaut," in *Histoire de l'Académie des sciences* (1765), pp. 144–159; Lesley Hanks, *Buffon avant l'"Histoire naturelle"* (Paris, 1966), p. 296 and *passim;* J. E. Montucla, *Histoire des mathématiques,* 2nd ed. (Paris, 1802; photographically repro., 1960), III, IV; Niels Nielsen, *Géomètres français du XVIIIème siecle* (Copenhagen-Paris, 1935), pp. 132–153; J. C. Poggendorff, *Histoire de la physique* (Paris, 1883), pp. 464–482; René Taton, *L'oeuvre scientifique de Monge* (Paris, 1951), pp. 106–108 and *passim;* Félix Tisserand, *Traité de mécanique céleste,* II (Paris, 1891); and Isaac Todhunter, *History of the Theories of Attraction and the Figure of the Earth,* I (London, 1873).

Works by Clairaut's father are listed in Taton's article in *Revue d'histoire des sciences et des techniques,* **6,** no. 2 (1953), 167. Works by his younger brother are "Méthode de former tant de triangles qu'on voudra, de sorte que la somme des quarrés des deux côtés soit double, triple, etc. . . . du quarré de la base, d'où suivent des quadratures de quelques espèces de lunules" (read before the Academy in 1730), in *Journal des sçavans* (1730), 273f. and (1733), 279; and *Diverses quadratures circulaires, élliptiques et hyperboliques par M. Clairaut le cadet* (Paris, 1731).

JEAN ITARD

CLARKE, SAMUEL (*b.* Norwich, England, 11 October 1675; *d.* London, England, 17 May 1729)

The son of Edward Clarke, an alderman of Norwich, and Hannah Clarke, Samuel Clarke attended the Norwich Free School and entered Gonville and Caius College, Cambridge, in 1690. He became a scholar of his college in 1691 and received the B.A. in 1695. His major interests were physics and theology, and he mastered the contents of Sir Isaac Newton's *Principia* while at Gonville and Caius. He was elected a fellow of the college in 1696 and retained the office until 1700.

The standard physics text used at Cambridge during this period was Théophile Bonnet's clumsy Latin translation of Jacques Rohault's *Physics.* Clarke's tutor, Sir John Ellis, urged him to prepare a more elegant version of the work. Making use of his familiarity with Newtonian physics, Clarke appended to his edition a series of notes that had the novel effect of turning a Cartesian treatise into a vehicle for disseminating the ideas of Newton. His translation remained the major text at Cambridge for over forty years and was translated into English at late as 1723, by Clarke's brother, John.

A chance meeting (in a Norwich coffeehouse) with the mathematician and Arian theologian William Whiston, in 1697, led to Clarke's introduction to Dr. John Moore, bishop of Norwich and Whiston's patron. In 1698 Clarke succeeded Whiston as Moore's chaplain and received his M.A. from Cambridge. His interests now turned to the primitive church, a subject of pivotal importance in the internecine quarrel between orthodox Anglicans, who accepted the Athanasian Creed, and Arian churchmen, who rejected it. Clarke's Arian bent did not hinder his rise in the church at this time. Bishop Moore appointed him rector of Drayton and granted him a parish within Norwich itself.

At Norwich, Clarke gained a reputation as a preacher of clear, learned sermons; this led him to be chosen to present the Boyle lectures for 1704.[1] He made such a favorable impression that he was asked to deliver an additional series the next year. The sixteen sermons were subsequently published as *The Being and Attributes of God.*[2] He opposed Descartes's idea that "motion is essential to all things" and his insistence on "an infinite *plenum.*" Clarke cited Newton's concept of the void to show that matter was no more "necessary" than motion, and it was clear that "The Self-existent and original Cause of All Things is Not a Necessary Agent, but a Being indued with Liberty and Choice." Liberty stood at the very roots of the universe, for without it there could be no "Cause, Mover, Principle, or Beginning of Motion anywhere."[3]

Thus the evidence of the physical world confuted the ideas of atheists. Clarke's sermons of 1705 were aimed at the deists; his vindication of natural religion demonstrated not merely God's existence but His presence in the world.

In 1706 Sir Isaac Newton commissioned Clarke to translate his *Opticks* into Latin for a broader audience. He was so satisfied with Clarke's "pure and intelligible Latin" that he paid him £500. In the same year Clarke was appointed to the rectory of St. Benet's in London, was introduced to Queen Anne, and was made one of her chaplains-in-ordinary.

Clarke's move to a London parish and his contact with the court involved him in two bitter controversies in which he defended Newton's ideas as well as his own. The first began with the High Church apologist Henry Dodwell, whose *Epistolary Discourse . . . that the Soul is . . . Naturally Mortal* was a high point of the Tory revival that marked Anne's reign.[4] Dodwell considered the soul as a material entity and appealed to the authority of Athanasius, Descartes, and Spinoza in support of his position. Had he been a man of lesser repute, and of worse connections, his work might have been ignored as a ridiculous attempt to cast doubt on both natural and revealed religion. His stature forced those who disagreed with him to reply, and "Mr. Clarke was thought the most proper person for the work."[5]

Clarke denied that the soul could be mortal, since it could not possibly be material. Matter was particulate; the soul was not, and thus was totally independent of matter. At the end of his treatise he cautioned Dodwell to reconsider the implication of his ideas, for Dodwell had furnished "A Weapon for the hands of skeptical men . . . to make profane men rejoice."[6]

The advice was sound but was given far too late. The materialist Anthony Collins now claimed to be Dodwell's defender. In his "Remarks on a (pretended) demonstration of the immateriality and natural immortality of the soul," he maintained that men were "meer machines," incapable of exercising free will.[7] Dodwell faded from the scene, and Collins emerged as Clarke's chief antagonist. In his initial response to Collins, Clarke sought to annihilate his adversary's basic argument by denying that matter could possibly think.[8] Collins replied that if soul existed, it needed extension; if it were extended, then it had to be corporeal.[9]

As the correspondence continued, Collins cited Descartes in support of his idea that consciousness was merely a "mode of motion," and Clarke turned to Newton's work in rebuttal. He accused Collins of having failed to perceive that "the present operations of nature, depending on Gravitation, cannot be Mechanical Effects of Matter in Constant Motion perpetually striking one Part against each other."[10] His final reply to Collins also revealed a debt to Newton in his assertion that the spirit makes use of space as its medium. Clarke's attack on Collins had succeeded in defending Newton's ideas in a metaphysical sense. Collins had had enough, and the dispute was over by 1710.[11]

During the course of this exchange, the queen had named Clarke rector of St. James's, Westminster, a most prestigious position. He was awarded the D.D.

by Cambridge at the same time (1709) and ably defended the thesis that "no article of faith is opposed to right reason."

Clarke's Arianism became obvious with the publication of his *Scripture Doctrine of the Trinity* in 1712. This unitarian work led to a long pamphlet war with such orthodox divines as Daniel Waterland[12] and to a complaint being made about it by the Lower House of Convocation in 1714. Clarke succeeded in defending himself before the Upper House and was not censured.[13] He did, however, agree to write and preach nothing further on this topic, a course of action of which the more outspoken Arians did not wholly approve.

George I's accession to the English throne upon the death of Anne in 1714 effectively destroyed the Tory party for fifty years. The Tory leader, Bolingbroke, who had attacked Clarke, was powerless, and the High Church faction was subdued. For Clarke, the most significant aspect of the Hanoverian succession lay not in these developments, however welcome, but in his meeting and subsequent friendship with the princess of Wales (later queen), Caroline. A close friend of Leibniz, the princess originally sought to have Clarke translate his *Theodicy*. Clarke refused, since the work contained an attack on Newton's concept of gravity. Impressed by Clarke's persuasive powers, Caroline sent copies of his works to Leibniz and asked for his opinion of them. His reply, shown by the princess to Clarke, sparked an exchange of letters that lasted until Leibniz's death in November 1716.

In the course of his five letters, Leibniz accused the Newtonians of having made "Natural religion itself . . . to decay [in England]," of turning God into a watchmaker who "wants to wind up his watch from time to time," of making gravity either an occult quality or a "perpetual miracle," and of having failed to understand the principle of "sufficient reason" by their belief in the vacuum, in atoms, and in the reality of space and time. Clarke undertook to answer these charges, drawing on the writings of Newton and occasionally obtaining his advice.[14] Thus, in his fourth paper Clarke cited not only Newton but the work of earlier experimenters to prove his contentions that the vacuum did exist, as did hard, impenetrable particles ("physical atoms"), or there could be "no matter at all in the Universe." Clarke also maintained that time and space were real entities and not merely the order of successive and coexistent phenomena, respectively, as suggested by his opponent.[15]

Clarke saw the conflict with Leibniz as involving not merely a differing interpretation of the physical universe and its phenomena but as a far more basic one implying a struggle between freedom and necessity. Leibniz's insistence on philosophical necessity always signified "absolute necessity" to Clarke, for Leibniz, no less than Collins, would have reduced men to "meer machines."[16]

Clarke's most direct contribution to physics during the course of this correspondence came in a footnote to his fifth paper, in which he considered the problem of computing the force of a moving body. He discussed the Newtonian position that such force could be expressed as the product of mass and velocity (mv) and that of the Leibnizians, who expressed it as the product of mass and the square of the velocity (mv^2). He saw the issue as one between the concepts of momentum and kinetic energy. He developed these ideas in his last published paper, a letter to Benjamin Hoadly, "Concerning the proportion of force to velocity in bodies in motion," in which he strongly advocated the Newtonian position.[17]

Despite Caroline's continuing favor, Clarke's heterodoxy had halted his rise in the church, and a bishopric, or an even higher position, escaped him.[18] He accepted only one further office: the mastership of Wigston Hospital, in Leicestershire, in 1718. He had powerful friends among the more latitudinarian clergy. During the 1720's George Berkeley, Benjamin Hoadly, and William Sherlocke met with him frequently at court. He retained his popularity as a preacher and was much in demand to deliver sermons away from St. James's until his death in May 1729.

Clarke used his talents as a translator to prepare editions of Caesar's *Commentaries* (dedicated to the duke of Marlborough) in 1712 and, by royal command, of the first twelve books of the *Iliad* in 1729. His political convictions were strongly Whiggish, for the Whigs were supporters of political liberty.[19]

Clarke married Katherine Lockwood and had five children who survived him. His son, Samuel, became a fellow of the Royal Society.

For twenty-five years Clarke had held to his position and had vindicated that of Newton. His contemporaries ranked him almost with Newton in the force of his intellect; certainly, of Newton's circle, Clarke was best fitted for the role of defender and publicist.

NOTES

1. Founded by the Honorable Robert Boyle "to assert and vindicate the great fundamentals of Natural Religion," the lectures consisted of eight sermons a year preached in a London church. The tone of the lectures was set by the first incumbent, Richard Bentley, who demonstrated how Newton's *Principia* gave proof of the existence of God and of free will.
2. "A Demonstration of the Attributes of God" and "A Discourse Concerning Natural Religion," in *A Defense of Natural and Revealed Religion: Being a Collection of Sermons at the Boyle Lectures*, vol. II.

3. *Ibid.*, pp. 12-32, *passim.*
4. By 1706 this movement was well under way. A long war abroad, the linking of the Whigs with the cause of dissent and broad church policies, and the queen's undoubted preference for the rituals of High Anglican tradition led to a realliance between the Tories and the extreme Episcopalians.
5. B. Hoadly, "Life of Clarke," prefixed to *The Works of Samuel Clarke*, I, v.
6. S. Clarke, "A Letter to Mr. Dodwell," *Works*, III, 749; *cf.* British Museum, Add. Mss 4370, fols. 1, 2.
7. A. Collins, "A Letter to the Learned Henry Dodwell," *Works*, III, 752 ff.
8. S. Clarke, "Defense of An Argument . . .," *Works*, III, 761.
9. A. Collins, "Reply to Clarke's Defense," *Works*, III, 775.
10. S. Clarke, "Third Defense," *Works*, III, 848.
11. Collins did reappear after the death of Leibniz with his *Philosophical Enquiry Concerning Human Liberty* (1717), and again Clarke answered him.
12. Clarke was aided by his brother, John, and by John Jackson; his opponents included Waterland, Edward Wells, and Joseph Clarke. The controversy is referred to briefly in H. G. Alexander, *The Leibniz-Clarke Correspondence*, pp. xli, xlii; and in detail in J. Rodney, *God, Freedom, and the Cosmos* (to be published).
13. The case is to be found in Clarke, *Works*, IV; *cf.* British Museum, Add. Mss 4370.
14. Cited in Alexander, *op. cit.*, *passim.*
15. *Ibid.*, pp. xiii, 100.
16. Clarke, "Fifth Reply," in Alexander, *op. cit.*, p. 110.
17. *Ibid.*, pp. 121-125; *Works*, IV, 737-740; reprinted in *Philosophical Transactions of the Royal Society* (1728).
18. Voltaire (*Oeuvres*, LV, 96) maintains that Caroline was prevented from appointing Clarke archbishop of Canterbury by Bishop Gibson's telling her that he had but one defect: "He was not a Christian."
19. The triumph of the Whigs in 1688 and in 1714 implies the acceptance politically of the philosophical tenet of human liberty. Clarke's political zeal may be seen in his willingness to dedicate his work to Marlborough at a time when the duke was out of favor; he remained a friend of Sarah, Duchess of Marlborough.

BIBLIOGRAPHY

I. Original Works. Clarke's translations of scientific works are *Jacobi Rohaulti, Physica: Latine vertit Samuel Clarke, recensuit et uberioribus, ex illustrissimi Isaac Newtoni philosophia maximam partem hausti, amplificavit et ornavit* (London, 1697); and *Optice: Sive de reflexionibus, refractionibus, inflexionibus & coloribus . . . authore Isaaco Newton, equite aurato, vertit Samuel Clarke* (London, 1706).

His writings on theological and philosophical topics, including the full texts of the correspondence with Dodwell, Collins, and Leibniz, as well as his letter to Hoadly, are brought together in *The Works of Samuel Clarke*, John Clarke, ed., 4 vols. (London, 1738).

II. Secondary Literature. The best contemporary biographical sketch is Benjamin Hoadly's "Some Account of the Life, Writings, and Character of [Samuel Clarke]," prefixed to the 1738 ed. of Clarke's *Works*. William Whiston's *Memoirs of the Life of Dr. Samuel Clarke* (London, 1730) is longer but far less reliable.

There is as yet no full-length modern study of Clarke. H. G. Alexander's *Clarke-Leibniz Correspondence* (Manchester, 1956) contains a brief sketch of Clarke's life and an analysis of the correspondence.

Modern articles on Clarke are equally scarce: John Gay's "Matter and Freedom in the Thought of Samuel Clarke," in *Journal of the History of Ideas* (1963), and J. Rodney's "Newton Revisited: Foes, Friends, and Thoughts," in *Research Studies, Washington State University*, **36** (1968), 351-360, are the most recent.

Joel M. Rodney

CLAUSEN, THOMAS (*b.* Snogbaek, Denmark, 16 January 1801; *d.* Dorpat, Estonia [now Tartu, Estonian S.S.R.], 23 May 1885)

Thomas Clausen was the eldest of the eight children of Claus Clausen and Cecilia Rasmussen Clausen. The elder Clausen was a poor peasant farmer in northern Schleswig. A local pastor, who was interested in the natural sciences and for whom young Clausen herded cattle, became interested in the young man and instructed him in Latin, Greek, mathematics, astronomy, and natural science over a seven-year period. On his own, Clausen studied French, English, and Italian. Upon the pastor's recommendation, H. C. Schumacher made Clausen his assistant at his Altona observatory in 1824. Clausen, a very individualistic man, had a falling out with his superior; and at the end of 1828 he moved to Munich as the appointed successor to Fraunhofer at the Joseph von Utzschneider Optical Institute. He held this position in name only, however; Utzschneider allowed Clausen to devote himself completely to his mathematical and astronomical calculations and publications, which soon gained him the attention and recognition of such authorities as Olbers, Gauss, Bessel, Steinheil, Hansen, Crelle, A. von Humboldt, Arago, and W. Struve.

In the middle of 1840, after a severe bout with mental illness, Clausen returned to Altona, where he spent two years in seclusion and reached the zenith of his scientific creativity. He also engaged in a mathematical argument with C. G. J. Jacobi. In 1842 he was appointed observer at the Dorpat observatory, and in 1844 he took his doctorate *honoris causa* under Bessel. On 1 January 1866 he was made director of the Dorpat observatory and professor of astronomy at Dorpat University. He went into retirement at the end of 1872. Clausen never married. In 1854 he received through Gauss a corresponding membership in the Göttingen Academy. In 1856 he received the same class of membership from the St. Petersburg Academy.

Like many astronomers of the first half of the nineteenth century, Clausen was a self-made man. He differed from most of his professional colleagues in that he was in a position to make a major contribution to those mathematical problems with which the leading intellectuals of his time were preoccupied. He possessed an enormous facility for calculation, a critical eye, and perseverance and inventiveness in his methodology. As a theoretician he was less inclined toward astronomy. Gauss soon recognized the "outstanding talents" of Clausen. The Copenhagen Academy awarded him a prize for his work "Determination of the Path of the 1770 Comet."[1] Bessel commented: "What a magnificent, or rather, masterful work! It is an achievement of our time which our descendants will not fail to credit him with."[2] Clausen's approximately 150 published works are devoted to a multitude of subjects, from pure and applied mathematics to astronomy, physics, and geophysics. He repeatedly solved problems that were posed to him publicly by other mathematicians or proved theories that had been published without proof, as was the custom at that time, and corrected mistakes and errors in others. Special mention should be made in this connection of the calculation of fourteen paths of comets, as well as of the theorem, named for Staudt and Clausen, dealing with Bernoullian numbers.[3] Fermat had hypothesized that all numbers of the form $F(n) = 2^{2^n} + 1$ were prime numbers. Euler disproved this hypothesis in 1732 by factoring Fermat's number $F(5) = 2^{2^5} + 1$. In 1854 Clausen factored $F(6) = 2^{2^6} + 1$ and thus proved that this number also is not a prime number. Clausen used as a basis his own new method—still unpublished—of factoring numbers into their prime factors.[4] There is substantial reason for believing that Clausen gained a deeper insight into the field of number theory than the material published by him would indicate.

NOTES

1. *Astronomische Nachrichten,* **19** (1842), 121-168.
2. *Ibid.,* pp. 335-336.
3. *Ibid.,* **17** (1840), 351-352.
4. *Journal für die reine und angewandte Mathematik,* **216** (1964), 185.

BIBLIOGRAPHY

I. Original Works. In addition to the works cited in the text, see *Astronomische Nachrichten, Journal für die reine und angewandte Mathematik, Archiv der Mathematik und Physik,* and *Publications de l'Académie impériale des sciences de St. Pétersbourg,* in which almost all of Clausen's works appeared. See also the bibliographical aids in the Biermann work cited below.

II. Secondary Literature. For a study of Clausen, see Kurt-R. Biermann's "Thomas Clausen, Mathematiker und Astronom," in *Journal für die reine und angewandte Mathematik,* **216** (1964), 159-198. This biography contains a virtually complete list (pp. 193-195) of the literature dealing with Clausen and a list of his MSS and unedited letters (pp. 191-193). Moreover, reference should be made to J. Gaiduk, "Thomas Clausen ja tema matemaatika-alane looming," in *Matemaatika ja kaasaeg,* **12** (1967), 116-122; and U. Lumiste, "Täiendusi Th. Clauseni biograafiale," *ibid.,* pp. 123-124.

Kurt-R. Biermann

CLAVIUS, CHRISTOPH (*b.* Bamberg, Germany, 1537; *d.* Rome, Italy, 6 February 1612)

Clavius entered the Jesuit order at Rome in 1555 and later studied for a time at the University of Coimbra (Portugal), where he observed the eclipse of the sun on 21 August 1560. He began teaching mathematics at the Collegio Romano in Rome in 1565, while still a student in his third year of theology; and for all but two of the next forty-seven years he was a member of the faculty as professor of mathematics or as scriptor. From October 1595 until the end of 1596, he was stationed in Naples.

In 1574 Clavius published his main work, *The Elements of Euclid.* (With the help of native scholars, Matteo Ricci, between 1603 and 1607, translated into Chinese the first six books of Clavius' *Elements.*) His contemporaries called Clavius "the Euclid of the sixteenth century." The *Elements,* which is not a translation, contains a vast quantity of notes collected from previous commentators and editors, as well as some good criticisms and elucidations of his own. Among other things, Clavius made a new attempt at proving the "postulate of parallels." In his *Elements* of 1557, the French geometer Peletier held that the "angle of contact" was not an angle at all. Clavius was of a different opinion; but Viète, in his *Variorum de rebus mathematicis responsorum* of 1593, ranged himself on the side of Peletier. In a scholion to the twelfth proposition of the ninth book of Euclid, Clavius objects to Cardanus' claim to originality in employing a method that derives a proposition by assuming the contradictory of the proposition to be proved. According to Clavius, Cardanus was anticipated in this method by Euclid and by Theodosius of Bithynia in the twelfth proposition of the first book of his *Sphaericorum.*

As an astronomer, Clavius was a supporter of the Ptolemaic system and an opponent of Copernicus. In his *In Sphaeram Ioannis de Sacro Bosco commentarius* (Rome, 1581) he was apparently the first to accuse Copernicus not only of having presented a physically absurd doctrine but also of having contradicted numerous scriptural passages. The friendship between Clavius and Galileo, according to their correspondence, began when Galileo was twenty-three and remained unimpaired throughout Clavius' life. In a report of April 1611 to Cardinal Bellarmine of the Holy Office, Clavius and his colleagues confirmed Galileo's discoveries, published in the *Sidereus nuncius* (1610), but they did not confirm Galileo's theory.

In his *Epitome arithmeticae practicae* (Rome, 1583), Clavius gave a distinct notation for "fractions of fractional numbers," but he did not use it in the ordinary multiplication of fractions. His $\frac{3}{5} \cdot \frac{4}{7} \cdot$ means $\frac{3}{5}$ of $\frac{4}{7}$. The distinctive feature of this notation is the omission of the fractional line after the first fraction. The dot cannot be considered as the symbol of multiplication. He offered an explanation for finding the lowest common multiple, which before him only Leonardo Fibonacci in his *Liber abaci* (1202) and Tartaglia in his *General trattato di numeri et misure* (1556) had done. In his *Astrolabium* (Rome, 1593) Clavius gives a "tabula sinuum," in which the proportional parts are separated from the integers by dots. However, his real grasp of that notation is open to doubt, and the more so because in his *Algebra* (Rome, 1608) he wrote all decimal fractions in the form of common fractions. Apart from that, his *Algebra* marks the appearance in Italy of the German plus (+) and minus (−) signs and of algebraic symbols used by Stifel. He was one of the very first to use parentheses to express aggregation of terms. As symbol of the unknown quantity, he used the German radix (𝔄). For additional unknowns he used 1*A*, 1*B*, etc.; for example, he wrote 3𝔄 + 4*A*, 4*B* − 3*A* for $3x + 4y$, $4z - 3y$. In his *Algebra,* Clavius did not take notice of negative roots, but he recognized that the quadratic $x^2 + c = bx$ may be satisfied by two values of x. His geometrical proof for this statement was one of the best and most complete. The appendix of his commentary on the *Sphaericorum* of Theodosius (Rome, 1586)—containing a treatise on the sine, the tangent, and the secant—and the rules for the solutions of both plane and spherical triangles in the *Astrolabium,* the *Geometria practica* (Rome, 1604), and the *Triangula sphaerica* (Mainz, 1611) comprehend nearly all the contemporary knowledge of trigonometry; in the *Astrolabium,* for example, is his treatment of the so-called prosthaphaeresis method, by which addition and subtraction were substituted for multiplication, as in

$$\sin a \sin b = \frac{1}{2}[\cos(a - b) - \cos(a + b)].$$

In this he also gives a graphic solution of spherical triangles based on the stereographic projection of the sphere.

Mention must also be made of Clavius' improvement of the Julian calendar. Pope Gregory XIII brought together a large number of mathematicians, astronomers, and prelates, who decided upon the adoption of the calendar proposed by Clavius, which was based on Reinhold's *Prussian Tables.* To rectify the errors of the Julian calendar it was agreed to write in the new calendar 15 October immediately after 4 October of the year 1582. The Gregorian calendar met with a great deal of opposition from scientists such as Viète and Scaliger and from the Protestants.

BIBLIOGRAPHY

Clavius' collected works, *Opera mathematica,* 5 vols. (Mainz, 1611/1612), contain, in addition to his arithmetic and algebra, his commentaries on Euclid, Theodosius, and Sacrobosco; his contributions to trigonometry and astronomy; and his work on the calendar.

The best account of Clavius' works and their several editions can be found in C. Sommervogel, *Bibliothèque de la Compagnie de Jésus,* II (Brussels–Paris, 1891). Some information on his life and work can be found in B. Boncompagni, "Lettera di Francesco Barozzi al P. Christoforo Clavio," in *Bollettino di bibliografia e storia delle scienze matematiche e fisiche,* **17** (1884), 831–837; A. von Braunmühl, *Vorlesungen über Geschichte der Trigonometrie,* I (1900), 189–191; F. Cajori, "Early 'Proofs' of the Impossibility of a Fourth Dimension of Space," in *Archivio di storia della scienza,* **7** (1926), 25–28; J. Ginsburg, "On the Early History of the Decimal Point," in *American Mathematical Monthly,* **35** (1928), 347–349; O. Meyer, "Christoph Clavius Bambergensis," in *Fränkisches Land,* **9** (1962), 1–8; J. E. Montucla, *Histoire des mathématiques,* 2nd ed., I (Paris, 1799), 682–687; E. C. Philips, "The Correspondence of Father Christopher Clavius S. I.," in *Archivum historicum Societatis Iesu,* **8** (1939), 193–222; and J. Tropfke, "Zur Geschichte der quadratischen Gleichungen über dreieinhalb Jahrtausend," in *Jahresbericht der Deutschen Mathematikervereinigung,* **44** (1934), 117–119.

H. L. L. BUSARD

CLEBSCH, RUDOLF FRIEDRICH ALFRED (*b.* Königsberg, Germany [now Kaliningrad, U.S.S.R.], 19 January 1833; *d.* Göttingen, Germany, 7 November 1872)

In 1850 Clebsch entered the University of Königsberg, where the school of mathematics founded by Jacobi was then flourishing. His teachers included the mathematical physicist Franz Neumann and the mathematicians Friedrich Richelot and Ludwig Otto

Hesse, both pupils of Jacobi. After graduation, in 1854, he went to Berlin, where he was taught under the direction of Karl Schellbach at various schools. Clebsch's academic career began in 1858, when he became *Privatdozent* at the University of Berlin. Soon afterward he moved to Karlsruhe, where he was a professor at the Technische Hochschule from 1858 to 1863. From 1863 to 1868 he was professor at the University of Giessen, collaborating with Paul Gordan. From 1868 until his death, he was professor at the University of Göttingen and in the forefront of contemporary German mathematics. In 1868 he and his friend Carl Neumann, son of Franz Neumann, founded the *Mathematische Annalen.*

Clebsch's doctoral dissertation at the University of Königsberg concerned a problem of hydrodynamics, and the main problems considered in the first period of his scientific career were in mathematical physics, especially hydrodynamics and the theory of elasticity. His book on elasticity (1862) may be regarded as marking the end of this period. In it he treated and extended problems of elastic vibrations of rods and plates. His interests concerned more the mathematical than the experimental side of the physical problems. He soon moved on to pure mathematics, where he achieved a dominant place.

Clebsch's first researches in pure mathematics were suggested by Jacobi's papers concerning problems in the theory of variation and of partial differential equations. He had not known Jacobi personally but collaborated in the edition of his *Gesammelte Werke.* For general problems in the calculus of variations, Clebsch calculated the second variation and promoted the integration theory of Pfaffian systems, surpassing results that Jacobi had obtained in these fields.

Although in these analytical papers Clebsch already proved himself to be highly skilled in calculus, his fame as a leader of contemporary scientists was first gained through his contributions to the theory of projective invariants and algebraic geometry. In the nineteenth century these fields were called modern geometry and modern algebra. The term "modern" or "new" geometry was applied to the projective geometry developed in synthetic form by Poncelet, Steiner, and Staudt, and in analytical form by Plücker and Hesse. Clebsch wrote a biographical sketch of Plücker, giving evidence of the author's deep insight into mathematical currents of the nineteenth century. In numerical geometry we still speak of the Plücker-Clebsch principle of the resolubility of several algebraic equations.

The name "modern algebra" was applied to the algebra of invariants, founded by the English mathematicians Cayley, Salmon, and Sylvester. One of the first German contributors to this discipline was Aronhold. It was especially the papers of Aronhold that incited Clebsch to his own researches in the theory of invariants, or "algebra of quantics," as it was called by the English. The results in the theory of invariants are to be interpreted by geometric properties of algebraic curves, surfaces, and so on. This connection between algebra and geometry attracted Clebsch in a special way. He was soon a master of the difficult calculations with forms and determinants occurring in the theory of invariants. In this he surpassed his teacher Hesse, whose ability and elegance in analytical geometry were praised at the time.

Clebsch completed the symbolic calculus for forms and invariants created by Aronhold, and henceforth one spoke of the Clebsch-Aronhold symbolic notation. Clebsch's own contributions in this field of algebraic geometry include the following. With the help of suitable eliminations he determined a surface of order $11n - 24$ intersecting a given surface of order n in points where there is a tangent that touches the surface at more than three coinciding points. For a given cubic surface he calculated the tenth-degree equation on the resolution of which the determination of the Sylvester pentahedron of that surface depends. For a plane quartic curve Clebsch found a remarkable invariant that, when it vanishes, makes it possible to write the curve equation as a sum of five fourth-degree powers. At the end of his life Clebsch inaugurated the notion of a "connex," a geometrical object in the plane obtained by setting a form containing both point and line coordinates equal to zero.

The general interest in the theory of invariants began to abate somewhat in 1890, when Hilbert succeeded in proving that the system of invariants for a given set of forms has a finite basis. In 1868 Gordan had already proved the precursory theorem on the finiteness of binary invariants. The theory of binary invariants thus being more complete, Clebsch published a book on this part of the theory (1872), giving a summary of the results obtained.

In the last year of his life Clebsch planned the publication of his lectures on geometry, perhaps to include those on n dimensions, results by no means as self-evident then as now. After Clebsch's death his pupil Karl Lindemann published two volumes of these lectures (1876–1891), completed with his additions but confined to plane and three-dimensional geometry. Between 1906 and 1932 a second edition of volume I, part 1 of this work appeared under the name of both Clebsch and Lindemann. The first volume contained almost all of the known material on plane algebraic curves and on Abelian integrals and invariants connected with them.

In 1863 Clebsch began his very productive collaboration with Gordan by inviting him to Göttingen. In 1866 they published a book on the theory of Abelian functions. Papers by Clebsch alone on the geometry of rational elliptic curves and the application of Abelian functions in geometry may be regarded as ancillary to the book. All these works are based on Riemann's fundamental paper (1857) on Abelian functions. In this celebrated work Riemann based the algebraic functions on the Abelian integrals defined on the corresponding Riemann surface, making essential use of topological ideas and of the so-called Dirichlet principle taken from potential theory.

Riemann's ideas were difficult for most contemporary mathematicians, Clebsch included. In the following years mathematicians sought gradually to eliminate the transcendental elements from the Riemann theory of algebraic functions and to establish the theory on pure algebraic geometry. Clebsch's papers were an essential step in this direction. The application of Abelian functions to geometry in his principal paper (1865) is to be understood as the resolution of contact problems by means of Abel's theorem, i.e., the determination of systems of curves or surfaces touching a curve in a plane or in space in given orders, such as the double tangents of a plane quartic curve.

Clebsch and Gordan's book had the following special features: (*a*) use of homogeneous coordinates for the points of an algebraic curve and for the Abelian integrals defined on it and (*b*) definition of the genus p for a plane algebraic curve of order n possessing as singularities only d double points and s cusps. They were the first to define the genus p by the expression

$$p = \frac{(n-1)(n-2)}{2} - d - s,$$

whereas Riemann had defined this expression as the topological genus of the corresponding Riemann surface. Also, as the title indicates, the transcendental point of view is prevalent in the book. It treats the Jacobian problem of inversion, introduces the theta functions, and so on. On the whole, to a modern reader a century later, the book may seem old-fashioned; but it must be remembered that it appeared long before Weierstrass' more elegant lectures on the same object.

As successors to Clebsch there arose the German school of algebraic geometry, led by Brill and M. Noether, both regarded as his pupils. At the end of the nineteenth century, algebraic geometry moved to Italy, where particular attention was paid to the difficult theory of algebraic surfaces. But the beginnings of the theory of algebraic surfaces go back to Cayley, Clebsch, and Noether, for Clebsch described the plane representations of various rational surfaces, especially that of the general cubic surface. Clebsch must also be credited with the first birational invariant of an algebraic surface, the geometric genus that he introduced as the maximal number of double integrals of the first kind existing on it.

BIBLIOGRAPHY

Among Clebsch's works are *Theorie der Elastizität fester Körper* (Leipzig, 1862); "Über die Anwendung der Abelschen Funktionen auf die Geometrie," in *Journal für die reine und angewandte Mathematik,* **63** (1865), 189–243; *Theorie der Abelschen Funktionen* (Leipzig, 1866), written with Gordan; "Zum Gedächtnis an Julius Plücker," in *Abhandlungen der Königliche Gesellschaft der Wissenschaften zu Göttingen* (1871); *Theorie der binären algebraischen Formen* (Leipzig, 1872); and *Vorlesungen über Geometrie,* Karl Lindemann, ed., 2 vols. (Leipzig, 1876–1891). Karl Lindemann brought out a 2nd ed. of vol. I, pt. 1 in 3 sections (1906, 1910, 1932).

On Clebsch, see "Rudolf Friedrich Alfred Clebsch, Versuch einer Darstellung und Würdigung seiner wissenschaftlichen Leistungen, von einigen seiner Freunde," in *Mathematische Annalen,* 7 (1874), 1–40.

WERNER BURAU

CLIFFORD, WILLIAM KINGDON (*b.* Exeter, England, 4 May 1845; *d.* Madeira, 3 March 1879)

Clifford is perhaps most widely remembered as a popular writer on mathematics and physics, his work being colored by highly personal philosophical overtones. He played an important part, nevertheless, in introducing the ideas of G. F. B. Riemann and other writers on non-Euclidean geometry to English mathematicians. Clifford added a number of his own ideas to the subject, and these were highly regarded at the time, as were his papers on biquaternions, the classification of loci, and the topology of Riemann surfaces.

The son of William Clifford, Clifford was educated at a small private school in Exeter until, at the age of fifteen, he was sent to King's College, London. In October 1863 he took up a minor scholarship to Trinity College, Cambridge, where he read mathematics. Clifford was second wrangler in the mathematical tripos, and second Smith's prizeman, in 1867. A year later he was elected professor of applied mathematics at University College, London, and in 1874 he became a fellow of the Royal Society.

Clifford was a first-class gymnast, whose repertory

apparently included hanging by his toes from the crossbar of a weathercock on a church tower, a feat befitting a High Churchman, as he then was. His health began to fail, however, when Clifford was barely thirty, and the lectures for which he had earned some celebrity gave way to a series of popular review articles, concerned especially with the interrelation of metaphysics, epistemology, and science. The *jeux d'esprit* and (according to Stephen) "strong sense of the ridiculous" characterizing his lectures—often given before distinguished audiences—are evident in these writings, as well as in the published versions of the lectures themselves. Philosophically speaking, he was something of a Spinozist and argued that the mind is the one ultimate reality. An early liking for Aquinas was dispelled by his reading Darwin and Spencer. He was always hostile to those who put ecclesiastical system and sect above humanity.

In 1875 Clifford married Lucy Lane, of Barbados. His health deteriorated rapidly, and despite long visits to Spain, Algeria, the Mediterranean, and finally Madeira, he died of pulmonary tuberculosis before he was thirty-four. His wife and two daughters survived him, and Mrs. Clifford subsequently became well-known as a novelist and dramatist.

In mathematics, Clifford was first and foremost a geometer; as an undergraduate at Cambridge, and as a member of a club known as the Apostles, he had inveighed against the current Cambridge bias towards analysis. At a later date he was atypical in arguing—under the influence of Riemann and Lobachevski—that geometrical truth is a product of experience. It is significant that Clifford, through a translation published in *Nature* (1873), should have drawn attention in England to Riemann's famous *Über die Hypothesen welche der Geometrie zugrunde liegen* (1854). (This had been delivered before a nonmathematical audience, and hence was shorn of the underlying analysis.) Riemann had broadly indicated a way in which matter might be regarded as an efficient cause of spatial structure, and Clifford went further in making matter (and its motion), electrical phenomena, and so forth a manifestation of the varying curvature of space. (See *The Common Sense of the Exact Sciences,* chap. 4; "On the Space-Theory of Matter," in *Proceedings of the Cambridge Philosophical Society,* **2** [1876], 157-158.)

Clifford's writings in geometry were largely on projective geometry; but in non-Euclidean geometry he did some of his best work, investigating the consequences of adjusting the definitions of parallelism (especially by abandoning the condition of coplanarity). Thus he found that parallels not in the same plane can exist (within current non-Euclidean terms) only in a Riemannian (elliptic) space, and that they do exist. (See "Preliminary Sketch of Bi-quaternions" [1873], in his *Mathematical Papers,* pp. 181-200.) He showed how a certain three parallels define a ruled second-order surface that has a number of interesting properties. The properties of such "Clifford's surfaces," as they were later known, were not investigated very deeply by Clifford himself, but Bianchi and Klein made much of them, considering especially an interpretation under which the geometry of the surface was Euclidean.

Elsewhere in his geometrical writings Clifford left memorable results, as in his investigations of the geometrical consequences of extending a method of Cayley's for forming a product of determinants, in his research into quaternion representations of the most general rigid motion in space, and in his application of the techniques of higher-dimensional geometry to a problem in probability. Simultaneously with Max Noether he proved (1870) that a Cremona transformation may be regarded as a compound of quadratic transformations, and toward the end of his life (1877) he established some important topological equivalences for Riemann surfaces. In all this, Clifford justifies the commonly expressed belief of contemporaries that his early death deprived the world of one of the best mathematicians of his generation.

BIBLIOGRAPHY

I. ORIGINAL WORKS. Most of Clifford's writings were published posthumously. *The Common Sense of the Exact Sciences* (London, 1885) was edited and completed by Karl Pearson. *Elements of Dynamics* (London, 1879; 1887), *Lectures and Essays* (London, 1879), and *Science and Thinking* (London, 1879) were all popular treatments. *Lectures and Essays* has an introduction by Sir Frederick Pollock, with a brief biography. The *Mathematical Papers,* edited by R. Tucker (London, 1882), has an introduction by H. J. S. Smith, and a good bibliography.

II. SECONDARY LITERATURE. See also Sir Leslie Stephen's biography in *Dictionary of National Biography* for personal detail—it apparently was written, however, more for Clifford's widow than for posterity. See also A. Macfarlane, *Lectures on Ten British Mathematicians of the Nineteenth Century* (New York, 1916).

JOHN D. NORTH

COCHRAN, WILLIAM GEMMELL (*b.* Ruthglen, Scotland, 15 July 1909; *d.* Orleans, Massachusetts, 29 March 1980)

Cochran was the son of Thomas and Jeannie Cochran. Thomas Cochran, the eldest of seven children, at age thirteen had to take a job with a railroad company. The Cochrans moved several times, finally settling in Glasgow, where in 1927 William was first in the Glasgow University Bursary Competition; this award enabled him to finance his studies at the university, from which he received an M.A. with first-class honors in mathematics and physics in 1931. He shared the Logan Medal for being the most distinguished graduate of the Arts Faculty. As a result he secured a scholarship for graduate work in mathematics at Cambridge.

John Wishart had transferred from the Rothamsted Experimental Station to Cambridge in 1931; fortunately for statistics, Cochran elected to take Wishart's course in mathematical statistics, followed by his practical statistics course in the School of Agriculture. Cochran wrote his important paper presenting "Cochran's theorem" (1934) under Wishart. In the same year he was offered a position at Rothamsted that had become available when R. A. Fisher left to accept the Galton chair in eugenics at University College, London, and Frank Yates had moved up to become head of the statistics department. Cochran had to decide whether he would complete his doctorate at Cambridge or accept the Rothamsted position. He later confided that it was not a difficult decision, because Great Britain (like the rest of the world) was in the throes of the Great Depression and few positions of this caliber were open. He did receive an M.A. from Cambridge in 1938. In his biographical sketch on Cochran, G. S. Watson states that Yates remarked, ". . . it was a measure of his good sense that he [Cochran] accepted my argument that a Ph.D., even from Cambridge, was little evidence of research ability, and that Cambridge had at that time little to teach him in statistics that could not be much better learnt from practical work in a research institute."

Cochran stayed at Rothamsted for five years. During that time he worked closely with Yates on experimental designs and sample survey techniques and had many opportunities to discuss problems with Fisher, who continued to spend much time at Rothamsted. By the time he left, Cochran had published twenty-three papers and had become a well-known statistician. One of his most exhaustive projects was a review of the long-term series of field experiments at the Woburn Experimental Station. Cochran and Yates collaborated on research on the analysis of long-term experiments and groups of experiments; here Cochran initiated his illustrious research on the chi-squared distribution and the analysis of count data. On 17 July 1937 Cochran married Betty I. M. Mitchell, who had a Ph.D. in entomology. The Cochrans were a popular couple, participating in many social activities. They had two daughters and a son. Cochran visited the Iowa State Statistical Laboratory in 1938 and accepted a position there in 1939 to develop a graduate program in statistics (it was part of the mathematics department until 1947). There he and Gertrude Cox initiated their collaboration that culminated in their famous book *Experimental Designs* (1950).

Late in 1943 Cochran took leave from Iowa State to join S. S. Wilks's Statistical Research Group at Princeton University as a research mathematician working on army-navy research problems for the Office of Scientific Research and Development. Much of his work there was devoted to an analysis of hit probabilities in naval combat that utilized little of his statistical background. In 1945 he was asked to serve on a select team of statisticians to evaluate the efficacy of the World War II bombing raids.

In 1946 Cochran joined the newly created North Carolina Institute of Statistics (directed by Gertrude Cox) to develop a graduate program in experimental statistics at North Carolina State College (now University); Harold Hotelling was to develop a graduate program in mathematical statistics at the University of North Carolina at Chapel Hill. Cochran was a member of the organizing committee for the International Biometric Society, which was founded in 1947 at Woods Hole, Massachusetts. His major contribution at North Carolina State was setting a firm foundation for a graduate program balanced in theory and practice and well coordinated with the more theoretical program at Chapel Hill.

In January 1949 the Cochrans moved to Baltimore, where he chaired the biostatistics department in the School of Hygiene and Public Health at the Johns Hopkins University. Since he was faced with medical rather than agricultural problems there, he had to develop procedures to obtain reliable information from observations rather than from experimental data, an area that became his dominant interest for the rest of his life. In 1963 he published *Sampling Techniques*.

Cochran remained at Johns Hopkins until 1957, when he joined the faculty at Harvard University to help Fred Mosteller and others develop the department of statistics. He continued to work closely with research workers at the Medical School and School of Public Health but also did his own research on a variety of topics. In 1967 Cochran was coauthor with G. W. Snedecor of the sixth edition of the latter's *Statistical Methods*. He retired from Harvard in 1976. Despite a dozen years of serious health problems, Cochran continued a wide range of professional activities and was working on the seventh edition of *Statistical Methods* and a book on observational studies until shortly before his death.

Cochran was president of the Institute of Mathematical Statistics (IMS) in 1946 and the American Statistical Association (ASA) in 1953; he served as editor of the *Journal of the ASA* (1945–1950). He was president of the Biometric Society (1954–1955) and of the International Statistical Institute (1967–1971); he was vice president of the American Association for the Advancement of Science (AAAS) in 1966. Cochran was elected to the National Academy of Sciences in 1974. He was a fellow of the ASA, the IMS, the AAAS, and the Royal Statistical Society, and was a Guggenheim fellow (1964–1965). He served on a number of scientific investigatory panels, including those concerned with the Kinsey Report, the efficacy of the Salk polio vaccine, the effects of radiation at Hiroshima, and the surgeon general's report on smoking. He wrote more than one hundred scientific articles (which are classified in Anderson).

Probably Cochran's greatest contributions to the scientific community were his guidance of students (he directed more than forty Ph.D. dissertations) and his textbooks. He had the ability to present complicated material in a format that could be understood by anyone who had an interest in collecting and analyzing data. He could explain where the usual assumptions might fail and take steps to ameliorate the effects of these failures. Cochran was quite willing to modify his statistical techniques when faced with such contingencies and often advocated approximate procedures, even though they might violate some of the accepted norms. Although he realized that there are many imperfections in the collection of data, the fact that an ad hoc statistical technique might modify (in an unknown way) the accepted probability levels did not deter him from using it. This pragmatic approach to the collection and analysis of data is held by many to be his most important contribution.

Cochran was that rarity, a man with both a keen mind and the desire to use it for the benefit of mankind. His office was always open to the struggling student, nonplussed scientist, or inquiring citizen.

BIBLIOGRAPHY

I. Original Works. A bibliography of Cochran's works is part of Morris Hansen and Frederick Mosteller, "William Gemmell Cochran," in *Biographical Memoirs. National Academy of Sciences*, **56** (1987) 61–89. His books are *Fifty Years of Field Experiments at the Woburn Experimental Station* (London, 1936), written with E. J. Russell and J. A. Voelcker; *Experimental Designs* (New York, 1950; 2nd ed., 1957), written with Gertrude Cox; *Sampling Techniques* (New York, 1963; 3rd ed., 1977); *Statistical Problems of the Kinsey Report* (Washington, D.C., 1954), written with Frederick Mosteller and John W. Tukey; *Statistical Methods* (6th ed., Ames, Iowa, 1967; 7th ed., 1980), written with G. W. Snedecor; *William G. Cochran: Contributions to Statistics*, Betty I. M. Cochran, comp. (New York, 1982); and *Planning and Analysis of Observational Studies*, Lincoln E. Moses and Frederick Mosteller, eds. (New York, 1983).

Cochran's papers include "The Distribution of Quadratic Forms in a Normal System," in *Proceedings of the Cambridge Philosophical Society*, **30** (1934), 178–191; "Long-Term Agricultural Experiments," in *Journal of the Royal Statistical Society*, supp. **6** (1938), 104–148; "The Use of the Analysis of Variance in Enumeration by Sampling," in *Journal of the American Statistical Association*, **34** (1939), 492–510; "Some Consequences When the Assumptions for the Analysis of Variance Are Not Satisfied," in *Biometrical Bulletin*, **3** (1947), 22–38; "The X^2 Test of Goodness of Fit," in *Annals of Mathematical Statistics*, **23** (1952), 315–345; "The Combination of Estimates from Different Experiments," in *Biometrics*, **10** (1954), 101–129; "Some Methods for Strengthening the Common X^2 Tests," *ibid.*, 417–451; "The Planning of Observational Studies of Human Populations," in *Journal of the Royal Statistical Society*, **128** (1965), 234–265; and "Errors of Measurement in Statistics," in *Technometrics*, **10** (1968), 637–666.

II. Secondary Literature. Works on Cochran and/or his contributions are Richard L. Anderson, "William Gemmell Cochran, 1909–1980. A Personal Tribute," in *Biometrics*, **36** (1980), 574–578; Theodore Colton, "Bill Cochran: His Contributions to Medicine and Public Health and Some Personal Recollections," in *American Statistician*, **35** (1981), 167–170; Arthur P. Dempster, "Reflections on W. G. Cochran, 1909–1980," in *International Statistical Review*, **51** (1983), 321–322; Arthur P. Dempster and Frederick Mosteller, "In Memoriam William Gemmell Cochran (1909–1980)," in *American Statistician*, **35** (1981), 38; H. O. Hartley, "In Memory of William G. Cochran," in D. Krewski, R. Platek, and J. N. K. Rao, eds., *Current Topics in Survey Sampling* (New York, 1981); Poduri S. R. S. Rao, "Professor William Gemmell Cochran: Pioneer in Statistics, Outstanding Scientist and a Noble Human Being," *ibid.*; Poduri S. R. S. Rao and J. Sedransk, eds., *W. G. Cochran's Impact on Statistics* (New York, 1984); and G. S. Watson, "William Gemmell Cochran 1909–1980," in *Annals of Statistics*, **10** (1982), 1–10.

Richard L. Anderson

CODAZZI, DELFINO (*b.* Lodi, Italy, 7 March 1824; *d.* Pavia, Italy, 21 July 1873)

Codazzi first taught at the Ginnasio Liceale of Lodi; then at the *liceo* of Pavia; and, from 1865 to his death, at the University of Pavia as professor of complementary algebra and analytic geometry and, for a while, of theoretical geodesics. His best-known paper, on the applicability of surfaces, was written as an entry in a prize competition sponsored in 1859 by the French Academy. All three entries in the contest—those of Edmond Bour, Ossian Bonnet, and Codazzi—have been very valuable. Bour's and Bonnet's papers were published long before that of Codazzi, which appeared in 1883; however, its main ideas were incorporated in a paper in *Annali di matematica pura ed applicata* (1867–1872). Here we find the formulas that Bonnet (1863) called "les formules de M. Codazzi." They were not new, for Codazzi's colleague at Pavia, Gaspare Mainardi, had derived them in his paper "Su la teoria generale delle superficie" (1856); however, Codazzi's formulation was simpler and his applications were wider. Bonnet (1867) used Codazzi's formulas to prove the existence theorem in the theory of surfaces.

Codazzi also published on isometric lines, geodesic triangles, equiareal mapping, and the stability of floating bodies.

BIBLIOGRAPHY

Codazzi's papers are in *Annali di scienze matematiche e fisiche*, **7** (1856) and **8** (1857), continued in *Annali di matematica pura ed applicata*, **1** (1858) and 2nd ser., **1-5** (1867–1872). His best-known paper is "Mémoire relatif à l'application des surfaces les unes sur les autres," in *Mémoires présentés par divers savants à l'Académie des sciences de l'Institut de France*, **27**, no. 6 (1883), 29–45; its main ideas are incorporated in the paper "Sulle coordinate curvilinie d'una superficie e dello spazio," in *Annali di matematica pura ed applicata*, 2nd ser., **1** (1867–1868), 293–316, **2** (1868–1869), 101–119; **3** (1869–1870), 269–287; **4** (1870–1871), 10–24; **5** (1871–1872), 206–222.

The only biographical material on Codazzi seems to be U. Amaldi, in *Enciclopedia italiana*, app. I (Rome, 1938), 438; and E. Beltrami, a biographical notice, in *Memorie per la storia dell'Università di Pavia*, ser. Ia (1878), 459. On the history of Codazzi's formulas see G. Darboux, *Leçons sur la théorie générale des surfaces*, II (Paris, 1889), 369, n. 1. Codazzi's formulas were derived in Gaspare Mainardi, "Su la teoria generale delle superficie," in *Giornale del R. Istituto lombardo*, **9** (1856), 385–398. Bonnet's relevant papers are "Note sur la théorie de la déformation des surfaces," in *Comptes rendus hebdomadaires des séances de l'Académie des sciences*, **57** (1863), 805–813; and "Mémoire sur la théorie des surfaces applicables sur une surface donnée," in *Journal de l'École polytechnique*, **42** (1867), 1–151.

Some of the data in this article were supplied by professors A. Pensa and S. Cinquini of the University of Pavia.

DIRK J. STRUIK

COLE, FRANK NELSON (*b.* Ashland, Massachusetts, 20 September 1861; *d.* New York, N.Y., 26 May 1926)

Cole was the third son of Otis and Frances Maria Pond Cole. He was graduated from Harvard College with an A.B. in 1882, second in a class of 189. Awarded a traveling fellowship, he spent two years at Leipzig studying under Felix Klein. In 1885 Cole returned to Harvard as a lecturer in the theory of functions. The next year he received his Ph.D. from Harvard; his dissertation was entitled "A Contribution to the Theory of the General Equation of the Sixth Degree." Cole's mathematical enthusiasm, according to W. F. Osgood, who, with M. Bocher, was among Cole's students, was contagious enough to inaugurate a new era in graduate instruction at Harvard.

In the fall of 1888 Cole went to the University of Michigan; he remained there until 1895, when he went to Columbia University. He was to have retired from Columbia in October 1926 but died the preceding May, survived by his wife and three children. He had married Martha Marie Streiff of Göttingen in 1888, but he had largely isolated himself from his family since 1908. At the time of his death Cole lived in a rooming house under the name of Edward Mitchell and claimed to be a bookkeeper.

Cole's most productive years were those at Ann Arbor. His research dealt mainly with prime numbers, number theory, and group theory. He was a leader in the organization of the American Mathematical Society and active in its affairs until his death. He was its secretary from 1896 to 1920 and a member of the editorial staff of its *Bulletin* from 1897 to 1920. His appreciation of scholarship and his literary skill exerted a great influence on the *Bulletin*, which in turn did much to establish the American Mathematical Society as an important scientific organization. In 1920, when Cole resigned as secretary and as editor, he was given a purse commemorating his long service to the society. He contributed this money to help establish the Frank Nelson Cole prize in algebra. A second prize in theory of numbers was established in Cole's name by the society in 1929. The *Bulletin* for 1921 was dedicated to Cole, and his portrait was the frontispiece.

 COLLINS

BIBLIOGRAPHY

I. ORIGINAL WORKS. Cole revised and translated, with the author's permission, E. Netto's *The Theory of Substitutions and Its Applications to Algebra* (Ann Arbor, Mich., 1892). Twenty of his articles are listed in R. C. Archibald, *A Semicentennial History of the American Mathematical Society, 1888–1938* (New York, 1938), p. 103. See also his reports as secretary of the American Mathematical Society, in *Bulletin of the American Mathematical Society,* **3–27** (1896–1920).

II. SECONDARY LITERATURE. Cole and his work are discussed in R. C. Archibald, *A Semicentennial History of the American Mathematical Society, 1888–1938* (New York, 1938), pp. 100–103 and *passim;* T. S. Fiske, in *Bulletin of the American Mathematical Society,* **33** (1927), 773–777; and D. E. Smith, in *National Cyclopaedia of American Biography* (1933), p. 290. See also *American Men of Science,* 3rd ed. (1921), p. 137; "Class of 1882," in *Harvard College Alumni Report* (1883–1926); *New York Times* (27 May 1926), p. 25; (28 May 1926), p. 1; (29 May 1926), p. 14; (31 May 1926), p. 14; (3 June 1926), p. 24; (7 June 1926), p. 18; and *Who's Who in America* (1920–1921).

MARY E. WILLIAMS

COLLINS, JOHN (*b.* Wood Eaton, near Oxford, England, 5 March 1625; *d.* London, England, 10 November 1683)

Removed from local grammar school after the death of his father, a "poore Minister," orphaned him, Collins was briefly apprenticed (at thirteen) to an Oxford bookseller "who failing I lived three yeares at Court [as kitchen clerk] and in this space forgot the Latin I had." From 1642, on the outbreak of the Civil War, he spent seven years in the Mediterranean as a seaman "in the Venetian service against ye Turke." On his return to London he set himself up as "Accountant philomath" (mathematics teacher). After the Restoration in 1660 Collins held a variety of minor government posts, notably "in keeping of Accompts" in the Excise Office, and for fifteen years managed the Farthing Office, but after its closure became once more a lowly accountant with the Fishery Company. He thought long about becoming a stationer but lacked the necessary capital; yet in a private capacity he did much to revive the London book trade after the disastrous 1666 fire, using to the full his own limited resources and the foreign contacts his employment gave him. Although he had "no Universitie education," he was deservedly elected fellow of the Royal Society in 1667.

On his own assessment Collins' mathematical attainments were "meane, yet I have an ardent love to these studies . . . endeavouring to raise a Catalogue of Math^{ll} Bookes and to procure scarce ones for the use of the Royall Society and my owne delight." His published works—*Merchants Accompts, Decimal Arithmetick, Geometricall Dyalling,* and *Mariners Plain Scale,* among others—are essentially derivative but reveal his competence in business arithmetic, navigational trigonometry, sundial construction, and other applications of elementary mathematics; his papers on theory of equations and his critique of Descartes's *Géométrie* are uninspiring.

Collins' scientific importance lies rather in his untiring effort, by correspondence and word of mouth, to be an efficient "intelligencer" of current mathematical news and to promote scientific learning: with justice, Isaac Barrow dubbed him "Mersennus Anglus." Between 1662, when he first met Barrow, and 1677, when the deaths of Barrow and Oldenburg (following on that of James Gregory in 1675), coupled with a growing reluctance on the part of Newton and Wallis to continue a letter exchange and the worries of his own straitened financial circumstances, effectively terminated it, Collins carried on an extensive correspondence with some of the finest exact scientists of his day, not only with his compatriots but with Bertet, Borelli, and (through Oldenburg) with Huygens, Sluse, Leibniz, and Tschirnhausen. Further, deploying his specialized knowledge of the book trade to advantage, Collins saw through press in London such substantial works as Thomas Salusbury's *Mathematical Collections,* Barrow's *Lectiones* and *Archimedes,* Wallis' *Mechanics* and *Algebra,* Horrocks' *Opera posthuma,* and Sherburne's *Manilius.* He sought likewise, but in vain, to have several of Newton's early mathematical works published. For the modern historian of science, Collins' still-intact collection of some 2,000 books and uncounted original manuscripts of such men as Newton, Barrow, and Halley is a major primary source.

BIBLIOGRAPHY

I. ORIGINAL WORKS. "The first thing I published was about a quire of Paper concerning Merchants Accompts [a rare folio broadsheet (London, 1652), repr. in G. de Malyne, *Consuetudo: vel, Lex Mercatoria* (London, 1656)] which upon later thoughts I found myself unable to amend and was reprinted in May last" (to Wallis, 1666). This reappeared in augmented form as *An Introduction to Merchants-Accompts* (London, 1674).

Next Collins wrote "a despicable treatise of quadrants [*The Sector on a Quadrant . . . Accomodated* [*sic*] *for Dyalling: For the Resolving of All Proportions Instrumentally* (London, 1659), a revision of his *Description and Use of a General Quadrant* (London, 1658)]. . . . And among these Luxuriances I met with a Dyalling Scheame of Mr Fosters and commented upon y^{t} [*Geometricall Dyalling* (London, 1659)] which it is too late to wish undone." Also in 1659 he issued his *Mariners Plain Scale New Plain'd* and *Navigation by the Mariners Plain Scale.*

Posthumously there appeared his *Decimal Arithmetick, Simple Interest, &c* (London, 1685), an augmentation of his rare 1669 single-sheet equivalent, "Compendium for a Letter Case." Of his other nonscientific publications his monograph *Salt and Fishery* (London, 1682) deserves mention for its passages on salt refining and fish curing. In addition, the *Philosophical Transactions* has several unsigned reviews by Collins and four short articles—**2**, no. 30 (Dec. 1667), 568–575; **4**, no. 46 (Apr. 1669), 929–934; **6**, no. 69 (Mar. 1675), 2093–2096; **14**, no. 159 (May 1684), 575–582—dealing with topics in arithmetic and algebra.

His correspondence is preserved in private possession (Shirburn 101.H.1–3), except for a group of letters relating to Newton's invention of fluxions deposited from it, at Newton's request, in the Royal Society's archives in 1712 (now, with some losses, MS LXXXI [Collins' Descartes critique is no. 39]) and smaller collections in the British Museum, the University of St. Andrews, and Cambridge University library.

II. Secondary Literature. Edward Sherburne, in his *Sphere of Manilius Made an English Poem* (London, 1675), app., pp. 116–118 (also found as a separate broadsheet), gives a creditable contemporary impression of Collins' work up to 1675. Brief sketches by Agnes M. Clerke, in *Dictionary of National Biography,* XI (1887), 368–369; and H. W. Turnbull, in *James Gregory Memorial Volume* (London, 1939), pp. 16–18, must serve in place of a standard biography. Collins' letters are printed in Newton's *Commercium Epistolicum* (London, 1712); S. P. Rigaud's *Correspondence of Scientific Men of the Seventeenth Century* (Oxford, 1841); and in modern editions of the letters of Newton, James Gregory, and Oldenburg.

D. T. Whiteside

COMMANDINO, FEDERICO (*b.* Urbino, Italy, 1509; *d.* Urbino, 3 September 1575)

The little that is known about Commandino's life is derived mainly from a brief biography written by a younger fellow townsman who knew him well for many years toward the end of his career.

Descended from a noble family of Urbino, Commandino studied Latin and Greek for some years with a humanist at Fano. When Rome was sacked on 6 May 1527 by the army of Charles V, the Orsini, a leading noble clan, fled to Urbino. For one of their sons they procured a tutor proficient in mathematics, who also taught Commandino. After this tutor became a bishop on 6 June 1533, he obtained for Commandino an appointment as private secretary to Pope Clement VII. However, the pontiff died on 25 September 1534, and Commandino went to the University of Padua. There he studied philosophy and medicine for ten years, but he took his medical degree from the University of Ferrara.

Returning to his birthplace, Commandino married a local noblewoman, who died after giving birth to two daughters and a son. Commandino resolved not to marry a second time. After his son's death he put the girls in a convent school (and later found husbands for them). Withdrawing from the general practice of medicine, he turned to his true vocation: editing, translating, and commenting on the classics of ancient Greek mathematics. Gaining renown thereby, Commandino was designated the private tutor and medical adviser to the duke of Urbino. The duke, however, was married to the sister of a cardinal; and the latter persuaded Commandino to be his personal physician in his intellectually stimulating household in Rome.

Commandino had been translating into Latin and commenting on Archimedes' *Measurement of the Circle* (with Eutocius' commentary), *Spirals, Quadrature of the Parabola, Conoids and Spheroids,* and *Sand-Reckoner.* Besides the first printed edition of the Greek text of these five works and an earlier Latin translation of them (Basel, 1544), he had access also to a Greek manuscript in Venice, where his patron was residing when Commandino published this Archimedes volume in 1558.

During the previous year Commandino had heard complaints about the difficulty of understanding Ptolemy's *Planisphere,* which showed how circles on the celestial sphere may be stereographically projected onto the plane of the equator. Although the Greek text of the *Planisphere* is lost, it had been translated into Arabic, and from Arabic into Latin. This Latin version, done at Toulouse in 1144, and Jordanus de Nemore's *Planisphere,* both of which had been printed at Basel in 1536, were edited by Commandino and, together with his commentary on Ptolemy's *Planisphere,* were published at Venice in 1558.

Ptolemy's *Analemma* explained how to determine the position of the sun at a given moment in any latitude by an orthogonal projection using three mutually perpendicular planes. Again, as in the case of Ptolemy's *Planisphere,* no Greek text was available to Commandino (a portion was later recovered from a palimpsest); but an Arabic version had been translated into Latin. This was edited from the manuscript by Commandino (Rome, 1562). Besides his customary commentary, he added his own essay *On the Calibration of Sundials* of various types, since he felt that Ptolemy's discussion was theoretical rather than practical.

Commandino's only other original work, dealing with the center of gravity of solid bodies, was published in 1565 at Bologna, of which his patron had become bishop on 17 July of the preceding year. Commandino's interest in this topic was aroused by Archimedes' *Floating Bodies,* of which he had no Greek text, unlike the five other Archimedean works he had previously translated. Since his time a large part of the Greek text of *Floating Bodies* has been recovered, but he had only a printed Latin translation (Venice, 1543, 1565), which he commented on and corrected (Bologna, 1565). In particular the proof of proposition 2 in book II was incomplete, and Commandino filled it out. One step required knowing the location of the center of gravity of any segment of a parabolic conoid. No ancient treatment of such a problem was then known, and Commandino's was the first modern attempt to fill the existing gap.

Archimedes' *Floating Bodies* assumed the truth of some propositions for which Commandino searched in Apollonius' *Conics.* Of the *Conics'* eight books only the first four are extant in Greek, and he had access to them in manuscript. An earlier Latin translation (Venice, 1537) was superseded by his own (Bologna, 1566), to which he added Eutocius' commentary, the relevant discussion in Pappus' *Collection* (book VII), the first complete Latin translation (from a Greek manuscript) of Serenus' *Section of a Cylinder* and *Section of a Cone,* and his own commentary.

Overwork and the death of his patron on 28 October 1565 greatly depressed Commandino; and he returned to Urbino, where he could live quietly, for many months on a salt-free diet. He resumed his former activities, however, after being visited by John Dee, who gave him a manuscript Latin translation of an Arabic work related to Euclid's *On Divisions* (of figures), of which the Greek original is lost. Commandino published this Latin translation and added a short treatise of his own to condense and generalize the discussion in the manuscript (Pesaro, 1570).

At the request of his ruler's son, Commandino translated Euclid's *Elements* into Latin and commented on it extensively (Pesaro, 1572). Also in 1572 he published at Pesaro his Latin translation of and commentary on Aristarchus' *Sizes and Distances of the Sun and Moon,* with Pappus' explanations (*Collection,* book VI, propositions 37–40).

For those of his countrymen who did not know Latin, Commandino supervised a translation of Euclid's *Elements* into Italian by some of his students (Urbino, 1575). His own Latin translation of Hero's *Pneumatics* (Urbino, 1575) was seen through the press by his son-in-law immediately after his death. From a nearly complete manuscript, needing three months' work at most, his faithful pupil Guidobaldo del Monte published Commandino's Latin translation of and commentary on Pappus' *Collection,* books III–VIII (Pesaro, 1588).

In the sixteenth century, Western mathematics emerged swiftly from a millennial decline. This rapid ascent was assisted by Apollonius, Archimedes, Aristarchus, Euclid, Eutocius, Hero, Pappus, Ptolemy, and Serenus—as published by Commandino.

BIBLIOGRAPHY

A list of Commandino's publications is available in Pietro Riccardi, *Biblioteca matematica italiana,* enl. ed., 2 vols. (Milan, 1952), I, cols. 42, 359–365; II, pt. 1, col. 15; II, pt. 2, col. 117; II, pt. 5. cols. 9, 49–50; II, pt. 6, col. 189; II, pt. 7, cols. 25–26. Riccardi omits *Conoids and Spheroids* (I, col. 42); misattributes the Italian translation of Euclid's *Elements* to Commandino himself (I, col. 364); and misdates Pappus' *Collection* as 1558 (correct date, 1588; II, pt. 1, col. 15). To Riccardi's list of writings about Commandino (I, col. 359; II, pt. 1, col. 15) add Edward Rosen, "The Invention of the Reduction Compass," in *Physis,* **10** (1968), 306–308; and "John Dee and Commandino," in *Scripta mathematica,* **28** (1970), 321–326.

Bernardino Baldi's biography of Commandino, completed on 22 November 1587, was first published in *Giornal de' letterati d'Italia,* **19** (1714), 140–185, and reprinted in *Versi e prose scelte di Bernardino Baldi,* F. Ugolino and F.-L. Polidori, eds. (Florence, 1859), pp. 513–537.

EDWARD ROSEN

COMTE, ISIDORE AUGUSTE MARIE FRANÇOIS XAVIER (*b.* Montpellier, France, 19 January 1798; *d.* Paris, France, 5 September 1857)

The eldest of the three children born to Louis Auguste Xavier Comte and Rosalie Boyer, Comte came from a Catholic and royalist family, his father being a civil servant of reasonable means. An exceptional and rebellious youth, Comte at an early age repudiated the Catholicism of his parents and took up the republican cause in politics. He entered the École Polytechnique in 1814, took part in the disturbances connected with the defense of Paris, and was one of many "subversive" students expelled in the royalist reorganization of the school in 1816. From 1817 to 1823 he was private secretary to Claude Henri de Rouvroy, comte de Saint-Simon, an intellectual association that was profoundly to affect Comte's later development. In 1825 he married a prostitute named Caroline Massin, a most unhappy union that was dissolved in 1842.

Comte's economic position was always an unstable one; he never acquired a university post and survived largely on money earned from the public lectures he gave in Paris, from school examiner's fees, and from the benevolence of admirers (such as Mill and Grote), who were periodically called on to subsidize Comte's researches. In 1830 he founded the Association Polytechnique, a group devoted to education of the working classes. In the early 1840's, he met Mme. Clothilde de Vaux, an intellectual and emotional experience which—even more profoundly than his earlier association with Saint-Simon—was to change his intellectual orientation. In 1848 he founded the Société Positiviste, devoted to the promulgation of the "Cult of Humanity." The last years of his life were spent in developing a godless religion, with all the institutional trappings of the Catholicism that he had repudiated as an adolescent. Abandoned by most of his friends and disciples (usually because of his abuse of them), Comte died in relative poverty and isolation.

Comte's writings exhibit a remarkable scope and breadth, ranging from mathematics to the philosophy of science, from religion and morality to sociology and political economy. What unifies them all is Comte's concern with the problem of knowledge, its nature, its structure, and the method of its acquisition. Positivism, the official name Comte adopted for his philosophy, was primarily a methodological and epistemological doctrine. Traditionally, writers on the theory of knowledge had adopted a psychologistic approach in which the nature and limitations of the human mind and the senses were examined and knowledge treated as a function of certain mental states. Comte's approach to this locus of problems was substantially different. Believing that knowledge could be understood only by examining the growth of knowledge in its historical dimension, he insisted that it is the collective history of thought, rather than the individual psyche, that can illuminate the conditions and limits of human knowledge. It was not knowledge in its static dimension which interested Comte, but the dynamics of man *qua* knower, the progressive development of knowledge. In general outline, this approach was inspired (as Comte acknowledges) by Condorcet and Saint-Simon. What Comte added to this tradition was a firm commitment to studying the history of scientific knowledge, since science was for him (as it was for Whewell) the prototypical instance of knowledge.

The most famous result of this approach is Comte's law of three states. The importance of this law to Comte's theory is crucial, for not only does it provide him with a solution to the problem of the growth of knowledge, but it also serves as an example of the fruitfulness of applying scientific methods to the study of human development. In Comte's eyes the law of three states is as valid—and on the same footing—as the laws of the inorganic world.

Basically, the law (first formulated in 1822) states that human thought, in its historical development, passes successively through three distinct phases: the theological (or fictional) state, the metaphysical (or abstract) state, and the positive (or scientific) state. In the theological state, man explains the world around him in anthropomorphic terms, reducing natural processes to the whims of manlike gods and agencies. Final causes are especially symptomatic of this stage. In the metaphysical state, deities are replaced by powers, potencies, forces, and other imperceptible causal agencies. The positive state repudiates both causal forces and gods and restricts itself to expressing precise, verifiable correlations between observable phenomena. While Comte believes that the theological and metaphysical states are based on a misconception of natural processes, he insists that they were essential preliminaries to the emergence of positive knowledge. Thus, the theological state is a natural one for a civilization which has neither the mathematical nor the experimental techniques for investigating nature, and its importance is that it provides a pattern, however crude, for introducing some element of order into an otherwise capricious world. The metaphysical state, which is purely transitional, contains positive elements which it clothes in the language of powers and forces so as not to offend the sensibilities of theologically inclined minds.

It is not only knowledge in general but every branch of knowledge which evolves through these three states. Different forms of knowledge evolve at different rates, however, and one of Comte's major critical tasks was to assess the degree of progress toward the positive stage in each individual science, a task that occupies most of the six-volume *Cours de philosophie positive* (1830–1842).

This task of assessment led immediately to Comte's hierarchy of sciences. No mere taxonomical exercise, his classification of the sciences is meant to reflect several important characteristics. While most other schemes (for example, those of Aristotle, Bacon, and Ampère) had classified the sciences with respect to their generality or relations of logical inclusion and reduction, Comte arranged the sciences in the hierarchy according to the degree to which they have attained the positive state. On this ranking, the sciences (in order) are (1) mathematics, (2) astronomy, (3) physics, (4) chemistry, (5) biology, and (6) sociology (or "social physics"). Of these, Comte believed that only mathematics and astronomy had reached full positive maturity, while metaphysical and theological modes of thought were still prominent in the others.

Although Comte's classification is based on the "degree of positivity" of the various sciences, it also captures other important characteristics. Neglecting mathematics, the sequence from astronomy to sociology represents an increasing complexity in the phenomena under investigation. Thus, the astronomer is concerned only with motions and positions, the physicist needs forces and charges as well, while the chemist also deals with configurations and structures. The Comtean hierarchy of the sciences reflects moreover important methodological characteristics of each science. Astronomy has only the method of observation, physics can both observe and experiment, and the biologist employs comparison and analogy as well as observation and experiment. It was necessary for Comte to establish the fact that different sciences utilize different methods, since his conception of sociology required a unique method (the "historical method") which none of the other sciences exemplify. Comte was manifestly not a reductionist in the sense of using a classificatory scheme to render one science logically subordinate to another. His scientific beliefs, as well as his insistence on the diversity of methods, made him an outspoken critic of reductionism. The unity of the sciences was not, for Comte, to be found in the identity of concepts, but rather in the positive mentality which he hoped would unite the sciences.

Comte's major impact on his contemporaries was methodological. The *Cours de philosophie positive* is simultaneously a methodological manifesto and an incisive critique of the science of the early nineteenth century. Comte was convinced that a careful analysis of the logic of science would lead him to far-reaching insights into the character of positive (that is, scientific) method. In practice, however, most of his methodological strictures derive from the doctrine of the three states rather than from an objective study of scientific procedures.

Comte claimed that discussion of scientific method had too long been dominated by the naïve division between what he called empiricists and mystics—the former purporting to derive all scientific concepts from experience and the latter from a priori intuition of the mind. He wanted a middle course which recognized the active, acquisitive role of the mind but which at the same time put rigid empirical checks on the conjectures that the mind produces. His approach to this problem was singularly perceptive.

Comte's quarrel with the empiricists had two aspects. By requiring that the scientist must purge his mind of all preconceived ideas and theories in order to study nature objectively, the empiricists demanded the impossible. Every experiment, every observation has as its precondition a hypothesis in the mind of some experimenter. Without theories, Comte insisted, scientific experiments would be impossible. He also urged that the empiricists misunderstood the place of experience in the scientific scheme. The function of experiments is not to generate theories but to test them. It is by subjecting theories to the scrutiny of empirical verification that they are established as scientific.

The stress on verification is a persistent theme in Comte's writings. It is a fundamental principle of the positive philosophy that any idea, concept, or theory that has any meaning must be open to experimental verification. Verification has been the vehicle whereby progress has been made from the metaphysical to the positive state. The forces, powers, and entelechies of the metaphysical epoch were repudiated precisely because they were finally recognized to be unverifiable. Comte's repeated criticisms of many of the physical theories of his own day (for instance, fluid theories of heat and electricity) were grounded largely in his requirement of verifiability. Although Comte was not the earliest writer to stress empirical verification, there is no doubt that it was largely through his influence (especially on such figures as Claude Bernard, J. S. Mill, Pierre Duhem, and C. S. Peirce) that the doctrine of verifiability enjoys the wide currency it has had in recent philosophy and science.

Closely connected with the requirement of verification was another important and influential dogma of Comte's methodology: the unambiguous assertion that the "aim of science is prediction." Since genuinely positive science offers only correlations between phenomena rather than their causes (in the Aristotelian sense of efficient causes), a theory is positively valid only insofar as it permits the scientist to reason from known phenomena to unknown ones. The sole object of the theoretical superstructure of science is to put the scientist in a position to predict what will happen, to substitute ratiocination for direct experimental exploration. The ideal science, for Comte, is one which, given certain empirically determined initial conditions, can deduce all subsequent states of the system. Clearly, it is the science of Laplace and Lagrange rather than that of Buffon or Fourcroy upon which Comte modeled his theory of science.

On other questions of scientific method and the philosophy of science, Comte's views were more traditional. He insisted on the invariability of physical law, argued that scientific knowledge was relative rather than absolute, and believed that scientific laws were approximate rather than precise (a point Duhem was to develop seventy years later). His treatment of the problem of induction, particularly in his *Discours sur l'esprit positif* (1844), is taken largely from Mill's *System of Logic* (1843).

Insofar as Comte identified himself as a natural scientist, it was mathematics which he knew best. Having been a tutor in mathematics for the École Polytechnique in the 1830's, Comte published two straightforward scientific works, the *Traité élémentaire de géométrie* (1843) and the *Traité philosophique d'astronomie populaire* (1844). Both were popular works that grew out of his public lectures in Paris.

Of considerably greater significance was Comte's examination and critique of scientific theories in his *Cours de philosophie positive.* Having laid a solid methodological foundation in the early parts of the *Cours,* Comte devoted the second and third volumes of that work to a scrutiny of the "inorganic" sciences.

Among all the empirical sciences astronomy was closest to the positivist ideal. Concerning themselves exclusively with the position, shape, size, and motion of celestial bodies, astronomers (more from necessity than choice) had restricted themselves to studying the observable properties of the heavens. Astronomy had achieved this positive state because it was not concerned with speculation on the internal constitution of the stars, their elemental composition, or their genesis. (No doubt Comte would have viewed the rise of spectral analysis of stellar objects as a retrograde development, representing the incursion of a metaphysical spirit into an otherwise positive science.) Comte went so far as to assert that astronomy should limit its domain to the solar system—which lends itself to precise mathematical analysis—and should forgo any attempt at the construction of a sidereal astronomy.

If Comte was generally satisfied with the state of contemporary astronomy, his attitude to the physical theories of his day was generally antagonistic. He saw lurking in every elastic fluid and subtle medium a vestige of the metaphysical state. In electricity, heat, light, and magnetism, natural philosophers were attempting to explain observable phenomena by resorting to unobservable, unverifiable, and unintelligible entities. To Comte such entities were not only inconceivable but unnecessary. Since the laws of phenomena are the object of science, only those laws are necessary and causal theories may be dispensed with as Fourier's treatment of heat had demonstrated. Phenomenal laws are valid independently of the theories from which they might be derived. In chemistry, on the other hand, Comte was willing to allow—even to insist on—the use of the atomic hypothesis, which, in many respects, seems as nonphenomenal as an optical ether. The difference between the two is that the properties which the atomic theory attributes to atoms are well-defined and coherent, while the properties attributed to the ether (for example, imponderability) are both inconceivable and unverifiable.

Comte believed chemistry to be in a state of "gross imperfection" with chemists having no clear sense of the aims or the limitations of their science. He believed that organic chemistry was a branch of biology rather than chemistry and that much of what we should now call physical chemistry was in fact physics. The sole function of chemistry, in his eyes, was to study the laws governing the combinations of the various elemental bodies. He likened chemists to the empiricists who were so interested in haphazardly synthesizing new compounds that they completely ignored the rational and theoretical side of the discipline.

Consistent with his classification of the sciences, Comte believed that biological processes (or at least a subset of them known as vital processes) could not be explained by means of physicochemical concepts. Biology, properly conceived, would integrate physiology and anatomy by relating structure to function. Moreover, a legitimate biological theory must study the connection between the organism and its environment, its milieu. He stated the basic problem of biology in the formula, "Given the organ, or the organic modification, find the function or the action, and vice versa."

Methodologically, Comte places biology on a very different footing from the higher sciences. One major difference concerns the amenability of biological phenomena to mathematical treatment. Comte says that life processes are generally too complex to treat quantitatively. This is compensated, however, in that biology has more methods at its disposal than astronomy, physics, or chemistry. Specifically, the biologist can utilize the method of comparison which, in order to understand the life processes in a given organism, successively compares that organism with similar ones of less complexity. If the function of the lungs in man is difficult to ascertain, their function can perhaps be determined by studying the function of lungs or lunglike organs in simpler species. For the method of comparison to have any validity, it is necessary to have a sequence of organisms whose differences from one to the next are very minor. Clearly, an accurate biological taxonomy is crucial to the utilization of this method. Like Cuvier, Comte maintained the fixity of the species, although he confessed that this doctrine was not fully established.

Comte found biology, like physics and chemistry,

to be still dominated by the metaphysical mode of thought. Theories of spontaneous generation, mechanistic physiology, materialism, and spiritualism are all manifestations of a prepositive mentality.

The last element in the chain of the sciences is "social physics" or, as he called it after 1840, sociology. Indeed, Comte is often considered the founder of sociology, and his treatment of this topic is his most original and probably his most influential. In his view previous thought about man's social nature had been speculative and a priori, rather than cautious and empirical. Certain moral perspectives and prejudices had stood in the way of an objective philosophy of history, and the subject had been dominated by crude theological and metaphysical perspectives. While social statics had been treated by such writers as Aristotle (especially in the *Politics*) and Montesquieu, social dynamics had been almost completely ignored. The birth, growth, and general life-cycle of a social ensemble were what Comte made the subject matter of sociology. In part, of course, the characteristics of a society (for instance, its family structure, politics, institutions, and so forth) are a function of the biological and physiological characteristics of the men who compose the society. To this extent, sociology is dependent on biology.

But there is another important dimension of sociology that has nothing to do with man's biology—the historical component. What distinguishes the social entity from the physical and biological is that it is uniquely a product of its own past. The structures and institutions of any society—intellectual, political, and economic—are determined by the previous conditions of the society. History thus becomes the heart of sociology, and the aim of the sociologist becomes that of determining the laws of human social progress by an empirical study of the evolution of human institutions. To understand the present and to predict the future, we must know the past. The sociologist seeks to find predictive laws by working in two directions simultaneously—he studies history in order to discover empirical generalizations about social change; while at the same time he attempts to explain these generalizations by deducing them from known laws of human nature, whether biological or psychological. This in essence is the famous "historical method" that Comte advocates in the fourth volume of his *Cours de philosophie positive.*

The basic social unit was, in Comte's view, the family, for the family is the main source of social cohesion. But the basic concept of sociological analysis was that of progress. Comte's theory of progress, while dependent upon the Enlightenment theory of progress, was nonetheless very different from it. He criticized Condorcet for thinking that man was infinitely perfectible and that continuous progress could occur if man would simply decide that he wanted it. Comte, on the contrary, maintained that progress is governed by strict laws, which are inviolate. The churchmen of the middle ages could not have discovered Newtonian astronomy even if they had set their minds to it, for the general social, moral, and intellectual conditions of the Latin West were not capable of embracing such a positive theory. Again, the law of the three states functions as the basic determinant of social change. The primary cause of social change is neither political nor economic, but intellectual. Sophisticated and complex economic and political institutions are possible only when man's intellectual progress has reached a certain level of maturity. To this extent, the sociology of knowledge is the cornerstone of sociological theory.

For most of the last twenty years of Comte's life, he was preoccupied with the problem of formulating the tenets of a "positive religion." Convinced that Christianity was doctrinally bankrupt, he felt nonetheless that formal, organized religion served a vital social and even intellectual function. He believed that egoism must be subordinated to altruism and maintained that this could be achieved only by a "religion of humanity." Such a religion, founded essentially on a utilitarian ethic, dispenses entirely with a deity, substituting mankind in its place. Otherwise, the trappings of traditional religion remain more or less intact. Churches are formed, a priesthood is trained, and sacraments, prayer, and even the saints are preserved, although in a very different guise.

Comte's fanaticism in this matter was a cause of profound dismay to many scientists and men of learning who had been greatly influenced by him in the 1830's and 1840's. It also made it easier for Comte's critics to discredit his earlier ideas by *ad hominem* arguments against the cult of humanity. In spite of his growing estrangement from the intellectual community, however, Comte persisted in his religious speculations, and established more than a hundred positivist congregations in Europe and North America.

The question of Comte's place in history, both as regards the influences on him and his influence on others, is still largely a matter of undocumented conjecture. Certain influences on Comte are virtually undeniable. Comte himself admitted to having learned much from the *philosophes* (especially Condorcet) and from the physiologist Barthez. Of equal authenticity was the role Saint-Simon played in directing Comte's attention to the problem of intellectual progress and its relevance to a philosophy of science. At a less explicit, but probably more pervasive, level of influence was the French tradition of analytic physics. The physics of Laplace and Lagrange, of Fourier and Ampère, was thoroughly positivistic in spirit, with its emphasis on quantitative correlations of phenomena (at the expense of abandoning microreductive theories). Comte himself often suggested that his mission was to extend the methods of mathematical astronomy and physics to the other sciences, especially social physics.

Comte's influence on his contemporaries and successors is a more complicated problem. In his own time, he had numerous disciples, including the literary figures Harriet Martineau, John Stuart Mill, G. H. Lewes, and É. Littré, as well as such scientists as Dumas, Audiffrent, and Claude Bernard, who were sympathetic to Comte's analysis. At the end of the nineteenth century, Comtean positivism became a powerful force in the philosophical critique of the sciences, represented by such figures as J. B. Stallo, Ernst Mach, Pierre Duhem, and A. Cournot. In certain respects, the twentieth-century movement known as logical positivism was a continuation of the philosophical tradition Comte founded.

BIBLIOGRAPHY

I. ORIGINAL WORKS. There is no collected edition of Comte's writings, nor even a full bibliographical list. Among Comte's more important works are *Appel aux conservateurs* (Paris, 1883; English trans. London, 1889); *Calendrier positiviste* (Paris, 1849; English trans. London, 1894); *Catéchisme positiviste* (Paris, 1852; English trans. London, 1858); *Cours de philosophie positive,* 6 vols. (Paris, 1830-1842; partial English trans. in 2 vols., London, 1853); *Discours sur l'ensemble du positivisme* (Paris, 1848; English trans. London, 1865); *Discours sur l'esprit positif* (Paris, 1844; English trans. London, 1903); *Essais de philosophie mathématique* (Paris, 1878); *Opuscules de philosophie sociale 1819-1828* (Paris, 1883); *Ordre et progrès* (Paris, 1848); *The Philosophy of Mathematics,* W. M. Gillespie, trans. (New York, 1851); *Synthèse subjective* (Paris, 1856; English trans. London, 1891); *Système de politique positive* (Paris, 1824); *Système de politique positive, ou Traité de sociologie,* 4 vols. (Paris, 1851-1854; English trans. London, 1875-1877); *Testament d'Auguste Comte* (Paris, 1884; English trans. Liverpool, 1910); *Traité élémentaire de géométrie analytique* (Paris, 1843); and *Traité philosophique d'astronomie populaire* (Paris, 1844).

Comte was a prolific correspondent and many of his letters have been preserved and published. The most important editions of Comte's correspondence are *Correspondance inédite d'Auguste Comte* (4 vols., Paris, 1903); *Lettres à des positivistes anglais* (London, 1889); *Lettres d'Auguste Comte . . . à Henry Edger et à M. John Metcalf* (Paris, 1889); *Lettres d'Auguste Comte . . . à Richard Congreve* (London, 1889); *Lettres d'Auguste Comte à Henry Dix Hutton* (Dublin, 1890); *Lettres d'Auguste Comte à John Stuart Mill, 1841-1846* (Paris, 1877); *Lettres d'Auguste Comte à M. Valat . . . 1815-1844* (Paris, 1870); *Lettres inédites à C. de Blignières* (Paris, 1932); and *Nouvelles lettres inédites* (Paris, 1939). A chronological list of almost all Comte's correspondence has been compiled by Paul Carneiro and published as a supplement to the *Nouvelles lettres.*

II. SECONDARY LITERATURE. The most important studies of Comte's biography are Henri Gouhier, *La vie d'Auguste Comte* (Paris, 1931) and *La jeunesse d'Auguste Comte et la formation du positivisme,* 3 vols. (Paris, 1933-1941), of which vol. III contains a list of Comte's writings before 1830, 421 ff. Other biographical works include H. Gruber, *Auguste Comte . . . sein Leben und seine Lehre* (Freiburg, 1889); C. Hillemand, *La vie et l'oeuvre d'Auguste Comte* (Paris, 1898); H. Hutton, *Comte's Life and Work* (London, 1892); F. W. Ostwald, *Auguste Comte: Der Mann und sein Werk* (Leipzig, 1914); and B. A. A. L. Seilliera, *Auguste Comte* (Paris, 1924).

The most valuable general works on Comte's philosophy are Jean Delvolvé, *Réflexions sur la pensée comtienne* (Paris, 1932); Pierre Ducassé, *Essai sur les origines intuitives du positivisme* (Paris, 1939); P. Ducassé, *Méthode et intuition chez Auguste Comte* (Paris, 1939); L. Lévy-Bruhl, *The Philosophy of Auguste Comte* (New York, 1903); É. Littré, *Auguste Comte et la philosophie positive* (Paris, 1863); and J. S. Mill, *Auguste Comte and Positivism* (London, 1865).

Specialized studies of various aspects of Comte's works include J. B. G. Audiffrent, *Appel aux médicins* (Paris, 1862); E. Caird, *The Social Philosophy and Religion of Comte* (Glasgow, 1893); G. Dumas, *Psychologie de deux messies positivistes: Saint-Simon et Auguste Comte* (Paris, 1905); F. von Hayek, *The Counter-Revolution of Science* (London, 1964); Jean Lacroix, *La sociologie d'Auguste Comte* (Paris, 1956); L. Laudan, "Towards a Reassessment of Comte's 'Méthode Positive'," in *Philosophy of Science,* **37** (1970); G. H. Lewes, *Comte's Philosophy of the Sciences* (London, 1853); F. S. Marvin, *Comte: the Founder of Sociology* (New York, 1937); George Sarton, "Auguste Comte, Historian of Science," in *Osiris,* **10** (1952); and Paul Tannery, "Comte et l'Histoire des Sciences," in *Revue générale des sciences,* **16** (1905).

Comte's influence on later science and philosophy has been studied by D. Charlton, *Positivist Thought in France During the Second Empire, 1852-1870* (Oxford, 1959); L. E. Denis, *L'oeuvre d'A. Comte, son influence sur la pensée contemporaine* (Paris, 1901); R. L. Hawkins, *August Comte and the United States, 1816-1853* (Cambridge, Mass., 1936); *Positivism in the United States, 1853-1861* (Cambridge, Mass., 1938); and R. E. Schneider, *Positivism in the United States* (Rosario, Argentina, 1946).

As an intellectual movement, positivism generated numerous journals and periodicals, many of which contain lengthy discussions of various aspects of Comte's work. Chief among these are *Philosophie positive* (Paris, 1867-1883), *El Positivismo* (Buenos Aires, 1876-1877 and

1925–1938), *The Positivist Review* (London, 1893–1923), *Revue occidentale* (Paris, 1878–1914), and *Revue positiviste internationale* (Paris, 1906–1940). Most of Comte's still unpublished manuscripts are kept in the library of the Archives Positivistes in Paris.

LAURENS LAUDAN

CONDORCET, MARIE-JEAN-ANTOINE-NICOLAS CARITAT, MARQUIS DE (*b.* Ribemont, France, 17 September 1743; *d.* Bourg-la-Reine, France, 27[?] March 1794)

Condorcet's family came originally from the Midi. Although converted at the beginning of the Reformation, the Caritat family renounced Protestantism during the seventeenth century; most of the young men of the family led lives typical of provincial noblemen, becoming either clergymen or soldiers. One of Condorcet's uncles was the bishop of Auxerre and later of Lisieux; his father, Antoine, was a cavalry captain stationed in the tiny Picardy village of Ribemont when he married Mme. de Saint-Félix, a young widow of the local bourgeoisie. It was there that the future marquis was born a few days before his father was killed during the siege of Neuf-Brisach. Raised by an extremely pious mother and tutored in his studies by his uncle the bishop, he was sent to the Jesuits of Rheims and subsequently to the Collège de Navarre in Paris, from which he graduated with a degree in philosophy in 1759, having written a thesis in Latin on mathematics;[1] d'Alembert was a member of the board of examiners.

Condorcet's mathematical ability asserted itself even though his family would have preferred that he pursue a military career. He took up residence in Paris, where he lived on a modest sum provided by his mother. He worked a great deal and became better acquainted with d'Alembert, who introduced him into the salons of Mlle. de Lespinasse and Mme. Helvétius; at the first salon he met Turgot, who subsequently became his close friend. In 1765 Condorcet published a work on integral calculus and followed it with various mathematical *mémoires* that earned him the reputation of a scientist. He was elected to the Académie des Sciences as *adjoint-mécanicien* (adjunct in mechanics), succeeding Bezout (1769), and later as an associate in the same section. He thereafter became closely involved with scientific life. As assistant secretary (1773) and then permanent secretary of the Académie des Sciences (1776), Condorcet published a great many mathematical *mémoires* and, in 1785, the voluminous *Essai sur l'application de l'analyse à la probabilité des décisions rendues à la pluralité des voix.* Simultaneously he wrote his *éloges* of deceased academicians, essays that are often remarkable for his fairness of judgment and broadness of view; he also tried, but in vain, to organize scientific activity in France along rational lines.[2]

In the 1770's, however, another of Condorcet's interests came to the surface, possibly as a result of a meeting with Voltaire at Ferney. The notion of a political, economic, and social reform to be undertaken on scientific bases was its most recurrent subject. From it stemmed, in the theoretical domain, his calculus of probabilities and, in the practical domain, the numerous applied-research projects he had set up or carried out as inspector of the mint (1776) and director of navigation under the ministry of Turgot. To that end he also participated, beginning in 1775, in the movement of political and social dissent from the regime through the publication of various pamphlets. On the eve of the Revolution, Condorcet was inspector of the mint, permanent secretary of the Académie des Sciences, and a member of the Académie Française (1782); in 1786 he married Sophie de Grouchy, whose salon at the Hôtel des Monnaies (the mint) had taken the place of the salons of Mlle. de Lespinasse and Mme. Helvétius. In 1776 he was entrusted with the articles on analysis for Panckoucke's *Supplément* to the *Encyclopédie,* and in 1784 he revised and rewrote, with Lalande and Bossut, the mathematical part of that work, recast as the *Encyclopédie méthodique.* Thus he can be considered one of the most representative personages of the Enlightenment and, so far as France is concerned, one of the most influential.

After 1787 Condorcet's life is scarcely of interest to the historian of science. He then stood forth as an advocate of calling a national assembly that would reform the regime according to the views of the liberal bourgeoisie. After twice failing to be elected to the States-General (from Mantes-Gassicourt, where he had landholdings, and then from Paris), he was elected representative from his quarter of Paris to the Municipal Council, sitting in the Hôtel de Ville, and founded, in association with Emmanuel Sieyès, the Society of 1789. In September 1791 he succeeded in becoming a delegate to the Legislative Assembly and later to the Convention of 1792. In the Assembly he concentrated his efforts mainly on the work of the Commission of Public Instruction, for which he was suited by virtue of the *mémoires* that he had published in the *Bibliothèque de l'homme public* (1791–1792). At the convention he drew up the draft of a constitution (1793), but it was not adopted. A friend of Jacques Brissot and closely linked to the political battle waged by the Girondists, Condorcet came under suspicion following their expulsion from the convention on 2 June 1793; when the draft constitution that had been substituted for his own by the Committee of Public Safety was voted on, he published *Avis aux français.* This pamphlet was the cause of his downfall. An order was issued for his arrest on 8 July, but he managed to escape and found refuge in a house in the present Rue Servandoni. He hid there until 25 March 1794, and there he composed the work that constitutes his philosophical masterpiece, the *Esquisse d'un tableau des progrès de l'esprit humain.* On the latter date, fearful of being discovered, he left on foot for Fontenay-aux-Roses, where he had friends. However, they managed not to be at home when he arrived. On 27 March he was arrested in Clamart under a false name and was taken to the prison of Bourg-la-Reine. The next morning he was found dead in his cell. It has never been possible to verify the rumor, originating as early as 1795, that he committed suicide by poison.

Condorcet seems to have had the character of a systematic and passionate intellectual. Described by d'Alembert as a "volcano covered with snow," he was praised by Mlle. de Lespinasse for his great kindness; and accusations of avarice and social climbing sometimes directed at him have never been corroborated by documentary evidence. He was the typical Encyclopedist and perhaps the last of them. All fields of knowledge fascinated him, as is shown by the equal care and competence that he devoted to his *éloges* of Euler as well as Buffon, d'Alembert as well as Jean de Witt, Frénicle as well as Pascal. He was thoroughly convinced of the value of science and of the importance of its diffusion as a determining factor in the general progress and well-being of mankind. That is why his interest never flagged in the applications of science,[3] or in the organization of scientific education,[4] or in the establishment of a universal scientific language.[5] His entire concept of scientific knowledge is essentially probabilist: "We give the name of mathematical certitude to probability when it is based on the content of the laws of our understanding. We call physical certitude the probability that further implies the same constancy in an order of phenomena independent of ourselves, and we shall reserve the term probability for judgments that are exposed to other sources of uncertainty beyond that" (*Essai sur l'application de l'analyse,* p. xiv). The concept of a science based on human actions, intrinsically probabilist, therefore seemed to him to be just as natural as a science of nature, and he attempted to establish a portion of such a science by proposing a theory of votes based on the calculus of probability. Thus, despite his reputation as a mathematician, much exaggerated in his lifetime, it is the novelty, the boldness, and the importance of this attempt that today seem to constitute his just claim on the attention of the historian of scientific knowledge.

Let us, nevertheless, briefly examine his work in pure mathematics before summarizing his work on probability and his application of analysis to the theory of votes.

Differential equations. Condorcet's scientific *mémoires* of the type contained in the principal periodicals of the academies have not been collected in book form. To those he did write may be added a few works that have not been republished and several unpublished manuscripts. It must be acknowledged that reading Condorcet's mathematical works is a thankless task and often a disappointing one. The notation is inconsistent, the expression of ideas often imprecise and obscure, and the proofs labored. This is certainly what Lagrange was complaining about when he wrote to d'Alembert on 25 March 1792: "I would like to see our friend Condorcet, who assuredly has great talent and wisdom, express himself in another manner; I have told him this several times, but apparently the nature of his mind compels him to work in this way: we shall have to let him do so. . . ."[6]

Nevertheless, the esteem expressed by good judges, such as Lagrange himself, leaves the contemporary reader perplexed; and one suspects that sometimes friendship and sometimes the respect due to the influential secretary of the Académie des Sciences may have somewhat dulled the critical sense of the mathematicians of his day. Indeed, it now seems that the mathematical part of Condorcet's work contributed nothing original and that it deserves to be considered by the historian merely as evidence of the manner in which a man highly educated in that science could comprehend it and keep abreast of its progress. Wishing to introduce into the theory of differential equations general concepts that would be capable of systematizing it, he prematurely outlined a philosophy of mathematical notions that failed to issue in any coherent or practical organization.

Although he seemed ahead of his time when in an unpublished and incomplete *traité*[7] he defined a function as any relation whatever of corresponding values, he nevertheless thought it possible to propose a systematic and exhaustive classification of all functions. The main idea of the construction of classes of functions was, however, interesting in itself: it was the idea of a procedure of iteration that allows for definitions by recurring algorithms. What he did emphasize was the supposed closed-system character of all analytical entities. He exhibited this intention in an even more dogmatic manner in his *Lettre à d'Alembert* appended to the *Essais d'analyse* of 1768, in which he affirmed that all transcendental functions could be constructed by means of a circle and hyperbola; and he actually expressed himself in many of his *mémoires* as if any nonalgebraic function were of a trigonometric, logarithmic, or exponential nature.

The manner in which Condorcet conceived of the problem of the integration of differential equations or partial differential equations arose from the same tendency to generalization, which appeared a bit hasty even to his contemporaries.[8] Most of his *mémoires* and analytical works deal with this problem: to find conditional equations by relating the coefficients of a differential equation in such a manner as to render it integrable or at least such that its order may be lowered by one degree. Once the existence of solutions was proved, he hoped to be able to determine their form a priori, as well as the nature of the transcendental functions included; a calculation identifying the parameters would thus complete the integration. (See, e.g., "Histoire de l'Académie des sciences de Paris," "Mémoires" [1770], pp. 177 ff.). At least, therefore, he must be credited with having clearly conceived and stated that it is normal for an arbitrary differential equation not to be integrable.

Let us limit ourselves to indicating the approach by which Condorcet proceeded, as set forth in the 1765 text *Du calcul intégral* and resumed in the *traité* of 1786. Given the differential expression of any order $V\,(x, y, dx, dy, d^2x, d^2y, \cdots, d^nx, d^ny)$, the question is under what conditions it might be the differential of an expression B, such that

$$V = dB\,(x, y). \tag{1}$$

Let us say $dx = p$, $dy = q$, $d^2y = dq = r$, $d^3y = dr = s$, x being taken as an independent variable, $d^2x = 0 = dp$. The differential of V, dV, has the form $dV = Mdx + Ndy + Pd^2y + Qd^3y + \cdots$, or

$$dV = Mp + Nq + Pr + Qs + \cdots. \tag{2}$$

The coefficients M, N, P, Q are functions calculable from V.

Condorcet next differentiated the two sides of equation (1):

$$dV = d^2B = d\left(\frac{\partial B}{\partial x}\right)p + d\left(\frac{\partial B}{\partial y}\right)q + \left(\frac{\partial B}{\partial y} + d\left[\frac{\partial B}{\partial q}\right]\right)r + \cdots. \tag{3}$$

The terms of the right-hand side of equations (2) and (3) are then

$$M = d\left(\frac{\partial B}{\partial x}\right) \tag{4}$$

$$N = d\left(\frac{\partial B}{\partial y}\right) \tag{5}$$

$$P = \frac{\partial B}{\partial y} + d\left(\frac{\partial B}{\partial q}\right) \tag{6}$$

$$Q = \frac{\partial B}{\partial q} + d\left(\frac{\partial B}{\partial r}\right). \tag{7}$$

Obtaining the differential of $P, Q, \ldots$

$$dP = d\left(\frac{\partial B}{\partial y}\right) + d^2\left(\frac{\partial B}{\partial q}\right) \tag{8}$$

$$d^2Q = d^2\left(\frac{\partial B}{\partial q}\right) + d^3\left(\frac{\partial B}{\partial r}\right), \tag{9}$$

by successive addition and subtraction of (5), (8), (9), . . . , we obtain

$$N - dP + d^2Q - \cdots = 0, \tag{10}$$

which is the condition of existence of an integral B.

Condorcet then generalized his example by abandoning the hypothesis $d^2x = 0$, i.e., by supposing that there is no constant difference. He noted that the equations of these conditions are the same ones that determine the extreme values of the integral of V, as established by Euler and Lagrange.

Nowhere in Condorcet's various *mémoires* and other works, whether they deal with differential equations or equations with partial derivatives or equations with finite differences, can any results or methods be found that are truly creative or original relative to the works of Fontaine, d'Alembert, Euler, or Lagrange.

Calculus of probability. In the calculus of probability also, Condorcet did not bring any significant perfection to the resources of mathematics; he did, however, discuss and explain in depth an interpretation of probability that had far-reaching consequences in the applications of the calculus. First of all, he made a very clear distinction between an abstract or "absolute" probability and a subjective probability serving merely as grounds for belief. An example of the former is probability, in throwing an ideal die, that a given side will appear. Condorcet attempted to justify the passage from the first to the second by invoking three axiomatic principles that in effect reduced to the simple proposition "A very great absolute probability gives 'grounds for belief' that are close to certainty." (See "Probabilités," in *Encyclopédie méthodique; Éléments du calcul des probabilités,* art 4.) As for passage from observed frequencies to "grounds for belief," this is effected through an estimated abstract probability; and the instrument for this estimation was Bayes's theorem, which had recently been reformulated by Laplace (*Mémoires par divers savants,* **6**, 1774). Condorcet made a very shrewd study of this.

In the fourth "Mémoire sur le calcul des probabilités" (published in 1786), he noted that Bayes assumed the a priori law of probability to be constant, whereas it was actually possible to exhibit experimental variations of that law whether or not it depended on the time factor. Let us examine the latter case by means of an example. In a series of urns everything happens as if the drawings were made each time from an urn selected at random from a group, the numerical order of the drawing having no influence upon the choice. Thus, let $N = m + n + p + q$ decks of mixed cards. The first draw produces m red cards and n black ones from $(m + n)$ decks. We are asked the probability of drawing p red ones and q black ones from the $(p + q)$ remaining decks. Bayes's simple scheme (from a single deck of N cards, $m + n$ drawings have already been made, yielding m red and n black) furnishes the value calculated by Laplace for the probability wanted:

$$\frac{(p+q)! \int_0^1 x^{m+p}(1-x)^{n+q}\,dx}{p!q! \int_0^1 x^m(1-x)^n\,dx}$$

The hypothesis of a variable law led Condorcet to the alternative value

$$\frac{(p+q)! \iiint \cdots \left[\sum \frac{x_i}{N}\right]^{m+p} \left[1 - \sum \frac{x_i}{N}\right]^{n+q} dx_1\,dx_2 \cdots dx_N}{p!q! \iiint \cdots \left[\sum \frac{x_i}{N}\right]^{m} \left[1 - \sum \frac{x_i}{N}\right]^{n} dx_1\,dx_2 \cdots dx_N}$$

the multiple integrals being taken, for each variable, between 0 and 1 and x_i being the a priori probability assigned to the first deck of cards.

It is not correct to say, as Todhunter does (p. 404), that such an improvement on Laplace's formula was purely "arbitrary"; it must, nevertheless, be admitted that even though the main idea presupposes a thorough analysis of the requirements of a probabilistic model, it is no less true that the result is a complication offering no real utility.

"Social mathematics." Condorcet's most significant and fruitful endeavor was in a field entirely new at the time. The subject was one that departed from the natural sciences and mathematics but nevertheless showed the way toward a scientific comprehension of human phenomena, taking the empirical approach of natural science as its inspiration and employing mathematics as its tool. Condorcet called this new science "social mathematics." It was apparently intended to comprise, according to the "Tableau général de la science qui a pour objet l'application du calcul aux sciences physiques et morales," *Journal d'instruction sociale* (22 June, 6 July 1795; *Oeuvres,* I, 539–573), a statistical description of society, a theory of political economy inspired by the Physiocrats, and a combinatorial theory of intellectual processes. The great work on the voting process, published in 1785, is related to the latter.

Condorcet there sought to construct a scheme for an electoral body the purpose of which would be to determine the truth about a given subject by the process of voting and in which each elector would have the same chance of voicing the truth. Such a scheme was presented exactly like what is today called a model. Its parameters were the number of voters, the majority required, and the probability that any particular vote voices a correct judgment. Condorcet's entire analysis consisted, then, of calculating different variable functions of these structural parameters. Such, for example, was the probability that a decision reached by majority vote might be correct. An interesting complication of the model is introduced by the assumption that individual votes are not mutually independent. For example, the influence of a leader might intervene; or when several successive polls are taken, the electors' opinions may change during the voting process. On the other hand, the problem of estimating the various parameters on a statistical basis was brought out by Condorcet, whose treatment foreshadowed very closely that employed by modern users of mathematical models in the social sciences. The mathematical apparatus may be reduced to simple theorems of addition and multiplication of probabilities, to binomial distribution, and to the Bayes-Laplace rule.

Here is an example of this analysis. Let v be the individual probability of a correct judgment. The probability that a collective decision having obtained q votes might be correct is

$$\frac{v^q}{v^q + (1-v)^q}.$$

If one requires a majority of q with n voters, the probability that it will be attained and will furnish a correct decision is given by the sum

$$v^n + \sum_{i=1}^{n-q} C_n^i v^{n-i}(1-v)^i.$$

In the case of a leader's influence, if a voters out of n shared his opinion in a prior vote, the a posteriori probability of a voter's following the leader is, according to Bayes's rule, $a + 1/n + 2$; if v' represents the probability of any individual's holding a correct opinion and v'' is the same probability for the leader, then the probability of a voter's fortuitously holding the same opinion as the leader is

$$v'v'' + (1 - v')(1 - v'').$$

Condorcet then proposed to measure the magnitude of the leader's influence by the difference between the probabilities:

$$\frac{a+1}{n+2} - (v'v'' + [1 - v'][1 - v'']).$$

Along the way he encountered a completely different problem, the decomposition and composition of electoral decisions in the form of elementary propositions on which voters pronounce either "Yes" or "No." He then anticipated, without being aware of it, the logical import of this problem, which was the theory of the sixteen binary sentence connectives, among which he emphasized the conditional. He showed that a complex questionnaire could be reduced to a sequence of dichotomies and that constraints implicitly contained in the complex questionnaire are equivalent to the rejection of certain combinations of "Yes" and "No" in the elementary propositions. This is literally the reduction into normal disjunctive forms as practiced by contemporary logicians (*Essai,* pp. xiv ff.). He therefore brought to light, more completely and more systematically than his predecessor Borda,[9] the possible incoherence of collective judgment in the relative ordering of several candidates.

If there are three candidates to be ranked and sixty voters, the voting may be done on the three elementary propositions p, q, r:

p: A is preferable to B
q: A is preferable to C
r: B is preferable to C.

Since the choice of each voter is assumed to be a coherent one—namely, determining a noncyclical order of the three candidates A, B, and C—an individual choice such as "p and not-q and r" is excluded.

However, let us assume that the results of the vote were as follows:

"p and q and r"	order A-B-C	23	votes
"not-p and not-q and r"	B-C-A	17	votes
"not-p and q and r"	B-A-C	2	votes
"not-p and not-q and not-r"	C-B-A	8	votes
"p and not-q and not-r"	C-A-B	10	votes

If we calculate the votes by opinion, then it is the order A-B-C that wins. But if we calculate the votes according to elementary propositions, the following is obtained: "p," 33 votes; "not-q," 35 votes; "r," 42 votes. These are the majority propositions and define a cyclical order, and therefore an incoherent collective opinion. This is the paradox that Condorcet pointed out, one that poses the problem, taken up again only in modern times, of the conditions of coherence in a collective opinion.

No doubt the results obtained in the *Essai d'application de l'analyse* were modest ones. "In almost all cases," Condorcet said, "the results are in conformity with what simple reason would have dictated; but it is so easy to obscure reason by sophistry and vain subtleties that I should feel rewarded if I had only founded a single useful truth on a mathematical demonstration" (*Essai,* p. ii). One must nevertheless recognize, in this work dated 1785, the first large-scale attempt to apply mathematics to knowledge of human phenomena.

NOTES

1. We believe we can identify a fragment of it with the MS at the Institut de France, fol. 222–223, carton 873.
2. See Baker's excellent "Les débuts de Condorcet . . .."
3. He became interested in hydraulics together with the Abbé Bossut ("Nouvelles expériences sur la résistance des fluides," in *Mémoires de l'Académie des sciences,* 1778); he became interested in demographic statistics together with Dionis du Séjour and Laplace ("Essai pour connaître la population du royaume," *ibid.,* 1783–1788). The *Mémoires* (1782) contains a curious report on a proposal for a rational distribution of taxes using geographical, economic, and demographic data as a basis; it was formulated in collaboration with two physicists (Bossut and Desmarest), an agronomist (Tillet), and an astronomer (Dionis du Séjour).
4. In the five *mémoires* on public instruction (1791–1792) and in the draft decree of 20 April 1792, he proposed to replace the old literary instruction at the *collèges* with truly modern humanistic subjects including four categories of study: the physical and mathematical sciences, the moral and political sciences, the applications of science, and letters and fine arts.
5. See the fragment of the MSS published in Granger, "Langue universelle . . ."; also *Esquisse,* O. H. Prio, ed. (Paris, 1937), p. 232.
6. *Oeuvres de Lagrange,* XIII (Paris, 1882), 232.
7. Pt. 1, sec. 1. The handwritten MS is at the Institut de France (cartons 877–879) with the first 152 pages in printed form. Printing was suspended in 1786; the MS was composed in 1778.
8. For example, Lagrange wrote to d'Alembert, on 6 June 1765, that he wanted Condorcet "to explain in more detail the manner in which he arrived at the various integrals to which a single differential equation was susceptible." The reference here is to Condorcet's first work, *Du calcul intégral.* Likewise, on 30 September 1771, Lagrange pointed out to Condorcet that he had tried to apply one of his methods of approximation to an equation already studied, and that the result obtained was inaccurate.
9. Charles de Borda's "Mémoire sur les élections au scrutin" was published in the *Mémoires de l'Académie des sciences* (1781), 657–665, but it had been presented to the Academy in 1770 and Condorcet knew of it.

BIBLIOGRAPHY

The *Oeuvres,* 12 vols., pub. by Mme. Condorcet-O'Connor and François Arago (Paris, 1847–1849), do not contain the scientific writings. A bibliography and a chro-

CONON OF SAMOS

nology of the latter will be found in Henry, "Sur la vie et les écrits . . ." and in Granger (see below).

Condorcet's MSS are at the library of the Institut de France; the scientific writings are for the most part found in cartons 873–879 and 883–885.

On Condorcet see K. M. Baker, "An Unpublished Essay of Condorcet on Mechanical Methods of Classification," in *Annals of Science,* **18** (1962), 99–123; "Les débuts de Condorcet au Secrétariat de l'Académie royale des sciences," in *Revue d'histoire des sciences,* **20** (1967), 229–280; "Un 'éloge' officieux de Condorcet: Sa notice historique et critique sur Condillac," in *Revue de synthèse,* **88** (1967), 227–251; and "Scientism, Elitism and Liberalism: The Case of Condorcet," in *Studies on Voltaire and the 18th Century* (Geneva, 1967), pp. 129–165; L. Cahen, *Condorcet et la Révolution française* (Paris, 1904), with bibliography; Gilles Granger, "Langue universelle et formalisation des sciences," in *Revue d'histoire des sciences,* **7**, no. 4 (1954), 197–219; and *La mathématique sociale du Marquis de Condorcet* (Paris, 1956), with bibliography; Charles Henry, "Sur la vie et les écrits mathématiques de J. A. N. Caritat Marquis de Condorcet," in *Bollettino di bibliografia e storia delle scienze matematiche,* **16** (1883), 271 ff.; and his ed. of "Des méthodes d'approximation pour les équations différentielles lorsqu'on connaît une première valeur approchée," *ibid.,* 292–324; F. E. Manuel, *The Prophets of Paris* (Cambridge, Mass., 1962); René Taton, "Condorcet et Sylvestre-François Lacroix," in *Revue d'histoire des sciences,* **12** (1959), 127–158, 243–262; and I. Todhunter, *History of the Mathematical Theory of Probability From Pascal to Laplace* (Cambridge, 1865), pp. 351–410.

GILLES GRANGER

CONON OF SAMOS (*b.* Samos; *fl.* Alexandria, 245 B.C.)

Conon made astronomical and meteorological observations in Italy and Sicily before settling in Alexandria, where he became court astronomer to Ptolemy III (Ptolemy Euergetes). He became the close friend of Archimedes, who was in the habit of sending him mathematical propositions that he believed to be true but had not yet succeeded in proving. He is famous chiefly for his identification of the constellation *Coma Berenices,* named in honor of Ptolemy's consort. This must have taken place about 245 B.C.; and since he predeceased Archimedes by a considerable number of years, he must have died well before 212. His friend Dositheus took his place as Archimedes' correspondent. To Vergil and Propertius, Conon became a symbolic figure for the astronomer, probably through Callimachus' elegy on the discovery of *Coma Berenices,* which Catullus translated into Latin.

Apollonius relates that Conon, in a work sent to Thrasydaeus, treated the points of intersection of conic sections with each other and with a circle—but inaccurately, so that he was rightly attacked by Nicoteles of Cyrene. Pappus states that Conon enunciated "the theorem on the spiral" proved by Archimedes, but this contradicts what Archimedes himself says. For Archimedes tells Dositheus that he had sent Conon three groups of propositions which were subsequently proved in his treatises *On the Sphere and Cylinder, On Conoids and Spheroids,* and *On Spirals* —as well as two on sections of a sphere that were not correct—and Conon died before he was able to inquire into them sufficiently.

Claudius Ptolemy's *Risings of the Fixed Stars* attributes seventeen "signs of the seasons" to Conon. He clearly played a notable part in the development of the *parapegma,* the Greek astronomical and meteorological calendar. Seneca testifies that Conon diligently studied the records of solar eclipses kept by the Egyptians. The poetic assessment of his work in Catullus (66.1–4)—that he "discerned all the lights of the vast universe, and disclosed the risings and settings of the stars, how the fiery brightness of the sun is darkened, and how the stars retreat at fixed times"—seems, therefore, a fair summary. Probus' commentary on Vergil's *Eclogues* (3.40) ranks Conon with the great astronomers of antiquity; and the Bern scholiast to this passage calls him *mathematicus, stellarum peritissimus magister* ("a mathematician and most skilled master of the stars").

Conon's chief claim to fame shows, however, his talent as a courtier rather than as an astronomer. Berenice had vowed to dedicate a lock of her hair in the temple of Arsinoë Zephyritis if her newly married husband returned victorious from the Third Syrian War, which had begun in 246 B.C. He quickly returned, and she duly fulfilled her vow. The following day the lock of hair disappeared; and Conon professed to see it in some stars between Virgo, Leo, and Boötes that have been known ever since as Βερενίκης πλόκαμος, *Coma Berenices.*

BIBLIOGRAPHY

According to Probus, Conon left a work in seven books, *De astrologia.* As noted above, Apollonius, *Conics,* IV, pref., records that he wrote a treatise, Πρὸς Θρασυδαῖον, on the points of intersection of conic sections with each other and with a circle. It is a fair deduction from Seneca, *Quaestiones naturales,* VII. iii, 3 that he wrote a book on eclipses of the sun. None of these works has survived.

The fullest modern account is Albert Rehm's article "Konon, 11," in Pauly-Wissowa, XI, 1338–1340. See also Gerald L. Geison, "Did Conon of Samos Transmit Babylonian Observations?," in *Isis,* **58,** pt. 3, no. 193 (1967), 398–401.

IVOR BULMER-THOMAS

COOLIDGE, JULIAN LOWELL (*b.* Brookline, Massachusetts, 28 September 1873; *d.* Cambridge, Massachusetts, 5 March 1958)

Coolidge was the son of John Randolph Coolidge, a lawyer, and his wife, the former Julia Gardner. He received the B.A. at Harvard in 1895 and the B.Sc. at Oxford in 1897. From 1897 to 1899 he taught at the Groton School, then became an instructor at Harvard and in 1902 joined its faculty. From 1902 to 1904 he studied abroad, where his work with Corrado Segre at Turin and Eduard Study at Bonn decisively influenced his scientific career. In 1904 he received the Ph.D. at Bonn with a thesis entitled *Die dual-projektive Geometrie im elliptischen und sphärischen Raume.*

Back at Harvard, Coolidge became assistant professor in 1908 and full professor in 1918. During 1918–1919 he was a liaison officer to the French general staff, and in 1919 he organized courses at the Sorbonne for American servicemen. He returned to the Sorbonne in 1927 as exchange professor. From 1929 until his retirement in 1940 he was master of Lowell House at Harvard. He married Theresa Reynolds; they had two sons and five daughters.

Coolidge's mathematical career can be followed through his books (all, except his thesis, published by the Clarendon Press, Oxford). Four are in the tradition of the Study-Segre school, with many original contributions: *The Elements of Non-Euclidean Geometry* (1909), *A Treatise of the Circle and the Sphere* (1916), *The Geometry of the Complex Domain* (1924), and *A Treatise on Algebraic Plane Curves* (1931). In a class by itself is *Introduction to Mathematical Probability* (1925), one of the first modern English texts on this subject.

The last three books, *A History of Geometrical Methods* (1940), *A History of the Conic Sections and Quadric Surfaces* (1943), and *The Mathematics of Great Amateurs* (1949), reflect the interest that Coolidge, in his later years, showed in the history of mathematics.

Coolidge was an enthusiastic teacher with a flair for witty remarks. He was also a distinguished amateur astronomer.

BIBLIOGRAPHY

I. ORIGINAL WORKS. Coolidge's books are mentioned in the text. Among his papers are "Quadric Surfaces in Hyperbolic Space," in *Transactions of the American Mathematical Society,* **4** (1903), 161–170; "A Study of the Circle Cross," *ibid.,* **14** (1913), 149–174; "Congruences and Complexes of Circles," *ibid.,* **15** (1914), 107–134; "Robert Adrain and the Beginnings of American Mathematics," in *American Mathematical Monthly,* **33** (1926), 61–76; "The Heroic Age of Geometry," in *Bulletin of the American Mathematical Society,* **35** (1929), 19–37; and "Analytical Systems of Central Conics in Space," in *Transactions of the American Mathematical Society,* **48** (1940), 354–376.

II. SECONDARY LITERATURE. On Coolidge or his work, see M. Hammond et al., "J. L. Coolidge," in *Harvard University Gazette* (26 February 1955), 136–138; and Dirk J. Struik, "J. L. Coolidge (1873–1954)," in *American Mathematical Monthly,* **62** (1955), 669–682, with bibliography.

DIRK J. STRUIK

COSSERAT, EUGÈNE MAURICE PIERRE (*b.* Amiens, France, 4 March 1866; *d.* Toulouse, France, 31 May 1931)

Cosserat first studied at Amiens. When he was seventeen, he was accepted at the École Normale Supérieure. His scientific career was spent in Toulouse: he was assigned to the observatory in 1886, became professor of differential calculus at the Faculty of Sciences in 1896 and of astronomy in 1908, and was director of the observatory from 1908 until his death. A reserved, kindly man and a diligent worker, Cosserat was one of the moving forces of the University of Toulouse for thirty-five years. He was a *membre non-résident* of the Académie des Sciences (1919) and a corresponding member of the Bureau des Longitudes (1923).

For the first ten years Cosserat divided his time between his duties at the observatory, where he made equatorial observations of double stars, planets, and comets, and his research in geometry. His doctoral thesis (1888), which deals with an extension of Plücker's concept of the generation of space by means of straight lines, considers the infinitesimal properties of space created by circles. The congruences and complexes of straight lines are the main subject of his later works, in which he remained a disciple of Darboux.

In studying the deformation of surfaces Cosserat was oriented toward the theory of elasticity and the general problem of continuous mediums. These studies were done between 1885 and 1914 in collaboration with his older brother François, who was chief engineer of the Service des Ponts et Chaussées. François was the main participant in tests on synthesis and philosophical concepts, the mathematical framework of the research being furnished by Eugène.

The most practical results concerning elasticity were the introduction of the systematic use of the movable trihedral and the proposal and resolution, before Fredholm's studies, of the functional equations of the sphere and ellipsoid. Cosserat's theoretical research, designed to include everything in theoretical physics that is directly subject to the laws of mechanics, was founded on the notion of Euclidean action combined with Lagrange's ideas on the principle of extremality and Lie's ideas on invariance in regard to displacement groups. The bearing of this original and coherent conception was diminished in importance because at the time it was proposed, fundamental ideas were already being called into question by both the theory of relativity and progress in physical theory.

The Toulouse observatory participated in the international undertaking of formulating the Carte du Ciel. Having become director, Cosserat organized the important work of meridian observations, photography, and computation of positions in order to make systematic determination of the proper motions of the stars. He personally supervised the details of these operations, including the computations, and was completely occupied with this task for the last fifteen years of his life.

Cosserat was particularly concerned with accuracy: he used his original research, which later appeared as notes in the now-classic works of Darboux, Koenigs, Appell, and Chwolson. Thus, although his name seldom appears in modern works, his influence on them was far-reaching.

BIBLIOGRAPHY

I. Original Works. In geometry and analysis, Cosserat's main works were published in *Annales de la Faculté des sciences de Toulouse:* "Sur le cercle considéré comme élément générateur de l'espace," **3** (1889), E1-E81, his doctoral thesis; "Formes bilinéaires," *ibid.,* M1-M12; "Courbes algébriques dans le voisinage d'un de ses points," **4** (1890), O1-O16; "Congruences de droites et la théorie des surfaces," **7** (1893), N1-N62; "Déformations infinitésimales d'une surface flexible et inextensible," **8** (1894), E1-E46; and "Travaux scientifiques de T. J. Stieljes," **9** (1895), [1]-[64]; in *Mémoires de l'Académie des sciences de Toulouse:* "Classe de complexes de droites," **4** (1892), 482-510; and "Théorie des lignes tracées sur une surface," **7** (1895), 366-394; in *Comptes rendus de l'Académie des sciences,* some twenty notes (1888-1908), most notably "Sur les courbes algébriques à torsion constante et sur les surfaces minima . . .," **120** (1895), 1252-1254; and "Sur la théorie des équations aux dérivées partielles du deuxième ordre," in G. Darboux, *Leçons sur la théorie des surfaces,* IV (Paris, 1896), 405-422.

In mechanics he wrote, with his brother François: "Théorie de l'élasticité," in *Annales de la Faculté des sciences de Toulouse,* **10** (1896), I1-I116; "Note sur la cinématique d'un milieu continu," in G. Koenigs, *Leçons de cinématique* (Paris, 1897), pp. 391-417; "Note sur la dynamique du point et du corps invariable," in O. Chwolson, *Traité de physique,* I (Paris, 1906), 236-273; "Note sur la théorie de l'action euclidienne," in P. Appell, *Traité de mécanique rationnelle,* III (Paris, 1909), 557-629; and "Note sur la théorie des corps déformables," in O. Chwolson, *Traité de physique,* II (Paris, 1909), 953-1173, also published separately (Paris, 1909).

In astronomy he wrote "Sur quelques étoiles dont le mouvement propre annuel dépasse 0″5," in *Comptes rendus de l'Académie des sciences,* **169** (1919), 414-418; and "Déterminations photographiques de positions d'étoiles," in *Annales de l'Observatoire de Toulouse,* **10** (1933), 1-306.

II. Secondary Literature. On Cosserat or his work, see P. Caubet, "E. Cosserat; ses vues générales sur l'astronomie de position," in *Journal des observateurs,* **14** (1931), 139-143; and L. Montangerand, "Éloge de Cosserat," in *Annales de l'Observatoire de Toulouse,* **10** (1933), xx-xxx.

Jacques R. Lévy

COTES, ROGER (*b.* Burbage, Leicestershire, England, 10 July 1682; *d.* Cambridge, England, 5 June 1716)

Cotes was the second son of the Reverend Robert Cotes, rector of Burbage. His mother was the former Grace Farmer, of Barwell, Leicestershire. He was educated first at Leicester School, where he showed such a flair for mathematics that at the age of twelve his uncle, the Reverend John Smith, took him into his home to supervise his studies personally. Cotes later went to St. Paul's School, London, where he studied mainly classics while keeping up a scientific correspondence with his uncle. He was admitted as a pensioner to Trinity College, Cambridge, in 1699, graduating B.A. in 1702 and M.A. in 1706. He became fellow of his college in 1705 and a fellow of the Royal Society in 1711, and was ordained in 1713. In January 1706, Cotes was named the first Plumian professor of astronomy and natural philosophy at Cambridge on the very strong recommendation of Richard Bentley, master of Trinity. Cotes, who never married, died of a violent fever when only thirty-three. His early death caused Newton to lament: "Had Cotes lived we might have known something."

On his appointment as professor, Cotes opened a subscription list in order to provide an observatory for Trinity. This, with living quarters for the professor, was erected on the leads over King's Gate. Cotes spent the rest of his life here with his cousin Robert Smith, who was his assistant and successor. The observatory was not completed in Cotes's lifetime and was demolished in 1797.

Concerning his astronomical work Cotes supplied, in correspondence with Newton, a description of a heliostat telescope furnished with a mirror revolving by clockwork. He recomputed the solar and planetary tables of Flamsteed and J. D. Cassini and had intended to construct tables of the moon's motion, based on Newtonian principles. According to Halley (1714), he also observed the total solar eclipse of 22 April 1715, noticing the occultation of three spots.

Cotes formed a school of physical sciences at Trinity in collaboration with William Whiston. The two performed a series of experiments beginning in May 1707, the details of which can be found in a posthumous publication, *Hydrostatical and Pneumatical Lectures by Roger Cotes* (1738). These demonstration classes indicate a simple, straightforward style that is both stimulating and thorough. There was no thought of practical work by students at this time.

In 1709 Cotes became heavily involved in the preparation of the second edition of Newton's great work on universal gravitation, the *Philosophiae naturalis principia mathematica.* The first edition of 1687 had few copies printed. In 1694 Newton did further work on his lunar and planetary theories, but illness and a dispute with Flamsteed postponed any further publication. Newton subsequently became master of the mint and had virtually retired from scientific work when Bentley persuaded him to prepare a second edition, suggesting Cotes as supervisor of the work.

Newton at first had a rather casual approach to the revision, but Cotes took the work very seriously. Gradually, Newton was coaxed into a similar enthusiasm; and the two collaborated closely on the revision, which took three and a half years to complete. The edition was limited to only 750 copies, and a pirated version printed in Amsterdam met the total demand. Bentley, who had borne the expense of the printing, took the profits and rewarded Cotes with twelve free copies for his labors. Newton wrote a preface, remarking that in this edition the theory of the moon and the precession of the equinoxes had been more fully deduced from the principles, the theory of comets confirmed by several observations, and the orbits of comets computed more accurately. His debt to Cotes for these improvements cannot be estimated.

Cotes's original contribution to this book was a short preface. He suggested to Newton that he write a description of the scientific methodology used and demonstrate, in particular, the superiority of these principles to the popular idea of vortices presented by Descartes. Cartesian ideas were still vigorous, not only on the Continent but also in England, and continued to be taught at Cambridge until 1730 at least. In particular, Cartesian critics alleged that Newton's idea of action at a distance required the conception of an unexplained, occult force. Newton and Bentley agreed that Cotes should write a preface defending the Newtonian hypothesis against the theory of vortices and the other objections.

Cotes began his preface by considering three possible methods of approaching celestial phenomena. The first, used mainly by the Greeks, was to describe motions without attempting a rational explanation; the second was to make hypotheses and, out of ignorance, to relate them to occult qualities; and the third was to use the method of experiment and observation. He vigorously asserted that Newton's approach belonged only to the third category. Illustrating this by means of the inverse-square law of gravitation, he quoted Newton's discovery that the acceleration of the moon toward the earth confirms this theory and that Kepler's third law of motion, taken in conjunction with Huygens' rule for central forces, implies such a law. He asserted that the paths of comets could be observed as conics with the sun as focus and that in both planetary and cometary motion the theory of vortices conformed neither to reason nor to observation. Cotes concluded that the law of gravitation was confirmed by observation and did not depend on occult qualities.

> But shall gravity be therefore called an occult cause, and thrown out of philosophy, because the cause of gravity is occult and not yet discovered? Those who affirm this, should be careful not to fall into an absurdity that may overturn the foundations of all philosophy. For causes usually proceed in a continued chain from those that are compounded to those that are more simple; when we are arrived at the most simple cause we can go no farther. . . . These most simple causes will you then call occult and reject them? Then you must reject those that immediately depend on them [*Mathematical Principles,* p. xxvii].

Cotes proceeded positively to imply the principle of action at a distance. "Those who would have the heavens filled with a fluid matter, but suppose it void of any inertia, do indeed in words deny a vacuum, but allow it in fact. For since a fluid matter of that kind can noways be distinguished from empty space, the dispute is now about the names and not the natures of things" (*ibid.,* p. xxxi).

Leibniz later condemned Cotes's preface as "pleine d'aigreur," but it can be seen that Cotes argued powerfully and originally in favor of Newton's hypothesis.

Cotes's major original work was in the field of

COTES

mathematics, and the decline in British mathematics that followed his untimely death accentuated his being one of the very few British mathematicians capable of following on from Newton's great work.

His only publication during his life was an article entitled "Logometria" (1714). After his death his mathematical papers, then in great confusion, were edited by Robert Smith and published as a book, *Harmonia mensurarum* (1722). This work, which includes the "Logometria" as its first part, gives an indication of Cotes's great ability. His style is somewhat obscure, with geometrical arguments preferred to analytical ones, and many results are quoted without explanation. What cannot be obscured is the original, systematic genius of the writer. This is shown most powerfully in his work on integration, in which long sequences of complicated functions are systematically integrated, and the results are applied to the solution of a great variety of problems.

Cotes first demonstrates that the natural base to take for a system of logarithms is the number which he calculates as 2.7182818. He then shows two ingenious methods for computing Briggsian logarithms (with base 10) for any number and interpolating to obtain intermediate values. The rest of part 1 is devoted to the application of integration to the solution of problems involving quadratures, arc lengths, areas of surfaces of revolution, the attraction of bodies, and the density of the atmosphere. His most remarkable discovery in this section (pp. 27–28) occurs when he attempts to evaluate the surface area of an ellipsoid of revolution. He shows that the problem can be solved in two ways, one leading to a result involving logarithms and the other to arc sines, probably an illustration of the harmony of different types of measure. By equating these two results he arrives at the formula $i\phi = \log(\cos\phi + i\sin\phi)$ where $i = \sqrt{-1}$, a discovery preceding similar equations obtained by Moivre (1730) and Euler (1748).

The second and longest part of the *Harmonia mensurarum* is devoted to systematic integration. In a preface to this section Smith explains that shortly before his death Cotes wrote a letter to D. Jones in which he claimed that any fluxion of the form

$$\frac{d\dot{z}z^{\theta n+(\delta/\lambda)n-1}}{e+fz^n}$$

where d, e, f are constants, θ an integer (positive or negative), and δ/λ a fraction, had a fluent that could be expressed in terms of logarithms or trigonometric ratios. He claimed, further, that even fluxions of the forms

$$\frac{d\dot{z}z^{\theta n+(\delta/\lambda)n-1}}{e+fz^n+gz^{2n}}$$

and

$$\frac{d\dot{z}z^{\theta n+(\delta/\lambda)n-1}}{e+fz^n+gz^{2n}+hz^{3n}}$$

had fluents expressible in these terms.

Returning to the text, Cotes then proceeds to evaluate the fluents of no fewer than ninety-four types of such fluxions, working out each individual case as θ takes different values. His calculation was aided by a geometrical result now known as Cotes's theorem, which, expressed in analytical terms, is equivalent to finding all the factors of $x^n - a^n$ where n is a positive integer. The theorem is that if the circumference of a circle is divided into n equal parts OO^1, O^1O^{11}, $\cdots$ and any point P is taken on a radius OC, then $(PC)^n - (OC)^n = PO \times PO^1 \times PO^{11} \times \cdots$ if P is outside the circle and $(OC)^n - (PC)^n = PO \times PO^1 \times PO^{11} \times \cdots$ if P is inside the circle. This result was proved by J. Brinkley (1797).

The third part consists of miscellaneous works, including papers on methods of estimating errors, Newton's differential method, the construction of tables by differences, the descent of heavy bodies, and cycloidal motion. There are two particularly interesting results here. The essay on Newton's differential method describes how, given n points at equidistant abscissae, the area under the curve of nth degree joining these points may be evaluated. Taking A as the sum of the first and last ordinates, B as the sum of the second and last but one, etc., he evaluates the formulas for the areas as

$$\frac{A+4B}{6} \text{ if } n = 3$$

$$\frac{A+3B}{8} \text{ if } n = 4$$

$$\frac{7A+32B+12C}{90} \text{ if } n = 5, \text{ etc.}$$

A modernized form of this result is known as the Newton-Cotes formula.

In describing a method for evaluating the most probable result of a set of observations, Cotes comes very near to the technique known as the method of least squares. He does not state this method as such; but his result, which depends on giving weights to the observations and then calculating their centroid, is equivalent. This anticipates similar discoveries by Gauss (1795) and Legendre (1806).

BIBLIOGRAPHY

I. Original Works. Cotes's writings are the preface to Isaac Newton, *Philosophiae naturalis principia mathematica,* 2nd ed. (Cambridge, 1713), trans. by Andrew Motte as *Sir Isaac Newton's Mathematical Principles* (London, 1729) and repr. with a historical and explanatory appendix by Florian Cajori (Cambridge, 1934); "Logometria," in *Philosophical Transactions of the Royal Society,* **29** (1714), 5–47; "A Description of the Great Meteor Which Was on the 6th of March 1716 . . .," *ibid.,* **31** (1720), 66; *Epistola ad amicum de Cotesii inventis, curvarum ratione, quae cum circulo & hyperbola,* R. Smith, ed. (London, 1722); *Harmonium mensurarum, sive Analysis et synthesis per rationum et angulorum mensuras promotae: Accedunt alia opuscula mathematica per Rogerum Cotesium,* R. Smith, ed. (Cambridge, 1722); and *Hydrostatical and Pneumatical Lectures by Roger Cotes A.M.,* R. Smith, ed. (London, 1738).

II. Secondary Literature. On Cotes or his work see the anonymous "An Account of a Book, Intituled, 'Harmonia mensurarum,'" in *Philosophical Transactions of the Royal Society,* **32** (1722), 139–150; D. Brewster, *Memoirs of Sir Isaac Newton,* I (Edinburgh, 1855), 332; J. Brinkley, "A General Demonstration of the Property of the Circle Discovered by Mr. Cotes Deduced From the Circle Only," in *Transactions of the Royal Irish Academy,* **7** (1797), 151–159; A. De Morgan, in *Penny Cyclopaedia,* **8** (1837), 87; and *ibid.,* **13** (1839), 379; J. Edleston, *Correspondence of Sir Isaac Newton and Professor Cotes* (London–Cambridge, 1850); R. T. Gunther, *Early Science in Cambridge* (Oxford, 1937), pp. 78, 161; Edmund Halley, "Observations of the Late Total Eclipse of the Sun on the 22nd of April Last Past . . .," in *Philosophical Transactions of the Royal Society,* **29** (1714), 253–254; A. Kippis, in *Biographia Britannica,* IV (London, 1789), 294–297; A. Koyré, "Attraction, Newton, and Cotes," in *Archives internationales d'histoire des sciences,* **14** (1961), 225–236, repr. in his *Newtonian Studies* (Cambridge, Mass., 1965), pp. 273–282; J. E. Montucla, *Histoire des mathématiques,* III (Paris, 1758), 149, 154; S. P. Rigaud, *Correspondence of Scientific Men of the Seventeenth Century,* I (Oxford, 1841), 257–270; N. Saunderson, *The Method of Fluxions Together With the Demonstration of Mr. Cotes's Forms of Fluents in the Second Part of His Logometria* (London, 1756); C. Walmesley, *Analyse des mesures* (Paris, 1753), a commentary on the *Harmonia mensurarum;* and W. Whiston, *Memoirs of the Life and Writings of Mr. William Whiston* (London, 1749), pp. 133–135.

J. M. Dubbey

COURNOT, ANTOINE-AUGUSTIN (*b.* Gray, France, 28 August 1801; *d.* Paris, France, 31 March 1877)

Of Franche-Comté peasant stock, Cournot's family had belonged for two generations to the *petite bourgeoisie* of Gray. In his *Souvenirs* he says very little about his parents but a great deal about his paternal uncle, a notary to whom he apparently owed his early education. Cournot was deeply impressed by the conflict that divided the society in which he lived into the adherents of the *ancien régime* and the supporters of new ideas, especially in the realm of religion. One of his uncles was a conformist priest, the other a faithful disciple of the Jesuits, having been educated by them.

Between 1809 and 1816 Cournot received his secondary education at the *collège* of Gray and showed a precocious interest in politics by attending the meetings of a small royalist club. He spent the next four years idling away his time, working "en amateur" in a lawyer's office. Influenced by reading Laplace's *Système du monde* and the Leibniz-Clarke correspondence, he became interested in mathematics and decided to enroll at the École Normale Supérieure in Paris. In preparation, he attended a course in special mathematics at the Collège Royal in Besançon (1820–1821) and was admitted to the École Normale after competitive examinations in August 1821. However, on 6 September 1822 the abbé Frayssinous, newly appointed grand master of the University of France, closed the École Normale. Cournot found himself without a school and with only a modest allowance for twenty months. He remained in Paris, using this free time—which he called the happiest of his life—to prepare at the Sorbonne for the *licence* in mathematics (1822–1823). His teachers at the Sorbonne were Lacroix, a disciple of Condorcet, and Hachette, a former colleague of Monge. A fellow student and friend was Dirichlet.

In October 1823, Cournot was hired by Marshal Gouvion-Saint-Cyr as tutor for his small son. Soon Cournot became his secretary and collaborator in the editing and publishing of his *Mémoires.* Thus, for seven years, until the death of the marshal, Cournot had the opportunity to meet the many important persons around the marshal and to reflect on matters of history and politics. Nevertheless, Cournot was still interested in mathematics. He published eight papers in the baron de Férussac's *Bulletin des sciences,* and in 1829 he defended his thesis for the doctorate in science, "Le mouvement d'un corps rigide soutenu par un plan fixe." The papers attracted the attention of Poisson, who at that time headed the teaching of mathematics in France. When, in the summer of 1833, Cournot left the service of the Gouvion-Saint-Cyr family, Poisson immediately secured him a temporary position with the Academy of Paris. In October 1834 the Faculty of Sciences in Lyons created a chair of analysis, and Poisson saw to it that Cournot was appointed to this post. In between, Cournot translated and adapted John Herschel's *Treatise on Astronomy* and Kater and Lardner's *A Treatise on Mechanics,* both published, with success, in 1834.

From then on, Cournot was a high official of the French university system. He taught in Lyons for a year. In October 1835 he accepted the post of rector at Grenoble, with a professorship in mathematics at the Faculty of Sciences. Subsequently he was appointed acting inspector general of public education. In September 1838, Cournot married and left Grenoble to become inspector general. In 1839 he was appointed chairman of the Jury d'Agrégation in mathematics, an office he held until 1853. He left the post of inspector general to become rector at Dijon in 1854, after the Fortoul reform, and served there until his retirement in 1862.

In the course of his long career as administrator, Cournot, who was extremely scrupulous in fulfilling his duties, was able to exert a strong influence on the teaching of mathematics in the secondary schools and published a work on the institutions of public instruction in France (1864). At the same time he pursued a career as scientist and philosopher. While rector at Grenoble, he published *Recherches sur les principes mathématiques de la théorie des richesses* (1838). Between 1841 and 1875 he published all his mathematical and philosophical works.

Unassuming and shy, Cournot was considered an exemplary civil servant by his contemporaries. His religious opinions seem to have been very conservative. In politics he was an enthusiastic royalist in 1815, only to be disappointed by the restoration of the monarchy. In the presidential elections following the 1848 Revolution, he voted for Louis Eugène Cavaignac, a moderate republican. In 1851, sharply disapproving the organization of public instruction as directed by Louis Napoleon, he decided to become a candidate in the legislative elections in Haute-Saône; this election, however, was prevented by the coup d'état of 2 December.

Cournot's background and his education made him a member of the provincial *petite bourgeoisie* of the *ancien régime.* But as a civil servant of the July monarchy and the Second Empire, he became integrated into the new bourgeoisie of the nineteenth century. Of certainly mediocre talents as far as pure mathematics was concerned, he left behind work on the philosophy of science, remarkably forceful and original for its period, that foreshadowed the application of mathematics to the sciences of mankind. Nobody could express better and more humorously Cournot's importance than he himself when he reported Poisson's appreciation of his first works: "He [Poisson] discovered in them a philosophical depth—and, I must honestly say, he was not altogether wrong. Furthermore, from them he predicted that I would go far in the field of pure mathematical speculation but (as I have always thought and have never hesitated to say) in this he was wrong" (*Souvenirs,* p. 154).

Cournot's mathematical work amounts to very little: some papers on mechanics without much originality, the draft of his course on analysis, and an essay on the relationship between algebra and geometry. Thus, it is mainly the precise idea of a possible application of mathematics to as yet unexplored fields that constitutes his claim to fame. With the publication in 1838 of his *Recherches sur les principes mathématiques de la théorie des richesses* he was a third of a century ahead of Walras and Jevons and must be considered the true founder of mathematical economics. By reducing the problem of price formation in a given market to a question of analysis, he was the first to formulate the data of the diagram of monopolistic competition, thus defining a type of solution that has remained famous as "Cournot's point." Since then, his arguments have of course been criticized and amended within a new perspective. Undoubtedly, he remains the first of the important pioneers in this field.

Cournot's work on the "theory of chance occurrences" contains no mathematical innovation. Nevertheless, it is important in the history of the calculus of probability, since it examines in an original way the interpretation and foundations of this calculus and its applications. According to Cournot, occurrences in our world are always determined by a cause. But in the universe there are independent causal chains. If, at a given point in time and space, two of these chains have a common link, this coincidence constitutes the fortuitous character of the event thus engendered. Consequently, there would be an objective chance occurrence that would nevertheless have a cause. This seeming paradox would be no reflection of our ignorance.

This objective chance occurrence is assigned a certain value in a case where it is possible to enumerate—for a given event—all the possible combinations of circumstances and all those in which the event occurs. This value is to be interpreted as a degree of "physical possibility." However, one must distinguish between a physical possibility that differs from 0 (or 1) only by an infinitely small amount and a strict logical impossibility (or necessity).

On the other hand, Cournot also insisted on the necessary distinction between this physical possibility, or "objective probability," and the "subjective probability" that depends on our ignorance and rests on the consideration of events that are deemed equiprobable[1] since there is not sufficient cause to decide otherwise. Blaise Pascal, Fermat, Huygens, and Leibniz would have seen only this aspect of probability. Jakob I Bernoulli, despite his ambiguous vocabulary, would have been the first to deal with objective probabilities that Cournot was easily able to estimate on the basis of frequencies within a sufficiently large number of series of events.

To these two ideas of probability Cournot added a third that he defined as "philosophical probability." This is the degree of rational, not measurable, belief that we accord a given scientific hypothesis. It "depends mainly upon the idea that we have of the simplicity of the laws of nature, of order, and of the rational succession of phenomena" (*Exposition de la théorie des chances,* p. 440; see also *Essai,* I, 98–99). Of course, Cournot neither solved nor even satisfactorily stated the problem of the logical foundation of the calculus of probability. But he had the distinction of having been the first to dissociate—in a radical way—various ideas that still were obscure, thus opening the way for deeper and more systematic research by more exact mathematicians. He also was able to show clearly the importance of the applications of the calculus of probability to the scientific description and explanation of human acts. He himself—following Condorcet and Poisson—attempted to interpret legal statistics (*Journal de Liouville,* **4** [1838], 257–334; see also *Exposition de la théorie des chances,* chs. 15, 16). But he also warned against "premature and abusive applications" that might discredit this ambitious project.

More than for his mathematical originality, Cournot is known for his views on scientific knowledge. He defined science as logically organized knowledge, comprising both a classification of the objects with which it deals and an ordered concatenation of the propositions it sets forth. It claims neither the eternal nor the absolute: "There can be nothing more inconsistent than the degree of generality of the data with which the sciences deal—data susceptible to the degree of order and the classification that constitute scientific perfection" (*Essai,* II, 189). Therefore, the fundamental characteristic of the scientific object must be defined differently. "What strikes us first of all, what we understand best, is the *form,*" Cournot wrote at the beginning of the *Traité de l'enchaînement des idées,* adding, "Scientifically we shall always know[2] only the form and the order." Thus, it was from this perspective that he interpreted scientific explanation and stressed the privilege of mathematics—the science of form par excellence. Even though establishing himself as forerunner of a completely modern structural concept of the scientific object, Cournot did not go so far as to propose a reduction of the process of knowledge to the application of logical rules. On the contrary, he insisted upon the domination of strictly formal and demonstrative logic by "another logic, much more fruitful, a logic which separates appearance from reality, a logic which connects specific observations and infers general laws from them, a logic which ranks truth and fact" (*Traité,* p. 6).

This discerning and inventive power orients and governs the individual steps of the strictly logical proof; it postulates an order in nature and its realization in the simplest ways.[3] This suggests the opposition Leibniz saw in the laws of logical necessity and the architectonic principles that make their application intelligible (see, e.g., Leibniz' "Specimen dynamicum," in his *Mathematische Schriften,* Gerhardt, ed., VI, 234–246). Cournot also declared himself, on several occasions, a great admirer of Leibniz. But to him the reason that governs the discovery of natural laws was not due to divine wisdom—he was always careful to separate religious beliefs (to which, incidentally, he adhered) from philosophical rationality. Reason, within scientific knowledge, denoted the ineluctable but always hazardous contribution of philosophical speculation. "Everywhere," he assures us, "we must state this twofold fact, that the intervention of the philosophical idea is necessary as a guideline and to give science its dogmatic and regular form; it also must insure that the progress of the positive sciences is not hindered by the indecision of philosophical questions" (*Essai,* II, 252). Thus philosophy, as research on the most "probable" hypotheses regarding the assumption of a maximum of order and a minimum of complexity, becomes an integral part of scientific practice. But if philosophical reason guides the organization of hypotheses, it is the role of logic, obviously, to exhibit consequences and of experience to provide the only evidence that can be decisive in their favor.[4]

From this analysis one must conclude that science cannot be defined as a pure and simple determination of causes. For Cournot the word "cause" meant the generative antecedent of a phenomenon. He wanted science to add to the designation of causes the indication of reasons, i.e., the general traits of the type of order within which the causes act. And since the indication of reasons stems from philosophical speculation, it can only be probable—within a probability that itself is philosophical—that knowledge will advance to the extent that hypotheses are refined and corrected on the basis of experience.

In this sense, Cournot's epistemology is a probabilism. And it is probabilism in another sense, too—since it insists upon the indissoluble connection between the "historic data" and the "theoretical data" in the sciences. Fortuitous facts, in the sense defined above, appear in our experience—by its very nature—and not through our ignorance of causes. These facts appear as knots of contingency within the tissue of theoretical explication and, according to Cournot, cannot be entirely removed from it.

The connection between science and history is defined more precisely by the classification of the sciences proposed in chapter 22 of the *Essai.* According to Cournot, the system of the sciences must show an order that his predecessors had vainly tried to reduce to one dimension. In order to describe this system, we need a double-entry table (Figure 1) that vertically approximates Comte's system of division: mathematical sciences, physical and cosmological sciences, biological and natural sciences, noological and symbolic sciences, political and historical sciences. Horizontally there are three series: theoretical, cosmological, and technical. The technical series gives a special place and autonomous status to certain applied disciplines the importance and development of which "depend upon various peculiarities of the state of civilized nations and are not in proportion to the importance and philosophical standing of the speculative sciences to which they should be linked" (*Essai,* II, 266).

The distinction between the theoretical and the cosmological series corresponds to the separation of a historic and contingent element. This element will always be present in the sciences, even in the theoretical sciences (with the exception, perhaps, of mathematics), and will become more and more dominant as one passes from the physical sciences to the natural sciences (see *Traité,* p. 251). But if the very nature of the process of scientific knowledge demands that the philosophical element cannot be "anatomically" separated, it allows for the establishment of sciences in which the historic element controls the contents and the method of knowing.

Another kind of separation appears in the system of the sciences that Cournot set forth and developed in his works following the *Essai.* This separation is the radical distinction between a realm of physical nature and a realm of life.

For Cournot, the scientific explanation of the phenomena of life requires a specific principle that, in the organism, must control the laws of physics and chemistry. As for man's role among the living beings, it seems that Cournot linked it with the development of community life, for "the superiority of man's instincts and the faculties directly derived from it . . . would not suffice to constitute a distinct realm within Nature, a realm in contrast with the other realms" (*Traité,* p. 365). On the other hand, he adds, "When I see a city of a million inhabitants . . . I understand very well that I am completely separated from the state of Nature . . ." (*ibid.,* p. 366).

This separation from the state of nature is accomplished by man in the course of a development that causes him to cultivate successively the great organizational forms of civilized life: religion, art, history, philosophy, and science. Cournot was careful not to interpret such a development as a straight and continuous march, yet he did not fail to stress that only scientific knowledge could be the sign of great achievement and alone was truly capable of cumulative and indefinitely pursued progress.

	Theoretical Series	Cosmological Series	Technical Series
Mathematical sciences	Theory of numbers, etc.		Metrology, etc.
Physical and cosmological sciences	Physics Physical chemistry, etc.	Astronomy Geology, etc.	Engineering sciences, etc.
Biological and natural sciences	Anatomy Experimental psychology	Botany Linguistics, etc.	Agronomy Medicine, etc.
Noological and symbolic sciences	Logic Natural theology, etc.	Mythology Ethnography, etc.	Grammar Natural law, etc.
Political and historical sciences	Sociology Economics, etc.	Political geography History, etc.	Judicial sciences, etc.

FIGURE 1

NOTES

1. Cournot's definition of an objective probability as the quotient of the number of favorable cases divided by the number of possible cases also entails a hypothesis of equiprobability of these various cases (*Essai,* ch. 2). Cournot does not seem to have noticed this difficulty, which later concerned Keynes and F. P. Ramsey.
2. According to Cournot, order is a fundamental category of scientific thought that can be deduced neither from time nor from space, which it logically precedes. Moreover, it cannot be reduced to the notion of linear succession. Without proceeding to a formal analysis, Cournot very often showed that by "order" he meant any relationship that can be expressed by a multiple-entry table.
3. But Cournot rebelled against the reduction of the principle of order to a maxim postulating the stability of the laws of nature (*Essai,* I, 90).
4. Cournot was always very careful to distinguish between philosophy and science. The following text shows a very rare lucidity, considering when it was written:

   In a century when the sciences have gained so much popularity through their applications, it would be a vain effort to try to pass off philosophy as science or as a science. The public, comparing progress and results, will not be fooled for long. And since philosophy is not—as some would have us believe—a science, one could be led to believe that philosophy is nothing at all, a conclusion fatal to true scientific progress and to the dignity of the human spirit [*Considérations,* II, 222].

BIBLIOGRAPHY

I. Original Works. Cournot's principal works are *Recherches sur les principes mathématiques de la théorie des richesses* (Paris, 1838, 1938); *Traité élémentaire de la théorie des fonctions et du calcul infinitésimal,* 2 vols. (Paris, 1841); *Exposition de la théorie des chances et des probabilités* (Paris, 1843); *De l'origine et des limites de la correspondance entre l'algèbre et la géométrie* (Paris, 1847); *Essai sur les fondements de la connaissance et sur les caractères de la critique philosophique,* 2 vols. (Paris, 1861, 1911); *Traité de l'enchaînement des idées fondamentales dans les sciences et dans l'histoire,* 2 vols. (Paris, 1861, 1912); *Considérations sur la marche des idées et des événements dans les temps modernes,* 2 vols. (Paris, 1872, 1934); *Matérialisme, vitalisme, rationalisme* (Paris, 1875); and *Souvenirs,* edited, with intro. and notes, by E. P. Bottinelli (Paris, 1913).

II. Secondary Literature. On Cournot or his work, see E. P. Bottinelli, *A. Cournot, métaphysicien de la connaissance* (Paris, 1913), which contains an exhaustive bibliography of Cournot's work; E. Callot, *La philosophie biologique de Cournot* (Paris, 1959); A. Darbon, *Le concept du hasard dans la philosophie de Cournot* (Paris, 1911); F. Mentré, *Cournot et la renaissance du probabilisme au XIXe siècle* (Paris, 1908); and G. Milhaud, *Études sur Cournot* (Paris, 1927). *Revue de métaphysique et de morale* (May 1905) is a special number devoted to Cournot; of special note are Henri Poincaré, "Cournot et les principes du calcul infinitésimal"; G. Milhaud, "Note sur la raison chez Cournot"; and H. L. Moore, "A.-A. Cournot," a biographical study.

G. Granger

COUTURAT, LOUIS (*b.* Paris, France, 17 January 1868; *d.* between Ris-Orangis and Melun, France, 3 August 1914)

From early childhood Couturat displayed an exceptional mixture of intellectual and artistic talent, and at the *lycée* his precocity brought him many prizes. He was to become a master of ancient literature, as well as an outstanding critic in the logic of theoretical and applied sciences. Logic was his basic concern, and even his writings on aesthetics show his preoccupation with logical foundations.

When not yet twenty-two Couturat was honored with the *lauréat du concours général* in philosophy and in science. During his fourth year at the École Normale Supérieure he studied mathematics under Jules Tannéry and then continued under Picard and Jordan, also taking courses with Poincaré. He received his licentiate in mathematics on 25 July 1892. Thus prepared to handle problems in the philosophy of science, he published a paper on the paradox of Achilles and the tortoise in the *Revue philosophique.*

His Latin thesis for the doctorate was a scientific study of the Platonic myths in the *Dialogues.* For the French thesis he devoted himself to a study of the mathematical infinite. Couturat finished both theses by 12 May 1894, while serving at Toulouse as lecturer on Lucretius and Plato. He defended them at the Sorbonne in June 1896 and again was awarded top honors. In *De l'infini mathématique* he brought to metaphysicians and logicians the theories of the then new mathematics. His treatment of basic concepts served to invalidate the Kantian antinomies, for in the treatment of number and of continuity Couturat adopted a Cantorian stance with respect to an infinite that is defined with logico-mathematical precision. He maintained that a true metaphysics can be founded exclusively on reason. In *De mythis Platonicis,* he showed that the set of mythical passages does not represent the real thought of Plato as represented in the dialectical passages.

A leave of absence enabled Couturat to continue his scientific studies in Paris, where he audited the lectures of Edmond Bouty and Victor Robin. He was called to the University of Caen on 27 October 1897, to lecture on mathematical philosophy.

In October 1899 he returned to Paris on a second leave of absence for research on Leibniz' logic, which, in the various editions, had appeared in fragmentary form only. Couturat believed that Leibniz' metaphysics was a unique product of his logical principles. While in Hannover in 1900–1901 he had access at last to the unpublished works of Leibniz in the Royal Library. His researches resulted in the publication of *La logique de Leibniz* and another volume of more than 200 new Leibnizian fragments, *Opuscules et fragments inédits de Leibniz*, on which he based his theory of Leibniz' logic.

The Leibniz studies brought Couturat into contact with Bertrand Russell and led to his influential edition (1905) of Russell's *Principia mathematica*, with analytical commentary on contemporary works on the subject. Bergson then chose Couturat as his assistant in the history of logic at the Collège de France (1905–1906).

Influenced by Leibniz' thoughts on the construction of a logical universal language, Couturat became a prime mover in the development of an auxiliary international language. On 1 October 1907 delegates from 310 societies throughout the world met and elected a committee to modify Esperanto. Couturat and Léau were the secretaries. With the collaboration of the Akademie di la Lingue Internaciona Ido, created in 1908, Couturat constructed the complete vocabulary of Ido, a language derived from Esperanto with reforms growing out of scientific linguistic principles. Couturat stood firmly for the application of his own logical principles, despite opposition from many quarters to changes in the already established forms of Esperanto.

Couturat never completed this work. At the age of forty-six and at the height of his intellectual power, he was killed while en route from Ris-Orangis to Melun on the very day Germany declared war on France. A twist of fate brought the speeding automobile carrying the French orders for mobilization into collision with the carriage in which Couturat, a noted pacifist, was riding.

BIBLIOGRAPHY

I. Original Works. Couturat's books include *De l'infini mathématique* (Paris, 1896); *De mythis Platonicis* (Paris, 1896; Hildesheim, 1961); *La logique de Leibniz* (Paris, 1901); *Opuscules et fragments inédits de Leibniz* (Paris, 1903); *Histoire de la langue universelle* (Paris, 1903), written with Léopold Léau; *L'algèbre de la logique* (Paris, 1905, 1914; Hildesheim, 1965); *Les principes des mathématiques* (Paris, 1905; Hildesheim, 1965), *Étude sur la dérivation en Esperanto* (Coulommiers, 1907); *Les nouvelles langues internationales* (Paris, 1908), sequel to the *Histoire;* and *Étude sur la dérivation dans la langue internationale* (Paris, 1910).

His interest in languages is shown in *Dictionnaire internationale-français* (Paris, 1908), in collaboration with L. de Beaufront; *International-English Dictionary, English-International Dictionary* (London, 1908), in collaboration with L. de Beaufront and P. D. Hugon; *International-deutsches Wörterbuch, Deutsch-internationales Wörterbuch* (Stuttgart, 1908), in collaboration with L. de Beaufront and R. Thomann; *Internaciona matematikal lexiko, en ido, germana, angla, franca ed italiana* (Jena, 1910); and *Dictionnaire français-international* (Paris, 1915), in collaboration with L. de Beaufront.

A complete bibliography of his numerous papers is given in André Lalande, "L'oeuvre de Louis Couturat," in *Revue de métaphysique et de morale*, **22**, supp. (Sept. 1914), 644–688.

II. Secondary Literature. Additional information is in Louis Benaerts, "Louis Couturat," in *Annuaire de l'Association amicale de secours des anciens élèves de l'École normale supérieure* (Paris, 1915); Robert Blanché, "Couturat," in *Encyclopedia of Philosophy* (New York, 1967), II, 248–249; and Ernst Cassirer, "Kant und die moderne Mathematik. Mit Bezug auf Russells und Couturats Werke über die Prinzipien der Mathematik," in *Kantstudien* (1907).

Carolyn Eisele

CRAIG, JOHN (*b.* Scotland, second half of seventeenth century; *d.* London, England, 1731)

Little is known of Craig's early life; even the place of his birth is not known with certainty. He was a pupil of David Gregory, who in 1683 had succeeded his uncle, James Gregory, as professor of mathematics at Edinburgh. Most of his life, however, was spent in Cambridge, where he attracted the notice of Newton. He maintained an extensive correspondence with many Scottish mathematicians, including Gregory, the noted mathematician and astronomer Colin Campbell, and later Colin Maclaurin.

Craig lived in an age that was witnessing spectacular advances in the development of mathematics. The Royal Society, of which Craig was elected a fellow in 1711, had already, under the guidance of Newton, established itself as one of the foremost scientific societies in Europe; and its members included many who were to leave their mark upon the progress of mathematics. Living in an age of such intellectual giants, Craig was rarely able to tower above his contemporaries; this is scarcely to be wondered at when it is recalled that they included Leibniz, Johann I and Jakob I Bernoulli, Halley, Moivre, Hooke, and Cotes.

Nevertheless, Craig was unusually gifted, and his writings covered a wide range. He had been received into holy orders, becoming in 1708 prebendary of Salisbury; and he made contributions of value to his adopted profession. It is, however, for his contributions to mathematics that he deserves to be remembered.

Of the vast fields that were thrown open to mathematicians at the close of the seventeenth century, none proved richer than the newly invented calculus; and it was to the extension and application of this that the mathematicians of the period directed their attention. Newton had outlined his discovery in three tracts, the first of which, *De analysi per aequationes numero infinitas,* although it did not appear until 1711, was compiled as early as 1669, and was already known to a number of his contemporaries. Meanwhile, Leibniz had contributed to the *Acta eruditorum* for October 1684 his famous paper "Nova methodus pro maximis et minimis, itemque tangentibus . . . et singulare pro illis calculi genus." For a time the new methods appear to have made surprisingly little impact upon English mathematicians, possibly because when Newton's monumental *Principia* first appeared (1687), there was scarcely any mention of the calculus in its pages; thus, it might well be thought that the calculus was not really necessary. On the Continent, however, Leibniz' great friends, the Bernoullis, lost no opportunity of exploring the new methods. Of the few Englishmen who realized the vast possibilities of the tool that had been placed in their hands, none showed greater zeal than did Craig.

Apart from a number of contributions to the *Philosophical Transactions of the Royal Society,* Craig compiled three major works (the titles are translated):

(1) "Method of Determining the Quadratures of Figures Bounded by Curves and Straight Lines" (1685). In this work Craig paid tribute to the work of Barrow, Newton, and Leibniz. Of great importance is the fact that its pages contain the earliest examples in England of the Leibnizian notation, *dy* and *dx*, in place of the "dot" notation of Newton.

(2) "Mathematical Treatise on the Quadratures of Curvilinear Figures" (1693). Here the symbol of integration $\int$ appears.

(3) "On the Calculus of Fluents" (1718), with a supplement, "De optica analytica." Apart from its importance, this work is particularly interesting because on the first page of its preface Craig gives an account of the steps that led to his interest in the fluxional calculus. Translated, it reads:

> You have here, kindly reader, my thoughts about the calculus of fluents. About the year 1685, when I was a young man I pondered over the first elements of this. I was then living in Cambridge, and I asked the celebrated Mr. Newton if he would kindly look over them before I committed them to the press. This he willingly did, and to corroborate some objections raised in my pages against D. D. T. [Tschirnhausen] he offered me of his own accord the quadratures of two figures; these were the curves whose equations were $m^2y^2 = x^4 + a^2x^2$, and $my^2 = x^3 + ax^2$. He also informed me that he could exhibit innumerable curves of this kind, which, by breaking off under given conditions, afforded a geometrical squaring of the figures proposed. Later, on returning to my fatherland I became very friendly with Mr. Pitcairne, the celebrated physician, and with Mr. Gregory, to whom I signified that Mr. Newton had a series of such a kind for quadratures, and each of them admitted it to be quite new.

In addition to the above works, Craig contributed a number of papers to the *Philosophical Transactions of the Royal Society.* The titles of the most important of these, translated into English, are (1) "The Quadrature of the Logarithmic Curve" (1698), (2) "On the Curve of Quickest Descent" (1700), (3) "On the Solid of Least Resistance" (1700), (4) "General Method of Determining the Quadrature of Figures" (1703), (5) "Solution of Bernoulli's Problem on Curvature" (1704), (6) "On the Length of Curved Lines" (1708), and (7) "Method of Making Logarithms" (1710).

This is an impressive list and one that bears eloquent testimony to the range and variety of Craig's interests. Nevertheless, he has fared ill at the hands of the historians of mathematics—particularly in his own country—few of whom even mention him and still fewer of whom make any attempt to assess the value of his contributions. French and German historians have treated him more generously.

BIBLIOGRAPHY

An exhaustive account of Craig's contributions to mathematics can be found in Moritz Cantor, *Vorlesungen über Geschichte der Mathematik*, III (Leipzig, 1896), *passim*, esp. pp. 52, 188; and J. P. Montucla, *Histoire des mathématiques,* II (Paris, 1799), 162.

J. F. Scott

CRAMER, GABRIEL (*b.* Geneva, Switzerland, 31 July 1704; *d.* Bagnols-sur-Cèze, France, 4 January 1752)

Gabriel was one of three sons born to Jean Isaac Cramer, whose family had moved from Holstein to Strasbourg to Geneva in the seventeenth century, and his wife, Anne Mallet. The father and one son, Jean-Antoine, practiced medicine in Geneva. The other two sons, Jean and Gabriel, were professors of law and of mathematics and philosophy, respectively. All three sons were also active in local governmental affairs.

Gabriel Cramer was educated in Geneva and at the age of eighteen defended a thesis dealing with sound. At twenty he competed for the chair of philosophy at the Académie de Calvin in Geneva. The chair was awarded to the oldest of the three contestants, Amédée de la Rive; but the magistrates making the award felt that it was important to attach to their academy two such able young men as Cramer and Giovanni Ludovico Calandrini, the other contestant, who was twenty-one. To do this they split off a chair of mathematics from philosophy and appointed both young contestants to it. This appointment provided that the men share both the position's duties and its salary. It was also provided that they might take turns traveling for two or three years "to perfect their knowledge," provided the one who remained in Geneva performed all the duties and received all the pay. Calandrini and Cramer, called Castor and Pollux by their friends, secured permission for the innovation of using French rather than Latin, not for courses *ex cathedra* but for recitations, "in order that persons who had a taste for these sciences but no Latin could profit." Calandrini taught algebra and astronomy; Cramer, geometry and mechanics. In 1734 Calandrini was made professor of philosophy and Cramer received the chair of mathematics. In 1750 he was made professor of philosophy when Calandrini entered the government.

Cramer's interests and activities were broad, both academically and in the daily life of his city. He wrote on such topics as the usefulness of philosophy in governing a state and the added reliance that a judge should place on the testimony of two or three witnesses as compared with one. He wrote against the popular idea that wheat sometimes changed to tares and also produced several notes on the history of mathematics. As a citizen Cramer was a member of the Conseil des Deux-Cents (1734) and Conseil des Soixante (1749) and was involved with artillery and fortification. He instructed workers repairing a cathedral and occupied himself with excavations and the search of archives. He was reported to be friendly, good-humored, pleasant in voice and appearance, and possessed of good memory, judgment, and health. He never married.

The encouragement to travel played an important role in Cramer's life. From 1727 to 1729 he traveled, going first to Basel, where he spent five months with Johann I Bernoulli and his students, including Daniel Bernoulli and Leonhard Euler. From Basel he went to England, Leiden, Paris, meeting Nicholas Saunderson, Christopher Middleton, Halley, Sloane, Moivre, James Stirling, s'Gravesande, Fontenelle, Réaumur, Maupertuis, Buffon, Clairaut, and Mairan. In 1747 Cramer visited Paris again with the young prince of Saxe-Gotha, whom he had taught for two years. During the trip he was invited to salons frequented by Réaumur, d'Alembert, and Fontenelle. The friendship with the Bernoullis, formed during the first trip, led to much of Cramer's later editorial work, and the acquaintanceships formed during his travels produced an extended correspondence in which he served as an intermediary for the spread of problems and as a contributor of questions and ideas.

Cramer's major publication, *Introduction à l'analyse des lignes courbes algébriques,* was published in 1750. During the previous decade he had edited the collected works of Johann I and Jakob I Bernoulli, Christian Wolff's five-volume *Elementa,* and two volumes of correspondence between Johann I Bernoulli and Leibniz. Overwork and a fall from a carriage brought on a decline in health that resulted in his being bedridden for two months. The doctor then prescribed a rest in southern France. Cramer left Geneva on 21 December 1751 and died while traveling.

Cramer received many honors, including membership in the Royal Society of London; the academies of Berlin, Lyons, Montpellier; and the Institute of Bologna. In 1730 he was a contestant for the prize offered by the Paris Academy for a reply to the question "Quelle est la cause de la figure elliptique des planètes et de la mobilité de leur aphélies?" He was the runner-up (*premier accessit*) to Johann I Bernoulli.

This last fact is perhaps typical of Cramer's status in the history of science. He was overshadowed in both mathematics and philosophy by his contemporaries and correspondents. He is best-known for Cramer's rule and Cramer's paradox, which were neither original with him nor completely delineated by him, although he did make contributions to both. His most original contributions are less well-known: the general content and organization of his book on algebraic curves and his concept of mathematical utility.

In the preface to the *Introduction à l'analyse,* Cramer cites Newton's *Enumeration of Curves of the Third Order,* with the commentary by Stirling, as an "excellent model" for the study of curves. He comments particularly on Newton's use of infinite series and of a parallelogram arrangement of the terms of an algebraic equation of degree v in two unknowns. He also refers to a paper by Nicole and one on lines of the fourth order by Christophe de Bragelogne. Cramer gives credit to Abbé Jean Paul de Gua de Malves for making Newton's parallelogram into a triangular arrangement in the book *L'usage de l'analyse de Descartes pour découvrir . . . les propriétés des lignes géométriques de tous les ordres* (1740).

Cramer also says that he would have found Euler's *Introductio in analysin infinitorum* (1748) very useful if he had known of it earlier. That he made little use of Euler's work is supported by the rather surprising

CRAMER

fact that throughout his book Cramer makes essentially no use of the infinitesimal calculus in either Leibniz' or Newton's form, although he deals with such topics as tangents, maxima and minima, and curvature, and cites Maclaurin and Taylor in footnotes. One conjectures that he never accepted or mastered the calculus.

The first chapter of the *Introduction* defines regular, irregular, transcendental, mechanical, and irrational curves and discusses some techniques of graphing, including our present convention for the positive directions on coordinate axes. The second chapter deals with transformations of curves, especially those which simplify their equations, and the third chapter develops a classification of algebraic curves by order or degree, abandoning Descartes's classification by genera. Both Cramer's rule and Cramer's paradox develop out of this chapter. The remaining ten chapters include discussions of the graphical solution of equations, diameters, branch points and singular points, tangents, points of inflection, maxima, minima, and curvature. Cramer claims that he gives no example without a reason, and no rule without an example.

The third chapter of Cramer's *Introduction* uses a triangular arrangement of the terms of complete equations of successively higher degree (see Fig. 1) as the basis for deriving the formula $v^2/2 + 3v/2$ for the number of arbitrary constants in the general equation of the vth degree. This is the sum of v terms of the arithmetic progression $2 + 3 + 4 + \cdots$ derived from the rows of the triangle by regarding one coefficient, say a, as reduced to unity by division. From this he concludes that a curve of order v can be made to pass through $v^2/2 + 3v/2$ points, a statement that he says needs only an example for a demonstration. In his example Cramer writes five linear equations in five unknowns by substituting the

DES DIFFERENS ORDRES

&c. &c. &c. &c. &c. &c. &c.

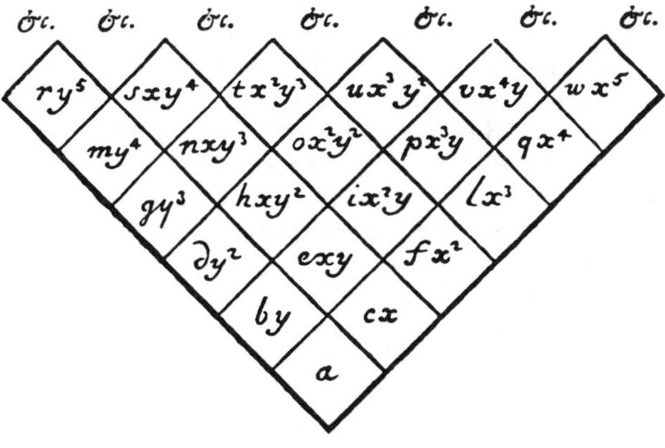

FIGURE 1

coordinates of five points into the general second-degree equation. He then states that he has found a general and convenient rule for the solution of a set of v linear equations in v unknowns; but since this is algebra, he has put it into appendix 1. Figure 2 shows the first page of this appendix. The use of raised numerals as indices, not exponents, applied to co-

Soient plusieurs inconnues z, *y*, *x*, *v*, &c. & autant d'équations

$$A^1 = Z^1z + Y^1y + X^1x + V^1v + \&c.$$
$$A^2 = Z^2z + Y^2y + X^2x + V^2v + \&c.$$
$$A^3 = Z^3z + Y^3y + X^3x + V^3v + \&c.$$
$$A^4 = Z^4z + Y^4y + X^4x + V^4v + \&c.$$
$$\&c.$$

où les lettres A^1, A^2, A^3, A^4, &c. ne marquent pas, comme à l'ordinaire, les puissances d'*A*, mais le prémier membre, supposé connu, de la prémiére, seconde, troisiéme, quatriéme &c. équation. De même Z^1, Z^2, &c. sont les coëfficients de *z*; Y^1, Y^2, &c. ceux de *y*; X^1, X^2, &c. ceux de *x*; V^1, V^2, &c. ceux de *v*; &c. dans la prémiére, seconde, &c. équation.

Cette Notation supposée, s'il n'y a qu'une équation & qu'une inconnue z; on aura $z = \frac{A^1}{Z^1}$. S'il y a deux équations & deux inconnues z & *y*; on trouvera $z = \frac{A^1Y^2 - A^2Y^1}{Z^1Y^2 - Z^2Y^1}$, & $y = \frac{Z^1A^2 - Z^2A^1}{Z^1Y^2 - Z^2Y^1}$. S'il y a trois équations & trois inconnues z, *y*, & *x*; on trouvera

$$z = \frac{A^1Y^2X^3 - A^1Y^3X^2 - A^2Y^1X^3 + A^2Y^3X^1 + A^3Y^1X^2 - A^3Y^2X^1}{Z^1Y^2X^3 - Z^1Y^3X^2 - Z^2Y^1X^3 + Z^2Y^3X^1 + Z^3Y^1X^2 - Z^3Y^2X^1}$$

$$y = \frac{Z^1A^2X^3 - Z^1A^3X^2 - Z^2A^1X^3 + Z^2A^3X^1 + Z^3A^1X^2 - Z^3A^2X^1}{Z^1Y^2X^3 - Z^1Y^3X^2 - Z^2Y^1X^3 + Z^2Y^3X^1 + Z^3Y^1X^2 - Z^3Y^2X^1}$$

$$x = \frac{Z^1Y^2A^3 - Z^1Y^3A^2 - Z^2Y^1A^3 + Z^2Y^3A^1 + Z^3Y^1A^2 - Z^3Y^2A^1}{Z^1Y^2X^3 - Z^1Y^3X^2 - Z^2Y^1X^3 + Z^2Y^3X^1 + Z^3Y^1X^2 - Z^3Y^2X^1}$$

FIGURE 2

efficients represented by capital letters enabled Cramer to state his rule in general terms and to define the signs of the products in terms of the number of inversions of these indices when the factors are arranged in alphabetical order.

Although Leibniz had suggested a method for solving systems of linear equations in a letter to L'Hospital in 1693, and centuries earlier the Chinese had used similar patterns in solving them, Cramer has been given priority in the publication of this rule. However, Boyer has shown recently that an equivalent rule was published in Maclaurin's *Treatise of Algebra* in 1748. He thinks that Cramer's superior notation explains why Maclaurin's statement of this rule was ignored even though his book was popular. Another reason may be that Euler's popular algebra text gave Cramer credit for this "très belle règle."

Cramer's paradox was the outgrowth of combining the formula $v^2/2 + 3v/2$ with the theorem, which

Cramer attributes to Maclaurin, that *m*th- and *n*th-order curves intersect in *mn* points. The formula says, for example, that a cubic curve is *uniquely* determined by nine points; the theorem says that two *different* cubic curves would intersect in nine points. Cramer's explanation of the paradox was inadequate. Scott has shown that Maclaurin and Euler anticipated Cramer in formulating the paradox and has outlined later explanations and extensions by Euler, Plücker, Clebsch, and others. Plücker's explanation, using his abridged notation, appeared in Gergonne's *Annales des mathématiques pures et appliquées* in 1828.

Cramer's work as an editor was significant in the preservation and dissemination of knowledge and reflects both the esteem in which he was held and the results of his early travel. Cantor says he was the first scholar worthy of the name to undertake the thankless task of editing the work of others. Johann I Bernoulli authorized Cramer to collect and publish his works, specifying that there should be no other edition. At the request of Johann, Cramer also produced a posthumous edition of the work of Jakob I Bernoulli, including some unpublished manuscripts and additional material needed to understand them. He also edited a work by Christian Wolff and the correspondence between Johann I Bernoulli and Leibniz.

Throughout his life Cramer carried on an extensive correspondence on mathematical and philosophical topics. His correspondents included Johann I Bernoulli, Charles Bonnet, Georges L. Leclerc, Buffon, Clairaut, Condillac, Moivre, Maclaurin, Maupertuis, and Réaumur. This list shows his range of interests and the acquaintanceships formed in his travels and is further evidence of his function as a stimulator and intermediary in the spread of ideas. For example, a letter from Cramer to Nikolaus I Bernoulli is cited by Savage as evidence of Cramer's priority in defining the concept of utility and proposing that it has upper and lower bounds. This concept is related to mathematical expectation and is a link between mathematical economics and probability theory. Cramer's interest in probability is further revealed in his correspondence with Moivre, in which he at times served as an intermediary between Moivre and various Bernoullis.

Cramer was a proposer of stimulating problems. The Castillon problem is sometimes called the Castillon-Cramer problem. Cramer proposed to Castillon (also called Castiglione, after his birthplace) that the problem of Pappus, to inscribe in a circle a triangle such that the sides pass through three given collinear points, be freed of the collinearity restriction. Castillon's solution was published in 1776. Since then analytic solutions have been presented and the problem has been generalized from a triangle to polygons and from a circle to a conic section.

Gabriel Cramer deserves to have his name preserved in the history of mathematics even though he was outshone by more able and single-minded contemporary mathematicians. He himself would probably have accepted the rule, if not the paradox, as meriting his name but would regret that his major work is less well-known than it merits.

BIBLIOGRAPHY

I. ORIGINAL WORKS. Cramer's chief and only published book is *Introduction à l'analyse des lignes courbes algébriques* (Geneva, 1750). Speziali (see below), pp. 9, 10, refers to two unpublished manuscripts: "Éléments d'arithmétique," written for the young prince of Saxe-Gotha, and "Cours de logique," which was sold in London in 1945 under the mistaken idea that it was by Rousseau.

Two source books have excerpts from Cramer's *Introduction* that present Cramer's rule and Cramer's paradox, respectively: Henrietta O. Midonick, *The Treasury of Mathematics* (New York, 1965), pp. 269–279; and D. J. Struik, *A Source Book in Mathematics* (Cambridge, Mass., 1969), pp. 180–183.

Cramer's minor articles, published chiefly in the *Mémoires* of the academies of Paris (1732) and Berlin (1748, 1750, 1752), include two on geometric problems, four on the history of mathematics, and others on such scattered topics as the aurora borealis (in the *Philosophical Transactions of the Royal Society*), law and philosophy, and the date of Easter. These are listed by Isely, Le Roy, and Speziali.

As editor, Cramer was responsible for the following: Johann I Bernoulli, *Opera omnia*, 4 vols. (Lausanne–Geneva, 1742); Jakob I Bernoulli, *Opera*, 2 vols. (Geneva, 1744), which omits *Ars conjectandi; Virorum celeberr Got. Gul. Leibnitii et Johan. Bernoullii commercium philosophicum et mathematicum* (Lausanne–Geneva, 1745), edited with Castillon; and Christian Wolff, *Elementa matheseos universae*, new ed., 5 vols. (1743–1752). Cantor and Le Roy also give Cramer credit for the 1732–1741 edition.

There is a portrait of Cramer by Gardelle at the Bibliothèque de Genève as well as a collection of 146 letters, many unpublished, according to Speziali. Many of Cramer's letters may be found published in the works of his correspondents. His correspondence with Moivre is listed in Ino Schneider, "Der Mathematiker Abraham de Moivre (1667–1754)," in *Archive for History of Exact Sciences*, **5** (1968/1969), 177–317.

II. SECONDARY LITERATURE. The best and most recent account of Cramer's life and works is M. Pierre Speziali, *Gabriel Cramer (1704–1752) et ses correspondants*, Conférences du Palais de la Découverte, ser. D, no. 59 (Paris, 1959). A short account of his life is to be found in Georges Le Roy, *Condillac, lettres inédites à Gabriel Cramer* (Paris, 1953). L. Isely, *Histoire des sciences mathématiques dans la Suisse française* (Neuchâtel, 1901), gives an extended account of Cramer, beginning on p. 126.

Probably the best account of Cramer's *Introduction* is that in Carl B. Boyer, *History of Analytic Geometry* (New York, 1956), pp. 194-197. Extended discussions are also to be found in Moritz Cantor, *Vorlesungen über Geschichte der Mathematik*, 2nd ed. (Leipzig, 1901), pp. 605-609, 819-842; and Gino Loria, *Storia delle mathematiche* (Milan, 1950), pp. 739-741.

See also Carl B. Boyer, "Colin Maclaurin and Cramer's Rule," in *Scripta mathematica*, **27** (Jan. 1966), 377-379; Leonard J. Savage, *The Foundations of Statistics* (New York, 1954), pp. 81, 92-95; and Charlotte Angas Scott, "On the Intersections of Plane Curves," in *Bulletin of the American Mathematical Society*, **4** (1897-1898), 260-273.

PHILLIP S. JONES

CRELLE, AUGUST LEOPOLD (*b*. Eichwerder, near Wriezen, Germany, 11 March 1780; *d*. Berlin, Germany, 6 October 1855)

A son of Christian Gottfried Crelle, an impoverished dike reeve and master builder, Crelle was trained as a civil engineer and became a civil servant with the Prussian building administration. He finally obtained the rank of *Geheimer Oberbaurat* and was made a member of the Oberbaudirektion, under the Prussian Ministry of the Interior. During the years 1816-1826 Crelle was engaged in the planning and construction of many new roads throughout the country. He also worked on the railway line from Berlin to Potsdam, the first to be opened in Prussia, which was built in 1838.

Crelle, who always had been interested in mathematics but lacked the funds to enroll at a university, acquired appreciable knowledge in this field by independent study. At the age of thirty-six he obtained the doctorate from the University of Heidelberg, having submitted a thesis entitled "De calculi variabilium in geometria et arte mechanica usu."

In 1828 Crelle transferred from the Ministry of the Interior to the Ministry of Education, where he was employed as advisor on mathematics, particularly on the teaching of mathematics in high schools, technical high schools, and teachers colleges. During the summer of 1830, on an official tour to France, he studied the French methods of teaching mathematics. In his report to the ministry Crelle praised the organization of mathematical education in France but criticized the heavy emphasis on applied mathematics. In line with the neo-humanistic ideals then current in Germany, he maintained that the true purpose of mathematical teaching lies in the enlightenment of the human mind and the development of rational thinking.

Nevertheless, to the journal for which he is best remembered Crelle gave the name *Journal für die reine und angewandte Mathematik*. He founded it in 1826 and edited fifty-two volumes. From the very beginning it was one of the leading mathematical journals and even today is universally known as *Crelle's Journal*.

Although not a great mathematician himself, Crelle had a unique sensitivity to mathematical genius. He immediately recognized the abilities of such men as Abel, Jacobi, Steiner, Dirichlet, Plücker, Moebius, Eisenstein, Kummer, and Weierstrass and offered to publish their papers in his journal. He also used his influence as ministerial advisor and his acquaintance with Alexander von Humboldt and other important persons to further their careers. It is for this lifelong, unselfish intercession that Crelle deserves a place in the history of science.

Crelle wrote many mathematical and technical papers, textbooks, and mathematical tables and translated works by Lagrange and Legendre. Except for his *Rechentafeln*, these are now mostly forgotten. Also, for many years he published *Journal für die Baukunst*.

Although beginning in the 1830's his health declined until he was hardly able to walk, Crelle continued to further the course of mathematics, even at great personal sacrifice. He was survived by his wife, the former Philippine Dressel.

Crelle was elected full, corresponding, or foreign member of the Prussian Academy of Sciences in Berlin; of the academies of sciences in St. Petersburg, Naples, Brussels, and Stockholm; of the American Philosophical Society; and of the Mathematical Society of Hamburg.

BIBLIOGRAPHY

I. ORIGINAL WORKS. Crelle's works include *Theorie des Windstosses in Anwendung auf Windflügel* (Berlin, 1802); *Rechentafeln, welche alles Multipliciren und Dividiren unter Tausend ganz ersparen*, 2 vols. (Berlin, 1820; latest ed., Berlin, 1954); *Sammlung mathematischer Aufsätze*, 2 vols. (Berlin, 1821-1822); *Lehrbuch der Elemente der Geometrie*, 2 vols. (Berlin, 1825-1827); *Handbuch des Feldmessens und Nivellirens* (Berlin, 1826); and *Encyclopädische Darstellung der Theorie der Zahlen* (Berlin, 1845).

His German translations are A. M. Legendre, *Die Elemente der Geometrie* (Berlin, 1822; 5th ed., 1858); and J. L. Lagrange, *Mathematische Werke*, 3 vols. (Berlin 1823-1824).

He edited *Journal für die reine und angewandte Mathematik*, **1-52** (1826-1856), still being published; and *Journal für die Baukunst*, **1-30** (1829-1851).

His numerous papers on mathematics and engineering were published in these two journals and in the *Abhandlungen* and *Monatsbericht der Berliner Akademie der Wis-*

senschaften (1828–1853). A selection is in Poggendorff, I, 496–497, and VI, pt. 1, 491.

II. SECONDARY LITERATURE. On Crelle or his work see the following (listed chronologically): Moritz Cantor, in *Allgemeine Deutsche Biographie,* IV (Leipzig, 1876), 589–590; Wilhelm Lorey, "August Leopold Crelle zum Gedächtnis," in *Journal für die reine und angewandte Mathematik,* **157** (1927), 3–11; Otto Emersleben, "August Leopold Crelle (1780–1855) zum 100. Todestag," in *Wissenschaftliche Annalen . . .,* **4** (1955), 651–656; and Kurt-R. Biermann, "A. L. Crelles Verhältnis zu G. Eisenstein," in *Monatsbericht der Deutschen Akademie der Wissenschaften zu Berlin,* **1** (1959), 67–92; and "Urteile A. L. Crelles über seine Autoren," in *Journal für die reine und angewandte Mathematik,* **203** (1960), 216–220, with a previously unknown portrait of Crelle.

CHRISTOPH J. SCRIBA

CREMONA, ANTONIO LUIGI GAUDENZIO GIUSEPPE (*b.* Pavia, Italy, 7 December 1830; *d.* Rome, Italy, 10 June 1903)

Cremona was the eldest child of Gaudenzio Cremona and his second wife, Teresa Andereoli. One of his brothers, Tranquillo, attained some fame as an artist.

Luigi was educated at the *ginnasio* in Pavia. When he was eleven, the death of his father threatened to interrupt his schooling; his stepbrothers came to his support, however, and he was enabled to continue his education. He was graduated first in his class with special recognition for his work in Latin and Greek, and entered the University of Pavia.

In 1848 Cremona joined the "Free Italy" battalion in the revolt against Austrian rule and attained the rank of sergeant. He took part in the unsuccessful defense of Venice, which capitulated on 24 August 1849. Because of the gallantry of the defenders, they were permitted to leave the city as a unit, with honors.

When Cremona returned to Pavia, he discovered that his mother had died. With the help of the family he reentered the university. On 27 November 1849 he was granted permission to study civil engineering. Here he came under the influence of A. Bordoni, A. Gabba, and especially Francesco Brioschi. Cremona was always grateful to Brioschi, later writing: "The years that I passed with Brioschi as pupil and later as colleague are a grand part of my life; in the first portion of those years I learned to love science and in the other how to transfer it to a large circle of auditors" (Gino Loria, "Luigi Cremona et son oeuvre mathématique," p. 129).

On 9 May 1853 Cremona received the doctorate in civil engineering and architecture, and on 4 August of the following year he was married. His record of military service against Austrian rule prevented him from obtaining an official teaching post in the educational system, so his first employment was as a private tutor to several families in Pavia.

On 22 November 1855 Cremona was granted permission to teach on a provisional basis at the *ginnasio* of Pavia, with special emphasis on physics. He was already engaged in the mathematical research for which he is so well known. His first paper, "Sulle tangenti sfero-conjugate," had appeared in March 1855.

On 17 December 1856 Cremona was appointed associate teacher at the *ginnasio* in recognition of his good work and his mathematical activity: his second paper, "Intorno al un teorema del Abel" had appeared in May 1856. On 17 January 1857 he was appointed full teacher at the *ginnasio* in Cremona.

He remained in Cremona for nearly three years, during which time he wrote a number of articles. Some were merely answers to problems proposed in the *Nouvelles annales de mathématique,* but at least four contained original results, including his method of examining curves by projective methods: "Sulle linee del terz' ordine a doppia curvatura—nota" (1858); "Sulle linee del terz' ordine a doppia curvatura—teoremi" (1858); "Intorno alle superficie della seconda classe inscritte in una stessa superficie sviluppabile della quarta classe—nota" (1858); and "Intorno alle coniche inscritte in una stessa superficie del quart' ordine e terza classe—nota" (1859).

On 28 November 1859 the Italian government of newly liberated Lombardy appointed Cremona a teacher at the Lycée St. Alexandre in Milan, and on 10 June 1860 he received his first college appointment. A royal decree appointed him ordinary professor at the University of Bologna, where he remained until October 1867.

Cremona's most important original research into transformations in the plane and in space was published while he was at Bologna. His first paper, "Introduzione ad un teoria geometrica della curve piane," appeared in December 1861. The first statement of his general theory for transformations involving plane curves was "Sulle trasformazione geometriche della figure piane" (1863). In March 1866 he published his second paper on transformations, "Mémoire de géométrie pure sur les surfaces du troisième ordre." This earned Cremona half of the Steiner Prize for 1866, the other half going to Richard Sturm. Both papers on transformations were translated into German by Curtze and published as *Grundzüge der allgemeinen Theorie der Oberflächen in synthetischer Behandlung* (1870). It was during this period at Bologna that

Cremona developed the theory of birational transformations (Cremona transformations). Besides being a creative mathematician, Cremona was an excellent lecturer: calm, rigorous, yet interesting and even exciting.

In October 1867 Cremona was transferred by royal decree, and on the recommendation of Brioschi, to the Technical Institute of Milan, to be in charge of the courses in higher geometry. He received the title of ordinary professor in 1872. During this period Cremona continued to produce mathematical articles that appeared in many Italian and French journals. His paper "Sulle trasformazione razionale . . . nello spazio. . ." (1871), which extended his transformation theory to space curves, supplemented and completed the main outlines of the theory of birational transformations.

The period at Milan, where he remained until 1873, was the time of Cremona's greatest creativity. He wrote articles on such diverse topics as twisted cubics, developable surfaces, the theory of conics, the theory of plane curves, third- and fourth-degree surfaces, statics, and projective geometry. He also turned out a number of excellent texts, including *Le figure reciproche nella statica grafica* (1872), *Elementi di geometria projettiva* (1873), and *Elementi de calcolo grafico* (1874).

In 1873 Cremona was offered a political post as secretary-general of the new Italian Republic by the minister of agriculture, but he refused. On 9 October of that year Cremona was appointed, by royal decree, director of the newly established Polytechnic School of Engineering in Rome. He was also to be professor of graphic statics. Administrative and supervisory work took up so much of Cremona's time during this period that it effectively ended his creative work in mathematics.

In November 1877 Cremona was appointed to the chair of higher mathematics at the University of Rome, and on 16 March 1879 he was appointed a senator. The duties entailed by this position put a complete stop to his research activities. On 10 June 1903, after leaving a sickbed to act on some legislation, Cremona succumbed to a heart attack.

Cremona's main contributions to mathematics lie in the areas of birational transformations, graphic statics, and projective geometry.

The earliest modern use of one-to-one transformations appears to have been that of Poncelet in 1822. Bobillier used them in 1827–1828, and in 1828 Dandelin used double stereographic projections. The algebraic approach seems to have been used first by Plücker in 1830, and in 1832 Magnus used noninvolutory transformations. Cremona combined all these developments and added much of his own material to create a unified theory. The clarity and polish of his presentation did much to publicize and popularize birational transformations.

The theory of birational transformations is basically as follows: Given a plane curve, $f(x,y) = 0$, which is irreducible and of degree m in x and n in y. Suppose also that $x' = \varphi_1(x,y)$, $y' = \varphi_2(x,y)$ are rational functions in x and y. The eliminant of the three equations yields a new equation, $F(x',y') = 0$, which may be easier to examine and more revealing than the original, $f(x,y) = 0$.

If we solve the transformation equations $x' = \varphi_1(x,y)$ and $y' = \varphi_2(x,y)$ for x and y thus

$$x = \theta_1(x',y'),\ y = \theta_2(x',y'),$$

and if these are rational functions in x', y', then we say that the transformation $x' = \varphi_1(x,y)$, $y' = \varphi_2(x,y)$ is birational.

Transformations of this nature are called Cremona transformations when there is a one-to-one reciprocal relation between the sets (x,y) and (x',y'). Geometrically, suppose the curve $f(x,y) = 0$ to be on the plane P and the curve $F(x',y') = 0$ to be on the plane P'. Then we seek a one-to-one correspondence between the sets of points. A very simple example would be that of a curve $f(x,y) = 0$ on P and its projection by a central perspectivity onto the plane P'.

One of the simplest examples of a Cremona transformation is the homographic transformation

$$x' = \frac{ax + by + c}{px + qy + r},\ y' = \frac{a'x + b'y + c'}{px + qy + r}.$$

If homogeneous coordinates are used, we may write

$$x':y':z' = (ax+by+c):(a'x+b'y+c'):(px+qy+r).$$

Another example of a birational transformation is the Bertini transformation: $x':y':z' = xy:xz:yz$.

Cremona transformations have been used for studying rational surfaces, for the resolution of singularities of plane and space curves, and for the study of elliptic integrals and Riemann surfaces. They are effective in the reduction of singularities of curves to double points with distinct tangents.

Cremona's main contribution to graphic statics seems to have been the skillful use of the funicular diagram, or the reciprocal figure. This is defined as follows: Let P be a planar polygon with vertices A, B, C, $\cdots$, K, and let V be a point in the plane not on any side. Let VA, VB, VC, $\cdots$, VK be drawn. Construct a polygon whose sides are parallel to VA, VB, VC, $\cdots$, VK. This polygon, P', is called the polygon reciprocal to P, or the funicular diagram.

By a theorem of Maxwell, "If forces represented in magnitude by the lines of a figure be made to act between the corresponding lines of the reciprocal figure, then the points of the reciprocal figure will all be in equilibrium under the action of these forces."

Geometers will probably recognize Maxwell's theorem more readily in the following simplified form.

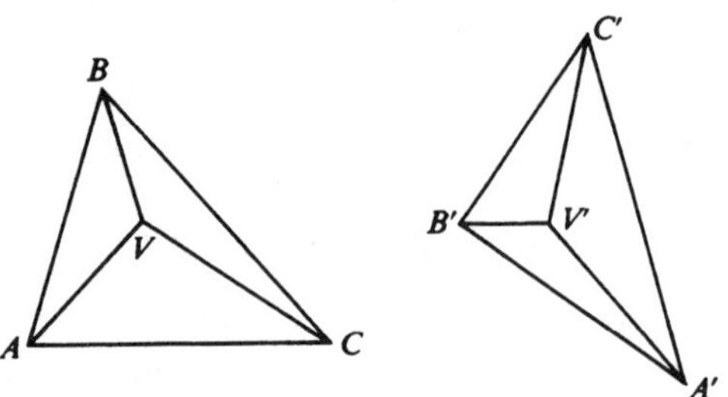

Given $\triangle ABC$, and V any point in the plane of the triangle; let lines VA, VB, BC be drawn. In $\triangle A'B'C'$, $B'C'$ is parallel to VA, $C'A'$ is parallel to VB, and $A'B'$ is parallel to VC. Now draw a line through A' parallel to BC, through B' parallel to AC, and through C' parallel to AB. These lines will be concurrent.

Note that each diagram is the reciprocal of the other, and that forces applied at any node of one are parallel to and proportional to the sides of the other. Note also that three forces in equilibrium in one figure, and therefore represented by a triangle, have as their images in the reciprocal figure three concurrent lines. It is this property that makes reciprocal figures so useful.

Again, the clarity and elegance of Cremona's presentation helped to disseminate and popularize the theorem and its consequences. Moreover, he collated results obtained by others and made them more readily available. Thus, his *Graphical Statics* contains not only signed lines and signed angles, which are fairly well known, but also the concept of signed and weighted areas. The development of the concepts of centroids of figures is elegant and clear.

The third area to which Cremona contributed was that of projective geometry; in fact, this discipline pervades all his work. Birational transformations arose from the concept of a curve and its projection onto another plane, and graphic statics makes extensive use of projective techniques. It is true that Cremona made no startling discoveries in this area; but he did derive many properties of projectively related figures, and he did present the subject to his classes in a manner calculated to clarify and bring out relationships most simply.

Cremona made use of Euclidean geometry when he thought it most effective, and it may be said that this introduced extraneous factors into projective geometry. It must be remembered, however, that his training and temperament favored the use of intuitive rather than strictly postulational methods.

As an organizer and popularizer of those areas of mathematics in which he did his work, Cremona has had few peers. His works may still be read with profit and enjoyment.

BIBLIOGRAPHY

I. Original Works. Cremona's works include "Sulle tangenti sfero-conjugate," in *Annali scienti di matematica,* **6** (Mar. 1855), 382–392; "Intorno al un teorema del Abel," *ibid.,* **7** (May 1856), 97–105; "Sulle linee del terz' ordine a doppia curvatura—nota," in *Annali di matematica pura ed applicata,* **1** (Apr. 1858), 164–174; "Sulle linee del terz' ordine a doppia curvatura—teoremi," *ibid.* (Oct. 1858), 278–295; "Intorno alle superficie della seconda classe inscritte in una stessa superficie sviluppabile della quarta classe—nota," *ibid.,* **2** (Dec. 1858), 65–81; "Intorno alle coniche inscritte in una stessa superficie del quart' ordine e terza classe—nota," *ibid.* (Feb. 1859), 201–207; "Introduzione ad una teoria geometrica della curve piane," in *Memorie della R. Accademia delle scienze dell'Istituto di Bologna,* **12** (Dec. 1861), 305–436; "Sulle trasformazione geometriche della figure piane" (1863); "Mémoire de géométrie pure sur les surfaces du troisième ordre," in *Journal für die reine und angewandte Mathematik,* **68** (Mar. 1866), 1–133; Curtze's translation of the two preceding papers, *Grundzüge der allgemeinen Theorie der Oberflächen in synthetischer Behandlung* (Berlin, 1870); "Sulle trasformazione razionale . . . nello spazio . . .," in *Memorie della R. Accademia delle scienze dell'Istituto di Bologna,* 3rd ser., **1** (1871), 365–386; *Le figure reciproche nella statica grafica* (Milan, 1872); *Elementi di geometria projettiva* (Turin, 1873); and *Elementi de calcolo grafico* (Turin, 1874). English translations of his works include *Graphical Statics,* trans. by Thomas H. Beare (Oxford, 1890); and *Elements of Projective Geometry,* trans. by Charles Leudesdorf (Oxford, 1893). An edition of his works is *Opera matematiche di Luigi Cremona,* Luigi Bertini, ed., 3 vols. (Milan. 1905).

II. Secondary Literature. Cremona's work is discussed in P. Appell and E. Goursat, *Théorie des fonctions algébriques,* I (Paris, 1929), 266–292; Hilda P. Hudson, *Cremona Transformations in Plane and Space* (Cambridge, 1927); Gino Loria, "Luigi Cremona et son oeuvre mathématique," in *Bibliotheca mathematica* (1904), 125–195; and Ganesh Prasad, *Some Great Mathematicians of the Nineteenth Century,* II (Benares, 1934), 116–143.

Samuel Greitzer

CROUSAZ, JEAN-PIERRE DE (*b.* Lausanne, Switzerland, 13 April 1663; *d.* Lausanne, 22 February 1750)

The second son of Abraham de Crousaz and Elisabeth Françoise Mayor, Crousaz belonged to one of the oldest and most noble families of Lausanne, which was then ruled by Bern. Destined at first for a military career by his father, who was a colonel, he eventually obtained permission to study philosophy and Reformed theology at the Academy of Lausanne and then at the Academy of Geneva. At the age of nineteen he went to Leiden and to Rotterdam, where he met the philosopher Pierre Bayle, and from there to Paris. Returning home in 1684, he commenced a theological career, married Louise de Loys, by whom he had three sons and four daughters, and gave private lessons in ancient languages and in the sciences. In 1700 Crousaz became a professor of philosophy and mathematics at the Academy of Lausanne; in his classes he abandoned the traditional use of Latin in favor of French. He was elected rector in 1706 and held this position for three more terms.

Crousaz's existence was arduous: he was a minister; besides his large family, he had in his home boarders, sons of foreign and local noblemen, for whose education and instruction he was responsible; and he wrote books, such as the treatise *Logique* (which first appeared in two volumes, then underwent numerous alterations and had many editions—the fourth, in 1741, reached six volumes) and the *Traité du beau* (first in one volume, then in two). Receptive to all the intellectual currents of the age, a great correspondent, and a virulent polemicist, Crousaz poured into his writings, which he continued to produce throughout his life, all of his immense knowledge and enriched them with reflections and comments that are still of interest.

Mysterious intrigues, tenacious jealousies, and a growing hostility annoyed Crousaz and wounded his pride, although it must be admitted that humility and resignation were certainly not the dominant traits in his character. Having decided to leave Lausanne, he accepted a chair of philosophy and mathematics at the University of Groningen, where he stayed from September 1724 until March 1726 with his wife, two of his daughters, and a large retinue. He then accepted a call from the house of Hesse-Kassel to direct the education of the young heir, Prince Frederick. Crousaz had acquired a solid pedagogical reputation through his *Nouvelles maximes sur l'education des enfants,* published at Amsterdam in 1718, and especially through the *Traité de l'education des enfants,* published in two volumes at The Hague in 1722. (Rousseau had read these two works before writing *Émile.*) His self-esteem flattered by the titles "counselor of the court" and "governor of the prince," Crousaz began a new life that, despite many obligations, left him leisure for his own work—especially since his family had returned to Lausanne. During this period he wrote *Examen du Pyrrhonisme,* a large work in which he refutes the philosophy of Bayle. The stay at Kassel lasted until 1733, when Crousaz was seventy years old; the landgrave of Hesse then granted him a life pension.

He returned to the Academy of Lausanne, where he once more held the chair of philosophy, a post that, thanks to his exceptional health, he did not relinquish until 1749, a year before his death. In this last prolific period he wrote *De l'esprit humain,* a harsh critique of Leibniz's preestablished harmony, which presupposed a determinism denying free will. (Mme. du Châtelet wrote him a long letter, dated 9 August 1741, defending Leibniz.) Before the end of his long life Crousaz had the satisfaction of following the brilliant scientific career of his grandson Philippe de Loys de Chéseaux (1718–1751). Previously, upon returning from Kassel, he had the pleasure of finding his eldest son, Abraham, as rector of the Academy of Lausanne.

During the first half of his life Crousaz was a follower of Cartesianism, but he later became a defender of the ideas of Newton. It appears, however, that in each case his choice was dictated solely by philosophical and moral arguments, since he placed philosophy, theology, and pedagogy above mathematics and physics. His attacks on Leibniz, moreover, were directed only against the *Théodicée,* for the simple reason that he saw in this system a danger to religion. He had furnished proof of this courageous attitude in his youth while at the Academy of Lausanne, during the period when the teaching of Cartesianism was suspected of undermining orthodoxy.

As for his scientific work, Crousaz was certainly prolific, even prolix, and his treatises on elementary mathematics must have been of some interest and utility in his time. They offer, however, little that is really original; style is often neglected, with a great many repetitions; and the calculations contain errors. In analysis the work that made him famous is the *Commentaire sur l'analyse des infiniment petits,* a large quarto volume of 320 pages, with four plates, which appeared in 1721—three years after the work of l'Hospital, the contents of which Crousaz examines step by step. Long, superfluous passages and excessively elementary detail result in a certain lack of balance in the exposition, in which, nevertheless, one can find new examples. Crousaz had fully assimilated infinitesimal calculus, and he no doubt taught it correctly to his students. Despite its errors and insufficiencies, his book proves this, as does the welcome accorded it by contemporary scientists, Johann I Bernoulli excepted. Indeed, on 15 July 1722 the latter wrote Crousaz a long, very harsh letter filled with criticisms and more or less veiled reproaches. Bernoulli states, however (which is at least curious), that he has read only the preface and the preliminary discourses; he thus allows one to infer that he did not find his name in these pages. The reproach is justified, but if Bernoulli had continued reading, he would have found, on page 303, his name and some kind remarks about himself.

In any case, it is certain that this book contributed in great part to the nomination of Crousaz, in 1725, as associate foreign member of the Académie des Sciences of Paris. He had already received from this academy, in 1720, first prize in the annual competition for a memoir on the theory of movement. Regarding this work, Johann I Bernoulli criticized him (in the letter mentioned above) for being too Cartesian and for having, like Descartes, made "the essence of bodies consist in extension alone and that of movement in the successive application of their surfaces to the surfaces of contiguous bodies." Crousaz was also three times (1721, 1729, 1735) a laureate of the Académie des Sciences of Bordeaux for his memoirs on the causes of elasticity, on the nature and propagation of fire, and on the different states of matter. In December 1735 he was elected a member of that academy.

Crousaz was also a great letter writer. Some 1,800 letters sent or received by him are preserved at Lausanne, and others are at Geneva, Basel, Paris, London, Leiden, Kassel, and elsewhere; they are almost all unpublished. Among his correspondents were Réaumur, Abbé Nollet, Mairan, Maupertuis, Jacques Cassini, Fontenelle, Bernoulli, and Maclaurin. With Réaumur he obviously discussed natural history, particularly certain shellfish found near Neuchâtel; with Nollet, it was electricity; Mairan was his closest confidant; to Maclaurin he addressed, in 1721, a memoir dealing with optics that, revised, was presented to the Academy of Bordeaux in 1736 under the title "Propagation de la lumière." The secretary of this academy, Sarrau, announced his agreement with the Cartesian conclusions proposed by Crousaz.

Long called "the celebrated professor," Crousaz appears to have had an encyclopedic mind—a mind representative of his age, of his country, and of Europe in the eighteenth century. His merit, if one accepts the *éloge* delivered by Grandjean de Fouchy, "seems to have been less excellence and superiority in a certain genre than universality of knowledge and of literary talents."

BIBLIOGRAPHY

I. ORIGINAL WORKS. Crousaz's scientific writings are *Réflexions sur l'utilité des mathématiques et sur la manière de les étudier, avec un nouvel essai d'arithmétique démontrée* (Amsterdam, 1715); *La géométrie des lignes et des surfaces rectilignes et circulaires*, 2 vols. (Amsterdam, 1718; Lausanne, 1733); *Commentaire sur l'analyse des infiniment petits* (Paris, 1721); *Discours sur le principe, la nature et la communication du mouvement* (Paris, 1721); *De physicae origine, progressibus ejusque tractandae methodo...* (Groningen, 1724); *De physicae utilitate dissertatio philosophica* (Groningen, 1725); *Essai sur le mouvement, où l'on traitte de sa nature, de son origine...* (Groningen, 1726); *Traité de l'algèbre* (Paris, 1726); *Dissertation sur la nature, l'action et la propagation du feu* (Bordeaux, 1729); and *Dissertation sur la nature et les causes de la liquidité et de la solidité* (Bordeaux, 1735).

II. SECONDARY LITERATURE. The following, listed chronologically, deal with Crousaz or his work: "Éloge de M. de Crousaz," read 14 Nov. 1750, in Grandjean de Fouchy, *Éloges des Académiciens*, I (Paris, 1761), 100–122; Rudolf Wolf, *Biographien zur Kulturgeschichte der Schweiz*, II (Zurich, 1859), 57–70; Eugène Secrétan, *Galerie suisse, Biographies nationales...*, I (Lausanne, 1879), 591–599; Henri Perrochon, "Jean-Pierre de Crousaz," in *Revue historique vaudoise* (1939), 281–298; Suzanne Delorme, *À propos du bicentenaire de la mort de Jean-Pierre de Crousaz: Ses relations avec l'Académie royale des sciences* (Paris, 1954); Jacqueline E. de La Harpe, *Jean-Pierre de Crousaz et le conflit des idées au siècle des lumières* (Geneva, 1955), which is indispensable for the life and literary and philosophical works of Crousaz and contains a complete list of his works; and Marianne Perrenoud, *Inventaire des archives Jean-Pierre de Crousaz* (Lausanne, 1969). A thorough study of his scientific work has yet to be published, and the same is true of his scientific correspondence.

PIERRE SPEZIALI

CULMANN, KARL (*b*. Bergzabern, Lower Palatinate, Germany, 10 July 1821; *d*. Zurich, Switzerland, 9 December 1881).

After preliminary schooling by his father, an evangelical clergyman, Culmann enrolled at the engineering and artillery school in Metz (an uncle was professor there) to prepare for entrance to the École Polytechnique in Paris. He learned of the graphical methods introduced by J. V. Poncelet and studied in Metz before a case of typhoid fever caused him to return home. Following a long convalescence, he attended the Polytechnikum at nearby Karlsruhe. On graduation in 1841 he joined the Bavarian civil service as cadet bridge engineer and was assigned to the Hof railway construction division; he continued to study under the guidance of Schnürlein, a student of

Gauss's. To prepare for a study trip abroad, he arranged in 1847 for transfer to the railway bureau in Munich, in order to extend his mathematical training and perfect his English.

Taking leave in 1849, Culmann visited England, Ireland, and the United States, returning in 1851 with detailed observations for two reports. The first dealt with the wooden bridges of the United States, the second with iron bridges in England and America. These reports present what is probably the most complete story of American bridges of the first half of the nineteenth century: American achievement lay in the largely empirical design of wooden bridges. To compare American and European designs Culmann developed new methods for the analysis of truss systems and approximate procedures for indeterminate structures, such as the Town lattice-truss and Burr arch-truss bridges.

Culmann was called to Zurich in 1855 as professor of engineering sciences at the newly founded polytechnic institute (the present ETH), a post he held until his death twenty-six years later, declining an offer to move to the Munich Polytechnikum in 1868. From 1872 to 1875 he was also director of the institute.

As a teacher Culmann drew high praise for his rich experience, excellent theoretical knowledge, and sympathetic understanding; but it is on his principal work, *Die graphische Statik* (1866), that his fame now rests. His youthful exposure to the developments of Poncelet and other French geometers is reflected in his reports on American bridge practice, in which his independent extensions of graphical methods are already evident. It was the custom to analyze a particular design with equations; but Culmann chose another route to the solution, geometric constructions of a fundamental and widely applicable nature.

Culmann presented the graphical calculus as a symmetrical whole, a systematic introduction of graphical methods into the analysis of all kinds of structures—beams, bridges, roof trusses, arches, and retaining walls. Among other things, he introduced the general use of force and funicular polygons, the method of sections, and the diagram of internal forces based on the equilibrium conditions of successive joints.

The methods, first used by his students, were quickly assimilated by bridge and structural designers, who appreciated the time saving of the graphical methods over the current procedures involving simultaneous equations of analytical mechanics. The contents of the first edition of *Die graphische Statik* was thus known when it was published, and the book was eagerly accepted by a wide circle. For example, graphical analysis was applied to the Eiffel Tower by its structural designer, Maurice Koechlin, a student of Culmann's. Further advances appeared in the first part of the second edition (1875), with more planned for the second volume, which was never published because of Culmann's death. His work was carried forward by a Zurich colleague, W. Ritter (who is not to be confused with his contemporary A. Ritter, a prominent structural engineer who was also professor of mechanics at the Polytechnikum in Aachen). Further developments came from E. Winkler, O. Mohr, L. Cremona, and H. Müller-Breslau, among others.

In his work on beams Culmann showed how the stresses at any point can be analyzed graphically and developed a stress circle for the uniaxial shear state, a particular case of the more general, and later, Mohr circle (1882). With this he was able to draw the stress trajectories of flexural members.

On seeing sections of human bones prepared by Hermann von Meyer, professor of anatomy at the University of Zurich, Culmann noted that in some the trabeculae forming the cancellous tissue (spongiosa) followed the principal stresses on assuming beam loading of the bone, as in the head of the femur. Just how this arrangement is related to the mechanical conditions of loading is not yet clear, even though Meyer's trajectorial theory of bone formation has been the subject of discussion since 1867.

Although modern structural analysis is no longer governed by graphical methods, Culmann's work was fundamental to the present analytical procedures that represent complements and extensions of the older, physical approach.

BIBLIOGRAPHY

I. Original Works. Culmann's writings are "Der Bau der hölzernen Brücken in den Vereinigten Staaten von Nordamerika," in *Allgemeine Bauzeitung* (Vienna), **16** (1851), 69–129; "Der Bau der eisernen Brücken in England und Amerika," *ibid.*, **17** (1852), 163–222; "Bericht über die Untersuchung der schweizerischen Wildbäche in den Jahren 1858–1863," in *Vierteljahrsschrift der Naturforschenden Gesellschaft in Zürich* (1864); *Die graphische Statik* (Zurich, 1866; 2nd ed., pt. 1, 1875); and "Ueber das Parallelogram und über die Zusammensetzung der Kräfte," in *Vierteljahrsschrift der Naturforschenden Gesellschaft in Zürich* (1870).

II. Secondary Literature. On Culmann's work see A. J. du Bois, *Graphical Statics* (New York, 1875); F. G. Evans, *Stress and Strain in Bones* (Springfield, Ill., 1957); H. von Meyer, "Die Architektur der Spongiosa," in *Archiv für Anatomie, Physiologie und wissenschaftliche Medizin*, **47** (1867); W. Ritter, *Anwendungen der graphischen Statik* (Zurich, 1888); and D'Arcy W. Thompson, *On Growth and*

Form, repr. of 2nd ed. (Cambridge, 1952), pp. 975–979, 997.

Obituaries are in *Zeitschrift für Bau- und Verkehrswesen* (17 Dec. 1881); and *Vierteljahrsschrift der Naturforschenden Gesellschaft in Zürich*, **27** (1882).

Biographical sketches are C. Matschoss, *Männer der Technik* (Berlin, 1925); W. Ritter, in *Allgemeine deutsche Biographie*, XLVII (1903); M. Rühlmann, *Vorträge über Geschichte der technischen Mechanik* (Berlin, 1885); Fritz Stüssi, in *Neue deutsche Biographie*, III (1957); S. Timoshenko, *History of Strength of Materials* (New York, 1953); and *Vierteljahrsschrift der Naturforschenden Gesellschaft in Zürich*, **41** (1896), Jubelband 1.

R. S. HARTENBERG

CUNHA, JOSÉ ANASTÁCIO DA (*b*. Lisbon, Portugal, 1744; *d*. Lisbon, 1 January 1787)

The son of Lorenzo da Cunha, a painter, and his wife, Jacinta Ignes, da Cunha learned grammar, rhetoric, and logic at the Lisbon school of the Congregation of the Oratory; he also studied mathematics and physics on his own. At the age of nineteen he volunteered as a lieutenant in the artillery and spent nearly ten years at Valença do Minho. At this time Portugal was experiencing antifeudal and anticlerical reforms, which were carried out by the marquis of Pombal, minister of King Joseph I. Da Cunha belonged to a group of freethinking intellectuals who supported Pombal and disseminated ideas of the Enlightenment; and he became known as a progressive thinker, talented poet, and author of an original memoir on ballistics. In 1773 Pombal appointed da Cunha as a geometry professor at the Faculty of Mathematics of Coimbra University. Da Cunha's university career was short. In 1777, after the death of Joseph I, reactionaries returned to power and Pombal was dismissed, then exiled. In the same year da Cunha was arrested and imprisoned by the Inquisition. Charged with supporting heretical doctrines, in October 1778 he was sentenced by the General Council of the Inquisition in Lisbon to three years in prison. Freed at the beginning of 1781, da Cunha, under the protection of a high official, obtained a mathematical professorship at the College of São Lucas and resumed his scientific research. His health had been weakened in jail, however, and he died before his forty-fourth birthday.

Da Cunha's main scientific work was *Principios mathemáticos*, published serially beginning in 1782 and as a complete book in 1790. Intended to be a textbook, this work is a concise encyclopedia of mathematics in twenty-one parts that embrace all basic branches of the science, from geometry and arithmetic to the solution of differential equations and problems in the calculus of variations.

Excessive conciseness was the pedagogical deficiency of this exposition, which contained many fresh and fruitful ideas. The most striking feature was da Cunha's tendency to rigorous exposition of mathematics in general and of the calculus in particular. Needless to say, not all of his attempts in this direction were successful.

In book IX of *Principios* da Cunha presented a new theory of the exponential function that anticipated the methods of the modern theory of analytic functions and that was based on the use of solely convergent series (a very uncommon restriction at that time). The convergence of series in question was tested by comparing the given series with a convergent geometric series with each term greater than the series. Let a be a (positive) number $a = 1 + c + \frac{c^2}{2!} + \frac{c^3}{3!} + \cdots$, which series is seen to converge for all values of c. Then the exponential function a^x to the base a is defined for all values of x as the sum of the series $1 + cx + \frac{(cx)^2}{2!} + \frac{(cx)^3}{3!} + \cdots$; to that end da Cunha demonstrated that every positive number a may be represented by the series $1 + c + \frac{c^2}{2!} + \frac{c^3}{3!} + \cdots$. From this definition the laws of exponents were derived. The binomial theorem—the power-series expansion of the function $(1 + x)^n$—was obtained in a very ingenious way: da Cunha represented both $1 + x$ and $(1 + x)^n$ in the form of the exponential expansions, a device also used in the modern theory of complex functions.

In book XV, devoted to the elements of the calculus, the fundamental concepts were those of infinitely great and infinitely small variables; the concept of limit was not explicitly used. Following Leibniz' notations, da Cunha profited to some extent from Newton's terminology; for instance, for the differential he adopted the symbol d but called it, as did some other mathematicians, "fluxion," a word that Newton used to designate the velocity of change of the variable or fluent. The definition of "differential" given by da Cunha was remarkable. During the eighteenth century the differential of a function, $y = f(x)$, was generally understood to be, and was defined as, its infinitely small increment, $dy = \Delta y$; but in practice dy was calculated as a part of the increment linear with respect to Δx, a distinction that was one of the sources of paradoxes and endless discussions. The definition proposed by da Cunha legitimated the procedures of differential calculus and was equivalent to one introduced in the nineteenth century following the works of Cauchy: If the increment $\Delta y = f(x + \Delta x) - f(x)$ can be represented as $\Delta y = A\Delta x + \epsilon\Delta x$, where A does not depend on Δx and ϵ approaches zero together with Δx, then $A\Delta x$ is called the differential of function $y, dy = A\Delta x$. In this way da Cunha deduced some formulas of the differential calculus.

Da Cunha was one of the main precursors of the reform of the foundations of infinitesimal calculus, initiated in the first decades of the nineteenth century. Neither the Portuguese nor the French edition of his *Principios* had a wide circulation, however, and they did not greatly influence the development of mathematics. Da Cunha's manuscripts on the problems of mathematics and its foundations are briefly mentioned in the preface to the French edition of *Principios*, but their subsequent fate is unknown.

BIBLIOGRAPHY

I. Original Works. Da Cunha's main writings are *Principios mathemáticos para instrucçao dos alumnos do Collegio de São Lucas, da Real Casa Pio do Castello de São Jorge* (Lisbon, 1790), French trans. by J. M. d'Abreu as *Principes mathématiques de feu Joseph-Anastase da Cunha* (Bordeaux, 1811; repr. Paris, 1816); and *Ensayo sobre os principios da mechanica obra posthuma de J. A. da Cunha, dada à luz por D. D. A. de S. C. possuidor do MS autographo* (London, 1807; Amsterdam, 1808).

II. Secondary Literature. See the following, listed chronologically: T. Braga, *Historia da Universidade de Coimbra*, III (Lisbon, 1898), 500–619; F. G. Teixeira, *História das matemáticas em Portugal* (Lisbon, 1934), 255–256; J. V. Gonçalves, "Análise do livro VIII dos *Principios mathemáticos* de José-Anastácio da Cunha," in *Congresso do mundo português*, I (n.p., 1940), 123–140; and A. P. Youschkevitch, "J. A. da Cunha et les fondements de l'analyse infinitésimale," in *Revue d'histoire des sciences et de leurs applications*, XXVI (1973), 3–22.

A. P. Youschkevitch

CURTZE, E. L. W. MAXIMILIAN (*b.* Ballenstedt, Harz, Germany, 4 August 1837; *d.* Thorn, Germany [now Torun, Poland], 3 January 1903)

Curtze was the son of Eduard Curtze, a physician, and of Johanna Nicolai-Curtze. He attended the Gymnasium in Bernburg and from 1857 to 1860 studied in Greifswald, primarily under Johann August Grunert. After he passed the teaching examination in 1861, he taught at the Gymnasium in Thorn, where one of his colleagues was the Copernicus scholar Leopold Prove.

Curtze had an excellent knowledge of the current mathematical literature and an unusual talent for languages; he translated many valuable mathematical works from Italian into German, an outstanding example being Schiaparelli's *Precursori di Copernico nell'antichità* (1876). He did not publish a comprehensive work on his main field—the editing of medieval manuscripts, especially those in the rich collection of the library of Thorn—but he did publish valuable reports on the treasures of this library (1871; 1873–1878). He was also responsible for editions of Oresme's *Algorismus proportionum* (1868) and of his mathematical writings (1870), the *Liber trium fratrum de geometria* (1885), Peter of Dacia's commentary on Sacrobosco's *Algorisms* (1897), and Anaritius' commentaries on Euclid's *Elements* (1899). Other publications are the collection *Urkunden zur Geschichte der Mathematik im Mittelalter und der Renaissance* (1902) and a carefully researched biography of Copernicus (1899).

Curtze contributed many essays to mathematical journals and journals of the history of science. His work was greatly aided by his skill in deciphering hard-to-read handwriting and by visits to libraries in Uppsala and Stockholm (1873) and central Germany (1896). He began corresponding with Moritz Cantor in 1865 but did not meet him until 1896.

In his time Curtze was the outstanding expert on medieval mathematical texts. Through his careful editions he pointed out new paths in a field that was then little investigated.

BIBLIOGRAPHY

I. Original Works. Curtze's writings include *Die Gymnasialbibliothek zu Thorn* (Thorn, 1871); *Die Handschriften und seltenen Drucke der Gymnasialbibliothek zu Thorn*, 2 vols. (I, Thorn, 1873; II, Leipzig, 1878); a biography of Copernicus (Leipzig, 1899); and *Urkunden zur Geschichte der Mathematik im Mittelalter und der Renaissance* (Leipzig, 1902). Among his translations is that of G. V. Schiaparelli's *Precursori di Copernico nell'antichità* (Leipzig, 1876). Curtze was responsible for editions of Nicole Oresme's *Algorismus proportionum* (Berlin, 1868) and of his mathematical writings (Berlin, 1870); of the *Liber trium fratrum de geometria* (Halle, 1885); of Peter of Dacia's *In algorismum Johannis de Sacro Bosco commentarius* (Copenhagen, 1897); and of Anaritius' *In decem libros elementorum Euclidis commentarii* (Leipzig, 1899).

II. Secondary Literature. Obituary notices are Moritz Cantor, "Maximilian Curtze," in *Jahresbericht der Deutschen Mathematiker-Vereinigung*, **12** (1903), 357–368, with portrait, and *Biographisches Jahrbuch und deutscher Nekrolog für das Jahr 1903,* (1904), 90–94; and S. Günther, "Maximilian Curtze," in *Bibliotheca mathematica,* 3rd ser., 4 (1903), 65–81, with portrait and bibliography.

J. E. HOFMANN

CUSA, NICHOLAS, also known as **Nikolaus von Cusa, Nicolaus Cusanus** (*b.* Kues, Moselle, Germany, *ca.* 1401; *d.* Todi, Umbria, Italy, 11 August 1464)

Nicholas was the son of a well-to-do Moselle fisherman, Johann Cryffts (or Krypffs, or Krebs), and his wife Katharina Römer. He may have received his early education at Deventer, in the Netherlands, in the school kept by the Brothers of the Common Life; he would thus have been early influenced by the *devotio moderna* movement. (This reform movement, which strove for a practical, Christocentric religious practice, was spread throughout the low countries and the Rhineland at that period.) Nicholas then entered the University of Heidelberg (he went as companion to Count Ulrich von Manderscheid) and presumably took the introductory course in philosophy there.

In 1417 Nicholas went on to the University of Padua, where he studied canon law with Prosdocimo de Comitibus and others; in 1423 he earned the degree *doctor decretalium.* At Padua, Nicholas met the physician Toscanelli—with whom he attended the lectures on astrology of Prosdocimo Beldomandi—and the humanist educators Guarino da Verona and Vittorino da Feltre. He also attended the penitential sermons of the Franciscan Bernardino of Siena.

In 1425 Nicholas entered the service of Elector Otto von Ziegenhain, archbishop of Trier. In 1426, he was in Cologne, where he had presumably come as a teacher of canon law (although he may have studied theology there in 1425). In Cologne, Nicholas began his independent researches into original source materials, probing deep into the annals of Germanic law; he was thus able to prove that the Donation of Constantine was in fact an eighth-century forgery. He also found copies of Latin writings long believed to be lost; the most important of these were the *Natural History* of Pliny the Elder and twelve comedies of Plautus. His fame spread; in 1428 and again in 1435 he was offered a post as teacher of canon law at the newly established University of Louvain, but he turned it down in each instance.

It was at this period that Nicholas became associated with Heimeric von Campen, who led him into closer acquaintance with the Scholastics as well as introducing him to Proclus' commentary on Plato's *Parmenides* and to the writings of Ramón Lull (whose work Nicholas annotated and, around 1428, copied out in part with his own hand).

Nicholas was ordained priest *ca.* 1430. In this year, too, the archbishopric of Trier was claimed by Ulrich von Manderscheid. In the contest that followed, Nicholas acted as Ulrich's representative in pleading his case before the Council of Basel, convened in 1431. (It was later reconvened in Ferrara and then in Florence.) He did not succeed in getting the council to grant Ulrich's request, but he was recognized as a participant and became one of the leading spokesmen for the conciliar faction. Nicholas dedicated his book *De concordantia catholica* (1433) to his fellow councillors; in it he based his arguments on the thesis that the authority of an ecumenical council was superior to that of a pope and elaborated a comprehensive system of government and society. He stressed the church as the supreme earthly society, and found a divine pattern for priestly concord. (That he could be more realistic as a politician is shown by his 1433 proposal for negotiations with the Hussites.) While in Basel, Nicholas met the humanist Piccolomini, who in 1440 became secretary to Pope Felix V and in 1458 himself became Pope Pius II.

In 1436 the council received an appeal from Christian Byzantium, then sorely pressed by the Turks. The prospect of union of the eastern and western churches triggered stormy arguments in Basel, in which Nicholas sided with the pope's party. In 1437 he took part in an embassy sent to Constantinople to bring the princes of the Byzantine church and the emperor John VIII Palaeologus to the west. Nicholas knew some Greek; he also brought from Constantinople manuscripts containing reports on the councils of Constantinople and Nicaea which shed new light on the doctrinal dispute that centered on the text of the Creed. (Although formal unification of the two churches was achieved in 1437 it was not recognized by Constantinople.)

Through his new alliance with the papal minority Nicholas was given other diplomatic missions. During 1438 and 1439 he was engaged in constant negotiations with the German princes, most of whom either supported the majority conciliar position or wished to remain neutral. It was in part through Nicholas' efforts that these princes agreed to recognize the authority of Pope Eugene IV and his successor Nicholas V. Coincident with his diplomatic work, Nicholas had begun his major philosophical treatise, *De docta ignorantia,* finished in 1440 (by his own account he had struck upon its key notion, the *coincidentia oppositorum,* on his way back from Constantinople).

Nicholas' work puts mathematics and experimental science at the service of philosophy in his attempt to describe the limits of human knowledge. In the *De docta ignorantia* he made new interpretations of those philosophically oriented introductory books of mathematics with which he was acquainted, most notably Boethius' *Institutio geometrica* and Thomas Bradwardine's *Geometria speculativa.*

Trained in the methods of Aristotelian logic, Nicholas found them inadequate to his purpose, since he considered them applicable only to finite phenomena. The Divine, being infinite, is inaccessible to the mind of man, but may be approached through a method of symbolic visualization which resolves apparent antitheses; necessarily, however, at the end of the process man must acknowledge his ignorance. Thus, if the truth is probably inaccessible to the mind of man, man can intellectually get closer and closer to it through the sum of his private knowledge—without ever quite reaching it, since the truth represents an absolute, unchanging maximum limit beyond the scope of man's understanding.

Nicholas made extensive use of geometric figures in his *visio intellectualis;* he chose them because the rational language of demonstration was not suited to explain *intellectus*—the power of knowing that is superior to human reason. Thus one could, for example, increase the number of vertices of a regular polygon until, in infinity, it was transformed into a circle; and while triangles, squares, and circles differed from each other on a finite level, they were resolved beyond it on the infinite scale—although man, of course, could never know such ultimate resolution, being bound by finity to approximations only. Likewise, the contradiction of opposites of a straight line and a circle may be resolved in infinity, since a circle of infinitely long radius has a straight line for its circumference.

As understood by Nicholas, the infinite could take two forms, the infinitely large and the infinitely small. No contradiction was here implied, however, since the infinitely large and the infinitely small could both be contained in the concept of maximum; the largest possible thing was of maximum largeness, while the smallest possible thing was of maximum smallness. The concept of maximum admitted one absolute maximum (God) which could also be seen as unifying absolute maximum and absolute minimum, being infinite and therefore without degree.

Such geometrical examples are the essence of the *coincidentia oppositorum,* by means of which Nicholas hoped to resolve all problems formerly considered insoluble. Since apparent contradictions are united in infinity, the largest possible number must coincide with the smallest possible—one—and since numbers are discrete entities, all are contained in the ultimate unity and can be produced from that unity, which is also the measure of all intermediary quantities. Pursuant to this reasoning Nicholas referred to Anaxagoras and assumed that each entity is present in every other entity. In geometry, continuous forms correspond to numbers; the point stands alone as the smallest initial unit and generates lines, surfaces, and solid forms. The most perfect geometric forms—the infinitely large circle and the infinitely large sphere—are at the same time coincident with their generating point.

In cosmology, the application of the *coincidentia oppositorum* led Nicholas to determine that there could be no cosmic mechanism or center point for the motions of the heavens, since such a point of necessity included the whole universe. The universe mirrors God and is a relative maximum, since it contains all things except God, in Whom all is contained; therefore, the universe has no fixed center and no circumference, being relatively infinite. Therefore, the earth is not the center of the universe, nor is it stationary; it moves, as do all other bodies in space, with a motion that is not absolute but relative to the beholder. Nicholas further suggests by analogy that the earth may not be the only body that supports life. Moreover, the earth is not completely round, there is no maximum movement of the other heavenly bodies as opposed to the fixity of the earth, and no possible movement of bodies in diametrically opposite directions (such as up and down). Nicholas' cosmological reasoning, although garbed in theological language, here anticipates scientific discovery; his later treatise on the subject, *De figura mundi* (1462) is unfortunately lost.

Also lost is an earlier work, *De conjecturis,* of which only a later, much revised version of some time prior to 1444 exists. In the *De docta ignorantia,* Nicholas makes several specific corrections to the earlier version, from which some indication of its contents may be gained; he draws upon earlier notions of what is knowable, which he restates. It is also clear that the earlier book made the same extensive use of symbolic reasoning as the later, although its purport was more clearly metaphysical. Nicholas' earlier cosmology drew upon the Neoplatonic notions of the hierarchy of God-angel-soul-body and united it with the four elements to produce a metaphysics of unity, to which he assigned analogous mathematical values—i.e., he assigned the numbers 1, 10, 100, and 1,000 to the four elements and maintained the Pythagorean relation $1 + 2 + 3 + 4 = 10$ as a symbol of the *arithmetica universalis.* He paid special attention to the relationship of oneness and otherness, which he represented as two opposed quadratic pyramids, conjoined so that each had its vertex at the center point of the other's base plane. One pyramid stood for light, the other for darkness, one for the male principle, the other for the female, and so on. In the *De docta ignorantia* Nicholas was able to use his newly formulated doctrine of the *coincidentia oppositorum* to resolve these contradictions and to develop his theory of a unity in which each form partakes of and mirrors every other form.

Although the *De docta ignorantia* was both respected and influential, such speculations left Nicholas open to attack from his political enemies for pantheistic teachings and other damnable heresies. Johannes Wenck acted as spokesman for Nicholas' detractors in publishing *De ignota litteratura,* against which Nicholas defended himself with his *Apologia doctae ignorantiae* (1449), quoting at length from Dionysius and Areopagite and the Church Fathers.

Following the publication of the *Apologia doctae ignorantiae* Nicholas undertook further diplomatic missions for the Curia and did not expound or develop his system in more extensive writings. He did, however, dictate a number of short treatises which were copied down and circulated among his friends. In addition, some 300 of his sermons, dating from 1431 on, were recorded in the form of brief notes. (These sermons, given in both Latin and vernacular German, were at first devotional exercises preached on holidays, but later Nicholas began to introduce his own philosophical tenets into them, and by 1444 the mystical influence of Meister Eckhart is apparent in them.) The sermons provided the bases for Nicholas' later tracts, including *De quaerendo Deum* (1445), an orthodox devotional guide; and *De filiatione Dei* (1445), *De ultimis diebus* (1446), *De genesi* (1447), and *De Deo abscondito* (1450[?]), which derive in part from ideas set forth in *De conjecturis* and *De docta ignorantia.* His *De dato patris tris luminum* (1445 or 1446) and *De visione Dei* (1458) both argue against his alleged pantheism.

Nicholas' services to the Curia were rewarded in 1446 when Pope Eugene IV appointed him a cardinal *in petto;* in 1448 Pope Nicholas V made him a full cardinal, with the titular see of St. Peter in Vincoli. Nicholas received the red hat in 1450 and was named bishop of Brixen, where the cathedral chapter recognized him only reluctantly. At the end of 1450 he was appointed legate for Germany; as such he undertook a journey through Germany, Belgium, and the Netherlands where he preached reform and worked for compromise and conciliation in secular and ecclesiastical disputes. He soon became embroiled in violent quarrels with the nobility; Duke Sigismund of Tirol intervened and threatened to use force.

In 1458 Nicholas went to Rome, where his friend Piccolomini had been elected Pope Pius II. On his return to Germany in 1460, he was immediately locked up in Bruneck castle by Duke Sigismund's mercenaries; eventually Nicholas capitulated to the secular forces and returned to Rome. He was there appointed a papal representative.

During this period, in addition to his sermons, Nicholas undertook brief works on mathematics, to which he sought to apply some of the new insights that he had reached philosophically. His principal aim was to transform a circle into a straight line and a square; he confined himself to approximations. In *Transmutationes geometricae* (1445) he displays familiarity with simpler Euclidean theorems and appears to rely heavily on Bradwardine's *Geometria speculativa,* which he never mentions, however. He further refers to a fragment of the writings of Pappus, and shows considerable knowledge of the practical geometries available to him, drawing upon them for his many examples of applied geometry.

Nicholas' *Complementa arithmetica* may also date from 1445, although the exact year of its first publication is not known and it now exists only in a corrupted form. In it, Nicholas first expressed the idea that the difference between the radii of a series of circles inscribed in a series of regular polygons is proportional to the difference in area between the inscribed circle and its corresponding regular polygon.

In his *De circuli quadratura* (1450) Nicholas used a computational approach similar to that employed in his *Transmutationes geometricae;* it is uncertain what earlier authors may have influenced this work. The *De circuli* is remarkable for its discussion of the disputed intermediate value theorem, derived from Aristotle, and of the angle-of-contingence problem and the problem of exactly squaring a circle. Two of Nicholas' *Idiota* dialogues, *De sapientia* and *De mente* (both 1450) are the philosophical synthesis of his mathematical work at this time: in them, a layman who recognizes God's work in nature is given an opportunity, in the form of Platonic dialogues, to explain Cusan philosophy—especially its mathematicizing tendencies—to an Aristotelian scholar. (A third such dialogue, *Idiota de staticis experimentis,* of the same year, has a more practical bias, and contains numerous methods for determining physical parameters through the use of such apparatus as scales and a water clock—for example, the work tells in detail how to determine the humidity of air by measuring the weight of wool.)

In 1452 Nicholas read Jacob of Cremona's translation of the works of Archimedes, and was much impressed with the latter's indirect method of deduction, which he erroneously associated with his own *coincidentia oppositorum.* He had by now thought through his earlier ideas, and set them down systematically in a series of works, beginning with the *Complementa mathematica* (1453; expanded in 1454), which contained many more approximations than the earlier books (although these dealt largely with special cases, and provided no new insights), and the *Complementum theologicum,* a continuation that pertained primarily to symbolic interpretations. Nicholas presented an important variation of the approximation proportion in the *Perfectio mathematica* (1458)—which, more importantly, also contained the notion that the method of *visio intellectualis* could yield an infinitely small arc of a circle and its corresponding chord (although inadequately expressed by Nicholas, this anticipated an infinitesimal concept of great significance). The *Aurea propositio in mathematicis* (1459) contains the final refinement of these ideas.

During the 1450's, Nicholas continued to apply his doctrine of *coincidentia oppositorum* to religious, as well as mathematical, problems. The shattering event of the year 1453—the fall of the Byzantine empire—led him to write *De pace fidei,* published in that year. In it, he presents a dialogue among seventeen articulate representatives of different nations and faiths and calls for mutual tolerance. Although he maintains the superiority of Christianity, he proposes that the differences among faiths are largely those of ritual and stresses the unifying factor of monotheism. He further undertook a thorough and critical investigation of Islam; his *Cribatio Alkoran* (published in 1461) is, however, based upon a poor translation of the Koran.

Nicholas' later works also include a number of relatively short treatises in which simple physical or mathematical examples are expanded into philosophical symbols. In *De beryllo* (1458) he compares the *visio intellectualis* to the effect of a magnifying glass; and in *De possest* (1460) he uses the example of a circular disc rotating at infinite speed within a stationary ring to show that all points of the circumference of the disc are at all points of the interior of the ring simultaneously—hence, motion and rest are identical, and thus time unfolds from the present and thus the single instant and eternity are the same in infinity. In *De ludo globi* (1463) he moves on to discuss the spiral motion of a partially concave sphere, and in *De non aliud* (1462) he reverts to dialogue form for a critical conversation with Aristotle, Plato, and Proclus. *De venatione sapientiae* (1463) stands in relation to his philosophy as the *Aurea proposito in mathematicis* does to his mathematics; it is a retrospective summation of his earlier attempts to illuminate for others his private intellectual world.

As a philosopher, Nicholas was chiefly concerned with knowing the ways of God; his mystical and symbolic approach was calculated to encourage man to seek the unity of all things and the end of antitheses in light of his insight that the Divine could not be known directly. He rejected the rationalism of the Schoolmen, and revitalized Neoplatonism in his time. That he failed always to be understood and appreciated by his contemporaries is due in part to the peculiarity of his language, neither medieval nor humanistic and flawed by inadequately defined words and concepts.

That he failed also to reach the ideal of conciliation that he preached may be attributed, too, to his character, since he was frequently hot-headed, temperamental, and inclined to arbitrary decisions. Despite his demonstrated skill as an imaginative diplomat, Nicholas spent the last years of his ecclesiastical career in Rome in a series of squabbles with the Italian clique and in ineffectual attempts to reform the clergy, the orders, and the Curia.

Only in the nineteenth century did the importance of Cusan thought begin to become clear, and only in the twentieth century was any thorough study of it begun. Precise study has been made possible through the happy circumstance that the home for the aged in Kues, generously endowed by Nicholas, has survived the ravages of time and war; its library, a chief source for Cusan scholars, has, except for minor losses, remained intact.

BIBLIOGRAPHY

I. Original Works. Nicholas' *Opera* were widely reprinted, including the editions of Martin Flach (Strasbourg, 1488; repr. in 2 vols. as *Nikolaus von Kues, Werke,* Berlin, 1967); Benedetto Dolcibelli (Milan, 1502); Jodocus Badius (Paris, 1514; three-volume facsimile repr. Frankfurt am Main, 1962); and Henricus Petri (Basel, 1565).

The modern edition prepared by the Heidelberger Akademie der Wissenschaften includes E. Hoffmann and R. Klibansky, eds., *De docta ignorantia* (Leipzig, 1932); R. Klibansky, ed., *Apologia doctae ignorantiae* (Leipzig, 1932); L. Bauer, ed., *Idiota de sapientia, de mente, de staticis experimentis* (Leipzig, 1937); B. Decker and C. Bormann, eds., *Compendium* (Hamburg, 1954); P. Wilpert, ed., *Opuscula I* (Hamburg, 1959); G. Kallen and A. Berger, eds., *De concordantia catholica,* 4 vols. (Hamburg, 1959–1968); and J. Koch, ed., *De conjecturis* (in preparation).

German translations of many individual works are available in the series *Schriften des Nikolaus von Cues* (Leipzig or Hamburg, various dates).

II. Secondary Literature. Works on Nicholas include M. de Gandillac, *La philosophie de Nicolas de Cues* (Paris, 1942), which was translated into German by K. Fleischmann (Düsseldorf, 1953); K. Jaspers, *Nikolaus Cusanus* (Munich, 1964); A. Lübke, *Nikolaus von Kues* (Munich, 1968); J. Marx, *Verzeichnis der Handschriftensammlung des Hospitals zu Cues* (Trier, 1907); E. Meuthen, *Nikolaus von Kues 1401-1464. Skizze einer Biographie* (Münster, 1964); P. Rotta, *Il cardinale Niccolò de Cusa* (Milan, 1928); E. Vansteenberghe, *Le cardinal Nicolas de Cues (l'action-la pensée)* (Paris, 1920).

Mitteilungen und Forschungsbeiträge der Cusanus Gesellschaft, Mainz, published since 1961, contains many individual articles on Nicholas and his works as well as a running bibliography of Cusan studies from 1920 on.

J. E. HOFMANN

DANDELIN, GERMINAL PIERRE (*b.* Le Bourget, France, 12 April 1794; *d.* Brussels, Belgium, 15 February 1847)

Dandelin's father was French; his mother, Anne-Françoise Botteman, was from Hainaut (now part of Belgium). The father, after the transfer of Belgium to France, occupied administrative functions in that country. Dandelin studied at Ghent, volunteered in 1813 for the defense of Walcheren against the British, and in the same year entered the École Polytechnique in Paris. He was wounded in action at Vincennes on 30 March 1814 and in 1815, during the Hundred Days, was attached to the Ministry of Interior under Carnot. After Waterloo, Dandelin returned to Belgium, where in 1817 he became a citizen of the Netherlands and *sous-lieutenant* in the corps of military engineers. In 1825 he was elected to the Royal Academy of Sciences in Brussels, and from 1825 to 1830 he was professor of mining engineering in Liège. He then served until 1835 as an officer in the Belgian army, taking part in the Revolution of 1830. He afterward held educational and engineering posts (building fortifications) in Namur, Liège, and (from 1843) Brussels. At the time of his death he was *colonel de génie* in the Belgian army.

Dandelin's early work was in geometry, in which he worked in the same spirit as his Belgian colleague Adolphe Quetelet. The theorem named for him, of great use in descriptive geometry, states that when a cone of revolution is intersected by a plane in a conic, its foci (or focus, in the case of a parabola) are (is) the points (point) where this plane is touched by the spheres that are inscribed in the cone. It is published in "Mémoire sur quelques propriétés remarquables de la focale parabolique" (1822). In "Sur l'hyperboloide de révolution et sur les hexagones de Pascal et de Brianchon" (1826) he proved that the theorem also holds for a hyperboloid of revolution and showed the relationship between the Pascal and Brianchon hexagons and the skew hexagon formed by generators of the hyperboloid.

These investigations were closely related to Dandelin's theory of stereographic projection of a sphere on a plane, presented in "Mémoire sur l'emploi des projections stéréographiques en géométrie" (1827). This led him to inversions, by which points P on a line OP connecting them with a fixed pole O are transformed into points P' on OP' such that the product of OP and OP' is constant. He thus found a rational circular cubic curve as the inverse of a conic with the pole on the conic.

Dandelin also wrote on statics, algebra, astronomy, and probability. In his "Recherches sur la résolution des équations numériques" (1823) he outlined in the second supplement a method (already suggested by Edward Waring in 1762) of approximation of the roots of an algebraic equation with roots α_i by determining the coefficients of equations with roots $\alpha_i^2, \alpha_i^4, \alpha_i^8, \ldots$ This method, named for Dandelin and C. H. Gräffe, was also proposed by Lobachevski in 1834.

BIBLIOGRAPHY

I. ORIGINAL WORKS. Two books by Dandelin are *Leçons sur la mécanique et les machines* (Liège, 1827) and *Cours de statique* (Paris, 1830). Among his papers are "Mémoire sur quelques propriétés remarquables de la focale parabolique," in *Nouveaux mémoires de l'Académie royale de Bruxelles,* **2** (1822), 171-200; "Recherches sur la résolution des équations numériques," *ibid.,* **3** (1823), 7-71; "Sur l'hyperboloide de révolution et sur les hexagones de Pascal et de Brianchon," *ibid.* (1826), 1-14; "Mémoire sur l'emploi des projections stéréographiques en géométrie," *ibid.,* **4** (1827), 13-47; "Sur la détermination des orbites cométaires," *ibid.,* **13** (1841), 1-23; and "Sur quelques points de métaphysique géométrique," *ibid.,* **17** (1844), 1-44, which misses the geometries of Bolyai and Lobachevski. There are also papers in Quetelet's *Correspondance mathématique et physique* (1825-1839).

II. SECONDARY LITERATURE. A biography is A. Quetelet, "C. P. Dandelin," in *Biographie nationale,* XIV (Brussels, 1873), 663-668. On Dandelin's theorem and its generalizations, see M. Chasles, *Aperçu historique sur l'origine et le développement des méthodes en géométrie* (Paris, 1837; 3rd ed., 1889); and E. Kötter, "Entwicklung der synthetischen Geometrie von Monge bis auf von Staudt," in *Jahresbericht der Deutschen Mathematikervereinigung,* **5**, pt. 2 (1901), 60-64. On the Dandelin-Gräffe method, see F. Cajori, *A History of Mathematics* (New York, 1938), p. 364; and C. Runge, *Praxis der Gleichungen* (Berlin-Leipzig, 1921), pp. 136-158.

DIRK J. STRUIK

DANTI, EGNATIO (PELLEGRINO RAINALDI) (*b.* Perugia, Italy, April 1536; *d.* Alatri, Italy, 1586)

Danti's father, Giulio, and his grandfather, Pier Vincenzio, were very well-read in Italian literature and in astronomy. The Danti family was originally named Rainaldi, but contemporaries of the grandfather, admiring his talents, began to call him Dante or Danti. The new name was taken by Giovanni Battista, Pier Vincenzio's brother, who was well-known for his work in mathematics and mechanics and who, according to contemporary reports, in 1503 made what appears to have been a successful flight.

At the age of thirteen Danti, having changed his name from Pellegrino to Egnatio, entered the Dominican order. His reputation as a scholar in science and the arts reached Cosimo I de' Medici, perhaps through his brother Vincenzio, a well-known sculptor at the court of the grand duke toward the end of 1562 or early in 1563. Cosimo I ordered him to prepare maps for his collection and a large terrestrial globe, which is still in existence. Cosimo's admiration for his cosmographer later grew to the point that, in 1571, he wrote to the general of the Dominican order, requesting permission for Danti to reside in the palace. While preparing the maps, Danti also did other work; and Cosimo I commissioned him to study reform of the calendar, which was later carried out by Gregory XIII.

Ever since the seventh and eighth centuries chronologists had noted that the length of the year as determined by Julius Caesar, which was the basis of the calendar then in use (the Julian calendar), did not correspond to the true course of the sun. In 45 B.C., Caesar, at the suggestion of the Alexandrian astronomer Sosigenes, had determined that the year should be 365 days, five hours, forty-eight minutes, and forty-six seconds. The value was eleven minutes greater than the true one, and by the time of Danti the error, which had been increasing for sixteen centuries, amounted to eleven days. The vernal equinox and the summer solstice should have fallen, respectively, on 21–22 March and 21–22 June. In order to establish the displacement in days, Danti, with the permission of the grand duke, constructed on the façade of the church of Santa Maria Novella an astronomical quadrant and an equinoctial armillary. By means of the latter Danti was able to observe the vernal equinox of 1574 and found that it fell on 11 March. Danti had also wanted to construct a large gnomon in Santa Maria Novella, but the death of Cosimo I prevented him from completing the work.

In 1569 Danti published the *Trattato dell'uso et della fabbrica dell'astrolabio,* which was reprinted in 1578. In 1579 he published the *Sphere* of Sacrobosco, translated by his grandfather, which he enlarged with his own comments. His Italian translation of Proclus' *Sphere* appeared in 1573. These were the earliest astronomical treatises in Italian.

Cosimo I had commissioned Danti to give public lectures in the mathematical sciences, but he was obliged to abandon this assignment in 1574, following the death of Cosimo I, when he lost the favor of the new grand duke, Francesco. Within twenty-four hours of the succession he was transferred to Bologna, where a year later he became professor of mathematics. In Bologna he was able to construct a large gnomon in the church of San Petronio, where he made observations on the exact date of the spring equinox.

In 1577 Danti returned to Perugia, where he was commissioned to draw up the topographical map of Perugia and the surrounding countryside. The pope later appointed him to enlarge the map to include all the papal states: Emilia-Romagna, Umbria, Latium, and Sabina. In 1580, Pope Gregory XIII called Danti to Rome to reform the calendar; and at the Vatican Danti constructed a meridian inside the Torre de' Veneti, in the room that later became known as the Calendar Room. In the same year Pope Gregory ordered him to depict in the Belvedere Gallery the various regions of Italy, in thirty-two large panels. On the completion of this work in November 1583, the pope appointed Danti bishop of Alatri. Even with this new office Danti found time to prepare, with corrections and additions, the second edition of Latino Orsini's *Trattato del radio latino.* In the same year Pope Sixtus V called Danti to Rome, to assist the architect Domenico Fontana in raising the obelisk in St. Peter's Square. On his return from Rome, Danti, although unwell, left Alatri for the transfer of a monastery. He contracted pneumonia, of which he died at the age of forty-nine.

BIBLIOGRAPHY

I. ORIGINAL WORKS. Among Danti's writings, editions, and translations are *Trattato dell'uso et della fabbrica dell' astrolabio con l'aggiunta del planisfero del Rojas* (Florence, 1569), repr. as *Dell'uso et fabbrica dell'astrolabio et del planisfero. Nuovamente ristampato ed accresciuto in molti luoghi con l'aggiunta dell'uso et fabbrica di nove altri instromenti astronomici* (Florence, 1578); *La sfera di Proclo Liceo tradotta da maestro Egnatio Danti. Con le annotazioni et con l'uso della sfera del medesima* (Florence, 1573); *La prospettiva di Euclide . . . tradotta* ([*dal greco*]) *da r. p. m. Egnatio Danti. Con alcune sue annotazioni dei luoghi più importanti* (Florence, 1573); *Usus et tractatio gnomonis magni, quem Bononiae ipse in Divi Petroni templo conferit anno d. 1576* (Bologna, n. d.); *Le scienze matematiche ridotte in tavole* (Bologna, 1577); *Anemographia. In anemoscopium verticale instrumentum ostensorem ventorum. His accessit ipsium instrumenti constructio* (Bologna, 1578); *Le due regole della prospettiva pratica di m. Jacomo Berozzi da Vignola con i commentari del R. P. M. Egnatio Danti* (Rome, 1583); and *Trattato del radio latino, instrumento giustissimo et facile più d'ogni altro per prendere qual si voglia misura, et positione di luogo, tanto in cielo come in terra . . . di Orsini Latino. Con i commentari del R. P. M. Egnatio Danti* (Rome, 1586).

II. SECONDARY LITERATURE. On Danti or his work, see J. del Badia, *Egnazio Danti. Cosmografo e matematico e le sue opere in Firenze* (Florence, 1898); Pietro Ferrate, "Recensione e critica di due lettere del Danti in data 23 novembre 1577 e 15 febbraio 1578," in *Giornale di erudizione artistica,* **2** (1873), 174–175; M. Fiorini, *Sfere terrestri e celesti di autori italiani* (Rome 1899), pp. 72 ff.; V. Palmesi, "Ignazio Danti," in *Bollettino della R. deputazione di storia patria per l'Umbria,* **5** (1899); G. Spini, *Annotazioni intorno al trattato dell'astrolabio e del planisfero universale del R. P. Ignazio Danti* (Florence, 1570); and G. B. Vermiglioli, "Elogio di Ignazio Danti detto in Perugia nel giorno 26 Dicembre 1819," in *Opuscoli letterari di Bologna,* III (Bologna, 1820), 1; "Ignatio Danti," in *Biografie degli scrittori perugini e notizie delle opere loro,* I (Perugia, 1829), 366–370.

MARIA LUISA RIGHINI-BONELLI

DANTZIG, DAVID VAN (*b.* Rotterdam, Netherlands, 23 September 1900; *d.* Amsterdam, Netherlands, 22 July 1959)

At the age of thirteen, Van Dantzig wrote his first mathematical paper, which was published in a Dutch mathematical periodical. After high school he studied chemistry, which he did not like; he soon stopped, owing to family circumstances that obliged him to take various odd jobs to support himself. At night he prepared for a sequence of state examinations in mathematics, which he passed in 1921, 1922, and 1923. After a short time at Amsterdam University he passed the *doctoraalexamen* (roughly equivalent to a master's degree). In 1927 he became an assistant to Jan A. Schouten at Delft Technical University. After a brief stay at a teacher training institution, Van Dantzig returned to Delft, where he became a lecturer in 1932, an extraordinary professor (roughly equivalent to associate professor) in 1938, and an ordinary professor (roughly equivalent to full professor) in 1940. He had received a Ph.D. degree at Groningen in 1932.

During the German occupation he was dismissed and obliged to move with his family from the Hague to Amsterdam. In 1946 he was appointed a professor at Amsterdam University and was a cofounder of the Mathematisch Centrum, a research and service institution. Until his death he played a leading role at this institution while retaining his chair at the university.

During his short period of study at Amsterdam University, Van Dantzig was strongly influenced by one of his mathematics professors, Gerrit Mannoury (1867–1956), whose personality had a great impact on many people (including L. E. J. Brouwer). With Mannoury, Van Dantzig shared the disbelief in mathematical certainty—intuitionist or formalist—and even more than Mannoury he stressed the social responsibility of the mathematician as a teacher and a researcher, which he expressed in a number of publications.

As an assistant to and collaborator of Schouten, Van Dantzig took up Schouten-style differential geometry and its applications, in particular projective and conformal differential geometry, and electromagnetism and thermodynamics, independent of Riemannian geometry. Unfortunately, he never elaborated on his idea of a statistical explanation of Riemannian metrics.

After the war Van Dantzig turned to probability and statistics, mainly by stimulating research in this field. After the flood of 1953 he took a part in the research preparing the now completed "Delta Works."

The most important part of Van Dantzig's work lies in topological algebra, a term coined by him. Although published in the 1930's, it was probably conceived in the late 1920's. His Groningen Ph.D. dissertation, "Studiën over topologische Algebra" (1931), is a fine example of mathematical style: it consists of a concise string of definitions and theorems organized in such a way that in this context each theorem is obvious and none needs a proof. He elaborated on this theme in a series of papers titled "Zur topologischen Algebra" that dealt with questions of metrization and completion of groups, rings, and fields, and eventually classified the fields with a nontrivial locally compact topology. In the course of these studies Van Dantzig discovered the solenoids as completions of the additive group of real numbers. These strange homogeneous spaces led to a problem on connected metric homogeneous spaces in general, solved by Van Dantzig and B. L. van der Waerden, showing that conjugacy classes of the fundamental group of such spaces must be finite.

BIBLIOGRAPHY

I. ORIGINAL WORKS. Van Dantzig's writings include "Studiën over topologische Algebra," (Ph.D. diss.,

Groningen, 1931), "Zur topologischen Algebra. I: Komplettierungstheorie," in *Mathematische Annalen*, **107** (1932), 587–626, " . . . II: Abstrakte b_v-adische Ringe," in *Compositio mathematica*, **2** (1935), 201–223, and " . . . III: Brouwersche und Cantorsche Gruppen," *ibid.*, **3** (1936), 408–426; and "Über metrisch homogene Räume," in *Abhandlungen der mathematische der Seminar Hamburgischen Universität*, **6** (1928), 367–376, written with B. L. van der Waerden. A complete bibliography is in *Statistica neerlandica*, **13** (1959), 422–432.

II. SECONDARY LITERATURE. On Van Dantzig's work see Hans Freudenthal, "L'algèbre topologique, en particulier les groupes topologiques et de Lie," in *Revue de synthèse*, 3rd ser., **89** (1968), 223–243. Memorial articles are Hans Freudenthal, "Levensbericht van David van Dantzig," in *Jaarboek Kon. Ned. Akademie van wetenschappen* (1959–1960), 295–299, and "In memoriam David van Dantzig," in *Nieuw archief voor wiskunde*, 3rd ser., **8** (1960), 57–73 (in Dutch); and J. Hemelrijk, "In memoriam Prof. Dr. D. van Dantzig," in *Statistica neerlandica*, **13** (1959), 416–421 (in Dutch).

HANS FREUDENTHAL

DARBOUX, JEAN-GASTON (*b.* Nîmes, France, 14 August 1842; *d.* Paris, France, 23 February 1917)

After having studied at the lycées at Nîmes and Montpellier, Darboux was admitted in 1861 to both the École Normale Supérieure and the École Polytechnique in Paris; in both cases he placed first on the entrance examinations. This—and the fact that he selected the École Normale—brought him a good deal of publicity. While a student at the École Normale, he published his first paper on orthogonal surfaces, which he studied in more detail in his doctoral thesis, *Sur les surfaces orthogonales* (1866).

From 1867 to 1872 Darboux taught in secondary schools. In the latter year his growing fame brought him a teaching position at the École Normale that he held until 1881. From 1873 to 1878 he held the chair of rational mechanics at the Sorbonne as *suppléant* of Liouville. In 1878 he became *suppléant* of Chasles at the Sorbonne, and two years later succeeded Chasles in the chair of higher geometry, which he held until his death. From 1889 to 1903 Darboux served as dean of the Faculté des Sciences. In 1884 he became a member, and in 1900 the *secrétaire perpétuel,* of the Académie des Sciences. A representative figure, Darboux was a member of many scientific, administrative, and educational committees and held honorary membership in many academies and scientific societies: Lebon (see below) lists more than a hundred.

Darboux was primarily a geometer but had the ability to use both analytic and synthetic methods, notably in the theory of differential equations. Conversely, his geometrical way of thinking enabled him to make discoveries in analysis and rational mechanics. Thus he followed in the spirit of Gaspard Monge, and Darboux's spirit can be detected in the work of Élie Cartan. This characteristic of Darboux's approach to geometry is fully displayed in his four-volume *Leçons sur la théorie générale des surfaces* (1887–1896), based on his lectures at the Sorbonne. This collection of elegant essays on the application of analysis to curves and surfaces is held together by the author's deep understanding of the connections of various branches of mathematics. There are many, sometimes unexpected, applications and excursions into differential equations and dynamics. Among the subjects covered are the applicability and deformation of surfaces; the differential equation of Laplace,

$$f_{uv} = A(u,v)f_u + B(u,v)f_v$$

and its applications; and the study of geodesics (these also in connection with dynamic systems) and of minimal surfaces. Typical is the use of the moving trihedral. Relying on the classical results of Monge, Gauss, and Dupin, Darboux fully used, in his own creative way, the results of his colleagues Bertrand, Bonnet, Ribaucour, and others.

In his *Leçons sur les systèmes orthogonaux* (1898), he returned to his early love, with new results: the cyclids, the application of Abel's theorem on algebraic integrals to orthogonal systems in n dimensions, and other novel types of orthogonal systems. Earlier than these two books was *Sur une classe remarquable de courbes algébriques* (1873), in which he made an analytic and geometric investigation of the cyclids, of which an early example had been given by Dupin and which can be obtained by inversion from quadrics. Full use is made of imaginary elements, in the tradition of Poncelet and Chasles.

Darboux also did research in function theory, algebra, kinematics, and dynamics. His appreciation of the history of science is shown in numerous addresses, many given as *éloges* before the Academy. He also edited Joseph Fourier's *Oeuvres* (1888–1890).

BIBLIOGRAPHY

I. ORIGINAL WORKS. Darboux's writings include "Remarques sur la théorie des surfaces orthogonales," in *Comptes rendus de l'Académie des sciences,* **59** (1864), 240–242; *Sur une classe remarquable de courbes algébriques et sur la théorie des imaginaires* (Paris, 1873); *Leçons sur la théorie générale des surfaces et les applications géométriques du calcul infinitésimal,* 4 vols. (Paris, 1887–1896; I, 2nd ed., 1914; II, 2nd ed., 1915); his ed. of Fourier's *Oeuvres,* 2 vols. (Paris, 1888–1890); and *Leçons sur les systèmes orthogonaux et les coordonnées curvilignes* (Paris, 1898, 1910). He also wrote many papers pub. in *Comptes rendus de l'Académie des sciences, Annales de l'École normale,* and other periodicals, including *Bulletin des sciences mathématiques,* which he founded in 1870. His *Éloges académiques et discours* (Paris, 1912) contains essays on Bertrand, Hermite, Meusnier, and others. He provided notes for Bourdon's *Applications de l'algèbre à la géométrie* (Paris, 1880; 9th ed., 1906), pp. 449–648.

II. SECONDARY LITERATURE. E. Lebon, *Gaston Darboux* (Paris, 1910, 1913), is a descriptive bibliography. *Éloges académiques et discours* (Paris, 1912) was collected to honor his scientific jubilee. See also Y. Chatelain, *Dictionnaire de biographie française,* X (1962), 159–160; L. P. Eisenhart, "Darboux's Contribution to Geometry," in *Bulletin of the American Mathematical Society,* **24** (1918), 227–237; D. Hilbert, "Gaston Darboux," in *Acta mathematica,* **42** (1919), 269–273; G. Prasad, *Some Great Mathematicians of the Nineteenth Century,* II (Benares, 1934), 144–182, with an analysis of some of Darboux's works; and J. J. Weiss, in *Journal des débats* (20 Nov. 1861).

DIRK J. STRUIK

D'ARCY (or **D'ARCI**), **PATRICK** (*b.* Galway, Ireland, 27 September 1725; *d.* Paris, France, 18 October 1779)

D'Arcy's father, Jean, and his mother, Jeanne Linch, were of noble birth. In 1739, to escape the English persecution of Catholics, he was sent to Paris, where he was cared for by an uncle. He lived in the same quarter as Jean Baptiste Clairaut, a mathematician who tutored him. D'Arcy became a good friend of Clairaut's son, the far more famous Alexis Claude, the pioneer in France of Newtonian mathematical astronomy. D'Arcy was somewhat of a mathematical prodigy and presented two memoirs on dynamics to the Paris Academy of Sciences at about the age of seventeen.

The elder Clairaut normally tutored a number of young military officers. Influenced by this association, d'Arcy entered the army as a captain and served in Germany and Flanders. He participated in an expedition to the coast of Scotland in 1746, was captured, and was later repatriated because of his reputation as a mathematician. D'Arcy reentered the military in 1752 as a colonel and served for the rest of his life, advancing to the rank of *maréchal-de-camp* in 1770. He was admitted to the Academy of Sciences on 12 February 1749 as *adjoint mécanicien* and advanced through its ranks, becoming *pensionnaire géomètre* on 20 February 1771. Profits from mining interests, his military pensions, and a legacy from his uncle left d'Arcy a rather rich man. He married his niece in 1777, just two years before his death from cholera.

A staunch patron of Irish refugees, d'Arcy enjoyed good relations with the English scientific community in spite of his hatred for the English king. His character has been described by Condorcet as "firm, independent, and quick to anger." This is reflected in d'Arcy's polemics with Maupertuis, d'Alembert, and others. He was tall and well built, and his active military career and social interests furthered his tendencies toward being something of a scientific gadfly.

D'Arcy did work in rational mechanics, military technology, and physics. In the *Mémoires* of the Academy of Sciences for 1747 he presented his principle of conservation of areas, stating the moments of bodies with respect to a given axis thus: "The sum of the products of the mass of each body by the area that its radius vector describes around a fixed center, . . . is always proportional to the time." In opposition to Maupertuis's principle of least action, d'Arcy extended his principle to what he called the principle of conservation of action: The sum of the products of the masses, velocities, and perpendiculars (drawn from the center toward the bodies) is a constant. In the extension of his principle to the problem of the precession of the equinoxes, d'Arcy criticized d'Alembert's work and was in turn criticized by both d'Alembert and Lagrange.

In 1751 d'Arcy presented a memoir on the physics and chemistry of gunpowder mixtures, the dimensions and design of cannon, and the placement of the charge in cannon. This work was continued in *Essai d'une théorie d'artillerie* (1760). He had the chemist Antoine Baumé conduct chemical analyses of gunpowder and showed that the physical mixing procedure, rather than the chemical content, was most important in obtaining a good product. In measuring the recoil and power of cannon he invented a momentum pendulum that was adopted by the Régie des Poudres.

In 1749 d'Arcy and Jean Baptiste Le Roy developed a floating electrometer. In it a float in water supported a metal rod and plate. A second, charged plate was brought near it. Weights needed to restore the floating plate to its original level measured the electrostatic force. This device never proved very successful in practice, however. In 1765 d'Arcy presented an interesting memoir, "Sur la durée de la sensation de la vue." His eyesight had been damaged in an accident; and he was forced to use an observer while conducting the experiment, in which he attempted to measure the optical persistence of visual images. For example, in moving a light in a small circle, he found that above seven revolutions per second, the single light gave the appearance of a continuous circle. This hastily performed experiment bears out a further remark of Condorcet's about d'Arcy's tendency to begin a project and leave it unfinished, for although he raised a number of important questions relating to the physiology of vision, d'Arcy never completed the work.

BIBLIOGRAPHY

I. ORIGINAL WORKS. Most of d'Arcy's memoirs are printed in the *Mémoires de l'Académie royale des sciences* for 1747–1765. A fairly complete list of these is given in Poggendorff, I, 58. His first memoir on the principle of conservation of areas is "Principe général de dynamique, qui donne la relation entre les espaces parcourus et les temps, quel que soit le système de corps que l'on considère, et quelles que soient leurs actions les unes sur les autres," in *Mémoires de l'Académie royale des sciences, année 1747* (1752), 348–356. Several of his Academy memoirs were also printed separately, and a partial list of these is given in the entry for d'Arcy in the general catalog of the Bibliothèque Nationale, Paris. His *Essai d'une théorie d'artillerie* was published in Paris (1760) and Dresden (1766).

II. SECONDARY LITERATURE. The best *éloge* of d'Arcy is by Condorcet, in *Histoire de l'Académie royale des sciences, année 1779* (1782), 54–70. J. B. A. Suard utilizes the Condorcet article but adds comments on d'Arcy's relationship with Condorcet in "Patrice d'Arcy," in *Biographie universelle,* II (Paris, 1811), 389. A discussion of the principle of conservation of areas is given in Ernst Mach, *The Science of Mechanics,* 6th Eng. ed. (La Salle, Ill., 1960), pp. 382–395. An excellent critical discussion of this principle and of the evolution of the general law of moment of momentum is C. Truesdell, "Whence the Law of Moment of Momentum?," in *Mélanges Alexandre Koyré, I. L'aventure de la science,* no. 12 of the series Histoire de la Pensée (Paris, 1964), pp. 588–612. The controversy between Maupertuis and d'Arcy over the principle of least action is discussed in P. Brunet, *Maupertuis—l'oeuvre et sa place dans la pensée scientifique et philosophique du XVIIIe siècle* (Paris, 1929), ch. 5.

C. STEWART GILLMOR

DARWIN, CHARLES GALTON (*b.* Cambridge, England, 19 December 1887, *d.* Cambridge, 31 December 1962)

Darwin was the grandson of Charles Darwin and the son of George Darwin. His contributions to science were in three different, although related, areas of activity: (1) theoretical research in optics (particularly X-ray diffraction), atomic structure, and statistical mechanics (in collaboration with R. H. Fowler); (2) educational and scientific administration; (3) world sociological and technical problems, with special reference to population.

Darwin was educated at Cambridge University, where he held a major scholarship in Trinity College and took an honors degree in the mathematical tripos in 1910. His training in applied mathematics was particularly strong, although there was little emphasis on contemporary developments in theoretical physics. After leaving Cambridge, Darwin became a postgraduate student with Ernest Rutherford at Manchester. He began research on the absorption of alpha rays and for a time showed interest in the dynamics of Rutherford's nuclear atom model. He soon turned to X-ray diffraction as a subject on which he could exercise his mathematical powers and, after some experimental work with H. G. J. Moseley, produced a series of papers which laid the foundation for all subsequent interpretation of X-ray diffraction by crystals. In these he anticipated by many years the classic work of P. P. Ewald. These researches were probably Darwin's most important contribution to theoretical physics.

After service in World War I, in which he engaged in some early work on acoustic gun ranging, Darwin was appointed fellow and lecturer of Christ's College, Cambridge, a post he held until 1922, when he spent a year in the United States as visiting professor at the California Institute of Technology. The principal fruit of his Cambridge appointment was the collaboration with Fowler on a new method of developing statistical mechanics. Known since this time as the Darwin-Fowler method, it differs from the Maxwell-Boltzmann and Gibbs approaches by calculating directly the averages of physical quantities over assemblies of systems by the method of steepest descents. It served as a particularly effective foundation for the later quantum statistics. For this work and his earlier researches, Darwin was elected a fellow of the Royal Society in 1922.

From 1924 to 1936 Darwin served as Tait professor of natural philosophy at the University of Edinburgh, where his colleagues were E. T. Whittaker in mathematics and J. G. Barkla in physics. Darwin turned his attention to quantum optics and published several papers, particularly in magneto-optics. After a visit to Niels Bohr's institute in 1927, he became interested in the new quantum mechanics and developed a quantum mechanical theory of the electron that proved to be an approximation to P. A. M. Dirac's later relativistic electron theory. This was another high point in Darwin's scientific career. In a sense it marked the termination of his creative investigations in theoretical physics, although during the rest of his life he continued to return to the examination of physical problems that happened to excite his interest.

In 1936 Darwin became master of Christ's College, Cambridge, and devoted himself primarily to educational administration. Presumably he would have been happy to devote the remainder of his professional life to this form of activity. But the approach of war and the resignation of Sir Lawrence Bragg from the directorship of the National Physical Laboratory put pressure on Darwin to take on this important national post. He served in this capacity throughout the war and did not retire until 1949. Darwin's administrative talents were demonstrated by his reorganization of the laboratory both before and after the war. The exigencies of wartime interfered to some extent with his program, since he was engaged in scientific liaison work in the United States during 1941–1942.

The last fifteen years of Darwin's life were devoted largely to the problems of science and society. He paid much attention to genetics and eugenics and to the sociological implications of the population explosion. He became a neo-Malthusian and developed a pessimistic attitude toward man's future on the earth, in spite of obvious technological progress. This view was presented in detail in his well-known book *The Next Million Years.* Here his theory of man as the last "wild" animal is skillfully although rather grimly worked out and has produced much healthy controversy.

Darwin traveled widely, especially in his later years, and showed great interest in international cooperation in science and culture generally. He was a gifted lecturer and knew how to present difficult ideas in simple fashion. Knighted in 1942, he was also honored for his accomplishments by many institutions in Britain and in other countries throughout the world.

BIBLIOGRAPHY

I. Original Works. A complete bibliography is in Thomson (see below).

Books. Darwin's two books are *The New Conceptions of Matter* (London, 1931); and *The Next Million Years* (London, 1952).

Articles. Of the ninety-three articles the following are representative: "A Theory of the Absorption and Scattering of the α-rays," in *Philosophical Magazine,* 6th ser., **23** (1912), 901; "The Reflexion of the X-Rays," *ibid.,* **26** (1913), 210, written with H. G. J. Moseley; "The Theory of X-Ray Reflexion," *ibid.,* **27** (1914), 315; "The Theory of X-Ray Reflexion," *ibid.,* 675; "The Collisions of α-Particles with Hydrogen Nuclei," *ibid.,* **41** (1921), 486; "On the Reflexion of X-Rays From Imperfect Crystals," *ibid.,* **43** (1922), 800; "On the Partition of Energy," *ibid.,* **44** (1922), 450, written with R. H. Fowler; "On the Partition of Energy, Part II: Statistical Principles and Thermodynamics," *ibid.,* 823, written with R. H. Fowler; "A Quantum Theory of Optical Dispersion," in *Proceedings of the National Academy of Sciences,* 1st ser., **9** (1923), 25–30; "Fluctuations in an Assembly in Statistical Equilibrium," in *Proceedings of the Cambridge Philosophical Society,* **21** (1923), 4, written with R. H. Fowler; "The Optical Constants of Matter," in *Transactions of the Cambridge Philosophical Society,* **23** (1924), 137–167; "The Intensity of Reflexion of X-Rays by Crystals," in *Philosophical Magazine,* 7th ser., **1** (1926), 897, written with W. L. Bragg and R. W. James; "The Constants of the Magnetic Dispersion of Light," in *Proceedings of the Royal Society,* **114A** (1927), 474, written with W. H. Watson; "The Electron as a Vector Wave," *ibid.,* **116A** (1927), 227; "Free Motion in the Wave Mechanics," *ibid.,* **117A** (1927), 258; "The Wave Equations of the Electron," *ibid.,* **118A** (1928), 654; "The Electromagnetic Equations in the Quantum Theory," in *Nature,* **123** (1929), 203; "Examples of the Uncertainty Principle," in *Proceedings of the Royal Society,* **130A** (1931), 632; "The Diamagnetism of the Free Electron," in *Proceedings of the Cambridge Philosophical Society,* **27** (1931), 1; "Thermodynamics and the Lowest Temperatures," in *Journal of the Institute of Electrical Engineers,* **87** (1940), 528, the thirty-first Kelvin Lecture; "A Discussion on Units and Standards," in *Proceedings of the Royal Society,* **186A** (1946), 149; "Atomic Energy," in *Science Progress,* **135** (1946), 449; "Electron Inertia and Terrestrial Magnetism," in *Proceedings of the Royal Society,* **222A** (1954), 471; "Energy in the Future," in *Eugenics Review,* **46** (1955), 237; "Forecasting the Future," in *New Zealand Science Review,* **14** (1956), 6; "The Value of Unhappiness," in *Eugenics Review,* **49** (1957), 77; "Population Problems," in *Bulletin of the Atomic Scientists,* **14** (1958), 322; "Can Man Control His Numbers?" in *Perspectives in Biology and Medicine* (1960), 252; "The Future Numbers of Mankind," in *Annales Nestle, Humanity and Subsistence Symposium in Vevey* (1960).

II. Secondary Literature. A biographical sketch written by Sir George Paget Thomson appears in *Biographical Memoirs of Fellows of the Royal Society,* **9** (1963), 69–85.

See also T. S. Kuhn, J. L. Heilbron, P. Forman, and L. Allen, *Sources for History of Quantum Physics* (Philadelphia, 1960), pp. 30 f. There is an obituary notice by G. B. B. M. Sutherland in *Nature,* **198** (1963), 18.

R. B. Lindsay

DARWIN, GEORGE HOWARD (*b.* Down House, Kent, England, 9 July 1845; *d.* Cambridge, England, 7 December 1912)

Darwin was the fifth child of Charles Robert Darwin and Emma Wedgwood. His greatgrandfather was Erasmus Darwin; his middle name commemorates Erasmus Darwin's first wife, Mary Howard. The Darwin family was comfortably settled in

Kent, where George Howard Darwin began his education at the private school of the Reverend Charles Pritchard (who was afterward Savillian professor of astronomy at Oxford). Darwin went on to attend Trinity College, Cambridge, from which he graduated second wrangler and Smith's prizeman in 1868. Darwin did not immediately embrace a scientific career, but rather studied law for six years and was admitted to the bar in 1874, although he never practiced that profession.

Darwin was elected fellow of Trinity College in October 1868, but did not return there for good until October 1873. There, in 1875, he began the series of mathematical papers that were eventually to form the four large volumes of his *Scientific Papers.* In 1879 he was elected fellow of the Royal Society and in 1883 he was elected Plumian professor of astronomy and experimental philosophy at Cambridge, to succeed James Challis.

Darwin held the Plumian professorship for the rest of his life. The chair bore no necessary connection with the observatory, and practical astronomy formed no part of his duties. His lectures on theoretical astronomy were poorly attended, but among his students were Ernest W. Brown and Sir James Jeans. During this tenure, Darwin received several honors and distinctions, including, in 1905, a knighthood (knight commander of the Bath) through the offices of his college friend Arthur Balfour. In 1912 he served as president of the International Congress of Mathematicians at Cambridge. This was his last public function; he died of cancer shortly thereafter, and was buried in Trumpington Cemetery, near Cambridge. He was survived by his widow, the former Maud Du Puy of Philadelphia, whom he had married in 1884, and four children, of whom the eldest, Charles Galton Darwin, was also a scientist.

Darwin's paper "On the Influence of Geological Changes on the Earth's Axis of Rotation," published in 1876, marked the beginning of his investigations of essentially geophysical problems. This work was directly inspired by Lord Kelvin, whose great interest in the young Darwin may be said to have been the chief influence in his decision to make science his career. Another group of papers, dated from 1879 to 1880, are concerned with the tides in viscous spheroids, and still show the influence of both Kelvin and Laplace, although their scope is more general. In his paper of this series, "On the Precession of a Viscous Spheroid and on the Remote History of the Earth" (1879), Darwin proposed the "resonance theory" of the origin of the moon, according to which the moon might have originated from the fission of a parent earth as the result of an instability produced by resonant solar tides. His monumental paper "On the Secular Changes in the Elements of the Orbit of a Satellite Revolving About a Tidally Distorted Planet" was published in 1880.

Following his accession to the Plumian chair Darwin delved even more deeply into the problems of the origin and evolution of the solar system, making numerous investigations of the figures of equilibrium of rotating masses of fluid and, later, making extensive studies of periodic orbits in the restricted problem of three bodies, carried out with special reference to cases obtaining for the particular values of the mass ratio of the two finite bodies of 1:10 and 1:1048 (the latter approximating the mass ratio of Jupiter to that of the sun).

Darwin's most significant contribution to the history of science lies in his pioneering work in the application of detailed dynamical analysis to cosmological and geological problems. That many of his conclusions are now out of date should in no way diminish the historical interest of his experiments, nor the important service that he rendered cosmogony by the example he gave of putting various hypotheses to the test of actual calculations. Darwin's method remains a milestone in the development of cosmogony, and subsequent investigators have favored it over the merely qualitative arguments prevalent until that time.

That Darwin's scientific work is homogeneous is apparent from glancing at the titles of the more than eighty papers collected in the four volumes of his *Scientific Works.* After publishing some short notes on a variety of subjects, he devoted himself steadfastly to the problems of mathematical cosmogony, departing from them only to undertake problems of pressing practical concern (as, for example, in his work on oceanic tides). The greatest part of his work is devoted to the explanation of the various aspects of the history of the double stars, the planetary system, and satellite systems. His papers on viscous spheroids (including those on tidal friction), on rotating homogeneous masses of fluids, and even those on periodic orbits are means to this end.

Darwin's work is further marked by the virtually complete absence of investigations undertaken out of sheer mathematical interest, rather than in the elucidation of some specific problem in physics. Indeed, he was an applied mathematician of the school of Kelvin or Stokes and was content to study physical phenomena by the mathematical methods most convenient to the purpose, regardless of their novelty or elegance. Should the problem fail to yield to analysis, Darwin resorted to computation, never hesitating to embark upon onerous and painstaking numerical work (such as marks his investigations of the stability of pear-shaped figures of equilibrium or of periodic orbits in the restricted problem of three bodies). Indeed, it would seem that he actually preferred quantitative rather than qualitative results, although he seldom carried his calculations beyond pragmatic limits. That this approach was sometimes too blunt is illustrated by Darwin's 1902 investigation of the stability of a rotating pear-shaped figure, which he found to be stable; shortly after publication of Darwin's results, Aleksandr Liapunov announced his proof of the instability of the pear-shaped figure, and several years later Darwin's pupil Jeans showed that Liapunov was indeed correct.

In his speech to the Fifth International Congress of Mathematicians at Cambridge in 1912, Darwin summed up his method, speaking of his work on the problem of three bodies and comparing his technique to that of Poincaré, to whom he had often paid tribute:

> My own work . . . cannot be said to involve any such skill at all, unless you describe as skill the procedure of a housebreaker who blows in a safe door with dynamite instead of picking the lock. It is thus by brutal force that this tantalising problem has been compelled to give up a few of its secrets; and, great as has been the labour involved, I think it has been worth while. . . . To put at their lowest the claims of this clumsy method, which may almost excite the derision of the pure mathematician, it has served to throw light on the celebrated generalisations of Hill and Poincaré.
>
> I appeal, then, for mercy to the applied mathematician, and would ask you to consider in a kindly spirit the difficulties under which he labours. If our methods are often wanting in elegance and do but little to satisfy that aesthetic sense of which I spoke before, yet they constitute honest attempts to unravel the secrets of the universe in which we live.

BIBLIOGRAPHY

I. Original Works. Darwin's books are *The Tides and Kindred Phenomena in the Solar System* (London, 1898), based on a series of popular lectures delivered in Boston in 1897, and *Scientific Papers* (London, 1907–1916). Among his most important articles are "On the Influence of Geological Changes on the Earth's Axis of Rotation," in *Philosophical Transactions of the Royal Society*, **167A** (1876) 271–312: "On the Precession of a Viscous Spheroid and on the Remote History of the Earth," *ibid.*, **170A** (1879), 447–538; "On the Secular Changes in the Elements of the Orbit of a Satellite Revolving About a Tidally Distorted Planet," *ibid.*, **171A** (1880), 713–891; and "On a Pear-Shaped Figure of Equilibrium," *ibid.*, **200A** (1902), 251–314. Darwin's presidential address presenting the medal to Poincaré is in *Monthly Notices of the Royal Astronomical Society*, **60** (1900), 406–415.

II. Secondary Literature. A memoir of Darwin's life by his brother, Sir Francis Darwin, is affixed to vol. V of his *Scientific Papers* (London, 1916).

Obituaries include those by F. J. M. Stratton in *Monthly Notices of the Royal Astronomical Society*, **73** (1913), 204–210; and S. S. Hough, in *Proceedings of the Royal Society*, **89A** (1914), i–xiii.

ZDENĚK KOPAL

DASYPODIUS, CUNRADUS (*b.* Frauenfeld, Thurgau, Switzerland, *ca.* 1530; *d.* Strasbourg, France, 26 April 1600)

Cunradus was the son of the Swiss humanist Petrus Dasypodius; his family name was Rauchfuss (rough-foot, hare). He studied in Strasbourg at the famous academy of Johannes Sturm and became professor there in 1558.

The greater part of Dasypodius' work was destined to be schoolbooks for his students: his editions of Euclid, his *Volumen primum* and *Volumen secundum*, and his *Protheoria* with the *Institutionum mathematicarum erotemata* (in the form of questions and answers) demonstrate his pedagogical interests. These books show that in Strasbourg, under the influence of Sturm, mathematics was studied far more extensively than in many of the universities of the time. Worthy of special mention is his *Analyseis geometricae* (1566). This book, written with his teacher Christian Herlinus, contains the proofs of the first six books of Euclid's *Elements* analyzed as their syllogisms; it was intended to facilitate the study of mathematics for students trained in dialectics.

Confident that the mathematics of his time was far below the Greek level, Dasypodius desired, as did many of his contemporaries (e.g., Commandino and Ramus), publication of all Greek mathematical works. Since he himself owned several manuscripts, he was able to make a beginning in that direction. He edited and translated works of Euclid (partly with and partly without proofs), some fragments of Hero, and (in his *Sphaericae doctrinae propositiones*) the propositions of the works of Theodosius of Bythinia, Autolycus of Pitane, and Barlaamo. His textbooks, too, show his knowledge of Greek mathematics.

Dasypodius' fame is based especially on his construction of an ingenious and accurate astronomical clock in the cathedral of Strasbourg, installed between 1571 and 1574. From his description of this clock it is clear that Dasypodius was influenced by Hero in many details.

BIBLIOGRAPHY

I. ORIGINAL WORKS. See J. G. L. Blumhoff, *Vom alten Mathematiker Dasypodius* (Göttingen, 1796). The following is a short-title bibliography, with location of copies and some additions to Blumhoff (L = Leiden, Univ.; B = Basel, Univ.; P = Paris, Bibl. Nat.). Place of publication is Strasbourg, unless stated otherwise. Dasypodius edited, with a Latin translation, the following works of Euclid: *Catoptrica* (1557, B); *Elementorum primum* (1564, B); *Elementorum II* (1564, B); *Propositiones reliquorum librorum* (1564, B); *Elementorum primum* and *Heronis vocabula geometrica* (1570, B; repr. 1571, B); *Propositiones Elementorum 15, Opticorum* (1570, B); and *Omnium librorum propositiones* (1571, B). He was also responsible for editions of Caspar Peucer, *Hypotyposes orbium coelestium* (1568, L); *Sphaericae doctrinae propositiones* (1572, P); and *Isaaci Monachi scholia in Euclid* (1579, L). With Christian Herlinus he published *Analyseis geometricae sex librorum Euclidis* (1566, L). He also wrote *Volumen primum* (1567, B), partly repr. in an ed. of M. Psellus, *Compendium mathematicum, aliaque tractatus* (Leiden, 1647); *Volumen II. Mathematicum* (1570, L); *Lexicon* (1573, L); *Scholia in libros apotelesmaticos Cl. Ptolemaei* (Basel, 1578, L); *Brevis doctrina de cometis* (1578, P), also a German ed.; *Oratio de disciplinis mathematicis* and *Heron* and *Lexicon* (1579, P); *Heron mechanicus* and *Horologii astronomici descriptio* (1580, L); *Wahrhafftige Auslegung und Beschreybung des astronomischen Uhrwercks zu Straszburg* (1580, B); *Protheoria mathematica* (1593, B); *Institutionum mathematicarum erotemata* (1593, B); and *Erotematum appendix* (1596, B).

II. SECONDARY LITERATURE. On Dasypodius or his work, see A. G. Kästner, *Geschichte der Mathematik*, I (Göttingen, 1796), 332–345; Wilhelm Schmidt, "Heron von Alexandria, Konrad Dasypodius und die Strassburger astronomische Münsteruhr," in *Abhandlungen zur Geschichte der Mathematik*, **8** (1898), 175–194; and E. Zinner, *Entstehung und Ausbreitung der Coppernicanischen Lehre* (Erlangen, 1943), p. 273.

J. J. VERDONK

DAVENPORT, HAROLD (*b.* Huncoat, Lancashire, England, 30 October 1907; *d.* Cambridge, England, 9 June 1969)

Davenport was the only son of Percy Davenport, first office clerk and later company secretary of Perseverance Mill, and of Nancy Barnes, the mill owner's daughter. From Accrington Grammar School he won a scholarship in 1924 to Manchester University, from which he graduated with first-class honors in 1927, at the age of nineteen. Davenport proceeded to Cambridge University with a scholarship to Trinity College, where he graduated with a B.A. in mathematics in 1929, again with the highest honors in each part of the final examination. He wrote his Ph.D. dissertation under J. E. Littlewood. In 1931 he was Rayleigh prizeman, and in 1932 he became a research fellow at Trinity College.

In 1944, while he was professor of mathematics at the University College of North Wales, Bangor, Davenport married a colleague in modern languages, Anne Lofthouse; they had two sons. In 1938 Davenport received the Cambridge Sc.D., in 1940 he was elected a fellow of the Royal Society, and in 1941 he won the Adams Prize of Cambridge University. He won the senior Berwick Prize of the London Mathematical Society in 1954, and from 1957 to 1959 he was president of that society. He was elected an ordinary member of the Royal Society of Sciences in Uppsala in 1964, and in 1967 he was Sylvester medalist of the Royal Society. In 1968 he received an honorary degree from the University of Nottingham.

When Davenport embarked on research in mathematics under the supervision of Littlewood, he was not yet committed to any one branch of the subject. Among the problems from analysis and number theory that Littlewood proposed to him, however, was a question about the distribution of quadratic residues that attracted him; virtually all his subsequent work was devoted to the theory of numbers. The topic of Davenport's first piece of research led him directly to the study of character sums and exponential sums, which were then (and still are) central to many of the most profound inquiries in higher arithmetic, and influenced many of his own later researches.

This work brought Davenport to the attention of Louis J. Mordell and of Helmut Hasse; the latter invited him to Marburg for a long visit during 1931. Davenport learned fluent German during this time, and he and Hasse wrote an important paper that still is influential; also, it might be said that Hasse was led by their association to his proof of the Riemann hypothesis for elliptic curves. The natural culmination of this strand of ideas—Weil's proof in 1948 of the Riemann hypothesis for algebraic curves in general by deep methods from algebraic geometry—was at this time far in the future, and Davenport was probably ready for a change of direction.

During his travels in Germany, Davenport met H. Heilbronn, Edmund Landau's last assistant in Göttingen; the two soon became friends and embarked on several new lines of research, including one in the general area of Waring's problem via the celebrated circle method of Hardy, Littlewood, and Ramanujan. Their association deepened when Heilbronn joined Davenport at Cambridge in 1933; they

DAVENPORT

wrote many joint papers over the years, the last appearing in 1971.

Working with Heilbronn or alone, Davenport made several novel adaptations of the circle method and also developed some important technical refinements that led to improved results for Waring's problem itself. While much of this work retains interest, its main importance derives from the fact that it prepared Davenport for the greatest mathematical achievements of his life: the adaptation, starting in 1956, of the circle method (which was invented to deal with additive problems) to nonadditive problems concerning values taken by quadratic and cubic forms in many variables. A critical feature of this adaptation was the use of ideas and results from the geometry of numbers, a branch of number theory that had originated with Hermann Minkowski.

In 1937, at the termination of his Cambridge fellowship, Davenport was appointed by Mordell to an assistant lectureship at the University of Manchester and, under his influence, took up the study of the geometry of numbers. This subject dominated his mathematical activities until 1956, by which time he had become a dominant figure in number theory, not only in the United Kingdom but also in most of the world. In 1941 Davenport, by then a fellow of the Royal Society, moved to a full professorship at the University College of North Wales at Bangor. In 1945 he was appointed Astor Professor of Mathematics at University College, London. In 1950 he became head of the department.

It was during the period 1945 to 1958 that Davenport achieved his full stature. His mathematical prose had been distinguished from the beginning by unusual grace and lucidity, and he now brought these gifts to the classroom and to the supervision of graduate students. Davenport was a superb teacher and an inspiring director of research, and his number theory seminar at University College became a mecca for aspiring number theoreticians from all over the world. It was here that Freeman Dyson conceived his remarkable proof of Minkowski's conjecture for the product of four nonhomogeneous linear forms, that C. A. Rogers developed his deep researches in the theory of packing space, that K. F. Roth was led to his theorem on rational approximations to algebraic numbers, and that D. A. Burgess reported on his dramatic improvement of Ivan M. Vinogradov's estimate of the least quadratic nonresidue. Many other fine pieces of mathematics, not least many of Davenport's own results, first saw the light of day here.

Davenport had an unusually well-organized mind, and was ever ready to make available to his students and associates the wisdom he had gleaned from his mathematical experiences. Like Littlewood he was punctilious about having research problems available for his students, though he was also quick to encourage promising initiatives of their own. Davenport was always eager to discuss mathematics and more than willing to help fellow mathematicians with difficulties. No query ever went unanswered, and he conducted a voluminous correspondence.

Davenport's research activity never flagged, and therefore his expository writing was not on the scale that his literary powers warranted, although he did produce *The Higher Arithmetic* (1954), a small, elegant book that has gone through several editions.

In 1958 Davenport returned to Cambridge as Rouse Ball Professor. He was at the height of his powers, a worthy successor of Hardy, Littlewood, and Mordell, and the unquestioned leader of the British school of number theory. His research went from strength to strength. The original work on forms in many variables had overlapped in a number of ways with that of D. J. Lewis and B. J. Birch, and he embarked on a vigorous collaboration with both these mathematicians. His association with Lewis was especially close and endured for the rest of his life. He was a frequent visitor to Lewis at Ann Arbor; and his two other books, *Analytic Methods for Diophantine Equations and Diophantine Inequalities* (1962) and *Multiplicative Number Theory* (1967), grew out of graduate courses he presented there.

Davenport's activities as research director continued unabated. Among his students were A. Baker, J. H. Conway, P. D. T. A. Elliott, M. N. Huxley, and H. L. Montgomery. The talented young Enrico Bombieri came to his notice, and Davenport brought him to Cambridge for the first of several fruitful visits. Bombieri reawakened Davenport's interest in prime number theory, and they wrote several important joint papers. Baker and Bombieri both won Fields medals in later years. In this last period Davenport also collaborated with A. Schinzel of the Polish Academy of Sciences on properties of polynomials and with W. Schmidt of the University of Colorado on Diophantine approximation. Many achievements and honors seemed still ahead of him when lung cancer set in with awful suddenness and brought his life to an untimely end.

Davenport was shy and reserved, and his outlook on life was at all times conservative. Despite this his organizational gifts, and his willingness to help all who came to him for advice and to render service to the institutions and learned societies with which he was associated, made him a natural academic leader and one of the most influential mathematicians of his time.

BIBLIOGRAPHY

I. ORIGINAL WORKS. A bibliography of Davenport's works is in *Acta arithmetica*, **18** (1971), 19–28. His writings were brought together as *Collected Works of Harold Davenport*, B. J. Birch, H. Halberstam, and C. A. Rogers, eds., 4 vols. (New York, 1977). His writings include "Die Nullstellen der Kongruenzzetafunktionen in gewissen zyklischen Fällen," in *Jahrbuch für Mathematik*, **172** (1934), 171ff., written with Helmut Hasse; *The Higher Arithmetic* (London, 1954; 5th ed., Cambridge and New York, 1982); *Analytic Methods for Diophantine Equations and Diophantine Inequalities* (Ann Arbor, 1962); and *Multiplicative Number Theory* (Chicago, 1967), rev. ed., Hugh L. Montgomery, ed. (New York, 1980).

II. SECONDARY LITERATURE. Articles on Davenport and his work are L. J. Mordell, "Harold Davenport" and "Some Aspects of Davenport's Work," in *Acta arithmetica*, **18** (1971), 1–4 and 5–11; C. A. Rogers, "A Brief Survey of the Work of Harold Davenport," *ibid.*, 13–17; and C. A. Rogers, B. J. Birch, H. Halberstam, and D. A. Burgess, "Harold Davenport," in *Biographical Memoirs of Fellows of the Royal Society*, **17** (1971), 159–192.

H. HALBERSTAM

DAVIDOV, AUGUST YULEVICH (*b.* Libav, Russia, 15 December 1823; *d.* Moscow, Russia, 22 December 1885)

Davidov, the son of a physician, enrolled in 1841 at Moscow University. He graduated in 1845, and was retained at the university in order to prepare for a teaching career. In 1848 he defended his dissertation, *The Theory of Equilibrium of Bodies Immersed in a Liquid,* and received the master of mathematical sciences degree. Davidov's dissertation was devoted to the exceptionally pressing problem of the equilibrium of floating bodies.

Although Euler, Poisson, and Dupin had worked extensively on the problem they had far from exhausted it, and new, major results were obtained by Davidov. He was the first to give a general analytic method for determining the position of equilibrium of a floating body, applied his method to the determination of positions of equilibrium of bodies, explained the analytical theory by geometric constructions, and investigated the stability of equilibrium of floating bodies.

In 1850 Davidov began teaching at Moscow University, and in 1851 he successfully defended his doctoral dissertation, *The Theory of Capillary Phenomena.* Shortly thereafter he was appointed a professor at Moscow University, where he worked until the end of his life. Both of his dissertations were awarded the Demidovskoy prize by the Petersburg Academy of Sciences.

Of the other valuable mathematics studies done by Davidov mention should be made of those on equations with partial derivatives, elliptical functions, and the application of the theory of probability to statistics. He also compiled a number of excellent texts for secondary schools. Of these, the geometry and algebra textbooks enjoyed special success and were republished many times. Through the next half century the geometry text underwent thirty-nine editions and the algebra text twenty-four.

Davidov conducted much scientific organizational work. For twelve years he was head of the physics and mathematics faculty; for thirty-five years he taught various courses in mathematics and mechanics at the university and prepared two generations of scientific workers and teachers. Along with N.D. Brashman, Davidov was a founder of the Moscow Mathematical Society and was its first president (1866–1885).

BIBLIOGRAPHY

Davidov's works, all in Russian, are *The Theory of Equilibrium of Bodies Immersed in a Liquid* (Moscow, 1848); *The Theory of Capillary Phenomena* (Moscow, 1848); *Elementary Geometry* (Moscow, 1864); *Beginning Algebra* (Moscow, 1866); *Geometry for District Schools* (Moscow, 1873).

See also "Reminiscences of A. Y. Davidov," in *News of the Society of Lovers of Natural Science, Anthropology, and Ethnography,* **51** (1887); and *Reminiscences of A. Y. Davidov. A Speech and Account, Read at the Meeting of Moscow University on 12 January 1886* (Moscow, 1886).

A. T. GRIGORIAN

DEBEAUNE (also known as **Beaune), FLORIMOND** (*b.* Blois, France, 7 October 1601; *d.* Blois, 18 August 1652)

Truly representative of a time of intense communication among intellectuals, Debeaune enjoyed great fame although he himself never published anything.

His renown was due entirely to Descartes. The *Notes brèves* that Debeaune wrote on the *Géométrie* were translated and added during his lifetime to the first Latin edition, published by Schooten in 1649. The second Latin edition (1659–1661) also contained two short papers on algebra, edited by Erasmus Bartholin, that are Debeaune's only posthumous publication. The letters published by Clerselier between 1657 and 1667 revealed to a wider public the esteem in which Descartes held his disciple from Blois.

Undoubtedly this was the reason why, in 1682, a chronicler concerned with celebrities of his province wrote a paper on Debeaune, drawing his information from sources close to the family while this was still possible. At the end of the nineteenth century a scholar from Blois confirmed the information by locating various documents in archives, and the great critical edition of Descartes's *Oeuvres* once again brought attention to Debeaune. Paul Tannery had the good fortune to discover a great many handwritten letters in Vienne, which enabled him to gain a great deal of scientific clarity.

On the basis of his interpretation of the signature of these letters, Tannery committed an error in insisting on the spelling "Debeaune," by which he is most frequently cited. Florimond's father, also named Florimond, was undoubtedly the natural son of Jean II de Beaune, brother of the archbishop Renaud de Beaune; but he was legitimized and his titles of nobility assured to his descendants.

A few accurate dates can be furnished for Debeaune. He was baptized on 7 October 1601. He married his first wife, Philiberte Anne Pelluis, on 21 December 1621. She died in August 1622, and he remarried on 15 December 1623. His second wife was Marguerite du Lot, who bore him three sons and one daughter. His burial certificate, designating him as Seigneur de Goulioust, is dated 18 August 1652.

Like Descartes, Debeaune at first did military service, but following a mysterious accident he had to lead a less strenuous life. Taking advantage of his law studies, he bought the office of counselor to the court of justice in Blois. The many years that he divided between this famous city on the banks of the Loire and his nearby country estate, excelling in both jurisprudence and mathematical research, bring Fermat to mind. However, Fermat does not appear on the list of correspondents that the chronicler of 1682 saw among the family papers, a list of which only a small part has been preserved.

Debeaune left his provincial retreat only for business trips to Paris. However, he had many visitors. The first part of Monconis' diary mentions observatory instruments made by him. An inventory made after Debeaune's death confirmed statements in parts of letters that have been preserved: he had built for his own use a shop for grinding lenses. He also had a magnificent library, worthy of a humanist of the preceding century.

Afflicted with various and painful infirmities, particularly gout, Debeaune resigned as counselor around 1648 and withdrew to a town house, the upper floor of which faced due south. There he had—at least for a time—an observatory at his disposal. However, his failing eyesight deteriorated rapidly, and he died shortly after having a foot amputated.

When he was very ill, Debeaune was visited by Erasmus Bartholin, whom he entrusted with arranging for the publication of several of his manuscripts. Despite the intervention of Schooten and Huygens in 1656, Bartholin fulfilled his obligations only partially. Of the manuscripts with which he was entrusted, only "La doctrine de l'angle solide construit sous trois angles plans" was discovered, in 1963. The "Méchaniques" mentioned by Mersenne, and the "Dioptrique" that Schooten knew in 1646 are still missing and may be lost.

This situation is unfortunate, for it deprives us of elements valuable for judging the origin of purely mathematical problems that Debeaune formulated in 1638 and that Paul Tannery analyzed fully according to the correspondence he discovered. According to Beaugrand, the first of these problems—which in the present state of textual study appears to concern itself only with the determination of the tangent to an analytically defined curve—interested Debeaune "in a design touching on dioptrics." As to the second of these problems, the one that has been particularly identified with Debeaune[1] and that ushered in what was called at the end of the seventeenth century the "inverse of tangents"—i.e., the determination of a curve from a property of its tangent—Debeaune told Mersenne on 5 March 1639 that he sought a solution with only one precise aim: to prove that the isochronism of string vibrations and of pendulum oscillations was independent of the amplitude. This statement, which is not easily justified except in the language of differential and integral calculus, was fifty years ahead of scientific developments and—by itself—reveals Debeaune's singular ability to translate physical questions into the abstract language of mathematical analysis, despite the inadequacies of the operative means of his time.

It is not surprising that Debeaune, aware of these inadequacies, eagerly seized upon anything that could possibly be of help in overcoming them. As he had once adopted and assimilated Herigone's algebra (the *Cursus mathematicus,* 1635–1637), he welcomed Descartes's *Géométrie;* and Descartes was right in believing that none of his contemporaries had better understood it. Debeaune's *Notes brèves* clarify and conveniently illustrate some of the difficult passages of the *Géométrie* and played a role in the belated spread of Cartesian mathematics.

As Paul Tannery has shown, Descartes's method for tangents misled Debeaune, at least initially. This purely algebraic method, which consists of determining the subnormal by writing that the equation obtained as a result of an elimination is to have two equal roots, is not susceptible of supporting a process of inversion. But if Debeaune, victim of a misconception that nevertheless bears the stamp of his mathematical genius, could give *his* problem (the first integration problem of a first-order differential equation) only an incorrect solution, he was nevertheless the only one to comprehend the remarkable solution to which it had led Descartes, a solution that anticipated the use of series. This was a remarkable solution that Leibniz, fifty years later, failed to recognize when he replaced it with the aid of new algorithms and the logarithmic function.

Undoubtedly the nature of the various problems posed by Debeaune becomes clearer when translated into the language of Leibnizian calculus, for Debeaune's language, based on the form of the triangle constructed on the ordinate and the subnormal, is without immediacy. Nevertheless, we should remember the man who dared to pose the inversion problem of tangents at a time when mathematicians had difficulty understanding the direct problem.

The example of Debeaune reminds us that mathematics is sustained more by the perception of profound logical structures than by the invention and use of languages that find acceptance in the structures only with time. As Debeaune wrote to Mersenne (5 March 1639), "I do not think that one could acquire any solid knowledge of nature in physics without geometry, and the best of geometry consists of analysis, of such kind that without the latter it is quite imperfect."[2]

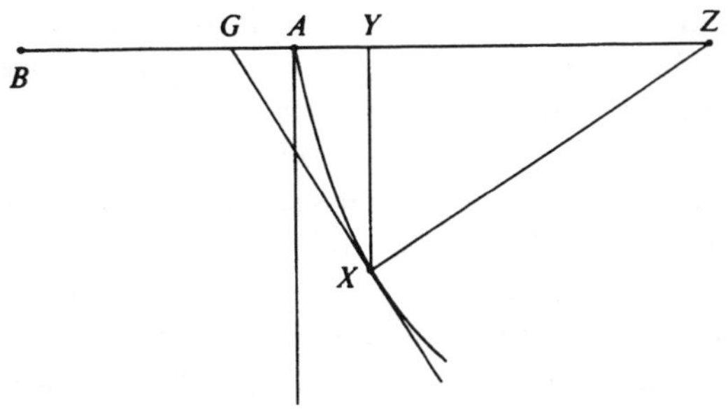

DEBEAUNE'S CURVE

NOTES

1. Find the curve such that ZY is to YX as a given AB is to the difference between YX and AY (letter of 16 October 1638). Descartes presented a solution in letters to Mersenne and Debeaune of 20 February 1639. There is a transformation of the statement by Descartes in a letter to an unknown person dated June 1645. This statement was followed up by Leibniz and Johann I Bernoulli, who formulated it by means of

$$\frac{dy}{dx} = \frac{a}{y - x}.$$

In a letter to Debeaune on 30 April 1639, Descartes congratulates himself for having taken the time to consider the proposed curve lines, stating that he has learned a great deal thereby.

2. "Je ne pense pas qu'on puisse acquérir aulcune cognoissance solide de la nature en physique sans la géometrie, et le plus excellent de la géométrie consiste en l'analyse, en sorte que sans cela elle est fort imparfaicte."

BIBLIOGRAPHY

I. ORIGINAL WORKS. The *Notes brèves* appeared in *Geometria a Renato Descartes anno 1637 edita, nunc autem cum notis Florimundi de Beaune* (Leiden, 1649) and in its 2nd ed., the title of which concludes *Florimundi de Beaune duo tractatus posthumi alter de natura et constitutione, alter de limitibus aequationum, ab Erasmio Bartholino edita* (Amsterdam, 1659–1661). "Notes briefves sur la méthode algébraique de Mr D. C.," the original French text, based on MSS in London and Paris, Charles Adam and G. Milhaud, eds., *Descartes—Correspondance,* III (Paris, 1941), pp. 353–401. "La doctrine de l'angle solide construit sous trois angles plans," handwritten, is at the Secretariat of the Academy of Sciences, Paris. Some of Debeaune's correspondence may be found in *Oeuvres de Descartes,* Charles Adam and Paul Tannery, eds., II and V; and in *Correspondance de Mersenne,* Centre National de la Recherche Scientifique, ed., VIII.

II. SECONDARY LITERATURE. On Debeaune or his work, see Charles Adam and G. Milhaud, eds., *Descartes—Correspondance,* I (Paris, 1931), 436–438; Jean Bernier, *Histoire de Blois* (Paris, 1682), pp. 563–568; Pierre Costabel, "Le traité de l'angle solide de Florimond de Beaune," in *Actes du XIe Congrès international d'histoire des sciences,* III (Warsaw, 1965–1968) pp. 189–194; Paul Tannery, "Pour l'histoire du problème inverse des tangentes," in *Verhandlungen der III Internationalen Mathematiker-Kongresses* (Leipzig, 1904), repub., with additions, in Tannery's *Mémoires scientifiques,* VI (Paris, 1926); and Adrien Thibaut, "Florimond de Beaune," in *Bulletin de la Société des sciences et lettres du Loir et Cher,* **4,** no. 6 (Mar. 1896), 13–29.

PIERRE COSTABEL

DECHALES, CLAUDE FRANÇOIS MILLIET (*b.* Chambéry, France, 1621; *d.* Turin, Italy, 28 March 1678)

Not much is known of Dechales's personal life. For some time he was a Jesuit missionary in Turkey. He was well liked in Paris, where for four years he read public mathematics lectures at the Collège de Clermont. After teaching at Lyons and Chambéry, he moved to Marseilles, where he taught the arts of navigation and military engineering and the practical applications of mathematics to science. From Marseilles he went to Turin, where he was appointed professor of mathematics at the university. He died there at the age of fifty-seven.

Although not a first-rate mathematician, Dechales was rather skillful in exposition; Hutton has observed that "his talent rather lay in explaining those sciences [mathematics and mechanics] with ease and accuracy . . . that he made the best use of the production of other men, and that he drew the several parts of the mathematical sciences together with great judgment and perspicuity."

Dechales is best remembered for his *Cursus seu mundus mathematicus,* a complete course of mathematics, including many related subjects that in his day were held to belong to the exact sciences. The first volume opens with a description of mathematical books arranged chronologically that, as De Morgan remarks, is well done and indicates that Dechales had actually read them. This is followed by his edition of Euclid's *Elements* (bks. I–VI, XI, and XII). Arithmetic computation, algebra, spherical trigonometry, and conic sections are of course included. Of the algebraic material, Hutton observes that it is "of a very old-fashioned sort, considering the time when it was written." The algebra of Dechales is imbued with the spirit of Diophantus; as Moritz Cantor points out, Dechales rarely mentions the work of Mydorge, Desargues, Pascal, Fermat, Descartes, or Wallis. Among other subjects included in the *Cursus* are practical geometry, mechanics, statics, geography, magnetism, civil architecture, military architecture, optics, catoptrics, perspective, dioptrics, hydrostatics, hydraulic machinery, navigation, pyrotechnics, gnomonics, astronomy, astrology, meteoritics, the calendar, and music, as well as a section entitled "A Refutation of the Cartesian Hypothesis." Indeed, in his history of mathematics, Cantor gives a detailed description of the *Cursus* both because it was a popular and widely used textbook and because it reflected the totality of mathematical knowledge as possessed by dilettantes or amateur mathematicians of the time who were fairly competent interpreters or expounders of the subject. Thus, while according Dechales due credit for his efforts, Cantor is nevertheless critical of much of the mathematical content of his work, deploring Dechales's failure to make full use of such available contemporary source materials as the first-hand works of mathematicians, their correspondence, and so on.

Dechales's separate edition of Euclid, long a favorite in France and elsewhere on the Continent, never became popular in England.

BIBLIOGRAPHY

I. Original Works. Dechales's works are *Cursus seu mundus mathematicus,* 3 vols. (Lyons, 1674), also ed. by Amati Varcin, 4 vols. (Lyons, 1690); *L'art de fortifier, de défendre et d'attaquer les places, suivant les méthodes françoises, hollandoises, italiennes & espagnoles* (Paris, 1677); *L'art de naviger demontré par principes & confirmé par plusieurs observations tirées de l'expérience* (Paris, 1677); and *Les principes généraux de la géographie* (Paris, 1677). His edition of Euclid, *Les élémens d'Euclide, expliquez d'une manière nouvelle & très facile. Avec l'usage de chaque proposition pour toutes les parties des mathématiques* (Lausanne, 1678, 1683), appeared in revised editions by Ozanam (Paris, 1730) and Audierne (Paris, 1753) and in English translation by Reeve Williams (London, 1685).

II. Secondary Literature. On Dechales or his work, see Moritz Cantor, *Vorlesungen über die Geschichte der Mathematik,* III (Leipzig, 1913), 4–6, 15–19; Augustus De Morgan, *Arithmetical Books From the Invention of Printing to the Present Time* (London, 1847), pp. xv, 53; Charles Hutton, "History of Algebra," in *Tracts on Mathematical Philosophical Subjects,* II (London, 1812), tract no. 33, p. 301; and *Philosophical and Mathematical Dictionary,* I (London, 1815), 395–396; and *The Penny Cyclopaedia of the Society for the Diffusion of Useful Knowledge,* VIII (London, 1837), 343.

William Schaaf

DEDEKIND, (JULIUS WILHELM) RICHARD (*b.* Brunswick, Germany, 6 October 1831; *d.* Brunswick, 12 February 1916)

Dedekind's ancestors (particularly on his mother's side) had distinguished themselves in services to Hannover and Brunswick. His father, Julius Levin Ulrich Dedekind, the son of a physician and chemist, was a graduate jurist, professor, and corporation lawyer at the Collegium Carolinum in Brunswick. His mother, Caroline Marie Henriette Emperius, was the daughter of a professor at the Carolinum and the granddaughter of an imperial postmaster. Richard Dedekind was the youngest of four children. His only brother, Adolf, became a district court president in

Brunswick; one sister, Mathilde, died in 1860, and Dedekind lived with his second sister, Julie, until her death in 1914, neither of them having married. She was a respected writer who received a local literary prize in 1893.

Between the ages of seven and sixteen Dedekind attended the Gymnasium Martino-Catharineum in Brunswick. His interest turned first to chemistry and physics; he considered mathematics only an auxiliary science. He soon occupied himself primarily with it, however, feeling that physics lacked order and a strictly logical structure. In 1848 Dedekind became a student at the Collegium Carolinum, an institute between the academic high school and the university level, which Carl Friedrich Gauss had also attended. There Dedekind mastered the elements of analytic geometry, algebraic analysis, differential and integral calculus, and higher mechanics, and studied the natural sciences. In 1849–1850, he gave private lessons in mathematics to his later colleague at the Carolinum, Hans Zincke (known as Sommer). Thus, when he matriculated at the University of Göttingen at Easter 1850, Dedekind was far better prepared for his studies than were the majority of graduates from the academic high school. At Göttingen, a seminar in mathematics and physics had just been founded, at the initiative of Moritz Abraham Stern, for the education of instructors for teaching in the academic high school. The direction of the mathematics department was the duty of Stern and Georg Ulrich, while Wilhelm Weber and Johann Benedict Listing directed the physics department. Dedekind was a member of the seminar from its inception and was there first introduced to the elements of the theory of numbers. A year later Bernhard Riemann also began to participate in the seminar, and Dedekind soon developed a close friendship with him. In the first semester, Dedekind attended lectures on differential and integral calculus, which offered him very little new material. He attended Ulrich's seminar on hydraulics but rarely took part in the physics laboratories run by Weber and Listing; Weber's lectures on experimental physics, however, made a very strong impression on him throughout two semesters. Weber had an inspiring effect on Dedekind, who responded with respectful admiration. In the summer semester of 1850, Dedekind attended the course in popular astronomy given by Gauss's observer, Carl Wolfgang Benjamin Goldschmidt; in the winter semester of 1850–1851, he attended Gauss's own lecture on the method of least squares. Although he disliked teaching, Gauss carried out the assignment with his usual conscientiousness; fifty years later Dedekind remembered the lecture as one of the most beautiful he had ever heard, writing that he had followed Gauss with constantly increasing interest and that he could not forget the experience. In the following semester, Dedekind heard Gauss's lecture on advanced geodesy. In the winter semester of 1851–1852, he heard the two lectures given by Quintus Icilius on mathematical geography and on the theory of heat and took part in Icilius' meteorological observations. After only four semesters, he did his doctoral work under Gauss in 1852 with a thesis on the elements of the theory of Eulerian integrals. Gauss certified that he knew a great deal and was independent; in addition, he had prophetically "favorable expectations of his future performance."

Dedekind later determined that this knowledge would have been sufficient for teachers in secondary school service but that it did not satisfy the prerequisite for advanced studies at Göttingen. For instance, Dedekind had not heard lectures on more recent developments in geometry, advanced theory of numbers, division of the circle and advanced algebra, elliptic functions, or mathematical physics, which were then being taught at the University of Berlin by Steiner, Jacobi, and Dirichlet. Therefore, Dedekind spent the two years following his graduation assiduously filling the gaps in his education, attending—among others—Stern's lectures on the solution of numerical equations.

In the summer of 1854, he qualified, a few weeks after Riemann, as a university lecturer; in the winter semester of 1854–1855 he began his teaching activities as *Privatdozent,* with a lecture on the mathematics of probability and one on geometry with parallel treatment of analytic and projective methods.

After Dirichlet succeeded Gauss in Göttingen in 1855, Dedekind attended his lectures on the theory of numbers, potential theory, definite integrals, and partial differential equations. He soon entered into a closer personal relationship with Dirichlet and had many fruitful discussions with him; Dedekind later remembered that Dirichlet had made "a new man" of him and had expanded his scholarly and personal horizons. When the Dirichlets were visited by friends from Berlin (Rebecca Dirichlet was the sister of the composer Felix Mendelssohn-Bartholdy and had a large circle of friends), Dedekind was invited too and enjoyed the pleasant sociability of, for example, the well-known writer and former diplomat, Karl August Varnhagen von Ense, and his niece, the writer Ludmilla Assing.

In the winter semester of 1855–1856 and in the one following, Dedekind attended Riemann's lectures on Abelian and elliptic functions. Thus, although an instructor, he remained an intensive student as well. His own lectures at that time are noteworthy in that he probably was the first university teacher to lecture on Galois theory, in the course of which the concept of field was introduced. To be sure, few students attended his lectures: only two were present when Dedekind went beyond Galois and replaced the concept of the permutation group by the abstract group concept.

In 1858, Dedekind was called to the Polytechnikum in Zurich (now the Eidgenössische Technische Hochschule) as the successor to Joseph Ludwig Raabe. Thus Dedekind was the first of a long line of German mathematicians for whom Zurich was the first step on the way to a German professorial chair; to mention only a few, there were E. B. Christoffel, H. A. Schwarz, G. Frobenius, A. Hurwitz, F. E. Prym, H. Weber, F. Schottky, and H. Minkowski. The Swiss school counsellor responsible for appointments came to Göttingen at Easter 1858 and decided immediately upon Dedekind—which speaks for his power of judgment. In September 1859, Dedekind traveled to Berlin with Riemann, after Riemann's election as a corresponding member of the academy there. On this occasion, Dedekind met the initiator of that selection, Karl Weierstrass, as well as other leaders of the Berlin school, including Ernst Eduard Kummer, Karl Wilhelm Borchardt, and Leopold Kronecker.

In 1862, he was appointed successor to August Wilhelm Julius Uhde at the Polytechnikum in Brunswick, which had been created from the Collegium Carolinum. He remained in Brunswick until his death, in close association with his brother and sister, ignoring all possibilities of change or attainment of a larger sphere of activity. The small, familiar world in which he lived completely satisfied his demands: in it his relatives completely replaced a wife and children of his own and there he found sufficient leisure and freedom for scientific work in basic mathematical research. He did not feel pressed to have a more marked effect in the outside world; such confirmation of himself was unnecessary.

Although completely averse to administrative responsibility, Dedekind nevertheless considered it his duty to assume the directorship of the Polytechnikum from 1872 to 1875 (to a certain extent he was the successor of his father, who had been a member of the administration of the Collegium Carolinum for many years) and to assume the chairmanship of the school's building commission in the course of the transformation to a technical university. Along with his recreational trips to Austria (the Tyrol), to Switzerland, and through the Black Forest, his visit to the Paris exposition of 1878 should also be mentioned. On 1 April 1894 he was made professor emeritus but continued to give lectures occasionally. Seriously ill in 1872, following the death of his father, he subsequently enjoyed physical and intellectual health until his peaceful death at the age of eighty-four.

A corresponding member of the Göttingen Academy from 1862, Dedekind also became a corresponding member of the Berlin Academy in 1880 upon the initiative of Kronecker. In 1900, he became a correspondent of the Académie des Sciences in Paris and in 1910 was elected as *associé étranger.* He was also a member of the Leopoldino-Carolina Naturae Curiosorum Academia and of the Academy in Rome. He received honorary doctorates in Kristiania (now Oslo), in Zurich, and in Brunswick. In 1902 he received numerous scientific honors on the occasion of the fiftieth anniversary of his doctorate.

Dedekind belonged to those mathematicians with great musical talent. An accomplished pianist and cellist, he composed a chamber opera to his brother's libretto.

In character and principles, in style of living and views, Dedekind had much in common with Gauss, who also came from Brunswick and attended the Gymnasium Martino-Catharineum, the Collegium Carolinum, and the University of Göttingen. Both men had a conservative sense, a rigid will, an unshakable strength of principles, and a refusal to compromise. Each led a strictly regulated, simple life without luxury. Cool and reserved in judgment, both were warm-hearted, helpful people who formed strong bonds of trust with their friends. Both had a distinct sense of humor but also a strictness toward themselves and a conscientious sense of duty. Averse to any excess, neither was quick to express astonishment or admiration. Both were averse to innovations and turned down brilliant offers for other professorial chairs. In their literary tastes, both numbered Walter Scott among their favorite authors. Both impressed by that quality called modest greatness. Thus, it is not astonishing to find their similarity persisting in mathematics in the same preference for the theory of numbers, the same reservations about the algorithm, and the same partiality for "notions" above "notations." Although considerable, significant differences existed between Gauss and Dedekind, what they had in common predominates by far. Their kinship also received a marked visible expression: Dedekind was one of the select few permitted to carry Gauss's casket to the funeral service on the terrace of the Sternwarte.

Aside from Gauss the most enduring influences on Dedekind's scientific work were Dirichlet and Riemann, with both of whom he shared many inclinations and attitudes. Dedekind, Dirichlet, and Riemann were all fully conscious of their worth, but with a modesty bordering on shyness, they never let their associates feel this. Ambition being foreign to them, they were embarrassed when confronted by the brilliance and elegance of their intellect. They loved thinking more than writing and were hardly ever able to satisfy their own demands. Being of absolute integrity, they had in common the same love for plain, certain truth. Dedekind's own statement to Zincke is more revelatory of his character than any description could be: "For what I have accomplished and what I have become, I have to thank my industry much more, my indefatigable working rather than any outstanding talent."

When Dedekind is mentioned today, one of the first associations is the "Dedekind cut," which he introduced in 1872 to use in treating the problem of irrational numbers in a completely new and exact manner.

In 1858, Dedekind had noted the lack of a truly scientific foundation of arithmetic in the course of his Zurich lectures on the elements of differential calculus. (Weierstrass also was stimulated to far-reaching investigations from such observations in the course of preparing lectures.) On 24 October, Dedekind succeeded in producing a purely arithmetic definition of the essence of continuity and, in connection with it, an exact formulation of the concept of the irrational number. Fourteen years later, he published the result of his considerations, *Stetigkeit und irrationale Zahlen* (Brunswick, 1872, and later editions), and explained the real numbers as "cuts" in the realm of rational numbers. He arrived at concepts of outstanding significance for the analysis of number through the theory of order. The property of the real numbers, conceived by him as an ordered continuum, with the conceptual aid of the cut that goes along with this, permitted tracing back the real numbers to the rational numbers: Any rational number a produces a resolution of the system R of all rational numbers into two classes A_1, A_2 in such a way that each number a_1 of the class A_1 is smaller than each number a_2 of the second class A_2. (Today, the term "set" is used instead of "system.") The number a is either the largest number of the class A_1 or the smallest number of the class A_2. A division of the system R into the two classes A_1, A_2, whereby each number a_1 in A_1 is smaller than each number a_2 in A_2 is called a "cut" (A_1, A_2) by Dedekind. In addition, an infinite number of cuts exist that are not produced by rational numbers. The discontinuity or incompleteness of the region R consists in this property. Dedekind wrote, "Now, in each case when there is a cut (A_1, A_2) which is not produced by any rational number, then we *create* a new, *irrational* number α, which we regard as completely defined by this cut; we will say that this number α corresponds to this cut, or that it produces this cut" (*Stetigkeit*, § 4).

Occasionally Dedekind has been called a "modern Eudoxus" because an impressive similarity has been pointed out between Dedekind's theory of the irrational number and the definition of proportionality in Eudoxus' theory of proportions (Euclid, *Elements*, bk. V, def. 5). Nevertheless, Oskar Becker correctly showed that the Dedekind cut theory and Eudoxus' theory of proportions do not coincide: Dedekind's postulate of existence for all cuts and the real numbers that produce them cannot be found in Eudoxus or in Euclid. With respect to this, Dedekind said that the Euclidean principles alone—without inclusion of the principle of continuity, which they do not contain—are incapable of establishing a complete theory of real numbers as the proportions of the quantities. On the other hand, however, by means of his theory of irrational numbers, the perfect model of a continuous region would be created, which for just that reason would be capable of characterizing any proportion by a certain individual number contained in it (letter to Rudolph Lipschitz, 6 October 1876).

With his publication of 1872, Dedekind had become one of the leading representatives of a new epoch in basic research, along with Weierstrass and Georg Cantor. This was the continuation of work by Cauchy, Gauss, and Bolzano in systematically eliminating the lack of clarity in basic concepts by methods of demonstration on a higher level of rigor. Dedekind's and Weierstrass' definition of the basic arithmetic concepts, as well as Georg Cantor's theory of sets, introduced the modern development, which stands "completely under the sign of number," as David Hilbert expressed it.

Dedekind's book *Was sind und was sollen die Zahlen?* (Brunswick, 1888, and later editions) is along the same lines; in it he presented a logical theory of number and of complete induction, presented his principal conception of the essence of arithmetic, and dealt with the role of the complete system of real numbers in geometry in the problem of the continuity of space. Among other things, he provides a definition independent of the concept of number for the infiniteness or finiteness of a set by using the concept of mapping and treating the recursive definition, which is so important for the theory of ordinal numbers. (Incidentally, Dedekind regarded the ordinal number and not the cardinal number [*Anzahl*] as the original concept of number; in the cardinal number he saw only an application of the ordinal number [letter to Heinrich Weber, 24 January 1888].) The demonstration of the existence of infinite systems given by Dedekind—similar to a consideration in

Bolzano's *Paradoxien des Unendlichen* (Prague, 1851, §13)—is no longer considered valid. Kronecker was critical because Dedekind, agreeing with Gauss, regarded numbers as free creations of the human intellect and defended this viewpoint militantly and stubbornly. Weierstrass complained that his own definition of a complex quantity had not been understood by Dedekind. Hilbert criticized his effort to establish mathematics solely by means of logic. Gottlob Frege and Bertrand Russell criticized Dedekind's opinion that the cuts were not the irrational numbers but that the latter produced the former. However, even his critics and those who preferred Cantor's less abstract procedure for the construction of real numbers agreed that he had exercised a powerful influence on basic research in mathematics.

Just as Kronecker and Weierstrass had edited the mathematical works of those to whom they felt obligated, so Dedekind worked on the erection of literary monuments to those who had stood close to him. Making accessible the posthumous works of Gauss, Dirichlet, and Riemann occupied an important place in his work. In doing this, he gave proof of his congeniality and the rare combination of his productive and receptive intellectual talents.

Publishing the manuscripts of Gauss on the theory of numbers (*Werke*, vol. II [Göttingen, 1863]) gave him the opportunity of not only making available to wider circles the papers of a man he so greatly respected, but also of commenting on them with deep understanding. Dirichlet's *Vorlesungen über Zahlentheorie* (Brunswick, 1863, and later editions) was edited by him. If, as has been said, Dirichlet was the first not only to have completely understood Gauss's *Disquisitiones arithmeticae* but also to have made them accessible to others, then the same is true, to a great extent, of Dedekind's relationship to Dirichlet's lectures on the theory of numbers. Finally, he collaborated in editing the *Werke Bernhard Riemanns* (Leipzig, 1876; 2nd ed., 1892) with his friend Heinrich Weber and with his accustomed modesty placed his name after Weber's.

The editing of Dirichlet's lectures led Dedekind into a profound examination of the theory of generalized complex numbers or of forms that can be resolved into linear factors. In 1871 he provided these lectures with a supplement, in which he established the theory of algebraic number fields, or domains, by giving a general definition of the concept of the ideal—going far beyond Kummer's theory of "ideal numbers"—that has become fruitful in various arithmetic and algebraic areas. In several papers Dedekind then, independently of Kronecker and with his approval, established the ideal theory that is held to be his masterpiece. Its principal theorem was that each ideal different from the unit ideal R can be represented unambiguously—with the exception of the order of factors—as the product of prime numbers. In his treatises concerning number fields, Dedekind arrived at a determination of the number of ideal classes of a field, penetrated the analysis of the base of a field, provided special studies on the theory of modules, and stimulated further development of ideal theory in which Emmy Noether, Hilbert, and Philipp Furtwängler participated. Paul Bachmann, Adolf Hurwitz, and Heinrich Weber in their publications also disseminated Dedekind's thoughts and expanded them.

That Dedekind did not stand completely apart from the applications of mathematics is shown by a treatise, written with W. Henneberg, which appeared as early as 1851 and concerns the time relationships in the course of plowing fields of various shapes, and also by the completion and publication of a treatise by Dirichlet concerning a hydrodynamic problem (1861).

Finally, we are indebted to Dedekind for such fundamental concepts as *ring* and *unit*.

It was indicative of the great esteem in which Dedekind was held even in foreign countries that, shortly after his death, in the middle of World War I, Camille Jordan, the president of the Académie des Sciences in Paris, warmly praised his theory of algebraic integers as his main work and expressed his sadness concerning the loss.

Although the association of mathematicians' names with concepts and theorems is not always historically justified or generally accepted, the number of such named concepts can provide an indication, albeit a relative one, of a mathematician's lasting accomplishments in extending the science. By this standard, Dedekind belongs among the greatest mathematicians; approximately a dozen designations bear his name.

BIBLIOGRAPHY

I. Original Works. For a bibliography of Dedekind's writings, see Poggendorff, I (1863), 534, 1555; III (1898), 340; IV (1904), 305; V (1926), 269; and VI (1936), 538.

His works include *Gesammelte mathematische Werke,* R. Fricke, E. Noether, and O. Ore, eds., 3 vols. (Brunswick, 1930–1932), with a bibliography in III, 505–507; and *Briefwechsel Cantor-Dedekind,* E. Noether and J. Cavaillès, eds. (Paris, 1937). Extracts from his works appear in Oskar Becker, *Die Grundlagen der Mathematik in Geschichtlicher Entwicklung* (Freiburg–Munich, 2nd ed., 1964), pp. 224–245, 316.

II. Secondary Literature. On Dedekind and his work, see Kurt-R. Biermann, "Richard Dedekind im Urteil der

Berliner Akademie," in *Forschungen und Fortschritte,* **40** (1966), 301-302; Edmund Landau, "Richard Dedekind," in *Nachrichten von der Königlichen Gesellschaft der Wissenschaften zu Göttingen, Geschäftliche Mitteilungen* (1917), pp. 50-70, with a bibliography on pp. 66-70; Wilhelm Lorey, *Das Studium der Mathematik an den deutschen Universitäten seit Anfang des 19.Jahrhunderts* (Leipzig-Berlin, 1916), with personal recollections of Dedekind on pp. 81-83; Karl Mollenhauer, "Julie Dedekind," in *Braunschweigisches Magazin,* **21** (1916), 127-130; Richard Müller, "Aus den Ahnentafeln deutscher Mathematiker: Richard Dedekind," in *Familie und Volk,* **4** (1955), 143-145; Nikolaus Stuloff, "Richard Dedekind," in *Neue Deutsche Biographie,* **3** (1957), 552-553; Hans Zincke ("Sommer"), "Erinnerungen an Richard Dedekind," in *Braunschweigisches Magazin,* **22** (1916), 73-81; "Die Akademien zu Paris und Berlin über Richard Dedekind," *ibid.,* 82-84; and "Julius Wilhelm Richard Dedekind," in *Festschrift zur Feier des 25-jährigen Bestehens des Gesellschaft ehemaliger Studierender des Eidgenössischen polytechnischen Schule in Zürich* (1894), pp. 29-30.

KURT-R. BIERMANN

DEE, JOHN (*b.* London, England, 13 July 1527; *d.* Mortlake, Surrey, England, December 1608)

Dee was the son of Roland Dee, a London mercer, and his wife, Johanna Wilde. He was educated at St. John's College, Cambridge, receiving the B.A. in 1545 and the M.A. in 1548. He was a fellow of St. John's and a foundation fellow of Trinity College (1546). He traveled to Louvain briefly in 1547 and to Louvain and Paris in 1548-1551, studying with Gemma Frisius and Gerhardus Mercator. Throughout his life Dee made extended trips to the Continent and maintained cordial relations with scholars there.

For more than twenty-five years Dee acted as adviser to various English voyages of discovery. His treatises on navigation and navigational instruments were deliberately kept in manuscript; most have not survived, and are known only from his later autobiographical writings. His "fruitfull Praeface" to the Billingsley translation of Euclid (1570), on the relations and applications of mathematics, established his fame among the mathematical practitioners. Although translated by Billingsley, the Euclid is unmistakably edited by Dee, for the body of the work, especially the later books, contains many annotations and additional theorems by him.

Although Dee was a man of undoubted scientific talents, his interests always tended toward the occult. His favor in court circles was due largely to his practice of judicial astrology. His interest in alchemy and the search for the philosopher's stone led to the gradual abandonment of other work. His last scientific treatise was a reasoned defense of calendar reform (1583). From that time on, he retreated almost wholly into mysticism and psychic research. Dee was certainly duped by his medium, Edward Kelley, but he himself was sincere. He felt that he had been ill rewarded for his many years of serious study and looked for a shortcut to the secrets of the universe through the assistance of angelic spirits.

BIBLIOGRAPHY

I. ORIGINAL WORKS. A more extensive list is in Thompson Cooper's article in *Dictionary of National Biography,* V, 721-729. *Monas hieroglyphica* (Antwerp, 1564) is presented in annotated translation by C. H. Josten in *Ambix,* **12**, nos. 2 and 3 (1964). "A very fruitfull Praeface . . . specifying the chief mathematical sciences," in H. Billingsley, trans., *Euclid* (London, 1570), was reprinted in *Euclid's Elements,* T. Rudd, ed. (London, 1651) and, with additional material by Dee, in *Euclid's Elements,* J. Leeke and G. Serle, eds. (London, 1661). *Parallaticae commentationis praxosque* (London, 1573) contains trigonometric theorems for determining stellar parallax, occasioned by the nova of 1572. "A plain discourse . . . concerning the needful reformation of the Kalendar" (1583) is in the Bodleian Library, Oxford, MS Ashmole, 1789, i. "The Compendious Rehearsal of John Dee" (1592), BM Cotton Vitellius C vii, 1, is available in "Autobiographical Tracts of Dr. John Dee," James Crossley, ed., *Chetham Miscellanies,* I (Manchester, 1851); it is the main source of biographical information but must be read with caution, since it was written as a request for compensation for injury to Dee's library and reputation. *The Private Diary of John Dee, 1577-1601* was edited by J. O. Halliwell as vol. XIX of Camden Society Publications (London, 1842); a corrected version of the Manchester portions, 1595-1601, was edited by John E. Bailey as *Diary, for the Years 1595-1601* (London, 1880).

II. SECONDARY LITERATURE. There is still no adequate biography of Dee. Both Charlotte Fell-Smith, *John Dee* (London, 1909), and Richard Deacon, *John Dee* (London, 1968), stress Dee's nonscientific activities. The latter has revived the theory, originating with Robert Hooke, that Dee's conversations with the angels were intelligence reports in code. Frances A. Yates, *Theatre of the World* (Chicago, 1969), considers Dee as a Renaissance philosopher in the Hermetic tradition. The book contains interesting discussions of Dee's library and of the mathematical preface to Euclid. It is argued that a revival of interest in Vitruvius was spread among the middle classes of London by Dee's Vitruvian references in the preface.

The best assessment of Dee's scientific work may be found in the books of E. G. R. Taylor, especially *Tudor Geography* (London, 1930) and *Mathematical Practitioners of Tudor and Stuart England* (Cambridge, 1954).

Dee had a remarkable library, and many MSS owned

by him are extant. M. R. James, "Lists of MSS Formerly Owned by John Dee," a supplement to *Transactions of the Bibliographical Society* (1921), is the basic work, but many others have been located. See, for example, A. G. Watson, *The Library of Sir Simonds D'Ewes* (London, 1966).

JOY B. EASTON

DE GROOT, JAN CORNETS, also known as **Johan Hugo De Groot** or **Janus Grotius** (*b.* near Delft, Netherlands, 8 March 1554; *d.* Delft, 3 May 1640)

The son of Hugo Cornelisz and of Elselinge Van Heemskerck, De Groot (or perhaps a namesake) entered the University of Leiden on 5 February 1575, its opening day. He was a master of liberal arts and philosophy at Douai. Belonging to the Delft patriciate, he was a councillor, and from 1591 to 1595 was one of the mayors. From 1594 to 1617 he was a curator of the University of Leiden, which in 1596 awarded him the doctorate of law. After 1617 he served as adviser to the Count of Hohenlohe.

In 1582 De Groot married Alida Borren, from Overschie. One of their five children was the jurist known as Hugo Grotius.

De Groot was a distinguished amateur scientist, acquainted with the best minds in the Netherlands. Stevin, with whom he collaborated in the construction of windmills, praised him as a man well versed in the whole of philosophy, mentioning Euclid, Alhazen (Ibn al-Haytham), Witelo, music, and poetry. De Groot is best known through the experiment he performed with Stevin, in which they proved that lead bodies of different weights falling on a board traverse the same distance in the same time. This anti-Aristotelian experiment, published by Stevin in his *Waterwicht* (1586, p. 66), anticipated Galileo's famous, but apocryphal, experiment at the Leaning Tower of Pisa. De Groot also befriended Ludolph Van Ceulen, on whose behalf he translated Archimedes' *Measurement of the Circle* from the Greek into Dutch and who submitted to him his approximation of π to 20 decimal places (1586). Van Roomen, in his *Ideae mathematicae* (1593), praises De Groot as one of the better mathematicians of his time.

BIBLIOGRAPHY

Only some Latin and Greek poems, correspondence with his son Hugo—*Hugonis epistolae* (Amsterdam, 1607)—and some MS letters in the library of the University of Leiden are extant.

Secondary literature is C. de Waard, "Groot, J. H. de," in *Nieuw Nederlandsch biographisch Woordenboek,* II (1912), cols. 528, 529, with bibliography; and *The Principal Works of Simon Stevin* (Amsterdam, 1955–1966), esp. vols. I, V.

DIRK J. STRUIK

DE GROOT, JOHANNES (*b.* Garrelsweer, Netherlands, 7 May 1914; *d.* Rotterdam, Netherlands, 11 September 1972)

De Groot was the son of Maria Margaretha (née Kuylman) and Johannes de Groot, a minister who later became professor of Near Eastern languages at the University of Groningen and subsequently professor of theology at the University of Utrecht. De Groot attended Christelijk Gymnasium in The Hague for two years, and Willem Lodewijk Gymnasium in Groningen for two years. In 1933 he enrolled at the University of Groningen to study mathematics, with minors in physics and philosophy. He was awarded the doctorate in 1942 with a dissertation titled *Topologische Studiën*. His supervisor was G. Schaake.

For the next several years de Groot taught mathematics at secondary schools in Coevorden and The Hague. In 1946 he became a researcher at the Mathematical Center in Amsterdam. In 1947 and 1948 he was lecturer of mathematics at the University of Amsterdam, from 1948 to 1952 professor of mathematics at the Delft Technical University, and from 1952 until his death he was professor of mathematics at the University of Amsterdam. From 1960 to 1964 he was head of the Pure Mathematics Department of the Mathematical Center.

De Groot held guest positions at several universities in the United States: in 1959 and 1960 at Purdue University, in 1963 and 1964 at Washington University in St. Louis, and in 1966 and 1967 at the University of Florida at Gainesville. From 1967 he combined his professorship at Amsterdam with a position of graduate research professor at the University of Florida at Gainesville. In 1969 de Groot became a member of the Royal Dutch Academy of Sciences.

De Groot's early research dealt with general topology and with problems in algebra, mainly in group theory. His early topological research was strongly influenced by Hans Freudenthal. This is noticeable in his dissertation, in which he obtained a number of results in compactification theory and introduced the interesting cardinal invariant's compactness deficiency and compactness degree. In group theory de Groot obtained results on equivalence of Abelian groups and effective construction of indecomposable abelian groups and rigid groups. Rigid structures, that is, structures with only trivial automorphisms, interested him; he later constructed rigid graphs and rigid spaces.

Subsequently, de Groot concentrated his attention on topology, although around 1960 he made good use of his group-theoretical expertise in several papers on groups of homeomorphisms of topological spaces. In the same period he introduced some new topological cardinal invariants, height and spread, which have turned out to be quite useful in set-theoretic topology.

In the last ten years of his life, de Groot was involved with new general approaches, mainly in set-theoretic topology. His early work in compactness and its generalizations, combined with new interest in Baire spaces, led him to introduce concepts like subcompactness, cocompactness, and cotopological properties in general. He elaborated a new compactification method through the use of so-called superextensions. He introduced and studied topological operators that change a given topology into another one by assigning as a closed subbase for the new topology all sets in the first topology with a specific property (for instance, all compact sets, or all connected closed sets). In his last few years, de Groot also began to do research in infinite-dimensional topology and in the topology of manifolds.

De Groot had many students and coworkers. Twelve dissertations were prepared under his supervision, and many of his papers were written with others. A number of his ideas and several of his conjectures were later taken up by others, while he himself, after launching them, went on to new fields. De Groot's influence on his coworkers and students, and through them on the development of general topology, was considerable.

BIBLIOGRAPHY

I. ORIGINAL WORKS. De Groot published about ninety papers, including *Topologische Studiën* (Assen, Netherlands, 1942), his dissertation; "Decompositions of a Sphere," in *Fundamenta mathematicae*, **43** (1956), 185–194, written with T. J. Dekker; "Rigid Continua and Topological Group Pictures," in *Archiv der Mathematik*, **9** (1958), 441–446, written with R. J. Wille; "Groups Represented by Homeomorphism Groups I," in *Mathematische Annalen*, **138** (1959), 80–102; "Discrete Subspaces of Hausdorff Spaces," in *Bulletin de l' Académie polonaise des sciences*, ser. Sciences Mathématiques, astronomiques et physiques, **13** (1965), 537–544; and "Inductive Compactness as a Generalization of Semicompactness," in *Fundamenta mathematicae*, **58** (1966), 201–218, written with T. Nishiura.

II. SECONDARY LITERATURE. A complete list of de Groot's papers and a survey of his scientific work is in P. C. Baayen and M. A. Maurice, "Johannes de Groot, 1914–1972," in *General Topology and Its Applications*, **3** (1973), 3–32. De Groot's contributions to algebra are more fully discussed in L. C. A. Leeuwen, "Some Problems and Results in Abelian Group Theory," in *Niuw archief voor wiskunde*, **22**, no. 2 (1974), 143–155.

P. C. BAAYEN

DEHN, MAX (*b.* Hamburg, Germany, 13 November 1878; *d.* Black Mountain, North Carolina, 27 June 1952)

Dehn studied at Göttingen under the direction of David Hilbert and received his doctorate in 1900. He then taught at several schools, served in the army, and was a professor of pure and applied mathematics at Frankfurt University from 1921 to 1935, when the Nazi regime forced him to leave. In 1940 he emigrated to the United States, where he taught at the University of Idaho, Illinois Institute of Technology, St. Johns College (Annapolis), and, from 1945 to 1952, at Black Mountain College, North Carolina. He was a member of the Norwegian Academy of Science, the Strassburger Naturforschung Gesellschaft, and the Indian Mathematical Association.

Dehn was an intuitive geometer. Stimulated by Hilbert's work on the axiomatization of geometry, Dehn showed in his dissertation that without assuming the Archimedean postulate, Legendre's theorem that the sum of the angles of a triangle is not greater than two right angles is unprovable, whereas a generalization of Legendre's theorem on the identity of the sums of angles in different triangles is provable. Following this work, Dehn solved the third of the twenty-three unsolved problems that Hilbert had presented in his famous address to the International Congress of Mathematicians in 1900. This problem concerned the congruence of polyhedra, the geometric properties of which Dehn spent much time studying.

In 1907 Dehn and P. Heegaard contributed a report to the *Encyklopädie der mathematischen Wissenschaften* on the topic of analysis situs (now called topology or algebraic topology), which had become prominent as a result of the works of Poincaré. The article was one of the early systematic expositions of this subject. In 1910 Dehn proved an important theorem concerning topological manifolds that became known as Dehn's lemma. In 1928, however, Kneser showed that the proof contained a serious gap; a correct proof was finally given by C. D. Papakyriakopoulos in 1957.

Following Poincaré, Dehn became interested in the groups that are generated in attempts to characterize topological structures. He formulated the central problems of what was to become an important mathematical field: the word, the transformation, and the isomorphism problems. In the case of fundamental groups these have direct topological significance.

Besides his numerous contributions to the field of fundamental groups, Dehn wrote papers on statics, on the algebraic structures derived from differently axiomatized projective planes, and on the history of mathematics. He supervised the work of eight doctoral candidates in Germany and three in the United States.

BIBLIOGRAPHY

A bibliography of Dehn's works may be found in Wilhelm Magnus and Ruth Moufang, "Max Dehn zum Gedächtnis," in *Mathematische Annalen,* **127** (1954), 215–227. See also C. D. Papakyriakopoulos, "Some Problems on 3 Dimensional Manifolds," in *Bulletin of the American Mathematical Society,* **64** (1958), 317–335.

C. S. FISHER

DELAMAIN, RICHARD (*fl.* London, England, first half of the seventeenth century)

Delamain was a joiner by trade, and after studying mathematics at Gresham College, London, he supported himself by teaching practical mathematics in London. Later he became mathematical tutor to King Charles I, for whom he fashioned a number of mathematical instruments. He was a pupil of William Oughtred, and in the early days of their association the two men became close friends. Unhappily this did not last, and later they quarreled violently over priority in the invention of the circular slide rule, which Delamain described in his *Grammelogia, or the Mathematicall Ring.*

Delamain's fame rests mainly on this essay, a pamphlet of thirty-two pages. The manuscript was sent to the king in 1629, and the work was published the following year. The king retained Delamain's services as tutor at a salary of £40 per annum. A few years later Delamain petitioned for an engineer's post at a salary of £100 per annum. Following an interview with the king at Greenwich in 1637, he was granted a warrant for making a number of mathematical instruments.

The appearance of the *Grammelogia* was the signal for the beginning of the quarrel. Oughtred had invented the rectilinear slide rule as early as 1622, but his *Circles of Proportion,* which contained a description of the circular slide rule, was not made public until 1632—by which time the *Grammelogia* had been in circulation for two years. William Forster, a friend and pupil of Oughtred, translated from the Latin and published the *Circles of Proportion,* the preface to which contains some ungenerous references to Delamain, who, it states, purloined the design of the circular slide rule from Oughtred. Delamain retaliated vigorously, attacking both Forster and Oughtred; the latter replied with a pamphlet, *The Apologeticall Epistle,* in which he refers to the "slåunderous insimulations of Richard Delamain in a Pamphlet called *Grammelogia, or the Mathematicall Ring*" and maintains that the latter's horizontal quadrant is no other than the horizontal instrument he had invented thirty years earlier.

Delamain perished in the Civil War sometime before 1645. Oughtred lived until 1660, but his last years were embittered by the dispute with his former friend and pupil.

Delamain was a competent mathematician whose genius lay in the practical realm. He excelled in the construction of a number of mathematical instruments. It is thought that the silver sundial which the king always carried with him and, at his execution, entrusted to Mr. Herbert to be given to the young duke of York, was one of Delamain's creations.

> He likewise commanded Mr. *Herbert* to give his son, the Duke of *York,* his large Ring Sundial of silver, a Jewel his Majesty much valued: it was invented and made by *Rich. Delamaine* a very able Mathematician, who projected it, and in a little printed book did shew its excellent use in resolving many questions in Arithmetick and other rare operations to be wrought by it in the Mathematicks [Wood, *Athenae Oxonienses. History of Oxford Writers,* II, 1692, 525].

BIBLIOGRAPHY

I. ORIGINAL WORKS. Delamain's writings are *Grammelogia, or the Mathematicall Ring* (London, 1630); and *The Making, Description and Use of a Small Portable Instrument for the Pocket . . . Called a Horizontal Quadrant* (London, 1632).

II. SECONDARY LITERATURE. On Delamain or his work, see Florian Cajori, *William Oughtred. A Great Seventeenth Century Teacher of Mathematics* (London–Chicago, 1916), *passim; Dictionary of National Biography;* and E. G. R.

Taylor, *The Mathematical Practitioners of Tudor and Stuart England* (Cambridge, 1954), p. 201.

J. F. SCOTT

DELSARTE, JEAN FRÉDÉRIC AUGUSTE (*b.* Fourmies, France, 19 October 1903; *d.* Nancy, France, 28 November 1968)

Delsarte was the oldest of three children of the head of a textile factory. After the German invasion in 1914, his father remained in Fourmies to preserve what he could of the factory, while the rest of the family fled to unoccupied France.

Delsarte entered the École Normale Supérieure in 1922. After graduating in 1925 and completing his military service, he was granted a research fellowship, and in a little more than one year he had written his dissertation. Although university teaching jobs were very scarce at that time, Delsarte obtained one at the University of Nancy immediately after receiving the doctorate in 1928; he remained there for the rest of his life, and was dean of the Faculty of Sciences from 1945 to 1949. In 1929 he married Thérèse Sutter; they had two daughters.

In mathematics Delsarte had a predilection for what has been called "hard" analysis, in the tradition of Leonhard Euler, Carl Jacobi, and G. H. Hardy. Like them, he was a superb calculator with a remarkable talent for seeing his way through a maze of computations. His ideas were strikingly original, and his work was completely uninfluenced by the mathematical fashions of his time. Since Delsarte had very few students, he did not receive the recognition he deserved; several of his pioneering ideas were rediscovered much later without his being given credit. Such was the case with his extension of the Möbius function to abelian groups and its use in enumeration problems, and with the generalization to Fuchsian groups of the formula giving the value of the number of lattice points within a ball.

Delsarte's main results in mathematical analysis stem from a common theme: the expansion of a function f by a series

$$S(f) \sim \sum_i L_i(f)\phi_i \tag{1}$$

where the ϕ_i are functions independent of f and the L_i linear functionals. The Taylor series with $\phi_k(x) = x^k/k!$ and $L_k(f) = D^k f(0)$ is the "classical" example, but many other types were known and were studied in George Watson and Edmund Whittaker's *A Course of Modern Analysis* and Watson's *Treatise on the Theory of Bessel Functions*, which were Delsarte's most cherished books. These works had convinced him that a good understanding of the formal properties of such expansions was necessary to a fruitful study of their domain of definition and their mode of convergence. This was the course he followed with remarkable success, opening up new fields of research that are still far from having been thoroughly explored.

The starting point is a vector space E of complex valued functions, which for simplicity one may assume to be defined in a neighborhood I of 0 in **R**, and to be C^∞.

(A) There is given an endomorphism D of E that has a continuous spectrum. This means that for every $\lambda \in \mathbf{C}$, there is a function $j_\lambda \in E$ for which

$$Dj_\lambda = \lambda j_\lambda. \tag{2}$$

(B) Each j_λ has a formal expansion

$$j_\lambda \sim \sum_{n=0}^{\infty} \lambda^n \phi_n, \tag{3}$$

where the ϕ_n are polynomials belong to E and $\phi_0 = 1$, so that

$$D\phi_n = \phi_{n-1} \quad \text{for} \quad n \geqslant 1. \tag{4}$$

(C) Delsarte introduces the formal series depending on a parameter $y \in I$

$$T^y f \sim \phi_0(y)f + \phi_1(y)Df + \cdots + \phi_n(y)D^n f + \cdots; \tag{5}$$

these operators satisfy the relation

$$T^y T^z = T^z T^y \qquad \text{for} \quad y, z \in I, \tag{6}$$

and if $\Phi_f(x, y) = (T^y f)(x)$ for x, $y \in I$,

$$D_x \Phi_f(\cdot, y) = D_y \Phi_f(x, \cdot). \tag{7}$$

This is in general a partial differential equation, and its integration with the initial condition $\Phi_f(x, 0) = f(x)$ yields $T^y f$. With the initial condition $\Psi(x, 0) = 0$, the equation

$$D_y \Psi(x, \cdot) - D_x \Psi(\cdot, y) = D_x^{n+1} f(x)\phi_n(y) \tag{8}$$

similarly yields the "remainder," the difference between $T^y f$ and the first n terms in (5). In the classical case, $\Phi_f(x, y) = f(x + y)$. A more interesting example (among many others studied by Delsarte) corresponds to

$$D = \frac{d^2}{dx^2} + \frac{1}{x}\frac{d}{dx}, j_\lambda(x) = J_0(ix\sqrt{\lambda}), \phi_n(x) = \frac{1}{(n!)^2}\left(\frac{x}{2}\right)^n, \tag{9}$$

for which Delsarte shows that

$$\Phi_f(x, y) = \frac{1}{\pi}\int_0^\pi f(\sqrt{x^2 + y^2 - 2xy\cos\phi})\,d\phi. \tag{10}$$

(D) Delsarte's main interest in these expansions was in the study of linear endomorphisms U of E that commute with all the T^y for $y \in I$. In the classical case with $E = D(\mathbf{R})$, this condition and minimal continuity properties characterize the convolution operators $f \mapsto f * \mu$, where μ is a measure or distribution with compact support. In general,

$$(U \cdot f)(x) = \langle T^y f, \alpha \rangle \qquad (11)$$

where α is a linear form on E; this implies

$$U \cdot j_\lambda = X(\lambda) j_\lambda \text{ with } X(\lambda) = \langle j_\lambda, \alpha \rangle. \qquad (12)$$

(E) The introduction of these generalized convolution operators U leads to the subclasses J_U of functions $f \in E$ such that $U \cdot f = 0$.

In the classical case, in which μ is the difference of two Dirac measures $\mu = \delta_a - \delta_0$, J_U consists of the functions of period a. For an arbitrary μ, Delsarte called J_U a space of mean-periodic functions; in the general case, he spoke of "J-mean periodic" functions. In many cases, $X(\lambda)$ is an entire function of λ with a sequence of zeroes $\lambda_1, \lambda_2, \cdots, \lambda_n, \cdots$; with each J-mean periodic function is associated a formal expansion

$$f(x) \sim \sum_n c_n j_{\lambda_n}(x), \qquad (13)$$

for which Delsarte gave a general method of computing the c_n; it is similar to the Fourier series, to which it reduces for $U \cdot f = f * (\delta_a - \delta_0)$. If $X(0) \neq 0$, the Taylor series $j_\lambda(x)/X(\lambda)$ introduces polynomials that generalize the Bernoulli polynomials. Delsarte also gave a generalized Euler-Maclaurin formula with explicit remainder using these polynomials.

Earlier, Delsarte had made a thorough study of the case $U \cdot f = f * \mu$; then X is the Fourier transform of μ, and therefore an entire function, and the j_{λ_n} have the form $P_n(x) \exp(2\pi i \lambda_n x)$, with P_n a polynomial. Delsarte investigated the convergence of such expansions, and his results were extended in the later work of Laurent Schwartz and Jean-Pierre Kahane. For the operator D defined in (9), he also showed how, for different choices of U, the expansions (13) became various known expansions in Bessel functions, where usually the coefficients c_n were computed by ad hoc devices but Delsarte's general process applied in every case.

After 1950 Delsarte greatly enlarged the scope of these ideas. The classical translation operators generalize naturally to the operators S^y and T^y defined by $S^y f: x \mapsto f(yx)$ and $T^y f: x \mapsto f(xy)$ in any Lie group. Delsarte considered the more general situation of a Lie group G with a compact group A of automorphisms of G. The operators S^y and T^y are defined by

$$S^y f: x \mapsto \int_A f(y^\sigma x) d\sigma, \; T^y f: x \mapsto \int_A f(xy^\sigma) d\sigma \qquad (14)$$

and reduce to translations when A reduces to the identity element 1_G. In general those operators still satisfy $S^y T^z = T^z S^y$ and depend only on the orbit $\bar{y}$ of y under A, so that they operate on functions on the space of orbits G/A. When G is the additive group $\mathbf{R}^2$ and A the group of rotations, G/A can be identified with the positive reals, and the function on $(G/A) \times (G/A)$,

$$\Phi_f(\bar{x}, \bar{y}) = (T^y f)(x) = (\check{S}^x f)(y), \qquad (15)$$

is given by (10). When $A = \{1_G\}$, the relation (7) for Φ_f on $G \times G$ still holds when D is an invariant vector field (element of the Lie algebra of G). Delsarte showed that such equations still exist in general, but for invariant differential operators, which in general will be of order > 1, as (9) shows. He considered this result as the beginning of an analog of Lie theory for G/A. This point of view was developed by B. Lewitan, and probably more remains to be done.

The fact that the operators (5) may be obtained by integrating the partial differential equation (7) led Delsarte to consider more generally, for two different differential operators D and D', the equation

$$D_x F(x, y) = D'_y F(x, y), \qquad (16)$$

which yields what he called "transmutation" operators, changing D into D'. This was developed by Delsarte in collaboration with J.-L. Lions, and later was used by Lewitan and others for the Sturm-Liouville problem.

The same ideas enabled Delsarte to prove one of his most elegant and unexpected results. It has been known since Gauss that if a C^∞ function f in $\mathbf{R}^n$ has at each point x a value equal to its mean value on every sphere of center x, it is a harmonic function. Delsarte showed that the conclusion still holds if $f(x)$ is equal to its mean value on only two spheres of center x and radii $a > b > 0$, provided the ratio a/b is not a number in a finite set depending only on n.

From 1950 on, Delsarte often lectured at institutes and universities in India and North and South America. After 1960 his eyesight, which had always been poor, began to deteriorate. At the end of his life he could read and write only with great difficulty. From 1962 to 1965 he was director of the Franco-Japanese Institute in Tokyo.

BIBLIOGRAPHY

Delsarte's works are collected in *Oeuvres de Jean Delsarte*, 2 vols. (Paris, 1971), which includes brief essays on his life and work. His writings also include *Lectures on Topics in Mean Periodic Functions and the Two-Radius Theorem* (Bombay, 1961).

JEAN DIEUDONNÉ

DEMOCRITUS (*b.* Abdera, Thrace, *fl.* late fifth century B.C.)

There were two main chronologies current in antiquity for Democritus. According to the first, which was followed by Epicurus among others, Democritus was the teacher of the Sophist Protagoras of Abdera and was born soon after 500 B.C. and died about 404 B.C. The other chronology puts his birth about 460 B.C., making him a younger contemporary of Socrates and a generation or more younger than Protagoras; in this case, the tradition that he lived to a great age would bring his death well into the fourth century B.C. According to Democritus' own words, he was a young man when Anaxagoras was old, and he may actually have said that he was younger by forty years. Although there was also more than one ancient chronology for Anaxagoras, this statement probably supports the later dates for Democritus, and these have usually been accepted by modern scholars. The question is an important one for our understanding of the history of thought in the fifth century B.C., and it is unfortunate that the occurrence of the name Democritus, presumably as a magistrate, on a fifth-century tetradrachm of Abdera does not help to settle the question, because we cannot be certain that it is the name of the Democritus here discussed nor can the tetradrachm be dated with certainty earlier than 430 B.C. (this would fit with either chronological scheme).

Most of the stories about Democritus are worthless later inventions, but it is probable that he was well-to-do, and stories of extensive travels may have a foundation in fact. He is reported to have said that he visited Athens, but no one knew him there, and from Cicero and Horace we learn that—at least in their time—he was known as the "laughing philosopher" because of his amusement at the follies of mankind. His only certainly attested teacher was Leucippus. The titles of more than sixty writings are preserved from a catalog that probably represented the holdings of the library at Alexandria. Of these we have only some 300 alleged quotations, many of which may not be genuine. More valuable for the understanding of Democritus' theories are the accounts given by Aristotle, Theophrastus, and the later doxographic tradition. Democritus left pupils who continued the tradition of his teachings and one of them, Nausiphanes, was the teacher of Epicurus. Epicureanism represents a further elaboration of the physical theories of Democritus, and surviving writings of Epicurus and others provide further interpretations and sometimes specific information about earlier atomist doctrines.

According to Posidonius in the first century B.C., the theory of atoms was a very old one and went back to a Phoenician named Mōchus, who lived before the Trojan War, in the second millennium B.C. According to others, Democritus was a pupil of Persian magi and Chaldean astrologers, either as a boy in his native Abdera or later in Egypt. Both stories seem to have originated only in the third century B.C. and to be part of the wholesale attempts to derive Greek thought from Oriental sources that followed the "discovery" of the East resulting from the establishment of Alexander's empire. More intriguing is the fact that certain Indian thinkers arrived at an atomic explanation of the universe, which is expounded in the Vaiśeṣika Sūtra and is interpreted by the aphorisms of Kanada. However, the Vaiśeṣika atoms are not quality-free but correspond to the four elements; nor is soul made from these atoms. Moreover, the date of the first appearance of the doctrine in India is probably subsequent to the founding of the Greek kingdom of Bactria, so that coincidences could be due to Greek influences on Indian thought. There is no early evidence of external sources for Democritus' thought; these are not needed, because the doctrines can be shown to have arisen naturally and almost inevitably as a result of the way in which the problems of explaining the physical universe had been formulated by Democritus' immediate predecessors among the pre-Socratics, who were of course Greeks. Consequently, Aristotle is probably right (*De generatione et corruptione,* 325a23 ff.) in explaining his views as developed in reply to the doctrines of the Eleatics. This need not exclude the possibility that the atomists were also influenced by what is sometimes called Pythagorean number-atomism, although whether this preceded or arose only after the time of Leucippus remains uncertain, and it is clear that Democritus did not invent atomism but received the essentials of the doctrine from Leucippus.

By the middle of the fifth century B.C., it seemed to many thinkers that Parmenides, the founder of the Eleatic school, had proved that nothing can come into being out of that which is not, and that anything which is cannot alter, because that would involve its becoming that which is not. Previous attempts to

 DEMOCRITUS

explain the physical universe as derived from one or more primary substances were thus doomed to failure, as they all involved change in the primary substances and so violated Parmenides' conclusions. Anaxagoras, at least in one view of his doctrine, made a heroic attempt to escape from the difficulty by supposing that all substances were always present in all other substances and that apparent change was simply the emergence of the required substance—which had been present unnoticed all the time. The atomism of Democritus was similar in its approach but went further in depriving the primary constituents of most, but not all, of the qualities apparent in objects derived from them. Moreover, Leucippus had boldly accepted empty space or void—the existence of which the Eleatics regarded as impossible because it would be that which is not—as necessary to make movement possible.

Atoms and void are the bases of Democritus' system for explaining the universe: solid corporeal atoms, infinite in number and shape, differing in size, but otherwise lacking in sensible qualities, were originally scattered throughout infinite void. In general, the atoms were so small as to be invisible. (They were all invisible for Epicurus, but later sources raise the possibility that for Democritus some exceptional atoms may have been large enough to be seen or even that an individual atom might be as big as the cosmos.) The atoms are physically indivisible—this is the meaning of the name *atomos,* which, while not surviving in the fragments of Democritus, must certainly have been used by him. Whether the atoms were conceptually or mathematically indivisible as well as physically is a matter of dispute. But they were certainly extended and indestructible, so that if he thought about it Democritus ought not to have denied mathematical divisibility, especially as the atoms' variety of shape implied the concept of parts within each physically indivisible atom. They are homogeneous in substance, contain no void and no interstices, and are in perpetual motion in the infinitely extended void, probably moving equally in all directions.

When a group of atoms becomes isolated, a whirl is produced which causes like atoms to tend toward like. Within a kind of membrane or garment, as it were, woven out of hook-shaped atoms, there develops a spherical structure which eventually contains earth, sky, and heavenly bodies—in other words a spherical cosmos. The only detailed description of the process ascribes it to Leucippus (Diogenes Laertius, IX, 30 ff.), but there is no reason to doubt that it was repeated by Democritus. There is no limit to the number of atoms nor to the amount of void, and so not one cosmos but many are formed. Some dissolved again before the formation of our cosmos; others coexist with ours, some larger and some smaller, some without sun or moon, and some without living creatures, plants, or moisture. From time to time a cosmos is destroyed by collision with another.

Our earth and everything in it, like everything elsewhere, is compounded of atoms and void, and there are no other constituents of the universe of any kind. Apart from differences in shape, atoms differ in arrangement and position. As Aristotle says, the letter *A* differs from *N* in shape; *AN* from *NA* in arrangement; and *Z* from *N* in position, although both have the same shape. We must add, although Aristotle does not say so here, that the spacings between atoms may vary from the zero space of actual contact through increasing distances apart. Soft and yielding bodies and bodies light in weight contain more void than heavier or harder objects of equal extent. Iron is lighter than lead because it has more void, but it is harder because it is denser than lead at particular points, the void not being distributed evenly throughout, as is the case with lead. It is probable that for Democritus the atoms when entangled do not cease to be in motion (their individual movement is naturally less extensive), but they participate in movements of the object of which they are a part. It appears that atoms were not regarded as possessing weight in their own right; this was Epicurus' innovation. But physical objects possess weight, and according to Aristotle, atoms are heavier in proportion to their excess of bulk. Objects as a whole are heavier the greater the proportion of atoms to void. It may be that weight operates only in a developed world and is the result of a tendency of compound objects to move toward the center of a whirl. For Democritus all movement and all change are due to "necessity," but this is an internal cause and not an agency operating from without: it is the necessary result of the natural movement of the atoms. All events are determined, and if Cicero is right at all in saying Democritus attributed events to chance, this can have meant only that they could not be predicted, not that they were not determined.

The perceived qualitative differences between objects depend upon the nature and arrangement of the relevant atoms and void. The importance and novelty of this doctrine were fully appreciated by Theophrastus, who discussed it at some length in his surviving *De sensibus.* It might have seemed sufficient answer to Parmenides' challenging argument to have said that secondary qualities such as colors and tastes were produced by the appropriate arrangement of atoms in the sense that they were present in any object possessing the appropriate atomic configuration and would be altered or disappear when the configuration changed. But Theophrastus complains that Democritus is inconsistent on this point and that, while explaining sensations causally in terms of configurations, he insists that the perceived qualities depend upon the state of the percipient—for example, his health—to such an extent that the qualities exist not in the object but only in the percipient at the time he is perceiving them. According to Sextus Empiricus, Protagoras, in his "Man is the measure" doctrine, had held that there are present in actual objects multiple qualities which are selectively perceived by different percipients. Democritus is said (fr. 156) to have criticized the doctrine of Protagoras at great length, and it could be that he carried the relativism of Protagoras one step further by supposing that secondary qualities did not exist in the configuration of atoms which constitute a thing but only in the consciousness of the percipient. But not all accept Sextus Empiricus' account of Protagoras on this point.

We lack details of many aspects of Democritus' cosmology. The earth is flat and elongated—twice as long as it is broad. Although earlier it strayed about, it is now stationary at the center of the universe. The angle between zenith and celestial pole is explained by the tilting of the earth because the warmer air to the south—under the earth—offered less support than that in the north. Earthquakes are caused by heavy rain or drought changing the amount of water in the cavities of the earth. While some explanations of meteorological phenomena were offered in terms of the theory of atoms (for example, the attraction of like atoms to like as an explanation of magnetism), in general Democritus seems to have followed traditional explanations drawn from earlier pre-Socratics, above all from Anaximander. Unlike Leucippus, who put the sun's orbit outermost in the heavens, Democritus had the normal order of fixed stars, planets, sun, Venus, moon. The moon, like the earth, contained valleys and glens, and its light was derived from the sun.

Two particularly quick-moving constituents of the universe, fire and soul, were for Democritus composed of spherical atoms. Spherical atoms are not themselves either fire or soul but become such by the suitable aggregation of a number of themselves. Such aggregation cannot be by entanglement, which is not possible with spherical atoms, but only by the principle of the attraction of like to like. Whereas air, water, and perhaps earth, and things containing them, were regarded as conglomerations of atoms of all shapes, only the one shape seems to have occurred in fire and soul. Aristotle more than once speaks as if soul and fire were identical, and he adds that the soul can be fed by breathing in suitable atoms from the air around us. In this way, losses of soul atoms from the body can be replaced. When we can no longer breathe, the pressure from the atmosphere outside continues to squeeze out the soul atoms from the body and death results. A slight excess of loss over replacement produces sleep only and not death. Even when death results, the loss of soul atoms takes time, so that some functions, such as growth of hair and nails, continue for a while in the tomb; a certain degree of sensation may also continue for a time, and in exceptional cases, even resuscitation may be possible. We do not know the contents of the work *On Those in Hades,* attributed to Democritus, except that it included reference to such resuscitations.

Within the living body, soul atoms are distributed throughout the whole in such a way that single atoms of the soul and body alternate, and it has sometimes been said that this involves treating isolated atoms as soul atoms and so reintroducing qualities into individual atoms. But such an alternation could be achieved within a lattice pattern of one kind or another for the soul atoms, so that there is no actual inconsistency. These soul atoms are the immediate source of life, warmth, and motion in a living body. In addition to the soul atoms dispersed throughout the body, there is another part of the soul, the mind, located in one part of the body, namely the head.

Sensation for Democritus was based upon touch and was due to images entering the sense organs from outside and producing alterations in the percipient. Sensation is thus the result of the interaction of image and organ. In the case of flavors, there is always a multitude of configurations of atoms present in what is tasted, but the preponderant configuration exerts the greatest influence and determines the flavor tasted, the result being influenced also by the state of the sense organs. In the case of sight, images continually stream off the objects, which are somehow imprinted —by stamping, as it were—on the intervening air. This imprinted air is then carried to the eyes, where its configuration produces the sensation of color. A similar analysis seems to have been offered for hearing and perhaps for smell. Taste, however, entails direct contact between organ and object: large, rough, polygonal shapes produce astringent flavors, and so on.

Thought, like sensation, is the result of a disturbance of the soul atoms by configurations of atoms from outside; it is what occurs when the soul achieves a fresh balance after the movement which is sensation. The details of the process are obscure, and the text of Theophrastus' description is uncertain. But there is no sure evidence to suggest that Democritus held the later theory of Epicurus that it is possible for certain externally originating images to bypass the senses and secure direct access to the mind in thought. For Democritus, thought follows after sensation, and we may believe that Democritus expressed his real view when he said (fr. 125) that the mind takes its evidence from the senses and then seeks to overthrow them, but that the overthrow is a fall for the mind also. Nonetheless, in an important fragment (fr. 11) Democritus did claim that there were two kinds of knowledge, one genuine or legitimate, and the other bastard. To the bastard belong the senses; genuine knowledge operates on objects too fine for any sense to grasp. This must surely refer to our knowledge of the atomic theory, including the imperceptible atoms and void of which things are composed, but we do not know what mechanical procedure, if any, Democritus envisaged for the acquisition of such knowledge.

It follows from the above view of the soul and the way it leaves the body at death that there is no survival of the individual soul, although the soul atoms themselves survive because, like all atoms, they are indestructible. It might have been expected that this approach would shed doubt on the existence of gods and spirits, especially since we are told that Democritus attributed early man's fear of the gods to his misunderstanding of natural phenomena such as lightning and eclipses. But he accepted that images of beings both beneficent and maleficent, destructible and yet able to foretell the future while being seen and heard, come to men apparently out of the air itself, without any more ultimate source. We do not know what doctrine lies behind this, but it is likely that there was no external source posited for these images other than the soul atoms at large in the air.

The list of Democritus' writings contains the titles of a number of works on mathematics, and it is clear from the few surviving scattered references that his mathematical interests were not inconsiderable. Protagoras had argued that the tangent touches the circle not at one point but over a distance. Democritus treated the sphere as "all angle," and Simplicius explained this as meaning that what is bent is an angle and the sphere is bent all over. It is inferred that he supposed that the sphere is really a polyhedron with imperceptibly small faces, presumably because a physical sphere involves atoms which cannot be further broken down. In such a case he would be in agreement with Protagoras as to the actual relation between tangent and circle while in disagreement as to the apparent relation. But with atoms in an infinite variety of shapes. there is no reason why Democritus could not have posited a perfect physical sphere made up of atoms of indivisible magnitude but with curved faces. In any case Democritus could probably distinguish a physical from a mathematical sphere well enough.

Of very great interest is Democritus' discussion of the question whether the two contiguous surfaces produced by slicing a cone horizontally are equal or unequal. If equal, it might seem that the cone is a cylinder, while if unequal, the cone becomes steplike and uneven (fr. 155). Chrysippus the Stoic, when discussing Democritus' doctrine, declared that Democritus was unaware of the true answer—namely, so he claimed, that the surfaces are neither equal nor unequal. Unfortunately what Democritus' view was remains in doubt. Some suppose that he argued for a stepped physical cone; others that he regarded the dilemma as genuine; and still others that he considered them equal, at least as far as mathematics was concerned. Archimedes records that Democritus was concerned with the ratios of size between cylinders, pyramids, and prisms of the same base and height. While this is evidence of further interest in problems associated with cones of the kind that were so important for the subsequent history of mathematics, we do not actually know the nature of Democritus' discussions concerning them.

Tantalizing references to individual doctrines and the titles of a number of his writings have suggested to some that Democritus' biological work rivaled Aristotle's in both comprehensiveness and attention to detail. The indications that survive do not for the most part suggest that he made any very particular application of atomic theories to biology, and it is probable that his clearly extensive writings were essentially within the general framework of Ionian speculation. More we cannot say through lack of positive information.

Later writers—as well as some from the fifth and fourth centuries B.C.—preserve details which all seem to come from a single account of the origins and development of human civilization. They have in common not only various particular points but also a basic conception—namely, that civilization developed from lower levels to higher, which contrasted strongly with the dominant view that human history represented a continuous decline from an original golden age. The clearest version of this history of culture survives in the *Bibliotheca historica* of Diodorus (bk. I, ch. 8), written in the age of Cicero. It is clear that Democritus held a similar view, and it is possible, although by no means certain, that he originated the whole tradition. Certain features of it, however, are already in Aeschylus' picture of Prometheus and probably in the writings of Protagoras summarized in Plato's dialogue named after the

Sophist. Part of Democritus' treatment of the evolution of culture concerned the origin and development of language, taking the view that names were not natural but conventional.

Special problems affect the reconstruction of Democritus' ethical doctrines, to which a very large part of the surviving fragments relate. Many of these are attributed in the manuscript tradition not to Democritus but to an otherwise unknown Democrates, so that their authority for the reconstruction of the views of Democritus is uncertain. Most of the fragments are extremely commonplace, and hardly any are related to atomic theory. The doxographic tradition does, however, suggest that he had a general theory of *euthymia* ("cheerfulness" or "contentment") as the end of ethics. It was based on a physical state, the actual constitution of the body at any one time, of which the external expression is pleasure or enjoyment when the state itself is satisfactory. Even this much is a matter of conjecture, and we do not know how it was all worked out by Democritus.

Most of the fragments dealing with what we would call political questions are as traditional in content as those dealing with ethics. He seems to have had no doubts about the importance of law, although its function was limited to preventing one man from injuring another. It is inferior to encouragement and persuasion, but "it is right to obey the law, the ruler and the man who is wiser" (fr. 47). Democritus had declared that secondary qualities of perception, such as sweetness, existed only by *nomos,* not in reality, and *nomos,* which means "custom" or "convention," is also the word used for "law." It is perhaps not going too far to say that in ethics and politics, just as in physics, Democritus was searching for a truth and a reality behind or beyond the world of appearances; but at the same time, he wished to reaffirm the importance of changing phenomena as the product of an unchanging reality. It is probable that political obedience to the law was regarded as rooted in the well-being of the soul, just as wrongdoing is not to be justified by the thought that one will escape discovery.

BIBLIOGRAPHY

The fragments and testimonia are collected in H. Diels and W. Kranz, *Die Fragmente der Vorsokratiker,* 6th ed., 3 vols. (Berlin, 1951–1952), vol. II. There is a translation of the fragments by K. Freeman, *Ancilla to the Pre-Socratic Philosophers* (Cambridge, Mass., 1966), and the most important are translated and discussed in G. S. Kirk and J. E. Raven, *The Presocratic Philosophers* (Cambridge, 1957).

For discussions of Democritus, see V. E. Alfieri, *Gli atomisti* (Bari, 1936) and *Atomos idea, l'origine del concetto dell'atomo nel pensiero greco* (Florence, 1953); C. Bailey, *The Greek Atomists and Epicurus* (Oxford, 1928); T. Cole, *Democritus and the Sources of Greek Anthropology,* American Philological Association Monograph (1967); W. K. C. Guthrie, *History of Greek Philosophy,* vol. II (Cambridge, 1965), ch. 8; A. B. Keith, *Indian Logic and Atomism* (Oxford, 1921); H. Langerbeck, *Doxis Epirhysmie, Studien zu Demokrits Ethik und Erkenntnislehre* (Berlin, 1935); S. Luria, *Zur Frage der materialistischen Begründung der Ethik bei Demokrit* (Berlin, 1964); J. Mau, *Zum Problem der Infinitesimalen bei den antiken Atomisten,* 2nd ed. (Berlin, 1957); P. Natorp, *Die Ethik des Demokritos, Texte und Untersuchungen* (Marburg, 1893); W. Schmid, *Geschichte der griechischen Literatur,* V (Munich, 1948), 236–350; G. Vlastos, "Ethics and Physics in Democritus," in *Philosophical Review,* **54** (1945), 578–592, and **55** (1946), 53–63.

G. B. KERFERD

DE MORGAN, AUGUSTUS (*b.* Madura, Madras presidency, India, June 1806; *d.* London, England, 18 March 1871)

De Morgan's father was a colonel in the Indian Army; and his mother was the daughter of John Dodson, a pupil and friend of Abraham de Moivre, and granddaughter of James Dodson, author of the *Mathematical Canon.* At the age of seven months De Morgan was brought to England, where his family settled first at Worcester and then at Taunton. He attended a succession of private schools at which he acquired a mastery of Latin, Greek, and Hebrew and a strong interest in mathematics before the age of fourteen. He also acquired an intense dislike for cramming, examinations, and orthodox theology.

De Morgan entered Trinity College, Cambridge, in February 1823 and placed first in the first-class division in his second year; he was disappointed, however, to graduate only as fourth wrangler in 1827. After contemplating a career in either medicine or law, De Morgan successfully applied for the chair of mathematics at the newly formed University College, London, in 1828 on the strong recommendation of his former tutors, who included Airy and Peacock. When, in 1831, the college council dismissed the professor of anatomy without giving reasons, he immediately resigned on principle. He resumed in 1836, on the accidental death of his successor, and remained there until a second resignation in 1866.

De Morgan's life was characterized by powerful religious convictions. While admitting a personal faith in Jesus Christ, he abhorred any suspicion of hypocrisy or sectarianism and on these grounds refused an

M.A., a fellowship at Cambridge, and ordination. In 1837 he married Sophia Elizabeth Frend, who wrote his biography in 1882. De Morgan was never wealthy; and his researches into all branches of knowledge, together with his prolific output of writing, left little time for social or family life. However, he was well known for his humor, range of knowledge, and sweetness of disposition.

In May 1828 De Morgan became a fellow of the Astronomical Society; he was elected to the council in 1830, serving as secretary (1831–1838; 1848–1854). He helped to found the London Mathematical Society, becoming its first president and giving the inaugural lecture in 1865. He was also an influential member of the Society for the Diffusion of Useful Knowledge from 1826. De Morgan was a prolific writer, contributing no fewer than 850 articles (one-sixth of the total production) to the *Penny Cyclopaedia* and writing regularly for at least fifteen periodicals.

De Morgan exerted a considerable influence on the development of mathematics in the nineteenth century. As a teacher he sought to demonstrate principles rather than techniques; and his pupils, who included Todhunter, Routh, and Sylvester, acquired from him a great love of the subject. He wrote textbooks on the elements of arithmetic, algebra, trigonometry, calculus, complex numbers, probability, and logic. These books are characterized by meticulous attention to detail, enunciation of fundamental principles, and clear logical presentation.

De Morgan's original contributions to mathematics were mainly in the fields of analysis and logic. In an article written in 1838, he defined and invented the term "mathematical induction" to describe a process that previously had been used —without much clarity—by mathematicians.

In *The Differential and Integral Calculus* (1842) there is a good discussion of fundamental principles with a definition of the limit which is probably the first precise analytical formulation of Cauchy's somewhat intuitive concept. The same work contains a discussion of infinite series with an original rule to determine convergence precisely when simpler tests fail. De Morgan's rule, which is proved rigorously, is that if the series is given by

$$\sum \frac{1}{\phi(n)},$$

then if

$$e = \lim_{n\to\infty} \frac{n\phi'(n)}{\phi(n)},$$

the series converges for $e > 1$ but diverges for $e \leq 1$.

Among his other mathematical work is a system that De Morgan described as "double algebra." This helped to give a complete geometrical interpretation of the properties of complex numbers and, as Sir William Rowan Hamilton acknowledged, suggested the idea of quaternions.

De Morgan's greatest contribution to scientific knowledge undoubtedly lay in his logical researches; and the subsequent development of symbolic logic, with its powerful influences on both philosophy and technology, owes much to his fundamental work. He believed that the traditional method of argument using the Aristotelian syllogism was inadequate in reasoning that involved quantity. As an example De Morgan presented the following argument:

In a particular company of men,
most men have coats
most men have waistcoats
∴ some men have both coats and waistcoats.

He asserted that it was not possible to demonstrate this true argument by means of any of the normally accepted Aristotelian syllogisms.

The first attempt to extend classical logic by means of quantifying the predicate and reformulating logical statements in mathematical terms was made by George Bentham in 1827. He rephrased the statement "Every X is a Y" into the equation "X *in toto* = Y *ex parte*" with the algebraic notation "$tX = pY$." It was more usual at this time, however, for logicians to make more classical attempts to broaden the Aristotelian syllogistic; and De Morgan's work, which commenced in the 1840's, can be seen as the bridge between this older approach and Boole's analytical formulation. Boole acknowledged his debt to De Morgan and Hamilton in the preface to his first logical work, *The Mathematical Analysis of Logic* (1847).

The Scottish philosopher Sir William Hamilton (not to be confused with Sir William Rowan Hamilton) worked out a system for quantifying the predicate a short time before De Morgan did and unjustly accused him of plagiarism. He had no shred of evidence to support his charge, and De Morgan's work was superior to his in both analytical formulation and subsequent development.

De Morgan invented notations, which he sometimes varied, to describe simple propositions. Objects with certain properties were denoted by capital letters $X, Y, Z, \cdots$ and those without this property by the corresponding small letters $x, y, z, \cdots$. One of his notations was

A	Every X is a Y	as	$X)Y$
E	No X is a Y	as	X.Y
I	Some X's are Y's	as	XY

O Some X's are not Y's as $X:Y$,

the symbols A, E, I, O, having their usual Aristotelian meaning. He then worked out rules to establish valid syllogistic inferences. Such results were then written in the form

$$X)Y + Y)Z = X)Z$$
$$Y{:}X + Y)Z = Z{:}X$$
$$X)Y + Z)Y = xz,$$

and so on. This notation was superseded by Boole's more algebraic one, but it helped De Morgan to establish valid inferences not always obtainable through the traditional rules. Using the notation of Boolean algebra, the two equations $(A \cap B)' = A' \cup B'$ and $(A \cup B)' = A' \cap B'$ are still referred to as the De Morgan formulas.

De Morgan was also the first logician to present a logic of relations. In a paper written in 1860 he used the notation $X..LY$ to represent the statement that X is one of the objects in the relation L to Y, while $X.LY$ meant that X was not any of the L's of Y. He also presented the idea $X..(LM)Y$ as the composition of two relations L,M, and of the inverse relation L^{-1}. This extension of the idea of subject and predicate was not adopted by any of De Morgan's successors, and the idea lapsed until Benjamin Peirce's work of 1883.

De Morgan was steeped in the history of mathematics. He wrote biographies of Newton and Halley and published an index of the correspondence of scientific men of the seventeenth century. He believed that the work of both minor and major mathematicians was essential for an assessment of mathematical development, a principle shown most clearly in his *Arithmetical Books* (1847). This work describes the many arithmetical books in the author's possession, refers to the work of 1,580 arithmeticians, and contains detailed digressions on such subjects as the length of a foot and the authorship of the popular *Cocker's Arithmetick.* De Morgan's book was written at a time when accurate bibliography was in its infancy and was probably the first significant work of scientific bibliography. Despite a lack of means, he collected a library of over 3,000 scientific books, which is now at the London University library.

De Morgan's peripheral mathematical interests included a powerful advocacy of decimal coinage; an almanac giving the dates of the new moon from 2000 B.C. to A.D. 2000; a curious work entitled *Budget of Paradoxes,* which considers, among other things, the work of would-be circle squarers; and a standard work on the theory of probability applied to life contingencies that is highly regarded in insurance literature.

BIBLIOGRAPHY

I. ORIGINAL WORKS. De Morgan's books include *The Elements of Arithmetic* (London, 1830); *Elements of Spherical Trigonometry* (London, 1834); *The Elements of Algebra Preliminary to the Differential Calculus, and Fit for the Higher Classes of Schools etc.* (London, 1835); *The Connexion of Number and Magnitude: An Attempt to Explain the Fifth Book of Euclid* (London, 1836); *Elements of Trigonometry and Trigonometrical Analysis, Preliminary to the Differential Calculus* (London, 1837); *An Essay on Probabilities, and on Their Application to Life Contingencies and Insurance Offices* (London, 1838); *First Notions of Logic, Preparatory to the Study of Geometry* (London, 1839); *Arithmetical Books From the Invention of Printing to the Present Time. Being Brief Notices of a Large Number of Works Drawn up From Actual Inspection* (London, 1847), repub. (London, 1967) with a biographical introduction by A. R. Hall; *The Differential and Integral Calculus* (London, 1842); *Formal Logic: or The Calculus of Inference, Necessary and Probable* (London, 1847); *Trigonometry and Double Algebra* (London, 1849); *The Book of Almanacs With an Index of Reference, by Which the Almanac May Be Found for Every Year . . . up to A.D. 2000. With Means of Finding the Day of Any New or Full Moon From B.C. 2000 to A.D. 2000* (London, 1851); *Syllabus of a Proposed System of Logic* (London, 1860); and *A Budget of Paradoxes* (London, 1872).

Articles by De Morgan can be found in *Quarterly Journal of Education* (1831–1833); *Cambridge Philosophical Transactions* (1830–1868); *Philosophical Magazine* (1835–1852); *Cambridge Mathematical Journal* (1841–1845); *Cambridge and Dublin Mathematical Journal* (1846–1853); *Quarterly Journal of Mathematics* (1857–1858); *Central Society of Education* (1837–1839); *The Mathematician* (1850); and *British Almanac and Companion* (1831–1857). He also contributed to *Smith's Classical Dictionary, Dublin Review, Encyclopaedia Metropolitana,* and *Penny Cyclopaedia.*

II. SECONDARY LITERATURE. On De Morgan or his work, see I. M. Bochenski, *Formale Logik* (Freiburg–Munich, 1956), pp. 306-307, 345–347, *passim;* S. De Morgan, *Memoir of Augustus De Morgan . . . With Selections From His Letters* (London, 1882); G. B. Halsted, "De Morgan as Logician," in *Journal of Speculative Philosophy,* **18** (1884), 1-9; and an obituary notice in *Monthly Notices of the Royal Astronomical Society,* **32** (1872), 112–118.

JOHN M. DUBBEY

DENJOY, ARNAUD (*b.* Auch, Gers, France, 5 January 1884; *d.* Paris, France, 21 January 1974)

Denjoy was the son of Jean Denjoy, a wine merchant in Perpignan, and of a woman surnamed Jayez, who was from Catalonia. After secondary education at Auch and Montpellier, in 1902 he entered the École Normale Supérieure in Paris, where he studied under Émile Borel, Paul Painlevé, and Charles Picard, and graduated first in his class. In 1905 he received a Fondation Thiers fellowship for a three-year period. Denjoy completed his dissertation ("Sur les produits canoniques d'ordre infini") in 1909 and was named *maître de conférences* at Montpellier University, where he taught until 1914. Poor eyesight kept him from military service during World War I. In 1917 he received a professorship at Utrecht, and in 1922 he accepted a position at the University of Paris, where he remained until his retirement in 1955.

On 15 June 1923 Denjoy married Thérèse-Marie Chevresson; they had three sons.

Denjoy led a quiet life, working most of the day at home. During the summers he enjoyed cycling on forest trails or walking along rivers and lakes. His death resulted from a fall in his home.

Elected to the Académie des Sciences in Paris on 15 June 1942, Denjoy was also a member of several other academies, including the Academy of Sciences of Amsterdam, the Société des Sciences et Lettres of Warsaw, and the Société Royale des Sciences of Liège. He was vice president of the International Mathematical Union in 1954. Although he did not write joint papers, he maintained contact with most of the great mathematical analysts, especially those from Russia, Poland, the Netherlands, and Germany.

Denjoy's weak voice and bad eyesight did not make him a notable lecturer, but in private talks he was very entertaining. His written work displayed his gift for brilliant metaphors to convey mathematical discoveries. He coined many illuminating mathematical terms, such as *clairsemé*, *gerbe*, *résiduel*, *plénitude*, and *épaisseur*.

Denjoy was an atheist, but tolerant of others' religious views; he was very interested in philosophical, psychological, and social issues. Throughout his life he wrote about them in his (unpublished) diary. In 1964 he published some of his thoughts in *Hommes, formes et le nombre*, which deals mainly with mathematical discoveries and concepts and with men of science. He liked neither the Bourbaki approach to mathematics nor its style, and at the time of his death he was planning a sharp account of his criticisms.

His activity in the Radical-Socialist Party, at the time headed by Édouard Herriot, led to Denjoy's election to the Montpellier town council in 1912 and to the Gers county council in 1920, and he served on the latter until 1940. From 1949 to 1950, just before François Duvalier became dictator, Denjoy held a cultural diplomatic position in Haiti. In 1960 he joined the Comité d'Honneur de l'Union Rationaliste, which aims to spread the spirit of science and the experimental method, and to fight dogmatism and fanaticism.

Denjoy was the youngest of the prestigious quartet of French mathematicians—the others were Émile Borel, René Baire, and Henri Lebesgue—that devised the theory of functions of real variables at a time when analytic functions $f(z)$ were more commonly studied.

By the time Denjoy completed his dissertation in 1909, Borel had introduced a theory of countably additive measure, divergent series, scales of growth and zero measure, and monogenic functions. Baire had initiated a new approach to real functions by introducing semicontinuity sets of the first category and the transfinite scale of (Baire) functions. Lebesgue had firmly established the notion of measure and his theory of integration. With those ingredients Denjoy realized a synthesis combining topological and metric tools: topology to reduce problems to basics, and metric notions for the final blow.

Denjoy had a strong classical background in complex function theory, differential equations, and continued fractions that permeated all his work. His dissertation, for instance, presented results concerning the series $\Sigma A_n/(z - a_n)$, canonical Weierstrass products for integral functions, asymptotic values of integral functions of finite order, and boundary behavior of conformal representation. Although some of these results are now considered among his best contributions, he wrote in 1934 that he considered his achievements to be (1) the integration of derivatives, (2) the computation of the coefficients of any converging trigonometric series for which the sum is given, (3) his theorem on quasi-analytic functions, and (4) differential equations on a torus.

Posterity has not always confirmed this hierarchy. For instance, the fourth achievement, which completely clarifies the "last Poincaré theorem," has grown into a vast field involving dynamical systems. His theorem concerning quasi-analytical functions (related to Borel monogeneity) and the Denjoy conjecture were the source of many subsequent studies (for example, Benoit Mandelbrot's). The first two are sometimes considered more feats of intellectual strength than sources of practical applications. It remains true, however, that they both had profound implications and that they were needed. It is likely that nobody but Denjoy could have achieved the computation of the coefficients, the results of which were first published (as were most of Denjoy's theorems) as notes in the *Comptes rendus* of the Academy of Sciences (1921). When confronted with growing skepticism, he published the complete proofs in five volumes (1941–1949). They contain much more than was required for the proofs and are an explosion of beautiful theorems and examples. Denjoy's *Leçons sur le calcul des coefficients d'une série trigonométrique* was for a long time recommended reading for research students at Moscow University. It contains, in addition to the Denjoy integral, a wealth of tangential properties of continuous functions that have inspired considerable research by Andrew Bruckner. Some of the properties were generalized by Frédéric Roger and Gustave Choquet.

BIBLIOGRAPHY

The best guide to Denjoy's works is "Arnaud Denjoy, évocation de l'homme et de l'oeuvre," in *Astérisque*, nos. 28–29. See also his *Leçons sur le calcul des coefficients d'une série trigonométrique*, 5 vols. (Paris, 1941–1949); *L'énumération transfinie*, 5 vols. (Paris, 1946–1954); *Mémoire sur la dérivation et son calcul inverse* (Paris, 1954); *Articles et mémoires*, 2 vols. (Paris, 1955); *Un demi-siècle de notes*, 2 vols. (Paris, 1957); and *Hommes, formes et le nombre* (Paris, 1964).

GUSTAVE CHOQUET

DEPARCIEUX, ANTOINE (*b.* Clotet-de-Cessous, France, 28 October 1703; *d.* Paris, France, 2 September 1768)

Deparcieux's father, Jean-Antoine, was a farmer; his mother was Jeanne Donzel. Orphaned in 1715, he was educated by his brother Pierre, who sent him at fifteen to the Jesuit college at Alès. In 1730, after finishing his studies, Deparcieux went to Paris, where he became a maker of sundials. He also investigated problems of hydraulics and conceived a plan for bringing the water of the Yvette River to Paris, which was carried out after his death. In 1746 he was admitted to membership in the Academy of Sciences.

In his *Nouveaux traités de trigonométrie rectiligne et sphérique* (Paris, 1741) Deparcieux gives a table of sines, tangents, and secants calculated to every minute and to seven places, and a table of logarithms of sines and tangents calculated to every ten minutes and to eight places. He also gives the formula for tan $a/2$ in the form of two proportions:

$$\sin s : \sin (s-c) = \sin (s-b) \sin (s-a) : x^2$$
$$\sin (s-a) : r = x : \tan \frac{A}{2},$$

but he did not use the words "cosine" and "cotangent." After long investigations of tontines, individual families, and religious communities, Deparcieux published his results in the famous *Essai sur les probabilités de la durée de la vie humaine* (Paris, 1746; suppl., 1760), one of the first statistical works of its kind. It consists of treatises on annuities, mortality, and life annuities. Deparcieux showed a real progress in his theoretical explanation of the properties of the tables of mortality. However, his tables, which were for a long time the only ones on life expectancies in France, indicated too small a value for the probable life expectancy at every age. He also made further inquiries on the concept of the mean life expectancy.

BIBLIOGRAPHY

On Deparcieux or his work, see J. Bertrand, *L'Académie des sciences et les académiciens de 1666 à 1793* (Paris, 1869), pp. 167, 168, 288, 289; A. von Braunmühl, *Vorlesungen über Geschichte der Trigonometrie,* II (Leipzig, 1903), 90; and G. F. Knapp, *Theorie des Bevölkerungs-Wechsels* (Brunswick, 1874), pp. 68–73.

H. L. L. BUSARD

DESARGUES, GIRARD (*b.* Lyons, France, 21 February 1591; *d.* France, October 1661)

One of the nine children of Girard Desargues, collector of the tithes on ecclesiastical revenues in the diocese of Lyons, and of Jeanne Croppet, Desargues seems to have studied at Lyons, where the family lived. The first evidence of his scientific activity places him in Paris on 9 September 1626, when, with another Lyonnais, François Villette, he proposed to the municipality that it construct powerful machines to raise the water of the Seine, in order to be able to distribute it in the city. Adrien Baillet, the biographer of Descartes, declares that Desargues participated as an engineer at the siege of La Rochelle in 1628 and that he there made the acquaintance of Descartes, but there is no evidence to confirm this assertion. According to the engraver Abraham Bosse (1602–1676), a fervent disciple of Desargues, the latter obtained a royal license for the publication of several writings in 1630. It was about this time that Desargues, living in Paris, seems to have become friendly with several of the leading mathematicians there: Mersenne, Gassendi, Mydorge, and perhaps Roberval. Although it is not certain that he attended the meetings at Théophraste Renaudot's Bureau d'Adresses (commencing in 1629), Mersenne cites him, in 1635, as one of those who regularly attended the meetings of his

Académie Parisienne, in which, besides Mersenne, the following participated more or less regularly: Étienne Pascal, Mydorge, Claude Hardy, Roberval, and soon Carcavi and the young Blaise Pascal.

In 1636 Desargues published two works: "Une méthode aisée pour apprendre et enseigner à lire et escrire la musique," included in Mersenne's *Harmonie universelle* (I, bk. 6), and a twelve-page booklet with one double plate that was devoted to the presentation of his "universal method" of perspective. The latter publication bore a signature that reappeared on several of Desargues's important works: S.G.D.L. (Sieur Girard Desargues Lyonnais).

Moreover, after presenting his rules of practical perspective, Desargues gave some indication of the vast program he had set for himself, a program dominated by two basic themes: on the one hand, the concern to rationalize, to coordinate, and to unify the diverse graphical techniques by his "universal methods" and, on the other, the desire to integrate the projective methods into the body of mathematics by means of a purely geometric study of perspective, several elements of which are presented in an appendix. This publication appears not to have excited a great deal of immediate interest among artists and draftsmen, who were hardly anxious to change their technique; in contrast, Descartes and Fermat, to whom Mersenne had communicated it, were able to discern Desargues's ability.

The publication in 1636 of Jean de Beaugrand's *Geostatice,* then of Descartes's *Discours de la méthode* in May 1637, gave rise to ardent discussions among the principal French thinkers on the various problems mentioned in the two books: the definition of the center of gravity, the theory of optics, the problem of tangents, the principles of analytic geometry, and so on. Desargues participated very actively in these discussions. Although he made Beaugrand his implacable enemy, his sense of moderation, his concern to eliminate all misunderstandings, and his desire to comprehend problems in their most universal aspect won him the esteem and the respect of Descartes and Mersenne, as well as of Fermat, Roberval, and Étienne Pascal. His letter to Mersenne of 4 April 1638, concerning the discussion of the problem of tangents, illustrates the depth of the insights with which he approached such questions and, at the same time, his inclination to synthesis and the universal. Even though Descartes had prepared for him an introduction to his *Géométrie,* designed to "facilitate his understanding" of it, Desargues did not follow Descartes in his parallel attempts to algebraize geometry and to create a new system of explaining all the phenomena of the universe.

Desargues's goal was at once to breathe new life into geometry, to rationalize the various graphical techniques, and, through mechanics, to extend this renewal to several areas of technique. His profound intuition of spatial geometry led him to prefer a thorough renewal of the methods of geometry rather than the Cartesian algebraization; from this preference there resulted a broad extension of the possibilities of geometry. The *Brouillon project* on conics, of which he published fifty copies in 1639, is a daring projective presentation of the theory of conic sections; although considered at first in three-dimensional space, as plane sections of a cone of revolution, these curves are in fact studied as plane perspective figures by means of involution, a transformation that holds a place of distinction in the series of demonstrations. But the use of an original vocabulary and the refusal to resort to Cartesian symbolism make the reading of this essay rather difficult and partially explain its meager success.

Although he praised the unitary conception that inspired Desargues, Descartes doubted that the use of geometry alone could yield results as good as those that a recourse to algebra would provide. As for Fermat, he reserved his judgment, and the only geometer who really comprehended the originality and breadth of Desargues's views was the young Blaise Pascal, who in 1640 published the brief *Essay pour les coniques,* inspired directly by the *Brouillon project.* But since the great *Traité des coniques* that Pascal later wrote has been lost, Desargues's example survived only in certain of the youthful works of Philippe de La Hire and perhaps in a few essays of the young Newton. The rapid success of the Cartesian method of applying algebra to geometry was certainly one of the basic reasons for the poor diffusion of Desargues's ideas. In any case the principles of projective geometry included in the *Brouillon project* were virtually forgotten until the publication in 1820 of the *Traité des propriétés projectives* of J. V. Poncelet—who, moreover, rendered a stirring homage to his precursor, although he knew his work only from a few brief mentions.

In July 1639 Beaugrand criticized Desargues's work, asserting that certain of his demonstrations can be drawn much more directly from Apollonius. Irritated that Desargues, in an appendix to his study of conic sections, had discussed the principles of mechanics and had criticized Beaugrand's conception of geostatics, Beaugrand wrote in July 1640, a few months before his death, another violent pamphlet against the *Brouillon project.*

In August 1640, Desargues published, again under the general title *Brouillon project,* an essay on techniques of stonecutting and on gnomonics. While refining certain points of his method of perspective presented in 1636, he gives an example of a new graphical method whose use he recommends in stonecutting and furnishes several principles that will simplify construction of sundials. He cites the names of a few artists and artisans who have already adopted the graphical methods he advocates: in particular the painter Laurent de La Hire and the engraver Abraham Bosse. In attempting thus to improve the graphical procedures employed by many technicians, Desargues was in fact attacking an area of activity governed by the laws of the trade guilds; he also drew the open hostility of all those who were attached to the old methods and felt they were being injured by his preference for theory rather than practice.

At the end of 1640 Desargues published a brief commentary on the principles of gnomonics presented in his *Brouillon project;* this text is known only through several references, in particular the opinion of Descartes, who found it a "very beautiful invention and so much the more ingenious in that it is so simple." Since 1637 Descartes had conducted an indirect correspondence with Desargues that had been established through Mersenne, and the two men had exchanged ideas on a number of subjects; in this way Desargues took an active part in the discussions that preceded the definite statement and the publication of Descartes's *Méditations.*

At the beginning of 1641 Desargues had Mersenne propose to his mathematical correspondents that they determine circular sections on cones having a conic for a base and any vertex. He himself had a general solution obtained solely by the methods of pure geometry, a solution that is known to us through Mersenne's comments (in *Universae geometriae mixtaeque mathematicae synopsis* [Paris, 1644], the preface to Mydorge's *Coniques,* pp. 330–331). Roberval, Descartes, and Pascal were interested in the problem, which Desargues generalized in his investigation of the plane sections of cones satisfying the above conditions. References in publications of the period seem to indicate that around 1641 Desargues published a second essay on conic sections, cited sometimes under the title of *Leçons de ténèbres.* But since no copy of this work has been found, one may suppose that there may be some confusion here with another work, either the *Brouillon project* of 1639 or with a preliminary edition of certain manuscripts on perspective that were later included in Bosse's *Manière universelle de Mr Desargues pour pratiquer la perspective* . . . (Paris, 1648). Yet a work that appeared later, Grégoire Huret's *Optique de portraiture et de peinture* . . . (Paris, 1670), specifies (pp. 157–158) that the *Leçons de ténèbres* is based on the principle of perspective that inasmuch as the sections of a cone with a circular base and any vertex are, for all cones, circles for two specific orientations of the cutting plane, therefore in general the projective properties of the circle may be extended to various types of conics, considered as perspectives of circles. This systematic recourse to considerations of spatial geometry obviously does not permit the identification of this work with either the *Brouillon project* of 1639 or the geometric texts of 1648 (mentioned below). But, in the absence of the decisive proof that would be provided by the rediscovery of a copy of the *Leçons de ténèbres,* no definite conclusion can be reached.

Desargues strove to spread the use of his graphical methods among practitioners and succeeded in having them experiment with his stonecutting diagrams without encountering very strong resistance. At the beginning of 1642, however, the anonymous publication of the first volume of *La perspective pratique* (written by the Jesuit Jean Dubreuil) gave rise to bitter polemics. Finding that his own method of perspective was both copied and distorted in this book, Desargues had two placards posted in Paris in which he accused the author and the publishers of this treatise of plagiarism and obtuseness. The publishers asserted that they had drawn his so-called "universal" method from a work by Vaulezard (*Abrégé ou raccourcy de la perspective par l'imitation* . . . [Paris, 1631]) and from a manuscript treatise of Jacques Aleaume (1562–1627) that was to be brought out by E. Migon (*La perspective spéculative et pratique* . . . *de l'invention de feu Jacques Aleaume* . . . *mise au jour par Estienne Migon* [Paris, 1643]). Desargues having replied with a new attack, Tavernier and l'Anglois, Dubreuil's publishers, brought out in 1642 a collection of anonymous pamphlets against Desargues's various writings on perspective, stonecutting, and gnomonics, to which they added the *Lettre de M. de Beaugrand* . . . of August 1640, which was directed against his projective study of conics.

Desargues, greatly affected by these attacks, which concerned the body of his work and put his competence and his honesty in question, entrusted to his most fervent disciple, the engraver Abraham Bosse, the task of spreading his methods and of defending his work. In 1643 Bosse devoted two treatises to presenting Desargues's methods in stonecutting and in gnomonics: *La pratique du trait à preuves de Mr Desargues, Lyonnois, pour la coupe des pierres en l'architecture* . . . and *La manière universelle de Mr Desargues, Lyonnois, pour poser l'essieu et placer les heures et autres choses aux cadrans au soleil.* Preceded by an "Acknowledgment" in which Desargues states he has given Bosse the responsibility for the spread of his methods, these works are clearly addressed to a less informed audience than the brief essays that Desargues had published on the same subjects. Their theoretical portion is greatly reduced and more elementary, and numerous examples of applications are handled in a very didactic and often prolix manner. Although only fifty copies of Desargues's essays had been printed, and had been distributed mainly in scientific circles, Bosse's writings were given large printings and were translated into several languages; consequently, they contributed to the diffusion of Desargues's graphical methods among practitioners.

In 1644, however, new attacks were launched against Desargues's work. They originated with a stonecutter, J. Curabelle, who violently criticized his writings on stonecutting, perspective, and gnomonics, as well as the two treatises Bosse published in 1643, claiming to find nothing in them but mediocrity, errors, plagiarism, and information of no practical interest. A very harsh polemic began between the two men, and Desargues published the pamphlet *Récit au vray de ce qui a esté la cause de faire cet escrit,* which contains a number of previously unpublished details on his life and work. He also attempted to sue Curabelle, but the latter seems to have succeeded in evading this action.

Although Desargues apparently gave up publishing, Abraham Bosse wrote an important treatise on his master's method of perspective, commenting in detail on a great many examples of the graphical processes deriving from the "universal method" outlined in 1636. This *Manière universelle de Mr Desargues pour pratiquer la perspective par petit-pied, comme le géométral, ensemble les places et proportions des fortes et foibles touches, teintes ou couleurs* (Paris, 1648) was directly inspired by Desargues and contains, in addition to a reprint of the *Exemple de l'une des manières universelles*. . . of 1636, several elaborations designed "for theoreticians" and others that are purely geometrical. These elaborations, which include the statement and proof of the famous theorem on perspective triangles, should be considered (at least those relating to the theorem should be) as having been written by Desargues. Certain remarks seem to indicate that these theoretical developments may have been the subject of an earlier version published in 1643, under the title of *Livret de perspective,* but no definite proof has yet been established. In 1653 Bosse completed this work with an account of perspective on planes and on irregular surfaces, which included several applications to his favorite technique, copperplate engraving. Desargues's influence is again evident, at least in the first part of this work, but it is less direct than in the *Manière* of 1648.

Meanwhile, relations between the two men had become less close. While continuing his work as an engraver and an artist, Bosse, since 1648, had been teaching perspective according to Desargues's methods at the Académie Royale de Peinture et de Sculpture. He continued to teach there until 1661, when the Academy, following a long and violent polemic in which Desargues intervened personally in 1657, barred him from all his duties, thus implicitly condemning the use and diffusion of the methods of perspective to which it had accorded its patronage for thirteen years. But Bosse continued, through his writings, to conduct a passionate propaganda campaign for his methods.

As for Desargues, after 1644 evidence of his scientific and polemic activity becomes much rarer. Besides the "Acknowledgment" (dated 1 October 1647) and the geometric elaborations inserted in Bosse's 1648 treatise on perspective, Descartes's correspondence (letter to Mersenne of 31 January 1648) alludes to an experiment made by Desargues, toward the end of 1647, in the context of the debates and investigations then being conducted by the Paris physicists on the nature of the barometric space. It seems that while remaining in close contact with the Paris scientists, Desargues had commenced another aspect of his work, that of architect and practitioner. There was no better reply to give to his adversaries, who accused him of wanting to impose arbitrary work rules on disciplines that he understood only superficially and theoretically. Probably, as Baillet states, he had already been technical adviser and engineer in Richelieu's entourage, but he had not yet had any real contact with the graphical techniques he wished to reform. It seems that his new career as an architect, begun in Paris about 1645, was continued in Lyons, to which he returned around 1649–1650, then again in Paris, to which he returned in 1657. He remained there until 1661, the year of his death.

In Paris the authors of the period attribute to Desargues, besides a few houses and mansions, several staircases whose complex structure and spectacular character attest to the exactitude and efficacy of his graphical stonecutting procedures. It also seems that he collaborated, for the realization of certain effects of architectural perspective, with the famous painter Philippe de Champaigne. In the region of Lyons, Desargues's architectural creations were likewise quite numerous; he participated in the planning of several private and public buildings and of rooms whose architecture was particularly delicate. Of Desargues's accomplishments as an engineer, which seem to have been many, only one is well known and is worth mentioning: a system for raising water that he installed near Paris, at the château of Beaulieu. This system, based on the use, until then unknown, of epicycloidal wheels, was described and drawn by Huygens in 1671 (*Oeuvres de Huygens,* VII, 112), by which time the château had become the property of Charles Perrault. Philippe de La Hire, who had to repair this mechanism, wrote about it (see *Traité de méchanique* [Paris, 1695], pp. 10, 368–374).

To complete this description of Desargues's activity, it is necessary to mention the private instruction he gave at Paris in order to reveal his different graphical procedures. Even before 1640 he had several disciples at Paris, as well as at Lyons, where, Moreri states, he was "of great assistance to the workmen . . . to whom he communicated his diagrams and his knowledge, with no motive other than being useful" (*Le grand dictionnaire historique,* new ed., I [Paris, 1759], 297).

In 1660 Desargues was again active in the intellectual life of Paris, attending meetings at Montmor's Academy, such as one on 9 November 1660, at which Huygens heard him present a report on the problem of the existence of the geometric point and sharply discuss the matter with someone who contradicted him. This is the last trace of his activity; the reading of his will at Lyons on 8 October 1661 revealed only that he had died several days before, without stating the date or place of his death, concerning which no document has yet been found.

A geometer of profoundly original ideas, sustained at the same time by a sense of spatial reality, by a much more precise knowledge of the great classic works than he admitted, and by an exceptional familiarity with the whole range of contemporary techniques, Desargues, in his geometrical work, introduced the principal concepts of projective geometry: the consideration of points and straight lines to infinity, studies of poles and polars, the introduction of projective transformations, the general definition of focuses, the unitary study of conics, and so on. Unfortunately, his work, burdened by a too original vocabulary and the absence of symbolism, and known only in a very limited circle, did not receive the audience it deserved. The disappearance of the essential portion of the work of his chief disciple, Blaise Pascal, and the sudden vogue of analytic geometry and infinitesimal calculus prevented the seventeenth century from witnessing the revival of geometry for which Desargues had laid the foundations. His few known forays into other areas of mathematics and mechanics attest to a perfect mastery of all the problems then under discussion and make us regret the absence of any publication by him. In the field of graphical techniques his contribution is of major importance. Between Dürer and Monge he marks an essential stage in the rationalization of the ensemble of these techniques, as much by the improvements he made in the various procedures then in use as by his concern for unity, for theoretical rigor, and for universality. But in this vast area, too, his innovations were bitterly contested and often rejected with contempt, even though the goal of their author was to reduce the burden of the practitioners through a closer and more trusting collaboration with the theorists.

After the reception, often reserved and sometimes malicious, that it received in his time and the oblivion that it experienced subsequently, Desargues's work was rediscovered and fully appreciated by the geometers of the nineteenth century. Thus, like that of all precursors, his work revealed its fruitfulness much more by its remote extensions than by its immediate repercussions.

BIBLIOGRAPHY

I. Original Works. Desargues's works, most of them published in editions of a small number of copies, are very rare. N. Poudra republished most of them in *Oeuvres de Desargues réunies et analysées* . . ., 2 vols. (Paris, 1864), but they are imperfect. The purely mathematical texts have been republished in an improved form by René Taton, as *L'oeuvre mathématique de Desargues* (Paris, 1951), pp. 75–212, with a bibliography of Desargues's writings and their editions, pp. 67–73. Aside from the polemic writings, prefaces, acknowledgments, and such, listed in the bibliography mentioned above, Desargues's main works and their most recent editions are the following: "Une méthode aisée pour apprendre et enseigner à lire et escrire la musique," in Mersenne's *Harmonie universelle,* I (Paris, 1638), bk. 6, prop. 1, pp. 332–342, repr. in photocopy (Paris, 1963); *Exemple de l'une des manières universelles du S.G.D.L. touchant la pratique de la perspective* . . . (Paris, 1636), also in Abraham Bosse, *Manière universelle de Mr Desargues pour pratiquer la perspective* . . . (Paris, 1648), pp. 321–334 (incorrect title), and in N. Poudra, *Oeuvres de Desargues,* I, 55–84, which follows the Bosse version; *Brouillon project d'une atteinte aux événemens des rencontres du cone avec un plan,* followed by *Atteinte aux événemens des contrarietez d'entre les actions des puissances ou forces* and an *Avertissement* (errata) (Paris, 1639), also in Poudra, I, 103–230, which includes omissions and errors, and in Taton, pp. 87–184, where the original version is reproduced without the figures; *Brouillon project d'exemple d'une manière universelle du S.G.D.L. touchant la practique du trait à preuves pour la coupe des pierres en l'architecture* . . . (Paris, 1640), also in Poudra, I, 305–358, with incorrect plates; original plates repub. by W. M. Ivins, Jr., in *Bulletin of the Metropolitan Museum of Art,* new ser., **1** (1942), 33–45; *Leçons de ténèbres* (Paris, 1640 [?]), which has not been found but may exist; *Manière universelle de poser le style aux rayons du soleil* . . .

(Paris, 1640), which has not been found but whose existence is definite, partly reconstructed in Poudra, I, 387-392; and *Livret de perspective adressé aux théoriciens* (Paris, 1643 [?]), which has not been found but is perhaps identical with the last part of Abraham Bosse's *Manière universelle de Mr Desargues pour pratiquer la perspective*... (Paris, 1648), pp. 313-343.

II. SECONDARY LITERATURE. Desargues directly inspired three works by Abraham Bosse: *La manière universelle de Mr Desargues, Lyonnois, pour poser l'essieu et placer les heures et autres choses aux cadrans au soleil* (Paris, 1643), also trans. into English (London, 1659); *La pratique du trait à preuves de Mr Desargues, Lyonnois, pour la coupe des pierres en l'architecture* (Paris, 1643), also trans. into German (Nuremberg, 1699); and *Manière universelle de Mr Desargues pour pratiquer la perspective* . . ., 2 vols. (Paris, 1648-1653), also trans. into Dutch, 2 vols. (Amsterdam, 1664; 2nd ed., 1686).

A lengthy bibliography of secondary literature is given in Taton's *L'oeuvre mathématique de Desargues.* The most important works cited are the following (listed chronologically): A. Baillet, *La vie de Monsieur des Cartes,* 2 vols. (Paris, 1691), *passim;* R. P. Colonia, *Histoire littéraire de la ville de Lyon* . . ., II (Paris, 1730), 807 f.; L. Moreri, *Le grand dictionnaire historique,* new ed., I (Paris, 1759), 297; J. V. Poncelet, *Traité des propriétés projectives* (Paris, 1822), pp. xxxviii-xxxxiii; M. Chasles, *Aperçu historique sur l'origine et le développement des méthodes en géométrie* . . . (Brussels, 1837), see index; and *Rapport sur les progrès de la géométrie* (Paris, 1870), pp. 303-306; G. Poudra, "Biographie," in *Oeuvres de Desargues* ..., I, 11-52; and *Histoire de la perspective* (Paris, 1864), pp. 249-270; G. Eneström, "Notice bibliographique sur un traité de perspective publié par Desargues en 1636," in *Bibliotheca mathematica,* **1** (1885), 89-90; "Die 'Leçons de ténèbres' des Desargues," *ibid.,* 3rd ser., **3** (1902), 411; "Über dem französischen Mathematiker Pujos," *ibid.,* **8** (1907-1908), 97; and "Girard Desargues und D.A.L.G.," *ibid.,* **14** (1914), 253-254; S. Chrzasczewski, "Desargues Verdienste um die Begründung der projectivischen Geometrie," in *Archiv der Mathematik und Physik,* 2nd ser., **16** (1898), 119-149; E. L. G. Charvet, *Lyon artistique. Architectes* . . . (Lyons, 1899), pp. 120-122; F. Amodeo, "Nuovo analisi del trattato delle coniche di Gerard [*sic*] Desargues e cenni da J. B. Chauveau," in *Rendiconti dell'Accademia delle scienze fisiche e matematiche* (Naples), ser. 3a, **12** (1906), 232-262; and *Origine e sviluppo della geometria proiettiva* (Naples, 1939), *passim;* J. L. Coolidge, *The History of Geometrical Methods* (Oxford, 1940), pp. 90, 109; and *The History of Conic Sections and Quadric Surfaces* (Oxford, 1949), pp. 28-33; M. Zacharias, "Desargues Bedeutung für die projektive Geometrie," in *Deutsche Mathematik,* **5** (1941), 446-457; W. M. Ivins, Jr., "Two First Editions of Desargues," in *Bulletin of the Metropolitan Museum of Art,* n.s. **1** (1942), 33-45; "A Note of Girard Desargues," in *Scripta mathematica,* **9** (1943), 33-48; *Art and Geometry. A Study in Space Intuition* (Cambridge, Mass., 1946), pp. 103-112; and "A Note on Desargues's Theorem," in *Scripta mathematica,* **13** (1947), 202-210; and F. Lenger, "La notion d'involution dans l'oeuvre de Desargues," in *IIe Congrès national des sciences, Bruxelles* . . ., I (Liège, 1950), 109-112.

Some more recent studies that should be noted are the following (listed chronologically): P. Moisy, "Textes retrouvés de Desargues," in *XVIIe siècle,* no. 11 (1951), 93-95; R. Taton, "Documents nouveaux concernant Desargues," in *Archives internationales d'histoire des sciences,* **4** (1951), 620-630; and "Sur la naissance de Girard Desargues," in *Revue d'histoire des sciences,* **15** (1962), 165-166; A. Machabey, "Gérard [*sic*] Desargues, géomètre et musicien," in *XVIIe siècle,* no. 21-22 (1954), 346-402; P. Costabel, "Note sur l'annexe du Brouillon-Project de Desargues," in *7° Congrès international d'histoire des sciences. Jérusalem, 1953* (Paris, n.d.), pp. 241-245; A. Birembaut, "Quelques documents nouveaux sur Desargues," in *Revue d'histoire des sciences,* **14** (1961), 193-204; and S. Le Tourneur, in *Dictionnaire de biographie française,* X (1964), 1183-1184.

RENÉ TATON

DESCARTES, RENÉ DU PERRON (*b.* La Haye, Touraine, France, 31 March 1596; *d.* Stockholm, Sweden, 11 February 1650)

Fontenelle, in the eloquent contrast made in his *Éloge de Newton,* described Descartes as the man who "tried in one bold leap to put himself at the source of everything, to make himself master of the first principles by means of certain clear and fundamental ideas, so that he could then simply descend to the phenomena of nature as to necessary consequences of these principles." This famous characterization of Descartes as the theoretician who "set out from what he knew clearly, in order to find the cause of what he saw," as against Newton the experimenter, who "set out from what he saw, in order to find the cause," has tended to dominate interpretations of both these men who "saw the need to carry geometry into physics."[1]

Descartes was born into the *noblesse de robe,* whose members contributed notably to intellectual life in seventeenth-century France. His father was *conseiller* to the Parlement of Brittany; from his mother he received the name du Perron and financial independence from property in Poitou. From the Jesuits of La Flèche he received a modern education in mathematics and physics—including Galileo's telescopic discoveries—as well as in philosophy and the classics, and there began the twin domination of imagination and geometry over his precocious mind. He described in an early work, the *Olympica,* how he found "in the writings of the poets weightier thoughts than in those of the philosophers. The reason is that the poets wrote through enthusiasm and the power of imagination." The seeds of knowledge in us, "as in a flint," were brought to light by philosophers "through reason; struck out through imagination by poets they shine forth more brightly."[2] Then, after graduating in law from the University of Poitiers, as a gentleman volunteer in the army of Prince Maurice of Nassau in 1618 he met Isaac Beeckman at Breda. Beeckman aroused him to self-discovery as a scientific thinker and mathematician and introduced him to a range of problems, especially in mechanics and acoustics, the subject of his first work, the *Compendium musicae* of 1618; published posthumously in 1650. On 26 March 1619 he reported to Beeckman his first glimpse of "an entirely new science,"[3] which was to become his analytical geometry.

Later in the year, on 10 November, then in the duke of Bavaria's army on the Danube, he had the experience in the famous *poêle* (lit. "stove," "well-heated room"), claimed to have given direction to the rest of his life. He described in the *Discours de la méthode* how, in a day of solitary thought, he reached two radical conclusions: first, that if he were to discover true knowledge he must carry out the whole program himself, just as a perfect work of art or architecture was always the work of one master hand; second, that he must begin by methodically doubting everything taught in current philosophy and look for self-evident, certain principles from which to reconstruct all the sciences. That night, according to his seventeenth-century biographer Adrien Baillet, these resolutions were reinforced by three consecutive dreams. He found himself, first, in a street swept by a fierce wind, unable to stand, as his companions were doing, because of a weakness in his right leg; second, awakened by a clap of thunder in a room full of sparks; and third, with a dictionary, then a book in which he read *Quid vitae sectabor iter?* ("What way of life shall I follow?"), then verses presented by an unknown man beginning *Est et non*; he recognized the Latin as the opening lines of two poems by Ausonius. Before he finally awoke he had interpreted the first dream as a warning against past errors, the second as the descent of the spirit of truth, and the third as the opening to him of the path to true knowledge. However this incident may have been elaborated in the telling, it symbolizes both the strength and the hazards of Descartes's unshakable confidence and resolve to work alone. But he did not make his vision his life's mission for another nine years, during which (either before or after his tour of Italy from 1623 to 1625) he met Mersenne, who was to become his lifelong correspondent, and took part in scientific meetings in Paris. The next decisive incident, according to Baillet, was a public encounter in 1628 in which he demolished the unfortunate Chandoux by using his method to distinguish sharply between true scientific knowledge and mere probability. Among those present was the influential Cardinal de Bérulle, who a few days later charged him to devote his life to working out the application of "his manner of philosophizing . . . to medicine and mechanics. The one would contribute to the restoration and conservation of health, and the other to some diminution and relief in the labours of mankind."[4] To execute this design he withdrew, toward the end of the year, to the solitary life in the Netherlands which he lived until his last journey to Stockholm in 1649, where, as Queen Christina's philosopher, he died in his first winter.

The primarily centrifugal direction of Descartes's thought, moving out into detailed phenomena from a firm central theory (in contrast with the more empirical scientific style of Francis Bacon and Newton), is shown by the sequence of composition of his major writings. He set out his method in the *Rules for the Direction of the Mind,* left unfinished in 1628 and published posthumously, and in the *Discours de la méthode,* written in the Netherlands along with the *Météores, La dioptrique,* and *La géométrie,* which he presented as examples of the method. All were published in one volume in 1637. At the same time his investigation into the true ontology led him to the radical division of created existence into matter as simply extended substance, given motion at the creation, and mind as unextended thinking substance. This conclusion he held to be guaranteed by the perfection of God, who would not deceive true reason. How these two mutually exclusive and collectively exhaustive categories of substance could have any interaction in the embodied soul that was a man was a question discussed between Gassendi, Hobbes, and Descartes in the *Objections and Replies* published with his *Meditations on First Philosophy* in 1641.

It was from these first principles that he had given an account in *Le monde, ou Traité de la lumière* of cosmogony and cosmology as products simply of matter in motion, making the laws of motion the ultimate "laws of nature" and all scientific explanation ultimately mechanistic. This treatise remained unpublished in Descartes's lifetime. So too did the associated treatise *L'homme,* in which he represented animals and the human body as sheer mechanisms, an idea already found in the *Rules.* He withheld these essays, on the brink of publication, at the news of Galileo's condemnation in 1633, and instead published his general system of physics, with its Copernicanism mitigated by the idea that all motion is relative, in the *Principles of Philosophy* in 1644. Finally, he brought physiological psychology within the compass of his system in *Les passions de l'âme* in 1649. This system aimed to be as complete as Aristotle's, which it was designed to replace. It was not by chance that it dealt in the same order with many of the same phenomena (such as the rainbow), as well as with others more recently investigated (such as magnetism).

A comparison of Descartes's performance with his program of scientific method presents a number of apparent contradictions. He made much of the ideal of a mathematically demonstrated physics, yet his fundamental cosmology was so nearly entirely qualitative that he came to fear that he had produced nothing more than a beautiful "romance of nature."[5] His planetary dynamics was shown by Newton to be quantitatively ridiculous. He wrote in the *Discours,* "I noticed also with respect to experiments [*expériences*] that they become so much the more necessary, the more we advance in knowledge,"[6] yet his fundamental laws of nature, the laws of motion and impact, had to be dismantled by Huygens and Leibniz for their lack of agreement with observation. These apparent contradictions may be resolved in the contrast between Descartes's theoretical ideal of completed scientific knowledge and the actual process and circumstances of acquiring such knowledge. For the modern reader to pay too much attention to his mechanics and to the *Principles,* a premature conception of completed science, can obscure Descartes's firm grasp of the necessity for observation and experiment already expressed in the *Rules* in his criticism "of those philosophers who neglect experiments and expect truth to rise from their own heads like Minerva from Jupiter's."[7]

No other great philosopher, except perhaps Aristotle, can have spent so much time in experimental observation. According to Baillet, over several years he studied anatomy, dissected and vivisected embryos of birds and cattle, and went on to study chemistry. His correspondence from the Netherlands described dissections of dogs, cats, rabbits, cod, and mackerel; eyes, livers, and hearts obtained from an abattoir; experiments on the weight of the air and on vibrating strings; and observations on rainbows, parahelia, and other optical phenomena. Many of his scientific writings reflect these activities and show sound experimental knowledge, although the extreme formalism of his physiological models obscures the question of his actual knowledge of some aspects of anatomy. Attention to the whole range of his scientific thought and practice shows a clear conception not only of completed scientific knowledge but also of the roles of experiment and hypothesis in making discoveries and finding explanations by which the body of scientific knowledge was built up.

Descartes's conception of completed scientific knowledge was essentially that envisaged by Aristotle's true scientific demonstration. It was the geometers' conception of a system deduced from self-evident and certain premises. He wrote,

> In physics I should consider that I knew nothing if I were able to explain only how things might be, without demonstrating that they could not be otherwise. For, having reduced physics to mathematics, this is something possible, and I think that I can do it within the small compass of my knowledge, although I have not done it in my essays.[8]

His optimism about the possibility of achieving such demonstrations seems to have depended on which end of the chain of reasoning he was contemplating. When considering the results of his analysis reducing created existence to extension (with motion) and thought, he seems to have been confident that it would be possible to show that from these "simple natures" the composite observed world must follow. It may be argued that his treatment of motion failed just where his a priori confidence led him to suppose that his analysis (of what was soon seen to be an insufficient range of data) placed his first principles beyond the need for empirical test. But when considering the chain lower down, nearer this complex world, he was more hesitant. He wrote to Mersenne:

> You ask me whether I think what I have written about refraction is a demonstration. I think it is, at least as far as it is possible, without having proved the principles of physics previously by metaphysics, to give any demonstration on this subject . . . as far as any other question of mechanics, optics, or astronomy, or any other question which is not purely geometrical or arithmetical, has ever been demonstrated. But to demand that I should give geometrical demonstrations of matters which depend on physics is to demand that I should do the impossible. If you restrict the use of "demonstration" to geometrical proofs only, you will be obliged to say that Archimedes demonstrated nothing in mechanics, nor Vitellio in optics, nor Ptolemy in astronomy, etc., which is not commonly maintained. For, in such matters, one is satisfied that the writers, having presupposed certain things which are not obviously contradictory to experience, have besides argued consistently and without logical fallacy, even if their assumptions are not exactly true.[9]

The paradox of Descartes as a natural scientist is that his grasp improved the more hopeless he found the immediate possibility of deducing solutions of detailed problems from his general first principles. Standing amidst the broken sections of a chain that he could not cast up to heaven, the experimentalist and constructor of hypothetical models came to life. In Descartes's letter prefaced to the French translation

DESCARTES

of the *Principles* (1647), he wrote that two, and only two, conditions determined whether the first principles proposed could be accepted as true: "First they must be so clear and evident that the mind of man cannot doubt their truth when it attentively applies itself to consider them"; and secondly, everything else must be deducible from them. But he went on to admit, "It is really only God alone who has perfect wisdom, that is to say, who has a complete knowledge of the truth of all things."[10] To find the truth about complex material phenomena man must experiment, but as the sixth part of the *Discours* shows, the need to experiment was an expression of the failure of the ideal.

As well as being demonstrative, scientific knowledge had to be explanatory; for Descartes the two went together. He wrote, "I have described . . . the whole visible world as if it were only a machine in which there was nothing to consider but the shapes and movements [of its parts]."[11] To such a mechanism it was possible to apply mathematics and calculation, but it was the mechanism that explained. His insistence that even mathematical science without fundamental explanations was insufficient appears in his interestingly similar criticisms of Harvey for starting simply with a beating heart in explaining the circulation of the blood and of Galileo for likewise failing to reduce the mathematical laws of moving bodies to their ultimate mechanisms. He commented on the latter that "without having considered the first causes of nature, he has only looked for the reasons for certain particular effects, and that thus he has built without foundation."[12] By this insistence Descartes here again extracted from the failure of his ideal a fundamental contribution to scientific thinking. He became the first great master to make the hypothetical model, or "conjecture," a systematic tool of research.

Current natural philosophy accepted Aristotle's absolute ontological distinction between naturally generated bodies (inanimate and animate) and artificial things made by man. Hence, in principle no humanly constructed imitation or model could throw real light on the naturally endowed essence and cause of behavior. This distinction had become blurred in the partial mechanization of nature made by some philosophers. Descartes's innovation was to assert the identity of the synthesized artificial construction with the naturally generated product and to make this identification an instrument of scientific research:

> And certainly there are no rules in mechanics that do not hold also in physics, of which mechanics forms a part or species [so that all artificial things are at the same time natural]: for it is not less natural for a clock, made of these or those wheels, to indicate the hours, than for a tree which has sprung from this or that seed to produce a particular fruit. Accordingly, just as those who apply themselves to the consideration of automata, when they know the use of some machine and see some of its parts, easily infer from these the manner in which others which they have not seen are made, so, from the perceptible effects and parts of natural bodies, I have endeavoured to find out what are their imperceptible causes and parts.[13]

This reduction made the principles of the mechanistic model the only principles operating in nature, thus bringing the objectives of the engineer into the search for the nature of things and throwing the entire world of matter open to the same form of scientific inquiry and explanation. Research, whether into cosmology or physiology, was reduced to the discovery and elucidation of mechanisms. He could construct in distant space the imaginary world of *Le monde* and *L'homme,* and later the world of the *Principles,* as explicitly and unambiguously hypothetical imitations of our actual world, made in accordance with the known laws of mechanics. The heuristic power of the model was that, like any other theory advanced in anticipation of facts, its own properties suggested new questions to put to nature. The main issue in any historical judgment of Descartes here is not whether his own answers were correct but whether his questions were fruitful. In insisting that experiment and observation alone could show whether the model corresponded with actuality, he introduced further precision into his theory of demonstration.

Descartes used the word *demonstrer* to cover both the explanation of the observed facts by the assumed theory and the proof of the truth of the theory. When challenged with the criticism that this might make the argument circular, he replied by contrasting two kinds of hypothesis.[14] In astronomy various geometrical devices, admittedly false in nature, were employed to yield true conclusions only in the sense that they "saved the appearances." But physical theories were proposed as true. He was persuaded of the truth of the assumption that the material world consisted of particles in motion by the number of different effects he could deduce, as diverse as the operation of vision, the properties of salt, the formation of snow, the rainbow, and so on. Thus he made range of application the empirical criterion of truth. He wrote in the *Discours:*

> If some of the matters of which I have spoken in the beginning of the *Dioptrique* and the *Météores* should, at first sight, shock people because I have called them suppositions, and do not seem to bother about their proof, let them have the patience to read them carefully

right through, and I hope that they will find themselves satisfied. For it seems to me that the reasonings are so interwoven that as the later ones are demonstrated by the earlier which are their causes, these earlier ones are reciprocally demonstrated by the later which are their effects. And it must not be thought that in this I commit the fallacy which logicians call arguing in a circle, for, since experience renders the majority of these effects very certain, the causes from which I deduce them do not so much serve to prove them as to explain them; on the other hand, the causes are proved by the effects.[15]

The test implied precisely by the criterion of range of confirmation was the *experimentum crucis.* This is the most obvious feature in common between Descartes's logic of experiment and that of Francis Bacon. Descartes described its function in the *Discours:*

> Reviewing in my mind all the objects that have ever been presented to my senses, I venture truly to say that I have not there observed anything that I could not satisfactorily explain by the principles I had discovered. But I must also confess that the power of nature is so ample and so vast and that these principles are so simple and so general, that I have observed hardly any particular effect that I could not at once recognize to be deducible from them in several different ways, and that my greatest difficulty is usually to discover in which of these ways it depends on them. In such a case, I know no other expedient than to look again for experiments [*expériences*] such that their result is not the same if it has to be explained in one of these ways as it would be if explained in the other.[16]

It was a logician rather than an experimenter who seems to have been uppermost in Descartes's application of this criterion in the same way to very general assumptions, such as the corpuscularian natural philosophy, and to questions as particular as whether the blood left the heart in systole or in diastole. Descartes argued in *La description du corps humain* (1648–1649) that whereas Harvey's theory that the blood was forced out of the heart by a muscular contraction might agree with the facts observed so far, "that does not exclude the possibility that all the same effects might follow from another cause, namely from the dilatation of the blood which I have described. But in order to be able to decide which of these two causes is true, we must consider other observations which cannot agree with both of them."[17] Harvey replied in his *Second Disquisition to Jean Riolan.*

As the great optimist of the scientific movement of the seventeenth century, Descartes habitually wrote as if he had succeeded in discovering the true principles of nature to such an extent that the whole scientific program was within sight of completion. Then, as Seth Ward neatly put it, "when the operations of nature shall be followed up to their staticall (and mechanicall) causes, the use of induction will cease, and syllogisme succeed in place of it." But Descartes would surely have agreed with Ward's qualification that "in the interim we are to desire that men have patience not to lay aside induction before they have reason."[18]

NOTES

1. Fontenelle, *Oeuvres diverses,* new ed., III (The Hague, 1729), 405–406.
2. Part of the *Olympica* incorporated in the *Cogitationes privatae* (1619–1621); see *Oeuvres,* X, 217.
3. *Oeuvres,* X, 156.
4. Baillet, II, 165.
5. *Ibid.,* preface, p. xviii.
6. *Oeuvres,* VI, 63.
7. Rule V; see *Oeuvres,* X, 380.
8. Letter to Mersenne, 11 Mar. 1640; see *Oeuvres,* III, 39. The "Essays" were the volume of 1637.
9. Letter to Mersenne, 27 May 1638; see *Oeuvres,* II, 141–142.
10. *Oeuvres,* IX, pt. 2, 2–3.
11. *Principia philosophiae,* IV, 188; *Oeuvres,* VIII, pt. 1, 315 (Latin); IX, pt. 2, 310 (French, alone with passage in square brackets).
12. Letter to Mersenne, 11 Oct. 1638; see *Oeuvres,* II, 380. For his comments on Harvey, see *Discours V.*
13. *Principia philosophiae,* IV, 203; *Oeuvres,* VIII, pt. 1, 326 (Latin); IX, pt. 2, 321–322 (French, alone with passage in square brackets).
14. Letter to J.-B. Morin, 13 July 1638; see *Oeuvres,* II, 197–202; cf. his letters to Vatier, 22 Feb. 1638, *ibid.,* I, 558–565, and to Mersenne, 1 Mar. 1638, *ibid.,* II, 31–32.
15. *Oeuvres,* VI, 76.
16. *Ibid.,* pp. 64–65; cf. *Principia philosophiae,* III, 46; VIII, pt. 2, 100–101; and IX, pt. 2, 124–125.
17. *Oeuvres,* XI, 241–242; cf. the comments on this controversy by J. B. Duhamel, "Quae sit cordis motus effectrix causa," in *Philosophia vetus et nova.* II, *Physica generalis,* III.ii.2 (Paris, 1684), 628–631.
18. *Vindiciae academiarum* (Oxford, 1654), p. 25.

BIBLIOGRAPHY

Descartes's complete works can be found in *Oeuvres de Descartes,* C. Adam and P. Tannery, eds., 12 vols. (Paris, 1897–1913), together with the revised *Correspondance,* C. Adam and G. Milhaud, eds. (Paris, 1936–). Besides these, primary sources for Descartes's life are Adrien Baillet, *La vie de Monsieur Descartes,* 2 vols. (Paris, 1691), which should be read with C. Adam, *Vie et oeuvres de Descartes* (in *Oeuvres,* XII); Isaac Beeckman, *Journal tenu . . . de 1604 à 1634,* C. de Waard, ed., 3 vols. (The Hague, 1939–1953): Marin Mersenne, *Correspondance,* C. de Waard, R. Pintard, B. Rochot, eds. (Paris, 1932–).

For Descartes's philosophy and method and their background, see E. Gilson, *Index scolastico-cartésien* (Paris, 1912); *Études sur le rôle de la pensée médiévale dans la formation du système cartésien* (Paris, 1930); *Discours de la méthode: texte et commentaire* (Paris, 1947); Alexandre Koyré, *Entretiens sur Descartes* (Paris–New York, 1944);

G. Milhaud, *Descartes savant* (Paris, 1921); L. Roth, *Descartes' Discourse on Method* (Oxford, 1937); H. Scholz, A. Kratzer, and J. E. Hofmann, *Descartes* (Münster, 1951); and Norman Kemp Smith, *New Studies in the Philosophy of Descartes* (London, 1952).

Specific aspects of Descartes's scientific method are discussed in A. Gewirtz, "Experience and the Non-mathematical in the Cartesian Method," in *Journal of the History of Ideas*, **2** (1941), 183–210; and A. C. Crombie, "Some Aspects of Descartes' Attitude to Hypothesis and Experiment," in Académie Internationale d'Histoire des Sciences, *Actes du Symposium International des Sciences Physiques et Mathématiques dans la Première Moitié du XVIIe Siècle: Pise-Vinci, 16–18 Juin 1958* (Paris, 1960), pp. 192–201. An indispensable bibliography is G. Sebba, *Descartes and His Philosophy: A Bibliographical Guide to the Literature, 1800–1958* (Athens, Ga., 1959).

A. C. CROMBIE

DESCARTES: Mathematics and Physics.

In this section, Descartes's mathematics is discussed separately. The physics is discussed in two subsections: Optics and Mechanics.

Mathematics. The mathematics that served as model and touchstone for Descartes's philosophy was in large part Descartes's own creation and reflected in turn many of his philosophical tenets.[1] Its historical foundations lie in the classical analytical texts of Pappus (*Mathematical Collection*) and Diophantus (*Arithmetica*) and in the cossist algebra exemplified by the works of Peter Rothe and Christoph Clavius. Descartes apparently received the stimulus to study these works from Isaac Beeckman; his earliest recorded thoughts on mathematics are found in the correspondence with Beeckman that followed their meeting in 1618. Descartes's command of cossist algebra (evident throughout his papers of the early 1620's) was perhaps strengthened by his acquaintance during the winter of 1619–1620 with Johann Faulhaber, a leading German cossist in Ulm.[2] Descartes's treatise *De solidorum elementis,* which contains a statement of "Euler's Theorem" for polyhedra ($V + F = E + 2$), was quite likely also a result of their discussions. Whatever the early influences on Descartes's mathematics, it nonetheless followed a relatively independent line of development during the decade preceding the publication of his magnum opus, the *Géométrie* of 1637.[3]

During this decade Descartes sought to realize two programmatic goals. The first stemmed from a belief, first expressed by Petrus Ramus,[4] that cossist algebra represented a "vulgar" form of the analytical method employed by the great Greek mathematicians. As Descartes wrote in his *Rules for the Direction of the Mind* (*ca.* 1628):

> . . . some traces of this true mathematics [of the ancient Greeks] seem to me to appear still in Pappus and Diophantus. . . . Finally, there have been some most ingenious men who have tried in this century to revive the same [true mathematics]; for it seems to be nothing other than that art which they call by the barbarous name of "algebra," if only it could be so disentangled from the multiple numbers and inexplicable figures that overwhelm it that it no longer would lack the clarity and simplicity that we suppose should obtain in a true mathematics.[5]

Descartes expressed his second programmatic goal in a letter to Beeckman in 1619; at the time it appeared to him to be unattainable by one man alone. He envisaged "an entirely new science,"

> . . . by which all questions can be resolved that can be proposed for any sort of quantity, either continuous or discrete. Yet each problem will be solved according to its own nature, as, for example, in arithmetic some questions are resolved by rational numbers, others only by irrational numbers, and others finally can be imagined but not solved. So also I hope to show for continuous quantities that some problems can be solved by straight lines and circles alone; others only by other curved lines, which, however, result from a single motion and can therefore be drawn with new forms of compasses, which are no less exact and geometrical, I think, than the common ones used to draw circles; and finally others that can be solved only by curved lines generated by diverse motions not subordinated to one another, which curves are certainly only imaginary (e.g., the rather well-known quadratrix). I cannot imagine anything that could not be solved by such lines at least, though I hope to show which questions can be solved in this or that way and not any other, so that almost nothing will remain to be found in geometry.[6]

Descartes sought, then, from the beginning of his research a symbolic algebra of pure quantity by which problems of any sort could be analyzed and classified in terms of the constructive techniques required for their most efficient solution. He took a large step toward his goal in the *Rules* and achieved it finally in the *Géométrie.*

Descartes began his task of "purifying" algebra by separating its patterns of reasoning from the particular subject matter to which it might be applied. Whereas cossist algebra was basically a technique for solving numerical problems and its symbols therefore denoted numbers, Descartes conceived of his "true mathematics" as the science of magnitude, or quantity, per se. He replaced the old cossist symbols with letters of the alphabet, using at first (in the *Rules*) the capital letters to denote known quantities and the lowercase letters to denote unknowns, and later (in the *Géométrie*) shifting to the *a,b,c; x,y,z* notation still in use today. In a more radical step, he then removed the last vestiges of verbal expression (and the conceptualization that accompanied it) by replacing the words "square," "cube," etc., by numerical superscripts. These superscripts, he argued (in rule XVI), resolved the serious conceptual difficulty posed by the dimensional connotations of the words they replaced. For the square of a magnitude did not differ from it in kind, as a geometrical square differs from a line; rather, the square, the cube, and all powers differed from the base quantity only in the number of "relations" separating them respectively from a common unit quantity. That is, since

$$1:x = x:x^2 = x^2:x^3 = \cdots$$

(and, by Euclid V, ratios obtain only among homogeneous quantities), x^3 was linked to the unit magnitude by three "relations," while x was linked by only one. The numerical superscript expressed the number of "relations."

While all numbers are homogeneous, the application of algebra to geometry (Descartes's main goal in the *Géométrie*) required the definition of the six basic algebraic operations (addition, subtraction, multiplication, division, raising to a power, and extracting a root) for the realm of geometry in such a way as to preserve the homogeneity of the products. Although the Greek mathematicians had established the correspondence between addition and the geometrical operation of laying line lengths end to end in the same straight line, they had been unable to conceive of multiplication in any way other than that of constructing a rectangle out of multiplier and multiplicand, with the result that the product differed in kind from the elements multiplied. Descartes's concept of "relation" provided his answer to the problem: one chooses a unit length to which all other lengths are referred (if it is not given by the data of the problem, it may be chosen arbitrarily). Then, since $1:a = a:ab$, the product of two lines a and b is constructed by drawing a triangle with sides 1 and a; in a similar triangle, of which the side corresponding to 1 is b, the other side will be ab, a line length. Division and the remaining operations are defined analogously. As Descartes emphasized, these operations do not make arithmetic of geometry, but rather make possible an algebra of geometrical line segments.

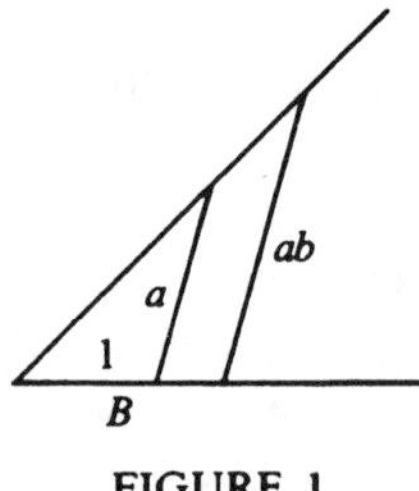

FIGURE 1

The above argument opens Descartes's *Géométrie* and lays the foundation of the new analytic geometry contained therein, to wit, that given a line x and a polynomial $P(x)$ with rational coefficients it is possible to construct another line y such that $y = P(x)$. Algebra thereby becomes for Descartes the symbolic method for realizing the second goal of his "true mathematics," the analysis and classification of problems. The famous "Problem of Pappus," called to Descartes's attention by Jacob Golius in 1631, provides the focus for Descartes's exposition of his new method. The problem states in brief: given n coplanar lines, to find the locus of a point such that, if it is connected to each given line by a line drawn at a fixed angle, the product of $n/2$ of the connecting lines bears a given ratio to the product of the remaining $n/2$ (for even n; for odd n, the product of $(n + 1)/2$ lines bears a given ratio to k times the product of the remaining $(n - 1)/2$, where k is a given line segment). In carrying out the detailed solution for the case $n = 4$, Descartes also achieves the classification of the solutions for other n.

Implicit in Descartes's solution is the analytic geometry that today bears his name. Taking lines *AB, AD, EF, GH* as the four given lines, Descartes assumes that point *C* lies on the required locus and draws the connecting lines *CB, CD, CF, CH.* To apply algebraic analysis, he then takes the length *AB,* measured from the fixed point *A,* as his first unknown, x, and length *BC* as the second unknown, y. He thus imagines the locus to be traced by the endpoint *C* of a movable ordinate *BC* maintaining a fixed angle to line *AB* (the axis) and varying in length as a function[7] of the length *AB.* Throughout the *Géométrie,* Descartes chooses his axial system to fit the problem; nowhere does the now standard—and misnamed—"Cartesian coordinate system" appear.

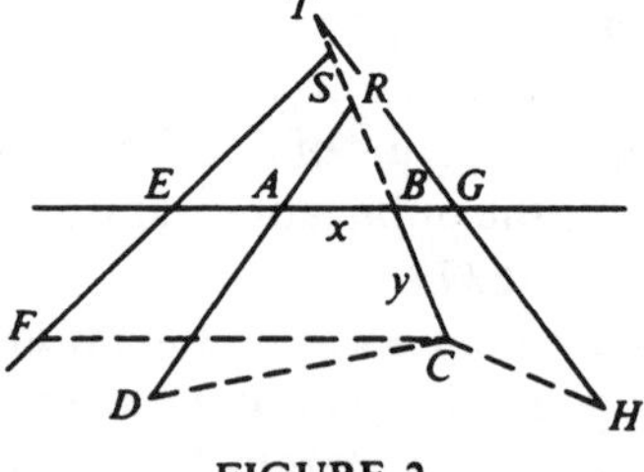

FIGURE 2

The goal of the algebraic derivation that follows this basic construction is to show that every other connecting line may be expressed by a combination of the two basic unknowns in the form $\alpha x + \beta y + \gamma$, where α, β, γ derive from the data. From this last result it follows that for a given number n of fixed lines the power of x in the equation that expresses the ratio of multiplied connecting lines will not exceed $n/2$ (n even) or $(n - 1)/2$ (n odd); it will often not even be that large. Hence, for successive assumed values of y, the construction of points on the locus requires the solution of a determinate equation in x of degree $n/2$, or $(n - 1)/2$; e.g., for five or fewer lines, one need only be able to solve a quadratic equation, which in turn requires only circle and straightedge for its constructive solution.

Thus Descartes's classification of the various cases of Pappus' problem follows the order of difficulty of solving determinate equations of increasing degree.[8] Solution of such equations carries with it the possibility of constructing any point (and hence all points) of the locus sought. The direct solvability of algebraic equations becomes in book II Descartes's criterion for distinguishing between "geometrical" and "nongeometrical" curves; for the latter (today termed "transcendental curves") by their nature allow the direct construction of only certain of their points. For the construction of the loci that satisfy Pappus' problem for $n \leq 5$, i.e., the conic sections, Descartes relies on the construction theorems of Apollonius' *Conics* and contents himself with showing how the indeterminate equations of the loci contain the necessary parameters.

Descartes goes on to show in book II that the equation of a curve also suffices to determine its geometrical properties, of which the most important is the normal to any point on the curve. His method of normals—from which a method of tangents follows directly—takes as unknown the point of intersection of the desired normal and the axis. Considering a family of circles drawn about that point, Descartes derives an equation $P(x) = 0$, the roots of which are the abscissas of the intersection points of any circle and the curve. The normal is the radius of that circle which has a single intersection point, and Descartes finds that circle on the basis of the theorem that, if $P(x) = 0$ has a repeated root at $x = a$, then $P(x) = (x - a)^2R(x)$, where $R(a) \neq 0$. Here a is the abscissa of the given point on the curve, and the solution follows from equating the coefficients of like powers of x on either side of the last equation. Descartes's method is formally equivalent to Fermat's method of maxima and minima and, along with the latter, constituted one of the early foundations of the later differential calculus.

The central importance of determinate equations and their solution leads directly to book III of the *Géométrie* with its purely algebraic theory of equations. Entirely novel and original, Descartes's theory begins by writing every equation in the form $P(x) = 0$, where $P(x)$ is an algebraic polynomial with real coefficients.[9] From the assertion, derived inductively, that every such equation may also be expressed in the form

$$(x - a)(x - b) \cdots (x - s) = 0,$$

where $a, b, \cdots, s$ are the roots of the equation, Descartes states and offers an intuitive proof of the fundamental theorem of algebra (first stated by Albert Girard in 1629) that an nth degree equation has exactly n roots. The proof rests simply on the principle that every root must appear in one of the binomial factors of $P(x)$ and that it requires n such factors to achieve x^n as the highest power of x in that polynomial. Descartes is therefore prepared to recognize not only negative roots (he gives as a corollary the law of signs for the number of negative roots) but also "imaginary" solutions to complete the necessary number.[10] In a series of examples, he then shows how to alter the signs of the roots of an equation, to increase them (additively or multiplicatively), or to decrease them. Having derived from the factored form of an equation its elementary symmetric functions,[11] Descartes uses them to eliminate the term containing x^{n-1} in the equation. This step paves the way for the general solution of the cubic and quartic equations (material dating back to Descartes's earliest studies) and leads to a general discussion of the solution of equations, in which the first method outlined is that of testing the various factors of the constant term, and then other means, including approximate solution, are discussed.

The *Géométrie* represented the sum of mathematical knowledge to which Descartes was willing to commit himself in print. The same philosophical concepts that led to the brilliant new method of geometry also prevented him from appreciating the innovative achievements of his contemporaries. His demand for strict a priori deduction caused him to reject Fermat's use of counterfactual assumptions in the latter's method of maxima and minima and rule of tangents.[12] His demand for absolute intuitive clarity in concepts excluded the infinitesimal from his mathematics. His renewed insistence on Aristotle's rigid distinction between "straight" and "curved" led him to reject from the outset any attempt to rectify curved lines.

Despite these hindrances to adventurous speculation, Descartes did discuss in his correspondence some problems that lay outside the realm of his *Géométrie*. In 1638, for example, he discussed with Mersenne, in connection with the law of falling bodies, the curve now expressed by the polar equation $\rho = a\lambda^{\vartheta}$ (logarithmic spiral)[13] and undertook the determination of the normal to, and quadrature of, the cycloid. Also in 1638 he took up a problem posed by Florimond Debeaune: (in modern terms) to construct a curve satisfying the differential equation $a(dy/dx) = x - y$. Descartes appreciated Debeaune's quadrature of the curve and was himself able to determine the asymptote $y = x - a$ common to the family, but he did not succeed in finding one of the curves itself.[14]

By 1638, however, Descartes had largely completed his career in mathematics. The writing of the *Meditations* (1641), its defense against the critics, and the composition of the magisterial *Principia philosophiae* (1644) left little time to pursue further the mathematical studies begun in 1618.

Optics. In addition to presenting his new method of algebraic geometry, Descartes's *Géométrie* also served in book II to provide rigorous mathematical demonstrations for sections of his *Dioptrique* published at the same time. The mathematical derivations pertain to his theory of lenses and offer, through four "ovals," solutions to a generalized form of the anaclastic problem.[15] The theory of lenses, a topic that had engaged Descartes since reading Kepler's *Dioptrica* in 1619, took its form and direction in turn from Descartes's solution to the more basic problem of a mathematical derivation of the laws of reflection and refraction, with which the *Dioptrique* opens.

Background to these derivations was Descartes's theory of light, an integral part of his overall system of cosmology.[16] For Descartes light was not motion (which takes time) but rather a "tendency to motion," an impulsive force transmitted rectilinearly and instantaneously by the fine particles that fill the interstices between the visible macrobodies of the universe. His model for light itself was the blind man's cane, which instantaneously transmits impulses from the objects it meets and enables the man to "see." To derive the laws of reflection and refraction, however, Descartes required another model more amenable to mathematical description. Arguing that "tendency to motion" could be analyzed in terms of actual motion, he chose the model of a tennis ball striking a flat surface. For the law of reflection the surface was assumed to be perfectly rigid and immobile. He then applied two fundamental principles of his theory of collision: first, that a body in motion will continue to move in the same direction at the same speed unless acted upon by contact with another body; second, that a body can lose some or all of its motion only by transmitting it directly to another. Descartes measured motion by the product of the magnitude of the body and the speed at which it travels. He made a distinction, however, between the speed of a body and its "determination" to move in a certain direction.[17] By this distinction, it might come about that a body impacting with another would lose none of its speed (if the other body remained unmoved) but would

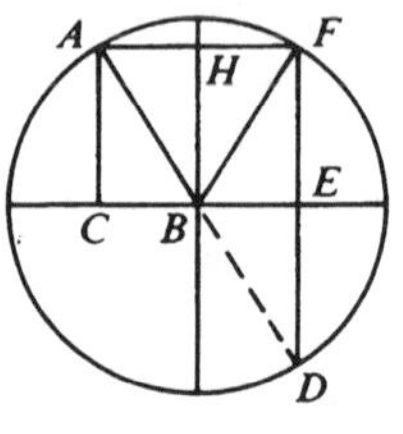

FIGURE 3

receive another determination. Moreover, although Descartes treated speed as a scalar quantity, determination was (operationally at least) always a vector, which could be resolved into components.[18] When one body collided with another, only those components of their determinations that directly opposed one another were subject to alteration.

Imagine, then, says Descartes, a tennis ball leaving the racket at point A and traveling uniformly along line AB to meet the surface CE at B. Resolve its determination into two components, one (AC) perpendicular to the surface and one (AH) parallel to it. Since, when the ball strikes the surface, it imparts none of its motion to the surface (which is immobile), it will continue to move at the same speed and hence after a period of time equal to that required to traverse AB will be somewhere on a circle of radius AB about B. But, since the surface is impenetrable, the ball cannot pass through it (say to D) but must bounce off it, with a resultant change in determination. Only the vertical component of that determination is subject to change, however; the horizontal component remains unaffected. Moreover, since the body has lost none of its motion, the length HF of that component after collision will equal the length AH before. Hence, at the same time the ball reaches the circle it must also be at a distance $HF = AH$ from the normal HB, i.e., somewhere on line FE. Clearly, then, it must be at F, and consideration of similar triangles shows that the angle of incidence ABH is equal to the angle of reflection HBF.

For the law of refraction, Descartes altered the nature of the surface met by the ball; he now imagined it to pass through the surface, but to lose some of its motion (i.e., speed) in doing so. Let the speed before collision be to that after as $p:q$. Since both speeds are uniform, the time required for the ball to reach the circle again will be to that required to traverse AB as $p:q$. To find the precise point at

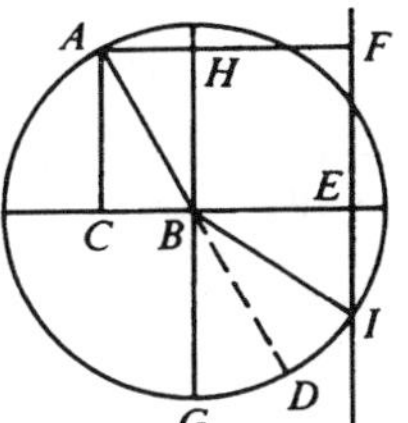

FIGURE 4

which it meets the circle, Descartes again considered its determination, or rather the horizontal component unaffected by the collision. Since the ball takes longer to reach the circle, the length of that component after collision will be greater than before, to wit, in the ratio of $p:q$. Hence, if $FH:AH = p:q$, then the ball must lie on both the circle and line FE. Let I be the common point.

The derivation so far rests on the assumption that the ball's motion is decreased in breaking through the surface. Here again Descartes had to alter his model to fit his theory of light, for that theory implies that light passes more easily through the denser medium. For the model of the tennis ball, this means that, if the medium below the surface is denser than that above, the ball receives added speed at impact, as if it were struck again by the racket. As a result, it will by the same argument as given above be deflected toward the normal as classical experiments with air-water interfaces said it should.

In either case, the ratio $p:q$ of the speeds before and after impact depended, according to Descartes, on the relative density of the media and would therefore be constant for any two given media. Hence, since

$$FH:AH = BE:BC = p:q,$$

it follows that

$$\frac{BE}{BI}:\frac{BC}{AB} = \sin \angle AHB : \sin \angle IBG$$
$$= p:q = n \text{ (constant)},$$

which is the law of refraction.

The vagueness surrounding Descartes's concept of "determination" and its relation to speed makes his derivations difficult to follow. In addition, the assumption in the second that all refraction takes place at the surface lends an ad hoc aura to the proof, which makes it difficult to believe that the derivation represented Descartes's path to the law of refraction (the law of reflection was well known). Shortly after Descartes's death, prominent scientists, including Christian Huygens, accused him of having plagiarized the law itself from Willebrord Snell and then having patched together his proof of it. There is, however, clear evidence that Descartes had the law by 1626, long before Golius uncovered Snell's unpublished memoir.[19] In 1626 Descartes had Claude Mydorge grind a hyperbolic lens that represented an anaclastic derived by Descartes from the sine law of refraction. Where Descartes got the law, or how he got it, remains a mystery; in the absence of further evidence, one must rest content with the derivations in the *Dioptrique.*

Following those derivations, Descartes devotes the remainder of the *Dioptrique* to an optical analysis of the human eye, moving from the explanation of various distortions of vision to the lenses designed to correct them, or, in the case of the telescope, to increase the power of the normal eye. The laws of reflection and refraction reappear, however, in the third of the *Essais* of 1637, the *Météores.* There Descartes presents a mathematical explanation of both the primary and secondary rainbow in terms of the refraction and internal reflection of the sun's rays in a spherical raindrop.[20] Quantitatively, he succeeded in deriving the angle at which each rainbow is seen with respect to the angle of the sun's elevation. His attempted explanation of the rainbow's colors, however, rested on a general theory of colors that could at the time only be qualitative. Returning to the model of the tennis ball, Descartes explained color in terms of a rotatory motion of the ball, the speed of rotation varying with the color. Upon refraction, as through a prism, those speeds would be altered, leading to a change in colors.

Mechanics. Descartes's contribution to mechanics lay less in solutions to particular problems than in the stimulus that the detailed articulation of his mechanistic cosmology provided for men like Huygens.[21] Concerned with the universe on a grand scale, he had little but criticism for Galileo's efforts at resolving more mundane questions. In particular, Descartes rejected much of Galileo's work, e.g., the laws of free fall and the law of the pendulum, because Galileo considered the phenomena in a vacuum, a vacuum that Descartes's cosmology excluded from the world. For Descartes, the ideal world corresponded to the real one. Mechanical phenomena took place in a plenum and had to be explained in terms of the direct interaction of the bodies that constituted it, whence the central role of his theory of impact.[22]

Two of the basic principles underlying that theory have been mentioned above. The first, the law of inertia, followed from Descartes's concept of motion as a state coequal with rest; change of state required a cause (i.e., the action of another moving body) and in the absence of that cause the state remained constant. That motion continued in a straight line followed from the privileged status of the straight line in Descartes's geometrical universe. The second law, the conservation of the "quantity of motion" in any closed interaction, followed from the immutability of God and his creation. Since bodies acted on each other by transmission of their motion, the "quantity of motion" (the product of magnitude and speed) served also as Descartes's measure of force or action and led to a third principle that vitiated Descartes's theory of impact. Since as much action was required for motion as for rest, a smaller body moving however fast could never possess sufficient action to move a larger body at rest. As a result of this principle, to which Descartes adhered in the face of both criticism and experience, only the first of the seven laws of impact (of perfectly elastic bodies meeting in the same straight line) is correct. It concerns the impact of two equal bodies approaching each other at equal speeds and is intuitively obvious.

Descartes's concept of force as motive action blocked successful quantitative treatment of the mechanical problems he attacked. His definition of the center of oscillation as the point at which the forces of the particles of the swinging body are balanced out led to quite meager results, and his attempt to explain centrifugal force as the tendency of a body to maintain its determination remained purely qualitative. In all three areas—impact, oscillation, and centrifugal force—it was left to Huygens to push through to a solution, often by discarding Descartes's staunchly defended principles.

Descartes met with more success in the realm of statics. His *Explication des engins par l'aide desquels on peut avec une petite force lever un fardeau fort pesant,* written as a letter to Constantin Huygens in 1637, presents an analysis of the five simple machines on the principle that the force required to lift a pounds vertically through b feet will also lift na pounds b/n feet. And a memoir dating from 1618 contains a clear statement of the hydrostatic paradox, later made public by Blaise Pascal.[23]

NOTES

1. Cf. Gaston Milhaud, *Descartes savant* (Paris, 1921), and Jules Vuillemin, *Mathématiques et métaphysique chez Descartes* (Paris, 1960).
2. Cf. Milhaud, pp. 84–87.
3. Defending his originality against critics, Descartes repeatedly denied having read the algebraic works of François Viète or Thomas Harriot prior to the publication of his own *Géométrie.* The pattern of development of his ideas, especially during the late 1620's, lends credence to this denial.
4. In his *Scholarum mathematicarum libri unus et triginta* (Paris, 1569; 3rd. ed., Frankfurt am Main, 1627), bk. I (p. 35 of the 3rd ed.). Descartes quite likely knew of Ramus through Beeckman, who had studied mathematics with Rudolph Snell, a leading Dutch Ramist.
5. *Regulae ad directionem ingenii,* in *Oeuvres de Descartes,* Adam and Tannery, eds., X (Paris, 1908), rule IV, 376–377.
6. Descartes to Beeckman (26 Mar. 1619), *Oeuvres,* X, 156–158. By "imaginary" curve, Descartes seems to mean a curve that can be described verbally but not accurately constructed by geometrical means.
7. Both the term and the concept it denotes are certainly anachronistic. Descartes speaks of the indeterminate equation that links x and y as the "relation [*rapport*] that all the points of a curve have to all those of a straight line" (*Géométrie,* p. 341). Strangely, Descartes makes no special mention of one of the most novel aspects of his method, to wit, the establishment of a correspondence between geometrical loci and indeterminate algebraic equations in two unknowns. He does discuss the correspondence further in bk. II, 334–335, but again in a way that belies its novelty. The correspondence between determinate equations and point constructions (i.e., section problems) had been standard for some time.
8. For problems of lower degree, Descartes maintains the classification of Pappus. Plane problems are those that can be constructed with circle and straightedge, and solid problems those that require the aid of the three conic sections. Where, however, Pappus grouped all remaining curves into a class he termed linear, Descartes divides these into distinct classes of order. To do so, he employs in bk. I a construction device that generates the conic sections from a referent triangle and then a new family of higher order from the conic sections, and so on.
9. Two aspects of the symbolism employed here require comment. First, Descartes deals for the most part with specific examples of polynomials, which he always writes in the form $x^n + a_1x^{n-1} + \cdots + a_n = 0$; the symbolism $P(x)$ was unknown to him. Second, instead of the equal sign, =, he used the symbol ∞, most probably the inverted ligature of the first two letters of the verb *aequare* ("to equal").
10. One important by-product of this structural analysis of equations is a new and more refined concept of number. See Jakob Klein, *Greek Mathematical Thought and the Origins of Algebra* (Cambridge, Mass., 1968).
11. Here again a totally anachronistic term is employed in the interest of brevity.
12. Ironically, Descartes's method of determining the normal to a curve (bk. II, 342 ff.) made implicit use of precisely the same reasoning as Fermat's. This may have become clear to Descartes toward the end of a bitter controversy between the two men over their methods in the spring of 1638.
13. Cf. Vuillemin, pp. 35–55.
14. *Ibid.,* pp. 11–25; Joseph E. Hofmann, *Geschichte der Mathematik,* II (Berlin, 1957), 13.
15. The anaclastic is a refracting surface that directs parallel rays to a single focus; Descartes had generalized the problem to include surfaces that refract rays emanating from a single point and direct them to another point. Cf. Milhaud, pp. 117–118.
16. The full title of the work Descartes suppressed in 1636 as a result of the condemnation of Galileo was *Le monde, ou Traité de la lumière.* It contained the basic elements of Descartes's cosmology, later published in the *Principia philosophiae* (1644). For a detailed analysis of Descartes's work in optics, see A. I. Sabra, *Theories of Light From Descartes to Newton* (London, 1967), chs. 1–4.
17. "One must note only that the power, whatever it may be, that causes the motion of this ball to continue is different from that which determines it to move more toward one direction than toward another," *Dioptrique* (Leiden, 1637), p. 94.
18. Cf. Descartes to Mydorge (1 Mar. 1638), "determination cannot be without some speed, although the same speed can have different determinations, and the same determination can be combined with various speeds" (quoted by Sabra, p. 120). A result of this qualification is that Descartes in his proofs treats

speed operationally as a vector.

19. See the summary of this issue in Sabra, pp. 100 ff.
20. Cf. Carl B. Boyer, *The Rainbow: From Myth to Mathematics* (New York, 1959).
21. For a survey of Descartes's work on mechanics, which includes the passages pertinent to the subjects discussed below, see René Dugas, *La mécanique au XVIIe siècle* (Neuchâtel, 1954), ch. 7.
22. Presented in full in the *Principia philosophiae*, pt. II, pars. 24–54.
23. Cf. Milhaud, pp. 34–36.

BIBLIOGRAPHY

I. Original Works. All of Descartes's scientific writings can be found in their original French or Latin in the critical edition of the *Oeuvres de Descartes,* Charles Adam and Paul Tannery, eds., 12 vols. (Paris, 1897–1913). The *Géométrie,* originally written in French, was trans. into Latin and published with appendices by Franz van Schooten (Leiden, 1649); this Latin version underwent a total of four eds. The work also exists in an English trans. by Marcia Latham and David Eugene Smith (Chicago, 1925; repr., New York, 1954), and in other languages. For references to eds. of the philosophical treatises containing scientific material, see the bibliography for sec. I.

II. Secondary Literature. In addition to the works cited in the notes, see also J. F. Scott, *The Scientific Work of René Descartes* (London, 1952); Carl B. Boyer, *A History of Analytic Geometry* (New York, 1956); Alexandre Koyré, *Études galiléennes* (Paris, 1939); E. J. Dijksterhuis, *The Mechanization of the World Picture* (Oxford, 1961). See also the various histories of seventeenth-century science or mathematics for additional discussions of Descartes's work.

Michael S. Mahoney

DESCARTES: Physiology.

Descartes's physiology grew and developed as an integral part of his philosophy. Although grounded at fundamental points in transmitted anatomical knowledge and actually performed dissection procedures, it sprang up largely independently of prior physiological developments and depended instead on the articulation of the Cartesian dualist ontology, was entangled with the vagaries of metaphysical theory, and deliberately put into practice Descartes's precepts on scientific method. Chronologically, too, his physiology grew with his philosophy. Important ideas on animal function occur briefly in the *Regulae* (1628), form a significant part of the argument in the *Discours de le méthode* (1637), and lie behind certain parts of the *Principia philosophiae* (1644) and all of the *Passions de l'âme* (1649). Throughout his active philosophical life, physiology formed one of Descartes's most central and, sometimes, most plaguing concerns.

Descartes hinted at the most fundamental conceptions of his physiology relatively early in his philosophical development. Already in the twelfth *regula,* he suggested (without, however, elaborating either more rigorously or more fully) that all animal and subrational human movements are controlled solely by unconscious mechanisms. Just as the quill of a pen moves in a physically necessary pattern determined by the motion of the tip, so too do "all the motions of the animals come about"; thus one can also explain "how in ourselves all those operations occur which [we] perform without any aid from the reason." Closely associated in the *Regulae* with this notion of animal automatism was Descartes's belief that human sensation is a two-step process consisting, first, of the mechanical conveyance of physical stimuli from the external organs of sense to a common sensorium located somewhere in the body and, second, of the internal perception of these mechanically conveyed stimuli by a higher "spiritual" principle.

Implicit in these two notions and seeming to tie them together is the assumption, evident in broader compass but in as terse a formulation as elsewhere in the *Regulae,* that all phenomena of the animate and inanimate world, with the sole exception of those directly connected with human will and consciousness, are to be explained in terms of mathematics, matter, configuration, and motion.

The fuller working out of his physiological ideas occupied Descartes in the early 1630's, when he was concerned generally with the development of his ontological and methodological views. In 1632 he several times referred to physiological themes and projects in his correspondence, and in June he informed Mersenne that he had already completed his work on inanimate bodies but still had to finish off "certain things touching on the nature of man." The allusion here was to the *Traité de l'homme,* which with the *Traité de lumière* was meant to form *Le monde.* Along with the *Traité de lumière,* however, the *Traité de l'homme* was suppressed by Descartes after the condemnation of Galileo in 1633, and although it thus had to await posthumous publication in the 1660's, his writing of the *Traité de l'homme* proved extremely important in the further maturation of Descartes's physiological conceptions.

The *Traité de l'homme* begins and ends with a proclamation of literary and philosophical license. In the *Traité,* Descartes writes, we deliberately consider not a real man but a "statue" or *machine de terre* expressly fashioned by God to approximate real men as closely as possible. Like a real man, the *machine de terre* will be imagined to possess an immaterial soul and a physical body, and, also like a real man, its physical body will consist of a heart, brain, stomach, vessels, nerves, *et al.* But since we are considering only an artificial man—a contrivance fashioned more perfectly but on the same principles as a clock or water mill—we will not be tempted to attribute the motions and activities of this man to special sensitive or vegetative souls or principles of life. Nothing more than a contained rational and immaterial soul and "the disposition of organs, no more and no less than in the movements of a clock or any other automaton" will be needed to comprehend the active functioning of this special contrivance formed by God and operated thereafter by the principles of mechanical action. We are to bear in mind, of course, that the man of the *Traité* is remarkably like men we know, but our literary and philosophical license allows us to hypothesize and analogize freely.

Descartes fully exercises his self-proclaimed license in the rest of the *Traité.* He first surveys various physiological processes, giving for each of them not the traditional or neoclassical account of such recent physiological writers as Fernel or Riolan but mechanistic details by which the particular function is performed automatically in the *homme.* Each of Descartes's explanations borrows something from traditionalist physiological theories, but in each case Descartes wields Ockham's razor to strip away excess souls, faculties, forces, and innate heats from the corpuscular or chemical core of explanation.

Digestion, for example, is for Descartes only a fermentative process in which the particles of food are broken apart and set into agitation by fluids contained in the stomach. Chyle and excremental particles are then separated from one another in a filtration performed merely by a sievelike configuration of the pores and vascular openings in the intestines. Chyle particles go through another filtration and fermentation in the liver, where they thereby—and only thereby—acquire the properties of blood. Blood formed in the liver drips from the vena cava into the right ventricle of the heart, where the purely physical heat implanted there quickly vaporizes the sanguinary mass. The expansion of this sanguinary vapor pushes out the walls of the heart and arteries. Expansion with rarefaction is succeeded by cooling; and, as the vapor condenses, the heart and arteries return to their original size. The heart is fitted with a perfect arrangement of valves, and in addition the *homme* is served by a perpetual circulation of blood. (Descartes had read William Harvey's *De motu cordis,* as is also clear from his prior correspondence, but apparently took seriously only the part on circulatory motion rather than on cardiac action.) Cardiac and arterial pulsation is thus continually and automatically repeated throughout the life of the automaton by mechanical means, not under the control of an active diastolic faculty. And while the sanguinary particles are coursing through the vessels, certain of them separate off into special pores, which accounts for both nutrition and the sievelike production of such secretions as bile and urine.

After this mechanistic survey of general physiology, Descartes moves to the nervous system, which he treats in considerable detail. The nerves are said to be a series of essentially hollow tubes with a filamentous marrow and are similar in operation to the water-filled pipes of those hydraulically controlled puppets and mechanical statues found "in the grottoes and fountains in the gardens of our Kings." Filling the spaces in the nerves is a fine, material substance, the animal spirits. These spirits are actually the most quickly moving particles of the blood that have traveled through the arteries in the shortest, straightest path from the heart to the brain. Once conveyed to the brain according to the laws of mechanics and then mechanically separated from the coarser parts of the blood, these most agile particles become "a wind or very subtle flame."

This spiritual wind can flow into the muscles, which are directly connected with the neural tubes. When a particular muscle is inflated by the influx of animal spirits, its belly distends as if by wind billowing a canvas sail, and the ends or insertions of the muscle are necessarily pulled more closely together. The pulling together of the muscular insertions constitutes muscle contraction. Gross movements in the *homme* (including breathing and swallowing) are produced, therefore, as the necessary mechanical effects of animal spirits discharged to one or another muscle group.

The movement of animal spirits is also controlled, however, by the action of the pineal gland in the brain. The rational soul is itself most closely associated with this gland located centrally in the substance of the cerebral marrow, and by directly causing this gland to move, no matter how slightly, the immaterial, willful soul of man can redirect the animal spirits from one set of nervous channels to another. Redirection of animal spirits results, in turn, in the production of different gross muscle movements. The pineal gland can also be, and often is, directly and unconsciously affected by a whole array of supervening influences, among the most important of which are the sensory. In animals, of course, only the supervening influences operate. Since Descartes has already gotten into a discussion of sensation, he now discusses that subject in great detail. He devotes much attention to the external organs of sense, concentrating to a large degree on the visual apparatus. For his discussion here, Descartes was able to draw upon the prior work of sixteenth-century anatomists and natural philosophers that had culminated in Kepler's fine account of the eye as a camera-like optical system. Yet Descartes inserts his optical account of the eye into his already developed physiological system; for once the image is formed on the retina, Descartes explains, the nerves—and with them Descartes's general physiology—take over. Rays of light focused on particular points of the retina cause specific nerves to jiggle slightly. Since the solid, filamentous part of the nerve is continuous from the sense organ to the brain, the externally caused jiggle is immediately transmitted, like the tug on a bell rope, to the interior of the brain as an internal jiggle. Internal jiggles directly control the streaming of animal spirits in the brain, and the rational soul, operating only at the pineal gland, interprets the patterns of the streams as particular sensations. The soul works "in the dark" this way, too, in all other sensations and in the difficult activity of multilevel perception. The soul "reads" various motions produced in the brain by the nerves and spirits, and interprets particular combinations of motions as taste, odor, color, or even distance.

Descartes moves from this complicated discussion of the five external senses of his *homme* to a consideration of certain internal feelings which it also experiences. The physiology (and psychology) is here, too, based on the manner by which the soul "reads" the messages delivered through the nerves by the spirits, messages which depend, in this instance, upon the internal functioning of the various parts of the body. Thus, when the blood entering the heart is purer and more subtle than usual, it vaporizes very easily in the cardiac chambers, and, as a consequence, it stimulates the nerves placed in the heart in a manner that the soul will associate with joy. All sorts of moods, feelings, and what might be generally labeled chains of somatopsychic effects (Descartes usually calls these "passions") are schematically accounted for in this same manner—by imagining a passive immaterial soul interpreting the varied motions of the spirits as they stream pass the pineal gland.

As a logical extension of his consideration of the "passions," Descartes turns, finally, to a discussion of sleep, dreams, memory, and imagination—other consequences of the interaction of the soul with internal neurophysiology. All these latter psychological phenomena are said to depend on the special motion of animal spirits, sometimes through favored pathways created by habitual or normal daytime activity.

With this discussion (and with his restatement of literary and philosophical license) Descartes terminates the *Traité.* It was obviously written as a full working out of the physiological hints included in the *Regulae* and elaborated in the light of his own philosophical development. A clearly stated dualist ontology runs through the *Traité,* while mechanistic details analogous to those of the *Traité de lumière* are evident at almost every turn.

But the *Traité de l'homme* served not only to clarify and develop Descartes's physiological views; it also quickly became a rich fund of ideas upon which he drew throughout the rest of his intellectual life. In 1637, for example, Descartes published two important works: *Discours de la méthode* and *Dioptrique.* In both he uses physiological ideas from the unpublished *Traité* at important points in his argument. Specifically, in part V of the *Discours,* Descartes employs a summary of his cardiovascular physiology to illustrate how the newly discovered laws by which God orders his universe are sufficient to explicate certain of the most important human functions, and the *Dioptrique* includes a summary of his general theory of sensation as a preliminary to a detailed study of image formation and visual perception. In the 1640's, too, Descartes drew heavily upon the unpublished *Traité.* The complicated arguments of the *Passions de l'âme,* published near the end of that decade, rest firmly on the extensive survey of basic Cartesian physiology incorporated in part I, while Descartes's unruffled assertiveness in his correspondence and later philosophical writings on the "beast-machine" makes full sense only against a background provided by the *Traité*'s automaton.

Descartes, however, had left one major physiological problem untreated in the *Traité:* the reproductive generation of animals and men. He had insisted for reasons of methodological circumspection that the *homme* of the *Traité* was directly contrived by God. The Cartesian program, of course, was to explain all but rational, deliberately willful, or self-conscious behavior in terms of mere mechanism. He had eliminated the souls, principles, faculties, and innate heats of traditional physiology and had systematically replaced them with hypotheses and analogies of purely physical nature. But generation had escaped, and its explanation in mechanistic terms was clearly needed for the logical completion of his system. Recently proposed theories of animal generation had left the subject replete with Galenic faculties and Aristotelian souls, and even William Harvey was soon to show himself content with innate principles and plastic forces as the controlling agents of embryonic development. Descartes, to be consistent, could not accept these explanatory devices and had, therefore, to formulate some alternative.

His correspondence and certain manuscript remains show that Descartes had actually been deeply concerned with the problem of animal generation for a considerable period of time. Earliest references in the former occur in 1629, and snippets of the latter reveal fitful grapplings with the problem, some of them even leading to direct anatomical investigations undertaken, apparently, as a means for providing clues to the processes involved. Descartes's ideas on the subject really seem to have crystallized, however, in the late 1640's, when he triumphantly announced his "solution" to the long-plaguing problem in a series of enthusiastic letters to Princess Elizabeth. The ideas alluded to in these letters appear to be those published as the *De la formation du foetus,* which Descartes completed not long before his death.

First published by Clerselier in 1664, the *Formation* is a curious essay. Unlike the *Traité de l'homme,* which much preceded it in date of composition, the *Formation* consists mainly of bald assertions and only the vaguest mechanisms. Generation commences when the male and female seeds come together and mutually induce a corpuscular fermentation. The motion of certain of the fermenting particles forms the heart, that of others the lungs. Streaming of particles as the process continues furrows out the blood vessels; later, membranes and fibers are formed which ultimately weave together to construct the solid parts. The formation of the bodily parts is described in these vague terms (no mechanism of organ or vascular development is ever made more precise than this), yet Descartes apparently felt satisfied with his results. For by describing generation in chemical and corpuscular, rather than vital or teleological, terms Descartes had, at least in his own mind, completed the mechanistic program for physiology. Everything in the animal's life, from its first formation to its final decay, now had an automatic, mechanical explanation.

The impact of the Cartesian physiological program, once it was publicly known, was enormous. In two ways—philosophically and physiologically—Descartes transformed long-standing beliefs about animals and men. Philosophically, of course, his notions of mind-body dualism and animal automatism had extremely important implications that were not lost on Henry More, Malebranche, Spinoza, and Leibniz, along with many others in the seventeenth century. The "beast-machine" idea also had continuing ramifications in the eighteenth century, leading, at least according to Aram Vartanian, directly to La Mettrie's *L'homme machine.* Also, according to Vartanian, Descartes's posthumously published views on human function and animal generation exerted important philosophical influence, contributing greatly to the eighteenth-century concern with these biological subjects by many of the *philosophes.* But physiologically, too, Descartes's conceptions had an impact that in many ways was even more impressive than the philosophical influence, because it affected the actual course of contemporary science.

Almost as soon as Descartes published his *Discours de la méthode,* a few professors of medicine began to react to specific Cartesian physiological ideas and to the general Cartesian program. Plempius at Louvain and Regius at Utrecht were among the first. Although Plempius proved relatively hostile to Cartesian ideas (his objections were not unlike those William Harvey was to raise a few years later), Regius became so enthusiastic that for a time he entered into something of a student-teacher relationship with Descartes. As their correspondence for 1641 makes clear, Regius would send his students' theses to Descartes for comment and correction. Descartes would then return them with such specific excisions of classical residues as "In the first line of the Thesis I would get rid of these words: vivifying heat."

The intimate contact between Descartes and Regius marked the beginning of the direct influence of Cartesian ideas and modes of thought on seventeenth-century physiology. That influence was deliberately continued later, even more vigorously after Descartes's death, by such influential figures as Thomas Bartholin and Nicholas Steno. These men, especially Steno, tried to wed the Cartesian method of mechanistic explanation to careful anatomical investigation. Steno was particularly highly regarded by contemporaries for his perfection of the mechanical theory of muscular contraction in his *Elementorum myologiae specimen* (1667) and for his defense of the Cartesian physiological methodology in his anatomically sound *Discours sur l'anatomie du cerveau* (1669).

Many other prominent seventeenth-century physiological writers were influenced by the Cartesian program, either directly by reading Descartes's writings or indirectly through such followers as Steno. Among those deeply influenced by Cartesian physiology were Robert Hooke, Thomas Willis, Jan Swammerdam, and Giovanni Alfonso Borelli. These men saw in Cartesian physiology exactly what Descartes had intended it to be: a method of mechanistic formulation by which traditional categories of physiological explanation could be circumvented. Without Descartes, the seventeenth-century mechanization of physiological conceptions would have been inconceivable.

BIBLIOGRAPHY

The main primary sources—letters, MSS, and published works—are all handsomely printed in the Adam-Tannery *Oeuvres de Descartes*; vol. XI contains the largest sample of relevant works.

Useful secondary studies of Descartes's philosophy which seriously consider his physiological writings range from Étienne Gilson's *Études sur le rôle de la pensée médiévale dans la formation du système Cartésien* (Paris, 1930) to Norman Kemp Smith's *New Studies in the Philosophy of Descartes* (New York, 1966). Two older monographic studies are also useful: Bertrand de Saint-Germain's *Descartes considéré comme physiologiste* (Paris, 1869) and Auguste-Georges Berthier's "Le mécanisme Cartésien et la physiologie au XVIIe siècle," in *Isis,* **2** (1914), 37–89, and **3** (1920), 21–58. Some of the background to Descartes's treatment of vision is made clear in A. C. Crombie, "The Mechanistic Hypothesis and the Scientific Study of Vision," in *Proceedings of the Royal Microscopical Society,* **2** (1907), 3–112; fundamental aspects of his mechanistic philosophy are discussed in Georges Canguilhem, *La formation du concept de réflexe aux XVIIe et XVIIIe siècles* (Paris, 1955); while the seventeenth-century impact of Cartesian ideas is studied by Berthier (*op. cit.*) and in two helpful general works, Paul Mouy, *Le développement de la physique Cartésienne* (Paris, 1934) and vol. I of Thomas S. Hall, *Ideas of Life and Matter* (Chicago, 1969).

A sense of the influence of Cartesian ideas and methods can also be gleaned from Michael Foster, *Lectures on the History of Physiology* (Cambridge, 1901); and Gustav Scherz's various studies of Nicholas Steno. Finally, see Aram Vartanian, *Diderot and Descartes* (Princeton, 1953) and *La Mettrie's "L'homme machine"* (Princeton, 1960).

THEODORE M. BROWN